A HISTORY OF THE COUNTY OF GLOUCESTER

EDITED BY N. M. HERBERT

VOLUME IV

THE CITY OF GLOUCESTER

PUBLISHED FOR

THE INSTITUTE OF HISTORICAL RESEARCH

BY

OXFORD UNIVERSITY PRESS

1988

Distributed by Oxford University Press until 1 January 1991
thereafter by Dawsons of Pall Mall

CONTENTS OF VOLUME FOUR

CONTENTS

LIST OF PLATES

For permission to reproduce material in their possession thanks are offered to Gloucester Divisional Library for items in the Gloucestershire Collection, to Gloucester Museum, to Gloucestershire Record Office, and to the Royal Commission on Historical Monuments (England) for items in the National Monuments Record (N.M.R.). Plate 35 is reproduced by permission of Gloucester Newspapers Ltd. and plate 59 by permission of Selwyn school, Matson.

Plates between pages 232 and 233:

PLATES

LIST OF MAPS, PLANS, AND OTHER TEXT FIGURES

Figures 1–3, 16, and 25 were drawn by Philip Moss and figures 4, 8, and 26 by Peter Dening and Janette Walker of the Gloucestershire County Planning Department; original drafts were prepared by N. M. Herbert, A. R. J. Juřica, and Carolyn Heighway. Figure 21 was drawn by A. P. Baggs and Figure 24 by Patricia A. Tattersfield. Figures 2, 4, 8, and 16 are based on O.S. Maps 1/2,500 (1886 edn.) and Figures 25–6 on O.S. Maps 6″ (1880s edn.). For permission to reproduce material in their possession thanks are offered to Gloucester Divisional Library, Gloucestershire Record Office, and Cambridge University Library.

Fig.

EDITORIAL NOTE

Although numbered Four, the present volume is the seventh to be published of the *Victoria History of Gloucestershire* and the sixth since the revival of the Gloucestershire History in 1958. An outline of the structure and aims of the *Victoria History* as a whole, as also of its origin and progress, is included in the *General Introduction* (1970), and the arrangements by which the Gloucestershire County Council and the University of London collaborate to produce the Gloucestershire History are indicated in the Editorial Note to *Gloucestershire*, Volume Six. Once again it is the General Editor's pleasure to record the University's gratitude for the generosity displayed by the County Council.

The County Council's Recreation and Leisure Committee has continued to supervise the compilation of the *Victoria History of Gloucestershire*. Cllr. P. M. Robins was succeeded as chairman of that committee in 1985 by Cllr. K. J. S. Hammond, who was succeeded in the same year by Cllr. J. Bartlett.

The authors and editors of the volume, as of all similar volumes, have drawn widely on the help, information, and advice of many people and bodies, too numerous all to be mentioned here but named in the footnotes to the articles with which they helped. They are all most cordially thanked. Professor Clark's chapter on Early Modern Gloucester is based on research which was generously funded by the Economic and Social Science Research Council and for which valuable assistance in research was provided by Dr. P. Morgan and Dr. A. Foster. Mr. M. A. Handford generously made available notes on the *Gloucester Journal* for part of the 18th century, and Mr. A. Done his detailed notes of Gloucester references from the *Gloucester Journal* for the whole of the 19th century. Mr. B. C. Frith gave generous help on many aspects of Gloucester's history, and among others who helped with particular aspects were Mrs. Evelyn Christmas, Mr. A. H. Conway-Jones, Miss Susan Reynolds, Mr. J. F. Rhodes, curator of Gloucester Museum, Mr. P. J. G. Ripley, and Mr. H. R. T. Shackleton, chief executive of Gloucester City Council. For access to records in their possession grateful acknowledgement is made to the Dean and Chapter of Gloucester, whose librarian Canon D. C. St. V. Welander gave valuable help with the account of the cathedral, and to the archivist of the United Reformed Church provincial archives, Leamington Spa. The Gloucestershire County Record Office has continued to give its indispensable aid, and in thanking the County Archivist, Mr. D. J. H. Smith, and his staff it is appropriate to mention in particular Mrs. Margaret Richards, former senior cataloguer, for her knowledge and careful cataloguing of the Gloucester Borough Records. The extensive use of the material for the city in the Gloucestershire Collection has made the help of the Gloucester Divisional Library of the county library service even more important in the present volume than in previous ones, and the librarian, Mr. G. R. Hiatt, and his staff in the reference and local history sections are sincerely thanked.

LIST OF CLASSES OF DOCUMENTS
IN THE PUBLIC RECORD OFFICE
USED IN THIS VOLUME
WITH THEIR CLASS NUMBERS

Clerks of Assize
ASSIZES 5 Oxford Circuit, Indictments

Chancery

		Proceedings
C	1	Early
C	2	Series I
C	3	Series II
		Six Clerks Series
C	5	Bridges
C	6	Collins
C	7	Hamilton
C	66	Patent Rolls
C	78	Decree Rolls
C	81	Warrants for the Great Seal, Series I
C	93	Commissioners for Charitable Uses, Inquisitions and Decrees
C	115	Masters' Exhibits, Duchess of Norfolk Deeds (including Llanthony cartularies and registers)
		Inquisitions post mortem
C	133	Series I, Edw. I
C	136	Ric. II
C	139	Hen. VI
C	140	Edw. IV and V
C	142	Series II
C	145	Miscellaneous Inquisitions

Court of Common Pleas
CP 25(1) Feet of Fines, Series I
CP 43 Recovery Rolls

Exchequer, King's Remembrancer
E 122 Customs Accounts
Decrees and Orders
E 123 Series I
E 126 Series IV
E 134 Depositions taken by Commission
E 142 Ancient Extents
Inquisitions post mortem,
E 150 Series II
E 159 Memoranda Rolls
E 179 Subsidy Rolls, etc.
E 190 Port Books

Exchequer, Augmentations Office
E 301 Certificates of Colleges and Chantries
E 315 Miscellaneous Books

Exchequer, First Fruits and Tenths Office
E 337 Plea Rolls

Exchequer, Lord Treasurer's Remembrancer and Pipe Office
E 372 Pipe Rolls

Ministry of Education
ED 7 Public Elementary Schools, Preliminary Statements

Registry of Friendly Societies
FS 2 Indexes to Rules and Amendments, Series I

Home Office
HO 107 Census Returns 1841 and 1851
HO 129 Ecclesiastical Returns

Justices Itinerant
JUST 1 Eyre Rolls, Assize Rolls, etc.
JUST 2 Coroners' Rolls

Ministry of Agriculture, Fisheries, and Food
MAF 68 Agricultural Returns: Parish Summaries

Privy Council
PC 2 Registers

Prerogative Court of Canterbury
PROB 11 Wills

British Transport Historical Records
RAIL 829 Gloucester and Berkeley Canal Company
RAIL 864 Sharpness New Docks & Gloucester & Birmingham Navigation Company
RAIL 1112 Reports and Accounts: Canal, Dock, and Harbour Undertakings

Court of Requests
REQ 2 Proceedings

Special Collections
SC 2 Court Rolls
SC 6 Ministers' Accounts
SC 12 Rentals and Surveys, Portfolios

Court of Star Chamber
Proceedings
STAC 5 Eliz. I
STAC 8 Jas. I

State Paper Office
State Papers Domestic
SP 12 Eliz. I
SP 14 Jas. I
SP 16 Chas. I
SP 29 Chas. II

War Office
WO 30 Miscellanea

SELECT LIST OF ACCUMULATIONS
IN THE GLOUCESTERSHIRE RECORD OFFICE

NOTE ON ABBREVIATIONS

Among the abbreviations and short titles used the following may require elucidation:

Acreage Returns, 1905	Board of Agriculture Acreage Returns of 1905, from a MS. copy in possession of the editor, V.C.H. Glos.
Acts of P.C.	*Acts of the Privy Council of England* (H.M.S.O. 1890–1964)
Ag. H.R.	*Agricultural History Review*
Atkyns, *Glos.*	R. Atkyns, *Ancient and Present State of Glostershire* (1712)
Austin, *Crypt School*	R. Austin, *Crypt School, Gloucester, 1539–1939* (Gloucester, 1939)
B. & G. Par. Rec.	*Guide to the Parish Records of the City of Bristol and County of Gloucester*, ed. I. Gray and E. Ralph (B.G.A.S. 1963)
B.G.A.S.	Bristol and Gloucestershire Archaeological Society
B.L.	British Library (used in references to documents transferred from the British Museum)
Bd. of Health Map (1852)	Plan of Gloucester, surveyed by Ordnance Survey Dept. for the Gloucester board of health, 1851 (accepted by board 1852): in possession of Glouc. city engineer's dept. (photocopy in Glos. R.O., Ph 1086/1–14)
Bibliotheca Glos.	*Bibliotheca Gloucestrensis: Collections of Scarce and Curious Tracts Illustrative of and Published during the Civil War* (2 vols. Gloucester, priv. print. 1825)
Bigland, *Glos.*	*Historical, Monumental, and Genealogical Collections Relative to the County of Gloucester, Printed from the Original Papers of Ralph Bigland* (3 vols. 1791–1889, issued in parts; vol. iii is unpaginated)
Bk. of Fees	*Book of Fees* (3 vols. H.M.S.O. 1920–31)
Bryant, *Map of Glos.* (1824)	A. Bryant, *Map of the County of Gloucester in the years 1823 & 1824* (1824)
C.J.	*Journals of the House of Commons*
Cal. Chart. R.	*Calendar of the Charter Rolls preserved in the Public Record Office* (H.M.S.O. 1903–27)
Cal. Close	*Calendar of the Close Rolls preserved in the Public Record Office* (H.M.S.O. 1892–1963)
Cal. Cttee. for Compounding	*Calendar of the Proceedings of the Committee for Compounding, etc.* (H.M.S.O. 1889–92)
Cal. Fine R.	*Calendar of the Fine Rolls preserved in the Public Record Office* (H.M.S.O. 1911–62)
Cal. Inq. Misc.	*Calendar of Inquisitions Miscellaneous (Chancery) preserved in the Public Record Office* (H.M.S.O. 1916–68)
Cal. Inq. p.m.	*Calendar of Inquisitions post mortem preserved in the Public Record Office* (H.M.S.O. 1904–74)
Cal. Inq. p.m. Hen. VII	*Calendar of Inquisitions post mortem, Henry VII* (H.M.S.O. 1898–1955)
Cal. Pat.	*Calendar of the Patent Rolls preserved in the Public Record Office* (H.M.S.O. 1891–1982)
Cal. S.P. Dom.	*Calendar of State Papers, Domestic Series* (H.M.S.O. 1856–1972)
Camd. Misc. xxii	*Camden Miscellany*, xxii (Camden 4th ser. i), including 'Charters of the Earldom of Hereford, 1095–1201', ed. D. Walker

Cat. Anct. D.	*Descriptive Catalogue of Ancient Deeds in the Public Record Office* (H.M.S.O. 1890–1915)
Cat. of Glos. Colln.	*Catalogue of the Gloucestershire Collection in the Gloucester Public Library*, compiled by R. Austin (Gloucester, 1928)
Causton, *Map of Glouc.* (1843)	A. Causton, *Map of City and Borough of Gloucester from an Actual Survey made in 1843* (London, 1844)
Char. Com.	Charity Commission
Ciren. Cart.	*Cartulary of Cirencester Abbey*, ed. C. D. Ross and M. Devine (3 vols. 1964, 1977)
Clarke, *Archit. Hist. of Glouc.*	J. Clarke, *Architectural History of Gloucester* (Gloucester [*c.* 1850])
Close R.	*Close Rolls of the Reign of Henry III preserved in the Public Record Office* (H.M.S.O. 1902–75)
Cole, *Map of Glouc.* (1805)	Map of *Gloucester*, drawn by G. Cole (London, 1805), republished in G. Cole, *British Atlas* (London, 1810)
Complete Peerage	G. E. C[ockayne] and others, *Complete Peerage* . . . (2nd edn., 13 vols. 1810–59)
Compton Census, ed. Whiteman	*Compton Census of 1676: a critical edition*, ed. A. Whiteman (British Academy Records of Social and Economic History, new ser. x, London, 1986)
Conway-Jones, *Glouc. Docks*	H. Conway-Jones, *Gloucester Docks: an Illustrated History* (Gloucester, 1984)
Counsel, *Glouc.*	G. W. Counsel, *History and Description of the City of Gloucester* (Gloucester, 1829)
D.N.B.	*Dictionary of National Biography*
Davis, *Glos. Brasses*	C. T. Davis, *Monumental Brasses of Gloucestershire* (1899)
Delineations of Glos.	J. and H. S. Storer and J. N. Brewer, *Delineations of Gloucestershire, being Views of the Principal Seats of Nobility and Gentry* (London, 1825–7)
Diary of a Cotswold Parson	*Diary of a Cotswold Parson: the Revd. F. E. Witts, 1783–1854*, ed. D. (C. W.) Verey (Dursley, 1978)
Dugdale, *Mon.*	W. Dugdale, *Monasticum Anglicanum*, ed. J. Caley and others (6 vols. 1817–30)
E.H.R.	*English Historical Review*
Eccl. Misc.	*Ecclesiastical Miscellany* (B.G.A.S. Records Section, xi, 1976), including 'Survey of Diocese of Gloucester, 1603', ed. A. C. Percival and W. J. Sheils
Educ. Enq. Abstract	*Education Enquiry Abstract*, H.C. 62 (1835), xli
Educ. of Poor Digest	*Digest of Returns to the Select Committee on Education of the Poor*, H.C. 224 (1819), ix (1)
Feud. Aids	*Inquisitions and Assessments relating to Feudal Aids preserved in the Public Record Office* (H.M.S.O. 1899–1920)
Finberg, *Early Charters of W. Midlands*	H P. R. Finberg, *Early Charters of the W. Midlands* (Leicester, 1961)
Finberg, *Glos. Studies*	*Gloucestershire Studies*, ed. H. P. R. Finberg (1957)
Fosbrooke, *Glos.*	T. D. Fosbrooke, *Abstracts of Records and Manuscripts Respecting the County of Gloucester, Formed into a History* (2 vols. Gloucester, 1807)
Fosbrooke, *Glouc.*	T. D. Fosbrooke, *Original History of the City of Gloucester almost Wholly Compiled from New Materials . . . including also the Original Papers of Ralph Bigland* (London, 1819)
G.B.R.	Gloucester Borough Records (see page xvii)
G.D.R.	Gloucester Diocesan Records (see page xviii)
Gent. Mag.	*Gentleman's Magazine* (1731–1867)
Glos. Ch. Bells	M. Bliss and F. Sharpe, *Church Bells of Gloucestershire* (Gloucester, 1986)

Glos. Ch. Notes	*Gloucestershire Church Notes*, by S. R. Glynne, ed. W. P. W. Phillimore and J. Melland Hall (1902)
Glos. Ch. Plate	*Church Plate of Gloucestershire*, ed. J. T. Evans (B.G.A.S. 1906)
Glos. Colln.	The Gloucestershire Collection, in Gloucester Divisional Library, comprising printed works, manuscripts, prints and drawings, etc.
Glos. N. & Q.	*Gloucestershire Notes and Queries* (10 vols. 1881–1914)
Glos. R.O.	Gloucestershire Record Office (see page xvii)
Glos. Subsidy Roll, 1327	*Gloucestershire Subsidy Roll I Edw. III, 1327* (priv. print. by Sir Thos. Phillipps [? 1856])
Glouc. Cath. Libr.	Gloucester Cathedral Library
Glouc. Corp. Rec.	*Calendar of the Records of the Corporation of Gloucester*, ed. W. H. Stevenson (Gloucester, 1893)
Glouc. Jnl.	*Gloucester Journal* (established 1722)
Glouc. Rental, 1455	*Rental of All the Houses in Gloucester A.D. 1455 . . . Compiled by Robert Cole, Canon of Llanthony*, ed. W. H. Stevenson (Gloucester, 1890)
H.L. Papers	*House of Lords Papers* (new ser. 1900–53)
H.M.S.O.	Her (His) Majesty's Stationery Office
Hall and Pinnell, *Map of Glouc.* (1780)	*Plan of the City of Gloucester, Surveyed and Delineated 1780 by R. Hall and T. Pinnell* (1782)
Hist. & Cart. Mon. Glouc. (Rolls Ser.)	*Historia et Cartularium Monasterii Sancti Petri Gloucestriae*, ed. W. H. Hart (Rolls Series, no. 33, 3 vols. 1863–87
Hist. MSS. Com.	Royal Commission on Historical Manuscripts
Hockaday Abs.	The 'Hockaday Abstracts', being abstracts of ecclesiastical records relating to Gloucestershire, compiled by F. S. Hockaday mainly from diocesan records, in Gloucester Divisional Library
Inq. Non. (Rec. Com.)	*Nonarum Inquisitiones in Curia Scaccarii*, ed. G. Vandersee (Record Commission, 1807)
Inq. p.m. Glos	*Abstracts of Inquisitiones post mortem for Gloucestershire, 1236– 1413, 1625–42* (6 vols. issued jointly by the British Record Society, Index Library vols. xxx, xl, xlviii, and ix, xxi, xlvii, and the B.G.A.S. 1893–1914)
Kirby, *Cat. of Glouc. Dioc. Rec.*	Diocese of Gloucester: vol. i, *Catalogue of the Records of the Bishop and Archdeacons* (Gloucester Corporation, 1968); vol. ii, *Catalogue of the Records of the Dean and Chapter* (Glos. County Council, 1967); compiled by I. M. Kirby
L. & P. Hen. VIII	*Letters and Papers, Foreign and Domestic, of the Reign of Henry VIII* (H.M.S.O. 1864–1932)
L.J.	*Journals of the House of Lords*
Lond. Gaz.	*London Gazette*
Manual of Glos. Lit.	*Bibliographer's Manual of Gloucestershire Literature*, ed. F. A. Hyett and W. Bazeley (3 vols. Gloucester, priv. print. 1895–7)
N.M.R.	National Monuments Record, of the Royal Commission on Historical Monuments (England)
Nat. Soc. files	Schools files of the National Society, Church House, Westminster
Nat. Soc. *Inquiry, 1846–7*	*Result of the Returns to the General Inquiry made by the National Society* (1849)
P.N. Glos. (E.P.N.S.)	*Place-Names of Gloucestershire* (English Place-Name Society vols. xxxviii– xli, 1964–5)
P.R.O.	Public Record Office (see page xvi)
Pat. R.	*Patent Rolls of the Reign of Henry III preserved in the Public Record Office* (H.M.S.O. 1901–3)
Payne, *Glos. Survey*	G. E. Payne, *Gloucestershire: a Survey* (Gloucester [?1946])
Pipe R.	*Pipe Rolls*

Plac. de Quo Warr. (Rec. Com.)	*Placita de Quo Warranto . . . in Curia Receptae Scaccarii Westm. asservata*, ed. W. Illingworth and J. Caley (Record Commission, 1818)
Pleas of the Crown for Glos. ed. Maitland	*Pleas of the Crown for the County of Gloucester, 1221*, ed. F. W. Maitland (1884)
Poor Law Abstract, 1804	*Abstract of Returns Relative to the Expense and Maintenance of the Poor* (printed by order of the House of Commons, 1804)
Poor Law Abstract, 1818	*Abstract of Returns to Orders of the House of Commons Relative to Assessments for Relief of the Poor*, H.C. 294 (1820), xii
Poor Law Com. 1st Rep.	*First Report of the Poor Law Commission*, H.C. 500-I (1835), xxxv
Poor Law Returns (1830–1)	*Account of the Money Expended for the Maintenance and Relief of the Poor for the five years ending 25th March 1825, 1826, 1827, 1828, and 1829*, H.C. 83 (1830–1), xi
Poor Law Returns (1835)	*Accounts of the Money Expended, 1830, 1831, 1832, 1833, and 1834*, H.C. 444 (1835), xlvii
Reg. Bransford	*Calendar of the Register of Wolstan de Bransford, Bishop of Worcester 1339–49*, ed. R. M. Haines (Worcs. Hist. Soc. 1966)
Reg. Cobham	*Register of Bishop Thomas de Cobham, 1317–27*, ed. E. H. Pearce (Worcs. Hist. Soc. 1930)
Reg. Giffard	*Register of Bishop Godfrey Giffard, 1268–1302*, ed. J. W. W. Bund (Worcs. Hist. Soc. 1902)
Reg. Ginsborough	*Register of Bishop William Ginsborough, 1303–7*, ed. J. W. W. Bund (Worcs. Hist. Soc. 1907)
Reg. Mon. Winch.	*Landboc, sive Registrum Monasterii de Winchelcumba*, ed. D. Royce (2 vols. Exeter, 1892–1903)
Reg. Orleton	*Calendar of the Register of Adam de Orleton, Bishop of Worcester 1327–33*, ed. R. M. Haines (Worcs. Hist. Soc. 1979)
Reg. Reynolds	*Register of Bishop Walter Reynolds, 1308–13*, ed. R. A. Wilson (Worcs. Hist. Soc. 1927)
Reg. Sede Vacante	*Register of the Diocese of Worcester during the Vacancy of the See*, ed. J. W. W. Bund (Worcs. Hist. Soc. 1893–7)
Reg. Wakefeld	*Calendar of the Register of Henry Wakefeld, Bishop of Worcester 1375–95*, ed. W. P. Marett (Worcs. Hist. Soc. 1972)
14th Rep. Com. Char.	*14th Report of the Commissioners Apppointed to Enquire Concerning Charities* (Lord Brougham's Commission), H.C. 382 (1826), xii
16th Rep. Com. Char.	*16th Report . . . Concerning Charities*, H.C. 22 (1826–7), ix (1)
Rep. Com. Mun. Corp.	*First Report of the Commissioners Appointed to Enquire into the Municipal Corporations of England and Wales*, App. I, H.C. 116 (1835), xxiii (1)
Richardson, *Wells and Springs of Glos.*	L. Richardson, *Wells and Springs of Gloucestershire* (H.M.S.O. 1930)
Ripley, 'Glouc. 1660–1740'	P. J. G. Ripley, 'City of Gloucester 1660–1740' (Bristol Univ. M. Litt. thesis, 1977)
Roper, *Glos. Effigies*	Ida M. Roper, *Monumental Effigies of Gloucestershire and Bristol* (Gloucester, 1931)
Rot. Hund. (Rec. Com.)	*Rotuli Hundredorum temp. Hen. III & Edw. I in Turri Londinensi, et in Curia Receptae Scaccarii Westm. asservati*, ed. W. Illingworth and J. Caley (2 vols. Record Commission, 1812–18)
Rot. Litt. Claus. (Rec. Com.)	*Rotuli Litterarum Clausarum in Turri Londinensi asservati, 1204–27*, ed. T. D. Hardy (2 vols. Record Commission, 1833–44)
Rot. Litt. Pat. (Rec. Com.)	*Rotuli Litterarum Patentium in Turri Londinensi asservati, 1201–16*, ed. T. D. Hardy (Record Commission, 1835)
Rot. Parl.	*Rotuli Parliamentorum* (6 vols. [1783])
Rudder, *Glos.*	S. Rudder, *New History of Gloucestershire* (Cirencester, 1779)
Rudge, *Agric. of Glos.*	T. Rudge, *General View of the Agriculture of the County of Gloucester* (Gloucester, 1807)

Rudge, *Glouc.*	T. Rudge, *History and Antiquities of Gloucester from the Earliest Period to the Present Time* (Gloucester, 1811)
Rudge, *Hist. of Glos.*	T. Rudge, *History of the County of Gloucester* (2 vols. Gloucester, 1803)
Smith, *Men and Armour*	*Names and Surnames of All the Able and Sufficient Men in Body Fit for His Majesty's Service in the Wars, within the County of Gloucester, Compiled by John Smith, 1608* (1902)
Speed, Map of Glouc. (1610)	Inset to map of Gloucestershire, first published 1610, republished in J. Speed, *Theatre of the Empire of Great Britaine* (London, 1611)
Taylor, *Map of Glos.* (1777)	I. Taylor, *Map of the County of Gloucester* (1777), republished in *Gloucestershire and Bristol Atlas* (B.G.A.S. 1961)
Tax. Eccl. (Rec. Com.)	*Taxatio Ecclesiastica Angliae et Walliae auctoritate P. Nicholai IV circa A.D. 1291*, ed. S. Ayscough and J. Caley (Record Commission, 1802)
Trans. B.G.A.S.	*Transactions of the Bristol and Gloucestershire Archaeological Society*
Univ. Brit. Dir.	*Universal British Directory of Trade, Commerce, and Manufacture*, ed. P. Barfoot and J. Wilkes (5 vols. 1791–8)
V.C.H.	*Victoria County History*
Valor Eccl. (Rec. Com.)	*Valor Ecclesiasticus temp. Hen. VIII auctoritate regia institutus*, ed. J. Caley and J. Hunter (6 vols. Record Commission, 1810–34)
Verey, *Glos.*	D. C. W. Verey, *Gloucestershire*: vol. i, *The Cotswolds;* vol. ii, *The Vale and the Forest of Dean* (The Buildings of England, ed. N. Pevsner, 1970)
Visit. Glos. 1623	*Visitation of the County of Gloucester, 1623*, ed. J. Maclean and W. C. Heane (Harleian Society xxi, 1885)
Visit. Glos. 1682–3	*Visitation of the County of Gloucester, 1682, 1683*, ed. T. FitzRoy Fenwick and W. C. Metcalfe (Exeter, priv. print. 1884)
Williams, *Parl. Hist. of Glos.*	W. R. Williams, *Parliamentary History of the County of Gloucester* (Hereford, priv. print. 1898)
Worc. Episc. Reg.	Worcester Episcopal Registers (in Worcestershire Record Office)

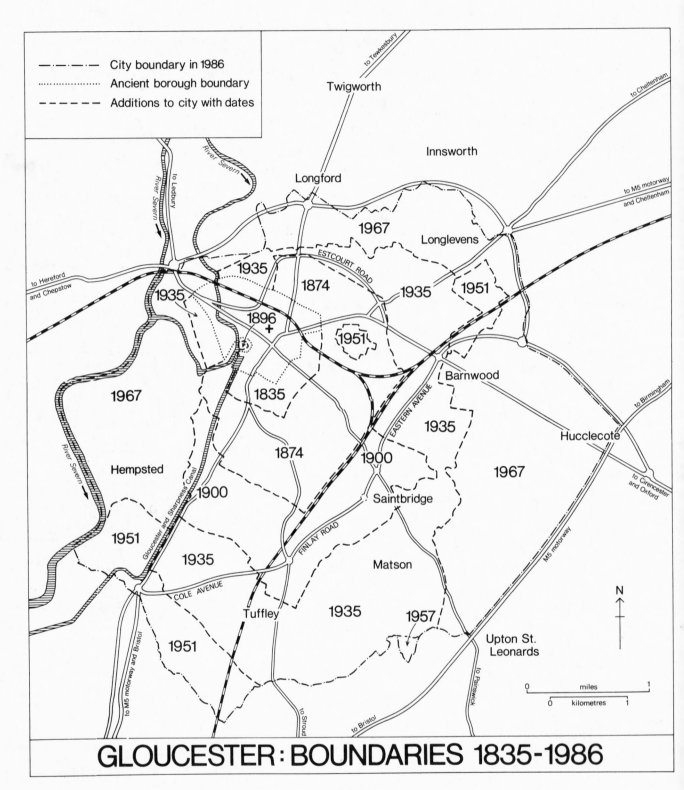

GLOUCESTER: BOUNDARIES 1835-1986

Fig. 1

THE CITY OF GLOUCESTER

THIS volume describes the history of Gloucester in most of its aspects from the late 7th century A.D. to the 1980s.[1] The institutional history of the religious houses and the history of the grammar schools to the late 19th century will be found in Volume Two of the county set, and some other matters, including the history of the canals and railways and the history of the county administration based in Gloucester, are intended to be more fully described in articles to be published later. Gloucester during the prehistoric, Romano-British, and pagan-Saxon periods is reserved for inclusion in a volume dealing with the archaeology of the county as a whole.

The boundaries of the medieval borough of the Gloucester, first found described in a perambulation of 1370,[2] enclosed 680 a. (275 ha.),[3] including a considerable area outside the town walls. Apart from a few, probably man-made, ditches, the boundaries were unrelated to physical features and followed a series of regular alignments; those on the north and north-west represent ancient divisions of meadowland and parts of the meadows left outside the boundary remained attached to the parishes of Gloucester churches. The fairly regular shape of the borough was disturbed only on the south-west where a peninsula of land intruded to enclose the site of Gloucester castle, later the county gaol.

Lying outside the borough were the hamlets of Twigworth, Longford, Kingsholm, Wotton, Barton Street, and Tuffley, and a number of extraparochial places, all of them having boundaries of great complexity. The hamlets were connected ecclesiastically with the parishes of Gloucester churches, and administratively they were attached to the city between 1483 and 1662 as part of the hundred of Dudstone and King's Barton and for a period in the earlier 18th century for poor-law purposes.

Gloucester's ancient boundary was first extended in 1835 and further extensions followed in 1874, 1900, 1935, 1951, 1957, and 1967.[4] By 1967, when the new boundary enclosed 8,239 a. (3,334 ha.),[5] the city had absorbed the bulk of the outlying hamlets, all but small parts of the ancient parishes of Barnwood, Matson, and Hempsted, a large part of Hucclecote parish (originally a hamlet of Churchdown), and parts of the ancient parish of Upton St. Leonards. The area covered by this volume is Gloucester city within its 1967 boundary, together with the modern civil parishes of Longford, Twigworth, Innsworth, and Hucclecote, which in 1986 included most of the land of the former hamlets and Hucclecote still outside the city, and a part of Quedgeley civil parish which had formerly belonged to Hempsted. Some former detached parts of the old hamlets and absorbed parishes remain outside that area, and those, which apart from a former part of Matson at Pope's wood near

[1] This introduction was written in 1986.
[2] Hist. & Cart. Mon. Glouc. (Rolls Ser.), iii. 256–7; the boundary is shown on Hall and Pinnell, Map of Glouc. (1780), and Parl. Representation: Boundary Rep. Pt. 1, H.C. 141 (1831–2), xxxviii, facing p. 191.
[3] Census, 1831.
[4] Fig. 1; below, Glouc. 1835–1985, city govt.
[5] Census, 1971.

Prinknash are very small, are reserved for treatment with their new parishes in later volumes.

Gloucester, which was the shire town of Gloucestershire from the late Anglo-Saxon period, was sometimes styled *civitas* in the 11th and 12th centuries. Later it was always styled a town or borough until 1541, when on the founding the see of Gloucester, it was made a city by charter. In 1483 the town and the surrounding hundred of Dudstone and King's Barton had been given the status of a separate county, or inshire, and placed under the administration of the Gloucester aldermen as J.P.s, and the city remained a separate county after 1662 when the hundred was removed from its jurisdiction and returned to Gloucestershire. Gloucester became a county borough in 1889 and retained that status until 1974 when it was made a district, though keeping the style of a city.

The Roman settlement at Gloucester, whose walls later provided the basis for the defences of the east part of the medieval town, was established near a crossing-point of the river Severn on a low rise at *c.* 15 m. The land there is formed by the Lower Lias clay, which has a cap of gravel where the central crossroads of the town were established, and a larger covering of gravel east of the walls including the Barton Street area. The west side of Gloucester and the adjoining meadowland are formed by alluvium.[6]

The decayed Roman town retained some significance as an administrative and religious centre in early Anglo-Saxon times, and *c.* 679 A.D., when it formed part of the Mercian under-kingdom of the Hwicce, it was chosen as the site of a minster church. It was not, however, until the early 10th century that Gloucester began to emerge as an important commercial centre, probably under the influence of Ethelfleda of the Mercians who founded the new minster of St. Oswald there. By Edward the Confessor's reign the kings of England had a palace at nearby Kingsholm and Gloucester was a regular meeting place of the royal council.

Under the Normans Gloucester's strategic position, commanding the route across the river Severn into South Wales, was recognized by the building of a strong castle. The town continued to benefit from royal attention, and it played a part in national events until the 13th century. The former minster of St. Peter grew to be one of the greatest Benedictine abbeys of England, and a number of new churches and other religious foundations were added, notably in 1137 the richly-endowed Llanthony Priory. Partly under the influence of the religious houses, new suburbs developed outside the town walls. The town's economic prosperity was based on its manufactures, notably ironworking, its market for agricultural produce, a limited role in overseas and inland trade, and its function as a centre for the supply of goods and services to the surrounding market towns, among which it established a pre-eminence that went unchallenged until the beginning of the 19th century.

A wealthy class of merchants and tradesmen, ambitious for control of their own affairs, had emerged by the later 12th century and secured the right to farm the town in 1165 and the right to elect bailiffs to govern it in 1200. The further development of a communal identity and more complex institutions culminated in 1483 with a charter of incorporation, which gave the town a mayor and aldermen and control of the inshire. Gloucester shared in the economic problems that troubled many English towns during the 15th century but was able to maintain its traditional economic roles and in the early 16th century enjoyed a revival of trade, led by clothmaking and capping. The religious aspirations of the leading townsmen of the late Middle Ages

---

[6] Geol. Surv. Map 1/9,500, drift, sheet 234 (1972 edn.).

were expressed in the foundation of chantries and religious guilds, and they sometimes adopted an aggressive attitude towards the monastic houses, whose dissolution in the late 1530s was a major landmark in the town's history.

In the late 16th century and the early 17th Gloucester endured a period of considerable difficulty, to which the decline of its textile trades, outbreaks of plague, and the burden of pauperism all contributed. It remained, however, a significant marketing and distribution centre, and its leather trades and malting industry flourished. The shipping of grain and malt down river gave it a significant share in the Severn trade, although the creation of a separate port of Gloucester in 1580 proved to be an irrelevance before the 19th century when the city finally freed itself from dependence on Bristol for most of its overseas trade. The management of charitable institutions became a principal concern of the city corporation, the medieval hospitals being augmented and reorganized. Other medieval institutions, such as the trade companies and the ancient city courts, had a dwindling role, as a small oligarchy, embodied in the bench of aldermen, tightened its grip on city government.

In the early 17th century Gloucester's rulers adopted puritan views, and at the outbreak of the Civil War the city became a stronghold of the parliamentary cause; the stubborn resistance of the inhabitants to a determined siege by a large royalist army in 1643 was widely regarded as the turning point of the war. The consequences for the city at the Restoration included the loss of the inshire, long a cause of friction between the corporation and neighbouring county gentry, and the purge of anti-royalist elements on the corporation. The city government continued to be disturbed by party conflict until the Revolution of 1688. There was, however, an improvement in Gloucester's economic fortunes, to which the growth of the pinmaking industry and the establishment of the city as a social centre for the county gentry contributed. It was a smaller place in the late 17th century, having lost large parts of its suburbs at the time of the siege, and nearly half of its eleven medieval parish churches had been demolished, but its main streets were steadily modernized by the refronting in brick of the old timber houses.

During the 18th century its markets, the river trade which brought the products of the West Midlands industrial area and Bristol imports to be distributed inland, a central position for road transport, its pinmaking and woolstapling industries, and, from the end of the century, the development of banking, gave Gloucester a moderately successful economy. Activity was such, however, as to generate only a very small growth in population and there was little new building, though considerable improvements to the streets and public buildings were carried through in the second half of the century. Within the limits of the closed, self-perpetuating system the city corporation was representative of the needs of the community as a whole, while a larger number of citizens shared in government through bodies set up to administer poor relief and street improvements. The city escaped serious problems of poverty and unrest and a philanthropic spirit prevailed, exemplified among other projects in the establishment of a county infirmary in 1755 and the promotion and support of Sunday schools from 1780.

The physical growth of the city began again after the Napoleonic Wars. It was stimulated in part by the development of a spa, though the rise of the neighbouring leisure resort of Cheltenham had by then diminished prospects of the development of the city as a social or residential centre. Its future lay with commercial activity, and in that field its opportunities were transformed by the opening in 1827 of the Gloucester and Berkeley ship canal, which gave direct and easy access to maritime trade. After the building of the railways in the 1840s Gloucester became a busy port for the distribution of foreign corn and timber to the Midlands, and docks, warehouses, railway sidings, mills, and timber yards developed at the head of the canal. The railways and the trade at the docks stimulated the growth of industry, which included flour milling, shipbuilding, and the manufacture of railway rolling stock and matches. The city was massively enlarged, its population increasing from c. 12,000 in 1831 to c. 48,000 by 1901, following three boundary extensions. In the mid Victorian period the building of churches and schools for the new suburbs became the main preoccupation of city churchmen, among whom the evangelical tradition was firmly rooted. Nonconformity, since the late 17th century only a minor element in city life, re-emerged as a significant force. The attendant social problems of growth, including epidemics and the decline of some older parts of the city into slums, were tackled by voluntary effort and by the array of stututory bodies which provided sewerage, water supply, and other services for the city and the adjoining suburbs. The city corporation, reformed as an elective body in 1835, took a leading part in the provision of such services after 1849 when it assumed the powers of a local board of health, and it acquired additional responsibilities in the fields of public health, education, housing, and public assistance in the late 19th century and the early 20th.

The trade at the docks had begun to decline by the late 19th century, but the established manufactures, joined by new engineering firms and, from the 1920s, by aircraft production, continued to provide employment on a large scale until the mid 20th century. In the later 20th century employment was increasingly provided by the institutions of local government, the civil service, and service industries, and office workers, drawn from a fairly wide surrounding area, comprised the bulk of those working in the city in the 1980s. Between the two wars slum clearance schemes in some inner city areas and new council housing estates on the outskirts further altered the appearance of Gloucester. Large private housing schemes were carried out from the 1960s, and by 1986 the greater part of the adjoining hamlets and absorbed parishes was built over. In the central streets of the city, where the basically Georgian character had been diluted by some large new banks and public buildings in the Victorian period, there was much redevelopment in the 1960s and 1970s. In 1986 the former abbey church with its elaborate perpendicular architecture and the dock basin with its ranges of 19th-century warehouses were the two most substantial reminders of the city's varied history.

The chapters that form the first part of this volume give the general economic, administrative, social, and topographical history of Gloucester over five main periods; they are followed by a series of articles which describe in detail and in a manner designed for ready reference particular topics, institutions, and groups of buildings; and in the final part the history of the adjoining hamlets and absorbed parishes (excepting those aspects directly related to the city's later industrial and suburban expansion) is recounted.

ANGLO-SAXON GLOUCESTER
c. 680–1066

ANY account of Anglo-Saxon Gloucester must begin with some reference to the Roman town which preceded it.[1] Although there was no continuous urban life to link the 4th century with the 10th, the physical framework of the Roman colony necessarily affected later development.[2]

The earliest Roman occupation, the fort built in the 60s A.D. north of Gloucester at Kingsholm, was abandoned after a decade.[3] The Roman fortress, the precursor of the medieval town, was built in the 70s A.D. in a position commanding the crossing of the river Severn. The river then flowed closer to the town than it does today, in or near the channel later known as the Old Severn and crossed by the Foreign bridge. After the fortress became a colony in the 2nd century, stone walls and gates were provided, as well as a stone quay and quayside retaining wall. The Roman north and east gates survived until the 11th century and the quayside wall until the 12th, while the east, south, and part of the north lengths of the Roman circuit still defended the city in the 17th century.[4] A suggestion that the riverside retaining wall was, by the 4th century, the western limit of Gloucester's defences has not yet met with general acceptance,[5] though there is some evidence that the original west wall of the Roman fortress had gone by the 10th century.[6] The massive public buildings of the Roman town also influenced, though in a less striking way than the walls, the shape of the later settlement.

After the early 5th century the very limited surviving archaeological evidence for Gloucester provides no record of trade or industry and even suggests that until the 10th century or later much of the urban area was used for agriculture.[7] Gloucester was still, however, regarded as an administrative centre in 577,[8] and there may have been institutional links between the Roman and the late Anglo-Saxon town. On the Continent, such a connection was provided by the Christian religion, and many late-Roman suburban cemeteries, from being used for Christian burial, acquired chapels which ultimately became parish or even episcopal churches.[9] At Gloucester it is significant that a Roman cemetery became the site of the late Anglo-Saxon minster of St. Oswald,[10] and that the church of St. Mary de Lode, which became the parish church for the estates of St. Peter's Abbey around Gloucester, had its origins in a small post-Roman burial chapel or mausoleum, which was aligned, perhaps deliberately, on the Roman house beneath.[11] Another Roman cemetery, at Kingsholm,

[1] This chapter was written in 1984 and revised in 1986.

[2] Glouc. before the late 7th cent. will be covered in another volume of V.C.H. Glos., dealing with the early hist. and archaeol. of the county.

[3] Jnl. Roman Studies, xxxii. 39–52; Trans. B.G.A.S. lxxxi. 14–16; Britannia, i. 186; Antiq. Jnl. lv. 267–94.

[4] Antiq. Jnl. lii. 24–69; liv. 8–52; C. Heighway, Gates of Glouc. (Bristol, 1983); H. Hurst, Glouc.: Roman and Later Defences (1986); and for the quayside wall, also. P. Garrod and C. Heighway, Garrod's Glouc. (Bristol, 1984), site 28/79.

[5] Garrod and Heighway, Garrod's Glouc. intro.; Hurst,

Glouc. Defences, 115.

[6] Garrod and Heighway, Garrod's Glouc. intro.; and for the alternative view that the whole fortress circuit remained intact until the late 11th cent., Hurst, Glouc. Defences, 129–32.

[7] Antiq. Jnl. liv. 33; Trans. B.G.A.S. xciii. 30; ci. 108.

[8] A.-S. Chron. ed. D. Whitelock (1961), 14.

[9] M. Biddle, 'Towns', Arch. of A.-S. Eng. (1976), 110–11; C. Thomas, Christianity in Roman Britain (1981), 157–63, 170–80.   [10] Antiq. Jnl. lx. 208.

[11] Ibid. 219; Glevensis, xiv. 4–12.

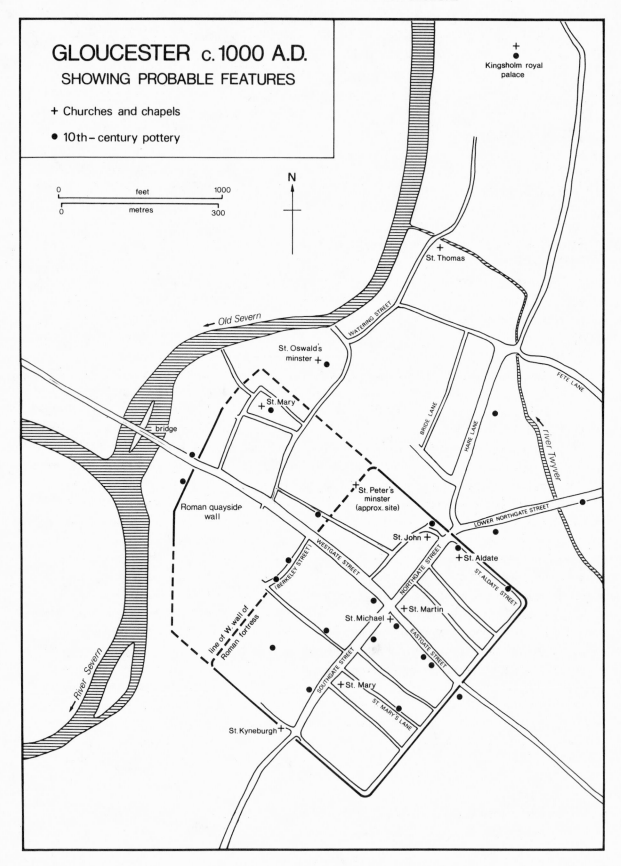

GLOUCESTER c. 1000 A.D.
SHOWING PROBABLE FEATURES

+ Churches and chapels

● 10th–century pottery

Fig. 2

which included late-Roman burials of high status, became the site of a late Anglo-Saxon royal palace, whose chapel might, if investigated, prove to have Roman origins.[12] It is also significant that the remains of the palace complex have a Roman alignment.[13]

Besides containing centres of religious significance, post-Roman Gloucester probably kept its reputation and function as an administrative centre. In 577, when it was captured by the Anglo-Saxon invaders after the battle of Dyrham, it was regarded as the head of a district,[14] and the foundation of a minster c. 679 indicates a similar status. It has been suggested that in 679 the old Roman land tax might still have been in operation.[15] The fabric of the Roman town was still impressive, but it was decaying and ruined; nothing better demonstrates that than the fact that the Roman street grid vanished entirely. Only the cardinal streets, controlled as they were by openings in the Roman walls, maintained a line that approximated to the Roman grid. Westgate Street diverged more than the others; in the early sub-Roman period it was rerouted through a ruined public building, the columns of which, originally some 30 ft. high, survived for many centuries.[16] Another surviving feature may have been the open area of the Roman *forum*. Even in the 10th century buildings in that area had not acquired the alignment of the later street frontage[17] and the concentration of 9th-century deposits[18] implies that it was a useful open space.

By the mid 7th century Gloucester had come within the influence of the kingdom of the Hwicce, which passed into the control of Mercia, possibly in 628, with the aid of Northumbrian warlords.[19] Links with Northumbria are a persistent theme in the history of the town and its shire, culminating in 909 with the translation of the bones of St. Oswald, king of Northumbria, to a final resting place in Gloucester.[20]

The 9th-century town was not a prepossessing place. Preserved organic material from the *forum* area demonstrates only domestic and agricultural activity. In contrast to 8th-century mercantile centres such as Southampton, Gloucester received few imports from far afield. The economy, on the evidence, which is admittedly limited, can hardly be termed urban.[21]

In 877 the remnants of a Danish army camped in the town.[22] A Mercian council of 896 was held at Gloucester, perhaps in a great hall at Kingsholm, and during the proceedings a priest 'of the inhabitants of the *ceastor*', presumably meaning the walled Roman town of Gloucester, was mentioned.[23]

In the 10th century Gloucester acquired, apparently quite suddenly, an administrative and military status which it is tempting to equate with the revival of towns elsewhere in southern England.[24] Although not listed in the surviving records as a Mercian *burh*, Gloucester was organized for defence by 914, and the failure of the Mercian register to mention the refortification of Gloucester between 902 and 914 may imply that it was fortified before that period[25] by Ethelfleda of Mercia. By 909

[12] The chapel was dedicated to St. Nicholas (*Bk. of Fees*, i. 377; ii. 1339), which is not usually considered an early dedication, but it could have been renamed.

[13] *Antiq. Jnl.* lv. 274; H. Hurst, *Kingsholm* (1985), 19–20, 133.

[14] *A.-S. Chron.* 14; Bath and Cirencester controlled other districts.

[15] Finberg, *Early Charters of W. Midlands*, p. 163; *Glos. Studies*, 14–16.

[16] *Britannia*, xi. 84.

[17] *Med. Arch.* xxiii. 160, fig. 1.

[18] C. Heighway, 'A.-S. Glouc. to A.D. 1100', *Studies in late A.-S. Settlement*, ed. M. Faull (1984), 35–54.

[19] *Trans. Worcs. Arch. Soc.* N.S. ii. 20–5; Finberg, *Early*

Charters of W. Midlands, pp. 167–80.

[20] *A.-S. Chron.* 61; *Die Heiligen Englands*, ed. F. Liebermann (Hanover, 1889), 9–10.

[21] *Med. Arch.* xxiii. 159–213.

[22] *A.-S. Chron.* 48 n.

[23] Finberg, *Early Charters of W. Midlands*, p. 50; *Eng. Hist. Doc.* i (1st edn.), pp. 56, 108–9, where it is suggested that the *ceastor* was Worcester, but Glouc., where the order was given and where Roman walls survived, is more likely.

[24] M. Biddle and D. Hill, 'A.-S. Planned Towns', *Antiq. Jnl.* li. 70–85.

[25] *A.-S. Chron.* 63; Radford, 'Pre-Conquest Boroughs', *Proc. Brit. Academy*, lxiv. 131–53.

she had founded in the town the new minster of St. Oswald, a sign of special royal favour towards the town, and by then the town also had a mint.[26] The royal palace mentioned in the 11th century may have been in existence as the centre of a royal manor, a *villa regalis, in the* 10th century. When Ethelfleda died at Tamworth in 918 it was not in that traditional centre of Mercia that she was buried, but at Gloucester.[27]

Ethelfleda's attention to Gloucester may also be demonstrated by the street pattern. There is a striking similarity between the east part of the pattern, with its grid of streets running back to the walls and intramural street, and the *burhs* of Wessex fortified by Ethelfleda's father Alfred in the late 9th century.[28] Nevertheless, good evidence is lacking for the date of that street layout. No Gloucester street has a documentary reference before the 12th century,[29] and archaeological sections produce inadequate or unhelpful dating evidence; for example, the second surface of St. Mary's Lane was of the 12th century.[30] The distribution of 10th-century pottery[31] emphasizes the importance of the four principal streets; if the side streets existed, they were not densely built up. There is, however, some evidence that St. Aldate's Street was laid down in the 10th century.[32] An intra-mural street of that date would strengthen the case for regarding Gloucester as a *burh* in the Alfredian tradition.

Curiously enough, it is the western part of the town that has produced the best evidence for 10th-century streets. It has been suggested that the Anglo-Saxon *burh* simply used all the walls of the Roman fortress,[33] but Berkeley Street, which straddles the line of the west wall of the Roman fortress, is now known to have been laid down during the 10th century, and the extension of the precinct of the old minster westwards across the same Roman line had also occurred by the end of that century. The archaeological evidence so far available suggests that the *burh* extended to the old course of the river and so was probably defended by the Roman riverside wall, which was not demolished until the 12th century.[34] How that part of the town was defended to the north and south is not known, but possible lines for the defences are indicated on the plan.[35] Included in the western part of the Anglo-Saxon *burh* were houses which were recorded as being destroyed soon after the Conquest to make way for the first Norman castle[36] and probably also a group of dwellings around St. Mary de Lode church on land belonging to the old minster.[37] At least two lanes in the lower Westgate Street area adjoining the Old Severn, Myende Lane and Powke Lane, had Old English names.[38]

As has been suggested,[39] substantial suburbs were probably built on the north side of the town in the late Anglo-Saxon period. Streets with Old English names existed north of the town on the road to the royal palace at Kingsholm. Hare Lane (from *here straet*, 'military road')[40] is assumed to have followed the line of the Roman road out of the north side of Gloucester, though that is not certain. The street layout in the area suggests an element of planning; Hare Lane is a double street, having Back Hare Lane (later Park Street) running parallel, while a third parallel street, Bride Lane, formerly

[26] *Trans. B.G.A.S.* x. 31.
[28] *Antiq. Jnl.* li. 70–85; lii. 66–8.
[29] Below, Street Names.
[30] *Trans. B.G.A.S.*, xciii. 30.
[31] Fig. 2.
[32] Glouc. Mus. Cat. A 1515–16; pottery re-identified by A. G. Vince.
[33] *Antiq. Jnl.* lxii. 36–7; lxiv. 13; Hurst, *Glouc. Defences*, 129–31.
[34] Garrod and Heighway, *Garrod's Glouc.* sites 19/79; 12/77; 28/79. Hurst, *Glouc. Defences*, 115, emphasizes that the

[27] *A.-S. Chron.* 67.

riverside wall was not a Roman defence but only a retaining wall.
[35] Fig. 2.
[36] *Dom. Bk.* (Rec. Com.), i. 162.
[37] Below, Medieval Glouc., topog.
[38] *P.N. Glos.* (E.P.N.S.), ii. 131; *Glouc. Corp. Rec.* p. 262; *Glouc. Rental, 1455*, 51; Glouc. Cath. Libr., Reg. Abb. Braunche, p. 156.
[39] 'Gloucester', *Historic Towns*, ed. M. D. Lobel, i (1969), 3.
[40] *P.N. Glos.* (E.P.N.S.), ii. 129.

existed further west.[41] Hare Lane itself has the shape of an extramural market,[42] with Alvin gate[43] at its head, though no documentary or archaeological evidence for that has been found.

Also forming part of the northern suburbs in the late Anglo-Saxon period were probably Watering (later St. Catherine) Street running north from St. Oswald's minster and later occupied wholly by its tenants;[44] lower Northgate Street between the north gate and the northern branch of the river Twyver; and Fete Lane leading between the London road and Alvin gate.[45]

It has been suggested that the extent of the Anglo-Saxon *burh* is indicated by those tenements which later paid landgavel.[46] In a rental of the town in 1455 about the same number of tenements rendered landgavel as *c.* 1100.[47] The Gloucester landgavel differs, however, from that in some other towns in that it is not a unitary rent but varies with the value of the property: that may mean that it is a later version of the tax.[48] Furthermore, the landgavel distribution suggests an 11th- or even 12th-century assessment. For example, it was levied on properties west of the Foreign bridge, an area which both archaeological and documentary evidence suggest was not colonized before the 12th century; the name of the bridge also suggests that it was once the limit of the borough.[49] It seems that at Gloucester the landgavel payments were altered and updated until the 12th century at least; that they do not represent a pre-Conquest situation; and that the coincidence between the surveys of 1455 and *c.* 1100 is accidental.

The palace of Kingsholm existed by 1051, and various customary dues rendered in the king's hall and chamber are mentioned in Domesday Book.[50] It is possible that there was a palace at Gloucester by 896 when the Mercian council met in or near the town.[51] The later royal manor or liberty of King's Barton seems to have had its origin in an estate which was appropriated to the palace in the late Anglo-Saxon period to supply the royal household with food and administrative services.[52] A hoard of early 11th-century coins, said to have been found at Kingsholm, was so large that it must represent the taxes of a wide region[53] and implies a significant administrative centre. Excavations at Kingsholm have uncovered evidence of large timber buildings dating to the 11th century or earlier.[54]

The old minster of St. Peter, the mother church of Gloucester, was founded by Osric, under-king of the Hwicce, *c.* 679 and probably had a continuous existence in some form[55] until it underwent a Benedictine reform *c.* 1022.[56] Its church was rebuilt and its site moved in 1058,[57] but it remained a small establishment until the time of the first Norman abbot, Serlo.[58] St. Oswald's minster was founded *c.* 900 by Ethelfleda, Lady of the Mercians,[59] and in 909 it received the relics of King Oswald of Northumbria. The endowing of more than one of Ethelfleda's royal boroughs with a minster and important relics may have been part of a political policy aimed at

[41] *Glouc. Rental, 1455*, p. xvi; G.B.R., J 4/1, at end.

[42] Cf. St. Giles, Oxford: Keene, 'Suburban Development', *Plans and Topography of Medieval Towns* (1976), 71–3.

[43] Also an O.E. name: *P.N. Glos.* (E.P.N.S.), ii. 126.

[44] Below, Medieval Glouc., topog.

[45] Its name is from the O.E. female name 'Feta': *P.N. Glos.* (E.P.N.S.), ii. 128–9.

[46] *Trans. Inst. Brit. Geographers* N.S. ii (3), 267–8; cf. J. Tait, *Medieval Eng. Borough* (1936), 89.

[47] *Glouc. Rental, 1455.*

[48] Cf. F. Hill, *Medieval Lincoln* (1948), 58.

[49] Heighway, 'A.-S. Glouc. to A.D. 1100', figs. 5–6; *Antiq. Jnl.* liv. 49; *Glouc. Rental, 1455*, 53–4, 59.

[50] *Vita Edwardi*, ed. F. Barlow, 21; *Dom. Bk.* (Rec. Com.), i. 162.

[51] Finberg, *Early Charters of W. Midlands*, p. 50.

[52] Cf. below, Outlying Hamlets, agric.; Medieval Glouc., Crown and boro.; military hist.

[53] *Brit. Numis. Jnl.* xxix. 70–80.

[54] *Antiq. Jnl.* lv. 274; Hurst, *Kingsholm.*

[55] Finberg, *Early Charters of W. Midlands*, pp. 153–66.

[56] The date is problematic: *Hist. & Cart. Mon. Glouc.* (Rolls Ser.), i. 8 ascribes the foundation to Wulfstan, bp. of Worc., with the consent of Cnut. Wulfstan was jointly abp. of York and bp. of Worc. 1003–1016, but after 1016 abp. of York only.

[57] *A.-S. Chron.* 134.

[58] *V.C.H. Glos.* ii. 53–4.

[59] Wm. of Malmesbury, *Gesta Pontificum* (Rolls Ser.), 293.

conciliation of Mercia during the 'Reconquest' of the Danelaw.[60] The church was always closely connected with the royal administrative centre at Kingsholm, whose chapel it served. St. Oswald's was later a royal free chapel, and probably had that status from its foundation. Its parish was very large and fragmented and was entangled with the parish of St. Mary de Lode, which itself appears to represent the remnants of the parish of the old minster. The two parishes together, with dependent chapels taken into account, cover a large part of the hundred of Dudstone and King's Barton, and may represent a survival of the original territory with which the old minster was endowed c. 679.[61]

Without extensive archaeological investigation, it is impossible to tell which of Gloucester's churches were in existence in the Anglo-Saxon period; the earliest documentary record for most of them comes in the 12th century.[62] There were ten churches by c. 1100,[63] a total which presumably included those which were technically chapels. A number of the churches may have been recent foundations: even in London very few churches were built before the late 10th century.[64] The fact that nearly all Gloucester churches acquired burial rights only in the 14th or 15th centuries, if then, is a reminder of the supreme importance of the old minster, which, with its church of St. Mary de Lode, was the parish church of town and suburbs until well after the Norman Conquest. It is clear from a dispute of 1143 about the burial of Miles, earl of Hereford, that the abbey claimed burial rights over the whole town within the walls (as well as the castle precinct), though in that case an exception was made and Miles was buried at Llanthony Priory. By 1197 Lanthony Priory had apparently won partial burial rights over its parishes of St. Mary de Crypt and St. Owen.[65] The exceptional status of St. Mary de Lode is shown by the fact that it had burial rights by the 11th century.[66] St. Oswald's minster had burials from its foundation.[67]

Apart from St. Peter, St. Mary de Lode, and St. Oswald, there were probably other Anglo-Saxon churches, without right of baptism or burial but neverthless maintained by their local communities. The earliest of those churches are likely to be those with the largest parishes and with land outside the town walls,[68] that is, St. John, St. Kyneburgh, St. Michael, and, probably, St. Mary de Crypt. The centre of a royal estate would certainly have had a chapel, and it is very likely that the chapel at Kingsholm was founded by the time of Edward the Confessor, though there is no documentary evidence for it before the early 13th century.[69]

St. Mary de Crypt parish lay inside the walls, but an extramural portion may have been assigned by the mid 11th century to St. Kyneburgh.[70] St. Michael's parish included an extramural area at Barton Street east of the town. St. Mary de Crypt and St. Michael, together with All Saints, a chapel to St. Mary de Crypt, later belonged to the bishop of Exeter[71] and presumably formed part of an estate that Bishop Osbern held in the town in 1086 and a man called Edmarus before the Conquest.[72] When St. Michael's church was pulled down in the 1950s excavation produced fragmentary remains of what was almost certainly a Saxon church.[73] It was in an area of 9th- and 10th-century organic material which had collected in the Roman *forum*.[74] The chapel

[60] *Northern Hist.* xviii. 211.
[61] *Antiq. Jnl.* lx. 219–20.
[62] Below, Churches and Chapels.
[63] *Glouc. Rental, 1455*, p. xv.
[64] C. Brooke and G. Kier, *London: the Shaping of a City* (1975), 128–9.
[65] *Hist. & Cart. Mon. Glouc.* i, pp. lxxv–viii.
[66] *Glevensis*, xiv. 8–9.   [67] *Antiq. Jnl.* lx. 217.

[68] *Jnl. Brit. Arch. Assoc.* xxxv. 50. For par. boundaries in Glouc., Causton, *Map of Glouc.* (1843).
[69] Below, Churches and Chapels, non-par. chapels.
[70] Below.
[71] Below, Churches and Chapels.
[72] *Dom. Bk.* (Rec. Com.), i. 162.
[73] *Trans. B.G.A.S.* lxxx. 59–74.
[74] *Med. Arch.* xxiii. 159–213.

10

of St. Martin, which belonged to St. Michael's in the 13th century, bore a dedication which suggests that it was another of the early churches. All Saints, which like St. Michael and St. Martin stood at the central crossroads of the town,[75] has been claimed as a Saxon building, though it could equally well belong to the late 11th century. When it was excavated in the 1890s one of the discoveries was a bear's head in stone which may be Saxon work.[76]

The chapel of St. Kyneburgh at the south gate was given to St. Owen's church after the Conquest and to Llanthony Priory in 1137.[77] A mid 12th-century list of the priory's endowments included 'the chapel of St. Kyneburgh and the whole of the parish inside and outside the south gate'.[78] The wording implies that the parish and chapel were connected. The parish boundary of St. Owen reinforces that impression: it comprised an extramural area and a small area inside the south gate which included St. Kyneburgh's chapel. It seems likely that St. Owen's parish had formerly belonged to St. Kyneburgh, to which a parish may still earlier have been assigned out of that of St. Mary de Crypt. The dedication to the legendary princess Kyneburgh[79] is clearly apocryphal, but the invention may hide a genuine early dedication to the Kyneburgh who became first abbess of the old minster c. 679. The position of the chapel, sited over the Roman gate, may also imply an early date. Other Roman gates of the town survived until the 11th century[80] and it is possible that there was an Anglo-Saxon gate-chapel set in the Roman structure. The later alignment, both of the western portion of the chapel and of the almshouses which replaced the rest of it in the mid 16th century, was close to a true east–west alignment[81] and was not a Roman one, but that is likely to have resulted from a rebuilding of the chapel c. 1147.[82]

The parish of St. Aldate in the north-east part of the walled area may have housed the 30 burgesses who at Domesday belonged to the church of St. Denis, Paris,[83] for St. Aldate's church later belonged to Deerhurst Priory, which had been granted to St. Denis by Edward the Confessor.[84] Its parish boundary, which followed the backs of the tenements on the side streets, was probably not established before the 12th century but the church, in view of its connection with Deerhurst, may well have had a pre-Conquest origin.

The physical appearance of Gloucester in the late Anglo-Saxon period seems to have been that of any small urban community. We know of no stone houses of the 10th and 11th centuries. Domestic buildings were of timber in the 9th and 10th centuries, either built of posts hammered into the ground and interwoven wattle[85] or of more solid construction. A 10th-century building at the top of Westgate Street incorporated a cellar constructed of a series of upright posts linked by sill-beams.[86] Such timber cellars were probably more common by the 11th century.[87] The houses above the cellars were undoubtedly timber-framed, and, like buildings of similar type in other towns, could have had more than one storey.[88]

It should be possible to chart by the development of crafts and trades the growth of Gloucester from the small, sub-urban or proto-urban settlement of the 9th century to the developed small town which appears in the late 11th century; but insufficient archaeological work has been done. The economy of the 9th-century settlement was purely domestic, including extensive use (and therefore probably manufacture) of

[75] Below, Churches and Chapels.
[76] *Trans. B.G.A.S.* xix. 142–58.
[77] Below, Churches and Chapels, non-par. chapels.
[78] *Camd. Misc.* xxii, p. 43.
[79] *Hist. & Cart. Mon. Glouc.* i, pp. lxiv–ix.
[80] Heighway, *Gates of Glouc.*
[81] Hall and Pinnell, *Map of Glouc.* (1780).

[82] *Hist. & Cart. Mon. Glouc.* i, p. lxvii n.
[83] *Dom. Bk.* (Rec. Com.), i. 166.
[84] Below, Churches and Chapels; *V.C.H. Glos.* ii. 103.
[85] *Med. Arch.* xxiii. 167–9; *Antiq. Jnl.* lii. 58–61.
[86] *Med. Arch.* xxiii. 167–8.
[87] *Antiq. Jnl.* lii. 44.
[88] *Arch. Jnl.* cxxxvi. 70; *Arch. of A.-S. Eng.* (1976), 49–98.

wooden objects and leather working. There was no pottery, and no iron nails or other iron objects; by contrast, the late 11th-century town rendered to the Crown a payment of '36 *dicras* of iron, and one hundred rods of ductile iron for making nails for the king's ships'.[89] The 10th-century town produced its own pottery, objects of silver, and glass.[90] Apart from that, economic activity in the town was little different in the 10th century from what it had been in the 9th. The quantity of 10th-century pottery was very small, and its distribution was confined to the principal streets. The true economic upturn seems to have occurred in the 11th century, when pottery becomes more abundant and its types more varied.[91] It was also in the 11th century that the frontages of the subsidiary streets began to be built up, though only in the 12th do they show signs of being fairly densely occupied.[92]

It is possible to see as one of the causes of the economic improvement the increase of royal attention. In the 10th century no significant events are recorded after the death of Athelstan at Gloucester in 939,[93] but 11th-century Gloucester saw a number of royal visits and councils. Edmund Ironside was at Gloucester in 1016[94] and Harthacnut came to the town at least once.[95] Under Edward the Confessor Gloucester was the meeting place of the council nine times between 1043 and 1062.[96] Those gatherings, some of considerable size, are likely to have been held in the hall at Kingsholm. The strategic importance of Gloucester, the result of the positioning of the original Roman fortress, was also evident in the 11th century. In 1051 Edward the Confessor assembled forces at Gloucester against Godwin's revolt;[97] in 1055 levies of troops gathered there to meet Earl Alfgar's revolt;[98] and in 1063 Gloucester was the starting point of Harold's expedition against the Welsh.[99]

There is, therefore, a contrast between the economic evidence, as provided by archaeology, and the topographical and historical implications of an early 10th-century foundation. Gloucester in the 10th century was economically a minor centre but the attention of Ethelfleda of Mercia gave it the status and pattern of a *burh* and provided it with a new minster richly endowed in relics and property. The town had its royal palace and its mint. Its administrative importance is shown by the fact that it became, perhaps by the early 11th century, the shire town.[1] Like 9th-century Winchester, 10th-century Gloucester had an adminstrative importance belied by its status as judged by trading activity.[2] The truth seems to be that the patronage of Ethelfleda provided the initial impetus for economic growth, which, though not entirely extinguished by her death, began to bear fruit only a century or more later.

[89] *Dom. Bk.* (Rec. Com.), i. 162.
[90] *Med. Arch.* xxiii. 201, 205.
[91] A. G. Vince, *Medieval Pottery* (Brit. Arch. Rep. S 120). 300–22.   [92] Heighway, 'A.-S. Glouc. to A.D. 1100'.
[93] Stenton, *A.-S. Eng.* (1947), 352; *A.-S. Chron.* 70.
[94] Wm. of Malmesbury, *Gesta Regum* (Rolls Ser.), 217.
[95] Symeon of Durham, *Hist. Eccl. Dunelm.* (Rolls Ser.), i. 85–6.
[96] T. J. Oleson, *Witenagemot in Reign of Edward the*

Confessor (1955), 71, 159–60.
[97] *A.-S. Chron.* 118.
[98] Ibid. 131.
[99] Ibid. 136.
[1] C. Taylor, 'Origin of the Mercian Shires', Finberg, *Glos. Studies*, 17–51; Stenton, *A.-S. Eng.* 293.
[2] M. Biddle, 'Winchester: the Development of an early Capital', *Vor und Frühformen der europäischen Stadt in Mittelalter* (Gottingen, 1973), 247.

MEDIEVAL GLOUCESTER
1066–1547

Gloucester 1066–1327

A T the time of the Norman Conquest Gloucester was already well established as an urban community and had acquired many of the features that were to govern its fortunes during the next few centuries.[1] A royal borough in which 300 burgesses, possibly about half the total, held their land directly from the Crown[2] and the site of a royal palace set at the centre of a large agricultural estate, Gloucester enjoyed a close relationship with the rulers of England. It was unchallenged as the focus of shire administration and was also the trading centre for a wide region; within its county Bristol and Winchcombe were probably the only other places with urban characteristics. The industry which was to be the most significant in the next two or three centuries, the working of iron from the Forest of Dean, was already established.[3] The town's mint was among the thirteen or so main producers of coin in England.[4] It was also a religious centre with two monastic houses and possibly as many as eight churches and chapels. Its established position as a shire town, as well perhaps as its Roman origins, was reflected in the term *civitas* which was applied to it in the 11th and 12th centuries;[5] later, as that term became restricted to places with cathedrals, Gloucester was styled a town or borough until it was made a city by charter at the founding of Gloucester diocese in 1541.[6]

Gloucester's most obvious importance to the new rulers of England was its strategic position in relation to South Wales. The crossing of the Severn controlled by the town was rapidly secured by a castle, which was rebuilt on a more substantial scale in the early 12th century.[7] The castle was entrusted by the Norman kings to a notable family of royal servants who, as hereditary castellans and sheriffs of the county, were dominant in the history of Gloucester for a century after the Conquest.[8]

The continuing royal interest in Gloucester that its strategic importance ensured, as well as its inherent strength as a trading centre, were needed to overcome a period of disruption and depopulation in the years following the Conquest. A survey dating from between 1096 and 1101 records that of the 300 royal burgages that had existed in Edward the Confessor's reign 82 were uninhabited and another 24 had been removed to make way for the castle; half of the remainder had changed hands since the Conquest, many of the new tenants being Normans. In addition to the core of royal burgesses there were 314 who held from other landlords. The total of 508 burgesses[9] perhaps indicates a total population of about 3,000. The farm owed from the town, which had been £36 with various renders and customs in Edward the Confessor's reign and £38 4s. (presumably also with the traditional renders) in the time of Roger

---

[1] This chapter was written in 1982–3.
[2] *Glouc. Rental, 1455*, pp. xiv–xv.
[3] *Dom. Bk.* (Rec. Com.), i. 162.
[4] Stenton, *A.-S. Eng.* (1947), 529–30.
[5] *Dom. Bk.* (Rec. Com.), i, 162; *Glouc. Rental, 1455*, pp. xiv–xv; *Hist. & Cart. Mon. Glouc.* (Rolls Ser.), i. 14–15,

22; cf. F. W. Maitland, *Dom. Bk. and Beyond* (1907), 183 n.
[6] *Glouc. Corp. Rec.* p. 20.
[7] Below, Glouc. Castle.
[8] Below, Crown and boro.; military hist.
[9] *Glouc. Rental, 1455*, pp. xiv–xv.

of Gloucester as sheriff soon after the Conquest, had been fixed at £60 by 1086; *c.* 1100, however, only £51 4*s.* appears to have been received.[10]

Domesday Book and the later survey reveal a complex pattern of landholding in the town, one that presumably dated in many of its essentials from before the Conquest. Apart from the Crown 25 other lords had burgesses *c.* 1100, the largest holdings being the archbishop of York's 60, held in right of St. Oswald's minster, and Gloucester Abbey's 52. The smaller estates included 6 burgesses of Samson, bishop of Exeter, apparently the remnant of a significant estate in the Southgate Street area which his predecessor Bishop Osbern had held, and the 15 burgesses of Walter of Gloucester, the hereditary sheriff and castellan. The other estates were mostly attached to outlying manors,[11] 17 of which had burgesses in Gloucester in 1086.[12] The largest holdings were attached to two important pre-Conquest estates in the neighbourhood: Deerhurst Priory, which became a possession of the abbey of St. Denis, Paris, after the Conquest, had 30 burgesses in Gloucester in 1086, while Tewkesbury manor had 8;[13] *c.* 1100 36 burgesses were attached to Deerhurst, while Robert FitzHamon, lord of Tewkesbury, had 22.[14] Two other manors with large holdings were Bisley with 11 burgesses in 1086 and Kempsford with 7.[15] The generally accepted explanation for such burgages attached to outlying manors, that they provided the parent manor with a foothold for conducting trade and business in the county town, is supported in the case of Gloucester. Most of the places concerned were distant Cotswold manors for which some such arrangement would be most useful; and for two of them, Quenington, which had a smith owing a cash rent and another burgess owing a rent in ploughshares, and Woodchester, which had a burgess owing a rent in iron,[16] the arrangement was a means of taking advantage of Gloucester's ironworking industry.

The century following the Norman Conquest saw major additions to Gloucester's complement of religious institutions. The survey of *c.* 1100 records that there were already 10 churches in Gloucester[17] and, as suggested above, most of them were probably founded before 1066.[18] Those added after the Conquest almost certainly included St. Owen's church, outside the south gate, which was probably founded by the first hereditary sheriff, Roger of Gloucester, whose son Walter added further endowments. Other late foundations were possibly the three churches with small compact parishes straddling the main market area, All Saints at the Cross and St. Mary de Grace and Holy Trinity in upper Westgate Street. The advowsons of the two last churches belonged to the Crown in the early 13th century and they were perhaps royal foundations, further manifestations of the interest shown in Gloucester by the early Norman kings. Another possibility is that they were built by wealthy townsmen, whose estates later escheated to the Crown. A total of 11 churches, all in existence by the later 12th century, exercised parochial functions in the town and its adjoining hamlets and there were also a number of non-parochial chapels.[19]

The two oldest religious houses of the town enjoyed very different fortunes after the Conquest. Under the rule of the able and energetic Abbot Serlo from 1072, Gloucester Abbey became one of the leading Benedictine houses of England. Its alienated property was recovered and additional gifts were attracted, the church was

---

[10] *Dom. Bk.* (Rec. Com.), i. 162; *Glouc. Rental, 1455*, p. xv. The Dom. Bk. account of Glouc. confines itself mainly to listing burgages that had been alienated from the royal demesne or were attached to outlying manors.

[11] *Glouc. Rental, 1455*, pp. xiv–xv.

[12] The list given in Taylor, *Dom. Glos.* 128, omits Brimpsfield and has Wheatenhurst for Woodchester.

[13] *Dom. Bk.* (Rec. Com.), i. 163, 166.

[14] *Glouc. Rental, 1455*, p. xiv.

[15] *Dom. Bk.* (Rec. Com.), i. 166v., 169.

[16] Ibid. 167v., 170v.

[17] *Glouc. Rental, 1455*, p. xv.

[18] Above, A.-S. Glouc.

[19] Below, Churches and Chapels.

rebuilt, and the community was much enlarged.[20] The abbey's possessions in the town and immediate neighbourhood gave it a major involvement in town affairs in succeeding centuries, sometimes bringing it into conflict with the burgess community.[21] The minster of St. Oswald passed under the control of the archbishop of York and was later weakened by disputes between the archbishop and the bishop of Worcester and archbishop of Canterbury about jurisdiction. Although reconstituted *c.* 1150 as a priory of Augustinian canons, St. Oswald's remained a relatively poor house.[22] In wealth and property, as well as in influence in the town and locality, it was outstripped by the new Augustinian priory of Llanthony Secunda, which was established on land on the south side of the town by Miles of Gloucester in 1137.[23] Three hospitals for the sick were founded at the approaches to the town in the 12th century. The leper hospital of St. Mary Magdalen, also called the hospital of Dudstone, was established on the London road at Wotton, probably by Walter of Gloucester in the early 12th century; Roger of Gloucester, earl of Hereford, augmented the endowment in the early 1150s[24] and the hospital was subsequently controlled by the family's foundation, Llanthony Priory.[25] Another leper hospital, St. Margaret, originally St. Sepulchre,[26] had been established on a nearby site by the mid 12th century; Gloucester Abbey then controlled it[27] but in the late Middle Ages it was managed by the burgess community of Gloucester.[28] A third hospital, St. Bartholomew, at the western approach to the town, between the Foreign and Westgate bridges, was according to tradition founded in Henry II's reign in connection with a rebuilding of Westgate bridge. It was reconstituted under the rule of a prior after Henry III endowed it with St. Nicholas's church in 1229.[29]

Gloucester's varied collection of religious foundations provided objects of piety to suit all tastes and a stream of gifts of land and rents was directed towards them by the burgesses of the 12th and 13th centuries. Some burgesses preferred to endow external religious houses, and Cirencester,[30] Flaxley,[31] Winchcombe,[32] Godstow (Oxon.),[33] and Eynsham (Oxon.)[34] were among those to acquire property in the town. An alternative form of pious donation, the founding of chantries in the parish churches, had begun by the mid 13th century.[35]

Another community established in Gloucester after the Conquest was formed by the Jews, who had their quarter in Eastgate Street.[36] Jews are recorded in the town from 1168, when they were alleged to have carried out the ritual murder of a boy,[37] and a Gloucester Jew was advancing money to those going to Ireland with Strongbow's expedition in 1170.[38] A prosperous member of the community at that period was Moses le Riche, whose heir owed the Crown 300 marks in 1192 for the right to have his debts.[39] In the early years of the 13th century Gloucester Jews were financing local magnates, such as Henry de Bohun, earl of Hereford, and Roger de Berkeley,[40], and their activities among the burgess community at the same period are revealed by sales of property to pay off debts owed to the Jews or to redeem

[20] *V.C.H. Glos.* ii. 53–4.
[21] Below, town and religious communities.
[22] *V.C.H. Glos.* ii. 84–6.   [23] Ibid. 87.
[24] E.J. Kealey, *Medieval Medicus* (1981), 112.
[25] *Glouc. Corp. Rec.* p. 119; P.R.O., C 115/K 2/6684, f.90v.
[26] *Glouc. Corp. Rec.* pp. 71, 75, 77.
[27] *V.C.H. Glos.* ii. 121; cf. Kealey, *Medieval Medicus*, 133; Glouc. Cath. Libr., Reg. Abb. Froucester B, pp. 228–9, where the abbey described it as 'our hospital'.
[28] Below, town and religious communities.
[29] *V.C.H. Glos.* ii. 119–20.
[30] *Ciren. Cart.* ii, pp. 388–98.
[31] *Flaxley Cart.* ed. A.W. Crawley-Boevey (Exeter, 1887),

pp. 113, 156, 173, 195–6.
[32] *Reg. Mon. Winch.* i. 74–5, 116–20.
[33] *Godstow Reg.* (E.E.T.S. orig. ser. 142), i, pp. 139–50.
[34] *Eynsham Cart.* i (Oxford Hist. Soc. xlix), pp. 204, 228–9.
[35] Below, Churches and Chapels, ancient par. ch.; *Reg. Mon. Winch.* i. 116–20.
[36] *Ciren. Cart.* ii, p. 397; *Glouc. Corp. Rec.* p. 303.
[37] *Hist. & Cart. Mon. Glouc.* i. 20–1.
[38] *Pipe R.* 1170 (P.R.S. xv), 78.
[39] Ibid. 1191 & 92 (P.R.S. N.S. ii), 292.
[40] Ibid. 1205 (P.R.S. N.S. xix), 98; 1207 (P.R.S. N.S. xxii), 216.

mortgages.[41] Some 13th-century Jews acquired considerable property outside the Jewish quarter, among them Ellis of Gloucester (d. c. 1216)[42] and Jacob Coprun (d. c. 1265).[43] The Jews of Gloucester had a grant of royal protection in 1218 and were placed in the custody of 24 burgesses.[44] The Jews' chest for keeping the chirographs of debts, in the custody of a Christian and a Jew, was mentioned in 1253.[45] The tallage levied on the Jews in 1255, when those at Gloucester were assessed at 30 marks, suggests that the community was then among the 18 leading Jewries of England.[46] The Gloucester Jews were removed to Bristol in 1275 at the insistence of the lady of the borough, Queen Eleanor, who had been promised that the towns she received in dower should not contain any Jews.[47]

The proliferation of Gloucester's religious institutions and the attraction to it of a large Jewish community are among indications of the economic vitality of the town during the 12th and 13th centuries. Aids raised from the English towns during Henry II's reign suggest that Gloucester may then have ranked about ninth in order of prosperity, well behind such great regional centres as York and Norwich but among the leading county towns, on a par with such places as Oxford and Winchester.[48] No equivalent information survives at that period, however, for Bristol, the town which over succeeding centuries was to dominate the region in which Gloucester lay and exert a significant influence over its economic fortunes. When a levy of men for service overseas was made in 1212 Gloucester and Bristol both had to supply 30,[49] but an aid of 1210, when Gloucester was assessed at 500 marks and Bristol at 1,000,[50] probably provides a more accurate indication of their relative size and prosperity. Within the northern half of Gloucestershire, however, Gloucester was not seriously challenged as the trading and administrative centre. Among neighbouring settlements Tewkesbury and Cirencester became market towns soon after the Norman Conquest, but both remained much smaller than Gloucester. Of the many other places which gained markets between the late 12th and early 14th centuries several in the immediate area of Gloucester, including Newent, Cheltenham, Painswick, and Newnham, were moderately successful and made some impact on its market trade but in the expanding economic climate of the period looked to Gloucester as the centre for the supply of manufactured and imported goods.

Gloucester's trading connections with the smaller market towns of its region and its own local market area were among the diverse elements that provided its livelihood. It had an industrial base supplied in particular by ironworking, for which it was widely known at that period, and by clothmaking; it played a part in the trade of the river Severn and, mainly through Bristol, in overseas trade; and its control of the trade routes out of South Wales benefited it from before the time of the Edwardian conquest.[51] The general impression to be gained from the available information is of a steadily prospering economy, though the local financial records needed to endorse such an impression do not survive. An isolated bailiffs' account roll, for 1264–5, records the fairly substantial sum of £49 18s. 5d. produced by the tolls on trade and that at a time when the local economy was disrupted by fighting in and around Gloucester.[52]

[41] e.g. *Glouc. Corp. Rec.* pp. 95, 121, 133; Glouc. Cath. Libr., Reg. Abb. Froucester B, p. 453; P.R.O., C 115/K 1/6681, ff. 99v., 105v.

[42] *Rot. Litt. Claus.* (Rec. Com.), i. 283, 317.

[43] *Close R.* 1264–8, 68, 235.

[44] *Rot. Litt. Claus.* (Rec. Com.), i. 354.

[45] *Select Pleas from Exchequer of Jews* (Selden Soc. xv), 28; *Close R.* 1264–8, 42–3.   [46] *Cal. Pat.* 1247–58, 441–4.

[47] *Select Pleas from Exchequer of Jews* (Selden Soc. xv), 85.

[48] C. Stephenson, *Borough and Town* (1933), 225.

[49] *Rot. Litt. Claus.* (Rec. Com.), i. 130.

[50] *Pipe R.* 1210 (P.R.S. N.S. xxvi), 143.

[51] Below, trade and ind. 1066–1327.

[52] G.B.R., F 3/1; cf. below, Crown and boro.; military hist.

Gloucester also benefited from its role as an administrative centre. From its castle the sheriff carried on the county government, while the town was also the venue for the justices in eyre, visiting commissions, and inquisitions of all kinds. Such events brought many people regularly to Gloucester, including inhabitants of Bristol before that town won separate county status in 1373.[53] Religious houses such as Winchcombe Abbey found it advisable to maintain lodgings for use when business brought the monks to Gloucester.[54] The town remained the site of a mint at least until the recoinage of 1248,[55] probably losing that role at a reorganization of mints in 1279.[56] Its status was also enhanced and its economy benefited by the regular visits of king and court, which continued until the mid 13th century, and by a role as a supply base during royal campaigns in Wales. Less beneficial to its economic well-being was the part its strategic position led it to play in the upheavals of the reigns of Stephen, Henry III, and Edward II.[57]

In the later 12th century the townspeople of Gloucester emerged as a community with political objectives and the wealth to acquire them from the Crown. The town secured its first charter at the beginning of Henry II's reign and in 1165 became one of the earliest places to be given the right of fee farm. An attempt soon afterwards by a group of leading burgesses to gain greater freedom from royal control was suppressed and the achievement of the right to elect bailiffs, under a charter of 1200, was the next major advance. Following that the exclusion of the county sheriff and other royal officials from interfering in their affairs remained a goal.[58] The government of the town, carried on until 1483 by the two bailiffs, acting mainly through the hundred court, settled into an oligarchical pattern; the bailiffs were drawn from a recognized class of wealthier burgesses,[59] apparently composed in the 13th century and the early 14th by the leading merchants in wine and wool and the principal wholesalers, such as mercers and drapers.[60]

Under the influence of its varied economic and administrative functions Gloucester expanded, its progress only temporarily disrupted by fires which devastated its main trading streets on several occasions in the late 12th century and the early 13th.[61] From the later 12th century suburban growth was recorded on monastic land outside the north, east, and south gates.[62] A clause in the town's charter of 1227 protecting absconded villeins who had been in the town for a year and a day from being reclaimed by their lords[63] suggests that numbers of immigrants were then being attracted to Gloucester. Surnames of 13th-century inhabitants that derived from place-names show that such immigration was mainly from a local area of north Gloucestershire villages; a few men had come from a greater distance, from Midland towns such as Ludlow, Kidderminster, Banbury, Warwick, and Northampton, and from Brecon and Abergavenny,[64] places on the main route into Wales which Gloucester commanded.

Other immigrants attracted to the town at the period were the friars: the Franciscans and Dominicans founded communities in the 1230s and the Carmelites in the 1260s.[65] The establishment of friaries in the 13th century has been seen as an index of the status of towns; Gloucester was one of 20 towns in England, but one of

[53] *Bristol Charters* (Bristol Rec. Soc. i), 119.
[54] *Reg. Mon. Winch.* i. 119.
[55] *Chron. Johannis de Oxenedes* (Rolls Ser.), 319.
[56] Cf. Powicke, *13th Cent.* (1962), 633.
[57] Below, Crown and boro.; military hist.
[58] Below, achievement of liberties.
[59] Below, town govt. 1200-1483.
[60] Below, trade and ind. 1066-1327.

[61] *Hist. & Cart. Mon. Glouc.* i. 22, 24, 26.
[62] Below, topog.
[63] *Glouc. Corp. Rec.* p. 9.
[64] The main sources for 13th-cent. surnames are property deeds in ibid. pp. 70-294; P.R.O., C 115/K 1/6681; and Glouc. Cath. Libr., Reg. Abb. Froucester B.
[65] *V.C.H. Glos.* ii. 111-12.

only 4 in the western half of the country, which attracted three or more different orders.[66]

The population of Gloucester during the period is difficult even to guess at, with the 1327 subsidy, for which 257 people were assessed, providing the first indication after the record of *c*. 1100. The total population in the early 14th century was perhaps around 4,000. The total sum for which Gloucester was assessed in 1327 was £28 4s. 8¼d.,[67] compared with Bristol at £80 12s. and Cirencester and Tewkesbury at £13 4s. 2¼d. and £10 3s. 6d. respectively.[68] Among English towns as a whole Gloucester then ranked about 16th in order of wealth.[69]

The Crown and the Borough; Military History

After the Conquest the royal borough of Gloucester retained the close connexion with the Crown that had been established under the Anglo-Saxon kings. Continuing royal interest was ensured by the town's strategic position, which made it an obvious site for a castle and gave it a significant role in most of the upheavals of the earlier Middle Ages. By 1086 and until the beginning of Henry I's reign Gloucester was the accepted venue for the Christmas crown-wearing of the Norman kings, one of three held at the great festivals of the year; in practice William I and his son seem to have kept as many Christmases at Westminster as at Gloucester.[70] It was at the Christmas council at Gloucester in 1085 that William I gave the order for the compilation of Domesday Book.[71] William II's visits included that in Lent 1093 when he almost died of an illness and another later the same year when he delivered the snub to Malcolm, king of Scotland, which broke the truce between the two kingdoms.[72] The Norman kings may have continued to use the palace at Kingsholm, and for the support of their household they kept in hand the large royal manor of King's Barton adjoining the town. It was presumably for ease of carrying on the government from Gloucester that a king's scribe held a house in the town in the late 11th century and the earlier 12th[73] and that six tenants of King's Barton held by the serjeanty of writ-carrying.[74]

For a few years immediately following the Conquest, probably while the first castle was being constructed, Gloucester was held at farm by William FitzOsbern (d. 1071), earl of Hereford, and so was attached to the great lordship created to secure the southern Marches.[75] In that period or soon afterwards the new castle was placed in the charge of Roger of Gloucester (or de Pîtres), whose family, as hereditary castellans and sheriffs of the county, was to dominate Gloucester for the next 100 years.[76] Roger died before 1086 when his offices and his estates in the county were held by his brother Durand. They passed before 1100 to Roger's son Walter of Gloucester who rebuilt the castle on a more substantial scale[77] and added the office of royal constable to the family's responsibilities. By 1126 Walter had become a monk at Llanthony Prima (Mon.) and been succeeded by his son Miles, who acquired extensive Welsh estates and founded Llanthony Secunda at Gloucester in 1137.[78]

During Stephen's reign Gloucester became one of the principal strongholds of the Angevin cause following Miles of Gloucester's declaration of support for the Empress

---

[66] S. Reynolds, *Intro. to Hist. of Eng. Med. Towns* (1977), 51, 63.
[67] *Glos. Subsidy Roll, 1327*, 1–2.
[68] Ibid. 4, 37.
[69] W. G. Hoskins, *Local Hist. in Eng.* (1972), 238.
[70] M. Biddle, 'Seasonal Festivals and Residence' (TS. of a paper given at C.B.A. conference, Apr. 1975).
[71] *A.-S. Chron.* ed. D. Whitelock (1961), 161.
[72] Ibid. 170.

[73] *Dom. Bk.* (Rec. Com.), i. 162; *Camd. Misc.* xxii, pp. 14–15.
[74] *Hist. & Cart. Mon. Glouc.* iii. 69.
[75] *Dom. Bk.* (Rec. Com.), i. 162.
[76] The account of the fam. given here is based on D. Walker, 'Miles of Glouc., Earl of Heref.', *Trans. B.G.A.S.* lxxvii. 66–84.
[77] Below, Glouc. Castle.
[78] *V.C.H. Glos.* ii. 87.

Maud. Miles, who was created earl of Hereford in 1141, escorted the empress to Gloucester on her arrival in England in 1139. She was at Gloucester again in February 1141 when Stephen was brought there after his capture at the battle of Lincoln and she retired there later the same year after her expulsion from London. On one of her visits the empress is recorded as exercising her rights in the borough by alienating part of the landgavel,[79] but for most of the period the local autonomy enjoyed by Miles and his son Roger, who succeeded on his death in 1143, made them in effect lords of the borough; they appear to have dealt as they wished with the royal demesne lands in the borough[80] and Earl Roger's control of the town is reflected in a grant of protection he made to the monks of Cirencester Abbey when they came on business.[81] Earl Roger's rebellion against Henry II in 1155 lost for the family its hereditary offices but his successors to the earldom of Hereford retained their connection with Gloucester, particularly as patrons of Llanthony Priory.

Henry II, who presumably was well disposed towards Gloucester as a result of the part it had played in the struggle against Stephen, granted the town its first charter of liberties and allowed the burgesses to farm the royal revenues for a period of 10 years.[82] During his reign and that of his successor Gloucester's military importance was as a supply base for operations against the Irish and Welsh. At the time of the Irish expedition of 1171 it was one of the assembly points for men and provisions and its iron industry provided much equipment for the army.[83] During the campaigns against Rhys ap Gruffudd in the early years of Richard I's reign men and supplies passed through Gloucester into South Wales.[84]

From King John the burgesses of Gloucester secured one of the most significant advances in their liberties, a charter of 1200 giving them the right to elect bailiffs, though they also suffered from shifts in the royal favour.[85] John was a fairly frequent visitor in the later years of his reign,[86] but his son, whose first coronation, in 1216, took place at Gloucester,[87] was perhaps the medieval king who had the closest connection with the town. During the first half of his reign Henry III was a regular visitor, coming three or four times in some years,[88] usually residing at the castle.[89] Several great councils met at Gloucester during the period, including that in 1233 when measures were taken to meet the threat from Richard Marshal, earl of Pembroke, and that in 1240 when David ap Llywelyn, ruler of Gwynedd, was reconciled to the king.[90] The town also continued its military role. The king ordered men and equipment to be sent from Gloucester when he was campaigning in mid Wales in 1228,[91] and in 1246 and 1247 the bailiffs of Gloucester were ordered to organize the carriage of provisions to the castles at Builth and Painscastle.[92] The army for the planned Irish expedition of 1233 was ordered to muster at Gloucester and requisitioned river craft were assembled there.[93]

Gloucester's strategic position ensured for it a prominent role in the period of the barons' war and the ascendancy of Simon de Montfort. It was involved in an early incident in the disturbances when, in 1263, John Giffard of Brimpsfield, Roger de Clifford, and other local dissidents successfully laid siege to the castle in an attempt to

[79] P.R.O., C 115/K 1/6681, f. 76v.
[80] Camd. Misc. xxii, pp. 14–15, 29.
[81] Ciren. Cart. iii, p. 739.
[82] Below, achievement of liberties.
[83] Pipe R. 1171 (P.R.S. xvi), 84, 87–8; 1172 (P.R.S. xviii), 119, 122.
[84] Ibid. 1190 (P.R.S. N.S. i), 4, 53; 1193 (P.R.S. N.S. iii), 148.
[85] Below, achievement of liberties.
[86] T. D. Hardy, Description of the Patent Rolls (and) Itin. of King John (Rec. Com.), passim.
[87] Rot. Litt. Claus. (Rec. Com.), i. 360.
[88] 'Itin. of Hen. III' (1923, TS. at P.R.O.).
[89] e.g. Rot. Litt. Claus. (Rec. Com.), i. 359; ii. 91; Close R. 1237–42, 57; 1247–51, 476.
[90] Powicke, 13th Cent. 53–4, 58, 60, 398; Close R. 1237–42, 437.
[91] Cal. Lib. 1226–40, 115.
[92] Ibid. 1245–51, 67, 104
[93] Close R. 1231–4, 317, 542.

remove the French knight Maci de Bezille from his office as county sheriff.[94] The castle was later garrisoned for the Crown by Roger de Clifford who, having returned to his allegiance, was given custody of it at the end of 1263.[95] The following February, as forces led by de Montfort's sons moved westwards to attack the lands of Roger Mortimer in the Marches, Clifford was ordered to fortify and hold the bridge at Gloucester, while all other bridges on the Severn were to be destroyed.[96] John Giffard and another local knight John de Balun gained entrance to the town in disguise and secured it for the Montfortian forces but the castle held out until Edward, the king's son, came to its relief at the beginning of March and concluded a truce with the rebels under which they withdrew from Gloucester. The prince is said to have imposed heavy fines on the burgesses for having allowed the rebels in.[97] Gloucester was once more at the centre of events in the spring of 1265 when Simon de Montfort came there with the king in an attempt to reach an agreement with Gilbert de Clare, earl of Gloucester, who, with John Giffard, took refuge in the Forest of Dean. There was a further siege in June of that year when, during the campaign that ended in the battle of Evesham, Edward captured the town from a garrison left by de Montfort.[98] The town and surrounding countryside apparently suffered considerably during the events of the period. In 1266 arrears owed by Gloucester Abbey in the farm of King's Barton manor were attributed to losses during the wars[99] and the poverty-stricken state of St. Bartholomew's Hospital in 1270 was said to result from the same cause.[1]

During the next two reigns the Crown's connections with the town were loosened. Edward I and Edward II were infrequent visitors,[2] though the former held parliament there in 1278 when the statute named from the town was promulgated.[3] After Henry III's death in 1272 the lordship of the borough passed in dower to Queen Eleanor (d. 1291), who was also given Gloucester castle and King's Barton manor.[4] The same rights passed on Edward I's death in 1307 to Queen Margaret.[5] After her death in 1318 the lordship was kept in hand by the kings, though the annual fee farm paid by the burgesses was usually alienated. Among those later granted the farm were Thomas de Bradeston, constable of the castle, who held it from 1330 until his death in 1360,[6] and two queens consort, Anne of Bohemia, first wife of Richard II,[7] and Joan of Navarre, second wife of Henry IV.[8].

In Edward II's reign Gloucester was once more heavily involved in disputes between Crown and barons. In July 1312, shortly after the execution of Gaveston, the king took steps to secure the town by granting custody and the role of 'keeper of the peace' there to Maurice de Berkeley, Lord Berkeley, ordering the townspeople to aid him in repairing the town's defences.[9] That appointment seems to imply not only the temporary suspension of Queen Margaret's rights but also an invasion of the liberties of the burgesses, and it presumably led the latter to seek the royal confirmation of one of their most important legal privileges that was granted a few weeks later.[10] The king held council at Gloucester in March 1321 when measures were taken to combat the military preparations of some of the Marcher lords.[11] In the last days of 1321 or the

[94] *Metrical Chron. of Rob. of Glouc.* (Rolls Ser.), ii. 736–8.
[95] Glos. R.O., D 4431 (no. 24006).
[96] *Close R.* 1261–4, 374.
[97] *Metrical Chron. of Rob. of Glouc.* ii. 740–6.
[98] Powicke, *13th Cent.* 199–202.
[99] *Close R.* 1264–8, 200–1.
[1] Ibid. 1268–72, 217.
[2] 'Itin. of Edw. I' (1935, TS. at P.R.O.); 'Itin. of Edw. II' (n.d., TS. at P.R.O.).

[3] *Statutes at Large*, i. 64.
[4] *Cal. Pat.* 1232–47, 394; 1272–81, 27; 1281–92, 444.
[5] Ibid. 1292–1301, 452; cf. ibid. 1317–21, 1.
[6] Ibid. 1330–4, 6, 43; *Cal. Inq. p.m.* x, pp. 478–9.
[7] *Cal. Pat.* 1381–5, 126; 1385–9, 55, 519.
[8] Ibid. 1401–5, 234.
[9] Ibid. 1307–13, 480, 484.
[10] *Glouc. Corp. Rec.* p. 11.
[11] *Cal. Close*, 1318–23, 364.

first of 1322 the town and castle were seized by local opponents of the Despensers led by John Giffard and Maurice de Berkeley, but the king recovered them early in February after his successes against the rebels in the Marches. It was at Gloucester that John Giffard, captured at the battle of Boroughbridge, was executed in May 1322.[12] Some of the leaders of the burgess community had sympathized with the rebels, among them the wealthy Robert of Goldhill, who was fined £100 as a result of his activities,[13] and John the tanner,[14] bailiff of the town in several previous years.[15] After the rising the town was once more placed under military government for a period: Gilbert Talbot was acting as 'keeper' of the town, castle, and King's Barton manor in November 1322 when the younger Hugh le Despenser was appointed to exercise superior custody.[16]

In October 1326 an order for forces from Wales and the Marches to muster at Gloucester to resist the invasion by Queen Isabella and Roger Mortimer was overtaken by events when the invaders themselves arrived there to be joined by dissident barons and their forces.[17] The burial of Edward II in Gloucester Abbey church in 1327[18] secured the favour of the new king for the town as well as the abbey: while in the town in December 1328, Edward III confirmed the borough charters 'in honour of the body of our father which lies buried at Gloucester'.[19] For the first few years of the new reign, however, Gloucester was secured for Mortimer's party: the castle was granted for life to Queen Isabella in 1327 and held by her until 1330.[20]

In the later Middle Ages Gloucester made much more occasional appearances at the centre of national affairs. It was once more the seat of government in the autumn of 1378 when parliament met in Gloucester Abbey,[21] and parliaments were again held there in 1406 and 1407. Once more, in 1403 during Owen Glendower's revolt, it saw a muster of troops to meet a threat from Wales.[22] The castle and the farm of the town were granted in 1462 to the infant Richard, duke of Gloucester, but the grant was apparently rescinded within a few years[23] and the castle was held during Edward IV's reign by successive constables Thomas Herbert the elder and Richard Beauchamp.[24] Beauchamp, aided by other Yorkist sympathisers in the town, made a decisive contribution to the campaign of 1471 when he prevented Queen Margaret's army from crossing the Severn at Gloucester in an attempt to reach supporters in Wales, forcing it to continue up river to be caught by the Yorkist army at Tewkesbury. A large body of townspeople was said, however, to have then supported the Lancastrians,[25] and it was presumably to some more recent service that Richard III referred in September 1483 when, shortly after visiting the town, he gave it a major grant of liberties in return for 'the good and faithful actions of the bailiffs and burgesses in causes of particular importance to us'. He gave specific orders that no fine should be exacted for the charter and also reduced the farm of the borough from £65 to £20,[26] a measure that was reversed by Henry VII.[27]

By the early 16th century the appearance of royalty in the town had ceased to be a familiar occurrence, and visits by Princess Mary in 1525 and by Henry VIII and Anne

[12] R. F. Butler, 'The Last of the Brimpsfield Giffards and the Rising of 1321-2', *Trans. B.G.A.S.*. lxxvi. 83-90.

[13] *Cal. Pat.* 1321-4, 79; cf. below, trade and ind. 1066-1327.

[14] *Cal. Close,* 1318-23, 460.

[15] Below, Bailiffs of Glouc. 1200-1483.

[16] *Cal. Pat.* 1321-4, 214.

[17] *Cal. Close,* 1323-7, 651; McKisack, *14th cent.* (1959), 85.   [18] *Hist. & Cart. Mon. Glouc.* i. 44-5.

[19] G.B.R., I 1/22.

[20] *Cal. Pat.* 1327-30, 69; 1330-4, 6.

[21] *Hist. & Cart. Mon. Glouc.* i. 52-4; *Cal. Close,* 1377-81, 216.

[22] *Cal. Pat.* 1401-5, 440.

[23] Ibid 1461-7, 197. The farm was back in the king's hand by 1465: ibid. 467; *Cal. Close,* 1461-8 345.

[24] *Cal. Pat.* 1461-7, 15; 1467-77, 183, 465; *Cal. Close,* 1468-76, p. 185.

[25] *Historie of the Arrival of Edw. IV in Eng.* (Camd. Soc. [1st ser.], i), 26-7.

[26] G.B.R., I 1/22; cf. P.R.O., C 81/1392, m.2.

[27] *Glouc. Corp. Rec.* p. 19; cf. ibid. pp. 61-2.

Boleyn in 1535 were made the occasions of much ceremonial by the borough corporation.[28]

Trade and Industry 1066–1327

The economy of medieval Gloucester was based on its indigenous industries, particularly ironworking, clothmaking, and the leather trades, and on a local trading area confined principally to neighbouring villages in the Vale of Gloucester but extended by connections with lesser market towns. An extra dimension was provided by the river trade on the Severn, and the town also benefited from some of the main currents of overland trade, particularly that from South Wales into England, and had a limited share in the overseas trade in wine, wool, and corn. During the two and a half centuries following the Norman Conquest those varied functions, together with the intermittent stimulants of the use of the town as a supply base for military operations and the frequent visits of king and government, brought Gloucester fairly steady prosperity.[29]

Such evidence as survives for Gloucester's involvement in overseas commerce in the 12th and 13th centuries suggests that, as with other towns, the Gascon wine trade played an important role in enriching its leading merchants. Ailwin the mercer, the wealthiest burgess of his day and the man who took the lead in the town's political aspirations, was trading in wine in 1183,[30] and another leading burgess of that period, Wascio (Gascon) the cook, whose daughter or close kinswoman married Ailwin,[31] was probably also involved in that trade. Richard the burgess the younger, who was selling wine in Gloucester in 1200,[32] was possibly the man who later became mayor of the borough.[33] Three others mentioned as dealing in wine in the early 1220s[34] all served as bailiffs of the borough, among them David Dunning who served the office in at least four years and was a considerable property-owner in the town.[35] Nine men of the town were presented for offences against the assize of wine in 1287;[36] six of them served as bailiff at some time, including Alexander of Bicknor, Walter Sevare, and Philip the spicer (or apothecary) who were regularly re-elected to the office. Another who traded in wine in the late 13th century was presumably the Gascon merchant William de Riouns who settled in the town,[37] probably by 1295 when he took a long lease of property there.[38] The town's wine merchants in the 13th century frequently had their business disrupted by having to give up their wine to stock the castle cellars against the king's coming,[39] though presumably the regular needs of the royal household ultimately benefited the trade.

Some Gloucester men were also involved in the export of wool in the 13th century and the early 14th. Philip the spicer was among four Gloucester merchants recorded as sending wool overseas during the early 1270s when a licensing system was in force.[40] Alexander of Bicknor was probably another with a share in that trade, for he was employed by the Crown to buy wool in 1297.[41] The import of cloth from Flanders concerned other Gloucester men, including probably William Payn who was

[28] G.B.R., B 2/1, ff. 119, 120v.–122.

[29] The general evidence for Gloucester's economic fortunes at the period is discussed above, Glouc. 1066–1327.

[30] Pipe R. 1183 (P.R.S. xxxii), 95.

[31] Ibid. 1173 (P.R.S. xix), 154; P.R.O., C 115/K 1/6681, f. 118.

[32] Pipe R. 1200 (P.R.S. N.S. xii), 123.

[33] Below, town govt. 1200–1483.

[34] Pleas of the Crown for Glos. ed. Maitland, p. 109; Rot. Litt. Claus. (Rec. Com.), i. 580. For those mentioned in this section as bailiffs, below, Bailiffs of Glouc. 1200–1483.

[35] Glouc. Rental, 1455, 31–5, 43, 51, 63, 101, 113.

[36] P.R.O., JUST 1/278, rot. 66.

[37] He served as bailiff in 1303, and he or another of the same name was assessed for subsidy in 1327: Glos. Subsidy Roll, 1327, 1.

[38] P.R.O., C 115/K 1/6681, f. 41v.

[39] e.g. Rot. Litt. Claus. (Rec. Com.), i. 580; Close R. 1227–31, 479, 499, 596.

[40] Cal. Pat. 1266–72, 557, 692, 704; 1272–81, 38.

[41] Ibid. 1292–1301, 300.

recorded as selling cloth in the town in 1287[42] and trading with Flanders in the 1290s.[43] Robert de Honsum was mentioned as bringing two boatloads of cloth, wine, and fish up river from Bristol to Gloucester in 1284,[44] and Adam Honsum, presumably of the same family, was importing cloth and silver from Antwerp in 1303.[45] The reference from 1284 suggests that, as later, much of Gloucester's overseas trade was done through Bristol, the goods being transhipped to smaller vessels there or else carried overland.

Gloucester men were apparently trading with Ireland in 1130;[46] Thomas Myparty of Gloucester was engaged in that trade in 1234;[47] and in 1301 John the Cornishman (le Cornwaleys) of Gloucester, described as a king's merchant, was ordered to transport victuals from Ireland to Scotland for Edward I's army.[48] Opportunities nearer at hand were provided by the Welsh campaigns of the 13th century; four Gloucester men were victualling the army there in 1277[49] and such activities may have helped to lay the basis for the penetration of South Wales by merchants of the town in later and more peaceful times. One trade that was to remain a feature of Gloucester's connections with Wales was already established before the Edwardian conquest: by the 1250s Welsh cattle were brought regularly for sale in the town or neighbourhood or to be driven on towards London.[50]

For the part that Gloucester played in long-distance trade within England in the early Middle Ages evidence is almost entirely lacking. Men from Salisbury were apparently regular traders in the town in 1229,[51] possibly helping to maintain trading links with Southampton, which were important in the late Middle Ages. A smith from Northamptonshire recorded in the town before 1287[52] was perhaps involved in the trade in iron, which, as mentioned below, was one Gloucester product that was widely dispersed throughout England.

From an early date the river trade on the Severn played a significant, though never a dominant, role in the town's economy. The use of the river was well established by the late 12th century when cargoes of military and other supplies were regularly shipped to and from Gloucester.[53] The importance of the Severn for carrying fuel for Gloucester's smithies is reflected in Henry II's grant c. 1170 of free passage to men of the town bringing wood and coal downstream,[54] and in the 13th century the river was apparently the usual means of bringing to Gloucester the Forest of Dean oaks that the Crown donated to religious houses of the town for their building operations or assigned for the works at Gloucester castle.[55] The timber trade on the river appears to have involved a number of the leading burgesses at the period, for Philip the spicer and Robert of Putley[56] were among those who supplied timber for the works at the castle in 1264. Stone for the same works was brought by boat, some of it from Denny, in Minsterworth,[57] and that was another commodity for which river transport was naturally used where possible; in 1298 and 1302 stone was shipped from Elmore for use by the town muragers.[58] Any obstruction to free passage on the river was a matter of concern to the town: in 1247 complaints were made that a monk of Gloucester Abbey had placed obstructions in the river, apparently for a fish weir, stopping boats

[42] P.R.O., JUST 1/278, rot. 66.
[43] *Cal. Pat.* 1292–1301, 247.
[44] Ibid. 1281–92 201.
[45] *Cal. Close,* 1302–7, 110.
[46] *Pipe R.* 1130 (H.M.S.O. facsimile), 77.
[47] *Cal. Pat.* 1232–47, 46.
[48] Ibid. 1292–1301, 591–2.
[49] Ibid. 1272–81, 224.
[50] *Ag. H.R.* ii. 12–14.

[51] *Close R.* 1227–31, 237–8.
[52] P.R.O., JUST 1/278, rot. 65.
[53] *Pipe R.* 1171 (P.R.S. xvi), 84; 1182 (P.R.S. xxxi), 24; 1190 (P.R.S. N.S. i), 53.
[54] *Glouc. Corp. Rec.* p. 4.
[55] *Cal. Lib.* 1251–60, 16, 21, 313–14.
[56] Cf. above and below.
[57] Glos. R.O., D 4431 (no. 24006).
[58] G.B.R., F 2/1.

from reaching the town,[59] and in 1277 two Gloucester men were appointed together with two Worcester men to supervise the alteration of weirs that were impeding navigation.[60] There are occasional references to mariners and watermen among the 13th-century inhabitants of Gloucester[61] but their rarity suggests that, as in later centuries, the bulk of the trade that came to the town's quay was carried in boats belonging to other towns on the river.

Evidence for the extent of the local market area that Gloucester served is not forthcoming until the late 14th century and is discussed below.[62] It is possibly not a reliable guide for the situation in earlier centuries, for the establishment of other markets nearby during the 13th century and the early 14th must have gradually restricted Gloucester's role as a mart for agricultural produce. The two nearest places to be successfully established as markets at that period were Painswick and Newent, which both had charters in 1253,[63] and the impact of Newent was being felt by 1258 when complaints were made that it had taken from Gloucester market the corn trade of the Newent area. It was, however, also noted that the chapmen of Newent still went to Gloucester to buy fish, hides, and salt[64] and later evidence shows that Painswick and Newent, as well as more distant market towns, remained important customers of Gloucester for its manufactured goods and for goods it imported from Bristol, London, and elsewhere.

In the 12th and 13th centuries an important factor in extending Gloucester's influence as a market centre was the network of Gloucester Abbey manors scattered throughout the county. When the abbey cultivated its manorial demesnes and brought much of the produce to supply the abbey or sell locally, services of carrying to Gloucester, sometimes as regularly as 15 times a year, were owed by the tenants of manors as far distant as Clifford Chambers and Eastleach Martin, and some carrying services continued to be required even when local markets could be used more conveniently for some of the produce.[65] Those tenants would tend to look to Gloucester as a source of manufactured goods as well as a market for the produce of their own holdings, while tenants from closer at hand, particularly from the compact group of abbey manors that lay just across the Severn, were even more firmly orientated towards Gloucester. The Gloucester Abbey tenants were evidently an important element among Gloucester's market traders in the 1240s when a dispute over their tolls arose between abbey and town.[66]

The produce brought in from the surrounding countryside to the market in 1273 included apples and pears from the Severnside orchards.[67] Honey was another product of the immediate neighbourhood which was brought in considerable quantities; on the Gloucester Abbey manors across the Severn, Churcham, Hartpury, and Upleadon, there were tenants in the 1260s who held their land in return for renders of honey.[68] Another regular item of the incoming trade, from rather further afield, is suggested by the abbey records: the monks owned rights in a salt well at Droitwich and carrying services were required from some tenants of manors near Gloucester.[69] Robert the salter, a Gloucester man who was among those who supplied timber for the castle works in 1264,[70] may have combined the carriage of Droitwich salt with the trade in timber on the river.

[59] P.R.O., JUST 1/274, rot. 13d.
[60] Cal. Pat. 1272–81, 195.
[61] Glouc. Corp. Rec. pp. 109, 113, 261, 278.
[62] Below, trade and ind. 1327–1547.
[63] Cal. Chart. R. 1226–57, 428, 435.
[64] Ag. H.R. ii. 12–14.
[65] Hist. & Cart. Mon. Glouc. iii. 52, 54, 56, 61, 190, 199.
[66] Ibid. p. xxiii. [67] G.B.R., G 8/1.
[68] Hist. & Cart. Mon. Glouc. iii. 78, 128, 136–7.
[69] Ibid. 68, 80, 129.
[70] Glos. R.O., D 4431 (no. 24006); cf. Glouc. Cath. Libr., Reg. Abb. Froucester B, p. 489.

An important item in Gloucester's local trade was fish, supplied both from fishing weirs adjoining the town and by villagers from riverside parishes downstream. Local fisheries included royal weirs, which were held with the castle in the 1250s,[71] Cokeyn weir and Castle weir just below the town, owned by Llanthony Priory, and Gloucester Abbey's Pool weir above Westgate bridge.[72] Fishermen or fishmongers (the distinction was not usually made at the period) were recorded fairly regularly in the town[73] and included a man who was bailiff at least three times in the mid 13th century. The regular supply of lampreys for the royal table by the burgesses had begun by King John's reign[74] and continued under his successor,[75] to be eventually formalized in the presentation of lamprey pies to the Crown.[76] The bailiffs were also regularly called upon to provide Henry III with Severn salmon and shad.[77] The fish trade was also stimulated by the requirements of the local religious houses. In 1277 a leading burgess Walter Sevare made an agreement with Gloucester Abbey to act as their buyer of fish;[78] Walter appears to have been a merchant involved in overseas trade[79] and so was probably expected to supply not only fish from local sources but also the salted fish which was imported to the Severn from Ireland and elsewhere.

The nature of other goods brought for sale in the town was governed by the needs of its principal industries. One of the most regular items of the incoming local trade was presumably iron carried from the Forest of Dean, which was perhaps also the main source of oak bark for the town's tanneries. Packs of leather were among goods being brought to the town in 1273, and the importance of the leather trade is suggested by the fact that the leather market was then held in the Boothall,[80] though perhaps, as later, sharing the building with the wool market. Wool, both for the town's own clothworkers and for the export trade, was apparently brought to Gloucester in quantity in the 13th century. The disguise as woolmongers adopted by two leaders of the rebels in 1264 in order to gain entrance to the town has been cited as an indication of the commonplace nature of such commerce at the period,[81] and six men involved in buying or selling wool in the town figure in the trade offences presented in 1273.[82]

In a mid 13th-century list of English towns and their characteristic products or other associations Gloucester is represented by the phrase 'iron of Gloucester'.[83] Its control of the land routes out of the Forest of Dean made Gloucester the natural centre for working the iron produced by that region, and ironworking remained one of the town's most important industries throughout the Middle Ages. It was an industry that was stimulated by the military and naval requirements of the Crown, as indicated by the earliest record, the 36 *dicras* of iron and 100 rods of ductile iron for nails for the king's ships owed as part of the farm in 1066.[84] In the years 1171–3 equipment supplied to Henry II, mainly for the Irish expedition, and allowed for in the Gloucester reeve's account, included nails, horseshoes, mattocks, ironwork for spades, arrows, 'engines', and kitchen utensils;[85] in 1212 and 1214 the sheriff of the

[71] *Close R.* 1247–51, 482–3; 1254–6, 111, 256, 326.

[72] P.R.O., C 115/K 2/6685, ff. 10, 55v.; G.B.R., B 2/2, ff. 21, 145; *Trans B.G.A.S.* lxii. 148.

[73] *Glouc. Corp. Rec.* pp. 86, 324; P.R.O., C 115/K 1/6681, f. 36v.; G.B.R., G 8/1.

[74] *Pipe R.* 1201 (P.R.S. N.S. xiv), 46; 1207 (P.R.S. N.S. xxii), 215.

[75] e.g. *Rot. Litt. Claus.* (Rec. Com.), i. 388; ii. 164; *Close R.* 1242–7, 155, 395.

[76] Glos. Colln. NQ 18.2.

[77] e.g. *Close R.* 1231–4, 349; 1237–42, 7; 1256–9, 365; *Cal.*

Lib. 1226–40, 455; 1240–5, 11, 126; 1245–51, 41, 114; 1260–7, 87, 162.

[78] *Hist. & Cart. Mon. Glouc.* ii. 239–41.

[79] Above.

[80] G.B.R., G 8/1.

[81] J. J. Powell, *Gloucestriana* (1890), 7.

[82] G.B.R., G 8/1.

[83] *Eng. Hist. Doc.* iii. 882.

[84] *Dom. Bk.* (Rec. Com.), i. 162.

[85] *Pipe R.* 1171 (P.R.S. xvi), 87–8; 1172 (P.R.S. xviii), 122; 1173 (P.R.S. xix), 156.

county acquired for the king, probably from Gloucester craftsmen, anchors and crossbow bolts;[86] in 1228 the bailiffs of the town sent two smiths and other workmen with axes, mattocks, and iron for making rock-cutting tools to Henry III at Kerry (Mont.) where he was on a campaign against the Welsh;[87] and in 1242 the king ordered the men of Gloucester to make 10,000 horseshoes and 100,000 nails and deliver them at Portsmouth within 20 days.[88] Gloucester castle was also an important source of employment in times of unrest: in the early months of 1264 numbers of smiths, as many as eight in one week, were put to work making crossbow bolts for the garrison.[89] The products of Gloucester's iron industry were also used by the Crown for its building operations. In the 1170s large quantities of nails were sent for use on houses under construction at Winchester;[90] in 1224 stocks of 'good Gloucester iron', kept at Southampton and Northampton, were ordered for the king's works at Bedford;[91] and Gloucester iron was used in 1261 for the works at Windsor.[92].

The strength of the metal-working industry is reflected in the surviving deeds from the late 12th century to the early 14th, which mention numerous smiths and farriers and, less often, representatives of specialized crafts, including locksmiths,[93] cutlers,[94] lorimers,[95] a buckler,[96] a knifesmith,[97] and three combmakers (*pectifabri*),[98] presumably making combs for use in the town's woollen industry. One of the most famous Gloucester trades is recorded from the later 13th century with mentions of Thomas the bellfounder in 1274[99] and Hugh the bellfounder at about the same date.[1]

By the beginning of the 13th century the smiths' forges had given the name of the smiths' street[2] to the later Longsmith Street in the south-west quarter of the town, and the sign of the Bolt inn which later gave that street the alternative name of Bolt Lane[3] presumably recalled the manufacture of crossbow bolts. A street leading off the smiths' street had become known as Broadsmith Street (later Berkeley Street) by the early 14th century,[4] and a lane off the main market area, formerly Craft's Lane, acquired the name Ironmongers' Row, at least two dealers in iron being resident there in 1333.[5] Some ironworkers also settled in the suburbs of the town: in the mid 13th century two smiths and three farriers were among inhabitants of the Newland and Fete Lane area outside the north gate.[6]

Clothmaking was the only industry that came near to rivalling ironworking. It was established in the town by the later 12th century: Wulward the fuller was one of the wealthiest burgesses in 1173[7] and a fuller and three weavers were recorded among the inhabitants of St. Nicholas's parish at the same period.[8] It was in the riverside areas of that parish that the industry naturally became concentrated, a street near the quay becoming known as the fullers' street. About 1230 eight different dyers were recorded as occupying land, or witnessing deeds of land, in that street or the surrounding area,[9] and in 1247 three dyers were presented for encroachments on the river bank.[10] At the

[86] Ibid. 1212 (P.R.S. N.S. xxx), 142; 1214 (P.R.S. N.S. xxxv), 55.
[87] *Cal. Lib.* 1226–40, 115.
[88] Ibid. 1240–5, 118.
[89] Glos. R.O., D 4431 (no. 24006).
[90] *Pipe R.* 1172 (P.R.S. xviii), 122; 1173 (P.R.S. xix), 156.
[91] *Rot. Litt. Claus.* (Rec. Com.), i. 610, 635.
[92] *Cal. Lib.* 1260–7, 57.
[93] *Glouc. Corp. Rec.* pp. 135, 158; P.R.O., C 115/K 1/6681, f. 100.
[94] *Hist. & Cart. Mon. Glouc.* i. 184; *Glouc. Corp. Rec.* p. 209; Glouc. Cath. Libr., Reg. Abb. Froucester B, pp. 250–1.
[95] *Glouc. Corp. Rec.* pp. 70, 209, 319; P.R.O., C 115/K 1/6681, f. 118v.
[96] Glouc. Cath. Libr., Reg. Abb. Froucester B, p. 465.
[97] P.R.O., C 115/K 1/6681, f. 101.

[98] Ibid. f. 98.
[99] P.R.O., CP 25(1)/75/30, no. 13.
[1] *Glouc. Corp. Rec.* p. 251.
[2] Ibid. p. 94; cf. *Cal. Lib.* 1240–5, 318, where, in 1245, one wall of Glouc. castle was said to face the town's forges.
[3] Rudder, *Glos.* 86.
[4] P.R.O., C 115/K 1/6681, f. 165; cf. *Glouc. Rental, 1455,* p. xvi.
[5] P.R.O., C 115/K 1/6681, f. 133v.; cf. *Glouc. Rental, 1455,* 33.
[6] Glouc. Cath. Libr., Reg. Abb. Froucester B, pp. 227–9, 244.
[7] *Pipe R.* 1173 (P.R.S. xix), 154.
[8] *Glouc. Corp. Rec.* p. 72.
[9] Ibid. pp. 122–3, 131, 136–7, 139–41, 152.
[10] P.R.O., JUST 1/274, rot. 13d.

same period and later, dyers and fullers held land near lower Northgate Street and Brook Street on the north-east fringes of the town, evidently making use of the water of the river Twyver.[11] The dyers were the most prosperous of the clothworkers, being most often mentioned in the surviving sources, which are mainly property deeds. The weavers of the town were numerous enough to have some collective identity by the 2160s when they were paying an annual sum of 20s. to the bailiffs,[12] but whether for the right to have a trade organization or for some other trading privilege is not known.

In 1287 ten people recorded as having sold cloth in Gloucester were said to have also made it. Little is known of those named. The absence of trade surnames among them suggests that they were not themselves dyers or fullers; nor did they include any men who can be identified as leading merchants or drapers and only one, James of Longney, attained the office of bailiff. They may represent a class of small capitalists which controlled the industry, contracting with the dyers and other clothworkers. Five others recorded at the same time as selling cloth but not making it seem to have been from a rather wealthier class of tradesman, for they included William Payn, mentioned above as being involved in the Flanders trade, John the draper, who served regularly as bailiff at the period, and Henry the draper, who also traded in wine.[13]

Among other industries in the town leather working was strongly represented. A part of Northgate Street was established as the cordwainers' quarter by 1223,[14] and Hare Lane was known as the tanners' street in the 1230s.[15] Leather working produced a number of fairly wealthy men. In 1327[16] the tanner John of Boyfield, assessed at 7s.,[17] was the 13th highest payer of the subsidy and two tawyers, paying 5s. each,[18] were also fairly prosperous. At least four other tanners, less wealthy men, were listed for the subsidy that year. Other leather workers, recorded in the mid 13th century, were sheathers,[19] skinners, and beltmakers, the last two groups being sufficiently numerous to have areas of the town named from them.[20]

Masons, plumbers,[21] soapmakers,[22] a horner (c. 1200),[23] a parchment maker (c. 1260),[24] and a potter, who had land at Fete Lane outside the north gate in the mid 13th century,[25] were among other varied trades recorded in the town during the period. Of the masons the most significant was the king's mason John of Gloucester (d. 1260), who was employed on works at Westminster Abbey, the Tower of London, and Gloucester castle.[26] Martin of Spoonbed, a mason who took a lease of property in the town from Llanthony Priory in 1319 or 1320,[27] may, his name suggests, have worked quarries in Painswick parish for the priory.[28]

The fragmentary nature of the surviving records makes it impossible to establish satisfactorily what trades provided the governing class of Gloucester at the period. The merchants, though few in number, played a prominent role: most of those men recorded as trading in wine and wool in the 13th century and the early 14th figure as bailiffs of the town and some, like Alexander of Bicknor and Walter Sevare, held the

[11] Glouc. Cath. Libr., Reg. Abb. Froucester B, pp. 247, 256, 299; Glouc. Corp. Rec. p. 98, B.L. Campb. Ch. xviii. 14.
[12] G.B.R., F 3/1.
[13] P.R.O., JUST 1/278, rot. 66.
[14] Hist. & Cart. Mon. Glouc. i. 26; cf. P.R.O., C 115/K 1/6681, f. 104v.   [15] Ciren. Cart. ii, p. 391.
[16] Glos. Subsidy Roll, 1327, 1–2.
[17] Cf. P.R.O., C 115/K 1/6681, f. 155.
[18] Hen. Patrick and John of Leominster, for whom cf. G.B.R., J 1/866.
[19] Ciren. Cart. ii, p. 397.
[20] Glouc. Cath. Libr., deeds and seals, x, ff. 18, 20; Reg. Abb. Froucester B, pp. 458–9.

[21] Glouc. Corp. Rec. pp. 87, 108, 260.
[22] Glouc. Cath. Libr., Reg. Abb. Froucester B, p. 256; P.R.O., C 115/K 1/6681, f. 142.
[23] Glouc. Cath. Libr., Reg. Abb. Froucester B, p. 231.
[24] Glouc. Corp. Rec. pp. 211–12.
[25] Glouc. Cath. Libr., Reg. Abb. Froucester B, pp. 227, 231.
[26] Harvey, Eng. Med. Architects (1954), 114–15; Cal. Lib. 1251–60, 284, 313. He witnessed Glouc. deeds c. 1250 (Glouc. Corp. Rec. pp. 194, 208) and had a grant of a shop there in 1258–9: Glouc. Cath. Libr., deeds and seals, ix, f. 2.
[27] P.R.O., C 115/K 1/6681, f. 136.
[28] Cf. V.C.H. Glos. xi. 67, 78.

office in as many as eight years. The men who distributed cloth, fabrics, and other goods locally appear to have also enjoyed a consistently prominent position. John the draper was bailiff at least four times in the early 13th century and another man of that name at least seven times in the later years of the century. The mercers of the town, whose shops occupied one of the prime trading positions, adjoining the main market area in upper Westgate Street,[29] included a number of wealthy burgesses who served as bailiffs in the mid 13th century: among them were Herbert the mercer, whose property at his death *c.* 1268 included 5 houses and 11 shops,[30] Richard Francis, described variously as mercer and merchant, who acquired much property in the town and gave some of it to Llanthony Priory and St. Bartholomew's Hospital,[31] and Robert of Putley, a benefactor of Gloucester Abbey.[32]

In 1327 when the subsidy assessment[33] provides the earliest complete list of the leading men of the town there can be identified among the 21 highest payers (those assessed at 6*s.* or more) 3 merchants,[34] the tanner John of Boyfield, a tavern keeper,[35] a dyer, a goldsmith, and a draper. The highest payer, Robert Pope assessed at 20*s.*, was presumably a draper, for in that and the following year he supplied Winchcombe Abbey with cloth to the value of £76,[36] and the second highest, Peter of the hill assessed at 13*s.* 4*d.*, had a son who was a draper.[37] Another leading payer, Robert of Goldhill assessed at 10*s.*, is one of the few Gloucester burgesses known to have owned property outside the town at the period. Before 1327 he bought the wardship of Lasborough manor during the minority of the heirs,[38] and in 1334, when he made a will which benefited many religious institutions and many individuals including his two apprentices, he also occupied farmland at Down Hatherley.[39]

The Achievement of Liberties

For a century after the Conquest the town of Gloucester was administered for the Crown by a royal reeve, though the powers of that office were presumably much inhibited by the dominant role played by the family of hereditary sheriffs.[40] The reeve of Gloucester was mentioned *c.* 1100, when he was in receipt of a stipend of 40*s.*,[41] and again in 1139, when his duties evidently included collection of the landgavel.[42]

Soon after his accession Henry II granted a charter to the burgesses giving them the customs and liberties that London and Winchester had enjoyed in the time of Henry I.[43] In 1165 the burgesses were allowed to farm the royal revenues arising in the town, Gloucester becoming only the fourth place to be given that major privilege by Henry II.[44] An agreement made the same year between the burgesses and a man called Ailwin the mercer, for which a fine of 100 marks was paid to the Crown, presumably settled the arrangements for the burgesses' assumption of the fee farm. Ailwin the mercer was probably the wealthiest burgess of the time, being himself responsible for 10 marks of the fine[45] and paying 7½ marks of a royal aid of 100 marks levied on the borough in 1173;[46] he may have been the head of the merchant guild, an organization

[29] *Close R.* 1264–8, 235; *Glouc. Rental, 1455,* 27.

[30] P.R.O., CP 25(1)/74/28, no. 632.

[31] P.R.O., C 115/K 1/6681, ff. 83v.-84, 87v., 98v., 100 and v.; C 115/K 2/6682, f. 180 and v.

[32] Glouc. Cath. Libr., Reg. Abb. Froucester B, pp. 8–9.

[33] *Glos. Subsidy Roll, 1327,* 1–2.

[34] Wm. Crisp, Steph. Brown, and John of Marcle: Glouc. Cath. Libr., Reg. Abb. Froucester B, p. 469; *Cal. Pat.* 1330–4, 232, 514; another merchant, Owen of Windsor, appears as one of the sub-assessors: *Glouc. Corp. Rec.* p. 339.

[35] Edw. of Ley: below, Bailiffs of Glouc. 1200–1483.

[36] *Reg. Mon. Winch.* i. 262–3.

[37] *Glouc. Corp. Rec.* p. 323.

[38] *V.C.H. Glos.* xi. 287.

[39] G.B.R., J 1/873.

[40] Above, Crown and boro.; military hist.

[41] *Glouc. Rental, 1455,* p. xv.

[42] P.R.O., C 115/K 1/6681, f. 76v., notification by Empress Maud to Miles, earl of Heref., and the reeve of Glouc. of a grant of part of the landgavel.

[43] *Glouc. Corp. Rec.* pp. 3–4.

[44] Cf. J. Tait, *Medieval Eng. Borough* (1936), 173–4.

[45] *Pipe R.* 1165 (P.R.S. viii), 14.

[46] Ibid. 1173 (P.R.S. xix), 154.

for which there is, however, no definite evidence before 1200.[47] Following the grant of the fee farm a group of burgesses tried to take fuller political control of the borough by the formation of a commune, or sworn association, which the royal government deemed subversive. Heavy amercements for that action were imposed in 1170, Ailwin the mercer owing £100 and other burgesses, apparently 26 in all, a total of £80 13s. 4d.; another offender fled and suffered forfeiture of his chattels.[48]

The fee farm, fixed at £55 in 1165, continued to be separately accounted for at the Exchequer by a man called Osmund the reeve (or Osmund Keys) until 1176,[49] and the borough was later described as having been at that period 'in the hands of the burgesses'.[50] The collection of the royal revenues, the landgavel, profits of court, and market tolls, implied a considerable degree of control over the borough administration, but it seems unlikely, in view of the fact that Osmund held his office throughout the period, that the burgesses had also gained the important privilege of electing their own reeve. Although certainly chosen from the burgess community — he contributed to the aid of 1173,[51] held property, including selds, in the town, and was the nephew of a Gloucester lorimer[52] — Osmund was probably a royal appointee. His responsibilities seem to have included presiding over the hundred court, the chief borough court, for he headed the list of witnesses to a grant made in the court at the period.[53]

In 1176 the right to farm was revoked by Henry II and returned to the county sheriff,[54] though separate royal reeves, among them Osmund's son Henry Keys, continued to administer the borough.[55] The farm was restored by Richard I by charter of 1194, for which the burgesses paid £100 and accepted an increase of the farm to £65.[56] In 1200, in return for another 200 marks,[57] they received from King John confirmation of the farm and a new charter which gave them the right to elect two bailiffs and four coroners, confirmed their freedom from tolls, and, among various legal franchises, established their freedom from pleading in courts outside the borough except in cases that concerned land held outside.[58] The charter marked a very significant advance in the burgesses' liberties, though it did not in the short term free them from the vagaries of royal favour. In 1201 or 1202 John returned the farm to the sheriff;[59] in 1204 the burgesses paid a fine of 25 marks for the king's protection;[60] and in 1206, after payment of a further 100 marks, they recovered the farm.[61]

From that time the borough retained, in theory at least, uninterrupted possession of its liberties, freedom from direct royal administration, and control of its revenues, court, and trade. Its liberties were not, however, secure against future challenges from the Crown or lesser authorities. The two bailiffs who administered the borough still exercised their office in the king's name, being referred to as the king's bailiffs of Gloucester[62] (or, in the period when Queens Eleanor and Margaret had the lordship, as the queen's bailiffs),[63] and the extent to which the king felt able to intervene in the

---

[47] *Glouc. Corp. Rec.* p. 6. The term guildhall, used in *Pipe R.* 1192 (P.R.S. N.S. ii), 285, is probably not definite evidence: cf. S. Reynolds, *Eng. Med. Towns* (1977), 83.

[48] *Pipe R.* 1170 (P.R.S. xv), 79; cf. Tait, *Medieval Eng. Borough*, 177.

[49] *Pipe R.* 1165 (P.R.S. viii), 12, 14; 1166 (P.R.S. ix), 77, 80; and later rolls. For Osmund, cf. P.R.O., C 115/K 1/6681, f. 82; C 115/K 2/6684, f. 164.

[50] *Pipe R.* 1178 (P.R.S. xxvii), 56–7.

[51] Ibid. 1173 (P.R.S. xix), 154.

[52] P.R.O., C 115/K 1/6681, f. 82 and v.

[53] Glouc. Cath. Libr., Reg. Abb. Froucester B, pp. 256–7.

[54] *Pipe R.* 1176 (P.R.S. xxv), 130; 1177 (P.R.S. xxvi), 41; 1178 (P.R.S. xxvii), 56–7.

[55] Ibid. 1184 (P.R.S. xxxiii), 62; Glouc. Cath. Libr., deeds and seals, i, f. 8; P.R.O., C 115/K 1/6681, ff. 87v., 118; *Flaxley Cart.* ed. A.W. Crawley-Boevey (1887), pp. 150–1, 173.

[56] *Glouc. Corp. Rec.* pp. 4–5; *Pipe R.* 1194 (P.R.S. N.S. v), 232, 238.

[57] *Pipe R.* 1199 (P.R.S. N.S. x), 28.

[58] *Glouc. Corp. Rec.* pp. 6–9.

[59] *Pipe R.* 1201 (P.R.S. N.S. xiv), 40; 1202 (P.R.S. N.S. xv), 172–3.

[60] Ibid. 1204 (P.R.S. N.S. xviii), 151.

[61] Ibid. 1206 (P.R.S. N.S. xx), 15–16.

[62] e.g. *Cal. Pat.* 1317–21, 439; P.R.O., C 115/K 1/6681, f. 169.

[63] Glouc. Cath. Libr., Reg. Abb. Froucester B, p. 506; *Cal. Close*, 1313–18, 42.

burgesses' affairs was a matter for his interpretation rather than theirs. Military requirements could result in a town of such strategic importance having its liberties temporarily suspended, as seems to have happened at least twice during Edward II's reign,[64] while the proximity of the castle, seat of the county administration, made the townsfolk particularly vulnerable to incursions on their liberties by the sheriff and to acts of petty tyranny by him or the constable of the castle.

The charter of 1200, which was described in 1391 as that which granted the town and fee farm to the bailiffs and community,[65] remained the basis of Gloucester's liberties for the next 283 years. The liberties it gave were, however, supplemented and clarified by a number of later charters, which reflect in particular the burgesses' concern to exclude the county sheriff from their affairs and to uphold the jurisdiction of the borough court against the claims of external courts. In 1227 they secured from Henry III freedom from interference by the sheriff in any plea in the borough court, and in 1256 another charter confirmed to them the right to return writs and excluded the sheriff from executing summons or distraint in the borough.[66] The king had continued to use the sheriff on occasion after 1200 for some executive functions within the borough, sometimes in ways which seem to have been a slight on the bailiffs' authority, as in 1216 and 1217 when the sheriff was ordered to give seisin of houses in the town[67] and in 1247 when he was the agent for dealing with illegal purprestures.[68] Even after the charter of 1256 there remained some judicial processes in which the sheriff could be involved: in 1276 he presided with the bailiffs and coroners in the hundred court over an inquisition into a felon's goods,[69] and at the same period he took possession of the goods of any outsiders who abjured the realm before the borough coroners.[70]

The charter of 1256 also protected the burgesses against being made to answer on any matter concerning their liberties in any but a royal court; a charter of 1312 confirmed that individual burgesses could be convicted only by a jury of their fellow burgesses; and another of 1328 made a special confirmation of the clause in the charter of 1200 concerning external pleading and protected the burgesses against any loss of liberties on the grounds of non-usage.[71] The last two charters evidently followed some severe incursions on the borough's liberties during the disturbances of Edward II's reign,[72] and the need to emphasize the borough's status was probably also reflected in the style of 'bailiffs of *the liberty* of the town of Gloucester' adopted by the bailiffs when witnessing deeds in the late 1320s and early 1330s[73] but not apparently used at any other period.

Further legal privileges were conferred in 1398 by Richard II who gave the bailiffs the powers of justices of the peace, labourers, and artificers, as well as re-affirming the jurisdiction of the court over all pleas arising in the town.[74] The borough's liberties in the latter respect were successfully upheld by the burgesses in 1405 when the abbot of Gloucester attempted to bring an action of novel disseisin against two burgesses before the assize justices[75] and again in 1407 when the Marshalsea court meeting at Cheltenham claimed to hear cases involving Gloucester burgesses.[76] The importance attached to freedom from external pleading is also reflected by the fact that it was

[64] Above, Crown and boro.; military hist.
[65] *Cal. Pat.* 1388–92, 444.
[66] *Glouc. Corp. Rec.* pp. 9–10; cf. M. T. Clanchy, 'Franchise of Return of Writs', *Trans R.H.S.* [5th ser.], xvii. 64–7.
[67] *Rot. Litt. Claus.* (Rec. Com.), i. 283, 317, 319.
[68] P.R.O., JUST 1/274, rot. 13d.
[69] *Cal. Inq. Misc.* i, p. 319.
[70] P.R.O., JUST 1/278, rot. 65 and d.
[71] *Glouc. Corp. Rec.* pp. 10–12.
[72] Above, Crown and boro.; military hist.
[73] e.g. P.R.O., C 115/K 1/6681, ff. 39v., 166; G.B.R., J 1/864, 877.
[74] *Glouc. Corp. Rec.* pp. 13–14.
[75] Glouc. Cath. Libr., Reg. Abb. Froucester B, p. 341.
[76] G.B.R., I 1/15.

enshrined in a clause in the freeman's oath which was in use in the early 16th century.[77].

Confirmation of the borough charters was obtained from each king after Richard II on or soon after his accession,[78] but no further liberties were added until 1483.

Town Government 1200–1483

Although the basic constitution for the government of the borough was created under the charter of 1200, there was a further, but short-lived, innovation. Over a period of at least eight years a man called Richard the burgess witnessed deeds as mayor of Gloucester[79] and evidently derived his authority from a royal order of 1228 appointing him as 'superior ex parte domini regis' in the town, to hold custody of it during pleasure.[80] Richard the burgess was a major property owner in the town,[81] and, if he was the same person who acted as deputy to the county sheriff between 1210 and 1214,[82] a man of considerable administrative experience; his apparently significant surname was probably acquired by an ancestor who served as reeve of Gloucester in the mid 12th century.[83] Richard was twice recorded as performing the representative function of the mayor as leader of the burgess community: he led the burgesses in a commoning dispute with Gloucester Abbey in 1236[84] and a few years later he advised on arrangements for an endowment made to St. Bartholomew's Hospital.[85] The order of 1228 evidently envisaged that he would also head the borough administration and his functions probably included presiding with the bailiffs over the hundred court. After Richard the burgess there is no further evidence for the existence of the office of mayor until its revival in 1483, and, though the surviving administrative records are few, the absence of any mention of a mayor as witness to any of the many property deeds seems to preclude the possibility that the office survived Richard.[86] The fact that his office originated in a royal order and was apparently non-elective, rather than evolving organically from the headship of the guild as seems to have been the case in some other towns, may have made it obnoxious to the burgesses.

The failure of the office of mayor to establish itself left the two bailiffs[87] in an unchallenged position both as heads of the borough administration and as chief representatives of the burgess community. Under the charter of 1200 the bailiffs were to hold office during the burgesses' pleasure, but the office was made annually elective (at Michaelmas) from that time or very soon afterwards.[88] Its duties included collecting and accounting for the fee-farm revenues,[89] presiding over the hundred court,[90] and taking responsibility for a wide range of executive and administrative functions, such a seisin and escheat of property, custody of prisoners, and summons

[77] G.B.R., B 2/2, at front.
[78] L. & P. Hen. VIII, i (1), p. 197.
[79] Below, Bailiffs of Glouc. 1200–1483.
[80] Pat. R. 1225–32, 182.
[81] Glouc. Rental, 1455, 27, 31, 33, 61, 69.
[82] Pipe R. 1210 (P.R.S. N.S. xxvi), 140; and later rolls.
[83] Another Ric. the burgess was a leading inhabitant of the town in the later 12th cent. and referred in a deed to his father, Ralph the reeve: P.R.O., C 115/K 1/6681, f. 87v.; and see ibid, f. 64v.; Glouc. Cath. Libr., Reg. Abb. Froucester B, pp. 203–4; Pipe R. 1172 (P.R.S. xviii), 119.
[84] Hist. & Cart. Mon. Glouc. iii, 240–1.
[85] Glouc. Corp. Rec. pp. 164–5.
[86] Orders from the central government were later very ocasionally addressed to 'the mayor and community' or 'the mayor and bailiffs' but that probably resulted merely from

ignorance on the part of the Chancery clerks: Cal. Pat. 1367–70, 188; Cal. Close, 1313–18, 217; 1337–9, 143; 1399–1402, 239.
[87] In the earlier 13th cent. they are termed both prepositi and ballivi; in later periods the second term is almost always used.
[88] Below, Bailiffs of Glouc. 1200–1483.
[89] Bailiffs' accounts survive for four years: G.B.R., F 3/1 (damaged; dated to 1264–5 by a payment to the widow of Gilb. de Rue and mention of the king's visits: Cal. Pat. 1258–66, 135; 'Itin. of Hen. III' (1923), TS. at P.R.O.); F 3/2 (1393–4); F 3/3 (damaged; probably soon after 1403, as the farm is payable to the queen: Cal. Pat. 1401–5, 234); F 3/4 (1408–9).
[90] Glouc. Corp. Rec. p. 14; Glouc. Cath. Libr., Reg. Abb. Froucester B, pp. 191, 341; G.B.R., G 8/1; F 3/4.

and distraint, some of which were, however, performed by deputies. The fee-farm revenues were drawn principally from the landgavel, the amercements levied by the hundred court and views of frankpledge, and the profits of trade, which included the market tolls and the annual payments made by unfranchised traders in the borough.[91] Out of those revenues the bailiffs had to meet the annual farm, for which they were required to account personally at the Exchequer in 1256[92] but by 1393 employed an attorney, and various fees and expenses involved in running the borough. They themselves drew a stipend of £4 in 1264.[93] The bailiffs were also used by the Crown to carry out and fund from the farm various administration tasks not directly connected with the running of the borough. They were sometimes required, for example, to supply provisions for the royal household[94] or the army,[95] oversee repairs to the castle,[96] and convey prisoners across country.[97] The paramount status of the bailiffs in the borough administration was recognized by the possession of their own seal distinct from the communal seal.[98]

The office of bailiff naturally devolved on the wealthiest members of the community, many of whom were elected for a number of terms.[99] As many as seven or eight terms were served by William of Cheltenham and John Payn in the mid 13th century and by John the draper and the merchants Alexander of Bicknor and Walter Sevare in the later years of the century, and many of the other bailiffs had three or four terms. In the 13th and 14th centuries there was none of the reluctance to serve that was later shown by some of the wealthier burgesses: of the 21 highest payers of the subsidy of 1327 14 served the office at least once.[1] Until the early 15th century men were often re-elected for a number of years, including at that period Roger Ball who (assuming it was the same man throughout) served in 14 years between 1394 and 1422. As the 15th century progressed, however, most of the leading burgesses seem to have become reluctant to take on the office for more than one or two terms. That probably reflects the declining economic fortunes of the town, bringing problems in collecting sufficient revenue to meet the fee farm, the bailiffs of the year being made personally responsible for any shortfall. In 1447 the burgesses claimed that the bailiffs were having to make up £20 of the farm out of their own pockets.[2]

The impression gained from the lists of bailiffs that town government was oligarchic is reinforced by a complaint to the Crown in 1290 that the *potentes* of the town were levying immoderate tallages on the other inhabitants,[3] and by an agreement made with Gloucester Abbey about fishing rights in 1368 which gave preferential treatment to the bailiffs and leading burgesses (*valentiores burgenses*).[4] The leading inhabitants may have been embodied in some formal organization under the borough constitution, as at Ipswich, one of four boroughs which had similar charters to Gloucester's from King John in 1200: there the inhabitants assumed under their charter the right to appoint 12 burgesses, including, and as an advisory body to, the bailiffs and coroners.[5] It is not impossible that such a body existed at Gloucester from 1200, unrecorded in the sparse administrative records that have survived. The earliest suggestion found of such a body is in the later 14th century when on two occasions a group of 12 burgesses — the 2 bailiffs, the 4 stewards, and 6 others —

91 G.B.R., F 3/1; C 9/1–5.
92 *Glouc. Corp. Rec.* p. 10.
93 G.B.R., F 3/1–4.
94 e.g. ibid. 1; *Close R. 1231–4*, 349, 451.
95 *Close R. 1231–4*, 317.
96 *Rot. Litt. Claus.* (Rec. Com.), i. 359; *Cal. Lib. 1245–51*, 107, 138, 336.
97 *Close R. 1251–3*, 83; *Cal. Pat. 1374–7*, 489.
98 *Glouc. Corp. Rec.* p. 326; *Trans. B.G.A.S.* xiii. 389–90.
99 Below, Bailiffs of Glouc. 1200–1483.
1 *Glos. Subsidy Roll, 1327*, 1–2.
2 *Cal. Pat. 1446–52*, 70–1.
3 *Rot. Parl.* i. 47.
4 P.R.O., C 115/K 2/6682, f. 76v.; and for date of the agreement, G.B.R., B 2/2, ff. 21, 145.
5 C. Stephenson, *Borough and Town* (1933), 174–6.

were named as acting for the town.[6] Those records may be of isolated instances in which the authority of six leading burgesses was thought necessary to support the officers; they may on the other hand record a formal consultative body, convened regularly to act with the officers in actions taken on behalf of the community.

Apart from the bailiffs, coroners were the only borough officers whose election was provided for by the charter of 1200. Four were to be elected by the burgesses and, besides keeping the crown pleas and answering for them before the eyre, their office was seen as a check on the power of the bailiffs: they were to see that the bailiffs treated the inhabitants impartially in their government of the town.[7] The names of the coroners recorded in the late 13th century and the 14th[8] show that they were mostly drawn from the class of wealthy burgess that provided the bailiffs and so would presumably have had the authority to act in that way. Election of the coroners by the burgesses evidently gave way to appointment by the justices in eyre; at the 1287 eyre all four were replaced by the justices.[9] The development of the office at Gloucester in the later medieval period is obscure. Its role was presumably diminished by the bailiffs' assumption of the powers of justices of the peace under the charter of 1398[10] and the office may actually have been absorbed in that of the bailiffs; in 1440 one of the bailiffs was also serving as a coroner.[11]

Other officers who probably existed from 1200, thought not found recorded before 1264, were the two serjeants or under-bailiffs. The serjeants, who were provided with gowns each year,[12] and by the late 14th century carried official maces,[13] deputized for the bailiffs in their administrative functions and were involved particularly in performing such tasks for the hundred court as empanelling juries, summoning defendants, and collecting amercements.[14] In 1287 one is recorded as acting as keeper of the town gaol,[15] also a function performed by delegation from the bailiffs.[16] At the beginning of the 16th century and probably from an earlier date the serjeants were required to execute a bond at the beginning of their annual term of office as a guarantee of faithful service to the bailiffs.[17] Porters of the town gates had existed from at least 1143[18] and were receiving a regular stipend from the bailiffs in 1264[19] but were later paid by the muragers.[20] More than one clerk was employed by the bailiffs in the 1260s.[21] Separate officials were appointed to levy and apply the murage from at least 1298, apparently holding office for the term of the current royal grant.[22] The office survived until at least 1410 but by the 1390s the muragers had become merely collectors, handing the balance of the fund over to the borough stewards to be applied by them.[23]

The principal organ of government in the borough was the hundred court, which was so called by the late 12th century,[24] Gloucester claiming the status of a separate hundred.[25] The court met, probably weekly, in the building called the Boothall or guildhall,[26] and frankpledge sessions of the court were held twice a year.[27] No

[6] *Glouc. Corp. Rec.* pp. 360–1, 368; and cf. ibid. p. 380.
[7] Ibid. p. 8.
[8] P.R.O., JUST 1/274, rot. 13d.; JUST 1/278, rott. 65–6; JUST 2/34, rott. 15–16; JUST 2/35/2–3; JUST 2/36/2; JUST 2/38, rott. 7–8.
[9] P.R.O., JUST 1/278, rott. 65–6.
[10] *Glouc. Corp. Rec.* p. 14; cf. R.F. Hunnisett, *Medieval Coroner* (1961), 197–9.
[11] *Cal. Pat.* 1441–6, 134.
[12] G.B.R., F 3/1–4.
[13] P.R.O., C 115/K 2/6684, f. 159.
[14] Glouc. Cath. Libr., Reg. Abb. Froucester B, p. 342; G.B.R., G 10/1, *passim*.
[15] P.R.O., JUST 1/278, rot. 65d.

[16] *Cal. Pat.* 1385–9, 359–60; *Cal. Close*, 1392–6, 320; 1396–9, 4.
[17] G.B.R., G 10/1, pp. 187, 332.
[18] P.R.O., C 115/K 1/6681, f. 76v.
[19] G.B.R., F 3/1.
[20] Ibid. F 2/3–4.
[21] Ibid. F 3/1.
[22] Ibid. F 2/1; cf. *Cal. Pat.* 1292–1301, 352; 1301–7, 68.
[23] G.B.R., F 2/3–4; F 4/1.
[24] Glouc. Cath. Libr., Reg. Abb. Froucester B, pp. 256–7.
[25] G.B.R., B 8/4; *Feud. Aids*, ii. 263–4.
[26] *Glouc. Corp. Rec.* p. 14; Glouc. Cath. Libr., Reg. Abb. Froucester B, p. 341.
[27] G.B.R., G 8/1; Glos. Colln. 11664, no. 1.

hundred court records survive until 1502, after the major reorganization of the borough constitution in 1483, so it is not clear to what extent its functions went beyond the hearing of pleas. It certainly had a role in property transactions, many of which were witnessed by the court[28] and at least some enrolled there.[29] Regulations for the butchers' company in 1454 and for the cooks' company in 1482 were approved at the view of frankpledge and the former record also implies that admissions to the freedom of the borough took place in the court before the bailiffs.[30] It seems probable that up to 1483 the hundred court was the main forum for administrative business and that the promulgation of bylaws for the regulation of trade and the general running of the borough, and perhaps also the election of officers, were among its functions.

The court's jurisdiction in purely legal matters was defended and enhanced by the provisions in the various royal charters that protected the burgesses against pleading in external courts and upheld the authority of ancient customs of the borough in determining pleas heard there. Its fullest extent, as defined by Richard II's charter of 1398, included the hearing of assizes of novel disseisin and mort d'ancestor.[31] The legal franchises claimed by the burgesses in 1287 included infangthief, the use of the gallows being shared with the county sheriff,[32] but in 1306 they appear to have been claiming to execute justice on all perpetrators of felonies within the borough.[33] The right to take the goods of felons, together with those of fugitives and outlaws, was not secured until 1398.[34]

If there was any organ of government apart from the court it may have been some form of guild meeting. At the beginning of the 16th century it was recorded that at a 'merchants' guild' held on St. Thomas's day (21 December) each year the balance of a sum of £500 left to the town by Thomas Gloucester (d. 1447) was handed over by four 'conservators' to their successors.[35] If such meetings were convened before 1483 they presumably provided another forum for discussion and decision on communal matters, for the terminology employed by the charter of 1200 and by later documents makes it clear that the guild comprised all those inhabitants who had full burgess rights. The charter granted both legal and trading franchises to 'the burgesses of Gloucester of the merchants' guild',[36] and the common seal of the borough that was in use c. 1240 bore the legend: 'sigillum burgensium de gilda mercatorum Gloucestrie'.[37] In 1409 and later those acquiring the freedom were sworn in as 'burgesses' to the 'merchants' guild'.[38]

An important development in the borough administration before 1483 was the emergence of an organization for administering those communal funds which were not appropriated to the fee farm and not therefore the direct responsibility of the bailiffs. A growing body of property and rents came to the community through new buildings, or extensions to existing buildings, on the waste land of the borough, and there were also lands given to it for certain communal purposes or held in trust for the hospitals or for other charitable or pious uses. Four stewards of the borough, apparently elected annually, were recorded from 1357 acting with the bailiffs in administering and leasing communal and trust property,[39] and there was presumably a separate treasury for receiving the profits from communal property in 1364 when a distinction was made between the landgavel rent owed from a piece of land to the

---

[28] e.g. *Glouc. Corp. Rec.* pp. 101, 144; Glouc. Cath. Libr., Reg. Abb. Froucester B, pp. 191, 504.
[29] *Glouc. Corp. Rec.* pp. 330 n., 375 n.
[30] Glos. Colln. 11664, no. 1; G.B.R., B 1/1.
[31] *Glouc. Corp. Rec.* pp. 6–7, 11–14.
[32] *Plac. de Quo Warr.* (Rec. Com.), 241.
[33] P.R.O., JUST 1/286, rot. 7.

[34] *Glouc. Corp. Rec.* p. 13.
[35] G.B.R., B 2/1, ff. 208v.–224; cf. *Glouc. Corp. Rec.* p. 398.
[36] *Glouc. Corp. Rec.* pp. 6–7.
[37] *Trans. B.G.A.S.* xiii. 385–6.
[38] G.B.R., F 4/1–2; C 9/6.
[39] *Glouc. Corp. Rec.* pp. 353, 361, 364, 368–9 sqq.

bailiffs and stewards and a rent owed to the stewards alone;[40] the communal treasury was recorded by that term in 1412 when the filing of deeds was among its functions.[41] The rents received by the stewards from the communal property amounted to £12 3s. 2d. by 1409,[42] and by 1455 the property comprised c. 25 burgage tenements and various shops and other parcels of land.[43] The stewards' other main source of income was the fines paid by those admitted to the freedom. Out of their income they were required to maintain the common property, including the Boothall, and by the early 15th century they were also administering the funds raised by virtue of royal grants of pavage and murage.[44] Their responsibility for maintaining the pipes and conduits of the public water supply probably dated from 1438 when the community acquired the system.[45]

The number of the stewards suggests that each had particular responsibility within one of the four wards into which the town was divided. The wards, named from the cardinal points and apparently based on the four main streets, were recorded from the mid 13th century when their inhabitants were responsible for taking felons and for supplying members of coroner's inquests.[46] In 1327 they were also being used as units for tax assessment.[47]

Gloucester in the Late Middle Ages

In the late Middle Ages Gloucester experienced the economic problems that affected many English towns at the period, but the inherent strength of its position as a centre of trade, administration, and communications brought it through them without any dramatic change in its fortunes. Among English towns it rated in terms of wealth at 16th in 1334, 15th in 1377, and 17th in 1523.[48]

The only direct evidence of the impact of the Black Death on Gloucester concerns the canons of Llanthony Priory who (in a record of a century later) were said to have lost two thirds of their number, 19 out of 30, at the first outbreak of the plague in 1349.[49] Gloucester Abbey appears to have lost about a quarter of its complement of monks.[50] In 1377 2,239 adults were assessed for the poll tax in Gloucester,[51] so the total population was presumably well above 3,000.

The available evidence for the late 14th century and early 15th suggests that the town was still enjoying reasonable prosperity, based on a continuance of its traditional economic roles. There was some export trade, particularly in corn, and goods were imported through Bristol, Southampton, and London and distributed, together with Gloucester's own manufactured goods, to the lesser towns of the region. Gloucester also benefited from its position on trade routes into South Wales and between the Midlands and Bristol, though its role in the trade of the river Severn was limited by competition from other towns. The metal working and clothmaking industries maintained their importance, as did the marketing of agricultural produce for surrounding villages.

In the late 14th century and the early 15th the town had a group of wealthy men, mostly merchants and drapers, who bought property, endowed chantries, and monopolized the office of bailiff.[52] Their willingness repeatedly to undertake that

[40] Ibid. p. 357.
[41] G.B.R., J 1/1069 (endorsement).
[42] Ibid. F 4/1.
[43] Glouc. Rental, 1455, passim.
[44] G.B.R., F 4/1.
[45] Ibid. 2; Glouc. Corp. Rec pp. 391–2.
[46] P.R.O., JUST 1/274, rot. 13 and d.; JUST 1/278,

rot. 65.
[47] Glos. Subsidy Roll, 1327, 1–2.
[48] Hoskins, Local Hist. in Eng. 238–9.
[49] P.R.O., C 115/K 2/6685, f. 12v.
[50] V.C.H. Glos. ii. 58.
[51] Hoskins, Local Hist. in Eng. 238–9.
[52] Below, trade and ind. 1327–1547.

office indicates that the fee-farm revenues, drawn from tolls, landgavel, and profits of justice, were producing adequate sums; the bailiffs were made responsible for making up any shortfall. In 1397 the burgesses were able to lend £200 to the Crown, a large sum compared to that offered by other towns,[53] and in 1404 a further £100 was lent.[54] That St. Mary de Crypt church, the greater part of St. Nicholas, and the chancel of St. Michael were rebuilt at the period could also be mentioned as indications of prosperity, but the disappearance of most of the other nine medieval churches makes such evidence difficult to put in its proper perspective.[55]

In the mid and later 15th century there is mounting evidence of a decline in prosperity. It exists most obviously in a series of appeals addressed by the townspeople to the central government. In an appeal for aid in 1447 they said that the town was depopulated by plague and that hardly £40 of the annual fee farm of £60 could be collected.[56] In 1455 when seeking paving powers they mentioned their great poverty.[57] Similar complaints were no doubt part of the negotiations that led to the granting of the charter of 1483, which reduced the fee farm to £20.[58] The farm was restored to its original amount by Henry VII, who was petitioned for a reduction in 1487 or 1488; the burgesses then claimed that 300 houses were in decay, that their walls and bridges were in disrepair, and that many of the wealthier inhabitants had left town to avoid serving the office of bailiff.[59] Again, in 1505, when presenting their case for levying tolls on the river trade, the burgesses spoke of the decay of the town and the difficulty of meeting the burdens of repairing Westgate bridge and the quay.[60]

As has often been said, such statements must be viewed with caution because of their context. In attempts to gain financial relief from the central government the worst possible picture was given and such petitions from towns, which are fairly common at the period, often follow a set formula;[61] in the suit over tolls in 1505 the final petitions of Gloucester and its fellow defendant, Worcester, were couched in almost identical terms.[62] Sometimes the petitioners resorted to manipulation of the facts. In 1455 the burgesses said that they had no communal property that they could use to finance street paving,[63] whereas the community had by then acquired a substantial holding of houses in the town.[64] In 1505 they said that their annual fee-farm revenues did not 'in certainty' produce more than £9;[65] they were presumably referring to the landgavel which produced £10 15s. 7½d. in 1455[66] and was indeed the only fixed sum, but there were also the variable sources of income, the tolls and amercements.

The picture of economic decline given by the appeals to the Crown can not, however, be discounted entirely, and it is supported by other evidence, though some of it of a negative kind. The wealthy merchants and drapers of the late 14th century and the early 15th were not followed by any prosperous descendants and there is very little evidence of any wealthy trading burgesses in the mid 15th century. The decline in the fee-farm revenues seems to be reflected in the fact that fewer men were then prepared to be elected as bailiff for more than one or two terms.[67]

There is also more concrete evidence in the reduction by the late 15th century in the number of unfranchised inhabitants and foreigners who paid for trading rights in the

[53] *Cal. Pat.* 1396–9, 179.
[54] Ibid. 1401–5, 417.
[55] Below, Churches and Chapels.
[56] *Cal. Pat.* 1446–52, 70–1.
[57] *Rot. Parl.* v. 338.   [58] *Glouc. Corp. Rec.* p. 16.
[59] Ibid. pp. 61–2.
[60] *Select Cases in Star Chamber*, i (Selden Soc. xvi), 211–13.

[61] Cf. R. B. Dobson, 'Urban Decline in Late Medieval Eng.' *Trans. R.H.S.* (5th ser.), xxvii. 10–12.
[62] *Select Cases in Star Chamber*, i (Selden Soc. xvi), 213–15.
[63] *Rot. Parl.* v. 338.   [64] Above, town govt. 1200–1483.
[65] *Select Cases in Star Chamber*, i (Selden Soc. xvi), 212.
[66] *Glouc. Rental, 1455*, 115.
[67] Above, town govt. 1200–1483.

town. Rolls for 1396, 1398, and 1423 list 285, 283, and *c.* 252 names, respectively, while one for 1481 lists only 108; in those rolls the numbers who can be definitely identified as traders from outside the town are respectively 87, 108, 98, and 33.[68] The figures for the outsiders may be the more significant indication of a decline in trade, for the reduction in the numbers of inhabitants on the rolls could mean that more were acquiring the wealth to purchase the freedom. Stewards' accounts for 1493 provide another indication of decline, showing that out of a total rental of £29 19s. 1½d. from communal property in the town £7 8s. 8d. had lapsed.[69]

It would be unwise to draw too definite conclusions from such isolated survivals of what were runs of annual records but the balance of the evidence is that, like other towns at the period, Gloucester underwent a period of decline in the mid and later 15th century. The wide-ranging nature of its functions in trade, administration, and communications within its region enabled it to survive without permanent dislocation, and in the early 16th century there was a revival in its fortunes, helped probably by the growth of the capping industry and a revival in its corn trade. Wealthy tradesmen are once more in evidence, including merchants, cappers, tanners, clothiers, and, most numerous, mercers and drapers.[70]

Late-medieval Gloucester no longer figured regularly at the centre of national affairs[71] but it retained its importance in local administration. That was reflected in the number of successful lawyers who played a part in town life at the period. Employment by the courts and administrations of county and borough was supplemented by work for the local monastic houses. One of the earliest lawyers to achieve prominence in the town was Robert Gilbert, who married the widow of a wealthy Gloucester merchant, John Banbury.[72] He was being employed by the townspeople to defend their liberties in 1409,[73] served as bailiff at least twice,[74] and by 1417 and until at least 1434 held the post of steward of Llanthony Priory's estates.[75] A similar example at a later date was Walter Rowden (d. 1514),[76] who was three times mayor of the town[77] and served as steward of Gloucester Abbey's manors.[78] Probably less closely involved in the town were other lawyers who became county gentry. In 1455 among a total of six lawyers who owned or occupied property in Gloucester[79] were John Edwards who became lord of Rodmarton manor in the early 1440s,[80] Thomas Deerhurst who probably owned Field Court manor in Hardwicke,[81] and Sir William Nottingham who was attorney-general 1451–61 and amassed considerable estates in the county.[82] One incentive for such men to buy property in the town and serve borough offices was apparently the opportunity of a seat in parliament: all five of the men mentioned above sat as M.P. for the borough.[83]

The opportunities for lawyers in Gloucester were increased by the duplication of the machinery of county administration under the town charter granted in 1483. The charter, which made Gloucester and the adjoining Dudstone and King's Barton hundred into a separate county, incorporated the town, and give it a mayor and

[68] G.B.R., C 9/2–5.
[69] Ibid. F 4/2.
[70] Below, trade and ind. 1327–1547.
[71] Above, Crown and boro.; military hist.
[72] Glos. R.O., P 154/14/CH 1/3, 15.
[73] G.B.R., I 1/15.
[74] Below, Bailiffs of Glouc. 1200–1483.
[75] P.R.O., C 115/K 2/6682, ff. 121, 245.
[76] Hockaday Abs. cciii, 1514.
[77] Fosbrooke, *Glouc.* 208.
[78] Glouc. Cath. Libr., Reg. Abb. Newton, f. 48 and v.,

where, in 1512, another man was appointed to hold the office jointly with him, probably because of his age or illness.
[79] *Glouc. Rental, 1455,* 7, 53, 75, 77, 89, 93; the rental also mentions (pp. 65, 93) three other lawyers, including Rob. Gilbert, as recent owners or occupiers.
[80] *V.C.H. Glos.* xi. 236.
[81] Ibid. x. 184.
[82] *Trans. B.G.A.S.* l. 185–99.
[83] J. T. Driver, 'Parl. Burgesses for Bristol and Glouc. 1422–37', *Trans. B.G.A.S.* lxxiv. 68–9, 81–4, 87–9; Williams, *Parl. Hist. of Glos.* 186–8.

aldermen, was the major landmark in the history of the town's government in the late Middle Ages.[84] An earlier, probably more gradual, development was the appearance of separate machinery for administering the property acquired by the community and financing public works.[85] That development was one expression at the period of the communal identity of the townspeople, which was also apparent in the aggressive attitude they displayed from the late 14th century over the jurisdictionary claims of the two large monastic houses, Gloucester Abbey and Llanthony Priory.[86]

The focus of communal life and the centre of the borough administration was the Boothall, or guildhall, in Westgate Street, and two other buildings, the Tolsey at the Cross and a council house at the east gate, came into use at the end of the period.[87] For other business, mainly of an incidental or private nature, much use was made of the town's churches. A bond entered into in 1396 was to be redeemed in St. Mary de Lode,[88] and in 1417 arbitration of a dispute was convened in Blackfriars and adjourned to St. Mary de Grace.[89] Llanthony Priory held a court for its town tenants in St. Owen's church[90] and the court of the honor of Hereford met in St. Mary de Crypt.[91] In St. Mary de Lode the first letters patent of Lord Chancellor Richard Scrope were sealed in October 1378 when parliament was meeting in Gloucester Abbey.[92]

An additional support to Gloucester's economy was its role in road communications. By 1455 at least 10 inns in its main streets catered for those visiting the town for trade or other business or passing through. Inns identified by name in 1455 were the New Inn in Northgate Street, recently rebuilt on a substantial scale by Gloucester Abbey, the St. George in Southgate Street (which had closed by 1509), and Savage's inn (by 1502 called alternatively the Catherine Wheel) in the later Berkeley Street; among others mentioned were an inn at the Boothall, another nearby, called the Bear in 1528 (later the Old Bear), and one at the quay kept by William Boatman, presumably that called Boatman inn in 1503.[93] In 1509 were mentioned the Swan in Northgate Street and the Lion in Westgate Street.[94] Between 1525 and 1544 were recorded the Ram in Northgate Street, which was rebuilt by Gloucester Abbey about that period; a great inn owned by the abbey in St. Mary de Grace parish in upper Westgate Street, probably the later Fleece;[95] the Bull in Northgate Street; the Crown and the George (later the Lower George), both in lower Westgate Street;[96] and the Bell on the east side of Southgate Street.[97] In 1583 most of the above mentioned were among twelve establishments distinguished as 'ancient' inns of the city.[98]

The importance to the town of its major roads presumably encouraged leading townsmen to choose them as an object of pious gifts. Gifts for repairing roads around the town were a regular item in wills from the late 14th century, with sums of £20 from John Ruseby (d. c. 1395)[99] and Robert Swansea (d. 1411)[1] among the more substantial. In 1401 there was a papal exhortation for alms for the repair of the London road at Wotton,[2] and in 1422 the bishop of Worcester offered indulgences for

[84] Below, town govt. 1483–1547.
[85] Above, town govt. 1200–1483.
[86] Below, town and religious communities.
[87] Below, Public Buildings.
[88] P.R.O., C 115/K 2/6684, f. 189v.
[89] Ibid. C 115/K 2/6682, f. 160.
[90] Ibid. C 115/K 1/6681, ff. 38, 56; C 115/K 2/6685, f. 11.
[91] Ibid. E 142/32, rot. 3; C 115/K 2/6685, f. 11.
[92] Cal. Close, 1377–81, 216.
[93] Glouc. Rental, 1455, 7, 9, 13, 39, 41, 47, 51, 63, 81, 85, 127; and for the George, G.B.R., J 5/3; for the Bear, Glouc. Corp. Rec. p. 428; for the Catherine Wheel, Glouc. Cath. Libr., Reg. Abb. Braunche, p. 53; and for Boatman inn, G.B.R., G 10/1, p. 48.

[94] G.B.R., J 5/3.
[95] Glouc. Cath. Libr., Reg. Abb. Malvern, i, f. 244; ii, f. 82v. An inscr. on the doorhead of the Ram (now in Glouc. Folk Museum) records its rebuilding by the town monk, the abbey official responsible for its property in the town.
[96] G.B.R., J 5/4; J 3/16, ff. 9v., 50v.–51; Austin, Crypt Sch. 149.
[97] G.B.R., J 5/5.
[98] Ibid. B 1/1.
[99] Hockaday Abs. ccxix, 1394; cf. P.R.O., C 115/K 2/6684, f. 185v.
[1] Hockaday abs. ccxvii.
[2] Cal. Papal Reg. v. 390.

the repair of the Bristol road between Cambridge, in Slimbridge, and Gloucester.[3] Of equal importance to the town was the road coming from South Wales and Hereford by way of the causeway and bridges west of the town, which attracted many bequests in the late Middle Ages. The roads from Painswick and Tewkesbury were also much travelled and, like the three mentioned above, entered the town by official gateways manned by porters.[4] Roadside chapels outside the town are an indication of the amount of travelling. A hermit occupied a chapel at Saintbridge on the Painswick route in the early 16th century and probably collected alms for road repairs.[5] A chapel at Highnam on the South Wales road was used by travellers at the same period,[6] and there may have been another chapel on the Tewkesbury road at Longford, where a wayside cross attracted offerings from travellers.[7]

It has sometimes been suggested that many of the visitors to Gloucester in the late Middle Ages came there on pilgrimage. The Gloucester Abbey chronicler states that Edward II's tomb in the abbey church was attracting visitors from all over England within a few years of his burial in 1327 and that their offerings financed some of the rebuilding work at the church in the mid 14th century.[8] In 1391, however, when the monks had licence to appropriate Holy Trinity church and its chapel of St. Mary de Grace the profits were needed for providing lights and ornaments around the tomb,[9] so it may be that the popularity of the cult was short lived. The tradition that the rebuilding of the New Inn in the mid 15th century was to provide lodging for pilgrims was not recorded before the 18th century[10] and the fact that it was the abbey which rebuilt the inn may alone have been enough to promote it. Offerings no doubt continued at the king's tomb and at the shrine of St. Kyneburgh, whose remains were ceremonially retranslated by Llanthony Priory to her chapel at the south gate in 1390,[11] while the relics of St. Oswald still attracted an occasional bequest in wills of the early 16th century.[12] The donors were probably for the most part people who were in the town for reasons of trade or business rather than those specifically making pilgrimage.

Apart from its shrines Gloucester offered many other objects for pious bequests. Gifts of land to the larger monastic houses had all but ceased by the late 14th century but the smaller houses, the hospitals and friaries, still benefited from cash bequests. Religious devotion was centred mainly on the parish churches. In the later 14th century and the earlier 15th at least nine endowments were made to found or augment chantries.[13] Other chapels in the churches were maintained by the religious guilds, of which five were recorded in the town in 1455. The most important was apparently the Holy Trinity guild, attached to St. Mary de Lode church,[14] which had been founded by 1420;[15] in the 1530s the name of its master, usually one of the aldermen, was recorded each year with the chief borough officers on the freemen's rolls.[16]

Another form of association for religious as well as social purposes was the trade companies, recorded in the town from the mid 15th century.[17] The weavers' company[18] and the tanners' company maintained chantry chapels, and ordinances for

[3] Worc. Episc. Reg., Reg. Morgan, ii. f. 8v.
[4] Below, Bridges, Gates, and Walls.
[5] Hockaday Abs. ccxvi, 1506; Glouc. Cath. Libr., Reg. Abb. Malvern, ii, f. 41v., a lease of the hermitage in 1531, which obliged the lessee to spend an annual sum on repairs to the road.   [6] V.C.H. Glos. x. 26–7.
[7] Below, Outlying Hamlets, intro.
[8] Hist. & Cart. Mon. Glouc. i. 46–7.
[9] Cal. Pat. 1388–92, 406.
[10] Bodl. MS. Top. Glouc. c.3, f. 45, which says that New

Inn Lane was formerly called Pilgrims Lane; cf. Rudder, Glos. 86.
[11] P.R.O., C 115/K 2/6684, f. 135.
[12] Worcs. R.O., Worc. dioc. wills, file I, no. 52.
[13] Below, Churches and Chapels.
[14] Glouc. Rental, 1455, 23, 31, 79, 81, 99.
[15] Hockaday Abs. ccxv.
[16] G.B.R., C 9/6.
[17] Below, regulation of trade and ind.
[18] Hockaday Abs. ccxix, 1485.

the tanners made in 1542 illustrate the various roles played by the companies in addition to regulating their trades. Pensions were provided for impoverished members; the whole company attended funerals of members; masses for dead members were held in the company's chapel in St. John's church; and twice a year the members, in their livery, attended the mayor and sheriffs in the king's watch, afterwards holding a 'drinking' in their hall in Hare Lane.[19]

A Lollard priest preached at Gloucester in 1383[20] but there is no further evidence of dissatisfaction with the traditional forms of religion until 1448 when two Gloucester men, William Fuer, a weaver, and William Grainger (or Skay), renounced their heresy before the bishop of Worcester. Fuer had learnt his opinions from some Bristol weavers and had spoken against landownership by the Church, begging by friars, and the veneration of relics.[21] In 1510 William Huntley of Gloucester was excommunicated for persistently denying the 'keys' (claves) of the Church.[22] The arrival of protestant ideas was causing dissension in the town in 1536. One of the sheriffs, Thomas Bell the younger, then complained to the bishop of London of the views of some of the chaplains who had been admitted to serve in Gloucester by Bishop Latimer. The following year Thomas Bell the elder, then mayor, was accused by two other leading townsmen, John Huggins and John Rastell, of calling Latimer a heretic[23] and there was trouble in Holy Trinity parish over the views of the curate, Hugh Rawlings.[24] In 1540 efforts to reconcile the opposing parties in the town were made by Thomas Evans, a confidant of Thomas Cromwell,[25] but later that year a weaver from Stonehouse read from an English bible in St. Mary de Crypt church and denied the doctrine of purgatory, much to the annoyance, it was said, of the congregation.[26]

The major change in the life of the town at the end of the period was that brought about by the dissolution of its monastic houses. St. Oswald's Priory was surrendered in 1536, the three friaries in 1538, Llanthony Priory in 1539, and Gloucester Abbey at the beginning of 1540.[27] The creation of the new bishopric of Gloucester in September 1541 made those events a less severe dislocation than they might have been. The great abbey church became the cathedral and, with most of its associated monastic buildings, was preserved; a group of cathedral clergy replaced the monks in residence there; and the abbey's extensive holding of property in the town was transferred to the dean and chapter.[28]

At the sales of the other monastic property in the town the main purchaser was the elder Thomas Bell, a wealthy capper, who thus became the largest private landowner. He bought Blackfriars and some Llanthony Priory property for £240 in 1539,[30] more Llanthony property for £100 in 1542,[31] and the bulk of the Llanthony property together with property of other monastic houses for £627 in 1543.[32] His later purchases included some of the chantry property in 1548, by which time he had acquired a knighthood.[33] The bulk of the former chantry property was bought in 1549 by Richard Pate, later recorder of Gloucester, and Thomas Chamberlayne, some of it passing from them to the corporation and to St. Bartholomew's Hospital.[34]

[19] Glos. Colln. 28652, no. 4.   [20] V.C.H. Glos. ii. 21.
[21] Ibid. 22; Worc. Episc. Reg., Reg. Carpenter, i, ff. 58–9.
[22] Hockaday Abs. cciii.
[23] L. & P. Hen. VIII, x, p. 463; xii (1), pp. 139–40; cf. Fosbrooke, Glouc. 208. The two Bells were described as brothers (perhaps actually step or half brothers) in 1525: Glouc. Cath. Libr., Reg. Abb. Malvern, i, f. 231v.
[24] L. & P. Hen. VIII, xii (1), pp. 313, 484.
[25] Ibid. xv, pp. 66–7.
[26] Hockaday Abs. ccclv.

[27] V.C.H. Glos. ii. 60, 86, 90, 111–12.
[28] Glouc. Corp. Rec. pp. 19–26; L. & P. Hen. VIII, xvi, p. 572.
[29] Cf. Glouc. Cath. Libr., Reg. Abb. Malvern, ii, f. 111v.
[30] L. & P. Hen. VIII, xiv (1), p. 590.
[31] Ibid. xvii, p. 265.
[32] Ibid. xviii (2), pp. 51–2.
[33] Cal. Pat. 1548–9, 40–1.
[34] Trans. B.G.A.S. lvi. 206–8; Glouc. Corp. Rec. pp. 438–40, 444–5.

Gloucester entered the early modern period under a new style: it was declared to be a city as a result of the foundation of the bishopric in 1541.[35]

Trade and Industry 1327–1547

In the late Middle Ages Gloucester continued to play a limited role in the import and export trade and enjoyed an apparently significant share of the down-river trade in corn. The basis of its economy remained, however, its industries, to which the new trades of pinning and capping were added, and its function as a local market centre and distributor of goods to the surrounding market towns. In common with many English towns it suffered a slump in prosperity in the 15th century, but its varied sources of livelihood enabled it to surmount its problems by the early years of the 16th.[36]

The wine trade evidently retained its importance. In the 1330s deputy customers were appointed to collect duty on wine imported to Gloucester,[37] and in 1404 the burgesses were allowed to recoup a £100 loan to the Crown out of the customs duties they owed on wine and other merchandise.[38] The murage collected in the town in 1394 included that on 101 tuns of wine.[39] Some Gloucester merchants probably also had a share in the growing export trade in English cloth, particularly as clothmaking remained one of the town's main industries; the appointment in 1347 of a deputy customer for cloth exported from Gloucester and the other 'creeks' of the lower Severn is, however, the only evidence found for that trade.[40] The considerable trade in herring and other fish from Ireland to the Severn[41] was another branch in which Gloucester men probably had a share, though no record of their involvement has been found before 1536.[42] The export of fruit and cider down river and as far as Cornwall, recorded in the 1580s,[43] is likely to have formed another part of the town's trade from the late Middle Ages.

One branch of waterborne trade in which Gloucester played a significant role was that in corn. The town was evidently a centre for the collection of corn from the Vale of Gloucester and from further up river, to be sent for export or to supply Bristol and South Wales. In the 1330s three Gloucester men were granted export licences for corn, two of them to ship it to the continent and the third to ship it to Wales and Ireland,[44] and in 1347 some men of the town complained that the amount exported from the Gloucester area was causing a shortage locally.[45] In the early 16th century, perhaps by long established practice, much of the corn brought in from the surrounding countryside for sale was carted directly to the town quay.[46]

In the late 14th century Gloucester's trade in corn, wine, and other merchandise enriched a small but influential group of merchants. Probably the most significant was John Banbury (d. c. 1404) who was exporting corn in 1386.[47] Other merchants of the period were John Monmouth, who became lessee of the demesne of Elmstone Hardwicke manor in 1373;[48] Thomas Pope (d. 1400),[49] who was bailiff in three years in the 1390s and founded a chantry in Holy Trinity church;[50] John Head (or Anlep),

[35] *Glouc. Corp. Rec.* p. 20.
[36] For a general discussion of the town's fortunes in the period, above, Glouc. in late Middle Ages.
[37] *Cal. Pat.* 1330–4, 166, 197; 1334–8, 23.
[38] Ibid. 1401–5, 417.
[39] G.B.R., F 2/3.
[40] *Cal. Pat.* 1345–8, 277.
[41] Cf. P.R.O., E 122/19/14, ff. 25–6.
[42] *L. & P. Hen. VIII*, xi, p. 572.
[43] G.B.R., B 2/1, ff. 92v.–92A; P.R.O., E 134/25 Eliz.

Hil./3.
[44] *Cal. Pat.* 1330–4, 232, 509, 514; 1338–40, 81.
[45] *Cal. Close*, 1346–9, 281.
[46] G.B.R., B 2/1, f. 22.
[47] Glos. R.O., P 154/14/ CH 1/1–19; *Cal. Pat.* 1385–9, 128; 1396–9, 496; 1401–5, 148.
[48] *Cal. Pat.* 1370–4, 366; Westm. Abb. Mun. 32755.
[49] Hockaday Abs. ccxiii; *Cal. Close*, 1389–92, 482–3.
[50] Below, Churches and Chapels; Bailiffs of Glouc. 1200–1483.

who was described as a draper in 1382[51] and was possibly involved in the export of cloth at his death in 1391 when he had goods overseas and left 20 marks for the upkeep of the quay;[52] and, probably, William Heyberare, who served as bailiff in six years between 1361 and 1384, gave a number of religious endowments,[53] and was employed by the Crown on various commissions, including an inquiry into smuggling on the South Wales coast in 1389.[54] Some of those men made considerable investments in property both within and outside the town. Banbury made the first of many purchases of house property in Gloucester in 1378 and also acquired an estate at Horsemarling, in Moreton Valence parish.[55] In 1389 Head held 8 houses and 10 shops in the town and an estate of 2 ploughlands outside it and Heyberare held 4 houses, 6 shops, and an outlying estate of 1 ploughland.[56]

Thomas Pope, John Head, and William Heyberare were from families that had been prominent in the town since the early 14th century[57] but there is no record of the families of any of the late 14th-century merchants occupying a prominent position later, a fact that presumably reflects the declining fortunes of the town in the 15th century. It may be that the grain trade on the Severn suffered a decline in the middle years of the century; that situation could lie behind the Crown's response in 1447 to a request for measures to halt the town's decline — permission to build two corn mills at Westgate bridge.[58] During the 15th century very few Gloucester men can be identified as merchants. One of the few was Philip Monger, who had the major share in overland trade from Southampton in the 1440s, bringing in woad and madder, used as dyestuffs in Gloucester's clothmaking industry, and some wine.[59] Monger was apparently a man of some wealth, for he and his wife rebuilt the chapel of St. Thomas outside the north gate.[60] Other merchants were Walter Spring (fl. 1444),[61] Henry Dood,[62] bailiff in 1446, and probably the wealthy burgess Richard Manchester who died in 1454.[63] By the end of the 15th century, when a revival of trade seems to have begun, the merchant Garet van Eck, presumably a Fleming by origin, was established in the town as one of its aldermen.[64] Another Gloucester man, David Vaughan, was importing goods into Bristol in 1502 in a 100-ton ship, built to his order.[65] Merchants who occur later included Robert Hawardine, who probably traded in wine, for he was lessee of the New Inn in 1508,[66] and Aldermen Robert Poole (d. 1545)[67] who built an 80-ton ship, the *Mary Fortune*, at Gloucester and traded with it to Spain and Portugal.[68]

Gloucester's lack of a large merchant class reflected the fact that it was mainly dependent on Bristol for the trade it conducted with the continent. An order made in 1387, commissioning two Gloucester men to check smuggling, stated that goods were shipped overseas directly from the town,[69] but other evidence, though fragmentary, suggests that the town's merchants usually transhipped their goods at Bristol. Nicholas Birdlip of Gloucester joined some Bristol merchants in a venture in the Baltic trade in 1389[70] and John Rawlings of Gloucester granted a Bristol ship, with his

[51] Glouc. Cath. Libr., Reg. Abb. Froucester B, p. 481.
[52] Hockaday Abs. ccxiii, 1390; *Cal. Close*, 1389–92, 483.
[53] *Cal. Pat.* 1361–4, 459; 1385–9, 338; 1388–92, 407.
[54] Ibid. 1381–5, 598; 1388–92, 60, 126.
[55] Glos. R.O., P 154/14/ CH 1/4, 8–10, 12, 14, 16–17.
[56] *Inq. p.m. Glos.* 1359–1413, 157–8.
[57] Below, Bailiffs of Glouc. 1200–1483; *Glos. Subsidy Roll, 1327*, 1–2.   [58] *Cal. Pat.* 1446–52, 70–1.
[59] *Brokage Bk. of Southampton, 1439–40* (Southampton Rec. Soc. xl), 77, 113, 136, 143, 148, 155–6, 159, 162; *1443–4*, i (Southampton Rec. Ser. iv), 7, 12, 20, 28–9, 57; ii (Southampton Rec. Ser. vi), 153, 200, 222–3, 240, 266, 322–7.

[60] *Glouc. Rental, 1455*, 99.
[61] *Cal. Close*, 1441–7, 383.
[62] *Glouc. Rental, 1455*, 47.
[63] *Glouc. Corp. Rec.* pp. 399–402.
[64] Below, Aldermen of Glouc. 1483–1835; Hockaday Abs. ccxvi, 1506.
[65] *Cal. Pat.* 1494–1509, 270.
[66] Glouc. Cath. Libr., Reg. Abb. Braunche, p. 175.
[67] Below, Aldermen of Glouc. 1483–1835.
[68] P.R.O., E 134/25 Eliz. Hil./3.
[69] *Cal. Fine R.* 1383–91, 178.
[70] *Overseas Trade of Bristol in the Later Middle Ages* (Bristol Rec. Soc. vii), pp. 28–9.

goods in England and overseas, to Thomas Pope in 1391.[71] John Banbury carried on at least part of his trade through Bristol,[72] as did David Vaughan.[73] Gloucester's dependence on Bristol was emphasized by its inclusion for customs purposes in the Bristol port area, though in the mid 14th century the town and the creeks below, such as Newnham, Gatcombe (in Awre parish), Frampton on Severn, and Berkeley, were controlled by separate deputy customers,[74] an arrangement that prefigured the creation of the port of Gloucester in 1580.

Although the narrows and shallows of the stretch of river immediately below Gloucester were presumably less of an obstacle to navigation in medieval times, when seagoing vessels were still very small, than they were in later centuries, they were already a factor that contributed to the use of Bristol and the creeks on the lower Severn for shipping and landing goods for Gloucester. Among the creeks, Gatcombe in particular was firmly established as a principal outlet for Gloucester's maritime trade by the 1580s[75] and probably had been used as such from an early date; an inhabitant of Gatcombe, James Whaley, who had property in the town before 1509,[76] was possibly involved in that trade.

Few occupations concerned with the river or maritime trade figure in the records of late-medieval Gloucester: a roll of non-freeman inhabitants in 1423 lists a single trowman[77] and entrants to the freedom in the period 1535–45 included two boatmen, a waterman, and a mariner.[78] As in later centuries, Gloucester men probably provided a regular connexion with Bristol by trows, but much of the trade with other places on the river was in the hands of outsiders. In 1411 the townspeople joined Bristol in a complaint that they were being forced to hire at extortionate prices trows belonging to men of Bewdley (Worcs.), Shropshire, and Wales for carrying their goods on the upper part of the river; that was disrupting in particular their supplies of firewood, and a group of Gloucester men bringing wood past Bewdley on some kind of raft had been attacked and their cargo lost.[79] Four Bewdley trowmen with seven vessels between them were trading regularly to Gloucester in 1481.[80] Coal, two grades of which were on sale in the town in 1500,[81] and timber, the sale of which at the quay was regulated in 1514,[82] continued to bulk large in the cargoes brought to the town from further up the Severn in the early 16th century. The supply of salt to the town, which was being maintained by Droitwich salters in the 1390s and 1481,[83] may also have come by river.

The greatest part of the trade on the Severn was, however, carried on between places up river and Bristol, a fact that caused jealousy in the Gloucester burgesses and aggravated the resentment at their dependence on Bristol. Their attempts to profit from that passing trade, a recurrent feature of the town's history over several centuries, were recorded from 1400 when complaints were made that the bailiffs had arrested boats carrying victuals down to Bristol.[84] The following year they were also accused of levying tolls on boats carrying victuals up river and forcing them to sell their cargoes in the town,[85] and a similar complaint was made in 1411 that Gloucester, Worcester, and Bridgnorth (Salop.) were exacting toll on wine, oil, and other

[71] *Cal. Close*, 1389–92, 482–3.
[72] Glos. R.O., P 154/14/ CH 1/6. He should not be confused with a contemporary Bristol merchant of the same name: *Great Orphan Book and Book of Wills*, ed. T.P. Wadley (B.G.A.S. 1886), 70–1; cf. Glos. R.O., P 154/14/ CH 1/3, 18.
[73] Above.
[74] *Cal. Pat.* 1345–8, 277; cf. ibid. 1330–4, 166, 197.
[75] G.B.R., B 2/1, ff. 90v., 91v.; P.R.O., E 134/25 Eliz. Hil./3.
[76] G.B.R., J 5/3.

[77] Below, Table I.
[78] Below, Table II.
[79] *Rot. Parl.* iii. 665–6.
[80] G.B.R., C 9/5.
[81] Ibid. B 2/1, f. 16v.
[82] Ibid. f. 22 and v.
[83] Ibid. C 9/2–3, 5.
[84] *Cal. Close*, 1399–1402, 146–7.
[85] *Cal. Pat.* 1399–1401, 516.

merchandise carried up river.[86] In 1505, following an Act of the previous year that declared the Severn a toll-free river, Gloucester and Worcester registered claims to tolls and were opposed by the trowmen of Tewkesbury, Bewdley, and other places further up river; their opponents complained that the Gloucester burgesses, in attempting to exact 6d. for each ton of merchandise landed at the quay or merely passing Westgate bridge, shot arrows and threw stones in order to force them to come in to the bank and sometimes made them sell their goods in the town.[87] The hostility of the Tewkesbury trowmen probably reflected a long standing trading rivalry between the two towns, particularly over the corn trade on the river, in which Tewkesbury's share was a substantial one.[88] In 1401 Tewkesbury was one of several towns in Gloucestershire and Worcestershire which Gloucester complained were interfering with those coming to sell corn in its market.[89] The attempt by Gloucester to exact toll from Tewkesbury men had evidently had a long history before 1483 when a special clause in the new borough charter established Tewkesbury's claim to be free of all tolls and customs in Gloucester.[90]

Although Gloucester's relationship to Bristol inhibited its economic development, it did gain some benefit from its position on trade routes to that city. Merchants from towns of the Midlands and Welsh Marches which looked to Bristol as their main export outlet[91] traded goods in Gloucester and used it as a staging post as they came down the river or along the main road routes through the town. Among regular visitors were merchants from Coventry: three Coventry men were trading in the town in 1481[92] and in 1498 its mayor complained that Gloucester was levying toll illegally on its merchants.[93] A Chester man had a dispute with the town authorities in 1398, perhaps over toll.[94] Men from Leominster (Herefs.) and Ludlow (Salop.) were among regular traders to the town in 1423,[95] and the latter place, which shipped its goods at Bewdley, was at law with Gloucester over the tolls charged at the quay in 1493 or 1494.[96] In the early 16th century Manchester merchants were apparently frequent visitors and on more than one occasion were forced by the town authorities to substantiate their claim to be free of toll as inhabitants of the duchy of Lancaster.[97]

One direction in which Gloucester continued to extend its influence through overland trade was into South Wales. In 1378 it was among the chief towns of the Marches which complained that their traders who travelled in Wales were being unjustly distrained,[98] and in 1438 a Gloucester man was one of two commissioners appointed to arrest traders coming out of Wales in reprisal for the imprisonment of a Bristol merchant.[99] Richard Barret, a wealthy draper[1] who was reported in 1394 to have been attacked on the road through Monmouth and Usk,[2] was probably one of many Gloucester men who traded into Wales. Traders from Brecon were often in Gloucester: as many as six paid the bailiffs for the right of trading in the town in 1423 and a carrier was journeying between the two towns in 1481. From further along the main road into South Wales the town of Llandovery (Carms.) sent six traders in 1481, two of them drapers and another a dealer in the cloth known as Welsh friezes.[3] Probably

[86] Rot. Parl. iii. 663.
[87] Select Cases in Star Chamber, i (Selden Soc. xvi), 209–26; ii (Selden Soc. xxv), 285–7.
[88] V.C.H. Glos. viii. 141.
[89] Cal. Pat. 1399–1401, 516.
[90] Glouc. Corp. Rec. p. 19; cf. G.B.R., I 1/41 (Furney's cal. of corp. rec. 1720), f. 25, which lists two mid 15th-cent. documents (now lost) referring to the dispute.
[91] Cf. Studies in Eng. Trade in 15th Cent. ed. E. Power and M. M. Postan (1933), 187–8.
[92] G.B.R., C 9/5.

[93] Coventry Leet Bk. (E.E.T.S.), 592.
[94] G.B.R., B 8/2.
[95] Ibid. C 9/4.
[96] Ibid. F 4/2.
[97] Ibid. B 2/1, f. 148v.; Glos. N. & Q. ii. 213–14.
[98] Rot. Parl. iii. 45.
[99] Cal. Pat. 1436–41, 198.
[1] Ibid. 1388–92, 415; Hockaday Abs. ccxix, 1401; G.B.R., C 9/1.
[2] Cal. Pat. 1391–6, 432.
[3] G.B.R., C 9/4–5.

Gloucester had regular links with other towns on the same route, such as Monmouth, Abergavenny (Mon.), and Carmarthen, but those towns were presumably able to establish their freedom from toll and so do not figure in the lists of 'foreign' traders which provide the main evidence for Gloucester's trading connexions at the period. The more southerly trading route, along the South Wales coast, appears also to have been of importance to Gloucester, for the Gloucester capper John Falconer left £40 for the rebuilding of Chepstow bridge at his death in 1545.[4] The cattle trade out of Wales presumably continued throughout the period, though a Welsh cowherd who was listed in the roll of traders in 1396[5] is the only evidence found. Its Welsh trade was one of the most stable elements in Gloucester's economic history and the bridge over the Severn, described by the burgesses in 1505 as that by which 'all the king's subjects have their passage between England and Wales with their goods and chattels and all other merchandise',[6] was prized by the town as one of its major assets.

Other long distance overland trade included the regular connexion with Southampton, mentioned above, and a ropemaker from Bridport (Dors.) who was trading in the town in 1396.[7] There was also a regular trade with the capital, dealings between Gloucester men and London mercers and other wholesalers being frequently recorded.[8] Such trade made long distance carrying a source of employment for some of the town's inhabitants, an early example being Reynold the carter, owner of a wagon, loaded with wine, and a team of eight horses which met with an accident at Coates in 1381. That particular wagon was probably on its way from Southampton but the fact that men of Oxford and Tetsworth (Oxon.), places on one of the London routes, acted as Reynold's mainpernors suggests that he also operated a service to the capital.[9] Four carriers were mentioned in Gloucester in 1455[10] and three carriers and a haulier were admitted as freemen in the late 1530s.[11]

The trade in wool was one that continued to draw some of the merchants from more distant parts who appeared in Gloucester. Men from Coventry and Stratton St. Margaret (Wilts.) were buying and selling wool in Gloucester in 1380, and two woolmongers were listed among the unfranchised inhabitants of the town that year.[12] Oliver Wulman of Wootton Bassett (Wilts.), who was listed in 1481, was presumably also involved in that trade.[13] A Cirencester wool merchant, trading in the town in 1380,[14] and a wool buyer of Tormarton, to whom a Gloucester capper was indebted in 1505,[15] may represent regular links between the town and the main Cotswold wool-raising area. The wool market, held in the Boothall, was obviously a significant part of the market business in the early 16th century; detailed regulations for it were enacted in 1527. Wool was also traded at the annual fairs, and under regulations made in 1514 the rules preventing 'foreigners' from buying from one another were relaxed at those times. In spite of Gloucester's own clothmaking industry, visiting merchants appear also to have brought finished cloth for sale in the town,[16] but one piece of evidence for that trade, the appearance on the roll of traders for 1481 of no fewer than 12 men described as 'kendalman',[17] is difficult to interpret. They appear to have all been 'foreigners' and were presumably dealers in the type of cloth made in Kendal (Westmld.), but the large number is surprising, particularly in view of the fact that

[4] Hockaday Abs. ccxix, 1545.
[5] G.B.R., C 9/2.
[6] Select Cases in Star Chamber, i (Selden Soc. xvi), 211-12. [7] G.B.R., C 9/2.
[8] e.g. Cal. Pat. 1370-4, 147; 1377-81, 316, 322; 1388-92, 451; 1416-22, 92; 1467-77, 498; Cal. Close, 1476-85, p. 21; G.B.R., G 10/1, p. 147.
[9] Cal. Close, 1377-81, 455-6.

[10] Glouc. Rental, 1455, 9, 13, 15, 29.
[11] G.B.R., C 9/6.
[12] Ibid. 1.
[13] Ibid. 5.
[14] Ibid. 1.
[15] Ibid. G 10/1, p. 246; cf. ibid. p. 257.
[16] Ibid. B 2/1, ff. 13v.-14, 22.
[17] Ibid. C 9/5.

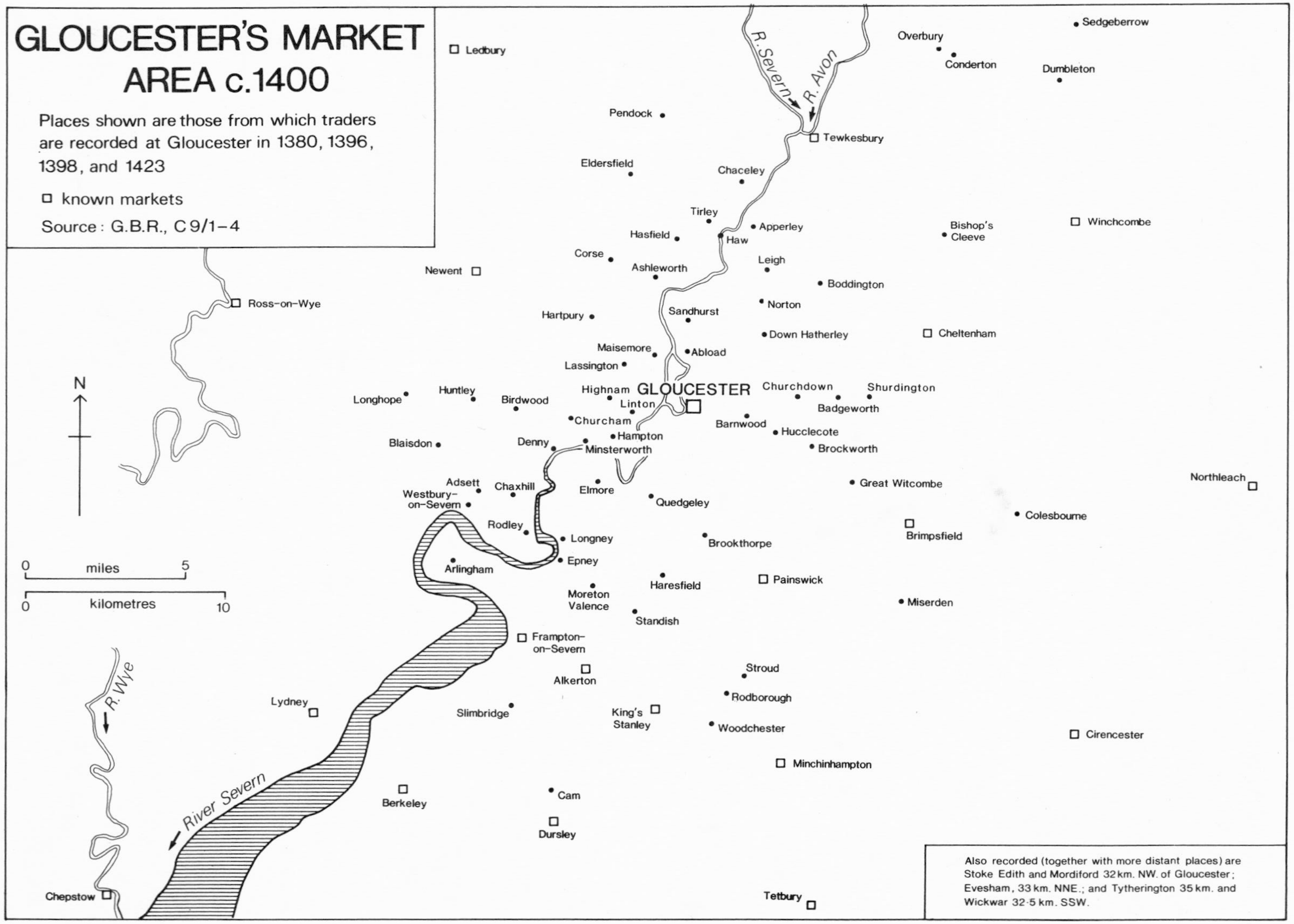
GLOUCESTER'S MARKET AREA c.1400
Places shown are those from which traders are recorded at Gloucester in 1380, 1396, 1398, and 1423
□ known markets
Source: G.B.R., C 9/1–4
N
0 miles 5
0 kilometres 10
R. Severn
R. Avon
River Severn
R. Wye
Ledbury
Pendock
Eldersfield
Chaceley
Tewkesbury
Overbury
Conderton
Sedgeberrow
Dumbleton
Winchcombe
Bishop's Cleeve
Tirley
Apperley
Haw
Hasfield
Corse
Ashleworth
Leigh
Boddington
Newent
Ross-on-Wye
Norton
Hartpury
Sandhurst
Down Hatherley
Cheltenham
Maisemore
Abload
Lassington
Highnam
GLOUCESTER
Linton
Churchdown
Shurdington
Badgeworth
Longhope
Huntley
Birdwood
Churcham
Barnwood
Hucclecote
Brockworth
Blaisdon
Denny
Hampton
Minsterworth
Adsett
Westbury-on-Severn
Chaxhill
Elmore
Quedgeley
Great Witcombe
Northleach
Colesbourne
Brimpsfield
Rodley
Longney
Brookthorpe
Arlingham
Epney
Painswick
Haresfield
Moreton Valence
Miserden
Standish
Frampton-on-Severn
Alkerton
Stroud
Rodborough
Lydney
Slimbridge
King's Stanley
Woodchester
Cirencester
Minchinhampton
Berkeley
Cam
Dursley
Chepstow
Tetbury
Also recorded (together with more distant places) are Stoke Edith and Mordiford 32 km. NW. of Gloucester; Evesham, 33 km. NNE.; and Tytherington 35 km. and Wickwar 32·5 km. SSW.

Fig. 3

the only other record of a trade in that commodity appears to be a bequest of Kendal cloth in the will of John Kendal, a Gloucester lawyer who died in 1447.[18]

More significant for Gloucester, however, was the local trade with the villages of the surrounding countryside and the neighbouring market towns. The evidence for the nature and extent of that trade in the late Middle Ages comes from five surviving rolls which listed (together with unfranchised residents) the 'foreigners' who traded regularly in the town in return for an annual fine or composition paid to the bailiffs;[19] the total numbers of those identified as foreigners were 87 and 108 in 1396 and 1398 respectively and 98 in 1423,[20] but some men for whom no address was given on the rolls may also have been foreigners. The rolls show that the villages from which men came regularly to trade in Gloucester's market lay within a relatively small surrounding area of the Vale and Severnside, most of them within or close to the well-known limit of 6⅔ miles (c. 11 km.) given by Bracton for the usual day's market journey.[21] Beyond that limit a ring of smaller market towns was effective in restricting Gloucester's influence, at least as a market for agricultural produce. In particular Gloucester appears to have had little impact as a market centre above the Cotswold ridge, where Cirencester and to a lesser extent Painswick and Minchinhampton provided market services.

The roll for 1380, more informative than the later ones, specifies the commodities brought for sale by some of the villagers, bread and ale being most often mentioned while six men from places west of the Severn brought honey. Fish from the Severnside parishes was evidently an important part of the incoming produce: two Longney men selling fish were listed in 1380 and another two in 1481, and fishmongering presumably explains the appearance on the rolls of men from such small riverside hamlets as Epney, in Moreton Valence,[22] and Denny, in Minsterworth.[23] Other produce of the Severnside parishes is suggested by the man surnamed Fowler from the Haw, in Tirley, who came in 1396. One group of regular traders who were particularly important to the town's industry was represented in 1380 by six men who brought iron to the town; no places of origin were given for them but all came in by the west gate and were evidently from the Forest of Dean. Two King's Stanley men given the description 'askeberner' in 1396 were possibly charcoal burners supplying the town's smiths.

Only one or two traders from each of the surrounding villages were listed each year. Many may have been general dealers who bought and sold on behalf of other villagers, men who came regularly enough to the market to warrant playing an annual composition rather than tolls on each load of produce and who possessed sufficient capital to be able to pay it. It can be assumed that many other villagers from those same places also used Gloucester as their market.

Higher numbers of traders were recorded from the two nearest market towns, Painswick at 9.5 km. and Newent at 13.5 km., which were evidently satellites of Gloucester for trade purposes. In 1396 and 1398 respectively 7 and 9 traders came from Painswick and 7 and 5 from Newent, though in two other years, 1380 and 1423, the numbers were smaller. The relationship to Tewkesbury, further out at c. 16 km. and more of a manufacturing town and rival to Gloucester, is less easy to assess. It sent five traders in 1423 but only one in each of the three other years mentioned

---

[18] Hockaday Abs. cciii, 1447.
[19] For what follows, G.B.R., C 9/1–5; Fig. 3.
[20] The rolls are each for a year running from Mich., but for convenience they are identified here only by the year in which

they begin.
[21] Bracton, *De Legibus et Consuetudinibus Anglie* (Rolls Ser.), iii. 585.
[22] Cf. *V.C.H. Glos.* x. 206. [23] Cf. Rudder, *Glos.* 552.

TABLE I: TRADES OF NON-FREEMEN AND 'PORTMEN'

	1396–7	1398–9	1423–4	1481–2
Metal Workers				
ironmongers			2	
farriers		1	1	
smiths	5	4	2	1
braziers			2	
locksmiths	1	1		
bladesmiths	2		1	
cutlers	1		8	
spoonmakers			1	
pinners	2	1	1	2
wiredrawers	2		3	1
lorimers				1
spurriers	1		1	
nailers	1			
pewterers	2			
latten makers		1		
bellmakers		1		
furbishers			2	
goldsmiths	1		1	
Textile Workers				
dyers	1		1	
walkers	1		1	
weavers	5	4	3	1
shearmen			2	1
chaloners	1	1	5	1
cardmakers	3	2		1
woadmen			1	
Leather Workers				
tanners	4	4	3	2
skinners	2	1	1	
curriers		2		
whittawers		4		
cordwainers	14	10	8	4
saddlers	3	1	1	
sheathers			1	
Clothing Trades				
tailors	7	5	6	1
hosiers			1	
cappers				1
glovers	5		3	1
pursers				2

GLOUCESTER: TRADE AND INDUSTRY 1327–1547

	1396–7	1398–9	1423–4	1481–2
Distributive Trades				
drapers		1		
mercers		1	1	
retailers		1		
tranters	1			4
chapmen			3	
Sellers of Food and Drink				
butchers	7	3	3	1
bakers	3	6		3
fishmongers		3	5	
brewers	1	3	1	1
maltmakers				1
salters	1			
spicers			1	
cooks			1	2
innkeepers	1		1	
Transport				
trowmen			1	
carriers			1	
Building and Allied Trades				
masons		2		
carpenters		1	2	
turners		1	1	1
glaziers	1		1*	
painters			1	
Other Trades				
wheelwrights	1	1	1	
hoopers		1	2	1
ropers	1			
bowyers	2			
fletchers	1			
sieve makers			1	2
patten makers				1
?charcoal burners (*askeberner*)	1		1	
barbers			3	1
millwards			1	

Sources: G.B.R., C 9/2–5.

above; the number listed may have depended on the success of Tewkesbury men in upholding their claim to freedom from tolls.

Beyond the basic market area various scattered villages sent traders regularly to Gloucester. Villagers who came from the Stroud area were mainly it seems clothworkers.[24] Another group, whose presence is more difficult to explain, came from villages between Tewkesbury and Evesham, c. 24 km. from Gloucester: men from Overbury in 1396 included a maltman and a man who was probably a slater working a quarry on Bredon Hill. There were also some more distant villages, such as Stoke Edith and Mordiford, near Hereford, and Tytherington, some way down in the Vale, whose presence on the rolls is probably explained by the trade in some particular commodity. Most of the more distant places which appear on the rolls are, not surprisingly, other towns. A ring of market towns within c. 30 km. of Gloucester, including Northleach, Cirencester, Tetbury, Berkeley, Lydney, Ross-on-Wye (Herefs.), and Ledbury (Herefs.), are represented. Most sent only one or two traders each year, the main exception being Ross, at a distance of 24 km. but standing on Gloucester's main trading route into Wales: 6 men came from Ross in 1380, 4 and 3 respectively in 1396 and 1398, and 8 in 1423.

For the market towns around Gloucester the trade in fish was evidently of some significance. Three of the Ross men who came in 1380 were selling fish, as was a man from Chepstow (Mon.). The same year two Cheltenham men were buying fish, while men from Evesham (Worcs.) and Winchcombe surnamed 'Fisher', who were listed in 1396, were probably fish buyers, as perhaps was a Cirencester man surnamed 'Heryng' in 1423. Gloucester appears to have been acting as a centre for distributing inland the fish caught in the Severn and Wye fisheries and perhaps also the saltwater fish that the Irish trade brought to the Severn.

Supplying Gloucester's leather workers with their raw material was another trade in which some of the market towns were involved. Men selling leather came from Newent, Painswick, and Ross in 1380 and a tanner was among the traders from Ross in 1423. Some of the goods taken out of the town may be indicated by the appearance on the rolls of a Tewkesbury draper and a Ross mercer, while a Minchinhampton man recorded in 1380 as buying and selling bread but described as a smith in the poll-tax returns of the following year[25] perhaps carried back iron or ironware to his town. A Tetbury man, one of those described as 'using his craft' in Gloucester in 1380, was a hosteler[26] and perhaps acted as a carrier and general dealer for his town.

Gloucester's traditional industries maintained their strength in the late-medieval period. The main evidence is provided by the occupations given in the surviving lists of unfranchised tradesmen, analysed above, but it should be remembered that those lists included only a proportion, perhaps a minority, of the town's tradesmen and tended to emphasize the poorer trades at the expense of the richer ones, whose members mostly had the freedom. Also there are other people on the lists whose trade is not specified (see Table I). At the end of the period further evidence for the relative strength of the town's trades is provided by the records of entrants to the freedom in the 1530s and 1540s (see Table II).

[24] Below.
[25] Rob. Smyth: P.R.O., E 179/113/35A, rot. 8.
[26] John Burbage: ibid. rot. 7.

TABLE II: TRADES OF FREEMEN ADMITTED MICHAELMAS 1535 TO MICHAELMAS 1545

Metal Workers

smiths	3
wiredrawers	3
cutlers	2
pewterers	2
goldsmiths	2

Textile Workers

weavers	22
dyers	2
clothiers	2
tuckers	1

Leather Workers

cordwainers	17
tanners	8
saddlers	2

Clothing Trades

tailors	16
cappers	8
hosiers	4
glovers	2
hatmakers	1

Distributive Trades

mercers	7
drapers	4
merchants	4

Sellers of Food and Drink

brewers	9
bakers	6
butchers	5
innkeepers	2
cooks	1

Transport

carriers	3
boatmen	2
watermen	1
mariners	1

Building and Allied Trades

carpenters	4
sawyers	3
turners	2
masons	2
tilers	2
glaziers	1

Other Trades

wheelwrights	1
ropers	1
mattress makers	1
barbers	1

Agricultural

yeomen	18
labourers	3
husbandmen	2

gentlemen	3
undifferentiated	13

Source: G.B.R., C 9/6.

Metal working retained its strength and variety and seems still to have been regarded as the most characteristic Gloucester industry in the late-medieval period: horseshoes and nails, which appeared as devices on the seal for merchant debts acquired in 1348 under the Statute of Acton Burnell of 1283, were used again on the mayor's seal that was made soon after 1483[27] and on the coat of arms granted to the town in 1538.[28] Seventeen different metal-working trades were recorded in the late 14th century and the early 15th. A new one, later to become one of Gloucester's most important trades, was the manufacture of pins, which was recorded from 1396 when 2 pinners and 2 wiredrawers were listed; it was well established by the beginning of the 16th century, when 6 pinners and 2 wiredrawers occur in the hundred court records for the years 1502–7.[29] Among the other trades the making of cutlery appears to have been particularly strong during the 15th century: 8 cutlers were listed among the unfranchised inhabitants in 1423 and 12 were mentioned as tenants in a rental of 1455.[30] Bellfounding was probably one branch that was maintained continuously throughout the period. Gloucester founders included John of Gloucester who cast bells for Ely cathedral in 1346,[31] Henry Prince, recorded as a bellmaker in the town in 1398,[32] apparently Robert Hendley, whose name appears on a bell made for St. Nicholas's church c. 1500;[33] William Henshaw (d. 1522),[34] who served as mayor in five years between 1503 and 1520,[35] and Richard Atkyns (d. 1530).[36] In 1507 Gloucester also had a clocksmith, William Green (or Chimemaker), who contracted with Llanthony Priory to keep its clock, chimes, and bells in repair.[37]

The continuing strength of the clothmaking industry is shown in particular by the number of weavers recorded. The weavers had formed themselves into a trade company by the late 15th century[38] and in the earlier 16th were one of the most numerous groups of tradesmen, 22 being admitted to the freedom between 1535 and 1545. All the other main branches of clothmaking continued to be carried on in Gloucester, with dyers, fullers, and shearmen all recorded throughout the period, but it is possible that some part of the finishing work for the Gloucester industry was already being done in the mills of the Stroud valleys. Men from villages in that area who figured on the rolls of traders included a Woodchester fuller in 1380,[39] a King's Stanley dyer in the 1390s,[40] and a Stroud fuller in 1481.[41] In the earlier 16th century the clothier John Sandford, who worked a fulling mill at Stonehouse but was settled in Gloucester as a leading burgess by 1544,[42] provides the most obvious connexion between the industry in the two places. Another connexion may be the purchase in 1524, perhaps as more than just an investment, of a fulling mill at Ebley, in Stonehouse parish, by the wealthy mercer John Cooke.[43]

Another branch of the woollen industry, the knitting of woollen caps, appears to have been an important contributor to Gloucester's economic recovery in the earlier 16th century. It had been established in the town by 1481, and nine cappers were mentioned in the period 1502–7.[44] By the 1530s, when the main cappers were John

27 Trans. B.G.A.S. xiii. 390–2; Cal. Pat. 1348–50, 14.
28 Below, Arms, Seals, Insignia, and Plate.
29 G.B.R., G 10/1.
30 Glouc. Rental, 1455, 9, 11, 19, 33, 35, 37, 57.
31 V.C.H. Glos. ii. 205.   32 G.B.R., C 9/3.
33 Trans. B.G.A.S. xviii. 238–9; Glos. Ch. Bells, 35.
34 Below, Aldermen of Glouc. 1483–1835.
35 Fosbrooke, Glouc. 208.
36 Hockaday Abs. ccxix, 1530.
37 P.R.O., C 115/L 2/6691, f. 20.
38 Below, regulation of trade and ind.
39 G.B.R., C 9/1: Rob. Brymor, for whose occupation,

P.R.O., E 179/113/35A, rot. 8.
40 G.B.R., C 9/2–3.
41 Ibid. 5. Also in 1481 there were two Woodchester men, John Barnfield and Thos. Bennett, whose surnames suggest that they were from clothworking families: cf. V.C.H. Glos. xi. 196, 228.
42 V.C.H. Glos. 281, which wrongly dates his move to Glouc. as after 1549; cf. G.B.R., B 2/2, f. 34 and v.; below, Aldermen of Glouc. 1483–1835.
43 Glouc. Corp. Rec. p. 427; Glos. R.O., D 2957/289.21, 24; cf. V.C.H. Glos. x. 278.
44 G.B.R., G 10/1.

Falconer and Thomas Bell, it was probably the town's principal industry.[45] Bell was said to employ over 300 people in 1538.[46]

Gloucester's leather trades continued to flourish during the period. Nine tanners were mentioned in the hundred court records for the years 1502–7[47] and the trade produced some wealthy men;[48] the tanners and the cordwainers were among the earliest groups of tradesmen to form themselves into trade companies.[49] Cordwainers were particularly numerous: 14 were listed among the unfranchised tradesmen in 1396, and 17 were admitted as freemen between 1535 and 1545.

Among more specialist craftsmen were the masons who built and maintained the many churches and religious houses and found employment in the surrounding region. Gloucester masons included Nicholas Wishanger, who was employed to build Arlingham church tower in 1372[50] and three years later was retained by Llanthony Priory as its chief mason,[51] and John Hobbs, who built a new chapel at Blackfriars, Worcester, in 1475.[52] John Hoggs (or Deacon) of Gloucester, described as a carpenter and carver, contracted to work for Llanthony c. 1510.[53] The specialist trade of shipbuilding seems to have been carried on only intermittently, at least in the early 16th century. The building of the 80-ton *Mary Fortune* at Gloucester c. 1540 was later remembered as an exceptional event, while one or two smaller vessels commissioned by Gloucester men at that period were built down river at places like Elmore and Minsterworth.[54]

Although a small group of wealthy merchants is identifiable in the late 14th century[55] and the significant role played by lawyers is evident in the 15th,[56] it is probable that the mercers and drapers, the men who sustained the town's function of supplying imported goods and its own cloth and other products to the region, were always an important element in late-medieval Gloucester. For the 100 years up to 1483 the occupations of only 24 of the men who held office as bailiffs have been identified; that very small and random sample was made up of 6 mercers, 4 lawyers, 4 merchants, 3 drapers (one also a hosier), 3 brewers, a fishmonger, a dyer, a chaloner, and a brazier.[57] For the late 15th century and the earlier 16th the fuller surviving records show that the mercers and drapers were then the dominant trades. That is underlined in particular by the composition of the town's inner governing body, the twelve-strong bench of aldermen, which at that period included almost all the most wealthy men.[58] Between 1483 and 1547 the occupations of roughly half of all the men who attained the bench of aldermen are known: they were 9 mercers, 8 drapers, 4 merchants, 4 cappers, 3 tanners, 2 clothiers, a dyer, a brewer, a cutler, a wiredrawer, a goldsmith, a bellfounder, and a lawyer.[59] In 1513 the 11 wealthiest townsmen, judged on their assessment at a muster, included 5 mercers and a draper, but some of the manufacturing trades also produced individuals of great wealth. William Henshaw, the bellfounder, shared the highest rate of assessment with the mercers John Cooke and William Cole in 1513, and at the subsidy of 1524 the tanners William Matthews and John Allen, the dyer William Hazard, and the clothier Thomas Tayloe were among the top 7 payers, and two representatives of the rising trade of capping, John Falconer and Ralph Sankey, were among the top 12. John Cooke was by far the

[45] Below, Aldermen of Glouc. 1483–1835; P.R.O., E 134/25 Eliz. Hil./3.
[46] *L. & P. Hen. VIII*. xiii (1), p. 548.
[47] G.B.R., G 10/1.
[48] Below.
[49] Below, regulation of trade and ind.
[50] Harvey, *Eng. Med. Architects* (1954), 311.
[51] P.R.O., C 115/L 1/6688, f. 89.
[52] Harvey, *Eng. Med. Architects*, 135–6.
[53] P.R.O., C 115/L 2/6691, f. 39.
[54] Ibid. E 134/25 Eliz. Hil./3.
[55] Above.
[56] Above, Glouc. in late Middle Ages.
[57] Below, Bailiffs of Glouc. 1200–1483.
[58] Of the 12 men given the highest assessments for the subsidy of 1524, 9 were on the bench: P.R.O., E 179/113/189; cf. below, Aldermen of Glouc. 1483–1835.
[59] Below, Aldermen of Glouc. 1483–1835.

wealthiest man in 1524, his assessment of £300 being more than twice that of anyone else. He died in 1528 and his pre-eminent position in the town was probably matched later only by the capper Thomas Bell, who in 1524 was just beginning his career, a man of moderate wealth[60] serving his first term as sheriff.[61]

Town Government 1483–1547

The charter granted by Richard III in 1483 remodelled the constitution of the town and gave it important additional liberties and status. It made Gloucester together with the surrounding parishes and hamlets of Dudstone and King's Barton hundred into a separate county, to be called 'the county of the town of Gloucester', gave the town a mayor and aldermen, and incorporated the burgess community under the style of 'the mayor and burgesses of the town of Gloucester'. The mayor was to perform the offices of clerk of the market, steward and marshal of the king's household, and escheator within the new county, and he and the aldermen were to exercise full magisterial powers there; the two bailiffs were to perform the office of sheriffs in the new county.[62] The creation of a common council as the governing body of the town was apparently implied by the charter, though not mentioned in it. Such a body existed by 1484[63] and comprised 40 members — the mayor and his fellow 11 aldermen, the 2 sheriffs, the 4 stewards, and 22 other burgesses.[64]

The charter gave formal expression to the oligarchical system of government that had existed previously and laid the basis for the 'closed corporation' that ran Gloucester for the next 3½ centuries. The aldermen were to hold office for life and vacancies were to be filled by the surviving aldermen. Later, and perhaps from the first, new recruits to the bench were drawn from among the senior common councilmen, while new councilmen were elected, also for life, by vote of the full council. Of the annual appointments, the mayor was to be chosen from among the aldermen by his fellows and 12 leading burgesses, who in later practice were all councilmen. The charter stated that the election of the bailiffs should be as formerly accustomed, without giving details. It does specify that a bailiff dying before the end of his term should be replaced by election of 'the burgesses of the town',[65] so possibly for them a wider electorate was envisaged; but in later practice in their election, too, no one outside the common council was involved.

Although making them sheriffs of the new county, the charter lessened the status and authority of the bailiffs[66] within the town government. The mayor, before whom they were required to take their oath of office,[67] took over their role as figurehead and chief representative of the burgess community and joined them in the presidency of the hundred court.[68] The mayor's status was emphasized in the charter by the right to have a sword carried before him,[69] and a separate seal of office was struck for his use.[70] His authority as president of the common council was bolstered by regulations made in 1522.[71] The sheriffs after 1483 were mainly executive officers, subject to the discipline of the common council which by 1500 had assumed the power to fine them

[60] G.B.R., B 2/1, ff. 225v.–226v.; P.R.O., E 179/113/189; cf. below, Aldermen of Glouc. 1483–1835. For Cooke and Bell, below, Plates 5–6.

[61] Fosbrooke, *Glouc.* 208.

[62] G.B.R., I 1/22 (the original charter, kept at Guildhall, Glouc., in 1982; it is paraphrased in *Glouc. Corp. Rec.* pp. 16–19).

[63] *Glouc. Corp. Rec.* p. 414.

[64] G.B.R., B 2/1, f. 1.

[65] Ibid. I 1/22.

[66] In all references in this volume to those officers at a period after 1483 they will be termed 'sheriffs', though their full style was 'bailiffs and sheriffs of Gloucester'.

[67] G.B.R., I 1/22.

[68] Ibid. G 10/1, pp. 21, 58, 72.

[69] Ibid. I 1/22.

[70] *Trans. B.G.A.S.* xiii. 390–2.

[71] G.B.R., B 2/1, ff. 14v.–15.

for failure to carry out its ordinances.[72] The office became a step in the borough hierarchy which councilmen were required to serve for two terms before being eligible for the aldermanic bench.[73] Its burdensome nature was emphasized in the years immediately following the new charter by the continuing shortfall of the fee-farm revenues: c. 1487 it was said that some recent sheriffs had been required to make up as much as £30 and that some of the wealthier burgesses had left the town to avoid serving the office.[74]

The common council rapidly emerged as the chief organ of government in the town, diminishing in the process the role of the hundred court and its frankpledge jury. The council was making ordinances for the regulation of trade in the town by 1499,[75] and in the following year regulations covering a wide range of matters though initiated by the frankpledge jury required the confirmation of the council.[76] The council was also recorded, by 1494, as authorizing items of the stewards' expenditure[77] and, before 1509, making regulations for procedure in the hundred and piepowder courts.[78]

The charter of 1483 provided for a single coroner to be elected by, and hold office during the pleasure of, the mayor and aldermen;[79] by the 1530s, when the office was annually elective, it was always filled by one of the aldermen.[80] The period also saw the growth of the office of town clerk, which was restricted to an individual by 1500,[81] and the creation, before 1534, of the office of recorder.[82] Of the minor borough officers, the charter increased to four the number of serjeants, who from that time were styled serjeants-at-mace, and assigned two to serve the mayor and two the sheriffs. By 1486 the office of mayor's sword bearer had been created at a salary and an allowance for gowns; in 1493, when the common council appointed to the office, it was decided that it should be held during pleasure.[83] The office of town bellman was recorded from 1542.[84] The relative status of the various borough officers at the end of the period is indicated by a scale of fees agreed in 1540 for their attendance at the annual visitation of the Crypt school: the mayor was to receive 4s., the recorder 3s. 4d., each alderman 2s., each sheriff 20d., the town clerk 16d., each steward 12d., the sword bearer 12d., each serjeant-at-mace 8d., and each porter 4d.[85]

Records of the ordinary sessions of the hundred court which survive for the years 1502-7[86] show it to have been by that period concerned solely with the hearing of pleas, pleas of debt predominating. Although some parts of the process, including the requirement to produce pledges *de prosequendo*, had become a formality, actions in the court still proceeded through the various stages of essoin, summons, plea, and verdict by a rigid process, governed by a body of ancient borough customs such as one recorded in 1503 concerning the disposal of goods taken in distress in a plea of debt;[87] the correct form of words for making a plea or defence was still insisted on.[88] Compurgation was still used to an extent almost equal to jury verdicts, but many cases were settled out of court by arbitration. The court sat weekly on a Monday, and every Michaelmas, at the start of the borough year, a special court was held at which all property owners in the town, including the various religious houses, were required to

[72] Ibid. ff. 19v., 22.
[73] Cf. Fosbrooke, *Glouc.* 208.
[74] *Glouc. Corp. Rec.* pp. 61-2.
[75] G.B.R., B 2/1, ff. 13, 21v.-22v.
[76] Ibid. ff. 16-21.
[77] Ibid. F 4/2.
[78] Ibid. B 2/1, f. 3.
[79] Ibid. I 1/22.
[80] Ibid. C 9/6.
[81] Ibid. B 2/1, f. 20v.
[82] *L. & P. Hen. VIII*, vii, p. 535.
[83] G.B.R., B 2/1, ff. 1-2.
[84] Glos. Colln. 28652, no. 4.
[85] Austin, *Crypt Sch.* 155-6.
[86] G.B.R., G 10/1.
[87] Ibid. p. 36.
[88] e.g. ibid. pp. 6, 14, 45.

perform suit.[89] The separate piepowder court, offering litigants a speedier procedure, is first recorded in 1504,[90] though it had presumably existed from much earlier times.

The increasing complexity of the borough administration at the period is reflected in the volume of records it produced, including the steadily lengthening accounts of the four stewards (called alternatively chamberlains), a 'red book' for common council ordinances kept from 1486,[91] a roll of admissions to the freedom from 1534 (not, of course, the earliest),[92] and a book in which deeds and leases concerning corporation property were entered from 1540.[93]

Among the communal responsibilities for which the stewards accounted were the maintenance of public buildings, street paving and cleaning, the upkeep of the town water supply, the expenses of the members of parliament, and the costs of litigation in which the town engaged with other communities or individuals over such matters as the charging of tolls.[94] Other concerns of the town government at the period were illustrated by ordinances made by the frankpledge jury in 1500 for the regulation of trade[95] and for the upkeep of public order and morality. Strumpets were to be carted around the town and, together with those who consorted with them, put on public display in the market place. Only town officers were to wear swords or long knives in the town; no inhabitant of the town was to be retained by any county gentleman, a practice said to have caused much trouble; and beggars were to be registered at the Boothall by the town clerk.[96] The problem of beggars was mentioned in 1493 when the mayor received a royal command to keep watch for vagabonds,[97] and in 1504 all paupers were ordered to leave town except for 36 people, mainly women, who had been registered and badged.[98]

Property management was another growing preoccupation of the officers. The annual rental of communal property in the town had risen to £29 19s. 1½d. by 1494 (though untenanted property then meant that over £7 was not being received).[99] An outlying estate of agricultural land came to the corporation in 1515 by John Capel's gift of the lease of White Barn farm for the upkeep of the bridge and quay,[1] and in 1540 it took responsibility for its first large trust estate, Podsmead and other lands given by Joan Cooke as the endowment of the Crypt school.[2] In 1542 it made a deliberate, and apparently speculative, venture into property, laying out £493 14s. 2d. in the purchase of some former Gloucester Abbey and Llanthony Priory lands around Gloucester and lands in Herefordshire formerly of Aconbury Priory;[3] the Herefordshire lands and much of those around Gloucester were sold off over the next few years,[4] though the demesne lands of Abbot's Barton manor were retained.

The first entry in the new council minute book in 1486 concerned the allowances to be paid to the borough officers for the public dinners which then and for many years later marked the main events of the civic year. Dinners were held at the election of the officers, which took place on the Monday after Michaelmas as laid down by the charter of 1483, and twice a year at the 'lawdays', the sessions of the frankpledge jury. Also held were a 'keziard' dinner at Michaelmas and 'drinkings' at Midsummer and the eve of St. Peter.[5] A procession to the west gate on Easter Day, followed by a banquet, was mentioned in 1527,[6] and the annual perambulation of the town

[89] Ibid. pp. 58, 136, 222.
[90] Ibid. p. 89.
[91] Ibid. B 2/1; and see ibid. f. 148v.
[92] Ibid. C 9/6; cf. ibid. f 4/2.
[93] Ibid. B 2/2, f. 16.
[94] Ibid. F 4/2–3.
[95] Below, regulation of trade and ind.
[96] G.B.R., B 2/1, ff. 17, 19 and v., 20v.
[97] Ibid. F 4/2.
[98] Ibid. B 2/1, f. 233v.
[99] Ibid. F 4/2.
[1] Ibid. B 2/1, ff. 237v.-239; cf. ibid. f. 26v.
[2] Austin, Crypt Sch. 147–58.
[3] Glouc. Corp. Rec. pp. 26–9.
[4] G.B.R., B 2/2, ff. 33–38v., 85–86v.
[5] Ibid. 1, f. 1.
[6] Ibid. f. 13v.

boundaries by the mayor and other burgesses just before Michaelmas may have been instituted at the period.[7] Even the annual visitation of the Crypt school by the borough officers after 1540 was made the occasion of a procession, covering the short distance from the Cross to the schoolhouse beside St. Mary de Crypt church.[8]

The Regulation of Trade and Industry

It seems to have been from an early date that the various commercial and legal privileges granted by the borough charters or sanctioned by ancient custom were restricted to a particular group rather than being enjoyed by the inhabitants or householders at large. The restriction may have been already implied by the terminology of the charter of 1200, which granted rights to 'the burgesses of the guild of merchants', a body which later comprised those who had been admitted to full burgess rights as freemen of the borough.[9] The style 'burgess of Gloucester' presumably had some particular significance c. 1230 when it began to be used by some parties to deeds,[10] though it was not used at all frequently until the early 14th century. Admission to the freedom by a special ceremony was recorded from the late 13th century: in 1311 a witness to an inquisition was able to recall the date of birth of an heir to one of the Berkeley family, in 1289, because his own admission as a burgess occurred a few months later.[11]

By the 15th century the freedom was gained by purchase, by serving an apprenticeship, or by patrimony. The purchase price of the freedom was £1 in 1409 and remained at that sum in the 1530s, when those admitted by apprenticeship had to pay 4s.; sons of burgesses were admitted free of charge.[12] Fifteen new burgesses were admitted by purchase in the borough year 1409–10[13] and 17 by purchase or patrimony in 1493–4;[14] between 1535 and 1545 the annual admissions averaged 20.[15]

Other inhabitants of the town under the style of 'portmen' (portmanni) enjoyed a more limited form of privilege, probably sharing only in some of the trading rights enjoyed by the full burgesses.[16] The separate category of portmen apparently existed by the 1260s,[17] and in the late 14th century and early 15th the portmen — as many as 92 in one year — each paid 6d. to the bailiffs as an entry fine to that state.[18] No record of portmen has been found after the early 16th century.[19]

A much larger number of people, comprising both unfranchised inhabitants and 'foreigners' from the surrounding villages or other towns, traded in Gloucester in return for an annual payment made to the bailiffs; lists of those payers survive for five years: 1380–1, 1396–7, 1398–9, 1423–4, and 1481–2.[20] The annual payments, which were evidently reassessed each year, varied between 6d. and 1 mark but were usually in the range of 1–2s. They were presumably made as a composition for the various market tolls to which the payer would be liable in the course of the year, as well as for the basic right of dealing in goods or practising a craft within the town, and probably did not give access to any of the privileges enjoyed by the freemen. The tradesmen listed on the rolls are each distinguished by 'north', 'south', 'east', or 'west', which in

[7] P.R.O., E 134/31 Eliz. East./15.
[8] Austin, Crypt Sch. 155.
[9] Above, town govt. 1200–1483.
[10] Glouc. Corp. Rec. pp. 133, 137.
[11] Cal. Inq. p.m. v, p. 164.
[12] G.B.R., F 4/1; C 9/6. Admission by apprenticeship was recorded from 1454: Glos. Colln. 11664, no. 1.
[13] G.B.R., F 4/1.
[14] Ibid. 2.
[15] Ibid. C 9/6.

[16] Suggested by the fact that they are listed on the same rolls which record the payments made for trading in the borough by unfranchised inhabitants and foreigners (ibid. C 9/1–4) and by the inclusion in the portmen's oath of a clause against 'covering' the goods of strangers: ibid. B 2/2, note at front.
[17] Ibid. F 3/1.
[18] Ibid. C 9/1–4.
[19] Ibid. B 2/2, note at front.
[20] Ibid. C 9/1–5.

the case of the foreigners evidently indicated the gate by which they entered (on one roll an abbreviation which apparently stands for Alvin gate is also used) and in the case of the unfranchised residents presumably indicated the ward in which they lived. The porters of the gates apparently collected, or else took pledges for, the tolls or annual composition money. Henry of Blackwell, who was presented by the frankpledge jury in 1273 for allowing 'men to enter and leave the gate for trade without giving a token',[21] was perhaps a porter; and a system was recorded in 1527 under which incoming wool merchants gave the porter a pledge which they could redeem only by handing over a token, apparently as proof that they had sold their wool in the approved market at the Boothall weighing beams and paid toll on it.[22] It was thus efficient toll collection, as well as security, that dictated the restriction of access to the town to approved main gates. One of a series of complaints made by the bailiffs against Llanthony Priory in 1392 concerned a doorway that the priory maintained near St. Kyneburgh's chapel; by means of it, they said, many traders entered without paying toll.[23]

Before 1483 the regulation of the town's industry and trade was apparently enforced mainly by the jury at the biannual views of frankpledge, making its presentments under those articles of the view that concerned prices, the quality of goods, and market offences. The jury was still making a wide range of ordinances for the provision trades, including fixing the bread and ale assizes, in 1500,[24] but responsibility for such measures was by then passing increasingly to the common council.

The sale of goods away from the open market presented the usual problem to the borough authorities. In 1273 the frankpledge jury reported forestalling by dealers in a wide range of provisions, including all the sellers of fresh fish, who were buying outside the town; other traders were presented for dealing outside the approved market hours. Concern over the activities of tradesmen in the suburbs beyond the borough boundary is also shown in the presentments for that year: a man living in Barton Street was said to intercept and buy leather from those coming through the suburb on their way to the market,[25] In the 1450s the canons of Llanthony claimed that a regular trade was carried on at the priory by merchants anxious to avoid the heavy tolls charged in the borough,[26] and from 1465 the annual fair established in Barton Street by Gloucester Abbey provided a more official venue for extramural trading.[27] In the early 16th century sales of wool in private houses instead of at the wool market in the Boothall and dealing in corn without its being pitched in the market place were among practices that the authorities attempted to check. In 1514 protective measures designed to maintain the privileged position of freemen included restricting to them the right of buying corn for resale, merchandise brought by boats to the quay, and wool or cloth brought to the town by 'foreigners'.[28] Freemen's use of their privileges for dealing on behalf of outsiders was a matter of particular concern in the early 16th century, when the oaths taken by new freemen and portmen included a clause forswearing that practice.[29]

Part of the responsibility for regulating trade and industry and protecting freemen's privileges was undertaken by the trade companies, which were first recorded in the

---

[21] The presentment apparently referred to a token given for toll or for some other purpose ('absque signo pacando tam de teoloneo . . .'); the end is now illegible: ibid. G 8/1.

[22] Ibid. B 2/1, f. 13v.

[23] P.R.O., C 115/K 2/6684, f. 159v.

[24] G.B.R., G 8/1; B 2/1, ff. 16–18.

[25] Ibid. G 8/1.

[26] P.R.O., C 115/K 2/6685, ff. 11v., 13.

[27] Below, Markets and Fairs.

[28] G.B.R., B 2/1, ff. 13 and v., 21v.–22.

[29] Ibid. 2, note at front.

second half of the 15th century. By the 1480s at least five groups of tradesmen had been formed into companies.

The butchers' company was formed in 1454 when an agreement, made with the bailiffs and stewards, empowered the butchers to elect two wardens to supervise the trade, present frauds and deception to the bailiffs, and enforce the apprenticeship qualification for butchers admitted as a freemen. At the same time the butchers were granted a parcel of land near the quay for disposing of the garbage from their trade,[30] which by its nature was one that posed the most serious environmental problems. Street-cleaning regulations of 1500 were largely directed at the butchers[31] and in 1517 the killing of pigs near the shambles in upper Westgate Street caused a dispute with local inhabitants.[32]

The tanner's company was probably formed in 1461 when a group of trustees, including at least five tanners, took possession of a building in Hare Lane, apparently the same one that the master and wardens held as the company's hall in 1540;[33] the chantry of St. Clement in St. John's church, which the company later supported and had presumably founded, existed by 1473.[34] A new set of ordinances for the tanners' company was approved in 1542.[35]

The cooks' company had been constituted by 1482, when ordinances were made for it,[36] and the cordwainers' company by 1483; in 1503 the master and wardens of the latter brought a suit in the hundred court in defence of the apprenticeship qualification for those carrying on the trade in the town.[37] The master weavers' company had been constituted with a master and wardens by 1485 and received new ordinances in 1508.[38] Two others which probably had their origins at the same period were the bakers' company, which existed by 1550,[39] and the tailors' and hosiers' company, which in 1587 was said to have existed from time immemorial.[40]

The Town and the Religious Communities

In Gloucester and its suburbs were nine religious houses.[41] Their interests and involvement in the town affected many individual townspeople and sometimes brought them into conflict with the burgess community as a whole.

The largest religious house, the great Benedictine abbey of St. Peter, was the one most heavily involved in town affairs. It became the principal landlord there after the Crown. In the late 12th century and the 13th its holding of burgages and rents was augmented by many gifts (and in some cases sales) from burgesses,[42] while suburban development on its lands outside the north and east gates added further to the proportion of townspeople who were its tenants.[43] By 1291 its rents from property in the town amounted to £54 19s. 4d.[44] and at the Dissolution, to £155 3s. 5d.[45] The abbey was also a major landlord in the immediate neighbourhood, holding a number of manors in the outlying hamlets and across the Severn; it increased its influence in the area by securing grants of the hundred of Dudstone in 1316[46] and the liberty of

[30] Glos. Colln. 11664, no. 1.
[31] G.B.R., B 2/1, ff. 16–17.   [32] Ibid. f. 3v.
[33] Glos. Colln. 28652, nos. 1–2; though not there so described, Nic. Hert, John Aleyn, and John Hyman were also tanners: cf. *Glouc. Rental, 1455*, 57, 71, 109.
[34] Glos. Colln. 28652, no. 4; Hockaday Abs. ccxv, 1473.
[35] Glos. Colln. 28652, no. 4.
[36] G.B.R., B 1/1.
[37] Ibid. G 10/1, p. 47, where the reference to the bailiffs making regulations for the company shows that it existed before 1483.

[38] Hockaday Abs. ccxix, 1485; G.B.R., B 1/3.
[39] G.B.R., B 2/1, ff. 50–52v.
[40] Glos. R.O., D 177/1/1, ff. 209–10.
[41] For the hist. of Gloucester's religious houses, *V.C.H. Glos.* ii.
[42] For the grants to the abbey, *Hist. & Cart. Mon. Glouc.*; Glouc. Cath. Libr., Reg. Abb. Froucester B; ibid. deeds and seals.
[43] Below, topog.   [44] *Tax. Eccl.* (Rec. Com.), 231.
[45] *Valor Eccl.* (Rec. Com.), ii. 417.
[46] *Cal. Fine R.* 1307–19, 304.

King's Barton (which it had held for periods in the 13th century) in 1345.[47] It was closely involved in the parochial life of the town, where it had the patronage of two churches, St. Mary de Lode and St. John, from ancient times and secured that of St. Michael in 1285 and of Holy Trinity and its chapel of St. Mary de Grace in 1391.[48]

Such a formidable presence in their midst was not always welcome to the burgesses and provided many causes of tension. There were certain matters of dispute which emerged regularly, though it should not be assumed that they permanently vitiated relations between the monks and the burgesses. There was presumably much unrecorded co-operation. A reasonable working relationship seems to have evolved over the management of the abbey's property in the town, with the bailiffs and leading burgesses witnessing its leases and leading burgesses joining its master of the works in his surveys of houses.[49] The bailiffs were called in as witnesses when the abbey made an escheat for rent arrears in 1344[50] and they sealed and witnessed an agreement about rent arrears made by another abbey tenant in 1382.[51] There were also, no doubt, family ties which acted as a curb on conflict between the two communities. John Thoky,[52] John Boyfeld,[53] and William Farley,[54] three abbots in the later Middle Ages, may have been from Gloucester families.

Among recurrent sources of dispute were the meadows north-west of the town in which the burgesses shared commoning rights with the abbey and its Maisemore tenants. In 1236 a large body of burgesses was involved in a dispute with the abbey, which subsequently recognized their rights in return for a payment of 35 marks,[55] but abbey and town were apparently again at law over the meadows in 1292 and 1347.[56] The southern branch of the river Twyver, or Full brook, was another recurrent cause of dispute, partly because before flowing through the abbey precinct it was tapped at the north-east corner of the town for filling the town moat. The abbey secured confirmation of its right to use the stream from at least three kings during the 12th century. In 1221 it complained that a burgess had diverted the stream[57] and the town's frankpledge jury made a similar claim against the abbey in 1273.[58] In 1374 the abbey secured another royal confirmation and an order that nobody should obstruct or divert the stream.[59] Other disputes arose over fishing rights in the Severn[60] and over responsibility for the walls which divided the precinct from the town.[61] Potentially more significant was a dispute in 1247 or 1248 over the bailiffs' right to levy tolls on abbey tenants from outside the town when they came in to trade,[62] for abbey manors accounted for a large part of Gloucester's local market area. Tension over that question was reflected in 1266 in the abbot's insistence that murage for which his tenants were liable was to be collected by him separately.[63]

In the late 14th century and the early 15th jurisdiction over abbey personnel and its walled precinct became a major issue between the two communities, apparently because of a more agressive attitude adopted by the town authorities. The precinct had probably caused difficulties in policing the town from earlier times; c. 1247 a suspected murderer against whom the hue was raised took refuge in the abbey, which closed its gates against his pursuers.[64] In the town charter of 1398 the abbey secured a

[47] Below, Outlying Hamlets, man.
[48] Below, Churches and Chapels.
[49] Glouc. Cath. Libr., Reg. Abb. Froucester B, p. 350.
[50] Ibid. p. 469.
[51] Ibid. pp. 480–1.
[52] Ibid.
[53] P.R.O., C 115/K 1/6681, f. 169; C 115/K 1/6682, f. 76v.
[54] Below, Bailiffs of Glouc. 1200–1483.
[55] Hist. & Cart. Mon. Glouc. iii. 240–1.
[56] G.B.R., B 8/6, a copy of the agreement of 1236 which is endorsed with notes of legal terms in 1292–3 and 1347.
[57] Hist. & Cart. Mon. Glouc. i. 78; Pleas of the Crown for Glos. ed. Maitland, p. 109.
[58] G.B.R., G 8/1.
[59] Glouc. Cath. Libr., Reg. Abb. Froucester A, ff. 17v.–18.
[60] P.R.O., C 115/K 2/6682, f. 76v.
[61] G.B.R., B 2/1, ff. 195v., 198.
[62] Hist. & Cart. Mon. Glouc. iii, p. xxiii.
[63] Close R. 1264–8, 180–1.
[64] P.R.O., JUST 1/274, rot. 13.

clause exempting its tenants and servants from the bailiffs' power to attach by the body when distrainable goods were lacking,[65] and in 1414 it complained to the Crown that the burgesses were challenging its right to hold a court for its tenants and servants and that the borough officers carrying their maces had entered the precinct to make executions in cases where they had no jurisdiction.[66] Arbitrators chosen in 1429 ruled that the bailiffs and serjeants could enter the precinct but reaffirmed the clause of 1398.[67] A further wide-ranging agreement between the two parties was found necessary in 1447. The monks then accepted that the precinct was a part of the town and within its jurisdiction but the town officers' powers of execution there were limited to cases of felony and treason and to the holding of coroners' inquests; the monks also agreed not to give sanctuary in the precinct to fugitives from justice. The exemption from attachment was confirmed for the monks themselves, and procedures for dealing with cases concerning tenants and dependants were laid down. Other matters of dispute, including the carrying of soil away from the common meadows and the taking of water from the Full brook, were also covered by the agreement.[68]

Tension between the town and the abbey led to an outbreak of violence at the beginning of the 16th century, the immediate cause being a recurrence of the ancient commoning dispute. During disturbances which extended over several weeks following the hay harvest of 1513 armed mobs, with the support of the mayor and aldermen, drove off the abbey's cattle, attacked its servants, and dug a ditch across the meadows. Later that year an agreement to end the dispute attempted to set up a system of arbitration.[69] but another detailed agreement was required in 1518. Among other things it gave the abbey the right to build a new bridge across the Old Severn, guaranteed it access across the meadows to its manors west of the Severn, and confirmed the abbot's right to buy victuals in the town and trade there as a burgess.[70] The power of the townspeople to besiege the monks in their precinct and starve them of supplies had evidently been demonstrated or at least threatened.

Matters of a similar nature were liable to disrupt relations between the burgess community and Llanthony Priory, a smaller house than the abbey but one that was almost as closely involved in the life of the town. In the 12th and 13th centuries the priory like the abbey was a popular object of pious gifts from individual burgesses, and men pre-eminent in the community, such as Osmund Keys, reeve in the 1170s, were among its benefactors.[71] Such gifts made the priory a major property owner within the town walls, while a considerable suburban population settled on the land of its original endowment, the area called the Hide south of the town.[72] The rents from its property at Gloucester amounted to £10 in 1291[73] and to £72 14s. 8½d. in 1535.[74] The priory also had rights as patron in three of the parish churches.[75]

Disputes over matters of jurisdiction between the town and Llanthony Priory were prompted in 1377 or 1378 by a new perambulation of the town boundaries made by the bailiffs. The canons objected to the inclusion of land in St. Owen's parish, anciently the property of their founder Miles of Gloucester, and apparently claimed that it lay within the jurisdiction of the view of frankpledge that they held at Llanthony for their tenants. Such a claim probably had no more justification in earlier practice than did the counter claim of the burgesses to exercise jurisdiction over land

[65] *Glouc. Corp. Rec.* p. 14.
[66] *Cal. Chart. R.* 1341–1417, 471.
[67] G.B.R., B 2/1, f. 195v.
[68] Ibid. ff. 196–8.
[69] *Hist. & Cart. Mon. Glouc.* iii, pp. xxxix–xlvii.
[70] *Glouc. Corp. Rec.* pp. 421–6.

[71] For the grants to the priory, P.R.O., C 115/K 1/6681, ff. 35–169.
[72] Below, topog.
[73] *Tax. Eccl.* (Rec. Com.), 232.
[74] *Valor Eccl.* (Rec. Com.), ii. 430.
[75] Below, Churches and Chapels.

beyond St. Owen's parish in the Hide and in the priory precinct itself. At different times in the late 14th century the borough officers attempted to collect subsidy and hold a coroner's inquest in the precinct,[76] and on more than one occasion the serjeants entered it carrying their official maces. The burgesses also objected to a court which the priory held in St. Owen's church for its town tenants, claiming it was a recent invasion of their liberties, though it had existed from the early 13th century at least.[77]

Questions of jurisdiction between the town and the priory were raised in a suit of 1391, the immediate cause of which was a dispute over a plot of land adjoining St. Kyneburgh's chapel. The priory also complained of other matters: the burgesses had exacted toll from its Hempsted tenants, refused to let it exercise full burgess rights when buying provisions in the town, and generally oppressed its tenants and servants and the pupils of its school in the town. The burgesses countered with their own list of grievances against the priory.[78] Such matters continued to rankle in the mid 15th century when various disputes over land and over the payment of landgavel from property in the town were also in progress.[79] It was perhaps in an attempt to resolve some of those questions that an elaborate rental of the landgavel was prepared in 1455; it was drawn up, apparently with the co-operation of the borough authorities, by a canon, Robert Cole, the 'renter' of the priory's town property.[80] The following year, however, grievances between the two communities were once more being aired and an agreement to accept the decision of arbitrators was made.[81]

Such disputes were sometimes carried on with much bitterness, as in 1391 when the bailiffs were said to have organized armed attacks on the priory's property and servants.[82] They did not, however, prevent close contacts between the two communities. It was possible for the lawyer Robert Gilbert to hold at the same time the offices of steward of the priory and bailiff of the town, while as arbitrator on their part in a property dispute of 1417 the priory chose John Hamlyn, a leading burgess.[83] John Hayward, who became prior of Llanthony in 1457, was a native of the town, as probably were several other canons at that period.[84]

The records of St. Oswald's Priory, if they survived, might reveal similar disputes. It was, however, a poorer house than the abbey or Llanthony and less substantially involved in the town. Its property there produced rents of only £7 13s. 4d. in 1535.[85] It exercised parochial rights over a suburban parish on the north side of the town.

With the friars who settled in the town the burgesses appear to have had consistently good relations, particularly with the Franciscans, the site of whose friary was vested in the borough community at their arrival in the town c. 1230.[86] It was the Franciscans who, 'on account of their sincere and mutual affection and esteem for the bailiffs, burgesses, and community of Gloucester' and in return for 'the many benefits' conferred on them by the burgesses, provided the town with a piped water supply in 1438.[87] Several leading burgesses, including the merchant John Banbury (d. c. 1404),[88] chose to be buried in Greyfriars church, while others, including the merchant Thomas Pope (d. 1400)[89] and the mercer Thomas Moore (d. 1421),[90] were

[76] P.R.O., C 115/K 2/6685, ff. 9–13.
[77] Ibid. C 115/K 2/6684, f. 159 and v.; and for the ct., cf. ibid. C 115/K 1/6681, ff. 38, 51v., 56.
[78] Ibid. C 115/K 2/6684, ff. 139–41, 144–6, 151–2, 159 and v.
[79] Ibid. C 115/K 2/6685, ff. 9–16v.
[80] Glouc. Rental, 1455, 3.
[81] P.R.O., C 115/K 2/6685, f. 17.
[82] Ibid. C 115/K 2/6684, f. 145.
[83] Ibid. C 115/K 2/6682, ff. 121, 160, 245; cf. below,

Bailiffs of Glouc. 1200–1483.
[84] P.R.O., C 115/K 2/6685, f. 7; the canons Wm. Saunders and Wal. Banknot mentioned then had namesakes among the leading burgesses: below, Bailiffs of Glouc. 1200–1483.
[85] Valor Eccl. (Rec. Com.), ii. 487.
[86] Glouc. Corp. Rec. p. 154.
[87] G.B.R., J 1/1112.
[88] Glos. R.O., P 154/14/CH 1/19; cf. ibid. 3, 16.
[89] Hockaday Abs. ccxiii, 1400.
[90] Ibid. cciii, 1421.

buried in Blackfriars. Legacies to all three orders of friars in Gloucester were a regular item in the wills of burgesses of the 15th century and early 16th, where significantly the larger religious houses were very rarely mentioned.[91]

Other regular recipients of charity were the three hospitals in the town. The leper hospital of St. Margaret at Wotton appears to have come under the control of the burgess community by the late 14th century: a leading burgess occupied the post of master of the hospital and the chief borough officers and other burgesses were involved in the management of its property.[92] There were close connexions, too, with St. Bartholomew's Hospital. About 1240 arrangements for the application of a recent endowment were made on the advice of the mayor Richard the burgess and sealed with the borough seal,[93] and at about the same date a grant of land by the hospital was made with the assent of the burgess community.[94]

Topography

The basic plan of Gloucester owes much to its Roman origins, but its street pattern was laid down in the Anglo-Saxon period, with possibly a planned development in the early 10th century.[95] Infilling and suburban expansion continued throughout the 11th and 12th centuries. By the 13th century, when a clear picture begins to emerge from the documentary evidence, the town had already acquired the form that has its earliest visual representation in Speed's map of 1610;[96] with few exceptions, the streets and side lanes can all be traced in the 13th-century records.[97] Medieval Gloucester took shape, therefore, in centuries for which there is little written record and, until fuller archaeological evidence becomes available, its development must remain largely a matter for conjecture.

In the immediate post-Conquest period one of the most significant changes was the provision of stronger defences.[98] Using the foundations of the Roman walls and water from the southern branch of the river Twyver (also called the Full brook), a circuit of walls with gates and a moat was built to enclose on three sides the inner eastern part of the town. On the north side of the town two outer gates were built on the northern branch of the Twyver to mark the limits of the suburbs which had grown up in late Anglo-Saxon times on Hare Lane and along the London road. In the north-west part of the town the inner defences were provided by the precincts of Gloucester Abbey, which were walled and extended between 1104 and 1113 and again extended in the early 13th century,[99] and the precincts of St. Oswald's minister. In the south-west part of the town the defences were strengthened soon after the Conquest by the building of a castle, which involved the removal of several houses. The first motte-and-bailey structure, incorporating the mound later known as the Barbican, was replaced in the first years of the 12th century by a more elaborate castle.[1]

On its west side Gloucester was defended by the river Severn, which flowed past the town in three channels. Apart from the western channel flowing by Over on the far side of the tract of low-lying meadowland called Alney Island,[2] two channels ran close to the town. The middle channel was thought to be man-made; a tradition recorded at

[91] For the P.C.C. wills for the period, Hockaday Abs., vols. for Glouc. pars.

[92] *Glouc. Corp. Rec.* pp. 360, 370, 376, 386, 407, 429; G.B.R., C 9/6, freemen's roll from 1534, which records the name of the master each year with those of the chief borough officers. [93] *Glouc. Corp. Rec.* pp. 164–5.

[94] P.R.O., C 115/K 2/6682, f. 105; cf. ibid. f. 180 and v.

[95] Above, A.-S. Glouc.

[96] Speed, *Map of Glouc.* (1610).

[97] For references to street names in this section, below, Street Names.

[98] For the town's defences, below, Bridges, Gates, and Walls.

[99] Below, Glouc. Cath. and Close.

[1] Below, Glouc. Castle.

[2] Glos. Colln. prints GL 65.27.

the beginning of the 18th century attributed its creation to an unspecified date in antiquity when the monks of St. Oswald's persuaded the townspeople to dig it in the hope of preventing flooding of their minster from the channel near the town.[3] The name Old Severn was in use for the easternmost channel in the early 16th century[4] and Leland described it as the chief arm of the river.[5] It was, however, the middle channel which carried the greater volume of water in the late Middle Ages: in 1370 and again in 1475 it was referred to as the Great Severn and the easternmost channel as the Little Severn,[6] and the surviving records suggest that Westgate bridge, spanning the middle channel, was much more of a burden to repair than the Foreign bridge, spanning the easternmost.[7]

Within its defences the core of the Anglo-Saxon *burh*, where most of the 300 royal burgesses of Edward the Confessor's reign had lived,[8] was based on the four main streets which met at the central crossroads where the town's high cross stood by the early 13th century.[9] Those four streets, named from the gates by which they entered the town, were sometimes distinguished as 'great' streets, as in 1473 when they alone were made subject to paving powers.[10]

The longest and most important street was Westgate Street. It was more usually known in the Middle Ages as Ebridge Street ('the street leading to the river bridge'),[11] for its importance resulted from the Severn bridges which gave Gloucester control of a route into South Wales. Along the street from west of the river also came much of the town's local market trade and the Forest of Dean iron that supplied its most significant industry. The upper part of Westgate Street was the main market place by the mid 12th century[12] and two churches, St. Mary de Grace and Holy Trinity, were built there with parishes that straddled the street.[13] Further down the street stood the Boothall or guildhall (recorded from 1192), which was both the administrative centre of the medieval town and its chief market hall,[14] and the mint which operated at Gloucester until the mid 13th century had premises near Holy Trinity church.[15]

Upper Westgate Street was presumably a much less constricted area when it first became the site of market trade. It may be only the remnant of an irregularly shaped market place, which occupied the whole area bounded on the north by the Gloucester Abbey precinct and which perhaps also included the west side of upper Northgate Street bounded by Grace (later St. John's) Lane, the eastern limit of the precinct. The irregular shape of the area bounded by upper Westgate Street, upper Northgate Street, and the precinct was governed partly by the fact that the main east–west route through Gloucester, that between London and South Wales, made a sharp turn in the centre of the town, entering by Northgate Street but leaving by Westgate Street; the ancient alignment of Ermin Street on the first Roman fort at Kingsholm, rather than on the later Roman town, had made Northgate Street, which joined Ermin Street at Wotton Pitch, the London road. If the irregular central area had once been an open market place, the infilling with the long and narrow burgage plots was early in date. A plot extending between Holy Trinity church and the precinct wall contained a house and three shops in 1176,[16] and the whole of the area adjoining the south and east sides

[3] Bodl. MS. Top. Glouc. c. 3, f. 6.
[4] Glouc. Cath. Libr., Reg. Abb. Malvern, ii, f. 8v.
[5] Leland, *Itin.* ed. Toulmin Smith, ii. 57–8.
[6] *Hist. & Cart. Mon. Glouc.* iii. 257; Worc. Episc. Reg., Reg. Carpenter, ii. f. 77 and v.
[7] For the bridges, below, Bridges, Gates, and Walls.
[8] *Glouc. Rental, 1455*, p. xiv.
[9] Below, Public Buildings.
[10] *Glouc. Corp. Rec.* p. 16; cf. ibid. pp. 267, 319; *Hist. &*

Cart. Mon. Glouc. i. 26.
[11] *P.N. Glos.* (E.P.N.S.), ii. 128.
[12] P.R.O., C 115/K 1/6681, f. 82; below, Markets and Fairs.
[13] For par. boundaries, Causton, *Map of Glouc.* (1843).
[14] Below, Public Buildings.
[15] P.R.O., C 115/K 1/6681, f. 110v.
[16] Ibid. C 115/K 1/6681, f. 82.

of the precinct was evidently closely built up by 1223 when fires raged from the Cross along the west side of Northgate Street and along both sides of Westgate Street as far as the present College Street.[17] The burgage plots laid out along the north side of upper Westgate Street remained separated from the abbey wall by a narrow lane running from Three Cocks Lane to St. John's Lane.[18] By the late Middle Ages other buildings, including houses and shops and the covered butter market called the King's Board, had been put up in the centre of upper Westgate Street, dividing it into two narrow lanes.[19]

Together with the routes from London and Wales, the third significant route into the town was that from Bristol which entered by Southgate Street. That street was a site of market trading by the early 13th century when it was the usual pitch for sellers of fish,[20] and by the beginning of the 16th century a covered wheat market stood near its north end.[21] The pillory stood nearby in 1455.[22] Though Southgate Street, like all the main streets, was closely built up for its full length by the 13th century, there had been little building behind the houses at its southern end; in the 1230s two friaries found sites there, the Franciscan house, on the east side, being given an extensive plot which occupied the whole south-east corner of the intramural area.[23] A side lane, later known as Blackfriars, was built c. 1246 to give access to the Dominican house on the west side of the street.[24]

Eastgate (or Ailesgate) Street was originally the least favoured of the four main streets, being the Jewish quarter until 1275.[25] It led out to the two bartons from which the royal and abbey estates adjoining the town were administered[26] and to the small market town of Painswick, but its importance as a route of commerce probably dated only from the end of the Middle Ages with the development of the Stroud Valley clothmaking area.

Of the principal side streets, those in the eastern half of the town running back from Northgate Street and upper Southgate Street to the town wall — St. Aldate Lane, Oxbode Lane (later also called Mitre Street), Grant or Rosse Lane (later New Inn Lane), and Travel (later Bell) Lane — have been suggested as the result of late Anglo-Saxon planning.[27] In the south-western part of the town the pattern was less regular. The main side street, the smiths' street (later Longsmith Street), led westwards from Southgate Street to the castle and was the seat of the ironworking industry. Gore (later Bull) Lane and Broadsmith (later Berkeley) Street linked the smiths' street to upper Westgate Street. From lower Westgate Street, Castle Lane led to the castle and to Bearland, an open space fronting the castle which was used to muster troops,[28] and the fullers' street (later Lower Quay Lane) gave access to the quay and the clothworking quarter adjoining it.

On the north side of Westgate Street lanes ran to the abbey precinct. Craft's Lane or Ironmongers' Row (later College Court) led to the small gate later called St. Michael's gate. Lich Lane (later College Street) gave access to the lich (later King Edward's) gate into the abbey churchyard, where, before the parish churches gained burial rights, many of the town's inhabitants were carried for burial. Further down,

[17] *Hist. & Cart. Mon. Glouc.* i. 26, where the street of the shoemakers and drapers is upper Northgate St. and the lich gate is the later King Edward's gate: cf. below.

[18] Glouc. Cath. Libr., Reg. Abb. Froucester B, pp. 1, 295; Bodl. MS. Top. Glouc. c. 3, f. 44v. For the position of the Portcullis inn mentioned in the second source, Glos. R.O., D 936/E 1, pp. 115, 117.

[19] Glouc. Cath. Libr., Reg. Abb. Malvern, i, f. 198v.; below, Public Buildings.

[20] *Abbrev. Plac.* (Rec. Com.), 92.

[21] Below, Markets and Fairs.

[22] *Glouc. Rental, 1455,* 7.

[23] Below, Sites of Religious Houses.

[24] *Cal. Lib.* 1245–51, 65.

[25] Above, Glouc. 1066–1327.

[26] Below, Outlying Hamlets, man.

[27] Above, A.-S. Glouc.

[28] *Cal. Pat.* 1370–4, 243, 293.

Abbey (later Three Cocks) Lane gave access to the abbey's west gate, St. Mary's, and by its continuation (later called Half Street) to St. Oswald's Priory and to the blind gate, which led into the northern suburb. Further west was Archdeacon's (later also called Leather Bottle) Lane which took its name from the residence of the archdeacon of Gloucester.[29]

Between Abbey Lane and Archdeacon's Lane was a block of Gloucester Abbey property, lying outside its main gate and grouped around its church of St. Mary de Lode.[30] That area, later known as St. Mary's Square, was evidently the site of the abbey's ancient burgage property, numbering 52 houses c. 1100.[31] From the west side of the square two lanes led down to the Old Severn, that on the north connecting with a crossing point, presumably the 'lode' from which St. Mary's church was named. In 1518 the river was crossed there by a footbridge, which the monks of Gloucester Abbey, who used it for access to their meadows across the river, planned to rebuild on a more substantial scale.[32] A large abbey barn, called Wood Barton, which stood nearby on the north side of the lane,[33] presumably provided storage for the hay crop from the meadows.

Development beyond the town's inner defences in late Anglo-Saxon times had apparently been confined to the north side. The Hare Lane suburb, on the route leading out to the royal palace at Kingsholm and to Tewkesbury, comprised three parallel lanes, Hare Lane, Back Hare Lane (later Park Street), and, some way to the west, the vanished Bride Lane.[34] Part of that suburb lay in St. Oswald's (later St. Catherine's) parish and some of the 60 houses held c. 1100 by the archbishop of York in right of St. Oswald's minster[35] were probably there. Most of the St. Oswald's property, however, lay along Watering (later St. Catherine) Street, which ran from the blind gate near the minster round to Alvin gate at the head of Hare Lane. Watering Street took its name from a place called the Wateringstead, which was situated on the Old Severn and was being used in the mid 14th century by townspeople for collecting water from the river.[36] In 1536 the St. Oswald's property in the northern suburbs comprised 28 houses and 6 cottages in Watering Street, 8 houses or cottages in Hare Lane, 6 cottages or houses in the street (later Pitt Street) which ran along the north wall of the abbey precinct, and a number of gardens, probably once the site of dwellings, in Hare Lane, Bride Lane, and on the Tewkesbury road just beyond Alvin gate.[37] On the London road another suburb, still described by that term in the 14th century,[38] stretched out beyond the inner north gate to the outer gate on the Twyver; it, too, seems to have been a pre-Conquest development.

On the west side of the town the extension of the built-up area across the Old Severn into the area known as the Island,[39] bounded by the middle channel of the Severn on the west and south and by an ancient ditch on the north,[40] may be no earlier than the 12th century.[41] The name Foreign bridge given to the bridge carrying Westgate Street over the Old Severn suggests that it once marked the limits of the borough and in 1220 or 1221 land in the Island was claimed as part of Maisemore

[29] Glouc. Corp. Rec, p. 282.
[30] Cf. Glos. R.O., D 1740/P 23, a copy of Causton, Map of Glouc. (1843) with chapter property marked on it.
[31] Glouc. Rental, 1455, p. xiv.
[32] Glouc. Corp. Rec. p. 424; cf. Speed, Map of Glouc. (1610).
[33] G.B.R., J 5/5; Glos. R.O., D 936/E 12/9, f. 253v.
[34] Glouc. Rental, 1455, p. xvi; cf. G.B.R., J 3/8, ff. 230v.-231.
[35] Glouc. Rental, 1455, p. xiv; cf. V.C.H. Glos. ii. 84.
[36] P.R.O., JUST 2/34, rot. 16d., which records the drow-

ning of a woman at 'le Watryngstud' while getting water from the Severn; cf. ibid. C 115/K 2/6682, f. 65v.; Glouc. Rental, 1455, p. xvi.
[37] P.R.O., SC 6/Hen. VIII/1212, rott. 4–5.
[38] Glouc. Cath. Libr., Reg. Abb. Froucester B, pp. 253, 261.
[39] Hall and Pinnell, Map of Glouc. (1780).
[40] Cf. P.R.O., C 115/K 1/6681, f. 94; Worc. Episc. Reg., Reg. Carpenter, ii, f. 77 and v.
[41] Above, A.-S. Glouc.

parish.[42] Development of the Island was apparently in progress in Henry II's reign, traditionally the date of the establishment of St. Bartholomew's Hospital there,[43] and the area was well built up by the mid 13th century.[44] The Island remained subject to flooding, which led to the rebuilding of St. Bartholomew's on a higher foundation in the early 16th century,[45] and the fact that it was ever developed at all is an indication of the importance of the western route into the town.

The borough boundary, as described in a perambulation of 1370, was fixed at roughly the centre point of Over causeway and marked by a stone cross,[46] but there was no attempt to build beyond Westgate bridge. Alney Island remained an area of periodically flooded meadows: those adjoining the town and partly within its boundaries were Common Ham (later Town Ham) and Pulle (Pool) Meadow, on the north side of the causeway, and Nun Ham and Priest Ham (later called respectively Oxlease and Portham) on the south side. Those meadows, together with Little Meadow, Meanham, and Archdeacon Meadow, north-west of the town between the Old Severn and the middle channel, belonged to Gloucester Abbey, but rights of common with the abbey and its Maisemore tenants were claimed there by the burgess community, a cause of continual disputes. In the early 16th century the borough pound was just east of Westgate bridge, giving its name to Pen Meadow.[47]

The main expansion of the town during the 12th century and the early 13th occurred on monastic land beyond the outer north, east, and south gates, creating the roadside suburbs which were largely destroyed at the siege of Gloucester in 1643. Beyond the outer north gate several parcels of Gloucester Abbey land were granted away in the period 1179–1224 at Newland on the south-east side of the London road near the borough boundary, at Fete Lane (later Alvin Street) on the north-west side of the road, and at Ladycroft between Fete Lane and the Twyver. As the abbey's land was usually granted in perpetuity at the period, being taken in hand again only as escheat or for rent arrears, the grants probably represent the earliest settlement of the area.[48] In the mid 1260s suburban growth in the area was represented by 23 houses in Newland and 10 in 'Lullescrofte', probably Ladycroft, which were held from the abbey's Abbot's Barton manor for cash rents and with no land attached. The abbey then had 10 houses in Brook Street,[49] which led out of the postern gate at the north-east corner of the town walls alongside the southern branch of the Twyver to Morin's Mill.[50] Soon afterwards the land between the London road and Brook Street was filled by the premises of the Carmelite friary founded c. 1269.[51]

The roadside suburb called Barton Street outside the east gate had also been formed by the 1260s: 24 houses without land owed cash rents and a few agricultural services to Abbot's Barton manor.[52] They were probably ranged along the street both within and without the borough boundary (marked there by a ditch called the Lawday ditch[53]) as far as the junction with a lane to Tuffley where the barton of the manor stood.[54] In 1455 there were a few abbey tenants south of the entrance to Barton Street on the lane (later Parker's Row) which ran along the outside of the town ditch[55] and

[42] *Hist. & Cart. Mon. Glouc.* i. 322.
[43] *Cal. Inq. Misc.* iii, p. 80.
[44] *Glouc. Rental, 1455*, 55, 57, 59.
[45] Leland, *Itin.* ed. Toulmin Smith, ii. 59; Austin, *Crypt Sch.* 138.
[46] *Hist. & Cart. Mon. Glouc.* iii. 256–7.
[47] Ibid. ii. 84–6; *Glouc. Corp. Rec.* pp. 421–6; for the positions of those meadows, Causton, *Map. of Glouc.* (1843); Glos. R.O., D 3269, bk. of plans of hosp. property 1826, nos. 10–11.
[48] Glouc. Cath. Libr., Reg. Abb. Froucester B, pp. 230–2,

244–8; significantly too, a clause valuing buildings on the premises, included in most other grants, is omitted. For those places, cf. P.R.O., E 134/31 Eliz. East./15; *Glouc. Rental, 1455*, 99–105; *Glouc. Corp. Rec.* pp. 265–6, 305, 438.
[49] *Hist. & Cart. Mon. Glouc.* iii. 154–6.
[50] Glouc. Cath. Libr., Reg. Abb. Froucester B, p. 320.
[51] *V.C.H. Glos.* ii. 112; Speed, *Map of Glouc.* (1610).
[52] *Hist. & Cart. Mon. Glouc.* iii. 156–8.
[53] *Glouc. Corp. Rec.* p. 417.
[54] Below, Outlying Hamlets, man.
[55] *Glouc. Rental, 1455*, 111.

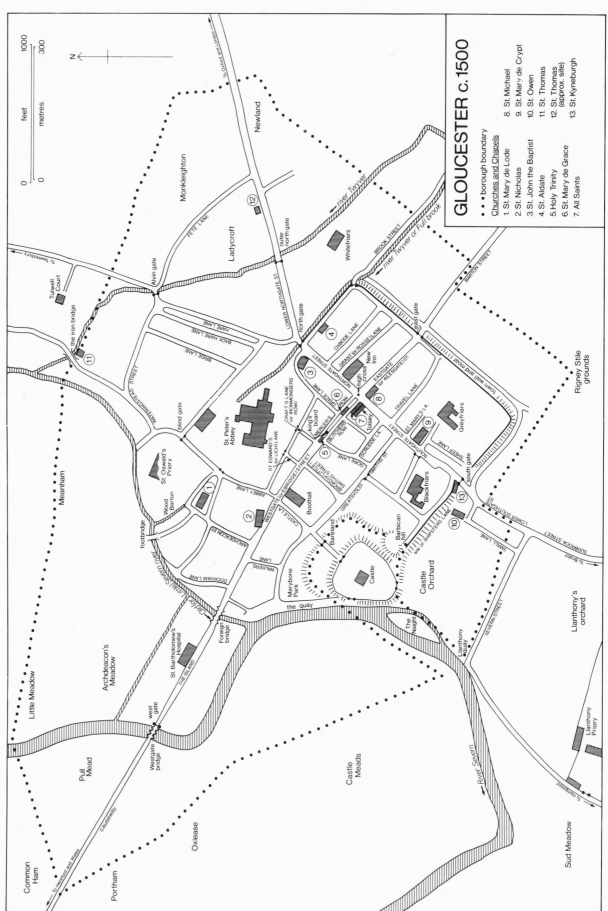

GLOUCESTER c.1500

•••• borough boundary

Churches and Chapels

1. St. Mary de Lode
2. St. Nicholas
3. St. John the Baptist
4. St. Aldate
5. Holy Trinity
6. St. Mary de Grace
7. All Saints
8. St. Michael
9. St. Mary de Crypt
10. St. Owen
11. St. Thomas
12. St. Thomas (approx. site)
13. St. Kyneburgh

Fig. 4

68

which had its equivalent (later Dog Lane) on the other side of Barton Street, leading along the ditch to Brook Street.[56]

On the south side of the town there was some early building just beyond the wall, in what became St. Owen's parish when that church was built outside the south gate in the late 11th century. All or most of the 15 burgesses who held their houses from Walter of Gloucester c. 1100[57] lived there. At the time when Walter built the new castle in the early years of the 12th century 13 houses (according to a later account) stood on Shipsters Lane which ran from the south gate westwards along the south wall and castle ditch; several were occupied by Walter's servants, including his huntsman, and kennels for his hounds stood by the Severn at the west end of the lane. Six of the houses in the lane were destroyed by the enlarging of the town ditch in the 1260s.[58]

By the mid 13th century there had been considerable building further south on land which formed part of Llanthony Priory's original endowment in 1137, both within St. Owen's parish and outside the borough boundary on the north part of land called the Hide.[59] Within the boundary houses were built along the part of the Bristol road later distinguished as lower Southgate Street, the houses on the west side backing onto a parallel back lane called Small Lane, running south from St. Owen's churchyard.[60] Also developed by the mid 13th century was Severn Street, which ran from the south end of lower Southgate Street to a quay on the Severn,[61] and at the same period was mentioned a new lane to Llanthony, running south of and parallel to Severn Street.[62] In 1539 at its dissolution Llanthony Priory's property included 13 houses and 5 cottages described as in Small Lane, but probably including those in lower Southgate Street, and 22 houses and 13 cottages in Severn Street.[63] Another street, called Sudbrook Street, on which cottages had been built by the late 14th century,[64] was apparently the roadside development later called Littleworth, along the Bristol road south of the junction with Severn Street.[65]

The principal trading area of the town in the Middle Ages remained around upper Westgate Street, the Cross, and upper Northgate Street. The houses and shops on the north side of upper Westgate Street were occupied mainly by the mercers, together with beltmakers and coifmakers, while on the south side were the butchers' shambles.[66] Shoemakers and drapers had their premises at the top of Northgate Street on the west side.[67] Shops clustered at the Cross around the churches of All Saints, St. Michael, and St. Martin.[68] There were, however, premises for trade along the length of the main streets and in the principal side lanes. Two shops outside the east gate at the entrance to Barton Street and two in the Island between the bridges were mentioned c. 1285, and seven shops fronting a tenement in the Island were mentioned in 1318. Oxbode Lane was lined with shops, fronting the tenements, in 1315.[69]

[56] Ibid. 103.
[57] Ibid. p. xiv.
[58] P.R.O., C 115/K 2/6685, ff. 9, 10v.
[59] Cf. ibid. C 115/K 2/6685, ff. 9v.–10; Dugdale, *Mon.* vi. 136.
[60] P.R.O., C 115/K 1/6681, ff. 47v., 49, 58v.; C 115/K 2/6684, ff. 63v., 181; cf. *Glouc. Rental, 1455*, p. xv; Speed, *Map of Glouc.* (1610).
[61] P.R.O., C 115/K 1/6681, ff. 35, 39, and v.; C 115/K 2/6685, f. 55v.; cf. ibid. E 134/31 Eliz. East./15. Severn St. survived until the building of the canal basin, though its houses were destroyed in the siege: Hall and Pinnell, *Map of Glouc.* (1780).
[62] P.R.O., C 115/K 2/6681, ff. 37v., 39v., 47v.
[63] Ibid. SC 6/Hen. VIII/1224, rott. 3–4d.; cf. *L. & P. Hen. VIII*, xviii (2), pp. 51–2, where in 1543 the former Llanthony property included 10 tenants in lower Southgate

St. and 51 tenants in Severn St.
[64] P.R.O., C 115/K 2/6684, ff. 39, 131v.–132, 153.
[65] Speed, *Map of Glouc.* (1610); Hall and Pinnell, *Map of Glouc.* (1780). Sudbrook St. was described in 1535 as running from the E. end of Severn St. to the wall of Llanthony's orchard (later called High Orchard): *Glouc. Rental, 1455*, p. xv.
[66] *Glouc. Rental, 1455*, pp. xvi, 27, 31; Glouc. Cath. Libr., Reg. Abb. Froucester B, p. 481; Reg. Abb. Malvern, i, f. 198v., where the positions of the high cross and St. Mary de Grace are given the wrong way round.
[67] *Glouc. Rental, 1455*, 67; *Glouc. Corp. Rec.* p. 207; Glouc. Cath. Libr., Reg. Abb. Froucester B, p. 480.
[68] e.g. *Cal. Pat.* 1247–58, 661; Glouc. Cath. Libr., Reg. Abb. Froucester B, p. 348; *Glouc. Corp. Rec.* p. 372; *Glouc. Rental, 1455*, 3.
[69] *Glouc. Corp. Rec.* pp. 277–8, 329, 309.

Craft's Lane on the north side of Westgate Street took its alternative name of Ironmongers' Row from premises of the ironmongers. The main industrial quarter near the centre of the town was formed by the smiths' forges in Longsmith Street and, presumably, Broadsmith Street. Other industrial activity took place on the outer fringes, with fulling and dyeing at the quay and by the Twyver, in the north-eastern suburbs, and tanning based in Hare Lane.[70]

Parish assessments of the early 16th century give some idea of the wealth of the different areas of the town at the end of the Middle Ages. St. Nicholas, a very populous parish comprising the central and lower parts of Westgate Street with the Island and the quay, was then the wealthiest, closely challenged by St. Michael, which included Eastgate Street and the inner part of the Barton Street suburb, and St. John, which had part of the central trading area in upper Northgate Street and some of the old inner suburbs on London road and Hare Lane. Holy Trinity, St. Mary de Grace, and All Saints, in upper Westgate Street, though the three smallest parishes were in the middle rank in terms of wealth, together with the large but fairly thinly populated parish of St. Mary de Crypt, based on Southgate Street. St. Oswald, with parts of the northern and north-eastern suburbs, was among the poorer parishes, together with St. Aldate and St. Mary de Lode, including small areas on the fringes of the town away from the main trading area, and St. Owen, made up of the lower Southgate Street suburb with a small area within the south gate. The great diversity in size and population between the 11 parishes makes detailed comparison pointless, but the figures do emphasise the relative wealth of Westgate Street and the central area around the Cross, as opposed to the outer fringes of the town and the suburbs where few wealthy men lived. Of 25 men in Gloucester who were assessed in 1513 on equipping two or more men for the muster, only one lived in the area covered by St. Owen, St. Oswald, St. Aldate, and St. Mary de Lode, while St. Nicholas and St. Michael had five each and All Saints four. The assessments given in Table III cover only the areas which lay within the borough boundary, or the liberty of the mace, as it was known, omitting the outlying hamlets which were attached to St. Mary de Lode, St. Oswald's, and St. Michael's parishes.

The fires which devastated large areas of Gloucester in 1122, 1190, 1214, 1222, and 1223[71] evidently occurred in a town of wooden houses, and timber framing was to remain the dominant building material until the mid 17th century. Stone-built houses were exceptional and were distinguished as such in early deeds: Gloucester Abbey owned one in Longsmith Street in the mid 12th century and there was another near Holy Trinity church in Westgate Street in 1215.[72] A house built in the 13th century on the east side of Hare Lane, later used as the hall of the tanners' company, is the only medieval domestic stone house in Gloucester of which any detail is known.[73] Stone-vaulted cellars were probably common features beneath the houses on the main streets. One, possibly of the 12th century, survives under the Fleece inn on the south side of Westgate Street and another under nos. 74–6 in the same street,[74] and there was formerly one of the 13th century under a house in Eastgate Street.[75] Other cellars were mentioned in 1379, running beneath a group of 11 shops at a place called Rotten Row east of St. Nicholas's church,[76] and in 1415 under a new-built house at the corner of Westgate Street and Bull Lane.[77] Stone in the form of re-used blocks of

[70] Above, trade and ind. 1066–1327.
[71] *Hist. & Cart. Mon. Glouc.* i. 14–15, 22, 24, 26.
[72] Glouc. Cath. Libr., Reg. Abb. Froucester B, pp. 1, 289.
[73] *Trans. B.G.A.S.* ci. 83–8.

[74] Nat. Mon. Rec. BB 72/5667, 5675.
[75] Glos. Colln. prints GL 37.5.
[76] P.R.O., C 115/K 2/6684, f. 40.
[77] Ibid. C 115/K 2/6682, f. 90.

TABLE III: PARISH ASSESSMENTS

	Muster 1513		*Subsidy 1534-5*			
	men equipped	*inhabitants assessed*		£	s.	d.
St. Nicholas	25½	31	St. Nicholas	10	5	0
St. John	20	29	St. Michael	9	18	5
St. Michael	20	24	St. John	8	0	4
Holy Trinity	16	23	Holy Trinity	6	0	3
St. Mary de Crypt	14	18	St. Mary de Grace	5	2	2
All Saints	14	10	St. Mary de Crypt	4	0	2
St. Mary de Grace	9	14	St. Oswald	2	19	11
St. Owen	3	1	All Saints	2	10	0
St. Oswald	2	5	St. Aldate	2	9	10
St. Aldate	1	3	St. Owen	1	10	0
St. Mary de Lode	0	0	St. Mary de Lode	1	10	0

Sources: 1513, G.B.R., B 2/1, ff. 225v.–226v.; 1534–5, ibid. f. 233.

ashlar, presumably of Roman origin, was also used for some party walls and passages at ground-floor level, for example at nos. 11 and 26 Westgate Street. Tile was the usual roof covering by 1273 when thatched roofs were being penalized as a fire risk.[78] Houses built at the beginning of the 13th century on a plot in Eastgate Street, each comprising a small hall, a chamber, and a kitchen, were described as of boards and plaster with tiled roofs.[79]

On the main streets the burgage plots, narrow-fronted and commonly running back 100 ft. or more, were an important determinant of the plans of the timber-framed houses. The houses were gabled to the street and extended back some distance along the plot, as with no. 68 Westgate Street and no. 3 Northgate Street (now demolished), both of the late 15th century.[80] They were generally of three storeys at the street end but might be lower at the back. Where the frontage was wider there might be a cross range parallel to the street and a ground-floor passage leading to a narrow court, as at the early 16th-century no. 84 Northgate Street (now demolished), formerly the Red Lion inn.[81] There were only a few large plots, most of them occupied by inns, having a courtyard and a wide passage from the street. The New Inn, built in the mid 15th century, has a galleried courtyard,[82] and a house which stood opposite St. John's church, built in the early 16th century as the Ram inn, had an open court approached through a central passage way.[83] The elevations of the principal houses had exposed close studding with mid rails to each storey, while elevations of lesser importance had box framing with prominent tension braces. Each storey, including the attic gables,

[78] G.B.R., G 8/1.
[79] *Cal. Inq. Misc.* i, pp. 57–8.
[80] E. Mercer, *Eng. Vernacular Houses* (1975), 159; *Glevensis*, no. 6, pp. 2–4.
[81] *Glevensis*, no. 9, pp. 24–7.
[82] W. A. Pantin, 'Medieval Inns', *Studies in Building Hist.* ed. E. M. Jope (1961); below, Plate 7.
[83] G. T. Robinson, *Picturesque Antiquities of Glouc.* (1849), 14–15; cf. Causton, *Map of Glouc.* (1843); Glos. Colln. 10962 (7).

was usually jettied on one elevation, and at the New Inn the jetties continued round two sides and had elaborately carved corner posts.

The character of the smaller cottages which lined the side lanes of the central area and the outer areas, such as St. Mary's Square, Hare Lane, and Watering Street (later St. Catherine Street),[84] is indicated by a building lease of 1413 for four tenements on the west side of Craft's Lane (later College Court). Each was to have a hall and shop on the ground floor and a solar on the jettied upper floor, while a lean-to penthouse (*shura*) with brick chimneys was to be built along the back of the tenements to house kitchens.[85]

By the end of the period many additions, in the form of penthouses,[86] posts to support jetties, and the occasional new chimney, had been made to houses on the principal streets and side lanes of the central area. The resulting encroachments, though an added source of income,[87] were sometimes a matter of concern to the town corporation, as in 1497 when it disputed alterations made by Gloucester Abbey to a house in the central row of buildings at the top of Westgate Street. Built wider and given cellar steps, steps up to the doorways, and shutters to the windows, it had narrowed the roadway on either side.[88]

[84] For the old cottages in those areas, almost all demolished by 1983, Glos. Colln. prints GL 40.19; Nat. Mon. Rec. BB 52/2159; BB 83/2447, 4494, 4496; below, Plates 1–2.

[85] P.R.O., C 115/K 2/6682, ff. 61v.–62, 120v.; the houses were possibly never built, for in 1420 the landowner, Llanthony Priory, was acting to compel the tenant to fulfil this agreement.

[86] Ibid. C 115/K 2/6682, f. 121; C 115/K 2/6685, f. 14.

[87] G.B.R., J 5/3.

[88] Ibid. B 8/5.

EARLY MODERN GLOUCESTER

1547–1720

GLOUCESTER 1547–1640

THE early Tudor period seems to have been a time of mild prosperity for Gloucester, but from the mid 16th century until the English Revolution it experienced considerable economic uncertainty. Its textile and capping industries declined and new crafts were slow to develop, though there was some expansion in its importance as a market and service centre. Meanwhile the city's control of the inshire hundred generated increasing conflict with the county landowners, particularly from the end of the 16th century. It was in that era of mounting economic and political tension that Gloucester emerged as an important puritan stronghold.[1]

Population

Estimates of town populations for the period are highly speculative, but it may be possible to discern the broad demographic trend at Gloucester. In 1548 the chantry commissioners counted 3,339 communicants, which might suggest a total population of *c.* 4,400 people, compared with *c.* 3,500, in 1524.[2] The diocesan census of 1563 enumerated *c.* 950 householders, indicating roughly 4,250 inhabitants; but that may be on the low side since the diocesan returns tend to under-register numbers.[3] In 1603 3,451 communicants were counted in the city, which points to a population of approximately 4,600. By the 1670s, if the hearth tax is any guide, the total number of townspeople was probably just over 5,000.[4]

From those assorted enumerations, it seems that Gloucester's population rose markedly during the early Tudor period and then more slowly in the late 16th century and the early 17th. Enumerations provide, however, only blurred snapshots of demographic trends, and the city's parish registers afford only limited help in trying to focus the picture. Records survive for only five of the parishes, mostly from the 1560s. Moreover, the surviving registers are mainly for the wealthier, commercial districts, the parishes of St. John, Holy Trinity, St. Nicholas, and St. Michael; the single poorer parish for which we have data is St. Aldate.[5] The general picture in the wealthier parishes is of a considerable surplus of baptisms over burials in most decades. In St. Aldate, however, there was an overall deficit with burials exceeding baptisms, and that may well have typified the situation in the poorer, peripheral parishes of the city, which were most vulnerable to food shortages and disease.

Epidemic disease was recurrent in Gloucester in the late 16th century and the early

---

[1] This chapter was written in 1983–4.
[2] *Trans. B.G.A.S.* viii. 253–61; P.R.O., E 179/113/189.
[3] Bodl. MS. Rawl. C.790, ff. 5v.–6v., where the figure for St. Nicholas's par. is omitted and has had to be estimated.

[4] *Eccl. Misc.* 68–9; P.R.O., E 179/247/14, rott. 29–31.
[5] Glos. R.O., P 154/4/IN 1/1; 6/IN 1/1; 9/IN 1/1; 14/IN 1/1; 15/IN 1/1.

17th. During Elizabeth I's reign the city was repeatedly swept by bubonic plague: there were epidemics in the years 1565, 1573, 1575–6, 1577–8, 1580, and 1593–4.[6] In 1565 the magistrates reported that the attack was mostly confined to the poorer suburbs and back lanes and that the main streets were free.[7] In 1593 the infection began about Midsummer; by 2 August 25 houses were affected and 47 people were dead, and later that month over 120 houses were stricken. Mortality remained high until the end of November, though 'some, more or less, died weekly till the Shrovetide following'.[8] The diocesan courts withdrew from the city, as did substantial numbers of traders and shopkeepers.[9] A further outbreak occurred in the summer of 1594.[10] There were apparently fewer irruptions during the early 17th century, but they may have been of greater severity. Particularly intense was the attack of 1604–5, almost certainly spread from Bristol where there was a major outbreak. One of the first households contaminated at Gloucester, in April 1604, was that of Alderman John Taylor who traded with Bristol. Taylor allegedly concealed the sickness of his servants, continued to perform his official duties, and so may have helped spread the bacillus.[11] About 350 died in 1604, nearly a twelfth of the city's population, and deaths continued into 1605. As usual there was an exodus of wealthier inhabitants, creating problems of poor relief and public order.[12] The city was again attacked by plague in the years 1625–6 and in 1637–8.[13] Less is known about the impact of other diseases like typhus and dysentery, though they probably recurred during the period. Food shortages may have caused the modest upturn in mortality rates in 1597.[14]

To offset the high mortality caused by disease and to expand its population, Gloucester relied very considerably on immigration. From the evidence of witnesses appearing before the church courts in the years 1595–1640, it appears that three-quarters of male citizens had moved at some time in their lives; nearly a quarter had come to Gloucester from the county; and over a quarter had travelled from outside the county. The picture was broadly the same for women.[15] The sons of countryfolk, mainly the offspring of yeomen and husbandmen, flocked to the city to become apprenticed to traders and craftsmen. Sizable numbers of apprentices, particularly those in poorer trades, never had their agreements formally recorded, but of those who did between 1595 and 1640, 69 per cent were born outside the city, the great majority in the county.[16] While apprenticeship migration tended to be localized, other newcomers came from further afield. Many were tramping poor. In 1615 the magistrates complained of the vagrants that swarmed in the city; further great numbers were reported in 1631.[17] Many poor labourers tramped to Gloucester from the northern and western uplands of the kingdom. Also recorded were occasional troupes of gypsies, itinerant entertainers, and quacks.[18] In 1636 and 1637 the city relieved a small contingent of German refugees, fleeing from the horrors of the Thirty Years War.[19]

[6] Heref. City Rec., misc. papers, vol. vi, no. 69 (I owe this reference to W. Champion); G.B.R., B 3/1, f. 58v.; F 11/2, 5; Glos. Colln. 29334; C. Creighton, *Hist. of Epidemics in Britain* (1965), i. 348; P.R.O., REQ 2/163/90.

[7] Heref. City Rec., misc. papers, vol. vi, no. 69.

[8] G.B.R., H 2/1, ff. 74–75v.; B 3/1, f. 144.

[9] Ibid. B 3/1, f. 143 and v.

[10] P. Ripley, 'Par. Reg. Evidence for Population of Glouc.', *Trans. B.G.A.S.* xci. 204.

[11] P.R.O., STAC 8/280/16; G.B.R., B 3/1, f. 203.

[12] P.R.O., STAC 8/4/9.

[13] G. S. Blakeway, *City of Glouc.* (1924), p. 82; G.B.R., B 3/2, pp. 80, 95, 105; G 3/SO 3, ff. 147v.–148.

[14] For high national mortality in 1596–7 due to famine and related diseases, P. Slack, 'Mortality Crises and Epidemic Disease in Eng. 1485–1610', *Health, Medicine and Mortality in 16th Cent.* ed. C. Webster (1979), 33–40.

[15] P. Clark, '"The Ramoth-Gilead of the Good": urban change and political radicalism at Glouc. 1540–1640', *Eng. Commonwealth 1547–1640*, ed. P. Clark et al. (1979), 168–9.

[16] G.B.R., C 10/1.

[17] Ibid G 3/SO 1, f. 34; P.R.O., SP 16/194, no. 11(1).

[18] G.B.R., F 4/3, ff. 72 sqq.; Creighton, *Epidemics*, i. 426–7.

[19] G.B.R., F 4/5, f. 40.

Economic Development

Like many other middle-rank county and cathedral towns in Tudor and early Stuart England, Gloucester had a mixed economy, depending on a medley of industrial, marketing, and service activities. Its economic structure was clearly more sophisticated than that of the two dozen or so small market towns in the shire, places like Stow-on-the-Wold, Tetbury, or Marshfield. According to the detailed muster returns of 1608, Gloucester had 68 different occupations, compared with the 20–25 found in the small centres. On the other hand, Gloucester did not completely dominate its area. There was strong economic competition from the larger market towns, as well as from Bristol in the south. Tewkesbury had an almost equally complex economy in 1608, with 67 different occupations listed, and at Cirencester the comparable figure was 58.[20] That may help to explain why there was considerable and growing economic instability at Gloucester from the end of the 16th century. The situation was particularly difficult during the 1620s and 1630s. In 1626 the magistrates lamented how compared with the past Gloucester was 'so much impoverished'. They put the blame on: 'the great fall of trade generally in this city by reason of the late great and yet continuing plague, the excessive number of poor, chiefly occasioned by the decay of clothing . . . besides the knights and gentlemen . . . within this county now for the most part residing in other places'.[21] Other complaints of economic hardship were voiced before 1640[22] and are confirmed by detailed evidence.

Up to the mid 16th century, the city's established industries of broadcloth production, capping, and metal working were still fairly prosperous. Thus persons belonging to the metal, textile, and clothing trades comprised nearly 40 per cent of all the city freemen admitted between 1535 and 1554.[23] In the 1550s the clothier and alderman John Sandford had an agency at Frankfurt am Main for the export of cloth to Germany.[24] In the earlier 16th century the successful cappers John Falconer and Sir Thomas Bell had kept 'great numbers of people at work on spinning and knitting of caps'.[25] By 1600, however, the textile and capping industries were in obvious decline. In 1582 it was said that the trade of cappers and clothiers was 'much decayed in Gloucester within 20 or 30 years past'.[26] The corporation's anxiety to revive the trade was evident in 1581 when it lent the first payment received by the city from the charity of Sir Thomas White to four clothiers, who were each required to add one loom to those they had in work. Another loan charity, given in 1585 by the Barton Street clothier Gregory Wilshire, also benefited those in the trade.[27] One of the last important clothiers was Lawrence Wilshire, who was mayor in 1606 and died six years later.[28] The muster rolls of 1608 listed only 4 clothiers, 29 weavers, and a handful of dyers and shearmen.[29] By the 1620s it was reported that there were only two or three clothiers whereas once there had been nearly '20 men of good estates who have kept great number of poor on work'.[30] In 1634 an elderly broadweaver bemoaned the fact that previously the city had had more than a hundred looms, but no more than six or seven looms were then at work. The weavers' company was in disarray and within a few years the last clothier had left Gloucester.[31] The collapse of capping was largely

[20] Smith, *Men and Armour*, 2–10, 121–7, 239–43.
[21] G.B.R., H 2/2, p. 67.
[22] Ibid. p. 127; P.R.O., E 134/11 Chas. I Mich./45.
[23] Clark, 'Ramoth-Gilead', 170.
[24] R. Perry, 'Glos. Woollen Ind. 1100–1690', *Trans. B.G.A.S.* lxvi. 112.   [25] P.R.O., E 134/25 Eliz. I Hil./3.
[26] G.B.R., B 2/1, f. 103v.

[27] Ibid. G 12/1, ff. 243–8v., 261v.–265; cf. below, Char. for Poor, city char.
[28] Rudder, *Glos.* 176.
[29] *Trans. B.G.A.S.* lxvi. 96.
[30] G.B.R., H 2/2, p. 67.
[31] P.R.O., E 134/11 Chas. I Mich./45; G.B.R., G 3/SO 2, f. 13v.

the result of a change in sartorial fashion, with the new popularity of hats, either imported or made in London. In the case of textiles, the decline stemmed from several factors: the vigorous competition of rural clothing in the Stroud valleys, aided by its exemption in 1557 from the Act against rural textiles;[32] the heavy dependence for sales on London merchants and the North European market, frequently disrupted by war; and the failure to take up the 'new draperies' which were increasingly adopted in the south-west by 1640 and exported to the Mediterranean. Several silk weavers worked in the city in the early 17th century and there was a municipal scheme in 1639 for making stuffs, but those new trades did not become established before the Civil War.[33]

Metal working may have fared better. Bellfounding faded away in the late 16th century, and in 1607 the city fathers declared that the metal trades were in decay.[34] Other crafts, however, were starting to expand before 1640, including pewtering,[35] wiredrawing,[36] and pinmaking. One or two pinmakers were working at Gloucester in 1608.[37] In 1627 the corporation loaned £20 to John Tilsley, a Bristol pinmaker, and furnished him with a house to set 30 boys on work[38]; by the 1630s he employed 80 boys and girls and was said to be worth over £2,000.[39] However, the growth of pinmaking into a major trade at Gloucester occurred mainly after the Restoration.[40]

In the period before 1640 one of the most buoyant crafts was tanning. In 1608 one in eight of the men whose occupations were listed in the muster returns belonged to leather trades, principally tanning.[41] Hides from the vale of Berkeley, Herefordshire, and Wales were processed in the city with oak bark from the Forest of Dean.[42] The leather was then shipped to Bristol and also up river to Bewdley (Worcs.) and so into the West Midlands as far as Lichfield (Staffs.)[43]. Shipbuilding probably disappeared at the time with the contraction of Gloucester's long-distance trade and the growing size of ships.[44] A newer, consumer trade was starch making, in which wheat was used. In 1594 the city obtained a government order against people converting corn into starch during the dearth.[45]

Starch production was undoubtedly linked with Gloucester's burgeoning importance in the late 16th and early 17th centuries as a centre for marketing and shipping grain. For the same reason the food-processing industries also prospered, providing for the increased population of the city and its hinterland. In 1608 the muster returns indicate that baking was one of the five largest occupations.[46] From the bakers' company records it is evident that the number of masters grew considerably in the eighty years before 1640. At the same time, production may have become concentrated in the hands of certain major bakers, with some masters working for their colleagues as journeymen, as well as keeping their own shops.[47] A similar increase both in output and the scale of production is also visible in brewing. Between the mid Tudor period and 1629 the number of common or wholesale brewers at Gloucester roughly doubled.[48] In addition there was considerable brewing by

[32] *Trans. B.G.A.S.* lxvi. 78 sqq., 97; Woollen Cloths Act, 4 & 5 Phil. and Mary, c. 5.

[33] *V.C.H. Glos.* ii. 190; P. Ripley, 'Trade and Social Structure of Glouc. 1600–1640', *Trans. B.G.A.S.* xciv. 118; G.B.R., B 3/2, pp. 125–6.

[34] *Trans. B.G.A.S.* xviii. 238, 243; Hist. MSS. Com. 27, *12th Rep. IX, Glouc. Corp.* p. 427.

[35] P.R.O., STAC 8/280/20. [36] Ibid. C 2/Jas. I/L 15/20.

[37] Smith, *Men and Armour*, 8.

[38] G.B.R., G 3/SO 1, f. 125.

[39] W.B. Willcox, *Glos. 1590–1640* (1940), 255.

[40] Below, Glouc. 1660–1720, econ. development.

[41] Smith, *Men and Armour*, 2–10.

[42] L. A. Clarkson, 'Leather Crafts in Tudor and Stuart Eng.', *Ag. H.R.* xiv. 29.

[43] *Documents illustrating the Overseas Trade of Bristol in the 16th Cent.* ed. J. Vanes (Bristol Rec. Soc. xxxi), 41–2; P.R.O., E 190/1284/5; E 134/4 Chas. I East./3.

[44] P.R.O., E 134/25 Eliz. I Hil./3.

[45] B.L. Lansdowne MS. 76, f. 103.

[46] Smith, *Men and Armour*, 2–10.

[47] Glos. Colln. 29334.

[48] P.R.O., E 134/18 & 19 Eliz. I Mich./10; G.B.R., B 3/1, ff. 529 sqq.

innkeepers and alehouse keepers.[49] The magistrates tried to limit brewing to the common brewers in 1548, 1573, and 1629[50], and in the 1630s their efforts were reinforced by the Crown's scheme to establish brewing monopolies.[51] By 1640 Gloucester had a cluster of prominent common brewers, including John Woodward whose estate was probably worth over £2,000 at his death in the 1640s.[52] Also affluent were maltsters. With at least six holding civic office between 1580 and 1600, they were the third largest occupational group on the corporation.[53] During the harvest failures of the 1590s there were allegations that leading maltsters were making malt and shipping it down river at a time when local inhabitants were short of food.[54] Further abuses in 1613 prompted the corporation to act against the maltsters, imprisoning 17 of them, including several civic leaders.[55] Most of the malt was transported to Bristol and the south-west.[56]

Malt was only one of the commodities shipped from the port in the decades before the Civil War. Shipping may have been encouraged by the establishment of a separate port at Gloucester in 1580, against the fierce opposition of Bristol.[57] The dimensions of the city's commerce cannot be plotted statistically because the port books do not differentiate sufficiently between trade out of Gloucester and that of the down-river creeks under Gloucester's jurisdiction.[58] Nonetheless, the impression is that some direct overseas commerce continued into Elizabeth I's reign, mainly shipments of grain to the Mediterranean in exchange for wine, citrus fruits, and oils.[59] That was, however, a diminishing element in Gloucester's trade. Only a small number of Gloucester merchants were members of the London-based French Company in James I's reign.[60] Nor apparently did Gloucester men play any significant part in the activities of the Bristol Merchant Adventurers.[61] Rather they turned to purchasing imported wares at Chepstow (Mon.), Neath (Glam.), and Bristol (increasingly dominant in the southern trades), mostly in return for wheat, barley, and malt.[62] By the late 16th century Gloucester had become the principal grain port on the river Severn, its business enhanced by the rise of specialist corn growing in the vales of Berkeley and Gloucester.[63] In 1582 it was said that 'Gloucester quay is the . . . place where three parts [in four], of all grain . . . is laden for Bristol, Devonshire, Cornwall, Wales, and Ireland'.[64] For the late Tudor period the Welsh port books confirm that Gloucester was a leading supplier of grain to Carmarthen and Pembrokeshire.[65] In the south-west Gloucester shipped wheat, malt, and peas to Barnstaple (Devon), St. Ives (Cornw.), and Padstow (Cornw.).[66] Other agricultural produce, including apples and cider, was transported coastwise from Gloucester.[67] The port was also the focus of activities like fishing, piracy, and smuggling.[68] In the 1580s it was claimed that the number of small boats based at Gloucester had increased to c. 40, varying between 15 and 30 tons in burden.[69] The muster returns of 1608

[49] P.R.O., E 134/18 & 19 Eliz. I Mich./10.

[50] Hist. MSS. Com. 27, *Glouc. Corp.* pp. 445–6; G.B.R., B 3/1, ff. 39, 529 sqq.

[51] G.B.R., B 1/5; G 3/SO 3, f. 10; cf. P. Clark, *Eng. Alehouse 1200–1830* (1983), 175.

[52] P.R.O., C 6/131/219.

[53] For principal occupations of the corp. élite, P. Clark, 'Civic Leaders of Glouc. 1580–1800', *Transformation of Eng. Provincial Towns 1600–1800*, ed. P. Clark (1984), 315.

[54] *Acts of P.C.* 1596–7, 154, 335–6.

[55] G.B.R., G 3/SO 1, f. 21v.

[56] P.R.O., E 190/1241/6; E 190/1284/5.

[57] G.B.R., B 2/1, ff. 95 sqq.; J. Latimer, *Sixteenth-Cent. Bristol* (1908), 44–5.

[58] P.R.O., E 190/1241/1, 5.

[59] Ibid. E. 134/27 & 28 Eliz. I Mich./17.

[60] G.B.R., G 12/1, f. 289v.

[61] *Rec. relating to Soc. of Merchant Venturers of the City of Bristol*, ed. P. McGrath (Bristol Rec. Soc. xvii).

[62] P.R.O., E 134/27 Eliz. I Trin./1; E 134/27 & 28 Eliz. I Mich./17; G.B.R., B 2/1, ff. 85v., 88v.

[63] P.R.O., E 134/25 Eliz. I Hil./3.

[64] G.B.R., B 2/1, f. 98v.

[65] *Welsh Port Books, 1550–1603*, ed. E. A. Lewis (Cymmrodorion Rec. Soc. xii).

[66] P.R.O., E 134/27 & 28 Eliz. I Mich./17; E 122/202/2.

[67] G.B.R., B 2/1, f. 103v.

[68] A. K. Longfield, *Anglo-Irish Trade in 16th Cent.* (1929), 45–6; *Acts of P.C.* 1578–80, 125.

[69] G.B.R., B 2/1, f. 86.

record few mariners actually resident in the city; most probably lived at Gatcombe, in Awre parish, and other creeks down river and only came to Gloucester to ply their trade.[70]

The port was an essential pillar of the city's role as a marketing and distribution centre. By the last part of Elizabeth I's reign that role was the most flourishing aspect of the urban economy. The city was described in the 1580s as a 'great market situated in the heart of the country where great concourse of people is'.[71] Forty years later John Taylor wrote that Gloucester's markets are 'always stored with abundance of varieties of all commodities'.[72] By ancient custom the city could hold markets every weekday, but in practice they took place only on Wednesdays and Saturdays.[73] The city's market region is difficult to plot, doubtless varying from one commodity to another. For cattle it extended into south Worcestershire,[74] while villagers from the Forest of Dean with its paucity of market towns came to trade in 'wood, coal, corn, and divers other necessary victuals'.[75] Most visitors, however, travelled from neighbouring parishes. By 1600 the market specialized in grain, fruit, and cattle, but there was also a lively trade in imported and consumer wares brought from Bristol, many no doubt purchased by farmers profiting from the high price of corn shipped down the Severn.[76] After the charter of 1605 the city had three fairs within its limits, a three-day fair in March, the ancient Midsummer fair lasting seven days, and a three-day fair in November. Barton Fair, held in September outside the city boundary, continued in private ownership following the dissolution of Gloucester Abbey.[77] The Midsummer fair was well known for cattle. Customers probably journeyed to the fairs from a large area of the Marches and the west.[78]

Before 1640, however, there are indications, as in other provincial towns, that the open markets were losing business to so-called private marketing. Merchants and farmers preferred to trade in the greater comfort, security, and privacy of inns, taverns, and similar premises. In 1617 the common council denounced the sale of linen and woollen cloth and other merchandise in city inns and other houses[79]; two years later the meal sellers were condemned for deserting the meal market.[80] To combat the problem the corporation tried to improve the facilities of the city's market houses,[81] but the trend away from open marketing was inexorable. By the early Stuart period there was also strong competition from the mercers, goldsmiths, and other distributive traders, who now boasted permanent retail shops on the London model and catered for the gentry and prosperous farmers of the shire.[82] Their shops were stocked with a mixture of imported and metropolitan wares.[83] Trade with the capital grew steadily before the Civil War. In 1602 Alderman John Browne the elder was said to have 'returned' up to £20,000 to London for himself and other Gloucester mercers, primarily to cover purchases of goods.[84] Several Gloucester traders had relatives and friends acting for them in the capital.[85]

With marketing and distribution so important in the economy, it is not surprising to find mercers, drapers, and goldsmiths playing a prominent part in city life. Distributive traders held well over a third of the seats on the corporation between

[70] Smith, *Men and Armour*, 2–10.
[71] G.B.R., B 2/1, f. 86.
[72] 'John Taylor's Last Voyage', 27, in J. Taylor, *Works*, ii (Spencer Soc. 1873).
[73] Below, Markets and Fairs.
[74] G.B.R., I 1/32. [75] P.R.O., C 2/Eliz. I/G 12/7.
[76] G.B.R., B 2/1, f. 89v.
[77] Below, Markets and Fairs.
[78] G.B.R., I 1/32; P.R.O., C 2/Eliz. I/G 12/7.

[79] G.B.R., B 3/1, f. 449.
[80] Ibid. f. 467v.
[81] Rudder, *Glos.* 89–90; G.B.R., B 3/1, f. 467v.
[82] *Com. for Eccl. Causes within the Dioceses of Bristol and Glouc. 1574*, ed. F. D. Price (B.G.A.S. Rec. Section, x), 135–6; Bodl. MS. Eng. Misc. E 6, *passim*.
[83] e.g. G.D.R. invent. 1587/41.
[84] P.R.O., REQ 2/275/13.
[85] Ibid. E 134/22 Jas. I Mich./31.

1580 and 1600. A number, men like Thomas Machen or John Browne the elder, were tycoons by Gloucester standards.[86] At the same time, the service sector was also expanding, albeit at a slower rate. How far the city suffered from the loss of pilgrimage and other religious traffic as a result of the Reformation is difficult to say; but there was some compensation with the establishment of the new diocese at Gloucester in 1541, whose church courts attracted substantial numbers of litigants and witnesses to the city.[87] By 1600 Gloucester was also a significant centre for Crown administration. With the general expansion of local government under the Tudors, assizes, county quarter sessions, muster meetings, and similar shire gatherings brought justices, gentry, and other country people to the city in unprecedented numbers.[88] In 1592 the Council in the Marches kept Trinity term in the cathedral close, sitting in the chapter house.[89]

Among the beneficiaries of the influx of visitors were the city's inns, taverns, and alehouses. A country cleric complained in 1580 that because 'lodging in the assizes time was scant' he was forced to share his bed at a Gloucester inn with four strangers.[90] By 1583 the major inns numbered 12 and the corporation recognized their importance by setting up a company of innkeepers and cooks.[91] Grandest of the inns was the New Inn, which had its own tennis court in James I's reign.[92] Inns with their numerous servants and extensive stabling served mostly the wealthier classes. A visitor to Gloucester in the 1630s remarked how the New Inn was 'much frequented by gallants, the hostess there being as handsome and gallant as any other'.[93] In such establishments gentry and merchants might lodge, feast, drink wine, and do business. As well as inns, Gloucester had about four taverns.[94] They sold wine to more respectable customers, though without usually providing accommodation. They were substantial premises: Edward Barston's tavern had 16 customers when it was closed in 1604 because of plague.[95] Far more numerous than either the inns or taverns were the alehouses which seem to have multiplied at Gloucester in the 16th century as elsewhere. In 1575 the Privy Council censured the excessive number in the city[96] and the corporation tried repeatedly to control them. In 1548 the magistracy appointed special overseers to supervise alehouse keepers and issued other regulations, anticipating the Licensing Act of 1552.[97] Most alehouses were rudimentary establishments selling ale and beer and a little food, with perhaps a bed for the itinerant. Their clients came largely from the lower orders. Under Edward VI the city fathers complained of the many poor craftsmen and journeymen resorting to them to drink and play at dice, cards, and other unlawful games.[98]

Professional men took advantage of the influx of country visitors and the increased demand for their services in the period before the Civil War. In the last decades of the 16th century about 20 lawyers are known to have been operating in the city. A certain number were eccclesiastical lawyers working in the church courts; one or two were barristers, such as Henry Robins, later town clerk and counsel to Sir Arthur Porter;[99] the majority were attorneys, generally not officers of the London courts, though several served the Council in the Marches. As well as advising and acting for town and country clients in lawsuits, attorneys helped draft wills and leases and worked as manorial stewards and surveyors. In addition, Gloucester had a small group of

[86] Clark, 'Civic Leaders', 315, 318–19.
[87] Cf. F. S. Hockaday, 'Consistory Court of the Diocese of Glouc.', *Trans. B.G.A.S.* xlvi. 197–287.
[88] G.B.R., B 2/1, f. 86; B 3/1, f. 248 and v.
[89] Ibid. H 2/1, f. 63.
[90] G.D.R. vol. 45 (Salway versus Orchard).
[91] G.B.R., B 1/1.   [92] P.R.O., STAC 8/4/8.
[93] *Glos. N. & Q.* iii. 366.
[94] G.B.R., B 3/1, f. 149.
[95] P.R.O., STAC 8/4/9.
[96] *Acts of P.C.* 1575–7, 20.
[97] G.B.R., B 2/1, ff. 44 sqq.
[98] Hist. MSS. Com. 27, *Glouc. Corp.* p. 446.
[99] P.R.O., C 2/Jas. I/P 20/55.

medical practitioners — physicians, apothecaries, and surgeons, as well as a larger number of traditional healers and quacks. John Smyth of North Nibley, steward of the Berkeleys, regularly consulted Gloucester men about his health.[1] Most medical men are shadowy figures, but John Deighton was a prominent surgeon in Charles I's reign and was chosen as city sheriff in 1620 and 1624.[2]

Despite some growth of its service sector, Gloucester never emerged as an important social centre in the decades before 1640. Only a handful of minor landowners are known to have been residing there in 1625, and the following year the city fathers pointed to the absence of county magnates.[3] In 1628 to attract visitors the corporation encouraged the opening of a fashionable bowling green at the Long Butts outside the south wall.[4] Nevertheless the landowners of the shire stayed obstinately away. In large measure that reflected the deteriorating political relations between the city and county over Gloucester's control of the inshire.[5] The mounting political hostility of the gentry had a serious effect on the city's economic performance as it tried to diversify away from its failing industries. As one local landowner confirmed, the city was 'hindered and depressed in [its] trades and subsistence by those of the county'.[6]

Full participation in the urban economy was in theory, and to a considerable extent in practice, confined to the freemen. Between 1534 and 1554 an average of 23 were admitted each year to the freedom; by the mid 17th century the annual number was roughly 50 per cent higher.[7] The total freeman body may have numbered about 400–500 at any one time in the early 17th century.[8] The principal routes to the freedom were through apprenticeship and patrimony. Freedom by purchase was increasingly expensive for outsiders: the typical fine rose from about £2 in the 1570s to over £10 in the 1630s.[9]

Freemen belonged to the trade companies. In 1634 there were officially 14 companies — the mercers, weavers, bakers, tanners, haberdashers, innkeepers, tailors, butchers, shearmen, glovers, shoemakers, barbers, metal men, and joiners; of those the shearmen's company was defunct.[10] According to a rate for 1573–4 the tailors were the wealthiest company with the weavers, butchers, and mercers next in rank.[11] Almost certainly the mercers grew in importance over the next decades, but little is known about that development. Evidence for the companies is patchy and it seems unlikely that they ever played the major role in civic life at Gloucester that they did in other provincial towns.

After the dissolution of the chantries in 1548 the wider religious and social activities of the companies declined and some of their lands were lost.[12] New civic ordinances for the butchers and bakers in 1549 and 1550 emphasized the companies' role as economic agencies.[13] The common council intervened more and more in their affairs, controlling and reorganizing them.[14] Social corporateness survived to some extent. In the 1630s the weavers' company still met every St. Anne's day at its hall and elected its officials. 'From thence in decent manner with a great cake consisting of a bushel of wheaten meal decked with flowers, garlands, silk ribbons, and other

[1] Bodl. MS. Eng. Misc. E 6, ff. 39v., 44.
[2] P.R.O., C 5/602/26; Glos. R.O., D 381; E. A. Barnard and L. F. Newman, 'John Deighton of Glouc., Surgeon', Trans. B.G.A.S. lxiv. 71–88.
[3] P.R.O., SP 14/181, no. 35; G.B.R., H 2/2, p. 67.
[4] P.R.O., C 5/7/60; and for its site, G.B.R., J 5/6; cf. Speed, Map of Glouc. (1610).
[5] Below, city govt. and politics.
[6] Autobiography of Thos. Raymond and Memoirs of Fam. of

Guise, ed. G. Davies (Camd. 3rd ser. xxviii), 104.
[7] G.B.R., C 9/6–7.
[8] P.R.O., STAC 5/A 1/15; G.B.R., B 8/12.
[9] G.B.R., B 3/1–2, passim.
[10] Ibid. G 3/SO 2, f. 5.
[11] Ibid. F 4/3, ff. 155 sqq.
[12] P.R.O., E 134/11 Chas. I Mich./45.
[13] Hist. MSS. Com. 27, Glouc. Corp. pp. 448–52.
[14] Ibid. pp. 522 sqq.; G.B.R., B 3/1, passim.

ornaments carried before them with music', company members processed the streets of Gloucester to the new master's house. By that time, however, the weavers' company was declining fast owing to the collapse of the cloth industry.[15] Indeed, the decades before 1640 saw Gloucester's companies confronted with serious difficulties. First, there was the failure of the textile trades, which swept the dyers, shearmen, cappers, and finally the weavers into oblivion. The metal workers also had to be reorganized as a company in 1607 because several trades were in decay.[16] Second, tension developed within companies, such as the bakers, which was fostered in part by the growing power of the leading masters. About 1602 the journeymen weavers set up their own rival company, which was recognized by the common council though it soon disappeared.[17] Internal divisions may help to explain the frequent refusals to serve as company officials by the 1630s.[18] Even more menacing to the Gloucester companies was a third problem: competition from outsiders. From the late 16th century non-free inhabitants, unable or unwilling to afford to become burgesses, were constantly trying to breach company monopolies. In 1581 the shoemakers' company denounced sundry men aged about 30, never apprenticed, some of them labourers or smallholders, who had set up in the trade.[19] The city was also invaded by country craftsmen and tradesmen who sold in and out of the markets, taking advantage of the upsurge of private trading.[20] The bakers' company repeatedly prosecuted foreign retailers; legal costs imposed a severe burden on the company.[21] Protectionism in lesser occupations like shoemaking and baking was virtually impossible. Only modest capital and skill were needed to enter the trade and there were large numbers of poorer townsmen and villagers eager to work. By 1640 Gloucester's trading institutions, along with the urban economy as a whole, were in a state of flux and depressed uncertainty.

Social Structure

As in other English towns during the 16th century and the early 17th, the social order at Gloucester was steeply graduated, as shown by the subsidy assessment of 1524.[22] The basic pyramid shape of the social structure continued, so far as one can judge, into the late 17th century. Within that relatively stable framework, however, significant changes can be observed during the late Tudor and early Stuart era. Members of the élite, particularly those engaged in the prosperous distributive trades, almost certainly gained in wealth and social standing. By the early 17th century they displayed their prosperity in new or enlarged houses, usually located in one of the central parishes like St. Michael or in the riverside parish of St. Nicholas. They also indulged in more elaborate household furnishings and in other forms of conspicuous expenditure like book-ownership. They aspired to gentility, styling themselves gentlemen and acquiring country estates: in 1624 at least five of the aldermen had houses in the inshire.[23]

Much less is know about the fortunes of middle-rank craftsmen and small traders. Some, like the shoemaker John Milton who died in 1633, were reasonably prosperous with a modest array of joined furniture, a carpet, and a few pieces of plate[24], but most

[15] P.R.O., E 134/11 Chas. I Mich./45.
[16] Hist. MSS. Com. 27, *Glouc. Corp.* pp. 427–30.
[17] G.B.R., B 1/6; G 3/SO 1, f. 154; Glos. Colln. 12120; 29334; Hist. MSS. Com. 27, *Glouc. Corp.* pp. 416–18.
[18] Glos. Colln. 28652, no. 18; 29334.
[19] G.B.R., B 3/1, f. 86.

[20] Ibid. G 3/SO 1, f. 95.
[21] Glos. Colln. 29334.
[22] P.R.O., E 179/113/189.
[23] Clark, 'Civic Leaders', 319; Blakeway, *Glouc.* map at pp. 48–9.
[24] G.D.R. invent. 1633/30.

probably suffered from the instability of the urban economy. At the bottom end of the social spectrum there was a growing incidence of poverty. The number of poor people relieved in St. Aldate's parish, for instance, advanced from *c.* 8 in the late 1570s to over 20 in the 1630s[25]; those relieved comprised only a small proportion of the needy. There are frequent references to the large groups of impoverished folk in the city. The problem was most acute in peripheral parishes like St. Catherine and areas like St. Mary de Lode, which were close to the river and so vulnerable to flooding.[26] Poverty in Gloucester was generated by the growth of population which the urban economy was unable to absorb. It was also imported from the countryside through an inflow of unskilled landless labourers and unemployed migrants. The long term problems were aggravated by short term difficulties, such as harvest failure in the years 1585–6 and 1594–7,[27] trade depression in 1586 and the 1620s[28], and plague in the years 1592–3 and 1604–5.[29]

Social distress and tension erupted in disorder during 1586. After a bad harvest the previous year, food prices began to rise sharply in March and April. At the time 'work was very scant for poor people, very small utterance of cloth by reason of the wars in Flanders'; some folk claimed that they 'were driven to feed their children with cats, dogs, and roots of nettles'. At Easter 'great numbers of weavers, tuckers, and other persons', allegedly up to 600 strong (but probably fewer), assembled by the Severn near the city and seized two boats laden with malt for Wales and Bristol. Some of the rioters were prosecuted at the next sessions.[30] There was further disorder in the city in July 1586 because of fresh attempts to ship malt down river[31], though the official response is not known. During the great plague outbreaks of 1604 and 1638 more disturbances occurred[32] and social unrest may also have contributed to the disturbances during the parliamentary election of 1604.[33]

In general, however, popular protest was relatively muted at Gloucester in the years before 1640. One reason was the growing scale and sophistication of poor relief. There was nothing particularly radical or adventurous about Gloucester's measures, but by the early 17th century they were implemented with greater efficiency than before. Traditional neighbourly almsgiving to widows, the sick, and the elderly remained an important ingredient in relief. In 1594 one Swayne was described as 'a very poor woman and lives by the alms of the parish and begs from door to door'.[34] About 1550 the common council tried to restrict begging of that sort to a fixed number of local people.[35] Another traditional mechanism for aiding the impoverished was the hospital or almshouse. None of the city's medieval hospitals proved very effective at coping with the rising tide of poverty. St. Bartholomew's Hospital, by then ruinous, was granted by the Crown in 1564 to the corporation, which repaired and enlarged it. St. Mary Magdalen's Hospital was in decay in 1598 when the corporation was granted the patronage, taking full control in 1617 following an augmentation of the endowment. The administration of St. Bartholomew, St. Mary Magdalen, and St. Margaret's Hospital (which had been under civic control since the late Middle Ages) was reorganized by the common council in 1636 with the establishment of a common board of officials drawn from the magistracy. In addition to the old establishments, a

25 Glos. R.O., P 154/6/OV 1/1, 12–13.

26 G.B.R., F 11/9; G 3/SO 4, Mich. 1640.

27 Ibid. B 3/1, ff. 97v., 99v.; H 2/1, f. 79.

28 P.R.O., SP 12/188, no. 47; Hist. MSS. Com. 27, *Glouc. Corp.* pp. 476–7.

29 G.B.R., H 2/1, ff. 74–75v.; P.R.O. STAC 8/4/9.

30 Hist. MSS. Com. 27, *Glouc. Corp.* pp. 458–60; G.B.R., B 3/1, f. 97v.; P.R.O., SP 12/188, no. 47.

31 G.B.R., B 3/1, f. 98v.

32 P.R.O., STAC 8/4/9; G.B.R., G 3/SO 3, f. 162v.

33 P.R.O., STAC 8/228/30; STAC 8/207/25.

34 G.D.R. vol. 79 (Wiseman versus Richardson).

35 G.B.R., F 4/3, ff. 19 sqq.

new hospital, St. Kyneburgh's, was founded by Sir Thomas Bell in the 1560s and passed to the corporation in 1603, and a few small almshouses, mostly short lived, were founded before 1640. Their overall impact on poverty was limited, however. In 1640 there were probably no more than 90 almsplaces available in the city,[36] satisfying only a fraction of the demand. Moreover, town hospitals provided only selective help, mainly to elderly and sick citizens and their widows, rather than to the growing numbers of poor labourers and distressed migrants and their families.

From the early 1570s, if not before, Gloucester's parishes offered statutory poor relief. Here some labouring poor and migrants benefited from weekly doles and occasional handouts, though the sick and aged were the principal recipients.[37] At Gloucester there are signs that parish relief was being co-ordinated by the corporation from the late 16th century[38]; by the 1620s and 1630s such relief was having a growing, though still limited, impact on poverty. During difficult times city leaders took other steps to relieve the needy. Special funds were set aside to supplement parish and charitable support. During plague outbreaks pest houses were erected and rates levied to help the victims and their families.[39] In years of dearth imported grain was purchased at Bristol, London, and abroad and sold in the city at subsidized prices to poorer inhabitants. A city grain stock was in operation under Edward VI[40] and was re-established at the end of the 16th century. In 1597 the corporation bought 400 quarters of Polish corn at Bristol and more was obtained later.[41] Poorer folk also faced fuel shortages in winter time, and the corporation, like other towns, maintained a civic stock to supply them at cheap rates.[42]

Less successful were attempts to set the unemployed on work. Loans or grants to various masters to employ poor children and others were usually unsuccessful.[43] The house of correction, first established c. 1579,[44] provided work in theory but was essentially a punitive institution harassing the idle, prostitutes, and the tramping destitute. Other weapons were also mobilized against the vagrant poor. In the 1550s there were civic overseers of the poor who prevented begging by newcomers.[45] Poor immigrants were rounded up by special beadles and ejected from the city, often after a whipping.[46] Inhabitants were fined for lodging outsiders.[47] In the 1630s provost marshals were appointed to act against vagrants.[48]

Rigorous measures were likewise employed against the local labouring poor on occasion. In 1591 over 100 were shipped abroad to fight in the English army in France.[49] Under Charles I considerable numbers of poor boys were transported to the West Indies.[50] The puritan leaders of early Stuart Gloucester also sought to enforce a reformation of manners on the lower classes. Alehouses, the popular meeting place of labourers, petty craftsmen, and newcomers, came under fierce attack from the authorities.[51] Almsfolk were required to attend church daily and a special lectureship was set up to preach godly obedience to the poor.[52] The magistracy dealt sharply with unmarried couples and others offending against the sexual mores of the ruling classes.[53]

Gloucester in the period was a city under considerable strain, but one where the

---

[36] Below, Char. for Poor, almshouses.
[37] G.B.R., F 11/1–17.
[38] Ibid. 9.
[39] Ibid. 9, 11, 15, 18; B 3/1, ff. 109, 143–4; F 4/5, ff. 45v.–46.
[40] Ibid. F 4/3, ff. 19 sqq.
[41] Ibid. B 3/1, ff. 165v.–167, 174v.
[42] Ibid. f. 240v.; 2, p. 3.
[43] Ibid. 2, pp. 109, 126; G 3/SO 1, f. 51v.
[44] Ibid. B 2/1, f. 79.

[45] Ibid. F 4/3, ff. 19 sqq.
[46] Ibid. B 3/1, f. 164v.
[47] Ibid. G 3/SO 2, f. 6 and v.
[48] Ibid. B 3/1, f. 550; G 3/SO 4, p. 2.
[49] Ibid. H 2/1, f. 58.
[50] Ibid. F 4/5, ff. 54, 70v.
[51] Ibid. G 3/SO 1, f. 39.
[52] P.R.O., C 93/20/25; Clark, 'Ramoth-Gilead', 176; Glos. Colln. NQ 12.1, pp. 18–20, 32 sqq.
[53] G.B.R., G 3/SO 1, f. 66, et passim.

pressures were contained and assuaged by growing poor relief and other mechanisms of social control.

City Government and Politics

The institutional arrangements for city government in the late 16th century and the early 17th remained those laid down by the charter of 1483. The charter had effectively concentrated power in the hands of town leaders headed by the mayor and aldermen. No less important was the provision that the city should have jurisdiction over the inshire,[54] a jurisdiction which steadily poisoned relations between Gloucester and the county in the decades before 1640. Subsequent charters prior to the Civil War made relatively minor changes to the governmental framework.[55]

Among Gloucester's courts, the hundred court met every Monday, swore in constables, freemen, and officers of the trade companies, and tried civil actions involving citizens.[56] From the mid 16th century, however, the court was in decline.[57] More active was the piepowder court held at the Tolsey by the sheriffs on market days. That was the main court of pleas in the city, hearing a good deal of litigation and with a number of attorneys in attendance.[58] The frankpledge jury continued to meet twice a year, and issue, or re-affirm, detailed bylaws concerning paving and other routine administrative matters.[59] A new body instituted by charter in 1561 was the orphans' court, which was modelled on the London institution.[60] Through it the mayor and aldermen administered the estates of freemen whose heirs were minors, checking wills and inventories, loaning out funds from minors' estates to citizens at interest, and reimbursing the 'orphans' when they achieved majority. There were, however, recurrent disputes over the court's working and it had almost fallen into disuse by 1640.[61]

The most important city institution was the common council, whose members were co-opted from the freemen. By custom the number of councillors was 40, but the figure fluctuated, depending on whether the aldermen were included in the total. In 1605 James I appears to have reduced the number of the council to 30,[62] but the membership was restored to 40 under Charles I's charter of 1627.[63] The common council elected certain city officers, such as the four stewards or chamberlains, the town clerk, and the recorder. It also made leases of town lands, regulated the commons, levied taxes, and issued ordinances for the general welfare and good rule of the community. During the 16th century the council expanded its authority at the expense of the frankpledge jury.

By 1600, however, the full council was increasingly overshadowed by the mayor and aldermanic bench. The path to aldermanic power was steep and difficult. An ambitious man had first to enter the council (usually in his late 30s), then serve twice in the costly and burdensome offices of steward and sheriff. After perhaps a dozen years' service on the council he might then be considered for co-option to the bench. Most aldermen were in their late 40s when they were elevated, wealthy men belonging to the top score of taxpayers in the city and frequently associated with the distributive trades, the most prosperous sector of the economy.[64]

[54] Above, Medieval Glouc., town govt. 1483–1547.
[55] For abstracts of the charters granted in the period, *Glouc. Corp. Rec.* pp. 29–45.
[56] G.B.R., G 10/2; P.R.O., STAC 5/A 20/11.
[57] G.B.R., B 2/1, f. 43 and v.; G 10/2.
[58] Ibid. G 6/1.
[59] Ibid. G 8/3.
[60] Ibid. G 12/1; cf. C. Carlton, *Court of Orphans* (1974), 13, *et passim*.
[61] G.B.R., B 3/1, ff. 103v., 160v.; P.R.O., C 3/247/26.
[62] *Glouc. Corp. Rec.* pp. 36–40.
[63] Ibid. pp. 40–5.
[64] Clark, 'Civic Leaders', 315, 317; below, Aldermen of Glouc. 1483–1835.

The aldermanic bench increasingly took the initiative in city government. By 1600 it was meeting at least once a week at the Tolsey to deal with pressing administrative matters and also, it seems likely, to agree on policy.[65] It had a powerful and often decisive voice in city appointments and the award of leases and did its best to manipulate parliamentary elections.[66] Though the aldermen were ex officio J.P.s under the charter of 1483, James I in 1605 confirmed their authority by granting them the power to hold quarter sessions for the city and inshire.[67] By 1640 quarter sessions, with its control over poor relief and public order, had become a major force in city and inshire government.[68]

The growth of oligarchic rule at Gloucester, as in most corporate towns, was encouraged by the Crown, which preferred to deal with small groups of loyal worthies. Under Elizabeth I the Privy Council intervened to support the decisions and orders of the aldermen.[69] James I's charter of 1605 significantly weakened the position of the ordinary councillors, though their powers were mostly restored in 1627.[70] Crown intervention was not the only cause of the ascendancy of oligarchy. With the mounting economic and social difficulties in the city, leading inhabitants came to regard restricted civic rule as essential for the maintenance of public order. Gloucester's common council observed in 1584 how 'experience has taught us what a difficult thing it has always been to deal in any matter where the multitude of burgesses have voice'.[71] No less influential was the enhanced economic importance of leading citizens and the ever-expanding volume of city administration. The central government and parliament imposed more and more duties on local officials, from setting up workhouses and plague prevention to regulating apprentices and suppressing vagrancy. There was an inevitable need for a standing committee of leading citizens such as the aldermanic bench.[72]

Advising and assisting the city leadership and acting as clerk of the peace, steward of the orphans' court, hundred court, and court of piepowder was the town clerk, who by the early Stuart period was starting to emerge as an important figure in urban politics.[73] Several of the town clerks before 1640 were barristers, trained at the inns of court, and were leading lawyers in the city and its region.[74] The choice of a new town clerk was hotly contested on several occasions before 1640.[75] The recorder, established as the principal legal officer by the charter of 1561, which confirmed in the post the wealthy and influential Richard Pate, was less closely involved in town administration.[76] Nonetheless the recorder was an increasingly significant figure, as the city became embroiled in legal disputes with citizens, the gentry of the inshire, and later the Crown. In 1638 William Lenthall, the future Speaker of the Long Parliament, was elected recorder of Gloucester.[77]

In the century before the Civil War Gloucester experienced mounting political problems. City finances deteriorated, moving from an annual surplus for most of the 1550s to an average annual deficit of £150 in the 1590s.[78] There were continuing deficits up to 1640 together with a large cumulative debt,[79] caused by inflation and expanded administrative activity: expenditure rose four-fold between the reigns of

[65] G.B.R., B 3/1, f. 188.
[66] Clark, 'Civic Leaders', 320–1.
[67] Glouc. Corp. Rec. p. 38.
[68] G.B.R., G 3/SO 3–4.
[69] e.g. Acts of P.C. 1587–8, 291–3.
[70] Glouc. Corp. Rec. pp. 37, 41.
[71] Hist. MSS. Com. 27, Glouc. Corp. p. 457.
[72] Cf. P. Clark and P. Slack, Eng. Towns in Transition 1500–1700 (1976), 129, 131–2.

[73] G.B.R., B 3/1, ff. 153v.-154.
[74] P.R.O., C 2/Jas. I/P 20/55.
[75] e.g. 1613–14: G.B.R., B 3/1, ff. 252–3, 259v.
[76] Glouc. Corp. Rec. p. 33; G.B.R., B 3/1, f. 196v.; and for Pate, A. L. Browne, 'Ric. Pates (sic), M.P. for Glouc.', Trans. B.G.A.S. lvi. 201–25.
[77] G.B.R., B 3/2, p. 88.
[78] Ibid. F 4/3.
[79] Ibid. 5.

Edward VI and Charles I. While rental income advanced as well, notably in the early 17th century, other sources of revenue such as freedom fines and tolls were less lucrative. Recurrent deficits forced the city to rely on borrowing, from outsiders,[80] from members of the bench[81], and from the city stewards. During the later decades of the 16th century it became established that the four incoming stewards lent the city chamber a sum sufficient to clear the current deficit; they were then reimbursed by the succeeding stewards.[82] That procedure created major difficulties. In 1579, 1584, and 1598 one or more stewards refused to pay; on such occasions the city came close to bankruptcy.[83] The heavy burden on the stewards deterred middle-rank men from entering or staying on the common council.[84]

The financial plight of the city contributed to a second problem, that of political factionalism. City leaders who helped fund the administration with loans or cash from their own pocket sought compensation from sales of office, bribes, and peculation. Corruption and abuse were widespread in city government at the end of the Tudor period. In 1596 and 1597 several aldermen were engaged in the fraudulent management of the municipal corn stock; one of the culprits allegedly made a profit of *c.* £150.[85] During the plague outbreak of 1604 the mayor, Thomas Rich, was said to have sold over-priced shrouds and winding sheets for the poor.[86] Abuse fuelled conflict and division within the ruling élite. It also encouraged mounting popular hostility towards the oligarchy. In the years 1586–7 there was a dispute over the election of a new recorder with a successful attempt by Richard Pate to nominate his successor William Oldisworth, who may have bought the office from Pate.[87] In the parliamentary election of 1588 the two more populist candidates, Thomas Atkyns and Luke Garnons, were elected.[88] Political factionalism was recurrent during the late 1590s. At the election of M.P.s in 1597 it was alleged that the bench had deliberately excluded from the poll numerous freemen who were supporters of Atkyns.[89] The corporation was divided between an establishment group, led by Alderman Thomas Machen and his son-in-law Thomas Rich, which was sympathetic towards puritan ideas, and a more populist faction, led by Alderman Garnons and Alderman John Jones, which endeavoured to mobilize the freeman vote and had stronger ties with the cathedral close (Jones was diocesan registrar under eight bishops).[90] When Rich became mayor in 1603 it was said he spent 'the greatest part of his time and study that year to be revenged upon his enemies and such as were not of his faction, to weaken, charge, and defame them'.[91] It was further alleged that he tried to rig the council meetings. The elections to parliament in December 1603 were particularly turbulent. Rich and his allies on the corporation tried to delay the execution of the election writ in order to prevent the return of Jones. In the meantime Jones canvassed freeman support, promising to get more fairs for the city and the redress of various popular grievances. When Jones was eventually chosen Rich tried to hold another poll, though without success.[92] Disputes continued through 1604, and in 1605 a series of cases involving leading members of the corporation was heard in Star Chamber and the Exchequer.[93] Further outbreaks of factionalism occurred in 1608[94] and the 1610s,[95]

[80] Ibid. B 3/1, f. 246.
[81] Ibid. H 2/1, f. 16.
[82] Clark, 'Ramoth-Gilead', 176.
[83] G.B.R., B 3/1, ff. 67v. sqq., 86v.–87v., 92, 175v.–176.
[84] Clark, 'Civic Leaders', 317.
[85] G.B.R., B 3/1, ff. 174v.–175; P.R.O., STAC 8/254/23.
[86] P.R.O., STAC 8/4/9.
[87] J. E. Neale, *Elizabethan House of Commons* (1949), 264–5.
[88] Ibid. 265.

[89] P.R.O., STAC 5/A 20/11; Neale, *Commons*, 267–9.
[90] Clark, 'Civic Leaders', 321.
[91] P.R.O., STAC 8/4/9.
[92] Ibid. STAC 8/228/30; STAC 8/207/25.
[93] Ibid. STAC 8/4/8–9; STAC 8/228/30; STAC 8/254/23; E 134/3 Jas. I Mich./3.
[94] *Les Reportes del Cases in Camera Stellata 1593 to 1609*, ed. W. P. Baildon (1894), 372–3, 413.
[95] G.B.R., B 3/1, ff. 252 sqq.

but they were on a lesser scale. During the second half of James I's reign there are signs that the magistracy, by then dominated by committed puritans, sought to curb internal conflict and consolidate oligarchic power by restraining abuses in city government.[96]

Nonetheless, although civic factionalism subsided in the years before 1640, the city fathers were beset with other problems. Disputes over jurisdiction were commonplace in corporate towns during the late 16th century and the early 17th, particularly in cathedral cities with their ecclesiastical liberties. In the years 1583–4 the city clashed with the dean and chapter of Gloucester over their respective powers in the close. The corporation won a decisive victory, thereafter levying taxes in the precincts.[97] There were also minor clashes with local gentlemen over the privileges of the castle liberty.[98] More serious were conflicts with outside bodies. On a number of occasions the Council in the Marches intervened in town affairs. In 1597 the mayor, Grimbald Hutchins, was imprisoned by the Council for flouting its orders and seven years later it acted to secure the restoration of an alderman after his dismissal from the bench.[99] In the two or three decades before the Civil War, however, the Council was a waning force.

A greater challenge to civic autonomy was posed by the county gentry. During Elizabeth I's reign and later county landowners were busy extending their power and authority in provincial England, frequently at the expense of borough privileges. In Gloucestershire rivalry between the city and gentry was exacerbated by Gloucester's control over the inshire. Not only was that regarded as a humiliating affront to county pride, but there were allegations that the city abused its position by imposing a disproportionate burden of taxes and other levies upon the inshire. In addition, there was anger over the way that the gentry and substantial men of the inshire were denied any voice in city government or in the election of Gloucester's M.P.s.[1]

There was tension between the city and county over the inshire in the mid 16th century,[2] but conflict escalated from the last years of Elizabeth I's reign. In 1595 there were disputes with the county over the levying of troops in the inshire.[3] In the parliamentary election of 1597 the populist candidate Atkyns sought to exploit the grievances of the inshire.[4] The frustration of the inshire exploded in 1624. Sir William Guise of Elmore held meetings of its leading inhabitants and charged the mayor and aldermen 'with want of good education, with ignorance, partiality, malice, wrong justice, oppression, and with unlawful [taxes]'. Parliament was petitioned to let the inshire have its own M.P.s.[5] At the same time Sir William, with his son William Guise of Brockworth and Sir Robert Cooke of Highnam, obtained a special commission of association from the Crown, which gave them authority to sit as justices of the peace.[6] At Midsummer 1624 the new J.P.s tried to take their seats at the city sessions. The city fought back fiercely, bringing actions against Sir William Guise in Star Chamber and trying to mobilize support at Court, albeit with limited success. The corporation protested that the gentry's action threatened 'a settled and constant government' which had continued for many years 'whereby an ill example will be given for knights and gentlemen to infringe and invade the liberties of all the cities of England'. In the end the city outmanoeuvred the gentry, offering concessions which it later withdrew.

[96] Clark, 'Civic Leaders', 321.
[97] G.B.R., B 3/1, ff. 86 sqq.; P.R.O., SP 12/171/24; R. Beddard, 'Privileges of Christchurch, Canterbury', *Archaeologia Cantiana*, lxxxvii. 99–100.
[98] P.R.O., E 134/10 Chas. I Mich./55.
[99] G.B.R., B 3/1, ff. 167v., 170, 203v., 206.

[1] Ibid. B 8/12.
[2] Ibid. B 2/1, f. 228v.
[3] Ibid. H 2/1, ff. 79v.–80.
[4] P.R.O., STAC 5/A 20/11.
[5] G.B.R., B 3/1, ff. 497–498v.; B 8/12; Glos. R.O., D 326/Z 2.
[6] G.B.R., B 3/1, f. 510v.; B 8/12.

Charles I's charter of 1627 confirmed Gloucester's jurisdiction over the inshire,[7] but the issue was far from settled and within a decade there was renewed conflict.[8]

Controversy over the inshire affected wider relations with the county of Gloucestershire. In the years 1587–8 there was a clash over whether the lord lieutenant, Lord Chandos, could muster troops in Gloucester.[9] The county reacted by delaying its contribution to the ship money.[10] In 1595 the gentry denounced Gloucester maltsters for exporting malt during the dearth and banned shipments down river.[11] When a conference was arranged between the city and county magistrates to resolve their differences, the county magistrates kept the mayor and aldermen waiting and then left town without talking to them.[12] In James I's reign the corporation refused to agree to leases of rights to gentry.[13] After further friction in the 1620s and over ship money in the years 1635–6,[14] the county raised a paltry sum to aid Gloucester inhabitants afflicted by the plague outbreak of 1638.[15]

With a growing tribe of enemies in the county, Gloucester needed powerful allies at Court to protect its interests. Under Elizabeth I Gloucester had a staunch patron in William Cecil, Lord Burghley, the lord treasurer, who secured the status of a port for the city in 1580 and supported it over the disputes with the county in 1588.[16] There was some local opposition to Crown levies in the 1590s, but that did not seriously harm city relations with the government.[17] Robert Cecil, earl of Salisbury, succeeded his father as high steward of Gloucester.[18] By the 1620s, however, relations with the Court were becoming more remote. Puritan magistrates were worried by the religious conservatism at Whitehall, by the pusillanimous support they received over the inshire dispute, and by the military levies and other exactions imposed between 1624 and 1628, at a time of severe economic and social difficulty in the city.[19] In 1629 one of the city's M.P.s, Alderman John Browne, criticized royal attempts to levy tunnage and poundage without parliamentary consent.[20] The crucial deterioration in relations between Gloucester and the Crown occurred during the 1630s, principally as a result of Archbishop Laud's attack on various aspects of the puritan regime in the city.[21] In 1639 the Privy Council complained of prolonged arrears of ship money at Gloucester, while about that time leading inhabitants may have had indirect contact with the Scottish rebels.[22]

By contrast with many boroughs, Gloucester retained control of its representation in parliament during the late 16th century and the early 17th.[23] Despite its financial problems, the city continued to pay its M.P.s up to 1610.[24] The aldermen rejected attempts by the earl of Leicester to nominate parliamentary burgesses in 1580 and 1584.[25] Gentlemen sat for Gloucester on only four occasions in the period 1559–1640; the majority of the city's M.P.s were merchants, with a number of lawyers (generally the recorder or town clerk). The considerable size of the freeman electorate, divisions in the magistracy, and popular and inshire discontent led to several tumultuous elections, particularly in 1597 and 1603.[26] Afterwards, it seems, the bench kept tighter control. Four candidates stood in the elections to the Short Parliament in

[7] Ibid. B 8/12; *Glouc. Corp. Rec.* p. 40.

[8] P.R.O., PC 2/45, p. 209; PC 2/46, p. 179; *Cal. S.P. Dom. 1635*, 470.

[9] G.B.R., B 3/1, f. 110v.; H 2/1, f. 3.

[10] Ibid. B 3/1, ff. 113v.–114; H 2/1, f. 16.

[11] Ibid. H 2/1, f. 79v.; B 3/1, f. 152v.

[12] Ibid. H 2/1, ff. 79v.–80.

[13] P.R.O., SP 14/54, no. 34 (1).

[14] Ibid. SP 16/94, no. 57; PC 2/44, pp. 265–6.

[15] *P.C. Reg.* iv, pp. 423–4.

[16] G.B.R., B 2/1, f. 79; B 3/1, f. 118; H 2/1, ff. 3, 14v. sqq.

[17] Ibid. H 2/1, f. 56 and v.; P.R.O., STAC 8/297/21.

[18] G.B.R., B 3/1, f. 200v.

[19] Ibid. H 2/2, f. 28, *et passim*; P.R.O., SP 16/94, no. 57; SP 16/77, no. 30; Hist. MSS. Com. 27, *Glouc. Corp.* pp. 478–9, 486.

[20] G.B.R., G 5/1; *Commons Debates for 1629*, ed. W. Notestein and F.H. Relf (1921), 201.

[21] Below, religious and cultural life.

[22] *P.C. Reg.* v. 205; *Cal. S.P. Dom. 1639*, 519–21.

[23] Cf. Williams, *Parl. Hist. of Glos.* 189–94.

[24] G.B.R., B 3/1, f. 232.

[25] Hist. MSS. Com. 27, *Glouc. Corp.* p. 460; G.B.R., B 3/1, f. 92v.

[26] Neale, *Commons*, 268; P.R.O., STAC 8/228/30.

1640: Alderman William Singleton, a moderate puritan and well respected for his work as mayor during the plague of 1638; the puritan recorder William Lenthall; Henry Brett, a gentleman related to several aldermanic families; and the radical puritan Thomas Pury, an attorney. Singleton and Brett were returned.[27] Later in 1640 Pury and Brett were elected to serve in the Long Parliament.[28]

Religious and Cultural Life

Religion remained the dominant motif in the cultural life of the community before 1640. Following the Reformation and the Dissolution of the Monasteries, the suppression of the chantries in 1548 dealt a serious blow at the guilds and fraternities which had played a lively part in the religious and ritual activities of the city.[29] One casualty was the Trinity guild in St. Mary de Lode whose officers had included leading citizens.[30] The trade companies became confined to a largely economic function. The radical protestant John Hooper was appointed bishop of Gloucester in 1551, but little is known about his activity in the city. It is likely, however, that the pace of religious change accelerated at the parish level from about that time. The churchwardens' accounts for St. Michael record the removal of the rood loft in 1550 or 1551, together with the sale of liturgical and other church items.[31] With Mary's accession St. Michael's parish conformed fairly rapidly to the restored Catholic order, probably like most city parishes,[32] and at least nine Gloucester clergy were deprived in 1554 for being married.[33] Hooper was burnt at Gloucester in February 1555, and there is a later report, impossible to confirm, that Mary was angered by Gloucester's protestant sympathies at the time.[34]

During the first half of Elizabeth I's reign there is little evidence that the citizens were zealous advocates of an evangelical protestant order. In 1576 a family of sectaries was prosecuted in the church courts, but that was an isolated instance.[35] The next decade saw action against a small number of Catholics from the city.[36] During the last years of Elizabeth's reign committed puritanism gained support. A city lectureship was instituted in St. Michael's church in 1598 and occupied by William Groves and, subsequently, Thomas Prior and John Workman.[37] By the 1630s several weekly lectureships had been established, including one on Sundays specifically for the poor.[38] The trade companies patronized puritan preachers.[39] From the end of the 16th century magistrates were promoting a godly reformation of manners with an emphasis on the sanctity of the sabbath and a determined campaign against drunkenness and alehouses.[40] A puritan conventicle was meeting at the New Inn at the turn of the century.[41]

The main impetus for the puritan movement in the city apparently derived from a number of city leaders, concerned to strengthen their own authority and to create a sense of godly, communal solidarity at a time when the city faced many stresses. There was also growing support among middle-rank inhabitants, who may well have been influenced by their contacts through trade with puritan centres like London,

[27] P.R.O., SP 16/448, no. 79.
[28] Williams, *Parl. Hist. of Glos.* 194–5.
[29] *Trans. B.G.A.S.* viii. 253–61.
[30] Hatfield House, Cecil Papers, 207/2.
[31] Glos. R.O., P 154/14/CW 1/5.
[32] Ibid. 7–8. [33] *Glos. N. & Q.* iii. 42–3.
[34] J. Foxe, *Acts and Monuments*, ed. J. Pratt and J. Stoughton (Lond. n.d.), vi. 653–9; Glos. Colln. NF 12.56.
[35] *Com. for Eccl. Causes*, ed. Price, 103–5, 107–8.
[36] J. N. Langston, 'Rob. Alfield, Schoolmaster of Glouc., and his Sons', *Trans. B.G.A.S.* lvi. 148 sqq.; *Eng. Martyrs*, ed. J. H. Pollen (Catholic Rec. Soc. v), 108–9, 140, 289.
[37] G.B.R., B 3/1, ff. 176v.–177, 236, 466, 467.
[38] Ibid. ff. 560, 561; 2, pp. 33, 79.
[39] Glos. Colln. 29334.
[40] G.B.R., B 3/1, f. 147; G 3/SO 1, f. 39.
[41] G.D.R. vol. 89 (office versus Simons).

Bristol, and the towns of the south-west.[42] Another important factor was the lamentable state of the established church at Gloucester. In 1603 six of the city's eleven parishes were too poor to have incumbents.[43] In the late 16th century the cathedral failed to provide any spiritual leadership: non-residence was rife and the diocesan establishment was racked by conflict and corruption.[44] During the early Stuart period, however, city puritans were encouraged by the sympathetic attitude of a number of cathedral divines: Miles Smith, bishop 1612–24, was especially favourable.[45]

The first reverse for the city's puritan leaders came in 1617. William Laud, newly appointed dean of Gloucester, moved the communion table from the middle of the cathedral choir to the east end.[46] A libel denouncing the innovation and calling on the prebendaries and city preachers to resist it was published in St. Michael's church and distributed throughout the city with cries that 'Popery was coming in'. Several of those involved in the opposition to Laud were summoned before High Commission.[47] In the 1620s, however, with Laud's departure relations between city and cathedral improved. In 1625 the city lecture was preached in the cathedral.[48] The crypto-Catholic Godfrey Goodman, who was consecrated bishop in 1625, was paradoxically on good terms with the puritan aldermen; the two sides united in their hostility to Laud (after 1633 archbishop of Canterbury).[49]

The 1630s, however, saw Gloucester puritans under severe pressure. In 1633 the city lecturer John Workman was tried by High Commission for preaching before the assize judges against images, denouncing dancing, and allegedly calling for the election of ministers.[50] When the corporation continued to pay Workman's stipend, city leaders were prosecuted and forced to submit.[51] At the metropolitan visitation in 1635 the seats of aldermen's wives were removed from the cathedral,[52] and two years later the management of the city hospitals was called into question, after it was claimed that an 'inconformable minister' had been presented to a hospital living.[53] In 1640 an attempt to remove the conservative John Bird as master of the Crypt school and to replace him with the distinguished puritan John Langley was rebuffed by Laud.[54] Puritan activists may have contemplated emigration to the New World.[55] In 1639 one of the city curates, Thomas Wynell, went to Scotland and may have been in touch with the Covenanters there.[56]

The changing religious climate led to a reorientation of the ritual world of the community. The important civic watches on Midsummer eve and St. Peter's eve, in which the trade companies had taken part, faded away after the middle of Elizabeth I's reign; the feast after the Midsummer watch ended about 1550. Company rituals may have survived longer, but were affected by the companies' economic decline.[57] By 1640 the main civic ceremonies were mostly associated with celebrating the power of the élite, for instance on the mayoral election day or in the magisterial processions to the courts.[58] As for popular rituals, country lords or abbots of misrule disappeared

[42] Clark, 'Ramoth-Gilead', 183–4.
[43] Eccl. Misc. 68–9.
[44] F. D. Price, 'Bishop Bullingham and Chancellor Black-leech: a diocese divided', Trans. B.G.A.S. xci. 175–98.
[45] P. Heylyn, Cyprianus Anglicus (Dublin, 1719), part i. 44–5; T. Prior, Sermon at the Funerall of the late Lord Bishop of Glouc. (Lond. 1632), 302–4.
[46] Heylyn, Cyprianus, 44; B. Taylor, 'William Laud, Dean of Glouc. 1616–21', Trans. B.G.A.S. lxxvii. 87–8.
[47] Heylyn, Cyprianus, 44–5; Trans. B.G.A.S. lxxvii. 88–90.
[48] G.B.R., B 3/1, f. 508.
[49] Ibid. B 9/2; Trans. B.G.A.S. xxiv. 299, 302; D.N.B. s.v.

Goodman, Godfrey.
[50] H.L. Papers, N.S. xi, pp. 418–19; W. Laud, Works (1847–60), iv. 233–4, 236.
[51] G.B.R., B 3/2, pp. 18, 23, 25, 38; Laud, Works, iv. 236.
[52] Laud, Works, v. 480.
[53] P.R.O., SP 16/379, no. 88.
[54] G.B.R., B 3/2, p. 148.
[55] P.C. Reg. x. 509.
[56] Ibid. vii. 629; Cal. S.P. Dom. 1639, 519–21.
[57] Clark, 'Ramoth-Gilead', 178; G.B.R., F 4/3, f. 20, et passim.
[58] Clark, 'Ramoth-Gilead', 178.

in the city after the 1560s.[59] Old fashioned morality plays probably vanished a couple of decades later.[60] In the 1610s the magistracy suppressed popular games.[61] Under Laud's sympathetic influence parish rituals may have revived a little in the 1630s, but the revival was short lived.[62]

Among respectable citizens there was a new preoccupation in the decades before 1640 with a more private and educated cultural world. John Aubrey tells the story of having visited as a boy the home of Alderman William Singleton, the city's M.P. in the Short Parliament. Singleton had in the parlour over the chimney 'the whole description of the funeral' of Sir Philip Sidney; it was 'engraved and printed on papers pasted together' which stretched the length of the room and was 'turned upon two pins that turning one of them made the figures march all in order'. Sidney, one of the heroes of Elizabeth I's war against Spain, had an obvious appeal to a puritan like Singleton.[63] Other puritan citizens had collections of books. John Deighton had about 160 different works, including medical books, chronicles, puritan tracts, and John Foxe's martyrology[64]; in the 1620s he was out in the county following up Foxe's account of some local Marian martyrs.[65] During Charles I's reign Gloucester had its own specialist bookseller, the puritan Toby Jordan.[66] The literate did not need to purchase all their books, for several city parishes had small libraries.[67] Moreover in 1629 Bishop Goodman sought to found a library in the cathedral whereby 'every private man [who] cannot furnish himself . . . might be supplied out of our common storehouse'; one of the librarians was the puritan John Langley.[68]

The increased availability of books was closely linked with rising literacy. In the period 1595–1640 64 per cent of Gloucester men appearing as witnesses in the diocesan courts were able to write their own names. As might be expected, illiteracy was lowest among the professional and distributive groups. Among women, however, the vast majority (96 per cent) were unable to write their names.[69] Educational skills were disseminated by parents, by masters teaching their apprentices, and by schooling. Relatively little can be discovered about the petty or primary schools in the city, though there were probably several by 1600. Some were taught by clergy or women[70]; on occasions the pupils came from the adjoining countryside.[71] John Taylor, the 'water poet', who was born in Gloucester about 1580, attended a petty school there in Elizabeth I's reign.[72]

The children of wealthier parents progressed to one of the two grammar schools in the city, the College school at the cathedral and the Crypt school. The College school had rather uncertain fortunes in the late 16th century, but prospered in succeeding decades.[73] John Langley, master 1617–c.1635, was particularly successful. He was later described as 'an excellent linguist and grammarian, historian, cosmographer, an artist, but [also] a most judicious divine and great antiquary in the most memorable things of this nation'.[74] In 1628 the puritan town of Dorchester tried to entice him away to teach there. The corporation in regard of 'his careful teaching and educating the youth of the city and . . . the sons of divers noblemen and gentlemen to the great grace of this city' agreed to supplement his stipend if he stayed.[75] Langley was driven

[59] Hist. MSS. Com. 27, *Glouc. Corp.* pp. 465, 469.
[60] R. Willis, *Mount Tabor* (Lond. 1639), 111–13.
[61] B.L. Royal MS. 12A. lxx, ff. 9v. sqq.
[62] Glos. R.O., P 154/14/CW 1/41; *Glos. N. & Q.* ii. 449.
[63] *Aubrey's Brief Lives*, ed. A. Clark (1898), ii. 249.
[64] Glos. R.O., D 381.
[65] B.L. Harl. MS. 425, f. 121.
[66] H. R. Plomer, *Dict. of Booksellers and Printers 1641–1667* (1907), 108.
[67] Glos. R.O., P 154/14/CW 1/41; 6/CW 1/10A.

[68] B.L. Sloane MS. 1199, ff. 92v.–93.
[69] Figures tabulated in Clark, 'Ramoth-Gilead', 182–3.
[70] Glos. R.O., D 326/Z 1; G.D.R. vol. 89 (Hallowes versus Trotman).
[71] Glos. R.O., D 326/Z 1.
[72] Austin, *Crypt Sch.* 78–9.
[73] *V.C.H. Glos.* ii. 323–5.
[74] Rudder, *Glos.* 170; E. Reynolds, *Sermon Touching the Use of Humane Learning* (Lond. 1658), 29.
[75] G.B.R., B 3/1, f. 521v.

out by the ecclesiastical climate of the 1630s, but in 1639 the city tried to appoint him as master of the Crypt school; the next year he became high master of St. Paul's, London.[76] The city's Crypt school had a mixed career. It prospered under Gregory Downhale in the 1570s and had the puritan William Groves as master 1589–1603.[77] In 1611, however, it was in disarray due to the master's meagre stipend.[78] John Bird, master in Charles I's reign, caused growing friction with the corporation because of his support for Laud and the alleged neglect of his duties; he was removed in 1641, after the onset of the English Revolution.[79]

GLOUCESTER 1640–60

Gloucester was renowned during the Civil War and afterwards as a parliamentary and puritan stronghold. In 1642 the Presbyterian Richard Baxter praised the inhabitants as 'a civil, courteous, and religious people',[80] while Thomas Pury, one of the city's M.P.s, was a prominent zealot in the Long Parliament.[81] During the summer of 1643 the city successfully withstood the king's army in a protracted siege, a victory which Bishop Goodman declared marked 'the turning of the wheel, for ever after the parliament-forces prevailed'.[82] Subsequently Gloucester was a leading garrison town against the royalists, controlling important military operations in the west. After Oliver Cromwell's victory over the Scots at the battle of Worcester in 1651, the city elected him high steward,[83] and the city's loyalty to the 'Good Old Cause' remained unquestioned until 1659. That had major economic, social, and political repercussions. At the Restoration Gloucester was, not surprisingly, singled out for retribution by the Crown.[84]

The City and the English Revolution

The elections to the Long Parliament in November 1640 opened a new era for the city. The M.P.s were Henry Brett, who had served in the previous parliament, and the radical Alderman Thomas Pury.[85] Within a few months the corporation was petitioning parliament for church reform, asking for several of the poorer parishes to be united to provide a preaching ministry, and seeking confirmation of its powers over the hospitals and Crypt school, powers which had recently been disputed by Archbishop Laud.[86] The following months witnessed the reinstatement of puritans harried by the Laudian regime. Thomas Wynell, previously in trouble over his visit to Scotland, returned to the curacy of St. Michael and was compensated for his trouble.[87] In May 1641 John Bird was dismissed from the Crypt school and replaced by the future Socinian John Biddle.[88] In September that year the city joined with county radicals in petitioning parliament against episcopacy.[89] With mounting fears of political and military conflict the city started to take steps for its defence; in early 1642

[76] Reynolds, *Sermon*, 30; G.B.R., B 3/2, p. 132.
[77] Austin, *Crypt Sch.* 47, 87–8.
[78] G.B.R., B 3/1, ff. 237v.-238.
[79] J. Bird, *Grounds of Grammer Penned and Published* (Oxford, 1639); G.B.R., B 3/2, pp. 143–4; below, Glouc. 1640–60, city and Eng. Revolution.
[80] Quoted in F. A. Hyett, *Glouc. in National Hist.* (Glouc. 1906), 98.
[81] M.F. Keeler, *Long Parliament 1640–1* (1954), 316–7.

[82] Quoted in Rudder, *Glos.* 110.
[83] G.B.R., B 3/2, p. 639.
[84] Below, Glouc. 1660–1720, city govt. and politics.
[85] Keeler, *Long Parliament*, 47.
[86] G.B.R., B 3/2, p. 172; above, Glouc. 1547–1640, religious and cultural life.
[87] G.B.R., F 4/5, ff. 150v. sqq.; B 3/2, p. 197. John Workman was also compensated: ibid. B 3/2, p. 167.
[88] Ibid. B 3/2, pp. 176–9.
[89] Glos. Colln. JF 4.13.

it purchased 40 muskets from London and 20 more from Bristol, together with four cannon.[90] In May the corporation and many leading citizens invested over £1,200 in the Adventure for the reconquest of Ireland, where the Catholics had recently risen in rebellion.[91] When the king raised his standard at Nottingham in August, Gloucester, according to the preacher John Corbet, 'determined not to stand neutral in action, but to adhere unto one party, with which they resolved to stand or fall'.[92]

Against a possible royalist attack the city's watch was doubled, the trained bands were put in readiness,[93] and a committee of defence was established to supervise the fortification work.[94] The parliamentary committee for the county, which included leading citizens, also held its meetings in the city.[95] That summer it was said that 'the parts about Gloucester . . . happened to be most unanimous for the parliament'.[96] Gloucester's strategic position on the Severn between Worcester and Bristol and on the high road to Wales was quickly recognized by parliament. In November 1642 two regiments of foot under Colonel Thomas Essex marched there from Worcester,[97] and shortly afterwards the earl of Stamford's troops arrived to garrison the city and Colonel Edward Massey was put in command.[98] With the king's forces increasingly successful in the west, Gloucester faced mounting pressure. Large sums were disbursed to maintain the garrison[99] and from February 1643 troops were quartered on the inhabitants.[1] In February Prince Rupert and his forces approached Gloucester but the city refused to surrender.[2] In March the situation was very tense with some of the garrison threatening to mutiny over pay.[3] Loyalists and neutrals were starting to leave the city, and corn prices were rising.[4] The city fought back: civic plate was sold off to pay for work on the fortifications;[5] provisions were purchased;[6] and a regiment was raised in the city and inshire for Gloucester's defence under the command of leading aldermen.[7] During the preceding year the town walls had been strengthened and the ditches flooded,[8] but the city was still vulnerable to attack, with an incomplete circuit of walls and extensive suburbs reaching up to the gates.[9] Action was taken to demolish some of the houses outside the walls.[10]

After the fall of Bristol in late July 1643, royalist armies converged on Gloucester, and the city, Corbet wrote, 'did stand alone without help and hope'.[11] On 29 July Massey informed parliament of the dismay in the town: the troops were discontented and melting away; 'Alderman Pury and some few of the citizens . . . are still cordial to us, but I fear ten for one incline the other way'.[12] Massey himself may have been in contact with the royalists about a possible surrender.[13] On 2 August loyalist gentry in the shire called on Gloucester to capitulate;[14] a dozen or so citizens tried to negotiate terms with the king's forces;[15] more royalists left.[16] On 10 August Charles I, according to Clarendon, 'ranged his whole army upon a fair hill in the clear view of the city and within less than two miles of it' and summoned the city to surrender.[17]

[90] G.B.R., G 3/SO 2, f. 24v.; B 3/2, p. 205.
[91] Ibid. B 3/2, pp. 213–15.
[92] *Bibliotheca Glos.* i. 6–7.
[93] G.B.R., B 3/2, pp. 220–1; G 3/SO 2, f. 27; *Bibliotheca Glos.* ii, pp. xxii–iii.
[94] J. K. G. Taylor, 'Civil Government of Glouc. 1640–6', *Trans. B.G.A.S.* lxvii. 67.
[95] G.B.R., H 3/3; G. A. Harrison, 'Royalist Organization in Glos. and Bristol, 1642–1645' (Manchester Univ. M.A. thesis, 1961), 41.
[96] R. Atkyns, *Vindication of Ric. Atkyns* (Lond. 1669), 18.
[97] *Trans. B.G.A.S.* lxvii. 84.
[98] Ibid. 84.
[99] Harrison, 'Royalist Organization', 46.
[1] *Trans. B.G.A.S.* lxvii. 85–6.
[2] *Bibliotheca Glos.* ii, p. xxxii.

[3] G.B.R., B 3/2, p. 245.
[4] Ibid.; ibid. G 3/SO 4, East. 1643.
[5] Ibid. B 3/2, p. 253.
[6] Ibid. pp. 249, 252.
[7] Ibid. p. 254.
[8] Ibid. p. 267.
[9] *Bibliotheca Glos.* ii, p. lviii.
[10] Hist. MSS. Com. 27, *Glouc. Corp.* pp. 511–12.
[11] Harrison, 'Royalist Organization', 82–3; *Bibliotheca Glos.* i. 39.
[12] Bodl. MS. Tanner 62, f. 197; cf. *Bibliotheca Glos.* i. 40.
[13] Clarendon, *Hist. of the Rebellion and Civil Wars in Eng.* ed. W. D. Macray (1888), iii. 144.
[14] Harrison, 'Royalist Organization', 84.
[15] Ibid. 85.   [16] *Bibliotheca Glos.* i. 41.
[17] Clarendon, *Hist.* iii. 132.

Despite all the pressure, the community rallied to defy the king. Two representatives were sent 'from the godly city of Gloucester' to the king, refusing to surrender except by 'the commands of his Majesty signified by both Houses of Parliament'.[18] The suburbs were then fired and over two hundred houses destroyed to drive off the advancing enemy.[19]

Confident of an easy success and anxious to avoid unnecessary bloodshed, the king, who made his headquarters at Matson, decided for an extended siege. The city was heavily bombarded and numerous public buildings, including the Tolsey, the Crypt school, and several churches, were damaged.[20] There were repeated attacks and counter sallies,[21] but there was only limited loss of life. City morale was increasingly strengthened by news of help coming from London. On 24 August the defenders again rejected the king's call to surrender.[22] On 5 September the earl of Essex's relief force, marching from London, reached the edge of the Cotswolds and signalled to the elated citizens.[23] The royalist forces withdrew into the shire. Gloucester remained on the alert for the next 18 months: the fortifications were repaired and improved[24] and special watches were kept. However, the king's army never mounted a fresh frontal assault. The most serious danger came in November 1643 when the royalists tried to bribe members of the garrison, though without success.[25]

Claims by puritans like John Corbet, who was Massey's chaplain, that Gloucester's inhabitants had espoused the parliamentary cause almost unanimously in 1642 and 1643 were undoubtedly exaggerated. A sizeable minority showed loyalist or neutral sympathies, particularly during the perilous summer of 1643.[26] However, Massey in his desperation that July overstated the importance of that group. Only a handful were significant members of the corporation, and quite a few left the city rather than support their cause. On crucial issues, such as the firing of the suburbs, there is little sign of serious opposition. There was a striking continuity of magisterial personnel during the 1640s.[27]

By 1645 the large garrison at Gloucester was causing serious difficulties, with soldiers protesting over lack of pay.[28] In early summer parliament removed Massey as governor because of suspicions over his loyalty,[29] but the city's commitment to parliament held firm. In November Gloucester elected as M.P. in place of Henry Brett, who had defected to royalist Oxford, John Lenthall, the son of the Speaker of the Long Parliament.[30] At the same time the corporation made renewed efforts to secure parliamentary approval for the reorganization of the city parishes.[31] There was also increasingly frantic lobbying for financial help. Parliament was asked to provide money for repairing the city and for paying off loans incurred during the military crisis.[32]

During the second Civil War the city and its garrison remained steadfast for parliament. In April 1648 parliament passed an Ordinance uniting most of the city parishes and setting up a preaching ministry.[33] Gloucester's M.P.s Pury and Lenthall survived Pride's Purge. In 1649 there was a government scheme for a citadel at

[18] Ibid. 133.

[19] *Bibliotheca Glos.* i. 211; Fosbrooke, *Glouc.* 70–1.

[20] G.B.R., B 3/2, pp. 291, 293–4; F 4/5, f. 212v., *et passim.*

[21] For detailed contemporary accounts of the siege, J. Corbet, 'Hist. Relation of the Military Government of Glouc.', *Bibliotheca Glos.* i. 39–59; J. Dorney, 'Brief and Exact Relation of the . . . Siege Laid before Glouc.', ibid. 207–32.

[22] Bodl. MS. Tanner 62, f. 298; A. R. Williams, 'Siege of Glouc. 1643', *Trans. B.G.A.S.* lxxxviii. 181.

[23] *Bibliotheca Glos.* i. 55; ii, p. lxviii.

[24] G.B.R., G 3/SO 4, Mich. 1644.

[25] *Bibliotheca Glos.* i. 76–86; ii, p. lxxxiii.

[26] Harrison, 'Royalist Organization', App. II–III.

[27] Below, city govt. and politics.

[28] *Letter Books of Sir Sam. Luke 1644–45*, ed. H. G. Tibbutt (Beds. Hist. Rec. Soc. xlii), 261.

[29] Hyett, *Glouc.* 125.

[30] Williams, *Parl. Hist. of Glos.* 195.

[31] G.B.R., B 3/2, p. 321.

[32] Ibid. p. 295.   [33] *Bibliotheca Glos.* i. 359–66.

Gloucester, possibly involving the rebuilding of the castle.[34] By the end of the year internal divisions within the community were more apparent, with disputes between Presbyterians and separatists and discontent over the continuing burdens caused by the garrison.[35] However, with the invasion of the Scottish army in 1651 Gloucester's leaders mobilized for war: fortifications were restored,[36] a city regiment was recruited,[37] and provisions were despatched to Cromwell's army.[38]

The garrison was withdrawn in 1653.[39] A year later Alderman Pury and William Lenthall were elected M.P.s to the first Protectorate parliament, though Lenthall chose to represent another seat and was replaced by Alderman Luke Nourse, a veteran of the siege.[40] In 1656 there was an abortive royalist plot to seize Gloucester.[41] The M.P.s elected to the second Protectorate parliament were Thomas Pury, the son of the alderman and former M.P., and the puritan alderman James Stephens. Stephens was re-elected to Richard Cromwell's parliament, along with Alderman Lawrence Singleton.[42]

With the break-up of the 'Good Old Cause', however, the city's loyalty to parliament was progressively eroded, some Presbyterians becoming openly disaffected.[43] In July 1659 Massey was in the west plotting to capture Gloucester for the royalists.[44] Alderman Pury and his son Thomas raised a force of 300 men for parliament and in the autumn three companies of foot were quartered in the city.[45] In January 1660 some of the soldiers began to threaten the inhabitants and the magistrates ordered precautionary measures.[46] The Quaker George Fox visited Gloucester during March and found it 'very rude and divided; for one part of the soldiers were for the king and another for the parliament'.[47] When Massey arrived at the end of the month he was welcomed by the mayor and aldermen, but threatened by a number of soldiers. A rumour that Massey had been murdered led to a riot. Massey, however, quietened the disorders and soon after was elected M.P. to the Convention Parliament, along with Alderman Stephens.[48] In May St. Michael's bells pealed out 'when the news came the king was voted in'.[49]

Population

The Civil War had a significant effect on Gloucester's population. The number of inhabitants was substantially increased by the presence between 1642 and 1652 of a garrison which at its peak probably had over 1,500 men.[50] The garrison not only enlarged the population by a quarter but altered the sex ratios in the community, with a higher proportion of men. During the early 1640s there was also an influx of other outsiders, including protestant refugees from Ireland, and puritan gentry, farmers, and others fleeing from the advancing royalist forces in the west;[51] in the spring of 1643 a contingent of Tewkesbury parliamentarians decamped to Gloucester.[52] More people came to the city as a refuge from the military destruction and dislocation in the

[34] *Cal. S.P. Dom.* 1649–50, 232.
[35] J. Dorney, *Certain Speeches* (Lond. 1653), 51, 55–6.
[36] Hist. MSS. Com. 27, *Glouc. Corp.* pp. 500–2.
[37] Ibid. p. 502. [38] Ibid. p. 505; *Bibliotheca Glos.* i. 406–7.
[39] *Bibliotheca Glos.* ii, p. cxxv.
[40] Williams, *Parl. Hist. of Glos.* 195–6.
[41] *Cal. S.P. Dom.* 1655–56, 344.
[42] Williams, *Parl. Hist. of Glos.* 196–9.
[43] *Cal. S.P. Dom.* 1659–60, 250.
[44] Clarendon, *Hist.* vi. 112.
[45] *Cal. S.P. Dom.* 1659–60, 195; Hist. MSS. Com. 27, *Glouc. Corp.* pp. 517–18.

[46] G.B.R., B 3/3, p. 124.
[47] *Jnl. of Geo. Fox*, ed. N. Penney (1911), i. 352.
[48] *Diurnal of Thos. Rugg*, ed. W. L. Sachse (Camd. 3rd ser. cxci), 68–9; *Letter from an Eminent Person in Glouc. to a Friend in London* (Lond. 1660), 1–4; Williams, *Parl Hist. of Glos.* 199–200.
[49] Glos. R.O., P 154/14/CW 2/2.
[50] *Trans. B.G.A.S.* lxvii. 84.
[51] G.B.R., F 4/5, f. 175v.; B 3/2, p. 209; *Letters of the Lady Brilliana Harley*, ed. T. T. Lewis (Camd. Soc. [1st ser.], lviii), 198.
[52] *Bibliotheca Glos.* ii, p. xxxiii.

countryside.[53] Less willing, over 1,500 royalist prisoners were confined there during March 1643.[54] Moving in the opposite direction was a smaller outflow of royalist sympathisers in search of districts under the king's control.[55]

Mortality may have been quite high in the 1640s, though the parish register evidence is fragmentary. The siege itself caused limited casualties with only *c*. 50 people killed.[56] There were, however, outbreaks of disease in 1641 and, more seriously, in 1645–6.[57] In 1646 Gloucester's town clerk spoke of 'so great a change in this place by reason of sicknesses'.[58] At St. Nicholas burials were then running at three or four times the normal rate.[59] During the 1650s Gloucester was apparently free of epidemics, but the population may well have declined with the departure of the garrison and the return to the countryside of many of the earlier refugees. During the war years 1642–4 there was a marked decline in the number of apprentices registered in the city, but with the advent of peace the figure returned to its normal level, and throughout the period the pattern of apprenticeship migration to the city remained broadly the same.[60]

Economic Development

Gloucester's rather fragile economy experienced further setbacks as a result of the war. In 1646 the city assessed the losses in goods and property due to the siege at over £28,000.[61] A few years later it was said that business there was dead.[62] In 1652 the report was that 'the trade of this city has been this last year under some eclipse', and shortly before the Restoration the mayor and aldermen complained to the Committee of Safety in London of 'the great decay of trading here' and the proliferation of the poor.[63] A number of wealthy royalist tradesmen left the city before and during the siege, depressing business, though some later returned.[64] At the same time, there is evidence that several puritan leaders suffered badly from the heavy burdens imposed by the war.[65]

Not all sectors of the economy were adversely affected. Pinmaking seems to have expanded; by the 1650s there were several important manufacturers.[66] Common brewers supplied the needs of the large garrison.[67] Broadcloth weaving finally disappeared, but the corporation made further attempts to introduce the new draperies to the city.[68] From the mid 1640s the corporation also encouraged the establishment of brickmaking at the Common (or Town) Ham on Alney Island.[69] However, if industrial activity was improving, marketing, one of the pillars of Gloucester's economy, was in difficulty, particularly during the early 1640s. Before and during the siege there were controls on the movement of grain and in August 1643 the king established a rival market at Matson.[70] Afterwards Gloucester's trade with the hinterland was disrupted because of continuing royalist activity.[71] Once parliament recovered Bristol the malt trade revived but with the bad harvests of the late 1640s the magistrates strictly regulated shipments of corn to allay popular unrest.[72] In

[53] Dorney, *Certain Speeches*, 27.
[54] *Bibliotheca Glos.* ii, p. xxxvii.
[55] P.R.O., C 6/192/25; C 6/8/136.
[56] *Bibliotheca Glos.* i. 56, 227, 279.
[57] G.B.R., G 3/SO 2, ff. 22v., 23v., 36; F 4/5, f. 318v.
[58] Dorney, *Certain Speeches*, 23.
[59] Glos. R.O., P 154/15/IN 1/1.
[60] G.B.R., C 10/1–2.
[61] Hist. MSS. Com. 27, *Glouc. Corp.* pp. 511–12.
[62] P.R.O., C 6/8/42.
[63] Dorney, *Certain Speeches*, 79; Hist. MSS. Com. 27,

Glouc. Corp. p. 517.
[64] P.R.O., C 6/8/136.
[65] Ibid. C 5/404/236; C 6/131/219.
[66] Ibid. C 5/179/35.
[67] Ibid. C 6/8/42.
[68] G.B.R., B 3/2, p. 316; F 4/5, f. 351.
[69] *Trans. B.G.A.S.* xcviii. 174.
[70] G.B.R., G 3/SO 2, f. 29; Harrison, 'Royalist Organization', 87.
[71] *Bibliotheca Glos.* i. 70.
[72] G.B.R., G 3/SO 5.

the longer run, commercial activity at Gloucester may well have been reduced by the economic difficulties of the inshire, which suffered military despoilment, and by the presence up to 1653 of the garrison, which deterred farmers and others from coming to the city.[73]

Those providing services likewise suffered. No assizes were held at Gloucester between 1642 and 1646 and the church courts more or less ceased to function after 1641, with a consequent diminution in the flow of litigants, witnesses, and others to the city.[74] Traffic was also discouraged by military dislocation. In any case, following the siege Gloucester was not one of the most attractive or appealing towns for the visitor. Many of the churches and other public buildings had been damaged by the royalist bombardment. The bowling green at the Long Butts, a fashionable amenity, was destroyed,[75] while large tracts of the suburbs had been laid waste. Moreover, as one citizen asserted in the 1650s, 'many of the gentry are much cooled in their affections to this city, because it has so constantly adhered unto . . . the parliament'; he saw that as one of the prime causes of Gloucester's decline.[76] The hostility of the gentry was exacerbated by fresh clashes over the inshire.[77]

The war brought some benefits. There was an influx of new men setting up in trade.[78] The number of freemen admitted roughly doubled in the late 1640s, with a third of them outsiders.[79] Some others set up in trade by right of having served in the parliamentary armies.[80] Over the period the trade companies saw a decline in their regulatory functions and became mainly restricted to social activities.[81] A more open urban economy was starting to evolve.

Social Problems

The war severely aggravated Gloucester's social difficulties. The influx of refugees swelled the ranks of the local poor. Those people made homeless by the firing of the suburbs in 1643 had to be maintained and found new accommodation.[82] The epidemic of the years 1645-6 caused serious distress,[83] while high food prices followed the bad harvests of the years 1647-9.[84] Together with those short-term problems, the depressed state of the urban economy generated more unemployment and underemployment. In August 1643 the poor rate had to be doubled in all the parishes.[85] Five years later the common council stressed the increase of poor people within the city.[86] During the 1650s there were repeated references to the growth of poverty.[87]

Gloucester's ability to cope with those difficulties was not aided by the state of the city's almshouses, which were so heavily in debt in 1641 that they were unable to pay their inmates.[88] The plight of the almshouses was compounded by the fall in their rental income because of the war.[89] In the late 1640s there was some attempt to revitalize them and expand their activities,[90] but the main burden of the poor during the Revolution was undoubtedly borne by the parishes. In St. Aldate's parish in the early 1640s the number of ratepayers more than doubled.[91] Statutory relief became

[73] *Trans. B.G.A.S.* lxvii. iii n.; Hist. MSS. Com. 27, *Glouc. Corp.* p. 508.
[74] *Trans. B.G.A.S.* lxvii. 100.
[75] P.R.O., C 5/7/60.
[76] Dorney, *Certain Speeches*, 80.
[77] Below, city govt. and politics.
[78] Dorney, *Certain Speeches*, 27.
[79] G.B.R., B 3/2, *passim*.
[80] Ibid. G 3/SO 2, f. 72.
[81] Glos. Colln. 28652, no. 18; 29334.

[82] G.B.R., G 3/SO 2, f. 35.
[83] Ibid. f. 36.
[84] Ibid. f. 56; ibid. SO 4-5.
[85] Ibid. B 3/2, p. 273.
[86] Ibid. p. 479.
[87] Ibid. 3, p. 61; Hist. MSS. Com. 27, *Glouc. Corp.* p. 517.
[88] *Trans. B.G.A.S.* lxvii. 104.
[89] Ibid. 104-5.
[90] G.B.R., B 3/2, p. 479.
[91] Glos. R.O., P 154/6/OV 1/16-21.

more effective after the union of parishes in 1648, which brought about the amalgamation of poorer areas like St. Aldate's with wealthier districts like St. Michael's parish: overseers were supervising the combined parishes by 1652.[92] In addition the inhabitants of the inshire were obliged by the bench to contribute generously towards city poor relief.[93] As well as statutory relief, there were other schemes for aiding and controlling the needy. In 1643 some of the poor were set to work on the fortifications.[94] Municipal foodstocks were operating in the early 1640s, but not later.[95] A provost marshal was reappointed in 1651 to drive out vagrants and in subsequent years parish authorities imposed swingeing fines on those inhabitants harbouring newcomers.[96] As in the past, there was also rigorous regulation of alehouses, the usual haunt of poor migrants and jobless labourers.[97]

City Government and Politics

The English Revolution caused less internal dissension and instability at Gloucester than in many other English towns. Despite the vicissitudes of war and upheavals of national government, Gloucester's civic leadership showed a striking continuity in its personnel during the period. There were only five recorded dismissals and retirements from the corporation in the years 1640–6. Unlike other towns, no purges took place in the late 1640s and the 1650s.[98] Death not political manoeuvring was the principal cause of changes in membership. In the early 1640s royalists and neutrals comprised only a small minority on the corporation.[99]

Civic government, as in the years before 1640, was dominated by the inner caucus of aldermen. In 1647 the city's rulers heard a paean to oligarchic rule on the mayoral election day.[1] The authority of the bench was underlined by parliament's appointment of most of the aldermen as deputy lieutenants at the start of the war.[2] Aldermen also played a leading part in the civic committee of defence which was established in August 1642 and in the more shadowy council of war which advised the governor.[3] Aldermen used their powers as J.P.s to maintain order and to intervene in most aspects of local administration.[4] Though a number of minor conciliar reforms were introduced, as in the leasing of city lands,[5] there is no evidence to suggest any significant liberalization of Gloucester's government during the period. Nor was there any opening-up of the narrow parish vestries.

So far as can be judged, civic administration underwent only limited dislocation in 1642 and 1643.[6] Quarter sessions and most of the other courts seem to have continued to function during the siege, though the volume of business was negligible.[7] The most pressing administrative problem, as before 1640, was finance. The city entered the revolutionary era with a debt of nearly £700.[8] Military preparations, the siege, and the garrison imposed tremendous burdens on the chamber. In the years 1642–3 over £4,000 was borrowed by the city, including £1,000 from Bristol,[9] £200 from a Manchester man,[10] and the rest locally at 6 or 8 per cent interest.[11] In 1644 parliament

[92] Ibid. 14/OV 2/1.
[93] G.B.R., G 3/SO 6, ff. 29v.–31v.; SO 5.
[94] Trans. B.G.A.S. lxvii. 81.
[95] G.B.R., B 3/2, p. 275.
[96] Ibid. G 3/SO 5; Glos. R.O., P 154/14/OV 2/1.
[97] G.B.R., G 3/SO 2, f. 67, et passim; SO 5.
[98] Trans. B.G.A.S. lxvii. 72; G.B.R., B 3/2, passim.
[99] Above, city and Eng. Revolution.
[1] Dorney, Certain Speeches, 31.

[2] Trans. B.G.A.S. lxvii. 75.
[3] G.B.R., B 3/2, p. 222; Trans. B.G.A.S. lxvii. 67–8, 76, 102.
[4] Trans. B.G.A.S. lxvii. 102.
[5] G.B.R., B 3/2, p. 587.
[6] Trans. B.G.A.S. lxvii. 97 sqq.
[7] G.B.R., G 3/SIb 1; SO 2; Trans. B.G.A.S. lxvii. 97–100.
[8] G.B.R., B 3/2, p. 146.
[9] Ibid. p. 222, et passim.
[10] Ibid. F 4/5, f. 346v.
[11] Ibid. 6, p. 142.

repaid £1,000 owed to the city and in 1648 granted it sequestered lands which raised £1,800 when sold.[12] In 1655–6 the accumulated debt still stood at about £2,000 and there was extra borrowing for military purposes in 1659.[13] The basic problem was that the city's usual sources of revenue barely covered ordinary expenditure, even less the exigencies of war. Annual deficits were recurrent throughout the period. Even so the corporation aggravated the financial position. In 1642 the corporation invested £200 in the Irish Adventure.[14] Though the city received a grant of Irish land, it never recouped any of its money until well after the Restoration.[15] Another heavy expense was on lobbying parliament for the union of parishes.[16] In 1649–50 Gloucester spent about £700 buying the fee farm from the government.[17]

On numerous occasions the financial situation was critical. In 1643 a number of councillors refused to serve in the post of steward.[18] Ten years later there was a scheme to sell off city houses and land.[19] Struggling to maintain control, the corporation appointed a salaried assistant to the stewards[20] and from 1650 the committee of auditors conducted a rigorous annual inspection of the stewards' accounts, putting forward proposals for reform.[21] No less important, the magistrates endeavoured to redeem their plight by heavy exactions on the inshire, which was made to pay at a much higher rate than the city towards parliamentary levies.[22]

As in other provincial towns, there was considerable friction between the city authorities and the governor. In 1644 Massey clashed with the local committee of safety appointed by parliament under the leadership of Alderman Pury.[23] Relations with Massey became acrimonious and other jurisdictional disputes broke out.[24] More serious, however, was the continuing conflict with the county gentry. In the 1640s the city had exploited its political credit with parliament after the siege to harass its enemies in the inshire.[25] Excessive taxes on the inshire led to serious opposition. In 1654 the county committee with the gentry dominant retaliated and proposed a draconian monthly assessment on Gloucester.[26] Four years later the shire gentry threatened a frontal attack in parliament on the city's jurisdiction over the inshire.[27]

In order to resist the challenge from the county and also achieve some of its cherished projects for the 'godly city', the magistracy did its best to keep on good terms with parliament and the army commanders. Relations were helped by the city's heroic defence in 1643 and by the support of William Lenthall, the city's recorder and Speaker of the Long Parliament. Despite persistent lobbying London never provided more than limited compensation for the losses of the Civil War. In other respects, however, Gloucester received favoured treatment. There was no interference in civic government or personnel;[28] the inshire was left under city control; and a number of religious reforms close to the city fathers' hearts was approved.

---

[12] Ibid. B 3/2, pp. 317–18, 477, 499, 514–15, 519.

[13] Ibid. F 4/6, pp. 142, 336 sqq.

[14] Ibid. 5, f. 176; B 3/2, p. 214.

[15] Below.

[16] G.B.R., F 4/5, f. 176.

[17] Ibid. f. 408v. Payment of the farm was resumed at the Restoration: Cal. S.P. Dom. 1660–1, 66; cf. G.B.R., F 4/6, p. 386.

[18] G.B.R., F 4/5, f. 235.

[19] Ibid. B 3/2, p. 744.

[20] Ibid. p. 378.

[21] Ibid. F 4/5, ff. 414v.–415v. sqq.

[22] Ibid. G 3/SO 2, f. 187.

[23] Trans. B.G.A.S. lxvii. 78.

[24] Luke Letter Books, ed. Tibbutt, 31–2, 382; Dorney, Certain Speeches, 4.

[25] Autobiography of Thos. Raymond and Memoirs of Fam. of Guise, ed. G. Davies (Camd. 3rd ser. xxviii), 124–5.

[26] G.B.R., F 4/6, p. 18; B 3/2, pp. 759, 769; Hist. MSS. Com. 27, Glouc. Corp. p. 509.

[27] G.B.R., F 4/6, pp. 298 sqq.

[28] Apparently there was no action by the cttee. for corporations in the 1650s against Glouc.: B. L. K. Henderson, 'Commonwealth Charters', Trans. R.H.S. (3rd ser.) vi. 129–61.

Religious and Cultural Life

The driving force behind Gloucester's commitment to the parliamentary cause during the English Revolution was a vision, shared by a substantial number of the aldermen, of the city as a godly, staunchly Calvinist stronghold. In 1643 the town clerk John Dorney declared that Gloucester was 'a free city . . . free from Popery and . . . free from tyranny . . . a famous city, famous . . . for constancy in the cause of God and of the commonwealth'.[29] Eight years later he lauded it as 'a city saved by the Lord, a maiden city'.[30] Shortly after the meeting of the Long Parliament Gloucester petitioned for the new modelling of its many small parishes to provide livings for learned preachers[31] and at the end of the siege it renewed its call.[32] In April 1648 parliament passed an Ordinance creating from ten of the eleven city parishes four enlarged parishes each with a godly divine; some dean and chapter lands were assigned to support the preachers.[33] Though the corporation probably exercised de facto control over the cathedral precincts from the late 1640s, it obtained official jurisdiction over them in 1657.[34]

In 1646 Dorney observed how 'instead of episcopacy (which seems to lie in the dust) a Presbytery is expected . . . and a spiritual instead of a formal and pompous service'.[35] Most of the ministers in the period were Presbyterians but there was no formal classis: congregational Presbyterianism was the rule. After 1648 the corporation appointed new ministers on the initiative of parishes.[36] As well as the four city preachers there were several parish lectureships, both civic and privately financed.[37] Parochial reform made possible the demolition or conversion to other uses of several churches, including those damaged by the siege. All Saints' church was incorporated in a new Tolsey to replace the old building which had been hit during the bombardment,[38] and St. Mary de Grace, St. Catherine, and St. Aldate were taken down in the mid 1650s; St. Owen had been demolished at the start of the siege.[39]

During the 1630s the magistracy had clashed with Laud over the grammar schools. After 1642 the masters of the College school as well as the Crypt school generally supported the corporation's puritan stance.[40] In 1648 the city approved the establishment of an English school in Trinity church.[41] The same year Thomas Pury the younger and other puritans re-established Bishop Goodman's library in the cathedral chapter house.[42] In 1657 the corporation took charge and began to equip it as a public library. In addition to books purchased by the chamber, donations of works came from leading citizens.[43] Moral reform had been a preoccupation of the magistracy since the start of the 17th century. During the Revolution controls were tightened. Action was taken against those disturbing the sanctity of the sabbath and against gamesters, players, and alehouse keepers.[44]

Though previously insignificant, separatism gained ground in the early 1640s, encouraged by the influx of outsiders.[45] Two preachers from Herefordshire, Robert Hart and a Mr. Vaughan, were among the first to gain a following for separatist views, and the sectary Robert Bacon later came from Bristol and, according to Richard

[29] Dorney, *Certain Speeches*, 2.
[30] Ibid. 71.
[31] G.B.R., B 3/2, p. 172; cf. Glos. Colln. JF 4.13.
[32] G.B.R., B 3/2, p. 321.
[33] *Bibliotheca Glos.* i. 359–66.
[34] *Glouc. Corp. Rec.* p. 45; *Bibliotheca Glos.* ii, p. cxxviii.
[35] Dorney, *Certain Speeches*, 20.
[36] G.B.R., B 3/2, pp. 455, 466.
[37] Ibid. p. 504; 3, p. 32; F 4/6, pp. 194, 256.
[38] Ibid. B 3/2, p. 459.

[39] Below, Churches and Chapels.
[40] *V.C.H. Glos.* ii. 327–30, 348–9.
[41] G.B.R., B 3/2, pp. 453, 801.
[42] S. M. Eward, *Cat. of Glouc. Cath. Libr.* (1972), p. vii; B.L. Add. MS. 33538, f. 61.
[43] Eward, *Cat. of Glouc. Cath. Libr.* pp. vii–viii; G.B.R., B 3/3, pp. 65–6, 97.
[44] G.B.R., G 3/SIb 1, p. 86; SO 2, ff. 64, 66, 80v.; SO 5; F 4/5, f. 411.
[45] *Bibliotheca Glos.* ii, pp. xci–ii.

Baxter, gained many adherents to his antinomian doctrines. In 1644 Bacon preached a sermon on the public fast day which provoked an outcry from the Presbyterian clergy. Bacon was examined by the governor, Massey, and urged to depart the city by the mayor but refused. After a disputation in the cathedral with Massey's chaplain Corbet, Bacon was expelled,[46] Hart and other clergy disassociating themselves from the expulsion. By then anti-Trinitarian views had also reached Gloucester: the master of the Crypt school, John Biddle, was accused before the magistrates of Socinianism, and in 1645 he was imprisoned and removed from the school.[47] John Knowles, a lay preacher who shared Biddle's views, was active in and around the city in 1646, and the following year another Socinian, John Cooper, became master of the Crypt school.[48] In 1647 John Dorney warned of the dangers of intolerance towards the sects and there may have been more religious dissension two years later.[49] Only a little is known about the separatists' activity in the 1650s and the impression is that their following was small.[50] In 1654 a Quaker disrupted a city sermon and the movement won some support.[51] Early in 1660 George Fox attended a meeting of Friends at Gloucester.[52] Over all, however, what is striking is the success of the city fathers in stamping their own broadly Presbyterian vision of a godly commonwealth on Gloucester during the Interregnum.

GLOUCESTER 1660–1720

The restoration of Charles II in May 1660 was celebrated at Gloucester with a display of official rejoicing. Wine ran out of the conduits and there were fireworks at night,[53] but the city had much to fear from the collapse of the parliamentary cause and the first years of the new reign were certainly inauspicious. Royalist retribution brought about the demolition of the town walls, the return of the inshire to the county, and the systematic purge of the corporation. Paradoxically, however, in the long run the later Stuart period saw Gloucester make a slow but steady recovery from the economic and social difficulties of the late 16th century and the early 17th. During Queen Anne's reign Sir Robert Atkyns, a county magnate, praised it as 'a handsome neat city' with 'a pleasant prospect . . . It is adorned with many beautiful towers and spires'.[54] Though other visitors like Celia Fiennes,[55] John Mackay,[56] and Daniel Defoe[57] were less fulsome, most commented favourably on the clean streets and fair public buildings, aspects of special interest to the gentry. For like other county towns in the period Gloucester benefited from its enhanced importance as a social centre for the landed classes who came in mounting numbers to shop and enjoy themselves. At the same time, the urban economy also prospered from the expansion of marketing activity and from the growth of specialist craft industries. The economic revival inevitably had important repercussions for the social, political, and cultural life of the community.

[46] R. Bacon, *Spirit of Prelacie Yet Working* (Lond. 1646); J. Corbet, *A Vindication of the Magistrates* (Lond. 1646): copies in Glos. Colln. (H) B.1 (2–3); W. Lloyd, *Hist of Barton Street Meeting Ho.* (priv. print. 1899), 35–8.
[47] G.B.R., G 3/SO 2, f. 38; *V.C.H. Glos.* ii. 349; H. J. McLachlan, *Socinianism in 17th-Cent. Eng.* (1951), 167–72.
[48] McLachlan, *Socinianism*, 255–7, 263–7.
[49] Dorney, *Certain Speeches*, 56.
[50] *Life and Death of Ralph Wallis the Cobler of Glouc.* (Lond. 1670), 5.
[51] G.B.R., G 3/SIb 2, f. 24; SO 6, ff. 55, 65.
[52] *Fox's Jnl.* ed. Penney, 352.
[53] G.B.R., F 4/6, p. 348.
[54] Atkyns, *Glos.* 82.
[55] *Journeys of Celia Fiennes*, ed. C. Morris (1947), 234.
[56] J. Mackay, *Journey through Eng. and Scotland* (Lond. 1722–3), ii. 128–30.
[57] D. Defoe, *Tour Through the Whole Island of Great Britain* (Everyman edn. 1962), ii. 41.

Population

The various population estimates for the period indicate that the city's demographic performance was generally sluggish with virtually no growth and possibly even a slight loss of inhabitants in the late 17th century. The hearth-tax assessment for 1672 listed about 1,100 houses, suggesting a population of just over 5,000.[58] According to Gregory King, the total was 4,756 in 1696,[59] while Atkyns c. 1710 counted 1,003 houses with c. 4,990 inhabitants.[60] By George II's reign the population was rising again, with 1,284 houses enumerated in 1743 and a population of c. 5,585.[61] The general picture, though tentative, is broadly in accord with what has been found for a number of middle-rank towns in the post-Restoration era.[62]

The parish register evidence is difficult to analyse but it sheds some light on the demographic stagnation. One problem is that after the Restoration an attempt was made to reverse the parochial reforms of the preceding regime and new parish arrangements were only completed c. 1676.[63] Even after that date double registration of baptisms and burials was not uncommon. Other complications arise from the inclusion in the registers of inhabitants of hamlets outside the city, and the omission of data for dissenters, a substantial group in post-Restoration Gloucester. Nevertheless evidence for the parishes of St. John, St. Nicholas, St. Mary de Lode, St. Michael, St. Mary de Crypt, and the cathedral provides a reasonable insight into the demographic trends.[64] In the first place, a steady increase in baptisms can be seen, particularly after the turn of the century. Second, burial rates were very high and in most decades exceeded baptisms. Though plague was absent after 1666, smallpox was a major killer. In 1687 it was said 'smallpox is very rife in this city', and there was another epidemic in the years 1712–13.[65]

With a running deficit of births against deaths, immigration remained a crucial element in the city's demographic matrix. Biographical information provided by Gloucester witnesses appearing in the church courts in the years 1660–85 indicates that c. 53 per cent of the male inhabitants and 60 per cent of the women had migrated there. Those were somewhat lower proportions than before the Civil War. Again, fewer than in the past had come long distances: only c. 13 per cent of the men had travelled from outside the county. Localized migration was particularly strong among women, where fewer than one in ten had travelled from outside the shire.[66] Many of them may have come to work in Gloucester as domestic servants or in the shops and victualling houses which were proliferating by 1700. In contrast to the century before the Civil War, there is declining evidence of vagrants and other poor migrants coming to Gloucester.[67]

Together with high mortality, the reduced level of migration almost certainly contributed to the static demographic position in post-Restoration Gloucester. At the same time, the higher incidence of female movement may have been an important factor in the unbalanced sex ratio in the city, with a surplus of women in all the parishes. The excess was particularly great in the wealthier areas like the cathedral close, St. Mary de Grace, and St. Nicholas, where there were substantial numbers

[58] P.R.O., E 179/247/14, rott. 29–31; Ripley, 'Glouc. 1660–1740', 11.

[59] G. King, 'Natural and Political Observations', *Earliest Classics*, ed. P. Laslett (1973), 70–1.

[60] Ripley, 'Glouc. 1660–1740', 11, 206.

[61] Ibid. 206; Glos. R.O., D 327, p. 4.

[62] Cf. *Country Towns in Pre-industrial Eng.* ed. P. Clark (1981), 16.

[63] Ripley, 'Glouc. 1660–1740', 13–14.

[64] Glos. R.O., P 154/4/IN 1/1; 9/IN 1/1–5; 11/IN 1/1–2; 12/IN 1/1; 14/IN 1/1–3; 15/IN 1/1–2; Glouc. Cath. Libr., vols. 37–8.

[65] Glos. R.O., Q/SO 2, f. 127; Ripley, 'Glouc. 1660–1740', 23.

[66] G.D.R. vols. 205, 211, 219, 221, 232.

[67] Above, Glouc. 1547–1640, population.

of domestic servants working in the houses of the gentry and other well-to-do citizens.[68]

Economic Development

After the Restoration Gloucester consolidated and enlarged its traditional role as a market town and river port, a role which had been adversely affected by the Civil War. Even more important, it began to prosper as a social and service centre, winning a growing following among the county gentry, now reconciled to the city by their victory in the matter of the inshire. Finally, there was the steady growth of industries like pinmaking, glassmaking, and possibly hosiery. All the signs are that by the early 18th century Gloucester was increasing its lead over the other market towns in the county, although, as ever, it was overshadowed by Bristol, which was rapidly advancing as a regional capital and Atlantic port.[69]

Visiting the city in the early 1720s, John Mackay noted that Gloucester had 'two markets a week on Wednesdays and Saturdays, well supplied both with flesh and fish; and four fairs yearly, viz Lady day, Midsummer day, the 17th of September, and the 17th of November'.[70] Corn remained one of the principal commodities traded at Gloucester. Grain was brought in from the Severn Vale and from Herefordshire and then shipped down river, principally to supply the growing demand of Bristol, whose population more than doubled between the 1670s and 1730s.[71] As before the Civil War, there was a lively trade in malt. A maltsters' company was set up in 1717[72] and probate inventories survive for a number of wealthy maltmen, such as Robert Elmes who died in 1681 with personal property and assets worth *c.* £811.[73] Some of the malt may have been used by local brewers and innkeepers, but most probably went to Bristol.[74] Other specialist agricultural trades were also growing. By the early 18th century Gloucester was a major market for the cheese which was increasingly produced in the Severn Vale: the September fair, Barton Fair, became famous as a cheese fair.[75] Part of the cheese was carted overland to Lechlade and Cricklade (Wilts.) and so down the Thames to the capital; more probably was shipped down river to Bristol and also to London.[76] Market gardening developed in Barton Street and Kingsholm. William Bennett, for instance, was growing beans, carrots, and onions in Barton Street during the 1670s, possibly manuring his ground with night soil from the city; the produce was sold locally and probably also sent down river.[77]

As in the past, the authorities tried to restrict trading to the traditional markets and fairs. A new wheat market house was erected;[78] certain market days were announced in the Gloucester newspapers as specializing in particular commodities;[79] and orders were renewed against the sale of goods outside the market.[80] By 1700, however, a considerable amount of business had departed the open markets and fairs for good. Inns and the larger alehouses clearly profited, expanding as important centres of private trading.[81] Country people brought goods to the victualling house to sell and itinerant traders found customers in its drinking rooms. In addition, by the early 18th

[68] King, 'Natural Observations', 70–1; cf. D. Souden, 'Migrants and the Population Structure of later 17th-Cent. Provincial Cities and Market Towns', *Transformation of Eng. Provincial Towns*, ed. P. Clark (1984), 154.

[69] Cf. W. E. Minchinton, 'Bristol–Metropolis of the West in the 18th Cent.', *Trans. R.H.S.* (5th ser.) iv. 69–87.

[70] Mackay, *Journey*, ii. 129–30.

[71] *H.L. Papers*, N.S. ii. 202; T. S. Willan, *Eng. Coasting Trade 1660–1750* (1938), 83–4.

[72] G.B.R., B 3/9, ff. 15–16.

[73] G.D.R. invent. 1682/73; cf. ibid. 1687/249.

[74] *Glouc. Jnl.* 24 June 1723; 10 Dec. 1728.

[75] G.B.R., B 3/7, f. 194v.

[76] R. B. Westerfield, *Middlemen in Eng. Business* (New Haven, 1915), 205.

[77] G.D.R. invent. 1677/140.

[78] G.B.R., B 3/3, p. 162.

[79] *Glouc. Jnl.* 10 Dec. 1728.

[80] G.B.R., G 8/3, f. 7v.; *Glouc. Jnl.* 2 Aug. 1725.

[81] G.B.R., G 8/3, f. 8.

century the city had a good selection of specialist retail shops on the London model, the most fashionable in Westgate and upper Northgate Streets. They catered for the gentry and other well-to-do folk who came to the city. By the 1720s shopkeepers were advertising their wares in the *Gloucester Journal*.[82] The grocer Peter Haynes (d. 1696) carried an enormous stock of goods from rice to currants, spirits to best London tobacco, and Holland tapes to Manchester cottons, which he stored in three warehouses and a cellar; his total personal wealth was appraised at £1,884.[83] John Rodway, a mercer who died a few years before, had an almost equally valuable array of fine cloths including silks, cambrics, Hollands, silver lace, and numerous types of 'new drapery'.[84] Probate inventories suggest that the distributive traders were the wealthiest occupational group in Gloucester. Not that all the inhabitants were easily impressed. In 1697 Giles Blethin declared that 'he did know Scotchmen that carried better packs at their backs than Mr. Alderman Rodway's shop of goods was worth' (the alderman was Giles, younger brother of John Rodway).[85] But it is clear that by 1700 Gloucester's shopkeepers were doing a good business, not only selling by retail but also enjoying a busy wholesale trade with the smaller towns of the region. Thus Gideon Palmer of Pershore (Worcs.), mercer, was a regular customer of the Gloucester draper Daniel Lysons during Charles II's reign, buying from him 'sundry cloths, goods, wares, and merchandises'.[86] Some Gloucester tradesmen had branch shops in the market towns.[87]

Gloucester's shopkeepers bought large quantities of wares from London wholesalers. In the 1670s Edward Lewis, a London ironmonger, had 'great dealings' with Francis Singleton, a Gloucester ironmonger, and sent him 'divers parcels and faggots of steel and other things usually sold by country ironmongers'.[88] Quite often the goods, particularly if they were valuable, were transported by carrier overland. By the early 1720s there was a twice weekly coach service to the capital.[89] Though road conditions may have been improving generally in the late 17th century, communications undoubtedly received some encouragement from the spread of turnpikes at the turn of the century: the Gloucester to Birdlip part of the London road was first turnpiked in 1698 and became a very busy route.[90] However, overland carriage was expensive. Edward Lewis sent some items by carrier to Gloucester but preferred to transport others by ship from London to Bristol and so up river, 'carriage that way being much cheaper than by land'.[91]

Gloucester's port continued to be a mainstay of the city's marketing role in the post-Restoration era. By then the city had lost virtually all of its overseas commerce to Bristol,[92] but it was much involved in the Severn trade. The quay was substantially improved in the early years of the 18th century.[93] As well as carrying Gloucester's agricultural and industrial exports down river, mainly to Bristol, and importing in exchange a great variety of consumer and other wares for sale in the city's markets and shops, trows and barges provided links with the expanding economy of the West Midlands. There was a flourishing trade with Bewdley (Worcs.), Worcester, and later Coalbrookdale (Salop.), aided by improvements to navigation on the upper reaches of the river. Iron and coal were brought down for use in the city's metal and glassmaking

[82] Ripley, 'Glouc. 1660–1740', 69.
[83] G.D.R. invent. 1696/176.
[84] Ibid. 1685/260.
[85] G.B.R., G 3/SR, Mich. 1697.
[86] P.R.O., C 6/66/43; C 5/503/89.
[87] H. R. Plomer et al., *Dict. of Printers and Booksellers 1668–1725* (1922), 228.

[88] P.R.O., C 5/516/12.
[89] *Glouc. Jnl.* 2 Dec. 1723.
[90] E. Pawson, *Transport and Economy* (1977), 58–9, 90; *H.L. Papers*, N.S. v. 461–2.
[91] P.R.O., C 5/516/12.
[92] Atkyns, *Glos.* 89.
[93] G.B.R., B 3/8, p. 509.

industries.[94] Attempts by the city authorities to levy tolls on the trowmen passing by or landing at Gloucester were contested and had partly lapsed by 1700.[95]

Gloucester's resurgent prosperity as a marketing and commercial centre after the setbacks of the Interregnum was undoubtedly related to the rising living standards of many urban and rural inhabitants, as a consequence of falling food prices and rising real wages. It was also encouraged by the city's closer ties with the landed gentry, some of whom joined the corporation,[96] and by transport improvements. Similar factors contributed to the major expansion of the service sector in the post-Restoration city. The professions did especially well. Already fairly numerous before the Civil War, lawyers became prominent city figures after the Restoration. With the decay of the church courts, ecclesiastical lawyers diminished in importance, but there was a large cluster of powerful attorneys in their place. As well as being involved in local and London litigation and probate work, they acted as rent collectors, estate agents, manorial stewards, and money lenders.[97] Benjamin Hyett (d. 1712) loaned up to £6,000, mainly to country people, on mortgages in the later Stuart period;[98] some of the money had probably been put on deposit with him by widows and others with surplus funds. Thomas Pearce, another Gloucester lawyer, was said in 1693 to have been 'very much employed . . . in placing forth of . . . moneys . . . by many other persons . . . as well great as small'.[99] The statute merchant records for the later Stuart period confirm that Gloucester was quite an important centre for money lending in south-west England, though only a small proportion of the borrowers and creditors were Gloucester men.[1] That financial importance may help in part to explain the early establishment of a bank of Gloucester c. 1716 by James Wood, a city mercer.[2]

Compared with the period before 1640, a greater number of the Gloucester attorneys had official links with the Westminster courts: Thomas Pearce, for instance, was one of the masters extraordinary of Chancery.[3] At the provincial level, city attorneys frequently had close ties with county administration, serving as under-sheriffs, deputy clerks of the peace, county treasurers, and clerks of the peace.[4] In that way they brought urban and rural society closer together. Along with the score or so of attorneys in Gloucester at the close of the 17th century, there was a smaller group of barristers, including Sir John Powell, who was town clerk in the years 1674–85 and 1687–92 and a justice of Common Pleas, and his brother Thomas, who succeeded him as clerk.[5] Over all the period was one of mounting prosperity and social recognition for the city's lawyers.

Second only to the lawyers were the medical men. Gloucester at the time had a number of successful physicians, including Henry Fowler, who became mayor in 1670, 1671, and 1679. Apothecaries, who included William Jordan, mayor in 1685,[6] were also prominent.[7] As for the surgeons, most still coupled their art with barbering and were relatively unimportant, but several were starting to prosper: John Shipton who died in 1684 left personal goods worth over £350.[8] By the later part of the 17th century Gloucester also had a group of talented schoolmasters like Maurice Wheeler

[94] S. W. Davies, 'An Econ. Hist. of Bewdley before c. 1700' (London Univ. Ph.D. thesis, 1981), 249 sqq.; P.R.O., E 134/4 Wm. and Mary Mich./50; B. Trinder, *Ind. Revolution in Shropshire* (1973), 104, *et passim*.
[95] P.R.O., E 134/4 Wm. and Mary Mich./50; E 134/1 Geo. II. Hil./4.
[96] Below, city govt. and politics.
[97] e.g. P.R.O., E 134/13 Wm. III East./34; C 6/277/76; P. Clark, 'Civic Leaders', 324.
[98] P.R.O., C 5/329/17; C 5/205/48.
[99] Ibid. C 5/109/18.

[1] G.B.R., G 9/1.
[2] Glos. Colln., Hannam-Clark papers, TS. notes on Glouc. bankers.
[3] P.R.O., C 5/522/6.
[4] Clark, 'Civic Leaders', 325.
[5] Fosbrooke, Glouc. 211; *D.N.B.*, s.v. Powell, John.
[6] Below, Aldermen of Glouc. 1483–1835; Fosbrooke, Glouc. 209–10; cf. G.D.R. wills 1685/180; invent. 1713/119.
[7] J. Blanch, *Hoops into Spinning-Wheels* (Glouc. 1725), 15.
[8] G.D.R. invent. 1684/3.

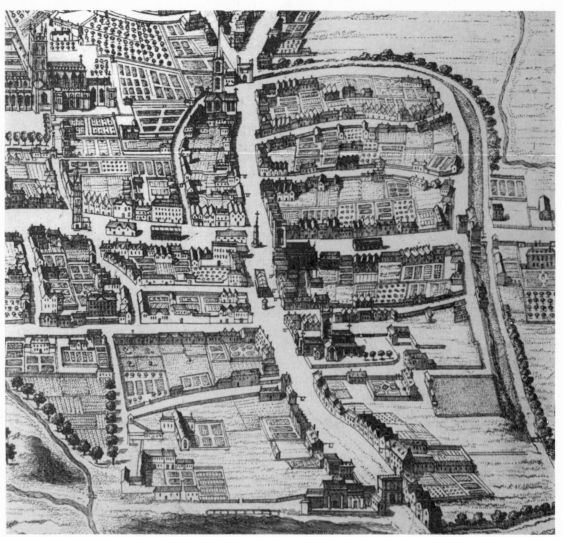

Fig. 5. The city centre from the south, *c.* 1710: features shown include the north, south, and east gates, Trinity tower in Westgate Street, the high cross, the market houses in three of the main streets, and St. Kyneburgh's Hospital adjoining the south gate

and Abraham Hague, together with some lesser known boarding-school teachers who attracted the children of the gentry and other prosperous folk from the region.[9]

Inns and other larger victualling houses did a handsome trade from the influx of the rural upper classes. In 1672 the corporation agreed to an increase in the number of inns from about 14 to 23.[10] Fourteen years later a government survey of hostelries (mostly inns) in the county established that Gloucester had beds for 484 people and stabling for 759 horses, far greater than the provision in any other town in the shire: Cirencester by comparison had 109 beds and Tewkesbury only 26.[11] Already quite large in the 16th century, a number of the inns had become extensive complexes. The Bell in Southgate Street comprised the main inn, outhouses, stables, several shops, and land and a garden worth £130 a year in rent.[12] In the 1660s the New Inn was rated at 29 hearths in the hearth tax and was probably one of the largest buildings in the city.[13] By the 1720s the Saracen's Head in Eastgate Street had stables for 60 horses.[14] As well as lodging and refreshing the well-to-do, inns were also important commercial centres and places where wagons and coaches were boarded for London and

[9] Below, religious and cultural life.
[10] G.B.R., B 3/3, pp. 546–7, 554–5.
[11] P.R.O., WO 30/48.
[12] Ibid. C 7/174/46; C 7/174/60.
[13] G.B.R., G 3/SO 7, f. 77v.
[14] *Glouc. Jnl.* 13 May 1729.

elsewhere.[15] Not least important, Gloucester inns provided a fashionable social arena where the urban and rural élites came for cockfights, concerts, and other entertainments.[16] A number of innkeepers served on the corporation in the last decades of the century, and, if the surviving probate inventories are a guide, they frequently ranked among the wealthiest inhabitants.[17]

Taverns, where the prosperous came to drink wine, spirits, and coffee, also flourished in the later Stuart city. When the Fountain in Westgate Street was converted into a tavern and coffee house c. 1672 the work cost over £200.[18] William Warwick's tavern, the Raven, was quite elaborately furnished with paintings and plate.[19] There, as at the inns, a good deal of commercial, professional, and fashionable social activity took place.[20] Licensed alehouses likewise prospered, and the total number of licensed premises in the city rose from 50 in 1674 to 89 in 1710 and to 92 in 1719. At the same time, the illicit petty tippling houses, so numerous before the Civil War, tended to fade away.[21] Alehouse premises became larger and more respectable; rooms were given over to specialist purposes like the game of shove-halfpenny.[22] Landlords tended to be modestly prosperous, though far inferior to inn and tavern keepers. The alehouses catered principally for the lower classes, then enjoying a substantial rise in real wages. Such establishments sold a growing variety of drinks (beer, ale, cider, and spirits) and also provided a wide range of economic and social services.[23]

For fashionable visitors there were other attractions. A bowling green by the castle had its coterie of devotees in the 1680s,[24] and by 1714 another green, in the grounds of Greyfriars, was in use.[25] By the early 1720s horse races were being run on Sud Meadow for large prizes.[26] With the revived interest in Gothic antiquities the cathedral became a tourist landmark.[27] Landowners began to rent or own houses in or near the precincts; the Guises, for instance, had a house in the cathedral yard.[28] The less wealthy might stay at the upper-class lodging houses which existed in the city by the 1720s.[29] From at least 1718 the music meeting (later known as the Three Choirs festival), rotating between Gloucester, Worcester, and Hereford, brought a triennial invasion of gentry, clergy, and other professional folk and well-to-do, coming to the concerts and related social events.[30] Gloucester never became a specialist gentry town, like Winchester or Shrewsbury, in the period,[31] but its growing significance as a social centre undoubtedly gave impetus to its economic revival.

As for industrial activity, the largest of the new industries was pinmaking. About 1710 it was said that the 'pinmaking trade is . . . very considerable in this city and returns about £80 a week'.[32] Already well established before the Restoration, pinmaking may well have benefited from the decline of Dutch competition in the late 17th century.[33] By Charles II's reign the Gloucester industry was clearly expanding, attracting investment from the service sector and other trades. John Cromwell, a

[15] Ibid. 30 Nov. 1724.
[16] Ibid. 24 Aug., 14 Sept., 7 Dec. 1724; 9 Mar. 1731.
[17] G.D.R. invent. 1685/169; 1707/187; 1691/87.
[18] P.R.O., C 5/425/105.
[19] G.D.R. invent. 1692/118.
[20] P.R.O., C 5/122/15; *Life and Times of Anthony Wood*, ii. (Oxford Hist. Soc. xxi), 143.
[21] G.B.R., G 3/AV 1.
[22] G.D.R. invent. 1712/275; 1714/103.
[23] Clark, *Eng. Alehouse*, chaps. 9–10.
[24] Hist. MSS. Com. 29, *13th Rep. II, Portland*, ii, p. 295.
[25] Bodl. MS. Top. Glouc. c. 3, f. 61v.; cf. Glos. Colln. prints GL 60.46 (in both sources Greyfriars is wrongly called Whitefriars).

[26] *Glouc. Jnl.* 10 Sept. 1722.
[27] *Journeys of C. Fiennes*, 234–5; Hist. MSS. Com. 29, *Portland*, ii, p. 294.
[28] *Autobiography of Thos. Raymond and Memoirs of Fam. of Guise* (Camd. 3rd ser. xxviii), 145; P.R.O., C 5/528/18.
[29] *Glouc. Jnl.* 21 Oct. 1729; 6 Oct. 1730.
[30] H. W. Shaw, *Three Choirs Festival* (1954), 1–2; D. Lysons et al., *Origin and Progress of the Meeting of the Three Choirs* (Glouc. 1895).
[31] *Country Towns*, ed. Clark, 172 sqq.; A. Everitt, 'Country, County and Town: Patterns of Regional Evolution in Eng.', *Trans. R.H.S.* (5th ser.) xxix. 95–6.
[32] Atkyns, *Glos.* 119.
[33] J. Thirsk, *Econ. Policy and Projects* (1978), 83.

carrier and innkeeper, became a leading pinmaker, raising part of the capital through the fortuitous control (and possibly misappropriation) of a trust estate. In 1675 he formed a partnership with Sampson Bacon, a lawyer, Isaac Lumbard, a jerseycomber, and William Gibbs, a Worcester chapman; Cromwell invested £1,200 in the joint stock and the others £400 each. The company traded in pins in several parts of England, Scotland, and Ireland, but was adversely affected by the failure of one of its creditors and by the subsequent death of Cromwell, which led to protracted litigation.[34] However, Cromwell's share in the company was taken over by another pinmaker and the company probably continued to operate.[35] Also active in the trade was Samuel Willetts, whose business was carried on successfully by his widow 'who greatly improved her estate thereby'.[36] Between 1660 and 1740 over 100 pinmakers worked in the city, but the great majority were small masters, employing a couple of men. In the years 1680–1700 only one pinmaker, John Cromwell, sat on the common council.[37] The manufacture involved a high division of labour with much of the work performed by women and children. The raw metal probably came from London initially, but later from the ironworks of the West Midlands.[38]

Another, older metal craft which flourished in the late 17th century was bellfounding. John Barnard was a modestly affluent bellfounder at the Restoration with property in Grace (later St. John's) Lane, Bearland, and elsewhere.[39] Abraham Rudhall's bell foundry from 1684 served both local customers and others across the country:[40] in 1705 Rudhall cast eight bells for the rebuilt St. Mary's church, Warwick.[41] Gloucester also had a number of other specialist metal workers in the post-Restoration period, including cutlers, watchmakers, and gunsmiths, often no doubt selling to wealthy customers from the countryside.[42]

Celia Fiennes in the 1690s drew attention to the new textile trades in the city: 'here they follow knitting, stockings, gloves, waistcoats and petticoats, and sleeves, all of cotton and others spin the cottons'.[43] There seems to have been some involvement in silkweaving and also in the 'new draperies'. In 1691 the corporation proposed establishing a linen manufacture at Gloucester.[44] Evidence from probate inventories and apprenticeship and freeman records, however, makes it clear that textiles never recovered as a major occupation. Hosiery may have suffered fatally from the competition of the highly successful Tewkesbury industry.[45] More buoyant was glassmaking. About 1682 Thomas Baskerville remarked on the glasshouse at the lower end of town near the river 'where they make a great store of glass bottles selling 15 to the dozen'.[46] In 1694 a large new glasshouse was built near the north end of the quay by the partnership of Benjamin Hyett, Thomas Browne, and Henry Fowler.[47] One important use for the glass was in bottling cider, which by 1700 was produced on a commercial basis in Herefordshire and Gloucestershire and shipped in great quantities to Bristol and London.[48] Also linked with the growth of a consumer society was the establishment of one or two sugar refineries in the city, processing the growing imports of Caribbean sugar to Bristol which may have outrun the capacity of the Bristol refiners.[49]

[34] P.R.O., C 5/417/41; C 7/585/20; C 7/95/52.
[35] Ibid. C 7/95/52.
[36] Ibid. C 5/179/35.
[37] Ripley, 'Glouc. 1660–1740', 62.
[38] P.R.O., C 5/516/12; *Selection from the Rec. of Phil. Foley's Stour Valley Ironworks 1668–74: Pt. I* (Worcs. Hist. Soc. N.S. ix), 99.
[39] P.R.O., C 6/231/63; C 6/169/22.
[40] *Glos. Ch. Bells*, 57–60.
[41] Warws. R.O., CR 1618; WA 4.

[42] G.D.R. invent. 1662/12; 1695/139; 1736/77; 1686/132.
[43] *Journeys of C. Fiennes*, 234.
[44] Ripley, 'Glouc. 1660–1740', 65; G.B.R., B 3/7, f. 36.
[45] T. Rath. 'Tewkesbury Hosiery Ind.', *Textile Hist.* vii. 140 sqq.
[46] Hist. MSS. Com. 29, *Portland*, ii, p. 294.
[47] Glos. R.O., P 154/15/IN 1/1; cf. Bodl. MS. Top. Glouc. c. 3, f. 41.
[48] Cf. Clark, *Eng. Alehouse*, 210–11.
[49] Ripley, 'Glouc. 1660–1740', 70–1.

The spread of fashionable brick-built housing in the late 17th century encouraged the growth of brickmaking on the Common Ham. Philip Greene, who was making bricks there by 1659, had a thriving business in the early 1680s, digging clay at the Ham and possibly at Wainlode Hill, in Norton, and using coal brought by river to fire his kilns.[50] John Blanch later lauded the city's 'admirable bricks at six shillings a thousand'.[51] One enterprise which may have contracted in the second half of the period was wholesale brewing. Gloucester's common brewers appear to have been flourishing at the Restoration, selling in the Forest of Dean and up river at Tewkesbury.[52] John Woodward (d. 1667) was said to have had a personal estate in excess of £6,000, but his heir John Price, also a brewer, had only a few hundred pounds in personal property by the 1690s.[53] During the 1680s Baskerville observed that 'here the people are wise and brew their own ale, not permitting public brewers';[54] by 1712 the brewers' company had lapsed.[55] The decline in brewing was in marked contrast with other southern towns where the common brewers steadily enlarged their share of the drink market in the late 17th century.[56] It may reflect, as Baskerville thought, an increase of domestic brewing by householders who were exempt from the heavy excise duties. More important probably was competition from the affluent innkeepers, who seem from their inventories to have moved into brewing on a large scale.[57] The brewers' beer may also have faced competition from cider, which had become a popular drink in the city. Tanning was another industry which may have declined in the period.[58]

The new trades did not, of course, dominate Gloucester's industrial order. The freemen lists and apprenticeship records, increasingly unreliable though they are by the later 17th century, indicate that the traditional clothing trades (especially shoemaking and tailoring), food processing trades (including baking), and building crafts remained principal sources of employment. The new specialist industries, however, added a more profitable and dynamic element to the urban economy. The growth of those industries was almost wholly outside the old framework of the trade companies and may have contributed to their general decline. In 1665 the butchers' company was reportedly in great disorder through the neglect of certain of their customs.[59] A few years later the mercers' company complained of the invasion of the distributive trades by outsiders without formal training.[60] Detailed records which survive for the tanners' and butchers' companies suggest that by the second half of the 17th century there was a marked reduction in the level of their activity.[61] By George I's reign the majority of Gloucester's 12 companies had been reduced to a mainly formal role in the community, processing with the mayor on ceremonial occasions. One reason for their eclipse was the politicization of the freedom after the Revolution of 1688, with droves of freemen, including growing numbers of outsiders, being enfranchised at parliamentary election times.[62] Another related factor was the influx of outside traders and craftsmen, which the corporation, itself with a growing number of gentry intruders, was unwilling or unable to exclude. The decline of the trade companies, which had never been especially strong at Gloucester, was only one aspect of the slow liberalization of the economy. Equally important was the growth of private

[50] *Trans. B.G.A.S.* xcviii. 175; G.D.R. invent. 1685/147. The brickworks on the Ham are shown in a painting of the city, attributed to Jan Griffier (d. 1718): Glos. Colln. prints GL 90.25.

[51] Blanch, *Hoops*, 15.

[52] P.R.O., C 5/417/41; C 7/79/47; E 134/25 Chas. II East./15. [53] Ibid. C 5/74/22; C 5/71/35.

[54] Hist. MSS. Com. 29, *Portland*, ii, p. 295.

[55] Atkyns, *Glos.* 119.

[56] Clark, *Eng. Alehouse*, 183–4.

[57] G.D.R. invent. 1695/226; 1688/8.

[58] Ripley, 'Glouc. 1660–1740', 45, 47.

[59] Glos. Colln. 11664, no. 5.

[60] *Cal. S.P. Dom.* 1671, 419.

[61] Glos. Colln. 28652, nos. 16, 18; 29334.

[62] Below, city govt. and politics.

marketing and the partial cessation of the levying of tolls in the city. By the 1720s Gloucester had both a more prosperous and a more open urban economy.

Social Structure

Some idea of the social order and topography of the city after the Restoration is provided by the hearth-tax return for 1672, which is complete except for parts of the west ward and Barton Street. Of the 1,113 households listed, 794 paid the tax and 319 (29 per cent) were exempt as too poor, a figure broadly in line with other county towns at the time. Of those paying the tax, just over half were assessed at the lowest rates of one or two hearths and only 117 (15 per cent) at the higher rates of six or more hearths. So over all the social hierarchy remained quite steeply tapered. At the same time, the tax reveals considerable variations in the incidence of wealth within the community. Those households paying at the higher rates accounted for only 2.2 per cent of taxpayers in the Barton Street area and 2.8 per cent in St. Catherine's parish, both outer districts, whereas in the prosperous commercial area of the west ward and the increasingly fashionable cathedral close the respective figures were 17.2 per cent and 38.9 per cent. There was a not dissimilar pattern of poverty, as measured by the incidence of exemptions. St. Catherine, Barton Street, and St. Mary de Lode all had high proportions of exempt households, as high as 58 per cent in St. Catherine.[63]

Comparative data are not available for the early 18th century, but by then there were signs of changes in the social structure. The narrow élite was reinforced and enlarged by growing numbers of gentry and professional men. For the years 1680 to 1700 gentlemen made up 17 per cent of the aldermen (or future aldermen) on Gloucester corporation and 6 per cent of the councillors.[64] Some were leading shire gentry like Sir John Guise of Elmore[65] and Sir Duncombe Colchester of Westbury-on-Severn;[66] others were middling or lesser figures like the royalist soldier Henry Norwood of Tuffley (later of Leckhampton).[67] They typified the growing numbers of landowners who increasingly spent part of the year in the city and who regarded it as a civilized, tolerably fashionable refuge from the bucolic longeurs of the countryside. In turn the accession of affluent outsiders, often with links with London or the Court, helped integrate the urban upper classes into the wider provincial and national community.

Also important in that context was the growing presence of lawyers and other professional men in the city. As well as playing a lively part in the urban economy, a substantial contingent served on the corporation.[68] The lawyers in particular were often very wealthy by urban standards: the attorney William Windowe (d. c. 1670) reportedly had a personal estate in excess of £7,000.[69] They maintained close ties with the county, and as the 18th century progressed acquired increasingly professional connexions with London and national society. Other leading members of the Gloucester élite were the mercers, grocers, and similar distributive traders, who undoubtedly prospered from the renewed expansion of the city's marketing function. They held just under 40 per cent of all the seats on the corporation in the last two decades of the 17th century.[70] Like the lawyers they frequently styled themselves as gentlemen and with rising expenditure on housing and fashionable consumer comforts could affect a display of gentility.[71]

[63] P.R.O., E 179/247/14, rott. 29–31.
[64] Clark, 'Civic Leaders', 315.
[65] Glos. R.O., D 326/F 13, F 15.
[66] Ibid. D 36/F 8.   [67] Ibid. D 303/F 40.

[68] Clark, 'Civic Leaders', 313, 323–4.
[69] P.R.O., C 5/493/39.
[70] Clark, 'Civic Leaders', 315.
[71] e.g. Nic. Webb: G.D.R. invent 1691/109.

Less evidence can be obtained about the fortunes of middle-rank citizens such as master craftsmen and smaller shopkeepers. Probate inventories suggest that they were more affluent than in the past, their houses provided with a modest array of consumer goods. The city's bakers, for instance, seem to have been solidly prosperous, in many cases owning plate. One of them, Thomas Partridge (d. 1684), had various feather beds, carpets, striped curtains, a collection of leather chairs, and a silver tankard, bowl, and other plate worth £10.[72] John Hone, a tailor whose inventory was taken in 1723, owned numerous small pictures and a clock and case, along with the usual feather beds.[73] The growing prosperity and social self-confidence of the middling inhabitants gave a new stability to urban society.

On the other hand, poverty was a persistent and serious problem in the post-Restoration city, especially in the outer parishes. In 1669, for instance, the inhabitants of St. Catherine's parish complained that they were burdened with many poor and sought relief from other parishes.[74] There is no evidence for the overall incidence of poor in need of relief, but the overseers' accounts for St. Nicholas and St. Michael indicate that the numbers of people receiving parish pensions remained broadly stable in the late 17th century, though the former parish saw some increase at the start of the following century.[75] If that reflects a greater stability in the general level of impoverishment, then part of the explanation was the revival of the urban economy after the Restoration, together with rising real incomes for the lower orders. Also influential may have been the growing effectiveness of city controls over poor immigrants, especially after the Settlement Act of 1662. In 1679 and 1680 the St. Michael's overseers acted on a number of occasions 'in taking care that no inmates might inhabit amongst us and that them that did come might give security to the parish, which several did'. Weekly fines were rigorously imposed on landlords who housed inmates.[76] At the same time, there is a suggestion that the authorities may have been pursuing a more selective policy than in the past and excluding mainly unskilled males.[77] There was vigorous action against vagrants.[78]

For the local poor, however, relief was more generous. The selective provision of the four main established hospitals or almshouses was enlarged by Sir Thomas Rich, a London merchant and native of Gloucester, who left the corporation a house and £6,000 to erect a bluecoat school for 20 poor boys, with surplus income to be distributed to other needy inhabitants.[79] Most parishes by the early 18th century had several charity funds for the poor, though they were largest in the wealthier parishes where poverty was less serious.[80] In addition there were parish voluntary collections, which in St. Michael's parish in 1677 were assigned to help the poor 'that be sick and at winter when the poor has most need'.[81] By the later Stuart period, however, philanthropy was less important in assisting the poor than statutory parish relief. Though the parish reforms of the Interregnum were partially overturned at the Restoration, parochial relief seems to have been increasingly well organized and supervised. A substantial part of the expenditure was in the form of pensions to the elderly, sick, and local destitute. Payments *per capita* rose by 60 per cent in St. Michael between the 1640s and 1690s;[82] in St. Nicholas the increase was a more modest 12 per cent in the years 1681–1720.[83] At a time of falling prices the real value

[72] G.D.R. invent. 1684/241.
[73] Ibid. 1723/21.
[74] G.B.R., G 3/SO 7, ff. 77v., 139 and v.
[75] Glos. R.O., P 154/15/OV 2/1–2; 14/OV 2/1.
[76] Ibid. 14/OV 2/1.
[77] Ibid. 2.

[78] G.B.R., G 3/SO 7, ff. 92, 106, *et passim*.
[79] Below, Educ., Sir Thos. Rich's sch.
[80] Below, Char. for Poor, par. char.
[81] Glos. R.O., P 154/14/CW 1/42.
[82] Ibid. OV 2/1.
[83] Ibid. 15/OV 2/1–2.

of pensions rose substantially. In addition, there was a growing range of miscellaneous provision for the poor, including clothes, medical aid, schooling, and payment of rents, the last comprising up to one eighth of parish expenditure. Overseers might also pay the taxes of those on the borderline of poverty in order to keep them solvent and off the rates.[84] As elsewhere, there were complaints that the poor were being mollycoddled: in 1681 St. Michael's parish ordered that its pensioners should no longer be paid, since they were 'refractory to the parish and have too large allowance already'.[85] Certainly parish expenditure on relief grew markedly: in St. Michael it doubled between the 1660s and 1690s; St. Nicholas had a similar increase in the period 1682–1720.[86] The high cost of parochial relief was one factor behind the urban corporations of the poor founded about the turn of the century, the earliest at Bristol in 1696.[87] Gloucester's was established by statute in 1702, whereby from 1703 all the city poor were to be employed in a large workhouse under the control of a board of guardians, including the mayor, 3 aldermen, and 24 respectable citizens elected by wards;[88] lands left by Timothy Nourse were applied to support the establishment, which included a charity school.[89] In 1707, however, the workhouse lapsed through insufficient finance and the difficulty of confining and employing all the poor there, though it was revived in 1727.[90]

For most of the period, therefore, parish payments were the principal mechanism for routine poor relief. In emergencies, however, they were supplemented by subscription funds. In 1709, for instance, because of the bad harvest and high grain prices whereby 'the poor of this city have been of late very much increased', the common council proposed the opening of a subscription to aid the poor, with contributors having a say in how the money was distributed.[91] Subscription funds of that type were to be of growing significance in 18th-century towns in alleviating social distress. By contrast, the civic corn stocks which had been an important element in poor relief in the late 16th century disappeared in the 17th as corn prices declined.

In sum, the urban social order appeared more prosperous, stable, and harmonious than in the decades before the Civil War. One sign of that was the relative absence of popular disturbances in Gloucester during the period. Those riots and disorders which did occur were almost invariably in the context of the growing party strife between Whigs and Tories.

City Government and Politics

The Restoration had a dramatic effect on the political landscape at Gloucester. The government and royalist landowners moved decisively to bring to an end the city's fiercely defended autonomy, its extensive jurisdiction over the inshire, and the puritan ascendancy on the corporation. The Crown was motivated not just by a desire for revenge against a community which had so thwarted royalist designs in 1643, but by fears that Gloucester might serve as a focus for future risings by old, incorrigible supporters of the parliamentary cause. In October 1660 there were reports that Edmund Ludlow was at Gloucester and that an uprising was being planned.[92] The city figured in further rumours of radical sedition and agitation in November 1661 and in January 1664.[93] Francis Topp wrote from Gloucestershire in May 1662 that 'every

---

84 Ibid.; ibid. 14/OV 2/1–2.
85 Ibid. 14/CW 1/42.
86 Ibid. OV 2/1; 15/OV 2/1–2.
87 D. Marshall, *Eng. Poor in 18th Cent.* (1926), 127–8.
88 Rudder, *Glos.* 129; G.B.R., B 6/5.

89 Below, Educ., elem. educ., Poor's sch.
90 Glouc. Poor-Relief Act, 13 Geo. I, c. 19.
91 G.B.R., B 3/8, p. 333.
92 Cal. S.P. Dom. 1660–1, 310.
93 Ibid. 1661–2, 153; 1663–4, 434, 440, 446.

day there is preaching and rumour', which he hoped would be over soon after 'the dismantling of our neighbour the city of Gloucester and others in the west that withstood the late king'.[94]

Most of Gloucester's town walls were demolished in 1662 under the supervision of Lord Herbert, the lord lieutenant.[95] In 1661 a bill was introduced into parliament providing for the return of the inshire to the county.[96] The corporation spent over £160 defending its powers, and twice petitioned the king, but the measure was enacted in May 1662.[97] The same year the whole governing body of the city came under attack. Since 1660 a number of former parliamentarians like Alderman Thomas Pury and Edward Nourse had left Gloucester, mainly for the greater safety of the capital.[98] In July 1662 Lord Herbert and a contingent of county landowners, commissioners under the Corporations Act of 1661, visited the city and proceeded to eject 22 members of the corporation; nine more were dismissed in October 1662 and four more the following March.[99] The purge of three quarters of the ruling body appeared all the more drastic because during the 1640s and 1650s few members of the corporation had been deprived. Moreover 1662 and 1663 saw only the first wave of removals; there was further replacement of personnel in 1672, 1683, and under James II.

The Restoration saw a marked increase in the influence and involvement of county landowners in city politics, matching their mounting importance in the urban economy and society. The new power of the gentry in Gloucester's government continued after the purges under the Corporations Act. A new charter granted in 1664 merely confirmed earlier royal grants to the city, apart from ratifying the loss of the inshire and giving the king power to control the appointment of the recorder and town clerk.[1] However, another charter which replaced it in 1672 appointed a clutch of county landowners to the ruling élite, including Sir Duncombe Colchester of Westbury-on-Severn, William Cooke of Highnam, Henry Norwood of Tuffley, and William Selwyn of Matson.[2] Gentry became mayors in the years 1672–5, 1688, and 1690.[3] In 1686 leading members of the corporation went out to Badminton to hear a royal message from the duke of Beaufort.[4] Again, whereas parliamentary elections before and during the English Revolution had almost invariably returned Gloucester men as the city's M.P.s, a high proportion of those chosen between 1660 and 1715 were gentry from the shire.[5] During election contests after the Revolution of 1688 the city was riven by party feuding between Whigs and Tories, led by county landowners.

The growth of electoral conflict was only one aspect of the recurrent political instability and factionalism which was evident in post-Restoration Gloucester. The purges of 1662 and 1663 had drawn only some of the teeth of the old parliamentary party, which retained a considerable following. In the late 1660s there was a groundswell of hostility to the new political order, fuelled by the persecution of dissenters.[6] In 1668 Nicholas Haines, a hosier, denounced parliament saying, 'one half of them [were] feathermen and the other half of them were whoremasters and drunkards . . . and that the times would turn and honest men would rule again'.[7] By 1670 the old parliamentarians and dissenters were again asserting themselves on the

[94] Hist. MSS. Com. 29, *Portland*, ii, p. 144.
[95] G.B.R., F 4/6, p. 440.
[96] *C.J.* viii. 285, 287, 348, 351; *L.J.* xi. 373–4, 381, 473; G.B.R., B 3/3, p. 188.
[97] G.B.R., F 4/6, pp. 430 sqq.; B 3/3, p. 188.
[98] Ibid. B 3/3, pp. 224, 231.
[99] Ibid. C 8/1, ff. 7v.–8, 16 and v., 18v.–19.
[1] Ripley, 'Glouc. 1660–1740', 100.

[2] Rudder, *Glos*. App. p. v; cf. ibid. 521, 542; *V.C.H. Glos.* x. 19, 87; below, Outlying Hamlets, man.; Matson, man.
[3] Fosbrooke, *Glouc.* 209–10; cf. below, Aldermen of Glouc. 1483–1835.
[4] G.B.R., F 4/7, f. 396.
[5] Williams, *Parl. Hist. of Glos.* 199–207.
[6] G.B.R., G 3/SIb 2, pt. i, pp. 308, 328, 356.
[7] Ibid. p. 353.

corporation. That year, according to Sir William Morton, the recorder, the 'Presbyterian party' sought to prevent the election of the royalist Henry Fowler as mayor, choosing instead William Bubb, a man who had reportedly promised that once 'in power he will crush the royal interest' at Gloucester.[8] The king's order for the corporation to elect Fowler was opposed by five dissenting aldermen, 'ringleaders of the faction'.[9] Fowler's mayoralty was stormy. The dissenting aldermen blocked the filling of vacancies on the bench with men of loyalist sympathies, and plotted to get Bubb elected as the next mayor.[10] When Bubb was in fact chosen in 1671, the conservatives complained of improper proceedings and the king overturned the election and gave Fowler authority to continue in office.[11] In November 1671 the Privy Council decreed that the city had forfeited its privileges and ordered the surrender of the charter.[12] The new grant in April 1672 brought many changes. A majority of the members of the old corporation was removed and a cadre of royalist gentry appointed. County justices were given authority to act in the city and the Crown reserved the power to deprive civic rulers at will and to approve future officials.[13] With the city on the defensive the dean of Gloucester, Robert Vyner, exploited the opportunity to reclaim the jurisdiction over the close which the dean and chapter had yielded to the corporation in 1584; the bishop, dean, and two prebendaries also became J.P.s for the city.[14]

The charter of 1672 imposed a royalist hegemony in Gloucester politics which lasted until James II's reign. Apart from a minor political disturbance in 1679,[15] the city remained loyal to the king throughout the Exclusion Crisis. In 1681 the ruling body presented the king with an obsequiously loyal address and two years later when a Whig prebendary, Edward Fowler, later bishop of Gloucester, preached against the Popish Plot in the cathedral the magistrates protested and refused to attend his services.[16] The Tory ascendancy on the corporation was underlined in 1683 when three loyalists were elected at the insistence of the duke of Beaufort.[17] During the Exclusion Crisis the city's over-zealous persecution of local dissenters caused concern even to the government,[18] and between 1681 and 1685 there was a spate of prosecutions of dissenters at the assizes and quarter sessions.[19] In 1685 the Whig Sir John Guise was deprived of his rights as a freeman.[20]

Under James II, however, the Tory-dominated magistracy encountered growing problems. In 1686 the king dispensed John Hill, a Catholic, from the oaths under the Test Act on his election to the mayoralty.[21] The following year Anselm Fowler, apparently also a Catholic, was enfranchised and appointed to the aldermanic bench by royal directive.[22] The civic elections in the autumn of 1687 merely confirmed the king's nomination of Hill for a second term as mayor.[23] During James's visit to the city in August 1687[24] he used a Catholic chapel that Hill had fitted up in the Tolsey,[25] and in November 1687 13 of the leading Tories on the corporation were purged, together with the recorder, by the king's order.[26] They were replaced with a motley

[8] P.R.O., SP 29/278, no. 123.
[9] Ibid. SP 29/278, no. 204.
[10] Cal. S.P. Dom. 1671, 411–12, 429.
[11] Ibid. 489–90, 517, 525–6, 531; G.B.R., B 3/4, p. 305.
[12] P.R.O., SP 29/293, no. 113 (I–II); SP 29/294, no. 85.
[13] Rudder, Glos. App. pp. iv–xii.
[14] Ibid.; R. Beddard, 'Privileges of Christchurch, Canterbury', Archaeologia Cantiana, lxxxvii. 85–6, 93–5, 99–100.
[15] Hist. MSS. Com. 32, 13th Rep. VI, Fitzherbert, p. 20.
[16] Glos. Colln. NF 12.303; Cal. S.P. Dom. July–Sept. 1683, 326.   [17] G.B.R., B 3/3, p. 837.
[18] Cal. S.P. Dom. 1680–1, 45–6.

[19] P.R.O., ASSIZES 5/5; G.B.R., G 3/SIb 2, p. 196, et passim.
[20] G.B.R., B 3/3, p. 877.
[21] Ibid. p. 914.
[22] Ibid. 6, ff. 153–5; Ripley, 'Glouc. 1660–1740', 150.
[23] G.B.R., B 3/6, ff. 169–70.
[24] Ibid. F 4/7, pp. 426–7; cf. Rudder, Glos. 89 n., where, as in most old histories of the city, the date of the visit is given wrongly.
[25] G.B.R., F 4/7, pp. 426–7; B 3/6, f. 159v.; cf. Bodl. MS. Top. Glouc. c. 3, f. 40.
[26] G.B.R., B 3/6, f. 174v.

group of dissenters and Catholics led by the unpopular new recorder Charles Trinder.[27] The remaining Tories appear to have seceded from council meetings.[28] In March 1688 the corporation, not surprisingly, gave its support for the repeal of the penal laws.[29] By the summer, however, there was growing unrest at the Jacobitism of the city's leaders.[30] In October 1688 Anselm Fowler was elected mayor,[31] but within a few weeks, after William of Orange's invasion, the political situation deteriorated. A panic broke out over the report of an Irish attack;[32] the Tolsey chapel and Catholic houses were assailed;[33] Fowler was forced to resign and was replaced by the Tory landowner William Cooke;[34] and the Williamite Whig, Lord Lovelace, then in prison in Gloucester, was released to command troops to quell the disorder.[35] Over the following months the Jacobite sympathizers lost their seats in the council on one pretext or another.[36] In 1690 Sir John Guise, who had been in exile with William III, was chosen mayor.[37]

During the 1690s the city's governing body was fairly evenly divided between Whigs and Tories, with the former coming to dominate the aldermanic bench. There were fiercely fought contests in elections to civic office and also to parliament. In 1690 there was a complaint that one of the candidates for parliament, William Trye, a Tory, had mobilized the support of poorer freemen and secured his own return, although not enfranchised himself.[38] Conflict accelerated after the turn of the century. Five contests occurred in the seven parliamentary elections between 1701 and 1715.[39] Hundreds of freemen were created in 1702, 1708, and afterwards to swing the large freeman electorate (about 1,400 strong) behind one party or the other.[40] In 1703 the Whigs pushed through the election of Nicholas Lane as mayor despite the vociferous opposition of the Tories, and the Tories absented themselves from other civic elections.[41] With the Tory resurgence in national politics in the last part of Anne's reign, however, the Whig aldermanic caucus was under pressure.[42] In 1710 the city, unlike numerous other Gloucestershire towns, aligned itself against the rabid Tory Dr. Sacheverell,[43] but two years later Whig aldermen were being investigated by the authorities for their alleged obstruction over the impressment of troops.[44] In 1712 the Whig bishop, Edward Fowler, exclaimed 'that popery and slavery are coming in upon us, that we are undone'.[45] In 1715 the large Tory following in the freeman body returned two likeminded M.P.s.[46] Party conflict continued into the 1730s.[47]

The upsurge of political instability in the post-Restoration city was partly a reflection of growing national party conflict, especially after 1688. It was also linked with local factors: the growing intervention of county gentry in city politics, the continuing importance of dissent, and the survival of Civil War loyalties and antagonisms. At the same time, party conflict should not be exaggerated in its impact on city government. There was no breakdown of public order. Only briefly in 1672 and 1688 did political feuding spill over into social disorder or administrative instability.

[27] Ibid. f. 175 and v.
[28] Ibid. ff. 183v., 187.
[29] Ibid. f. 190.
[30] Ibid. f. 198.
[31] Ibid. f. 205 and v.
[32] Ibid. F 4/7, p. 483.
[33] H. Misson, *Memoirs and Observations in his Travels over Eng.* (Lond. 1719), 247; below, Roman Catholicism.
[34] G.B.R., B 3/6, f. 219 and v.
[35] Hist. MSS. Com. 6, *7th Rep. I, Denbigh*, p. 227; G.B.R., B 3/6, ff. 219v., 221v.
[36] G.B.R., B 3/6, ff. 238, 251, 273v.

[37] Ibid. ff. 275v.–276, 280.
[38] Glos. Colln. 6768 (26).
[39] W.A. Speck, *Tory and Whig* (1970), 128.
[40] G.B.R., B 3/8, p. 345, *et passim*; C 9/7.
[41] Ibid. B 3/8, pp. 110, 113, 116, 122–3.
[42] Ibid. pp. 305, 429–30.
[43] G. Holmes, *Trial of Dr. Sacheverell* (1973), 236.
[44] Hist. MSS. Com. 29, *Portland*, x, pp. 76–8.
[45] *Diary of Ralph Thoresby F.R.S.* ed. J. Hunter (1830), ii. 148.
[46] R. Sedgwick, *House of Commons 1715–54* (1970), i. 246.
[47] Below, Glouc. 1720–1835, parl. representation.

One buttress of governmental stability was the continuing dominance of civic oligarchy. While major changes of personnel occurred in the years 1662–3, 1672, and 1687–9, only under James II is there any indication of a broadening of the composition of the ruling élite and then on a minor scale.[48] All the major civic officers were pre-elected by the aldermanic bench on nomination day, before the formal elections.[49] Under the charter of 1672 the electoral college for civic posts was reduced from 24 to 20, curbing the number of ordinary councillors and strengthening the power of the aldermen.[50] The Friday court of aldermen at the Tolsey was by then an established and important institution for dealing with much of the regular business of city administration.[51] The aldermen as magistrates presided over quarter sessions, which heard a great variety of cases concerning the poor, alehouses, trade, civic improvement, nonconformity, and public order.[52] The old hundred court was virtually defunct.[53] Deliberations of the common council were progressively given over to more routine business, such as the awarding of town leases and the choice of minor town officials.[54] In 1693 it was agreed that the mayor might only summon the council with the consent of the aldermen.[55]

Administrative coherence was also aided by certain improvements in civic administration. Finance remained a serious problem at the Restoration, since the chamber was heavily encumbered with large debts, some dating back to the Civil War and some incurred more recently, including those for the defence of the inshire.[56] The traditional system of four stewards, never a satisfactory one, disintegrated with repeated refusals of councillors to serve, disputes among officials, and allegations of fraudulent accounting.[57] The difficulties came to a climax in 1671 with the disputed mayoral election.[58] The new charter of 1672 inaugurated a major reform of civic finances: a single, salaried, quasi-permanent chamberlain was chosen to replace the four stewards;[59] debts due the chamberlain were called in;[60] income was improved;[61] in 1679 the city's lands in Ireland were finally sold for £1,300;[62] and charity funds may have been diverted to pay off outstanding loans.[63] By the 1690s the city's finances were increasingly in balance.[64]

The town clerk, already important before the Civil War, became a pivotal figure in the administration. Two members of the Powell family, John and his brother Thomas, occupied the post for virtually all of the last quarter of the 17th century and provided invaluable continuity at a time of political flux.[65] In 1701 the town clerk's offices at the Cross were extended, presumably because of the growth of business.[66] With the decline of the traditional piepowder (sheriffs') and hundred courts, Gloucester obtained in 1689 a statutory court of conscience to hear small debt cases, particularly useful given the expansion of trade.[67] In addition, as noted above, a corporation of the poor was established in 1703. Both new institutions had their problems, however.[68] More vital for city government was the tightening up of administrative procedures, as, for instance, over alehouse licensing.[69] Another

[48] Clark, 'Civic Leaders', 322–5.
[49] G.B.R., F 4/7, *passim*.
[50] Rudder, *Glos*. App. p. vi.
[51] G.B.R., B 3/3, p. 766.
[52] Ibid. G 3/SIb 2; SO 7.
[53] Ibid. G 8/3–4.
[54] Ibid. B 3/8.
[55] Ibid. 7, f. 78A v.
[56] Ibid. F 4/6, pp. 336 sqq., 367, 374 sqq.
[57] Ibid. B 3/3, pp. 351, 354, 363, 376–7, 382; P.R.O., C 5/419/102.
[58] P.R.O., C 5/419/102.

[59] Rudder, *Glos*. App. pp. vi–vii; G.B.R., B 3/3, p. 506.
[60] G.B.R., B 3/3, pp. 503, 592.
[61] Ibid. pp. 554–5, *et passim*.
[62] Ibid. p. 730.
[63] P.R.O., C 5/631/6.
[64] G.B.R., F 4/7.
[65] Fosbrooke, *Glouc*. 211.
[66] G.B.R., B 3/8, p. 29.
[67] Hyett, *Glouc*. (1906), 192.
[68] Above, social structure; G.B.R., B 3/8, pp. 431–2.
[69] G.B.R., G 3/SO 7, ff. 149v., 205v., 225.

development was the growing power and effectiveness of parish vestries, select bodies whose members were quite frequently recruited from the city's ruling élite.[70]

During the post-Restoration period Gloucester's civic leaders became steadily more conscious of the need to promote urban improvement, not least to attract the patronage of the county gentry. In 1694 the council sought to supplement the supply of piped water from Robins Wood Hill by authorizing the erection of an engine below Westgate bridge to pump river water into the city.[71] A fire-engine house was built adjoining Trinity tower in 1702,[72] and the quay was enlarged in 1713.[73] By the early 18th century, following the London fashion, a variety of rather crude royal statues gazed down on the streets to impress the gentry.[74] It was a time of positive advances in urban government.

Religious and Cultural Life

At the Restoration the godly religious regime which had been established earlier in the 17th century was overturned. Some ministers conformed to the new Anglican order; others like James Forbes suffered ejection and harassment under the Uniformity and Conventicle Acts.[75] Most of the city's lectureships were phased out: that in St. Michael's church ceased in December 1661.[76] Pensions to puritan veterans like the widow of John Workman came to an end.[77] The cathedral and with it the city library was restored to the dean and chapter.[78]

In the late 1660s quarter sessions heard a number of cases against dissenters for non-attendance at church.[79] After the failure of Exclusion the Tory magistracy launched a systematic persecution of nonconformists.[80] Despite those onslaughts the evidence suggests that nonconformity survived as an influential force in Gloucester's religious life in the late 17th century. The Independent or Congregationalist church, led by James Forbes, had the largest following. In 1672 Forbes was licensed under the Declaration of Indulgence to hold a meeting at Sampson Bacon's house,[81] and in the late 1670s he was said to be 'preaching to at least a hundred auditors'.[82] About 1680 the Tory mayor arrested and imprisoned Forbes, but succeeded only in stirring up the dissenting interest.[83] Forbes was released after government intervention and moved outside the city, but continued to plague the authorities. Bishop Frampton denounced him in 1682 as 'the source of all the schisms that we have had in and about Gloucester'.[84] Forbes resumed his work in Gloucester in 1687 after James II's introduction of toleration.[85] As well as Forbes's group, there were several other Independent congregations in the city in the early 1670s, and the Baptists and the Quakers had small meetings after the Restoration.[86] About 1664 John Edmonds was charged with distributing Quaker tracts, and a few years later the wealthier Bristol meeting donated funds for the relief of the Gloucester Friends.[87] In 1670 a monthly meeting was established in the city and a number of Quakers were imprisoned in the early 1680s.[88]

[70] G.D.R. vol. 221 (churchwardens of St. Michael versus Freeman and Marshall); Clark, 'Civic Leaders', 325.
[71] G.B.R., B 3/7, ff. 57v., 86v., 100; below, Public Services.
[72] Below, Public Services.   [73] Below, Quay and Docks.
[74] Below, Public Buildings.
[75] Calamy Revised, ed. A.G. Matthews, 204–5.
[76] G.B.R., B 3/3, p. 214.   [77] Ibid. p. 258.
[78] Eward, Cat. of Glouc. Cath. Libr. p. viii.
[79] G.B.R., G 3/SIb 2, pt. i, pp. 360–1, 369.
[80] Ibid. pt. ii, p. 196, et passim.
[81] Original Rec. of Early Nonconf. ed. G. L. Turner

(1911), i. 600.
[82] G.D.R. vol. 221 (office versus Forbes).
[83] Cal. S.P. Dom. 1680–1, 45–6.
[84] Bodl. MS. Tanner 316, f. 251.
[85] Calamy Revised, ed. A. G. Matthews, 205.
[86] Original Rec. ed. Turner, i. 600; below, Prot. Nonconf.
[87] Extracts from State Papers Relating to Friends 1654–1672, ed. N. Penney (1913), 228; Minute Book of the Men's Meeting of the Soc. of Friends in Bristol 1667–1686 (Bristol Rec. Soc. xxvi), 33–4.
[88] Glos. R.O., D 1340/A 1/M 1; Cal. S.P. Dom. Jan.–June 1683, 133.

The continuing strength of dissent after the Restoration was partly due to the decay of the church courts.[89] Also, one of the leading clergy in the cathedral, Edward Fowler, was an avowed Whig and supporter of toleration.[90] Effective persecution was impeded by the fact that dissenters were elected to parish office in considerable numbers and formed a substantial minority on the corporation.[91] Sudden reversals of government policy, with the proclamation of toleration in 1672 and under James II, also brought campaigns against dissent to a halt.

After the Revolution of 1688 and the final advent of toleration James Forbes was the leading figure in city nonconformity. He sought to bring together the different groups; he opened his vast library to other dissenting ministers; and he educated young men for the ministry. In 1699 the Barton Street meeting house was built for him.[92] Already before his death in 1712 there were strains in the congregation and by 1716 a large part had seceded to form a separate church.[93]

The established church remained in the doldrums after the Restoration. The dean and chapter devoted much of their energy to recovering control of property in and out of the city which had been lost during the Interregnum;[94] they regained their jurisdiction over the close in 1672.[95] The parish unions made in 1648 were reversed but the five demolished churches were not replaced and the inhabitants of their parishes continued to attend the churches of larger parishes; a sixth church, Holy Trinity, was demolished, except for the tower, in 1699.[96] Pluralism was widespread,[97] and other abuses also reappeared. The large parish of St. Mary de Lode, which was impropriated to the dean and chapter and was reputedly worth £500 per annum, had a meagrely paid vicar who engaged in litigation with the chapter to try and obtain a share of the great tithes.[98]

A more lively element in the city's cultural life in the later Stuart period was education. There is little evidence for the petty or primary schools, but there may have been a sizeable number. John Collier, for instance, kept a writing school in the 1680s with various writing tables and forms in his house and a small collection of teaching books.[99] A charity school started by subscription in 1700 was teaching basic learning to over 80 children in 1711.[1] In 1666 the Londoner Sir Thomas Rich endowed a more advanced, bluecoat school on the model of Christ's Hospital to teach 20 poor boys.[2]

The principal endowed schools in the city remained the College school in the cathedral and the Crypt school. Abraham Hague was master of the Crypt from 1656 to 1696 and was said in 1675 to have 'bred several scholars, some whereof are now eminent men in the university'; on occasions other schools tried to lure him away to teach in them.[3] After Hague's death, however, there was a considerable turnover of masters and by 1719 the school was in 'such a condition that . . . parents though burgesses are obliged to send their children to other schools for education at great charges'.[4] At the College school the master from 1673 to 1684 was Oliver Gregory, a former usher of the Crypt. Gregory was a rigorous teacher with a particular gift for teaching Greek: according to one account 'he became famous in Greek by reading all

[89] Glos. Colln. 10633(76).

[90] D.N.B.; E. Fowler, Resolution of this Case of Conscience (Lond. 1683), 53–4.

[91] G.D.R. vol. 219 (churchwardens of St. Michael versus Freeman and Marshall); above, city govt. and politics.

[92] Calamy Revised, ed. A. G. Matthews, 205.

[93] Ibid.; G. F. Nuttall, 'George Whitefield's "Curate"', Jnl. Eccl. Hist. xxvii. 374 sqq.; below, Prot. Nonconf.

[94] P.R.O., C 6/155/110; C 6/230/73.

[95] Above, city govt. and politics.

[96] Below, Churches and Chapels.

[97] Glos. R.O., D 262, ff. 246–248v.

[98] P.R.O., C 5/140/19.

[99] G.D.R. invent. 1688/117.

[1] Below, Educ., elem. educ., Poor's sch.

[2] Ibid. Sir Thos. Rich's sch.

[3] Austin, Crypt Sch. 110–11; G.D.R. vol. 221 (office versus Littleton); for Hague, cf. P. Ripley, 'A Seventeenth-Century Consistory Court Case', Trans. B.G.A.S. c. 213–17.

[4] G.B.R., B 3/9, f. 57v.

authors, prose and verse, occasioned by his being overdone [beaten] once by an antagonist in Greek'.[5] His successor Maurice Wheeler, master until 1712, was even better known, attracting numerous sons of the gentry to the school from a wide area of the county.[6] In the 1670s it was described as 'a long, spacious, lightsome school'; the library was very extensive with a number of historical, geographical, and mathematical works.[7] In addition to the endowed grammar schools there were also various private establishments. In 1677 at least five private schools were operating in the city. Between 1708 and 1712 there was a dissenting academy with a number of students.[8] In George I's reign Mrs. Shelton advertised her school near the cathedral where 'young ladies may be boarded at reasonable rates and taught several sorts of work'.[9]

Literacy rates seem to have been rising. In the case of Gloucester men appearing as witnesses in the church courts in the years 1660–85, 88 per cent could sign their own names; among women the proportion was a third.[10] Evidence from wills also shows a fairly high level of literacy; 74 per cent of male testators between 1660 and 1739 could sign their names; the comparable figure for women was 49 per cent. On the other hand there remained important variations according to occupational grouping. Among testators in the period 1660–1739 virtually all the gentlemen and professional men could sign; the proportion was 64 per cent for tradesmen and artisans and 41 per cent for yeomen.[11] Much of the impetus for educational expansion came from the growth of internal trade and rising living standards among the middling and lower orders. Also significant, however, was the growing influence of the county gentry. Gloucester by the early 18th century was a tolerably civilized city. In addition to the cathedral library it had several booksellers, most notably Gabriel Harris, who also published various books.[12] The earliest detailed history of the city and county was compiled by a Gloucester man, Abel Wantner (d. 1714), parish clerk of St. John the Baptist.[13] The city's first newspaper appeared in 1722.[14]

The emergence of Gloucester as a social centre led to an efflorescence of cultural activities to entertain the gentry and other well-to-do folk. There were concerts of vocal and instrumental music at the Tolsey and elsewhere in the city with soloists from Bristol and Bath.[15] A music club flourished, holding its annual feast on St. Cecilia's day attended by a large number of ladies and gentlemen; there were also monthly gatherings and private rehearsals which were sometimes held at the deanery.[16] City printers published works by local musicians with long lists of Gloucester subscribers.[17] By 1718 the music meeting (later the Three Choirs festival) had been established.[18] Other fashionable entertainments included balls and assemblies at the Tolsey,[19] plays, usually performed by touring companies,[20] and early scientific exhibitions and lectures.[21] Civic rituals were increasingly oriented towards the gentry. Thus the nomination day feast was frequently attended by prominent landowners.[22] By the 1720s Gloucester enjoyed the economic, social, and cultural buoyancy of a reviving county town.

[5] Bodl. MS. Rawl. D.191, ff. 7v.–8, 18 and v.
[6] V.C.H. Glos. ii. 331.
[7] Bodl. MS. Corpus Christi 390/1, f. 142; 390/3, f. 205.
[8] G.D.R. vol. 220 (reversed); ibid. B 4/1/1056; below, Prot. Nonconf.
[9] Glouc. Jnl. 11 Feb. 1723.
[10] G.D.R. vols. 205, 211, 219, 221, 232.
[11] Ripley, 'Glouc. 1660–1740', 173.
[12] Glouc. Cath. Libr. MS. 71; Plomer et al., Dict. 1668–1725, 228, 246; H. R. Plomer et al., Dict. of Printers and Booksellers 1726–75 (1932), 116; Glos. Colln. NQ 4.33.
[13] Trans. B.G.A.S. xcix. 170–2; his MS. hist., which was never published, is in Bodl. MS. Top. Glouc. c. 3.
[14] Below, Glouc. 1720–1835, social and cultural life.
[15] Glouc. Jnl. 10, 17 Sept. 1722.
[16] Ibid. 30 Nov. 1725; 1 Dec. 1730.
[17] B. Gunn, Two Cantatas . . . Set to Musick (Glouc. 1736); Glos. Colln. 26048; A. M. Broadley, Wm. and Phil. Hayes: Cat. of their Compositions (Bridport, 1900), 4–5, 7.
[18] Shaw, Three Choirs Festival, 1–2.
[19] Glouc. Jnl. 30 Nov. 1724; 23 Aug. 1725.
[20] Ibid. 2 Nov. 1724; 7 Mar. 1727.
[21] Ibid. 4 June 1728.
[22] G.B.R., F 4/7, passim.

TOPOGRAPHY 1547–1720

During the first hundred years of the period there were no major changes in the plan or extent of Gloucester. In the early 17th century there was some new building in the cathedral close[23] and, as a result of a quickening of activity in the river trade, at the quay. Most of the houses and warehouses fronting the south part of the quay were built on land leased by the city corporation in 1610, 1620, and 1633.[24] Otherwise the main activity in the late 16th century and the early 17th was the rebuilding and embellishment of the city's timber-framed houses. One indication of that process was the increase in the number of purpresture rents payable to the corporation for encroachments on the common soil: *c.* 120 such rents were payable in 1630, about two thirds of them incurred since 1544. Many were for 'underbuildings', probably for new encroachments caused by jettying, and some specified new 'parlour windows'.[25] The city's houses remained almost exclusively of timber frame until the mid 17th century. The earliest house of brick found recorded was one built by John Hanbury *c.* 1633 on the north side of Bearland.[26]

Fig. 6. A house in Westgate Street (no. 26): the elevation to the side alley

Timber framing continued to be used for street fronts and for the less visible back elevations, and, as in the late medieval period, both close studding and box framing, with decorative bracing, remained fashionable; floors were often emphasized by overhanging jetties. Among the isolated examples that survived in 1984, no. 8 Hare Lane, which is perhaps of the late 16th century, has close studding, while no. 26 Westgate Street, which was built in several stages, probably in the earlier 17th century, has ovolo-moulded mullion and transom windows and a fireplace dated 1622.[27] The latter house is of four storeys with attics, but a more common height was

---

[23] Below, Glouc. Cath. and Close.
[24] G.B.R., J 3/1, ff. 37 and v., pp. 106–8, 193; 3, ff. 75v.–76.
[25] Ibid. J 5/6; cf. ibid. 5.
[26] Ibid. J 3/3, f. 81.
[27] *Trans. B.G.A.S.* ii. 192; above, Fig. 6.

two or three storeys. A house in lower Westgate Street (the folk museum) is of three storeys with prominent gables and shallow oriel windows beneath the jetties. The 'Golden Cross' in Southgate Street is a notable example of decorative box framing, but some of the framing was evidently redesigned in the 19th century when new fenestration was inserted. No. 9 Southgate Street, which has a carved wooden fireplace with the date 1650 and the arms of the Yate family of Arlingham,[28] has the most decorative timber front in the city.

The major changes in the city during the period occurred at the time of the Civil War and Interregnum. Most notably there was a sudden reduction in its size by the burning of the roadside suburbs outside the gates by the defenders at the start of the siege on 10 August 1643.[29] As John Dorney, the town clerk, described it, the city became 'as a garment without skirts, which we were willing to part with all, lest our enemies should sit upon them'.[30] Including some pulled down in the course of the siege, a total of 241 houses was lost, later valued together with their contents at £28,740. Outside the south gate 88 houses were destroyed in Severn Street, lower Southgate Street, and Small Lane, including most of the property of Gloucester's main private landowners, the Dennis family, who had succeeded to the former Llanthony Priory property acquired after the Dissolution by Sir Thomas Bell; beyond the east gate 67 houses were destroyed in the inner Barton Street suburb; beyond the outer north gate in Newland and Fete Lane, and in Brook Street, 69 houses; and beyond Alvin gate and in Kingsholm hamlet 17 houses.[31] The destruction outside the gates was probably not total, however: a few early timber cottages remained in inner Barton Street in 1984, while the Littleworth suburb on the Bristol road south of the junction with Severn Street may have escaped the burning.[32]

After the siege no effort was made to rebuild the suburbs, but a new development, intended to make up some of the loss,[33] was promoted by the corporation within the city on land north of the castle between the quay and the west end of Longsmith Street. In Marybone Park, a railed-off piece of waste ground between the quay and Castle Lane,[34] the corporation leased 11 plots for building in 1644, 1645, and 1647, and a row of new houses was built on them fronting the south side of Quay Street.[35] The largest house, standing at the corner with Castle Lane, was built by John Singleton, an innkeeper, in 1647 and became the New Bear inn.[36] The land east of Castle Lane, known as the Bearland, was traditionally a site of common dunghills,[37] and was still used for that purpose in 1631 when the dunghill used by the Boothall inn was required to be walled off from the roadway.[38] Five houses were built on the south side of the road at Bearland on land leased by the corporation in 1644, four of them on a plot taken by a carpenter, William Sparks.[39] Another house at Bearland (later known, imprecisely, as Marybone House) was built on a plot leased in 1651 to Walter Harris, a cordwainer; it was acquired before 1686 by Alderman Benjamin Hyett,[40] a lawyer, and was later enlarged, remaining a residence of the Hyett family for several generations.[41]

[28] Plate 9; cf. Visit Glos. 1682–3, 209.
[29] Bibliotheca Glos. i. 211.
[30] Dorney, Certain Speeches, 20–1.
[31] Ibid. 70–1; for the Dennis property, cf. G.D.R. wills 1566/150; Inq. p.m. Glos. 1625–42, i. 64–6.
[32] Cf. Trans. B.G.A.S. c. 217.
[33] Dorney, Certain Speeches, 21. Several of those given building leases in Marybone Park and Bearland had lost houses in the suburbs: cf. Fosbrooke, Glouc. 70.
[34] G.B.R., J 3/1, f. 37 and v.; 3, f. 83; Speed, Map of Glouc. (1610).
[35] G.B.R., J 3/3, ff. 205v.–6, 212–13, 223v.–8v., 230–2; 4, pp. 50–1, 53–5, 63.
[36] Ibid. 3, ff. 224v.–226; 4, pp. 53–5; 5, p. 799; cf. Atkyns, Glos. plate at pp. 82–3.
[37] Cal. Pat. 1370–4, 243, 293; G.B.R., J 5/3.
[38] G.B.R., J 3/3, ff. 40v.–41; cf. ibid. 1, f. 66v.
[39] Ibid. 3, ff. 206v.–206A, 214 and v.; 4, pp. 400–1, 406–7, 418–19.
[40] Ibid. 4, pp. 182–4; 5, pp. 146–7; 6, pp. 32–4.
[41] Trans. B.G.A.S. xcix. 123–5.

The Civil War and Interregnum also saw some major changes to the city's stock of public buildings, notably the loss of several of its churches. St. Owen's was taken down at the start of the siege; in 1648 the corporation rebuilt the Tolsey, incorporating the adjoining church of All Saints within it; and in the mid 1650s the churches of St. Aldate, St. Catherine, and St. Mary de Grace were all demolished.[42] There were, however, some improvements to the secular public buildings. Apart from the new Tolsey, new market houses were provided in Eastgate Street and Southgate Street in 1655 and 1660 respectively.[43]

Fig. 7. The Island and the quay from the south, *c.* 1710, with Westgate bridge on the left and the Old Severn and the Foreign bridge at the right centre; St. Bartholomew's Hospital stands north of the main road in the Island and the great glasshouse west of the mouth of the Old Severn

In the late 17th century and the early 18th, a period when Gloucester enjoyed a new popularity as a resort for the local gentry,[44] rebuilding of some of the houses with more fashionable brick fronts began to transform the appearance of the city's principal streets. Brick was made locally from the mid 1640s,[45] and most of the new houses in the Marybone Park and Bearland development were of brick, though at least one was of timber;[46] by the end of the century brick was also being imported from Worcester and other places on the river.[47] By 1714, though gabled timber fronts still predominated in the four main streets,[48] there were substantial numbers of the new brick façades[49] with their heavy cornices, long-and-short stone quoins, and sash windows.[50] In some cases the old timber houses were merely refronted rather than being completely rebuilt, as was the case with a house in Northgate Street, for which a

[42] Below, Churches and Chapels.
[43] Below, Markets and Fairs.
[44] Above, Glouc. 1660–1720, econ. development; religious and cultural life. [45] *Trans. B.G.A.S.* xcviii. 174–5.
[46] G.B.R., J 3/4, pp. 50–1, 53–5, 63, 745; 5, pp. 146–7.
[47] *Trans. B.G.A.S.* xcviii. 176.

[48] Atkyns, *Glos.* plate at pp. 82–3, detail reproduced above, Fig. 5.
[49] Bodl. MS. Top. Glouc. c. 3, ff. 43v.-44.
[50] The main surviving groups in 1984 were at the top of Northgate St. on the E. side and in Westgate St. above the entrance to Berkeley St.

builder's contract of 1701 specified a three-storeyed brick front with six sash windows.[51]

The largest of the new brick houses were detached dwellings built away from the main streets, presumably attracted to their sites by the availability of land for large gardens. One of the earliest, built soon after 1681 when the site was leased to Alderman John Webb,[52] was a house (later called Elton House) on the south side of the entrance to Barton Street; it had a hipped roof, mullioned and transomed windows, and prominent ornamental gatepiers.[53] About 1704 Ladybellegate House, with a tall façade with seven bays of sash windows, was built by Henry Wagstaffe on the north side of Longsmith Street.[54] Bearland House, opposite the south end of Berkeley Street, was also of late 17th- or early 18th-century origin, though extended and refronted later. Despite the new building much open land remained, much of it laid out as formal gardens, nurseries, and orchards.[55]

By the end of the period the growth of commercial activity connected with the river trade had caused new industrial building in the riverside area called the Island.[56] A great conical glasshouse was built just west of the entrance of Dockham ditch (or the Old Severn) in 1694 and a conical limekiln was built east of the ditch in 1696.[57] Another building shown on a view of c. 1710, by Dockham ditch north of the Foreign bridge, was probably a glasshouse,[58] and standing by the riverside was a tall structure of four storeys and attics, possibly built as a sugar refinery.[59] By the early 18th century the Island was also the site of a number of malthouses.[60]

[51] *Trans. B.G.A.S.* xcviii. 175–8.
[52] G.B.R., J 3/5, pp. 618–20; 6, f. 290 and v.
[53] *Jnl. of Garden Hist.* i (2), 170; Glos. Colln. prints GL 40.7. The house has been demolished.
[54] M. Rogers, *Ladybellegate House, Glouc., and Rob. Raikes* (1975, Glos. R.O.), 2.
[55] Atkyns, *Glos.* plate at pp. 82–3.

[56] For bldgs. mentioned in this para., ibid., detail reproduced as Fig. 7.
[57] Glos. R.O., P 154/15/IN 1/1.
[58] Cf. G.B.R., F 4/8, pp. 354, 359.
[59] Cf. *Glouc. Jnl.* 2 Sept. 1729; 4 Nov. 1760.
[60] Ibid. 24 June 1723; 31 May 1725.

GLOUCESTER 1720–1835

TO later historians the 18th century[1] seemed a placid, uneventful era for Gloucester. G.W.Counsel, writing in the 1820s, declared that 'no interesting event . . . occurred' between the visit of James II in 1687 and the visit of George III in 1788.[2] The apparently unremarkable nature of the period was emphasized both by the stirring events of the century that had preceded it and by the increased economic activity and growth in progress at the time when Counsel was writing.

There was certainly little evidence of growth during the first 70 or 80 years of the period covered by this chapter. Such new initiatives in the field of trade and industry as there were generally proved unsuccessful. There was hardly any physical expansion, and the population barely increased. The number of people living within the city boundary was estimated at c. 5,585 in 1743[3] compared with an estimate of c. 4,990 in about 1710.[4] It is suggested that the level of population, which was reduced periodically by outbreaks of disease, notably a smallpox epidemic which killed 99 people in 1726, was maintained during the earlier 18th century only by immigration from the surrounding area.[5] In the later 18th century there was a modest increase and a figure of 7,579 people was returned in 1801.[6] In spite of the lack of growth, however, the city during the 18th century performed a dominant and varied role in the trade, communications, and social life of its region; its government, though principally under the control of the non-elective corporation, was carried on responsibly and reasonably efficiently; and substantial improvements were made to its buildings and streets.

After the Napoleonic Wars there were at last signs of progress. New initiatives culminated in 1827 in the opening of the Gloucester and Berkeley canal, which gave the city a major role in seagoing trade and laid the basis for its commercial and industrial expansion in the Victorian era. There was new building on the outskirts of the city, associated in particular with the development of a spa after 1814. The population began a steady increase. Within the city boundary it rose from 8,280 in 1811 to 9,744 in 1821 and to 11,933 in 1831; in the adjoining hamlets, some of which were affected by new building, it rose from 1,819 in 1811 to 4,249 in 1831.[7]

Economic Development 1720–91

Gloucester's economy remained on a plateau during the 18th century. The city kept its dominance of the north Gloucestershire region, which it supplied with products acquired through the river trade and with services such as banking. It was also the hub of the developing road transport system of the region. Pinmaking remained the most significant manufacturing industry, though woolstapling and other industries also gave employment in the second half of the century. There was, however, little

---

[1] This chapter was written in 1983–4.
[2] Counsel, *Glouc.* 47.
[3] Glos. R.O., D 327, p. 4.
[4] Atkyns, *Glos.* 187–92, 195.

[5] Ripley, 'Glouc. 1660–1740', 23–6.
[6] *Census*, 1801.
[7] Ibid. 1811, 1821, 1831; in 1821 and 1831 Kingsholm was included in the figure for the city.

growth in the economy, and to some observers that seemed at variance with the city's geographical advantages: a visitor in the 1750s commented on the failure of the inhabitants 'to make the most of their advantageous situation for trade'.[8] Because of the problems of navigation on the lower Severn Gloucester remained under the commercial dominance of Bristol, and some new enterprises that were attempted were thwarted by competition from Bristol.

In the early 18th century most of Gloucester's inhabitants were employed in providing for the household needs of the city and its region.[9] In the decade 1720-9 half of all apprentices registered joined the clothing trades (28 per cent), the processors of food and drink (13 per cent), and those engaged in distributive trades and transport (9 per cent). Similarly, those categories accounted during the decade for 54 per cent of men admitted as freemen on completion of apprenticeship. The other main categories attracting apprentices were then metal working (18 per cent), mainly pinmaking, and the building and allied trades (14 per cent), boosted by the rebuilding of many houses in brick at the period.[10] The individual trades attracting the highest number of apprentices are listed in Table IV.

TABLE IV: APPRENTICESHIPS 1720-9

cordwainers	53	joiners	12	glovers	7
pinmakers	41	weavers	10	carpenters	7
bakers	25	mercers	9	coopers	7
tailors	23	grocers	9	blacksmiths	6
barber surgeons	18	apothecaries	8	feltmakers	5
butchers	12	bricklayers	8	gardeners	5

Source: Ripley, 'Glouc. 1660–1740', App. XIX.

The pattern of employment remained broadly similar throughout the century, though the further development of pinmaking and the establishment of woolstapling may have increased the proportion involved in manufacturing. A trades directory of 1791 (by no means a comparable source to the apprentice registers, for it listed only master craftsmen and tradesmen and included many trades outside the apprenticeship system) recorded the most numerous groups of tradesmen, as shown in Table V.

TABLE V: TRADESMEN LISTED IN 1791

victuallers	26	milliners	11	watchmakers	7
innholders	23	pinmakers	10	cabinet makers	7
grocers	20	woolstaplers	10	hatters	6
bakers	19	carpenters	10	plasterers	6
maltsters	18	mercers	9	wine merchants	5
shoemakers	17	hairdressers	9	ironmongers	5
attorneys	16	butchers	8	tea dealers	5
surgeons and apothecaries	14	coopers	8	smiths	5
		bankers	7		

Source: Univ. Brit. Dir. iii (1794), 192–5.

[8] B. Martin, Natural Hist. of Eng. (1759), 357.
[9] Ripley, 'Glouc. 1660–1740', 44–8.
[10] Ibid. App. XVIII–XIX.

A total of 120 different trades and professions was represented in 1791,[11] reflecting the wide-ranging functions of the city and its paramount position in the economy of Gloucestershire. The two middle-sized market towns, Cirencester and Tewkesbury, then mustered 70 and 60 different trades respectively, and the growing leisure resort of Cheltenham 50.[12]

At the start of the period members of the distributive trades still provided a high proportion of the most wealthy and influential citizens.[13] At the beginning of the civic year 1720–1 the bench of aldermen included 3 mercers, a draper, and an ironmonger, and the common councilmen included 4 mercers, 4 grocers, and a draper.[14] The dominance of that group was weakened in the middle of the century by the rise to prominence of men from the pinmaking and woolstapling industries, but it remained an important element in the city. John Blanch of Barton Street, who left £950 for local charitable and religious purposes at his death in 1756,[15] and Samuel Burroughs (d. 1763), who acquired a considerable fortune and lands in several surrounding parishes,[16] were among wealthy drapers of the mid century. Grocers were represented on the aldermanic bench by Richard Webb and his son John in the 1760s and 1770s.[17] It was mainly mercers and grocers who, in the late years of the century, established the city's banks.[18]

The city's function as a supplier of goods to its region and the livelihood of the leading wholesalers, particularly wine merchants, grocers, ironmongers, and timber merchants, depended largely on the trade on the river Severn. Much of the economic activity was linked directly to goods brought up river from Bristol and down river from the industrial West Midlands.

From Bristol were brought the traditional imports of that city, wine and citrus fruits from Spain and Portugal, sugar and tobacco from the West Indies, and timber from the Baltic, as well as Bristol's own products of brass wire (used in the pinmaking industry), lead shot, glass bottles, and occasionally Hotwells water. Also carried up the river to Gloucester, though for the most part transhipped at the creeks such as Gatcombe, were goods from South Wales, particularly coal from Neath (Glam.) and Tenby (Pemb.) used by the city's maltsters, and copper and iron from Neath and Swansea (Glam.). On their voyages down river to Bristol the Gloucester trows carried such local products as malt, cheese, cider, pins, and leather, together with some goods, including Manchester wares and pottery, from up river. Wool from the Cotswolds and further afield was another regular item in the cargoes; in 1747 a Gloucester wharfinger John Harmar was acting as agent for Kidderminster (Worcs.), Birmingham, Winchcombe, and Cirencester suppliers. In some years, depending on the state of the export trade, large quantities of grain were shipped down.[19]

In the cargoes brought down the Severn to Gloucester the principal item was coal from the Staffordshire and Shropshire colleries, then the city's main source of supply;[20] the relatively undeveloped Forest of Dean coalfield was resorted to only when navigation of the river was impeded by lack of water in times of drought or by

[11] *Univ. Brit. Dir.* iii (1794), 192–5 (the names of the corp. members given show that the inf. was collected in 1791).

[12] Ibid. ii (1791), 550–1, 563–5; iv (1798), 594–6.

[13] Ripley, 'Glouc. 1660–1740', 69–70, 78.

[14] Ibid. App. XXV; cf. G.B.R., B 3/9, f. 94v.

[15] *Glouc. Jnl.* 21 Dec. 1756; P.R.O., PROB 11/830 (P.C.C. 182 Herring), ff. 327–9.

[16] *Glouc. Jnl.* 7 Nov. 1763; P.R.O., PROB 11/893 (P.C.C. 497 Caesar), ff. 65v.-66v.

[17] Glos. R.O., D 936/E 12/12, f. 21; 13, ff. 124v., 280. For

references in this section to aldermen, below, Aldermen of Glouc. 1483–1835.

[18] Below.

[19] This para. is based generally on the Glouc. port bks. for coastal trade 1720–65, e.g. P.R.O., E 190/1261/10 and E 190/1264/5 (where Francis Owen and Ric. Lewis are Glouc. shippers); E 190/1265/5 (John Harmar, Wm. Coles, Thos. Yerbury); E 190/1267/7 (Perks & Hill, Wm. Coles, Ann Rawlings); E 190/1269/1 (Thos. Humphries).

[20] *Glouc. Jnl.* 8 Jan., 25 Feb. 1740; 3 Nov. 1747; *Glouc. Guide* (1792), 4.

icing in severe winters.[21] Coalyards at the quay and at some of the inns supplied both the city and its region; in 1744 a yard at the Black Spread Eagle, in lower Northgate Street, stocked coal for collection by wagons from the Cotswolds.[22] It was the city's role as a supplier of coal to the Cotswolds that caused the corporation to oppose the schemes for a Strondwater canal in 1730 and 1759.[23]

Other goods brought from the West Midlands were ironware from Coalbrookdale (Salop.), bricks and tiles from Stourbridge (Worcs.), Bewdley (Worcs.), and Worcester,[24] and Staffordshire pottery, which a man from Newcastle under Lyme was selling at the quay in 1773.[25] Droitwich salt was another regular item.[26] A Worcester trow owner was supplying it to country chapmen at the quay in 1727[27] and a Droitwich salt merchant set up business there in 1755.[28] Three salt merchants were trading in the city in 1791.[29] Manchester goods, for which a warehouse was opened at Gloucester in 1758,[30] were also brought down by the trows.

The sale of iron and ironwares, brought from Coalbrookdale, the Forest of Dean, and South Wales, provided a good livelihood for a number of Gloucester men, who usually acted also as general wharfingers. Rowland Pytt, who held ironworks at Lydney and Lydbrook on lease from the early 1740s,[31] traded as an ironmonger from Gloucester quay. Pytt (d. 1755) also had interests in tinworks in Glamorganshire, and his son-in-law William Coles,[32] one of two ironmongers based at the quay in 1757,[33] employed a number of vessels in bringing copper, pig iron, tinplate, and coal from Swansea and Neath and coal from Tenby. Coles later settled at Cadoxton, near Neath, but continued his trade to the quay,[34] which after his death in 1779 was taken on by his son John (d. 1799).[35] Other ironmongers included John Ellis (d. 1758), who was succeeded by his son Robert and grandson Anthony,[36] and John Quarington (d. 1790) and his two sons. Both the Ellises and Quaringtons were engaged to some extent in manufacture, employing men at Gloucester in nailmaking.[37]

Dealing in timber was another activity directly connected with the river trade. John Pasco, builder and deal merchant, and his partner, Barnabas Gunn, the cathedral organist, occupied a former sugar house beside the river in 1736,[38] and Pasco and Cornelius Gardiner were importing large quantities of timber from the Baltic in the 1750s.[39] The most durable business proved to be that founded by Morgan Price, who opened a warehouse in 1756 and with a partner was importing Baltic deals in 1771;[40] he was succeeded at his death in 1776 by his son William.[41] The timber merchants were also the city's chief builders at the period. Members of the Roberts family, timber merchants and carpenters,[42] were regularly employed by the corporation during the middle years of the century,[43] and William Price was employed in the 1780s to build new markets and St. Bartholomew's Hospital.[44]

[21] *Glouc. Jnl.* 8 Aug. 1785; 22 Dec. 1788; Glos. Colln. R 22.1, entry for 1 Feb. 1763.
[22] *Glouc. Jnl.* 10 Jan. 1744.
[23] G.B.R., B 3/9, ff. 274v., 275v.; 10, f. 254v.
[24] *Glouc. Jnl.* 25 Apr. 1732; 11 July 1768.
[25] Ibid. 18 Oct. 1773.   [26] Ibid. 8 Jan., 26 Feb. 1740.
[27] Ibid. 25 July 1727.   [28] Ibid. 5, 12 Aug. 1755.
[29] *Univ. Brit. Dir.* iii (1794), 193–5.
[30] *Glouc. Jnl.* 14 Feb. 1758.
[31] C. Hart, *Ind. Hist. of Dean* (1971), 76, 87.
[32] Glos. R.O., D 936/E 12/9, f. 252; D 3117/349–50; Fosbrooke, *Glouc.* 178; P.R.O., PROB 11/822 (P.C.C. 148 Glazier), f. 363 and v.
[33] *Glouc. Jnl.* 6 Dec. 1757.
[34] P.R.O., E 190/1267/7, 14; *Glouc. Jnl.* 2 Apr. 1764; 26 June 1775; Glos. R.O., D 936/E 12/12, f. 29.
[35] Glos. Colln. 13220, ff. 125–6; Glos. R.O., D 3117/350–

4; *Glouc. Jnl.* 3 Oct. 1785; 26 Sept. 1791.
[36] G.D.R. wills 1758/149; Glos. R.O., D 936/E 12/12, ff. 208v.–209; 16, f. 131v.; *Glouc. Jnl.* 3 Jan. 1758; Glos. R.O., D 1406, Surman and Wood fams.
[37] P.R.O., PROB 11/1195 (P.C.C. 396 Bishop), f. 172 and v.; *Glouc. Jnl.* 20 Feb., 28 May, 12 Nov. 1792; G.B.R., B 3/11, f. 51v.
[38] *Glouc. Jnl.* 12 Oct. 1736; cf. Glos. R.O., D 936/E 12/10, ff. 7–8v.; A1/6, p. 253.
[39] *Glouc. Jnl.* 2 July, 6 Aug. 1751; 19 Sept. 1752; 7 Sept. 1756; 18 Apr. 1758.
[40] Ibid. 31 Aug. 1756; 2 Sept. 1771.
[41] G.D.R. wills 1776/44; *Univ. Brit. Dir.* iii (1794), 194.
[42] G.D.R. wills 1744/5; 1773/188; *Glouc. Jnl.* 8 Jan. 1745; 16 Apr. 1754.
[43] G.B.R., F 4/10–12, s.v. 'general payments'.
[44] Ibid. B 3/11, f. 367 and v.; 12, ff. 84v.–85, 119.

The sale of imported wines and spirits supported a number of other Gloucester businesses. Benjamin Saunders, landlord of the King's Head, was trading in wine by 1731,[45] and was succeeded at his death in 1763 by his son Abraham; both became aldermen.[46] Four wine merchants and four brandy merchants were active in the city in 1791.[47]

Few imported goods or goods from coastal ports came directly to the quay. In 1732 Thomas Yerbury planned to operate a brig between London and Gloucester[48] and a brig with Tenby coal was at the quay in 1754,[49] but few seagoing craft came so far up river and by 1791 the voyage had come to be regarded as impossible.[50] Some goods for the city were transhipped at the creeks of the port of Gloucester: Gatcombe was used for the South Wales trade[51] and from the 1750s Newnham merchants carried goods to and from London for Gloucester tradesmen.[52] Chepstow (Mon.) was used as a transhipment port by Gloucester's timber merchants.[53] Most goods, however, passed through Bristol, with which Gloucester trow owners maintained a regular connexion. In the 1720s and 1730s the principal owners were Richard Lewis and Francis Owen, who made the voyage each month at the spring tide,[54] and a similar pattern evidently continued later.[55] Other Gloucester men operated barges and wherries (which carried passengers) up river to Worcester[56] but the more distant carrying up river was almost entirely in the hands of owners from such places as Bridgnorth (Salop.), Bewdley, and Stourport (Worcs.).[57]

The restrictions on foreign and coastal trade imposed by the problem of navigating the lower Severn prevented any major enlargement in Gloucester's trading position. Among new schemes which foundered was an attempt in 1723 by John Blanch of Wotton to make Gloucester a centre for marketing and shipping cloth produced in the Stroud and Dursley areas and in West Midland towns.[58] The almost total lack of foreign trade made the separate Gloucester port area appear merely a hindrance. Owners of vessels from up river objected to having to take out cockets to clear the port on their way to Bristol and Bridgwater (Som.), on the grounds that their voyages were not into the open sea; they secured legal opinions in their favour in 1789 and 1792.[59]

Road communications also had a significant role in Gloucester's economy, particularly in the later 18th century as the city began to benefit from the improvements achieved belatedly by local turnpike trusts. The original Act of 1698 for the Northgate roads had been allowed to expire and a new one was acquired in 1723 with the aid of a loan from the city corporation. Of the two important routes covered by the Act, that up Birdlip Hill, leading to Lechlade and Abingdon (Berks.), then still ranked as the main London road, but that up Crickley Hill, leading to Burford (Oxon.) and Oxford,[60] was used as an alternative way to London by the 1730s[61] and later became the main London coach road.[62] The other main roads leading from the city were brought under the turnpike system in 1726. One Act covered the western road towards Ross-on-Wye (Herefs.) and Hereford, with various branches towards

[45] *Glouc. Jnl.* 25 May 1731; G.B.R., G 3/AV 1.
[46] *Glouc. Jnl.* 5 Mar. 1764; Fosbrooke, *Glouc.* 182.
[47] *Univ. Brit. Dir.* iii (1794), 193, 195.
[48] *Glouc. Jnl.* 9 May 1732.
[49] Ibid. 11 June 1754.
[50] Ibid. 28 Nov. 1791; P.R.O., RAIL 829/4, p. 284.
[51] *Glouc. Jnl.* 2 Apr. 1764; 26 June 1775.
[52] *Trans. B.G.A.S.* xcvii. 93–100.
[53] *Glouc. Jnl.* 7 Sept. 1756; 18 Apr. 1758.
[54] P.R.O., E 190/1261/10; E 190/1262/6.
[55] For some of the later owners, see *Glouc. Jnl.* 4 Jan. 1737;

12 Aug. 1740; 14 Dec. 1742; 28 Mar. 1758; 26 June 1759; 30 Mar. 1762; 21 Sept. 1789.
[56] Ibid. 28 Aug. 1739; 20 June 1749.
[57] Cf. *Gent. Mag.* xxviii. 277–8.
[58] *Glouc. Jnl.* 9 Sept. 1723; cf. ibid. 19 July 1725.
[59] Ibid. 3 Aug. 1789; 8 Mar. 1790; Glos. Colln. NF 15.14.
[60] Glouc. Roads Act, 9 Geo. I, c. 32; G.B.R., B 3/9, f. 137v.
[61] Glos. Colln. prints GL 90.1.
[62] e.g. *Glouc. Jnl.* 29 Aug. 1785; 16 Jan. 1792; *Paterson's Roads* (1808), 97–101.

Chepstow, Newent, and Worcester (then reached through Upton upon Severn),[63] and another Act covered the southern road towards Bristol, with its branch towards Bath by way of Frocester Hill, and the eastern road through Upton St. Leonards to Painswick and Stroud.[64] An Act acquired in 1756 with the active support of the corporation turnpiked the Cheltenham road, branching out of the London road at Wotton Pitch, and the Tewkesbury road[65] which, out of various routes formerly used, became established as that via Prior's Norton and Coombe Hill.[66]

In their early years the local turnpike trusts were ineffective and the dissatisfaction of road users sometimes erupted in violence. The toll gate by Over bridge on the western road was pulled down on several occasions in the early 1730s,[67] and in 1734 a mob destroyed the gates at all the approaches to the city.[68] A more energetic policy by the trusts is evident from the 1760s. The new Northgate trustees under a renewal of the Act in 1761 experimented with new methods of roadbuilding and publicized their efforts through annual reports.[69] The trustees of the western roads were active in widening and altering parts of their routes in the late 1760s.[70] The roads also benefited in the late 18th century from more durable materials acquired by the trustees: slag from the Bristol copper works was introduced c. 1769,[71] and from c. 1783 roadstone from quarries in the Avon gorge near Bristol and the Wye near Chepstow became one of the main cargoes carried up river to Gloucester quay.[72]

In 1722 a coach ran from Gloucester to London once a week, taking three days on the journey. A mercer, John Harris, was the Gloucester partner in that concern[73] until 1753.[74] It was taken on by John Turner,[75] who was the leading Gloucester coachmaster during the next 25 years, though on his London route he had a rival in Thomas Pruen of the Bell inn by 1774.[76] Turner's business apparently passed to Paine & Co., who with Isaac Thompson, landlord of the King's Head, were partners in the first London mailcoach, introduced in August 1785. Within a few weeks, however, the contract was transferred to John Phillpotts, landlord of the Bell.[77] In 1791 the mail and a London coach of Paine & Co. ran on six days a week.[78]

Coaches to Bristol and Bath ran twice a week in the 1720s,[79] and in 1733 John Harris and a rival operator were running the Bristol coaches.[80] By the 1780s Bristol coaches left the city two or three times a day.[81] The first coach from Gloucester into Wales was apparently that to Brecon established by John Turner in 1756; its arrival in Abergavenny was greeted by the ringing of the church bells,[82] but the service proved unprofitable and was later discontinued, being revived c. 1764.[83] In 1785 John Phillpotts introduced a service to Milford Haven to connect with the Irish packets.[84] Worcester and Birmingham coaches were being run in 1773[85] and a Coventry coach was established in 1791.[86]

[63] Glouc. and Heref. Roads Act, 12 Geo. I, c. 13.
[64] Glouc. Roads Act, 12 Geo. I, c. 24; cf. the renewal Act in 1746 (19 Geo. II, c. 18), which confirmed the inclusion of the road from the east gate.
[65] Glouc. Roads Act, 29 Geo. II, c. 58; G.B.R., B 3/10, f. 176.
[66] Notes on Glos. turnpikes by Mr. A. Cossons, in possession of editor, V.C.H. Glos.
[67] Glouc. Jnl. 11 June 1734; Glos. R.O., D 204/2/2, min. 19 Nov. 1733.
[68] Glouc. N. & Q. iv. 493–4.
[69] Glos. R.O., D 204/3/1.
[70] Ibid. 2/4.
[71] Ibid. 3/1, mins. 16 Jan., 19 Sept. 1769; G.B.R., F 4/11, pp. 465–6; 12, p. 138; Rudge, Agric. of Glos. 335.
[72] Glos. R.O., D 204/1/1, accts. 1786–8; G.B.R., F 4/13,

pp. 119, 250; Rudge, Agric. of Glos. 334.
[73] Glouc. Jnl. 11 June 1722.
[74] Ibid. 30 Oct. 1753.
[75] Ibid. 25 Nov. 1755; 13 Apr. 1756.
[76] Ibid. 7 Mar. 1774; cf. ibid. 3 Oct. 1768.
[77] Ibid. 8, 15, 29 Aug., 26 Sept., 3 Oct. 1785.
[78] Univ. Brit. Dir. iii (1794), 189–90.
[79] Glouc. Jnl. 27 Apr. 1724; 5 Apr. 1725.
[80] Ibid. 16, 23 Jan., 1 May 1733.
[81] Ibid. 15 Apr. 1782; Univ. Brit. Dir. iii (1794), 189–90.
[82] Glouc. Jnl. 9 Nov. 1756.
[83] Ibid. 30 May 1758; 2 Apr. 1764.
[84] Ibid. 5 Sept. 1785.
[85] Ibid. 15 Feb. 1773.
[86] Ibid. 3 Oct. 1791.

Wagons to London, taking four days on the journey, were being run in 1729 by Robert Arnold.[87] His widow sold the business to Samuel Manning in 1755 when there were two other Gloucester carriers operating on the London route.[88] Manning was succeeded in 1787 by his book keeper Rowland Heane[89] who sent wagons to London twice a week in 1791 and also ran a weekly wagon into South Wales.[90] On more local routes, to Bristol, Worcester, and Ledbury (Herefs.), some carriers continued to operate with strings of packhorses until the middle of the century,[91] but by the 1740s there were also wagons, run by Samuel Manning, to Bristol, Worcester, Birmingham, and Coventry.[92] Connexions with the Stroud valleys, important for Gloucester's woolstaplers, were also regularly maintained. Manning's Bristol wagon went by way of Stroud and Minchinhampton in 1773.[93]

The city's inns benefited from the volume of travelling through the city. Apart from some of the larger inns which operated coach services, others found a specialized role in road transport. The Three Cocks claimed in 1724 to be the usual lodging place for clergy travelling between Oxford and South Wales;[94] the Lamb put up Hereford and Monmouth carriers on their weekly journeys to London;[95] and the Black Spread Eagle offered grazing for the cattle of passing Welsh drovers in 1744.[96] The custom of commercial travellers had significance for some inns by the 1770s and at least one, the Lower George, later concentrated on providing accommodation for that group.[97]

Gloucester's role as a market for produce and livestock also remained a steady source of livelihood. Many neighbouring villagers, including in the 1750s between 30 and 50 country butchers,[98] had their stalls and standings in the weekly produce markets, and congestion of the streets led to the building of two new market places in 1786. Gloucester remained the principal corn market for the county. The four annual fairs also continued, though the importance of Barton Fair for the sale of cheese from the Vale of Gloucester declined at the end of the period as travelling factors increased their operations.[99] Enough, however, was sold in the city to employ three cheesemongers in 1791.[1] The marketing of cider from Severnside orchards also employed some citizens during the period,[2] and Severn salmon continued to be sold through Gloucester in the 1750s when it was carried to London by fast fish-carts run by the coachmaster John Turner.[3] Market and nursery gardens, supplying the needs of the city, were a feature of the inner suburbs, in the London road, in lower Southgate Street, and at Chapel House.[4] James Wheeler, a Gloucester nurseryman who published the *Botanist's and Gardener's New Dictionary* in 1763,[5] was followed in the business by several generations of his family.[6]

Gloucester's chief manufacturing industry during the period was pinmaking.[7] In the early 18th century it was an expanding trade, attracting many new apprentices: 32 were registered in the years 1710–19, 41 in 1720–9, and 49 in 1730–9.[8] In 1744 it was said to bring c. £300 a week into the city, and in the early 1770s it was estimated that c. £20,000 a year was earned from sales in London,[9] the chief market for Gloucester pins. The later 18th century was probably the most profitable time for the industry,

[87] Ibid. 1 Apr. 1729.
[88] Ibid. 1 Apr. 1755.   [89] Ibid. 26 Feb. 1787.
[90] *Univ. Brit. Dir.* iii (1794), 190.
[91] *Glouc. Jnl.* 9 Sept. 1735; 9 Sept. 1740; 15 July 1755.
[92] Ibid. 29 Mar. 1743; 9 Apr. 1745.
[93] Ibid. 15 Feb. 1773; cf. ibid. 12, 19 July 1790.
[94] Ibid. 30 Nov. 1724.
[95] Ibid. 16 Oct. 1739.
[96] *Glouc. Jnl.* 10 Jan. 1744.
[97] Ibid. 26 Mar. 1770; 7 Dec. 1807.
[98] G.B.R., F 4/10, pp. 304, 521.

[99] Below, Markets and Fairs.
[1] *Univ. Brit. Dir.* iii (1794), 192–4.
[2] *Glouc. Jnl.* 4 Feb. 1752; 2 Dec. 1755; 15 June 1778.
[3] Ibid. 25 Nov. 1755; 5 Apr. 1757.
[4] Ibid. 15 Nov. 1748; 8 Mar. 1757; 21 Mar. 1785.
[5] Copy in Glos. Colln. 10028.
[6] e.g. Glos. R.O., D 936/E 12/16, f. 52; *Pigot's Dir.* (1822–3), 58.
[7] *Glouc. Jnl.* 29 Apr. 1735; *Univ. Brit. Dir.* iii (1794), 187.
[8] Ripley, 'Glouc. 1660–1740', 273.
[9] Rudder, *Glos.* 124.

indicated by the accession of five pinmakers to the bench of aldermen between 1768 and 1785. Among them were John Jefferies (d. 1778) and his son John, who were successively partners of Thomas Weaver[10] in one of the most successful firms; it was selected to be visited by George III when he came to the city in 1788.[11] Another business was run by the Cowcher family, including Alderman William Cowcher (d. 1785), and there were a number of smaller firms, making a total of nine in 1791.[12]

Gloucester's main contribution to the textile trades in the period was through woolstapling and woolcombing. Established on a small scale by the 1720s,[13] woolstapling was apparently a growing trade in 1752 when a house was advertised as suitable for a woolstapler,[14] and stapling and combing were mentioned in 1755 among the 'new trades' which were to be allowed to register apprentices in the same way as the old company trades.[15] Several men came to prominence through woolstapling, the first to become aldermen being John and Edward Baylis in 1760. The case of Alderman John Bush, who died in 1781 leaving over £8,000 among his relatives, indicates the substantial profits to be made in the trade at the period.[16] Nine woolstaplers and two woolcombers were in business in the city in 1791.[17]

Gloucester's involvement in the making of woollen cloth had almost lapsed by the early 18th century.[18] When a Woodchester clothier Benjamin Gegg began to operate new fulling and napping mills in Barton Street in 1741 there were hopes of a revival,[19] but his business is not found recorded later and was possibly the only venture into those branches of clothmaking during the period. A few weavers continued to work in the city, however,[20] and dyeing was being carried on at a dyehouse in the Island in 1755[21] and at Morin's Mill, in Brook Street, from 1782.[22]

The malting industry was of considerable importance. Numerous malthouses operated during the 18th century, many of them in the Island where they were conveniently situated for shipping malt to Bristol and for taking in supplies of Tenby malting coal.[23] Three city aldermen followed the trade in 1720[24] but there were no later recruits to the bench from it, though it remained a major industry. In 1791 there were 18 maltsters in the city, most combining the business with some other trade.[25]

Ropemaking and sackmaking provided some employment. Richard Evans, presumably a successor of the man of the same name recorded in the trade in 1731,[26] was carrying on an extensive ropemaking business at his death in 1781;[27] he was succeeded by his nephew Luke Church.[28] In 1791 ropemaking was listed with pinmaking, woolstapling, and malting as the city's chief trades, though the businesses of Church and another man were then the only two.[29] Brushmaking, established in the city by 1730,[30] was included among the new trades that were coming to the fore in 1755,[31] and there were three brushmakers in 1791.[32] The making of edgetools was introduced from Cirencester c. 1759 by William Cox.[33] Among older trades brickmaking continued in the meadows on Alney Island.[34] In the late 18th century

[10] Glos. R.O., D 3117/3953, 3955, 3957.
[11] Glouc. Jnl. 28 July 1788.
[12] Univ. Brit. Dir. iii (1794), 192-3, 195.
[13] Ripley, 'Glouc. 1660-1740', App. XVIII-XIX.
[14] Glouc. Jnl. 4 Feb. 1752.
[15] G.B.R., B 3/10, f. 200v.
[16] P.R.O., PROB 11/1078 (P.C.C. 286 Webster), ff. 357-358v.
[17] Univ. Brit. Dir. iii (1794), 192-5.
[18] Ripley, 'Glouc. 1660-1740', 65.
[19] Glouc. Jnl. 20 Jan. 1741; 9 Mar. 1742.
[20] Ripley, 'Glouc. 1660-1740', App. XVIII-XIX.
[21] Glouc. Jnl. 10 June 1755.
[22] Glos. R.O., D 3117/930.

[23] Ripley, 'Glouc. 1660-1740', 57.
[24] Ibid. App. XXV.
[25] Univ. Brit. Dir. iii (1794), 192-5.
[26] G.B.R., B 3/9, f. 294v.
[27] Glouc. Jnl. 8 Jan. 1781.
[28] Ibid. 10, 17 June 1782.
[29] Univ. Brit. Dir. iii (1794), 187, 193-4.
[30] G.B.R., B 3/9, f. 285.
[31] Ibid. 10, f. 200v.
[32] Univ. Brit. Dir. iii (1794), 193-5.
[33] Southgate chap. reg. (in possession of United Reformed Ch. provincial archives, Leamington Spa), baptisms 1759; Glouc. Jnl. 3 Feb. 1766; cf. Counsel, Glouc. 219.
[34] G.B.R., B 3/9, f. 230 and v.

bricklayers and builders owned a works at Pool Meadow and also dealt in bricks and tiles shipped from the West Midlands. Limekilns were operated at Pool Meadow[35] and at the quay.[36]

At the Gloucester bell foundry Abraham Rudhall (d. 1736) was joined by his son Abraham (d. 1735), and the business was later carried on by the younger Abraham's son Abel (d. 1760).[37] Francis Tyler ran the business for some years during the minority of Abel's son[38] Thomas, after whose death in 1783 the foundry in Oxbode Lane was run by his brother Charles and half-brother John.[39] The firm established a near monopoly of the local church trade as well as supplying bells further afield. In 1789 John Rudhall claimed that 4,000 church bells had been cast by the firm in its hundred years of existence.[40]

Industries which had a more spasmodic existence were glassmaking and sugar refining. Two glasshouses were apparently in production in the early 1720s, the large conical building at the quay and one north of the Foreign bridge; the latter was then occupied by a member of the Wilcox family, who had permission to take boats to it up Dockham ditch.[41] In 1740 the glasshouse at the quay was taken on by a partnership consisting of six Gloucester tradesmen (four of them grocers), Henry Powell, a Bristol bottle maker, and John Platt of Bristol who was to manage the business; the partners put a sum of £1,500 into the firm.[42] The following year glass bottles, pickling and butter pots, and melon glasses were being produced,[43] but the venture came to an end in 1744 after the death of Platt and some of the other partners.[44] The great glasshouse was evidently in production again in 1778 when a Gloucester wharfinger offered glass bottles for sale as cheap as at the glasshouse.[45] No later record of glassmaking has been found, and its failure to get firmly established was later attributed to Bristol competition.[46] A sugar house for refining imported sugar was in operation in the Island in 1722.[47] In 1729, however, the refiner John Pinfold moved his business to Bristol and a group of Bristol refiners took over the Gloucester premises for warehousing sugar destined for the Midlands.[48] In the late 1750s the sugar house was once more put to work refining,[49] but it was for sale in 1760[50] and that venture too was later said to have been ended by the manoeuvres of Bristol refiners.[51]

Another industry which failed to establish itself was shipbuilding. Three partners planned to open a yard at the quay for building trows and other vessels in 1755,[52] but the business is not recorded later and shipbuilding was not revived until the early 19th century.

The supply of luxury goods and services to the gentry of the surrounding countryside and to wealthy citizens employed many Gloucester tradesmen. They included booksellers (notably the aldermen Gabriel Harris (d. 1744) and his son Gabriel),[53] printers (of whom Robert Raikes and William Dicey, founders of the *Gloucester Journal* in 1722, are the earliest known),[54] sellers of musical instruments,[55] dancing masters, miniature painters, an engraver (Thomas Bonnor, fl. 1763,

[35] *Glouc. Jnl.* 17 Feb. 1761; 4, 11 July 1768; 7 Jan. 1782; cf. Hall and Pinnell, *Map of Glouc.* (1780).
[36] *Glouc. Jnl.* 12 July 1762; 23 Nov. 1789.
[37] *Glos. Ch. Bells*, 61–2.
[38] *Glouc. Jnl.* 8 Apr. 1760; 12 Jan. 1762.
[39] *Glos. Ch. Bells*, 63; *Glouc. Jnl.* 27 Oct. 1783.
[40] *Glouc. Jnl.* 12 Oct. 1789.
[41] G.B.R., F4/8, pp. 354, 359, 444, 449; cf. Atkyns, *Glos.* plate at pp. 82–3.
[42] Glos. R.O., D 3117/23.
[43] *Glouc. Jnl.* 19 May, 16 June 1741.
[44] Ibid. 1 May 1744.
[45] Ibid. 15 June 1778.
[46] Counsel, *Glouc.* 219.
[47] G.B.R., B 3/9, f. 119.
[48] *Trans. B.G.A.S.* lxxxiv. 130–1; lxxxv. 180–3.
[49] Martin, *Natural Hist. of Eng.* 357.
[50] *Glouc. Jnl.* 4 Nov. 1760.
[51] *Glouc. New Guide* (1802), 124.
[52] *Glouc. Jnl.* 18 Nov. 1755.
[53] P.R.O., PROB 11/732 (P.C.C. 94 Anstis), f. 357 and v.; *Glouc. Jnl.* 24 Apr. 1744.
[54] *Glouc. Jnl. Bicentenary Hist. Suppl.* (1922).
[55] *Glouc. Jnl.* 26 Feb. 1745.

1807), gunsmiths,[56] makers of hunting saddles,[57] and coach builders (including a business carried on for many years from the 1760s by the Marsh family);[58] there were also the more numerous watchmakers, wigmakers, milliners, and hairdressers.[59] Some men, including jewellers and silversmiths of the Jewish community established in the city from *c.* 1764,[60] travelled out into the surrounding area in search of customers. Henry Whittick, described in 1791 as a hairdresser, perfumer, and umbrella maker,[61] visited race meetings in the county and as far afield as Cardiff and Cowbridge (Glam.) with an assortment of luxury goods ranging from jewellery to guns.[62] The gentry attracted to Gloucester's own race meeting and the triennial music meeting increased the trade of such men and also brought an influx of hairdressers and other travelling tradesmen.[63]

At the end of the period banking became one of the principal services that Gloucester supplied to its region. James Wood's bank was continued after his death in 1761, together with his mercer's business, by his son Richard.[64] A goldsmith Thomas Price also acted as a banker in 1747 and until at least 1758.[65] The grocers Samuel Niblett and his son John were in business as bankers by 1783[66] and are said to have begun as travelling bankers, visiting markets and fairs in the region. In 1789 they were joined in partnership (in what was known as the Old Bank) by James Jelf, a man who, unusually, came into banking by apprenticeship rather than from another trade.[67] Another banker by 1785 was John Turner[68] who later took into partnership the mercer Edwin Jeynes. The mercer Merrot Stephens was also a banker by 1791, bringing the number of banks in the city to four.[69]

Lawyers continued to be a strong element in the city. Fourteen Gloucester attorneys were mentioned in the 1720s,[70] and 16 attorneys and 2 barristers were practising there in 1791.[71] The various administrative bodies which, besides private practice, gave employment to such men are indicated in the career of Thomas Stephens (d. 1723), who was registrar of the diocese, clerk of the peace for the county, and town clerk of the city.[72] Few lawyers, however, sought a role on the corporation at the period. An exception was William Lane who was deputy town clerk in the 1770s[73] and later became an alderman; he bought farms in Lea (Herefs. and Glos.) and English Bicknor and at his death in 1789 left £1,000 to endow a charity school in his native Mitcheldean.[74]

The medical needs of the inhabitants of the city and its region were supplied in the earlier 18th century mainly by apothecaries, who numbered at least ten in 1739; several achieved the rank of alderman. There were apparently no more than two qualified physicians in the earlier 18th century[75] but the number of physicians and surgeons increased later, encouraged partly by the founding of the Gloucester Infirmary in 1755.[76]

[56] *Univ. Brit. Dir.* iii (1794), 192–3; and for Bonnor, *D.N.B.*

[57] *Glouc. Jnl.* 1 Apr. 1755.

[58] *Univ. Brit. Dir.* iii (1794), 193–4; *Glouc. Jnl.* 27 Mar. 1820; 8 July 1837.

[59] e.g. *Univ. Brit. Dir.* iii (1794), 192–5; *Glouc. Jnl.* 2 May, 20 June 1749; 27 Jan. 1756; Glos. R.O., D 936/E 12/14, ff. 117v., 133.

[60] *Jewish Monthly*, ii (1948), 473; below, Other Religious Bodies.

[61] *Univ. Brit. Dir.* iii (1794), 195.

[62] *Glouc. Jnl.* 18 July 1785; 15 June 1807; 19 Sept. 1808.

[63] Ibid. 6 Sept. 1784.

[64] Glos. R.O., D 936/E 12/9, ff. 94v.–95; 13, f. 47v.; Fosbrooke, *Glouc.* 140.

[65] *Glouc. Jnl.* 6 Oct. 1747; 20 June 1758.

[66] G.B.R., B 3/11, ff. 339v.–340; cf. ibid. ff. 152v., 161v.

[67] Glos. Colln., Hannam-Clark papers, TS. notes on Glouc. bankers: 'Nibletts (later Evans and Jelf)'.

[68] G.B.R., B 3/12, f. 11.

[69] *Univ. Brit. Dir.* iii (1794), 189, 194–5.

[70] Ripley, 'Glouc. 1660–1740', 79.

[71] *Univ. Brit. Dir.* iii (1794), 192.

[72] Fosbrooke, *Glouc.* 211; G.B.R., B 3/9, f. 146.

[73] G.B.R., F 4/12, s.v. 'annuities, fees, and wages'.

[74] P.R.O., PROB 11/1191 (P.C.C. 193 Bishop), ff. 11v.–19v.; *Glouc. Jnl.* 21 Dec. 1789.

[75] *Glouc. Jnl.* 10 July 1739; 9 Sept. 1760.

[76] *Univ. Brit. Dir.* iii (1794), 192; cf. G. Whitcombe, *General Infirmary at Glouc.* (1903), 88–9.

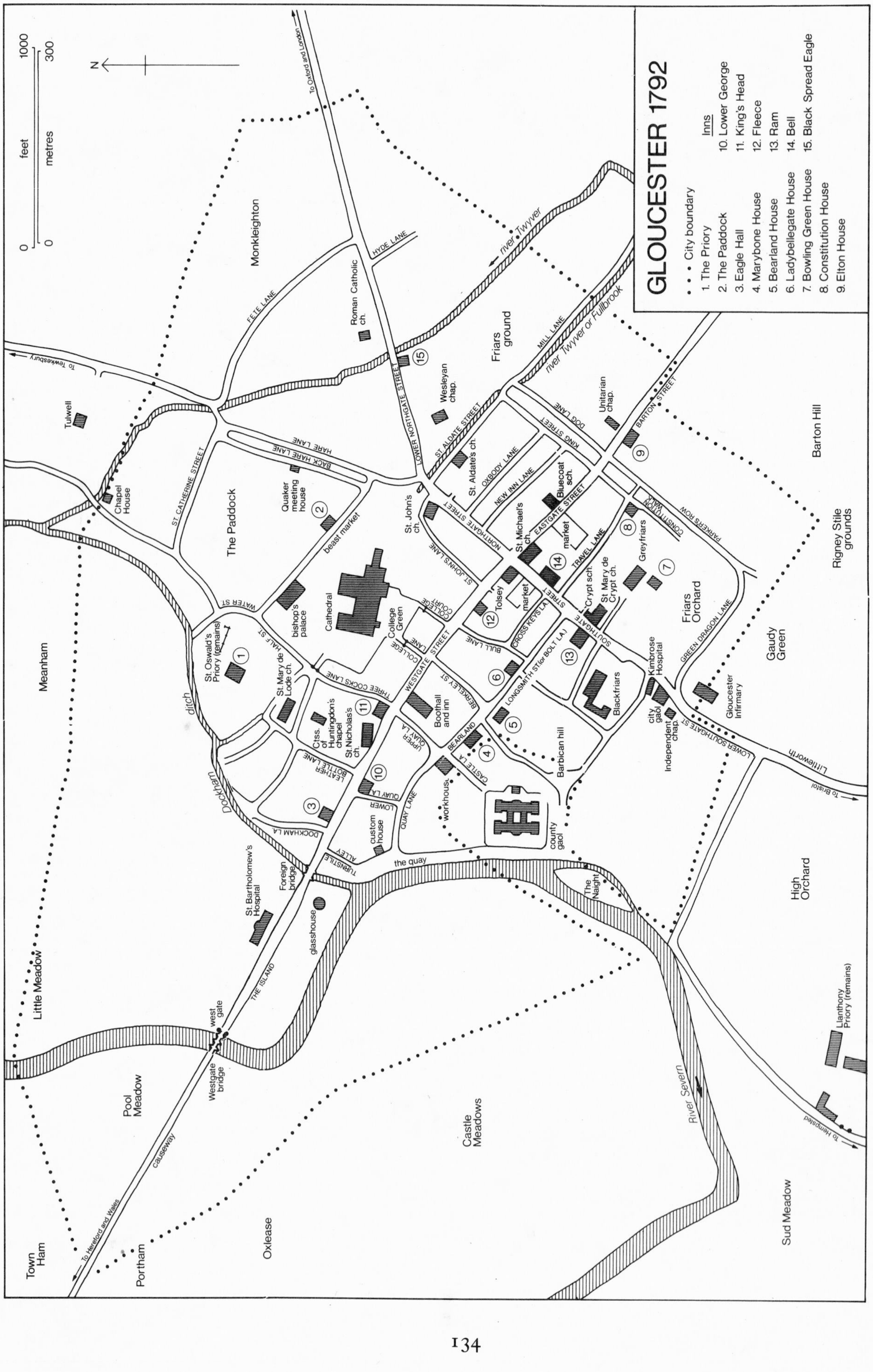
GLOUCESTER 1792
City boundary
1. The Priory
2. The Paddock
3. Eagle Hall
4. Marybone House
5. Bearland House
6. Ladybellegate House
7. Bowling Green House
8. Constitution House
9. Elton House
Inns
10. Lower George
11. King's Head
12. Fleece
13. Ram
14. Bell
15. Black Spread Eagle
feet
0
1000
metres
0
300
N
Monkleighton
Meanham
The Paddock
Little Meadow
Pool Meadow
Town Ham
Portham
Oxlease
Castle Meadows
Sud Meadow
High Orchard
Gaudy Green
Rigney Stile grounds
Barton Hill
Friars ground
Friars Orchard
Tulwell
Chapel House
To Tewkesbury
To Oxford and London
To Hereford and Wales
To Bristol
To Hempsted
FETE LANE
HYDE LANE
Roman Catholic ch.
HARE LANE
BACK HARE LANE
ST CATHERINE STREET
Quaker meeting house
beast market
WATER ST
St. Oswald's Priory (remains)
ditch
Dockham
bishop's palace
Cathedral
College Green
COLLEGE COURT
COLLEGE LANE
HALF ST
St. Mary de Lode ch.
THREE COCKS LANE
Ctss. of Huntingdon's chapel
St. Nicholas's ch.
LEATHER BOTTLE LANE
DOCKHAM LA
TURNSTILE ALLEY
custom house
LOWER QUAY LA
QUAY LANE
UPPER QUAY LA
Foreign bridge
St. Bartholomew's Hospital
glasshouse
THE ISLAND
west gate
Westgate bridge
causeway
the quay
workhouse
county gaol
The Naight
River Severn
WESTGATE STREET
BERKELEY ST
Boothall and inn
BEARLAND
CASTLE LA
Barbican hill
LONGSMITH ST (or BOLT LA)
BULL LANE
CROSS KEYS LA
Tolsey
market
St. John's ch.
ST. JOHN'S LANE
NORTHGATE STREET
LOWER NORTHGATE STREET
ST ALDATE STREET
St. Aldate's ch.
Wesleyan chap.
OXBODY LANE
NEW INN LANE
St. Michael's ch.
Bluecoat sch.
EASTGATE STREET
market
TRAVEL LANE
Crypt sch.
St. Mary de Crypt ch.
SOUTHGATE STREET
Blackfriars
Greyfriars
Kimbrose Hospital
city gaol
Independent chap.
Gloucester Infirmary
LOWER SOUTHGATE ST
GREEN DRAGON LANE
Littleworth
PARKERS ROW
CONSTITUTION WALK
KING STREET
DOG LANE
BARTON STREET
Unitarian chap.
MILL LANE
river Twyver
river Twyver or Fullbrook
Llanthony Priory (remains)

Fig. 8

Economic Development 1791–1835

In the last years of the 18th century a new spirit of enterprise, that would eventually transform Gloucester's economic fortunes, became evident. The most important potential development was the scheme for a canal to carry seagoing vessels past the most difficult stretch of the Severn. A plan was advanced in 1783 to link Gloucester with the Stroudwater canal, opened between Stroud and the river at Framilode in 1779, but it was given up when the new county gaol was built on the site planned for the terminus. A new scheme, for a canal between Gloucester and the river at Berkeley, was promoted from 1792 and an Act of Parliament was acquired the following year.[77] The scheme had strong local backing, with about 50 Gloucester men among the 129 original shareholders. Shareholders who stood to benefit directly from the canal included the leading wine merchants, the timber merchant William Price, and the wharfinger and ironmonger John Coles; it was also strongly supported by the city's bankers. Most of the other support came from places in the West Midlands which relied on the Severn navigation: among the 15 principal shareholders were the Shropshire ironmasters William Reynolds and John Wilkinson, members of the Skey family of merchants and bankers in Bewdley and Upton upon Severn (both Worcs.), William Russell, a former Birmingham merchant living near Gloucester, and men of Birmingham, Worcester, and Stourport (Worcs.).[78] In the event few of the original shareholders lived to see the canal completed; work began in 1794 but ceased in 1799 with only the basin and a few miles of the north end dug.[79]

In 1791, however, a direct overseas trade was opened up by way of the river when a brig with a cargo of Portuguese wine managed to sail up to the quay, where it received an enthusiastic welcome.[80] Regular voyages to Spain and Portugal to bring back wine, lemons, and cork were begun by two firms of merchants, which acquired their own vessels for the purpose;[81] one firm was that of Abraham Saunders (d. 1793) and his sons Abraham and David Arthur Saunders, and the other was formed by John Cooke, Edmund Stock, and Benjamin Sadler.[82] In 1820 the first cargo of French brandy brought direct to the quay was landed.[83] The direct foreign trade remained, however, subject to many difficulties, as was demonstrated in 1818 when a cargo of timber was delayed in the river for two weeks.[84] The timber trade, which was continued by William Price (d. 1815) and his son William[85] and by William Prosser,[86] was still carried on mainly through the creeks and Chepstow.[87]

Another development in waterborne commerce was the Herefordshire and Gloucestershire canal, which was promoted in 1789 and an Act acquired in 1791.[88] The scheme had the support of the city corporation, which paid part of the cost of the survey,[89] and a few Gloucester men, including William Price and Edmund Stock, were among the original shareholders, though the great majority was from

[77] C. Hadfield, *Canals of S. and SE. Eng.* (1969), 341–2.

[78] P.R.O., RAIL 829/14; and for Russell and the Skeys, Glos. Colln., Hannam-Clark papers, TS. notes on Glouc. bankers: 'Wilton & Co.'.

[79] Hadfield, *Canals of S. and SE. Eng.* 343–4.

[80] *Glouc. Jnl.* 28 Nov., 5 Dec. 1791.

[81] e.g. ibid. 19 Dec. 1791; 16 Jan., 23 Apr. 1792; 23 Sept. 1793; 10 Aug., 12 Oct. 1795; 13 Jan. 1800; 13 July, 3 Aug. 1807; 3 Aug. 1812; 3 July, 11 Sept. 1815; 15 Sept. 1817; 17 May, 9 Aug. 1819; 3 Dec. 1821.

[82] Cf. P.R.O., PROB 11/1239 (P.C.C. 570 Dodwell), ff.

72v.–73v.; *Glouc. New Guide* (1802), 148, 162; Glos. R.O., D 3117/815, 1637.

[83] *Glouc. Jnl.* 3 Apr. 1820.

[84] Ibid. 19 Oct., 2 Nov. 1818.

[85] Ibid. 4 Apr. 1891, obit. of W. P. Price; *Pigot's Dir.* (1822–3), 60.

[86] *Glouc. Jnl.* 24 Nov. 1806; Rudge, *Glouc.* 316.

[87] *Glouc. Jnl.* 5 Sept., 17 Oct. 1803; 21 Apr., 18 Aug. 1806; 29 June 1818.

[88] D. E. Bick, *Heref. and Glouc. Canal* (Newent, 1979), 8–9.

[89] G.B.R., B 3/12, ff. 124, 129v.

Herefordshire.[90] The canal was begun at Gloucester and reached Newent in 1795 and Ledbury in 1798. It raised hopes for a trade in coal from the Newent coalfield[91] and that Gloucester might replace Worcester as the chief market for fruit in the region,[92] but those hopes were not realized and the canal had little relevance for Gloucester's economic development. The stretch across Alney Island between the two branches of the Severn, providing a direct connexion with the quay, was soon abandoned and allowed to silt up.[93]

Although work on the Gloucester and Berkeley canal was suspended for many years, plans for completing it were continually discussed and helped to encourage new enterprise in the city.[94] Interest was seriously revived after 1811 when a horse tramroad was opened from Cheltenham to Gloucester, connecting with the quay and the new canal basin, and the basin was opened to the river in 1812.[95] In the following years John Upton, the clerk to the canal company, and a shareholder Mark Pearman of Coventry promoted efforts to restart work on the canal. David Arthur Saunders and the barrister John Phillpotts were among leading Gloucester men to give active support.[96] Digging finally began again in 1817,[97] and from the next year was financed in part by a loan from the Exchequer Bill Loan Commissioners. In 1820 the junction with the Stroudwater canal was made, enabling some vessels to enter the basin from the canal, but financial problems led to a further suspension of the works between 1820 and 1823.[98]

Meanwhile a considerable trade by river and coasting vessels continued at the quay and the basin. Coal began to come to Gloucester in large quantities from the Forest of Dean coalfield[99] after that was opened up in 1809–10 by the building of tramroads and docks at Bullo Pill and Lydney.[1] The traditional sources of supply from Staffordshire, Shropshire, and South Wales continued.[2] In 1822 10 coal merchants had yards at the basin, while others were based at or near the quay.[3] Mainly to accommodate that trade the canal company built a barge dock in 1825 with a series of coalyards connected to sidings of the Gloucester and Cheltenham tramroad.[4] The carriage of coal to Cheltenham was the main function of the tramroad and it also took there much roadstone, brought up river from Bristol. It brought to Gloucester building stone from the Leckhampton quarries and agricultural produce.[5] As Gloucester (and Cheltenham) expanded, building materials bulked large in the trade at the basin and quay. Welsh slate (an item recorded in Gloucester's trade from 1791),[6] Forest of Dean paving stones,[7] Stourbridge bricks, Broseley tiles, and 'Roman cement'[8] were landed. The carriage of imported goods from Bristol still employed at least one or two Gloucester trow owners,[9] and the trade in copper from South Wales also continued.[10] Leonard Darke (d. 1811) made direct sailings between Gloucester and Swansea in a small schooner, designed specifically to negotiate the shallows of the Severn estuary.[11]

[90] Notes on share reg. by M. J. Handford, in possession of editor, V.C.H. Glos.; cf. Heref. and Glouc. Canal Act, 31 Geo. III, c. 89.   [91] Bick, *Heref. and Glouc. Canal*, 8, 13–14.

[92] *Glouc. Jnl.* 9 Nov. 1795.

[93] Bick, *Heref. and Glouc. Canal*, 46.

[94] G.B.R., B 3/12, f. 372; *Glouc. Jnl.* 5 Sept. 1814.

[95] D. E. Bick, *Glouc. and Chelt. Railway* (1968, Locomotion Papers, no. 43), 9, 14, 16.

[96] Hadfield, *Canals of S. and SE. Eng.* 345; P.R.O., RAIL 829/4, pp. 405–6, 457–64, 470–1, *et passim*; RAIL 829/5, *passim*; and for Pearman, cf. RAIL 829/14; *Glouc. Jnl.* 28 Apr. 1827.

[97] P.R.O., RAIL 829/4, pp. 479, 489.

[98] Hadfield, *Canals of S. and SE. Eng.* 345–7.

[99] *Glouc. Jnl.* 24 Sept. 1810; 15 June 1812; 2 Sept. 1816;

17 Mar. 1817; 17 Aug. 1818; 3 July 1820.

[1] H. W. Paar, *Severn & Wye Railway* (1963), 20–2; *G.W.R. in Dean* (1965), 20–2.

[2] *Glouc. Jnl.* 11 Oct. 1819; 29 May 1820.

[3] *Pigot's Dir.* (1822–3), 57.

[4] Conway-Jones, *Glouc. Docks*, 24–5.

[5] Bick, *Glouc. and Chelt. Railway*, 9, 12, 14, 38.

[6] *Glouc. Jnl.* 26 Sept. 1791; 18 Nov. 1816.

[7] Ibid. 17 Mar. 1817.

[8] Ibid. 27 Dec. 1813; 1 May 1820; *Pigot's Dir.* (1822–3), 57.

[9] *Glouc. Jnl.* 16 Feb., 16 Mar. 1807; 8 July 1811; 1 Mar. 1819; 19 Feb. 1821.   [10] Ibid. 15 July 1805; Rudge, *Glouc.* 122.

[11] *Glouc. Jnl.* 8 July 1811; 29 June, 24 Aug. 1812; cf. *Glouc. New Guide* (1802), 139.

There was also a regular connexion by trow with Stroud, which had been instituted in 1779 with the opening of the Stroudwater canal.[12]

In 1825 a writer predicted that the day when the Gloucester and Berkeley canal was completed would be the most important in the city's history,[13] and when that day came, on 26 April 1827, it was marked with appropriate festivity. A convoy of vessels, decorated with flags and streamers and led by a large square-rigged ship and a brig, came up the canal while crowds lined the banks.[14] The canal, which could take ships of up to 600 tons,[15] gave Gloucester a role as a supplier of imported goods to Birmingham and a large area of the West Midlands.[16] Its effect on Gloucester's foreign trade was immediate and dramatic and a rapid growth in trade continued until the mid 1830s (Table VI).

TABLE VI: CUSTOMS RECEIPTS FOR THE PORT OF GLOUCESTER

1825	£12,711	1829	£ 57,400	1833	£106,751
1826	£19,006	1830	£ 90,282	1834	£131,118
1827	£28,550	1831	£ 94,155	1835	£160,484
1828	£45,428	1832	£109,657		

Source: Power's Glouc. Handbk. (1848), 66.

The number of ships using the canal was 4,272 in 1828 and 7,576 in 1832.[17] Corn, imported almost entirely from Ireland, rapidly became established as one of the principal imports.[18] In the late 1820s and early 1830s the first of the large brick warehouses for corn were built at the basin, where Joseph and Charles Sturge of Birmingham and George Lucy & Co. were among the earliest corn merchants.[19] Timber from Canada and the Baltic was the other chief import. William Price, who was by then in partnership with William Tupsley Washbourne, and the firm of Maurice and James Shipton of Birmingham had premises at the basin from 1827 and a third firm of timber importers had joined them there by 1830.[20] The established trade in wine and fruit from Spain and Portugal also continued. There were relatively few foreign exports, with Droitwich salt the only consistent item. In the coasting trade slate from Portmadoc (Caern.) and other Welsh ports became the most regular cargo landed at the basin, and the South Wales copper trade was continued, mainly by Brown & Sons. In 1827 a partnership including William Kendall, a prominent Gloucester wharfinger, instituted a regular service by brigs to London,[21] and vessels also came regularly with wool and corn from Bridgwater (Som.). The city already had a substantial group of merchants by 1831 when they formed the Gloucester Commercial Rooms, a society for promoting the trade of the port.[22]

Gloucester's economy also benefited from the continuing improvement of the roads. One new turnpike route out of the city, that through Whaddon and Pitchcombe to Stroud, was established in 1818,[23] and many other improvements were made by the local trusts during the 1820s. Two of the new ventures, however, the building of

[12] Glouc. Jnl. 6 Sept. 1779; 13 Dec. 1784; 30 Sept. 1805.

[13] Delineations of Glos. 17.

[14] Diary of a Cotswold Parson, 70; Glouc. Jnl. 28 Apr. 1827.   [15] Hadfield, Canals of S. and SE. Eng. 348.

[16] Counsel, Glouc. 233, 236-7.

[17] Rep. Com. Mun. Corp. 68.

[18] For the trade at the docks, see shipping listed on third page of Glouc. Jnl. from 1827.

[19] Conway-Jones, Glouc. Docks, 32, 36; Pigot's Dir. (1830), 374.

[20] P.R.O., RAIL 829/6, pp. 13, 15; Pigot's Dir. (1830), 376.

[21] Glouc. Jnl. 27 Oct., 24 Nov. 1827.

[22] G.B.R., Glouc. Commercial Rooms min. bk. 1831-4.

[23] Stroud and Glouc. Road Act, 58 Geo. III, c. 1 (Local and Personal); cf. Glos. R.O., Q/RUM 61.

bridges over the Severn at the Haw in 1825 and at the Mythe, at Tewkesbury, in 1826, threatened Gloucester's historic control of the routes to Hereford and South Wales;[24] in 1827 the city corporation campaigned strongly against plans by the Post Office to transfer the direct mail route to Hereford and Brecon to the Mythe bridge road.[25] The new routes across the Severn benefited Cheltenham,[26] which had already begun to rival Gloucester as a centre for road transport. By the beginning of the century some of the London coaches from Gloucester were being routed through Cheltenham.[27] By 1822 Cheltenham coach operators were running more services than those of Gloucester, though Gloucester was still a greater centre for the carrying trade.[28]

In the 1790s the principal Gloucester coach offices were the Bell inn and the lower Northgate Street coach office, where the Paine family was succeeded by Heath & Co.[29] In 1802 the Bell horsed both the London mail and the Bristol and Birmingham mail on the other mail route that came through Gloucester, while Heath & Co. horsed the Welsh mail and ran another London coach.[30] In the following years, in a climate of increasing rivalry among Gloucester operators, the Boothall inn, under John Spencer, emerged as one of the principal coach offices and posting houses.[31] Spencer's London coach acquired a reputation for providing Gloucester with the latest news, bringing word of the battle of Waterloo five hours before the mail.[32] The journey to London had by then been cut to 15 hours.[33] In 1822 five establishments, the Bell, Heath's office which then had the contract for the London and Welsh mails, the Boothall, the Ram, and the Lower George, were running coaches. Of the 37 services, most of them running daily, London accounted for 7 and there were others to Bristol, Bath, Birmingham, Coventry, and towns in South Wales as far as Milford Haven; there were 5 local coaches to Cheltenham.[34] In the late 1820s it was said that nearly 100 coaches a day passed through the city.[35]

The main London carrying business, that of the Heane family,[36] was taken over in 1817 by the Rodborough firm of Tanner and Baylis, which began fast fly-wagons to the capital.[37] In 1819 the firm also absorbed a carrying business formerly run by John Spencer of the Boothall.[38] In 1822, apart from the main services to London, Bath, Bristol, and Hereford, local carriers connected Gloucester to 24 market towns and villages in north Gloucestershire and adjoining counties,[39] an indication that the city's economic links with its traditional region remained as strong as ever.

The local market trade was one aspect of the economy to benefit from the improvement of the roads. The city's market area expanded at the expense of some of the lesser local markets, particularly that at Newent.[40] The markets for produce and for livestock, for which a large new market was opened in 1823, became an important source of revenue for the city corporation during the period.[41]

A number of attempts were made to establish new industry in the city, but some, before the completion of the canal, were unsuccessful. Sugar refining was re-established in the Island by Henry Ercks before 1799, when his premises were

[24] V.C.H. Glos. viii. 97, 115–16.
[25] G.B.R., B 3/14, ff. 80v.–81; Glouc. Jnl. 1, 8 Dec. 1827.
[26] Cf. Glouc. Jnl. 31 Mar., 15 Sept. 1827.
[27] Ibid. 23 May 1803.
[28] Pigot's Dir. (1822–3), 50–1, 60–1.
[29] Glouc. Guide (1792), App.; Glouc. Jnl. 17 Nov. 1794; Glouc. New Guide (1802), 152. Heath & Co. later moved to Southgate St.: Counsel, Glouc. 243.
[30] Glouc. New Guide (1802), 136–7; and for the mail routes, Paterson's Roads (1808), 97–101, 328–30.
[31] Glouc. Jnl. 23 May 1803; 11 July 1808; 16 Nov. 1818;

Paterson's Roads (1808), 22.
[32] Glouc. Jnl. 10 July 1815.
[33] Ibid. 15 Sept. 1817.
[34] Pigot's Dir. (1822–3), 61.
[35] Counsel, Glouc. 209.
[36] Glouc. Jnl. 8 Aug. 1803; 27 June 1808; Glos. R.O., DC/F 1/3, partnership deeds 1803, 1813.
[37] Glouc. Jnl. 28 July 1817.
[38] Ibid. 26 July 1819.
[39] Pigot's Dir. (1822–3), 60.
[40] Fosbrooke, Glouc. 213.
[41] Below, city govt.

devastated by fire. In 1801 Ercks found new partners but the partnership was dissolved the following year and he was later declared bankrupt.[42] In 1808 a brewery for porter and strong beer was built on the site of the sugar house.[43] It was for sale in 1812 and again in 1814[44] and had apparently closed by 1822, though there were then two other breweries in operation[45] and the city still had an extensive malting industry, carried on in 21 premises.[46] A steam flour mill, established by a group of shareholders c. 1801, was another short-lived venture.[47] More successful was an iron foundry started in the Island in 1802 by William Montague,[48] who had earlier been a partner in John Coles's ironmongery business.[49] In the late 1820s the foundry was producing castings of a high quality, using Forest of Dean iron from works at Cinderford and Parkend in which Montague had an interest.[50] He also continued to trade as a wholesale ironmonger in partnership with Charles Church.[51]

A new industry directly stimulated by the growth of waterborne commerce was shipbuilding. A yard opened at the canal basin in 1814 and in that year launched a 113-ton brig, the first vessel bigger than a Severn trow built at Gloucester within living memory.[52] The venture was apparently short lived but after the opening of the canal shipbuilding was resumed at the basin by William Hunt, who built small schooners. In 1818 John Bird of Stourport built a dry dock at the basin and subsequently he built Severn trows there as well as repairing craft.[53] By 1822 Edward Hipwood, also from Stourport, had opened a yard building small craft by the river at Westgate bridge.[54] Two sailmakers were in business at the quay in 1830.[55]

Of the old industries, pinmaking maintained its strength in the late 18th century, and in 1802 there were 11 firms, employing 1,500 people in the city and adjoining parts of the county;[56] the outworkers, who headed and packed the pins, included inmates of parish workhouses.[57] Over the next two decades the industry suffered a recession. At least four firms went bankrupt, including in 1817 the former Weaver & Jefferies firm carried on by Edward and Charles Weaver,[58] and other firms gave up trading. Only four remained in 1822[59] and only three in 1833 when they employed c. 330 people, excluding outworkers.[60] The surviving firms, which enjoyed a recovery in the trade in the 1820s, maintained warehouses in London where the large department stores were their main customers; from 1827 they operated a price-fixing ring for the London trade. In the early 1830s one of the firms, Hall, English, & Co., experimented with new machinery but the main breakthrough in mechanization was achieved in other centres than Gloucester.[61] Woolstapling suffered an earlier and more rapid decline, and by 1802 only four woolstaplers and two woolcombers remained in business in the city.[62] The industry survived at a reduced level, with five firms operating in 1830.[63]

In the late 1820s the loss of employment caused by the decline of the two main industries was said to have been made up to some extent by the growth of the rope and

[42] Glos. Colln., Hannam-Clark papers, deed 1805; *Glouc. Jnl.* 22 Apr. 1799; 11 Oct. 1802.

[43] *Glouc. Jnl.* 11 Apr. 1808; Rudge, *Glouc.* 121.

[44] *Glouc. Jnl.* 20 Apr. 1812; 7 Feb. 1814.

[45] *Pigot's Dir.* (1822–3), 57.

[46] Ibid. 56, 58.

[47] *Glouc. Jnl.* 13 Apr. 1801; 13 Feb. 1804; 15 Aug. 1808; Rudge, *Glouc.* 121.

[48] Counsel, *Glouc.* 213.

[49] P.R.O., RAIL 829/4, pp. 126, 139, 162.

[50] Counsel, *Glouc.* 214; Hart, *Ind. Hist. of Dean*, 121–2, 127–8.

[51] G.B.R., L 6/3/5; *Pigot's Dir.* (1822–3), 58; (1830), 374.

[52] *Glouc. Jnl.* 5 Sept., 31 Oct. 1814; 3 July 1815.

[53] Conway-Jones, *Glouc. Docks*, 22, 34.

[54] *Pigot's Dir.* (1822–3), 57; *Glouc. Jnl.* 30 Dec. 1899, obit. of Sam. Hipwood.

[55] *Pigot's Dir.* (1830), 375.

[56] *Glouc. New Guide* (1802), 10–12, 144–6, 148–9, 152–3, 157, 161, 165–6.

[57] *V.C.H. Glos.* x. 98, 152, 228.

[58] *Glouc. Jnl.* 27 June 1808; 1 Dec. 1817; 23 Mar. 1818; 20 Dec. 1819; 12 Nov. 1821.

[59] *Pigot's Dir.* (1822–3), 58.

[60] *Rep. Factory Com.* H.C. 450, B. 1, xx, pp. 27–8 (1833).

[61] S. R. H. Jones, 'Hall, English & Co., 1813–41', *Business Hist.* xviii. 35–65.

[62] *Glouc. New Guide* (1802), 10, 146–7, 149, 153, 166.

[63] *Pigot's Dir.* (1830), 376.

sackmaking trade, then carried on extensively by Luke Church's son Charles in partnership with James Taylor.[64] In 1833, however, the largest of the three firms in business, William Brimmell's, employed only 22 people on the premises.[65] Brushmaking was carried on by five firms, including that of Alderman Samuel Jones, in the 1820s,[66] and William Cox's edgetool making business was continued by his son-in-law James Buchanan.[67] Animal skins were dressed at a number of sites,[68] including one established since the mid 18th century by the Twyver at the north end of Hare Lane.[69] Higher up the Twyver a large new tannery was built *c.* 1811 behind the Black Dog inn in lower Northgate Street; the owner was bankrupted in 1816[70] but it was apparently one of the two tanneries working in the city in 1830.[71] The bell foundry was carried on by John Rudhall, who survived bankruptcy *c.* 1814[72] and died in 1835; his business was continued by Thomas Mears & Co. of the Whitechapel foundry.[73]

The expansion of the city that followed the Napoleonic Wars benefited the building trade, with men like William Hicks,[74] Henry Edwards,[75] and James Dewey[76] playing a leading role. In 1822, when the boom was at its peak, the city had 16 building firms.[77] Leading Gloucester architects of the period were John Wheeler (d. 1817), John Collingwood (d. 1831), and Thomas Fulljames, who all served successively as county surveyor.[78] Fulljames was the nephew of Thomas Fulljames (d. 1847) of Hasfield Court[79] who practised as a land surveyor in the city from *c.* 1797 and was commissioner for numerous Gloucestershire inclosure Acts.[80] Another Gloucester surveyor Elisha Farmer Sadler, who was much employed by the corporation in the 1820s, became an alderman in 1834.[81] Lawyers and surgeons were numerous and influential. In 1802 the city had 19 legal firms and 16 medical men.[82] The two professions accounted for a third of all new aldermen between 1800 and 1835, when the retiring bench included four surgeons.[83]

The economic development of the city and surrounding region enhanced Gloucester's role as a banking centre. Of the four banks, the Nibletts' Old Bank was carried on from the mid 1790s by the partnership of James Jelf, the barrister William Fendall (d. 1813), and the attorney Charles Evans;[84] John Turner carried on his bank in partnership with members of the Jeynes and Morris families;[85] Merrot Stephens (d. 1815) was succeeded by John Merrot Stephens;[86] and the bank of Richard Wood (d. 1792) passed to his son James ('Jemmy') Wood,[87] whose eccentricity, miserliness, and immense wealth made him one of the most celebrated Gloucester men of the period.[88] The bankers were prominent on the city corporation, including two aldermen and eight councillors in 1810,[89] and many of them owned land in the

[64] Counsel, *Glouc.* 219. *Pigot's Dir.* (1822–3), 59; 'Freemen of Glouc. 1653–1838', ed. P. Ripley (1984, TS. in Glos. R.O. Libr.), 175, 211, 221.
[65] *Rep. Factory Com.* (1833), pp. 27–8.
[66] *Pigot's Dir.* (1822–3), 57; (1830), 373; below, Aldermen of Glouc. 1483–1835
[67] Gell and Bradshaw, *Glos. Dir.* (1820), 37.
[68] *Glouc. New Guide* (1802), 145, 150–1.
[69] G.B.R., J 3/10, ff. 212v.–213; 12, pp. 339–40; 13, pp. 45–6; J 4/12, no. 60.
[70] Rudge, *Glouc.* 121; *Glouc. Jnl.* 17 June 1816.
[71] *Pigot's Dir.* (1830), 376. [72] *Glouc. Jnl.* 7 Feb. 1814.
[73] Ibid. 21 Feb., 2 May 1835.
[74] Glos. Colln. 18423(2); Counsel, *Glouc.* 188.
[75] G.B.R., B 3/13, ff. 292v.–293; *Glouc. Jnl.* 13 Nov. 1820.
[76] G.B.R., J 3/13, pp. 327–31; Glos. R.O., D 3117/19.
[77] *Pigot's Dir.* (1822–3), 56–7.
[78] Colvin, *Biog. Dict. Brit. Architects* (1978), 230, 881;

[79] *V.C.H. Glos.* viii. 284; P.R.O., PROB 11/2063 (P.C.C. 771), f. 160.
Glouc. Jnl. 3 Feb. 1817; 12 Mar. 1831; Glos. R.O., Q/SO 14, f. 224v.; 16, f. 231.
[80] Glos. R.O., index of inclosure maps; *Glouc. New Guide* (1802), 150; *Pigot's Dir.* (1822–3), 58.
[81] G.B.R., F 4/16, s.v. 'general payments'; cf. ibid. J 4/12.
[82] *Glouc. New Guide* (1802), 140–2.
[83] Below, Aldermen of Glouc. 1483–1835.
[84] *Glouc. Jnl.* 16 June 1794; Glos. R.O., D 3117/394, 784; *Glouc. New Guide* (1802), 141, 167.
[85] *Glouc. Jnl.* 10 Feb. 1794; 9 Mar. 1801; Glos. R.O., D 3117/1647, 1649.
[86] *Trans. B.G.A.S.* xc. 174.
[87] Fosbrooke, *Glouc.* 140–1; G.B.R., B 3/12, f. 199v.
[88] C. H. Savory, *Life and Anecdotes of Jemmy Wood* (Ciren. n.d.); Counsel, *Glouc.* 174; cf. below, Plate 11.
[89] G.B.R., B 3/13, f. 90v.

surrounding countryside. Samuel Niblett's purchase of estates at Haresfield and Colethrop established his descendants as prominent local landowners.[90] Charles Evans, before entering banking, had become a landowner by his marriage to the daughter of the former city M.P. Charles Barrow of Highgrove, Minsterworth,[91] and his partner William Fendall acquired an estate at Much Marcle (Herefs.).[92] The Morrises owned the Barnwood Court estate[93] and James Wood became a major landowner in Westbury-on-Severn in 1825 on the death of his cousin, the Gloucester ironmonger Anthony Ellis.[94]

The banking crisis of 1815 caused the failure of the Old Bank, which was thought to have been weakened by the involvement of Fendall and Jelf in the Bullo Pill tramroad and an abortive plan for a Severn tunnel at Newnham.[95] John Merrot Stephens failed later the same year.[96] A new bank was formed before 1820[97] by the solicitor Robert Pleydell Wilton, Thomas Washbourne, and Thomas Russell (later Russell and Skey),[98] but the next financial crisis, in 1825, closed the bank of Turner and Morris, an extensive business which included a branch in Cheltenham.[99] In the measures taken following the second banking crisis, one of the four new provincial branches of the Bank of England was opened at Gloucester in 1826.[1] The business of Russell and Skey was absorbed into the Gloucestershire Banking Co., an early joint-stock bank formed in 1831,[2] and in 1834 the National Provincial Bank opened a branch, its first in the provinces, at Gloucester.[3]

At the close of the period, despite some new industrial ventures and the beginning of the growth of the docks, Gloucester's economy was still dominated by its traditional role of distributing goods and providing services to its region. Its manufactures (though it was those that contemporary writers noted) remained a very small sector. In an analysis of the employment of adult males (over 20 years old) made in 1831 the two main industries, pinmaking and ropemaking, employed respectively c. 70 and 37; tanning employed 12, brushmaking 11, boatbuilding 8, ironfounding 8, brewing 7, and bellfounding 3. Most adult males worked as small craftsmen or in service and retail trades: they included 331 shoemakers, tailors, and other clothing makers, 295 in the bulding trades, 171 sellers of food and drink, 149 shopkeepers and other retailers, 87 smiths and other metal workers, 84 keepers of public houses, and 56 in road transport. A total of 1,663 adult males in the city was employed in manufacture, retailing, and handicrafts; another 731 were unskilled labourers; and 260 were classed as capitalists, bankers, and professional men.[4]

City Government

During the 18th century and the early 19th the corporation, particularly the aldermen in their role as magistrates, remained dominant in city government. Other citizens were able to play some part in government through the parish vestries, which elected representatives and levied rates for statutory bodies set up to administer poor relief and city improvements. Involvement of corporation members and supervision

[90] V.C.H. Glos. x. 191, 193, 235.
[91] Glouc. Jnl. 23 Mar. 1789; Fosbrooke, Glos. ii. 206.
[92] P.R.O., PROB 11/1550 (P.C.C. 591 Heathfield), ff. 136–138v.
[93] Below, Barnwood, man.
[94] Glos. R.O., D 1406, exec. papers of Ant. Ellis; V.C.H. Glos. x. 89.
[95] Glos. Colln., Hannam-Clark papers, TS. notes on Glouc. bankers: 'Nibletts (later Evans and Jelf)'.

[96] Trans B.G.A.S. xc. 174.
[97] Gell and Bradshaw, Glos. Dir. (1820), 98.
[98] Glos. Colln., Hannam-Clark papers, TS. notes on Glouc. bankers: 'Wilton & Co.'.
[99] Ibid. 'Turner and Morris'.
[1] Ibid. 'Bank of England'.
[2] Ibid. 'Glos. Banking Co.'.
[3] Glos. Local Hist. Bulletin, Spring 1984, 6–7.
[4] Census, 1831.

by the magistracy were important elements in the statutory bodies, and the local Acts which constituted them were promoted and fashioned by the corporation and city M.P.s with whom it had influence. Control by the corporation was, however, sometimes thwarted by the independent attitude of the parish vestries.

The corporation underwent no modification between the charter of 1672 and municipal reform in 1835. It remained a closed body, comprising the mayor and his fellow eleven aldermen, the two sheriffs, a maximum of 28 common councilmen, and the two largely honorary officers, the high steward and the recorder. The wider involvement of citizens in corporation decisions was limited to meetings called by the mayor to 'take the sense of the city' on matters of unusual importance, such as improvement Acts or possible threats to the city's trade.[5] Such weighty matters varied the usual round of common council business, made up of management of property, administration of the city almshouses and other charities, upkeep of the public buildings, management of the markets, and control of the freedom. Complex matters were usually referred to *ad hoc* committees.[6] From 1732 there was a standing committee to vet admissions to the freedom[7] and from 1740 there was another to survey property before leases were renewed.[8]

In the day-to-day administration of corporation business the two most important officers in the earlier 18th century were the town clerk and the chamberlain. The office of town clerk continued to be held by prominent city barristers until 1813 when an attorney was appointed for the first time.[9] The town clerk, who also acted as clerk to the magistrates,[10] was aided by a deputy from at least 1727.[11] The chamberlain, annually elected from among the senior common councilmen but usually continuing in office for a number of years,[12] had sole responsibility for the corporation's revenues until 1738. From 1738 a treasurer was appointed to hold office during pleasure and do the rent collecting and accounting, while the chamberlain (from that time one of the aldermen) retained the general supervision of property management.[13] The treasurer also served as rent collector and accountant for the three ancient almshouses and for Sir Thomas Rich's school,[14] and until 1827 the same man seems usually to have been appointed by the city magistrates in quarter sessions as treasurer for their 'county stock'.[15]

The annual corporation budget[16] which the chamberlain, and later the treasurer, administered amounted to *c.* £1,300 in the 1720s, rising to £5–6,000 by the early 1830s. As well as the revenues of the corporation in its own right, it included the revenues of St. Kyneburgh's Hospital, the Crypt school, and various minor charities; for the three ancient hospitals, under their board of governors,[17] and for Sir Thomas Rich's school the accounts were kept separately. The bulk of the income was drawn from property, which produced an annual rental rising during the period from *c.* £900 to *c.* £2,500. In addition a variable sum, £200–300 in some years, was produced by renewal fines for leases.

Apart from rents, the other consistent, though smaller, item in the corporation's income was made up of tolls on trade. In the 1720s they comprised various dues collected at the gates, the quay, and Westgate bridge, which had long formed part of

[5] e.g. *Glouc. Jnl.* 3 Feb. 1766; 16 Oct. 1780; 24 Jan. 1785.
[6] e.g. G.B.R., B 3/9, ff. 290, 316, 371.
[7] Ibid. ff. 325v.–326v.
[8] Ibid. f. 454.   [9] Ibid. 14, f. 61v.
[10] Ibid. B 4/1/5, ff. 31–2.
[11] *Glouc. Jnl.* 1 Aug. 1727.
[12] G.B.R., B 3/9 (annual elections of officers, Monday after Mich.).
[13] Ibid. ff. 426–7.
[14] Ibid. f. 427; 10, f. 125; 12, f. 284v.; Glos. R.O., D 3270/19669–70.
[15] G.B.R., B 4/1/5, f. 32 and v.; cf. Glos. R.O., P 154/11/OV 2/3, acct. 1782–3; 14/VE 2/1, min. 19 Sept. 1773.
[16] What follows on the corp. finances is based generally on the accounts for the period in G.B.R., F 4/8–16.
[17] Below, Char. for Poor, almshouses.

the fee-farm revenues, and in the early 18th century those tolls remained the responsibility of the sheriffs under an annual lease made to them by the corporation.[18] Difficulties of collection, however, made the sheriffs' office burdensome and dissuaded young men from entering the common council, and so in 1732 the tolls and responsibility for payment of the annual fee farm were transferred to the chamberlain's account, bringing to an end the historic distinction between the revenues of the sheriffs and the city chamber.[19]

After 1732 the former sheriffs' tolls were usually granted out among a number of lessees for short terms of years, though sometimes salaried collectors were used. The tolls formed four main categories, those on corn and other market produce brought into the city, those on cattle and other livestock brought to the markets and fairs or driven through the city, the water bailiff's dues charged on goods carried under Westgate bridge and landed at the quay, and 'wheelage' charged on laden wagons and packhorses entering the city.[20] In addition there were tolls which had long been leased with the Boothall inn; those collected at weights at the quay on wood and coal[21] were removed from the lease in 1742,[22] the innkeeper retaining the right to the profits of the weighing beams in the wool, yarn, and leather market in the great hall of the Boothall.[23]

For most of the period the tolls produced only small sums and were sometimes difficult to collect. Those from the Boothall weighing beams probably lapsed altogether in the mid 18th century as a result of the failure to control sales outside the market.[24] Attempts to enforce the levy of pontage charged for passing Westgate bridge apparently ceased in the mid 1720s with the failure of lawsuits brought against Severn trowmen by the sheriffs,[25] though it was still claimed later.[26] The lessee of the cattle tolls periodically encountered difficulties with the Welshmen who drove large herds through the city on their way to the fattening pastures in the Home Counties; in 1770 one drover was distrained for toll owed on 3,560 beasts.[27] Ancient exemptions, claimed by tenants of the duchy of Lancaster and freemen of the borough of Monmouth among others, also caused difficulties for the collectors.[28]

New facilities provided by the corporation enabled it, however, substantially to increase its profits from trade in the city. Shambles set up in Southgate Street from 1737 to accommodate butchers from the surrounding countryside on market days[29] produced rents of £110–20 a year in the 1740s and 1750s. A public weighing machine provided by the corporation in 1779[30] was leased at c. £50 in the 1780s; it was replaced by a new machine in Upper Quay Lane in 1815 and a second machine was installed near the Foreign bridge in 1825.[31] Cranes were provided at the quay in 1812 and 1828 for the use of the lessee of the weights there.[32] The most significant improvements were two new market places for produce opened in 1786 and a new cattle market opened in 1823.[33] At first the produce markets brought in c. £395 a year from tolls and rents of standings (including those of the country butchers who were installed there, but excluding tolls of corn which were separately leased); after 1814,

[18] G.B.R., F 10/5; B 3/9, ff. 114v., 135.
[19] Ibid. B 3/9, ff. 326v.–327v.; cf. ibid. f. 373v.
[20] Cf. ibid. f. 425v.; 10, ff. 33v., 47v., 116; 11, ff. 94, 106, 252v.; F 10/5, 7.
[21] Ibid. J 3/1, ff. 66v.–69v.; 6, ff. 255v.–256v.
[22] Ibid. F 4/9, p. 353.
[23] Ibid. J 3/9, ff. 75v.–77v.
[24] Glouc. Jnl. 19 June 1750; 18 June 1751; 24 Oct. 1752.
[25] G.B.R., B 3/9, ff. 191, 373v.; P.R.O., E 134/1 Geo. II Hil./4.
[26] G.B.R., B 3/10, f. 116; B 4/1/2, f. 91; Glouc. Jnl. 16 May

1803.
[27] G.B.R., F 4/11, p. 47; 12, pp. 20–1, 60–1; 13, p. 456; B 3/10, f. 268; 11, f. 152.
[28] Ibid. B 3/6, f. 208; 10, f. 241; 13, f. 19v.
[29] Ibid. 9, f. 394.
[30] Ibid. 11, f. 231; F 4/12, p. 375.
[31] Ibid. F 4/15, p. 296; F 10/7, lease 15 Sept. 1825; J 4/12, nos. 2, 7.
[32] Ibid. F 4/15, pp. 186–7; 16, pp. 175, 177; F 10/7, lease 26 Apr. 1830.
[33] Below, Markets and Fairs.

when the lease of the profits was publicly auctioned,[34] £700 a year was produced. The tolls of the new cattle market were usually let for c. £300 a year in the 1820s and 1830s.

The corporation's total revenue from trading activities in the city was £270 in the year 1742–3, made up of £133 from the former sheriffs' tolls, £20 from the quay weights, and £117 from the butchers' shambles, and it remained at much the same level until the 1770s. By 1790–1, after the provision of the new markets and the weighing machine, the revenue had risen to £583; by 1814–15, mainly due to the increased value of the produce markets, it had risen to £865; and by 1833–4, after the opening of the new cattle market and an increase in the tolls taken at the quay, it had risen to £1,360.

Another regular source of revenue was provided by freemen's fines, a modest total sum in most years. Usually no more than two or three men purchased the freedom each year at a fine which remained at £20 until c. 1812 when it was doubled, reverting to £20 c. 1830. The fines of 6s. 8d. and 2s. 8d. respectively for those taking up the freedom by apprenticeship or patrimony amounted to a noticeable sum only in years, such as 1726–7 and 1804–5, when a contested election encouraged registration.

The corporation's revenues generally proved adequate to meet its annual expenses, namely its charity obligations, the tax and chief rents owed on its property, the hospitality allowances made to the mayor and sheriffs, the salaries of the other officers, and (the largest items) tradesmen's bills for maintenance of the public buildings, pavements, and bridges. Only rarely did it have to resort to borrowing. The principal occasions were in 1785 when it found the £4,000 needed for the new markets by organizing a tontine among leading citizens and local gentry,[35] and in 1826 when recent expenditure of over £10,000 on the cattle market and substantial sums on other projects made it necessary to raise £8,000,[36] the bulk of which was borrowed from the treasurer Henry Hooper Wilton.[37]

Financial problems were threatened not so much by a shortfall of revenue as by lax rent collecting, accounting, and auditing. In 1779, when it was realized that the correct procedure for auditing the city and hospital accounts had been allowed to lapse in 1757, the common council made a determined effort to establish stricter supervision. A committee of inquiry was set up and, after considerable difficulty in extracting the books from the aged Alderman Gabriel Harris, who had served as treasurer since 1749, began a minute audit. It revealed that £2,639 in rent was in arrears and that several loans made under tradesmen's loan charities had not been recovered. Harris, judged to have been negligent rather than corrupt, was forced to resign and stricter procedures for auditing the accounts, authorizing disbursements, and granting leases were introduced.[38] The actions taken in 1779 may have been linked to the espousal of the cause of parliamentary reform by some corporation members and the withdrawal of support from the city M.P., George Selwyn; Gabriel Harris was a supporter of Selwyn and had acted as his election agent.[39] In 1801 as a further incentive to efficient rent collecting the treasurer's salary, then £30, was replaced by a commission of 6d. in the £ on all the money he received.[40]

After 1779 the committee of inquiry remained a permanent part of the administration, used to audit the annual accounts and to inquire and make recommendations to

[34] G.B.R., B 4/1/2, f. 148v.
[35] Ibid. B 8/23.
[36] Ibid. B 4/1/3, ff. 53v.–54; Rep. Com. Mun. Corp. 66–7.
[37] G.B.R., F 4/16, p. 70.
[38] Ibid. B 4/1/1.

[39] P. Clark, 'Civic Leaders of Glouc. 1580–1800', Transformation of Eng. Provincial Towns, ed. P. Clark (1984), 334–5.
[40] G.B.R., B 3/12, ff. 212v., 338v. The new system was suspended and a salary paid again between 1815 and 1825: ibid. 14, f. 25v.

full council on matters of particular complexity. From the early 1820s, under the style of committee of estates, it also became responsible for surveying property and recommending terms for leases.[41]

The composition of the aldermanic bench[42] and of the full council during the 18th century reflected fairly accurately the principal sources of wealth in the city: in the 1720s[43] the distributive trades still predominated, but in the mid 18th century the growing prosperity of the pinmakers and woolstaplers became evident and towards the end of the century that of the wine merchants and bankers. In the early 19th century, however, professional men, mainly surgeons and attorneys, played a disproportionate role compared to the tradesmen. Only occasional representatives of the local gentry served on the council and bench at the period. Members of the Selwyn and Guise families were introduced for political reasons, and one or two lesser gentry, such as Thomas Mee (d. 1812) of Tuffley[44] and Daniel Willey (d. 1817) of Moreton Valence,[45] also served.

Several families were represented on the corporation in two or more generations, with the tradesmen families of Webb, Jefferies, Weaver, Baylis, and Saunders particularly prominent. Towards the end of the period the most significant family in the city administration were the Wiltons.[46] The involvement of the family firm of solicitors dated from at least 1775 when Henry Wilton became steward of the court leet;[47] in 1779 he was appointed clerk to the new committee of inquiry, becoming city treasurer on Gabriel Harris's resignation,[48] and by 1786 he was also deputy town clerk.[49] Henry Wilton's son Henry (d. 1822) and grandson Henry Hooper Wilton followed him in the office of treasurer;[50] another son Robert Pleydell Wilton was town clerk from 1813 until his death in 1827, from which time Henry Hooper Wilton combined that office with the treasurership.[51] Two other members of the family, the surgeon John Pleydell Wilton and his son John William Wilton, became aldermen at the period.[52]

A strict order of precedence was maintained in the corporation according to length of service; members could be degraded for poor attendance and for other reasons.[53] Members who got into financial difficulty, particularly the aldermen with their magisterial duties, were expected to resign.[54] The most spectacular departure was that of Sir James Jelf, whose bank failed during his mayoralty in 1815.[55]

Civic ceremonial included attendance by the mayor and corporation at Sunday service in the cathedral. Between 1738 and 1751, however, a dispute with the chapter over seating led to the use of St. Nicholas's church and a chapel fitted up at the Tolsey and to the appointment of a corporation chaplain.[56] In 1782 some members were avoiding attendance at church because of the heavy and 'uncouth' gowns worn; new silk gowns in a more fashionable style were acquired.[57] Major national events, such as coronations and military successes, were marked by a procession of the full corporation, sometimes joined by the trade companies with their banners.[58] In August or September the city bounds were perambulated by the mayor, some corporation members, and the Bluecoat school boys; sometimes one of the boys was

[41] Ibid. B 4/1/1–4.
[42] For which, below, Aldermen of Glouc. 1483–1835.
[43] Ripley, 'Glouc. 1660–1740', App. XXV.
[44] Cf. below, Outlying Hamlets, man.
[45] V.C.H. Glos. x. 210; Glos. Colln. 13221, f. 8ov.
[46] For whom, see pedigree in Glos. Colln., Hannam-Clark papers, TS. notes on Glouc. bankers: 'Wilton, Skey, etc.'.
[47] G.B.R., G 8/5.
[48] Ibid. B 4/1/1, pp. 5, 110–11.
[49] Glouc. Jnl. 4 Dec. 1786.

[50] G.B.R., B 3/12, f. 96 and v.; 13, f. 325v.
[51] Ibid. 13, f. 138; 14, f. 62.
[52] Below, Aldermen of Glouc. 1483–1835.
[53] e.g. G.B.R., B 3/9, ff. 65v., 92 and v.; 12, ff. 8v.–9v.
[54] Ibid. 14, f. 136v.
[55] Ibid. 13, ff. 168, 178; cf. Glouc. Jnl. 8, 15 May 1815.
[56] G.B.R., B 3/9, f. 413; 10, ff. 6v., 9v., 18, 153–154v.
[57] Ibid. 11, ff. 315Av.–315B.
[58] Glouc. Jnl. 30 Oct. 1739; 14 Oct. 1746; 7 Feb. 1820; Glouc. Guide (1792), 23.

paid 1s. for swimming the river, while the rest of the party crossed in a hired barge.[59] From 1737 a dinner was held on the perambulation day,[60] adding to the array of dinners which marked the other landmarks in the civic year. In the early 18th century the mayor held one at his own expense and another, at general corporation expense, was held at his nomination in August; the sheriffs out of their traditional revenues then provided dinners at the four quarter sessions, at the two lawdays of the court leet, and at the election of the officers on the Monday after Michaelmas.[61] The most important of those events was the nomination dinner which in the 1720s and 1730s cost £50–80, the inn to provide it being chosen by vote of the common council.[62] In spite of periodic attempts to limit it, expenditure on the civic dinners remained considerable[63] until 1798 when the council decided to discontinue the nomination and perambulation dinners to enable it to make a grant of £500 to the national war effort.[64] Resumed after the war, the civic dinners were worth up to £300 a year to the corporation's favoured inn, the King's Head.[65]

The commissioners for municipal reform, on their visit to Gloucester in 1833, received many complaints about the functioning of the corporation: among matters raised were the use of its influence at parliamentary elections, the lack of energy in some aspects of administration, and the animosities and jealousies caused by the exclusion of some prominent citizens from the governing body. The commissioners' verdict was that the evils of the closed system were less developed than in many other towns, and particular charges of corruption were not substantiated.[66] During the period 1720–1835 the corporation appears to have been generally free of corruption, with the exploitation of its patronage at election times the only regular complaint made against it. It seems, too, to have been reasonably attentive to the needs of the city, defending the economy against possible threats, giving financial support to canal schemes and turnpike trusts, and actively promoting market and street improvements. Its administration of a wide range of city charities with extensive endowments was, by the standards of the period, reasonably efficient. The four main city almshouses and Sir Thomas Rich's Bluecoat school remained effective institutions; the occasional piece of muddled accounting, or failure to maintain a proper distinction between their funds and endowments and those held by the corporation in its own right, caused problems only after municipal reform, when the charities were placed under separate administration.[67] More serious was the corporation's failure to preserve the funds of the tradesmen's loan charities[68] or to halt the decline of the Crypt grammar school. The Crypt school had sunk from its previous high reputation to a condition described as 'fatal' in 1765, and in the early 19th century its masters taught only fee-paying pupils, refusing to take any boys on the foundation.[69] The obvious remedy of paying the master a living wage was not applied, presumably due as much to lack of concern on the corporation's part as to the restrictive terms of Joan Cooke's gift, which made it difficult to realize the value of Podsmead farm and the other endowments.[70]

Among other ancient institutions, the trade companies continued, with the support of the corporation, sporadic attempts to enforce their restrictive practices; the last

[59] e.g. G.B.R., F 4/8, pp. 492, 516; 13, pp. 27, 161; 14, pp. 397, 523; *Glouc. Jnl.* 27 Aug. 1821.
[60] G.B.R., B 3/9, f. 399.
[61] Ibid. ff. 8v., 71v.
[62] Ibid. ff. 148, 296, 366v.; F 4/8, pp. 516, 539.
[63] Ibid. B 3/9, f. 399; 11, ff. 339, 343v.
[64] Ibid. 12, ff. 283v.–284.
[65] Ibid. F 4/15, pp. 302, 378, 492, 623, 713 (payments to John Dowling); cf. *Pigot's Dir.* (1822–3), 58.

[66] *Rep. Com. Mun. Corp.* 62.
[67] G.B.R., B 3/15, min. 17 Jan. 1837; B 4/1/2, ff. 153–154v.; Glos. R.O., D 3270/19677, pp. 79, 190, 481, 521–2; 19678, pp. 319, 334–8.
[68] Below, Char. for Poor, city char.
[69] Austin, *Crypt Sch.* 71–3; *V.C.H. Glos.* ii. 349–50.
[70] Austin, *Crypt Sch.* 156–7; Glos. R.O., D 3270/C 32, C 71; cf. below, Hempsted, man.

occasion was perhaps in 1781 when the mercers abandoned a suit against an unfranchised linen draper for trading in the city.[71] In the 1760s and early 1770s at least five companies were active enough to seek new bylaws from the corporation.[72] In 1787, however, it was recognized that many companies had lapsed, at least for the purposes of regulating their trades, and a new system of registering freemen by apprenticeship was adopted.[73] The ceremonial and social functions probably lasted a bit longer. In 1792 it was said that 12 companies, the same number as had existed at the start of the 18th century, still accompanied the mayor on civic occasions,[74] but membership of some was probably very small. The tanners' company comprised only two members in 1801,[75] and in 1825 the mercers' company was said to have long since ceased to exist.[76]

Of the city's ancient courts, the ordinary sessions of the hundred court had degenerated by the 1720s to a single annual session, which, though held until at least 1796, did no business apart from occasionally taking the oaths of new officers of the trade companies.[77] The bi-annual views of frankpledge (usually called lawdays) continued to be held in the Boothall before the two sheriffs and seem to have been reasonably effective in rectifying minor public nuisances, which by the beginning of the period were the sole content of the jury's presentments. By the late 1780s, however, only one session a year was held and meetings later became more sporadic, with no business done in the last few recorded sessions up to 1819.[78] The piepowder court continued to be used until 1787 or later by tradesmen recovering debts of up to c. £10,[79] and a considerable volume of business was done throughout the period by the newer court of conscience, which met once a month before a group of aldermen at the Tolsey to deal with actions for debts of up to 40s.[80]

Among various statutory bodies which played a part in the government of Gloucester during the period the poor-relief corporation was the most important. It had a chequered history in the first part of the century. After the failure of the original workhouse scheme in 1707, the functions of the governor and guardians of the poor were confined to running a charity school and managing the property left by Timothy Nourse. Plans for reviving the workhouse were prompted partly by bequests made to the guardians, principally by Alderman John Hyett (d. 1711) and his son Joseph. A bill was promoted in 1722[81] and, after much debate in the city,[82] was passed in 1727. By the Act the governor and guardians were reconstituted to include the mayor and the five senior aldermen, the bishop of Gloucester, the dean with other cathedral clergy, the trustees of Nourse's will, and 31 members elected by the city's ten parish vestries and a meeting of residents in the close. The main differences from the system set up in 1703 by the original Act were that the outlying hamlets were included in the scheme, which made it necessary to substitute the parishes for the four city wards as the units for electing guardians; the voting qualification was changed from payment of 3d. a week in poor rates to occupancy of a house valued at £5 a year; and the elected guardians' term of office was lengthened from one year to six. The city corporation's distaste for the frequent elections held under the former system lay behind the last-mentioned change.[83]

[71] *Glouc. Jnl.* 17 Dec. 1734; 28 May 1764; 19 Mar. 1781; G.B.R., B 3/9, f. 100; 10, f. 243; 11, ff. 133v., 310.
[72] G.B.R., B 3/11, ff. 19, 36v., 85v., 107v., 149.
[73] Ibid. 12, f. 86.
[74] *Glouc. Guide* (1792), 23–4; Atkyns, *Glos.* 119.
[75] Glos. R.O., D 3117/3406.
[76] *14th Rep. Com. Char.* 33.
[77] G.B.R., G 10/3.

[78] Ibid. G 8/5–6.
[79] Ibid. G 6/8–12.
[80] Ibid. G 13/1–9.
[81] Glouc. Poor-Relief Act, 13 Geo. I, c. 19; Rudder, *Glos.* 129; G.D.R. wills 1711/212; 1713/42.
[82] G.B.R., B 3/9, ff. 142v.–143; J 1/1999A; Glos Colln. (H) F 1.2.
[83] Glouc. Poor-Relief Act, 13 Geo. I, c. 19.

The workhouse was opened in 1727 in the former New Bear inn[84] at the corner of Quay Street and Castle Lane,[85] and the able-bodied inmates were put to work at heading and packing pins under an agreement with a local manufacturer.[86] The finance from the parish rates was supplemented by the proceeds of land,[87] mainly the estate in Longford left by Timothy Nourse,[88] an estate in Taynton left by Dorothy Cocks, and an estate in Miserden bought in 1733 with part of the Hyetts' bequest.[89] The guardians also found it necessary on occasion to borrow money at interest.[90] Their main problem was in collecting the rate income from the parish officers. Particularly recalcitrant were some of the hamlets beyond the city boundary, where the situation was complicated by the fact that it was the county magistrates, rather than those of the city, who had to authorize and enforce collection.[91] In the late 1720s the total annual sum assessed on the parishes was £859, of which £209 came from the outlying hamlets;[92] an increase of one eighth on that sum in 1741, a time of high food prices, apparently raised the assessment to the limit imposed by the Act.[93] In 1755 the guardians were attempting to put the workhouse with its c. 160 inmates out to farm.[94] By 1757 they were in debt for £830 and, after some of the parishes had resisted a proposal to get parliamentary sanction for higher rates, the workhouse was closed. The poor were returned to the parishes,[95] two of the most populous of which, St. Nicholas and St. Michael, opened their own workhouses in 1760.[96]

In 1764, in spite of opposition from some of the parish vestries,[97] the city workhouse was revived by an amending Act of Parliament. The hamlets, except for Kingsholm, were excluded from the scheme and the city magistrates were given wider powers for enforcing payment of rates; however, the parishes were given greater control by a return to annual elections.[98]

After 1764 the workhouse functioned without further interruption. The poor were employed principally by arrangements with pinmakers, but in the early 19th century some were employed in ropemaking and flaxdressing, and children were offered as apprentices to cotton manufacturers.[99] In the year ending March 1803, a time of particular scarcity, 216 paupers were maintained in the house and 578 people were given out-relief.[1] In the period 1813–15 there were 70–100 adults in the house, c. 185 people each year received out relief, and occasional relief was given to numbers of others.[2] In the year ending March 1803 the guardians' expenditure, including the cost of their charity school and property expenses, was £2,290, while their income, made up of the assessments on the city parishes (c. £1,660), rents (£267), and interest from investments, was £2,335.[3] In 1813, after it had become apparent that the school was the sole object of the gifts by the Hyetts and Dorothy Cocks, the rents of the Miserden and Taynton estates were applied exclusively to a reorganized charity school.[4]

The cost of the city's poor was reasonably well contained until the difficult years at the end of the period. Between 1813 and 1827 the total annual sum required from the

---

[84] Glos. R.O., D 3270/19712, pp. 1, 28.
[85] Cf. G.B.R., J 3/8, ff. 251v.–252; Hall and Pinnell, *Map of Glouc.* (1780).
[86] Glos. R.O., D 3270/19712, pp. 27, 31–2, 207.
[87] Ibid. pp. 204, 211; Glouc. Poor-Relief Act, 13 Geo. I, c. 19.
[88] G.D.R. wills 1700/57.
[89] Below, Educ., elem. educ., Poor's sch.
[90] Glos. R.O., D 3270/19712, pp. 131, 144, 208, 308.
[91] Ibid. pp. 211, 297, 327, 334; Glouc. Poor-Relief and Lighting Act, 4 Geo. III, c. 60.
[92] Glos. R.O., D 3270/19712, pp. 72–7.
[93] Ibid. pp. 308, 327; cf. ibid. pp. 398, 401, 403.

[94] *Glouc. Jnl.* 4 Mar. 1755.
[95] Glouc. Poor-Relief and Lighting Act, 4 Geo. III, c. 60; Glos. R.O., P 154/11/CW 2/4; 14/VE 2/1.
[96] Glos. R.O., P 154/14/VE 2/1; 15/OV 2/4.
[97] Ibid. 11/OV 2/3; 14/VE 2/1.
[98] Glouc. Poor-Relief and Lighting Act, 4 Geo. III, c. 60.
[99] *Poor Law Abstract, 1804,* 186–7; *Glouc. Jnl.* 5 July 1802; 11 Jan. 1808; 11 Mar. 1816.
[1] *Poor Law Abstract, 1804,* 186–7.
[2] Ibid. *1818,* 158–9.
[3] Ibid. *1804,* 186–7.
[4] Below, Educ., elem. educ., Poor's sch.

parishes remained at c. £2,500, but by 1834 it had risen to £4,617;[5] as well as the sums raised for the workhouse, those figures included the cost of settlement and removal, for which the parishes were individually responsible and for which the larger parishes found it necessary to employ paid assistant overseers in the early 1830s.[6]

The burden of the poor on the guardians and the parishes was eased by the wide array of parish charities, and by the corporation almshouses, which supported c. 90 poor people.[7] In times of particular need, such as hard winters, food shortages, and the severe Severn floods of 1770, 1795, and 1809, when the western part of the city up to the cathedral close was inundated, relief funds were organized and were usually opened by substantial donations from the corporation.[8] On a regular basis the corporation also continued its supply of cheap coal for sale to the poor. Until 1829, when it was decided to give £20 to the poor at Christmas instead,[9] one of the city's wharfingers was given the use of a coalyard at the quay and an interest-free loan of £70 to stock it.[10]

Measures for city improvement during the period, when not directly carried out by the corporation, were administered and financed in a variety of ways. In 1740 a new water supply, though ostensibly a corporation venture, was provided by one of the city M.P.s, John Selwyn of Matson; street lighting, originally provided by some of the parishes, was made a statutory responsibility of the governor and guardians of the poor from 1764;[11] and in the early 19th century the rebuilding of Westgate bridge and Over causeway and the building of Worcester Street were financed by tolls on road users.[12] For other measures improvement commissioners were created by Act of Parliament.

Under the earliest improvement Act, that of 1750 for removing buildings in Westgate Street, a body comprising the whole corporation, the cathedral clergy, and various prominent citizens was empowered[13] and apparently financed its operations by raising subscriptions.[14] Later Acts authorized the levying of rates and linked the parish vestries with the corporation in an often uneasy partnership. Parish surveyors appointed from 1777 to supervise paving and street cleaning were chosen by the city magistrates from lists nominated by the vestries,[15] and a body of commissioners appointed in 1781 to remove some of the city gates and build a new gaol was composed equally of corporation members and parish representatives elected by the vestries.[16] An Act of 1821 established a night watch, to be chosen by the magistrates from lists nominated by the vestries;[17] earlier schemes for a watch had failed because of opposition from some of the parishes, though some had given their support.[18] The Act of 1821 also set up a body of street improvement commissioners, comprising the aldermen and elected parish representatives. It proved an ineffectual body, apparently because of the reluctance of the parish representatives to commit large sums from the rates. For the first three years its meetings dealt only with procedural matters and after another four years only two fairly minor projects had been completed.[19]

The independent character of the parish vestries became evident once again in their

[5] *Poor Law Abstract 1818*, 158–9; *Poor Law Returns* (1830–1), 72; (1835), 71.
[6] Glos. R.O., P 154/9/VE 2/1; 11/VE 2/1; 15/VE 2/1.
[7] Below, Char. for Poor.
[8] *Glouc. Jnl.* 22 Jan. 1740; 26 Nov. 1770; 16 Feb. 1795; 20 Oct. 1800; 30 Jan., 6 Feb. 1809; 18 Nov. 1816; G.B.R., F 4/9, p. 261; 11, p. 383; 12, p. 57; 13, pp. 118, 400; 15, p. 60; K 4/4.
[9] G.B.R., B 4/1/4, f. 39.
[10] Ibid. B 3/9, f. 304; 10, f. 113; 11, f. 260 and v.
[11] Below, Public Services.

[12] Below, Bridges, Gates, and Walls; Glos. R.O., D 204/1/2.
[13] Glouc. Improvement Act, 23 Geo. II, c. 15.
[14] *Glouc. Jnl.* 9 June 1752.
[15] Maisemore Bridge and Glouc. Improvement Act, 17 Geo. III, c. 68.
[16] Glouc. Gaol and Improvement Act, 21 Geo. III, c. 74.
[17] Glouc. Market and Improvement Act, 1 &2 Geo. IV, c. 22.
[18] Glos. R.O., P 154/11/VE 2/1; 12/VE 2/1; 14/VE 2/2.
[19] Glos. Colln. 22415.

attitude to the board of health set up by Privy Council order in May 1832 to deal with the cholera epidemic raging in the city. The 20-strong body included the mayor and four aldermen (three of whom were surgeons), some of the other city medical men, the bishop of Gloucester, and various gentry and clergy.[20] Some of the parishes gave unqualified support[21] but three of the most populous, St. Nicholas, St. Mary de Crypt, and St. Michael, were antagonized by the lack of parish representatives on the board and urged that the governor and guardians of the poor should act in its stead. The St. Michael's vestry appointed its own committee and health inspectors to carry out the recommended measures independently of the board.[22]

In their efforts to maintain law and order in 18th-century Gloucester the main concerns of the city authorities were discouragement of vagrants and control of alehouses. In the earlier part of the century some responsibility for enforcing the vagrancy laws was taken by the governor and guardians of the poor under powers given by the Act of 1703. They managed the city bridewell at the east gate and in 1727 also fitted up a house of correction at the new workhouse.[23] Following the vagrancy Act of 1740 the bench of magistrates (composed of the 12 aldermen, the recorder, the bishop of Gloucester, the dean, and two cathedral prebendaries) took sole responsibility for vagrancy, levying a separate rate on the parishes for that purpose.[24] The large number of alehouses in the city was identified as an encouragement to vagrants and a general cause of disorder in 1730, when the magistrates refused to relicence some of them. Undesirable characters expelled from the city could, however, find similar haunts just beyond the magistrates' jurisdiction, and the Gloucestershire magistrates were pressed to take parallel action against alehouses in the suburbs.[25] In 1747 the city magistrates launched a campaign to establish tighter control over the alehouses. Licences were to be granted only to city freemen; a limit of 90 was placed on the number of licensed houses, which were to be restricted to the more central parts of the city; and there were to be regular inspections of the houses and examinations into the character of their keepers.[26]

Vagrancy and the other petty offences that provided much of the business of the city quarter sessions were usually punished by public whippings through the streets on market days. In the 1760s a person characterized as 'idle and disorderly' might be whipped from the prison at the north gate round the wheat market near the entrance to Southgate Street, while a person convicted of a more serious offence, such as obtaining money by false pretences, might be whipped the length of Westgate Street and back. More persistent offenders were put to hard labour in the bridewell. The pillory and stocks in Southgate Street were still used occasionally in the early 19th century, but the usual punishment for petty crime was then imprisonment in the new city gaol,[27] built under an Act of 1781.[28] The new gaol, in Southgate Street south of St. Kyneburgh's Hospital,[29] was built with separate cells on the lines advocated by John Howard.[30] It was considerably enlarged to the west c. 1816 when a house of correction was built adjoining it and a treadwheel installed.[31]

In the later part of the period the magistrates, who by 1802 met twice a week at the

[20] *Glouc. Jnl.* 30 June 1832.
[21] Glos. R.O., P 154/9/VE 2/2; 12/VE 2/1.
[22] Ibid. 11/VE 2/1; 14/VE 2/2; 15/VE 2/1; Glos. Colln. 18747; cf. *Glouc. Jnl.* 25 Aug., 1 Sept. 1832.
[23] G.B.R., B 6/5; Glos. R.O., D 3270/19712, pp. 37, 48, 96, 133–4.
[24] Glos. R.O., P 154/11/OV 2/3; 15/OV 2/3.
[25] Ibid. D 3270/19712, pp. 137, 142–3.
[26] G.B.R., B 3/10, ff. 89v.–97.

[27] G.B.R., G 3/SO 8–10; and for use of the stocks, *Glouc. Jnl.* 10 July 1820.
[28] Glouc. Gaol and Improvement Act, 21 Geo. III, c. 74; G.B.R., F 4/13, pp. 50, 191.
[29] Cole, *Map of Glouc.* (1805).
[30] Fosbrooke, *Glouc.* 218; *Glouc. Guide* (1792), 85.
[31] G.B.R., F 4/15, pp. 351, 539; *Delineations of Glos.* 15; Counsel, *Glouc.* 172; cf. G.B.R., G 3/AG 1. The gaol is illustrated in copy of Fosbrooke, *Glouc.* in Glos Colln. 10675.

Tolsey, attempted more effective policing of the city.[32] A regular challenge for them and for the city police, comprising 12 ward constables and the minor corporation officers, was provided by the fairs, which encouraged an influx of disreputable characters. In the mid 1780s the magistrates began the practice of searching the cheap lodging houses on those occasions and rigorously excluding likely offenders; the *Gloucester Journal* co-operated by issuing warnings against pickpockets and tricksters and against the footpads who lay in wait on the outskirts of the city for farmers returning from the fairs.[33] In 1786 a system of rewards for arrests by the city police was introduced[34] and a night watch was instituted. The watch was not, however, established on a permanent basis until the Act of 1821[35] and even then was not found particularly effective. The funds to cover its expenses were severely restricted by a clause in the Act, and the problem of villains taking refuge beyond the city boundary remained, particularly as few county magistrates lived in the immediate vicinity.[36] Voluntary efforts to combat crime included a prosecution society, established by 1800.[37]

On the whole Georgian Gloucester was a peaceful place. The occasional riots reflected national political issues or regional unrest rather than internal tensions. In 1734 a mob destroyed all the turnpike gates outside the city;[38] during the bread riots of 1766 weavers from the Stroud area invaded the market in an attempt to lower the price of corn;[39] there were minor disturbances at elections, as in 1780 when reformist zeal was directed against the sitting member George Selwyn;[40] and in 1792 a 'Church and King' mob burnt Tom Paine in effigy.[41] In 1804 and 1811 some journeymen shoemakers were proceeded against under the Combination Acts for holding meetings to seek higher wages[42] but the radical movements of the early 19th century made little impact in the city, where there was only a small industrial workforce. At the autumn quarter sessions of 1819 the city magistrates congratulated themselves on the absence of disturbance in recent years.[43] The only riot of the early 19th century, in 1827 over tolls charged at Westgate bridge, had, it was said, the tacit support of many respectable inhabitants and the demands of the rioters were speedily conceded.[44]

As in other cities, public health did not become a cause for concern until the national cholera epidemic of 1832. A voluntary board of health formed in November 1831 to meet the threat found the city at risk through inadequate water supply, scavenging, and sewerage. Highlighted in particular was the state of some of the western districts — the Island, Archdeacon Street, and around the quay — where there were crowded courts of poor housing, whose inhabitants took water directly from the Severn. Those districts suffered most during the epidemic, which between July and September 1832 killed 123 people out of a total of 366 who contracted the disease. Measures taken by the voluntary board and the new board that succeeded it in May 1832 included the opening of an isolation hospital in Barton Street, the issue of regulations and advice, and the encouragement of subscriptions to a relief fund. The epidemic prompted the establishment of a society 'for bettering the condition of the industrious poor', which instituted a clothing and coal charity, but otherwise promoted only the vague aims of encouraging sobriety, industry, and cleanliness.[45]

[32] *Glouc. New Guide* (1802), 21; G.B.R., J 4/12, no. 1.
[33] *Glouc. Jnl.* 29 Nov., 6 Dec. 1784; 3 Oct. 1785.
[34] Ibid. 4 Dec. 1786.
[35] Below, Public Services.
[36] *Rep. Com. Mun. Corp.* 63–4.
[37] *Glouc. Jnl.* 30 Mar. 1801.
[38] *Glos. N. & Q.* iv. 493–4.

[39] *Glouc. Jnl.* 15 Sept. 1766.
[40] *Trans. B.G.A.S.* lxxviii. 149–50.
[41] *Glouc. Jnl.* 31 Dec. 1792.
[42] G.B.R., G 3/SO 9–10.
[43] *Glouc. Jnl.* 25 Oct. 1819.
[44] Ibid. 29 Sept., 6 Oct. 1827.
[45] Ibid. 29 Oct. 1831–3 Nov. 1832.

Concrete measures for improvement were not forthcoming, and at municipal reform in 1835 the city still awaited adequate systems for sewerage and water supply.

Parliamentary Representation

Gloucester was one of the largest freemen boroughs, with between 1,500 and 1,850 people voting in the most fiercely contested elections of the period.[46] For that reason it was never for long subject to the control of any particular interest, though at one time or another most of the important political families of the county involved themselves in its politics, usually acting in concert with the city corporation. The corporation's influence at elections derived mainly from its power to create honorary freemen, a cause of much controversy, particularly at the contest of 1727 when it was claimed that 140 honorary freemen had been created in one day. That practice was inhibited by an Act of 1786, though the number of freemen continued to show a sharp increase of between 300 and 400 at times of contested elections, as the rival parties encouraged those eligible by patrimony or apprenticeship to register.[47] The corporation also exercised influence through its control of the city charities, particularly the almsmen's places. Its large holding of property seems to have had little relevance, as almost all was granted on long leases. The expense of contested elections was much increased by the cost of tracing and canvassing the large number of outvoters, Gloucester freemen living in other parts of the country: of the 1,579 freemen who voted in 1816, only 562 lived in the city.

At the start of the period the Tories held both city seats and party rivalry was strong. After the fiercely contested election of 1727 a more placid period followed,[48] the representation being shared between the Tories and the Whig-dominated corporation, acting in concert with local landowners. During the next 53 years three members of the Selwyn family of Matson, Charles Selwyn, his brother John (d. 1751), and John's son the wit and eccentric George Augustus Selwyn, sat for the city and were all elected to the bench of aldermen. The family's influence was said to result partly from the waterworks on Robins Wood Hill, which John Selwyn built for the city. The Selwyns also had the support of Philip Yorke, Lord Hardwicke, who owned the nearby Hardwicke estate and was recorder of the city 1734–64. The other seat was held by the Tory Benjamin Bathurst for most of the period 1727–54, but in 1741 he was ousted by Benjamin Hyett, of a prominent Gloucester family, who stood as a 'pure Tory', opposed to Bathurst's willingness to share the representation with the Whigs. Charles Barrow of Highgrove, Minsterworth, was elected as a Tory candidate in 1751, and for the next 30 years he agreed with the Selwyns and the corporation to share the representation; in 1761, however, a contest was caused by the appearance of another Tory candidate.

In 1780 there was a major realignment of interests. The movement for parliamentary reform, promoted by the Yorkshire Association, was supported by the leading Whigs of the county and city, who formed a local association at Gloucester.[49] The corporation committed itself to the reform programme by a vote in February 1780,[50] a move that involved withdrawing their support from George Selwyn, who

---

[46] This section is based on J. A. Cannon, 'Parl. Representation of City of Glouc. (1727–90)', *Trans. B.G.A.S.* lxxviii. 137–52; G. L. Goodman, 'Pre-Reform Elections in Glouc. City, 1789–1831', ibid. lxxxiv. 141–60; Williams, *Parl. Hist. of Glos.* 207–15.

[47] *Parl. Representation: Voters Polled and Number of Freemen*, H.C. 112, p. 37 (1831–2), xxvi.

[48] Clark, 'Civic Leaders of Glouc.', 328.

[49] *Trans. B.G.A.S.* lxxv. 171–91.

[50] G.B.R., B 3/11, ff. 266v.–7.

held several sinecures and controlled the rotten borough of Ludgershall (Wilts.).[51] At the general election in September the corporation backed a new candidate, John Webb of Cote House, Westbury on Trym, and also endorsed Charles Barrow, who had been active in the county association;[52] Selwyn withdrew from the contest in the face of much local hostility. The corporation's attitude was dictated partly by the increasing influence in its affairs of one of the leading aristocratic supporters of reform,[53] Charles Howard, earl of Surrey, owner of the nearby Llanthony manor estate.[54] Howard, who became duke of Norfolk in 1786, remained a major influence in city politics until his death in 1815. He was elected an alderman in 1781 and served four terms as mayor, though the duties were usually performed by a deputy;[55] he was recorder of the city from 1792 to 1811 when he became its high steward.[56]

In 1789, when Charles Barrow died after representing the city for 38 years, the duke of Norfolk and the corporation attempted to secure the second seat, but their candidate, the duke's nephew Henry Howard, was opposed by the attorney John Pitt, the former steward of Lord Hardwicke but now a prominent opponent of the corporation in city affairs. After a fierce contest, in which the poll was kept open for 15 days, Pitt won by a single vote. He claimed that he had spent £10,000 and his opponents £20,000. Pitt's influence derived partly from a considerable holding of property in the northern suburbs of the city, built up by purchase, mainly during the 1760s;[57] he claimed to have 148 tenants in the city in 1768. Following the expensive 1789 election, Pitt and the Whigs agreed to share the representation and there were no more contests until Pitt's death in 1805. When John Webb died in 1795 Henry Howard (later Lord Henry Howard-Molyneux-Howard) replaced him as the Whig member and remained M.P. until 1818.

At the byelection of 1805 the banker Robert Morris of Barnwood Court was elected with the support of both the Pitt family and the Whigs, defeating an attempt by the duke of Beaufort to extend his influence into the city. After 1815 the duke of Norfolk was replaced as the principal Whig patron by Sir Berkeley William Guise, owner of the neighbouring Highnam estate and an alderman of the city since 1810.[58] After Robert Morris's death in 1816 his seat was taken by Edward Webb, Guise's brother-in-law and son of the former M.P. John Webb, who defeated Robert Bransby Cooper, another Tory candidate put forward by the duke of Beaufort. In 1818, however, Cooper was elected with Webb, when Maurice Frederick Berkeley, a son of the 5th earl of Berkeley, was an unsuccesful second Whig candidate.

In the 1820s another local independent candidate opposed to the influence of the county families emerged. The barrister John Phillpotts assiduously nursed the consistuency, promoting the building of Worcester Street and the new cattle market.[59] He and Edward Webb, both supporting parliamentary reform, defeated Cooper in 1830, but in 1831 Webb and M. F. Berkeley joined forces against him, backed by the Berkeley, Guise, and corporation interests. At the election following the 1832 Reform Act, however, Phillpotts was returned again with Webb.

The Reform Act, while extending the franchise to the £10 householders, disfranchised all freemen living more than seven miles from the city, and restricted the voting rights of future freemen to those qualifying by birth or apprenticeship.[60] At the

[51] *D.N.B.*
[52] *Trans. B.G.A.S.* lxxv. 180.
[53] I. R. Christie, *Wilkes, Wyvill and Reform* (1962), 194, 199.
[54] Below, Outlying Hamlets, man.
[55] G.B.R., B 3/11, ff. 293v., 349; 12, f. 292v.; 13, ff. 80, 177.

[56] Ibid. 12, f. 166; 13, f. 105v.
[57] Glos. R.O., D 2078, Goodrich fam., sched. of deeds 1849.
[58] G.B.R., B 3/13, f. 84v.
[59] Counsel, *Glouc.* 176, 192; below, Plate 20.
[60] Representation of the People Act, 2 & 3 Wm. IV, c. 45, ss. 27, 32.

same time the parliamentary borough was enlarged to include an additional part of Barton Street and the newly developed Spa by extending the boundary to the tramway and the later Parkend Road on the east and to the Sud brook on the south.[61] The disfranchisement of the large number of outvoters, however, brought about a net reduction in the total electorate: 1,600 people voted at the 1830 election and 1,197 (out of 1,300 on the new register) at that of 1832.

Social and Cultural Life

For most of the 18th century, until that function was reduced by the rise of the London season and the growth of the neighbouring resort of Cheltenham, Gloucester had some importance as a social centre for the county gentry. A few of the lesser county families maintained houses in the city, among them the Crawley-Boeveys of Flaxley, who had an old, gabled house in Eastgate Street,[62] and the Hyetts, who retained Marybone House in Bearland after they built a country residence at Painswick.[63] Most of those houses in the lower Westgate Street area which were later thought to have been the town houses of gentry families[64] were, however, probably never used as more than short-term lodgings by that class.

The main annual event which drew the county gentry to the city was a race meeting held in September, coinciding every third year with the music meeting of the three choirs of Gloucester, Hereford, and Worcester. During race week, assemblies, balls, and ordinaries were held at the principal inns, while the music meeting, which by the 1730s had begun to attract leading soloists from London, included evening concerts in the great hall of the Boothall as well as the choral services held in the cathedral.[65] Regular assemblies for the gentry and leading citizens took place throughout the year: in 1724 they were held at the Tolsey twice a month in winter and once a month in summer, and in 1744 they were held weekly at the Bell inn between October and March.[66] The leading city inns staged events to suit various tastes: advertised at the Bell in the spring of 1743 were a ball for the assizes, an inter-county cockfight between Shropshire and Monmouthshire, and a course of lectures on philosophy.[67] In the mid 1740s a society of 'gentlemen florists and gardeners' held its meetings and competitions at one of the inns.[68] The Boothall was used for performances by travelling showmen and theatre companies.[69] In 1763 a permanent theatre was fitted up in a building in Barton Street.[70] Samuel Ryley, its manager in 1784,[71] described it as 'a melancholy, inconvenient place, which, when filled, would not hold more than thirty-five pounds'.[72] Soon afterwards the building of a new theatre in St. Mary's Square was begun, but it was apparently never used for that purpose.[73] In 1791 John Boles Watson, who ran theatres in Cheltenham and several other towns, built a theatre on the north side of upper Westgate Street.[74]

During the first half of the period five or six of the city's inns seem to have been of equal importance as social centres. They included the King's Head, in Westgate

[61] Parl. Boundaries Act, 2 & 3 Wm. IV, c. 64, sched. (O); *Parl. Representation: Boundary Rep.* Pt. 1, H.C. 141, p. 191 (1831–2), xxxviii.

[62] Glos. R.O., D 3963/1; cf. Glos. Colln. prints GL 90.1.

[63] *Trans. B.G.A.S.* xcix. 124.

[64] Clarke, *Archit. Hist. of Glouc.* 99.

[65] *Glouc. Jnl.* 10 Sept. 1722; 20 Aug. 1734; 2 Sept. 1735; 6, 13 Sept. 1737; 22 Aug. 1738; 30 Sept. 1740; 20 Sept. 1748; 12 Aug. 1760; D. Lysons et al., *Origin and Progress of the Meeting of the Three Choirs* (Glouc. 1895), 14–17, 25, 30.

[66] *Glouc. Jnl.* 30 Nov. 1724; 2 Oct. 1744.

[67] Ibid. 1, 29 Mar., 17 May 1743.

[68] Ibid. 24 July 1744; 23 July 1745.

[69] Ibid. 24 Sept. 1734; 10 Nov. 1766; 19 Dec. 1768; 23 Mar. 1789.

[70] Glos. Colln. R 22.1, entry for 25 Nov. 1763.

[71] *Glouc. Jnl.* 31 May 1784.

[72] S. W. Ryley, *The Itinerant, or Memoirs of an Actor,* i (1808), 263–4.

[73] Rudge, *Glouc.* 336; *Power's Glouc. Handbk.* (1862), 67; cf. *Glouc. Jnl.* 29 Nov. 1784.

[74] T. Hannam-Clark, *Drama in Glos.* (1928), 113.

Street below the entrance to Three Cocks Lane,[75] which was generally chosen by the city corporation for its nomination dinner in the 1720s and 1730s;[76] the Boothall inn, fronting the county hall in Westgate Street, which also enjoyed the corporation's patronage later in the 18th century;[77] the Bell, on the east side of Southgate Street;[78] the Golden Heart, in Southgate Street, which was among the inns where social events in connexion with the races were held in the 1730s;[79] and the White Swan, in upper Northgate Street.[80] In 1791 the White Hart and the Ram, both in Southgate Street, the Lower George, in lower Westgate Street, and the Fleece, in upper Westgate Street, also ranked among the chief inns of the city.[81]

By the start of the 19th century, however, two inns, the Bell and the King's Head, had achieved a pre-eminent position.[82] The latter was by then the established venue for all corporation dinners[83] and was also used by the county magistrates.[84] The business rivalry between the two inns was heightened at election times when the Bell was the headquarters of the Tories and the King's Head of the corporation-backed Whig interest;[85] rival county political societies, a Pitt Club established by the Tories in 1814 and a Constitutional Whig Club established in 1816, held their annual meetings and dinners at the inns.[86] The landlords of the two inns were usually men of substance. Giles Greenaway, who kept the King's Head from 1758 until 1776 or 1777,[87] bought the manor of Little Barrington in 1779[88] and later acted as agent to the duke of Norfolk;[89] in 1789 he became a city alderman.[90] John Phillpotts, who kept the Bell from 1782 to 1791, was able to educate his sons for the professions: William became bishop of Exeter and John became a successful barrister and M.P. for Gloucester.[91]

Among inns of middle rank, occupying main-street sites but not major social or coaching[92] centres, were the Black Dog, the Black Spread Eagle, and the Horse and Groom, all in lower Northgate Street, the Greyhound and the Saracen's Head in Eastgate Street, the New Inn in Northgate Street, and the Talbot in Southgate Street.[93] Of those, the Spread Eagle, benefiting from the opening of the new cattle market nearby, joined the ranks of the leading inns at the close of the period; it was much improved by the corporation, which bought it in 1824,[94] and in the early 1830s it was the principal saleroom for the city.[95] The lesser public houses of the city were particularly numerous in the Island and around the quay, where such old-established houses as the Ship, the Star, and the Anchor benefited from the river trade and were often kept by men involved in it.[96] The total number of licensed houses in Gloucester rose rapidly from 66 in 1720 to 129 in 1747;[97] the magistrates then fixed a maximum

[75] For sites of leading inns, Fig. 8.

[76] G.B.R., B 3/9, ff. 148, 318, 366v., 383v.

[77] Ibid. F 4/10–13, s.v. 'general payments', where members of the Rayer fam. and Geo. Hinks are landlords of the Boothall and John Heath, Giles Greenaway, and Isaac Thompson are landlords of the King's Head: ibid. G 3/AV 4.

[78] Above.

[79] *Glouc. Jnl.* 6 Sept. 1737; 9 May 1758.

[80] Ibid. 27 July 1756; 12 Aug. 1760.

[81] *Univ. Brit. Dir.* iii (1794), 189.

[82] *Glouc. New Guide* (1802), 83.

[83] e.g. *Glouc. Jnl.* 12 Oct. 1807; 26 Sept. 1808; 1 Nov. 1813; 27 Aug., 8 Oct. 1821.

[84] Ibid. 16 Jan. 1809; *Diary of a Cotswold Parson*, 33.

[85] *Glouc. Jnl.* 2, 16 Feb. 1789; 29 June 1818.

[86] Ibid. 6 June 1814; 30 Sept. 1816; 19 Jan., 10 Aug. 1818; 21 Jan., 12 Aug. 1822; 30 Jan., 6 Feb. 1830; a True Blue Club, just for city Tories, also met at the Bell.

[87] Ibid. 25 Apr. 1758; G.B.R., G 3/AV 4.

[88] *V.C.H. Glos.* vi. 20; P.R.O., PROB 11/1565 (P.C.C. 80 Pakenham), ff. 169–72.

[89] P.R.O., RAIL 829/3, p. 33; RAIL 829/4, pp. 6, 79.

[90] G.B.R., B 3/12, f. 122.

[91] *D.N.B.*, s.v. Phillpotts, Hen.; *Glouc. Jnl.* 3 Oct. 1791; Williams, *Parl. Hist. of Glos.* 214. In 1799 the elder John was appointed land agent to the dean and chapter, whom the younger John and his partners, members of the Whitcombe fam., served as registrars: Glouc. Cath. Libr., Chapter Act bk. iv, pp. 292–292A; v, pp. 44, 80, 94.

[92] For the role of the inns in road transport, above, econ. development 1720–91; 1791–1835.

[93] *Glouc. New Guide* (1802), 83; Hall and Pinnell, *Map of Glouc.* (1780).

[94] G.B.R., F 4/15, pp. 669, 671; 16, pp. 33–9, 81–5.

[95] e.g. *Glouc. Jnl.* 9 Jan., 13 Feb. 1830.

[96] G.B.R., J 3/8, ff. 69v., 195v.–196, 208v.–209, 216v.; 9, ff. 48v., 63v.

[97] Ibid. G 3/AV 1–2.

limit of 90[98] and in the later 18th century and the early 19th the number was kept at *c.* 70.[99] A directory of 1822 distinguished 12 as inns, the rest being classed as taverns and public houses.[1]

Among the functions of the lesser public houses was as the meeting places of the friendly societies which had begun to appear in the city by 1775.[2] Five societies registered their rules in 1794 under a recent Act,[3] and by 1804 the city had 10 (three exclusively for women) with a total of 767 members.[4] The societies were still well supported in 1821 when their Whitsun processions and dinners were a notable event in the city year.[5] A savings bank was established in the city in 1818.[6]

Besides its inns, the city had five or six coffee houses in the later 18th century and the early 19th.[7] In 1802 the leading coffee house was at the Upper George in Westgate Street, where newspapers and a billiard table were provided.[8] In 1809 two new reading rooms, one with a circulating library, were opened in the city,[9] and a subscribing library was established in 1818.[10] Among clubs and societies in the city at the close of the period, a cricket club existed in 1816,[11] a horticultural society was founded in 1828,[12] and a natural history society, founded in 1829, organized lectures and supported a museum and library.[13] The Gloucester Commercial Rooms, founded by local merchants in 1831, maintained a library and reading room.[14]

In the later part of the period efforts were made to develop that most important requirement of an inland social resort, medicinal springs. The first spring apparently exploited in Gloucester was one in the garden of Eagle Hall (later Old Spa House) in lower Westgate Street.[15] In 1788 the lessee of the house, Thomas Lewis, a corn factor, built a pump room and opened the garden to subscribers, but the spa seems to have enjoyed only a brief popularity.[16] More significantly for Gloucester's development, springs were discovered in 1814 in Rigney Stile grounds on the south side of the city. The owner, Sir James Jelf, sank wells, built a pump room with hot and cold baths, and laid out walks. The spa was opened to subscribers in 1815.[17] Shortly afterwards Jelf was made bankrupt, but the potential importance of the spa to the city was already evident[18] and a group of shareholders raided £6,500 to buy it. They added to the amenities, sold off the adjoining land for building,[19] and in 1818 built a hotel.[20] The spa was at its most popular in the 1820s.[21] Lodgings in the new terraces built in the vicinity were taken by visitors,[22] some of them encouraged by John Baron, a physician at the Gloucester Infirmary, who recommended the waters for their iodine content.[23] Between 1826 and 1828 the spa company was able to lease the spa for £450 a year. A decline in its popularity was evident by 1829 when a new lessee agreed to take it at £350 a year for two years and £370 a year for five years after that; by 1835, partly as a result of the cholera epidemic of 1832, both he and the lessee of the Spa hotel were in financial difficulties.[24] Another resort frequented at the same period was

[98] Ibid. B 3/10, f. 93.
[99] Ibid. G 3/AV 4–5.
[1] *Pigot's Dir.* (1822–3), 58–60.
[2] *Glouc. Jnl.* 1 July 1822.
[3] G.B.R., G 3/SR, 1794.
[4] *Poor Law Abstract, 1804,* 186–7.
[5] *Glouc. Jnl.* 18 June 1821.
[6] Ibid. 22 Sept. 1817; 23 Feb. 1818.
[7] G.B.R., G 3/AV 4–5.
[8] *Glouc. New Guide* (1802), 84.
[9] *Glouc. Jnl.* 5 June 1809.
[10] Counsel, *Glouc.* 174; *Glouc. Jnl.* 9 Jan., 27 Mar. 1830.
[11] *Glouc. Jnl.* 27 May 1816.
[12] Counsel, *Glouc.* 175.
[13] Glos. Colln. 18707; *Glouc. Jnl.* 29 May 1830.

[14] G.B.R., Glouc. Commercial Rooms min. bk. 1831–4.
[15] Cf. Glos. R.O., D 3117/4138, 4144A.
[16] *Glouc. Jnl.* 7 July, 15 Sept., 3, 10 Nov. 1788; 5 July 1790; Glos. Colln. N 23.2.
[17] *Glouc. Jnl.* 5, 12 Sept., 21 Nov. 1814; 24 Apr., 8 May 1815. For the pump room, below, Plate 17.
[18] *Glouc. Jnl.* 12, 26 June 1815.
[19] Glos. Colln. 18420, 18423 (2–3).
[20] *Glouc. Jnl.* 25 May 1818.
[21] Ibid. 16 Aug. 1819; 26 June 1820.
[22] *Pigot's Dir.* (1830), 372.
[23] A. B. Granville, *Spas of England: Southern Spas* (1841), 330–1; Glos. Colln., Hannam-Clark papers, TS. notes on Glouc. bankers: 'Turner and Morris'.
[24] Glos. Colln. 18420.

Blenheim Gardens (renamed Vauxhall Gardens *c.* 1832) in outer Barton Street.[25] It was opened in 1812 by James Kimber as a bowling green and tea garden and staged events such as balls, pigeon-shooting matches, and, in its first years, firework displays to celebrate Peninsular War victories.[26]

Gloucester's spa and other social attractions were, however, increasingly overshadowed by the growth of the fashionable health resort only a few miles distant. Cheltenham, described by the Revd. Thomas Fosbrooke in 1819 as 'a very shouldering, unpleasant neighbour',[27] had matched Gloucester in population by 1811 and outstripped it by 1821.[28] The relative position of the two places as social centres was indicated in 1819 by the announcement by a new manager that Gloucester's theatre would open 'for an occasional night during the present Cheltenham season'.[29] The two most celebrated visitors during the period were seen in Gloucester only because they happened to be staying at Cheltenham: George III came in 1788 and was shown over the cathedral, the infirmary, the new county gaol, and a pin factory,[30] and in 1816 the duke of Wellington was given the freedom of the city, dined with the corporation at the King's Head, and laid the foundation stone of a new National school.[31]

Gloucester's race meeting, which from the mid 1740s appears to have been held only in the years when the music meeting was in the city, was discontinued in 1793[32] and not revived again until 1826.[33] The music meeting continued, however, to attract the local gentry in large numbers. In 1817, when the evening concerts were first held in the new Shire Hall, a Bow Street runner was employed to control the crowds,[34] and the meeting of 1823 was attended by numerous parties from Cheltenham. The next Gloucester meeting, in 1826, was equally crowded.[35] William Cobbett, who happened to arrive in the city during it, found he would 'run a risk of having no bed if I did not bow very low and pay very high' and continued on his way, making some predictably trenchant comments about such gatherings.[36]

In the religious life of Gloucester during the period the most notable development was the contribution made to the Sunday School movement. The Sunday schools started in the city in 1780 by the printer Robert Raikes and Thomas Stock, curate of St. John the Baptist and master of the College school, though certainly not the first, proved to be the most influential: the publicity given to the venture by Raikes through his newspaper, the *Gloucester Journal*, was the main impetus for the spread of the movement. Raikes's brand of Christian philanthropy, which was also directed towards the reform of the county gaol and to the general encouragement of charity,[37] was possibly not as unusual as might seem in the general climate of the 18th-century city, where the Gloucester Infirmary, supported from 1755 by subscriptions of the county gentry and leading citizens,[38] was an object of civic pride[39] and where collections for the relief of the poor in times of hardship met with a ready response.[40] Individual citizens were also concerned that adequate church services should be maintained. One of the parishes that had lost its church in the 17th century, St. Aldate, was provided with a new one, opened in 1756, as a result of a private benefaction. At the same

[25] Cf. *Glouc. Jnl.* 28 Apr. 1832; Causton, *Map of Glouc.* (1843).

[26] *Glouc. Jnl.* 27 Apr., 8 June 1812; 19 July, 16 Aug. 1813; 11 Apr. 1814; 7 June 1819; 23 June 1827.

[27] Fosbrooke, *Glouc.* 213.

[28] *Census*, 1811, 1821.

[29] *Glouc. Jnl.* 14 June 1819.

[30] Ibid. 28 July 1788.

[31] Ibid. 5 Aug. 1816.

[32] *Glouc. Jnl. passim*; Lysons et al., *Three Choirs*, 30.

[33] *Glouc. Jnl.* 1 July, 30 Sept. 1826; 22 Sept. 1827.

[34] Ibid. 22 Sept. 1817.

[35] *Diary of a Cotswold Parson*, 30–1, 65–6.

[36] Cobbett, *Rural Rides* (Everyman edn.), ii. 105.

[37] F. Booth, *Robert Raikes of Glouc.* (Redhill, 1980).

[38] Below, Hosp., general infirmaries.

[39] *Glouc. Jnl.* 28 July 1788; *Glouc. New Guide* (1802), 84–5.

[40] e.g. *Glouc. Jnl.* 22 Jan. 1740; 26 Nov. 1770; 20 Oct. 1800; 18 Nov. 1816; G.B.R., K 4/4.

period a number of citizens, including Richard Elly (d. 1755) and John Blanch (d. 1756), gave substantial endowments for sermons or additional services or else to augment the meagre incomes of the benefices.[41]

Among parish incumbents of the period Thomas Stock, who gave self-effacing and devoted service at St. John the Baptist from 1787 to 1803,[42] was perhaps as typical as the more worldly Thomas Rudge, rector of St. Michael 1784–1825 and archdeacon of Gloucester, who for 15 years was also master of the Crypt school, then effectively a private boarding school, and followed antiquarian and agricultural interests.[43] Though incumbents of the city churches often held livings in the surrounding countryside,[44] usually they seem to have resided in Gloucester, where the total complement of clergy, including the cathedral contingent and others who chose to reside in the city, was c. 30 in the 18th century.[45] The cathedral clergy of the period included some notable figures, such as Bishop Martin Benson, a popular and conscientious diocesan from 1735 to 1752, and Josiah Tucker, dean 1758–99, who was widely known for his writings on politics and economy.[46] In the more relaxed religious climate of the 18th century, however, the close was less directly involved in the life of the city than it had been in the 17th century.

The evangelical movement in the established church was already well represented among Gloucester citizens in 1812, when a branch of the British and Foreign Bible Society was formed,[47] and it gained much impetus after the appointment of Henry Ryder as bishop of Gloucester in 1815. Ryder was active in promoting lectures in the city churches and he took the lead in founding a National school in 1816 and a penitentiary for reforming prostitutes,[48] the Magdalen Asylum in a house in St. Mary's Square, in 1821.[49] His influence presumably also lay behind the formation of a Sunday observance society, which in 1817 was attempting to get city employers to pay their workers on Friday rather than Saturday night; payment on Saturday was thought to lead to shops opening on Sunday and to low attendance at services, following heavy drinking on Saturday night.[50] In 1818 the society was said to have almost put a stop to traffic on Sundays, even extending its objections to the use of velocipedes.[51] The provision of more church accommodation for the poor was also discussed at the period,[52] but in the event the first new church built in the 19th century was a proprietary church for the wealthy inhabitants of the Spa, opened in 1823.[53] A later bishop of Gloucester, James Monk, was active in similar fields, lending his support to a dispensary opened in 1831[54] and to a local branch of a national temperance society established in 1832.[55] Following the cholera epidemic of 1832 he formed a society for improving the condition of the poor.[56] Among evangelical clergy of the city at the period was the hymn writer John Kempthorne, a protégé of Bishop Ryder. Kempthorne, who held curacies before becoming rector of St. Michael's parish in 1826, preached against fairs and other public entertainments.[57]

Nonconformity was not a major element in the life of the city during the period. In

[41] Below, Churches and Chapels; Rudder, *Glos.* 199; P.R.O., PROB 11/830 (P.C.C. 182 Herring), f. 327v.
[42] Booth, *Rob. Raikes*, 78–9, 93, 177–8; Hockaday Abs. ccxv.
[43] I. Gray, *Antiquaries of Glos. and Bristol* (B.G.A.S. 1981), 72–3; *Glouc. Jnl.* 24 Mar. 1788.
[44] Hockaday Abs. ccxvi, ccxviii–xx.
[45] *Univ. Brit. Dir.* iii (1794), 191–2; *Glouc. New Guide* (1802), 142–3.
[46] *D.N.B.*
[47] *Glouc. Jnl.* 7, 21 Sept. 1812.
[48] W. J. Baker, 'Hen. Ryder of Glouc. 1815–24', *Trans.*

B.G.A.S. lxxxix. 139–40; Glos. R.O., P 154/VE 2/2, mins. 1821–3; Hockaday Abs. ccxv, 1820; ccxx, 1822.
[49] Counsel, *Glouc.* 178–9.
[50] *Glouc. Jnl.* 10 Mar. 1817.
[51] Ibid. 2 Nov. 1818; 10 May 1819.
[52] Ibid. 22 Feb. 1819.
[53] Below, Churches and Chapels.
[54] Glos. Colln. N 19.3; NF 19.1.
[55] T. Hudson, *Temperance Pioneers of the West* (1888), 74; *Glouc. Jnl.* 1 Dec. 1832.
[56] *Glouc. Jnl.* 3, 10 Nov. 1832.
[57] *N. & Q.* 11th ser. x. 401–3, 422–3; Glos. Colln. NQ 8.3.

1735 a total of 220 members, less than in several much smaller towns of the county,[58] was recorded for the three groups then established in the city. The most significant group was the Independents, under their minister Thomas Cole. Cole allied himself with George Whitefield, a native of Gloucester, who preached and established a following in the city in the late 1730s and early 1740s. The Countess of Huntingdon's Connexion and the Wesleyans built chapels in 1788, and in the early 19th century nonconformity was further expanded by the arrival of new groups and the growth of existing ones.[59] Roman Catholics established a mission in the city *c.* 1789.[60]

The life of the city during the period is reflected most comprehensively in the columns of the *Gloucester Journal* newspaper, which was begun in 1722 by Robert Raikes and William Dicey, who were already partners in a Northampton newspaper. Raikes, who carried on the paper alone from 1725 was succeeded at his death in 1757 by his son Robert, who, though using the paper to further his philanthropic aims, was a practical and successful businessman.[61] He sold the paper in 1802 to David Walker, printer of the *Hereford Journal*.[62] The *Gloucester Journal* acquired a wide circulation in the 18th century, extending into several adjoining counties and far into South Wales.[63] Within Gloucestershire it had no effective rival during the century, though at least two other papers were published in Gloucester for short periods: they were the *Gloucester Gazette and South Wales Advertizer* of 1782–4 and the *Gloucester Gazette*, published by John Selwyn Pytt from 1788 until 1796 or later. Of several other papers published in the early 19th century, the most successful was the *Gloucester Herald* which appeared from 1801 until 1828. The most enduring competitor of the *Gloucester Journal*, however, proved to be the *Gloucestershire Chronicle* started in 1833; it was backed by supporters of the Tory party, the *Journal* under David Walker and his two sons Alexander and David Mowbray Walker,[64] all of whom served as city aldermen, having become attached to the Whig interest.[65]

One of the earliest Gloucester men to take a serious interest in the city's history was the Revd. Richard Furney, who was master of the Crypt school in 1720 when the city corporation employed him to reorganize its archives. His detailed compilation on the city was used, largely unaltered, by Samuel Rudder in his county history of 1779. Histories of the city by the Revd. Thomas Rudge and the Revd. Thomas Fosbrooke, published in 1811 and 1819 respectively, were of a conventional antiquarian type, concerned mainly with the Roman and medieval periods and the Civil War events. Some rather more mundane detail was provided by the solicitor George Worrall Counsel in a short history published in 1829;[66] Counsel's anxiety to stress the orderly and efficient government of the city and its favourable economic prospects presumably reflected the fact that he was then its leading property developer.[67]

Topography

During the 18th century Gloucester's unspectacular economic performance was matched by the lack of physical growth. There was some new building in the inner part of Barton Street.[68] Houses just beyond the city boundary there were advertized in 1736 as advantageous for tradesmen, who could conduct their business without

[58] *Trans. B.G.A.S.* ci. 135.
[59] Below, Prot. Nonconf.
[60] Below, Roman Catholicism.
[61] Booth, *Rob. Raikes*, 32–3, 37, 41–62.
[62] *Glouc. Jnl. Bicentenary Hist. Suppl.* 8 Apr. 1922.
[63] Glos. Colln. NV 26.1.
[64] *Glouc. Jnl. Bicentenary Hist. Suppl.* 8 Apr. 1922.
[65] Below, Aldermen of Glouc. 1483–1835.
[66] Gray, *Antiquaries of Glos. and Bristol*, 59–60, 72–3, 75–6, 87–8.
[67] Cf. below, topog.
[68] Hall and Pinnell, *Map of Glouc.* (1780).

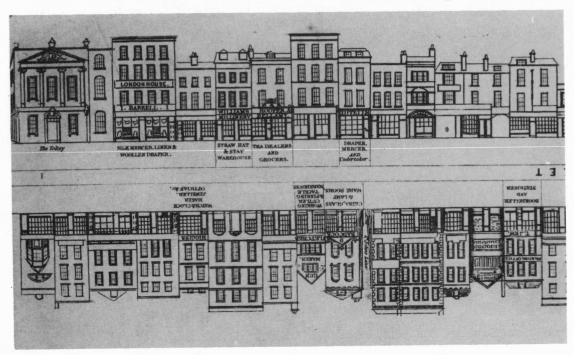

Fig. 9. Upper Westgate Street, *c.* 1841: the south side (*at the top*) includes the Tolsey

taking the freedom,[69] and soon after 1763 the woolstapler James Helps built new houses and workshops some way beyond the boundary adjoining the later Charlton House.[70] That and other new building led to the moving of the turnpike further out, to the junction with Barton Lane, *c.* 1779.[71] For the most part, however, the roadside suburbs destroyed in 1643 were not replaced: the earliest detailed map of the city, in 1780, showed only a few scattered houses on the London road, while Brook Street and Severn Street remained empty of buildings.[72] The modest population increase of the 18th century was accommodated mainly by subdividing existing buildings, including parts of Greyfriars and Blackfriars,[73] and by occasional new building on available waste land within the city. A new house was built before 1732 just beyond the east gate on the site of a former horsepool,[74] and after the demolition of the gate and adjoining buildings in 1778 new houses were built on the north and south sides of the street there;[75] a piece of waste on the south side of the Foreign bridge, adjoining Dockham ditch, was filled by three houses *c.* 1744;[76] and *c.* 1802 the bricklayer Daniel Spencer built a row of nine cottages on the culverted river Twyver on the north side of St. Aldate Street.[77]

The failure of the city to expand puzzled some of its citizens. 'While whole streets are building in other places, scarcely a single house rears its head in this' wrote one in 1792. He apparently attributed it to lack of initiative, refuting a popular view that the high proportion of leasehold, under the dean and chapter and the city corporation, was the main deterrent to new building. He pointed out that with chapter property, which was held on 40-year leases renewable every 14 years at a fine estimated at a years' value, the first renewal after any improvement was usually allowed at the old

[69] *Glouc. Jnl.* 29 June 1736.
[70] Glos. R.O., D 3117/3709–10, 3722; later the site of the public baths.
[71] G.B.R., B 3/17, min. 10 May 1852; cf. Hall and Pinnell, *Map of Glouc.* (1780).
[72] Hall and Pinnell, *Map of Glouc.* (1780).

[73] Below, Sites of Religious Houses.
[74] G.B.R., J 3/9, f. 1; cf. ibid. B 3/8, p. 231.
[75] Ibid. J 3/12, pp. 90–96, 194–5; below, Plate 16.
[76] G.B.R., J 3/9, f. 93v.; 10, pp. 96–7.
[77] Glos. R.O., D 936/E 12/17, f. 134; 18, ff. 57–60, 63–8; cf. G.B.R., J 4/12, no. 56.

value.[78] Similarly the corporation in an attempt to encourage new building as early as 1729 had offered the holders of its 41-year leases the chance of taking new leases at $1\frac{1}{4}$ years' value and renewing them after 14 years at the old rate.[79] When the necessary incentives for growth appeared after the Napoleonic Wars some of the new building, for example on hospital property in the London road, did take place on leaseholds.[80] Nevertheless expansion was helped by the fact that much of the land immediately adjoining the city, including Monkleighton grounds and Gaudy Green, had been sold by the chapter and the corporation for land-tax redemption in 1800.[81]

The old city did, however, change its appearance considerably during the mid and later 18th century. Rebuilding and refronting in brick continued in the main streets and in the cathedral close.[82] Most of the timber houses had gone or been masked by c. 1770 when the city was said to be built mainly of brick.[83] The new fronts of the mid 18th century were generally rather plain, decoration being limited to a dentilled cornice and perhaps keystones to the windows.[84] A few were more elaborate. Bearland House, in Longsmith Street, which was enlarged and refronted for an attorney William Jones,[85] and no. 100 Westgate Street both have details copied from the pattern books of Batty Langley.[86] Nos. 29 and 31 Southgate Street, later the premises of the Saunders family of wine merchants,[87] share a pedimented doorway, above which is a venetian window from a pattern book of W. and J. Halfpenny.[88] Other such details were presumably lost when shop fronts became ubiquitous in the main streets in the early 19th century.[89]

One street front which stood out, both for its architectural distinction and for the fact that it was in ashlar, was on a house on the north side of lower Westgate Street, which was rebuilt by Anthony Freeman soon after he bought it in 1724.[90] Called Eagle Hall in 1801, it was later known as Old Spa House, for a medicinal spring in its garden was briefly fashionable in the 1780s. Popularly it also because known as the Duke of Norfolk's House, Charles Howard, duke of Norfolk (d. 1815), having lodged there when visiting the city to cultivate his political interests.[91] The front was of three storeys and of five bays between Corinthian pilasters. The ground-floor windows had segmental pediments and those on the first floor triangular pediments; the parapet carried a large eagle and four urns.[92] The quality of the design suggests that it was the work of a Bristol or London architect.

Other fronts of a more architectural flavour added to the streets in the period were those of the public buildings and chief inns, including the Boothall inn of c. 1742, the Tolsey of 1751,[93] the Eastgate market portico of 1786,[94] and the long pedimented front of the Bell, probably of 1793.[95] The rise of banking gave its first notable addition to the street frontages c. 1801 when the firm of Fendall, Evans, and Jelf built premises in upper Northgate Street.[96] With its rusticated ground floor, pilastered upper floor,

[78] *Glouc. Jnl.* 16 Jan. 1792; cf. Rudge, *Glouc.* 109.
[79] G.B.R., B 3/9, f. 259v.
[80] Below.
[81] Glos. R.O., D 3117/75, 992; cf. below.
[82] For the close, below, Glouc. Cath. and Close.
[83] Rudder, *Glos.* 81.
[84] The extent of 18th-century rebuilding can now be appreciated only from Glos. Colln. 10962 (7), street elevations c. 1841, details reproduced as Figs. 9–10; cf. also, *Delineations of Glos.* plate facing p. 1, reproduced below, Plate 13.
[85] Glos. R.O., GMS 107.
[86] e.g. *Treasury of Designs* (1739), plate 40.
[87] P.R.O., PROB 11/1239 (P.C.C. 570 Dodwell), ff. 72v.–73v.; G.B.R., J 4/12, no. 37.
[88] *Modern Builders Assistant* (1747), plate 70.
[89] e.g. *Delineations of Glos.* plate facing p. 1; Glos. Colln.

10962 (7).
[90] Glos. R.O., D 3117/4126, 4138.
[91] Ibid. 4132, 4138, 4144A, 4154A; cf. *Glouc. Jnl.* 15 Sept., 3 Nov. 1788.
[92] For the house, which was demolished in 1971, *Glouc., a Pictorial Rec.* (John Jennings Ltd., n.d.), 50; *Rec. of Glouc. Cath.* ed. W. Bazeley, ii (1883–4), frontispiece.
[93] Plates 14, 38; below, Public Buildings.
[94] Fig. 10; below, Markets and Fairs.
[95] *Glouc. Jnl.* 28 Oct. 1793; R. Philip, *Life and Times of Revd. George Whitefield* (1842), frontispiece, showing the inn before it was again altered in the mid 19th cent., reproduced below, Plate 15.
[96] Glos. R.O., D 3117/1642–9; cf. Causton, *Map of Glouc.* (1843); it was later used successively by Turner and Morris and the Bank of England branch.

and balustraded parapet, the bank was very similar in design to the new Bluecoat school in Eastgate Street[97] built in the years 1806–8 and was possibly by the same architect, John Wheeler.[98]

Away from the main streets, one of the more imposing new houses of the period was Constitution House, at the east end of Bell Lane, built by a woolstapler, Richard Chandler, in 1750.[99] In the late 18th century and at the start of the 19th some large new houses were added around Greyfriars[1] and on inner Barton Street, where the barrister and banker William Fendall built an ashlar-faced, bow-fronted mansion (later Mynd House) c. 1800.[2]

Apart from the central area around the Cross, the city retained a fairly uncongested character until the early 19th century with large expanses of garden behind the houses.[3] Some gardens were highly ornamental in character. That behind Anthony Freeman's house in lower Westgate Street had an octagonal summer house with a painted ceiling in 1736, and in the 1740s Benjamin Hyett laid out a Chinese-style garden on the castle grounds behind Marybone House, including serpentine walks and a pagoda on a mount. An even more elaborate garden was formed by the physician Charles Greville at the house at the entrance to Barton Street (later Elton House) which he occupied by 1749; it included summer houses, arbours, and a central obelisk on a mount.[4] The more conventional style of landscape gardening was later represented in the city on a small scale. By 1780 John Pitt, owner of Paddock House in the later Pitt Street from 1758, had laid out a small park, including an ornamental pond, on land between the house and St. Catherine Street,[5] and in the early 19th century the former bowling green and adjoining land in the south-east angle of the city walls was planted by the owners of Bowling Green House.[6]

During the second half of the 18th century alterations were made to the city's main streets as the increase in wheeled traffic demanded thoroughfares uncluttered by obstacles and projections. Under an improvement Act of 1750 the buildings in the centre of Westgate Street, including Holy Trinity church tower and the King's Board, were removed, together with the high cross and some buildings in Northgate and Southgate Streets.[7] Other projecting buildings and obstructions were removed under an Act of 1777, which also enforced the repaving of the main streets and other improvements, such as the provision of guttering to the houses.[8] The city's east gate was taken down in 1778 and several of the other gates in 1781,[9] when further regulations were made for improving the state of the streets.[10] The entrance to Hare Lane, then the main Tewkesbury road, was widened in 1779;[11] the main road out to the west was widened in the 1780s when St. Bartholomew's Hospital in the Island was rebuilt;[12] and the entrance to Lower College Lane was widened at the joint expense of the corporation and dean and chapter in 1794 or 1795.[13] In 1786 the opening of new market places, off Eastgate Street and Southgate Street, removed the produce markets and butchers' shambles from the streets.[14] In the gradual modernisation of

[97] Glos. Colln. 10962 (7); *Glouc., a Pictorial Rec.* 47, 61; and for the Bluecoat sch., below, Plate 47.

[98] Colvin, *Biog. Dict. Brit. Architects* (1978), 881.

[99] G.B.R., J 3/9, f. 97v.; 10, f. 173 and v.; date on rainwater head.

[1] Below, Sites of Religious Houses.

[2] Glos. R.O., D 3117/394–6; in 1984 occupied by car saleroom of Page and Davies Ltd. and shops.

[3] Hall and Pinnell, *Map of Glouc.* (1780); Cole, *Map of Glouc.* (1805).

[4] J. Harris, 'Gardenesque: the Case of Charles Grevile's Garden at Glouc.', *Jnl. of Garden Hist.* i (2), 167–78.

[5] Hall and Pinnell, *Map of Glouc.* (1780); Glos. R.O., D

2078, Goodrich fam., sched. of deeds 1849.

[6] Below, Sites of Other Religious Houses, Greyfriars.

[7] Glouc. Improvement Act, 23 Geo. II, c. 15; Rudder, *Glos.* 204; below, Public Buildings.

[8] Maisemore Bridge and Glouc. Improvement Act, 17 Geo. III, c. 68; *Glouc. Jnl.* 27 Oct. 1777.

[9] Below, Bridges, Gates, and Walls.

[10] Glouc. Gaol and Improvement Act, 21 Geo. III, c. 74.

[11] G.B.R., B 3/11, f. 253.

[12] Ibid. 12, ff. 78v., 83v.

[13] Glouc. Cath. Libr., Chapter Act bk. iv, p. 247; Glos. R.O., D 936/A 1/9, p. 253; G.B.R., B 3/12, f. 223v.

[14] Below, Markets and Fairs.

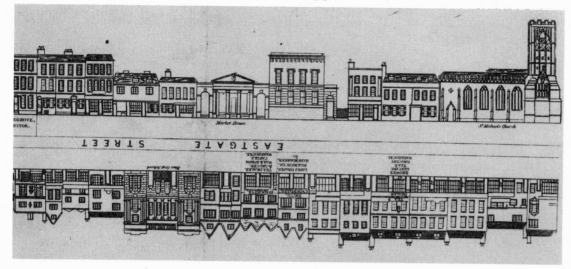

Fig. 10. Upper Eastgate Street, *c.* 1841: the south side (*at the top*) includes St. Michael's church, the market portico of 1786, and (*west of the portico*) the premises of the Gloucestershire Banking Co.

the city and its public buildings an important landmark was the removal of the old castle keep near the quay in 1787 to make way for the building of a new county gaol on model lines.[15] Another imposing medieval feature, the west gate, was demolished *c.* 1805 and the ancient bridge on which it opened was rebuilt a few years later.[16] The Boothall, the old timber-built county hall behind the Boothall inn in Westgate Street, remained in use, a picturesque but increasingly inconvenient survival, until 1816 when a new Shire Hall with a dignified classical street front was opened on an adjoining site.[17]

In a history of the city published in 1811 the Revd. Thomas Rudge applauded the effect of the late 18th-century street improvements, recalling a time when 'the whole north side of St. Michael's church was hid from view, by mean houses or shops; the rain dropped from the eaves of the buildings, directly on the heads of those who passed under; the butchers. . . slaughtered their beasts in public view, and the blood running down the open gutters, afforded a most filthy and nauseous spectacle; the pavement was incommodious to foot passengers, and the main street equally so for carriages and horses. . .'.[18] To the more antiquarian-minded Revd. Thomas Fosbrooke, however, early 19th-century Gloucester was 'merely a mutilated figure of its antique picturesque glory. The statue has been stripped of its limbs, such as were various churches, the castle, religious houses, walls, etc. Only the fine bust, the cathedral, remains partially unimpaired'.[19]

At the close of the Napoleonic Wars a period of expansion began for the city. One incentive was the better economic prospects provided by the revival of the scheme for the Gloucester and Berkeley canal. The canal basin, on the south side of the city, adjoining the river, had been dug in the 1790s, its construction involving the severing of the old Severn Street and the building of Llanthony Road as a link between the Bristol road and Hempsted Lane. The basin was opened in 1812 and, connected to a horse tramway from Cheltenham completed the previous year,[20] began the transformation of that part of the city into its main industrial quarter. A parallel stimulus was the exploitation after 1814 of medicinal springs on Rigney Stile grounds east of the Bristol road. New building on the fringes of the city reached a peak of activity in the

[15] Below, Glouc. Castle.
[16] Below, Bridges, Gates, and Walls.
[17] Below, Public Buildings.
[18] Rudge, *Glouc.* 115.
[19] Fosbrooke, *Glouc.* 216.
[20] Below, Quay and Docks.

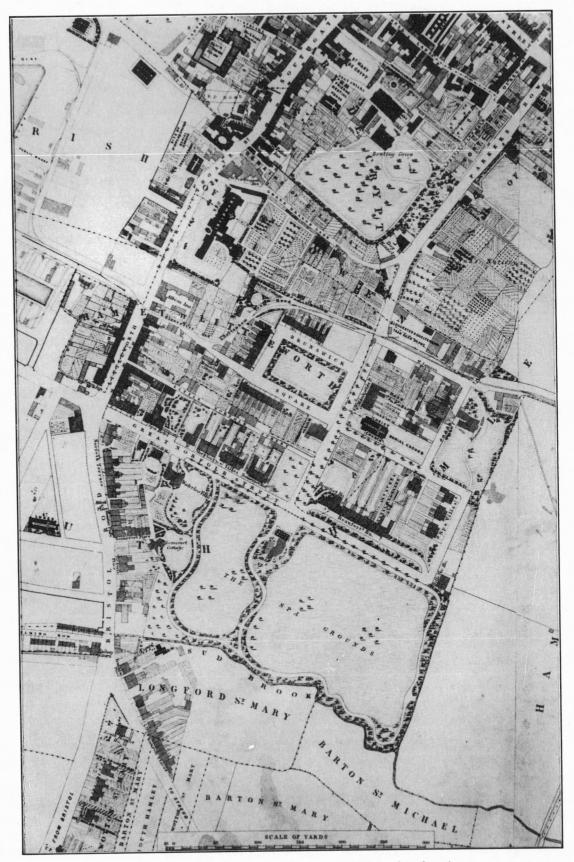

Fig. 11. The Spa and the south side of the city, 1843 (*north at the top*)

early 1820s when the columns of the *Gloucester Journal* carried many notices of the sale of building plots,[21] surveyors and architects advertised their services,[22] and the city corporation actively encouraged the process by offering building leases free of any fine at the first renewal.[23] New building was checked by the slump of 1825 but began again in the late 1820s.

Building around the new spa, in the area that was later known simply as the Spa, was encouraged by its position in the extraparochial and low-rated South Hamlet.[24] South Hamlet contained only seven inhabited houses in 1811; by 1821 the number had increased to 80, and by 1831 to 160.[25] Building began after 1816 when the company which took over the spa on the bankruptcy of its original promoter James Jelf[26] began selling off plots of land in a block lying north of the new pump room and walks. Prominent among the developers were the builder William Hicks, the attorney John Chadborn, and the barrister and later M.P. John Phillpotts.[27]

A new road laid out along the north side of the walks, was originally called Norfolk Street (later Spa Road) and access from it towards the city was opened by a street called Gloucester Place (later regarded as part of Brunswick Road).[28] On the north side of Norfolk Street, facing the walks, a row of substantial stuccoed villas in classical style with ornamental ironwork was built. The Spa hotel (later Ribston Hall), at the west end, was built by the spa company in 1818 as a boarding house for visitors to the spa.[29] The house adjoining (later Maitland House) was designed by Thomas Rickman for Alexander Maitland, a former London merchant.[30] Further east were two pairs of large semi-detached houses called Sherborne Villas, one pair built by John Chadborn.[31] On the other side of the entrance to Gloucester Place a long terrace called Beaufort Buildings was built in 1818,[32] and *c.* 1820 three pairs of small villas, called Spa Villas, and Bellevue House, the latter for Thomas Skipp, a Ledbury timber merchant, were built at the western edge of the spa company's land.[33] Further north a new church, Christ Church, was opened in 1823, fronting on Gloucester Place,[34] and north of it a terrace with ornamental plasterwork, called Montpellier Place, was built by James Pollard.[35] Further west a substantial house called Rignum Villa (later Rikenel) was built, apparently for the merchant William Price (d. 1838).[36] Waterloo House, west of the spa walks, was one of the many houses at the Spa for which William Hicks was the builder.[37]

The spa also stimulated building on land adjoining the plots sold off by the company. On the close called Gaudy Green a square (later named Brunswick Square) was developed from 1822 by Thomas Reece, an ironmonger; 19 houses in terraces had been built around it by 1825 when the owners agreed to preserve the central area as a garden.[38] Near the north-east corner of the spa company's development a short terrace called Rignum Place was begun beside the tramroad in 1821,[39] and the following year the city corporation built a new road (later called Park Road) alongside the tramroad to connect the Spa to Barton Street.[40] On the Bristol road below the

[21] *Glouc. Jnl.* 1820–22, *passim*.
[22] Ibid. 7 Feb. 1820; 8 Jan., 13 Aug. 1821.
[23] e.g. G.B.R., B 3/14, f. 68; B 4/1/3, f. 18.
[24] Counsel, *Glouc.* 189.
[25] *Census*, 1811–31.
[26] Above, social and cultural life.
[27] Glos. Colln. 18420, mins. 8 July, 9 Dec. 1816; 18423 (2); *Glouc. Jnl.* 2 June 1817.
[28] Glos. Colln. 18423 (2).
[29] *Glouc. Jnl.* 23 Feb., 25 May 1818. Causton, *Map of Glouc.* (1843) identifies the houses at the Spa mentioned here: see detail reproduced as Fig. 11.
[30] B.L. Add. Ms. 37793, ff. 68, 160; cf. *D.N.B.*, s.v. Mait-

land, Sam. Roffey.
[31] Counsel, *Glouc.* 188; cf. Glos. Colln. 18423 (2).
[32] *Glouc. Jnl.* 23 Feb. 1818.
[33] Glos. R.O., D 3117/2689A–90; cf. *Glouc. Jnl.* 6 Aug. 1821.
[34] Below, Churches and Chapels, mod. par. ch.
[35] Counsel, *Glouc.* 188; cf. Glos. Colln. 18423 (2).
[36] *Citizen*, 17 Nov. 1952; cf. *Glouc. Jnl.* 20 Oct. 1838.
[37] Counsel, *Glouc.* 188.
[38] Glos. R.O., D 3117/19, 75.
[39] Ibid. D 3013/2.
[40] G.B.R., B 4/1/3, f. 13v.; *Rep. Com. Mun. Corp.* 67.

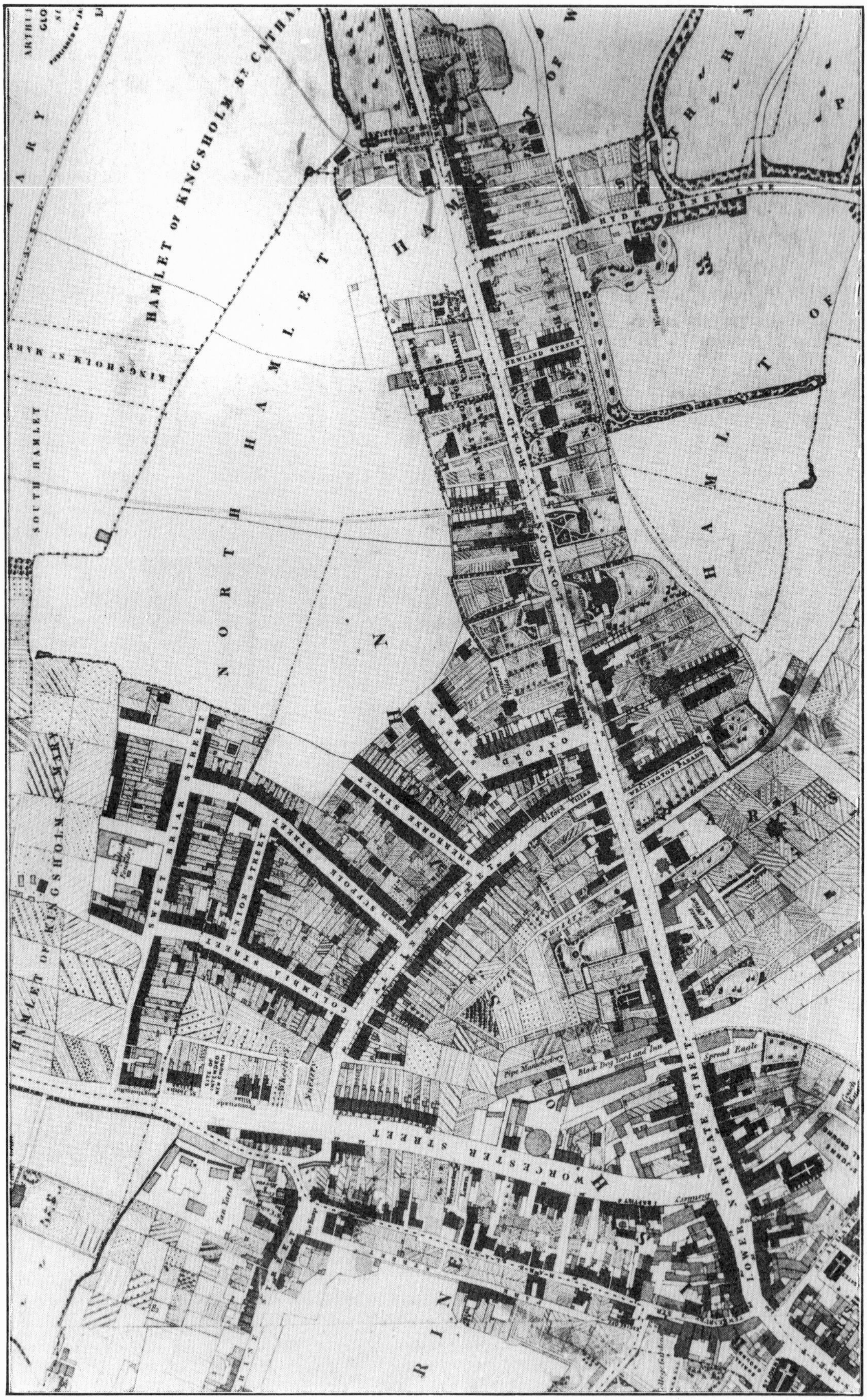

Fig. 12. The London Road and Worcester Street area, 1843 (*east at the top of the page*)

entrance to Norfolk Street, Norfolk Terrace was completed in the mid 1820s[41] and building continued down that side of the Bristol road into the entrance of the new Stroud turnpike road, which had been laid out in 1818.[42] South of the entrance to the Stroud road several houses of a more modest type were built in 1821 on Drakes Croft, a piece of the corporation's hospital land.[43] The future of the Bristol road as a fashionable residential area was compromised, however, by the rapid development of the docks after the completion of the canal in 1827. Already by 1831 a collection of 'wretched dwellings' of the poor had been established at High Orchard between the canal and the road; they were later removed for the Baker's Quay development.[44] The old Littleworth suburb, north of the entrance to Norfolk Street, remained an area of poorer housing and premises for trade; the rebuilding of the Squirrel inn, opposite the docks entrance, as the classical-style Albion hotel to designs of Thomas Fulljames in 1831[45] was one of the few improvements made there at the period.

The other area substantially affected by new building in the early 19th century was on the north and north-east fringes of the city. New developments there were chiefly responsible for an increase in the total number of inhabited houses within the city boundary from 1,509 in 1811 to 1,732 in 1821 and to 2,069 in 1831.[46]

In the inner part of the London road[47] building had begun by 1814 when Wellington Parade, a terrace built endways to the road, had been completed.[48] At the same period[49] some substantial detached stuccoed villas, including Claremont House and the three Newland Villas, were built further out. Coburg Place,[50] a pair of brick houses on the north side of the road, was described as new built in 1820[51] and several of the other houses near it had been built by 1821.[52] Wotton Lodge, some way south of the road, was built in the mid 1820s by John Michael Saunders, a former soapboiler.[53] Further out near Wotton, where the road was improved by a diversion in 1821,[54] land belonging to the two ancient hospitals was built on. The houses called Wotton Parade, east of St. Mary Magdalen's Hospital, were built on land leased in 1820 to John Phillpotts and the building partnership of Henry Edwards and Charles Copner.[55] In 1827 Joseph Roberts, a printer and lessee of land adjoining St. Margaret's Hospital, planned a terrace of 17 houses, each valued at £500, east of the hospital, and a terrace of 8 houses, each valued at £400, west of it. Roberts was not able to dispose of all the lots and only parts of the two terraces, called Hillfield Parade and York Buildings respectively, were completed.[56] On the opposite side of the road a large villa called Hillfield House, set in fairly extensive grounds, was built c. 1820 for the banker Thomas Turner.[57]

New building was most concentrated on the north side of the city and was prompted in part by the building of Worcester Street in 1822 as a new entrance for the Tewkesbury road, replacing the narrow Hare Lane route. The new road was promoted by John Phillpotts and carried out under the powers of the Tewkesbury road turnpike trustees.[58] Within a few years[59] it was built up for most of its length

[41] Counsel, *Glouc.* 192.

[42] Stroud and Glouc. Road Act, 58 Geo. III, c. 1 (Local and Personal); Glos. R.O., Q/RUm 61.

[43] G.B.R., B 3/13, ff. 308v.–309v.; Glos. R.O., D 3269, plans and corres. 1818–53.

[44] *Glos. Chron.* 26 Dec. 1891; *Glouc. Jnl.* 12 Nov. 1831.

[45] Glos. R.O., HO 19/11/4–5.   [46] Census, 1811–31.

[47] For that area in 1843, Fig. 12.

[48] *Glouc. Jnl.* 13 June 1814.

[49] Cf. Fosbrooke, *Glouc.* 220.

[50] Cf. Causton, *Map of Glouc.* (1843).

[51] *Glouc. Jnl.* 26 June 1820.

[52] Ibid. 12 Nov. 1821.

[53] Counsel, *Glouc.* 191; cf. *Pigot's Dir.* (1830), 372; G.B.R., J 3/12, pp. 545–6.

[54] Glos. R.O., D 204/3/3.

[55] G.B.R., B 3/13, ff. 292v.–293, 307v.–308; Glos. R.O., D 3269, plans and corres. 1818–53.

[56] G.B.R., B 3/14, f. 68; Glos. R.O., D 3269, plans and corres. 1818–53.

[57] *Delineations of Glos.* 195; cf. Glos. R.O., D 3117/1647–9.

[58] Glouc., Chelt., and Tewkes. Roads Act, 58 Geo. III, c. 5 (Local and Personal); Glos. R.O., D 204/1/2; Counsel, *Glouc.* 192.

[59] Cf. G.B.R., B 3/14, f. 32.

with plain brick and stucco terraces. Their commonest elaboration, as with other houses built in the city at the time, was prominent ashlar voussoirs, and some of the terraces had segmental-headed blind arcading framing the window bays. At the same period the attorney George Worrall Counsel[60] began laying out an estate of several hundred artisans' houses on his land called Monkleighton grounds, lying between Worcester Street and the London road and bounded on the south-west by Alvin Street (formerly Fete Lane).[61] The building up of Alvin Street, Sherborne Street, and Oxford Street was under way between 1823 and 1825, when the building slump temporarily halted the development and left many of the contractors in financial difficulties. Building had begun again by 1829 when Sweetbriar Street, just beyond the city boundary, was under way; Columbia Street was begun in 1831 and Union Street in 1833. Most of the area was developed in plots for one or two houses by a variety of small contractors, including plasterers, carpenters, and blacksmiths. Some streets were built up with houses with different plans and roof levels, as with one of the main surviving parts in 1984, on the south-west side of Alvin Street. Oxford Street, however, on a single large plot sold to the attorney John Bowyer in 1823, was built up with uniform stuccoed terraces.[62]

Further out on the Tewkesbury road there was scattered building around the old hamlet of Kingsholm at the same period.[63] A detached villa called Bijou had been built on the east of the road beyond the junction with Gallows Lane (later Denmark Road) by 1820[64] and several pairs of tall brick houses were put up nearby. The site of the old White Barn at the junction with Gallows Lane was offered in building lots by the corporation in 1823.[65]

There was also some new building in Barton Street on the east side of the city; 107 new houses were added between 1821 and 1831 in the hamlets of Barton St. Mary and Barton St. Michael beyond the city boundary.[66] At the point where the tramroad crossed the street (at the junction with Park Road, two rows of houses called Foley Place and Foley Cottages were built on land leased by the corporation in 1821.[67] More houses were added near the junction in the late 1820s and early 1830s, some on the site of the farm buildings of the old Abbot's Barton court house.[68] Further out, several new houses, probably including the pair of ornamental cottages called Gothic Cottages on the north side of the road, were built before 1822 near the place of entertainment called Blenheim Gardens.[69] There was also building in the early 1820s at the road junction by the India House inn,[70] and on the Tredworth road some way south of the junction Thomas Smith, a timber merchant, and others began the development of Barton Terrace (later called High Street).[71] At the close of the period, however, there were still only widely scattered buildings in outer Barton Street: Gothic Cottages were judged suitable for use as an isolation hospital in the cholera epidemic of 1832, and to go beyond the junction with Park Road was then regarded as 'going into the country'.[72]

Within the old city refronting in brick and some infilling proceeded in the 1820s, particularly in the western areas. Lower Westgate Street between Archdeacon Street

[60] *Pigot's Dir.* (1822–3), 56.
[61] For that estate, largely redeveloped in mid 20th cent., Causton, *Map of Glouc.* (1843), detail reproduced as Fig. 12.
[62] Glos. R.O., D 3117/463, 888–922, 931–41, 959–79, 999–1007, 1688–92, 1843–63; and for Oxford St., see also Counsel, *Glouc.* 191; *Pigot's Dir.* (1822–3), 56.
[63] e.g. Glos. R.O., D 3013/3; deeds in possession of Mrs. G. Sykes, of Westfield Terrace, Glouc.
[64] *Glouc. Jnl.* 8 May 1820; cf. O.S. Map 1/2,500, Glos.

XXV. 15 (1886 edn.).
[65] G.B.R., B 4/1/3, f. 18. [66] *Census*, 1821, 1831.
[67] G.B.R., J 3/13, pp. 327–36; 14, pp. 146–60; cf. Causton, *Map of Glouc.* (1843).
[68] G.B.R., B 4/1/4, ff. 24v.–25, 86; B 3/14, f. 262v.
[69] *Glouc. Jnl.* 22, 29 July 1822.
[70] Ibid. 21 May, 1 Oct. 1821.
[71] Glos. R.O., D 3117/1608–9; D 3963/3.
[72] Glos. Colln. 6587; cf. *Glouc. Jnl.* 11 Aug. 1832.

and the Foreign bridge was largely refronted or rebuilt at the period.[73] North of the Foreign bridge the area between White Swan Lane and Dockham ditch was filled with new houses in 1823,[74] while south of the bridge the corporation culverted Dockham ditch and made a new road through to the head of the quay in 1825.[75] In the Island there was some infilling with new houses by William Hicks, William Price, and others.[76] The western parts of the city were, however, becoming one of the poorest and most insanitary areas, as old houses were subdivided and cottages built on their back courts.[77] Three houses in Archdeacon Street were occupied as eight tenements in 1815,[78] and a long plot in the Island, formerly occupied by a single house and industrial premises, was subdivided after 1826 into 19 tenements.[79]

The last major development of the period within the city came in the years 1832–3 when the builder William Rees laid out, and began to build on, Clarence Street. It linked the city end of Barton Street to Mill Lane (formerly Brook Street),[80] where part of the Twyver was culverted,[81] and to the new cattle market opened in 1823.[82]

[73] For the N. side, entirely demolished in mid 20th cent., *Glouc., a Pictorial Rec.* 40.

[74] G.B.R., J 3/13, pp. 364–6, 424–31; 14, pp. 200–5; cf. J 4/12, nos. 14, 120–1.

[75] Ibid. J 3/13, p. 452; cf. *Rep. Com. Mun. Corp.* 67; G.B.R., J 4/12, no. 8.

[76] G.B.R., B 3/13, ff. 335, 342; 14, ff. 28 and v., 58v.; J

3/13, pp. 372–4; 14, pp. 166–7.

[77] *Glouc. Jnl.* 12 Nov. 1831; 21 July 1832; cf. Clarke, *Archit. Hist of Glouc.* 99.

[78] Glos. R.O., D 936/E 12/18, f. 52.

[79] Ibid. f.22; 19, ff. 10, 141.

[80] Ibid. D 4453, deeds 1758–1886.

[81] Ibid. D 936/E 12/19, ff. 78–9.

GLOUCESTER 1835–1985

OR Gloucester the Victorian period[1] was one of almost uninterrupted growth. In the mid 19th century the trade brought by the Gloucester and Berkeley canal was of primary importance to the economy, and the building of railways improved links with Gloucester's hinterland. The canal trade, which thrived on grain and timber imports and on coastal traffic, contributed to the expansion of the city's industry, and by the late 19th century, when its decline as a port began, Gloucester had become an important manufacturing centre. Timber yards, flour mills, engineering works, and manufactures ranging from railway wagons to matches were among its industries. The livestock market also increased in importance. The growth of a large working-class population had a decisive influence on the city's social and cultural life, which also reflected its status as a cathedral and county town. Municipal reform in 1835 vested the city corporation's powers in elected councillors and aldermen, but corruption became a feature of municipal as of parliamentary elections, resulting in Gloucester losing its representation in one parliament and one of its members in another. The reformed corporation's role in government was at first small, as most public services were outside its control and the administration of important almshouse and educational charities passed to a separate body of trustees. The corporation became more involved in government after 1849 when it acquired the powers of a local board of health, and in the early 1850s it provided the city with a sewerage and drainage system, the first of several major municipal schemes. In the late 19th and early 20th century the corporation assumed further functions in public health, education, and public assistance, and in 1889 the city, as a county of itself, was accorded county borough status. After the Second World War municipal control over many services disappeared and in 1974 the city was given the status of a district. Apart from the addition of aircraft production in the 1920s, Gloucester's industrial base was virtually unchanged until after 1945, when activity at the docks dwindled, distributive and service trades expanded, and the city became a major centre of employment for the region.

Gloucester's commercial and industrial expansion was accompanied by a rapid growth in population (see Table VII) and by suburban development. Older parts of the city lost population. In the mid and later 19th century new building took place mostly outside the municipal boundary in the outer Barton Street, Tredworth, and Bristol Road areas. There was also building at Kingsholm and Wotton, and between 1851 and 1871 the population of the hamlets immediately adjoining the city rose from c. 7,000 to 14,544.[2] To improve services in the suburbs the city boundary was extended in 1874 and 1900. The city continued to expand after the First World War, when the corporation began slum clearance in inner parts and building large housing estates on the outskirts, and after the Second World War the pace of growth quickened. In attempts to plan ahead the city boundary was extended several times, most considerably in 1935, 1951, and 1967.[3] The development of outlying settlements

---

[1] This chapter was written in 1984–5.
[2] *Census*, 1851–71, s.vv. Barton St. Mary, Barton St. Michael, Kingsholm St. Catherine, Kingsholm St. Mary,

Wotton St. Mary, vill of Wotton, North Hamlet, and South Hamlet.
[3] Below, city govt.

as suburbs began in the late 19th century. The population of Barnwood, Hempsted, Hucclecote, Longford, Matson, Tuffley, and Wotton St. Mary (Without) rose from 3,165 in 1881 to 6,382 in 1901, and in those parts not absorbed by the city in 1900, but excluding Tuffley, from 3,892 in 1901 to 7,049 in 1931.[4] After 1945 an even wider area outside the city was affected by residential development and between 1951 and 1961 the population of the parishes of Barnwood, Hempsted, Hucclecote, Longford, and Longlevens increased from 8,322 to 15,535. The boundary alterations of the mid 20th century included Barnwood, Hempsted, Matson, and most of Hucclecote in the city. Suburban development continued outside the boundary after 1967, and in 1971 it accounted for most of the population of 4,563 in the parishes of Hucclecote, Innsworth, Longford, and Twigworth.[5]

TABLE VII: POPULATION 1831–1981

The figures are for the municipal borough until 1881, the county borough 1891–1971, and the district in 1981, with those for the parliamentary borough in brackets.

1831	11,933	1881	36,521 (36,521)	1931	52,937
1841	14,497	1891	39,444 (39,444)	1951	67,280
1851	17,572	1901	47,955 (45,146)	1961	69,773
1861	16,512	1911	50,035 (46,112)	1971	90,232
1871	18,341 (31,844)	1921	51,330 (51,330)	1981	92,385

Source: Census, 1831–1981. The 1831 fig. includes Kingsholm. The parl. boundary was extended in 1868 and 1918. No reliable estimate of the 1941 population is available; the population of the area covered by the county borough between 1935 and 1951 rose from 55,886 in 1931 to 65,529 in 1951.

Economic Development 1835–1914

Gloucester remained an important market town and administrative centre after 1835, but as a social centre it had been eclipsed by Cheltenham. The Gloucester and Berkeley canal was the main stimulus to commercial activity in the city and encouraged the growth of industry, particularly engineering and manufacture which came to dominate the economy in the later 19th century when Gloucester's fortunes as a port were waning. Trading links with the port's hinterland, which included the industrial centres of Birmingham and the Black Country and the agricultural counties of Hereford and Worcester, were restricted before the advent of the railway by the insufficiency as waterways of the Severn and the canals to which it gave access at Worcester and Stourport (Worcs.).[6] Work to aid navigation on the river above Gloucester began only in 1842, two years after the city had obtained a railway link with the Midlands.[7]

Railway development consolidated Gloucester's position as a regional centre and as a junction of major routes from the Midlands to south-western England, and from London to South Wales.[8] The first railway to reach the city, the narrow-gauge line

[4] Census, 1891–1931. [5] Ibid. 1951–71. [7] Glos. Colln. MF 1.50.
[6] Glouc. Jnl. 3 Oct. 1835; 21 Jan. 1837. [8] For main railways, below, Fig. 14.

from Birmingham, opened in 1840 with a station east of the cattle market.[9] The Bristol – Gloucester line, made by extending the line of the Bristol and Gloucestershire company from Westerleigh, was completed in 1844. It used the broad gauge and from Standish ran over the tracks of the G.W.R. to a temporary platform north of the Birmingham company's terminus. The Bristol and Birmingham lines were worked together, and the inconvenience of the break between gauges at Gloucester[10] lasted until 1854 when the Midland Railway converted the Bristol line to the narrow gauge and built the Tuffley (or Barton) loop line.[11] The Cheltenham and Great Western Union company, formed under an Act of 1836 to provide a railway from Cheltenham and Gloucester to London by joining the broad-gauge G.W.R. at Swindon (Wilts.), lacked adequate funds. The track between Cheltenham and Gloucester was laid by the Birmingham and Gloucester company as part of its line, and in 1845 the G.W.R. finished the line from Swindon by way of Stroud and Standish to Gloucester. In 1847 the G.W.R. converted the line between Gloucester and Cheltenham as a mixed-gauge track and bypassed the city with a line near Barnwood linking the tracks from Standish and Cheltenham. A short line ran into the city from the T station on the bypassing line, which was abandoned in 1851 when the South Wales line opened.[12] That line used the broad gauge and was worked by the G.W.R., which in 1852 rebuilt its station. The line crossed the Severn's eastern channel by a swing bridge, designed by I. K. Brunel and replaced in 1958. The section between Gloucester and Grange Court in Westbury-on-Severn was constructed by the Gloucester and Dean Forest company,[13] which subscribed to the building of the Gloucester – Hereford line, making a junction at Grange Court. The latter, completed in 1855, was worked by the G.W.R.[14]

In 1851 there were 5,670 men and 2,877 women living in the city who were in employment and most employers had five or fewer workers. The presence of 485 bargemen and boatmen and 111 seamen indicates the overwhelming economic importance of the docks, which presumably accounted for many of the 146 messengers and porters. The railways, which had not made their full impact, employed 160 men and road transport 77, besides 63 grooms and stable workers and 22 coach builders. Apart from metal and engineering trades, in which at least 434 people worked, the city also depended heavily for employment on building, the provision of food and clothing, and domestic service. As many as 567 men worked in the building trades, including 197 carpenters and joiners, and another 185 people in timber industries. The distributive trades included 143 bakers and confectioners, 126 grocers, 84 drapers, and 81 butchers. In the clothing trades were 463 milliners and other hatmakers and 210 tailors, and shoemakers numbered 366 besides 135 women working with their husbands. More than 17 per cent of the employed population, including 44 per cent of women, was in domestic service and allied occupations such as inn servants and washerwomen. The professions accounted for 228 men and 89 women, mainly teachers (114) and lawyers (90). The courts, of which the assizes were in session when the figures were compiled, gave employment to another 53 men, and there were 117 officers of national and local government, including the customs service (37) and the police (19).[15]

Activity in the docks depended primarily on the traffic of the Gloucester and

[9] Glouc. Jnl. 7 Nov. 1840; Causton, Map of Glouc. (1843).
[10] C. Maggs, Bristol and Glouc. Railway (1969), 10–26; for illustrations of the break between gauges, Illustrated Lond. News, 6 June 1846, pp. 368–9, one reproduced below, Plate 33.
[11] Glouc. Jnl. 26 Mar. 1853; 3 June 1854.
[12] E. T. MacDermot, Hist. G.W.R. i (1964), 79–92.
[13] Ibid. 156–8, 454; Citizen, 20 Nov. 1956; 25 Mar. 1958.
[14] Railway Mag. xxiv. 305–12.
[15] Census, 1851; P.R.O., HO 107/1961–2; Glouc. Jnl. 5 Apr. 1851.

Berkeley canal and was controlled by the canal company. The greater cost of trading through Gloucester, which included pilotage charges levied by the port of Bristol, favoured other ports,[16] but the tonnage carried on the canal rose from 321,853 in 1832 to 654,714 in 1847.[17] In the late 1830s a schooner plied between Gloucester and Hamburg[18] and in 1841 eight foreign powers had consular representation in the city.[19] There was also considerable commerce with Welsh and Irish ports, and by 1845 regular steamer services to Chepstow and Swansea had been established.[20] Outside merchants and financiers, including several from Birmingham, figured prominently in Gloucester's trade and the development of its docks and railways.[21] One of the most active was Samuel Baker, a West Indies merchant from Bristol, who lived near Gloucester at Highnam Court until 1838 when he bought the Lypiatt Park estate in Stroud.[22] He was the first chairman of the Gloucester Chamber of Commerce, formed in 1839 to protect the port's interests.[23] The railways had an adverse effect on river traffic above the city but their impact on canal traffic was initially beneficial, though from the late 1840s they began to make inroads in the coasting trade.[24] The extension of the Herefordshire and Gloucestershire canal to Hereford in 1845 had little, if any, effect on Gloucester's commercial life.[25] The Birmingham and Gloucester railway company gained access to the docks in 1841 by bringing the Gloucester – Cheltenham tramway by a spur to its station. As a link between docks and railway the tramway proved unsuitable and in 1848 the Midland Railway completed a branch railway from the station to High Orchard and the docks. Where it ran next to the Sud brook the stream was straightened and culverted. From that time the tramway declined, a process hastened by the opening of the Forest of Dean railway, which gave Cheltenham direct access to coal supplies. The Midland Railway and the G.W.R. obtained powers to abandon the tramway in 1859 and sold the Gloucester depot and removed the lines in 1861.[26]

The staples of Gloucester's trade in the mid 19th century were timber and grain imports. The timber came mainly from the Baltic and Canada and the trade was dominated by local firms such as Price & Co., John Forster & Co., and Robert Heane & Co. in 1850,[27] when the Hull firm of Barkworth & Spaldin established a Gloucester branch.[28] Price & Co., the most important, later opened branches in Grimsby (Lincs.) and Barrow in Furness (Lancs.).[29] After William Price's death in 1838 the firm was headed by his son William Philip Price (d. 1891), who from his newly acquired Tibberton Court estate played an important part in the life of the city, from 1852 as one of its M.P.s. His extensive railway interests culminated in his appointment as chairman of the Midland Railway and in 1873 as a Railway Commissioner.[30] By the 1850s he was partnered in his timber business by Richard Potter, who lived at Standish House and became an industrial and railway magnate, holding the chairmanship of the G.W.R. between 1863 and 1865,[31] and by Charles Walker (d. 1877), who in 1873 purchased the Norton Court estate near Gloucester.[32]

[16] P.R.O., RAIL 829/7, pp. 381–4; *Port of Bristol 1848–84* (Bristol Rec. Soc. xxxvi), 22–3.

[17] *Suppl. to 56th Rep. Glouc. Chamber of Commerce* (1897), 15: copy in Glos. Colln. N 15.6.

[18] *Glouc. Jnl.* 25 Feb. 1837.

[19] *Bryant's Dir. Glouc.* (1841), 84.

[20] *Glouc. Jnl.* 3 Oct. 1835; 5 July, 13 Dec. 1845.

[21] Cf. Glos. R.O., D 3117/612.

[22] *Glouc. Jnl.* 7, 14 Jan. 1837; 4 Aug. 1838; *D.N.B.* suppl., s.v. Baker, Sir Sam. White.

[23] *Suppl. 56th Rep. Chamber of Commerce*, 3.

[24] *Glouc. Jnl.* 8 Mar. 1851; P.R.O., RAIL 1112/11.

[25] D. E. Bick, *Heref. and Glouc. Canal* (1979), 29–41.

[26] Bick, *Glouc. and Chelt. Railway* (1968, Locomotion Papers, no. 43), 24–9, 58; *Glouc. Jnl.* 4 Oct. 1848.

[27] Weekly shipping lists in *Glouc. Jnl.*

[28] Glos. Colln. NX 15.1.

[29] *Kelly's Dir. Glos.* (1856), 299; (1870), 571.

[30] *Glouc. Jnl.* 20 Oct. 1838; 4 Apr. 1891; Glos. R.O., D 4080/1; below, Plate 22.

[31] *Glouc. Jnl.* 9 Jan. 1892; MacDermot, *Hist. G.W.R.* ii (1964), 1–18.

[32] *Glouc. Jnl.* 13 Oct. 1877; 11 Nov. 1893; Glos. R.O., D 142/T 19.

The timber importers' yards, which from the later 1830s centred on High Orchard,[33] converted logs or deals for the building trades.[34] Gloucester's first steam-powered sawmill, built at High Orchard in 1838 by a company of merchants, was quickly abandoned[35] and manual sawing continued for many years. In 1836 the Anti-Dry-Rot Co. of London constructed kyanizing works at High Orchard. They closed in 1841 but several other firms took up timber preserving and creosote production.[36] In the late 1840s and early 1850s the timber trade and industry benefited from railway contracts, particularly those for lines from Oxford to Worcester, Wolverhampton, and Birmingham. From 1849 annual timber imports more than trebled to 106,377 tons in 1852 and then fell to 48,760 tons in 1856. New yards were opened in the Bristol Road area and the number of sawyers rose to more than 75 pairs in 1851. The chief employers were T. and W. Tredwell, Price & Co., and William Eassie.[37] Eassie, who established his works in Gloucester in 1849 and built some railway trucks, later specialized in prefabricated buildings, some of which were sent to Australia.[38] In 1854 and 1855, in association with Price & Co., he supplied huts and hospitals for the British and French armies in the Crimea. Those contracts were obtained by Richard Potter and employed as many as 1,000 men, working in shifts.[39]

In the late 1830s and 1840s the grain trade was still mainly Irish and coastal. Following the repeal of the Corn Laws in 1846 foreign imports, notably from the Ukraine, grew considerably and the docks were enlarged. In 1851 the city ranked third in the trade after London and Glasgow. The Irish and coastal commerce declined from the late 1840s but Irish imports remained significant until the late 1870s when Gloucester's grain trade was falling off generally.[40] Birmingham and Bristol merchants conducted much of the trade, notably the Birmingham firm of Joseph & Charles Sturge and the Bristol firm of Wait, James, & Co., but an important part was handled by local businesses, such as those started c. 1850 by John Robinson and Charles Lucy.[41] Robinson was joined by his cousin Thomas Robinson (d. 1897), who was head of the firm after John moved to Bristol and who became a prominent figure in Gloucester's commercial and public life.[42] William Charles Lucy (d. 1898), who continued his father's business from 1851, built Harescombe Grange on an estate he bought near the city in 1861.[43] Apart from timber and grain, imports covered a wide range of goods in the middle of the century, including metals, ores, Welsh slates and coal, wines, spirits, Irish porter, potatoes, animal feed, and fertilizers.[44]

The balance of trade, both foreign and coastal, heavily favoured imports.[45] The principal export was salt from Droitwich and Stoke Prior (both Worcs.), which was transhipped for markets at home and, to a lesser extent, abroad.[46] The trade survived despite Liverpool's considerable advantages for handling it,[47] and among merchants active in it was Gopsill Brown (d. 1867), who founded a sack-hiring business.[48] The lack of significant outward trade, which arose principally from Gloucester's failure to

[33] Below, topog.; Quay and Docks.

[34] *Suppl. 56th Rep. Chamber of Commerce*, 52–3.

[35] Glos. R.O., D 3117/2543–9.

[36] *Suppl. 56th Rep. Chamber of Commerce*, 29; *Slater's Dir. Glos.* (1852–3), 137; *Kelly's Dir. Glos.* (1863), 275.

[37] *Glouc. Jnl.* 9 Aug. 1851; 24 Jan., 29 May 1852; P.R.O., RAIL 1112/11, rep. Mar. 1854; *Suppl. 56th Rep. Chamber of Commerce*, 52–3.

[38] *Glouc. Jnl.* 29 May 1852; 28 Jan. 1854; 25 Aug. 1888.

[39] Glos. Colln. NR 15.40.

[40] *Suppl. 56th Rep. Chamber of Commerce*, 14, 16–18, 24–5; *Glouc. Jnl.* 24 Jan. 1852.

[41] *Pigot's Dir. Glos.* (1842), 111; *Slater's Dir. Glos.* (1852–3), 132; weekly shipping lists in *Glouc. Jnl.*

[42] *Glouc. Jnl.* 30 Oct. 1897; below, city govt.; parl. representation.

[43] *Glouc. Jnl.* 14 May 1898; Glos. R.O., D 177/III/7.

[44] Weekly shipping lists in *Glouc. Jnl.*

[45] *Glouc. Jnl.* 8 Mar. 1851.

[46] Conway-Jones, *Glouc. Docks*, 29–30; weekly shipping lists in *Glouc. Jnl.*

[47] *Glouc. Jnl.* 15 Apr. 1854.

[48] *Bryant's Dir. Glouc.* (1841), 28–9; *Glouc. Jnl.* 4 May 1867.

become a major outlet for Midlands industry, led many seagoing vessels to leave the port in ballast and take on return cargoes elsewhere.[49] There were several attempts to develop exports of Forest of Dean coal. The most ambitious, involving the construction of a branch railway from Over to a new wharf at Llanthony, was begun by the Gloucester and Dean Forest railway company in 1851 and completed by the G.W.R. in 1854 with a swing bridge over the Severn's eastern channel.[50] It failed, and coal-handling equipment at the wharf was dismantled in 1869.[51]

In the 1840s Gloucester, though not primarily a manufacturing town, had a great variety of small trades and a few larger industries, notably pinmaking and shipbuilding. Metal trades included those of brazier, cutler, gunsmith, tinplate worker, blacksmith, and whitesmith.[52] A small but growing number of foundries supplied castings for, among other things, sugar pans and mortars. The main works were William Montague's foundry in the Island and the Kingsholm foundry started in the early 1830s in Sweetbriar Street.[53] Agricultural and milling implements and machinery were produced in several places, including the Island foundry and works established at Westgate bridge by Thomas Webb in 1838.[54] J. G. Francillon had presumably opened his millstone works by 1850 when he was importing French burrs.[55] In the early 1840s the firm of Cox & Buchanan continued its edgetool manufacture, and nails and wire were made at a few sites,[56] including Whitegoose Mill outside the city boundary.[57] The metal trades and engineering benefited from expansion of the Forest of Dean coal industry and railway contracts in the early 1850s, and foundry facilities were increased.[58] Ironworks at High Orchard and in Quay Street, built for William & James Savory and for William Harris respectively, both dated from 1851.[59]

In its former staple industry of pinmaking, in which much female labour was employed, Gloucester faced strong competition from other places by the 1830s, and the removal of patent restrictions led to collapse.[60] Of the surviving firms one ceased production before 1841[61] and the other two in the 1850s.[62] That of Kirby, Beard, & Co., which employed 132 people in 1851, moved to Birmingham.[63] Another old industry disappeared c. 1849 with the closure by Thomas Mears & Co. of its Gloucester bell foundry.[64] Shipbuilding was represented in 1841 by William Hunt, who was launching schooners of 175 tons at the canal basin, and by three makers of smaller vessels, including Edward Hipwood at Westgate bridge.[65] The industry, which in 1851 employed 55 men from the city,[66] grew in the mid 19th century and new yards were opened on the canal.[67] Among craftsmen associated with the industry were a mast and block maker in 1842[68] and an anchor smith in 1851.[69] There were also firms making rope, sacking, and sailcloth, rope being produced at three sites in the

[49] *Glouc. Jnl.* 8 Mar. 1851; Conway-Jones, *Glouc. Docks,* 29–30.

[50] Glos. R.O., D 1950/E 8 (ii); *Glouc. Jnl.* 1 Nov. 1851; 1 Oct. 1853; 25 Mar. 1854.

[51] *Glouc. Jnl.* 11 Nov. 1854; 20 Feb. 1869.

[52] *Bryant's Dir. Glouc.* (1841), 57–69; *Pigot's Dir. Glos.* (1842), 107–15.

[53] *Pigot's Dir. Glos.* (1842), 107, 112; *Glouc. Jnl.* 5 July 1834.

[54] *Suppl. 56th Rep. Chamber of Commerce,* 30; *Bryant's Dir. Glouc.* (1841), 64; *Kelly's Dir. Glos.* (1856), 298, 300; cf. *Trans. B.G.A.S.* xcix. 157.

[55] *Slater's Dir. Glos.* (1852–3), 137; *Glouc. Jnl.* 25 May 1850.

[56] *Bryant's Dir. Glouc.* (1841), 60, 64, 70; *Pigot's Dir. Glos.* (1842), 115.

[57] Below, Outlying Hamlets, mills.

[58] Cf. *Glouc. Jnl.* 2 Dec. 1854.

[59] Ibid. 16 Aug. 1851; Glos. R.O., DC/F 34.

[60] S. R. H. Jones, 'Hall, English & Co., 1813–41', *Business Hist.* xviii. 35–59.

[61] *Bryant's Dir. Glouc.* (1841), 65.

[62] Cf. *Slater's Dir. Glos.* (1852–3), 134; (1858–9), 196; *Kelly's Dir. Glouc.* (1856), 296; (1863), 277.

[63] P.R.O., HO 107/1962; *Suppl. 56th Rep. Chamber of Commerce,* 29.

[64] *Glouc. Jnl.* 12 May 1849; *Slater's Dir. Glos.* (1852–3), 126.

[65] *Bryant's Dir. Glouc.* (1841), 56, 66; *Glouc. Jnl.* 25 June 1842; 6 Apr. 1844.

[66] *Census,* 1851.

[67] Cf. *Slater's Dir. Glos.* (1852–3), 130.

[68] *Pigot's Dir. Glos.* (1842), 115.

[69] *Census,* 1851.

early 1840s.[70] Gloucester also had three coachbuilding concerns in 1841[71] and new carriage and wheel works were opened in 1846.[72]

Leather trades were represented by curriers, fellmongers, a glover, saddlers, and numerous boot and shoemakers, of whom one had 24 employees in 1851.[73] Of the city's two tanneries one was producing sheepskin mats in 1841 and parchment in 1851.[74] Several businesses made brushes and three factories soap in 1841.[75] The decline of the malting trade saw the number of listed maltsters fall from 14 in 1842 to 6 in 1859.[76] The only brewery of any size, that of Charles Tolley and Edward Trimmer, moved to premises between Westgate and Quay Streets in 1837 and controlled 12 public houses in 1848.[77] The city also had a vinegar factory at that time.[78] A steam flour mill, opened near Westgate bridge in 1833, was worked in 1840 by Thomas McLean, a baker.[79] The growing volume of corn imports from the late 1840s stimulated Gloucester's development as a centre for the flour industry in 1850 with the building by Joseph and Jonah Hadley of City Mills in the docks.[80]

As Gloucester grew the building trades prospered and in 1851 builders were among the largest employers. The firm of William Wingate & Sons, the most important with 64 workers,[81] was connected with many city improvements of the mid and later 19th century.[82] Brickmaking in the meadows near the city expanded considerably after 1840 and works were extended, and new ones established, by the Severn on Alney Island, in Walham and Sandhurst, and at Llanthony and Lower Rea.[83] Local gravel beds were also worked, with important pits being opened, probably before 1875, between Barnwood and Hucclecote.[84] Associated with the docks and the building trades was the enamelled slate industry, which was introduced to Gloucester c. 1845 to dress imported slate to look like marble, granite, or wood.[85]

Gloucester's growing population and commerce increased the demand for shops and services, and professions and businesses catering for the wealthier classes flourished. In retailing, drapery stores were established by Robert Blinkhorn in Eastgate Street in 1843 and by Thomas Denton and a partner in Northgate Street in the early 1850s.[86] Cabinet makers and upholsterers, jewellers, clock and watch makers, and wine and spirit merchants were recorded in the mid 19th century,[87] and there were separate businesses making organs and pianos.[88] The printing industry was represented in the early 1840s by at least eight printers, including the owner of the *Gloucester Journal*,[89] and 54 printing and bookbinding workers lived in the city in 1851.[90] In 1842 the legal and medical professions were followed by 41 and 20 men respectively, the former figure reflecting Gloucester's role in civil and ecclesiastical administration.[91] Auctioneers and estate agents practising in the city were joined in

[70] *Bryant's Dir. Glouc.* (1841), 66; *Pigot's Dir. Glos.* (1842), 113.

[71] *Bryant's Dir. Glouc.* (1841), 59.

[72] *Kelly's Dir. Glos.* (1870), 1056.

[73] *Bryant's Dir. Glouc.* (1841), 57–66; *Pigot's Dir. Glos.* (1842), 111–13; P.R.O., HO 107/1962.

[74] *Bryant's Dir. Glouc.* (1841), 66, 69; Bd. of Health Map (1852).

[75] *Bryant's Dir. Glouc.* (1841), 57, 67.

[76] *Pigot's Dir. Glos.* (1842), 112; *Slater's Dir. Glos.* (1858–9), 195.

[77] *Glouc. Jnl.* 18 Mar. 1837; 7 Oct. 1848; Causton, *Map of Glouc.* (1843).

[78] *Pigot's Dir. Glos.* (1842), 115; *Slater's Dir. Glos.* (1852–3), 137.

[79] *Glos. Chron.* 31 Aug. 1833; *Glouc. Jnl.* 28 Mar. 1840.

[80] *Suppl. 56th Rep. Chamber of Commerce*, 25–6; *Glos. Hist. Studies*, xii. 3–4.

[81] P.R.O., HO 107/1962.

[82] *Glos. Chron.* 20 July 1867; Glos. Colln. NR 15.39.

[83] Cf. G.D.R., T 1/16, 156; O.S. Map 6″, Glos. XXV. NW. (1883 edn.); SE., SW.(1889 edn.); XXXIII. NW. (1888 edn.).

[84] Glos. R.O., D 292; O.S. Map 6″, Glos. XXXIII. NE. (1891 edn.); cf. *Glouc. Jnl.* 26 May 1894.

[85] *Suppl. 56th Rep. Chamber of Commerce*, 32.

[86] *Glouc. Jnl.* 3 Nov. 1888; 29 Aug. 1896.

[87] *Slater's Dir. Glos.* (1852–3), 131–7.

[88] P.R.O., HO 107/1962.

[89] *Bryant's Dir. Glouc.* (1841), 65.

[90] *Census*, 1851.

[91] *Pigot's Dir. Glos.* (1842), 109–10, 113–14.

1849 by Henry Bruton from Newent.[92] The main banks in 1835 were those of the Bank of England, the National Provincial Bank, and the Gloucestershire Banking Co. The Gloucester City and County Bank, which commenced trading that year, was taken over in 1836 by the new County of Gloucester Bank of Cheltenham. James Wood, the city's last private banker, died in 1836, and the Bank of England closed its branch and transferred its business to Bristol in 1849.[93]

There are numerous indications of economic hardship in Gloucester in the 1850s when many businesses, notably the vinegar factory and the edgetool firm of Cox & Buchanan, closed.[94] On the canal traffic plummeted from 634,520 tons in 1852, when railway contracts sustained much economic activity, to 418,470 tons in 1857. The Crimean war, which severely reduced both grain and timber imports, compounded the depression.[95] Unemployment, mitigated until 1855 by activity at William Eassie's works, led to a prevalence of pauperism and attendant social problems which persisted in some districts in 1859.[96] Nevertheless the late 1850s saw an improvement in Gloucester's economic fortunes with a revival in trade and industrial expansion.

Despite the recovery Gloucester's advantages as an inland port were jeopardized by the inability of larger seagoing vessels to use the canal and docks, by the increasing use of railway links between the Midlands and other ports, and by the lack of a strong export trade. The last factor led in turn to a shortage of railway wagons at Gloucester and to the diversion by 1865 of barley for the malting industry at Burton-upon-Trent (Staffs.) to Newport (Mon.).[97] Larger vessels transferred all or part of their cargoes bound for Gloucester to lighters at the Sharpness end of the canal by the early 1850s,[98] when a regular steam packet service on the canal was begun.[99] Although steam towage, introduced on the canal in 1860, reduced the cost of importing through Gloucester,[1] traffic carried on the canal had risen by 1872 to only 624,454 tons. New and larger docks opened at Sharpness in 1874 failed to halt the port's comparative decline, and deep water docks built at Avonmouth and Portishead (Som.) in the port of Bristol in the late 1870s attracted much of its business, particularly the grain trade. The loss of that trade was temporarily checked by an agreement of 1882 ending intense competition between the ports.[2] Gloucester's timber trade continued to prosper, 160,257 tons being imported in 1877, and William Nicks (d. 1885) became one of its more prominent local representatives.[3] During that period a trade in petroleum imports from America was established,[4] but a steamship company formed in 1874 to link Gloucester with Ireland was short lived.[5] The port's decline, which extended to the coasting trade, and the economic recession of the early 1880s led some merchants, including the firm of J. & C. Sturge, to leave the city.[6]

Gloucester's river trade was assisted by the regular employment of steam tugs on the Severn from the mid 1850s.[7] Dredging of the river above the entrance locks of the Gloucester and Berkeley and the Herefordshire and Gloucestershire canals, begun in

[92] Glos. Colln. N 15.7; *Slater's Dir. Glos.* (1852–3), 129.
[93] Glos. Colln., Hannam-Clark papers, notes on Glouc. bankers; Glos. R.O., D 2025, Co. of Glouc. Bank papers.
[94] *Glouc. Jnl.* 12 Mar., 18 June 1853; *Slater's Dir. Glos.* (1852–3), 137; (1858–9), 199.
[95] *Suppl. 56th Rep. Chamber of Commerce,* 15; P.R.O., RAIL 1112/11.
[96] *Glouc. Jnl.* 19 Nov. 1859.
[97] Conway-Jones, *Glouc. Docks,* 66–74; *Glouc. Jnl.* 7 Oct. 1865.
[98] *Glouc. Jnl.* 23 July 1853.
[99] Conway-Jones, *Glouc. Docks,* 60–1; cf. *Slater's Dir. Glos.*

(1858–9), 201.
[1] Glos. Colln. J 14.2.
[2] *Suppl. 56th Rep. Chamber of Commerce,* 15–16, 18; Conway-Jones, *Glouc. Docks,* 80–4.
[3] *Suppl. 56th Rep. Chamber of Commerce,* 52–6; *Glos. Chron.* 2 Jan. 1886.
[4] Conway-Jones, *Glouc. Docks,* 82–3; *Kelly's Dir. Glos.* (1885), 503.
[5] *Glouc. Jnl.* 29 Aug. 1874; 11 Sept. 1880.
[6] Glos. Colln. J 14.3, 14–15; Conway-Jones, *Glouc. Docks,* 87.
[7] *Glouc. Jnl.* 29 July 1854.

1842, proved inadequate as larger seagoing vessels replaced Severn trows, and to maintain the depth of water between the city and Tewkesbury new channels with locks and weirs were cut at Llanthony and Maisemore between 1869 and 1871.[8] Those works contributed, by changing the Severn's flow, to the virtual abandonment of the city quay and increased river traffic in the docks, where the Severn & Canal Carrying Co., formed in 1873 by a merger of Worcester and Stourport firms, transhipped goods.[9]

The railways and particularly their extension west of the Severn ended Gloucester's days as a coaching centre.[10] The Brecon mailcoach made its last run in 1854.[11] Although their advent reduced the work of the city's remaining woolstaplers,[12] the railways contributed to a growth in market trade. New markets for cheese, wool, and hides were established in the 1850s, and a new produce market and a corn exchange were built in 1856.[13] The business of the livestock market, through which 33,800 sheep, 21,276 cattle, 11,222 pigs, and 2,030 horses passed in 1861,[14] continued to grow after its improvement in 1863.[15] The mops or hiring fairs held after Barton Fair (28 September) attracted many farm hands and domestic servants and survived attempts to replace them by a registration society, formed in 1838 mainly by the efforts of John Curtis-Hayward of Quedgeley and revived in 1859.[16] The mops, which were attended by employers and servants from all over the county in the early 1870s,[17] later succumbed to the use of newspaper advertisements.[18] Gloucester's growing population provided a market for the agricultural produce of the surrounding countryside and there were extensive market and nursery gardens in the suburbs.[19] Notable were the nurseries of J. C. Wheeler, whose firm in 1859 received an order for fruit trees for Osborne House (I.W.) and Windsor.[20] Local carrying businesses, which flourished in the mid 19th century, maintained links between Gloucester and its traditional economic region, the towns and villages of north Gloucestershire and adjoining counties.[21]

Gloucester's industrial development, which from the mid 19th century centred principally on the docks and canal, became the most significant factor in economic activity after the slump of the mid 1880s. Industrialization created several major employers, the largest being the Gloucester Wagon Co., founded in 1860 by local businessmen to make, repair, and hire railway trucks. With Richard Potter as chairman the company built a factory in Bristol Road and by the end of 1860 employed 360 workers.[22] Owing much of its success to the first manager, Isaac Slater, it penetrated non-colonial overseas markets from 1867, when it obtained a Russian contract,[23] and it constructed large repair works near the former T station south-east of the city in 1869.[24] In 1874 the company had a workforce of c. 800.[25] The Bristol Road works stood next to William Eassie's joinery workshops,[26] and that business, continued after Eassie's death in 1861 by his sons, received an injection of capital from

[8] Glos. Colln. MF 1.50, pp. 7–9; Glos. R.O., D 2460, Severn Com., engineer's rep. bk. 1855–78.

[9] G.B.R., B 6/25/1, pp. 22, 53; Conway-Jones, *Glouc. Docks*, 108.

[10] Cf. G.B.R., L 6/4/2, mem. 8 Oct. 1867.

[11] *Glouc. Jnl.* 1 Apr. 1854.

[12] *Glos. Chron.* 14 Feb. 1885.

[13] Below, Markets and Fairs; *Glouc. Jnl.* 10 May 1851; 26 June 1852; 15 Apr. 1854.

[14] G.B.R., B 4/1/7, f. 265.

[15] Ibid. L 6/4/2, mem. 23 Mar. 1869; B 6/25/1, pp. 21, 59–63.

[16] S. Lysons, *Glos. Achievements* (1862), 19; *Glouc. Jnl.* 6 Aug. 1859; 6 Oct. 1860; 3 Oct. 1868.

[17] *Western Daily Press*, 9 Oct. 1872.

[18] *Glouc. Jnl.* 2 Oct. 1937.

[19] Causton, *Map of Glouc.* (1843); below, Outlying Hamlets, agric.

[20] *Glouc. Jnl.* 26 Mar. 1859.

[21] *Slater's Dir. Glos.* (1858–9), 200–1.

[22] Glos. R.O., D 4791, Glouc. Railway Carriage & Wagon Co., min. bk. 1860–4, pp. 1–18, 68–9.

[23] *Hist. Glouc. Railway Carriage & Wagon Co.* (1960), 6–8: Glos. Colln. 18581.

[24] Glos. R.O., D 4791, Glouc. Railway Carriage & Wagon Co., min. bk. 1868–71, pp. 5–6, 117–18, 165.

[25] G.B.R., B 6/25/1, p. 12.

[26] Ibid. L 6/4/2, mem. 26 Jan. 1864.

the wagon company's directors in 1866.[27] Production at Eassie & Co. was increasingly dominated by orders for the wagon company, which in 1875 bought the business, thereby doubling the size of its Bristol Road works.[28]

Foundry work and engineering grew and diversified. Samuel Fielding and James Platt, who in the later 1860s acquired the Atlas Ironworks, built at High Orchard in 1860, established the principal heavy engineering concern, specializing in hydraulic machine tools and gas engines.[29] The older High Orchard ironworks, one of several producing flour-milling machinery,[30] was acquired in 1881 by the heavy engineering firm of T. & W. Summers of Southampton. It constructed a machine shop in Bristol Road c. 1890.[31] William Gardner, who in 1861 took over J. G. Francillon's millstone factory, established a firm of milling engineers. He built a factory in Southgate Street in 1878 and moved to new and larger works in Bristol Road in 1894 when he took his sons into partnership.[32] In Quay Street J. J. Seekings from 1870 and William Sisson from 1889 developed a marine engineering business, which moved in 1905 to new works near Elmbridge Road, where it produced a wide range of high speed machinery.[33] Works catering for agriculture included those of the implement makers S., A., and H. Kell of Ross-on-Wye (Herefs.), who took over a foundry in Barton Street in 1856,[34] and H. S. Crump of Tewkesbury, who began a business in London Road after 1874.[35] Among older foundries that of William Montague was continued by Charles Montague and was closed in 1865.[36] An attempt to establish edgetool works in Kingsholm in the late 1850s was short lived.[37]

Gloucester's flour industry expanded in the 1860s. The number of mills rose from two in 1860, when City Mills was taken over by Joseph Reynolds and Henry Allen, to eight by the early 1870s. Albert Mills dated from a conversion in 1869 of a warehouse in the docks by James Reynolds, whose partners later included James Bruton. From the 1870s the industry was threatened by imported flour and by failure to introduce new technology. At least one mill closed before 1914 and at others animal feed was increasingly the main product. Only Albert and City Mills, which adopted the roller-milling process in the early 1880s, prospered as flour mills. City Mills was worked from 1886 by the firm of Priday, Metford, & Co.[38] Gloucester's role in supplying agricultural needs increased in the late 19th century. Fertilizer works were built near Hempsted bridge c. 1855,[39] but more important was the move by Foster Bros. of its seed-crushing business from Evesham (Worcs.) to a new mill at Baker's Quay in 1863.[40] The mill, which processed linseed from Argentina, India, and Russia, and cotton seed from Egypt, produced oil for markets at home and abroad and cake for sale in the Midlands as animal feed or fertilizer. Foster Bros. became a major employer with a workforce of 129 in 1897 and amalgamated with other firms in 1899 to form British Oil & Cake Mills Ltd.[41]

The shipbuilding industry thrived after 1859 when the Sunderland firm of

[27] Glouc. Jnl. 1 June 1861; Glos. Chron. 29 Sept. 1866.

[28] Glos. R.O., D 4791, Glouc. Railway Carriage & Wagon Co., min. bk. 1875–8, pp. 55–6, 78, 94, 143.

[29] Suppl. 56th Rep. Chamber of Commerce, 30; Glos. Colln. NQ 15.11; below, Plate 26.

[30] Kelly's Dir. Glos. (1870), 571.

[31] Glos. Chron. 14 Feb. 1885; Ind. Glos. 1904, 6: copy in Glos. Colln. JV 13.1.

[32] Glouc. Jnl. 16 Dec. 1916; Suppl. 56th Rep. Chamber of Commerce, 30.

[33] Glouc. Jnl. 7 Jan. 1899; Glos. R.O., IN 75.

[34] Suppl. 56th Rep. Chamber of Commerce, 30; Trans.

B.G.A.S. xcix. 157–66.

[35] Glos. Chron. 14 Feb. 1885; Who's Who in Glouc. (1910), 47.

[36] Kelly's Dir. Glos. (1856), 298; (1863), 280; Suppl. 56th Rep. Chamber of Commerce, 29.

[37] Slater's Dir. Glos. (1858–9), 199; Glouc. Jnl. 7 June 1862.

[38] Glos. Hist. Studies, xii. 3–5; Suppl. 56th Rep. Chamber of Commerce, 26–8; Ind. Glos. 1904, 49–50.

[39] Glos. R.O., P 173/VE 2/1, min. 12 Apr. 1855.

[40] Glouc. Jnl. 17 Jan., 21 Feb. 1863.

[41] Suppl. 56th Rep. Chamber of Commerce, 32; Ind. Glos. 1904, 51.

Pickersgill & Miller took over a yard.[42] A barque of 500 tons launched in 1860 was said to be the largest vessel built at Gloucester but was soon surpassed by several ships.[43] A few iron vessels were constructed by engineering firms, including Fielding & Platt which completed Gloucester's first seagoing steamer in 1868,[44] but with the replacement of wooden sailing ships the industry declined rapidly. After the late 1870s, when F. C. Hipwood launched two seagoing vessels into the river above Westgate bridge, it was devoted mostly to building and repairing river and canal craft.[45] The number of yards fell to three or four with a workforce of over 50 in 1911.[46] The decline was felt in ancillary trades such as ropemaking which had ceased by that time.[47]

The fortunes of Gloucester's other industries and trades varied in the late 19th century. Brushmaking survived and soapmaking, which had stopped in the early 1860s, was revived. Industrialization in the food and clothing trades produced several major employers. In 1870 John Stephens started a vinegar and pickle factory at the tannery at the north end of Hare Lane, which had closed a few years earlier. The factory extended production to jam and in 1897 employed 400 people.[48] A small mineral water and soft drinks factory was built in Commercial Road in the mid 1870s, incorporating part of the Blackfriars.[49] Several breweries were started[50] but most were closed after acquisition by larger concerns outside the city, principally by the Cheltenham brewery.[51] A successful malting business belonged to G. and W. E. Downing of Smethwick (Staffs.), whose maltings, built at High Orchard in 1876, were considerable enlarged by the early 20th century.[52] A shirt factory and a cuff and collar factory, built in 1887 and c. 1900 respectively, were among the largest employers.[53]

In the cabinet-making trade the most successful firm was started by J. A. Matthews in 1863. It produced a range of furniture, much of it from 1894 at a large new factory at High Orchard, and employed 200 people in 1897. A smaller company was created by Edwin Lea, who added extensive workshops to his retailing business in Northgate Street.[54] The enamelled slate industry prospered and in 1897 employed c. 200 people. One of its leading exponents by the mid 1860s was Jesse Sessions (d. 1894), who had begun as a builders' merchant in 1838. His successors built a factory at Baker's Quay in 1897 for the manufacture of chimney pieces and bathroom furniture.[55] Most of Gloucester's enamelled slate production ceased before 1918.[56] In the early 1890s G. T. Whitfield opened brickworks on the west side of Robins Wood Hill.[57] Prominent among Gloucester builders was Albert Estcourt (d. 1909), who, at first in partnership with his brother Oliver (d. 1871), worked throughout the country with leading architects.[58] Also known outside the city at the turn of the century was the sculptor Henry Frith, who with his brother W. S. Frith of London provided carvings for the Birmingham law courts.[59] The printing and stationery industry also prospered

[42] P.R.O., RAIL 1112/11; Conway-Jones, *Glouc. Docks*, 69–70.

[43] *Glouc. Jnl.* 10 Mar., 28 Apr. 1860; 3 Aug. 1861; 5 July 1862.

[44] Ibid. 7 Nov. 1868; 10 Oct. 1891; *Suppl. 56th Rep. Chamber of Commerce*, 29.

[45] *Glos. Chron.* 17 Jan. 1885; cf. *Glouc. Jnl.* 23 Jan., 16 July 1892.

[46] *Kelly's Dir. Glos* (1910), 442; (1914), 450; *Census*, 1911.

[47] *V.C.H. Glos.* ii. 199.

[48] *Suppl. 56th Rep. Chamber of Commerce*, 29–33.

[49] Glos. Colln. NR 15.39, pp. 23–4.

[50] *Glos. Chron.* 14 Feb. 1885.

[51] Glos. R.O., IN 18.

[52] *Glouc. Jnl.* 24 Mar. 1877; Glos. R.O., D 2460, plans 1/C/1–13; parts of the maltings are dated 1895 and 1901.

[53] *Suppl. 56th Rep. Chamber of Commerce*, 32; *Kelly's Dir. Glos.* (1902), 199; Glos. R.O., D 4014/4, p. 75.

[54] *Suppl. 56th Rep. Chamber of Commerce*, 31; Glos. Colln. NR 15.39.

[55] *Suppl. 56th Rep. Chamber of Commerce*, 31–2; *Glouc. Jnl.* 21 Apr. 1894; *Ind. Glos.* 1904, 46.

[56] Glos. Colln. NF 15.19.

[57] Glos. Colln. 40298; *Kelly's Dir. Glos.* (1894), 330.

[58] *Glouc. Jnl.* 20 Feb. 1909.

[59] Glos. Colln. NR 15.39, p. 38; *Ind. Glos.* 1904, 45.

and employed well over 300 people in 1901.[60] One of the largest employers was John Bellows, who started his business in 1858 and published a successful pocket French–English dictionary from 1872.[61] The firm of Wellington & Co., which began as paper merchants in the early 1850s and also manufactured paper bags and cardboard boxes, had a workforce of c. 160 in 1904.[62]

Matchmaking, an industry for which Gloucester became widely known, was introduced in 1867.[63] S. J. Moreland built a factory in Bristol Road the following year[64] and as his business expanded the factory was enlarged and a timber float was constructed on the canal at Two Mile Bend between Hempsted and Quedgeley. The firm's familiar England's Glory trademark, registered in 1891, copied a label produced in the 1870s at one of two match factories in the Island. In 1885 the industry employed over 1,000 outworkers, chiefly women and children, making match boxes. Moreland's factory, which had a workforce of 640 in 1907, was rebuilt on a larger scale in 1911;[65] the business was acquired by Bryant & May in 1913 but remained under the management of the Moreland family.[66] A successful chemicals business was started in 1869 by J. M. Collett, who in 1904 moved to a new factory near Bristol Road.[67] A lampblack factory in Millbrook Street, opened by 1870, was closed c. 1916.[68]

The general economic revival begun in the later 1880s was felt throughout Gloucester's economy. It supported a growth in banking[69] and in retail trade. Some stores were enlarged,[70] including the Bon Marché, a drapery business started by J. R. Pope in Northgate Street in 1889.[71] Chain stores opened branches in the city centre, including, by the First World War, Boots Cash Chemists and Home & Colonial Stores. The footwear business of George Oliver had premises there from the late 1870s.[72] The Gloucester Co-operative and Industrial Society, formed in 1860, opened retail outlets both in the centre and the suburbs, and by 1910 it had 18 shops, a bakery, and a depot in Gloucester. Between 1887 and 1900 it also had a dairy farm of 100 a. at Saintbridge.[73] The market trade flourished, with the cattle market being enlarged several times, and a wholesale fruit market was established in 1900.[74] The railway companies undertook works to accommodate increased traffic through Gloucester. In 1885 the G.W.R. opened a line to Ledbury (Herefs.) along the course of the Herefordshire and Gloucestershire canal, which had closed in 1881.[75] The company rebuilt its station following the opening of the Severn Tunnel in 1886.[76] To compete, the Midland Railway in 1896 replaced its terminus by a station which through trains could use without reversing. The new station (later Eastgate) was some way south-east of the old and was connected by a long footbridge to the G.W.R. station (later Central).[77] The G.W.R. relaid track on the line bypassing Gloucester near Barnwood in 1901.[78]

The port's trade benefited not only from the general economic recovery but also from a reduction in tolls and improvements in the river approach to Sharpness. By the

[60] Census, 1901.
[61] Suppl. 56th Rep. Chamber of Commerce, 32; D.N.B. 2nd suppl.
[62] Ind. Glos. 1904, 63.   [63] Glos. Chron. 14 Feb. 1885.
[64] G.B.R., B 4/5/2, min. 11 Oct. 1867; Glos. R.O., D 3117/3469.
[65] Glos. R.O., IN 50; Glos. Chron. 14 Feb. 1885; Conway-Jones, Glouc. Docks, 159.
[66] Glos. R.O., IN 83.
[67] Ind. Glos. 1904, 58; Glouc. Jnl. 29 Nov. 1924.
[68] Kelly's Dir. Glos. (1870), 568; (1914), 202; (1919), 190.
[69] Glos. Colln., Hannam-Clark papers, notes on Glouc. bankers.

[70] Ind. Glos. 1904, 77; Glos. R.O., D 4335/193.
[71] Glos. Colln. NR 15.10.
[72] Kelly's Dir. Glos. (1914), 196–214; Glos. R.O., AR/C/BA Glouc.
[73] F. Purnell and H. W. Williams, Jubilee Hist. of Glouc. Co-operative and Ind. Soc. Ltd. (1910), 157, 180–4.
[74] Below, Markets and Fairs; Glouc. Jnl. 15 Oct. 1892; Glos. Colln. NX 3.1, p. 4.
[75] Bick, Heref. and Glouc. Canal, 41, 58–9.
[76] Glouc. Jnl. 4 Dec. 1886; Glos. Chron. 9 Nov. 1889.
[77] Glouc. Jnl. 11, 18 Apr. 1896; Glos. Soc. for Ind. Arch. Jnl. (1975), 76–83.
[78] MacDermot, Hist. G.W.R. i. 92 n.

end of the century vessels with cargoes of 1,200 tons were navigating the canal, but most of Gloucester's overseas trade was transhipped at Sharpness. Canal-borne traffic rose from 594,772 tons in 1886 to 776,497 tons in 1896[79] and continued to grow after 1900.[80] With the port of Bristol continuing to take the bulk of the grain trade, the chief increase was in the timber trade. Timber imports, comprising a great variety of goods, rose from 107,714 tons in 1886 to 192,119 tons in 1896, when Gloucester was the ninth largest timber port in the country.[81] For the trade a dock and pond, with a branch line from the Midland railway, were constructed in Monk Meadow in the 1890s.[82] Most of the importers' yards were in the Bristol Road area[83] and the Price family business, re-formed in 1889 as Price, Walker, & Co. Ltd., moved to new premises there in 1894. The company, which took over several other businesses and in 1904 employed up to 700 people in its yard, dominated the trade.[84] A regular steamer service to Antwerp and Rotterdam, inaugurated in 1885, was later extended to Hamburg. Its main cargo comprised sugar imports. Gloucester retained a substantial trade with ports of the West Country, South Wales, and Ireland, and salt remained the chief export.[85] In 1887 Gloucester corporation rebuilt the city quay in an attempt to revive its trade with the port's hinterland,[86] but it opposed the deepening of the Severn between the city and Worcester, promoted by commercial interests in Cardiff and undertaken in the early 1890s.[87]

The late 19th and early 20th century saw further industrial expansion and diversification.[88] In 1888 the wagon company, which also made railway carriages, sold its **T** station works (known later as the Emlyn Works) and to overcome difficulties re-formed with reduced capital as the Gloucester Railway Carriage & Wagon Co. Ltd.[89] The new company enlarged the Bristol Road works[90] and with the purchase in 1893 of carriage and wheel works in the city began producing road vehicles, including during the Boer war ambulances.[91] The company reduced operations by closing its joinery and road-vehicle departments in 1900 and 1908 respectively, their work being continued by other companies.[92] In the early 20th century the local character of the wagon works was diluted by the inclusion of outsiders on the board; among them was Stanley Baldwin, with whose firm the company collaborated in the purchase of steelworks at Port Talbot (Glam.) in 1906.[93] In 1897 the wagon works, the largest firm in the city, employed 1,100 people. Nine other engineering firms employed 1,080 people; the most important were Fielding & Platt (500) and Summers & Scott (180). The latter, formerly T. & W. Summers,[94] passed into receivership c. 1907.[95] W. S. Barron & Son, an engineering firm noted for provender mill plant, started at Kingsholm in 1903.[96] New manufactures, which came to employ 100–150 people, included folding furniture at the Hatherley Works in Melbourne Street, opened in

[79] *Suppl. 56th Rep. Chamber of Commerce*, 6, 15–16; Glos. Colln. N 13.58 (12–18); Conway-Jones, *Glouc. Docks*, 98–100.

[80] C. Hadfield, *Canals of S. & SE. Eng.* (Newton Abbot, 1969), 352.

[81] *Suppl. 56th Rep. Chamber of Commerce*, 24, 52.

[82] Conway-Jones, *Glouc. Docks*, 91–4.

[83] Glos. Colln. NX 15.1.

[84] *Ind. Glos. 1904*, 32–4; Glos. Colln. NV 15.2.

[85] Conway-Jones, *Glouc. Docks*, 85–6, 98–100.

[86] *Suppl. 56th Rep. Chamber of Commerce*, 37.

[87] Glos. Colln. MF 1.50, pp. 10–12; Conway-Jones, *Glouc. Docks*, 91–2; G.B.R., L 6/11/32.

[88] Above.

[89] Glos. R.O., D 4791, Glouc. Railway Carriage & Wagon Co., min. bk. 1886–90, pp. 189–216, 250; cf. *Kelly's Dir. Glos.* (1894), 194.

[90] *Hist. Glouc. Railway Carriage & Wagon Co.* 21; *Glouc. Jnl.* 2 Sept. 1905. For the works in 1921, below, Fig. 13.

[91] Glos. R.O., D 4791, Glouc. Railway Carriage & Wagon Co., min. bk. 1890–4, pp. 243, 278–9; *Hist. Glouc. Railway Carriage & Wagon Co.* 24. For examples of vehicles produced, below, Plates 28–9.

[92] Glos. R.O., D 4791, Glouc. Railway Carriage & Wagon Co., min. bk. 1899–1904, pp. 34–5, 72; min. bk. 1904–9, p. 317; Glos. Colln. NX 3.1, p. 16.

[93] *Hist. Glouc. Railway Carriage & Wagon Co.* 41; *Glouc. Jnl.* 1 Sept. 1906.

[94] *Suppl. 56th Rep. Chamber of Commerce*, 30.

[95] Glos. R.O., D 4791, Glouc. Railway Carriage & Wagon Co., min. bk. 1904–9, p. 318.

[96] *Ind. Glos. 1904*, 11; *Milling*, 21 Aug. 1937, p. 207: copy in Glos. Colln. NV 15.3.

1885, and from 1892 hairpins and toys and games.[97] In the early 20th century motor cars and cycles were built in Gloucester on a small scale,[98] among others by the Cotton Motor Co., which made cycles for trials to a design patented in 1914.[99]

Trade unionism appeared in Gloucester before 1835[1] but made little progress before the 1850s when railwaymen, watermen, and shipwrights registered friendly societies.[2] In 1844 solicitors' clerks were among groups seeking a reduction in winter working hours similar to that introduced by some shopkeepers.[3] A branch of the Amalgamated Society of Engineers was formed before 1860.[4] In the 1860s and 1870s industrial relations were occasionally disrupted by strikes, notably by shipwrights, building workers, dock labourers, and railwaymen, the last forming a branch of the Amalgamated Railway Servants' Association in 1872.[5] The printing workers also became more organized, having their own branch of the Typographical Association from 1875.[6] In the late 19th century trade unionists were active in many industries, and on several occasions engineering employers resorted to lockouts.[7] Employment in the docks was sensitive to any disruption of trade by economic recession, war, and harsh weather,[8] and over 250 deal porters struck in 1881 over an attempt to reduce their wages. The formation of a branch of the Dock Labourers' Union in 1889 was followed by a strike of c. 1,300 men at Gloucester and Sharpness in sympathy with Bristol dockers and by friction over the employment of non-union labour.[9] In 1900 the grain and oil-seed importers formed an association to protect their interests and in 1902 employers in the port formed another to deal with labour matters.[10]

Gloucester's occupational structure in the early 20th century reflected the relative decline of the port, the growth in manufacturing industry and engineering, and the continuing importance of distributive trades. The railways employed more than 1,200 men in 1901 but among male workers engineering and building trades were even more dominant. The proportion of the population in domestic service had declined and the main areas of female employment included the clothing, toy, match, and jam and pickle industries. The number of people employed in the civil service and local government to administer the population of both city and county rose from 329 in 1901 to 502 in 1911.[11]

Economic Development 1914–85

The First World War greatly reduced Gloucester's foreign trade. Recovery was slow and traffic on the Gloucester and Berkeley canal did not return to its pre-war level until the 1930s,[12] though a service between the city and Norwegian ports had been restored by the early 1920s.[13] Activity in the docks continued to reflect the city's position as a centre for water, rail, and road transport and as a gateway to the Midlands, but grain and oil-seed imports were increasingly destined only for local

[97] Suppl. 56th Rep. Chamber of Commerce, 31–2; Ind. Glos. 1904, 17–18, 40, 42–3; Glos. and Avon Life, Aug. 1980, 57. [98] Citizen, 4 Mar. 1971.
[99] Glos. Colln. N 15.101; NV 15.7.
[1] Glouc. Jnl. 3 May 1834.
[2] P.R.O., FS 2/3, nos. 468, 684; FS 4/12, no. 550.
[3] Glouc. Jnl. 16 Nov. 1844.
[4] Purnell and Williams, Hist. Glouc. Co-Operative and Ind. Soc. 4.
[5] Glouc. Jnl. 27 Feb. 1864; 21 Apr., 9 June 1866; 15 July 1871; 6 Apr., 3, 17 Aug. 1872; 18 Sept. 1875; 11 Jan. 1879.
[6] Glos. R.O., D 3983/1.
[7] Glos. Colln. N 13.92; Glouc. Jnl. 1 Dec. 1888; 23 Feb. 1889; 28 Feb. 1891; 25 Sept. 1897; J. R. Howe, 'Political

Hist. of the Parl. Constituencies of Chelt., Glouc., and the Ciren. and Tewkes. Divisions of Glos. 1895–1914' (Bristol Univ. M.Litt. thesis, 1977), 43.
[8] Glouc. Jnl. 3 Feb. 1855; 26 Mar. 1864; 7 Jan. 1871; 7 May 1881; 6 Mar. 1886.
[9] Ibid. 9 July 1881; 28 Dec. 1889; 29 Mar., 19, 26 Apr. 1890.
[10] Glos. R.O., D 4828, Glouc. Grain & Oil-Seeds Importers Assoc., min. bk. 1900–4.
[11] Census, 1901–11; Rep. of Medical Off. of Health, 1911: copy in G.B.R., B 3/46.
[12] Paragraph based on Conway-Jones, Glouc. Docks, 126–4, and Glos. Colln. N 15.30, pp. 23–4, 48–50.
[13] G. S. Blakeway, City of Glouc. (1924), 127.

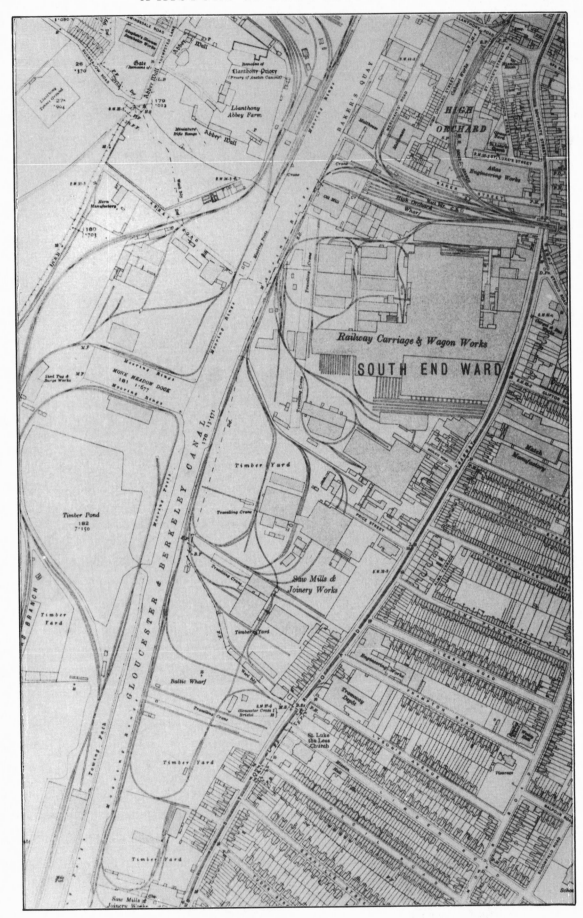

Fig. 13. The upper Bristol Road area, 1921 (*north at the top*)

industry and several warehouses were abandoned or put to other uses. Gloucester regained its role as a leading timber port, and other imports sent inland by river included cocoa beans, sugar, and chocolate crumb for the Cadbury Bros. factory at Bournville (Birmingham) and from the mid 1920s refined petroleum products. The Monk Meadow dock became a distribution point for the petroleum trade and was bordered by storage tanks.[14] Export trade remained much smaller and shipments of salt, which was usually brought to the docks by rail, became less frequent because of competition from Liverpool. Local traffic on the canal faced increasing competition from road transport, and in the early 1930s the regular steamer service between Gloucester and Sharpness was withdrawn.

During the First World War Gloucester industry was subordinated to military needs. Products of the wagon works included stretchers and shells.[15] The war led to an expansion in engineering, and the firm of Williams & James, founded in 1915, was one of several new enterprises.[16] At Hempsted c. 350 men were engaged between 1917 and 1920 in building six concrete barges, begun as part of the war effort.[17] Aeroplanes were assembled and tested at an airfield laid out by the Air Board in 1915 on the boundary of Hucclecote and Brockworth. A munitions factory in Quedgeley provided wartime employment for 6,000 hands, many presumably from the city,[18] and a munitions store was laid out by the canal in Monk Meadow.[19] Attempts to foster industry during the post-war slump were generally unsuccessful. The match industry, at that time hit by taxation and foreign competition,[20] was unable to sustain a new factory, built at Hempsted bridge in 1920 and closed in 1923.[21] More successful was a factory built at Llanthony in 1919 for the manufacture of incubators and poultry houses. It employed c. 125 men in 1932.[22] In the early 1920s the engineering works of W. Sisson & Co. were enlarged to make chocolate-rolling machinery for Cadbury Bros. Ltd.[23]

The Gloucester Railway Carriage & Wagon Co. relinquished its repairing and hiring operations in 1918 and 1920 respectively.[24] From 1922 it was closely associated with Alfred Danks Ltd., a local engineering firm which that year purchased the Emlyn Works and closed the Kingsholm foundry. The wagon works purchased Danks Ltd. in 1929 and had a large interest in the Gloucester Foundry Ltd., set up in 1930 to run the Emlyn Works, from which it had obtained malleable castings.[25] The wagon works narrowly avoided financial disaster in 1930 when a railway-wagon hiring business which it controlled went into liquidation. Following the appointment in 1931 as chairman of Harold Leslie Boyce, M.P. for Gloucester, the wagon works were reorganized, and their financial recovery was helped by orders in the late 1930s for re-armament projects and from the London Passenger Transport Board.[26] Boyce, who was knighted in 1944, died in 1955.[27]

Production at the wagon works continued throughout the General Strike of 1926. The strike was joined by dockers, railwaymen, tramway employees, and printers, but

[14] *Glouc. Jnl.* 11 Nov. 1922; *Waterways World*, Sept. 1976, 29; Oct. 1976, 33.

[15] *Hist. Glouc. Railway Carriage & Wagon Co.* (1960), 44: Glos. Colln. 18581.

[16] *Glouc. Official Guide* (1963), 123–5; Glos. R.O., D 4014/4, p. 39; IN 75.

[17] Glos. R.O., D 4325/1–3; *Glouc. Jnl.* 30 Nov. 1918; 20 Dec. 1919.

[18] D. N. James, *Gloster Aircraft since 1917* (1971), 5; *Glouc. Jnl.* 28 Dec. 1918.

[19] *Waterways World*, Oct. 1976, 33.

[20] Glos. Colln. N 15.21–2.

[21] Glos. R.O., D 4014/4, pp. 55, 60–1; IN 50.

[22] *Glouc. Jnl.* 27 Aug. 1932; *Citizen*, 10 July 1961.

[23] Glos. R.O., IN 75.

[24] *Glouc. Railway Carriage & Wagon Co. Ltd.* (1951), 6: Glos. Colln. 33041; ibid. NR 15.12.

[25] Glos. R.O., D 4791, Glouc. Railway Carriage & Wagon Co., min. bk. 1917–23, pp. 325–401; min. bk. 1923–9, pp. 90–1, 404–31; min. bk. 1929–33, pp. 73–88; *Glouc. Jnl.* 25 Feb. 1922.

[26] *Hist. Glouc. Railway Carriage & Wagon Co.* 47–8, 57.

[27] *Who Was Who, 1951–60,* 124.

economic activity was relatively undisturbed except in the docks where work halted for a fortnight.[28] In the later 1920s the Gloster Aircraft Co. gave a major boost to employment by transferring production from Cheltenham to Hucclecote, where it built a factory on the airfield. The company, which made military aircraft, had financial problems because of reduced orders in the early 1930s but it recovered and enlarged its factory after 1934 when Hawker Aircraft Ltd. secured control of it. G.A.C. continued to design and build its own products.[29]

Gloucester's major firms survived the depression of the early 1930s. The engineering firm of W. S. Barron & Son was building a factory in Bristol Road in 1934 when it started a collaboration with the milling engineers Henry Simon Ltd. of Stockport (Ches.).[30] The weaving of reversible carpets and rugs, introduced in 1915,[31] prospered and moved in the late 1930s to a factory at High Orchard.[32] In the late 1930s several new industries were established,[33] and among older ones to disappear was hairpin making.[34] The tannery in lower Northgate Street apparently closed in the early 1930s.[35] The clothing industry, which suffered a serious loss with the burning of a shirt factory in 1933,[36] employed fewer people. The number of employees in local government and public services such as gas, electricity, water, and transport doubled in the 1930s.[37]

From the later 1930s industry in and around Gloucester benefited from the re-armament programme.[38] The aircraft industry, including the Churchdown factory of Rotol Airscrews Ltd. formed in 1937,[39] became the principal employer. Between 1938 and 1943 it increased its workforce by 13,430 people, many of whom travelled to work from other areas. The Gloster Aircraft Co., which between 1938 and 1940 built a second factory, on the Brockworth side of the airfield, produced the Meteor, the country's first jet-propelled fighter, from 1943. A. W. Hawksley Ltd., a company formed in 1940, also built aircraft at the airfield.[40] During the Second World War many factories turned to military needs; the wagon works produced tanks, munitions, and Bailey bridges.[41] The number of people employed by national and local government, some administrative and military departments being moved to the area, and by the railways increased. The docks, which handled essential supplies for the industries and population of the Midlands, saw a revival in the corn trade and regular coal shipments to the new Castle Meads electricity generating station.[42] After the war industry quickly readjusted to peacetime production. Hawksley's factory prefabricated houses and bungalows for the Ministry of Supply.[43] In the early 1950s the aircraft industry accounted for the four largest employers in the area and for many of the 3,000 people travelling in each day for work. National and local government, public services, and the armed forces employed large numbers, and there were significant numbers engaged in professional services, notably nursing and teaching.[44]

After 1948, when the docks and associated waterways were acquired by the British Transport Commission,[45] the docks continued to handle a wide range of imports, including raw materials for industry, agricultural supplies, foodstuffs, and oil and petroleum.[46] Shell Mex & B.P. Ltd., whose needs outgrew its storage tanks at Monk

[28] *Trans. B.G.A.S.* xci. 207–13.
[29] James, *Gloster Aircraft*, 18–36.
[30] Inf. from sec., Simon-Barron Ltd., Glouc.
[31] Glos. R.O., D 4014/4, p. 83.
[32] *Citizen*, 27 Aug. 1975.
[33] Glos. Colln. NQ 15.35; *Glouc. Official Guide* (1980), 95.
[34] Glos. Colln. NF 15.66.
[35] Cf. *Kelly's Dir. Glos.* (1931), 213; (1935), 214.
[36] *Glouc. Jnl.* 28 Oct. 1933.
[37] Glos. Colln. 28622 (2), pp. 32–4.

[38] Paragraph based on Glos. Colln. 28622 (2), pp. 28–37.
[39] Glos. R.O., IN 96; *Kelly's Dir. Glos.* (1939), 116.
[40] James, *Gloster Aircraft*, 40–7.
[41] *Hist. Glouc. Railway Carriage & Wagon Co.* 58–9.
[42] Conway-Jones, *Glouc. Docks*, 144.
[43] Glos. Colln. NR 15.68, p. 44.
[44] *Census*, 1951.
[45] Transport Act, 1947, 10 & 11 Geo. VI, c. 49.
[46] Conway-Jones, *Glouc. Docks*, 146–53.

Meadow, opened a larger depot on the canal near Quedgeley in 1960, and the construction of a pipeline from the new depot to Worcester before 1967 ended the principal river traffic above Gloucester.[47] In the early 1960s a substantial trade in boxed car parts to Ireland passed through the docks,[48] but in general the period after the Second World War was one of steady decline for docks and canal. Goods, including timber, bound for the city and the Midlands were transferred at Sharpness or at other ports to the roads, particularly the motorways built in the 1960s and early 1970s.[49] The British Transport Commission and the British Waterways Board, to which the docks and canal were transferred in 1963,[50] improved and extended wharfage facilities, especially below Llanthony bridge. Those improvements stimulated some commercial activity,[51] and in 1967 the canal carried 547,686 tons, including timber, oil, and container traffic,[52] but the long-term decline was not halted and in 1980 only nine registered dockers were employed.[53] The decline was especially evident in the older part of the docks, where the surviving 19th-century warehouses were no longer suited to commercial needs and where goods traffic had been partly replaced by pleasure craft. Traffic passing into the river included wheat for a mill at Tewkesbury. The two graving docks maintained Gloucester's tradition of shipbuilding, mostly in repairing river and small seagoing craft, in the early 1980s.[54] Plans were then being discussed for reviving the docks as an area for trade, industry, leisure, and housing.[55]

Despite the decline of the timber trade after the Second World War, timber yards remained an important feature near the canal and several new ones were opened.[56] The firm of Price, Walker, and Co., which ceased to be independent in 1962, sold part of its yard in 1969 and employed 59 people in 1984.[57] A successful business to grow out of the trade was Permali Ltd., known until 1951 as the New Insulation Co. It was formed in 1937 to make 'permali', a reinforced electrical insulator obtained from wood veneer treated with synthetic resin, and leased the former tramways depot in Bristol Road. The company, which secured overseas markets and in 1957 opened a new factory in Bristol Road, developed a range of reinforced plastics, electrical insulation, and composite goods. Its factory space was enlarged after it became part of the B.T.R. Group in 1975.[58]

From the mid 1950s industrial estates were laid out on the outskirts of Gloucester, most of them near the bypass road. Initially they were intended for the relocation of badly sited firms,[59] but with the decline and disappearance of established manufactures, notably aircraft and railway rolling stock, they were used to encourage entirely new businesses.[60] Many Gloucester factories were closed by outside interests to benefit production elsewhere. The toy factory, which had been enlarged in the early 1930s to employ up to 750 people, was an early example. The Chad Valley Group, which acquired it in 1954, shut it with a loss of 198 jobs in 1956 and moved production to Birmingham. The jam and pickle factory also closed in 1956.[61] Bryant & May reduced the match factory of S. J. Moreland & Sons to branch status in 1972 and shut it with a loss of 280 jobs in 1976 to centre production on Liverpool and Glasgow.[62] The factory was reopened as a trading estate in 1978.

[47] Glos. R.O., IN 70; Waterways World, Sept. 1976, 29; V.C.H. Glos. x. 180.   [48] The Times, 6 Apr. 1965.
[49] Conway-Jones, Glouc. Docks, 153.
[50] Transport Act, 1962, 10 & 11 Eliz. II, c. 46. From c. 1963 the canal was called the Glouc. and Sharpness canal: Glos. R.O., CA 23.
[51] The Times, 6 Apr. 1965; Glouc. Official Guide (1980), 73.
[52] C. Hadfield, Canals of S. and SE. Eng. (Newton Abbot, 1969), 353.   [53] Citizen, suppl. 17 June 1980.
[54] Conway-Jones, Glouc. Docks, 154–8.
[55] Cf. Glouc. Jnl. 22 Nov. 1980.
[56] Conway-Jones, Glouc. Docks, 158; Glouc. Official Guide (1980), 99.
[57] Inf. from Mr. M. I. Phillips, director, Price, Walker, & Co. Ltd.   [58] Glos. Colln. N 15.88; NQ 15.35.
[59] Glos. Colln. 28622 (1), p. 2; Glouc. Official Guide (1963), 104.   [60] G.B.R., L 6/12/2, p. 75.
[61] Citizen, 20 Oct. 1956.   [62] Ibid. 27 Aug., 26 Sept. 1975.

In response to changes in defence policy the Gloster Aircraft Co. reorganized its research department in 1956 and a few years later switched part of its Hucclecote factory to the manufacture of automatic vending machines and forage harvesters. Aircraft production ceased in 1960 and the factory was sold in 1964 to Gloucester Trading Estates, which converted it as an industrial estate.[63] In 1972 the estate, which was outside the city, housed over forty firms. They included Gloster Saro Ltd.,[64] which as a new company within the Hawker-Siddeley Group had taken over production of vending machines, road tankers, and airfield refuellers in 1965.[65] The Gloucester Railway Carriage & Wagon Co. diversified its interests after 1948 by purchasing the Hatherley Works, the Gloucester Foundry, and William Gardner & Sons.[66] Because of a decline in orders for railway rolling stock the wagon works began production for the Winget Group of companies, which absorbed it in 1962. The works made specialist rolling stock and freight containers; contractors' plant, notably Muir-Hill dumpers, loaders, and tractors; and plant for the steel industry. At the same time production of machinery for chemicals, plastics, and food-processing industries was moved to the works from Gardners' factory, which was closed.[67] The companies within the Winget Group, which was itself acquired by the Babcock and Wilcox Group in the late 1960s, were reorganized several times before 1984.[68]

Despite the large number of men laid off at the aircraft works, the success of the Gloucester area in attracting new industry and the growth in service and distributive trades resulted in a shortage of labour in the early 1960s.[69] Many of the new factories were outside the city boundary, notably the light engineering works of the Dowty Group near Cheltenham[70] and the factory of British Nylon Spinners, opened on the site of the Brockworth aircraft works in 1960 and owned by I.C.I. Fibres Ltd. from 1964.[71] T. Wall & Son (Ice Cream) Ltd., which began a factory by the railway on the eastern boundary of the city in 1958, became a major employer. The factory, which in its first summer of full production, in 1961, had a workforce of 1,300,[72] was enlarged in 1984.

The natural recession in engineering and manufacturing led to a rise in unemployment in Gloucester from the later 1960s. The works of W. Sisson & Co., which had been acquired in 1958 by a Birmingham company, were closed with a loss of 160 jobs in 1968 and production moved to Bedford.[73] The decline in foundry work and engineering, which had been a major part of Gloucester's industry in the early 1960s,[74] became more pronounced from the later 1970s. The Gloucester Foundry, which had employed over 500 people, was shut in 1981 and replaced by a trading estate.[75] The workforce of Fielding & Platt fell from c. 500 in 1976 to 75 in 1983[76] and that of Williams & James, which in the early 1960s employed 350 people to make hydraulic and pneumatic machinery for the motor car industry,[77] also dropped. Simon-Barron Ltd., formed in 1963 by the merger of Barron & Son and the animal-feed section of Henry Simon Ltd., employed 500 people to manufacture animal-feed milling plant in the early 1970s but only 200 in 1984. Part of the reduction was accounted for by the formation in 1974 of a marketing company.[78] Kell & Co.,

[63] *Glouc. Official Guide* (1963), 113; James, *Gloster Aircraft*, 63–7.
[64] *The Times*, 12 May 1972.
[65] James, *Gloster Aircraft*, 66–7.
[66] *Hist. Glouc. Railway Carriage & Wagon Co.* 60–3.
[67] Glos. R.O., D 4791, Glouc. Railway Carriage & Wagon Co., rep. for 1959–60; *Glouc. Official Guide* (1963), 115–17; cf. *Kelly's Dir. Glouc.* (1959), 28; (1963), 31.
[68] Glos. R.O., D 4557, cat.
[69] *The Economist*, 20 Apr. 1963; *Municipal Jnl.* 29 Oct. 1965, pp. 3683–8.
[70] *Glouc. Official Guide* (1963), 121.
[71] Ibid. 111; *Citizen*, 2 Dec. 1964.
[72] *Citizen*, 22 Mar. 1958; Glos. Colln. RR 58.7.
[73] Glos. R.O., IN 75; *Citizen*, 13 June 1968.
[74] *The Economist*, 20 Apr. 1963.
[75] *Citizen*, 16 Sept. 1982; 25 Jan. 1983.
[76] *Citizen Centenary Suppl.* 1 May 1976; *Citizen*, 27 May 1983.
[77] *Glouc. Official Guide* (1963), 123.
[78] Inf. from sec., Simon-Barron Ltd.

which had ceased to make agricultural implements in the early 1950s when it was acquired by Helipebs Ltd., moved in the late 1960s to the former Sisson's works where it made a wide range of castings and machinery. The workforce in the foundry and machine shop fall to c. 82 in 1984.[79]

The decline in manufacturing and the resulting loss of jobs was only partly compensated for by new businesses. In addition to the match factory, closures included the Hatherley Works furniture factory in 1983[80] and the carpet factory at High Orchard, which had employed 250 people in 1975.[81] One successful venture was that started by G. R. Lane (d. 1964), who made health products and natural remedies from the 1930s. The business, which built up an export trade, employed nearly 100 people in 1984.[82] Another firm to prosper in the early 1980s was Mecanaids Ltd., which made equipment for hospitals and disabled people and in 1984 demolished the former jam and pickle factory for an extension of its works.[83]

Gloucester remained the market centre for north Gloucestershire and the adjoining parts of Herefordshire and Worcestershire. In the mid 1920s the livestock market near the railways handled c. 60,000 sheep, c. 52,500 pigs, c. 24,500 cattle, and c. 13,500 calves a year, with the September sheep sale at Barton Fair attracting buyers from Wales.[84] The volume of business was greater in the mid 1950s when the market was moved to a more convenient site on the bypass road. Horse sales had dwindled but the autumn sheep sales served a wide area in the Midlands, South Wales, and the West Country.[85] The fruit and vegetable market, which lost some of its trade to the Grange Court market started in Westbury-on-Severn in 1920,[86] sold over 6,000 tons of produce a year, as well as poultry and eggs, in the early 1930s and c. 10,000 head of live poultry in the mid 1950s.[87] In the early 1970s it was attended by buyers from Bristol and South Wales.[88] Organized corn dealing had apparently ceased by the mid 1950s.[89]

An important newcomer to Gloucester's animal feed industry was the West Midland Farmers' Association Ltd., an agricultural co-operative formed in 1909,[90] which acquired Island Mills in lower Westgate Street c. 1920.[91] British Oil & Cake Mills reduced operations at Baker's Quay after the Second World War[92] and West Midland Farmers' bought those premises in 1955 for its own compounding and milling activities. The association expanded in the 1970s, and in 1983, when it bought disused maltings at High Orchard, formerly the premises of G. and W. E. Downing, for grain storage, it traded and supplied farming services over a wide area and had 5,384 members and 383 employees.[93] The flour industry continued to shrink between the wars, and when Allied Mills Ltd. closed Albert Mills in 1977 only City Mills was left producing flour.[94] Priday, Metford, & Co. employed 55 people there in 1984.[95]

By the 1970s much of Gloucester's economic activity depended for transport on the developing road system,[96] which included the bypass, completed in 1959,[97] and attracted many new businesses to the city. The M5 motorway between the Midlands and south-western England opened east of the city in 1971.[98] The railways ceased to

[79] Inf. from managing director, Kell & Co. Ltd.
[80] *Citizen*, 3 May 1983. [81] Ibid. 27 Aug. 1975.
[82] Inf. from Mr. R. G. Lane, director, G. R. Lane Health Products Ltd.
[83] Cf. *Citizen*, 1 Mar. 1983.
[84] *Rep. on Midland Markets* (H.M.S.O. 1927), 12, 21, 156.
[85] Glos. Colln. NF 12.247; *Handbk. of Glouc. Corp. Markets* [? 1957], 23-37: copy in Glos. Colln. NF 12.246 (1).
[86] *Rep. on Midland Markets*, 33, 82; *V.C.H. Glos.* x. 95.
[87] Glos. Colln. N 3.11; NF 12.247.
[88] *The Times*, 12 May 1972.

[89] Cf. *Handbk. of Glouc. Corp. Markets* [? 1957], 11.
[90] *Glouc. Jnl.* 29 May 1909; 5 Mar. 1910.
[91] *Glos. Hist. Studies*, xii. 5; cf. *Milling*, 21 Aug. 1937, p. 213: copy in Glos. Colln. NV 15.3.
[92] Glos. Colln. NQ 15.8, 20.
[93] Inf. from general manager and sec., West Midland Farmers' Assoc. Ltd.
[94] *Glos Hist. Studies*, xii. 5-7.
[95] Inf. from sec., Priday, Metford, & Co. Ltd.
[96] *Glouc. Official Guide* (1980), 21, 74.
[97] Below, topog. [98] *Citizen*, 6 Apr. 1971.

be an important employer at Gloucester after the Second World War[99] and the local branch lines to Hereford and to Ledbury were closed in 1964.[1] The decline of the docks also reduced railway traffic, and most lines serving the docks had been removed by the 1970s.[2] With the closure of Eastgate station and the Tuffley loop line in 1975 and the building of a new station on the site of Central station's down platform Gloucester's railways reverted to much the same pattern as before 1854.[3] The municipal airfield in Churchdown, laid out in 1936,[4] had limited impact on the city's economic life.

Emphasis on Gloucester's role as an administrative and service centre from the 1950s contributed to the changing pattern of employment and to a growth in jobs,[5] which in 1976 numbered 44,309. The number of workers travelling into the city each day passed 7,260 in 1971.[6] Local government and public services provided many new jobs, and the expansion of educational and health services, for which Gloucester was a major centre, helped the growth of the professions.[7] The city council employed over 2,000 people in 1959[8] and, following local government reorganization in 1974, had 750 full-time employees. That figure fell to 650 in 1984,[9] when the county council employed c. 1,500 people at the Shire Hall.[10] The land registry's regional office, established at Elmbridge Court by 1964, moved in 1968 to an office block in Bruton Way, which was staffed by 672 people in 1976.[11] The number of jobs in insurance, banking, and postal and telecommunication services also rose.[12] The Trident Life and Ecclesiastical insurance companies moved their headquarters to Gloucester in 1974 and 1976 respectively,[13] Barclays Bank built a computer centre at Barnwood in the late 1970s,[14] and in 1974 the Central Electricity Generating Board completed at Barnwood the head office for its generation development and construction division,[15] which in 1984 employed 1,177 people.[16] Some civilians worked at R.A.F. Innsworth in Churchdown, opened in 1940. The station included from 1975 the R.A.F. personnel management centre, which had grown out of a merger in 1965 between the R.A.F. record and central pay offices. Those offices had been established in Eastern Avenue near Barnwood for several years, the record office opening a branch there in 1941.[17]

The growth of Gloucester in the 20th century benefited the building trades and increased the demand for shops as well as services. Between the wars more chain stores, including F. W. Woolworth & Co. in the early 1920s, opened branches in the city centre, and several established retailers extended their range of trade.[18] After the Second World War branches of chain stores became increasingly prominent in the principal shopping streets at the expense of local businesses,[19] notably Blinkhorn's which ceased trading in 1953 on its sale to F. W. Woolworth & Co.[20] The Bon Marché, acquired in the late 1920s by the Drapery Trust (later Debenhams Ltd.),[21] retained its traditional name until the early 1970s; the store employed 650 people in 1984.[22] The redevelopment of the city centre in the 1960s and 1970s, and particularly

[99] Cf. *Census*, 1951; 1971.
[1] *V.C.H. Glos.* x. 6, 16.
[2] Conway-Jones, *Glouc. Docks*, 158.
[3] *Citizen*, 1 Dec. 1975; for railways in mid 1980s, above, Fig. 1.   [4] Below, city govt.
[5] *The Economist*, 20 Apr. 1963.
[6] Glos. Colln. 40266, p. 4.
[7] *Census*, 1951–71.
[8] Glos. Colln. NQ 12.34.
[9] Inf. from personnel off., Glouc. city council.
[10] Inf. from sec. dept., Glos. co. council.
[11] Glos. Colln. N 12.331; *Glos. Co. Gazette*, 10 Apr. 1976.
[12] *Census*, 1951–71.
[13] *Glouc. Official Guide* (1980), 99; Glos. R.O., IN 83.
[14] *Citizen*, 25 Oct. 1977.
[15] *Architects' Jnl.* 30 June 1976, pp. 1269–86.
[16] Inf. from assistant public relations off., generation development and construction division, Central Electricity Generating Bd.
[17] *R.A.F. Innsworth Inf. Handbk.* (1984), 3–5.
[18] Glos. Colln. N 15.30, p. 43; cf. *Smart's Dir. Glouc.* (1927), 39.
[19] *Citizen Centenary Suppl.* 1 May 1976.
[20] *Citizen*, 5 Sept. 1953.
[21] Ibid. 22 Oct. 1964.
[22] Inf. from personnel manager, Debenhams, Glouc.

the completion of the King's Square and Eastgate shopping precincts, enhanced Gloucester's position as a retailing centre,[23] though the Severn Road Bridge opened in 1966 gave shoppers from west Gloucestershire access to Bristol.[24] In the early 1980s several large stores with their own car parks were built outside the city centre, including in 1982 one on the site of Eastgate railway station and another next to the former St. Bartholomew's Hospital in the Island. Others were on new housing estates, and in 1984 Tesco moved its supermarket from lower Northgate Street to a site outside the city in Quedgeley. The tourist trade depended mainly on the attraction of the cathedral and provided little employment. Hotel accommodation, which was limited in the city centre, especially after the closure of the Bell in 1967,[25] was increased with the opening of a large hotel on the Barnwood bypass in 1981.

City Government

Under the Municipal Corporations Act of 1835[26] the city was enlarged to cover the same area as the parliamentary borough, which included the Spa and an additional part of Barton Street.[27] The corporation's powers were vested in a council comprising 18 councillors, of whom six went out of office each year, six aldermen, of whom three were elected triennially in rotation by the council, and a mayor, elected annually by the council from among its members. The city was divided into three electoral wards, each represented by six councillors.[28] As a county of itself Gloucester retained one sheriff, chosen annually by the council. The city also retained, by royal grant in 1836,[29] a court of quarter sessions, with a recorder appointed no longer by the council but by the Crown. The council appointed a clerk of the peace and a coroner. The city's magistrates, nominated under a separate commission of the peace in 1836,[30] had their own clerk and in 1837 moved their petty sessions from the Tolsey to the Shire Hall.[31] The court of requests or conscience continued to be held and became a county court under the Small Debts Act of 1846.[32] The reformed corporation had a limited role in local government. Public services such as water supply, gas supply, and street lighting remained outside its control, as did supervision of street repairs and cleansing.[33] The almshouses and several other charities administered by the old corporation came under the control of newly appointed municipal charity trustees in 1836. The trustees, though many were council members, acted independently and in the 1840s and 1850s succeeded in several claims against the corporation. The corporation's refusal in 1844 to surrender the Crypt grammar school, which it had retained, led to a Chancery suit and, following a compromise of 1852, the trustees obtained control.[34]

The Municipal Corporations Act entitled 892 people to vote in civic elections in Gloucester,[35] and the municipal electorate in 1843 and 1851 numbered 1,158 and 1,366 respectively.[36] The first election under the Act, held in 1835 against a background of disunity among the Whigs or Liberals, ended the exclusion from office of the Tories or Conservatives. Only nine members of the old council stood as

[23] Municipal Jnl. 29 Oct. 1965, pp. 3687-9; Glouc. Official Guide (1980), 23.
[24] Cf. The Economist, 20 Apr. 1963.
[25] Municipal Jnl. 29 Oct. 1965, p. 3683; Citizen, 28 July 1967.
[26] Municipal Corporations Act, 5 & 6 Wm. IV, c. 76.
[27] Above, Glouc. 1720-1835, parl. representation; cf. Causton, Map of Glouc. (1843). For boundary extensions, above, Fig. 1.
[28] Lond. Gaz. 7 Dec. 1835, pp. 2334-5.

[29] G.B.R., B 3/15, min. 2 June 1836.
[30] Glos. R.O., D 3117/374.
[31] G.B.R., B 3/15, min. 23 Jan. 1837.
[32] Ibid. G 13/9-12; Bryant's Dir. Glouc. (1841), 12; Small Debts Act, 9 & 10 Vic. c. 95.
[33] Below, Public Services.
[34] Glos. R.O., D 3269, char. trustees' min. bks. 1836-88; cf. G.B.R., L 6/11/11; V.C.H. Glos. ii. 350.
[35] Glouc. Jnl. 14 Nov., 5 Dec. 1835.
[36] Glos. Colln. 7204.

candidates; six, including the retiring mayor, were defeated, and of the three returned only David Mowbray Walker, owner of the *Gloucester Journal*, had been an alderman. The electors chose thirteen Conservatives and five Liberals, and the former consolidated their advantage by almost total domination of the new aldermanic bench.[37] In contrast the new charity trustees represented a balance of political interests and the six magistrates appointed under the Act, all city men, were drawn equally from both factions.[38] Despite the wholesale change of personnel the new council made few significant innovations in civic affairs. Henry Hooper Wilton remained town clerk but was replaced as treasurer by William Matthews. Many other officials, including ceremonial officers, retained their positions and salaries. The town clerk was given a salary of £200, the treasurer £150, and the recorder £100. The new council, which appointed a high steward as before, abolished only the post of night bellman.[39] The civic ceremony of perambulating the city's boundaries continued,[40] but the custom of presenting provisions to the assize judges and lamprey pies to the king, bishop, high steward, town clerk, and recorder was ended.[41] The mayors of the new corporation were chosen from both councillors and aldermen. H.H. Wilton, partner in the largest solicitors' practice in the area, continued his wide involvement in city government after 1835. As town clerk and from 1849 as clerk to the local board of health he was energetic on the corporation's behalf,[42] and among other offices he held were those of clerk of the peace and clerk and treasurer to the municipal charity trustees. He gave up public office and private practice in 1851.[43]

Apart from the payment of its officials and the management of its property, financial demands on the new corporation were few. Its main duties were in the enforcement of law and order, notably in the provision of a city police force, which cost £851 in its first full year. Another major burden was the maintenance of the city gaol and lock-up in Southgate Street.[44] For a few years the council superseded the magistrates in regulating the gaol, and as the building was unsuitable on the grounds of size, security, and sanitation convicts were sent to the county gaol when accommodation there allowed.[45] The city gaol was closed in 1858.[46] The police force did not contain lawlessness,[47] and the council, unwilling to add to its financial commitments, did little to improve policing. In 1846 it dismissed a proposal for a police station in Archdeacon Street, a notoriously turbulent area.[48] The failings of the police service, which was described as 'rotten from beginning to end', and the prospect of financial support from central government convinced the council of the benefits of a merger of its force with that of the county in 1859.[49] Police salaries remained an item of considerable expenditure after that date. Other regular charges on the borough fund[50] were charities vested in the corporation, the city's contribution to the asylum at Wotton, until the late 1840s the contract[51] for repairing streets maintained by the corporation, and until the mid 1860s the tontine organized by the old corporation in the mid 1780s to fund the building of markets.[52]

[37] *Glouc. Jnl.* 2 Jan. 1836; cf. G.B.R., B 3/14, f. 277v.

[38] *Glos. Chron,* 4 Apr. 1885.

[39] G.B.R., B 3/15, mins. 1, 21 Jan., 11 Apr. 1836.

[40] Ibid. min. 19 Aug. 1836; *Glouc. Jnl.* 20 Oct. 1855; 19 Sept. 1857.

[41] G.B.R., B 4/1/5, f. 10; B 3/15, min. 15 Mar. 1836; the gift of a lamprey pie to the monarch was revived between 1893 and 1917 and again from 1953: Glos. R.O., D 3558/12, pp. 27–30; *Glouc. Municipal Year Bk.* (1964–5), 97.

[42] G.B.R., B 3/15–17, *passim*; N 2/1/1, pp. 4–334.

[43] *Glos. Chron.* 5 Nov. 1881.

[44] *Abstracts of Treasurer's Accts. 1836–41*: copies in Glos. Colln. NX 12.3.

[45] G.B.R., B 4/1/5, *passim*; 2/1, *passim*; B 3/15, min. 23 Jan. 1837; 16, pp. 266–76.

[46] Ibid. G 3/G 2/3.

[47] Cf. ibid. B 4/1/5, f. 57.

[48] Ibid. B 3/17, pp. 138–9; *Glouc. Jnl.* 20 June 1846.

[49] *Glouc. Jnl.* 31 Jan. 1857; below, Public Services.

[50] See *Abstracts of Treasurer's Accts. 1836–41, 1850–1, 1854–5, 1857–8, 1859–1945*: from 1850–1, copies in G.B.R.

[51] Cf. G.B.R., L 6/7/1.

[52] Below, Markets and Fairs.

Much of the corporation's income was supplied by rents, renewal fines, and tolls.[53] The income from the tolls, which were farmed, fluctuated and the corporation occasionally had difficulty in leasing them.[54] The most lucrative were those of the markets, particularly the cattle market after its improvement in the early 1860s.[55] The corn exchange opened in 1857 provided an income in rents for stands. The other tolls became less profitable from the middle of the century, the weighing machine in Upper Quay Street being abandoned in 1848 and the collection of wheelage and driftage ceasing in 1867.[56] Decline in the value of the quay tolls was not reversed by the abolition in 1874 of the exemption enjoyed by freemen of the city and residents of the duchy of Lancaster.[57] Both groups continued to be exempt from toll in the cattle market, the privilege of the latter being protected until 1958.[58] The corporation took the market and quay tolls in hand in 1888.[59] Before 1875 it also derived a small income from its management of the freemen's common rights.

As traditional sources of income did not meet the new corporation's financial obligations, from 1836 the council imposed a borough rate, collected with the poor rate by the overseers of the parishes and hamlets.[60] The borough fund was nevertheless usually run at a deficit, and in the 20 years following reform the corporation occasionally sold property to raise income. During that period legal fees and other payments arising from claims, among others, by officers of the old corporation for loss of office and by the municipal charity trustees added to the financial burdens on the corporation. In the mid 1850s it paid the charity trustees over £11,925, including rents taken between 1844 and 1852 from the Crypt school lands, which it relinquished in 1857.[61] The corporation also spent nearly £8,000 in an unsuccessful suit to obtain £200,000 from the executors of James Wood (d. 1836). Its claim, based on alleged codicils to Wood's will, was dismissed in the House of Lords in 1847. In 1844 the corporation had declined to abandon its action and accept £25,000.[62] After the discovery of errors in the treasurer's accounts the council in 1851 ordered an audit from the time the corporation was reformed. The treasurer's death a few days later delayed the examination of his books.[63]

The claims of the freemen to common rights were the cause of many disputes, particularly with the corporation, and in 1848 the freemen appointed a committee to look after their interests.[64] Later a few freemen, mostly butchers and cattle dealers, exercised common rights in Oxlease, Portham, and Town Ham on Alney Island and in Archdeacon Meadow, Little Meadow, and Meanham (later St. Catherine's Meadow) on the north-west side of Gloucester. In 1875 the corporation transferred the management of the meadows to the freemen's committee, though the appointment of the hayward remained with the corporation. The disputes between the corporation and freemen were finally resolved in 1899 and the corporation, which resumed the management of the meadows, extinguished the freemen's rights in Oxlease and Town Ham in 1900 and, following its purchase of the land, in Portham, Little Meadow, and the part of Archdeacon's Meadow south of the railway in 1901. Under an award of 1901 the corporation paid the freemen £7,095[65] which was invested for a charity, known under a Scheme of 1906 as the Freemen's Compensation Fund.[66] In 1931 the

[53] Two paragraphs based on *Abstracts of Treasurer's Accts*.
[54] Cf. G.B.R., L 6/2/5–11; B 4/1/5, ff. 43v., 46., 127v.; 6, pp. 155–61, 373–5; 7, ff. 1–3, 39–40.
[55] Cf. ibid. L 6/4/2, mem. 23 Mar. 1869.
[56] Ibid. B 4/1/6, p. 366; 8, min. 18 June 1867.
[57] Glouc. Extension and Improvement Act, 1874, 37 & 38 Vic. c. 111 (Local).
[58] Glouc. Corp. Act, 1911, 1 & 2 Geo. V, c. 92 (Local); 1958, 6 & 7 Eliz. II, c. 35 (Local).
[59] G.B.R., B 4/1/11, p. 140.
[60] Cf. ibid. B 3/23, rep. of off. duties cttee.
[61] Ibid. B 3/15–18, *passim*; L 6/4/2, *passim*.
[62] Ibid. B 3/15, min. 16 June 1836; 16, p. 390; 17, pp. 195–9.
[63] Ibid. B 4/1/7, ff. 20–3; B 3/17, f. 377.
[64] Glos. R.O., D 4430/1.
[65] G.B.R., L 6/11/35; Glos. R.O., D 4430/12/8, 10–11.
[66] Glos. Colln. NQ 12.5.

common rights in that part of St. Catherine's Meadow needed for a bypass road were extinguished, and the freemen surrendered their remaining common rights in 1940 and 1942.[67]

Statutory bodies other than the corporation retained a role in the government of the city after 1835. Some were ineffective, notably the parish surveyors appointed to superintend street repair and cleansing.[68] Administration of poor relief passed in 1835 from the corporation of the governor and guardians of the poor to the board of guardians of the newly formed Gloucester union, which also included all the suburbs and a large rural area beyond.[69] The new guardians built a workhouse off London Road in the years 1837–8 to designs by G. G. Scott and W. B. Moffatt.[70] The building was encroached on by the railway several times, including in 1850 when a new infirmary was built.[71] To ease the plight of vagrants in the city, the board of guardians continued the policy of supplying food and overnight accommodation in lodging houses until 1873, when it erected a block of casual or tramp wards and instituted a regime of hard work in return for food and shelter.[72] Under the Public Health Act of 1872 the board of guardians acted as sanitary authority in the suburbs outside the city boundary.[73] The former poor-relief corporation, which demolished its workhouse in Quay Street in 1839,[74] used the rents from its land at Longford until 1869 to reduce the burden on parishes in the old part of the city of poor rates levied by the board of guardians.[75] Among other rates collected by parishes and hamlets within the city were those levied before 1865 by the former poor-relief corporation for lighting the old part of Gloucester and by the improvement commissioners.[76] Under the Extraparochial Places Act of 1857 Littleworth and the city part of Pool Meadow became civil parishes, as did South Hamlet, which was mostly in the county. Anomalies in the boundaries of the civil parishes were removed in the mid 1880s.[77]

Local government in the later 1830s and 1840s was unequal to the needs of Gloucester with its growing population and commerce. Little was done to improve sanitary conditions, even in the squalid courts and lanes of the Island and Archdeacon Street areas where cholera had been rife in 1832.[78] In 1847 the death rate in those districts was higher than elsewhere in Gloucester. The use of the Severn and of streams, notably the Sud brook and Twyver, as sewers remained the greatest danger to public health, particularly in the areas liable to flood, which included most of the poorer housing. A Board of Health inquiry carried out in 1848 revealed poor sanitary conditions throughout the city, including the Spa. Adequate drainage and sewerage were lacking, and cesspools and privies were numerous. In Clare Street one privy was shared by c. 13 houses. The water supplied from Robins Wood Hill by a private company was pure but most domestic needs were supplied by wells contaminated by seepage from cesspools and dirty streets. The squalor was worse and life expectancy shorter in the suburbs where much of the newer housing was located. Because of the conditions rents in Oxford Street, which comprised better houses, were lowered to attract tenants.[79] The keeping of pigs by householders was an additional nuisance.[80] From 1847 the corporation, prompted by the threat of another cholera epidemic,

[67] *Glouc. Municipal Year Bk.* (1964–5), 83.
[68] *Rep. to General Bd. of Health of Sanitary Condition of Glouc.* (1849), 39, 41; below, Public Services.
[69] Glos. R.O., G/GL 8A/1, pp. 1–8, 99, 111.
[70] Ibid. pp. 318–57; 3, pp. 7–35, 289–315.
[71] Causton, *Map of Glouc.* (1843); Bd. of Health Map (1852); below, Hosp., general infirmaries.
[72] Glos. R.O., G/GL 8A/3, pp. 169–70; 13, ff. 82v.–84v., 138v.–139v.
[73] Public Health Act, 1872, 35 & 36 Vic. c. 79.

[74] Glos. R.O., D 3270/19713, mins. 17 Jan., 11 May 1839.
[75] *Rep. Sanitary Condition of Glouc.* (1849), 47–8; cf. Glos. R.O., D 3270/19713, *passim*; G/GL 8A/1, pp. 105–6.
[76] G.B.R., B 4/1/5, ff. 48 and v., 115v.–116; 2/1, *passim.*
[77] *Census*, 1861; 1891.
[78] G.B.R., B 4/6/1, min. 5 Nov. 1847.
[79] *Rep. Sanitary Condition of Glouc.* (1849), 10–33, 41–2, 51.
[80] *Glouc. Jnl.* 8 Jan. 1848; 16 June 1849.

attempted to improve conditions,[81] but until 1849, when it was constituted as the local board of health for the city,[82] it lacked effective powers to deal with sanitary matters and also to undertake the street repairs necessitated by increased traffic. Most burial grounds were full by 1848,[83] and the corporation, with the concurrence of the parish vestries, acquired powers as a burial board for the city in 1856 and opened a cemetery the following year.[84]

The assumption of the powers of a local board of health greatly increased the corporation's part in city government. The council preserved the distinction between its old and new functions in its committees and finances, and it first combined the offices of surveyor to the local board and city chamberlain in 1855.[85] The most pressing tasks for the corporation were the construction of a sewerage and drainage system and the provision of enough water for domestic use and flushing drains. Sewers were laid between 1853 and 1855, and to ensure the system's efficiency the corporation in 1854 purchased the water undertaking supplying the city and surrounding area and altered the supply to the public conduit in Southgate Street. Measures were taken to increase the city's water supply, upon which ever greater demands were placed, and the construction of works at Great Witcombe in the later 1850s and early 1860s was a major project. The corporation, which as a board of health became responsible for street repair and cleansing undertook few road improvements apart from the gradual macadamization of the city's streets,[86] but, to ease traffic congestion in the central area, in 1854 it built a road (later Priory Road) along the course of Dockham ditch between lower Westgate Street and St. Catherine Street.[87] Among its other public works was the creation of a park in the early 1860s.[88]

The improvements carried out by the corporation after 1847 were limited and too late to prevent outbreaks of cholera in 1849 and 1854. In 1849, when the disease returned to the slums of the Island and Archdeacon Street with their polluted water supplies, nearly 100 people died and the burial ground at Longford was reopened.[89] The 1854 outbreak, which began in the county gaol, was much less serious.[90] Although a reduction in the death rate for both the city and suburbs was reported in 1858, many nuisances prejudicial to public health were not removed, notably in the slums in the west of the city; St. Mary de Lode was the parish with the highest mortality.[91] A petition for the establishment of public baths and wash-houses was presented to the mayor in 1846,[92] but none were opened for many years and few people used the baths at the spa pump room, taken over by the corporation in 1861.[93] Air pollution by industry had become a problem by 1861.[94]

The corporation's powers as local board of health were extended by its acquisition of those of other statutory bodies and continued by its constitution under the Public Health Act of 1872 as sanitary authority for the city.[95] The improvement commissioners, who expended little energy on public works, continued to meet until 1860.[96] Their powers were transferred to the corporation in 1865, when the latter also became responsible for the city's street lighting.[97] The former poor-relief corporation,

[81] Below, Public Services, sewerage.
[82] G.B.R., N 2/1/1, p. 2.
[83] *Rep. Sanitary Condition of Glouc.* (1849), 36–40, 47, 54–5.
[84] Below, Public Services; G.B.R., B 3/18, pp. 30–2, 62–4.
[85] G.B.R., N 2/1/1–3, *passim*.
[86] Below, Public Services; *Glouc. Jnl.* 1 Oct. 1853; G.B.R., N 2/1/2, mins. 22, 29 June 1854.
[87] G.B.R., N 2/1/2, min. 29 June 1854; *Glouc. Jnl.* 28 Jan. 1854.
[88] G.B.R., N 2/1/3, min. 20 Feb. 1860; *Glouc. Jnl.* 2 Aug. 1862.

[89] G.B.R., B 4/6/1, min. 9 May 1849; *Glouc. Jnl.* 4 Aug. 1849.
[90] *Glouc. Jnl.* 9 Sept., 21 Oct. 1854.
[91] *Rep. on Sanitary Condition of Glouc. during 1858*: copy in Glos. Colln. NQ 12.51; G.B.R., B 4/5/1, min. 7 Oct. 1859.
[92] G.B.R., B 3/17, p. 110.
[93] Below, social and cultural life.
[94] G.B.R., B 4/5/1, min. 19 July 1861.
[95] Public Health Act, 1872, 35 & 36 Vic. c. 79.
[96] Glos. Colln. 22415.
[97] Local Govt. Supplemental Act, 1865 (No. 3), 28 Vic. c. 41.

stripped of its lighting functions, ran a school until 1899 and was dissolved in 1907.[98] The lighting commissioners for the suburbs provided street lights until at least the early 1950s.[99] The city corporation financed its activities as board of health and later as urban sanitary authority by levying a general district rate,[1] collected, unlike the borough rate, by its own officers.[2] In 1853 it raised a separate highway rate.[3] Water rates or charges were collected from 1854 by the manager of the Robins Wood Hill works and from 1856 with the general district rate.[4] Costly permanent works were funded by borrowing, and the waterworks accounted for the bulk of the loan debt. The debt and loan charges on the sewerage system were met by a special district rate. Pool Meadow, which was not served by the sewerage and water undertakings, paid only a general district rate from 1853, and between 1859 and 1870 only a highway rate.[5]

The Conservatives retained a numerical advantage in the council only until 1838. They won the mayoral and aldermanic elections of that year, conducted acrimoniously on party lines and with doubtful legality, but the new aldermen did not take part in council business[6] and were unseated in 1840 in favour of the Liberals' candidates.[7] The Liberals, who had gained control of the council in 1839,[8] included several nonconformists[9] but apparently few radicals, and their principal leader until the mid 1850s was D. M. Walker.[10] With their larger representation a few more former members of the old council came back into city government.[11] Party rivalry frequently surfaced in the mayoral elections but was absent from the choice of a Conservative in 1848. In 1854, when the Conservatives became the majority party, there was a particularly bitter byelection, and the council elected a Liberal as mayor to avoid party conflict but divided in its choice of sheriff.[12] In municipal elections seats were often filled without contests but such agreements were occasionally rejected by members of both parties.[13] Contests were usually accompanied by corruption, those of 1853 taking place, according to the *Gloucester Journal*, 'after the distribution of large quantities of beer and the incentives usually given to voters on these occasions.'[14] In the early 1850s parliamentary elections and concern about increasing corporation expenditure apparently fuelled party rivalry.[15] The Conservatives, who sold some corporation property to raise funds, paid the corporation's debts to the charity trustees and, in addition to board of health and burial board works, built a new produce market and a corn exchange, improved the cattle market,[16] and constructed part of Denmark Road outside the city. Under the leadership of Thomas Robinson, an ambitious and ruthless politician who became a councillor in 1858, the Liberals dominated the council again from 1865 and accused their opponents of mismanagement, particularly in the construction of the Great Witcombe waterworks and in funding the cattle market improvement by the issue of debentures.[17] Conservative representation between 1869 and 1871 was reduced to a single councillor, John

[98] Below, Educ., elem. educ., Poor's sch.; Glos. Colln. NF 17.13.
[99] Glouc. Corp. Act, 1894, 57 & 58 Vic. c. 91 (Local); G.B.R., L 22/5/2–8.
[1] Rest of paragraph based on *Abstracts of Treasurer's Accts. 1854–6, 1859–1945*: copies in G.B.R.
[2] G.B.R., B 3/23, rep. of off. duties cttee.
[3] Ibid. N 2/1/1, p 616.
[4] Ibid. 2, mins. 22 June 1854, 2 Jan. 1856.
[5] Ibid. L 22/8/6–101; 7/2.
[6] Ibid. B 3/15, mins. 9, 12 Nov. 1838; *Glouc. Jnl.* 3, 10 Nov. 1838.
[7] G.B.R., B 3/16, pp. 49–56.
[8] Ibid. pp. 1–2.

[9] T. Russell and W. and W. T. Washbourne were Unitarians (Glos. R.O., D 4270/4/1/13–15) and W. Higgs was a Wesleyan Methodist (*Glouc. Jnl.* 11 Jan. 1890).
[10] *Glouc. Mercury*, 15 July 1871; Glos. Colln. SR 24.1.
[11] For A. H. Jenkins, W. M. Meyler, and T. Russell, G.B.R., B 3/14, f. 277v.
[12] *Glouc. Jnl.* 11 Nov. 1848; 4, 11 Nov. 1854.
[13] Ibid. 7 Nov. 1840; 4 Nov. 1848; 4 Nov. 1865.
[14] Ibid. 5 Nov. 1853.
[15] Ibid. 4, 11 Nov. 1854; below, parl. representation.
[16] G.B.R., L 6/4/2, *passim*; below, Markets and Fairs.
[17] *Glouc. Jnl.* 5 Nov. 1864; 11 Nov. 1865; 30 Oct. 1886; *Glos. Chron.* 23 Oct. 1886. For Robinson, *Glouc. Jnl.* 30 Oct. 1897; below, Plate 21.

Ward.[18] The Liberals favoured economy with efficiency and generally avoided costly projects. They later portrayed that period as one of financial recovery.[19] By 1871 they had redeemed all the debentures[20] and between 1870 and 1874 they reduced the corporation's loan debt from £97,839 to £88,607.[21] Their most important achievements came after 1874 when they obtained an extension of the municipal boundary as a first step towards ameliorating conditions in the sprawling suburbs.[22]

The hamlets outside the city, where much of Gloucester's growth took place in the mid 19th century, lacked powers to deal with the problems of speculative building.[23] Sewers laid in the late 1850s and early 1860s by the corporation reduced the Sud brook nuisance south of the city[24] but conditions in the suburban terraced streets were generally squalid. To improve matters Barton St. Mary and Barton St. Michael took the powers of local boards of health for most of the south-eastern suburbs in 1863 and Kingsholm St. Catherine took similar powers for part of the northern suburbs in 1865. The major task for the boards was to construct sewerage and drainage systems, which they financed by borrowing and had completed by 1867,[25] but they had little impact on sanitary conditions.[26] The Barton boards, which acted in concert and shared officers, exercised no control over new housing.[27] The Kingsholm St. Catherine board, which put pressure on the corporation to reduce pollution of the Twyver in the city,[28] lacked adequate funds and its activity was further hampered by the fragmented area it covered. The complexity of hamlet and parish boundaries before the mid 1880s hindered effective measures for regulating the layout and repair of suburban streets.[29] In 1864 the city corporation acting as a landowner took legal action to compel Kingsholm St. Catherine to improve part of Denmark Road.[30] Responsibility for highway maintenance in the suburbs was exercised by several authorities, including the three boards and the Gloucester highway district formed in 1863.[31] The trusts administering the turnpike roads leading from the city lapsed in the 1870s.[32] The county council took responsibility for main roads in 1889 and the Gloucester rural district for lesser highways in 1899.[33]

By an Act of 1874 Kingsholm, part of Wotton, outer Barton Street, Tredworth, part of Stroud Road, and part of Bristol Road came within the municipal boundary, which became coterminous with that of the enlarged parliamentary borough. The county prison and asylum, though within the extended boundary, remained outside the municipality. Membership of the city council was increased to 36, including nine aldermen, and a fourth electoral ward, which returned nine councillors, was created in the south-eastern part of the city. The three suburban boards of health were abolished[34] and the corporation shouldered their loan debts and discharged the debt on the Kingsholm St. Catherine board's non-capital expenditure.[35] As a matter of urgency the council extended the city's sewers and water mains and repaired footways in the added areas, where it levied an additional district rate to pay for those works. The improvements greatly increased the corporation's loan debt, which between 1874

[18] *Glos. Chron.* 4 Apr. 1885.
[19] *Glouc. Jnl.* 11 Mar. 1871; 30 Oct. 1886.
[20] G.B.R., B 4/1/8, mins. 22 July, 26 Aug. 1868; 9, mins. 26 Aug. 1869, 14 July 1871.
[21] *Abstracts of Treasurer's Accts.*
[22] Glouc. Extension and Improvement Act, 1874, 37 & 38 Vic. c. 111 (Local).
[23] Cf. *Glouc. Jnl.* 5 Dec. 1857.
[24] G.B.R., N 2/1/2, mins. 17, 23 Nov. 1858; B 4/5/1, mins. 19 June, 11 Sept. 1863; 2, min. 26 Feb. 1864.
[25] Ibid. N 4/2, 12; N 5/2, 7; N 6/1–2.
[26] Ibid. B 6/25/1, p. 10.
[27] Cf. ibid. N 6/2, min. 2 Sept. 1873.

[28] Ibid. 1, min. 7 Oct. 1867; N 2/7/7.
[29] Ibid. N 6/2, mins. 7 Jan., 2 Sept. 1873.
[30] Ibid. L 6/11/26.
[31] *Lond. Gaz.* 24 Mar. 1863, pp. 1709–10.
[32] Below, Outlying Hamlets, intro.; Annual Turnpike Acts Continuance Act, 1878, 41 & 42 Vic. c. 62.
[33] Glos. R.O., HB 8/M 1/4, pp. 318–27; 6, p. 213.
[34] Glouc. Extension and Improvement Act, 1874, 37 & 38 Vic. c. 111 (Local); below, parl. representation; cf. O.S. Map 6", Glos. XXV. SE., SW. (1889 edn.); XXXIII. NE.(1891 edn.); NW. (1888 edn.).
[35] Local Govt. Bd. Order, 29 Nov. 1875: copy in Glos. Colln. NF 12.8.

and 1878 rose by over 45 per cent to £128,452.[36] The differential rating of the new parts of the city encouraged development beyond the boundary,[37] where the need to control growth and improve services led the corporation to seek a further extension of the boundary at the end of the century.[38] The city was enlarged in 1900 but the increase in area, from 1,441 a. to 2,315 a. by the addition of land in the Coney Hill, Saintbridge, Tuffley, and Bristol Road areas to the south and on the west side of the canal below Llanthony, was much smaller than the corporation had wanted. The old electoral wards were abolished and the city was divided into ten new wards, each represented by three councillors; the number of aldermen was increased to ten.[39]

The council remained under the influence of the Liberal Thomas Robinson until 1886. His leadership and use of municipal patronage sharply divided the parties[40] and most municipal elections were hotly disputed. An agreement by the parties to avoid contests after the 1874 boundary extension was quickly overturned and Conservative members boycotted council committees in retaliation.[41] Bribery remained ingrained in elections, and in 1880 candidates sponsored by an electoral reform association received few votes and failed to defeat councillors guilty of corruption in the parliamentary election earlier that year.[42] The Conservatives gained control of the council in 1886 with promises to reduce rates, particularly in the newest parts of the city, and by electing aldermen from outside the council they not only secured their majority but also unseated Robinson.[43] He reappeared as a councillor between 1889 and 1895.[44] After 1886 the council was much more active in initiating public works and providing services. Although changes of political control became more frequent, with the Liberals regaining power in 1889 and the Conservatives in 1894, both parties recognized the need for greater municipal enterprise.[45] As a result the corporation's loan debt, which had been gradually reduced from 1878, rose steadily after 1887 when it was £107,992.[46] To reduce the mounting burden of debt and interest repayments the corporation in 1895 consolidated most loans by an issue of £158,000 stock, which also funded the construction of new waterworks and other improvements.[47] In another reform the differential rating of the areas added in 1874 was ended in 1894.[48]

The corporation's range of activities widened in the late 19th and early 20th century and the council obtained from parliament several extensions of its powers.[49] In 1889 the city, as a county of itself, assumed county borough status and the council took over some administrative functions from the magistrates.[50] In 1896 the city took in the county prison and the council acquired the powers of the city's civil parishes, which were consolidated to form the civil parish of Gloucester.[51] For the new parish the council appointed four overseers from among its members and employed an assistant overseer.[52] The change equalized rating throughout the city.[53] The overseers' duties lapsed in 1927 when rating powers for poor relief in the city passed to the corporation.[54]

[36] *Abstracts of Treasurer's Accts.*
[37] *Suppl. to 56th Rep. Glouc. Chamber of Commerce* (1897), 40: copy in Glos. Colln. N 15.6.
[38] G.B.R., B 6/33/1.
[39] Local Govt. Bd.'s Provisional Orders Confirmation (No. 14) Act, 1900, 63 & 64 Vic. c. 183 (Local): *Census*, 1891–1901; cf. O.S. Map 6″, Glos. XXXIII. NE., NW. (1903 edn.).
[40] *Glos. Chron.* 4 Apr. 1885; 30 Oct., 6 Nov. 1886.
[41] *Glouc. Jnl.* 8, 15 May 1875.
[42] Ibid. 6 Nov. 1880; *Rep. Com. Corrupt Practices in Glouc.* [C. 2841], pt. I, pp. 13–15, H.C. (1881), xli.
[43] *Glos. Chron.* 6 Nov. 1886; *Glouc. Jnl.* 6, 13 Nov. 1886; 5 Nov. 1887.
[44] *Glouc. Jnl.* 30 Oct. 1897.

[45] J. R. Howe, 'Political Hist. of the Parl. Constituencies of Chelt., Glouc., and the Ciren. and Tewkes. Divisions of Glos. 1895–1914' (Bristol Univ. M.Litt. thesis, 1977), 4, 20.
[46] *Abstracts of Treasurer's Accts.*
[47] G.B.R., B 3/29, pp. 100–6, 170; cf. Glos. Colln. NR 12.62.
[48] Glouc. Corp. Act, 1894, 57 & 58 Vic. c. 91(Local).
[49] Ibid.; 1911, 1 & 2 Geo. V, c. 92 (Local).
[50] Local Govt. Act, 1888, 51 & 52 Vic. c. 41.
[51] Glouc. Corp. Act, 1894, 57 & 58 Vic. c. 91 (Local); *Census*, 1901.
[52] G.B.R., B 3/30, pp. 163–4.
[53] Ibid. 35, rep. of finance and gen. purposes sub-cttee.
[54] Glos. R.O., P 154/15/VE 2/3; G/GL 52A.

Gloucester's growing population increased pressure upon public services, notably the water and sewerage undertakings.[55] Despite improvements the sewers became overloaded in the early 20th century by extensions of mains to new parts of the city. By installing meters to detect waste in 1883 the council ensured a constant water supply until the early 1890s[56] and postponed heavy expenditure on new works. Additional works completed in 1896 and 1911 tapped sources some way from the city. As revenue from water charges increased, the undertaking became a very profitable trading concern and from the mid 1880s it contributed large sums to the general district fund.[57] Other improvements included works to ease the pollution and periodic flooding of streams, particularly the Sud brook in the south. To remove one obstacle the Wishing bridge carrying Parkend Road over the brook was rebuilt and the road raised and widened in 1880.[58] Street lighting and footways were improved in the later 1880s,[59] and road widening schemes included a major project in lower Westgate Street between 1902 and 1913.[60] The corporation also carried out important works in the cattle market and at the quay,[61] and in 1896 it moved its depot to a new building at the corner of Stroud and Seymour Roads.[62]

The medical officer of health,[63] first appointed in 1873, directed his efforts towards ensuring that houses had a clean water supply and proper drainage. Connexions were made to the city water mains and flushing boxes were compulsorily installed in water-closets, but progress was slow and was not helped in the late 1880s by the poor health of the inspector of nuisances.[64] There were attempts to improve lighting and cleanliness in the worst courts and alleys[65] but a house inspection in 1892 revealed numerous sanitary defects. Many dwellings in the Bristol Road area lacked adequate sanitation until 1897 when the new waterworks replaced a private supply. In the south-eastern part of the city gas from the old sewers posed a threat to public health. The council's policy for removing the nuisance in the early 1880s relied on property owners to connect drains to the new city sewers, but it was ineffective and in 1885 over 1,000 houses were connected to the new system at public expense.[66] Several ventilating shafts were erected at the same time and more later. In 1894 the corporation obtained extra powers to deal with the problem throughout the city of pockets of slum dwellings. Orders taken out against individual properties resulted principally in repairs in the Longsmith Street, London Road, and Barton Street areas. Following the Housing Act of 1909 the council was more active in enforcing improvements but, though many dwellings were demolished, there were no large-scale clearances and the work was interrupted by the First World War.[67]

From 1873 the council also acted as port sanitary authority in the docks at Gloucester and Sharpness and along the canal. The city supplied 45 per cent of the cost of that work and the riparian sanitary authorities the rest.[68] As Gloucester was an inland waterway centre the inspection of boats used as dwellings was an important task for council officials.[69] In 1885 the council built cholera hospitals at both ends of

[55] Below, Public Services.
[56] *Reps. of Medical Off. of Health, 1888, 1893*: copies in G.B.R., B 3/23, 28.
[57] *Glos. Chron.* 4 Apr. 1885; *Abstracts of Treasurer's Accts.*
[58] G.B.R., B 3/23, rep. on floods of 8 Mar. 1889; 31, rep. on sewerage system; 38, rep. of city surveyor; L 6/7/6.
[59] *Glos. Chron.* 19 Oct., 28 Dec. 1889.
[60] Below, topog.
[61] Below, Markets and Fairs; Quay and Docks.
[62] *Suppl. 56th Rep. Chamber of Commerce*, 42.

[63] Paragraph based on *Reps. of Medical Off. of Health, 1882–1914, 1919*: copies in G.B.R., B 3/22–49, 54, and Glos. Colln. N 12.141.
[64] G.B.R., B 3/23, rep. of off. duties cttee.
[65] *Glos. Chron.* 19 Oct. 1889.
[66] G.B.R., B 3/31, rep. on sewerage system.
[67] For the period 1911–15, also G.B.R., public health department, slum clearance rec.
[68] G.B.R., B 4/5/4, min. 27 Aug. 1873; *Abstracts of Treasurer's Accts.*
[69] G.B.R., B 3/23, rep. of off. duties cttee.

the canal.[70] It was constituted permanently as port sanitary authority in 1894 and continued as port health authority under the Public Health Act of 1936.[71]

Resistance to smallpox vaccination was marked among Gloucester's poor by 1858 when 69 people died from the disease there.[72] A serious outbreak of the disease lasted from May 1873 to February 1875 with 151 deaths.[73] In response the corporation built an isolation hospital in 1874,[74] but its inadequate design and the level of charges, which deterred people from seeking admission, rendered it ineffective in halting the spread of infections. Proposals for the urban and rural sanitary authorities to join in building a more suitable isolation hospital for both the city and suburbs came to nothing.[75] From the mid 1870s a local society led by Samuel Bland, proprietor of the newly founded *Citizen* newspaper, gained wider support for the anti-vaccination cause, and in 1887 the board of guardians suspended the enforcement of compulsory vaccination.[76] An outbreak of smallpox in 1895 assumed grave proportions in February 1896 when the disease spread among children at schools in New Street and Widden Street and then to many households in the southern part of the city. Children were moved from the union workhouse to Tuffley, schools in the infected areas were closed, and temporary buildings were put up at the isolation and cholera hospitals, but through the council's lack of organization infected houses went uninspected and victims were not isolated. The death rate was highest among patients in the isolation hospital.[77] The city was virtually in quarantine and the assize courts and county quarter sessions were transferred to Cheltenham.[78] In March the board of guardians reversed its policy and began enforcing vaccination,[79] and in April local opinion prevented the use of the East End tabernacle in Derby Road as a hydropathic hospital.[80] Unvaccinated children were for a time excluded from the schools, which were reopened in May[81] when the epidemic began to abate. The outbreak, which ended in July, was confined to the city, and children aged under 10 years accounted for 706 of the 1,979 notified cases and for 280 of the 434 fatalities. The council was severely criticized for its handling of the epidemic, specially for its hospital management.[82]

After the epidemic the strength of the anti-vaccination movement was reflected in elections to the city council, board of guardians, and school board and worked largely to the Liberals' advantage. The Conservatives lost control of the council for a while but the balance between the parties was complicated by divisions among the Liberals and by the election of several independents as anti-vaccinationists.[83] The latter included from 1898 Walter Robert Hadwen, a doctor and ardent anti-vivisectionist, who came to Gloucester to champion the anti-vaccination cause during the outbreak and remained as its leader.[84] From 1890 the Labour movement had its own voice in the Gloucester Trades' Council.[85] In the municipal elections of that year the trades' council helped in the defeat of the industrialist James Platt by Walter Madge,[86] who was the secretary of a Conservative working men's friendly society,[87] but in 1891 it failed to persuade the city council to require its contractors to pay recognized trade

[70] Below, Hosp., isolation hosp.
[71] *Glouc. Municipal Year Bk.* (1964–5), 78.
[72] *Rep. Sanitary Condition of Glouc. during 1858.*
[73] G.B.R., N 2/7/13.
[74] Ibid. B 4/5/4, min. 3 Feb. 1874; below, Hosp.
[75] *Glouc. Jnl.* 11 Aug. 1883; 30 Jan. 1897; 7 Jan. 1899.
[76] F. T. Bond, *Story of the Glouc. Epidemic of Smallpox* (1896): Glos. Colln. N 27.35; for Bland's involvement, *Glouc. Jnl.* 17 Apr. 1886.
[77] G.B.R., N 2/7/13; Glos. R.O., G/GL 8A/22, pp. 481–2; 23, p. 13. [78] Howe, 'Political Hist. 1895–1914', 55–6.

[79] Bond, *Glouc. Epidemic.*
[80] *Glouc. Jnl.* 25 Apr., 2 May 1896.
[81] Glos. R.O., SB 20/1/7, pp. 72–3, 78–9.
[82] G.B.R., N 2/7/13.
[83] Howe, 'Political Hist. 1895–1914', 56–60; *Glouc. Jnl.* 7 Nov. 1896.
[84] B. E. Kidd and M. E. Richards, *Hadwen of Glouc.* (1933), 99–124.
[85] Howe, 'Political Hist. 1895–1914', 43.
[86] *Glouc. Jnl.* 1, 8 Nov. 1890; Glos. Colln. N 13.92 (1).
[87] *Glos. Chron.* 22 Feb. 1908.

union wages.[88] Organized Labour made some advances, mostly by co-operation with Liberals, and from the mid 1890s it had limited representation on the city council, board of guardians, and school board. Abel Joseph Evans, local secretary of the dockers' union, sat as a councillor intermittently between 1896 and 1905 and was particularly associated with educational policy. After his estrangement from the trades' council he was elected to the city council as a Liberal from 1906. He became a magistrate the same year.[89]

In the elections of 1900, which were for all the seats on the enlarged council, the wards returned 15 Conservatives, 14 Liberals, and 1 independent, W. R. Hadwen. The Conservatives secured the mayoralty and aldermanries but the Liberals took control in 1901 when a councillor and the aldermen were unseated on petition, the former for involvement in a corporation contract, and the mayor resigned.[90] Although there were no clear differences between the municipal policies of the two parties, elections were keenly contested and sometimes corrupt in the early 20th century. The period was one of municipal progress, notably in the purchase and electrification of the city's tramways and in education, but the Liberals' popularity waned as city rates rose. After the Conservatives regained control of the council in 1909 party feeling in municipal matters declined. Because the Liberals were unable to field candidates fewer elections were contested and the Conservatives remained the majority party for many years.[91] One of their leaders, James Bruton, who was knighted in 1916, was elected mayor nine times between 1908 and 1919.[92]

The Education Act of 1870, which required elementary schooling to be available for every child, sparked off much debate in the city. The creation of a school board was initially favoured by the council, but encountered strong opposition from churchmen and ratepayers and, though the closure or reduction in size of several schools for want of funds illustrated the limitations of the voluntary system, was delayed[93] until introduced compulsorily in 1876.[94] Most of the triennial elections of the board's nine members were contested, and the main battle was between church and undenominational parties. The board was usually chaired by an Anglican clergyman, several times because the undenominational party, which comprised both churchmen and nonconformists, was unable to agree on a candidate. One nonconformist to occupy the chair was the Revd. John Bloomfield from 1891 until his death in 1895. The board always had several independent members, including Joseph Clay (d. 1901), who was elected from 1882 as the nominee of the co-operative society. Another trade unionist elected from 1894 was A. J. Evans, who chaired the board from 1900 when nonconformist members blocked the re-election of an Anglican clergyman. W. R. Hadwen was on the board from 1897 when he headed the poll of candidates.[95] The board, which built, with some reluctance, four large schools in the south-eastern and southern parts of the city, was dissolved when the city became the local education authority under the Education Act of 1902.[96] The city council had a limited involvement in secondary education from 1882 through its representation on the governing body of the Gloucester United Endowed Schools. Its role in technical education began in the early 1890s with financial support to classes and it assumed responsibility for such teaching in the city in 1896, when the corporation acquired the

[88] G.B.R., B 3/25, pp. 323–4; *Glouc. Jnl.* 31 Oct. 1891.
[89] Howe, 'Political Hist. 1895–1914', 43–5, 120–1, 150–1; *Glouc. Jnl.* 12 Dec. 1925.
[90] *Glouc. Jnl.* 3 Nov., 29 Dec. 1900; 28 Dec. 1901.
[91] Howe, 'Political Hist. 1895–1914', 59, 99–106, 138–43, 170–1.
[92] *Glouc. Jnl.* 4 Mar. 1933; below, Plate 23.
[93] *Glouc. Jnl.* 11 Mar. 1871; 17, 24 July, 30 Oct. 1875.
[94] *Lond. Gaz.* 11 July 1876, p. 3941.
[95] Glos. R.O., SB 20/1/1–9; *Glouc. Jnl.* 18 May 1895; 5 Dec. 1903.
[96] Below, Educ., elem. educ.; *Glouc. Jnl.* 5 Dec. 1903.

Schools of Science and Art. After 1903 education quickly became the corporation's costliest service[97] and in 1907 the mayor marked the opening of new schools in Derby Road with a plea for economy.[98]

The wider range of services provided by the council from the 1890s included a mortuary,[99] public baths,[1] playing fields, a museum, and a library.[2] The fire service became a municipal undertaking in 1912. For electricity supply the council rejected private schemes in favour of a municipal service. Inaugurated in 1900,[3] it quickly became a profitable concern.[4] Less successful was the corporation's involvement with the city's tramways. Horse-drawn trams had been part of the internal transport services from 1879. Although companies running the undertaking had had financial difficulties the corporation bought it in 1902, relaid the lines for electric traction, and extended the system. The corporation's service, which included trams to Hucclecote on rails laid by the county council, began in 1904.[5] Burdened by heavy debt and loan charges, the undertaking made considerable demands on the city rates.[6] After the 1896 epidemic the corporation decided to build a new isolation hospital at Over. The building, which was not for smallpox victims, was delayed and before it was opened in 1903 the corporation, following a requirement of the Local Government Board, made provision for a smallpox hospital.[7] To combat the spread of tuberculosis the city council joined the county council in 1912 in a joint committee, which opened a sanatorium at Standish House in 1922 and continued its work until the advent of the National Health Service in 1948.[8]

The corporation began building houses in 1919 and had completed 280 dwellings by 1922. It provided only some of the houses needed for Gloucester's growing population and after the Housing Act of 1930 it concentrated on slum clearance and rehousing. The first clearances were in the Archdeacon Street and Island areas, and in the later 1930s there were clearances throughout the city.[9] The corporation undertook many other improvements between the wars, including the formation of the Oxbode and King's Square in the late 1920s, a bypass road, running north and east of the central area, started in the early 1930s,[10] and works at the quay and the cattle market.[11] Education remained the city's most expensive service and it underwent several reorganizations. In 1933 the corporation resumed direct responsibility for technical education, which it had relinquished in 1906, and in 1937 it assumed greater control over secondary education.[12] In 1936 a municipal airport was established in Churchdown as a joint undertaking with Cheltenham corporation. Known as Staverton airport, it was first managed by a Gloucester company which had run an airfield nearby from 1932.[13]

In attempts to plan ahead the corporation began buying up land on the outskirts of the city,[14] and in 1935 the city's area was doubled to 4,582 a., mostly by the addition of land to the east in the Cheltenham Road, Wotton, and Coney Hill areas and to the

[97] Below, Educ., secondary educ. 1882–1984; higher educ.; *Abstracts of Treasurer's Accts.*

[98] *Glouc. Jnl.* 13 Apr. 1907.

[99] *Rep. of Medical Off. of Health, 1890*: copy in G.B.R., B 3/25.

[1] *Glouc. Jnl.* 25 July 1891.

[2] *Glouc. Municipal Year Bk.* (1964–5), 80–1; below, social and cultural life.

[3] Below, Public Services.

[4] *Abstracts of Treasurer's Accts.*

[5] P.W. Gentry, *Tramways of W. of Eng.* (1952), 75–82; *Glouc. Jnl.* 5 Nov. 1932.

[6] S.E. Webb, 'Glouc. Corp. Light Railways' (TS. in Glos. Colln. 37171); Howe, 'Political Hist. 1895–1914', 138–40, 171.

[7] *Glouc. Jnl.* 14 Aug. 1897; 28 Sept. 1901; 25 Apr. 1903.

[8] *Reps. of Medical Off. of Health, 1912–14, 1919–37*: copies in Glos. Colln. N 12.141; *V.C.H. Glos.* x. 207; Glos. R.O., HO 36/1/1–5.

[9] *Glouc. Municipal Year Bk.* (1964–5), 88–9; *Reps. of Medical Off. of Health, 1920–37, 1938–45*: copies in Glos. Colln. N 12.141 and NR 12.44.

[10] Below, topog.; cf. Min. of Health Provisional Orders Confirmation (No. 8) Act, 1925, 15 & 16 Geo. V, c. 84 (Local).

[11] Below, Quay and Docks; Markets and Fairs.

[12] Below, Educ., secondary educ. 1882–1984; higher educ.

[13] G.B.R., B 3/70(1), pp. 608–12; *Glouc. Jnl.* 18 July 1936.

[14] Below, Outlying Hamlets, man; Barnwood, man.; *V.C.H. Glos.* x. 219.

south at Matson, Tuffley, Lower Tuffley, and Podsmead.[15] The council's composition was unchanged but the wards' boundaries and names were altered.[16] Between the wars the Conservatives, whose leaders included John Owen Roberts,[17] remained the largest party group on the council. Although a former Liberal, William Levason Edwards, failed to retain his council seat as a Labour candidate at a byelection in 1919, the Labour party won two seats at the municipal elections later that year.[18] For many years Labour party representation, which by 1922 had risen to five councillors, suffered because of a lack of aldermen. From 1925 the Conservatives and Liberals worked jointly against Labour[19] and supplied alternate mayors until 1932 when Edwards became the city's first Labour mayor.[20] There were six Labour councillors in 1936. Interest in municipal elections waned in the early 1930s, and in 1935 only one ward was contested. Interest was revived the following year by a ratepayers' association, which won three seats.[21]

The most serious threat to public health between the wars was an outbreak of mild smallpox in 1923. The medical officer of health, who later resigned, believed it to be a chickenpox epidemic but the corporation, once advised by the Ministry of Health that it was smallpox, took prompt and efficient action. Additional medical help was engaged and a temporary hospital opened. Of 698 smallpox cases notified in 1923 only three were fatal.[22] From the 1920s the corporation supplied a range of health services, including motor ambulances. It relied on voluntary agencies to discharge maternity and child welfare services and it provided a maternity hospital from 1940.[23] In the late 19th and early 20th century general hospital accommodation in the city was divided between the Gloucester Infirmary and the poor-law union infirmary. In 1912 the board of guardians started a new infirmary opposite the workhouse and opened a new block of casual wards to increase overnight accommodation for wayfarers.[24] In 1930, on the abolition of the board of guardians, the city corporation became responsible for poor relief in the city,[25] and a joint committee of the council and of other local authorities in south-western England was established to deal with vagrancy.[26] The corporation's new duties involved a range of welfare services, and it took over the former union buildings, including the infirmary and two children's homes, and an estate in Tuffley.[27]

In its increasingly complex finances[28] the corporation continued to distinguish its functions as a sanitary authority until 1929, when the borough and general district funds and rates were consolidated.[29] Spending on police, education, and poor relief was covered largely by government grants, and non-capital expenditure on other municipal services was met out of the rates. The water undertaking and the markets yielded a surplus in relief of the rates.[30] In 1929 the corporation replaced most of the tramways with a motor bus service,[31] which did not require support from the rates,[32] and in 1936, in a major change of policy, it transferred the running of the bus service, which covered the city and outlying villages, to the Bristol Tramways & Carriage Co.

[15] *Census*, 1931 (pt. ii); cf. *Glouc. Official Guide* (1949), map at pp. 194–5.   [16] Glos. Colln. NQ 12.6.
[17] *Glouc. Jnl.* 19 Jan. 1935.   [18] Ibid. 8 Nov., 27 Dec. 1919.
[19] Ibid. 4 Nov. 1922; 7 Nov. 1925; 30 Mar. 1935.
[20] Ibid. 12 Nov. 1932.
[21] Ibid. 9 Nov. 1929; 26 Oct. 1935; 7 Nov. 1936.
[22] *Rep. Chief Medical Off. of Min. of Health, 1923*: copy in Glos. Colln. NQ 12.52.
[23] *Reps. of Medical Off. of Health, 1920–37*: copies in Glos. Colln. N 12.141; *Glouc. Municipal Year Bk.* (1964–5), 86; below, Hosp., maternity hosp.
[24] *Glouc. Jnl.* 17 Feb. 1912; below, Hosp.
[25] Local Govt. Act, 1929, 19 Geo. V, c. 17.
[26] Glos. R.O., G/GL 185/12.
[27] 'Rep. of Public Assistance Cttee. 1930–1' (TS in Glos. Colln. NF 12.383).
[28] Cf. G.B.R., B 3/35, rep. of finance and gen. purposes sub-cttee.
[29] *Abstracts of Treasurer's Accts.*; Rating and Valuation Act, 1925, 15 & 16 Geo V, c. 90.
[30] *Rep. of Finance Cttee. on Municipal Schemes* (1931): copy in Glos. Colln. N 12.99.
[31] Gentry, *Tramways of W. of Eng.* 83; Glouc. Corp. Act, 1928, 18 & 19 Geo. V, c. 73 (Local).
[32] *Rep. of Finance Cttee. on Municipal Schemes* (1931); cf. Webb, 'Glouc. Corp. Light Railways'.

(renamed the Bristol Omnibus Co. in 1957).[33] The water and electricity undertakings, which were both supplying outlying rural areas by the Second World War, continued to trade at a profit. In 1936 the corporation collaborated with Cheltenham corporation in a joint water undertaking, and in 1943 it opened a new electricity generating station.[34] Education, transport, public health, and the water, sewerage, and electricity undertakings required heavy capital investment in the early 20th century. The corporation's loan debt rose from £195,551 in 1900 to £360,334 in 1904 and to £456,775 in 1914. After 1918 there was also heavy capital expenditure on housing and roads and by 1940 the loan debt had reached £2,097,334. The corporation's debts were reorganized by further issues of stock in 1925 and 1929.[35]

After the Second World War Gloucester's growth was marked by several extensions of the city boundary. In 1951 land at Elmbridge to the east and at Lower Tuffley and Netheridge to the south was added and Wotton Vill, the island of the county formed by the Wotton asylum, was absorbed to give the city 5,272 a.[36] In 1957 the city took in 22 a. between Matson and Sneedham's Green to the south,[37] and in 1967 it added Longlevens and parts of Longford and Innsworth to the north, much of Barnwood and Hucclecote to the east, meadow land to the west, and Hempsted to the south-west to give it, after a minor adjustment, 8,239 a. (3,334 ha.). That extension moved the western boundary to the Severn's western channel and the eastern boundary to major roads, of which the Birmingham – Bristol motorway opened in 1971. The enlarged city was divided into eleven wards, each represented by three councillors, and the number of aldermen was increased to eleven.[38] The aldermanic bench was abolished at local government reorganization in 1974 when Gloucester lost its status as a county borough and became a district. It kept the title of city together with its mayor and sheriff.[39] Labour party representation on the council included several aldermen after 1945, when it held 17 of the 40 seats. The Liberals, who worked jointly with the Conservatives in the 1945 elections, were reduced to a handful[40] and for a period were without representatives.[41] Labour was in control between 1957 and 1966[42] and the Conservatives, who gained power in 1968, won a majority of the seats in the elections for the district council, taking over city government in 1974.[43]

From 1945 corporation expenditure grew rapidly as services were provided in new parts of the city and as older parts were redeveloped. Education services, which expanded under the Education Act of 1944, remained the largest single item in non-capital expenditure. New health and welfare services were created;[44] the corporation had opened three old people's homes, not all within the city, by 1954 and ran a residential nursery at Wallsworth Hall in Sandhurst from 1944 until 1953.[45] There was heavy capital expenditure on new school buildings, roads, and housing, which included new estates on the fringes of the city and, in the early 1960s, houses for sale.[46] A new sewerage system with a treatment plant was constructed.[47] Both the city and county library services catered for the areas of new housing.[48] The

[33] *Glouc. Municipal Year Bk.* (1964–5), 83; *People's Carriage 1874–1974* (1974), 68–9; cf. G.B.R., B 6/39/10.

[34] *Rep. of City Treasurer on Accts. 1933–4*: copy in Glos. Colln. NF 12.359(1); below, Public Services.

[35] *Abstracts of Treasurer's Accts.*; cf. G.B.R., B 3/59, pp. 203–7; 63, p. 281.

[36] Glouc. Extension Act, 1950, 14 Geo. VI, c. 51 (Local); *Census*, 1951; cf. *Glouc. Official Guide* (1952), map at pp. 192–3. Part of Wotton Vill had been absorbed by the city in 1910: *Census*, 1911.

[37] City of Glouc. (Extension) Order, 1957; *Census*, 1961; cf. *Glouc. Official Guide* (1961), map at pp. 208–9.

[38] Glouc. Order, 1966; *Census*, 1971.

[39] Local Govt. Act, 1972, c. 70; *Glouc. Official Guide* (1980), 26, 45.

[40] *Citizen*, 15 Dec. 1945; 23 May 1949.

[41] Ibid. 9 May 1958.

[42] Ibid. 10 May 1957; 13 May 1966.

[43] Ibid. 10 May 1968; 8 June 1973.

[44] *Rep. on City's Accts. 1946–50*: copy in Glos. Colln. NR 12.54.

[45] *Glouc. Municipal Year Bk.* (1964–5), 95–6.

[46] *Glouc. Official Guide* (1963), 67, 73, 101.

[47] Below, Public Services.

[48] Below, social and cultural life.

corporation's loan debt had risen by 1954 to over £6,300,000, more than half of which had been incurred in housing schemes,[49] and by 1960 to over £10,300,000,[50] and in 1970 its borrowing powers were increased.[51] The council's policy of making loans to house purchasers brought problems as arrears in repayments mounted, and in 1964 the ensuing financial and political difficulties led to the retirement of the city treasurer and the resignation of the town clerk.[52]

A development plan, drawn up by the corporation and implemented from 1954,[53] aimed to improve the city's layout, reduce areas of decay, relieve traffic congestion, and provide services for the city's expanding population. The corporation, which started comprehensive redevelopment of parts of Kingsholm and lower Westgate Street, obtained further powers for making improvements in 1958.[54] For the city centre the council commissioned the architect G. A. Jellicoe to design a comprehensive plan, which was presented in 1962, but later varied its details.[55] Major public works included the completion of the bypass road (1959), the construction of an inner ring road[56] (in progress 1985), and the building of a new cattle market (1955), fire station (1956), ambulance station (1961), antenatal and child welfare clinic (1962),[57] and bus station (1962).[58] New recreational facilities included a leisure centre (1974) and a country park on Robins Wood Hill.[59] Two shopping centres were developed by a property company and an insurance company in collaboration with the city council.[60] In the early 1980s the council replaced the development plan by a new district plan, which with the county council's structure plan became the basis for city planning.[61]

Municipal control over some services disappeared before the 1974 local government reorganization. Electricity generation and supply and some health services, including hospitals, were removed by nationalization in 1948, the two water undertakings were merged with others in 1965, and the fire service was merged with that of the county in 1972. In 1974 the county council took over the city's structural planning, education, libraries, refuse disposal, social services, trading standards, and major highways, and separate authorities most of its health services and its water supply and sewage disposal. The city council retained responsibility for most highways and transportation and for the sewerage system, by agreements respectively with the county council and the water authority, and for planning, housing, environmental health, refuse collection, cemeteries, and leisure services.[62] Staverton airport, which from 1957 had been run by the Gloucester and Cheltenham Joint Airport Committee and before 1974 had traded at a small profit, remained in the ownership of the Gloucester and Cheltenham councils.[63]

Parliamentary Representation

After 1835[64] Gloucester, which returned two members of parliament until 1885, was represented by political moderates, usually Whigs or Liberals. Maurice Frederick

[49] *Statement of Loans Fund, 1953–4*: copy in Glos. Colln. NX 12.13.

[50] Glos. Colln. N 12.334.

[51] Glouc. Corp. Act, 1970, c. 70 (Local).

[52] Glos. Colln. NR 12.53.

[53] *Citizen*, 4 Feb. 1954; for the plan, Glos. Colln. 28622 (1–3); NF 12.20, 25.

[54] Glouc. Corp. Act, 1958, 6 & 7 Eliz. II, c. 35 (Local).

[55] Jellicoe, *Comprehensive Plan for Central Area of Glouc.* (1961): copy in Glos. Colln. 33014; *Citizen*, 1 Feb. 1962. For a review of the plan in 1965, Glos. Colln. 39449.

[56] *Glouc. Official Guide* (1963), 101.

[57] *Glouc. Municipal Year Bk.* (1964–5), 76, 84, 86.

[58] Ibid. (1966–7), 85.

[59] Below, social and cultural life.

[60] *Municipal Jnl.* 29 Oct. 1965, pp. 3687–9.

[61] For the district plan, Glos. Colln. 40266; 40543; 41085.

[62] Below, Public Services; Hospitals; inf. from chief executive, Glouc. city council (1985).

[63] *Citizen*, 21 Jan. 1976; inf. from chief executive, Glouc. city council.

[64] Paragraph based on Williams, *Parl. Hist. of Glos.* 214–18.

Berkeley (M.P. 1835–7 and 1841–57) and his son Charles Paget Berkeley (M.P. 1862–5) belonged to a leading county family, but the influence of Whig landowners on Gloucester's parliamentary elections declined in the mid 19th century. The Guise family of Elmore continued to support Liberal candidates.[65] Most members, including John Phillpotts[66] (M.P. 1837–47), had significant city connexions. William Philip Price[67] of Tibberton Court (M.P. 1852–9 and 1865–73) was a leading timber importer and Unitarian, and the barrister Charles James Monk[68] (M.P. 1859, 1865–85 and 1895–1900) was the son of a former bishop of Gloucester. The Tory or Conservative Henry Thomas Hope of Deepdene (Surr.), a banker who owned the Hampnett estate near Northleach,[69] won a seat in 1835 and 1837, when M. F. Berkeley and Phillpotts, both supporters of parliamentary reform, were at loggerheads, and again in 1847 when Price, who came forward as candidate in place of Phillpotts, failed to join forces with Berkeley and withdrew before the poll.[70]

The electorate numbered 1,308 in 1835.[71] By 1859 it had risen to 1,518,[72] and in 1868 the parliamentary borough was enlarged to take in most of the suburbs, the new boundary including Dockham ditch on the north, the Wotton brook on the east, a disused railway line bypassing the city on the south-east, and watercourses, notably the canal, Still ditch, and the Severn, on the south and south-west.[73] The electorate, which was also increased by the extension of the franchise in 1867, rose from 4,040 in 1868[74] to 5,371 in 1880.[75]

With the exception of the 1847 election all general elections were contested and Conservative candidates, often only one at the beginning of the period, were usually men brought in from outside.[76] Improper electoral practices, encouraged by the conduct of municipal elections, were a prominent feature of parliamentary contests and occasionally, as in 1857, influenced the result. The electorate showed little interest in political debate and the venality of many voters, both freemen and householders, was disclosed in evidence before a Royal Commission in 1859. Both parties paid for men to register as freemen, thereby slowing the decline in the number of freemen voters, which fell from 800 in 1832 to 534, including 197 outvoters, in 1859. Hope's opponents attributed Conservative successes to his lavish expenditure, and after the election of 1837, which was particularly costly and corrupt, there was a petition against his return. He resigned and regained the seat the following year. In 1852 the three candidates agreed to avoid unnecessary and corrupt expenses and the election was conducted with remarkable purity. Hope, who lost his seat, unsuccessfully contested a byelection in 1853[77] when his supporters were accused of treating on a lavish scale.[78] That contest broke the convention of not opposing the re-election of members appointed to office under the Crown. In 1855 Price was unopposed in a byelection following his involvement in a government contract for supplying huts to the army in the Crimea.[79]

Although there were earlier party clubs to ensure the registration of supporters,[80] Gloucester's first permanent political organization was established by the Conserva-

[65] *Glouc. Jnl.* 1 Mar. 1862; 15 July 1865; 7 May 1873.

[66] For whom, above, Glouc. 1720–1835, parl. representation.

[67] For whom, above, econ. 1835–1914.

[68] Cf. C. J. Monk, *Reminiscences of Parl. Life* (priv. print. 1901).

[69] *Glos. Chron.* 6 Dec. 1862.

[70] *Glouc. Jnl.* 10 Jan. 1835; 29 July 1837; 31 July 1847.

[71] Williams, *Parl. Hist. of Glos.* 215.

[72] C. Jackson, 'British General Elections of 1857 and 1859' (Oxf. Univ. D. Phil. thesis, 1981), 314.

[73] Boundary Act, 1868, 31 & 32 Vic. c. 46, sched. 1.

[74] *Glouc. Jnl.* 21 Nov. 1868.

[75] *Rep. Com. Corrupt Practices in Glouc.* [C. 2841], pt. I, p. 14, H.C. (1881), xli.

[76] Willliams, *Parl. Hist. of Glos.* 215–20.

[77] *Rep. Com. Corrupt Practices in Glouc.* [2586], pp. v–vii, xvi–xvii, H.C. (1860), xxvii; Williams, *Parl. Hist. of Glos.* 215; *Glouc. Jnl.* 26 May 1838.   [78] *Glouc. Jnl.* 8 Jan. 1853.

[79] Williams, *Parl. Hist. of Glos.* 216–19; *Glouc. Jnl.* 18 July 1846; 31 Mar., 7 Apr. 1855; 28 May 1864.

[80] Cf. *Glouc. Jnl.* 13 Feb. 1836.

tives in 1853 to repair the loss of Hope's seat and to win control of the city council. For the parliamentary election of 1857 they brought in Sir Robert Carden, a wealthy London stockbroker, and secured his place at the top of the poll by extensive bribery and treating. The Liberals also resorted to corruption, though on a much smaller scale. Political issues were irrelevant to the result and Berkeley, who had supported Palmerston on the Chinese question, was beaten into third place. Petitions against Carden and Price were unsuccessful, but it was later found that at least 116 voters had been bribed, 109 of them by Carden's supporters. After the election the Liberals improved their organization by setting up a political club similar to the Conservative association and at the election in 1859 copied the methods used by their opponents two years earlier. The 1859 contest was consequently energetic and even more costly and corrupt, with 250 voters, a sixth of the electorate, taking bribes. The Liberals were also helped by the strong local ties of C. J. Monk, who had become their second candidate in Berkeley's place. Carden, who spent more than his two opponents together, was decisively beaten, but Price and Monk were unseated for bribery and a Royal Commission was appointed to investigate illegal practices.[81]

Gloucester remained unrepresented in parliament until 1862 when a writ for a new election was issued. The Liberal candidates, including the barrister John Joseph Powell, held off a challenge from Richard Potter of Standish House, a local industrialist and former Liberal who fought as a Conservative,[82] and they stood down at the next general election in 1865 to enable Price and Monk to resume their parliamentary careers.[83] Conservatism received greater support in Gloucester in the early 1870s, and in 1873 William Killigrew Wait, a Bristol corn merchant with business interests in Gloucester, defeated the local Liberal leader, the corn merchant Thomas Robinson, in a contest for the seat vacated by Price on his appointment as a Railway Commissioner. Robinson's campaign was not helped by his outmanoeuvring of Powell in his bid for the Liberal candidacy, but Powell was equally unsuccessful as a candidate in the general election of 1874[84] when both parties resorted again to widespread illegal practices. Corruption was on an even greater scale in 1880 when the Liberals, who in 1875 had improved their organization by establishing a party caucus chosen by ward meetings, redoubled their efforts to defeat Wait. Robinson and Monk were returned but were petitioned against for bribery. Robinson, who topped the poll, was unseated, but his willingness to stand down and the unwillingness of the Conservatives to continue proceedings against Monk and of Monk to claim his costs raised suspicions of collusion by the parties and led to the setting up of a Royal Commission to examine electoral practices.

Gloucester was among the most corrupt of the seven towns investigated at that time and 1,916 voters known to have taken bribes were disqualified for seven years. The Royal Commission concluded that bribery was the rule at all elections in the city, reckoned that c. 2,756 voters, over half of the electorate, had taken bribes in 1880, and blamed local politicians for most of the corruption; scheduled persons included 18 councillors and aldermen, 6 poor-law guardians, 3 magistrates, and 5 solicitors.[85] No new writ was issued for the seat vacated by Robinson[86] but a proposal to disfranchise the borough entirely came to nothing.[87] Gloucester's reputation for corrupt politics

[81] Rep. Corrupt Practices (1860), pp. vii–xxxix; Jackson, 'General Elections of 1857 and 1859', 314–32.
[82] Glouc. Jnl. 22 Feb., 1 Mar. 1862; Williams, Parl. Hist. of Glos. 218–19.
[83] Glouc. Jnl. 8, 15 July 1865.
[84] Williams, Parl. Hist. of Glos. 219–20; Glos. Chron. 3, 10

May 1873; Glouc. Jnl. 3, 7, 10 May 1873; 7 Feb. 1874. For W.K. Wait, Glos. Chron. 20 Dec. 1902.
[85] Rep. Corrupt Practices (1881), pt. I, pp. 1–34; Glouc. Jnl. 21 Mar. 1885.
[86] Williams, Parl. Hist. of Glos. 220.
[87] Monk, Reminiscences, 178–89.

lingered until the First World War, and allegations of corruption on a significant scale were made, notably in January 1910.[88]

In 1885 Gloucester's parliamentary representation was reduced to one member.[89] Because many voters were disqualified for corruption the electorate was then only 4,547. In 1900 it was 7,685[90] and in 1918, when the parliamentary borough was made coterminous with the larger county borough,[91] 25,006. It had grown to 34,786 by 1935.[92] In 1948 the constituency was enlarged to comprise the county borough and the parishes of Barnwood, Brockworth, Hempsted, Hucclecote, and Wotton Vill,[93] and in 1950 the electorate was 49,005. Several minor changes in the parliamentary boundary followed, and in 1970, when the parliamentary borough was again made coterminous with the county borough, that part outside the municipal boundary, namely the parishes of Brockworth and Hucclecote, was detached, leaving 61,164 voters.[94] In 1983 five parishes south of the city were added to the constituency to give an electorate of 74,316.[95]

In the late 19th century the Conservatives gained ground in Gloucester. They benefited from the antipathy of some Liberals towards Thomas Robinson, whose control of the Liberal party caucus ensured that he, and not the sitting member C. J. Monk, became the candidate for the single parliamentary seat in 1885.[96] Robinson, who was knighted in 1894, represented Gloucester between 1885 and 1895.[97] The Liberals were harmed more by the split over Home Rule in 1886,[98] and prominent among the Liberal Unionists were former M.P.s Price and Monk. Price's daughter-in-law, Margaret Price (d. 1911), remained a patron of the Gloucester Liberals, as did Sir William Wedderburn, a landowner at Meredith in Tibberton. Monk, who gained the support of the Conservative association, challenged Robinson for the parliamentary seat in 1892 and held it between 1895, when his opponent was an inexperienced and radical 'carpet-bagger', and 1900.[99]

In the 1890s there were occasional socialist gatherings in the city and a branch of the Independent Labour Party had been formed by 1896. Liberal candidates before the First World War broadly supported the demands of organized Labour, and Russell Rea, a Liverpool merchant and shipowner and a director of the Taff Vale Railway Company, regained Gloucester for the Liberals in 1900 with the backing of the railwaymen's national leader. Rea was defeated in January 1910 by a Conservative, and the Liberals failed by five votes to recapture the seat at the end of the year.[1] With few exceptions Gloucester's representatives in the 20th century lacked local ties. Of the four Conservatives holding the seat between 1910 and 1945[2] Sir James Bruton (1918–23) was prominent in local industry and commerce and in civic affairs[3] and James Nockells Horlick (1923–9) was the son of a county landowner.[4] The first Labour candidate, W. L. Edwards, stood in 1918 and gained 17 per cent of the vote.[5] In the early 1920s Labour gained from having an exceptionally popular candidate in

[88] J. R. Howe, 'Corruption in Brit. Elections in the Early Twentieth Cent.: Some Examples from Glos.' *Midland Hist.* v. 63–77.

[89] Redistribution of Seats Act, 1885, 48 & 49 Vic. c. 23.

[90] *Glouc. Jnl.* 28 Nov. 1885; 6 Oct. 1900.

[91] Representation of the People Act, 1918, 7 & 8 Geo. V, c. 64; *Glouc. Jnl.* 28 Dec. 1918.

[92] F. W. S. Craig, *Brit. Parl. Election Results 1918–49*, 137.

[93] Representation of the People Act, 1948, 11 & 12 Geo. VI, c. 65.

[94] Craig, *Brit. Parl. Election Results 1950–73*, 149; Parl. Constituencies (Eng.) Order 1970.

[95] Parl. Constituencies (Eng.) Order 1983; *Citizen*, 10 May, 10 June 1983.

[96] *Glouc. Jnl.* 21 Nov. 1885; Monk, *Reminiscences*, 227–36.

[97] *Glouc. Jnl.* 30 Oct. 1897. [98] Cf. ibid. 11 June 1887.

[99] J. R. Howe, 'Political Hist. of the Parl. Constituencies of Chelt., Glouc., and the Ciren. and Tewkes. Divisions of Glos. 1895–1914' (Bristol Univ. M. Litt. thesis, 1977), 18, 26–30, 41; Monk, *Reminiscences*, 249–79; *Glouc. Jnl.* 1 Apr. 1911.

[1] Howe, 'Political Hist. 1895–1914', 44, 64–6, 120–5, 149, 162–5, 174–82.

[2] Craig, *Election Results 1918–49*, 137.

[3] *Glouc. Jnl.* 4 Mar. 1933.

[4] *Who Was Who, 1971–80*, 382; cf. *V.C.H. Glos.* vii. 194.

[5] Craig, *Election Results 1918–49*, 137.

Morgan Philips Price, grandson and heir of the former Liberal M.P. and himself the prospective Liberal candidate before the First World War. Price, who as a journalist had reported political revolutions in Russia and Germany during the war and its aftermath,[6] won 36 per cent of the vote and came within 52 votes of defeating Bruton at the election of 1922. The Liberals, who from 1922 held third place, did not put up a candidate in 1931 or in 1935, when the Labour candidate won 43 per cent of the vote. Gloucester fell to Labour as part of the national swing in 1945 and the Conservatives recaptured the seat in 1970. The Liberals contested all but one election between 1945 and 1979,[7] and the Labour party retained second place in 1983 when a Social Democratic Party candidate represented the national alliance with the Liberals.[8]

Social and Cultural Life

Gloucester's development as a commercial and manufacturing centre in the mid and late 19th century and the growth of a large working-class population had a distinct influence on its social and cultural life. Although the social attractions of nearby Cheltenham were more popular with the gentry, the city's status as a cathedral and county town ensured that Gloucester was not totally abandoned by county landowners. Many such as William Henry Hyett of Painswick and Thomas Gambier Parry of Highnam figured prominently in its institutions.[9]

The growth of suburbs and of slums posed the greatest challenge to organized religion in Gloucester by the 1830s.[10] Missionary work among the poor was as much concerned with education and social conditions as with public worship and was fruitful for nonconformist groups, many of them new. Nonconformity, which also satisfied the aspirations of many leading merchants and industrialists, became a significant element in the life of the city. A British school was opened in 1841 and the principal groups, the Independents, Wesleyan Methodists, and Baptists, later displayed their wealth and confidence in large chapels with imposing street fronts.[11] Anglicans built several schools in the city in the 1830s and early 1840s, and in the 1840s they also provided churches and schools for the new working-class areas of Barton End (St. James), High Orchard (St. Luke), and Kingsholm (St. Mark).[12] Much of that work was initiated or sustained by clergymen, including John Kempthorne, rector of St. Michael 1826–38, who planned the church at Barton End, and Thomas Hedley, perpetual curate of St. James 1841–8, who built the school there.[13] More notable was Samuel Lysons, rector of Rodmarton, who built the church and school at High Orchard, an area inhabited by dock labourers near his Hempsted Court estate.[14] In the larger parishes or districts the parochial clergy were assisted by stipendiary curates.[15] Gloucester's importance as an ecclesiastical centre was diminished by the union of the sees of Gloucester and Bristol in 1836, following which the bishop, James Monk, left the city.[16] The dean, Edward Rice, who was also non-resident, took little interest in the life of the cathedral and city,[17] and a teacher training school and a church music school started in Gloucester in the 1840s were both short lived.[18]

[6] M. P. Price, *My Three Revolutions* (1969); Howe, 'Political Hist. 1895–1914', 196–8.

[7] Craig, *Election Results 1918–49*, 137; *1950–73*, 149; *Citizen*, 4 May 1979.

[8] *Citizen*, 10 June 1983.

[9] e.g. below, Hosp., eye, children's, and mental hosp.

[10] Cf. Glos. R.O., D 936/A 36.

[11] Below, Educ., elem. educ.; Prot. Nonconf.

[12] Below, Educ., elem. educ.; Churches and Chapels, mod.

par. ch.

[13] Hockaday Abs. ccxv; ccxix; *Glouc. Jnl.* 13 Oct. 1866; cf. obit. of Thos. Evans, in *Glouc. Jnl.* 21 Jan. 1854.

[14] *D.N.B.*; *Glos. N. & Q.* ii. 514–16; Nat. Soc. files, Glouc., St. Paul. [15] Hockaday Abs. ccxiii–ccxx.

[16] *Trans. B.G.A.S.* xcvii. 82–3; the union of the sees lasted until 1897: *V.C.H. Glos.* ii. 48.

[17] *Glos. Chron.* 23 Aug. 1862; *V.C.H. Glos.* vi. 95.

[18] *Bryant's Dir. Glouc.* (1841), 81; *Glouc. Jnl.* 22 May 1847.

Church life revived following the return to the city of a new bishop in the later 1850s[19] and the appointment of Henry Law as dean in 1862. Law (d. 1884), a prominent evangelical who played an active part in the city's philanthropic institutions, removed secular monuments from College Green. Under him the cathedral's fabric was restored[20] and its music improved by 1865 when the composer and instrumentalist Samuel Sebastian Wesley became organist.[21] Charles Ellicott, bishop from 1863, opened a theological college in Gloucester in 1869. It closed before his episcopate ended in 1905.[22] From the later 1860s parochial life flourished. Partly at the instigation of the merchant William Charles Lucy a new church was built for St. Catherine's parish, which had been without one since the mid 17th century.[23] The revival, which included the opening of new schools[24] and missionary work in Kingsholm,[25] Tredworth, Millbrook Street, Longlevens, and Tuffley,[26] owed much to clergymen such as John Emeris, perpetual curate of St. James 1848–72, and his curate John Alington.[27] In the late 19th century the established and nonconformist churches continued missionary work throughout Gloucester and in outlying places such as Coney Hill and Saintbridge but, although several churches and chapels and many more halls were built,[28] some areas remained without suitable places for worship. In one of his first acts Edgar Gibson, bishop 1905–22, appointed a commission which led to the provision of two more churches and a reorganization of the city's parishes.[29]

In general, relations between the established and nonconformist churches in Gloucester were good. The evangelical movement, which strongly influenced many aspects of life, brought members of different churches together for missionary work.[30] The levying of church rates aroused most controversy in St. Michael's parish in 1837.[31] In the mid 19th century the growing confidence of Roman Catholics, who rebuilt their church in Gloucester,[32] brought assertions of the city's protestant tradition, including the erection of an imposing memorial to the martyred Bishop John Hooper.[33] Within the established church High Church practices were observed for short periods at St. Aldate's church and St. Paul's church (consecrated 1883),[34] and the main centre of Anglo-Catholic worship was St. Lucy's Home of Charity,[35] founded in 1864 by Thomas Gambier Parry and closed in 1933.[36] Among the evangelical parish clergy John Luce, vicar of St. Nicholas 1877–1923, who ran a mission room in the Island from 1879, fostered particularly close ties with nonconformist groups.[37]

The eradication of crime and of the associated evils of drunkenness and prostitution attracted the energies of social reformers, in particular clergymen and members of the small Quaker meeting. As early as 1836 the town clerk reported that the growth in the port's trade had increased the incidence of crime in Gloucester.[38] Missionaries were active among seamen and boatmen frequenting the docks and the quay. The most

[19] Cf. *Trans. B.G.A.S.* xcvii. 83.
[20] *Glouc. Jnl.* 29 Nov. 1884; 28 Nov. 1863.
[21] Ibid. 9 Apr. 1864; 18 Feb. 1865; for Wesley, *D.N.B.*
[22] *Glouc. Jnl.* 21 Oct. 1905; 23 Jan. 1869.
[23] Below, Churches and Chapels; *Glos. N. & Q.* iv. 484–6.
[24] Below, Educ., elem. educ.
[25] *Glos. Chron.* 4 Dec. 1869; 16 Apr. 1870.
[26] Below, Churches and Chapels, mod. par. ch.
[27] Glos. R.O., P 154/8/IN 1/1–2; *Glouc. Jnl.* 13 Oct. 1866.
[28] Below, Churches and Chapels, mod. par. ch.; Prot. Nonconf.; for new mission rooms, *Glouc. Jnl.* 1 Dec. 1888; 28 Dec. 1889; 7 Feb. 1903.
[29] Below, Churches and Chapels; *Glouc. Jnl.* 15 Mar. 1924.
[30] e.g. *Glouc. Jnl.* 24 Apr. 1840.
[31] Glos. R.O., P 154/14/CW 2/4; VE 2/3; cf. *Glouc. Jnl.* 3 June, 26 Aug. 1837.
[32] Below, Roman Catholicism.
[33] *Glouc. Jnl.* 24 Apr. 1852; 9 Feb. 1855; below, Public Buildings.
[34] *Glouc. Jnl.* 29 June 1872; Glos. Colln. N 5.46.
[35] *Glouc. Jnl.* 21 Jan. 1871; J. N. Langston, 'Notes on St. Lucy's Home of Char.' (Glos. Colln. 18349).
[36] Below, Hosp., children's hosp.
[37] *Glouc. Jnl.* 25 Aug. 1923; 1 Nov. 1879.
[38] G.B.R., B 4/1/5, f. 57; for drunkenness and prostitution, *Glouc. Jnl.* 14 Sept. 1844; 27 Aug. 1870; 19 Aug. 1882.

successful centre for such evangelism was a mariners' chapel, built in the docks by private benefactors and opened in 1849. A mission to Norwegian seamen was provided with a chapel in 1878.[39] In the mid 1850s a lodging house within the shell of the Greyfriars church was a sailors' home.[40] The home, which moved to a new building in Ladybellegate Street in 1862,[41] was closed in 1879 because the number of ocean-going vessels entering the docks had declined.[42]

In the mid 19th century public houses, already plentiful in the older part of Gloucester, became more numerous near the docks and around the cattle market.[43] In 1877 the city had 121 alehouses and 86 beerhouses.[44] Many were in newer working-class areas, and soon afterwards the city magistrates shut some of the worst beerhouses, including several in Westgate Street.[45] The temperance movement, which attracted fierce opposition from the liquor trade,[46] was widely supported, and Bands of Hope promoted the abstainers' cause throughout the city.[47] The movement's leader was the merchant Samuel Bowly (d. 1884), who formed a temperance society with fellow Quakers and became president of the National Temperance League.[48] In the 1860s, after the closure of the public conduit in Southgate Street, private benefactors and the temperance society provided drinking fountains at the docks, Tolsey, park, and cattle market.[49] The success of a coffee house in the docks, opened by the mariners' chaplain in 1877, led to the formation of a company which by 1883 had opened five more coffee houses in the city.[50]

Many philanthropic organizations and individuals addressed problems caused by demoralization, poverty, and unemployment among the working classes. Members of most churches supported an industrial ragged school, built in 1852 in Archdeacon Street, one of the most deprived parts of the city, to turn children there from lives of crime.[51] In 1897 the Church Army opened a home in New Inn Lane to give work to destitute and unemployed men. It moved to London Road c. 1913.[52] The reform of prostitutes was undertaken in the Magdalen Asylum in St. Mary's Square, which closed in 1874.[53] A temporary refuge opened by 1870 was replaced in 1873 by a home built by Quakers led by Eliza Sessions, where girls were employed in domestic service and laundry work. Known as the Home of Hope, it stood east of the workhouse near London Road.[54] The Magdalen Asylum's work was revived in the late 1870s, and from c. 1900 it included a training institution in domestic and laundry work at Picton House in Wellington Parade, provided by William Long.[55] Missionary work among women was also undertaken by St. Lucy's Home of Charity, which ran a children's hospital from 1867, an orphanage from 1870, and a reformatory at Newark House, Hempsted, from the early 1880s,[56] and by a club founded in 1879 by Constantia Ellicott, wife of the bishop, to train factory girls for domestic service.[57] Outbreaks of

[39] Cf. below, Prot. Nonconf., undenominational missions; Churches and Chapels, non-par. chap.

[40] J. Hollins, *Pastoral Recollections* (1857), 26, 36; *Kelly's Dir. Glos.* (1856), 294; G.B.R., planning dept., file 1863/13.

[41] G.B.R., B 4/5/1, mins. 25 July, 31 Oct. 1862; *Kelly's Dir. Glos.* (1863), 274.

[42] *Glouc. Jnl.* 7 Feb. 1880.

[43] Cf. Causton, *Map of Glouc.* (1843); Bd. of Health Map (1852); O.S. Map 1/2,500, Glos. XXV. 14, 15 (1886 edn.); XXXIII, 2, 3 (1886 edn.).

[44] *Glouc. Jnl.* 15 Sept. 1877.

[45] Ibid. 27 Aug. 1870; 27 Jan. 1883.

[46] Ibid. 13 Oct. 1855; 7 Sept. 1872; 27 Jan., 17 Mar. 1883.

[47] Ibid. 30 Sept. 1876; 13 Oct. 1877; 20 May 1882.

[48] *D.N.B.*; J. Stratford, *Glos. Biog. Notes* (1887), 201–13; *Glouc. Jnl.* 29 Mar. 1884.

[49] G.B.R., N 2/1/3, min. 29 Mar. 1859; B 4/5/2, min. 2 Aug. 1867; *Glos. Chron.* 20 Oct. 1860; *Glouc. Jnl.* 13 July 1861; 28 May 1864.

[50] W. H. Whalley, *Mariners' Chap.* (1909), 43; Glos. R.O., D 3087.

[51] Glos. Colln. 24099; below, Educ., elem. educ.

[52] Glos. Colln. N 20.4; NR 20.1.

[53] A. J. Brewster, *One Hundred Years of Rescue Work in Glouc.* (1930), 6–10: Glos. Colln. NQ 20.4.

[54] *Kelly's Dir. Glos.* (1870), 552; *Glouc. Jnl.* 23 Aug., 20 Dec. 1873; Glos. Colln., J. J. Powell's newspaper cuttings 1873–8, 18.

[55] Brewster, *One Hundred Years of Rescue Work*, 10–12.

[56] Glos. Colln. 18349; *Glouc. and Bristol Dioc. Cal.* (1875) (2), 47; *St. John Baptist Clewer Mag.* Autumn 1884, 14.

[57] *Glouc. Jnl.* 8 Nov. 1879; 3 Oct. 1885; 28 Feb. 1914; Glos. Colln. N 20.17 (1).

hooliganism were frequent in the city in the later 19th century,[58] and organizations providing a recreational outlet for youths included branches of the Gordon League and of the Young Men's Christian Association formed in 1885 and 1895 respectively.[59] During the acute economic depression of the mid 1880s the city corporation provided some temporary employment.[60] The local politician, John Ward (d. 1895), whose beneficence enhanced his popularity among labourers, gave an annual Christmas dinner for the poor from 1884.[61]

A Chartist meeting in the city in 1839 drew a large crowd but more out of curiosity than commitment.[62] Although Gloucester was not associated with radical politics, numerous organizations were formed there for the benefit of the working classes, many by labourers themselves. Trade unions, which were active by 1835,[63] and other friendly societies, including branches of the Odd Fellows and by 1851 the Ancient Order of Foresters, increased in number.[64] Local institutions encouraging thrift included a savings bank, which closed in 1886,[65] and a penny bank, which was open from 1859 until 1905.[66] A co-operative society, started by railway and dock employees in 1860 for the purpose of retail trade, had 2,128 members in 1878 and 8,600 in 1910. In 1879 it began providing loans for house purchase and founded two scholarships at the School of Science. It also had a library until 1900.[67] The trades' council formed in 1890 also promoted workers' education,[68] and in 1908 a branch was formed of the Workers' Educational Association, founded by Gloucester-born Albert Mansbridge.[69]

A mechanics' institution, established in the late 1830s and sustained for several years by William Higgs, had a reading room and organized literary and scientific courses and musical entertainments.[70] It had been dissolved by 1852 when Higgs opened a short-lived public institute.[71] Higgs also took a prominent part in an evangelical society for young men which was organized by David Nasmith in 1839 and had its own library.[72] In 1855 a working men's institute was opened with the support of leading merchants, notably Joseph Sturge, in a new building in lower Southgate Street with lecture and reading rooms. Despite closure for several periods it was a centre for social gatherings and missionary work in the later 19th century.[73] Several other working men's clubs established at the turn of the century grew out of church missions, as in the parishes of St. James and St. Mark.[74] The institute in Southgate Street was largely superseded c. 1916 by a club in Barton Street run by the Gloucester Labour party.[75] The club, which occupied a former chapel acquired in 1904 by socialists,[76] moved to a new building there in 1983,[77] and the Labour party opened new offices there in 1963.[78]

From the 1850s the Conservatives and Liberals established a number of politico-benevolent associations for working people.[79] The most successful was the Gloucester

[58] *Glouc. Jnl.* 6 July 1872; 19 Sept. 1885.

[59] Ibid. 20 Oct. 1858; 27 Apr. 1861; 12 Dec. 1885; Glos. Colln. NQ 13.18.

[60] *Glouc. Jnl.* 6 Mar. 1886.

[61] Ibid. 27 Dec. 1884; *Glos. Chron.* 2 Jan. 1886; 9 Mar. 1895.

[62] *Glouc. Jnl.* 16 Mar. 1839.

[63] Above, econ. development 1835–1914.

[64] Glos. Colln. 10956 (2); P.R.O., FS 2/3, nos. 350, 417, 468, 471, 489, 510, 524, 550, 643, 658, 684, 710, 718, 725, 733, 747, 758, 773, 869, 890.

[65] *Glouc. Jnl.* 10 July 1886.

[66] Ibid. 18 Dec. 1858; 25 May 1905; for min. bk., G.B.R., L 6/26/1.

[67] *Glouc. Jnl.* 20 Oct. 1860; F. Purnell and H. W. Williams, *Jubilee Hist. of Glouc. Co-Operative and Ind. Soc. Ltd.* (1910), 1–6, 107, 157, 190–8, 201–4.

[68] Glos. Colln. N 13.92 (2).

[69] Ibid. N 13.105 (1–4); for Mansbridge, *Citizen,* 23 Aug. 1952.

[70] F. Bond, *Hist of Glouc.* (1848), 53; *Glouc. Jnl.* 29 May 1841; Glos. Colln. NF 20.1 (1, 3); for Higgs, *Glouc. Jnl.* 11 Jan. 1890.

[71] Glos. Colln. NR 20.3.

[72] Ibid. NF 20.1 (3); *Glouc. Jnl.* 20 Apr. 1839.

[73] *Glouc. Jnl.* 27 Jan. 1855; 8 June 1861; 17 Jan. 1863; 3 Oct. 1868; 19 Feb. 1870; 8 July 1871; H. Richard, *Memoirs of Joseph Sturge* (1864), 548.

[74] *Glouc. Jnl.* 30 Sept. 1899; 13 Apr. 1901.

[75] Cf. *Smart's Dir. Glouc.* (1914), 15, 45; (1918), 15, 45.

[76] *Glouc. Jnl.* 26 Mar., 2 Apr. 1904; 29 July 1882.

[77] *Citizen,* 8 Nov. 1983.

[78] Ibid. 21 Jan. 1963.

[79] *Rep. Com. Corrupt Practices in Glouc.* [2586], pp. vii, x, xxv, H.C. (1860), xxvii; P.R.O., FS 4/11, no. 12; FS 4/13, no. 1080.

Working Men's Conservative Benefit Association formed in 1880. It had over 7,000 members in the city and county by 1901 when it became the Gloucester Conservative Benefit Society.[80] The smaller Gloucester Liberal Benefit Society, founded in 1887 and renamed the Gloucester Mutual Benefit Society in 1936,[81] was among several provident institutions to lapse following the introduction of the National Health Service in 1948.[82] The Conservative society continued to flourish and in 1968 merged with its parent society in Stroud to form the Original Holloway Society,[83] which in 1985 ran two homes for old people at Tuffley.

The Liberals and Conservatives also established social clubs for leading townspeople and the county gentry. The Liberal club, formed in 1877 at Ladybellegate House and transferred in 1890 to Suffolk House, closed in 1927.[84] The Conservative club opened at Constitution House in 1883[85] and remained there in 1985. Other organizations catering for the social needs of leading citizens included freemasonry, which was revived in Gloucester in 1844 after a lapse of several years.[86] The Barton Street corporation, an ancient mock institution supported by gentlemen, met at the Vauxhall Gardens in 1835. It elected officers and held a court, and apparently lapsed in 1848 or 1850.[87] The county gentry had their own club in the city by 1870, but it was later amalgamated with the Gloucester Club, formed for business and professional men in 1874.[88] Women were admitted to membership from 1979.[89]

The newspapers published in the city in the mid 19th century reflected the division of political opinion in Gloucester. The *Gloucester Journal* and *Gloucestershire Chronicle*, the main papers, were respectively Liberal and Conservative in affiliation. After David Mowbray Walker's death in 1871 the *Gloucester Journal* was bought by Thomas Chance, who in 1879 formed a partnership with Samuel Bland, owner of the *Citizen*.[90] The *Citizen*, which was published daily from 1876, was the most successful of many newspapers started in the later 19th century.[91] Others with some success were the Liberal *Gloucester Mercury*, begun by Charles Jeynes in 1855 and published weekly until 1884, and the Conservative *Gloucester Standard and Gloucestershire News*, published weekly between 1870 and 1902.[92] The partnership started by Chance and Bland dominated newspaper publication in Gloucester until 1928 when Northcliffe Newspapers Ltd. bought the business and amalgamated the *Gloucestershire Chronicle* with the *Gloucester Journal*.[93] From 1981 the *Gloucester Journal* appeared as a weekly supplement to the *Citizen*.[94] In 1980 an independent radio station, Severn Sound, commenced broadcasting from Gloucester to the city and county.[95]

In the later 1830s the Bell hotel in Southgate Street and the King's Head hotel in Westgate Street were important social centres for prominent citizens and the county gentry, and were identified respectively with Conservative and Liberal interests.[96] The landlord of the King's Head, where corporation dinners were revived in 1838,[97] was John Dowling, who was elected mayor in 1844.[98] Of his sons John (d. 1841) was

[80] *Glouc. Jnl.* 19 Oct. 1901; Glos. Colln. NF 13.2.
[81] Glos. Colln. NF 13.4; *Glouc. Jnl.* 21 Mar. 1936.
[82] Cf. Glos. Colln. NF 13.22; below, Hosp., dispensaries.
[83] Glos. Colln. J 11.278; *Citizen*, 28 May 1975.
[84] *Kelly's Dir. Glos.* (1879), 654; *Glouc. Jnl.* 28 June 1890; 25 Apr. 1891; J. R. Howe, 'Political Hist. of the Parl. Constituencies of Chelt., Glouc., and the Ciren. and Tewkes. Divisions of Glos. 1895–1914' (Bristol Univ. M. Litt. thesis, 1977), 34 and n.
[85] *Kelly's Dir. Glos.* (1889), 783.
[86] Glos. R.O., D 3558/10.
[87] *Glouc. Jnl.* 10 Oct. 1835; Glos. Colln. 35369.
[88] *Kelly's Dir. Glos.* (1870), 552; (1879), 654; *Glouc. Jnl.* 2

May 1874.
[89] *Citizen*, 26 Mar. 1981.
[90] R. Austin, *Bicentenary Glouc. Jnl.* (1922), 54–61, 115.
[91] *Citizen* Centenary Suppl. 1 May 1976.
[92] Austin, *Bicentenary Glouc. Jnl.* 116–19; *Bretherton's Dir. Glouc.* (1873), 59; (1877), 55.
[93] *Glouc. Jnl.* 6 Oct. 1928. [94] *Citizen*, 16 Sept. 1981.
[95] Ibid. 22 Oct. 1980.
[96] *Glouc. Jnl.* 15 Oct. 1836; 29 July 1837; *Diary of a Cotswold Parson*, 124, 140–1; Glos. Colln. 7202, min. 14 Nov. 1835.
[97] *Glouc. Jnl.* 15 Dec. 1838.
[98] G.B.R., B 3/16, p. 434.

rector of St. Mary de Crypt and master of the Crypt school and James (d. 1885) bought Barnwood Court.[99] Among lesser inns the Lower George in lower Westgate Street retained some importance as a meeting place in the mid 19th century.[1] Like other coaching inns, including the Boothall inn in Westgate Street, the King's Head lost much of its trade to the railway and by 1865 its hotel had been closed.[2] The Spread Eagle hotel in lower Northgate Street, near the cattle market and railway stations, enjoyed a period as a major social centre[3] and was rebuilt by a company which bought it from the corporation in 1864.[4] It closed as a hotel in 1896[5] but the taproom facing the market remained open intermittently until 1972.[6] The Bell, which was acquired by a company in 1864, remained an important meeting place for many years and closed in 1967.[7]

In the mid 19th century the Shire Hall and the Tolsey were used for large public gatherings, as was the corn exchange opened in 1857.[8] The Shire Hall assembly room was the city's main concert hall and from 1849 it had an organ, paid for by a subscription organized by a choral society. The organ was rebuilt by subscription in 1910 when the composer Sir Charles Hubert Hastings Parry, Bt., owner of the nearby Highnam estate, paid for the rebuilding of the room's orchestra and the addition of a gallery.[9] Many smaller halls were opened in the later 19th century, including in the 1870s the Wellington Hall in Longsmith Street and the Glevum Hall in lower Southgate Street.[10] Frederick Goddard's piano factory and warehouse in lower Northgate Street were used as assembly rooms by 1881.[11] To mark the centenary of the Sunday School movement in 1880 a fund was launched to build a hall in memory of Robert Raikes. The project encountered many difficulties, during which in 1884 the Baptists built their own Raikes Memorial Hall in Brunswick Road, and the money raised was later used in the building of a public library.[12] Anglicans and Primitive Methodists commemorated the centenary of 1880 with new places of worship.[13]

In the early 1840s Gloucester had several libraries and reading rooms, including those of the mechanics' institution. A commercial library and reading room[14] remained open until the early 20th century.[15] The Gloucester Literary and Scientific Association, founded in 1838 by prominent citizens, local gentry, and clergymen, organized lectures and acquired the city's principal library.[16] In 1860 it opened a museum in Southgate Street, in accommodation provided by the poet Sydney Dobell, and the exhibits included items from the collections of Thomas Barwick Lloyd Baker and William Vernon Guise.[17] County landowners, notably Thomas Gambier Parry, also figured in the movement to open schools of art and science in the city. From 1872 the schools were housed in a new building in Brunswick Road, paid for mainly by subscriptions and vested in the Gloucester Science and Art Society. It also housed a museum, incorporating that of the literary and scientific association. In 1893 a hall, built for the science and art society by Margaret Price as a memorial to her husband William Edwin Price, was opened next to the schools. The city corporation, which

[99] *Glouc. Jnl.* 16 Jan. 1841; 27 June 1885; Austin, *Crypt Sch.* 117.

[1] *Glouc. Jnl.* 16 Jan. 1836; 26 Nov. 1853.

[2] G.B.R., L 6/4/2, mem. 8 Oct. 1867; letter 12 Feb. 1868; B 4/5/2, min. 14 Sept. 1865; the bldg. dating from the late 18th cent. was demolished in 1944: *Trans. B.G.A.S.* lxv. 222.

[3] *Glouc. Jnl.* 13 Apr. 1861; 22 Jan. 1870; 1 Jan. 1876; 15 Dec. 1888; 23 May 1891.

[4] G.B.R., L 6/4/2, mem. 26 Jan. 1864; B 4/5/2, min. 13 Oct. 1864.

[5] *Glouc. Jnl.* 7 Nov. 1896. [6] *Citizen,* 26 Sept. 1972.

[7] Ibid. 28 July 1967; Glos. R.O., D 3089.

[8] *Glouc. Jnl.* 18 Feb. 1854; 24 Mar. 1855; 19 Feb. 1859.

[9] T. Hannam-Clark, *Glouc. Choral Soc. 1845–1947* (1947), 2–3; *Glouc. Jnl.* 10 Sept., 31 Dec. 1910.

[10] *Glouc. Jnl.* 31 Oct. 1874; Glos. R.O., D 3117/1468–73.

[11] *Glouc. Jnl.* 19 Nov. 1881; cf. *Kelly's Dir. Glos.* (1879), 669.

[12] Glos. Colln. 15298; N 21.16; *Glouc. Jnl.* 22 Nov. 1884; 2 June 1900.

[13] Below, Churches and Chapels, mod. par. ch., St. Paul; Prot. Nonconf.

[14] *Pigot's Dir. Glos.* (1842), 112.

[15] *Smart's Dir. Glouc.* (1906–7), 435.

[16] Glos. Colln. 8850.

[17] *Glouc. Jnl.* 17 Mar. 1860; for Dobell, *D.N.B.*

took over the buildings and the running of the schools and museum in 1896, adapted the Price Memorial Hall for the museum in 1902.[18] In the later 19th century there were several attempts to run a free lending library at the working men's institute and in 1887 ratepayers rejected the idea of a free public library in a poll.[19] The city corporation, which in 1895 purchased the books of the literary and scientific association,[20] began a free library service in 1897.[21] From 1900 it was housed next to the Schools of Science and Art in a library built to mark Queen Victoria's Diamond Jubilee with funds raised by private benefactions for that and other purposes.[22] By that time Gloucester had become a centre for higher education in the county.[23]

As a county town and regional centre Gloucester was also the meeting place for many societies. One formed by landed interests in 1833 for the encouragement of agriculture, arts, manufactures, and commerce held an annual agricultural show in the city until 1855, when it merged with a body at Cirencester to form the Gloucestershire Agricultural Society.[24] A farmers' club founded in 1840 organized lectures and monthly discussions in Gloucester.[25] In the later 19th century and the early 20th the county agricultural society met several times in Gloucester,[26] where an annual root, fruit, and grain show and an annual rose show, both organized by county societies, were held from 1863 and 1888 respectively.[27] In 1853 the Royal Agricultural Society held its annual show at Gloucester. During the event, which brought a great influx of visitors, the city was decorated with triumphal arches and there were flower shows at the Spa and in Cheltenham.[28] The society returned to Gloucester for its show in 1909.[29] The Three Counties' Agricultural Society, formed in 1921 by the merger of the Gloucestershire and the Herefordshire and Worcestershire societies, met on the Oxlease several times before the Second World War.[30] Among professional bodies in Gloucester from 1888 was an engineering society, which had a library and a reading room.[31]

Gloucester's music festival, which had grown out of the triennial meeting of the choirs of Gloucester, Hereford, and Worcester cathedrals, was conducted on a larger scale from 1835 and lasted for four days from 1838. It drew large crowds to the city, particularly after the opening of the railway, and was usually supported by the county gentry. From the later 1840s local choirs participated in the festival, which included oratorio performances in the cathedral, secular evening concerts in the Shire Hall, and a ball. Clerical objections, particularly to the use of the cathedral, were voiced, most trenchantly by Francis Close, vicar of Cheltenham, and to allay criticisms the Gloucester meeting introduced choral services in 1853 and replaced the ball with a sermon in 1874. Such criticisms, which culminated at the Worcester meeting of 1875,[32] were heard again at Gloucester in 1925.[33] In the mid 19th century the timber merchants Price & Co. gave their employees money to pay for admission to concerts at the Gloucester meeting.[34] After the death of S. S. Wesley, the cathedral organist, in 1876, the meeting's repertoire was broadened. The standard of performances

[18] Glos. Colln. N 17.90; N 24.1; P. G. Rossington, 'Hist. Glouc. Technical Coll.' (c. 1962, TS. in ibid. NF 17.461), 12–43.

[19] Glos. Colln. 15149; *Glouc. Jnl.* 14 Feb. 1885; 5, 12 Mar. 1887.

[20] Glos. Colln. 20196: the literary and scientific assoc. was dissolved in 1896.

[21] *Glouc. Municipal Year Bk.* (1964–5), 81.

[22] *Glouc. Jnl.* 1 Jan. 1898; 2 June 1900.

[23] Below, Educ., higher educ.

[24] Glos. Colln. 7202; *Wilts and Glos. Standard,* 13 June 1914.

[25] Glos. Colln. N 13.81 (1–7).

[26] *Glouc. Jnl.* 1 Aug. 1868; 1 Aug. 1885; 31 Dec. 1904.

[27] Ibid. 21 Nov. 1863; 14 July 1888; *Smart's Dir. Glouc.* (1910–11), 435.

[28] *Glouc. Jnl.* 9 Apr., 18 June, 16 July 1853.

[29] Ibid. 26 June 1909.

[30] *Citizen Centenary Suppl.* 1 May 1976; *Glouc. Jnl.* 10 June 1922; *Glouc. Official Guide* (1937), 47.

[31] *Smart's Dir. Glouc.* (1893), 175; (1910–11), 436.

[32] *Stranger's Guide Through Glouc.* (1848), 92–4; D. Lysons et al. *Origin and Progress of the Meeting of the Three Choirs* (1895), *passim*; H. W. Shaw, *Three Choirs Festival* (1954), 47, 54.

[33] A. H. Brewer, *Memories of Choirs and Cloisters* (1931), 216–18.

[34] *Glouc. Jnl.* 17 Sept. 1859.

improved in the late 19th century, and from 1892 choirs from outside the three counties were no longer used. In the early 20th century the meeting was attended by leading British composers and several European figures, notably Camille Saint-Saëns in 1913 and Zoltán Kodály in 1928 and 1937.[35] The festival remained the principal musical event in the city in the mid 1980s, when there was also an annual festival of the arts in Barnwood, established in 1965.[36]

Life in Gloucester was enriched by a variety of musical and dramatic societies and clubs. Gloucester Choral Society, which originated with concerts organized by William Higgs from 1845 to promote the mechanics' institution, was formally constituted in 1848 and, following its disbanding, was re-formed in 1861.[37] Orchestral concerts were given by a philharmonic society, which had lapsed by 1864 when some members forced a new group.[38] In the early 1860s wagon works' employees formed a brass band.[39] The composer Alfred Herbert Brewer, a native of Gloucester and cathedral organist from 1896, was an important influence on musical activity. He conducted a male-voice choir, the Gloucester Orpheus Society, established in 1898, and he founded the Gloucestershire Orchestral Society in 1901. He was knighted in 1926 and died in 1928.[40] Gloucester had several dramatic societies in the later 19th century and the early 20th, including the Mynd Players founded in 1923.[41] Gloucester Operatic and Dramatic Society began as a light opera group in 1913 and performed drama from 1936. Following the closure of many halls in the city centre the society converted a Salvation Army citadel in King's Barton Street as a theatre, opened in 1963 and used until 1985.[42] A division within the society in 1920 led to the formation of the Caer Glow Amateur Operatic and Dramatic Society.[43] The poet William Ernest Henley (1849–1903) was the son of a Gloucester bookseller,[44] and the poet and composer Ivor Gurney (1890–1937) the son of a city tailor.[45] A story about another local tailor, John Prichard (d. 1934), apparently inspired the children's book *The Tailor of Gloucester* by Beatrix Potter.[46] Among local writers was the printer John Bellows (d. 1902), a Quaker whose interests included philology, archaeology, and foreign travel.[47]

Major national events, such as coronations, royal weddings, and military victories, were celebrated enthusiastically and in the mid 19th century were often marked by a procession of the corporation and Bluecoat schoolboys.[48] The traditional procession of Bluecoat boys to the cathedral ended in 1882.[49] Other public ceremonial centred on the cathedral benefited from a widening of College Street, the main approach to the close, in the early 1890s.[50] To mark Queen Victoria's Golden and Diamond Jubilees a beacon, forming part of a national chain, was lit on Robins Wood Hill.[51] The city received few royal visits and when Queen Victoria changed trains there in 1849 spectators pressed forward and became mixed up with her party. On a similar occasion in 1852 the public was excluded from the station's platforms.[52] Edward VII's presence in Gloucester in 1909 for the Royal Agricultural Society's meeting was the first formal visit by a reigning monarch since 1788.[53] Because of its regional

[35] Shaw, *Three Choirs Festival*, 62–77, 84–100.
[36] Glos. Colln. R 35.14.
[37] Hannam-Clark, *Glouc. Choral Soc.* 1–4; cf. Bond, *Hist. of Glouc.* 54.
[38] *Glouc. Jnl.* 19 Nov. 1864; 11 Nov. 1865.
[39] Ibid. 30 Apr. 1864.
[40] Ibid. 3 Mar. 1928; Brewer, *Memories of Choirs and Cloisters*, 66–81, 104–23.
[41] Hannam-Clark, *Drama in Glos.* (1928), 187–90; Glos. R.O., D 4856/3.
[42] Glos. R.O., D 4655.

[43] Hannam-Clark, *Drama in Glos.* 190.
[44] *D.N.B.* 2nd suppl.
[45] M. Hurd, *Ordeal of Ivor Gurney* (1978).
[46] *Glos. and Avon Life*, Aug. 1977, 50–1.
[47] *D.N.B.* 2nd suppl.
[48] *Glouc. Jnl.* 30 June 1838; 30 Apr. 1856; 14 Mar. 1863.
[49] Ibid. 16 Sept. 1882.
[50] Below, topog.; Glos. Colln. N 15.9.
[51] *Glouc. Jnl.* 25 June 1887; *Glos. Chron.* 26 June 1897.
[52] *Glouc. Jnl.* 6 Oct. 1849; 4 Sept. 1852; *Illustrated Lond. News*, 6 Oct. 1849. [53] *Glouc. Jnl.* 25 Dec. 1909.

importance Gloucester was in 1860 the location for a large review of volunteer troops from surrounding counties.[54] Among volunteer troops raised in the city in 1859 were two rifle corps, one being connected with the docks.[55] Although a militia regiment was stationed in Gloucester for many years[56] and the county yeomanry trained there in 1836 and 1837,[57] the city was not made a military centre in the reform of 1872.[58]

Gloucester's fortunes as a fashionable resort were not revived by improvements at the spa, where a billiard room and bowling green were opened in 1836.[59] The spa's attractions were noticeably diminished by the construction of a railway along the south side of the grounds in 1848,[60] and in 1861 its proprietors conveyed the spa to the city corporation for inclusion in a public park. The park, which also took in Rignum Stile Field and most of Lower Barton Hill, two fields east of the spa grounds,[61] was opened in 1862 and became Gloucester's principal recreation area. In 1863 private benefactors paid for a bandstand and the removal to the park of the Eastgate market fountain.[62] Under the corporation the spa was little patronized[63] and the Spa hotel, which the spa proprietors had sold in 1835[64] and which had been used as judges' lodgings, became a school in 1867.[65] The pump room baths, which were connected to the city's water mains,[66] fell into disrepair and were removed in 1894,[67] and the medicinal springs were closed, following contamination, in 1926.[68] The Vauxhall Gardens, the pleasure ground in Barton Street, were built on from 1863,[69] but a bowling green survived behind the Vauxhall inn until the mid 20th century.[70] In 1879 Thomas Dutton created the City Gardens in Dean's Walk as a public pleasure and recreation ground but the venture was unsuccessful.[71]

The opening of the park in 1862 encouraged popular sporting activity, particularly cricket and football,[72] and the spa grounds were used by several of Gloucester's many new sports clubs in the later 19th century.[73] Sports and games continued to be played on the meadows to the north and west of the city.[74] From the 1890s the corporation made greater provision for recreation. It opened playing fields in Kingsholm and Priory Road in 1894 and 1901 respectively,[75] and in 1900 it took over a recreation ground at Saintbridge, laid out by Upton St. Leonards parish council following the inclosure of open fields in 1897.[76] Gloucester Cricket Club had its ground at the Spa from 1863,[77] and a pavilion erected there in 1869 was replaced in 1883 by a larger building. County cricket was played there by 1884[78] and until 1923.[79] A gymnastic society formed in 1863 held athletics events at the Spa and swimming races in the Gloucester and Berkeley canal. It was apparently wound up in 1872[80] but later clubs organized athletic sports in the spa grounds.[81] A bowling and quoits club was

[54] Ibid. 22 Sept. 1860.
[55] Ibid. 25 June, 23 July 1859.
[56] Ibid. 30 Oct. 1852.
[57] Ibid. 15 Oct. 1836; 14 Oct. 1837.
[58] Ibid. 13, 20, 27 Apr. 1872.
[59] Glos. Colln. 18420; *Glouc. Jnl.* 21 May 1836; 27 Dec. 1856.
[60] D. E. Bick, *Glouc. and Chelt. Railway* (1968, Locomotion Papers, no. 43), 26; Bd. of Health Map (1852).
[61] G.B.R., B 3/18, pp. 369–70; B 4/5/1, *passim*; N 2/1/3, *passim*.
[62] Ibid. B 4/9/1, *passim*; *Glouc. Jnl.* 2 Aug. 1862; 19 Sept. 1863.
[63] Cf. F. T. Bond, *Glouc. Mineral Spa* (1905): Glos. Colln. NF 23.1.
[64] G.B.R., L 6/1/128.
[65] *Glouc. Jnl.* 7 May 1853; 29 Dec. 1866.
[66] G.B.R., B 4/9/1, mins. 22 Apr., 6 May 1862.
[67] Ibid. B 3/28, pp. 322, 330, 350.

[68] *Glouc. Jnl.* 1 May 1926.
[69] Glos. Colln. NV 28.1; Glos. R.O., D 1388/SL 6/19.
[70] Inf. from Mr. B. C. Frith, of Tuffley.
[71] *Glouc. Jnl.* 31 May, 14 June 1879; *Glos. Chron.* 5 Aug. 1893; cf. Glos. R.O., D 3117/3052.
[72] *Glouc. Jnl.* 5 Mar. 1864.
[73] G.B.R., B 4/9/1, *passim*.
[74] *Glouc. Jnl.* 14 July 1883; D. Robertson, *King's Sch., Glouc.* (1974), 127.
[75] *Glouc. Jnl.* 23 June 1894; 29 Dec. 1900; 30 Nov. 1901.
[76] G.B.R., B 3/35, p. 54; cf. Glos. R.O., P 347B/PC 10/1; Q/RI 149.
[77] *Glouc. Jnl.* 18 Apr. 1863.
[78] Ibid. 17 July 1869; 29 Dec. 1883; 31 May 1884.
[79] *Smart's Dir. Glouc.* (1893), 164; Glos. Colln. J 21.8 (4–5).
[80] *Glouc. Jnl.* 10 Sept. 1864; 1 July 1865; 15 June 1872.
[81] Ibid. 4 Sept. 1880; 9 Aug. 1924.

established there in 1866.[82] Bowling was very popular in the early 20th century and public greens were opened at the Spa in 1913 and 1922.[83] In 1924 there were at least eleven greens in the city, including one laid for the Liberal club at Suffolk House in Greyfriars in 1921.[84] Gloucester's first lawn tennis club was begun in 1878[85] and the spa grounds included several courts by the mid 1880s.[86] Public courts opened there in 1915 were replaced by new ones in Parkend Road in 1922.[86] A cycling track was opened in Tuffley Avenue in 1895.[87] Gloucester Golf Club, established in 1896, had links in Barnwood. In the early 20th century golf was also played in Churchdown[88] and in Brockworth, where the Gloucester club had a course from 1910 until the Second World War.[89] There were several shooting ranges in Gloucester in the 19th century and the early 20th.[90] The principal outdoor range for both city and county was nearby at Over. Opened in 1861, it was closed in 1895 and replaced by a range at Sneedham's Green in Upton St. Leonards in 1904.[91]

At a national level the city became identified with rugby union football through the successful Gloucester Football Club, formed in 1873. The club moved its ground from the Spa to Kingsholm in 1891, and since 1896 many members have obtained international honours.[92] In the 1970s the club won the national club championship several times.[93] Of clubs playing association football the most important was Gloucester City Association Football Club, originating in 1889 and re-formed in 1925. From 1935 it had its ground at Longlevens[94] and in 1964 it moved to a new stadium in Horton Road,[95] which was later also used for dog races.[96] A more important centre for greyhound racing was a track at Longlevens, opened in 1933 and closed in 1983.[97]

The Gloucester and Berkeley canal and the river Severn were used for recreation in the mid 19th century, when summer excursions along the canal were popular.[98] Several rowing clubs held races near the city before the formation in 1861 of Gloucester Rowing Club.[99] That club, which had a boathouse on the canal below Hempsted bridge, held an annual regatta on the canal from 1921, at first near Epney and later above Hempsted bridge.[1] A consortium formed in 1963 to solve the club's difficulties and including the city education committee and the King's school built a new boathouse and bought new craft, which were used by children attending secondary schools.[2] Male swimming and bathing in the canal continued after 1873[3] when James Blake built an outdoor pool by the river Twyver in Millbrook Street. In 1891 the corporation opened two indoor pools, one convertible as a gymnasium or skating rink, as part of the new public baths in Barton Street.[4]

Popular entertainment in the mid 19th century took a variety of forms, including touring circuses and menageries.[5] Public executions, the last of which was above the lodge of the county gaol in 1864, also attracted many spectators.[6] Gloucester's annual

82 Ibid. 19 May 1866.
82 Glouc. Municipal Year Bk. (1964–5), 87.
83 Glouc. Official Guide (1924), 98, 120–2; Glouc. Jnl. 6 May 1922.
84 Smart's Dir. Glouc. (1893), 165.
85 G.B.R., B 4/9/1, min. 28 Feb. 1884.
86 Glouc. Municipal Year Bk. (1964–5), 87.
87 Glouc. Jnl. 20 July 1895.
88 V.C.H. Glos. ii. 305; Glos. R.O., D 1277/1; 2/1–3.
89 Glos. Colln. R 58.1, 5; Glouc. Official Guide (1954), 69.
90 Glouc. Jnl. 10 Nov. 1860; Smart's Dir. Glouc. (1910–11), 430.
91 Glouc. Jnl. 26 Sept. 1861; 8 Oct. 1904; Glos. Colln. J 11.50.
92 Glos. Colln. N 13.16; Smart's Dir. Glouc. (1893), 165; (1910–11), 433.

93 Citizen, 13 May 1978.
94 Glos. Colln. N 13.184.
95 Citizen, 26 Aug. 1964.
96 Glouc. Official Guide (1980), 81.
97 Glouc. Jnl. 15, 22, 29 July 1933; Citizen, 17 Oct. 1983.
98 Conway-Jones, Glouc Docks, 61.
99 Glouc. Jnl. 4 July 1835; 4 July 1846; 22 Apr. 1865.
1 Ibid. 16 July 1921; Glouc. Official Guide (1949), 105; (1954), 69.
2 Glos. Colln. NF 17.204.
3 Glouc. Jnl. 16 July 1870; 9 Aug. 1873; 21 Aug. 1880; 29 July 1893.
4 Ibid. 28 June 1873; 25 July, 1 Aug. 1891; 23 Dec. 1893.
5 Ibid. 28 Sept. 1839; 27 Mar. 1847; 30 July 1859.
6 Ibid. 27 Aug. 1864; 13 Jan. 1872.

race meeting on the meadows near Over bridge[7] was deserted by the county gentry and was replaced in 1839 by a smaller event organized locally.[8] The larger meeting was revived several times, including in 1861 and 1870 when it took place in Meanham north of the railway,[9] but despite its popularity among the townspeople[10] it had no lasting success. To benefit from Gloucester's more central position the promoters of the Hereford races held an annual meeting in nearby Maisemore in the later 1880s.[11] The main regular entertainment was the pleasure fair held with Barton Fair and the hiring fairs. It drew large crowds from both town and country and survived several attempts to suppress it on the grounds of danger to public order and morality.[12] Carnivals were held in 1925, 1930, and 1936 to raise funds for the Gloucestershire Royal Infirmary,[13] and in the late 1950s the city corporation established an annual festival with a carnival procession.[14]

The theatre in Westgate Street, known as the Theatre Royal from the late 1830s,[15] was bought in 1857 by John Blinkhorn, a railway contractor.[16] He enlarged the building, which reopened as a theatre and assembly room in 1859. The theatre was run from 1873 by Thomas Dutton (d. 1893) and celebrated its centenary in 1891 with a performance by Henry Irving, Ellen Terry, and members of the Lyceum company in aid of local hospitals. Under Charles Poole, the owner from 1903, it was a variety theatre and picture house. It was partly demolished in 1922 during conversion as a store.[17] The old Boothall was used regularly for popular entertainments in the mid 19th century and became the Alhambra music hall in 1869.[18] It was more successful than a music hall in lower Southgate Street, opened the same year, but fire closed it in 1874, and from 1876 the building was used as a circus and skating rink, known as the Royal Albert Hall.[19] Later it was a variety theatre and from 1907 a picture house.[20] In 1909 Goddard's assembly rooms became a cinema called the Theatre de Luxe, and from 1911 a cinema club occupied a building in Eastgate Street, which was also used as a theatre and from 1915 was called the Hippodrome.[21] Roller-skating rinks were opened in a former tramways depot in India Road in 1909 and in a new building in Brunswick Road, on the side of St. Michael's Square, in 1910.[22] The latter became a drill hall for many years and was demolished in 1934.[23] At that time the George Street corn exchange was used also as a dance hall.[24] Gloucester had six cinemas in 1935 and four in 1960. Two in Barton Street later became bingo halls and in 1984 the only remaining cinema was that opened in King's Square in 1956.[25] One bingo hall was converted in 1985 by the Gloucester Operatic and Dramatic Society as a theatre.

After the First World War the corporation increased the number of public parks, ornamental gardens, and playing fields in the city.[26] It enlarged the Kingsholm playing field in 1929 and opened tennis courts and a putting green at the Oval, in the south end of the city, in 1931.[27] Some ornamental gardens had formerly been in private ownership, including that at Hillfield in London Road acquired by the

[7] *Diary of a Cotswold Parson*, 110.
[8] *Glouc. Jnl.* 18 Aug. 1838; 24 Aug., 14 Sept. 1839.
[9] Ibid. 26 Oct. 1861; 22 Oct. 1870; Cadle, *Map of Glouc.* (1877): Glos. R.O., D 4335/248.
[10] Cf. *Glouc. Jnl.* 14 Aug. 1852.
[11] *Glos. Chron.* 14 Dec. 1889.
[12] *Glouc. Jnl.* 1, 8 Oct. 1859; 29 Sept., 6 Oct. 1860; 18 Oct. 1862; 5 Oct. 1872; 4 Oct. 1879; 18 Oct. 1884; 2 Oct. 1937.
[13] Ibid. 4 July 1925; 5 July 1930; 4, 11 July 1936.
[14] *Glouc. Official Guide* (1972), 89; *Citizen*, 27 July 1957.
[15] Glos. Colln. NX 29.3.
[16] Glos. R.O., D 3364/1.

[17] Hannam-Clark, *Drama in Glos.* 120–4; *Glouc. Jnl.* 5 Mar. 1859; 5 Aug. 1893; 7 Oct. 1922.
[18] *Glouc. Jnl.* 4 Apr. 1840; 25 Feb. 1854; 18 Dec. 1869.
[19] Ibid. 27 Aug., 1 Oct. 1870; 30 May 1874; 5 Feb., 9 Sept. 1876.
[20] Hannam-Clark, *Drama in Glos.* 110.
[21] Glos. Colln. NR 29.30, 32.
[22] *Glouc. Jnl.* 11 Sept., 25 Dec. 1909; 5 Mar. 1910.
[23] Ibid. 28 July 1934.
[24] Glos. Colln. NZ 12.5.
[25] Ibid. NR 29.30–2.
[26] *Glouc. Official Guide* (1937), 79.
[27] *Glouc. Municipal Year Bk.* (1964–5), 80, 87.

corporation in 1933.[28] Playing fields were also provided outside the city boundary, notably by Hucclecote and Longlevens parish councils in the late 1930s.[29] The Plock Court playing fields at Longford, established by the city corporation at that time,[30] covered 22.66 ha. in the late 1970s. Many of Gloucester's sports clubs were connected with large factories and businesses in the mid 20th century.[31] A sports ground in Tuffley Avenue, laid out by the wagon works company after the First World War,[32] was the venue for county cricket in Gloucester from 1924[33] and was bought by the city council in the mid 1980s. The council also extended its museum and library services. A folk museum was opened in lower Westgate Street in 1935[34] and the former Bearland fire station was adapted as a transport museum in 1977.[35] A children's library, begun at Suffolk House in 1938,[36] moved in 1967 to Greyfriars House where it was joined by a music and gramophone record library started in 1963.[37] The Wheatstone Lecture Hall, opened at the Brunswick Road museum in 1947,[38] only partly compensated for the disappearance of many important public meeting places in the mid 20th century, notably the former corn exchange in 1938[39] and the Shire Hall assembly room in the early 1960s.[40] The city's memorial to its dead of the First World War was unveiled in the main park in 1933.[41]

From the 1920s the drift of population from the older parts of the city to the suburbs, evident in the mid 19th century, had a pronounced impact on social and cultural life.[42] Church and village halls were built in outlying areas, including Barnwood,[43] Longlevens, Hempsted, and Hucclecote,[44] and after the Second World War community associations were active in such places and a number of community centres were built.[45] Local voluntary organizations, many of them small, sustained a range of sporting and artistic activities throughout the city. From 1959 both the city and county library services established branches in the suburbs, where the first purpose-built library was opened in Matson in 1963. By 1974 libraries had also been built in Lower Tuffley and Hucclecote,[46] both as part of new community centres.[47] In the 1960s and 1970s the city council increased the opportunities for recreation. To the public baths in Barton Street it added a third swimming pool and a large leisure centre, opened in 1966 and 1974 respectively. The leisure centre included a hall, which was used for concerts as well as sports, a theatre, and a dance hall.[48] The council, which constructed a boating lake near Westgate bridge in 1975, continued to lay out new playing fields and other sporting facilities[49] and Beaufort school at Lower Tuffley, completed in the early 1970s, also served as a sports centre.[50] The traditional use by Gloucester people of Robins Wood Hill for recreation was confirmed in the 1970s when the council laid out part as a country park (96.32 ha.), opened in 1975,[51] and a country club catering for a range of sporting activities was established at Larkham Farm in Matson with two golf courses and an artificial ski slope.[52] The potential of the docks for recreation and leisure was acknowledged in plans for

[28] G.B.R., B 3/67 (2), pp. 800–1, 1341–2; cf. ibid. 70 (2), p. 1689.
[29] Glos. R.O., PA 183/1, pp. 282–4; Church Com. MSS., file 66698; deed 406337.
[30] G.B.R., B 3/70 (2), p. 1353; 71 (1), p. 990.
[31] *Glouc. Official Guide* (1980), 69–70, 81–3.
[32] Glos. Colln. NR 29.35.
[33] Ibid. J 21.8 (4–5).
[34] *Glouc. Municipal Year Bk.* (1964–5), 86–7.
[35] *Glouc. Jnl.* 29 Jan. 1977.
[36] *Glouc. Municipal Year Bk.* (1964–5), 82.
[37] Glos. Colln. 7944.
[38] *Glouc. Municipal Year Bk.* (1964–5), 82.
[39] Ibid. 78.

[40] *Citizen*, 11 June 1962.
[41] *Glouc. Municipal Year Bk.* (1964–5), 94–5.
[42] Below, topog.
[43] Cf. *Kelly's Dir. Glos.* (1931), 36; (1935), 35.
[44] *Glouc. Jnl.* 20 June 1925; 12 Oct. 1928; 4 Jan. 1930.
[45] *Glouc. Official Guide* (1980), 57.
[46] Glos. Colln. 7944; J 15.8.
[47] Cf. *Citizen*, 19 May 1970; 6 Mar. 1972; 8 June 1974.
[48] *Glouc. Official Guide* (1980), 57–61.
[49] Ibid. 69–70.
[50] *Citizen*, 19 Oct. 1973.
[51] *Glouc. Official Guide* (1980), 70; Glos. Colln. N 3.61.
[52] *Citizen*, 17 July 1967; 11 Oct. 1973; Glos. Colln. R 201.4.

redevelopment, and from 1978 an arts trust held concerts in a barge moored there.[53] One warehouse was converted as an antiques centre from 1979[54] and another included a museum of advertizing and packaging from 1984. Excursions along the canal continued.

Gloucester's cultural life diversified after the Second World War. A small Ukrainian community was established in and around the city and had its own church.[55] An Irish society was founded in 1964.[56] From the 1950s the arrival of immigrants from new Commonwealth countries, particularly from the West Indies, led to the growth of ethnic communities in the Barton Street area with their own clubs and places of worship.[57] Among them were Moslems who built two mosques.[58]

Topography

Although to one writer Gloucester in 1841 seemed unaffected by the building mania prevalent elsewhere,[59] the redevelopment and physical growth that would transform the city in the 19th and 20th centuries was then already under way. By 1850 the appearance of the main streets was dominated by brick and stucco fronts and large shop windows. A few timber fronts were visible, and among those to have disappeared was that of the New Inn in Northgate Street.[60] Prominent new buildings included those of the Gloucestershire Banking Co. in Eastgate Street and the County of Gloucester Bank in Westgate Street, at the corner of College Court, both built in the late 1830s in classical style.[61] Higher up Westgate Street the former house of the banker James Wood was replaced in 1843 by a building in a 14th-century Gothic style for the National Provincial Bank.[62] The city's architecture was also enriched by the rebuilding in 1847 and 1850 of chapels in Parker's Row (later Brunswick Road) and lower Southgate Street.[63] Buildings added to Worcester Street after 1835 included several houses,[64] a circular room erected in 1836 for a circus,[65] and a nonconformist chapel which on becoming an Anglican school in 1847 was given windows in a Gothic style.[66] In the west part of the city once fashionable houses, particularly in lower Westgate Street and Archdeacon Street, had been converted as lodgings and their back courts filled with cottages by 1850 to make the area one of the most congested in Gloucester. In lower Westgate Street Old Spa House, more popularly known as the Duke of Norfolk's House, had been subdivided and two projecting shop fronts added to the ground floor.[67] Industrial development continued in the Island and behind the quay,[68] but in Quay Street the site of the city workhouse demolished in 1839 remained empty until after 1850.[69] The area to the south was dominated by the county gaol.[70] The Gloucester poor-law union erected its workhouse on the east side of the city and outside the built-up area in 1837 and 1838.[71]

[53] *Cotswold Life*, June 1980, 32–3.
[54] *Glouc. Jnl.* 15 Oct. 1983.
[55] Below, Roman Catholicism.
[56] *Citizen*, 14 Apr. 1969.
[57] Below, Prot. Nonconf.
[58] Below, Other Religious Bodies.
[59] A. B. Granville, *Spas of Eng.* (1841), 333.
[60] Clarke, *Archit. Hist. of Glouc.* 62–3; for street elevation: c. 1841, Glos. Colln. 10962 (7), details reproduced above, Figs. 9–10.
[61] *Glouc. Jnl.* 1 July 1837; Granville, *Spas of Eng.* 340–2; Glos. Colln. NR 15.9. For Glos. Banking Co. bldg., above, Fig. 10.
[62] Glos. Colln. prints GL 1.1–2, 6, 10; *Glouc., a Pictorial Rec.* (John Jennings Ltd., n.d.) 59.

[63] Below, Prot. Nonconf., Baptists; Congregationalists and Independents. For Southgate chap., above, Plate 52.
[64] Glos. R.O., D 3117/3408–10.
[65] *Glouc. Jnl.* 17 Sept. 1836.
[66] Below, Prot. Nonconf., Baptists; *Brunswick Road Bapt. Ch. Mag.* (Sept. 1894): copy in 1981 in possession of the minister, Brunswick Bapt. ch., Glouc.
[67] Clarke, *Archit. Hist. of Glouc.* 98–9.
[68] *Glos. Hist. Studies*, xii. 3; *Power's Glouc. Handbk.* (1862), 73.
[69] Glos. R.O., D 3270/19713, mins. 17 Jan., 11 May 1839, 31 Dec. 1850.
[70] Causton, *Map of Glouc.* (1843); Bd. of Health Map (1852); for the gaol, below, Glouc. Castle.
[71] Above, city govt.

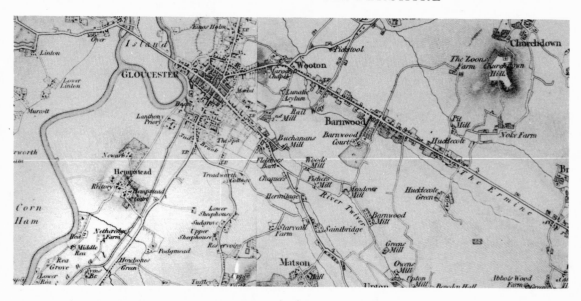

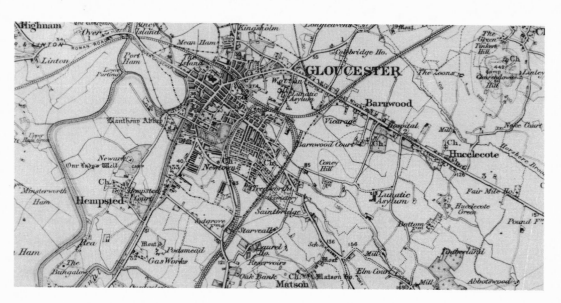

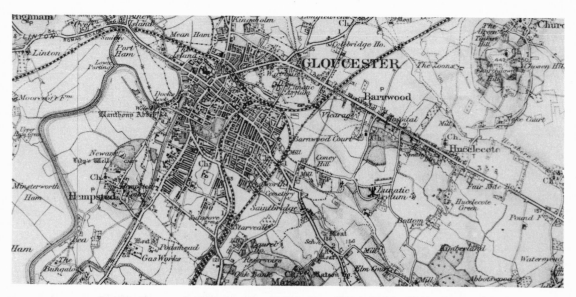

Fig. 14. The growth of Gloucester: *c.* 1830 (*top*); *c.* 1885 (*middle*); *c.* 1904 (*bottom*)

Few alterations were made to the city's streets in the mid 19th century. The improvement commissioners widened the entrance to Upper Quay Street from Westgate Street in 1839, and congestion at the Cross was eased in 1849 by the rebuilding of St. Michael's church and the removal of an obstacle in Southgate Street.[72] The only major improvement was the construction in 1847 of Commercial Road from Southgate Street to the docks and the new custom house. The new road, which replaced the narrow twisting route along Kimbrose Lane, was laid out by a private company. At the entrance, which the commissioners formed by demolishing a group of cottages projecting into Southgate Street at Pye Corner,[73] the prominent triangular site on the south side was filled in 1849 and 1850 by new offices for the Gloucester Savings Bank,[74] and the Black Swan inn (later the Yeoman) on the north side was rebuilt to a similar design.[75]

The leading local architects before 1850 were Thomas Fulljames, the county surveyor, and Samuel Whitfield Daukes.[76] Daukes, a pupil of the York architect J. P. Pritchett, had an office in Gloucester by 1834 and obtained commissions for new commercial buildings. On his departure in the late 1840s his associate James Medland, another of Pritchett's pupils, continued the practice, at first with J. R. Hamilton who had been Daukes's partner from 1841.[77] By the later 1840s Fulljames (d. 1874), also the diocesan surveyor, had taken into partnership his pupil F. S. Waller.[78] Another local architect of the period was John Jacques (d. 1868).[79]

Railway development took place mainly outside the old part of the city and caused little destruction. In the later 1840s Foley Cottages and part of Foley Place in Barton Street were demolished to make room for a branch line to High Orchard and the docks,[80] and several houses in London Road, Hare Lane, and St. Catherine Street were removed for the viaduct carrying the South Wales line.[81] The opening of railway stations east of the cattle market in the early 1840s[82] turned Eastgate Street into one of the busiest parts of the city.[83] In Clarence Street, which ran from Barton Street to the market and stations, development began in the late 1830s with a pair of substantial houses for professional men on the east side and continued sporadically.[84] The narrowness and steepness of its entrance from Northgate Street made St. Aldate Street a difficult route for traffic to the stations,[85] and an alternative way was provided in 1851 when Charles Church laid out George Street off lower Northgate Street.[86]

The development of the docks in the south-west corner of the city attracted industry and a large working-class population to that area.[87] On Barbican hill, north of the docks, buildings erected in the mid 1830s by the merchant Samuel Baker were used for commercial purposes, part being occupied from 1835 by the Gloucester Commercial Rooms.[88] South of the docks, building at High Orchard, between the Bristol road and the Gloucester and Berkeley canal, was begun in 1835 or 1836 by a company led by Baker, which removed existing huts and sold off land for commercial

[72] Glos. Colln. 22415; cf. Causton, *Map of Glouc.* (1843); Bd. of Health Map (1852).

[73] Glos. Colln. 22415; *Glos. Chron.* 26 Jan. 1861; cf. Causton, *Map of Glouc.* (1843).

[74] *Builder*, 23 Mar. 1850, pp. 138–9.

[75] G.B.R., N 2/1/1, p. 178.

[76] *Pigot's Dir. Glos.* (1842), 109; for later architects, below.

[77] *Trans. B.G.A.S.* xcii. 5–6; *Country Life*, 6 Dec. 1973, pp. 1914–16; 13 Dec. 1973, pp. 2016–18; *Glouc. Jnl.* 23 June 1894.

[78] *Glouc. Jnl.* 2 May 1874; 25 Mar. 1905; many plans of Fulljames and Waller are in Glos. R.O., D 1381 and D 2593.

[79] *Glouc. Jnl.* 25 Apr. 1868.

[80] D. E. Bick, *Glouc. and Chelt. Railway* (1968, Locomotion Papers, no. 43), 26–7; G.B.R., J 3/14, pp. 607–11.

[81] Glos. R.O., Q/RUm 303; Glos. Colln. JF 14.90 (1–2).

[82] Above, econ. development 1835–1914.

[83] F. Bond, *Hist. of Glouc.* (1848), 30.

[84] Glos. R.O., D 4453, deeds 1758–1886; cf. Bd. of Health Map (1852).

[85] G.B.R., B 3/16, pp. 90–1.

[86] *Glouc. Jnl.* 31 May 1851; 3 Dec. 1853; cf. Glos. Colln. 22415.

[87] Nat. Soc. files, Glouc., St. Paul; for the docks, below, Quay and Docks.

[88] Glos. R.O., D 177, deed 1839; *Glouc. Jnl.* 6 June 1835.

and industrial development. Several cottages, forming terraces in Anti-Dry-Rot Street (later Elming Row) and High Orchard Street, had been built by the early 1840s,[89] when the Revd. Samuel Lysons, owner of the nearby Hempsted Court estate, provided a church and a school for the area.[90] An inn called the Railway Tavern, built on the corner of Elming Row in the area known as Sudbrook, took its name from a railway begun there in 1839 but abandoned soon afterwards.[91] Residential development continued around the junction of the Bristol and Stroud roads, and a pilaster-fronted house at the corner of Llanthony Road had been completed by 1840.[92] East of the Bristol road and some way south of the entrance to the Stroud road and turnpike, Theresa Place, an imposing ashlar-fronted terrace, was begun in 1836. Built for Samuel Lysons to a design of Thomas Fulljames,[93] it was intended for prosperous residents but was later surrounded by artisans' houses and factories. Commercial development of the canal bank south of High Orchard had started by the later 1830s, but little building took place west of the canal before the 1850s.[94]

The floodlands of the river Severn restricted development on the north and west sides of Gloucester and the highest floods, notably that of 1852, covered low-lying parts of the built-up area.[95] As a result suburban growth was largely confined to areas south and east of the city centre,[96] and builders' reluctance to take leasehold land meant that development was piecemeal and sprawling and that land belonging to institutions was in general not built on early.[97] Streets were laid out by speculators and built up, sometimes over several decades, by small contractors developing plots for a few houses at a time.[98] The main building material was local brick, mostly from meadows by the Severn.[99]

Most of the residential development started after 1835 was for working-class housing, usually in terraces of two storeys, and was concentrated in new streets on the south-east side of Gloucester near the railway. The builder William Rees, one of the principal speculators, laid out Prince Street, Albert Street, and Cambridge Street at the east end of Mill Lane in 1839.[1] Further west he and the builder William Wingate formed Bedford Street, Whitfield Street, and the western part of Russell Street c. 1845.[2] On the south side of Barton Street a cul-de-sac called Hampden Place was apparently laid out by the surgeon James Peat Heane and built up in the early 1840s.[3] Further out on Barton Street many houses and workshops were built beyond the point where the Gloucester–Cheltenham tramway crossed the road.[4] The turnpike on the city side of the tramway was moved further out by public subscription in 1854 but the railway crossing formed there in 1848 remained a considerable obstacle to road traffic.[5] In 1843 there was also a turnpike in Goose Lane (later Millbrook Street), where further building took place by the railway from the early 1840s.[6] On the south

[89] Glos. R.O., D 3117/589–91, 612, 2536–58, 4038–9; D 4791, Glouc. Railway Carriage & Wagon Co., Elming Row deeds 1840–96; G.D.R., T 1/99; Glos. Chron. 26 Dec. 1891.

[90] Above, social and cultural life.

[91] Glouc. Jnl. 19 Oct. 1839; Pigot's Dir. Glos. (1842), 114; Conway-Jones, Glouc. Docks, 40.

[92] G.D.R., T 1/99; J. Stratford, Glos. Biog. Notes (1887), 203.

[93] Glos. R.O., D 3117/750–2; G.D.R., T 1/99.

[94] G.D.R., T 1/86, 99.

[95] Illustrated Lond. News, 27 Nov. 1852, pp. 464–5; cf. Glouc. Jnl. 20 Nov. 1875; 6 Jan. 1877; 22 May 1886.

[96] For 19th-cent. growth of Glouc., above, Fig. 14.

[97] G.B.R., L 6/4/2, mem. 26 Jan., 8 Apr. 1864.

[98] Cf. ibid. L 6/1/1–37, 41–57, 64–126; Glos. R.O., DC 2/1–42.

[99] Cf. G.D.R., T 1/16, 156; O.S. Map 6″, Glos. XXV. NW. (1883 edn.); SE., SW. (1889 edn.); XXXIII. NW. (1888 edn.).

[1] G.B.R., L 6/1/1, 7, 19, 32.

[2] Glos. R.O., D 4062/14–15, 20.

[3] Ibid. D 3462/1; D 3117/386, 778; Causton, Map of Glouc. (1843).

[4] G.B.R., B 3/17, min. 10 May 1852.

[5] Glouc. Jnl. 22 Apr., 16 Dec. 1854; 8 Jan. 1848; 14 Dec. 1867.

[6] Causton, Map of Glouc. (1843); Glos. R.O., D 3117/ 1372–5, 2777–8.

side of Barton Street Victoria Street was laid out for terraced housing by Richard Helps in 1837[7] and building began in the west part of Ryecroft Street before 1843.[8] Falkner Street was formed c. 1850 by the Birmingham corn merchant Joseph Sturge, whose firm built a row of semidetached cottages there for its employees.[9] Building also continued in the Barton End suburb around Barton Terrace (later the north part of Tredworth High Street),[10] and to the south-west a group of dwellings known as Newtown, mostly huts inhabited by the poor evicted from High Orchard, sprang up around a pipe factory in the late 1830s.[11] Some building took place near an old farmstead on Barton Lane (later Parkend Road), and by 1850 Samuel Bowly had erected two cottages in that area as part of an allotment scheme.[12]

On the north-east side of Gloucester the building of artisans' houses in the streets north-east of Alvin Street continued after 1835,[13] and the combination of overcrowding with poor drainage made the area around Sweetbriar Street the least sanitary in Gloucester.[14] In 1840 a small working-class development was begun south of London Road in Newland Street by William Lea and William Dawes.[15] In the early 1840s a few houses were built for more prosperous residents in the entrance to Gallows Lane (later Denmark Road) near Wotton Pitch.[16]

Gloucester's increasing importance as an industrial centre and its rapidly growing population stimulated considerable redevelopment in the older parts of the city and widespread building in outlying districts after 1850. In 1854 the construction of a sewerage system enabled the corporation to fill in and use the course of Dockham ditch between the Foreign bridge and St. Catherine Street for a new road (Priory Road) to reduce traffic at the Cross and in Three Cocks Lane.[17] The corporation also widened lower Westgate Street at the entrance to the Island in 1859[18] and carried out minor improvements in St. Mary's Square in 1865, after St. Mary de Lode parish had cleared its churchyard of secular buildings, including two former alehouses.[19] The corporation diverted the west part of Parliament Street northwards by demolishing the Green Dragon inn at the entrance to Southgate Street in 1869,[20] and it widened the entrance from Northgate Street to St. Aldate Street in 1882.[21]

Rebuilding and refronting continued in the city centre and several of the oldest buildings were replaced, including in 1865 the former Ram inn in Northgate Street.[22] The porticos of 1856 on the Eastgate market and corn exchange were among prominent additions to the main street fontages,[23] and the Bell hotel was refronted during extensive alterations, which began in 1864 and allowed a widening of the entrance to Bell Lane.[24] In the same year T. F. Addison, a lawyer, built a tower in the garden of a house south of Bell Lane as a memorial to Robert Raikes.[25] Notable additions to lower Northgate Street were the new Spread Eagle hotel of 1865 to a

[7] Glos. R.O., D 3117/1233.

[8] Causton, Map of Glouc. (1843).

[9] Glos. R.O., D 3963/2; D 3117/801; Glos. Chron. 3 Jan. 1885.

[10] Glouc. Jnl. 13 May 1848; Glos. R.O., D 3963/2, 4.

[11] Glos. R.O., D 3117/758–9; Pigot's Dir. Glos. (1842), 115; Bond, Hist. of Glouc. 33; Glos. Chron. 26 Dec. 1891.

[12] Glos. R.O., D 3117/759; Glouc. Jnl. 8 June 1850.

[13] Causton, Map of Glouc. (1843), detail reproduced above, Fig. 12; Bd. of Health Map (1852).

[14] Glouc. Jnl. 27 Dec. 1845; 24 Mar. 1849.

[15] Glos. R.O., D 127/1063; D 4062/13.

[16] Ibid. D 3117/464–5, 473–4; Causton, Map of Glouc. (1843).

[17] Glouc. Jnl. 5 Nov. 1853; 28 Jan. 1853; Glos. R.O., D 3117/2315.

[18] Glouc. Jnl. 4 Sept. 1858; 19 Mar. 1859; cf. Glos. Colln. 22415.

[19] G.B.R., B 4/5/2, min. 21 Sept. 1864; cf. Glos. R.O., P 154/12/IN 3/1; G.D.R., V 5/GT 25; Bd. of Health Map (1852).

[20] G.B.R., B 4/5/3, mins. 10 Dec. 1868, 2 Apr., 8 July 1869.

[21] Glouc. Jnl. 3 June 1882.

[22] Power's Glouc. Handbk. (1862), 94; G.B.R., B 4/5/2, min. 23 Nov. 1865.

[23] Below, Markets and Fairs. For Eastgate portico, above, Plate 30.

[24] Glos. R.O., D 3089; G.B.R., B 4/5/2, min. 21 Sept. 1864.

[25] Citizen, 23 Oct. 1970.

design of J. Medland and A. W. Maberly[26] and the Northgate chapel of 1877–8.[27] The influence of the cattle market and railway stations on that part of the city was particularly evident in George Street where early building included two hotels at the south end, the Wellington, on the west side, opening before the Gloucester opposite in 1854.[28] The building up of Clarence Street continued[29] and the north side of St. Aldate Street was gradually dominated by a range of workshops begun by 1874 for the furniture maker Edwin Lea.[30] Another industrial development in the central area was the building of a factory behind Eastgate House, between King Street and Dog Lane, in 1873 for the printer John Bellows.[31]

In the west part of the city industrial building continued in Quay Street,[32] and between 1854 and 1856 Castle Gardens north of the county gaol were covered by barracks in castellated Gothic style for the Royal South Gloucestershire Militia.[33] Among other buildings of that time was a Gothic-style probate registry office, built at the corner of Pitt Street and Park Street in 1858.[34] In Worcester Street a chapel was built in 1857,[35] and the older circular building was demolished in 1861 to make room for a school.[36] At the corner of Southgate Street and Kimbrose Lane the site occupied by the former city gaol, police station, and Kimbrose Hospital, all demolished in the early 1860s,[37] was built on from 1866.[38] During that period buildings were added to Commercial Road and Ladybellegate Street, where an orchard belonging to Bearland House was developed commercially from 1870.[39] Buildings were also added to the north part of Brunswick Road, beginning in 1867 with stores for the Gloucester Co-operative and Industrial Society. In 1877 the society also filled the angle formed with Barton Street by stores to a Gothic design by Medland and Son.[40] Other important developments in Brunswick Road were the Schools of Science and Art of 1871–2 to a Gothic design by F. S. Waller[41] and the Baptist chapel of 1872–3 and Raikes Memorial Hall of 1884.[42] Further south towards the Spa, St. Michael's Square was laid out in 1882 by Daniel Pidgeon of Putney (Surr.).[43]

The closure of the Gloucester–Cheltenham tramway in 1861 released land for building and a section north of Barton Street was replaced by a road leading into Mill Lane.[44] The site of the tramway depot at the corner of Brunswick Road and Park Road was used for commercial development.[45] East of the Spa, which had remained a fashionable residential area, several large houses were built facing the park opened in 1862.[46] Most were on the north side of Park Road, where development on Barley Close, over which the corporation laid out New Park Street (later Belgrave Road) in 1864, was delayed by the retention of ground rents.[47] The most prominent building was the Presbyterian church of 1870–2.[48]

[26] G.B.R., B 4/5/2, min. 13 Jan. 1865.
[27] Below, Prot. Nonconf., Wesleyan Methodists.
[28] *Glouc. Jnl.* 30 Sept. 1854; cf. G.B.R., N 2/1/1, p. 608.
[29] Glos. R.O., D 3117/4536.
[30] G.B.R., N 2/1/4, min. 16 Oct. 1874; for illustrations, Glos. Colln. NR 15.39, p.10; *Barrow's Glouc. and Dean Forest Guide* (1904), 14.
[31] *D.N.B.* 2nd suppl.
[32] Glos. R.O., D 3833/7; DC/F 34.
[33] Bd. of Health Map (1852); *Glouc. Jnl.* 25 Mar. 1854; 5 July 1856; cf. Glos. R.O., GPS 611/3.
[34] *Glouc. Jnl.* 1 May 1858; *Building News*, 3 May 1861, p. 371.
[35] Below, Prot. Nonconf., United Methodists and their Predecessors.
[36] *Glouc. Jnl.* 28 Sept. 1861.
[37] G.B.R., B 4/1/8, p. 21.

[38] Glos. R.O., D 3117/734–5, 1464–78.
[39] Ibid. 1521–9.
[40] *Glouc. Jnl.* 23 Nov. 1867; 22 Sept. 1877; above, Plate 31.
[41] *Glouc. Jnl.* 27 July 1872; above, Plate 48.
[42] *Glouc. Jnl.* 28 June 1873; 22 Nov. 1884.
[43] G.B.R., B 4/6/2, min. 8 Sept. 1882; Glos. R.O., D 3117/1795.
[44] Cf. Bd. of Health Map (1852); O.S. Map 1/2,500, Glos. XXV. 15 (1886 edn.); the new road, called Station Road, was widened in 1885: Glos. Colln. NQ 28.50.
[45] *Glouc. Jnl.* 13 July 1861; G.B.R., B 4/5/1, mins. 28 Feb., 7 Mar. 1862.
[46] Above, social and cultural life; cf. G.B.R., B 4/5/2, min. 19 Mar. 1866.
[47] G.B.R., L 6/4/2; Glos. Colln. NX 28.7.
[48] Below, Prot. Nonconf.

Though building slowed during periods of economic recession such as the later 1850s and early 1880s Gloucester's suburban growth in the later 19th century was extensive. New working-class housing was generally located on low ground south and south-east of the city, especially near the docks and Bristol Road which had become the main industrial quarter. The dwellings of the prosperous middle classes were on higher ground further south and east and in outlying settlements. With the growth of the suburbs the older, crowded parts of Gloucester became less populous, particularly in the 1850s when the city's population fell by over 1,000 as people moved to more open streets outside the boundary. In 1871 the parliamentary borough had a population of 31,844 while the municipal borough had one of only 18,341.[49] Building continued in the confined courts of the Island, though in general there was a drift of people away from the western part of the city.[50] Many of the new areas were taken into the city in 1874 but the corporation's rating policy in them encouraged development outside the new boundary.[51]

In the Bristol Road area industrial development spread southwards from High Orchard after the railway reached that area in 1848 by crossing the road at Sudbrook.[52] In response to the shortage of housing, Samuel Lysons in 1854, following the principles of the philanthropist Angela Burdett-Coutts, built 52 artisan dwellings behind Theresa Place in 12 pairs of cottages called Clarence Town (later the south side of Theresa Street) and a long terrace called Alma Place.[53] Several factories were established in Bristol Road in the 1860s and 1870s, notably the works of the Gloucester Wagon Co. opposite the junction of Stroud Road in 1860,[54] and from the late 1860s, when S.J. Moreland laid out two streets next to his match factory, speculative developments of terraced housing sprang up east of Bristol Road and north of Stroud Road.[55] Much further south, Tuffley Avenue was laid out between the two roads in 1874 on the former Sheephouse estate,[56] and by 1882 several streets had been started off Bristol Road.[57] Although some landowners opposed development of land fronting the canal,[58] timber yards covered much of the eastern bank as far as Hempsted bridge by 1854.[59] Further south gasworks were built on the Bristol road in the mid 1870.[60] At Llanthony, west of the canal, commercial development began in the early 1850s with the construction of a quay and railway,[61] the Hempsted road having been diverted to make room for a dock which was never built.[62] During the construction of the Llanthony lock and weir in the Severn's eastern channel c. 1870 the river was widened.[63]

In New Street, between Stroud Road and the Sud brook, over 60 houses had been built by 1871, most of them by Richard Cherrington, who began building terraced houses there in 1867[64] and was involved in the development of other parts of Gloucester. Further out on Stroud Road, Forest Terrace was built by Joseph Scudamore in 1870[65] and building in Castle Street (later the north part of Stanley

[49] *Census*, 1851–71.
[50] *Glouc. Jnl.* 22 Jan. 1853; 3 Sept. 1859; *Census*, 1861; Glos. R.O., D 3087, Glouc. Coffee Ho. Co., min. bk. 1877–84, min. 19 Apr. 1881.
[51] Above, city govt.
[52] *Glouc. Jnl.* 9, 16 Aug. 1851; for the Sudbrook railway crossing, ibid. 18 Mar. 1848.
[53] Glos. R.O., P 154/22/IN 3/2; P 173/VE 2/1; G.B.R., N 2/1/2, min. 7 Jan. 1856; G.D.R., V 6/130.
[54] O.S. Map 1/2,500, Glos. XXXIII. 2 (1886 edn.); above, econ. development 1835–1914.
[55] Glos. R.O., D 3117/3469; G.B.R., B 4/5/2–3; B 4/6/2.
[56] *Glouc. Jnl.* 30 May 1874; Glos. R.O., D 1740/T 49.

[57] O.S. Map 1/2,500, Glos. XXXIII. 2 (1886 edn.).
[58] Glos. Colln. (H) G 2.57.
[59] Below, Quay and Docks.
[60] Below, Public Services; O.S. Map 1/2,500, Glos. XXXIII. 6 (1886 edn.).
[61] Above, econ. development 1835–1914.
[62] Glos. R.O., Q/RUm 231; Glouc. and Dean Forest Railway Act, 1847, 10 & 11 Vic. c. 76 (Local and Personal); Glos. Colln. JF 14.90 (13).
[63] Glos. Colln. MF 1.50, p.9; Glos. R.O., D 2460, Severn Com., South Hamlet deeds 1869–75.
[64] G.B.R., B 4/5/2, min. 18 June 1867; 3, mins. 13 Feb. 1868, 27 Oct. 1871.
[65] Ibid. N 4/2, pp. 92, 101.

Fig. 15. The outer Barton Street and Tredworth area, 1883 (*north at the top*); Barton Street runs diagonally across at top right

Road) began in 1877.[66] Larger houses and villas were being built on the main road towards Tuffley by the late 1870s when the formation of Linden Road began.[67] Building at Tuffley during the period included several substantial houses on Robins Wood Hill with extensive views over the Vale of Gloucester. Oak Bank, one of the earliest, dates from the late 1860s.[68] A few smaller houses were built at the reservoirs on the north-west side of the hill.[69]

Most new building in the later 19th century took place on the south-east side of Gloucester, where inner Barton Street ceased to be a fashionable residential area and was surrounded by more streets. J. N. Balme released the land remaining south of Mill Lane (later Market Street) for building in 1853, but the square formed by his extension of Russell Street, Tanner Street (later St. Kilda Parade), and Nettleton Road was not filled with houses.[70] South of Barton Street, Wellington Street and Cromwell Street were begun in 1852, and the former, a continuation of Hampden Place into the road from the Spa to Barton Street (later Park Road),[71] was built up with terraces of three storeys for more prosperous residents. To the east King's Barton Street and Arthur Street were laid out in 1864 for working-class housing by Joseph Lovegrove, and the corporation shared in the formation of Arthur Street as part of its Barley Close development.[72] Lovegrove, who contributed to the growth of other parts of Gloucester, was a prominent local solicitor.[73]

Further out on Barton Street there was extensive new building. In 1854 A. G. D. Goodyere, the owner of Barton House, laid out several streets north of the road, including Widden Street[74] where Gloucester's first board school was built in 1878,[75] and Joseph Lovegrove started a small development south of the road after he bought Barton House in 1870.[76] The Vauxhall Gardens were covered with terraced housing from 1863.[77] A terrace had been built to face the gardens from Millbrook Street, where there was a surge of building in the later 1860s.[78] A considerable stimulus to development there was given by the construction in 1869 of wagon repair works near the former T station. The new works adjoined the Lower Barton House property of Isaac Slater, the Gloucester Wagon Company's manager, who laid out and built houses in Sidney Street.[79] The increased demand for housing was also met by building in India Road[80] and, by 1874, beyond the railway, at first along the Painswick road towards Saintbridge[81] and later at Coney Hill, where several streets in the Newton Avenue area had been formed in 1872.[82] In 1871 the solicitor James Bretherton, one of the developers of the Millbrook Street area, laid out a street north of the railway towards Wotton,[83] where development was dominated by a mental hospital. In the late 1870s building continued in and around Millbrook Street and India Road,[84] with All Saints' vicarage being by far the largest house.[85] The city's tramways inaugurated in 1879 ran to a depot in India Road.[86]

[66] Ibid. B 4/6/2, improvement cttee. 19 June 1877; O.S. Map 1/2,500, Glos. XXXIII. 3 (1886 edn.).
[67] Glos. R.O., D 4335/78, 114, 182; cf. O.S. Map 6", Glos. XXXIII. NE. (1891 edn.).
[68] Glos. R.O., D 3117/2100–3; D 2593, private, Geo. Whitcombe; *Kelly's Dir. Glos.* (1870), 662.
[69] Glos. R.O., D 3117/2072; O.S. Map 6", Glos. XXXIII. NE. (1891 edn.).
[70] Glos. R.O., D 1388/SL 4/13; O.S. Map 1/2,500, Glos. XXV. 15 (1886 edn.).
[71] Glos. R.O., D 3117/396, 778; cf. G.B.R., N 2/1/1, p. 342.
[72] G.B.R., L 6/4/2, mem. 8 Apr. 1864, rep. Mar. 1864; B 4/5/2, min. 21 July 1865.
[73] *Glos. Chron.* 13 Jan. 1883; cf. below, Outlying Hamlets, man.

[74] Glos. R.O., D 3117/2719; D 4453, sale partics. 1854.
[75] Below, Educ.
[76] Glos. R.O., D 3117/2719–20.
[77] Ibid. 1236, 3499A–B; Glos. Colln. NV 28.1.
[78] Glos. R.O., DC 2/1/1–48; D 3117/3465–7; D 3963/6; D 4062/12; G.B.R., N 4/2, p. 58.
[79] Glos. R.O., D 4791, Glouc. Railway Carriage & Wagon Co., min. bk. 1868–71, pp. 5–6, 165, 288–9; G.B.R., N 4/2, p. 68; B 4/5/5, min. 21 Sept. 1875.
[80] G.B.R., L 6/1/39–40, 59–62.
[81] Ibid. B 6/25/1, p. 13.
[82] *Glouc. Jnl.* 17 Feb. 1872; 3 Oct. 1874; O.S. Map 1/2,500, Glos. XXXIII. 3 (1886 edn.).
[83] G.B.R., L 6/1/64.
[84] Ibid. B 4/5/5–6; B 4/6/2.
[85] Below, Churches and Chapels, mod. par. ch.
[86] P. W. Gentry, *Tramways of W. of Eng.* (1952), 75–7.

New building was also concentrated in the High Street area of Tredworth, some way south of Barton Street, where more streets were laid out for terraced housing in the early 1850s.[87] The Gloucestershire Mutual Benefit Building Society, a land society founded in 1852 for the working classes by leading Gloucester Liberals, such as the temperance advocate Samuel Bowly, developed two estates in the area. The Barton Lane estate of 1853 was on the south side of Falkner Street, and the Painswick Road estate of 1854 was east of High Street and bounded on the south by the Sud brook and on the east by the railway. The society built several houses, including a row dated 1855 in Melbourne Street, but sold most plots to members. The estates were completed slowly, only 63 houses having been built by 1865,[88] and introduced villas and semidetached residences to the area, which became known as California and was described in 1871 as 'a strange mixture of neat villas, fragrant pigsties, and Newtown shanties'.[89] South of Tredworth Road two new streets were built up with terraced houses from 1870.[90]

The construction of water mains from Great Witcombe to the city in the late 1850s stimulated building on Ermin Street,[91] with many of the new houses on the south side of the road set in grounds running back to the Wotton brook. Wotton, where the local politician John Ward built Bohanam House for his residence in the later 1860s,[92] became a favoured middle-class suburb, but building in Barnwood, further out, slowed after the opening in 1860 of Barnwood House Hospital, which was to dominate the village for over a century.[93] Nearer the city several houses in London Road became residences for city clergymen,[94] and Hillfield was rebuilt for the timber merchant Charles Walker to an Italianate design of John Giles c. 1867.[95] Another important development there was the replacement of the ancient hospitals of St. Margaret and St. Mary Magdalen by a large new almshouse in the early 1860s.[96] Building on the Heathville estate north of London Road was delayed until after an improvement in 1865 of Gallows Lane, which had been renamed Denmark Road in 1863 when part was rebuilt by the city corporation.[97] Heathville Road was laid out first, followed in the late 1860s by Alexandra Road,[98] and by the early 1880s several large houses, including two terraces, had been built.[99] The streets formed west of Heathville Road from 1876 were filled with smaller houses.[1] East of Gloucester some building had taken place in the early 19th century beside the Gloucester–Cheltenham tramway, notably in the Armscroft Road area in the east of Wotton[2] and on the Cheltenham road at Longlevens.[3] The settlement at Longlevens, which comprised an inn and several cottages in 1851,[4] had begun to expand westwards along the north side of the Longford road by 1863[5] and took the name of former open-field land there.[6]

On the north side of Gloucester there was much building in parts of Kingsholm and the number of inhabited houses in the hamlets of Kingsholm St. Catherine and

[87] G.B.R., L 6/1/41, 45–6, 48, 51–2, 56; cf. above, Fig. 15.

[88] *Glouc. Jnl.* 4 Dec. 1852; 3 Sept. 1853; 20 May, 30 Dec. 1854; Glos. R.O., D 3117/605–8; Q/SRh 1859 D/1; the soc. was taken over by the Chelt. and Glos. Permanent Mutual Benefit Building Soc. in 1909: *Glouc. Jnl.* 7 Aug. 1909; 19 Feb. 1910.

[89] *Glouc. Jnl.* 11 Mar. 1871.

[90] Glos R.O., D 3117/779–80; D 3963/12; G.B.R., N 4/2, p. 149.

[91] Below, Public Services; G.B.R., B 6/33/1, p. 7.

[92] G.B.R., B 4/5/3, min. 19 Mar. 1869; *Glouc. Jnl.* 9 Mar. 1895.

[93] *Census*, 1851–81; below, Hosp., mental hosp.; Glos. R.O., D 3725, Barnwood Ho. Trust, rep. 1878–1973.

[94] Cf. O.S. Map 1/2,500, Glos. XXV. 15 (1886 edn.).

[95] G.B.R., B 4/5/2, min. 20 Dec. 1865; Glos. Colln. prints GL 40.23A.

[96] Below, Char. for Poor, almshouses.

[97] *Glouc. Jnl.* 4 Apr., 15 Aug. 1863; G.B.R., N 6/1.

[98] Glos. R.O., SL 539; D 1388/III/134.

[99] O.S. Map 1/2,500, Glos. XXV. 15 (1886 edn.).

[1] G.B.R., B 4/5/5, min. 7 July 1876; Cadle, *Map of Glouc.* (1877).

[2] Cf. O.S. Map 6", Glos. XXV. SE. (1889 edn.).

[3] Glos. R.O., D 204/1/2.

[4] P.R.O., HO 107/1961, s.v. Longford St. Mary.

[5] It was then called Springfield: *Kelly's Dir. Glos.* (1863), s.vv. Barnwood, Longford, and Wotton.

[6] Glos. R.O., D 1740/E 3, ff. 107–8; Q/RI 70 (map G, nos. 18–19); O.S. Map 6", Glos. XXV. SE. (1887 edn.).

Kingsholm St. Mary rose from 219 in 1851 to 383 in 1861.[7] In the early 1850s the working-class development north-east of Alvin Street was extended, with Joseph Lovegrove laying out Counsel Street,[8] and at the same time Worcester Parade, a stuccoed terrace, was built piecemeal on one of James Cheslin Wheeler's nurseries behind St. Mark's church.[9] Further north humbler terraces were begun in St. Mark Street and Edwy Parade (formerly Snake Lane) and several villas were built in the newly formed Kingsholm Square.[10] Part of Sebert Street had been built up by 1855.[11] North of Kingsholm on the Tewkesbury road towards Longford new building had included Westfield House, a large classical residence of c. 1840 which was enlarged in the mid 1880s when it became a school.[12] Nearby in Westfield Terrace two pairs of small villas were built c. 1850 and a third pair, to a different design, before 1865.[13] Nearer the city Greville House was built in the early 1860s for the timber merchant William Nicks[14] and a children's hospital opened on the opposite side of the road in 1867.[15] The turnpike was moved from Kingsholm out to Longford in 1858.[16]

The meadows north and west of Gloucester were little touched by development, though there was some building beyond Westgate bridge in Pool Meadow, which in 1843 had a boatbuilder's yard, an inn, and a pair of houses.[17] By 1861 the number of houses there had increased to 15 and by 1881 to 43.[18] Tabby Pitts Pool, a large pond created in the southern part of Meanham (later St. Catherine's Meadow) c. 1850 by brickmaking for the nearby railway viaduct, was filled in in 1889.[19] In the early 20th century parts of the meadows were adapted for public recreation, namely the Priory Road playing field in Little Meadow in 1901 and the Oxlease showground in 1904.[20]

The pace of building in Gloucester and outlying districts quickened with the economic revival of the later 1880s. In the city alone 27 streets, 1,789 houses, and 206 shops and factories were built between 1889 and 1899. Most new building was on the south and east sides of Gloucester and with the movement of people to the suburbs many houses in the western part of the city became derelict.[21] The city corporation carried out many street improvements,[22] and a private company widened the approach to the cathedral from Westgate Street in 1892 and 1893 by replacing the buildings on the east side of College Street by a uniform range of red brick shops with timber gables designed by Waller & Son.[23] In another major improvement Westgate Street was widened between Lower Quay Street and the Island between 1902 and 1913.[24] Road improvements and other developments involved the demolition of many ancient buildings, including several in Longsmith Street in the early 20th century.[25] There was some rebuilding in areas of housing just outside the city centre, such as Park Street and St. Catherine Street, and from 1909 the courts and lanes of the city centre and the 19th-century suburbs to the north-east and south-east were subject to sporadic slum clearance.[26]

By the early 20th century new public buildings, banks, and shops had transformed the appearance of the older part of the city.[27] The most prominent group was in

[7] Census, 1851–61.
[8] Glos. R.O., D 3117/1239.
[9] G.B.R., N 2/1/1, p. 79; Glos. R.O., D 3117/1133, 1594: according to date and inits. on S. end, part of terrace was built in 1851 by Hen. Weaver.
[10] Glos. R.O., D 3013/3; P 154/7/VE 1; Glouc. Jnl. 6 Mar., 3 Apr. 1852; 15 Oct. 1853.
[11] Glouc. Jnl. 5 May 1855.
[12] Glos. R.O., D 1388/SL 8/8; D 2299/456.
[13] Ibid. P 154/7/VE 1; D 1388/SL 4/97.
[14] Ibid. Q/SRh 1860 C/2; Kelly's Dir. Glos. (1863), 304.
[15] Below, Hosp.
[16] Glouc. Jnl. 12 June 1858.

[17] Causton, Map of Glouc. (1843).
[18] Census, 1851–81.
[19] Glos. Chron. 9 Nov. 1889.
[20] Glouc. Jnl. 28 Dec. 1901; 31 Dec. 1904.
[21] G.B.R., B 6/33/1, pp. 94, 180.
[22] Cf. Glos. Chron. 4 May, 19 Oct. 1889.
[23] Glos. R.O., D 2593, private, Cath. Approaches Co. Ltd.
[24] G.B.R., B 3/47, pp. 401–3.
[25] Photogs. in Glos. Colln. 29157; 31607; 37156.
[26] Reps. of Medical Off. of Health, 1909–14, 1919: copies in G.B.R., B 3/44–9, 54; cf. G.B.R., public health department, slum clearance rec.
[27] Ind. Glos. 1904, 77: copy in Glos. Colln. JV 13.1.

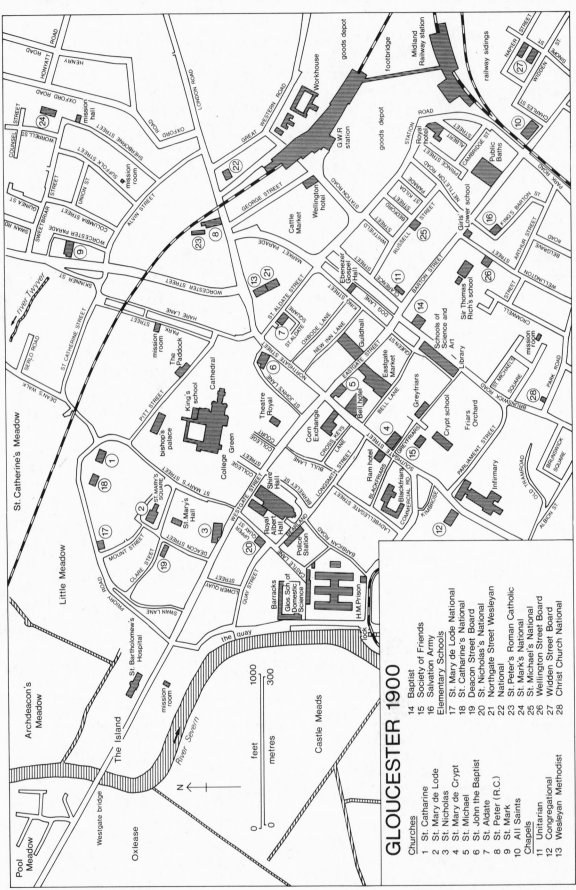

GLOUCESTER 1900

Churches
1 St. Catharine
2 St. Mary de Lode
3 St. Nicholas
4 St. Mary de Crypt
5 St. Michael
6 St. John the Baptist
7 St. Aldate
8 St. Peter (R.C.)
9 St. Mark
10 All Saints

Chapels
11 Unitarian
12 Congregational
13 Wesleyan Methodist
14 Baptist
15 Society of Friends
16 Salvation Army

Elementary Schools
17 St. Mary de Lode National
18 St. Catharine's National
19 Deacon Street Board
20 St. Nicholas's National
21 Northgate Street Wesleyan
22 National
23 St. Peter's Roman Catholic
24 St. Mark's National
25 St. Michael's National
26 Wellington Street Board
27 Widden Street Board
28 Christ Church National

Fig. 16

1. Houses on the corner of Park Street and St. Catherine Street, demolished *c.* 1957

2. The east side of Hare Lane in 1886

4. Gloucester cathedral: the choir from the west

3. Gloucester cathedral from the north-east

6. John Cooke (d. 1528) and his wife Joan (d. c. 1545), founders of the Crypt grammar school. Cooke, a mercer and alderman, was four times mayor

5. Sir Thomas Bell (d. 1566), alderman of Gloucester and three times mayor. A wealthy capper, he bought monastic property at the Dissolution and founded St. Kyneburgh's Hospital

7. The courtyard of the New Inn, Northgate Street, in 1892

8. The old Ram inn, Northgate Street, demolished in 1865

9. Overmantel at no. 9, Southgate Street, with the date 1650 and the arms of Yate family

10. Effigies of Alderman John Walton (d. 1626) and his wife Alice (d. 1620) on a monument in St. Nicholas's church

11. 'Jemmy' Wood's house and bank in upper Westgate Street, with Wood in the doorway

12. Gloucester from the south-west *c.* 1750, with a ship passing the Naight. Buildings shown include (*left to right*) Eagle Hall beyond the masts at the quay, St. Nicholas's spire, the castle keep, Marybone House, the cathedral, Trinity tower, and the Tolsey with St. John's spire beyond

13. View down Westgate Street, *c.* 1824, with St. Nicholas's church in the background

15. The Bell inn, Southgate Street, c 1830; it was remodelled in the 1860s and demolished in 1968

17. The pump room built at the Spa in 1814 and demolished in 1960

14. The Boothall Hotel, lower Westgate Street, c. 1905; it was demolished in 1957

16. Eastgate House, built c. 1780 after the removal of the east gate and demolished c. 1970

19. Gloucester cathedral: the nave in the early 19th century, with the screen inserted in 1741

18. Gloucester cathedral: the south walk of the great cloister with carrels on left

20. John Phillpotts (d. 1849), barrister and M.P. for the city

21. Sir Thomas Robinson (d. 1897), corn merchant and leader of the Liberals on the city council

22. William Philip Price (d. 1891), timber merchant and M.P. for the city

23. Sir James Bruton (d. 1933), nine times mayor of the city, wearing his chain of office

24. The Albert Mills from the Victoria dock, c.1900

25. Cox's Court, Hare Lane, before the buildings were removed under a slum clearance scheme in 1935

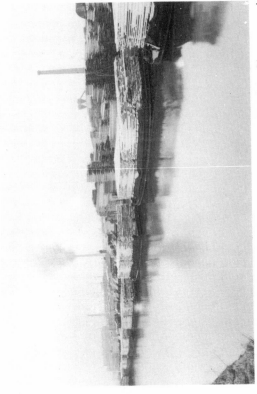

27. The timber yard of Price, Walker, & Co. on the east side of the Gloucester and Berkeley canal, c. 1925

29. A delivery van built by the Wagon Co. in 1896 for the Gloucester pickle factory

26. The works of Fielding & Platt: the gas-engine assembly shop, c. 1908

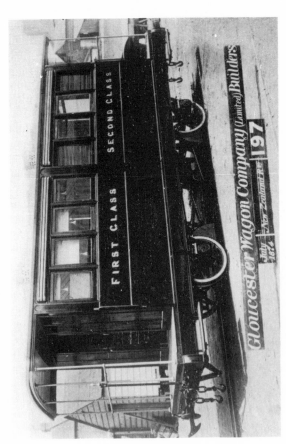

28. A carriage built by the Gloucester Wagon Co. in 1874 for New Zealand railways

31. The Gloucester Co-operative society's store, at the corner of Brunswick Road and Barton Street, built in 1877 and replaced in 1931

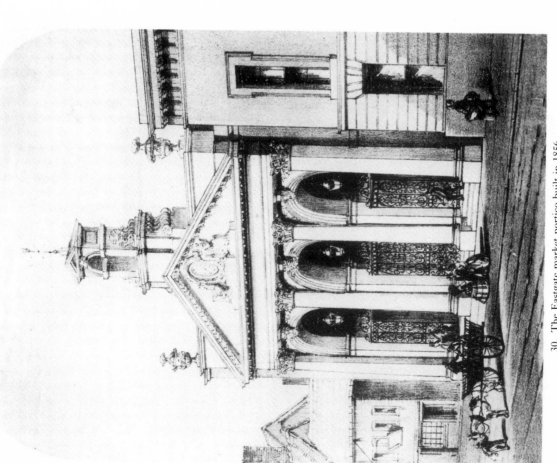

30. The Eastgate market portico built in 1856

32. Part of the docks, *c.* 1925: view towards the Victoria dock from south of the barge arm

33. The break in the gauges at Gloucester: cartoon of 1846 depicting the inconvenience caused

34. The main basin at Gloucester docks in 1883, with narrow boats, brigs and Severn trows; the warehouses on the west quay (*on the right*) were demolished in 1966

35. Gloucester docks from the south-east in 1985, with the barge arm and Victoria dock in the foreground and the main basin and the river beyond

36. The high cross before it was demolished in 1751, with the Tolsey on the left

37. The Boothall in 1847 when in use as stables

38. The Tolsey (as rebuilt in 1751) shortly before it was demolished in 1892

39. The King's Board after its removal to Hillfield gardens

40. Over bridge and causeway in 1734. In the background the conical glasshouse and limekiln are shown beyond Westgate bridge, boats are moored at the city quay to the right, and the ruins of Llanthony Priory are shown at the far right

41. The west gate and Westgate bridge in 1796

42. Blackfriars in 1721, with Bell's Place (the remodelled church) on the left and the claustral buildings on the right

43. Greyfriars in 1721, with the bowling green in the foreground; the towers are those of St. Mary de Crypt, the cathedral, and St. Michael

44. St. Michael's church, *c.* 1790, with the entrance to Southgate Street on the right

45. St. John's church, *c.* 1790, with the classical nave and aisles built in the 1730s

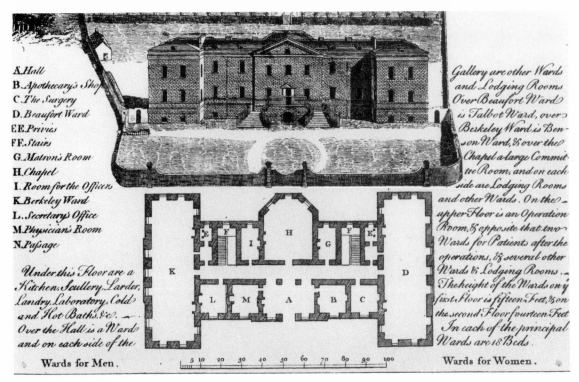

A. Hall
B. Apothecary's Shop
C. The Surgery
D. Beaufort Ward
EE. Privies
FF. Stairs
G. Matron's Room
H. Chapel
I. Room for the Officers
K. Berkeley Ward
L. Secretary's Office
M. Physician's Room
N. Passage

Under this Floor are a Kitchen, Scullery, Larder, Landry, Laboratory, Cold and Hot Baths, &c. — Over the Hall is a Ward and on each side of the

Gallery are other Wards and Lodging Rooms. Over Beaufort Ward is Talbot Ward, over Berkeley Ward is Benson Ward, & over the Chapel a large Committee Room, and on each side are Lodging Rooms and other Wards. On the upper Floor is an Operation Room, & opposite that two Wards for Patients after the operations, & several other Wards & Lodging Rooms. The height of the Wards on first Floor is fifteen Feet, & on the second Floor fourteen Feet. In each of the principal Wards are 18 Beds.

Wards for Men.

Wards for Women.

46. The Gloucester Infirmary in lower Southgate street, opened in 1761; it was demolished in 1984

47. The Bluecoat school in Eastgate Street, built in 1807 and replaced by the Guildhall in the early 1890s

48. The Schools of Science and Art in Brunswick Road, completed in 1872; the public library was later added on the left side, and the Price Memorial Hall (later the museum) on the right

49. St. James's National school at Barton End, opened in 1844

50. The Unitarian chapel, Barton Street, before alterations in 1893

51. The chancel of St. Catherine's church, built beside the ruins of St. Oswald's Priory in 1867–8 and demolished in 1921

52. Southgate Congregational church, opened in 1851 and demolished in 1981

53. St. Mark's church, Kingsholm, completed in 1847

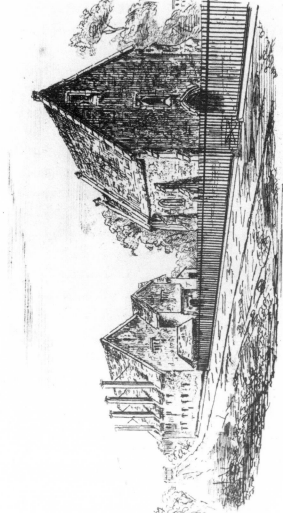

54. St. Kyneburgh's Hospital, demolished c. 1862

55. St. Margaret's Hospital and chapel, c. 1849; the almshouse building was demolished in 1862

56. The chapel of St. Mary Magdalen's Hospital before removal of the nave in 1861

57. St. Bartholomew's Hospital in 1929; the chimneys were removed c. 1966

58. Hempsted Court from the south *c*. 1700; the Newark is just visible in the left background

59. Matson House and the parish church from the south

Eastgate Street[28] and comprised the Guildhall, built in the early 1890s on the site of the early 19th-century Bluecoat school,[29] the National Provincial Bank, replacing in 1888 the former town house of the Crawley-Boevey family and having a stone front in a classical design by Charles Gribble of London,[30] and Lloyds Bank, a tall brick building of 1898 in a Renaissance style by F. W. Waller.[31] Ashmeade House between Dog Lane and Clarence Street was replaced by new offices and a showroom of the Gloucester Gaslight Co., opened in 1891.[32] In Southgate Street the Ram (later the New County) hotel was refronted in 1890[33] and the corn exchange portico was rebuilt flush with the street frontage in 1893.[34] At the Cross the Tolsey was replaced by a building for the Wilts and Dorset Banking Co., opened in 1895,[35] and a shop on the south-east corner in Southgate Street was rebuilt in 1901.[36] The north-west corner was remodelled between 1905 and 1907 when three shops gave way to a stone building for the London City and Midland Bank.[37] In the early 20th century new frontages in the principal streets were in a variety of styles, including timber framing and elaborate brickwork with shaped gables.[38] In Brunswick Road the block east of Queen Street was dominated by the co-operative society's stores, which were extended in 1883 and 1904.[39] The block east of Constitution Walk was completed in the 1890s, notably by the stone Price Memorial Hall of 1892–3, in a Renaissance design by F. W. Waller, and the public library of 1898–1900, designed by Waller as a southwards extension of the science and art schools.[40] Further south the new Crypt school was built at Friars Orchard in 1889.[41]

The railway and dock companies contributed substantially to Gloucester's development in the late 19th and early 20th centuries. In 1889 the lane leading from London Road to the workhouse was widened by the G.W.R. for goods traffic and was renamed Great Western Road.[42] The poor-law union began building on the east side in 1912.[43] The removal of the Midland Railway's passenger station to the east end of Market Street (renamed Station Road) in 1896[44] stimulated new building in that area, a prominent addition being the Royal hotel of 1898 designed by H. A. Dancey.[45] The move possibly contributed to the closure of the Spread Eagle hotel, the main part of which, acquired in 1898 for the Y.M.C.A., was converted with shops and offices on the ground floor and renamed Northgate Mansions.[46] The railway stations attracted further commercial development to George Street, with the Post Office gradually occupying most of the east side; its sorting office there incorporated from 1904 showrooms built for the Gloucester Railway Carriage & Wagon Co. in 1894. New buildings on the west side included an extension of the cattle market completed in 1899.[47] The corporation's electricity works opened in 1900 replaced several buildings in Commercial Road and Ladybellegate Street,[48] and developments in Bearland included the county magistrates' courts of 1908.[49]

[28] For a view of that part of street before 1888, *Glouc., a Pictorial Rec.* 61. [29] Below, Public Buildings.
[30] *Glouc. Jnl.* 3 Mar. 1888; Verey, *Glos.* ii. 249.
[31] Date on bldg.; *Glouc. Jnl.* 2 Dec. 1933.
[32] *Glos. Chron.* 27 Apr. 1889; Glos. Colln. N 15.30, p. 35; for the bldg., demolished during redevelopment, *Glouc. Official Guide* (1947), 126.
[33] G.B.R., B 3/24, p. 179; *Glouc. Jnl.* 14 June 1890.
[34] *Glouc. Jnl.* 29 Apr., 10 June 1893.
[35] Below, Public Buildings; *Suppl. to 56th Rep. Glouc. Chamber of Commerce* (1897), 13: copy in Glos. Colln. N 15.6.
[36] Date on bldg.; for the shop before rebuilding, *Glouc. As It Was* (Nelson, 1973), 5.
[37] *Glouc. Jnl.* 23 Feb. 1907.
[38] Cf. *Glouc., a Pictorial Rec.* 23, 51; dates 1909 and 1914

on gables of Debenhams (formerly Bon Marché) store, Northgate Street.
[39] *Glouc. Jnl.* 17 Feb. 1883; 1 Oct. 1904.
[40] Ibid. 25 Nov. 1893; 2 June 1900; Glos. Colln. N 24.1.
[41] Glos. R.O., D 3270/19655, pp. 430–534.
[42] *Glos. Chron.* 9 Nov. 1889; the road was extended *c.* 1895: *Glouc. Jnl.* 2 Feb. 1895.
[43] *Glouc. Jnl.* 17 Feb., 13 Apr. 1912.
[44] Ibid. 11 Apr. 1896.
[45] Ibid. 4 Nov. 1933; date on bldg.
[46] *Glouc. Jnl.* 7 Nov. 1896; 17 Dec. 1898; 13 Oct. 1900.
[47] Ibid. 22 June 1889; 5 Jan. 1895; 1 Apr. 1899; 19 Nov. 1904; cf. O.S. Map 1/2,500, Glos. XXV. 15 (1886 and later edns.).
[48] Below, Public Services; cf. Glos. R.O., D 3117/1520–34.
[49] *Glouc. Jnl.* 12 Sept. 1908.

In the suburbs the building up of streets and infilling proceeded as Gloucester continued to grow, and from the mid 1890s the city corporation encouraged the work of speculative builders by laying out streets for residential development on its land in the Stroud Road and Denmark Road areas.[50] In the late 19th century more factories were built at High Orchard and in Bristol Road and timber yards covered the remaining farmland between the road and canal. East of the road more streets were laid out[51] and building in those north of Tuffley Avenue led to a considerable rise in the population of Tuffley parish.[52] The city's tramways were extended along the road from Theresa Place to Tuffley Avenue in 1897 and a depot was built there.[53] In the north part of the area several terraces and streets disappeared under factory extensions before the end of the First World War[54] and the offices of the wagon works facing Stroud Road were rebuilt on a much larger scale in 1904 and 1905.[55] South of Tuffley Avenue the Bristol road was diverted and carried by a bridge over the new Monk Meadow branch railway in the late 1890s,[56] and there was further industrial building on that part of the road in the early 20th century. The opening of the Monk Meadow dock in 1892 stimulated further industrial development west of the canal at Llanthony, where several houses and a new street were also built.[57]

On the south-east side of Gloucester the land remaining in Barton Street and Tredworth west of the G.W.R. line was filled with new streets.[58] In Barton Street Lower Barton House was demolished after Isaac Slater's death in 1885 and Derby Road and several other streets were formed on its grounds.[59] In 1887 the co-operative society built a depot at the east end of India Road.[60] In Tredworth the Newtown huts had been removed by 1891.[61] Suburban development continued at Saintbridge and Coney Hill.[62] There was extensive building in the Stroud Road area in the south, where Linden and Seymour Roads were laid out in stages. Towards Tuffley the main road continued to be built up with larger houses, and development of the former Sheephouse estate, which by 1901 included two streets south of Tuffley Avenue, quickened in the early 20th century.[63] At Tuffley G. T. Whitfield built Fox Elms for his residence and many smaller houses for employees at the brickworks that he opened on Robins Wood Hill in the early 1890s.[64] May Hill Villas, four pairs of dwellings on the main road dated 1896 or 1897, were part of that development. The building up of Reservoir Road continued with large houses, and after the death of Henry Nice in 1912 streets were laid out on his land to the north, in the Northfield (later Southfield) Road area.[65]

There was further building at Kingsholm, notably in Dean's Walk where several houses were erected on the former City Gardens from the later 1880s.[66] The south part of the road, where building had begun by 1901,[67] was widened in the early 20th century,[68] and further north part of Dean's Way was laid out before the First World

[50] Glos. R.O., D 4453, sales partics.; D 3651/1–2; G.B.R., B 6/33/1, pp. 24, 48; *Abstracts of Treasurer's Accts.*: copies in G.B.R.

[51] Cf. O.S. Map 1/2,500, Glos. XXXIII. 2 (1886 and 1902 edns.); Glos. Colln. H (G) 2.57. For the area in 1921, above, Fig. 13, and for timber yards, above, Plate 27.

[52] *Census*, 1881–1901.

[53] Gentry, *Tramways of W. of Eng.* 77.

[54] *Glos. Chron.* 27 Jan. 1923; G.B.R., G 3/SRh 2–3.

[55] *Ind. Glos. 1904*, 5; *Glouc. Jnl.* 2 Sept. 1905.

[56] *Glouc. Jnl.* 23 Oct. 1897.

[57] O.S. Map 1/2,500, Glos. XXXIII. 2 (1886 and later edns.); *Ind. Glos. 1904*, 21, 58; above, econ. development 1835–1914.

[58] O.S. Map 1/2,500, Glos. XXXIII. 3 (1886 and later edns.).

[59] *All Saints' Par. Memories* (1925), 11: Glos. Colln. N 5.10; cf. G.B.R., B 4/5/7, pp. 57–8.

[60] F. Purnell and H. W. Williams, *Jubilee Hist. of Glouc. Co-Operative and Ind. Soc. Ltd.* (1910), 95.

[61] *Glos. Chron.* 26 Dec. 1891.

[62] Glos. Colln. RF 321.1, 3.

[63] Cf. O.S. Map 1/2,500, Glos. XXXIII. 2, 3 (1886 and later edns.).

[64] Glos. Colln. 40298; G.B.R., B 6/33/1, p. 12.

[65] Glos. R.O., D 3117/2073–84, 2362–3; D 2714, Northfield Road deeds 1878–1929; MA 73; O.S. Map 6", Glos. XXXIII. NE. (1891 and later edns.).

[66] Glos. R.O., D 3117/3011–14; *Glos. Chron.* 5 Aug. 1893.

[67] O.S. Map 6", Glos. XXV. SE. (1903 edn.).

[68] Glos. Colln. 31607 (14–15).

War.[69] Several new roads were also formed between Kingsholm and Wotton and large houses continued to be built in the Denmark Road area.[70] The settlements on Ermin Street were affected by considerable suburban development. In Wotton, where Egbert Horlick had laid out Wolseley Road in 1883,[71] there was much building in the Armscroft Road area.[72] The building of middle-class houses in Cheltenham Road and Oxstalls Lane was stimulated by the development of the Wotton Court estate north of Ermin Street from the late 1890s.[73] Sisson Road was formed to lead to engineering works opened east of Elmbridge Road in 1905.[74] In Barnwood houses, including 12 in Upton Lane, were built in the 1890s but development was discouraged by the Ecclesiastical Commissioners, lords of the manor, and by the proximity of two mental hospitals.[75] There was much more building in Hucclecote, which grew as a dormitory of Gloucester from the later 1890s. The village expanded eastwards along Ermin Street towards Brockworth, and Green Lane and several new roads were also built up, many of the houses being detached.[76] Between 1891 and 1901 the number of inhabited houses in Hucclecote rose from 98 to 142 and the population from 459 to 671. The opening of an electric tramway between the city and the village in 1904 encouraged further building, and by 1911 Hucclecote's population had risen to 1,103.[77] Much of the development was on land belonging to William Colwell, an insurance manager.[78]

In the later 19th and early 20th century many new institutional buildings such as churches, chapels, and schools accompanied Gloucester's growth. Some, notably the Linden Road board school of 1893–5 with its tall campanile,[79] were the most prominent features of their localities. The leading Gloucester architect was James Medland (d. 1894), who had started his long career before 1850 and was partnered between 1854 and 1868 by A. W. Maberly, a former pupil of S. W. Daukes. Medland, who was county surveyor 1857–89, designed many of Gloucester's public buildings and his work, which included churches, schools, shops, and factories, was continued by his son M. H. Medland (d. 1920), also county surveyor.[80] C. N. Tripp, the son of a Gloucester timber merchant and a pupil of the elder Medland, established his own practice in the early 1870s but his career was cut short by his early death in 1883.[81] The principal exponent of the Gothic style in Gloucester was F. S. Waller (d. 1905), whose career, beginning before 1850, included the position of cathedral architect. He and his son and sucessor F. W. Waller (d. 1933), who favoured the Renaissance style, designed many important buildings.[82] Significant contributions to Gloucester's architecture were also made by W. B. Wood (d. 1926), a partner of the Wallers, and by H. A. Dancey (d. 1933), who established their own practices in 1889 and 1897 respectively.[83] Col. N. H. Waller (d. 1961) was the third generation of his family employed as cathedral architect.[84]

In the thirty years before the First World War there was sporadic building beyond the suburbs in districts which were later transformed by housing estates,[85] including

[69] Cf. G.B.R., B 3/42, p. 80.
[70] O.S. Map 6″, Glos. XXV. SE. (1889 and 1903 edns.); XXXIII. NE. (1891 and 1903 edns.).
[71] Glos. R.O., Q/SRh 1884 D.
[72] Glos. Colln. R 35.8; G.B.R., B 6/33/1, p. 77.
[73] G.B.R., B 6/33/1, p. 47; Glos. Colln. (H) G 4.16; Glos. R.O., D 2299/5726.
[74] Glos. R.O., IN 75.
[75] Glos. Colln. JF 4.6, p. 43; R 35.8; G.B.R., B 6/33/1, pp. 60–1, 65, 70, 247, 260.
[76] G.B.R., B 6/33/1, pp. 65, 143–5; Glos. R.O., HB 8/M 1/6, pp. 74, 144; O.S. Map 6″, Glos. XXXIII. NE. (1891 and 1903 edns.).

[77] Census, 1891–1911; Gentry, Tramways of W. of Eng. 81–2.
[78] Who's Who in Glouc. (1910), 46; G.B.R., B 6/33/1, p. 143.
[79] Verey, Glos. ii. 254.
[80] Glouc. Jnl. 23 June 1894; Glos. Chron. 30 Oct. 1920.
[81] Glos. Chron. 1 Sept. 1883; Kelly's Dir. Glos. (1856), 300.
[82] Glouc. Jnl. 25 Mar. 1905; 2 Dec. 1933; for plans, Glos. R.O., D 2593.
[83] Glouc. Jnl. 30 Jan. 1926; 4 Nov. 1933.
[84] Citizen, 6 Jan. 1961.
[85] Paragraph based partly on personal observation.

Lower Tuffley[86] and Longlevens[87] south and north-east of Gloucester respectively. To the south-east beyond Saintbridge the inclosure of the open fields of Upton St. Leonards in 1897 released land for building,[88] one development comprising six pairs of cottages at Awefield Pitch, but Matson on the east side of Robins Wood Hill was largely untouched.[89] South-west of Gloucester a few houses were built in Hempsted village along the road to Hempsted bridge. Beyond the village towards the Severn a row of cottages had been built near brickworks at Lower Rea by 1882 and some cottages were erected at Upper Rea in the early 20th century.[90] North of the city Longford and Twigworth, which had been given a church and a school in the mid 19th century,[91] remained essentially rural. At Longford, the population of which rose between 1891 and 1901 from 521 to 673,[92] a short street of semidetached cottages laid out *c.* 1900 attracted artisans from the city.[93] There was little new building further out at Twigworth, whose population in the later 19th century usually stood at *c.* 180.[94]

After the First World War redevelopment of the city centre continued in a piecemeal fashion. The appearance of the main streets was governed almost entirely by commercial interests which replaced many buildings and shop fronts. Most rebuilding in the 1920s and 1930s was in Northgate and Eastgate Streets which contained the largest stores.[95] Part of the Northgate Street frontage of the New Inn, which included two shops, was restored in 1925.[96] There were several new developments at the west end of Barton Street where the co-operative society's stores on the corner of Brunswick Road were rebuilt in 1931.[97] Holloway House on the north side opened in 1936 as offices for the Gloucester Conservative Benefit Society.[98] At the west end of London Road several houses had been replaced by the early 1920s by the garage of the Bristol Tramways & Carriage Co., which was later enlarged and became the city's bus depot.[99] Several new cinemas appeared in the main streets and the Theatre de Luxe in lower Northgate Street was given a classical portico during alterations to designs by local architect William Leah in 1922.[1] Important buildings outside the principal streets included the employment exchange of 1935 in Commercial Road and the technical college of 1938–41 at Friars Orchard in Brunswick Road.[2]

As a result of commercial development several lanes and courts in the city centre disappeared, particularly in Northgate Street where Dolphin Lane leading to St. Aldate Square was closed in 1926.[3] In the largest scheme the Oxbode, leading off Northgate Street in the place of Oxbode Lane, and King's Square were formed between 1927 and 1929 by the demolition of shops and slum dwellings in an area also touching St. Aldate Street, King Street, and New Inn Lane.[4] The north side of the Oxbode was filled by a large building of 1928–31 to a design of Thomas Overbury of Cheltenham for the Bon Marché store,[5] and the south side by smaller shops beginning

[86] O.S. Map 6″, Glos. XXXIII. NW. (1888 and later edns.).
[87] Ibid. XXV. SE. (1889 and later edns.).
[88] Cf. Glos. R.O., Q/RI 149; Glos. Colln. RF 321.1, 3.
[89] O.S. Map 6″, Glos. XXXIII. NE. (1891 and later edns.).
[90] Ibid. NW. (1888 and later edns.).
[91] Below, Churches and Chapels, mod. par. ch., St. Matthew; Educ., elem. educ., voluntary sch.; cf. G.B.R., B 6/33/1, p. 244.
[92] *Census*, 1891–1901.
[93] Nat. Soc. files, Twigworth; O.S. Map 6″, Glos. XXV. SE. (1903 edn.).
[94] *Census*, 1851–1911.
[95] *Glouc. Jnl.* 25 Jan. 1936; 27 Mar. 1937; for Northgate Street, cf. Glouc. R.O., GPS 154/138–9.

[96] Glouc. Colln. NF 1.1; *Glouc. Jnl.* 2 May 1925.
[97] *Glouc. Jnl.* 14 Nov. 1931.
[98] Ibid. 5 Dec. 1936.
[99] O.S. Map 1/2,500, Glos. XXV. 15 (1902 and later edns.); G.D.R., F 4/6/14.
[1] Glos. Colln. NR 29.30–2; *Glouc. Jnl.* 22 Apr. 1922; for the Theatre de Luxe portico (demolished 1959) and interior (burnt 1939), Glos. Colln. 37156 (56); *Glouc. As It Was*, 39.
[2] *Glouc. Jnl.* 8 June 1935; *Glouc. Municipal Year Bk.* (1964–5), 81.
[3] G.B.R., G 3/SRh 4.
[4] *Glouc. Municipal Year Bk.* (1964–5), 93–4; Glos. Colln. NV 2.8; cf. Min. of Health Provisional Orders Confirmation (No. 8) Act, 1925, 15 & 16 Geo. V, c. 84 (Local); for photogs., Glos. Colln. 37156 (12–51).
[5] *Glouc. Jnl.* 14 Mar. 1931; Glos. Colln. NR 15.10.

in 1929 with Oliver's store at the entrance from Northgate Street.[6] At the east end of that range the city's central post office, opened in 1934,[7] faced King's Square, which was a car park and bus station until the 1960s. On the north side of the square a cinema planned before the Second World War was not completed until 1956.[8]

The pace of slum clearance increased in the 1930s, beginning under orders confirmed in 1932 with 150 houses in courts and lanes in the Archdeacon Street and Island areas. In the later 1930s there were clearance throughout the city, mostly in older areas such as Hare Lane, St. Catherine Street, Quay Street, and lower Southgate Street.[9] Slum clearances and commercial developments greatly reduced the population of the older part of the city and many people were rehoused in new estates on the outskirts.[10] The west part of the city continued to decay as the suburbs spread southwards and eastwards, and shops in lower Westgate Street closed in even greater numbers after the formation of the Oxbode and King's Square.[11]

The new schemes of the corporation and of commercial interests in the 20th century led to the demolition of many old buildings and, in the main streets, of prominent buildings of a more recent date, including the former corn exchange (1938) and the early and mid 19th-century banks. At the Spa the pump room was demolished in 1960.[12] In the mid 1930s two ancient buildings in lower Westgate Street, including the putative lodging of Bishop John Hooper before his execution, were restored as a folk museum[13] and Sir Philip Stott, Bt., saved the early 16th-century Old Raven Tavern in Hare Lane from destruction.[14] At the quay the Round House, the remains of the late 17th century glasshouse that had once been a notable landmark in the western prospect of Gloucester, was demolished in 1933.[15] From the late 1920s overhead electricity transmission lines on the meadows west of the city intruded into that prospect.[16] In Castle Meads, where a transforming station was completed in 1933,[17] the corporation's power station, a prominent feature built in the early 1940s,[18] was removed in the early 1970s. Gloucester suffered little bomb damage during the Second World War, the worst air raid destroying 18 houses and a mission church in the Millbrook Street area in 1941.[19]

To prevent traffic congestion in the city centre and to give work to the unemployed a bypass road, running north-east from Westgate bridge round three sides of the city to the Bristol road, was begun in the early 1930s. It incorporated Finlay Road, which had been built on the south-east side of the city between 1925 and 1927,[20] and, with the construction of St. Oswald's Road from the bridge to the Tewkesbury road north of Kingsholm, Estcourt Road linking the Tewkesbury and Barnwood roads, and Eastern Avenue running east of the railway line bypassing Gloucester, had been almost completed to the Stroud road at Tuffley by 1938.[21] It was finished in 1959 when Cole Avenue, completing the link between Tuffley and the Bristol road north of Quedgeley, was opened,[22] but traffic between South Wales and Bristol continued to follow the route along the quay and Commercial Road into Southgate Street.[23]

[6] Date on bldg.; cf. Glos. Colln. NV 28.2.
[7] *Citizen*, 13 June 1934.   [8] Glos. Colln. NR 29.30.
[9] *Reps. of Medical Off. of Health, 1931–45*: copies in Glos. Colln. N 12.141 (41–7) and NR 12.44.
[10] Glos. Colln. N 15.30, p. 67.
[11] Glos. Colln. 28622 (3), p. 7.
[12] Verey, *Glos.* ii. 244–52; *Glouc. Municipal Year Bk.* (1964–5), 78; *Glouc., a Pictorial Rec.* 19, 24, 47, 59.
[13] Glos. Colln. NF 1.3.
[14] *Rep. of Medical Off. of Health, 1935*: copy in Glos. Colln. N 12.141 (45); *Glouc. Jnl.* 4 Jan. 1936; G.B.R., public health department, slum clearance rec., photog. 14, reproduced above, Plate 25.

[15] *Glouc. Jnl.* 12 Aug. 1933.
[16] G.B.R., B 3/62, pp. 107–8, 131; Glos. Colln. JR 13.9.
[17] *Glouc. Official Guide* (1933), 93; (1956), 95.
[18] Below, Public Services; *Glouc. Official Guide* (1947), 127.
[19] *Citizen Centenary Suppl.* 1 May 1976.
[20] *Glouc. Jnl.* 18 May, 28 Sept. 1929; Glos. Colln. NF 12.16.
[21] O.S. Map 6″, Glos. XXV. SE., SW. (1938 edn.); XXXIII. NE. (1938 edn.).
[22] Glos. Colln. N 12.401 (1–5); for the bypass, above, Fig. 1.
[23] Cf. G.B.R., B 3/70 (1), p. 781.

By building 2,115 houses between 1919 and 1939 the city corporation contributed greatly to Gloucester's growth after the First World War. Large estates were created in the south, in the Linden Road, Tuffley Avenue, and Tredworth Road areas, and in the years 1924–5 several houses were built on a new section of the Painswick road at Saintbridge. From 1927 the corporation also built houses at Kingsholm and developed estates on the south-east side of the city at Finlay Road (602 houses between 1927 and 1931) and Coney Hill (474 houses between 1931 and 1939).[24] Many houses were built privately, most of them adjoining the Tewkesbury, Cheltenham, Barnwood, Painswick, and Hempsted roads in areas added to the city in 1935 and 1951. Before the Second World War most private development was in the Cheltenham Road area, where Estcourt Road and Oxstalls Lane were built up and many new roads formed, but the largest houses were sited at Tuffley on the side of Robins Wood Hill. Suburban development in Lower Tuffley began in 1939 with houses in the Randwick Road area, in the angle of Tuffley Lane and Grange Road, for staff of the R.A.F. maintenance unit in Quedgeley.[25] The suburbs also spread beyond the city boundary, particularly in Longlevens where building was under way on the Elmbridge Court estate in the later 1930s.[26] Outlying villages such as Longford, Barnwood, Hucclecote, and Hempsted became increasingly suburban in character. Among new houses in Barnwood were four pairs of cottages in Welveland Lane built between 1927 and 1935 for staff of Barnwood House Hospital.[27] Hucclecote's development, influenced by the construction of an airfield between the village and Brockworth in 1915 and even more by the establishment of an aircraft factory there in the later 1920s,[28] included in 1920 fourteen council houses at Dinglewell, one of the Gloucester rural district's first housing schemes.[29] During the Second World War army barracks were erected on the north-east side of Robins Wood Hill near Matson[30] and some non-residential building took place on the bypass in Eastern Avenue.

From the mid 1950s land near the bypass in St. Oswald's Road, Eastern Avenue, and Cole Avenue was used for industrial development and some firms moved there from the city centre.[31] The cattle market was moved to St. Oswald's Road between 1955 and 1958 and the offices of some public services were transferred to Eastern Avenue.[32] The four streets meeting at the Cross remained the centre of commercial activity, but the opening of a bus station on the former cattle market site in 1962[33] increased the trade of the shopping area between Northgate Street and Eastgate Street. There was some road widening at the Cross in the later 1950s, when the body of St. Michael's church was replaced by shops and the shops on the north-east corner were rebuilt.[34] To relieve traffic congestion in the surrounding streets an inner ring road was begun. The first section, running east of the bus station between London Road and Station Road and known as Bruton Way, was opened in 1962.[35] At the same time the Kimbrose was built from Southgate Street to Commercial Road as part of the ring road, which included the route along the quay[36] and joined the bypass in the Island by a gyratory road system, completed in 1961, around St. Bartholomew's

[24] *Glouc. Municipal Year Bk.* (1964–5), 88–9; G.B.R., L 6/12/4.

[25] G.B.R., B 3/72 (1), p. 1037; 73 (1), pp. 314, 369, 841; 73 (2), p. 1018.

[26] Ibid. 72 (1), pp. 130–1, 661–2; O.S. Map 6″, Glos. XXV. SE. (1938 edn.).

[27] Glos. R.O., D 3725, Barnwood Ho. Trust, rep. 1927–35.

[28] D. N. James, *Gloster Aircraft since 1917* (1971), 5, 18.

[29] Glos. R.O., DA 27/114/1, p. 14.

[30] Glos. Colln. N 3.61, pp. 27, 39.

[31] G.B.R., L 6/12/2, p. 75; *Glouc. Official Guide* (1963), 104.

[32] *Glouc. Municipal Year Bk.* (1964–5), 76, 86; *Citizen,* 10 July 1970.

[33] Glos. Colln. N 12.453.

[34] *Glouc. Jnl.* 22 Feb. 1958; *Citizen,* 14 May, 26 Sept. 1958.

[35] Glos. Colln. NV 12.29.

[36] *Citizen,* 8 May, 2 Nov. 1962; 5 July 1963.

Hospital.[37] Gloucester's traffic problem was eased by the opening in 1966 of the Severn Road Bridge linking Bristol and South Wales,[38] but Westgate bridge remained an obstacle until the early 1970s when Over causeway was replaced by a new western approach road and the gyratory system in the Island was improved. The opening in 1971 of the Birmingham–Bristol motorway east of the city reduced traffic on the bypass.[39] By 1975 the movement of road traffic in the city had also been helped by the closure of most of the railway level crossings, notably those at Sudbrook and in Barton Street.[40] Work on the inner ring road, proposals for which had been modified,[41] resumed in the early 1980s and in 1983 the section between Worcester Street and the park, incorporating parts of Station Road and the former Tuffley loop railway line, was completed. George Street was replaced in two stages by the ring road, and between 1970 and 1984 the Post Office transferred its operations from there to Eastern Avenue.[42]

In the 1960s and 1970s the main streets of the city centre, including lower Northgate Street, were increasingly dominated by branches of chain stores, bank, and building societies. The principal developments were connected with the formation of two pedestrian shopping precincts with car parking at roof level linked by bridges over Eastgate Street and Southgate Street. The Eastgate shopping centre, developed by an associate company of Land Improvements Ltd.,[43] was created between 1966 and 1974 by the reconstruction of an area touching Eastgate Street, Queen Street, Constitution Walk, Greyfriars, and Southgate Street and including the Eastgate market, Suffolk House, Bell Lane, and the Bell hotel. It incorporated a new market hall south of Bell Lane, which became a covered way, and a large new Woolworth's store fronting Eastgate and Southgate Streets. The market portico, which was moved, formed an entrance to the precinct from Eastgate Street. The remains of the Greyfriars church were restored and an area to the north was landscaped, and the Greyfriars bowling green was retained. Queen Street became a covered pedestrian way,[44] and Boots The Chemists Ltd. filled the area between it and Brunswick Road with a new store, opened in 1980. The other pedestrian precinct, developed by Norwich Union Insurance Societies,[45] centred on King's Square, where in the early 1960s the west side had been filled by an extension of the Bon Marché store[46] and showrooms had been built on the east side for the Midlands Electricity Board.[47] Beginning in 1969 the square was landscaped and new shops were built on the south and east sides and in King Street, which became a covered pedestrian way. The scheme, which also involved closing Dog Lane and rebuilding the west side of Clarence Street, was completed in 1972.[48] Rebuilding on the north side of the square was finished in 1984 under a different scheme, which included the south side of lower Northgate Street where several large stores had been built, notably the Tesco supermarket on the site of the Methodist chapel demolished in 1973.[49] As suggested by G. A. Jellicoe in his plan for the city centre, a pedestrian way called the Via Sacra was formed using some of the ancient streets to link the new shopping areas with historic buildings, including the cathedral.[50]

[37] *Glouc. Official Guide* (1963), 101.
[38] *Glouc. Planning Handbk.* (1972), 20.
[39] *Citizen*, 6 Apr. 1971.
[40] Ibid. 1 Dec. 1975; cf. Glos. Colln. 28622 (1), p. 4.
[41] Glos. Colln. NV 12.29; *Citizen*, 12 Nov. 1975.
[42] *Citizen*, 10 July 1970.
[43] *Municipal Jnl.* 29 Oct. 1965, p. 3685.
[44] *Glouc. Official Guide* (1980), 23; cf. *Citizen*, 28 Jan. 1964.
[45] *Municipal Jnl.* 29 Oct. 1965, p. 3689.
[46] *Citizen*, 22 Oct. 1964.
[47] *Trans. B.G.A.S.* lxxvii. 5–6; *Kelly's Dir. Glouc.* (1963), 103.
[48] *Glos. Co. Gazette*, 20 May 1972; *Glouc. Official Guide* (1980), 23.
[49] *Citizen*, 4 Mar. 1976; 22 Dec. 1983; 31 Jan. 1973.
[50] Glos. Colln. 33014; 39449.

During the same period many streets just outside the city centre were affected by office and commercial development and several prominent buildings were demolished, notably in 1984 the former infirmary in lower Southgate Street. Large extensions to the Shire Hall from the early 1960s replaced buildings on the east side of Upper Quay Street and south side of Bearland and Quay Street, including the former militia barracks.[51] In Spa Road, Waterloo House gave way in the later 1960s to offices called Cedar House for the city council's planning department. In Brunswick Road there were new buildings in the late 1960s and early 1970s for the technical college.[52] In Great Western Road, the east side of which was filled from the early 1960s with additional hospital buildings,[53] the Post Office erected an eight-storeyed block for its telecommunications services in the late 1960s on the site of the former workhouse, finally demolished in 1961.[54] South-east of the city centre building on abandoned railway land began with Twyver House, the land registry's offices opened in Bruton Way in 1968,[55] and continued after the closure of Eastgate station in 1975.[56] With the decline of the port and of older industries in the 1970s and early 1980s, parts of the docks and High Orchard were cleared and factories in several parts of the city were replaced by industrial or trading estates. New factories were built in the Bristol Road and Llanthony areas, which together remained the city's principal industrial quarter, and new industrial estates continued to be established along parts of the bypass road.[57] From 1967 the land between Barnwood and a new bypass road to the north was used largely for commercial development,[58] and outside the city factories and warehouses were built on the former airfield between Hucclecote and Brockworth from the early 1960s.

Slum clearance programmes from the mid 1950s were followed by the comprehensive redevelopment of parts of lower Westgate Street and Kingsholm.[59] In the Westgate Street scheme, which covered the area north of the street between the cathedral precinct and St. Oswald's Road, the buildings below St. Nicholas's church, many of them derelict shops, were replaced by council maisonettes and flats, beginning in 1956 with 64 dwellings at the corner of Archdeacon Street.[60] The Duke of Norfolk's House was demolished in 1971, and rebuilding east of the former Swan Lane finished in the early 1980s. Archdeacon Street was continued to the junction of St. Mary's Street and Pitt Street in 1961,[61] and in the late 1960s the area north of St. Mary's Square was built up with houses for clergy and flats for old people. On the south side of Westgate Street a block of flats on the corner of Lower Quay Street was completed in 1984. At Kingsholm the area north-east of Alvin Street was almost totally cleared and rebuilt with council maisonettes and flats in the 1960s, including an 11-storeyed tower block completed in 1963.[62] In 1983 the municipal charity trustees built a block of old people's flats in Sherborne Street. Other parts of the city were subject to sporadic clearance, and in the 1970s and early 1980s improvement schemes were carried out in the High Street, Alma Place, Millbrook Street, and Victoria Street areas.[63] In the Prince Street area most houses were demolished to make way for the

[51] Below, Public Buildings; *Citizen*, 4 Aug. 1962; 24 Jan. 1964.

[52] *Glouc. Official Guide* (1980), 49.

[53] Below, Hosp., general infirmaries; maternity hosp.

[54] *Citizen*, 18 Aug. 1970; Glos. Colln. NF 12.384.

[55] Glos. Colln. N 12.331; *Glouc. Official Guide* (1980), 25.

[56] *Citizen*, 1 Dec. 1975.

[57] *Guide to Ind. Estates in Glos.* (Glos. Co. Planning Dept., 1984).

[58] Glos. R.O., D 3725, Barnwood Ho. Trust, rep. 1966–73.

[59] Glos. Colln. 28622 (1–3).

[60] *Municipal Jnl.* 11 July 1958, pp. 1742–3; Glos. Colln. N 3.17.

[61] *Glouc. Official Guide* (1963), 101.

[62] *Architects' Jnl.* 6 Sept. 1964, pp. 643–5; *Glouc. Municipal Year Bk.* (1964–5), 92; G.B.R., L 6/12/4.

[63] *Glouc. Planning Handbk.* (1972), 29–30; (1977), 31; *Glouc. Official Guide* (1980), 55; Glos. Colln. 41085, p. 13.

leisure centre built between 1972 and 1974,[64] and in the 1970s a private developer replaced the houses between Whitfield Street and Bedford Street with new flats.

Gloucester's suburban development after the Second World War was on a vast scale. The corporation began building houses at Podsmead and Lower Tuffley in the south in 1946, at Elmbridge in the north-east in 1949, and at Matson in the south-east in 1951. By 1963 those estates comprised 487, 779, 380, and 1,717 dwellings respectively; the Lower Tuffley estate included houses and flats by the Stroud road south of Tuffley.[65] Piecemeal development, mostly private, continued beyond the city boundary, particularly in Longlevens, Barnwood, and Hucclecote, and included building at the Wheatridge between Saintbridge and Upton St. Leonards to the south-east.[66] Gloucester rural district council in 1956 resumed building in Hucclecote[67] and in the early 1950s built houses at Innsworth,[68] north-east of the city near the R.A.F. station in Churchdown, where later there was private development. The only suitable building land left in the city in the mid 1960s was at Lower Tuffley.[69] The boundary extension of 1967 added a large area to the east between the Painswick road and Barnwood and Hucclecote, which was used for extensive private housing, beginning in 1971 with the Heron Park estate (1,000 houses) between Saintbridge and Coney Hill Hospital[70] and including from 1980 the Abbeydale estate (3,500 houses proposed) between the Wheatridge and Hucclecote.[71] Most other houses built between 1967 and 1985, including extensive estates at Lower Tuffley and small infill schemes, were also private, but 378 houses on an estate which replaced the Robins Wood Hill barracks at Matson after 1974 were built by the city council.[72] Hempsted and Hucclecote villages, which had been absorbed by the city, were built up and in Barnwood most of Barnwood House Hospital was demolished in 1969 to make room for houses.[73] Outside the city suburban development continued at Innsworth and was stimulated at Longford by the construction in the early 1980s of an outer northern bypass. The traffic problem was also eased by the opening in 1966 of the Barnwood bypass, which ran north of Barnwood and Hucclecote between Eastern Avenue and Ermin Street,[74] and in 1972 of a link road between that bypass and the Cheltenham road at Elmbridge.[75] The outer northern bypass, which ran from Elmbridge and across the Tewkesbury road and Walham to a junction with the Chepstow and Ledbury roads on Alney Island, was completed in 1983.[76]

[64] *Glouc. Official Guide* (1980), 57.
[65] *Glouc. Municipal Year Bk.* (1964–5), 89–92; *Glouc. Official Guide* (1963), 101; cf. G.B.R., L 6/12/4.
[66] G.B.R., L 6/12/2, pp. 92–102.
[67] Ibid. 12/4.
[68] Glos. R.O., CP/M 3/4/1–2.
[69] *Glouc. Official Guide* (1963), 101; cf. G.B.R., L 6/12/2, p. 106.

[70] *Glouc. Planning Handbk.* (1972), 28–9.
[71] Glos. Colln. 40266, p. 23; *Citizen*, 1 Dec. 1983.
[72] *Glouc. Planning Handbk.* (1979), 25; Glos. Colln. N 3.61, p. 39.
[73] *Citizen*, 1 Oct. 1969; *Brockworth News*, 13 Aug. 1970.
[74] *Glouc. Official Guide* (1980), 21.
[75] *Glos. Echo*, 14 Oct. 1972.
[76] For main roads in mid 1980s, above, Fig. 1.

BRIDGES, GATES, AND WALLS

BRIDGES.[1] The main road out of Gloucester towards the west was carried across three branches of the river Severn and low-lying meadow by a series of bridges and a long causeway. The bridges and causeway evidently existed in some form by 1086 when Highnam manor at the western end was included in a hundred called 'Tolangebriges'.[2] 'Gloucester bridge' was a landmark in the perambulation of the Forest of Dean before Henry II's reign.[3] The history of Over bridge, spanning the western branch of the river, is given in another volume,[4] and a bridge across the eastern branch giving access to Gloucester castle is mentioned below.[5]

The easternmost branch of the river, known as the Old or Little Severn[6] and, later, Dockham ditch,[7] was crossed by the Foreign bridge. The name of the bridge, though not found recorded before 1493,[8] presumably derived from an early period when the Old Severn marked the western limit of the town's liberties. The bridge, which was repaired by the corporation out of the communal funds,[9] had seven stone arches c. 1540[10] and at the beginning of the 18th century was a substantial structure with cutwaters.[11] As a result of the filling in of the northern part of the Old Severn before the early 17th century[12] the volume of water under the bridge was much reduced and most of the arches rendered unnecessary; by the 1820s several had been built over and hidden from view.[13] Dockham ditch was culverted below the bridge in 1825[14] and north of the bridge the channel was filled in in 1853 as part of a programme of sanitary improvements in the city.[15] Further down Westgate Street beyond St. Bartholomew's Hospital a smaller bridge, of one or two arches, called Cole bridge, carried the road across Cole brook, a watercourse which drained the meadows.[16] It was demolished in the late 18th century or the early 19th.[17]

Westgate bridge, or the west bridge, crossed the central branch of the Severn at the western limit of the town. In 1355 it was stated that a chaplain called Nicholas Walred began building the bridge in Henry II's reign and that a house established nearby as lodgings for the workmen and for the care of the sick was the origin of St. Bartholomew's Hospital;[18] that record presumably related to a rebuilding, perhaps the building of the first stone structure. The brothers of St. Bartholomew's assumed responsibility for the upkeep of the bridge. They were described as the wardens and preachers of Gloucester bridge in 1221,[19] though at the same time the incumbent of St. Nicholas's church claimed the custody of the bridge;[20] if there was any dispute over the matter it was presumably resolved a few years later when the church was granted to the hospital. In 1264 Henry III gave four oaks to the hospital for the repair of the bridge, which had been broken down, presumably in the recent fighting in the town,[21] and the brothers were collecting alms for its repair in 1266.[22] In the late 1280s the archbishop of York granted an indulgence for those aiding further repairs, the brothers because of their poverty undertaking to use their own labour.[23] In 1456 a grant of protection was made on behalf of four representatives of the hospital who were journeying through the country seeking alms for repairs.[24] Walter Bridgeward, who lived in a house adjoining the bridge in 1451, was presumably employed by the hospital to supervise the works.[25]

By the beginning of the 16th century, however, the burgess community, for whose prosperity the bridge was vital, had accepted the greater part of the burden of repairing Westgate bridge. In 1505 the mayor and burgesses, in support of their claim to levy tolls on passing trows, said that they owned the bridge and were responsible for the repairs, having spent 300 marks on it during the previous three years.[26] The work on the bridge, and on Over causeway beyond it, was also aided at that period by bequests of money from many individual burgesses,[27] and there were more substantial endowments from some eminent inhabitants. Alderman John Capel (d. 1505) left his lease of White Barn farm at Kingsholm, from 10 years after his death, to the care of two burgesses chosen by the mayor, who were to use the profits to buy stone for the bridge; the labour was to be provided by the hospital and any surplus funds were to be used on stone for the Foreign bridge and the quay.[28] Joan Cooke charged the endowment she made in 1540 for the Crypt school with £5 a year for repairs to the bridge and Over causeway,[29] and Thomas Bell and his wife Joan in 1542 assigned property to the corporation from

---

[1] This article was written in 1982.
[2] *Dom. Bk.* (Rec. Com.), i. 165v.
[3] *Close R.* 1227–31, 99.
[4] *V.C.H. Glos.* x. 15–16.
[5] Below, Glouc. Castle.
[6] *Hist. & Cart. Mon. Glouc.* (Rolls Ser.), iii. 257; Glouc. Cath. Libr., Reg. Abb. Malvern, ii, f. 8v.; G.B.R., J 4/12, nos. 13, 125; Counsel, *Glouc.* 68, 153.
[7] G.B.R., F 4/3, f. 302v.; Causton, *Map of Glouc.* (1843).
[8] G.B.R., F 4/2.
[9] Ibid. 2; 3, f. 134.
[10] Leland, *Itin.* ed. Toulmin Smith, ii. 57–8.
[11] Atkyns, *Glos.* plate at pp. 82–3, detail reproduced above, Fig. 7.   [12] Below, Outlying Hamlets, intro.
[13] Counsel, *Glouc.* 68, 153.
[14] *Rep. Com. Mun. Corp.* 67; G.B.R., J 3/13, p. 452; J 4/12, nos. 7–8.

[15] G.B.R., N 2/1/1, p. 741.
[16] Leland, *Itin.* ed. Toulmin Smith, ii. 58; G.B.R., F 4/5, f. 398; J 3/16, ff. 4, 80; J 5/2.
[17] Rudder, *Glos.* 88; Fosbrooke, *Glouc.* 66.
[18] *Cal. Inq. Misc.* iii, p. 80.
[19] *Pat. R.* 1216–25, 320.
[20] *Hist. & Cart. Mon. Glouc.* i. 321–2.
[21] *Close R.* 1264–8, 9.   [22] *Cal. Pat.* 1258–66, 595.
[23] *Reg. Romeyn,* i (Surtees Soc. cxxiii), p. 10.
[24] *Cal. Pat.* 1452–61, 289.
[25] *Glouc. Corp. Rec.* p. 398.
[26] *Select Cases in Star Chamber,* i (Selden Soc. xvi), 211–12.
[27] e.g. Hockaday Abs. ccxiii, 1534; ccxvi, 1506, 1528; ccxix, 1522; ccxx, 1488, 1490, 1492.
[28] G.B.R., B 2/1, ff. 237v.–8; cf. ibid. f. 26v.
[29] Austin, *Crypt Sch.* 154–5.

after their deaths, to be used initially for repairing the bridge and causeway.[30] Full legal responsibility for the bridge (if it had not assumed it earlier) would have passed to the corporation when it took control of St. Bartholomew's Hospital in the 1560s.[31]

Westgate bridge was described as having four arches in 1447,[32] as a great bridge of freestone, arched and embowed, in 1505,[33] and as having five great arches c. 1540.[34] Part of the bridge was taken down and replaced by a drawbridge at the time of the siege of 1643,[35] and in 1727 it comprised two arches spanned with brick and stone and two spanned with planks of timber.[36] Later in the 18th century, when the bridge and the west gate leading on to it formed a favourite subject for artists, only one of the irregularly built arches was formed of timber.[37] Work on the bridge was a regular item of corporation expenditure in the 17th and 18th centuries.[38] Floods and ice often caused damage in the winter months, and in its disputes with the trowmen over tolls the corporation claimed that hooking and grappling in order to haul boats through the arches was another regular cause of damage.[39] A capstan for hauling boats through was installed at the bridge in 1569 or 1570[40] and was still in use in the 1720s.[41]

In 1806 an Act of Parliament empowered commissioners, including the full corporation, to levy tolls for rebuilding the bridge.[42] The work was carried out between 1813 and 1816[43] while traffic was diverted over a temporary wooden bridge built alongside. The new bridge, a single arch of stone, was designed by Robert Smirke, the commissioners having decided to employ an eminent architect rather than an engineer in the belief that 'the scientific principles, approved and acted upon by the ancient masters of architecture, and which have stood the test of ages' were the only ones to be relied on.[44] The tolls let for about £2,000 a year and the commissioners' expenditure would have been recouped within a few years had they not decided to go on to rebuild Over causeway, a decision that was challenged unsuccessfully in the courts. The continuance of the tolls caused much annoyance locally, culminating in the destruction of the tollhouse by a mob in September 1827. Workmen engaged on rebuilding Over bridge, who had to cross Westgate bridge on their way to and from work, began the disturbance but they were joined by many other

people, instigated, it was said, by some of the 'more respectable' townspeople. After detachments of troops had been called in to restore order, the commissioners agreed to end the tolls on foot passengers within a few weeks and all other tolls by the end of 1828.[45] Responsibility for repair of the bridge then reverted to the corporation,[46] which from 1859 until 1910 received £80 a year in aid of the maintenance of the bridge and causeway, paid in respect of Joan Cooke's bequest out of the Crypt school endowment.[47] In 1941 the arch of Westgate bridge was demolished and a steel Bailey bridge laid on the abutments.[48] That was replaced in the early 1970s by a pair of steel and concrete structures as part of a new western approach road.

Over causeway ran for c. 1,000 yd. across the meadows of Alney Island between Westgate bridge and Over bridge. By the 1540s[49] it was pierced at intervals by a series of double or single arches which allowed for the passage of water during the flooding by the river in winter. In the early 18th century there were about 17 arches in the whole length of the causeway.[50] The corporation repaired the eastern half which lay within the city boundary and had some responsibility for the other half through its administration of Joan Cooke's bequest, which applied to the whole length.[51] Responsibility for the western half was assumed in 1726 by the new Gloucester and Hereford turnpike trust. An Act of 1776 gave powers for raising and widening the causeway; the floods sometimes rose over the roadway, which on the arches was wide enough only for single-line traffic.[52] The Gloucester and Hereford trustees paid for widening and repairing seven arches and rebuilding two others in 1778, and in 1793, when a further scheme of improvement was under discussion, their half of the causeway was 12 ft. 6 in. in width and the corporation's half only 9 ft. 6 in.[53] In the early 1820s the causeway was described as ruinous and dangerous and in the years 1823–4 the Westgate bridge commissioners rebuilt the whole length with brick arches and parapet walls;[54] trees were planted along it at the corporation's expense.[55] In the early 1970s a new raised roadway was constructed on the western side of the city, based for part of its length on the existing causeway but leaving it to cross the western branch of the Severn by a new bridge upstream from Over bridge.[56]

[30] G.B.R., B 2/2, ff. 24v.–26v.
[31] V.C.H. Glos. ii. 121.
[32] Cal. Pat. 1446–52, 71.
[33] Select Cases in Star Chamber, i (Selden Soc. xvi), 211.
[34] Leland, Itin. ed. Toulmin Smith, ii. 58.
[35] G.B.R., B 3/2, pp. 317–18.
[36] P.R.O., E 134/1 Geo. II Hil./4.
[37] e.g. Glos. Colln. prints GL 5.2, 4, 8; above, Plate 41.
[38] G.B.R., F 4/5–14.
[39] Select Cases in Star Chamber, i (Selden Soc. xvi), 212; P.R.O., E 134/4 Wm. and Mary Mich./50.
[40] G.B.R., F 4/3, ff. 130v., 134.
[41] Ibid. 8, p. 493.
[42] Westgate Bridge Act, 46 Geo. III, c. 45 (Local and Personal).
[43] Glouc. Jnl. 1 Feb. 1813; 10 June 1816.
[44] Glos. R.O., D 204/4/1; and for an illustration, G.B.R., L 6/30/20.

[45] Glos. R.O., D 204/4/1; Glouc. Jnl. 29 Sept., 6 Oct. 1827.
[46] Westgate Bridge Act, 46 Geo. III, c. 45 (Local and Personal), s.49.
[47] Glos. R.O., D 3270/19679, pp. 59–60; Glos. Colln. NF 17.18, 21; NQ 17.2; in 1910 the payment was diverted to support an exhibition at the sch.
[48] Glouc. Municipal Year Bk. (1964–5), 76.
[49] Leland, Itin. ed. Toulmin Smith, ii. 58.
[50] Glos. Colln. prints GL 90.2; Glos. R.O., A 154/83, print of 1734, detail reproduced above, Plate 40.
[51] G.B.R., F 4/3, f. 30; 5, ff. 19v., 47v., 103.
[52] Maisemore Bridge and Glouc. Improvement Act, 17 Geo. III, c. 68.
[53] Glos. R.O., D 204/2/4.
[54] Ibid. 4/1.
[55] G.B.R., F 4/15, pp. 621, 625.
[56] Over bridge, closed to traffic, was preserved.

GATES AND WALLS. The inner defences of medieval Gloucester were based to a considerable extent on those of the Roman town; the walls enclosing the eastern half of the town rested on the remains of the Roman walls. On the south side the defences were continued westwards to the Severn by those of Gloucester castle and on the north side by the precinct walls of Gloucester Abbey and St. Oswald's Priory. The north wall of the abbey precinct was probably rebuilt further north in the early 13th century,[57] and whether it was the town wall or belonged to the abbey was in some doubt before 1447 when the burgess community released their claim to it, the abbey undertaking to repair it and promising not to make any new entrances in it.[58] In the inner circuit of defences there were six town gates. The road from Painswick and the Barton Street suburb entered by the east gate, or Ailes gate;[59] the Bristol road entered by the south gate; the road from Wales and Hereford entered across Westgate bridge through the west gate, which stood at the east end of the bridge; Water Street entered by the blind gate, so called by 1447,[60] at the north-west corner of the abbey precinct; the London road entered by the north gate; and Brook Street entered by the postern gate at the north-east corner of the walls. The walls around the eastern half of the town had an outer moat. Between the postern gate and the north gate the moat was provided by the southern branch of the river Twyver, and water diverted from the Twyver filled the ditch along the east and south walls. The ditch along the east wall was known as Goose ditch.[61]

On the north side of the town there were two outer gates built on the north branch of the Twyver at the limits of ancient suburbs. Alvin gate stood on the Tewkesbury road at the north end of Hare Lane and the outer north gate stood in the London road. No evidence has been found of there having been any additional defences apart from the Twyver to defend that outer area.

Archaeological evidence suggests that the town's defensive system was rebuilt soon after the Norman Conquest, the new work being based partly on the Roman defences, which may have been maintained in late Saxon times.[62] The documentary evidence for the defences begins in the next century; the north and south gates were

mentioned in the 1140s[63] and Alvin gate in 1181.[64] Murage for the upkeep of the walls and gates was granted at intervals between 1226 and the early 15th century, and the mid 13th century with grants in 1250, 1260, and 1265[65] saw a major programme of improvements. Excavation has shown that a substantial new east gate and a bastion in the wall north of the east gate were provided at that period,[66] and the postern gate at the north-east corner of the walls was apparently built c. 1250.[67] The southern half of the east wall was probably given similar defensive works at the same period, for a postern at the south end and a tower between it and the east gate were mentioned in 1509.[68] In 1266 or 1267 the burgesses, on the king's orders, enlarged the south ditch of the town, demolishing several houses in the process.[69] Much repair work was done at the end of the century under a murage grant of 1298.[70] In April 1360, when measures were being taken in response to the fear of French invasion, the walls were reported to be in a neglected state and the townspeople were ordered to repair them; when peace was made with France they left the work unfinished and a further order was made two months later.[71] The south ditch was further enlarged in 1377 when French raids on the English coast caused alarm.[72]

In the late Middle Ages five of the town gates — the east, south, west, outer north, and Alvin gates — were the official entrances for such purposes as collecting tolls and were manned by porters.[73] The inner north gate housed the main prison of the town by 1502.[74] In 1590 a gaoler's lodging was built on the east side of it, partly financed with 20 marks given by Richard Pate (d. 1588) for repairing the gates.[75] Two gates were in use as prisons in 1485;[76] the other one was probably the east gate, which housed women prisoners in 1560.[77] From at least 1613 until its demolition in the late 18th century the east gate was used as the bridewell, or house of correction.[78] The rooms in the various gates were also used in the late 16th century as meeting places for some of the trade companies.[79]

The gates were regularly repaired and maintained during the earlier 17th century.[80] During the siege of the city by the royalist army in 1643 the gates and walls provided the inner ring of defences. They were masked by an elaborate system of outer defensive works and strengthened

[57] Below, Glouc. Cath. and Close.

[58] G.B.R., B 2/1, f. 198.

[59] *Glouc. Corp. Rec.* p. 83; G.B.R., B 2/1, f. 121; for the gates, cf. above, Figs. 4–5.

[60] G.B.R., B 2/1, f. 198.

[61] *Glouc. Corp. Rec.* p. 130; G.B.R., F 4/3, f. 24v.

[62] C. Heighway, *E. and N. Gates of Glouc.* (Western Arch. Trust, 1983), 5.

[63] *Camd. Misc.* xxii, pp. 14–15; P.R.O., C 115/K 1/6681, f. 76v.

[64] Glouc. Cath. Libr., Reg. Abb. Froucester B, p. 200.

[65] *Pat. R.* 1225–32, 61, 479; *Cal. Pat.* 1232–47, 110, 225; 1247–58, 73; 1258–66, 67, 428; 1292–1301, 352; 1301–7, 68; 1307–13, 497; 1343–5, 563; 1358–61, 178; 1367–70, 188; G.B.R., F 2/3–4.

[66] Heighway, *E. and N. Gates of Glouc.* 6.

[67] A deed refers to the 'new east gate' adjoining land in St.

Aldate's parish: *Glouc. Corp. Rec.* p. 209.

[68] G.B.R., J 5/3.

[69] *Close R.* 1264–8, 343, 414; P.R.O., C 115/K 2/6685, f. 10v.

[70] G.B.R., F 2/1; *Cal. Pat.* 1291–1301, 352.

[71] *Cal. Close,* 1360–4, 25, 43.

[72] P.R.O., C 115/ K 2/6685, f. 12v.

[73] Above, Medieval Glouc., regulation of trade and ind.; Austin, *Crypt Sch.* 155. G.B.R., J 5/3 confirms that of the two N. gates it was the outer one that was manned.

[74] G.B.R., G 10/1, p. 4.

[75] Ibid. B 3/1, f. 124v.; G 12/1, f. 269.

[76] Hockaday Abs. cciii, 1485.

[77] G.B.R., F 4/3, f. 83.

[78] Ibid. B 3/1, f. 246v.; 2, p. 41; 12, ff. 104v.–105v.

[79] e.g. ibid. F 4/3, ff. 284, 302.

[80] Ibid. 5, *passim.*

against artillery fire by earth ramparts,[81] while as an additional defence on the north-west side the low-lying land of Little Meadow and Meanham was flooded.[82] Other modifications to the ancient defences at the time of the siege probably included the drawbridges at the main gates, recorded in the late 1640s.[83] Alvin gate was apparently destroyed during the siege,[84] and the south gate, battered by cannon shot, later collapsed and was rebuilt in 1644 with the inscription: 'A City Assaulted by Man, but Saved by God'.[85] In 1671 the royalist mayor Henry Fowler removed that inscription and placed the royal arms over the gate.[86] Great breaches were made in the walls under an order for slighting in 1662 and the wooden doors were taken down from the gates, most of them being given to Worcester city.[87]

As the 18th century progressed the gates were found to be obstacles to traffic. The east gate was taken down in 1778[88] and the north, outer north, and south gates were removed under an improvement Act of 1781.[89] The west gate, a substantial structure with four corner turrets,[90] was removed in 1805 or 1806 in preparation for the rebuilding of Westgate bridge.[91] The blind gate still stood in 1724[92] but in 1783 was said to have been pulled down many years previously.[93] Substantial parts of the city walls, mainly in the south-east quarter, remained until the late 19th century.[94] The sections enclosing Friars Orchard on the east and south were maintained by the owners of that property under a 100-year lease granted by the corporation in 1785,[95] and in 1888, when it conveyed Friars Orchard as the site of the Crypt school, the corporation insisted on the preservation of the wall as an object of historic interest.[96] Another section of the east wall in Constitution Walk and a section of the north wall near St. Aldate's church were still kept in repair by the corporation in the 1820s;[97] substantial remains at the former site were removed or obscured in the late 19th century when the science and art school and library were built.[98] In 1982 no part of the walls remained visible but substantial footings survived underground or in cellars.[99] The foundations of the east gate, excavated in the 1970s,[1] and those of the bastion north of it, first uncovered in 1873,[2] were preserved in viewing chambers.

GLOUCESTER CASTLE

A CASTLE[3] was built at Gloucester soon after the Norman Conquest, 16 houses having been demolished to make way for it.[4] It was placed in the custody of the sheriff of the county, Roger of Gloucester. That castle, distinguished as the old castle in 1143,[5] probably had as its motte the mound called Barbican hill, in the south-west part of the town at the south end of the later Barbican Road. Archaeological evidence, however, has led to the suggestion that the first structure was a ditched enclosure within the south-west corner of the old Roman town and that the Barbican hill motte was a later addition near the end of the 11th century.[6]

Before 1112 Walter of Gloucester built a new castle west of Barbican hill on a former garden of Gloucester Abbey, overlooking the Severn.[7] The hereditary sheriffs held Gloucester castle until 1155. Later it was retained by the Crown, passing with the borough lordship to the widows of Henry III and Edward I. Henry III often used it as a residence, and it played an important role in the barons' war of the 1260s.[8] Under the Crown the castle was the responsibility of the county sheriffs[9] and of constables appointed during pleasure or for life.[10] The perquisites of the constableship included Castle Meads, on the opposite bank of the river from the castle,[11] and a custom called the tyne of ale (later castle cowle) which was levied on the brewers of the town until the mid 16th

[81] *Bibliotheca Glos.* ii. 42–3, 214; cf. *Cal. S.P. Dom.* 1661–2, 447.   [82] Fosbrooke, *Glouc.* 71.

[83] G.B.R., F 4/5, ff. 367, 406v.–407, 434v.–435.

[84] Fosbrooke, *Glouc.* 71; cf. Glos. R.O., D 327, p. 147.

[85] G.B.R., F 4/5, ff. 237, 242v.; Rudder, *Glos.* 87.

[86] G.B.R., B 3/3, pp. 195, 478; 6, note at end; *Cal. S.P. Dom.* 1671, 419.

[87] *Cal. S.P. Dom.* 1661–2, 424, 447; Rudder, *Glos.* 88.

[88] G.B.R., B 3/11, ff. 228, 245.

[89] Glouc. Gaol and Improvement Act, 21 Geo. III, c. 74: G.B.R., F 4/13, pp. 50, 100.

[90] Glos. Colln. prints GL 5.2, 8, 12; above, Plate 41.

[91] G.B.R., F 4/14, p. 507.   [92] Ibid. B 3/9, f. 159.

[93] Ibid. F 4/13, p. 100;

[94] Cf. Rudder, *Glos.* 87; Clarke, *Archit. Hist. of Glouc.* 24.

[95] G.B.R., J 3/11, p. 403; Glos. R.O., D 3270/C 133, C 142.

[96] Glos. R.O., D 3270/19655, pp. 418, 427–8.

[97] G.B.R., F 4/15, p. 625; B 4/1/4, f. 24v.

[98] *Glouc. Jnl.* 29 Apr. 1870; *Trans. B.G.A.S.* liii, plate facing p. 272.

[99] Cf. *Trans. B.G.A.S.* liii. 267–84; lxxxvi. 5–9.

[1] Heighway, *E. and N. Gates of Glouc.*

[2] *Trans. B.G.A.S.* i. 153–5; liii. 273.

[3] This article was written in 1986.

[4] *Dom. Bk.* (Rec. Com.), i. 162.

[5] *Hist. & Cart. Mon. Glouc.* (Rolls Ser.), i, pp. lxxv–vii.

[6] H. Hurst, 'Arch. of Glouc. Castle', *Trans. B.G.A.S.* cii. 76–81. The suggestion depends partly on the theory that the Roman W. wall remained intact until the late 11th cent., which is not generally accepted: above, A.-S. Glouc.

[7] *Hist. & Cart. Mon. Glouc.* i. 235, 319; cf. *Cal. Inq. Misc.* i, p. 127.

[8] Above, Medieval Glouc., Crown and boro.; military hist.

[9] e.g. *Pipe R.* 1159 (P.R.S. i), 27; *Cal. Lib.* 1226–40, 114, 232, 312–13, 339; *Cal. Close,* 1271–9, 6.

[10] e.g. *Pipe R.* 1194 (P.R.S. N.S. v), 232; *Cal. Inq. Misc.* i, p. 127; *Rot. Litt. Pat.* (Rec. Com.), i. 71, 78; *Cal. Pat.* 1367–70, 377; 1388–92, 7; 1422–9, 5; 1441–6, 297.

[11] *Cal. Pat.* 1266–72, 209; 1441–6, 460; 1461–7, 15; *Cal. Inq. p.m.* xiii, p. 126.

century.[12] Part of the castle was being used as a gaol by 1185 and it was probably then the official county gaol, as it certainly was by 1228.[13]

A chapel in the castle and the offerings made there belonged to St. Owen's church, presumably by gift of Walter of Gloucester, and in 1137 were included in the endowment of Llanthony Priory.[14] The priory later exercised full parochial rights in the castle;[15] a claim by Gloucester Abbey to those rights was apparently not pursued after 1197.[16] The castle and its defences, together with Barbican hill which was probably maintained as an outwork, were excluded from the borough boundary in a peninsula of the county. In the post-medieval period the site formed part of the extraparochial North Hamlet.[17]

In the mid 13th century, when it had reached its fullest extent and strength, the castle and its defences covered *c.* 8 a. of the south-western sector of the town.[18] It was defended on the west by the Severn and on the other sides by moats, for most of the circuit a double line. There were three entrances. The main entrance on the north-east, leading to the town by way of Castle Lane, had inner and outer gatehouses and drawbridges over the moats. On the west a gateway opened on a bridge across the Severn, defended at its western end by a brattice; the bridge was rebuilt in 1222, and again in 1265 after its destruction in the siege of the previous year. On the south another gateway and drawbridge led to a road to Llanthony Priory. The curtain wall within the moats included towers and turrets with a tall tower over the inner gatehouse on the north-east. Within the wall were several baileys, one of which was attached to the office of county sheriff in 1222, and a vineyard and herb garden. The central feature was a massive square keep, evidently built by Walter of Gloucester in the early 12th century; it was heightened in the 1230s. A chapel adjoined the keep and was probably contemporary with it. The other buildings, most of them built in the 1240s and 1250s for Henry III and his family, included the king's and the queen's chambers, each with chapels, a great hall, and a kitchen. All of those buildings were apparently ranged round the curtain wall.

Although few additions were made to the castle after the 1260s, the defences were kept in full repair until the mid 15th century.[19] According to later tradition it was in Richard III's reign that the castle ceased to be maintained as a fortress, continuing in use later only as the county gaol.[20] The office of gaoler had become attached to the

constableship by the late 14th century,[21] and in the post-medieval period the constable, who held for life by letters patent and had custody of all of the castle buildings, usually sublet his rights to deputies, who acted as, or appointed, gaolers. In spite of early 16th-century statutes covering castles used as county gaols, the rights of the county sheriff in Gloucester castle remained vague and undefined, and in the late 17th century the constable claimed that the sheriff might house prisoners there only by agreement with him. In 1672, following a lawsuit, the sheriff established his right to use the inner yards and surviving buildings for the gaol,[22] and the constable, though his patents still included the whole site, was later required to grant leases of those parts to the county. From 1712 to 1810 the constableship was held by the Hyett family, tenants of Marybone House which adjoined the castle grounds on the north-east side.[23]

Parts of the castle buildings were demolished in 1489 and the stone used for road repairs.[24] In 1529 the city corporation was allowed to take stone from the castle for building the new Boothall, on condition that it left enough for repairs to the gaol,[25] and in the 1590s the corporation used much stone from the site for road repairs.[26] By the mid 17th century all the buildings around the curtain wall had apparently gone, leaving only the keep, used as the gaol, and the main gatehouse standing. Most of the wall itself was removed in the 1630s and 1640s, the stone being sold by the deputy constable for roadworks or burnt in a limekiln at the site. New low walls were built to enclose the gaol area, and *c.* 1650 the county authorities, who had temporarily asserted their rights against the constable, built a brick bridewell on the north side of the keep.[27] Thomas Baskerville, who visited the castle in 1683, said that the gaol was 'esteemed. . . the best in England, so that if I were forced to go to prison and make my choice I would come hither'; the prisoners' ample scope for fresh air and exercise was mentioned in 1714. The precincts included a flower garden kept by the gaoler's wife and a bowling green, used by inhabitants of the city[28] as well as by the gaoler and his prisoners.[29] The attractions of the area were enhanced in the 1740s when the constable Benjamin Hyett laid out an ornamental garden on the castle grounds to the east and south of the gaol.[30]

John Howard reported unfavourably on the county gaol in 1777, and from 1783 a leading county magistrate Sir George Onesiphorus Paul

[12] *Cal. Pat.* 1247–58, 457; 1441–6, 297; *Cal. Inq. p.m.* xiii, p. 126; P.R.O., E 134/18 & 19 Eliz. Mich./10.

[13] *Pipe R.* 1185 (P.R.S. xxxiv), 144; *Rot. Litt Pat.* (Rec. Com.), i. 78; *Pat. R.* 1225–32, 183.

[14] Dugdale, *Mon.* vi. 136.

[15] P.R.O., C 115/K 2/6685, f. 11v.; *Valor Eccl.* (Rec. Com.), ii. 430.

[16] *Hist. & Cart. Mon. Glouc.* i, pp. lxxv–viii.

[17] Ibid. iii. 257; Rudder, *Glos.* 577; Causton, *Map of Glouc.* (1843).

[18] This para. is based on Hurst, in *Trans. B.G.A.S.* cii. 81–111, a detailed account which publishes much of the documentary and visual evidence.

[19] *Cal. Pat.* 1446–52, 228; 1452–61, 415.

[20] Glos. R.O., D 326/X 3, Exchequer decree 1672.

[21] *Cal. Pat.* 1396–9, 113; 1401–5, 173; 1422–9, 226; 1485–94, 22, 390.

[22] Glos. R.O., D 326/X 3; P.R.O., E 134/24 Chas. II Mich./37.

[23] Glos. R.O., D 326/X 3; D 6/X 2, L 3; cf. *Trans. B.G.A.S.* xcix. 124.

[24] *Cal. Pat.* 1485–94, 298.

[25] G.B.R., B 2/1, f. 120.

[26] Ibid. F 4/3, ff. 307v.–308.

[27] P.R.O., E 134/17 Chas. I Trin./1; E 134/17 Chas. I Mich./1; E 134/24 Chas. II Mich./37; Glos. R.O., D 326/X 3.

[28] Hist. MSS. Com. 29, *13th Rep. II, Portland,* ii, pp. 294–5; Bodl. MS. Top. Glouc. c. 3, f. 45v.

[29] P.R.O., E 134/24 Chas. II Mich./37.

[30] *Jnl. of Garden Hist.* i (2), 168.

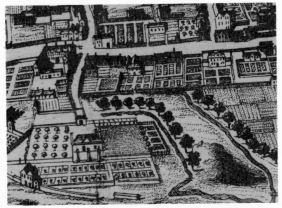

Fig. 17. Gloucester castle, *c.* 1710, with Castle Lane leading to Bearland on the north (*top*) and Barbican hill on the east

promoted its reform and rebuilding on lines advocated by Howard, including the provision of separate cells. An Act of 1785 empowered the county magistrates to build a new gaol, and they acquired for that purpose the central part of the castle site, buying out the Hyetts' interest.[31] Demolition of the castle keep began in 1787,[32] and the new gaol, designed by William Blackburn and completed under the supervision of John Wheeler,[33] was finished in 1791. The extensive, three-storeyed buildings were ranged around three quadrangles and housed a gaol, penitentiary, and house of correction; in the perimeter wall on the east side was a gatehouse.[34] In 1826, to the designs of John Collingwood, the perimeter walls were extended eastward to Barbican Road, a new debtors' prison was built east of the gatehouse of 1791, and a new gatehouse was built in the north-east part of the wall, opening on the Castle Lane approach.[35] In the years 1844–50 a new convict prison, originally organized on the 'Pentonville' separate system, was built east of the gaol of 1791. It incorporated the original gatehouse, to which large three-storey cell-blocks were added on the north and south, and on the west, linking it to the old prison, a block containing a chapel. A treadmill was built south of the old prison.[36] Among buildings added later in the mid 19th

century was a governor's house built in the south perimeter wall facing Commercial Road.[37]

In 1878, under the Prisons Act of the previous year, the buildings passed from the control of the county magistrates to become H.M. Prison, Gloucester.[38] The eastern ranges of the prison of 1791 were demolished in the late 19th century or the very early 20th, but its western range remained in use for female prisoners until *c.* 1915 when the prison became an all-male establishment. The western range was demolished *c.* 1920,[39] and in 1921 a terrace of eight houses for prison officers was being built at the north-west corner of the site, facing the road along the riverside and excluded from the secure area by an alteration in the perimeter wall.[40] In the years 1985–6 those houses and other buildings on the west part of the site were cleared and a new reception and administration block was built overlooking the road along the riverside. In 1986 the prison of the 1840s, relatively little altered since it was built, housed prisoners from the area covered by the Crown courts of Gloucester, Worcester, and Hereford, while a small new block east of it housed a unit for 'special category' prisoners, opened in 1971.[41] Of the earlier buildings the gatehouse of 1826 and the former debtors' prison, from which the top storey had been removed, still survived.

In 1816 commissioners for Crown lands sold some of the old castle grounds outside the walls of the county prison to John Phillpotts, tenant of Marybone House under the Hyetts, and Phillpotts apparently also had a grant of the constableship. Those lands included Barbican hill,[42] which was levelled *c.* 1819[43] and built over in the mid 1830s,[44] and a garden behind Marybone House, which was sold with the house when it became the police station in 1858[45] and was covered by the new police station and sessions courts in the 1960s. Castle Gardens, another part of the castle grounds lying north of the prison,[46] was used in the mid 1850s as the site for the militia barracks[47] and in the 1970s for a new wing of the Shire Hall. All the former castle grounds, except those occupied by the prison, were placed within the city boundary in 1874,[48] and the prison was included in the city in 1896.[49]

[31] J. R. S. Whiting, *Prison Reform in Glos. 1776–1820* (1975), 1–14; cf. Glos. R.O., Q/CL 1/3. The institutional hist. of the county gaol is reserved for an article on the county administration in another volume; the present article describes only the main alterations to the buildings.

[32] *Glouc. Jnl.* 9 Apr. 1787.

[33] Colvin, *Biog. Dict. Brit. Architects* (1978), 113, 881.

[34] Whiting, *Prison Reform*, 16–17, plates at pp. 90–1, and plans at front.

[35] Glos. R.O., Q/CL 1/7, 9; Counsel, *Glouc.* 173.

[36] *Glouc. Jnl.* 6 Jan. 1844; 19 Oct. 1850; F. Bond, *Hist. of Glouc.* (1848), 41–2; Bd. of Health Map (1852).

[37] Plan of prison, late 19th cent., in possession of admin. dept., H.M. Prison, Glouc.

[38] *Glouc. Jnl.* 13 Apr. 1878.

[39] Inf. from, and aerial photog. in possession of, Senior Off. B. White, H.M. Prison, Glouc.

[40] Copy of plan of 'proposed quarters', 18 Aug. 1921, in possession of works dept., H.M. Prison, Glouc.; cf. O.S. Map. 1/2,500, SO 8218 (1955 edn.).

[41] Inf. from Senior Off. White.

[42] Glos. R.O., DC/F 2/1; D 6/L 3; cf. G.B.R., J 3/13, pp. 403–4.

[43] Fosbrooke, *Glouc.* 62–3.

[44] Glos. R.O., Q/CL 1/9; above, Glouc. 1835–1985, topog.

[45] Glos. R.O., DC/SJ 2.

[46] Ibid. F 2/1.

[47] *Glouc. Jnl.* 25 Mar. 1854; 5 July 1856; cf. O.S. Map 1/2,500, Glos. XXV. 14 (1886 edn.).

[48] Glouc. Extension and Improvement Act, 37 & 38 Vic. c. 111 (Local); cf. O.S. Map 1/2,500, Glos. XXV. 14 (1886 edn.).

[49] *Census*, 1901.

BOOTHALL.[50] A building on the south side of Westgate Street, in the block between Berkeley Street and Upper Quay Lane, was the original seat of the government of the town as well as playing an important role in its commercial life. A building on or near the site was recorded as the guildhall in 1192 when the burgesses were licensed to use it for buying and selling,[51] and the Boothall was named in 1216.[52] A lease of land at the site c. 1230, granted on behalf of the guild merchant, suggests that separate parts of the same group of buildings were then known as the guildhall and the Boothall[53] but later the two names were used indiscriminately until the term guildhall lapsed altogether in the late Middle Ages. Described as 'the Boothall of the community of the town of Gloucester' in 1349,[54] the building was used for the sittings of the hundred court[55] and as a market hall; it was apparently the principal leather market in 1273,[56] and by 1396 wool was sold there and weighed on the official weighing beams.[57] In 1455, and apparently by the early 14th century, the buildings included an inn.[58]

In 1529 the corporation decided to rebuild the Boothall, using £80 of a bequest made to the town by Thomas Gloucester (d. 1447) for loans to tradesmen; the sum was to be repaid over the succeeding years out of the rents of the site and the profits of the weighing beams. The rebuilding was evidently completed before 1536.[59] Later the Boothall and the Boothall inn were granted on long leases by the corporation, which reserved the use of the main hall for sittings of the hundred court and the city assizes and quarter sessions and the use of a great chamber called the election chamber for the election of the city officers at Michaelmas (and perhaps also for the election of the M.P.s). By 1558, and perhaps from much earlier, the Boothall was also being used as the shire hall for Gloucestershire, the county assizes and quarter sessions being held there.[60] A new place for the sale of yarn was apparently provided in the building in the mid 1580s,[61] and work carried out in the years 1593–4 involved the building of a 'new hall'.[62] In 1607 the Boothall was to be rebuilt and enlarged and separate courtrooms created so that the assize courts for city and county could sit at the same time without disturbing each other.[63] In 1613 the rooms used for official purposes were the great hall and the election chamber, both described as newly built, and two other chambers, one used by the grand jury. The chambers, entered from a gallery,[64] apparently formed an upper storey at one end of the great hall, which occupied the full height of the building, its roof supported by a double row of wooden posts.[65] The south end of the hall was rebuilt in brick in 1761 following a fire,[66] but the rest of the building remained of close-studded timber-frame construction.[67] The Boothall inn, occupying the street frontage of the site,[68] was also a basically timber-framed building, but in the 18th century, apparently in the years 1742–3, it was refaced as seven bays with a central pediment, containing the city arms.[69]

From the mid 16th century the Boothall was used by visiting companies of players,[70] and concerts, plays, and performances by travelling showmen were regularly staged there in the 18th century and the early 19th.[71] The hall continued to house the wool and leather markets until at least the 18th century.[72] As courtrooms, however, the Boothall was found increasingly inadequate; by the 1770s the city quarter sessions had been moved to the Tolsey[73] and in the early years of the 19th century some of the business of the county sessions was done at the King's Head inn on the other side of Westgate Street.[74] The Boothall finally lost its role as a seat of justice in 1816 with the opening of the new Shire Hall on an adjoining site. The old hall was later used as a coach house and stables for the Boothall hotel,[75] and, following its sale by the corporation in 1868, it housed at various times a music hall, skating rink, theatre, and cinema.[76] It was largely rebuilt c. 1850[77] and again, following a fire, in the mid 1870s,[78] though sections of timber-framed walling survived the rebuildings.[79] The hall and the Boothall hotel were demolished in 1957[80] and the site was later incorporated in the extended Shire Hall.

[50] This article was written in 1982 and revised in 1986.

[51] *Pipe R.* 1192 (P.R.S. N.S. ii), 285.

[52] *Rot. Litt. Claus.* (Rec. Com.), i. 283.

[53] *Glouc. Corp. Rec.* p. 122.

[54] Ibid. p. 346.

[55] Ibid. p. 14; Glouc. Cath. Libr., Reg. Abb. Froucester B, p. 341; *Glouc. Rental, 1455,* 47.

[56] G.B.R., G 8/1.

[57] Ibid. C 9/2; B 2/1, ff. 13v.–14.

[58] *Glouc. Rental, 1455,* 47.

[59] G.B.R., B 2/1, ff. 14, 218v., 222v., 236; and for Gloucester's bequest, *Glouc. Corp. Rec.* p. 398.

[60] G.B.R., B 2/2, ff. 114–115v., 138–139v.; B 3/1, f. 201.

[61] Ibid. F 4/3, f. 233.

[62] Ibid. ff. 293v.–295v.

[63] Ibid. B 3/1, f. 220v.

[64] Ibid. f. 248 and v.; J 3/1, ff. 66v.–67.

[65] Ibid. J 4/12, no. 2; Counsel, *Glouc.* 169; *Illustrated Lond. News,* 23 Jan. 1847.

[66] G.B.R., B 3/11, f. 20; cf. Glos. R.O., GPS 154/468.

[67] Sketch in *Illustrated Lond. News,* 23 Jan. 1847, reproduced above, Plate 37.

[68] Causton, *Map of Glouc.* (1843).

[69] Glos. R.O., GPS 154/467; G.B.R., B 3/9, f. 464; F 4/9, pp. 374–5, 393; above, Plate 14.

[70] T. Hannam-Clark, *Drama in Glos.* (1928), 41–2.

[71] *Glouc. Jnl.* 10 Nov. 1766; 19 Dec. 1768; 23 Mar. 1789; 29 Dec. 1806.

[72] Ibid. 9 Apr. 1722; 19 June 1750; 24 Oct. 1752.

[73] Rudder, *Glos.* 89.

[74] *Glouc. Jnl.* 30 Sept. 1811.

[75] *Illustrated Lond. News,* 23 Jan. 1847.

[76] Hannam-Clark, *Drama in Glos.* 110; Glos. R.O., DC/F 24.

[77] *Power's Glouc. Handbk.* (1848), 90, says it had been rebuilt, but Bd. of Health Map (1852), shows only parts of the bldg. standing.

[78] *Glouc. Jnl.* 30 May 1874; 15 Jan., 30 May 1876.

[79] Glos. R.O., GPS 154/468–9; Hannam-Clark, *Drama in Glos.* 107.

[80] *Glouc. Jnl.* 18 May 1957. The arms from the hotel pediment, restored and regilded, were placed on a new bldg. at the entrance of Three Cocks Lane in 1961: plaque on bldg.

SHIRE HALL. The Shire Hall, east of the Boothall extending from Westgate Street through to Bearland, was begun in 1815 and opened the following year.[81] The cost was met by a county rate and the building was vested in the county magistrates but, as the city assizes and quarter sessions were also to use the new courtrooms, the corporation was made responsible for buying the houses that had to be cleared from the site.[82] The new building was designed by Robert Smirke. The front part, opening on Westgate Street by a tall Ionic portico said to be inspired by the temple on the river Ilissus in Greece, included a grand jury room, the office of the clerk of the peace (who had previously occupied a nearby house), and a large public room which was used for concerts during the Three Choirs festival. The rear part of the building comprised two semicircular courtrooms linked by offices and retiring rooms for the judges and counsel.[83] The front part was internally remodelled in 1896 to provide a county council chamber and new offices for the clerk of the peace, county treasurer, and county surveyor, and a substantial addition was made on its east side in the years 1909–11.[84] Various temporary buildings were put up on the west side of the Shire Hall after 1938.[85] During the early 1960s the front part of the original building was rebuilt except for the portico[86] and the whole complex was massively enlarged by blocks of offices added on the west side and extending over Bearland to connect with another new block which incorporated the county police headquarters. In the early 1970s another block was built south of Quay Street on the site of the old county militia barracks.

TOLSEY. A building which stood on the southwest corner of the Cross was presumably in use for town business by 1455 when it was owned and occupied by the stewards.[87] It was mentioned by the name Tolsey in 1507 in a context which suggests that it was the place where property deeds were filed.[88] It was rebuilt in the mid 1560s[89] and again in 1603. By the latter date it had become the venue for the meetings of the common council;[90] in 1509 and until at least 1594 the council held its meetings in a room at the east gate.[91]

In 1622 a new room was made in the Tolsey as an office for the town clerk who had previously worked from an adjoining building.[92] In 1648 there was a major rebuilding of the Tolsey when All Saints' church, which adjoined its north side, was incorporated within it. The upper floor of the new building was used for the council chamber and the ground floor for the sheriffs' court.[93] The former, in which sash windows were inserted in 1724, was jettied out over a colonnade and surmounted by a wooden balustrade.[94]

The Tolsey was rebuilt in 1751 as a two-storeyed classical building of brick with stone dressings, having a parapet surmounted by urns and, over the main front to Westgate Street, a pediment with a carving of the city arms and insignia.[95] By the later 19th century the building had become unsuitable for the increasingly complex city administration; by 1889 the town clerk and other city officers were housed in part of the nearby corn exchange,[96] and traffic noise from the streets was disturbing the councillors' meetings.[97] In 1892 the Tolsey was replaced by the new Guildhall. Sold by the corporation the following year, it was demolished and new premises for the Wilts and Dorset Banking Co. built on the site.[98] From 1843 until its sale part of the Tolsey had been used as the city post office.[99]

GUILDHALL. The new city hall, named the Guildhall, was begun in 1890 and opened in 1892 on the site on the north side of Eastgate Street formerly occupied by Sir Thomas Rich's school. The building was designed by G. H. Hunt. It extended back from Eastgate Street, on which it had a stone front in Renaissance style, as far as New Inn Lane and included offices for the town clerk, accountant, surveyor, and other officials on the ground floor and council chamber, committee rooms, mayor's parlour, and public hall on the first floor.[1] It remained in use for council meetings and as the chief executive's offices until 1985 when the council sold it to the Cheltenham and Gloucester Building Society and began moving its headquarters to a converted warehouse at the docks. Most of the city council administration was then housed in two modern office blocks, the planning and environmental departments in Spa Road and the treasurer's and housing departments on the north side of Barton Street.

CROSSES. A cross stood at the main crossroads in the centre of Gloucester by the mid 13th century.[2] In 1455, when it was known as the high cross, it was depicted as a structure with an

[81] *Glouc. Jnl.* 19 June 1815; 19 Aug. 1816.
[82] Glos. Shire Hall Act, 54 Geo. III, c. 175 (Local and Personal).
[83] *Glouc. Jnl.* 19 Aug. 1816; 22 Sept. 1817; Counsel, *Glouc.* 169–71; cf. Bd. of Health Map (1852).
[84] Glos. R.O., DC/F 6/1; *Kelly's Dir. Glos.* (1939), 183.
[85] Glos. R.O., DC/F 24–30; cf. *Glouc., a Pictorial Rec.* (John Jennings Ltd., n.d.), 40.
[86] Cf. *Glouc. Jnl.* 7 July 1962.
[87] *Glouc. Rental, 1455,* 3.
[88] G.B.R., G 10/1, p. 350.
[89] Ibid. F 4/3, ff. 114, 119, 122v.
[90] Ibid. B 3/1, ff. 196v., 198v.
[91] Ibid. J 5/3, 5; F 4/3, ff. 234 and v., 308v.; cf. ibid. J 3/1, ff. 79v.–80.

[92] Ibid. B 3/1, ff. 438v., 485v., 488v.
[93] Ibid. 2, pp. 459–60, 464; *Trans. B.G.A.S.* xix. 152–3.
[94] Glos. Colln. prints GL 20.6, reproduced above, Plate 36; G.B.R., B 3/9, f. 167v.
[95] G.B.R., B 3/10, ff. 147v.–148, 154 and v.; Glos. Colln. prints GL 7.25, reproduced above, Plate 38. The carpenter Wm. Roberts, who was paid for the work, may also have been the architect: G.B.R., F 4/10, ff. 249, 293.
[96] *Kelly's Dir. Glos.* (1889), 783.
[97] *Glouc. Jnl.* 16 July 1892.
[98] *Trans. B.G.A.S.* xix. 152–3; *Kelly's Dir. Glos.* (1894), 167.
[99] G.B.R., B 4/1/6, pp. 107, 334; Causton, *Map of Glouc.* (1843); *Glouc. Jnl.* 28 Nov. 1891.
[1] *Glouc. Jnl.* 16 July 1892.
[2] *Glouc. Corp. Rec.* p. 207.

octagonal plan and two storeys, surmounted by a spire; the upper storey had crocketed niches. The lower storey had by then been adapted as a conduit for the water supply brought by pipes from Robins Wood Hill.[3] The cross is said variously to have been rebuilt in the reigns of Henry VII and Henry VIII.[4] In 1635 it was repaired and railed off at the instigation of Bishop Godfrey Goodman who gave £20 towards the cost, and it was repaired and regilded in 1694 and 1712.[5] It was depicted in 1750 as a substantial structure, rising to over 34 ft. in height, with a lower storey of blind crocketed arches, an upper storey of eight crocketed niches containing statues of sovereigns, and an elaborate top stage with castellations and pennants. Apart from the top stage, the cross appears to have been mainly 14th-century work, though the details of the two lower storeys are difficult to reconcile with sketches made in 1455.[6] The statues on the cross were listed c. 1710 as those of King John, Henry III and Eleanor his queen, Edward III, Richard II, Richard III, Elizabeth I, and Charles I.[7] The original statue of the last sovereign, removed from the cross in 1650 or 1651 after some soldiers had defaced it, had been replaced by a new one at the Restoration.[8] The choice of John, Henry III, Richard II, and Richard III was presumably dictated by the charters of liberties granted by those kings, and of Queen Eleanor by her tenure of the lordship of the borough during her widowhood. The cross was demolished in 1751 as part of measures taken for clearing obstructions from the streets.[9]

Other medieval crosses in the town included one with a stepped plinth which stood by St. Kyneburgh's chapel at the south gate in 1455,[10] one recorded from the 13th century in the Island below St. Bartholomew's Hospital,[11] and one, mentioned in 1370, marking the borough boundary in the middle of Over causeway.[12] The cross by St. Kyneburgh had been removed by 1551, and in 1550 or 1551 two other crosses, at Alvin gate and at one of the abbey gates, were pulled down.[13] In 1647 a cross in the cathedral close, evidently a fairly large one, was demolished.[14]

KING'S BOARD. A structure known as the King's Board which stood in the middle of

Westgate Street above Holy Trinity church was, according to tradition, given to the town by Richard II[15] and on architectural grounds can be assigned to that period; the earliest documentary record found is in 1455.[16] The small size of the structure has led to the suggestion that its original function was as a preaching cross[17] but by the 1580s it was used as a butter market.[18] In 1693 its top was altered to accommodate a cistern for storing water pumped up from the Severn by the new water works built at Westgate bridge.[19] The King's Board was taken down under the improvement Act of 1750[20] and re-erected in the ornamental garden of the Hyett family on the castle grounds. When the site was taken for building the new county gaol in the 1780s the King's Board was moved to the garden of a house in Barton Street, from which it was moved by W. P. Price to the grounds of Tibberton Court in the mid 19th century.[21] In 1937 it was brought back and placed in the public gardens at Hillfield in London Road.[22]

The King's Board is decagonal on plan, having five bays of open arcading, the spandrels of the arches being carved with scenes from the life of Christ.[23] Effigies of heraldic beasts on the parapet and a pyramidal roof, surmounted by a cross, were taken down to make way for the cistern in 1693[24] and it is possible that further alterations to the form of the structure occurred during the later removals and reconstructions.

SCRIVEN'S CONDUIT. An elaborately carved conduit was put up in Southgate Street in 1636 at the cost of John Scriven and supplied with water from the Robins Wood Hill pipe.[25] It was taken down in 1784 or 1785 and moved to a garden in Dog Lane on the east side of the city. In the 1830s when that area was developed as the new Clarence Street it was moved by Edmund Hopkinson to the grounds of his house, Edgeworth Manor.[26] It was returned to Gloucester at the same time as the King's Board in 1937 and placed in the Hillfield gardens.[27]

Scriven's Conduit is an open octagonal structure in a mixture of Gothic and classical styles, having carved medallions, depicting the resources of the Vale of Gloucester, on the entablature. The

[3] *Glouc. Rental, 1455*, sketches; below, Public Services, water supply.
[4] Bodl. MS. Top. Glouc. c. 3, f. 18; Rudder, *Glos.* 88.
[5] C. H. Dancey, 'High Cross at Glouc.', *Trans. B.G.A.S.* xxiv. 299–301, 306–7.
[6] Glos. Colln. prints GL 20.6 (reproduced above, Plate 36), a print from a drawing made by Thos. Ricketts at the request of the Soc. of Antiquaries before the demolition of the cross: *Glouc. Jnl.* 5 Nov. 1751. *Trans. B.G.A.S.* xxiv. 303–4, suggests that the statues and some of the apparent medieval work shown in 1750 came from the cross in College Green demolished in the 1640s and supports the theory by the fact that the accounts for the 1635 work do not mention any statues; but those accounts appear to relate mainly to the addition of railings, a new plinth, and new water cocks, suggesting that the main part of the structure was left substantially untouched. [7] Atkyns, *Glos.* 190.
[8] G.B.R., F 4/5, f. 436v.; 6, pp. 367–8. Mr. Baldwin who carved the new statue and that of Chas. II put up soon afterwards was presumably Steph. Baldwin: Gunnis, *Dict. of Brit. Sculptors*, 36.

[9] G.B.R., B 3/10, f. 160; *Glouc. Jnl.* 5 Nov. 1751.
[10] *Glouc. Rental, 1455*, 19, and sketch no. 7.
[11] Ibid. 27, 57; P.R.O., C 115/K 1/6681, f. 94.
[12] *Hist. & Cart. Mon. Glouc.* (Rolls Ser.), iii. 257.
[13] G.B.R., F 4/3, f. 29v.
[14] Ibid. 5, ff. 341 and v., 347; B 3/2, p. 397.
[15] Bodl. MS. Top. Glouc. c. 3, f. 14.
[16] *Glouc. Rental, 1455*, 35.
[17] M. H. Medland, 'So-called King's Board at Tibberton Court', *Trans. B.G.A.S.* xxvi. 342–3.
[18] G.B.R., F 4/3, f. 238.
[19] Below, Public Services, water supply.
[10] Glouc. Improvement Act, 23 Geo. II, c. 15.
[21] *Trans. B.G.A.S.* xxvi. 339.
[22] *Glouc. Corp. Mins.* (1936–7), pp. 1855, 2022.
[23] Above, Plate 39.
[24] Bodl. MS. Top. Glouc. c. 3, f. 214 and v.
[25] G.B.R., B 3/2, p. 39.
[26] H. Medland, 'Scriven's Conduit', *Trans. B.G.A.S.* xiii. 242.
[27] *Glouc. Corp. Mins.* (1936–7), pp. 1851, 2022.

top, which may not be original, as it is said to have been rebuilt in 1705,[28] comprises an ogee-shaped open canopy, the finial carved with allegorical figures, one representing the river Severn.

STATUES. Several statues of sovereigns once adorned the main streets of the city. A statue of Charles II was set up in a niche on the north end of the wheat market house in Southgate Street in 1661 or 1662.[29] After the demolition of the market house in the 1780s, it was moved to the garden of a house at Chaxhill, Westbury-on-Severn.[30] In 1960 it was returned to Gloucester, damaged and badly weathered, and was set up in a new housing estate south of St. Mary's Square.[31] In 1686 the Catholic mayor John Hill set up a statue of James II on the conduit by Holy Trinity church, but after the Revolution of 1688 it was broken up and thrown into the Severn by soldiers quartered in the town.[32] In 1711 or 1712 a statue of Queen Anne, carved by John Ricketts, was put up near the top of Southgate Street.[33] About 1780 it was moved to the grounds of Paddock House, north of the later Pitt Street, and in 1839 to College Green.[34] In 1865 it was moved to the park at the Spa,[35] where it remained, much weathered, in 1986. A statue of George I in Roman dress, also by Ricketts, was put up in Westgate Street in 1720 and was moved to Eastgate Street near the barley market house in 1766;[36] its later history has not been traced.

In 1826 the place outside St. Mary's gateway where Bishop Hooper was burnt at the stake in 1555 was marked by a monument in the form of a small tomb, put up at the cost of J. R. Cleland of Rathgael House, co. Down.[37] A more substantial monument, paid for by public subscription, was begun in 1861 and completed in 1863. Designed by Medland and Maberly, it has an effigy of the bishop by Edward Thornhill[38] under a crocketed and pinnacled canopy. A statue of Robert Raikes, a replica of one on the Thames embankment in London, was set up in the park in 1930 to mark the third golden jubilee of the Sunday School movement.[39]

QUAY AND DOCKS

ACCORDING[40] to a tradition recorded in the early 1540s there was at one time a quay on the Old Severn near St. Oswald's Priory.[41] By the late Middle Ages most of Gloucester's river and maritime trade was conducted at the town's common quay. Vessels used the common (later the city) quay until the 20th century, but from the earlier 19th trade centred on docks and yards at the city end of the Gloucester and Berkeley canal. This account describes the development of the common quay and docks and the principal buildings connected with them. Their trade and the role which it played in Gloucester's economy are discussed in the general chapters on the city's history.

QUAY. Though not found recorded before 1390 the common quay,[42] a stone structure on the east bank of the eastern arm of the Severn below its confluence with the Old Severn (later Dockham ditch),[43] was presumably built by the burgess community at a much earlier date. It fronted waste land belonging to the borough, and in 1454 the bailiffs and stewards granted a parcel of that land by the quay's southern end to the butchers' company for the disposal of refuse.[44] About 1520 butchers, tanners, and glovers were ordered not to wash puddings, hides, and sheepskins at slipways on the quay;[45] the butchers' slip recorded in 1620 may have been on the bank just below the quay,[46] which itself had four slipways.[47] In 1505 the mayor and burgesses, in support of their claim to exact tolls on merchandise landed there, said that maintenance of the quay was a great charge,[48] and work on the quay was later a regular item of expenditure in the corporation's accounts.[49] The water bailiff, the officer responsible in 1586 for collecting the tolls on goods carried under Westgate bridge and landed at the quay, later kept the quay clean.[50] Weights kept there for assessing tolls on wood and coal were included in the lease of the Boothall inn in 1613.[51]

In 1580 the quay, known then as the king's

[28] Bodl. MS. Top. Glouc. c. 3, f. 41v.
[29] G.B.R., B 3/3, pp. 162, 222; F 4/6, p. 446.
[30] Cf. Glos. Colln. NR 1.4.
[31] Plaque on plinth.
[32] Bodl. MS. Top. Glouc. c. 3, f. 40 and v.; G.B.R., F 4/7, p. 425.
[33] G.B.R., F 4/8, p. 103; Rudder, Glos. 86.
[34] Gent. Mag. (1839) pt. i, 631.
[35] G.B.R., B 4/9/1, min. 12 June 1865.
[36] Ibid. B 3/9, ff. 73, 84v.; 11, f. 78v.; B. Martin, Natural Hist. of Eng. (1759), 354.
[37] Glouc. Jnl. 21 Sept. 1861 (suppl.); illustrated in Glos. Colln. prints GL 55.33.
[38] Glouc. Jnl. 21 Sept. 1861; 14 Feb. 1863.
[39] Ibid. 4 Oct. 1930.
[40] This article was written in 1986.
[41] Leland, Itin, ed. Toulmin Smith, ii. 57.
[42] Hockaday Abs. ccxiii.
[43] Select Cases in Star Chamber, i (Selden Soc. xvi), 212; Speed, Map of Glouc. (1610).
[44] Glos. Colln. 11664, no. 1.
[45] G.B.R., B 2/1, f. 22v.
[46] Ibid. J 3/1, p. 107; the slip was presumably at the butchers' refuse dump, in use until 1571 or later: Glos. Colln. 11664, no. 2.
[47] Speed, Map of Glouc. (1610).
[48] Select Cases in Star Chamber, i. 212; cf. G.B.R., F 4/2.
[49] G.B.R., F 4/3–16, passim.
[50] Ibid. B 3/1, ff. 101v., 218; 6, f.208; 8, pp. 117, 376; 9, ff. 69v., 114v., 425.
[51] Ibid. J 3/1, ff. 66v.–69v.

quay, was designated the principal landing place in the new port of Gloucester,[52] and the following year the city corporation built a custom house there.[53] Part was used as a warehouse by 1583,[54] and in 1630 the customs officers occupied the upper rooms and the corporation kept its stock of coal for sale to the poor at low prices in the warehouse underneath. The fuel was evidently dispensed at a penthouse standing in front of the building[55] and known by 1636 as Pennyless Bench.[56] By 1692 a merchant held the warehouse on lease from the corporation.[57] In 1610 the custom house was part of a range of buildings fronting the northern part of the quay from Dockham ditch to the entrance of the road later called Quay Street.[58] Three yards for wood and coal had been formed on the waste ground adjoining the southern part of the quay, where the building of warehouses had started by 1622 when two new houses occupied land formerly used as a dunghill.[59] Also in 1622 the corporation began constructing a second quay, probably by extending the first one southwards to the city boundary, beyond which were the castle precincts. That work was completed the following year.[60]

By the early 18th century warehouses and other buildings extended along the southern part of the quay as far as the castle precincts. In the late 17th century and early 18th several industrial buildings were erected on the waste ground near the quay's northern end, notably a large conical glasshouse west of the mouth of Dockham ditch in 1694. Building east of the ditch included a conical limekiln in 1696 and led to the formation of a narrow lane (later Turnstile Alley or Quay Court) between the quay and lower Westgate Street.[61] The mouth of Dockham ditch was dredged in 1713[62] when the corporation built a short quay there;[63] the new wharf apparently extended along the east side of the ditch up to the Foreign bridge.[64] In 1724 the custom office was enlarged by carrying the two storeys above the warehouse forwards on pillars over the site of Pennyless Bench.[65] The new building was faced in ashlar decorated with pilasters and a cornice. John Pitt, the collector of the customs, occupied the warehouse in 1779[66] and purchased it in 1799.[67] The

corporation provided new weights at the quay in 1741,[68] and between 1750 and 1771 the lessee of the weights also had charge of the yard at the quay for storing the corporation's stock of coal for the poor.[69] Several inns were opened on the quay in the 17th and 18th centuries, the earliest recorded being the Star which in 1630 stood next to the custom house.[70] At least three sites on or near the quay have been occupied by inns called at some time the Ship.[71]

The opening of a direct overseas trade by way of the river in 1791 gave impetus to the scheme for the construction of a ship canal terminating at a basin or dock on the south side of the city. That project was completed in 1827[72] but the city quay continued for several years to handle large numbers of vessels. In the early 19th century the custom office was transferred to a larger building nearby[73] and in the early 1830s from St. Mary's Square to Bearland.[74] Later it was moved to the docks. The quay provided the terminus of a horse tramway for transporting coal to Cheltenham. It was completed in 1811 and ran southwards along the river bank to the canal basin.[75] Among buildings erected behind the quay were the gasworks in Quay Street in 1819.[76] In 1812 the corporation erected a crane on the quay for the collector of its tolls and in 1828 it supplied a second crane for him.[77] In 1825 a new road was formed between the quay and lower Westgate Street by culverting Dockham ditch below the Foreign bridge, near which the corporation installed a weighing machine. During those improvements a wharf above the mouth of the ditch was extended at the corporation's expense.[78] A small building had been erected at the northern end of the quay for the corporation's weights by 1842.[79]

In the early 19th century the southern end of the quay incorporated a private wharf, which was occupied by the wharfinger John Walker and was owned with the warehouses lying behind it in the county.[80] To the south vessels were prevented from mooring along the river bank adjoining the new county gaol, completed in 1791 on the site of the castle, and the county magistrates thwarted attempts from 1796 to build a road and wharf along the bank between the quay and the canal

[52] *Glouc. Corp. Rec.* p. 35.
[53] G.B.R., B 3/1, f. 74v.; F 4/3, ff. 210, 213.
[54] Ibid. F 4/3, f. 218.
[55] Ibid. J 5/6.
[56] Ibid. J 3/3, f. 109v.
[57] Ibid. 6, ff. 146–7; cf. ibid. J 4/3, no. 31.
[58] Speed, *Map of Glouc.* (1610).
[59] G.B.R., J 3/1, f. 37 and v., pp. 106–8, 193; 3, ff. 75v.–76.
[60] Ibid. B 3/1, f. 491; cf. *Glouc. Corp. Rec.* p. 43; Hall and Pinnell, *Map of Glouc.* (1780); *Trans. B.G.A.S.* cii. 82.
[61] Atkyns, *Glos.* plate at pp. 82–3, detail reproduced above, Fig. 7; above, Early Mod. Glouc., topog.; below, Street Names, s.v. Turnstile Alley. A second limekiln was recorded near the first in 1716: G.B.R., J 3/8, ff. 77–78v.
[62] G.B.R., B 3/8, p. 509.
[63] Ibid. p. 385; F 4/8, pp. 157–8; Bodl. MS. Top. Glouc. c. 3, f. 42v.; P.R.O., E 134/1 Geo. II Hil./4.
[64] Cf. Hall and Pinnell, *Map of Glouc.* (1780).
[65] G.B.R., B 3/9, f. 167v.
[66] Ibid. J 4/3, no. 31; P.R.O., E 190/1268/5.
[67] G.B.R., J 6/3, f. 40.
[68] Ibid. B 3/9, f. 460.

[69] Ibid. F 4/10, pp. 73, 512; 11, p. 431; 12, pp. 105, 143; B 3/10, ff. 146, 195; 11, ff. 25, 128v., 137v.
[70] Ibid. J 5/6; J 3/3, f. 109v.
[71] Ibid. J 3/6, ff. 145–6; B 3/11, f. 169; Causton, *Map of Glouc.* (1843).
[72] Above, Glouc. 1720–1835, econ. development 1791–1835; below, docks.
[73] Rudge, *Glouc.* 117–18.
[74] *Pigot's Dir.* (1830), 376; Glos. R.O., DC/SJ 15; the excise off. remained in St. Mary's Square in the early 1840s: *Pigot's Dir. Glos.* (1842), 115.
[75] Glos. R.O., Q/RUm 26; D.E. Bick, *Glouc. and Chelt. Railway* (1968, Locomotion Papers, no. 43), 9.
[76] *Power's Glouc. Handbk.* (1862), 73; below, Public Services.
[77] G.B.R., F 4/15, pp. 186–7; 16, pp. 175, 177, 181; F 10/7, lease 26 Apr. 1830.
[78] Ibid. B 3/14, ff. 28, 32v.; F 10/7, lease 15 Sept. 1825; J 3/13, pp. 452–3; J 4/12, nos. 7–9; cf. *Rep. Com. Mun. Corp.* 67.
[79] G.B.R., B 4/1/6, p. 37; Bd. of Health Map (1852).
[80] G.B.R., J 4/12, nos. 111, 119; Glos. R.O., DC/F 2/1; cf. P.R.O., E 178/7000; G.B.R., G 3/RUm 2/1/3C.

basin. The canal company appropriated part of the bank at the entrance to its lock leading from the river to the basin in 1818 for a wall, and the road was formed under an agreement of 1827 between the city corporation and the magistrates.[81] The prohibition on mooring remained.[82]

The number of vessels using the city quay was evidently falling by the 1840s, and of the corporation's cranes one had been abandoned by 1844 and the other by 1854.[83] The quay's decline, which accelerated with the severing of the tramway at the docks in 1848 and the removal of the lines behind the county gaol,[84] was caused not only by the expansion of the docks and railways but also by the silting up of the river foreshore, particularly following the construction c. 1870 of weirs at Llanthony and Maisemore which reduced the tidal flow. Those works enabled seagoing vessels, which were replacing trows on the river, to pass through the lock into the docks throughout the year.[85] By the early 1870s the quay could be reached only by planks over the foreshore[86] and the wharf upstream of it had been extended forwards.[87] The private wharfage rights on the southern end of the quay apparently lapsed in or soon after 1864, a crane being removed and warehouses and other buildings behind demolished to make room c. 1870 for an extension of the militia barracks.[88] Industrial development behind the quay continued,[89] and among new buildings facing the river were offices built c. 1864 for the gasworks.[90] The gasworks closed in the mid 1870s.[91]

A major improvement was carried out at the city quay in 1887 by extending it over the foreshore to a new wall in line with the wharf upstream. Following the contractor's bankruptcy his work was completed in 1888 by Maynard Colchester-Wemyss, owner of the Westbury Court estate. The new quay had six slipways, and parts were fenced off for letting as yards, including the section north of Quay Street. The corporation, which took the tolls in hand,[92] installed a new crane and weighing machine on the quay.[93] The water bailiff, who looked after those and other fittings, regulated mooring.[94] In the late 19th century and the early 20th the buildings facing the quay were altered considerably,[95] the remains of the glasshouse being demolished in 1933;[96] Quay Court disappeared after 1901 in a remodelling of the area between the northern end of the quay and Westgate Street.[97] The river wall was extended from the quay to the canal lock in 1937 when the road along the quay and the river bank adjoining the prison was improved to carry traffic bypassing the city centre.[98] Trade at the quay had ceased by the mid 1960s when the road along it and the entrance to Commercial Road at the south-western corner of the prison were widened as part of an inner ring road.[99] In 1986, when the southern part of the area was dominated by the new block of the Shire Hall, built in the early 1970s, the old custom house was the only building to survive as a reminder of the trade once carried on at the quay.

DOCKS.[1] The first stage in the development of Gloucester's docks was the construction of a basin at the terminus of a ship canal bypassing the obstacles to navigation on the Severn below the city. The scheme for a basin, first advanced in 1783 but abandoned when the site chosen was included in that of the new county gaol, was revived in 1792 and building began in 1794. The new scheme, which was delayed many times by engineering and financial problems, placed the basin next to the Naight, a small island in the Severn a short way below the city quay,[2] with the canal running southwards to the river at Berkeley. To make the basin, the southern end of the river channel east of the Naight was blocked and the northern end was adapted as a double lock for trows and barges passing to and from the river. Soil removed from the basin was used to build up the river bank to the west or was dumped on land to the east. The construction of the basin and canal destroyed Severn Street, the old road leading from lower Southgate Street towards Sud Meadow and Hempsted, which the canal company replaced by a new road (Llanthony Road) further south and carried over the canal by a wooden swing bridge.[3] At the basin stone quays were built along the north and west sides and an earth bank was left on the east side where it was proposed to enlarge the dock later. In 1799 with the completion of the lock the basin was ready for use but work on the canal, which had been dug as far as Hardwicke, was halted. The basin was opened to vessels from the river in 1812 following the construction of the horse tramway between Gloucester and Cheltenham. The tramway ran east of the basin where it turned to cross lower Southgate Street.[4] A weighing machine erected

[81] Glos. R.O., Q/CL 1/3; cf. P.R.O., RAIL 829/5, pp. 25–7, 48–9; above, Glouc. Castle.

[82] Glouc. Extension and Improvement Act, 1874, 37 & 38 Vic. c. 111 (Local), s. 19.   [83] G.B.R., L 6/2/6–8.

[84] Conway-Jones, Glouc. Docks, 55; Bd. of Health Map (1852).

[85] Glos. Colln. MF 1.50, p. 9; Glos. R.O., D 2460, Severn Com., engineer's rep. bk. 1855–78, letter 8 Sept. 1860.

[86] G.B.R., B 6/25/1, pp. 22, 53.

[87] Ibid. J 3/15, pp. 182–92; cf. O.S. Map 1/2,500, Glos. XXV. 14 (1886 edn.).

[88] Glos. R.O., DC/F 2/1, 4; L/C 3/3; Glouc. Jnl. 8 Jan. 1870.

[89] Glos. R.O., DC/F 34; Glos. Hist. Studies, xii. 4–5; O.S. Map 1/2,500, Glos. XXV. 14 (1886 edn.).

[90] G.B.R., planning dept., file 1864/18.

[91] Below, Public Services.

[92] G.B.R., B 4/1/11, passim; L 6/7/12; Glos. R.O., D 2460,

Severn Com., Glouc. quay papers 1874–88; for Colchester-Wemyss, Burke, Land. Gent. (1937), 2401; V.C.H. Glos. x. 87–8.   [93] G.B.R., B 3/23, accts. p. 35; 24, accts. p. 35.

[94] Ibid. 23, rep. of off. duties cttee.

[95] Cf. J. Voyce, Glouc. in Old Photogs. (1985), 29, 74, 85; Glos. R.O., GPS 154/38, 40.

[96] Citizen, 12 Aug. 1933.

[97] Cf. O.S. Map 1/2,500, Glos. XXV. 14 (1902 and 1923 edns.).

[98] G.B.R., B 3/70 (1), p. 949; (2), p. 1082; 71 (2), pp. 1217, 1770.

[99] Citizen, 8 May 1962; Glos. R.O., GPS 154/38, 40, 42.

[1] Except where indicated this section is based on Conway-Jones, Glouc. Docks.

[2] Cf. Hall and Pinnell, Map of Glouc. (1780).

[3] P.R.O., RAIL 829/3, pp. 292, 312, 344; RAIL 829/4, pp. 124, 126, 162–3; cf. Glos. R.O., Q/RUm 15.

[4] Glos. R.O., Q/RUm 26.

there c. 1814 had an office in the Doric style.[5] A new road formed from Blackfriars by 1813[6] provided a better route between the city and the basin than the old road by Barbican hill.[7]

In the early 19th century there were several timber yards and a rope walk by the basin. A shipbuilding yard was opened there in 1814,[8] and in 1818 John Bird of Stourport (Worcs.) built a graving dock at the basin's south-western corner. As traffic in the basin grew the canal company divided the adjoining land into yards for letting to merchants and on the east side laid sidings connected to the tramway.[9] In 1817 work was resumed on the canal, for which a new course joining the Severn at Sharpness was agreed, and the completion of a junction with the Stroudwater canal at Saul in 1820 enabled vessels to enter the basin from that canal. In 1824 the company constructed a quay on the east side of the basin and a barge arm (known in the late 19th century as the Old Arm)[10] entered from the canal to the south-east. Around the barge arm, which was finished in 1825, yards with tramway sidings were laid out. They were used mainly by coal, stone, and slate merchants[11] and among their equipment were manually operated cranes.

In 1826 the canal company began building the first of the large warehouses which were to be the dominant architectural feature of the docks.[12] The other warehouses were added at intervals until the early 1870s by merchants for their own use or letting, but the company required them to conform in design and to be set back from the quay. The warehouses, which were mostly for grain, were all of brick and the earliest had three or four storeys over a high vaulted basement. Each floor was supported by wooden beams carried by cast iron pillars and had a central loading bay facing the quay. Ventilation was provided by numerous small windows fitted with metal bars. From the 1830s taller warehouses without basements and aligned at right angles to the quays were built.

The company's warehouses, a pair completed in 1827, formed a four-storeyed range facing the north quay and known later as the North Warehouse. They were built for letting and to designs prepared by Bartin Haigh, a Liverpool builder, for the development of the basin. After the opening of the canal in 1827 private warehouses were built on the west side of the basin. The first had only one storey, but following the company's adoption of leases for 63 years, the Birmingham corn merchants Joseph and Charles Sturge submitted plans for three-storeyed buildings, which became the model for a range of eight

warehouses erected along the length of the west quay between 1829 and 1831.[13] Two blocks were for a salt company and another replaced the smaller warehouse. In 1830 John Biddell, a Stroud miller,[14] built a warehouse on the east side of the basin, beside the barge arm. Its design, prepared by William Franklin of Stroud, included a hipped roof, windows with segmental arches, and loading bays facing both the basin and the barge arm.[15] As most of the land east of the basin was used for timber yards in the 1830s other warehouses had to be built elsewhere. In 1833 James Shipton, a timber merchant, built one in the yard behind Biddell's warehouse with the roof's gable end facing the barge arm, and in 1834 J. and C. Sturge one fronting the lock. The gap between the latter and the range on the west quay was filled in 1835 by a warehouse built by Samuel Baker and Thomas Phillpotts, the upper floors of which were carried over the quay on pillars to provide cover for perishable goods. In addition to its warehouses the canal company built an office on the site of the lock keeper's cottage at the main north-east entrance to the docks in 1830 and a steam engine, housed beside the graving dock, to pump river water into the basin in 1834. It enlarged the graving dock to take ships of 700 tons in 1837.[16]

Commercial development had started on the east side of the canal by the mid 1830s when two salt warehouses were built on the company's land above Hempsted bridge 2 km. from the basin. Both were long single-storeyed buildings and beside each the canal was widened and a quay constructed.[17] Nearer the basin major works were carried out immediately below Llanthony bridge where, under an agreement with the company in 1836, the canal was widened and a quay built in front of High Orchard by a partnership formed by Samuel Baker, Thomas Phillpotts, William Tupsley Washbourne, and two Birmingham bankers to develop the land for commercial and industrial use; the quay, though known as Baker's Quay, belonged to the canal company.[18] The northern part was in use by the end of 1837[19] and the southern part was completed after a dock had been formed there in 1839 or 1840 for the Birmingham and Gloucester railway company.[20] The railway company erected coke ovens in its yard by the dock but a branch line to its proposed terminus at Gloucester was abandoned after some rails had been laid.[21] Most of the land behind the quay was used for timber yards and related industry but Samuel Baker and James Shipton built a grain warehouse on the northern part[22] in 1838. It comprised two blocks[23] and, as the 1836 agree-

[5] P.R.O., RAIL 829/4, p. 418; Bd. of Health Map (1852).

[6] Glouc. Jnl. 11 Oct. 1813.

[7] Cf. Glos. R.O., Q/CL 1/3.

[8] Cf. Glouc. Jnl. 5 Sept. 1814.

[9] Cf. P.R.O., RAIL 829/4, p. 394; Bick, Glouc. and Chelt. Railway, 14.

[10] O.S. Map 1/2,500, Glos. XXV. 14 (1886 edn.).

[11] Bd. of Health Map (1852).

[12] For principal warehos., Conway-Jones in Glouc. Docks, 162–70, and Glos. Soc. for Ind. Arch. Jnl. (1977–8), 13–19.

[13] S. part of range shown above, Plate 34.

[14] V.C.H. Glos. xi. 127.

[15] It was given a simple pitched roof probably during repairs

c. 1864: Glos. Soc. for Ind. Arch. Jnl. (1977–8), 15.

[16] Cf. Glouc. Jnl. 16 Dec. 1837.

[17] Cf. Glos. R.O., D 2460, plans 1/P/7–8; 1/T/2; 10/I/10; P.R.O., RAIL 829/7, pp. 46, 66, 246.

[18] Glos. R.O., D 3117/589, 612; cf. G.D.R., T 1/99; Causton, Map of Glouc. (1843).

[19] Glouc. Jnl. 23 Dec. 1837.

[20] Cf. G.B.R., G 3/RUm 2/2/1A–B; P.R.O., RAIL 829/8, p. 98.

[21] Cf. Glouc. Jnl. 19 Oct. 1839.

[22] Causton, Map of Glouc. (1843); Glos. R.O., D 3117/590, 2543; G.D.R., T 1/99.

[23] Glouc. Jnl. 24 Mar. 1838.

ment allowed, the upper floors extended on pillars over the quay. South of High Orchard, to where John Bird had moved his boatbuilding yard c. 1834, a quay had been formed by 1838.[24] Further south were several other yards, of which at least one was occupied by slate merchants and another by the timber merchants Price & Washbourne.[25]

In 1839 work began on a small dock below the barge arm, but it was abandoned after disagreements between the developer and the canal company and the excavation filled in.[26] Building on the east side of the basin resumed in 1840 with two warehouses to the north of John Biddell's. Both were constructed sideways to the water, an alignment copied for later warehouses, and one, erected by J. and C. Sturge, comprised two blocks. More sidings were laid by the basin after the Birmingham and Gloucester railway company formed a connexion between the tramway and its station on the opposite side of the city in 1841,[27] and in 1844 the tramway was adapted to carry railway as well as tramway wagons between the docks and the station. In 1845 the custom office was moved to a new brick building near the basin. Designed by Sydney Smirke[28] it had a classical-style ashlar front to the road from Blackfriars, which in 1847 was incorporated in Commercial Road, formed as the principal thoroughfare between the city centre and the docks.[29]

In the later 1840s and early 1850s, as water-borne traffic grew, the docks area was enlarged and more warehousing was provided, together with a mariners' chapel completed in 1849.[30] In anticipation of the repeal of the Corn Laws three warehouses were built east of the basin in 1846 on a timber yard given up by Price & Co. The following year the canal company constructed a second barge dock and began work on a new ship dock. The barge dock was west of the canal in Berry Close, between the basin and Llanthony Road. Opposite it the canal was widened by Thomas Tripp, a timber and slate merchant,[31] who built a quay, known later as the Britannia Quay, in front of his yard there. The new ship dock, which was entered by a narrow cut in the east side of the basin and was bounded by stone quays, was opened in 1849[32] and was called the Southgate Street or Victoria dock.[33] Its excavation, which provided soil for a railway embankment near Over, severed the lines of the tramway. The northern end leading to the city quay was abandoned and railway sidings were laid around the new dock. Those sidings were connected to a branch line which the Midland Railway

completed to the docks by way of High Orchard in 1848. William Partridge, a wharfinger who carried goods on the river above Gloucester,[34] built two warehouses on the west side of the new dock, the Victoria at the northern end in 1849 and the Albert at the southern by the entrance in 1851,[35] and Joseph and Jonah Hadley built a flour mill to the north in Commercial Road in 1850. The mill, known as City Mills, had doubled in size by 1853.[36] The Berry Close dock, the sides of which had been left as earth banks, was filled in, probably during the preparations for a second and larger graving dock, which the canal company constructed in 1852 at the main basin near the first.[37] The engine house between them was altered in 1855 to accommodate a larger machine.

Following the completion of its branch line the Midland Railway abandoned the High Orchard dock and, presumably in the early 1850s, filled it in to form a goods yard behind Baker's Quay.[38] Below High Orchard, where the timber yard of Price & Co. had been enlarged in 1846 and the quay in front of it rebuilt and lengthened,[39] more timber yards and moorings were established[40] and in 1854 the Midland Railway laid sidings along the bank to a yard just above the salt warehouses at Hempsted bridge.[41] John Bird moved his boatbuilding works to a site beyond the bridge where he built a small graving dock in 1846. Commercial development on the western bank of the canal was begun in 1851 with the widening of the canal and the construction of Llanthony Quay opposite Baker's Quay for the export of coal. The project, started by the Gloucester and Dean Forest railway company and completed in 1854 by the G.W.R.,[42] included a branch line to Over but a planned dock, for which the Hempsted road was diverted, was never built.[43] A railway goods yard was created behind the quay.[44]

The construction of new quays and railway sidings in the docks resumed with the end of the economic depression of the mid and later 1850s, and William Partridge built two more warehouses, one of them in 1861 west of the Victoria dock. Most of the improvements took place north of Llanthony Road. The bridge over the canal was replaced by an iron structure to carry railway lines, and a quay was built in front of Berry Close, where sidings were laid and where in 1863 William Partridge's other new warehouse was built by the road. The Britannia Quay was extended northwards to the barge arm, where the quay on the south side was raised to enable railway sidings to be brought to it.[45] They

[24] Glos. R.O., D 3117/612, 2545.
[25] P.R.O., RAIL 829/7, pp. 28–9; G.B.R., L 22/1/111, pp. 55–6; G.D.R., T 1/86.
[26] Cf. G.D.R., T 1/99; Causton, Map of Glouc. (1843).
[27] Cf. Bick, Glouc. and Chelt. Railway, 24.
[28] Colvin, Biog. Dict. Brit. Architects (1978), 972.
[29] Causton, Map of Glouc. (1843); Glos. Colln. 22415.
[30] Below, Churches and Chapels, non-par. chap.
[31] Pigot's Dir. Glos. (1842), 115.
[32] Cf. Glouc. Jnl. 21 Apr. 1849.
[33] Lond. Gaz. 12 June 1849, p. 1917; Bd. of Health Map (1852).
[34] Cf. Kelly's Dir. Glos. (1856), 299.
[35] Cf. Bd. of Health Map (1852).
[36] Cf. Glouc. Jnl. 19 Mar. 1853.

[37] Cf. Glos. R.O., D 2460, plans 9/F/2–5; O.S. Map 1/2,500, Glos. XXV. 14 (1886 edn.).
[38] Cf. O.S. Map 1/2,500, Glos. XXXIII. 2 (1886 edn.).
[39] Glos. R.O., D 3117/4059/1.
[40] Cf. ibid. P 173/VE 2/1, mins. 7 Aug. 1851, 2 Feb. 1854.
[41] P.R.O., RAIL 1112/11; cf. G.D.R., V 6/130.
[42] Glouc. Jnl. 1 Nov. 1851; 1 Oct. 1853; 25 Mar. 1854; Glos. R.O., D 1950/E 8 (ii).
[43] Glos. R.O., Q/RUm 231; Glouc. and Dean Forest Railway Dock Act, 1847, 10 & 11 Vic. c. 76 (Local and Personal).
[44] Suppl. to 56th Rep. Glouc. Chamber of Commerce (1897), 48: copy in Glos. Colln. N 15.6.
[45] Cf. Glouc. Jnl. 2 Mar., 21 Sept. 1861; 18 Oct. 1862; 18 Apr., 17 Oct. 1863.

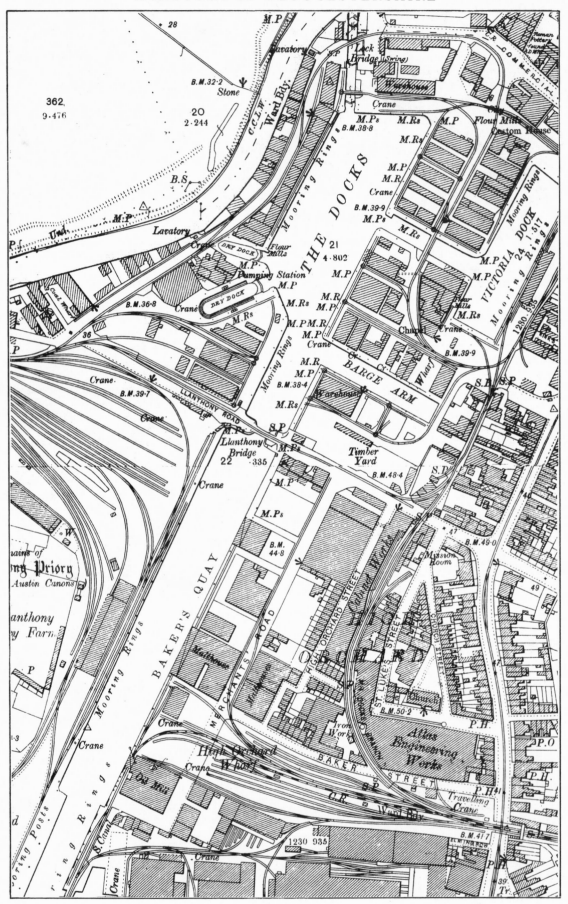

Fig. 18. Gloucester docks, 1901

replaced the tramway sidings which had been abandoned in 1861.[46] Transit sheds to store imported grain awaiting transfer to the railways were built, one east of the Victoria dock by the canal company in 1866 and another at the Midland Railway company's Baker's Quay yard in 1867.[47]

After the early 1860s there were few major works in the docks. Many seagoing vessels had become too large for them and for the canal and, beginning with docks opened in 1874, the canal company concentrated more on the development of facilities at Sharpness. In the Gloucester docks two new grain warehouses were provided in the early 1870s, one, south-west of the main basin, built by W. Fox of Rhyl (Flints.) for his sons in 1870, being rebuilt after a fire in 1875.[48] The other, built in 1873 for the firm of Wait, James, & Co., comprised two blocks south of the entrance to the barge arm.[49] The canal company, which was renamed the Sharpness New Docks & Gloucester & Birmingham Navigation Co. in 1874,[50] undertook some improvements at Gloucester. The most notable were to the railways on its land, which came more fully under its control in 1876, and included the construction in 1880 of an iron swing bridge to carry lines over the lock.[51] The lock was replaced in 1892 by a larger single chamber as part of improvements to navigation above the city.[52] Among new buildings was a store built by an importer of petroleum products in 1882. One of the salt warehouses at Hempsted bridge was converted as a petroleum store in 1881.

Industrial development around the docks and canal increased and diversified from the 1860s. Two more flour mills were established in the docks by the conversion of the southernmost warehouse on the west quay as St. Owen's Mills c. 1863 and of the Albert Warehouse in 1869.[53] An oil and cake mill built at the southern end of Baker's Quay in 1862[54] incorporated a wooden structure carried over the quay on pillars.[55] South of the quay part of Price & Co.'s yard was included in the works of Eassie & Co.[56] and from 1875 of the Gloucester Wagon Co.[57] A wooden church was built beside the canal there in 1878 for

Norwegian seamen visiting the docks.[58] Shipbuilding was revived near Hempsted bridge in the 1860s[59] and the graving dock there was enlarged in 1868.[60] Further south, moorings were created for the gasworks built on the Bristol road in the mid 1870s,[61] and in 1869 S. J. Moreland, the owner of a match factory, formed a timber float where the road touched the canal at Two Mile Bend between Hempsted and Quedgeley.[62] Later industrial developments included a malthouse (1888)[63] and the docks company's engineering workshops (1891–3) near the main basin. At Baker's Quay the site of the remaining timber yard was filled by a factory making enamelled slate and by maltings in 1897 and 1899 respectively. The maltings, which were completed in 1901,[64] formed a large addition to the High Orchard works of G. and W.E. Downing and extended over the quay on pillars.[65] The oil mill to the south had been rebuilt on a larger scale in 1893 following a collapse of the quay wall.[66] In 1917 a yard was established south of the graving dock at Hempsted bridge for building concrete barges as part of the war effort. After the completion of the barge contract the yard continued to operate as concrete works for many years.[67]

From the late 1880s a number of works were carried out below Llanthony bridge to benefit trade.[68] The docks company constructed a dock and a large pond for floating timber in Monk Meadow, west of the canal, in 1891 and 1896 respectively.[69] The new dock was served by sidings connected to the goods yard behind Llanthony Quay and to a branch line from Tuffley, which the Midland Railway began in 1897 and carried over the canal by a swing bridge north of Hempsted bridge.[70] Opposite Monk Meadow the timber merchants Price, Walker, & Co. enlarged their yard and mills in 1894[71] and at the wagon works to the north a small timber pond was constructed in 1899.[72] The installation of gantries to improve handling methods in some of the yards had started by the 1870s,[73] and at Llanthony Quay, the principal wharf for the larger steamers using the canal, the G.W.R. provided sheds and mobile steam cranes for the sugar trade;[74] hydrau-

[46] Cf. P.R.O., RAIL 1112/11; Bick, *Glouc. and Chelt. Railway*, 27–9.

[47] Cf. *Glouc. Jnl.* 20 Apr. 1867; O.S. Map 1/2,500, Glos. XXXIII. 2 (1886 edn.); Glos. R.O., D 2460, plans 1/U/6; for other railway bldgs., Glos. R.O., D 3039/11.

[48] *Glouc. Jnl.* 16 Apr. 1870; 9 Oct. 1875; *Glos. Chron.* 28 Aug. 1875; Glos. R.O., D 2460, plans 1/K/3.

[49] *Glos. Chron.* 17 Jan. 1874; *Glouc. Jnl.* 18 Aug. 1888.

[50] P.R.O., RAIL 1112/11. [51] Cf. *Citizen*, 25 Sept. 1962.

[52] Cf. Glos. Colln. MF 1.50, pp. 10–12; Severn Navigation Act, 1890, 53 & 54 Vic. c. 155 (Local), ss. 12–14.

[53] For Albert Mills, above, Plate 24.

[54] *Glouc. Jnl.* 26 Apr., 26 July 1862; 21 Feb. 1863.

[55] Photogs. in Conway-Jones, *Glouc. Docks*, 69, 78.

[56] Glos. R.O., D 3117/4059, 4061; G.B.R., J 3/15, pp. 193–8.

[57] Glos. R.O., D 4791, Glouc. Railway Carriage & Wagon Co., min. bk. 1875–8, pp. 55–6, 78.

[58] Ibid. min. bk. 1878–81, pp. 13, 23; below, Prot. Nonconf., undenominational missions.

[59] Cf. *Glos. Chron.* 17 Jan. 1885.

[60] Glos. R.O., D 2460, plans 9/E/2, 5; *Glouc. Jnl.* 10 Apr. 1869.

[61] *Glouc. Jnl.* 11 Mar. 1876.

[62] Ibid. 10 Apr. 1869; above, Glouc. 1835–1985, econ. development 1835–1914.

[63] For plans, Glos. R.O., D 4335/153–4.

[64] Date on bldg.

[65] *Glouc. Jnl.* 5 Aug. 1899; Glos. R.O., D 2460, plans 1/C/1–13.

[66] Glos. Colln. NQ 15.8, p. 43; Conway-Jones, *Glouc. Docks*, 125, 169.

[67] *Glouc. Jnl.* 30 Nov. 1918; 20 Dec. 1919; Glos. R.O., D 4325/1–3; D 2460, plan of Glouc. docks c. 1950.

[68] For features in that area, above, Fig. 13.

[69] Cf. Glos. R.O., D 2460, plans 10/B/2, 4; 9/I/2; *Glouc. Jnl.* 30 Apr. 1892.

[70] *Glouc. Jnl.* 10 July, 21 Aug. 1897; Glos. R.O., D 2460, plans 6/M/13.

[71] *Glouc. Jnl.* 26 Jan. 1895; above, Plate 27.

[72] Cf. Glos. R.O., D 2460, plans 9/H/2–5.

[73] O.S. Map 1/2,500, Glos. XXXIII. 2 (1886 and 1902 edns.); *Glouc. Jnl.* 26 Jan. 1895; cf. G.B.R., L 22/1/111, pp. 55–6.

[74] *Ind. Glos. 1904*, 77: copy in Glos. Colln. JV 13.1; cf. *Glouc. Jnl.* 21 Nov. 1896.

lic lifts handling coal there had been removed in 1869.[75]

Elsewhere in the docks warehousing and handling equipment were increasingly unsuited to commercial needs. Many of the principal warehouses continued to store grain and one was occupied by a firm hiring out sacks for bagging cargoes. The Severn & Canal Carrying Co. used the two warehouses on the north side of the barge arm, and warehousing firms rented space in several others to merchants.[76] In the early 20th century two warehouses near Llanthony bridge stored sugar.[77] Several fixed manually-operated cranes remained in use in the later 1920s, others having been replaced by steam-powered machines moving over the railways. The warehouse supported on pillars over the west quay was burnt down in 1917[78] and fire reduced that by Llanthony Road to a single storey in 1945. The North Warehouse, to which the plant of St. Owen's Mills was transferred in 1921,[79] was made a single unit by the insertion of doorways in the dividing wall.[80] City and Albert Mills, which used several warehouses for storage, were provided with additional buildings.[81] Before the Second World War some warehouses were taken over by builders' merchants and some were abandoned. During the war several were used again to store grain and in 1943 a silo was built beside the canal between Llanthony Quay and the Monk Meadow dock for processing local corn. The Monk Meadow dock, where a transit shed had been erected in 1921, had become a distribution point for refined petroleum products and from the mid 1920s several oil companies built storage tanks around it.[82]

The British Transport Commission, which acquired control of the docks and canal in 1948,[83] began a number of improvements in the late 1950s. They included replacing the swing bridges by single-leaf structures, Hempsted bridge being rebuilt in 1959 and the lock bridge in 1962,[84] and developing wharfage facilities below Llanthony bridge where ships of 750 tons could moor. At Llanthony Quay works completed in 1962 included the reconstruction of the quay and the provision of single-storeyed warehousing. The policy was continued by the British Waterways Board, the docks authority from 1963, with the building in 1965 of a quay for the timber trade below the entrance to the Monk Meadow timber pond.[85] The pond was later filled in and by 1985 the southern part of the new quay had been incorporated in a timber yard.

The older part of the docks above Llanthony bridge declined markedly as a commercial and industrial centre after the Second World War. Several warehouses were abandoned and those remaining on the west quay were pulled down in 1966.[86] The tall stack of the engine house nearby was demolished about the same time.[87] From the late 1970s many smaller buildings were demolished. The dismantling of the dock railways, which had begun south of Monk Meadow by the 1950s,[88] was carried out mostly in the 1960s and left only a line from Over to Llanthony serving a cement depot behind the quay and the silo to the south. Among railway buildings to disappear was the Victoria dock transit shed.[89]

From the late 1970s the older docks, which because of the survival of the mid 19th-century warehouses featured occasionally in historical films and television programmes, were increasingly used by pleasure craft. Some warehouses took on new uses, that by the lock housing an antiques centre from 1979[90] and the former Albert Warehouse a museum of advertizing and packaging from 1984. The custom house in Commercial Road was occupied from 1978 by the headquarters, and later by the museum, of the Gloucestershire Regiment.[91] The warehouse on the northern part of Baker's Quay was converted as offices and restaurants in 1983. To encourage revitalization of the older docks as a commercial, residential, and leisure area the city council in 1985 and 1986 refurbished the North Warehouse for its main administrative offices.[92] The area's industrial tradition was represented in 1986 principally at City Mills and the graving docks.

Although the canal lost much of its goods traffic to the roads, industrial and commercial development of the land adjoining it continued after the Second World War. Timber yards were opened near the new quay in Monk Meadow in the mid 1960s[93] and continued to dominate the eastern bank above Hempsted bridge, although some were replaced by factories and warehouses.[94] Of the former salt warehouses at Hempsted bridge one was a timber store and the other a packing case factory in the mid 1970s. Below the bridge industrial and trading premises were strung out along the eastern bank to just beyond Two Mile Bend, where the timber float had been filled in and its site used for concrete works.[95] Industrial development west of the canal centred on Llanthony, where in 1985 the former goods yard behind the quay was filled with buildings for a trading estate, and on Monk Meadow, where oil storage tanks remained around the dock.

[75] *Glouc. Jnl.* 11 Nov. 1854; 20 Feb. 1869.

[76] For warehousing firms in 1883, P.R.O., RAIL 864/3, pp. 63–5.

[77] *Ind. Glos.* 1904, 77; cf. Conway-Jones, *Glouc. Docks,* 169.

[78] *Glouc. Jnl.* 15 Dec. 1917.

[79] *Glos. Hist. Studies,* xii. 5.

[80] *Glos. Soc. for Ind. Arch. Jnl.* (1977–8), 15.

[81] *Glos. Hist. Studies,* xii. 7.

[82] Cf. *Glouc. Jnl.* 11 Nov. 1922; *Waterways World,* Oct. 1976, 33.

[83] Transport Act, 1947, 10 & 11 Geo. VI, c. 49.

[84] C. P. and C. R. Weaver, *Glouc. and Sharpness Canal* (W. Midlands Area of Railway and Canal Hist. Soc. 1967), 19.

[85] *Citizen,* 18 Sept. 1961; 1 Apr. 1965; *The Times,* 6 Apr. 1965; Transport Act, 1962, 10 & 11 Eliz. II, c. 46.

[86] For photog., Conway-Jones, *Glouc. Docks,* 33.

[87] Weaver, *Glouc. and Sharpness Canal,* 34.

[88] Glos. R.O., D 2460, plan of Gloucester docks c. 1950.

[89] For view of docks in 1985, above, Plate 35.

[90] *Glouc. Jnl.* 15 Oct. 1983.

[91] *Citizen,* 14 Nov. 1978.

[92] Inf. from chief executive, Glouc. city council.

[93] *Citizen,* 1 Apr. 1965.

[94] Cf. Glos. Colln. N 15.88.

[95] *Waterways World,* Oct. 1976, 34–5.

MARKETS AND FAIRS

GLOUCESTER'S market and fair trade and the role it played in the economy of the city are discussed in the general chapters on the city's history. This section gives an account of the institutional history of the markets and fairs and of the sites and buildings connected with them.[96]

MARKETS. Gloucester's market rights derived from ancient custom and were not specifically mentioned in any of the town charters or other grants, though in a suit concluded in 1590 the grant of the liberties of London and Winchester made by the earliest charters was used to support a claim that Gloucester was an open market on every weekday; the expenses of the defendant who was successful in that claim were partly met by the corporation.[97] In practice, however, from the mid 13th century or earlier the town authorities had limited market activities to Wednesdays and Saturdays.[98] Those were the two usual days for the sale of corn in 1514 and for the country butchers to bring meat for sale in 1549,[99] and they were the only two market days claimed by the mayor and burgesses at a *quo warranto* enquiry in 1553.[1] The two days came to differ in the type of business transacted: Wednesday was said to be the main market day for corn, butter, and cheese in 1588,[2] and it was presumably the usual day for the livestock market in 1729 when 'great markets' for stock were instituted on three Wednesdays in the year.[3] Saturday had become the usual day for the country butchers to come by the early 18th century[4] and for the corn market by 1756, when it was announced that corn sales would in future also be held on Wednesday.[5] The old claim to a market on every weekday was presumably revived later to justify the daily opening of part of the new produce markets after 1786 and the holding of cattle sales on other days than Wednesdays and Saturdays in the 20th century.

Market trading was probably carried on in all four of the main streets and some of the lesser ones from medieval times, but the greatest concentration of activity was in the upper part of Westgate Street where it was lined by the shops of the mercers and butchers. St. Mary de Grace church which stood there was sometimes called St. Mary in the market from the late 12th century,[6] and the King's Board, Gloucester's earliest known market building, was put up between it and Holy Trinity church in the 14th century[7] and was used for the sale of cheese and butter[8] until removed under the improvement Act of 1750.[9] In the mid 13th century the corn market was being held in Westgate Street.[10] In the lower part of the street, by St. Nicholas's church, fish was sold from carts in 1213 when, however, the sellers secured permission to move to a place in Southgate Street which they claimed was their traditional pitch.[11]

Upper Westgate Street was still the scene of much market trade in the early 18th century when it had a market house for the sale of bacon and was the site of the stalls and standings of the fishmongers and market gardeners;[12] a new market bell was installed in Trinity tower there in 1706.[13] The produce sales then extended into the other three streets all of which had been the site of covered markets for many years. In the northern part of Southgate Street a building for the wheat market had been provided by 1509[14] and was rebuilt in 1607[15] and again in 1660.[16] At the beginning of the 18th century the stalls for the country butchers were located at its southern end.[17] The barley market house stood in Eastgate Street near the gate[18] until 1655 when it was replaced by a new building halfway up the street. The new building, a substantial structure supported on columns, was built with materials from the churches of St. Mary de Grace and St. Catherine and paid for with £50 given by Margery Price, widow of an alderman.[19] A market house for the sale of meal, built or rebuilt in the years 1569–70,[20] adjoined the east end of St. John's church in upper Northgate Street; it went out of use *c.* 1657 and was removed at the rebuilding of the church in 1732.[21] Fruit and poultry were sold in other parts of that street at the beginning of the 18th century.[22] Market trading also extended into the area of the Cross, at the meeting of the four streets, but that was not a site approved by the common council which barred hucksters and apple sellers from standings near the Tolsey in 1646.[23]

Some reorganization of the produce markets was carried out during 1737, partly in an attempt

---

[96] This article was written in 1980.

[97] G.B.R., B 3/1, ff. 117, 124 and v.; I 1/32.

[98] *Ag.H.R.* ii. 13.

[99] G.B.R., B 2/1, ff. 21v., 48.

[1] *Glouc. Corp. Rec.* pp. 30–2.

[2] G.B.R., I 1/32.   [3] *Glouc. Jnl.* 8 July 1729.

[4] Bodl. MS. Top. Glouc. c. 3, f. 44.

[5] *Glouc. Jnl.* 7 Dec. 1756.

[6] P.R.O., C 115/K 1/6681, f. 82; Glouc. Cath. Libr., deeds and seals, viii, f. 6.

[7] Above, Public Buildings.

[8] Bodl. MS. Top. Glouc. c. 3, f. 44; G.B.R., B 3/10, f. 19; F 4/3, f. 238.

[9] Glouc. Improvement Act, 23 Geo. II, c. 15.

[10] *Ag.H.R.* ii. 13. 'Ebridge Street', there identified as *lower* Westgate Street, was a name used for the whole course of the street: below, Street Names.

[11] *Abbrev. Plac.* (Rec. Com.), 92; the move was to 'the cross' in Southgate Street, perhaps meaning the end of the street near the high cross.

[12] Bodl. MS. Top. Glouc. c. 3, f. 44.

[13] G.B.R., B 3/8, p. 224.

[14] Ibid. J 5/3.

[15] Ibid. B 3/1, f. 220v.

[16] Ibid. 3, p. 162; Rudder, *Glos.* 89.

[17] Bodl. MS. Top. Glouc. c. 3, f. 44.

[18] Rudder, *Glos.* 89.

[19] G.B.R., B 3/2, pp. 775, 815, 818, 855, 857, 859; J 3/3, ff. 156–7; Atkyns, *Glos.* plate at pp. 82–3, detail reproduced above, Fig. 5.

[20] G.B.R., F 4/3, f. 130v.

[21] Rudder, *Glos.* 90; G.B.R., B 3/1, f. 467v.

[22] Bodl. MS. Top. Glouc. c. 3, f. 44.

[23] G.B.R., B 3/2, p. 389.

to ease the congestion of the streets on market days: new standings for the country butchers were assigned on the east side of Southgate Street; the bacon market was moved into Southgate Street; an order was made to confine the standings of the city market gardeners to the vicinity of the King's Board and those of the country gardeners to the upper part of Eastgate Street; and there was a further prohibition on standings adjoining the Tolsey.[24]

The Boothall in the lower part of Westgate Street played an important role in the town's market trade from at least 1192 when the Crown gave the burgesses permission to use it for buying and selling.[25] It was being used for the sale of leather by 1273[26] and for the sale of wool by 1396 when the weighing beams and the tolls collected there were on lease.[27] The building continued as the official market for wool, leather, cloth, and other commodities brought by visiting merchants until at least the 1750s, the profits being included in the lease of the Boothall inn. Sales made outside the market in inns and private houses were, however, a constant problem for the authorities over the centuries.[28]

Although the pig market was held in upper Northgate Street until at least 1741,[29] the other livestock markets were presumably kept out of the congested central area of the town from an early date. Sheep Lane near the south gate, so called by the mid 13th century,[30] may have been used for the sale of sheep, while Bearland, where cattle were sold at the midsummer fair in 1500,[31] may have been the usual site for the cattle market. By the beginning of the 18th century, however, the sheep market was held in Three Cocks Lane, Half Street, and the adjoining part of St. Mary's Square,[32] and in 1779 the cattle market was held in the street behind the College walls (later Pitt Street).[33] The cattle market tended to spread beyond its restricted site: in 1798 an order was made to confine it to the College walls and Water Street,[34] and in 1807 local residents complained of cattle penned in St. Mary's Square and the surrounding streets.[35] In the early 19th century horse sales were held at the south end of Parker's Row (later Brunswick Road).[36] In 1823 all livestock sales were moved to a new cattle market.[37]

In the mid 1780s a major reorganization of the city's market facilities took the produce markets out of the streets. The old market houses were demolished,[38] and two new markets were built at the cost of £4,000, which the corporation raised from shareholders under a tontine agreement.[39] The new markets, opened in 1786,[40] were designed and built by William Price.[41] The Eastgate market extended from the south-west side of Eastgate Street, on which there was a Doric portico with iron gates, to Travel Lane (later Bell Lane) and comprised an open area for stalls and sittings and a covered building for the sale of corn;[42] the market was open on Wednesdays and Saturdays for corn, meat, pigs, poultry, fruit, vegetables brought by country market gardeners, and tradesmen's wares.[43] The new Southgate market on the north-west side of Southgate Street not far from the Cross[44] had a hall for dairy produce and space for the stalls of the fishmongers, the town market gardeners, and earthenware sellers; it was open daily.[45]

At another reorganization in the 1850s the Eastgate market was rebuilt to house a daily produce market. The new market, designed by James Medland and A. W. Maberly and opened in 1856, comprised one large hall with a massive pedimented portico with Corinthian columns and carvings of produce in the spandrels of the arches.[46] The end of the hall on Bell Lane was rebuilt in brick with a bell turret c. 1890.[47] The market came increasingly to be occupied by regular stallholders and by 1933 country people with baskets of produce had ceased to come.[48] The Eastgate market hall was taken down in the late 1960s during the redevelopment of that area of the city as a modern shopping centre, and a new market hall, opened in 1968,[49] was provided as part of the development. The old portico was re-erected (further down Eastgate Street than its original site) as the main entrance to the new shopping centre.

The Southgate market was rebuilt in 1856 (and opened in 1857) as a corn exchange. Designed by Medland and Maberly,[50] it had a tall Corinthian portico forming a semicircular bay and surmounted by a statue of Ceres.[51] In 1893, when it apparently ceased to be used as a corn exchange,[52] the front was rebuilt flush with the street frontage and part of the building was adapted as the post office.[53] From that time corn dealing was presumably carried on at the cattle market off

---

[24] Ibid. 9, ff. 394, 397v., 411.

[25] *Pipe R.* 1191 & 92 (P.R.S. N.S. ii), 285.

[26] G.B.R., G 8/1.

[27] Ibid. C 9/2.

[28] Ibid. B 2/1, f. 22; 2, ff. 114–115v.; B 3/1, f. 449; J 3/3, ff. 113–17; 9, ff. 75v.–77v.; *Glouc. Jnl.* 19 June 1750; 24 Oct. 1752.

[29] Bodl. MS. Top. Glouc. c. 3, f. 44; *Glouc. Jnl.* 6 Jan. 1741.   [30] Below, Street Names.

[31] G.B.R., B 2/1, f. 17v.

[32] Bodl. MS. Top. Glouc. c. 3, f. 44v.; Glos. R.O., D 936/E 12/10, f. 8v.; L 7, plan.

[33] G.B.R., B 4/1/1, p. 87; Hall and Pinnell, *Map of Glouc.* (1780).   [34] *Glouc. Jnl.* 23 Apr. 1798.

[35] G.B.R., B 3/13, f. 43; cf. *Glouc. Jnl.* 12 July 1813.

[36] *Glouc. Jnl.* 27 Apr. 1807.

[37] Below.

[38] Rudge, *Glouc.* 114–15.

[39] G.B.R., B 8/23.

[40] *Glouc. Jnl.* 27 Feb., 13 Mar. 1786.

[41] G.B.R., B 3/11, f. 367 and v.; B 4/1/1, p. 198; F 4/13, pp. 208–10.

[42] Ibid. B 8/25; Glos. Colln. prints GL 57.20; above, Fig. 10.

[43] G.B.R., B 4/1/1, pp. 230–4.

[44] Cole, *Map of Glouc.* (1805).

[45] G.B.R., B 4/1/1, pp. 230–4.

[46] Ibid. 7, ff. 122, 124–7; Glos. Colln. prints GL 57.8, reproduced above, Plate 30.

[47] Glos. Colln. prints GL 57.19; cf. ibid. GL 57.10.

[48] Glos. Colln. NZ 12.5.

[49] Plaque in bldg.

[50] G.B.R., B 4/1/7, ff. 49, 101, 151.

[51] Glos. Colln. prints GL 7.25; cf. Glos. R.O., D 4335/199.

[52] Cf. *Kelly's Dir. Glos.* (1889), 783; (1894), 167.

[53] *Glouc. Jnl.* 29 Apr., 10 June 1893; Glos. R.O., D 4335/199. The bldg. was demolished in 1938: *Glouc. Municipal Year Bk.* (1964–5), 78.

lower Northgate Street and in 1923 an exchange was opened in George Street adjoining the cattle market; the new exchange was, however, soon largely abandoned by the dealers in favour of sheds in the open market.[54]

Cheese was sold at the cattle market from 1851 in a market[55] established by a committee of subscribers and taken over by the corporation in 1866.[56] Another committee started a wool market, held on three days of the year, at the cattle market in 1852,[57] and a hide and skin market was started there in 1857.[58] Sales of cheese and wool were being held on one day a month in 1870.[59] In 1894 a privately-owned market for hides, skins, fat, and wool was being held daily at premises on the quay.[60] From 1900 a wholesale fruit market was held at the cattle market on one day a week; by 1928, when the corporation provided a new building, it was being held on three days a week and attracted business from a wide area.[61]

The new cattle market south of lower Northgate Street was built under an Act of 1821[62] and opened in 1823.[63] The leading promoter of the scheme was John Phillpotts. The new market, an open walled area,[64] was extensively remodelled in 1862–3,[65] and improvements were made several times in the late 19th century and the earlier 20th as the volume of business showed a steady increase, encouraged by the easy access from the railway. In 1933 the market had accommodation for 5,000 sheep, 2,000 pigs, and 1,000 cattle.[66] The first cattle auctions were begun there in 1862 by the two founders of the firm of Bruton, Knowles, & Co. and came gradually to replace dealing by private treaty. General stock sales were being held twice a week by 1910, on Mondays and Saturdays, and on Saturdays there was also a horse market and private dealing in Irish cattle.[67] Between 1955 and 1958[68] the cattle market was gradually moved to a 35–acre site adjoining St. Oswald's Road on the north-west outskirts of the city. The large new complex of buildings included traders' display units, shops, banks, a public house, and a restaurant, besides sale halls, covered accommodation for stock, an abattoir and meat market, and a large lorry park.[69] Gloucester market had by then become one of the leading stock markets in the country, known particularly for its pig and sheep sales, the latter attracting buyers from all over southern England.[70] In 1980, when the firm of J. Pearce Pope & Sons shared the conduct of the market business with Bruton, Knowles, & Co., the stock sales were held on Mondays and Thursdays.

FAIRS. In 1302 the Crown granted the burgesses a seven-day fair around the Nativity of St. John the Baptist (24 June).[71] James I's charter of 1605 granted the city two additional fairs, to be held on the Annunciation (25 March) and the two days following and on 17–19 November.[72] The three fairs, which came to be held for only one day each and, after the calendar change, took place on 5 April, 5 July, and 28 November,[73] appear to have been principally for cattle in the 18th century.[74] The November fair was also the main horse fair; the horse fair on that date was held in New Street (possibly the later Queen Street) near the east gate in the middle of the century.[75] After the opening of the new cattle market in 1823 special sales of cattle and horses took place there on the three days, and by 1910 the days of holding them had been fixed as the first Saturdays in April and in July and the last in November. The April fair had by then come to specialize in the sale of shorthorn bulls.[76]

There was another fair, Barton Fair, which did not belong to the corporation and was held outside the city boundary, factors which may have contributed to its growth into the most notable of the Gloucester fairs. In 1465 the abbot of Gloucester as fee farmer of King's Barton manor was granted the right to a fair on the eve, day, and morrow of St. Lambert (17 September).[77] In 1586 the Crown granted the rights in the fair to Edward Reed and William Hulbert[78] who sold them later that year to Thomas Evans. Evans sold the fair in 1599 to John Madock[79] (d. 1606),[80] whose grandson John Madock of Hartpury sold it in 1683 to Francis Wheeler of Bridgnorth (Salop.). Wheeler was succeeded by his nephew Robert Carpenter, whose widow Audrey settled the fair in 1725 on their daughter Susannah and her husband Strickland Lodge. Lodge and his wife both died in 1764 and their devisee Strickland Holden in 1765, and Holden's two sons sold the fair in 1765 or soon afterwards to Samuel Hayward,[81] later of Wallsworth Hall, Sandhurst. Hayward (d. 1790) was succeeded by his son-in-law Walter Wilkins, who sold his rights to the corporation in 1823.[82]

Barton Fair was described as a pig fair in 1586[83]

[54] Glos. Colln. NZ 12.5.

[55] G.B.R., B 4/1/7, f. 18.

[56] Ibid. 8, pp. 251, 261.

[57] Glouc. Jnl. 19, 26 June 1852.

[58] Ibid. 7 Feb. 1857. A plan for such a market in 1854 was presumably not implemented: ibid. 15 Apr. 1854.

[59] Kelly's Dir. Glos. (1870), 552.

[60] Glouc. Jnl. 26 May 1894.   [61] Ibid. 3 Nov. 1928.

[62] Glouc. Market and Improvement Act, 1 & 2 Geo. IV, c. 22.

[63] G.B.R., B 4/1/3, f. 19; F 4/15, pp. 596–7.

[64] Glos. Colln. prints GL 57.1.

[65] G.B.R., B 4/1/8, pp. 15, 55, 109.

[66] Glos. Colln. NF 12.249–51; NZ 12.5.

[67] Ibid. NR 12.42.

[68] Glouc. Municipal Year Bk. (1964–5), 76.

[69] Handbk. of Glouc. Corp. Markets [c. 1957], 14–20: copy in Glos. Colln. NF 12.246 (1).

[70] Ibid. 27, 29.

[71] Cal. Chart. R. 1300–26, 29.

[72] Glouc. Corp. Rec. p. 39.

[73] Gell and Bradshaw, Glos. Dir. (1820), 115.

[74] Glouc. Jnl. 8 Apr. 1765; Glos. Colln. R 22.1, entries for 5 Apr., 5 July 1763.

[75] Glouc. Jnl. 4 Nov. 1746.

[76] Kelly's Dir. Glos. (1863), 271; Glos. Colln. NR 12.42.

[77] Cal. Chart. R. 1427–1516, 206.

[78] G.B.R., J 1/1909.

[79] Glos. R.O., D 626, abs. of title to est. in Twigworth and Down Hatherley.

[80] P.R.O., C 142/297, no. 143.

[81] Glos. R.O., D 626, abs. of title to est. in Twigworth and Down Hatherley.

[82] G.B.R., F 4/15, p. 531; cf. V.C.H. Glos. vii. 204; Rudder, Glos. 638.

[83] G.B.R., J 1/1909.

but it later became widely known as a cheese fair, serving the rich dairying region of the Vale of Gloucester.[84] The volume of cheese brought to the fair declined towards the end of the 18th century as the practice of buying it directly from the farms became more common,[85] but the fair still attracted enough of that commodity for it to be described as 'our great cheese fair' in 1792,[86] and it was also fairly important as a livestock fair.[87] It also became the city's principal pleasure fair, attracting pedlars, gypsies, and travelling showmen in large numbers.[88] By the 18th century the fair had apparently become restricted to a single day (28 September after 1752), but by 1756 it had become the custom to hold two mops, or hiring fairs, in connexion with it, on the two Mondays following[89] and by 1808 mops were held on three Mondays.[90] The ancient site of the fair was in Barton Street.[91] In the 18th century and the early 19th the mops were held in a part of the street a short way beyond the city boundary.[92] The livestock fair was held on a field called Barton Hill, some way south of the street, in the early 19th century, and in 1823 the corporation moved it to the new cattle market.[93] In 1910 it dealt mainly in sheep and horses, with Irish hunters and unbroken Welsh ponies among the animals sold,[94] and by the 1950s it had become a major sheep fair attracting stock and buyers from a wide area and in some years dealing in as many as 10,000 animals.[95] Pleasure fairs continued in Barton Street on the days of Barton Fair and the three mops,[96] whose hiring function dwindled in the late 19th century.[97] In 1880 an attempt by the magistrates to move the fairs was resisted by local shopkeepers and others.[98] In 1904, however, the installation of equipment for the tramways caused the removal of the fairs to Oxlease by Over causeway.[99]

PUBLIC SERVICES

WATER SUPPLY.[1] The earliest piped water supplies were brought to Gloucester by the initiative of the religious houses. The copious springs rising on Robins Wood Hill, which provided the principal supply to the city until the 19th century, were exploited by Gloucester Abbey from the early 13th century. The sacrist Ellis of Hereford (d. 1237) was said to have built a fresh water supply for the abbey,[2] and it was presumably in connexion with his scheme that the owner of springs on the hill, William Geraud, granted the abbey the right to take water and to hold land on which a reservoir had been formed. The abbey's rights were confirmed before 1284 by a later owner, Philip, son of Philip of Matson.[3] William Geraud also granted rights in the springs to the Franciscan friars of Gloucester who later engaged in disputes with the abbey over the water; by a settlement made in 1357 after mediation by the prince of Wales the friars' pipe from the hill was limited to one third the size of the abbey's pipe.[4] The Carmelite friars also built a water supply for their house, laying a pipe from Goosewhite well on the east side of the city in the 1340s.[5]

In 1438 the Franciscans granted to the bailiffs and community of the town three quarters of the water coming through their Robins Wood Hill pipe together with the right to pipe it to the high cross or elsewhere in the town;[6] the cross had been adapted as a public conduit by 1446, when property was assigned for its upkeep.[7] By 1509 at least one house in the town had its own private pipe, for which the corporation was paid 20s. a year,[8] and the number of private pipes had proliferated by 1571 when they were causing shortages at the public conduit.[9] The corporation was retaining a town plumber to maintain the system in 1494,[10] and later it made contracts for terms of years with local plumbers for that purpose.[11] It bought the pipeline coming from Robins Wood Hill and the other quarter share of the water, together with the freehold of Greyfriars, in 1630.[12] The separate Gloucester Abbey pipeline continued to be used after the Dissolution by the dean and chapter,[13] who were associated with the corporation in an Act of Parliament of 1542 which gave the two bodies licence to exploit additional springs on the hill.[14] In the early 17th century the

[84] Atkyns, *Glos.* 255.   [85] Rudder, *Glos.* 207.
[86] *Glouc. Jnl.* 1 Oct. 1792.
[87] Ibid. 3 Oct. 1808; 30 Sept. 1816.
[88] e.g. ibid. 3 Oct. 1785; 29 Sept. 1794.
[89] Ibid. 21 Sept. 1756.
[90] Ibid. 10 Oct. 1808; cf. *Bretherton's Dir. Glouc.* (1867), 4.
[91] G.B.R., J 1/1909.
[92] *Glouc. Jnl.* 21 Sept. 1756; 10 Oct. 1808; cf. Glouc. and Stroud Road Act, 18 Geo. III, c. 98 (the turnpike referred to was then on or near the city boundary). Several lanes much further out, meeting S. of World's End, were known as Mop Lane in the late 18th cent. and early 19th but no connexion with the mop is known: Glos. R.O., Q/RI 70 (map R); D 3117/1101; D 9363/3; G.B.R., J 4/9, no. 15.
[93] Glouc. Market and Improvement Act, 1 & 2 Geo. IV, c. 22; cf. Hall and Pinnell, *Map of Glouc.* (1780).
[94] Glos. Colln. NR 12.42.
[95] *Handbk. of Markets*, 27.
[96] *Bretherton's Dir. Glouc.* (1867), 4; *Glouc. Jnl.* 3 July 1880.
[97] Above, Glouc. 1835–1985, econ. development 1835–1914.   [98] *Glouc. Jnl.* 3, 10 July, 7 Aug., 4 Sept. 1880.
[99] G.B.R., B 3/38, pp. 474, 481, 497, 517.
[1] This article was written in 1981 and revised in 1986.
[2] *Hist. & Cart. Mon. Glouc.* (Rolls Ser.), i. 28.
[3] *Trans. B.G.A.S.* lxxxvii. 117–18.
[4] *Glouc. Corp. Rec.* pp. 351–3.
[5] Ibid. p. 343; *Cal. Pat. 1340–3*, 255.
[6] *Glouc. Corp. Rec.* pp. 391–2.
[7] G.B.R., J 1/1936; cf. *Glouc. Rental, 1455*, sketches.
[8] G.B.R., J 5/3.   [9] Ibid. B 3/1, f. 31.
[10] Ibid. F 4/2.
[11] e.g. ibid. B 3/1, ff. 49, 488; 2, p. 445; 9, f. 56 and v.
[12] Ibid. 1, f. 546; cf. ibid. J 3/3, ff. 51v.–52.
[13] Ibid. B 3/3, p. 900.
[14] Glouc. Conduits Act, 33 Hen. VIII, c. 35.

chapter's tenant of the Ram inn, in Northgate Street, beneath which its pipeline ran, served as the 'aquaeductor', with responsibility for maintaining the pipeline and a wellhouse on the hill.[15]

During the 17th century efforts were made to improve the city's supplies of the Robins Wood Hill water. In 1623 the corporation shared with the parishioners of St. Mary de Grace the cost of building a conduit against the wall of that church,[16] and in 1636 John Scriven at his own cost built a conduit south of the market house in Southgate Street.[17] Another conduit which stood near Holy Trinity church by 1635[18] was dismantled c. 1690 and the cistern and pipes moved under the church tower.[19] Public wells continued to be used and in 1653 the corporation made grants to help parish ratepayers to improve two of them: an ancient well at the north gate, which had been in use in 1494, was reopened and a pump placed over it, and a pump in St. Mary de Lode parish was repaired. Orders made the same year for locking the public conduits at night were presumably part of a general concern about the adequacy of the city's supplies.[20]

In 1693 Thomas Nicholls, a Gloucester plumber who had taken over the maintenance of the Robins Wood Hill pipe for life in 1680,[21] devised a scheme for supplying the city with water from the river Severn. In partnership with Richard Lowbridge, an ironmonger of Stourbridge (Worcs.), and Daniel Denell, a carpenter of Handsworth (Staffs.), he built a pump house near Westgate bridge to pump water to a cistern installed in the top of the King's Board in upper Westgate Street and had licence from the corporation for piping supplies to householders who contracted with him. The works were completed in 1695, when three more shareholders were admitted, but the venture was not apparently a success, for of the six shares, each valued at £250 initially, one was sold for £60 in 1737 and another for £120 in 1741.[22] The company's area of supply was presumably limited to the lower part of Westgate Street and the Island. The system was abandoned with the removal of the King's Board under the improvement Act of 1750.[23]

The next major attempt to improve the city's supplies came in 1740 when an Act empowered the corporation to build new works on Robins Wood Hill.[24] The corporation made its powers over to John Selwyn, owner of the springs on the hill and one of the city M.P.s, who had paid the expenses of the Act.[25] Selwyn built two reservoirs and laid new pipes. In 1744 he was supplying c. 140 households in the city.[26] He and his successors at Matson continued to supply the city until 1836 when Viscount Sydney sold the works to the Gloucester Water company, constituted under an Act of that year with powers to build new works and supply an area which included the city and the hamlets and parishes immediately surrounding it.[27] The company's supply was fairly soon found inadequate for the growing city, particularly after 1849 when the corporation in its role of board of health began to exercise its powers to make householders connect to the supply[28] and began to put pressure on the company to extend its mains to the newer areas of the city.[29] In 1851 the company was supplying only about one seventh of the houses in the city.[30]

In 1854 the corporation acting as board of health bought the water company's undertaking.[31] Finding it possible to supply the city for no more than two days a week, the board adopted temporary measures to supplement the supply: new wells, most of which were in the event found to produce water unfit for use, were dug and water was pumped up from the Severn to the reservoirs.[32] In 1855 the board took powers for building new works at Great Witcombe and for a wider area of supply.[33] Supplies were taken directly from the Horsbere brook at Witcombe[34] until 1863 when two large new reservoirs, fed from the numerous springs in the area, were completed; a third reservoir was opened in 1870.[35] The distribution system within the city was also extended by the board and by the end of 1856 covered all parts of the city as then constituted.[36] By 1867 about five sixths of the houses within the boundary were connected to it.[37]

Regular extensions to the mains were required in subsequent years to keep pace with new building;[38] in 1879 535 applications for connexion were received.[39] Many of the old and new houses within the enlarged city still remained unconnected in 1887, however, when 1,294 were said to draw supplies from impure surface wells,[40] but the number dependent on well water had been reduced to 163 by 1893 and to only 12 by 1900.[41] From 1871 a part of the Bristol Road area, comprising 187 houses in 1893, was supplied from waterworks built at Hempsted by the Revd. Samuel Lysons; in 1897 those houses were connected to the city supply.[42]

[15] S. Eward, *No Fine but a Glass of Wine* (1985), 25.
[16] G.B.R., B 3/1, ff. 487v., 494v.
[17] Ibid. 2, p. 39.
[18] Ibid. F 4/5, f. 34.
[19] Bodl. MS. Top. Glouc. c. 3, ff. 40, 41; cf. G.B.R., B 3/8, p. 46.
[20] G.B.R., B 3/2, pp. 715, 735, 740; and for the 1494 reference, ibid. F 4/2.
[21] Ibid. B 3/3, p. 763.
[22] Ibid. B 8/17–21.
[23] Cf. B. Martin, *Natural Hist. of Eng.* (1759), 354.
[24] Glouc. Waterworks Act, 14 Geo. II, c. 11.
[25] Glos. R.O., D 149/E 33.
[26] Glos. Colln. NR 12.33; NX 12.2 (2); cf. Glos. R.O., Q/RI 70 (map P).
[27] Glouc. Waterworks Act, 6 & 7 Wm. IV, c. 67 (Local and Personal).

[28] G.B.R., N 2/1/1, pp. 7–8, 10 sqq.
[29] Ibid. pp. 26, 42, 87–8.
[30] Ibid. p. 338.
[31] Ibid. 2, min. 8 June 1854.
[32] Ibid. mins. 28, 31 Aug., 14 Sept., 24 Nov. 1854.
[33] Glouc. Waterworks Act, 18 & 19 Vic. c. 89 (Local and Personal).
[34] G.B.R., N 2/1/2, mins. 13 Apr. 1855, 19 Feb. 1856.
[35] *Proc. C.N.F.C.* xvii. 347–8.
[36] G.B.R., N 2/1/2, min. 18 Dec. 1856.
[37] *Glouc. Jnl.* 26 Oct. 1867.
[38] G.B.R., B 4/7/1, mins. 6 Dec. 1875, 22 Feb. 1877 sqq.
[39] Ibid. min. 23 Apr. 1880.
[40] Ibid. 6/3, min. 17 June 1887.
[41] *Rep. of Medical Off. of Health, 1893, 1900*: copies of the reps. are in Glos. Colln. N 12.141.
[42] Ibid. *1893, 1897*; G.B.R., B 4/5/3, min. 2 Mar. 1871.

By the early 1890s the Robins Wood Hill and Witcombe works were no longer sufficient for the city. While possible new schemes were examined, Severn water, introduced through a pumping and filtration works built at Walham in 1893 was used temporarily to supplement supplies.[43] In 1894 the corporation took powers for building what became known as its Newent works, involving a well and pumping station in Oxenhall parish and a reservoir at Madam's Wood near Upleadon. Those works were completed in 1896 and a second reservoir was built at Madam's Wood in 1901.[44] In 1911 the corporation built another well and pumping station at Ketford in Pauntley parish to increase supplies to Madam's Wood.[45] The need for yet further sources of supply led the corporation in 1936 to join with Cheltenham corporation in the formation of the Cheltenham and Gloucester joint water board.[46] The existing Cheltenham corporation works at Tewkesbury were much enlarged and water from the Severn was pumped up to reservoirs on Churchdown Hill. From 1942 that supply provided the bulk of Gloucester's needs, though the Witcombe, Newent, and Ketford sources continued to be used,[47] the Ketford works being modernized in 1951 and those at Oxenhall in 1957. Robins Wood Hill ceased to be used as a source of supply in 1924 but the reservoirs there remained in use for storage until 1946.[48] Some of the older outlying settlements adjoining the city were not connected to its supply until the mid 20th century: in 1930 Twigworth village was still wholly dependent on wells, while only 19 of the 130 houses in Longford parish and only 13 of the 115 houses in Hempsted parish had mains water.[49]

From the 1930s Gloucester corporation negotiated agreements for supplying adjoining rural areas and in 1938 began work on a scheme for the southern parishes of Gloucester rural district. In the mid 1940s a major scheme was built to provide supplies to the northern part of the Thornbury rural district.[50] The undertakings of the corporation and the joint board were taken over by the North West Gloucestershire water board in 1965 and that in its turn was absorbed by the Severn-Trent water authority in 1974. Under the new authority Gloucester continued to receive most of its water from the Tewkesbury works, supplemented by water brought from the river Wye through a new treatment works at Mitcheldean. The Witcombe, Newent, and Ketford sources continued in use for supplying some rural areas of the county.[51]

GAS SUPPLY. A gas company was formed in 1819 when powers to provide public gaslighting were granted to the governor and guardians of the poor. It built its works in Quay Street and was incorporated in the following year as the Gloucester Gaslight company.[52] Some street lamps and supplies to some private consumers were provided during 1820,[53] but the company encountered early difficulties and improvements to the original works were found to be necessary. By 1829, however, the system was working well.[54] In 1834 the company was given powers to raise additional capital for providing a supply for the suburbs.[55] In 1872 the limits of supply of the company were widened to cover an area lying within three miles of the original (pre-1835) city boundary and it was given powers for new gasworks,[56] which were built between 1874 and 1877 on the Bristol road near Podsmead.[57] A further extension in 1898 took the limits of supply to the outer boundaries of Hardwicke, Brockworth, and Down Hatherley parishes,[58] and another in 1935 included parts of Newent and East Dean rural districts.[59] After nationalization in 1948 the Gloucester works continued in use as one of the South West Gas Board's chief manufacturing stations until the 1960s when the region was supplied with gas made from oil products, replaced in the early 1970s by natural gas from the North Sea.[60]

ELECTRICITY SUPPLY. From 1889 onwards several companies put forward proposals for supplying the city with electricity, but the corporation decided to provide its own supply and took powers for doing so in 1896. Its works, built in Commercial Road, were opened in 1900 and the provision of street lamps and the connexion of private consumers to the supply began that year.[61] In 1927 the parishes of the Gloucester rural district were added to the corporation's area of supply.[62] In 1943 the works were replaced by a new power station built at Castle Meads with access for coal supplies from a branch railway and a jetty on the Severn. The undertaking was nationalized in 1948,[63] and the Castle Meads power station continued to supply the National Grid until it was closed in 1970.[64]

PAVING, CLEANING, AND LIGHTING. The town had regular grants of pavage from 1321;[65] in 1410 the administration of the fund was

[43] G.B.R., B 3/27, pp. 103–4, 121, 163, 195, 224, 281, 313; ibid. rep. on Glouc. water supply, 1893.
[44] Glouc. Corp. Act, 57 & 58 Vic. c. 91 (Local); *Proc. C.N.F.C.* xvii. 349–50.
[45] Glouc. Corp. Act, 1 & 2 Geo. V, c. 92 (Local).
[46] Cheltenham and Glouc. Joint Water Board Act, 26 Geo. V and 1 Edw. VIII, c. 29 (Local).
[47] Glos. Colln. NQ 12.83; *Glouc. Municipal Year Bk.* (1964–5), 77.
[48] *Glouc. Municipal Year Bk.* (1964–5), 77.
[49] Richardson, *Wells and Springs of Glos.* 102, 113, 164.
[50] Glos. Colln. NQ 12.83.
[51] *Glouc. Official Guide* (1980), 79–80.
[52] Glouc. Gas Act, 1 Geo. IV, c. 10 (Local and Personal);

cf. below, paving, cleaning and lighting.
[53] *Glouc. Jnl.* 31 Jan., 14 Feb. 1820.
[54] Counsel, *Glouc.* 182.
[55] Glouc. Gas Act, 4 Wm. IV, c. 52 (Local and Personal).
[56] Glouc. Gas Act, 35 & 36 Vic. c. 5 (Local).
[57] *Kelly's Dir. Glos.* (1889), 816.
[58] Glouc. Gas Act, 61 & 62 Vic. c. 69 (Local).
[59] *Index to Local and Personal Acts, 1801–1947*, 616, 656.
[60] *Glouc. Official Guide* (1966), 56; (1980), 78.
[61] G.B.R., B 6/31/1.
[62] Ibid. 38.
[63] *Glouc. Municipal Year Bk.* (1964–5), 82.
[64] *Citizen*, 2 Apr. 1969.
[65] *Cal. Pat.* 1317–21, 578.

the responsibility of the stewards who expended the considerable sum of £17 17s. in that year.[66] In 1473 the bailiffs and stewards petitioned the Crown about the poor state of repair of the paving in the town and secured an order that the householders in the four principal streets should make the pavement from the fronts of their houses to the middle of the street, the officers being given power to do the work if necessary and recover the cost from those responsible by distraint;[67] the obligation of tenants to repair the pavements created under the order was later a regular provision in leases of Gloucester Abbey's houses in the main streets.[68] An improvement Act of 1776 made all householders and property owners responsible for making up and keeping in repair the streets adjoining their houses, and to superintend and enforce the work it provided for the appointment of parish surveyors, to be chosen by the city magistrates each year from lists supplied by the vestries. Pitching was to be allowed only in the side streets. The four main streets were to be surfaced with flat paving stones and were to have side gutters and foot pavements 5 ft. wide.[69] Foot pavements may already have existed in some places, for an order by the common council in 1743 allowed householders to pave with broad stones up to 5 ft. from their doors provided that 12 ft. of roadway was left between.[70] The paving of the main streets under the Act was completed in 1778, and College Court was also paved by means of subscription.[71] Under an Act of 1781 the obligation to provide flat paving was extended to include the Island, lower Northgate Street, St. Mary's Square, and Three Cocks Lane.[72]

The city corporation through its ownership of the gates, quay, market houses, and other public buildings was liable to repair a considerable area of the main streets, and it took responsibility for the upkeep of all five of the main roads between the gates and the city boundary. On the Bristol road it also repaired beyond the boundary as far as the Sud brook, using an annual sum of £4 given by Sir Thomas Bell by deed of 1562, and from at least 1651, perhaps by virtue of its hospital property, it repaired the London road beyond the boundary as far as Wotton Pitch.[73] Repair of the public pavements and pitchings was consigned by the corporation to contractors for 21 years in 1705 and 1736,[74] and contracts for shorter terms were made later.[75] In 1798 a deficit in the corporation's

budget was attributed mainly to the recent heavy cost of street repairs.[76] In 1849 it was responsible for 40,886 yd. of the streets and private owners were responsible for 45,731 yd., while the Gloucester and Berkeley canal company and the spa company maintained streets laid out around their respective undertakings.[77] In that year the responsibilities of the parish surveyors under the improvement Acts passed to the corporation under its new powers as a board of health. From that date the board repaired the roadways out of the rates but the cost of repairing the foot pavements in the streets covered by the Acts remained the responsibility of the property holders until 1861.[78]

Some parts of the city streets had been macadamized by 1828,[79] but macadamization of the main streets was mostly done by the board of health in 1850. Later in that decade the old pitching of some of the minor streets and lanes was replaced by a macadamized surface and their old central gutters were at last done away with.[80]

Attempts by the town authorities to enforce street cleaning were recorded from the beginning of the 16th century, when butchers' refuse was the main cause for concern.[81] There was a common 'gorreour' responsible for clearing out the butchers' shambles in 1514; he was ordered to operate at night because of the stench that was caused.[82] The butchers' refuse was dumped on a piece of land near the quay, assigned for that purpose in 1454.[83] Bearland in the same area of the town was used for common dunghills from at least 1372 when complaints were made by the constable of the castle.[84] In the early 16th century there were other common dunghills at the south end of Hare Lane and at Goose ditch outside the east wall.[85] From 1600 the corporation periodically appointed scavengers but the post does not appear to have been established on a regular basis,[86] perhaps because of the problem, evident in the 1670s, of raising his salary by a special rate.[87] In 1641 the common council enacted that individual householders should clean once a week the parts of the paved streets for which they were responsible and instituted an inspection committee and fines for neglect.[88] In 1731 it ruled that distress might be taken from householders to enforce the removal of rubbish from outside houses.[89] In the 1760s at least two of the larger parishes employed scavengers for their own

[66] G.B.R., F 4/1.

[67] *Glouc. Corp. Rec.* pp. 15–16; a similar petition, for powers for all the streets of the town, had been made in 1455: *Rot. Parl.* v. 338.

[68] e.g. Glouc. Cath. Libr., Reg. Abb. Braunche, pp. 32, 34, 43, 53, 80.

[69] Maisemore Bridge and Glouc. Improvement Act, 17 Geo. III, c. 68.

[70] G.B.R., B 3/10, f. 23.

[71] *Glouc. Jnl.* 7 Sept. 1778.

[72] Glouc. Gaol and Improvement Act, 21 Geo. III, c. 74.

[73] G.B.R., J 3/6, ff. 364v.–365; B 8/22; F 4/5, ff. 22 and v., 48, 72, 79, 372, 431v.–433, 454v.; Bodl. MS. Top. Glouc. c. 3, f. 41 and v.; Glos. R.O., D 204/1/1, min. 30 Jan. 1798; *14th Rep. Com. Char.* 19.

[74] G.B.R., J 3/6, ff. 364v.–365; B 8/22.

[75] Ibid. B 3/11, ff. 278v.–289; B 4/1/4, ff. 23v., 111v.

[76] Ibid. B 3/12, f. 284.

[77] *Rep. to General Bd. of Health on Sanitary Condition of Glouc.* (1849), 38–9: copy in Glos. Colln. N 12.119.

[78] G.B.R., N 2/1/1, pp. 1–2, 304, 388; 3, min. 23 Apr. 1861; *Glouc. Jnl.* 20 Oct. 1860; 27 Apr. 1861.

[79] G.B.R., B 4/1/4, f. 23v.

[80] Ibid. N 2/1/1, pp. 69–70, 83, 110, 115–16, 139, 775; 2, mins. 9 May 1856, 8 May, 4 Sept. 1857.

[81] Ibid. B 2/1, ff. 17–18.

[82] Ibid. f. 22v.

[83] Ibid. f. 48v.; Glos. Colln. 11664, no. 1.

[84] *Cal. Pat.* 1370–4, 243, 293; cf. G.B.R., B 2/2, ff. 44v.–45; J 3/3, ff. 40v.–41.

[85] G.B.R., J 5/3.

[86] Ibid. B 3/1, ff. 185, 538; 2, pp. 198, 355, 746; 9, f. 75v.

[87] Ibid. 3, pp. 468, 516, 570, 595, 604.

[88] Ibid. 2, pp. 201–2.

[89] Ibid. 9, f. 308 and v.

areas,[90] and in 1769 the magistrates invoked powers given them under a recent statute and appointed two for the city.[91]

The duties of the parish surveyors appointed under the improvement Act of 1776 included organizing street cleaning twice a week, and the Act also required householders to sweep their parts of the footways every Saturday and laid down detailed penalties for leaving rubbish in the streets.[92] The system created by the Act was not working satisfactorily in 1812 when the corporation attempted a more rigid enforcement of the penalties for leaving rubbish in the streets and appointed an inspector of nuisances.[93] In the late 1840s, when each parish had its own scavenger who contracted with the surveyors, the work was very inefficiently done, and some of the newer streets, having not yet been adopted by the parishes, were not covered at all. Many householders found it necessary to make private arrangements for rubbish disposal.[94] The board of health on its appointment in 1849 at first intended to employ direct labour for scavenging and bought two horse-drawn sweeping machines, but it soon decided to use contractors, who were required to sweep the streets and remove night soil three times a week.[95] Carts for watering the streets were also acquired by the board.[96] Four sites outside the town were assigned as refuse tips in 1849,[97] and later, between 1902 and 1923, a refuse destructor incorporated in the city electricity works was in use.[98]

An early measure to provide street lighting was taken by the council in 1685 when it ordered all householders paying at least 2d. a week in poor rates to hang lanterns outside their doors on winter evenings.[99] St. Nicholas's parish was maintaining public oil lamps in the 1720s,[1] as was St. Mary de Crypt in 1734, when the governor and guardians of the poor decided to take responsibility for all the public lamps of the city.[2] That responsibility was returned to the parish vestries in 1755[3] but once more taken by the guardians under the Act reconstituting them in 1764.[4] By 1790 the guardians were maintaining c. 160 lights and employing a lamplighter.[5]

By an Act of 1819 the governor and guardians were empowered to provide gaslighting in the city, the rates levied by them to be authorized by the corporation. The newly formed gas company began to install gaslights in the streets the following year.[6] In the 1830s difficulties over securing a satisfactory contract with the company led the governor and guardians to contemplate purchasing the undertaking.[7] In 1834 commissioners, including the mayor and aldermen and the county magistrates, were appointed to light the suburbs lying within a mile from the city boundary.[8] The unequal rights levied by the two lighting authorities later caused dissatisfaction,[9] and in 1865 the lighting powers of the governor and guardians and those of the commissioners in the area added to the city in 1835 were transferred to the corporation as board of health.[10] The suburban commissioners lost a further area to the corporation under the boundary extension of 1874,[11] but in 1894 they were given powers over the suburbs within two miles of the then boundary[12] and, in the area left to them by later boundary extensions, continued to operate until the mid 20th century.[13] Electric lighting was introduced in the city streets from 1900.[14]

SEWERAGE. In 1831 the city corporation and the improvement commissioners were urged by the voluntary board of health, set up to meet the threat of the cholera epidemic, to take action on providing a sewerage system for Gloucester.[15] It was the approach of cholera to England in 1847 that once more aroused concern about the sanitary state of the city. A memorial by the city's doctors then stated that 'all the evils which arise from a total want of a system of sewerage exist here to a very serious extent' and urged the corporation to take measures for cleaning the streams and ditches surrounding the city, into which most of the sewage drained. A sanitary committee, formed by the corporation in response to that appeal, appointed an inspector of nuisances and made some attempt to improve the situation. The culverting of one of the most notorious ditches, on the city's northern boundary behind houses in Sweetbriar Street, carried out by the property owner Brasenose College at the committee's instigation, was regarded as an important improvement; but the measures taken were piecemeal and insufficient to prevent the arrival of cholera in 1849.[16] When the corporation assumed its powers as a board of health in 1849 it began culverting some more of the open ditches and improving surface drainage.[17] The building of a complete underground sewerage and drainage system, the planning of which was delayed until a detailed map of the city had been prepared by the Ordnance Survey, was begun by the board in

[90] Glos. R.O., P 154/11/OV 2/3, mins. 13 Jan. 1766, 2 Feb. 1767; 15/OV 2/4, min. 31 Oct. 1763.
[91] G.B.R., G 3/SO 8.
[92] Maisemore Bridge and Glouc. Improvement Act, 17 Geo. III, c. 68.
[93] Glouc. Jnl. 14 Sept. 1812.
[94] Rep. to General Bd. of Health on Glouc. (1849), 41.
[95] G.B.R., N 2/1/1, pp. 14, 30, 40, 44, 49, 242-3.
[96] Ibid. pp. 80, 104.
[97] Ibid. p. 36.
[98] Ibid. B 6/31/1; Glouc. Municipal Year Bk. (1964-5), 83.
[99] G.B.R., B 3/3, p. 896.
[1] Glos. R.O., P 154/15/OV 2/3.
[2] Ibid. D 3270/19712, pp. 229-31.
[3] Ibid. P 154/11/OV 2/3; 15/OV 2/3.
[4] Glouc. Poor-Relief and Lighting Act, 4 Geo. III, c. 60.

[5] Glouc. Jnl. 5 July 1790.
[6] Glouc. Lighting Act, 59 Geo. III, c. 69 (Local and Personal); above, gas supply.
[7] Glos. R.O., D 3270/19713.
[8] Glouc. Gas Act, 4 Wm. IV, c.52 (Local and Personal).
[9] G.B.R., B 6/21-2.
[10] Local Govt. Suppl. Act, 1865 (No. 3), 28 Vic. c. 41.
[11] Glouc. Extension and Improvement Act, 1874, 37 & 38 Vic. c. 111 (Local).
[12] Glouc. Corp. Act, 1894, 57 & 58 Vic. c. 91 (Local).
[13] G.B.R., L 22/5/2-8.
[14] Above, electricity supply.
[15] G.B.R., B 3/14, f. 180v.; Glouc. Jnl. 26 Nov. 1831.
[16] G.B.R., B 4/6/1; Glouc. Jnl. 24 Mar. 1849.
[17] G.B.R., N 2/1/1, passim.

1853 and completed in 1855.[18] The system was based on two main outfall sewers which emptied into the Severn at the north end of the quay.[19] Modifications and additions began almost immediately, including works carried out in 1858 and 1859 to prevent pollution of the Sud brook on the city boundary in the Spa area; in collaboration with three adjoining hamlets and the Gloucester and Berkeley canal company, a sewer was laid under the bed of the stream from Parkend Road to Bristol Road, where it was connected to the new city system.[20]

Sewering the outlying areas, as new building progressed rapidly in the mid and later 19th century, was a piecemeal process, hampered by friction between the various sanitary authorities, and it was many years before the problem of pollution of watercourses, including the Twyver, the Sud brook, and the Still ditch (the Sud brook west of the canal), was completely solved. In 1863 the local boards of health formed for Barton St. Michael and Barton St. Mary took over responsibility for the newly developed lower Barton Street area. That area relied for sewerage on a rudimentary system of culverted ditches connecting with the Twyver or with the Sud brook,[21] which the boards, acting jointly, culverted from above Tredworth High Street to Parkend Road. An annual payment made to the city board for allowing the sewage to drain into the city system through the Sud brook sewer was the cause of much dispute and renegotiation, leading the Barton boards to consider plans for a separate outfall in 1871.[22] The local board formed in 1865 for Kingsholm St. Catherine on the north side of the city tackled the pollution of the Twyver by building a new system of sewers, completed in 1867, with its own outfall pipe across Meanham to the eastern channel of the Severn. Later the Kingsholm board made repeated complaints to the Gloucester board about the continuing pollution of the Twyver from houses within the city boundary.[23] Following the enlargement of the boundary and the abolition of the suburban boards in 1874, the city system was extended into the added areas. New sewers were laid in the Barton area in the years 1876–7, though it was not until 1885 that all house drains were given direct connexions to them; the continuing use of the old culverts as part of the system caused the problem of a build-up of gas, making it necessary to install ventilation pipes.[24] The Kingsholm board's sewers were linked to the city system in 1879 and the old outfall abandoned.[25]

In 1876 the Gloucester union as a rural sanitary authority formed the East End special drainage district and planned a scheme for sewering the Saintbridge area; due to the refusal of the city authority to allow it to connect with the city system, it was never built,[26] and that area was not adequately sewered until after the boundary extension of 1900.[27] In the Bristol Road area on the south side of the city co-operation was found possible. The rural sanitary authority formed the South End special drainage district in 1883,[28] and in the years 1884–5 collaborated with the city in building a new main outfall sewer from Stroud Road to the Severn below Llanthony weir and in filling the offensive Still ditch.[29] In 1897 the Gloucester rural district council formed the North End special drainage district and in 1898 completed a scheme for the Hucclecote, Barnwood, and Wotton areas, with an outfall works east of Pleasure Farm at Longford.[30] In the mid 20th century the principal scheme benefiting areas remaining outside the city was a new one built by the rural district for its northern parishes in the years 1939–41, with a treatment works by the Horsbere brook in Longford.[31]

Among significant improvements to the city system was the re-laying and enlargement of the main sewer along Barton Street in 1898,[32] and in 1912 the extension of the main outfall for the old city area under the eastern channel of the Severn to discharge into the western channel.[33] With its continuing expansion into newly built-up areas the sewerage and drainage system became overloaded and periodic flooding resulted. To ease the problem the new housing estates built after the First World War were given separate drainage systems for dealing with surface water, discharging it into streams.[34] Plans for a new main sewerage and drainage scheme were drawn up by the corporation in 1933 but it was not until 1951 that work on building it began. The scheme included various new trunk sewers, a pumping station at Netheridge opened in 1956 with an outfall on the river bank nearby, and a treatment plant built next to the pumping station and opened in 1963.[35] The new system was substantially complete by 1967 and was extended to the new area taken into the city that year. In 1974 management of the system passed to the new Severn-Trent water authority.[36]

FIRE SERVICE. The acquisition and maintenance of fire engines, ladders, and buckets was a periodic preoccupation of the city's common council. In 1635 it maintained fire buckets at churches and other places in the city and firehooks at the barley market house. The buckets were

[18] Ibid. pp. 3, 404, 437–8, 595–6; 2, mins. 14 Feb. 1854, 29 Nov. 1855.
[19] Ibid. B 3/31, rep. on sewerage system, 1897.
[20] Ibid. N 2/1/2, mins. 14 May 1858 – 7 Feb. 1859; Glouc. Jnl. 20 Nov. 1858; 3 Aug. 1872.
[21] G.B.R., B 3/31, rep. on sewerage system, 1897.
[22] Ibid. N 5/2.   [23] Ibid. N 6/1.
[24] Ibid. B 3/31, rep. on sewerage system, 1897.
[25] Ibid.; cf. ibid. B 4/7/1, min. 18 Feb. 1879.
[26] Glos. R.O., DA 27/100/1, ff. 59v. sqq.
[27] Rep. on Suggested Extension of Boundaries (1899): copy in Glos. R.O., DA 27/100/4.

[28] Glos. R.O., DA 27/100/1, ff. 157 sqq.; 2, ff. 5–6v., 14v.
[29] G.B.R., B 4/7/2, mins. of joint cttee.; B 3/31, rep. on sewerage system, 1897.
[30] Glos. R.O., DA 27/100/3, ff. 88 sqq.; Glouc. Jnl. 31 Dec. 1898.
[31] Glos. R.O., DA 27/100/12, pp. 17–18, 124, 218; 13, pp. 99, 153.
[32] Rep. of Medical Off. of Health, 1898.
[33] Glos. Colln. NF 12.429.
[34] Glouc. Official Guide (1966), 59.
[35] Glos. Colln. NF 12.429.
[36] Glouc. Official Guide (1980), 80.

supplied out of a fund made up of fines from new burgesses.[37] In 1648 the council ordered a fire engine from London, the cost to be met from the bucket money.[38] A second engine was bought in 1652 and part of Holy Trinity church was adapted to house the engines in 1656.[39] In 1702 a new engine house was built adjoining the tower of the church.[40] In 1741, when it owned four engines, the corporation bought a new one, to Richard Newsham's design, capable of raising water to a height of 30 ft.[41] In 1748 the corporation appointed six firemen, who were required to practise with the equipment every six weeks.[42]

In 1836 the city firefighting equipment was placed in the care of the superintendent of the police force formed that year, and in 1838 it was decided that the force as a whole should be drilled and instructed as a fire brigade.[43] The force was provided with a new engine and more modern equipment in 1849.[44] By that time and until the early 20th century, however, the bulk of the firefighting in the city was carried out by insurance companies,[45] two of which maintained brigades there in 1841[46] and three in 1867.[47]

In 1912 the corporation formed a new city brigade, accepting the free offer of the equipment of the Norwich Union and the Liverpool and London and Globe insurance companies, which had decided to disband their brigades.[48] A motor fire engine was bought and a fire station, opened in 1913, was built in Bearland.[49] The new brigade also took over the city's fire float.[50] That vessel, based in the docks and supplied with sufficient hose for fighting fires up to ½ mile from the canal, had been provided in 1906 as a joint project of the local firms of corn and timber merchants, the docks company, and the corporation;[51] the last had assumed complete control of the float in 1910.[52] The city brigade was taken over by the National Fire Service in 1941 and returned to the control of the corporation in 1948.[53] In 1949 it had a full-time strength of 50 men, based at Bearland and at a second station in Barnwood.[54] A new fire station, built in Eastern Avenue, was opened in 1956.[55] In 1972 the city brigade was amalgamated with the Gloucestershire county brigade.[56]

WATCHING AND POLICE. The serjeants-at-mace, bellmen, and other minor corporation offi-

cers were assisted in their policing duties in the city by a body of constables; by 1690 there were two constables each to act in the east and south wards of the city and four each in the west and north wards.[57] From 1769 one of the serjeants-at-mace was appointed as high constable by the magistrates and acted as head of the city police. Early in 1786 the magistrates directed the constables to maintain a night watch for the next few months[58] but that appears to have been only a temporary measure. A plan to set up a regular night watch financed from the rates was supported by a public meeting in 1812 but met with opposition from some of the parish vestries, as did a revival of the plan in 1814,[59] and arrangements for watching were not placed on a regular basis[60] until 1821. An Act then required each parish to submit a list of three candidates each year to the magistrates who were to choose one man from each list to form the watch and make regulations for its procedure.[61]

In 1836 a full-time uniformed police force was formed for the city by the watch committee set up by the corporation under the provisions of the Municipal Corporations Act. The force comprised a superintendent, 3 sergeants, one of whom lived at the city lock-up in Southgate Street which became the police station, and 12 constables. The corporation officers and four watchmen employed by the Gloucester and Berkeley canal company were also sworn in as constables to enable them to assist the police when necessary.[62] The city police force was amalgamated with the Gloucestershire county force in 1859 when it was agreed that a force of 32 men should be stationed at Gloucester, 20 of them to be paid for by the city; the force was also to police a suburban area previously policed by a small county detachment stationed at Wotton.[63] The Gloucester force was increased to a strength of 40 after the extension of the city boundary in 1874,[64] and in 1906 it numbered 76, under the command of a deputy chief constable.[65] Marybone House in Bearland was bought for use as a police station in 1858[66] and a large new station was built on the site as part of the new Shire Hall complex in the early 1960s.

CEMETERIES. The corporation was constituted the burial board for the city in 1856 and laid out as a cemetery a 13-acre site at

[37] G.B.R., F 4/5, ff. 29, 32v.–33v.
[38] Ibid. B 3/2, pp. 447, 451.
[39] Ibid. pp. 679, 859.
[40] Ibid. 8, pp. 46, 292.
[41] *Glouc. Jnl.* 15 Sept. 1741; G.B.R., F 4/9, pp. 281, 301, 321; for Newsham, *D.N.B.*
[42] G.B.R., B 3/10, f. 121.
[43] Ibid. B 4/3/1.
[44] Ibid. 2.
[45] Cf. *Glouc. Jnl.* 28 Feb. 1885; 26 Nov. 1887; *Glouc. Official Guide* (1966), 85.
[46] *Bryant's, Dir. Glouc.* (1841), 87.
[47] *Bretherton's Dir. Glouc.* (1867), 59, 125.
[48] *Glouc. Corp. Mins.* (1911–12), pp. 25, 83–5, 149, 261–3.
[49] *Glouc. Jnl.* 19 July 1913.
[50] *Rep. of Chief Off. of Glouc. Fire Brigade* (1913): copy in Glos. Colln. N 12.66.
[51] *Glouc. Jnl.* 14 July 1906; *Glouc. Corp. Mins.* (1905–6), pp. 14–15.
[52] *Glouc. Corp. Mins.* (1909–10), pp. 392–3.
[53] *Glouc. Municipal Year Bk.* (1964–5), 85–6.
[54] *Rep. of Chief Off. and Glouc. Fire Brigade* (1949): copy in Glos. Colln. N 12.66.
[55] *Glouc. Municipal Year Bk.* (1964–5), 86.
[56] *Glouc. Official Guide* (1980), 51.
[57] Bodl. MS. Top. Glouc. c. 3, f. 47v.; G.B.R., G 3/SR, Trin. 1690; SIb 1, pp. 37, 114.
[58] G.B.R., G 3/SO 8.
[59] *Glouc. Jnl.* 20, 27 Jan. 1812; Glos. R.O., P 154/11/VE 2/1; 12/VE 2/1.
[60] Cf. *Glouc. Jnl.* 18 Dec. 1815; 17 Jan. 1820.
[61] Glouc. Market and Improvement Act, 1 & 2 Geo. IV, c. 22.
[62] G.B.R., B 4/3/1.
[63] Glos. R.O., Q/AP 10A.
[64] G.B.R., B 4/3/2, min. 23 Feb. 1875.
[65] *Kelly's Dir. Glos.* (1906), 178.
[66] Glos. R.O., DC/SJ 2.

Tredworth, which was opened in 1857 when burials in the old city churchyards ceased. Chapels for Anglicans and for nonconformists, linked by a central corridor surmounted by a tower and spire, were designed by the firm of Medland and Maberly.[67] The cemetery was

extended in 1875, 1909, and 1911, the final extension enlarging it to 35 a. A second city cemetery, at Coney Hill, was laid out in 1934[68] but not opened for burials until 1939. A crematorium, added to the cemetery chapel at Coney Hill, was opened in 1953.[69]

HOSPITALS

IN THE 18th and 19th centuries several hospitals were opened in and around Gloucester on private initiatives.[1] The most important, the Gloucester Infirmary, dated from 1755. In the early 19th century the county and city joined in the building of a lunatic asylum at Wotton and later the county built a second asylum in Barnwood. The city, which provided infectious diseases hospitals and in 1930 took over the infirmary of the Gloucester poor-law union, later built a maternity hospital. Before that a voluntary body had been the main provider of midwifery services in Gloucester. Anglican orders of nuns ran a children's hospital from 1867.

In 1948 the Gloucester, Stroud, and the Forest hospital management committee took control of the county and city general infirmaries, the maternity hospital, and an infectious diseases hospital at Over. The Horton Road and Coney Hill hospital management committee controlled the two mental hospitals from 1948 until 1965 when it amalgamated with the Gloucester, Stroud, and the Forest management committee.[2] A private hospital in Barnwood became an independent registered mental hospital and the work of two dispensaries was continued under the National Health Service in health centres provided by the city corporation, acting as local health authority. In the early 1960s a new general hospital was begun in Great Western Road and from the mid 1960s the city provided new buildings at Rikenel house in Montpellier as the centre for its health and welfare services.[3] At reorganization in 1974 the Gloucestershire area health authority took over the functions of both the hospital management committee and the local health authority, and in 1982 most of those functions devolved upon the Gloucester district health authority. A private hospital opened in the city in 1981.[4]

GENERAL INFIRMARIES. In the mid 1720s a hospital in Gloucester belonged to Mr. Sin-

gleton,[5] possibly Luke Singleton who later designed the Gloucester Infirmary.[6] Bishop Martin Benson collected subscriptions for an infirmary in the city and in 1752 left £200 for such a project. In 1754 a scheme for a dispensary in Stroud was extended to provide a county hospital at Gloucester. A subscription opened later that year[7] received wide support. The principal benefactors included Norborne Berkeley of Stoke Gifford, M.P. for the county, and the Revd. George Talbot of Temple Guiting. Benson's bequest was paid into the fund.[8]

In 1755 it was decided to build the Gloucester Infirmary outside the south gate and a temporary infirmary was opened at the Crown and Sceptre inn in lower Westgate Street. It was supported by voluntary contributions and the governors met every Thursday to manage it and admit patients. It was intended for patients from any country unable to pay for their keep and medicine. Admission was by subscriber's ticket and a donation of £20 conferred the same privileges as a subscription of £2 2s. Physicians and surgeons from the city gave their services free of charge and the resident staff included an apothecary, who had general care of the patients, a matron, and a secretary. Samuel Colborne, the first apothecary, came from London. In setting up the infirmary the governors took the Northampton Infirmary as their model and sent the matron and secretary to the Bristol Infirmary for instruction.[9]

In 1756 the governors acquired a lease of the site for the county infirmary[10] and George II gave timber from the Forest of Dean for building it.[11] Patients were admitted from 1761[12] and the temporary infirmary was closed. The infirmary in lower Southgate Street was built in brick to plans by Luke Singleton, approved after consultation with the Bath architect John Wood.[13] It had two storeys on a high basement and north and south wings contained the four principal wards, each with 18 beds. An extensive kitchen garden with orchard was laid out behind it.[14] In 1780 land

[67] G.B.R., B 4/1/7, ff. 134–5, 147, 158; *Building News*, 26 Mar. 1858, 325–6.
[68] *Kelly's Dir. Glos.* (1939), 183.
[69] *Glouc. Municipal Year Bk.* (1964–5), 78.
[1] This article was written in 1982 and revised in 1986.
[2] Glos. R.O., HO 22/26/4, 14.
[3] *Rep. of Medical Off. of Health, 1973*, 30–1: Copy in G.B.R., N 2/10/5.   [4] *Citizen*, 8 Feb. 1983.
[5] Glos. R.O., P 154/11/IN 1/2, burials 25 Aug. 1724, 7 Apr. 1725.
[6] *Glouc. Jnl.* 29 Aug. 1768.

[7] Ibid. 6 Feb. 1753; 12 Feb., 10 Sept. 1754; for Benson's will, P.R.O., PROB 11/797 (P.C.C. 249 Bettesworth), ff. 176–9.
[8] Glos. R.O., HO 19/8/1; cf. Rudder, *Glos.* 58, 699, 466.
[9] Glos. R.O., HO 19/1/1–2; 8/1; cf. ibid. D 3269, surv. bk. 1741–90, f. 65.
[10] Ibid. HO 19/11/1.
[11] Ibid. 1/2; 8/1, rep. 1762.
[12] *Glouc. Jnl.* 21 July 1761.
[13] Glos. R.O., HO 19/1/1–2; 8/1.
[14] Ibid. 8/1, rep. 1763, detail reproduced above, Plate 46.

behind the Independent chapel on the other side of the street was given to the infirmary for a burial ground, consecrated in 1781.[15] In 1788 George III, during his stay in Cheltenham, visited the infirmary.[16]

The infirmary's ordinary income was supplied by subscriptions. Extraordinary income came from many gifts and legacies, including a bequest of £10,000 stock from Martha Davies (d. 1871), collections, and amercements assigned by courts. Many parishes subscribed to provide treatment in the infirmary for their poor. Chedworth in 1760 was the first, and by 1788 forty, including two outside the county, were subscribing. Several endowed charities and benefactions ensured treatment for the poor of certain places in the county.[17]

From its beginning the infirmary was faced with abuse of its charity[18] and problems of overcrowding, rising costs, and insufficient ordinary income. In 1784 the governors appointed a committee to look into the state of the infirmary and its finances and in 1785 a trust fund was set up to augment ordinary income.[19] Part of the principal was later used to meet continuing deficits. In 1796 another committee investigated the finances and Sir George Paul, in a detailed analysis, observed that the root of the problems of overcrowding and finance was the increasing number of subscribers following the drop in real value of subscriptions.[20] From that time the recommending privileges of subscribers were limited[21] but financial problems continued and in the early 1840s invested funds were sold.[22]

In 1846 the governors elected a supervising committee and limited membership of the weekly board.[23] In 1866 a committee of investigation recommended considerable changes to increase the usefulness of the infirmary, which then had 118 beds, and improve its management, staffing, and facilities.[24] In 1867 the management was entrusted to a committee of governors which chose the weekly board from its members. At the same time the system of recommendation by ticket was relaxed to allow free admission for emergency cases. Subscribers' recommending rights were increased, particularly in the out-patient department which had been underused.[25] In the later 19th century the number of patients recommended by subscribers dwindled and the infirmary became more like a free hospital.[26] In 1878 the Gloucestershire Eye Institution amalgamated with the infirmary,[27] and Edward VII

granted the title of the Gloucestershire Royal Infirmary and Eye Institution in 1909.[28] From 1922 all in-patients paid for their keep according to means unless they were members of a contributory scheme.[29]

The first major enlargement of the infirmary was a south wing to designs by Thomas Rickman and Henry Hutchinson begun in 1825. It contained 54 beds in three wards.[30] On the north side a wing, built following a diversion of Parliament Street, opened in 1871. It was designed by A. W. Maberly and contained an out-patient department and two surgical wards. In 1885 it was enlarged and another ward created in it.[31] A nurses' home completed in 1904[32] was enlarged several times in the 1920s and 1930s. Following the opening in 1932 of a detached block with specialist departments and clinics and 16 beds for paying patients the infirmary had 216 beds and 3 operating theatres.[33]

On the introduction of the National Health Service in 1948 the infirmary was amalgamated with Gloucester City General Hospital and from 1949 was known as the Gloucestershire Royal Hospital.[34] In the early 1960s a new general hospital for the Gloucester district was begun in Great Western Road, and departments and clinics were moved from lower Southgate Street as buildings on the new site were completed.[35] The wards in Southgate Street were closed in 1975[36] and only a few services remained there in the early 1980s. In 1984 the main part of the old infirmary was demolished and the nurses' home was disused.

Gloucester City General Hospital was formerly the infirmary of the Gloucester poor-law union. The infirmary behind the union workhouse was demolished in 1850 to make way for the South Wales railway[37] and replaced by a detached building west of the workhouse, designed by the firm of John Jacques & Son and completed in 1852.[38] In 1912 the guardians began a 149-bed infirmary on a block system on the other side of Great Western Road.[39] Patients were transferred to the east block of the new building in 1914. The British Red Cross Society took over the west block for nursing war wounded in 1914 and the east block in 1915. The guardians completed the building after the war.[40] In 1930 the infirmary was transferred to the corporation and became known as Gloucester City General Hospital.[41] On the introduction of the National Health Service it was

[15] G. Whitcombe, *General Infirmary at Glouc.* (1903), 18; plan of Southgate chap. before Apr. 1850, among W. Midland provincial archives of United Reformed Ch., Leamington Spa.

[16] Whitcombe, *Gen. Infirmary*, 15.

[17] Glos. R.O., HO 19/8/1–2; Whitcombe, *Gen. Infirmary*, 27–36.

[18] Glos. R.O., HO 19/1/2, min. 15 Jan. 1756.

[19] Ibid. 5/1; 12/1.

[20] G. O. Paul, *Observations on state of Glouc. Infirmary 1796*.

[21] Ibid.; Glos. R.O., HO 19/1/7, min. 11 Aug. 1797; 10, min. 1 Sept. 1827.

[22] Whitcombe, *Gen. Infirmary*, 39–41.

[23] Glos. R.O., HO 19/8/1.

[24] Ibid. 1/19, rep. at pp. 191–2.   [25] Ibid. pp. 251–60.

[26] Ibid. 8/2, rep. 1876, 1880; 3, rep. 1894.

[27] Ibid. D 195/1/2.

[28] *Glouc. Jnl.* 26 June 1909.

[29] Glos. R.O., HO 19/8/6.

[30] Ibid. 1/10–11.

[31] Ibid. 8/1–2; Whitcombe, *Gen. Infirmary*, 20–2.

[32] Glos. R.O., HO 19/8/4.

[33] Ibid. 6–7.

[34] B. Frith, *Story of Glouc. Infirmary* (1961), 17.

[35] Glos. Colln. NR 19.9.

[36] *Cotswold Life*, Nov. 1975, 38.

[37] *Glouc. Jnl.* 28 Sept. 1850; cf. Causton, *Map of Glouc.* (1843).

[38] Glos. R.O., G/GL 8A/6, ff. 113v.–193v.; Bd. of Health Map (1852).

[39] *Glouc. Jnl.* 13 Apr. 1912.

[40] Glos. R.O., G/GL 185/2, 4, 5; ME 3, pp. 15 and n., 28.

[41] G.B.R., B 3/64, pp. 414–15, 634.

amalgamated with the Gloucestershire Royal Infirmary.[42] Later the Great Western Road buildings and the adjoining land, which included a maternity hospital and wooden huts erected in 1942 for treatment of war wounded, were chosen for the new Gloucestershire Royal Hospital, begun in the early 1960s. The first departments were opened in 1964 and others in succeeding years, including in 1975 the main feature of the new hospital, a tower block of 11 storeys.[43] Older buildings in the area, including the former Home of Hope,[44] continued in use in 1981 when the hospital had 618 beds, excluding those in the maternity hospital.[45]

MATERNITY HOSPITALS. In 1793 the surgeon Charles Brandon Trye and the Revd. Thomas Stock founded a lying-in charity for poor women. From 1800 it was supported by subscriptions and from 1813 it was supervised by the Revd. F. T. Bayley.[46] The charity provided the services of two surgeons at St. John's National school in Worcester Street in 1856 and at Christ Church National school at the Spa in 1870, and helped c. 100 patients a year in the mid 1880s.[47] From 1894 the charity made payments to the Gloucester District Nursing Society for its midwifery work. The society, a voluntary body founded in 1884 to provide trained nurses for the sick poor in their own homes, became an important provider of maternity and other services in and around the city and trained nurses and midwives. Its principal benefactor William Long (d. 1914) left it £10,000. In 1917 the society opened a ward with four beds for maternity cases in its premises at the corner of Clarence and Russell Streets, and in the following years extended its services, particularly after 1934 when it introduced a provident contributory scheme.[48] In 1927 Mary Fluck founded a convalescent home in Longford for women and children of the city and neighbourhood.[49]

From 1931 the Gloucester District Nursing Society attended maternity cases at the City General Hospital in Great Western Road. Also in conjunction with the city corporation the society ran an antenatal clinic begun in 1928,[50] provided a domiciliary midwifery service under the Midwives Act of 1936,[51] and ran a maternity hospital from 1940. That year the corporation requisitioned and fitted the Fluck convalescent home as a temporary maternity hospital while it built Gloucester Maternity Hospital, a single-storeyed

building which opened behind the City General Hospital in 1943.[52] The society continued to run the hospital and to provide services for the corporation under the National Health Service.[53] The corporation opened an antenatal and infant welfare clinic in Great Western Road in 1962.[54] In 1966 as part of the Gloucestershire Royal Hospital a new maternity hospital and midwives' home was opened behind the older hospital, which became a general practitioner maternity unit.[55] In 1981 the maternity hospital had 111 beds.[56] From 1963 the work of the Gloucester District Nursing Society for the corporation was reduced and in 1971 the society's agency agreement for running the maternity hospital was ended.[57] Under a Scheme of 1974 the society provided help for the sick poor of the city and adjoining parishes.[58] The Fluck convalescent home was used by the corporation as a children's home in the mid 1940s.[59] Under a Scheme of 1956 the endowments supported a fund, which helped poor convalescent women and children[60] and in 1971 had an income of £3,600.[61]

EYE HOSPITAL. Over 80 cases of eye disease were treated at the Gloucester Infirmary each year by 1866 when W. H. Hyett of Painswick took the lead in opening the Gloucestershire Eye Institution in Gloucester.[62] The eye hospital, which was for the poor of the Gloucester and Stroud areas and was supported by subscriptions and donations, was in a house in Clarence Street. At first out-patients were treated there two days a week and later four beds were provided for in-patients. Admission was by recommendation, and treatment was free for the poor and for mechanics contributing to provident schemes and their dependants. The hospital, which in its first year dealt with 425 cases, moved in 1867 to two houses in Market Parade.[63] It closed on its amalgamation with the Gloucester Infirmary in 1878.[64]

CHILDREN'S HOSPITAL. In 1866 a free hospital for children of the poor was begun next to St. Lucy's Home of Charity between Kingsholm and Longford. The home, a converted villa east of the Tewkesbury road, was occupied by the sisters of St. Lucy, an Anglican community founded in 1864 by Thomas Gambier Parry of Highnam to train nurses and tend the sick in their homes. By 1866 the sisters, who were sent to many parts of the country, nursed some patients in the home.[65]

[42] Frith, *Glouc. Infirmary*, 17.
[43] Glos. Colln. NR 19.9; *Cotswold Life*, Nov. 1975, 38–40.
[44] Cf. deeds in 1981 in possession of Glos. area health authority, Burlington Ho., Chelt.
[45] *Medical Dir.* (1981), ii. 137.
[46] D. Lysons, *Life of Chas. Brandon Trye* (1812), 7; *Glouc. Jnl.* 24 Jan. 1814.
[47] *Kelly's Dir. Glos.* (1856), 303; (1870), 555; (1885), 470.
[48] *Rep. Glouc. District Nursing Soc. 1885, 1894, 1900, 1915*: Glos. Colln. N 13.80; *Hist. Glouc. District Nursing Soc.* (1938), 7–15.   [49] *Glouc. Jnl.* 4 June 1927; Glos. Colln. N 20.18.
[50] *Rep. Glouc. District Nursing Soc. 1929, 1931*.
[51] G.B.R., B 3/70 (2), pp. 1790–1; 71 (1), pp. 336–8.
[52] *Hist. Glouc. District Nursing Soc.* (1960), 21; *Rep. of Medical Off. of Health, 1938–45*, 36: copy in G.B.R., N 2/10/5.

[53] *Hist. Glouc. District Nursing Soc.* (1960), 22–3.
[54] *Glouc. Municipal Year Bk.* (1964–5), 84.
[55] Glos. Colln. NR 19.9.   [56] *Medical Dir.* (1981), ii. 137.
[57] *Rep. of Medical Off. of Health, 1973*, 29–30.
[58] Glos. R.O., D 3469/5/67, file marked 'Glouc. District Nursing Soc.'
[59] *Rep. of Medical Off. of Health, 1938–45*, 36.
[60] Glos. R.O., D 3469/5/67, file marked 'Fluck Convalescent Fund'.
[61] Ibid. CH 21, Glouc. co. boro., p. 12.
[62] Ibid. D 195/3/3.
[63] Ibid. 1/1; 3/2, 7; Glos. Colln. N 19.11.
[64] Glos. R.O., D 195/1/2; 3/6.
[65] Ibid. D 177, St. Lucy's Home and children's hosp., trust deed 1875; *Glos. Chron.* 17 Dec. 1864; 15 Dec. 1866.

Gambier Parry also conceived the idea for the children's hospital in connexion with the home and paid much of the building costs. The hospital, a brick building designed by William Jacques, opened in 1867 with 22 beds. Children of the poor from any distance were admitted and out-patients were treated at a house in Bell Lane. The hospital was supported by subscriptions and donations.[66]

In 1872 the sisters of St. John the Baptist from Clewer (Berks.) took over the work of the sisters of St. Lucy.[67] In 1876 Gambier Parry moved the home to a large house at the corner of Hare Lane and Pitt Street.[68] The new home included a ward for fee-paying incurables from 1885[69] and adjoined the hospitals out-patient department, which occupied that building, known as College Gardens, from 1873[70] to 1905, when a new dispensary opened in the hospital's grounds.[71] In 1921 the sisters gave up their work at the hospital and the management committee made new arrangements, introducing payments for patients' keep according to means. Further changes in management came in 1928 when the Clewer sisters resumed their work, and from 1929 children sent by the Gloucestershire Royal Infirmary were admitted. The Clewer sisters were succeeded at the hospital in 1939 by the nursing sisters of St. John the Divine from Deptford (Kent). In 1941 accommodation was increased[72] but in 1947 the hospital was closed and sold to the city corporation.[73] The proceeds of the sale supported a fund for the relief of sick children. In 1951 the charity of George Peters, who by will proved 1909 had provided a bed in the hospital, was added to the fund,[74] which in 1971 had an income of £2,000.[75] The hospital, which was used by the Gloucestershire Royal Hospital as a nurses' home until the mid 1970s, was demolished in 1979.[76] St. Lucy's Home was closed in 1933 following the withdrawal of the Clewer sisters.[77]

DISPENSARIES. The Gloucester Dispensary and Vaccine Institution established in 1831 was supported by subscriptions and donations. It provided free advice and medicine to the poor upon the recommendation of subscribers.[78] Doctors gave their services free of charge and an apothecary was employed. He lived at the dispensary, which occupied a house within the shell of the Greyfriars church. To reduce costs, in 1850 the dispensary was closed and a chemist in Eastgate Street contracted to provide rooms and supply medicines. The dispensing was at a chemist's shop in Southgate Street in 1853 and until 1857, when a medical officer was employed to carry on the institution's work,[79] and by 1870 a dispensary had been opened in Blackfriars.[80] In 1872 the Gloucester Dispensary was reorganized as a provident society supported by members' payments and voluntary contributions, and a house in Longsmith Street was fitted as a dispensary.[81] In 1895 it was replaced by a house in Barton Street provided by William Long[82] (d. 1914), who left £3,000 for the society. A new dispensary was opened behind the house in 1921 and enlarged in the late 1920s. On the introduction of the National Health Service the buildings were let to the corporation for a health centre,[83] which included a dispensary and closed in 1963,[84] and the endowments, including the Barton Street premises, supported a fund for the sick poor of the city. That charity, which in 1969 became known as the Gloucester Relief in Sickness Fund,[85] had an income of £2,000 in 1971.[86]

The Gloucester Friendly Societies' Medical Association was formed in 1887 to retain the services of a doctor,[87] and from the early 1890s it ran a dispensary at Ladybellegate House, then the Foresters' hall, in Longsmith Street.[88] Following the introduction of the National Health Service the corporation purchased the house for a health centre. The centre, which had a dispensary, was transferred to Rikenel house in 1971.[89]

ISOLATION HOSPITALS. In 1637 the city corporation built a pest house outside the east gate,[90] where land between the city wall and Goose ditch was traditionally the place for accommodating the sick in times of plague,[91] and in 1638 there was also a pest house at St. Margaret's Hospital, Wotton, for city plague victims.[92] In 1832 the board of health dealing with an outbreak of cholera in Gloucester bought a house in Barton Street and fitted it as a temporary hospital.[93] The

[66] Glos. Chron. 21 Sept. 1867; 17 May 1873; Victoria Mag. Feb. 1870, 339–41.   [67] Glos. Colln. 18349.
[68] St. John Baptist Clewer Mag. Autumn 1884, 13.
[69] Glos. R.O., D 177, St. Lucy's Home and children's hosp., rep. St. Lucy's Home, 1888.
[70] Glos. Chron. 17 May 1873; cf. G.B.R., L 6/1/127.
[71] Glouc. Jnl. 29 July 1905.
[72] Rep. Children's Hosp. 1921, 1928–9, 1939, 1940–1: Glos. Colln. R 192.1.
[73] Glos. R.O., D 177, St. Lucy's Home and children's hosp., extracts from meetings of council of St. Lucy's Home; sched. of hosp. deeds.
[74] Ibid. D 3469/5/67, file marked 'Free Hosp. and Geo. Peters Fund'.
[75] Ibid. CH 21, Glouc. co. boro., p. 11.
[76] Ibid. GHO 5; Citizen, 6 Dec. 1979.
[77] Glos. R.O., D 177, St. Lucy's Home and children's hosp., mem. July 1934.
[78] Glos. Colln. N 19.3.
[79] Rep. Glouc. Dispensary, 1833, 1849–58: Glos. Colln. NF 19.1, N 19.4; Causton, Map of Glouc. (1843).

[80] Kelly's Dir. Glos. (1870), 552, 566.
[81] Rep. Glouc. Dispensary, 1871–3.
[82] Kelly's Dir. Glos. (1897), 171.
[83] Rep. Glouc. Dispensary, 1915, 1921, 1929, 1948; Glouc. Jnl. 19 Feb. 1921.
[84] Rep. of Medical Off. of Health, 1973, 27–8.
[85] Glos. R.O., D 3469/5/67, file marked 'Glouc. Dispensary 1948'.
[86] Ibid. CH 21, Glouc. co. boro., pp. 12–13.
[87] Glouc. Jnl. 26 Mar. 1887; cf. Kelly's Dir. Glos. (1889), 800.
[88] Kelly's Dir. Glos. (1894 and later edns.); Anct. Order of Foresters' Guide to Glouc. (1901).
[89] Rep. of Medical Off. of health, 1973, 27–8; cf. ibid. 1949, 22: copy in G.B.R., N 2/10/5.
[90] G.B.R., F 4/5, ff. 45v.–46; B 3/2, p. 80.
[91] Ibid. J 3/1, pp. 147–9.
[92] G.D.R. vol. 204, depositions 28 Feb.–2 Mar. 1639; wills 1638/97.
[93] Glouc. Jnl. 11 Aug. 1832; cf. ibid. 19 Nov. 1831; Glos. R.O., P 154/11/VE 2/1, min. 30 Aug. 1832.

house was later that pair of dwellings known as Gothic Cottages.[94]

In 1874, during an outbreak of smallpox, the corporation purchased a wooden hospital from the Cheltenham improvement commissioners and erected it south of the Stroud road as an infectious diseases hospital for 14 patients.[95] It was enlarged several times and in 1888 was largely of brick.[96] With the approach of cholera in 1885 the corporation, acting as port sanitary authority, erected small wooden hospitals, each with five beds, by the docks at Sharpness and Gloucester.[97] The latter was moved in 1891 to make way for the Monk Meadow dock.[98] During the smallpox epidemic of 1896 the corporation put up temporary buildings next to it and the Stroud Road hospital,[99] and in Hucclecote leading residents adapted a cottage as an isolation hospital.[1]

In 1897 the corporation began a new infectious diseases hospital outside the city at Over. The new hospital was not for smallpox and when it opened in 1903[2] the Stroud Road hospital was closed and many of its buildings were transferred to Field Farm near Longford as a smallpox hospital.[3] During the smallpox epidemic of 1923 the corporation adapted buildings on the airfield in Brockworth for the treatment of patients.[4] The Longford hospital, which had 18 beds,[5] was enlarged in 1926, by the addition of buildings from the Monk Meadow cholera hospital, and was closed in 1947.[6] The buildings were later removed. At the Over hospital a pavilion for tuberculosis patients was provided in 1915 by a joint committee of the city and county councils. Further building had taken place by 1981[7] when the hospital had 95 beds, some for geriatric and pre-convalescent cases.[8]

MENTAL HOSPITALS. In 1793 the governors of the Gloucester Infirmary opened a subscription for building an independent lunatic asylum at Gloucester. In 1794 the subscribers bought an inn and two houses south of the infirmary as a site for it and adopted a scheme of Sir George Paul modelled principally on the York asylum.[9] The asylum was to be supported by patients' payments, the patients divided into three classes, the wealthy, the poor on parochial relief, and the poor not on relief, and the classes and sexes segregated;

payments from the poor not on relief were to be reduced in proportion to the growth of a special fund derived from surplus payments by wealthy patients, benefactions, and legacies.[10] In 1811 the subscribers bought 8½ a. at Wotton for the building[11] and in 1813 sold the old site to the infirmary.[12]

In 1812 the subscribers, who lacked sufficient funds, invited the county and city magistrates to join in the project under an Act of 1808 to provide accommodation for paupers on parochial relief. Paul, who had played an important part in securing the Act, opposed county involvement on the ground that it would delay the building of the Shire Hall, but the three parties agreed to a union in 1813. The county was to pay eleven parts of the building and maintenance costs, the city one, and the subscribers eight. The county and city also made a separate agreement between themselves.[13] Building to a plan by William Stark of Edinburgh (d. 1813), modified by John Wheeler, began in 1814. Completion was delayed mainly by the financial problems of the subscribers,[14] and the asylum was opened in 1823.[15] It was built of brick and stucco and the central feature was a crescent of three storeys with a principal east elevation. North, south, and west wings of two storeys were connected to the crescent by single-storeyed day rooms.[16] The crescent contained accommodation for 24 wealthy patients and their servants and the wings for 60 paupers and 26 charity patients.[17] There were detached wards for noisy and violent patients.[18]

The asylum was governed by a committee of county and city magistrates and subscribers. It retained the main features of the subscribers' scheme, including the charity to reduce payments from poor patients not on parochial relief.[19] It was beset with problems, particularly the need of the county and city to house an increasing number of poor and the subscribers' lack of funds. Surplus payments from patients were small and were paid into the general account of the asylum until 1829 when they were divided between the three parties. Few charity patients were admitted and the county and city filled the charity wards with paupers.[20] In 1832 a fire damaged the building.[21] Samuel Hitch, resident medical superintendent 1828–45, was the principal founder of the Royal Medico-Psychological Association in 1841. He

[94] Glos. R.O., D 3270/19713, mins. 12 Mar., 8 Apr. 1839; Glos. Colln. 6587.

[95] G.B.R., B 4/5/4; *Glouc. Jnl.* 22 Aug. 1874.

[96] *Rep. of Medical Off. of Health, 1888, 1892*: copies in G.B.R., B 3/23, 27.

[97] G.B.R., B 4/6/3; B 4/7/2; *Rep. of Port Medical Off. of Health, 1907*: copy in ibid. B 3/42.

[98] *Rep. of Port Medical Off. of Health, 1891*: copy in ibid. B 3/26.

[99] G.B.R., B 3/30, pp. 113–90.

[1] Ibid. B 6/33/1, pp. 139–40.

[2] *Glouc. Jnl.* 23 Oct. 1897; 7 Jan. 1899; 25 Apr. 1903.

[3] G.B.R., B 3/37, pp. 180, 255–7, 293–4.

[4] Glos. Colln. NQ 12.52.

[5] *Kelly's Dir. Glos.* (1910), 372.

[6] *Glouc. Municipal Year Bk.* (1964–5), 84; *Rep. of Medical Off. of Health, 1925*: copy in G.B.R., B 3/60.

[7] *Rep. of Medical Off. of Health, 1914*: copy in G.B.R., B 3/49; *Glouc. Municipal Year Bk.* (1964–5), 83–4.

[8] *Medical Dir.* (1981), ii. 138.

[9] G.O. Paul, *Mins. of proc. relative to establishment of a general lunatic asylum near Glouc.* (1796); Glos. R.O., D 3725, Barnwood Ho. Trust, subscribers' min. bk 1794–1813; ibid. HO 19/11/5.

[10] *Scheme for a general lunatic asylum in or near Glouc.*: Glos. Colln. 13165 (5).

[11] Glos. R.O., D 3725, Barnwood Ho. Trust, subscribers' min. bk. 1794–1813.

[12] Ibid. HO 19/11/5, deed 23 Dec. 1831.

[13] Ibid. D 3725, Barnwood Ho. Trust, subscribers' min. bk. 1794–1813; *Trans. B.G.A.S.* li. 158–9; xc. 181–3.

[14] Glos. R.O., HO 22/1/1; cf. Colvin, *Biog. Dict. Brit. Architects* (1978), 776–7, 881.

[15] Glos. R.O., HO 22/8/1.

[16] Ibid. A 154/80; *Glouc. Jnl.* 28 Apr. 1832.

[17] Glos. R.O., HO 22/1/1.

[18] Counsel, *Glouc.* 177.

[19] Glos. Colln. (H) C 10.1.

[20] Glos. R.O., HO 22/8/1; HO 22/ 26/8–9.

[21] *Glouc. Jnl.* 28 Apr. 1832.

severed his connexion with the asylum in 1847 to open a private institution in Dowdeswell near Cheltenham.[22]

From 1838, when the Wotton asylum had 20 wealthy, 3 charity, and 167 pauper patients, the number of charity patients increased considerably. In 1843 the figures were 18, 47, and 191 respectively. The subscribers had all surplus payments from patients from 1842, and from 1843 each party maintained those parts of the asylum in its sole use and shared the costs of those in common use under a new agreement. The number of charity patients declined after 1846 and by 1855 the number of pauper patients had risen to 310. To meet the altered circumstances the parties divided the property in 1847 and agreed to a new union and division of costs.[23] Because of overcrowding admissions were halted several times in the early 1850s and patients sent to other asylums. Large new wings for paupers were opened in 1852 and 1855. In 1856 the union between county, city, and subscribers was dissolved and the county and city, which bought the subscribers' part of the asylum, converted the building for the exclusive use of paupers. The conversion, which included adding a third storey to the original wings, was interrupted by a serious fire in 1858.[24] From 1856 the county paid most of the costs and the asylum became known as the county asylum.[25]

In 1849 a chapel designed by the firm of Fulljames and Waller was built in front of the asylum.[26] It was replaced by a larger chapel, opened in 1873, on the site of the asylum's burial ground to the south. The new chapel, built of brick and designed by James Medland, was a single-cell building with south apse and east and west porches.[27]

Despite additions in the late 1860s and early 1870s there was a shortage of room at the asylum,[28] and in 1878 the county bought an estate in Barnwood, east of Coney Hill, for the site of a new asylum. The new institution, designed on a block system by the firm of John Giles and Gough,[29] was built between 1880 and 1884. It was governed by the county magistrates visiting the first asylum and was under the same medical superintendent. Surplus accommodation at the second asylum was used for paupers from other counties and until 1890 for private patients. In 1900 the asylums housed 1,059 patients. In the early 20th century there was further building at both, including a block opened at the second asylum in 1909.[30]

At the introduction of the National Health Service in 1948 the two county asylums became known as Horton Road Hospital and Coney Hill Hospital respectively.[31] During the 1950s more buildings were provided for both hospitals, including a house in Denmark Road opened as a day hospital in 1958,[32] and in the 1970s a unit for mentally handicapped patients was built at Coney Hill.[33] In 1981 the two hospitals had over 900 beds.[34]

When the union was dissolved in 1856 the subscribers to the Gloucester asylum were paid £13,000 and they removed the wealthy and charity patients. They supported nine of the latter in a private asylum in Fairford. In 1858 the subscribers, among whom W.H. Hyett was prominent, bought Barnwood House in Barnwood village for an asylum.[35] The house, a small early 19th-century villa of stuccoed brick with a symmetrical garden front with segmental bays rising the full three storeys and later east and west wings, was converted to a plan by the firm of Fulljames and Waller. Service buildings to the west were pulled down, the wings, from which the stucco was removed, were raised by the addition of a third storey and extended symmetrically by ranges which ended in towers, and a glass corridor was erected along the north side of the ground floor. The asylum, which opened in 1860 and was known later as Barnwood House Hospital,[36] was supported by voluntary contributions and patients' payments. The patients were from the upper and middle classes, and the less wealthy paid according to their means, some receiving free treatment.[37] A bequest of £10,000 stock to the Gloucester asylum by Martha Davies (d. 1871) was awarded by Chancery in 1872 to Barnwood House and was used to buy land in Barnwood.[38]

By 1864 the hospital, with 60 patients, was full. To increase accommodation many alterations were made and new buildings added in the later 19th and early 20th century. The central block, the original house which was used for offices and the medical superintendent's residence, was rebuilt in brick in 1896 and 1897. In 1869 a chapel designed by F. S. Waller was built in the grounds south of the Wotton brook; after a rebuilding in 1887, when a south aisle and vestry were added, the body had an apsidal and gabled east end, an east flèche, and a north porch. From 1884 a few patients were housed in a villa on the other side of the main road, and the hospital ran a sanatorium near Mitcheldean until 1919. Other houses in

[22] *Jnl. Mental Science*, cvii. 607–29.

[23] Glos. R.O., HO 22/8/1–2; deeds in 1981 in possession of Glos. area health authority.

[24] Glos. R.O., HO 22/8/2; HO 22/16/2–3; deeds in possession of Glos. area health authority; *Glouc. Jnl.* 3 July 1858.

[25] Glos. R.O., HO 22/8/2, 4.

[26] Ibid. 1/1, pp. 646–8; 8/2; plan in possession of Glos. area health authority.

[27] Glos. R.O., HO 22/1/2, p. 399; *Glouc. Jnl.* 9 Aug. 1873; Causton, *Map of Glouc.* (1843), shows a bldg. in the burial ground.

[28] Glos. R.O., HO 22/8/4.

[29] Ibid. HO 23/1/1, pp. 2–20.

[30] Ibid. HO 22/8/6–11.

[31] Ibid. HO 22/26/14.

[32] Ibid. HO 22/8/19.

[33] *Citizen*, 22 Apr. 1972.

[34] *Medical Dir.* (1981), ii. 136.

[35] Glos. R.O., D 3725, Barnwood Ho. Trust, min. bk. 1856–62; cf. ibid. min. 30 Jan. 1860.

[36] Ibid. plan of ho. 1810; photogs. of S. front before 1896; specification of works 1858; min. bk. 1856–62.

[37] Ibid. gen. regulations 1860; *Kelly's Dir. Glos.* (1870), 470.

[38] Glos. R.O., D 3725, Barnwood Ho. Trust, min. bk. 1862–77; for the Barnwood Ho. estate, below, Barnwood, man.

Barnwood were used for patients in the early 20th century and in 1938 a branch house opened in Badgeworth.[39]

After the introduction of the National Health Service in 1948 the hospital, which was left under the control of the governors, had financial problems and from the mid 1950s the number of patients fell. In 1968 the hospital was closed and its work continued on a much smaller scale at the Manor House to the east, which became a nursing home for geriatric and psychiatric cases and in 1977 a day home for the elderly disabled, for whom 18 bungalows were built in its grounds in 1981. In 1969 the hospital was sold and demolished, save for the central block which was converted for domestic use, and the grounds south of the brook were given to the corporation as a public park.[40]

GLOUCESTER CATHEDRAL AND THE CLOSE

THE MINSTER of St. Peter[41] was established by Osric, under-king of the Hwicce, on the north side of Gloucester c. 679. It became a Benedictine abbey in 1022, and Eldred, bishop of Worcester 1047–62, rebuilt the abbey church.[42] Eldred's church was said, in an account of c. 1600, to have been built 'nearer the side of the town' than its predecessor,[43] which has been variously interpreted as meaning that the new site was further north or further south than the old one. Eldred's church was probably on the same site as the great Norman church that replaced it in the late 11th century, built over the north-west angle of the old Roman walls. The Norman church and its claustral buildings were later remodelled and embellished, particularly in the 14th century, when perpendicular architecture of a novel and highly ornamental character was introduced, and in the 15th, when the massive central tower, Gloucester's dominant feature, was built. Gloucester Abbey was dissolved in 1540, and in 1541 its church became the cathedral of the new diocese of Gloucester and with its precinct and claustral buildings was placed in the custody of the newly incorporated dean and chapter.

The original bounds of the precinct are not known. About the time the Norman church was begun in 1089 the abbey extended its boundaries over land of St. Oswald's minster, presumably an enlargement northwards or north-westwards, and Peter, abbot 1104–13, built a stone wall around the precinct.[44] Shortly before 1218 a further extension was made on to land of St. Oswald's and a new stretch of wall built.[45] At its fullest extent the precinct enclosed 13 a. of the north-western sector of the town. It was bounded on the west by Abbey Lane and Half Street (parts of the later St. Mary's Street), on the north by the later Pitt Street, on most of the east by Grace (later St. John's) Lane, and on the south by a back lane to the burgage plots on the north side of Westgate Street.[46] Water and drainage were provided by the southern branch of the river Twyver, or Full brook, flowing westwards through the precinct, and from the early 13th century a supply of fresh water was piped from springs on Robins Wood Hill.[47]

Jurisdiction over the close was sometimes a cause of dispute between the abbey and the town authorities[48] and continued to be a source of friction after the Dissolution until 1672 when the bishop, dean, and two prebendaries were given the status of city magistrates.[49] Ecclesiastically the close remained separate after the Dissolution but for some civil purposes it was attached to the adjoining parish of St. Mary de Lode, to which the private residents, and the chapter and its officers at a fixed composition, paid poor rates. The close was included in the city scheme for a workhouse, first implemented in 1703.[50] It remained independent, however, of statutory measures for lighting, paving, and scavenging the city in the later 18th century,[51] and the dean and chapter continued to provide some public services for the close out of their own funds until the late 19th century.[52] Until the late 18th century the gates leading from the close into the city were maintained and manned by porters. After soldiers had caused disturbances in the close in 1762 stricter rules for closing the gates at night were enforced, leading to a bitter dispute between the chapter and a prominent resident, the attorney and later M.P. John Pitt, who organized the pulling down of the infirmary gate in 1766.[53] Other measures taken by the chapter to preserve the peace and separate character of the close

[39] Glos. R.O., D 3725, Barnwood Ho. Trust, min. bks. 1856–77; rep. 1878–1948; D 2953, public, Barnwood Ho. Hosp.

[40] Ibid. PA 35/3, pp. 25–38; inf. from sec., Barnwood Ho. Trust. (1982).

[41] This article was written in 1986.

[42] The institutional hist. of the abbey is given in V.C.H. Glos. ii. 53–61.   [43] Dugdale, Mon. i. 564.

[44] Hist. & Cart. Mon. Glouc. (Rolls Ser.), i. 13; ii. 65.

[45] Ibid. i. 25.

[46] For the bounds, S. Eward, No Fine but a Glass of Wine: Cath. Life at Glouc. in Stuart Times (1985), map at end; Causton, Map of Glouc. (1843).

[47] Above, Public Services.

[48] Above, Medieval Glouc., town and religious communities.

[49] Above, Glouc. 1547–1640, city govt. and politics; Glouc. 1660–1720, city govt. and politics.

[50] G.B.R., G 3/SO 8, Epiph. 1766; Glos. R.O., P 154/12/ VE 2/1; cf. above, Glouc. 1720–1835, city govt.

[51] Glouc. Poor-Relief and Lighting Act, 4 Geo. III, c. 60; Maisemore Bridge and Glouc. Improvement Act, 17 Geo. III, c. 68; cf. above, Public Services.

[52] Glos. R.O., D 936/A 1/8–14. The city corp. took over responsibility for lighting and scavenging in 1891: Glouc. Cath. Libr., Chapter Act bk. vii, pp. 411, 428, 430; G.B.R., B 3/24, p. 302.

[53] Glos. R.O., D 936/L 5–7.

CATHEDRAL ANTIQUITIES.

GLOUCESTER CATHEDRAL.
NAVE:—COMPARTMENT, INTERIOR & EXTERIOR.

Fig. 19. Gloucester cathedral: part of the nave arcade (north side) and elevation of a bay of the nave and the south aisle

included barring alehouses and premises for trade.[54] New building for private residents had increased the total population of the close to 227 in 51 households by 1743.[55] In 1986 the buildings, almost all of which were still owned by the chapter, were mainly occupied by cathedral and diocesan staff as residences or offices, by the King's school, and by professional firms.

ABBEY BUILDINGS. By the Dissolution the abbey church of *ST. PETER* comprised lady chapel with side chapels, choir with ambulatory and chapels over a crypt, central tower, north and south transepts with chapels, nave with north and south aisles and south porch, and an extensive range of claustral buildings on the north side. The whole was built of oolitic limestone from the Cotswolds.[56]

No remains of the churches built by Osric and Eldred have been discovered. In 1089[57] Serlo, the first Norman abbot, began building the large Romanesque church that remains the basis of the present structure. Work began with the crypt, presumably after the setting out of the church and cloister. The crypt has an ambulatory with three radiating chapels and a chapel on each side, below those of the transepts. Above the crypt the presbytery was of four bays with two further piers on the curve of the east end. In the crypt there are solid masses of masonry beneath the piers of the presbytery arcades but they soon proved to be an inadequate foundation for the weight that was placed upon them, and, following the deformation of the transverse arches of the ambulatory vault, supporting arches on large semicircular piers were inserted and the outer wall of the crypt was thickened. At the same time the central vaulted area, which probably originally had two aisles, was rebuilt with three aisles. Those alterations appear to have been completed before the presbytery aisles were vaulted.

It is likely that when the new church was consecrated in 1100 the building was roofed only as far as the crossing and transepts. The church suffered fires in 1102 and 1122, the second apparently destroying the roof of the completed nave.[58] It has been suggested that the early 12th-century nave was one bay longer before its west end was remodelled in the early 15th century,[59] but it had twin western towers over the ends of the aisles[60] and if they were supported by expanded piers then arcades of eight bays with an additional bay beneath the towers would fit the present length. The location of the towers, one of

which fell between 1163 and 1179,[61] within the existing plan is suggested by the thickening of the north and south walls and by a blocked 12th-century window in the west end of the north wall.

The location of the cloister on the north side of the church was probably dictated by the easy availability of water from the Full brook. While the claustral buildings were probably laid out in the first phase of the Norman rebuilding the presumed survival of the buildings of the old monastery implies that the erection of domestic buildings was not a matter of priority. The earliest surviving claustral buildings are the slype, next to the north transept, which is lined with early 12th-century arcading, and the lower part of the west wall of the chapter house. The arcading lining the north and south walls of the chapter house is of the later 12th century, suggesting a remodelling at that time.

The original dormitory probably occupied the conventional position north of the chapter house with the reredorter beyond that over the course of the Full brook. The early 12th-century refectory was 6 ft. narrower than that of the 13th century which replaced it and was the length of the whole of the north side of the cloister. It was raised on a vaulted undercroft with a central row of piers.[62] Most of the west side of the cloister was flanked by a range of buildings, presumably lodgings, but at its southern end was an early 12th-century tower *c.* 35 ft. square, which was probably the original accommodation for the abbot. The tower was separated from the north side of the nave by a vaulted ground-floor passage above which an abbot's chapel was built *c.* 1130. The guest range was possibly destroyed by a fire[63] which damaged the domestic buildings in 1190, and the abbot's lodging was given a western lobby behind an elaborate new front *c.* 1200.

Another fire destroyed some of the monastic offices on the west side of the precinct in 1222. Making good that damage must have been a great expense but the early 13th century was a period of considerable new building. Beginning in 1222 the sacrist, Ellis of Hereford (d. 1237), built a central tower on foundations which had been provided in the original plan and may have supported an earlier tower. The new tower carried a spire and had corner turrets.[64] Between 1224 and 1228 a lady chapel was built at the cost of Ralph of Willington of Sandhurst and his wife Olympia.[65] In 1232 Henry III gave 100 oaks and in 1233 10 more, perhaps for the completion of a new nave roof for which lead was being melted in 1234.[66] The church was dedicated again in 1239 and the

[54] Glouc. Cath. Libr., Chapter Act bk. iii, p. 159.
[55] Rudder, *Glos.* 180.
[56] Quarries in Painswick and Minchinhampton still provided stone for repairs to the fabric in the mid 20th cent. but from the early 1970s Lepine stone from Chauvigny, in France, was used: inf. from Mr. B. J. Ashwell, former cathedral architect.
[57] For the hist. of the building work up to the late 14th cent., *Hist. & Cart. Mon. Glouc.* i. 9–55.
[58] There are signs of calcination on the nave piers.
[59] W. H. St. John Hope, 'Notes on the Benedictine Abbey of St. Peter at Glouc.' *Arch. Jnl.* liv. 108.
[60] Marginal sketch from Geof. of Monmouth, *Hist. Regum*

Britannie, reproduced in D. Verey and D. Welander, *Glouc. Cath.* (1979), plate V.
[61] Giraldus Cambrensis, *Opera* (Rolls Ser.), vii. 64–5.
[62] *Arch. Jnl.* liv. 95–6; Soc. of Antiquaries MS. 785.4, St. John Hope notebk.
[63] There are signs of calcination on the W. face of the cloister.
[64] Verey and Welander, *Glouc. Cath.* plate V. Parts of the turrets survive incorporated in the fabric of the later tower: inf. from Mr. Ashwell.
[65] Cf. Glouc. Cath. Libr., Reg. Abb. Froucester B, pp. 486–8.
[66] *Close R.* 1231–4, 69, 178, 366.

Fig. 20. Gloucester cathedral: part of the north side of the choir

vaulting of the nave was finished by 1243.[67] The south-west tower, perhaps that which had fallen, was rebuilt in the years 1242–3 and the refectory in 1246. Like its predecessor the refectory was raised on a vaulted basement and close to its north side one of the contemporary buildings, which is a also on a vaulted basement, may have been the misericord.

Separated from the north-east corner of the refectory by a small cloister was the 13th-century infirmary, an aisled hall of six bays which included a chapel dedicated to St. Bridget,[68] probably at the east end. A fire which began in the great court of the abbey in 1300 destroyed a great chamber, the cloister, and a small bell tower. In 1303 work began on a new dormitory, and the building was completed in 1313. It was aligned east–west, perhaps so that it could be longer than its predecessor and so that a new reredorter could be located further away from the infirmary.

The appearance of the southern side of the church was changed in the earlier 14th century by the rebuilding of the old south aisle wall between 1318 and 1329 and the remodelling of the south transept, dedicated to St. Andrew, between 1329 and 1337. The windows of the aisle are richly ornamented with ballflower,[69] and the great south window of the transept is one of the first examples of the early perpendicular style. The work on the transept was paid for out of gifts by visitors to the tomb of Edward II, buried in the church in 1327, and those gifts also financed an extensive remodelling of the choir begun under Adam of Staunton, abbot 1337–51, and completed under his successor Thomas Horton (d. 1377). A great east window was put in, the two eastern piers of the ambulatory were removed, and the inner faces of the other piers were recut or built up and incorporated in the open stone screens which filled the arcades. The tracery of those screens was carried up into a new and richly decorated vault.[70] The east window was filled with painted glass depicting the Coronation of the Virgin with attendant apostles and saints and included a series of shields of knights who fought in the Crécy and Calais campaigns of 1346 and 1347.[71] The carved wooden choir stalls, made c. 1350, have a set of 44 misericords depicting domestic scenes, fabulous monsters, and folk tales.[72]

Writers on architectural history once saw Gloucester Abbey as the cradle of the perpendicular style. The style is now thought to have been invented by royal masons in London and transmitted to Gloucester. There, however, the monks and their masons developed it in original and highly ornamental forms which were later a major influence on the growth of the style in England.[73] Even more elaborate than their decoration of the choir is the fan vault which they used in the great cloister, where rebuilding began under Horton with the east range. Work on the other ranges of the cloister continued in a similar style until after the accession of Abbot Walter Froucester in 1381. The north range includes a separately vaulted lavatorium opposite the doorway to the refectory stairs and each of the 10 bays of the south range has two carrels beneath its window.[74] The north transept, dedicated to St. Paul, was reconstructed in the years 1368–73, largely at Horton's expense. At about that time the east end of the chapter house was rebuilt with a large window in place of the former apse, and a vestry and library were built above the slype, which was extended eastwards some distance beyond the line of the transept. During the 14th century most of the crypt chapels were refitted and chapels were fitted up in the triforium gallery around the choir and transepts.

The west front and two western bays of the nave were rebuilt by John Morwent, abbot 1420–37, who was said to have intended to complete the whole nave.[75] The new design of the west front omitted the towers which had been a feature of the old front but provided for a large west window. Morwent also built a new two-storeyed south porch[76] against the second bay from the west; it emphazised the importance of that side, which was close to the gate from the town, as an entry to the nave rather than the west doorway which opened on to the great court of the abbey. The building of a great central tower was begun by Thomas Seabrook, abbot 1451–7, and completed before 1460 by a monk, Robert Tully.[77] It is richly decorated with blind tracery and surmounted by delicate open-work parapets and corner turrets.[78] Other work carried out during the 15th century included the remodelling of the nave clerestory and the rebuilding of the little cloister at the north-east corner of the claustral ranges.

The last major work on the church was the lady chapel, which replaced that of the earlier 13th century; it was begun under Richard Hanley, abbot 1458–72, and completed under his successor William Farley (d. 1498).[79] A tall and richly vaulted building of five bays, it has small flanking chapels. The west end is set back from the great east window of the choir so as not to obstruct the light and the triforium gallery is continued into the chapel on covered bridges which are decorated with re-used chevron arches. Those bridges have the characteristics of a

[67] The new vault may have replaced one of the 12th cent.: M. Thurlby, 'Elevations of the Romanesque Abbey Churches of Tewkesbury and Glouc.', *Brit. Arch. Assoc. Conference Trans.* ix. 47.

[68] Glouc. Cath. Libr., Reg. Abb. Froucester B, p. 463.

[69] Cf. above, Fig. 19.

[70] Fig. 20, and above, Plate 4.

[71] T. D. Grimké-Drayton, 'E. Window of Glouc. Cath.', *Trans. B.G.A.S.* xxxviii. 69–97; G. McN. Rushforth, 'Great E. Window of Glouc. Cath.', ibid. xliv. 293–304. The first writer suggests that the window was given by Thos. de Bradeston in memory of Maur. de Berkeley who died at Calais in 1347.

[72] O. W. Clark, 'Misereres of Glouc. Cath.', ibid. xxviii. 61–85. Fourteen new ones were added when the choir was restored c. 1870.

[73] Verey, *Glos.* ii. 200–1; and for a discussion of Gloucester's place in the development of the style, J. H. Harvey, *Perpendicular Style* (1978).

[74] Above, Plate 18.

[75] Leland, *Itin.* ed. Toulmin Smith, ii. 61.

[76] Ibid.

[77] Dugdale, *Mon.* i. 564; Rudder, *Glos.* 138. Tully became bp. of St. Davids in 1460.

[78] Above, Plate 3.

[79] Leland, *Itin.* ed. Toulmin Smith, ii. 61.

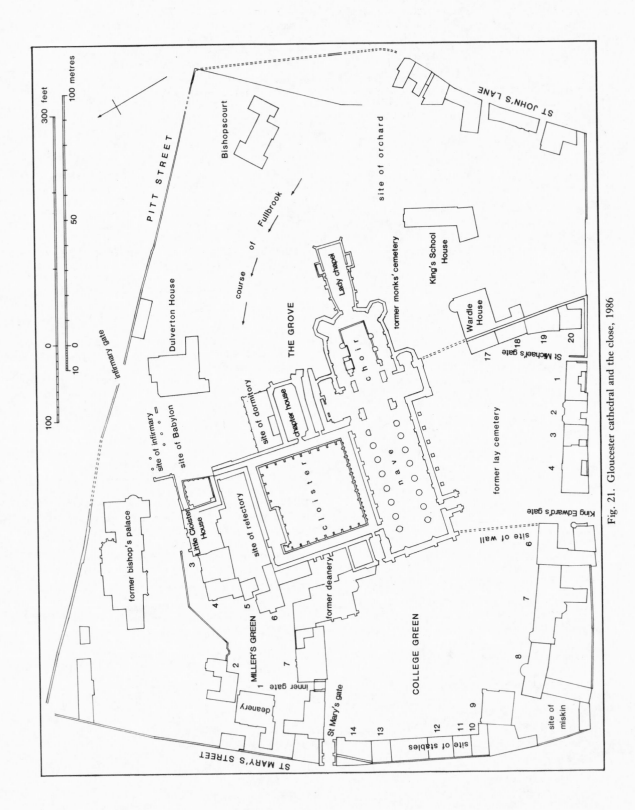

Fig. 21. Gloucester cathedral and the close, 1986

'whispering gallery', a widely known feature of the church by the early 17th century.[80] An early 13th-century stone screen placed across the north end of the north transept is thought to have been the narthex of the former lady chapel, moved there at the rebuilding.[81] Its original purpose has long puzzled visitors to the church who have described it variously as a prison, confessional, and reliquary.[82]

Among the principal monuments[83] placed in the church in medieval times is that to Robert, duke of Normandy (d. 1134), who was buried before the high altar.[84] The effigy of Irish oak, depicting him cross-legged with his hand on his sword, is dated by the style of the armour to Henry III's reign and the chest on which it rests is of the late 14th century or the 15th. The effigy was broken up by soldiers in the Civil War but the pieces were preserved by Sir Humphrey Tracy of Stanway and after the Restoration were repaired and replaced in the presbytery.[85] The monument was moved to the chapel off the north-east ambulatory in the mid 18th century,[86] returned to the presbytery in 1905, and moved to the south ambulatory in 1986. Fixed to the wall on the south side of the presbytery is the 13th-century stone effigy of a priest, depicted as founder holding a model church; though identified in most early accounts as Eldred,[87] it is more probably Abbot Serlo.[88] Edward II, whose body was brought to the church by Abbot John Thoky after his murder at Berkeley castle in 1327,[89] is buried on the north side of the presbytery, his alabaster effigy covered by an elaborately carved stone canopy. Set in the wall at the east end of the south aisle are the early 15th-century effigies of an unidentified knight and lady.[90] On the opposite side of the aisle, adjoining the screen, Abbot Thomas Seabrook (d. 1457), is depicted in effigy on a tomb in a small chapel. The last abbot of Gloucester, William Malvern (d. 1539),[91] built himself a chapel with a tomb and effigy north-west of the presbytery. Malvern also built a founder's tomb north-east of the presbytery for King Osric, and the king's remains were moved there from the lady chapel.[92] Most of the abbots of Gloucester were buried, like John Wyg-

more in 1337,[93] at the entrance to the choir, their tomb slabs being later removed or obscured,[94] and many members of the knightly families of the county are said to have been buried in the ambulatory and its chapels.[95]

Apart from the great east window of the choir, the main surviving medieval stained glass is in the east window of the lady chapel, where the pieces are disordered and include glass introduced from other windows, and in two north aisle windows where the glass was restored in 1865.[96] Much medieval glass was broken in the Civil War, and that in the west choir window, depicting the Trinity, was smashed by a Whig prebendary of the cathedral, Edward Fowler, in 1679.[97] The church had an organ by the early 16th century.[98] Several bells were cast for the church in the early 15th century and others, including a great bourdon, were apparently added when the new tower was built. In 1525 there was a ring of eight, as well as a set of chimes which a Gloucester blacksmith contracted to maintain.[99] Of the many costly objects lavished on the church in medieval times one of the few survivors is a richly decorated gilt candlestick given in the time of Abbot Peter, 1104–13.[1] A pair of medieval cope chests are preserved in the south ambulatory.

The circuit of walls around the abbey was completed in the early 13th century.[2] The main, western gate to the precinct was recorded from 1190[3] and was later known as St. Mary's gate from the parish and church of St. Mary de Lode which lay outside it. The gateway has a late 12th-century vault and its superstructure appears to be of the early 13th century. It stands not, as is often the case, in line with the west front of the church but at the centre of the west wall. The southern gateway, which opened on the lay cemetery, where many of the town's inhabitants were brought for burial in the early Middle Ages,[4] was recorded as the lich gate in 1223.[5] About 1600 it was known as King Edward's gate and was said to have been built and named from Edward I,[6] but the fact that in the early 16th century the lane leading to it, usually King Edward's Lane, was

[80] Rudder, *Glos.* 178; D. Defoe, *Tour through the Whole Island* (Penguin edn. 1971), 366.

[81] B. J. Ashwell, 'Some Notes on the So-called Reliquary in N. Transept' (1976, TS.); Verey, *Glos.* 206. Dr. P. Tudor Craig, in a lecture to Brit. Arch. Assoc. 12 Apr. 1981, argued that the evidence of the fabric shows the screen to be *in situ*.

[82] T. Bonnor, *Itinerary* (1796), 15; J. Britton, *Hist. and Antiquities of Abbey and Cath. Ch. of Glouc.* (1829), 53; *Murray's Handbk. of Glouc. Cath.* (1865), 24.

[83] For the monuments, Roper, *Glos. Effigies*, 231–57.

[84] *Hist. & Cart. Mon. Glouc.* i. 16.

[85] Atkyns, *Glos.* 184.

[86] B. Willis, *Survey of Caths. of York, Glouc., and Bristol* (1727), ii, plan at p. 692; Rudder, *Glos.* 175.

[87] e.g. Willis, *Surv.* ii. 696.

[88] As identified by Leland, *Itin.* ed. Toulmin Smith, ii. 60.

[89] *Hist. & Cart. Mon. Glouc.* i. 44–5.

[90] Identifications as Humph. de Bohun (d. 1361), earl of Heref. (e.g. Dugdale, *Mon.* i. 564), and John Bridges (d. 1437) are rejected by Roper.

[91] The tradition that he was not buried in the tomb apparently derives from the mistaken belief that at the dissol-

ution of the abbey in 1540 he was still living and was contumacious: *V.C.H. Glos.* ii. 60 n.; cf. *Rec. of Glouc. Cath.* ed. W. Bazeley, i (1882–3), 122–3.

[92] Leland, *Itin.* ed. Toulmin Smith, ii. 60.

[93] *Hist. & Cart. Mon. Glouc.* i. 47.

[94] Rudder, *Glos.* 175; *Glouc. Jnl.* 12 Mar. 1787.

[95] Dugdale, *Mon.* i. 564.

[96] *Trans. B.G.A.S.* xliii. 191–218; *Rec. of Glouc. Cath.* ii. (1883–4), 76–8; D. Welander, *Stained Glass of Glouc. Cath.* (1985), 86–7.

[97] S. Eward, *No Fine*, 159–61.

[98] H. Gee, *Glouc. Cath.: its Organs and Organists* (1921), 6: copy in Glos. Colln. N 4.60.

[99] *Glos. Ch. Bells*, 316–17; *Rec. of Glouc. Cath.* i. 129–30; below.

[1] *Glos. Ch. Plate*, 91–2, *frontispiece*. It was later given to Le Mans cath. and in 1986 was in the Victoria and Albert Mus.

[2] Above, intro.

[3] *Hist. & Cart. Mon. Glouc.* i. 22.

[4] Below, Churches and Chapels, ancient par. ch.

[5] *Hist. & Cart. Mon. Glouc.* i. 26; cf. Glouc. Cath. Libr., Reg. Abb. Froucester B, pp. 10–11.

[6] Dugdale, *Mon.* i. 564; Speed, *Map of Glouc.* (1610).

known alternatively as St. Edward's Lane,[7] suggests that both lane and gate had become popularly associated with Edward II and his burial in the abbey. The surviving portion of the gateway dates from a rebuilding by Abbot Malvern in the early 16th century,[8] and the small gate opening into the cemetery further east, called St. Michael's gate in 1649,[9] is of the same period. Their reconstruction may reflect a change in the relative importance and use of the gates into the precinct, the western gate continuing to be the principal entrance to the abbey but the southern ones providing more convenient access for visitors going from the town to the church. The three gates were apparently the only entrances through the precinct walls in the Middle Ages. The north wall formed part of the town's defences on that side and in 1447 a condition of the settlement of a dispute between abbey and town was that no breaches should be made in it.[10] Possibly the abbot had been pressing to make a more convenient entrance to his lodgings which adjoined the wall, for his only route from the main, western gate was through the service court and across the drains from reredorter and cloister.

Within the walls, the south-west part of the precinct was occupied by the great court of the abbey. To the north lay a smaller court divided from the great court by a range of buildings and entered by an inner gateway, which was rebuilt in the 14th century. The smaller court contained the service buildings including a mill, driven by the Full brook, at its north-west corner, the kitchen to the north-east adjoining the end of the refectory,[11] and probably the bakery and brewery mentioned in 1222.[12] South of the body of the church the lay cemetery was divided from the great court on the west by a wall running from below King Edward's gate to the south-west corner of the church and from the monks' cemetery on the east by a wall running from above St. Michael's gate to the south transept.[13] The monks' cemetery appears to have been bounded on the east by walls adjoining the end of the lady chapel and to have occupied land both north and south of the chapel.[14] The northern part would have been entered from the cloister by the parlour or slype and the southern part by the passage made below the east end of the lady chapel when the chapel was rebuilt on a larger scale in the late 15th century. The extensive area of land at the east end of the precinct was probably, as in the 17th century, occupied mainly by an orchard.[15]

The oldest surviving building adjoining the great court is the 12th-century block at the north-west corner of the church which was the abbot's lodgings until the early 14th century when new lodgings were built on another site.[16] On the north-west it is joined by a substantial 14th-century block which is possibly the great guest hall built by Thomas Horton, abbot 1351–77, and used for the sittings of the commons when parliament was held in the abbey in 1378. Those two blocks, which were apparently both parts of the hospitate at the time of the parliament,[17] were entered by a turret at the south-west angle where parts of a newel stair survive. In the late 15th century or the early 16th the upper part of the 14th-century block was rebuilt and the two blocks may then have become the prior's lodgings. To the north the 14th-century block abuts a range of building which has a 13th-century lower storey with a timber-framed upper storey (later called the Parliament Room) built on it in the late Middle Ages. That building evidently once extended further west and in the early 17th century, when it was occupied as part of the deanery, it was still adjoined on that side by an empty, ruinous range extending to the inner gate and known as the old workhouse and old schoolhouse.[18] The western range was apparently referred to c. 1600 as the 'long workhouse', the most ancient part of the abbey, where early kings were thought to have held councils or parliaments;[19] the building that replaced it on the site in the late 17th century was known as the Parliament House.[20]

A building on the west side of the inner gate, where a basement retains medieval walling, may have housed the cellarer or almoner. To the south-west St. Mary's gate lies within a range, partly of stone and partly timber-framed, which is still predominantly medieval but whose original function is not known. A stable mentioned in 1222 apparently adjoined the south end of that range[21] and perhaps, as in the 17th century, a range of stables extended along the precinct wall to the south-west corner of the outer court, where in the mid 17th century there was a walled miskin, or dungheap.[22] The buildings on the south side of the outer court are probably of medieval origin and may have been part of the accommodation for guests, but it is only at the western end, where there was a large upper room with an open roof and a fireplace, that early work can be seen. A building at the eastern end, adjoining the wall of the lay cemetery, was known in the 17th century as the sexton's house.[23] There is no evidence of medieval structures in the lay cemetery apart from a large cross which stood there until the 1640s.[24]

The abbot's lodgings adjoining the north wall of the precinct originated in a chamber built next to the infirmary garden shortly before 1329.[25] Surviving basement walls and a survey made

[7] Below, Street Names.

[8] Dugdale, *Mon.* i. 564.

[9] Glos. R.O., D 936/E 1, p. 256.

[10] G.B.R., B 2/1, f. 198.

[11] Eward, *No Fine*, 34, 36; for the mill, cf. P.R.O., E 315/494, p. 95.

[12] *Hist. & Cart. Mon. Glouc.* i. 26.

[13] Speed, *Map of Glouc.* (1610); Atkyns, *Glos.* plate at pp. 82–3.

[14] Cf. Glouc. Cath. Libr., Reg. Abb. Froucester B, p. 492, where the 13th-cent. lady chap. is said to stand in the abbey cemetery.

[15] Glos. R.O., D 936/E 1, pp. 260, 265.

[16] Below.

[17] *Hist. & Cart. Mon. Glouc.* i. 50–3.

[18] Glos. R.O., D 936/E 12/1, f. 249; cf. ibid. E 1, pp. 267–8, 281–2.

[19] Dugdale, *Mon.* i. 564.

[20] Eward, *No Fine*, 307–8.

[21] *Hist. & Cart. Mon. Glouc.* i. 26.

[22] Glos. R.O., D 936/E 1, pp. 246, 268.

[23] Ibid. pp. 270, 283.

[24] G.B.R., B 3/2, p. 397.

[25] *Hist. & Cart. Mon. Glouc.* i. 46.

before all but small parts of the buildings were demolished in the mid 19th century[26] suggest that the lodgings included at the west end a hall with private apartments, to which was added the chapel built by Abbot Horton in the mid 14th century.[27] The lodgings were extended in the 15th century and the early 16th. Abbot Malvern after 1514 enlarged the gate on the south side[28] and it was presumably he who added a gallery range on the north along the inside of the precinct wall. The gallery linked the hall block to an eastern block, which may in the late-medieval period have contained the private apartments of the abbot.

CATHEDRAL CHURCH FROM 1541.

In 1541 the abbey church became the cathedral of the *HOLY AND UNDIVIDED TRINITY*.[29] The ornaments and jewels which had enriched its interior were removed for the king's use,[30] and later many of its fittings were lost, particularly perhaps under John Hooper, bishop of Gloucester 1551–4, who went further than most of his contemporaries in ordering the removal of effigies, rood screens, and other such survivals.[31] Little is known of the fortunes of the cathedral during the later 16th century but it was in need of extensive repair in 1617 when the chapter, following the appointment of William Laud as dean, applied £60 a year to a maintenance fund. At Laud's first chapter meeting he ordered the most celebrated internal rearrangement in the history of the cathedral, the moving of the communion table from the centre of the choir to the east end, where new wooden altar rails were provided. Plans were also made to replace the existing decayed organs with a new instrument[32] but it was not until 1640 that a new organ, built by Robert Dallam, was installed in a loft on the south side of the choir.[33] The cathedral escaped serious damage in the siege of Gloucester in 1643 but later many of the windows were smashed by Scots soldiers, probably those of the earl of Leven's army which marched through the city in 1645.[34] After the sequestration of the building with the rest of the chapter property there is said to have been an attempt to demolish it and profit from the sale of the materials.[35] In 1652 it was described as being in danger of collapse and the town clerk of Gloucester, John Dorney, urged the corporation to help repair it.[36] In 1656 the corpor-

ation secured a grant of the cathedral[37] and organized repairs, raising some of the cost by an appeal for subscriptions.[38] After the return of the cathedral to the dean and chapter at the Restoration an extensive programme of reglazing was carried out in the early 1660s.[39] A new portable wooden font was made in 1663[40], and a new organ was built by Thomas Harris in 1665 and the loft in the choir rebuilt for it. The organ was later restored or reconstructed a number of times but retains its elaborately carved case and painted pipes.[41]

In the earlier 18th century there were some major alterations to the internal arrangement of the cathedral. At the beginning of the century sermons were preached in the east end of the nave, where the pulpit, provided by Bishop Henry Parry in 1609, stood against the third pier on the north side. The east end of the aisles, including the second piers of the arcades, were enclosed by wooden partitions, the enclosure on the north, called the mayor's chapel, containing the seats used by the city corporation and that on the south those used by the cathedral clergy. A medieval screen, adjoining the first piers of the arcades, crossed the full width of the church, its central portion surmounted by a loft and altar, apparently the *pulpitum* built by Abbot John Wygmore *c.* 1330.[42] In the years 1717–18 the dean, Knightly Chetwood, with the help of a grant from the corporation, refitted the choir for hearing sermons,[43] providing new box pews, placed rather awkwardly in front of the medieval stalls, and a portable pulpit. A wooden altarpiece in classical style,[44] carved by Michael Bysaak, had been installed in 1716.[45] In 1741 Bishop Martin Benson replaced the central portion of the screen at the east end of the nave with a new gothick screen, designed by William Kent, with three ogee arches.[46] The organ was placed on top of the screen, and the wooden partitions at the east end of the aisles were apparently removed at the same time. During Chetwood's alterations the old pews of the choir were moved to the lady chapel, which was later used for morning prayers. Bishop Benson later put a new stucco altarpiece in the chapel.[47]

The fabric of the cathedral was regularly maintained during the 18th century and the earlier 19th, there being few years in which a mason, plumber and glazier, and carpenter from the city

[26] *Arch. Jnl.* liv. 110 and plans and elevations facing (from G.D.R., A 13/10).   [27] *Hist. & Cart. Mon. Glouc.* i. 50.

[28] Dugdale, *Mon.* i. 564.

[29] *Glouc. Corp. Rec.* p. 25. The form 'Holy and Indivisible Trinity' was generally used by the 19th cent., and the dedication was changed *c.* 1963 to 'St. Peter and the Holy and Indivisible Trinity': *Glouc. Dioc. Year Bk.* (1962–3), 6; (1963–4), 6.

[30] Cf. P.R.O., E 315/494, p. 100; *Rec. of Glouc. Cath.* ii. 133.   [31] *Trans. B.G.A.S.* lx. 64–6.

[32] B. Taylor, 'Wm. Laud., Dean of Glouc. 1616–21', *Trans. B.G.A.S.* lxxvii. 86–94.

[33] Gee, *Glouc. Cath. Organs*, 11.

[34] Eward, *No Fine*, 160; G.B.R., F 4/5, f. 273.

[35] Rudder, *Glos.* 172.

[36] J. Dorney, *Certain Speeches* (Lond. 1653), 82.

[37] *Cal. S.P. Dom.* 1656–7, 3; *Glouc. Corp. Rec.* p. 45.

[38] G.B.R., B 3/2, pp. 873–5, 878–9, 881.

[39] Glos. R.O., D 936/A 24.

[40] Eward, *No Fine*, 125; *Trans. B.G.A.S.* xlvii. 180–1; it was presumably that shown on S. side of the nave in the 1720s but later it stood in the N. transept chap.: Willis, *Surv.* ii, plan at p. 692; Britton, *Cath. Ch. of Glouc.* plate XII.

[41] Gee, *Glouc. Cath. Organs*, 13–17, 25–44; *Rec. of Glouc. Cath.* iii (1885–97), 73–89.

[42] Rudder, *Glos.* 177; Willis, *Surv.* ii, plan at p. 692; G.B.R., B 3/2, p. 857; for the arrangement of screens, which in the Middle Ages had also included a rood screen adjoining the second piers, cf. *Arch. Jnl.* liv. 84–6.

[43] G.B.R., B 3/9, ff. 22v., 42v.

[44] Willis, *Surv.* ii, plan at p. 692; Bonnor, *Itin.* 14, plate 2.

[45] Glouc. Cath. Libr., Chapter Act bk. ii, f. 79.

[46] Glos. Colln. prints GL 102.8; above, Plate 19.

[47] Rudder, *Glos.* 172, 177; Bonnor, *Itin.* 13, 15; cf. T. H. Cocke, 'Bishop Benson and his Restoration of Glouc. Cath.', *Brit. Arch. Assoc. Conference Trans.* ix.

did not present substantial bills.[48] From 1738, in a measure that probably reflected Bishop Benson's concern for the upkeep and improvement of the building, the chapter applied the fines paid each year by prebendaries for non-residence to the fabric fund, and in 1740 Benson ordered that £20 a year, assigned by the cathedral statutes to the repair of roads and bridges on chapter property, should also be applied;[49] by the early 19th century, however, those sums were usually used on the general upkeep of the close. John Bryan of Gloucester and his partner and eventual successor, George Wood, were the cathedral masons in the late 18th century and the early 19th.[50] In the mid 1780s Bryan carried out a more than usually thorough restoration of the stonework[51] and, over a period of several years, he repaved most of the cathedral.[52]

In 1807 the altarpiece at the east end of the choir was replaced by a new stone one, designed by Robert Smirke,[53] and Benson's lady chapel altarpiece was removed in 1819, revealing once more the late-medieval reredos that survived there in a mutilated state.[54] In 1820 Benson's screen, by then regarded as thoroughly inconsistent with its surroundings, was replaced by a new screen, paid for and designed by a prebendary, James Griffith. At the same time the medieval screens across the aisles were removed.[55]

In 1855 the chapter commissioned a detailed report on necessary restoration work from the Gloucester architect F. S. Waller. He carried out a few of the proposed alterations during the next few years, including the clearing and restoration of the crypt, which had long been used as a bone hole, and the removal of soil and the insertion of drainage around the base of the walls, and in the early 1860s parts of the fabric were restored under the direction of his partner Thomas Fulljames.[56] In 1863 the sittings of the consistory court of the diocese, held since the beginning of the 18th century or earlier in a railed-off area at the west end of the south aisle, were removed to the chapter house.[57] During the late 1850s and the 1860s a series of stained glass memorial windows was introduced in the aisles and in the great cloister; most were by John Hardman or the firm of Clayton and Bell. The glass of the great west window of the nave, a memorial to Bishop James

Monk (d. 1856), was made at the workshops of William Wailes in 1859.[58]

In 1865 when Thomas Fulljames gave up the post of cathedral architect the chapter offered it to (Sir) George Gilbert Scott, who was empowered to draw up plans for an extensive restoration.[59] A restoration of the chapel of St. Andrew in the south transept was completed in 1868, its walls and ceiling being painted with frescoes by Thomas Gambier Parry.[60] The general restoration under Scott was begun later that year; it was financed mainly by subscriptions, and the cost of particular parts of the building and items of furnishing was met by prominent county families and Gloucester citizens. By 1871 work had been completed on the choir, where the floor was retiled, the vault painted, the north clerestory windows reglazed, mainly with new stained glass, new choir seats provided, and the sedilia recarved,[61] and on the south porch, where the stonework was largely renewed and new figures placed in the niches.[62] Later in the 1870s much of the interior and exterior stonework of the nave, aisles, and transepts was restored and the north aisle reroofed.[63] A new reredos was installed in 1873[64] and a new Romanesque-style font in 1878, both to designs by Scott.[65] After Scott's death in 1878 restoration of the fabric to his plans continued under the direction of F. S. Waller,[66] who had served as supervisor of the works since 1872 and succeeded Scott as cathedral architect. Most of the work was finished by the end of 1881 when Waller suggested that the chapter should make an appropriate reduction in his salary.[67]

During the 1880s and 1890s stained glass by C. E. Kempe was placed in the windows of the ambulatories.[68] Between 1893 and 1897 a thorough restoration of the fabric of the lady chapel was carried out, the work including the replacement of its parapet and pinnacles.[69] Stained glass by Christopher Whall was placed in the side windows of the chapel between 1898 and 1913.[70] A further extensive restoration of the tower, the fabric of the body of the cathedral, and the roofs was carried out between 1906 and c. 1914 under the direction of Waller's son and successor, F. W. Waller.[71] In the mid 1950s, under N. H. Waller, the third member of the family to serve as cathedral architect, and his partner B. J. Ashwell, the

[48] Glos. R.O., D 936/A 1/6–10.

[49] Glouc. Cath. Libr., Chapter Act bk. ii, ff. 152, 159v.; iii, pp. 1–2.   [50] Glos. R.O., D 936/A 1/8–10.

[51] Glouc. Cath. Libr., Chapter Act bk. iv, pp. 141, 151, 171.

[52] Ibid. p. 147; Glos. R.O., D 936/A 1/8, pp. 452, 496, 520.

[53] Counsel, Glouc. 100; Glos. R.O., D 936/A 1/9, p. 586.

[54] Britton, Cath. Ch. of Glouc. 75; cf. ibid. plate XX.

[55] Glouc. Cath. Libr., Chapter Act bk. v, pp. 111, 138, 160; Glouc. Jnl. 11 Sept. 1820.

[56] Glouc. Cath. Libr., Chapter Act bk. vi, pp. 308, 337, 351–2, 372–4; vii, pp. 19–21, 29–48; Builder, 8 Nov. 1856, 603; and for the crypt, cf. Bodl. MS. Top. Glouc. c. 3, f. 114; Britton, Cath. Ch. of Glouc. plate XIII.

[57] Bodl. MS. Top. Glouc. c. 3, f. 118v.; Bonnor, Itin. 13, plate 1; Trans. B.G.A.S. xlvi. 207.

[58] Welander, Stained Glass, 77–98.

[59] Glouc. Cath. Libr., Chapter Act bk. vii, p. 98; Glouc. Jnl. 20 Apr. 1867.

[60] Ecclesiologist, Aug. 1868, 210–11.

[61] Glouc. Jnl. 12 Aug., 2 Sept. 1871. Some of the old seats were moved to the E. end of the nave and the early 17th-cent. altar rails to the lady chap.

[62] Ibid. 2 Sept. 1871.

[63] Kelly's Dir. Glos. (1879), 652.

[64] Glos. Colln. NR 4.3.

[65] Glouc. Jnl. 27 Apr. 1878. It was kept in the crypt from the mid 20th cent. and a Norman lead font from Lancaut, placed on a new podium in the lady chap. in 1986, was used instead: cf. V.C.H. Glos. x. 77–8.

[66] Kelly's Dir. Glos. (1885), 467.

[67] Glouc. Cath. Libr., Chapter Act bk. vii, pp. 172, 238, 284.

[68] Welander, Stained Glass, 105–10.

[69] Glouc. Jnl. 26 Nov. 1892; 2 Oct. 1897; Trans. B.G.A.S. xxxiv. 100.

[70] Welander, Stained Glass, 115–30.

[71] Glos. Colln. (H) E 3.82, 84; Glouc. Cath. Libr., Chapter Act bk. viii, pp. 210, 235, 244 sqq.; for the Wallers, above, Glouc. 1835–1985, topog.

roofs of the nave, choir, north transept, and cloisters were reconstructed,[72] and in the mid 1960s a long programme of cleaning the begrimed exterior began, revealing once more the honey colour of the oolite.

In Tudor and Stuart times a number of substantial and ornate monuments were placed in the cathedral, commemorating among others prominent Gloucester citizens.[73] That to Richard Pate (d. 1588), recorder of the city, in the south transept had painted figures (hardly visible in 1986) of Pate, his wife, and children beneath a stone canopy. Against the wall at the east end of the north aisle painted effigies of Alderman Thomas Machen (d. 1614), in his mayoral robe, and his wife kneel on a canopied and painted tomb. A monument to Alderman John Jones (d. 1630), said to have been made under his direction, is fixed to the west wall of the south aisle, having been moved from its original position next to the west door;[74] Jones's half-length, upright effigy is surrounded by items of civic insignia and by bundles of deeds and other details recalling his long service as diocesan registrar. John Bower (d. 1614), a Gloucester apothecary,[75] is depicted with his wife and children on panels at the back of a large monument in the north transept. John Powell (d. 1713), town clerk of Gloucester, is commemorated in the lady chapel by a standing effigy by Thomas Green, depicting him in the robes of a judge of queen's bench. In the chapel on the south side of the lady chapel a monument to Thomas Fitzwilliams (d. 1579) comprises a painting on a mural slab and a plain table tomb. In the chapel opposite the painted effigy of Godfrey Goldsborough (d. 1604), bishop of Gloucester, lies on a table tomb, and two daughters of Bishop Miles Smith, Elizabeth Williams (d. 1622) and Margery Clent (d. 1623), are depicted in effigy on monuments near the west end of the lady chapel. Placed in the south transept but originally in the north aisle, where it was enclosed like Machen's monument in the mayor's chapel,[76] is a tomb with richly detailed alabaster effigies of Abraham Blackleech (d. 1639) and his wife; Blackleech, the son of a former chancellor of the diocese, was a prominent resident of the close.[77]

Of the many monuments fixed to the walls of the aisles in the Georgian period two of the most notable on artistic grounds are those to Sarah Morley (d. 1784) by John Flaxman and to Dame Mary Strachan (d. 1770) by John Ricketts the younger of Gloucester. Others commemorate prominent men of the city and county, including Ralph Bigland (d. 1784), herald and antiquary, Charles Brandon Trye (d. 1811), surgeon, the Revd. Thomas Stock (d. 1803), joint founder of the Gloucester Sunday schools, whose monument was erected c. 1840,[78] and the Revd. Richard Raikes (d. 1823), whose Gothic monument was designed by Thomas Rickman and Henry Hutchinson. In the south aisle a monument to Sir George Paul (d. 1820), prison reformer and county administrator, comprises a bust, carved by Robert Sievier, on a sarcophagus. Also by Sievier[79] is the figure of Edward Jenner (d. 1823), discoverer of smallpox vaccination, set on a pedestal beside the west door. There are monuments with medallion portraits to the two best known bishops of Gloucester of the period: that to Martin Benson (d. 1752) has been moved from the south transept to the south triforium gallery and that to William Warburton (d. 1779) is on the west wall of the north aisle.

A canopied Gothic sepulchre in the south ambulatory to John Kempthorne (d. 1838), rector of St. Michael's church, and a bronze, kneeling figure in the north aisle to Canon E. D. Tinling (d. 1897) are among the few monuments of the Victorian period, when the chapter encouraged the use of memorial windows instead.[80] Bishop Charles Ellicott (d. 1905) is commemorated by an alabaster effigy, carved by W. S. Frith,[81] on a tomb chest in the south ambulatory. There are plaques for Dorothea Beale (d. 1906), first principal of Cheltenham Ladies College, the musician Sir Hubert Parry (d. 1918), the poets Ivor Gurney (d. 1937) and Frederick Harvey (d. 1957), and Albert Mansbridge (d. 1952), founder of the Workers' Educational Association.

The oldest bells at the cathedral survive from the 15th century, and by the early 16th there was a ring of eight.[82] Individual bells of the ring were recast in 1598, 1626, 1686 (and again in 1810), 1736, and 1810. The ring, which was hung in a new oak frame in 1632,[83] often rang out over the city to mark events of national importance.[84] In 1956 it was augmented to 10 by the addition of two bells from St. Michael's church. In the years 1978–9, at the instigation of the dean, Gilbert Thurlow, an enthusiast for campanology, the ring was restored, augmented to 12, and rehung in a new frame by the Whitechapel foundry, London. The last five bells of the old ring were retained, three others recast, and four new bells cast, leaving the ring as follows: (treble and ii) 1978; (iii and iv) 1978, recastings of the former St. Michael's bells; (v and vi) 1978; (vii) 1978, recasting of a bell of 1810; (viii) 1810 by John Rudhall; (ix and x) early 15th century by a London foundry; (xi) 1626 by John Pennington of Exeter; (tenor) 1736 by Abel Rudhall. The two bells of the old ring not re-used were preserved in the bell chamber and are as follows: (old iii) 1598 by Robert Newcombe of Leicester; (old iv) mid 15th century by John Sturdy of London.[85]

A great bourdon bell, thought to be the largest medieval bell in existence, was made in the mid 15th century and bears the abbey's arms and the

[72] Verey and Welander, *Glouc. Cath.* 37.
[73] For the monuments, Roper, *Glos. Effigies*, 258–98.
[74] Bodl. MS. Top. Glouc. c. 3, f. 118v.; cf. Willis, *Surv.* ii, plan at p. 692.   [75] G.B.R., C 10/1, p. 140.
[76] Willis, *Surv.* ii, plan at p. 692. Its original site perhaps led to the mistaken belief that he was an alderman.
[77] Rudder, *Glos.* 163; Eward, *No Fine*, 329.
[78] Glouc. Cath. Libr., Chapter Act bk. vi, p. 25.

[79] Counsel, *Glouc.* 125, 127.
[80] Glouc. Cath. Libr., Chapter Act bk. vii, pp. 190–1, 379, 400.
[81] Ibid. viii, pp. 234, 287.   [82] *Rec. of Glouc. Cath.* i. 129–33.
[83] *Glos. Ch. Bells*, 318–20.
[84] Glos. R.O., D 936/A 1/6–10; cf. Glouc. Cath. Libr., Chapter Act bk. v, p. 250.
[85] *Glos. Ch. Bells*, 309–22.

inscription: 'Me fecit fieri conventus nomine Petri'. It hung in the ringing chamber, where a new frame for it was provided in the 17th century.[86] Ringing the bell, which was used mainly as a passing bell, required considerable skill and strength. In the late 17th century it was said to need 10 men to raise it and 6 to swing it.[87] 'Great Peter' was temporarily silenced in 1827 when the experienced ringers resigned after a disagreement with the chapter[88] and it was not swung at all after 1878. In 1927 it was rehung 'dead' and sounded by means of a rope attached to the clapper until 1979 when it was rehung to be swung by an electric motor. The cathedral's sanctus bell was brought from St. Nicholas's church in the 1970s and dates from the early 16th century.[89] The chiming mechanism, installed before 1525 to strike the hours and play two hymn tunes on the bells,[90] was renewed in 1762[91] and in the course of the centuries had a number of new tunes composed for it by cathedral organists or choristers. At the restoration of the bells a new electrically-operated chiming mechanism was installed to play the repertoire of seven tunes.[92]

After the Restoration the cathedral was provided with a new set of silver-gilt plate, comprising 2 chalices, 2 tankard flagons, and 3 patens, all dated 1660, and a pair of silver-gilt candlesticks dated 1661. Other pieces were added later, including a credence paten of 1705, given in 1905, and chalices of 1817 and 1862. A bishop's mace was given by Martin Benson in 1737.[93] In 1977 the cathedral plate, together with plate from other churches in the diocese, was put on permanent display in a treasury built in the slype adjoining the north transept.[94] The registers of christenings, marriages, and burials survive from 1662.[95]

BUILDINGS IN THE CLOSE FROM 1541.
On the creation of the see of Gloucester in 1541 the former abbot's lodgings were assigned to the bishop as his palace and the remainder of the close and the other abbey buildings to the dean and chapter.[96] The group of buildings at the north-west corner of the cathedral became the deanery and others were assigned as residences of the six prebendaries, the minor canons, the choristers, the masters of the College school run by the chapter, the almspeople maintained by it under its statutes of 1544, and other members of the establishment.[97] Some buildings were soon found superfluous and removed, and others were rebuilt or

remodelled in the 17th and 18th centuries to house the cathedral staff in greater comfort or for letting to private households.[98]

Among the abbey buildings demolished were the dormitory, the refectory, which was damaged by fire soon after 1540,[99] and parts of the infirmary. By the mid 17th century surviving parts of the infirmary were incorporated, together with the east side of the little cloister, in an extensive range of buildings, the upper rooms of which were known as the Babylon; divided into numerous little chambers, the buildings housed choristers, almspeople, and poor widows. Buildings east of the infirmary (later Dulverton House), perhaps originally the infirmarer's lodging, and west of the little cloister (later Little Cloister House), including the supposed misericord, were among those adapted as the houses of prebendaries. The other four prebendal residences were in the great court, in buildings adjoining the south wall (nos. 7–8 College Green), south of St. Mary's gate (no. 14 College Green), and west of the inner gate (later Community House). The great cloister was preserved intact together with the chapter house, which was fitted up as a library in 1648 by Thomas Pury the younger with the support of the city corporation and remained the cathedral library after the Restoration.[1] The former abbey library, at the top of the range between the chapter house and north transept, became the schoolroom of the College school, while the rooms on the floor below were used as vestries, the treasury, and for chapter meetings.[2] The former abbey mill in the inner court, known as Miller's Green (and, in the 19th century, Palace Yard), was leased as a working corn mill until the mid 18th century.

The old circuit of walls was apparently first breached on the east side near St. John's church where one of the tenants had permission to make a gateway in 1626,[3] and the walls on that side were removed later as the west side of St. John's Lane was built up. A new entrance with a wicket gate, known as the infirmary gate, had been made in the north wall, east of the bishop's palace, by 1673.[4] The room over King Edward's gate was leased as a dwelling until it was removed in 1805 or 1806, leaving only the piers standing.[5] The eastern pier had been removed by the early 1890s when its site and the house adjoining (no. 5 College Green) were taken for the widening of College Street.[6] St. Mary's gate, St. Michael's gate, the inner gate, and most of the walls around the west part of the close, in a much-repaired state, survived in 1986.

[86] Ibid. 311, 232–4.
[87] *Journeys of Celia Fiennes*, ed. C. Morris (1947), 235.
[88] Glouc. Cath. Libr., Chapter Act bk. v, pp. 250–1.
[89] *Glos. Ch. Bells*, 325–6.
[90] *Rec. of Glouc. Cath.* i. 129–30.
[91] Glouc. Cath. Libr., Chapter Act bk. iii, p. 139; Glos. R.O., D 936/A 1/8, p. 139.
[92] G. Thurlow, *Tower, Bells, and Chimes of Glouc. Cath.* (1979), 14–21.　[93] *Glos. Ch. Plate*, 92–4.
[94] Verey and Welander, *Glouc. Cath.* 81.
[95] Kirby, *Cat. of Glouc. Dioc. Rec.* 26.
[96] *Glouc. Corp. Rec.* pp. 22–5.
[97] Cf. Rudder, *Glos.* App. pp. xlii, xlvi.
[98] Where no other source is given the hist. of the buildings in the close during the 17th and 18th cents. is based on the detailed account in Eward, *No Fine*, 29–40, 295–329; on a map of the close c. 1762, reproduced in ibid. at end; and on a surv. of 1649, in Glos. R.O., D 936/E 1, pp. 243–82.
[99] P.R.O., E 315/494, p. 100.
[1] S. Eward, *Cat. of Glouc. Cath. Libr.* (1972), pp. vii–viii. The libr. was moved to the S. ambulatory of the cath. in 1743 and back to the chapter ho. in 1764: ibid. p. xi.
[2] Willis, *Surv.* ii, plan at p. 692; cf. Glouc. Cath. Libr., Chapter Act bk. vii, p. 45.
[3] Eward, *No Fine*, 70.
[4] Glos. R.O., D 936/L 6.
[5] Ibid. A 1/9, pp. 524, 560, 562; cf. Counsel, *Glouc.* 64.
[6] Glos. R.O., D 2593, private, Cath. Approaches Co. Ltd., notes by F.S. Waller.

Among the earliest new houses built for tenants was one in the east part of the close (later King's School House) of the late 16th century. In the same area the building of houses on the west side of St. John's Lane had begun by 1649. In the lay cemetery, known after the Dissolution as the upper churchyard and still used partly as a burial ground,[7] building had begun by 1616, and by 1649 there were houses ranged along its east wall and along the south wall between the two gates. In the great court, known as the lower churchyard or College Green, the two prebendal houses on the south side were remodelled in the 17th century.[8] In the late 17th century a number of new brick houses were built in the close, including the Parliament House (no. 7 Miller's Green) on the site of the old workhouse and schoolhouse c. 1670,[9] a house on the east side of Miller's Green (no. 6), one on the south side of the upper churchyard (no. 4 College Green), and one on the east side of its east wall (Cathedral, later Wardle, House) built c. 1680. One of the most imposing houses in the close was built c. 1707 at the south-west corner of College Green (no. 9) and is of three storeys and five bays with a central pediment and angle pilasters.[10]

There was another busy period of building and rebuilding in the mid 18th century. Under leases with imposing gate piers (no. 1) was built before 1741, and between c. 1746 and 1766 a number of other houses, including the eastern ones of the range at the south side of the upper churchyard, were rebuilt or remodelled.[12] The house adjoining the north side of St. Mary's gate (later Monument House) was rebuilt c. 1774 with a front with a gothick doorcase to St. Mary's Square,[13] and the prebendal house adjoining it on the east was rebuilt about the same time with a long front with a rusticated ground floor facing College Green. One of the last houses to be altered in the Georgian period was the former sexton's house on the west side of King Edward's gate (no. 6 College Green) which was extensively remodelled in 1813.[14]

The two principal residences in the close, those of bishop and dean, remained basically medieval buildings. The palace was altered c. 1740 by Bishop Benson[15] who added on ornate classical portico to the south end of the great hall. Then or at other times in the 18th century many of its windows were replaced, particularly those on the west side[16] facing the spacious garden which occupied the north-west corner of the close. The deanery in the 17th century had included the 12th-century block at the north-west corner of the cathedral, the adjoining 14th-century block,

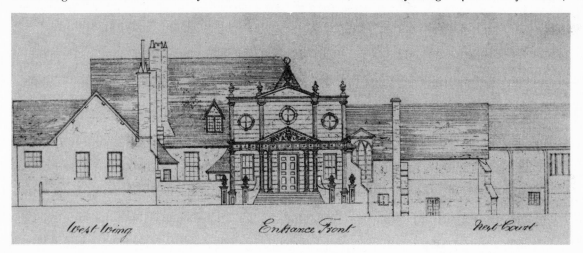

Fig. 22. The bishop's palace: the south side before rebuilding, with the portico added c. 1740

granted in 1735 and 1736 a timber merchant John Pasco in partnership with the cathedral organist Barnabas Gunn built a row of four houses (nos. 10 – 13) along the west wall of College Greeen on the site of the stables and coach houses of the bishop and dean. No. 12 includes a ground-floor assembly room with tall sash windows, which in the time of the first tenant, Alderman Benjamin Saunders, former landlord of the King's Head inn,[11] was used for concerts and social gatherings. On the west side of Miller's Green a tall house where there was some internal refitting in the early 17th century including new panelling in the main first-floor rooms, the attached block on the north containing the Parliament Room, and a range of building on the east side of the courtyard adjoining the cloister. The last-mentioned range was removed in or before the mid 1730s when a brick coach house and stable were built on part of its site. The Parliament Room ceased to be occupied as part of the deanery c. 1720,[17] and in the 1760s, called the club room, was apparently

[7] Hall and Pinnell, *Map of Glouc.* (1780).

[8] They were again altered in the late 19th cent.: cf. photog. c. 1865 in Glouc. Cath. Libr.

[9] For its original appearance, with dutch gablets and mullion and transom windows, Eward, *No Fine*, plate facing p. 215.

[10] A new doorcase was added in the mid 18th cent.

[11] Cf. G.B.R., G 3/AV 1.

[12] Ibid. SO 8, Epiph. 1766.

[13] Glos. R.O., D 936/L 7.

[14] Counsel, *Glouc.* 64; cf. Glos. R.O., D 936/E 12/18, f. 137.

[15] *Horace Walpole's Correspondence*, ed. W. S. Lewis, xxxv (1973), 153.

[16] G.D.R., A 13/10, elevations, one reproduced as Fig. 22.

[17] Glouc. Cath. Libr., Chapter Act bk. ii, p. 87.

used for social gatherings. The cloister garth served as the deanery garden. Dean Josiah Tucker spent considerable sums on the deanery c. 1760;[18] the new windows in various styles which the stair turret and the fronts towards College Green had before restoration in the mid 19th century[19] were presumably inserted during his long tenure.

By the mid 18th century College Green was landscaped, with walks lined with lime trees around the grassed central area.[20] The wall between it and the upper churchyard was removed in 1768[21] and later the name College Green was applied to the whole area. The east side of the close was mainly occupied by gardens, including those of the two large houses standing south-east of the cathedral,[22] both of which were remodelled in the early 19th century, Cathedral House being given a prominent bow on its north front. Land in the angle formed by the lady chapel and the east claustral range became known as the Grove after the late 17th century when Maurice Wheeler, master of the College school, organized his pupils in clearing and planting work.[23] In 1777 there was a fives court in the Grove which the chapter ordered to be broken up because it attracted a disorderly crowd of players.[24]

Alterations in the close during the 19th century affected mainly buildings on the north side of the cathedral. In 1849 a new schoolroom for the College school was built against the north side of the chapter house.[25] During 1857 and 1858 the cathedral library was moved from the chapter house to the former schoolroom in the adjoining range, the chapter house was restored for its original purpose, and the rooms below the former schoolroom were restored as sacristies.[26] Between 1860 and 1862 the bishop's palace was rebuilt to the designs of Ewan Christian as a massive Tudor-style mansion in Cotswold stone; west of the great hall, which was rebuilt on the old cellars, were business offices and to the east the bishop's private apartments.[27] Some of the buildings of the

Babylon on the east side of the little cloister had been demolished in 1831[28] and another part, then occupied by the headmaster of the College school, in 1854 or 1855 when the site became the school playground. At the rebuilding of the palace a house built into the end of the infirmary arcade and other buildings further west were removed to open up a public way through to Miller's Green in place of a covered walk under the north side of Little Cloister House.[29] Those various alterations left the north and east walks of the little cloister unroofed and the remains of the infirmary arcade exposed. Beginning in 1863 the deanery was restored and remodelled to the designs of Thomas Fulljames: the fronts to College Green were refaced and the fenestration renewed, the stair turret was rebuilt, and additions were made to the courtyard side of the 14th-century block.[30] In the mid 19th century landscaping work was carried out around the east end of the cathedral and at its south side,[31] where the burial ground was closed in 1857.[32]

One of the few additions to the close in the 20th century was a war memorial to the Royal Gloucestershire Hussars Yeomanry in lower College Green, unveiled in 1922; the design includes bronze panels depicting incidents from the regiment's campaigns in the Middle East.[33] In 1940 the dean's residence was moved to no. 1 Miller's Green. The south block of the old deanery, renamed Church House, became diocesan offices in 1948 and the upper rooms of the adjoining block were assigned for meetings and social events.[34] The bishop's palace became part of the King's (formerly College) school in 1954,[35] and a new house for the bishop (called Bishopscourt in 1986) was built at the north-east corner of the close. In the 1970s during redevelopment of the area at the east side of the close between Pitt Street and St. John's Lane a new pedestrian entrance was made and a slightly different boundary from the ancient one was adopted.[36]

SITES AND REMAINS OF RELIGIOUS HOUSES

LLANTHONY PRIORY.[37] The priory of Llanthony Secunda occupied a low-lying site south-west of the town, bounded on the west side

by the lane to Hempsted and on the south side by the Sud brook. The short period which elapsed between the gift of the priory's site in 1136 and

---

[18] Ibid. iii, pp. 105–6.

[19] Eward, *No Fine*, plate facing p. 215; Storer, *Hist. and Antiquities of Cath. Ch. of Glouc.* (1817), plate 3; photogs. of deanery during restoration, pasted in Glos. R.O., D 874, copy of J. Carter, *Some Account of Cath. Ch. of Glouc.* (1809).

[20] Eward, *No Fine*, plate facing p. 215.

[21] Glouc. Cath. Libr., Chapter Act bk. iii, p. 183.

[22] Atkyns, *Glos.* plate at pp. 82–3; Hall and Pinnell, *Map of Glouc.* (1780); Cole, *Map of Glouc.* (1805).

[23] Bonnor, *Itin.* 17–18.

[24] Glouc. Cath. Libr., Chapter Act bk. iv, p. 26; cf. Bonnor, *Itin.* plan at p. 1.

[25] D. Robertson, *King's Sch., Glouc.* (1974), 117.

[26] Eward, *Cat. of Glouc. Cath. Libr.* p. xiv; Glouc. Cath. Libr., Chapter Act bk. vi, pp. 330, 351–2, 372–4; vii, p. 45.

[27] *Glouc. Jnl.* 8 Feb. 1862; *Trans. B.G.A.S.* xcvii. 83.

[28] Glos. R.O., D 936/E 174; cf. Bd. of Health Map (1852).

[29] Glouc. Cath. Libr., Chapter Act bk. vi, p. 316; G.D.R., A 13/10, plan of precincts; cf. photog. of the bldg. in the infirmary arcade, pasted in Glos. R.O., D 874.

[30] G.B.R., planning dept., file 1863/6; Glouc. Cath. Libr., Chapter Act bk. vii, p. 59.

[31] Glouc. Cath. Libr., Chapter Act bk. vi, pp. 372–4.

[32] G.B.R., L 4/6/4.

[33] F. Fox, *Hist. of Royal Glos. Hussars* (1923), 323–4.

[34] *Country Life*, 13 Apr. 1951, pp. 1102, 1105.

[35] Robertson, *King's Sch.* 190.

[36] Cf. O.S. Map 1/2,500, Glos. XXV.15 (1886 edn.). A small part of the old precinct wall survived in that area in 1986, adjoining the former St. John's graveyard.

[37] This article was written in 1984 and revised in 1986. The institutional hist. of the religious houses was given in *V.C.H. Glos.* ii. For the buildings of the medieval hospitals, below, Char. for Poor, almshouses.

the dedication of its church the following year, and the fact that a return to the mother house in the Honddu valley (in the later Monmouthshire) was envisaged,[38] suggests that the original buildings were of a temporary nature. By the late 12th century, as architectural fragments found in 1846 indicate,[39] there was a substantial church at the site. In 1301 the church, described as having four bell towers, was burnt and the expense of its rebuilding presumably contributed to the priory's financial problems in the early 14th century. William of Cherington, prior 1377–1401, rebuilt a chapel of the Trinity, the cloister, and a granary. In 1518 the church was said to be ruinous.[40]

In 1540 the site of the priory was sold by the Crown to Arthur Porter[41] and it descended with his Llanthony manor estate until 1898.[42] The Porters and their successors, the Scudamores, used part of the buildings as a residence until at least 1697,[43] and during the 18th and 19th centuries the site was used as a farmstead.[44] In 1974 the site, subject to various tenancies and used partly for industrial purposes, was bought by the city council, which took possession in 1984 and began some clearing and landscaping work.[45]

Substantial remains of the priory, including part of the church, survived until the time of the siege of Gloucester in 1643. A tower, which could have been used by an enemy force to overlook the city, was pulled down before the siege,[46] and the buildings were further damaged during the siege as the city's defenders retaliated against royalist artillery sited there.[47] The church had probably been demolished completely by c. 1710 when Atkyns described the tombs of the de Bohun family as heaps of rubbish under the sky.[48] In the late 1790s the Gloucester and Berkeley canal was dug through the east side of the precinct, revealing foundations of a building c. 30 ft. wide, apparently part of the church.[49]

The surviving buildings and ruins are of the 15th century and the early 16th. Along the west side is a length of brick precinct wall with the ruins of a stone gatehouse. On the north side are the ruins of a large stone barn, which had two transeptal entrances and in the past was sometimes taken for the ruins of the church.[50] South of the barn, on a north–south alignment, ran a long range of stone building with a timber-framed upper storey; an addition, described in 1853 as a modern cottage, was later made at its south end.[51] Before

1882 the north part of the old range was demolished,[52] and the cottage was rebuilt. Other buildings, of two storeys, survive from a range which ran along the south side of the site and aligned on foundations discovered further east during the widening of the Gloucester and Berkeley canal and the building of a new wharf in 1852.[53] The priory church, of which the western end presumably still underlies the north-eastern part of the site, probably had a southern cloister, though that is unlikely to have connected with the surviving buildings to the west and south, which are more likely to have been lodgings or part of the farmery.

ST. OSWALD'S PRIORY. The minster (later priory) of St. Oswald, founded c. 900 A.D. by Ethelfleda of Mercia,[54] occupied a site north of the town, bounded on the north-west by the Old Severn, where remains of the precinct wall survived in the early 19th century,[55] and on the north-east and east by Water Street and Half Street. Detailed excavations[56] at the site of the church have shown that the 12th-century arcade, all that remained visible of the priory in 1984, was an insertion representing only one of a long series of alterations, a number of which pre-dated the Norman Conquest.

The first-period church, some of the stonework of which survives in the ruin, is assumed to be that built c. 900 A.D. It had a rectangular nave and chancel, north and south porticus, entered not by arches but by doorways, and a western apse. The last feature was presumably an imitation, on a small scale, of some Carolingian churches. Built into the first church were fragments of two 9th-century cross shafts[57] and two others were found near the site in the 19th century.[58] All the cross shafts may have been on the site before the church was built, or they may have been brought there with the many Roman architectural fragments which were re-used in the first church. In the second period a crypt or burial vault was added at the east end of the church; it had independent foundations and four internal piers, supporting an upper chapel. At the same time a crossing-wall was added in the nave; it was decorated with red-painted figures and foliate ornamentation. The crypt and its chapel may have been intended to house the relics of St. Oswald, which were translated to Gloucester in 909 A.D.[59]

[38] V.C.H. Glos. ii. 87–8.

[39] Glos. Colln. prints GL 60.14.

[40] V.C.H. Glos. ii. 89–90.

[41] L. & P. Hen. VIII, xvi, pp. 383–4.

[42] Rudder, Glos. 515; below, Outlying Hamlets, man.

[43] Inq. p.m. Glos. 1625–42, i. 128–9; Glos. R.O., P 173/IN 1/1, burials 1697.

[44] F. Grose, Antiquities of Eng. and Wales, i (1773), s.v. Llanthony Priory, plate II; Causton, Map of Glouc. (1843); G.D.R., T1/99.

[45] Inf. from Mr. J. F. Rhodes, curator of Glouc. Mus.

[46] J. Clarke, A Popular Account of the Interesting Priory of Llanthony (1853), 36–7.

[47] Bibliotheca Glos. ii. 219–20, 222, 226; Glos. R.O., D 327, p. 339. [48] Atkyns, Glos. 501.

[49] Clarke, Llanthony, 34, plan facing p. 35; Fosbrooke, Glouc. 147.

[50] Grose, Antiquities, i, s.v. Llanthony Priory, plate II;

Causton, Map of Glouc. (1843).

[51] Clarke, Llanthony, 33, sketch and plan facing p. 35.

[52] O.S. Map. 1/2,500, Glos. XXXIII. 2 (1886 edn.).

[53] Clarke, Llanthony, 34, plan facing p. 35; cf. Diary of a Cotswold Parson, 179. [54] Above, A.-S. Glouc.

[55] G. A. Howitt, Gloucester's Ancient Walls and Gate Houses (Glouc. 1890), 24.

[56] For what follows, C. Heighway et al., 'Excavations at Glouc.: St. Oswald's Priory, 1975–6', Antiq. Jnl. lviii (1), 103–32; C. Heighway, 'Excavations at Glouc.: St. Oswald's Priory, 1977–8', Antiq. Jnl. lx (2), 107–26; C. Heighway and R. Bryant, 'Reconstruction of the 10th Cent. Church at St. Oswald's, Glouc.' A.-S. Church (Council Brit. Arch. Research Rep. 1986), pp. 188–95.

[57] Antiq. Jnl. lx (2), plate XXIII.

[58] Glouc. Mus. A 2656, A 5075, A 6305; T. Kendrick, A.-S. Art to A.D. 900 (1938), 187, plate LXXXII.

[59] Above, A.-S. Glouc.

In the 11th century the crossing-wall was thickened, probably to take a tower. The new wall made use of stone taken from elsewhere in the building, including grave covers, with 10th-century foliate ornament, and a decorated doorhead.[60] Later the crossing-arch was widened, the door to the north porticus was replaced by a new wide arch, and clasping butresses were added to the crypt. At a later period the chancel was widened to align with the nave walls.

After the Norman Conquest there was a major rebuilding, dated by coins to 1086 or later. The north porticus was demolished and its arch blocked, a north transept was added further east, and a crossing-tower raised on the site of the old chancel. At the same rebuilding, or possibly earlier, the chancel was placed above the crypt. In the early 12th century, presumably part of work carried out by Thurstan, archbishop of York 1119–40, a north aisle was added, and in the mid 12th century, possibly in connexion with the conversion of the minster to a priory of Augustinian canons,[61] an arcade was inserted between the nave and aisle. Later, a pointed arch was inserted between the aisle and north transept, and a sunken-floored chapel was added on the east side of the transept to provide covered access to the Anglo-Saxon crypt. In the 13th century nave and aisle were extended by two bays and there was some rebuilding of the claustral buildings; the king gave timber for building at the priory in 1234, and in 1256 he made a grant of protection for those preaching in aid of the works there.[62]

After the Dissolution, the site of St. Oswald's Priory was sold by the Crown in 1540 to John Jennings (later knighted),[63] but the north aisle and transept of the church remained in use as the church of St. Catherine's parish.[64] The arches of the arcade were blocked and windows and a door inserted into the blocking; the nave was partly demolished and allowed to become ruinous. Most of the surviving church was pulled down in 1655–6.[65] Parts of the domestic buildings of the priory, south-west of the church, were incorporated in a dwelling house, later known as the Priory.[66] The Priory was the home of the Revd. John Newton c. 1770,[67] and later it was a private school.[68] The house, which comprised substantial ranges of buildings of stone and timber framing,[69] was demolished in 1823 or 1824.[70] North of the remains of the priory church a new church for St.

Catherine's parish was built in the years 1867–8 and demolished in 1921.[71]

BLACKFRIARS. The house of Dominican friars, founded c. 1239,[72] occupied a site west of Southgate Street, bounded on the south side by the town wall. The building of the friary, which was aided by numerous grants of money and materials from the Crown,[73] evidently continued over many years; the church was not consecrated until 1284.[74] A plot of land for enlarging the buildings was granted in 1365.[75]

In 1539 the buildings of the friary were sold to Thomas Bell, the wealthy Gloucester capper and clothier, and his wife Joan.[76] Bell put the claustral buildings to use for his trade,[77] and by 1545 he had remodelled the church as a dwelling house, known as Bell's Place.[78] Bell, who was knighted, died in 1566 and Joan the following year.[79] Blackfriars then passed to the Dennis family, which owned it until the end of the 17th century.[80] Among later owners of Bell's Place were, in the early 18th century, Samuel Cockerell and, from 1768, the woolstapler John Bush.[81] The claustral buildings were divided into dwellings in the early 18th century[82] and one part housed the workshop of the Bryan family of stonemasons from at least 1755 until 1802 when the business passed to George Wood.[83] In the early 19th century part of the west range was heightened and refronted to form three houses. By the 1930s Bell's Place was divided into two dwellings and the several tenants of the claustral buildings included firms of printers and mineral water manufacturers.[84]

Most of the surviving buildings at Blackfriars[85] reflect the building grants of the mid 13th century. Of that date are parts of the chancel and the nave and its arcades and most of the claustral ranges south of the church. The west range of the claustral buildings included at its south end the refectory, using the full height of the building, while the south range had the buttery and other rooms on the ground floor and a room lined with carrels, perhaps a library, on the first floor. The east range, mostly destroyed, apparently included the chapter house. In the 14th century the north aisle of the church was rebuilt. When the church was converted into Bell's Place c. 1540 the nave and chancel were shortened and the aisles, except for their eastern ends, were removed. Upper

[60] J. West, in *Studies in Med. Sculpture*, ed. F. H. Thompson (Soc. of Antiq. 1983), 41–53; *Antiq. Jnl.* lx (2), plate XXI A.

[61] *V.C.H. Glos.* ii. 85.

[62] *Close R.* 1231–4, 363; *Cal. Pat.* 1247–58, 490.

[63] *L. & P. Hen. VIII*, xv, p. 292; *Cal. Pat.* 1549–51, 303.

[64] Below, Churches and Chapels.

[65] G.B.R., B 3/2, pp. 815, 862–3.

[66] Hall and Pinnell, *Map of Glouc.* (1780).

[67] Rudder, *Glos.* 190.

[68] *Glouc. Jnl.* 19 Sept. 1796; Howitt, *Ancient Walls and Gate Houses*, 24.

[69] For illustrations, *Antiq. Jnl.* lviii (1), plate XLVII A; B.L. Add. MS. 36362.

[70] *Glouc. Jnl.* 5 Jan. 1824.

[71] Below, Churches and Chapels.

[72] *V.C.H. Glos.* ii. 111.

[73] *Arch. Jnl.* xxxix. 296–8.

[74] *Reg. Giffard*, p. 235.

[75] *Cal. Pat.* 1364–7, 121.

[76] *L. & P. Hen. VIII*, xiv (1), p. 590.

[77] Leland, *Itin.* ed. Toulmin Smith, ii. 58.

[78] G.B.R., B 2/2, ff. 44v.–45.

[79] Fosbrooke, *Glouc.* 165–6.

[80] G.D.R. wills 1566/150; P.R.O., C 142/323, no. 35; *Inq. p.m. Glos.* 1625–42, i. 64–6; G.B.R., J 3/6, ff. 148v.–149.

[81] Rudder, *Glos.* 194.

[82] Glos. R.O., D 327, p. 343.

[83] Rudge, *Glouc.* 315; *Glouc. Jnl.* 22 Apr. 1755; 5 Apr. 1802; 5 June 1807.

[84] *Trans. B.G.A.S.* liv. 197.

[85] W. H. Knowles, 'Black Friars at Glouc.', *Trans. B.G.A.S.* liv. 167–201, gives a detailed, illustrated account of the bldgs.; and for the bldgs. in 1721, above, Plate 42.

floors and stone-mullioned windows were inserted, and a semicircular bay was added on the north side of the former nave. About 1960 restoration of the Blackfriars buildings was begun by the Ministry of Works;[86] by 1984 work on the former church had been completed and it was open to the public.

There were formerly two gateways leading into the Blackfriars precinct. One, described as the great gate of the friars preacher in 1455, stood on Longsmith Street at the entrance to what became Ladybellegate Street,[87] and another, recorded in 1509, stood on Southgate Street at the entrance to the lane called Blackfriars.[88] By 1630 both those gates were known as Lady Bell's gate[89] after Joan Bell. The one on Southgate Street fell down in the mid 18th century,[90] and the one on Longsmith Street has not been found recorded after 1724.[91]

GREYFRIARS. The house of Franciscan friars was founded c. 1231 on a site east of Southgate Street. Additional land was given to the friars in 1239, 1285, and 1359,[92] and their property later extended to the town walls on the south and east.[93] In 1544 the Crown granted the site to John Jennings, who sold it a few weeks later to Alderman Thomas Payne.[94] In 1556 Payne granted a 500-year lease to Alderman Thomas Pury[95] and Greyfriars continued to be held under that lease, the occupants paying a chief rent of 30s. to the owners of the freehold, who from 1630 were the city corporation.[96] At the beginning of the 18th century Greyfriars was held by the town clerk, Judge John Powell, and his heirs, the Snell family of Guiting Power, held it for most of the rest of that century, together with various other leasehold and freehold properties in the Southgate Street area.[97]

Immediately after the Dissolution part of the church was converted into a brewhouse,[98] a purpose for which it was suited by its supply of piped water from Robins Wood Hill;[99] brewing apparently continued there until the mid 18th century.[1] A windmill which Thomas Pury mentioned among his possessions in 1577[2] was presumably that which stood on the north-east part of the friary property in 1610.[3] The buildings were severely damaged by artillery fire at the siege

in 1643,[4] and by 1721, though the nave and north aisle of the church survived largely intact, the chancel and most of the claustral ranges had vanished.[5] Later in the 18th century, before c. 1770, several dwelling houses were built within the shell of the church,[6] and about 1810 a substantial residence in classical style was built into the west end by Philo Maddy, a currier.[7] Another large house, later called Suffolk House, was built in the early 19th century, close to, but detached from, the east end of the church;[8] after housing a private school for many years, it became the Liberal club in 1890 and the children's library in 1938.[9] Its site was taken in the late 1960s for the new market hall and at the same time the remains of the church were restored, the large house at the west end was renovated as a new children's library, and the other houses were removed.

The shell of the church survives from a rebuilding carried out at the cost of Maurice Berkeley, Lord Berkeley, and begun c. 1518.[10] Nave and aisle, separated by a tall arcade of seven bays, are of equal height and almost equal width. Below and between the large windows much of the interior wall surface was decorated by blind panelling. The vanished chancel was of the same width, and probably the same height, as the nave. The cloister, which had a pentice roof, abutted the eastern six bays of the south wall of the nave.

By the early 18th century a bowling green had been laid out south-east of the remains of the church, and in 1747 a dwelling house called Bowling Green House, evidently incorporating some remains of the domestic buildings of the friary, adjoined the west side of the green.[11] That building with the green and adjoining land called Friars Orchard was alienated by the Snells before 1783. It was bought that year by Shadrach Charleton, an apothecary, who by 1790 had rebuilt Bowling Green House[12] as a classical-style mansion.[13] Charleton or one of the later owners, who included from 1804 the surgeon Charles Brandon Trye,[14] formed the land to the east and south of the house into a small park.[15] In 1888 the property was acquired for the Crypt school; the house (by then known as Friars Orchard) became the school's junior house and a new school building was built on the west part of the site.[16] The east part of the site was taken for the

[86] *Trans. B.G.A.S.* lxxxii. 169.
[87] *Glouc. Rental, 1455,* 19, 109; Speed, *Map of Glouc.* (1610).
[88] G.B.R., J 5/3.   [89] Ibid. 6.
[90] Rudder, *Glos.* 88; cf. G.B.R., J 3/9, f. 71.
[91] G.B.R., J 1/2001A.
[92] *V.C.H. Glos.* ii. 111–12; *Cal. Pat.* 1358–61, 257.
[93] *Cal. Pat.* 1370–4, 397; cf. *Glouc. Corp. Rec.* p. 441; Glos. R.O., D 3270/C 131A, C 142.
[94] *L. & P. Hen. VIII,* xix (1), pp. 41, 85.
[95] *Glouc. Corp. Rec.* pp. 441–2.
[96] Ibid. p. 450; P.R.O., C 142/160, no. 77; Glos. R.O., D 327, p. 346; D 4262/T 8; G.B.R., B 3/1, f. 546; F 4/12–13, s.v. 'city rent roll'.
[97] Glos. R.O., D 4262/E 2; G.B.R., F 4/13, pp. 524–5, 604–5.
[98] Leland, *Itin.* ed. Toulmin Smith, ii. 58; G.B.R., J 1/1255.   [99] Above, Public Services.
[1] Glos. R.O., D 214/T 20; cf. Rudge, *Glouc.* 314.
[2] Glos. R.O., D 214/T 20.

[3] Speed, *Map of Glouc.* (1610).
[4] Glos. R.O., D 327, p. 346.
[5] Glos. Colln. prints GL 60.46, where the friary is called Whitefriars, a mistake that was continued throughout the 18th cent.
[6] Rudder, *Glos.* 194; cf. Glos. Colln. prints GL 60.50.
[7] Rudge, *Glouc.* 314; cf. *Pigot's Dir.* (1822–3), 57.
[8] Glos. Colln. 33034; Causton, *Map of Glouc.* (1843).
[9] *Glouc. Jnl.* 21 Dec. 1867; *Citizen,* 23 Apr. 1948; Glos. Colln. N 21.36.
[10] *Trans. B.G.A.S.* liv. 120–1.
[11] Bodl. MS. Top. Glouc. c. 3, f. 61v.; Glos. Colln. prints GL 60.46, reproduced above, Plate 43; Glos. R.O., D 4262/E 2; cf. *Glouc. Guide* (1792), 86.
[12] Glos. R.O., D 3270/C 131A, C 133.
[13] The main, E. front was probably remodelled in the earlier 19th cent.: Glos. Colln. N 17.140.
[14] Glos. R.O., D 3270/C 134.
[15] Causton, *Map of Glouc.* (1843); Glos. Colln. N 17.140.
[16] Glos. R.O., D 3270/C 149; Glos. Colln. N 17.185.

technical college, built between 1938 and 1941,[17] and the former school buildings were removed during later extensions to the college. Another house which stood west of the site of Bowling Green House in the early 18th century apparently preserved the alignment of the west walk of the cloister.[18] It was replaced in the early 1860s when two terraces of houses called Priory Place and a larger house called Priory House were built.[19]

WHITEFRIARS. The house of Carmelite friars was founded c. 1268 near Brook Street, outside the walls at the north-east corner of the town.[20] The building of the church seems to have been in progress in 1290.[21] For enlarging its buildings the friary received 3½ a. of land and a house from two benefactors in 1343.[22] In 1543 the site was bought by two property speculators who sold it almost immediately to Thomas and Joan Bell.[23] Bell gave it in 1562 as part of the endowment of St. Kyneburgh's almshouse.[24]

Most of the Whitefriars buildings are said to have been demolished c. 1567.[25] In 1637 those surviving included a brick and stone building known as the founder's lodging, by then converted to a barn.[26] Further destruction occurred before the siege of 1643 when some of the materials were used for the fortifications, but the barn, housing one of the defenders' batteries, played a major part in the fighting.[27] The barn was pulled down in the late 17th century or the early 18th,[28] after which the name Friars Ground given to the site seems to have been the only reminder of the friary.[29] The north-west part of Friars Ground was used for the new cattle market in the early 1820s.[30]

CHURCHES AND CHAPELS

ANCIENT PARISH CHURCHES. Until the mid 17th century Gloucester had 11 churches with parochial functions.[31] Save for St. Owen's church, established by the late 11th century, little is known of their origins. Archaeological evidence shows that there was a pre-Conquest church on the site of St. Mary de Lode. It was closely connected to Gloucester Abbey and served a large parish in the outlying hamlets of Gloucester, where the parochial division of lands indicates that the church of St. Michael was also an early foundation. The priory church of St. Oswald (formerly a royal free chapel) exercised parochial functions in the late 12th century and part of it remained a parish church, under the dedication of St. Catherine, after the Dissolution. St. Mary de Lode and St. Oswald both had burial rights in the 11th century.[32] Other churches and chapels built before 1066 may have included St. Aldate, which became parochial, and St. Kyneburgh, which possibly had a parish until it was given to St. Owen.

At the end of the 11th century there were said to be 10 churches in the king's soke at Gloucester.[33] They included the later parish church of St. John the Baptist. Five other churches mentioned by the end of the 12th century (All Saints, Holy Trinity, St. Mary de Crypt, St. Mary de Grace, and St. Nicholas) became parochial and another (St. Martin) a chapel to St. Michael. In 1143 Gloucester Abbey claimed burial rights within the town but by 1197 it had conceded some, chiefly in respect of the parishes of St. Mary de Crypt and St. Owen, to Llanthony Priory,[34] though St. Owen, which was outside the walls, had a graveyard before that time. St. Michael acquired burial rights in the mid 14th century, St. Aldate,[35] St. John, St. Mary de Crypt,[36] and St. Nicholas had them by the early 15th, and All Saints, Holy Trinity, and St. Mary de Grace[37] by the early 16th. In the Middle Ages chantries were founded in all the parish churches. Except where otherwise noted, their endowments were sold in 1549 to two speculators, Thomas Chamberlayne and Richard Pate.[38]

Gloucester Abbey acquired the patronage of five churches and Llanthony Priory that of three. Vicarages were ordained for Holy Trinity, St. Mary de Lode, and St. Owen. The livings were poorly endowed and only St. Mary de Lode, St. Michael, and St. Owen took tithes from land outside Gloucester. In 1584 the city clergy were

[17] Glouc. Municipal Year Bk. (1964–5), 81.
[18] Atkyns, Glos. plate at pp. 82–3; cf. Hall and Pinnell, Map of Glouc. (1780).
[19] G.B.R., planning dept., file 1862/10, 15. The southern terrace was demolished in the 1970s.
[20] V.C.H. Glos. ii. 112; Speed, Map of Glouc. (1610).
[21] Cal. Close, 1288–96, 72.
[22] Cal. Pat. 1343–5, 142.
[23] L. & P. Hen. VIII, xviii (1), pp. 529, 541.
[24] Below, Char. for Poor, almshouses.
[25] Glos. R.O., D 327, p. 347.
[26] G.B.R., J 3/3, ff. 117–18v.
[27] Glos. R.O., D 327, p. 348; Bibliotheca Glos. ii. 215, 219, 222.
[28] G.B.R., J 3/8, f. 148; Bodl. MS. Top. Glouc. c. 3, f. 61v., which calls the friary Greyfriars.
[29] Rudge, Glouc. 317; cf. Hall and Pinnell, Map of Glouc. (1780).
[30] G.B.R., F 4/15, pp. 596–7; Glos. Colln. prints GL 57.1.
[31] This account was written in 1980 and revised in 1986.
[32] Above, A.-S. Glouc.
[33] Glouc. Rental, 1455, p. xv.
[34] Hist. & Cart. Mon. Glouc. (Rolls Ser.), i, pp. lxxv–lxxviii.   [35] Glouc. Rental, 1455, 73.
[36] Hockaday Abs. ccxvi, 1406.
[37] Ibid. ccxiii, All Saints, 1503; Holy Trinity, 1534; ccxvii, 1542.
[38] Cal. Pat. 1548–9, 260–7.

all said to be very poor,[39] and at least six livings (All Saints, St. Aldate, St. Catherine, St. John, St. Mary de Crypt, and St. Owen) were vacant through poverty in 1603[40] and another (St. Michael) in the early 1620s.

In 1648 the city corporation, which claimed that most parishes were served by unscholarly and dissolute singing men, obtained a parliamentary Ordinance for a reorganization of the city's parishes and the appointment of preaching ministers. Four parishes were created, served from the churches of St. John, St. Mary de Crypt, St. Michael, and St. Nicholas by ministers appointed by the corporation and paid stipends to augment their livings. The churches made redundant, including St. Owen which had been taken down just before the siege of 1643, were given to the corporation for public use.[41] The reorganization did not include the largely extra-mural parish of St. Mary de Lode. In the early 1650s its church lacked a minister[42] and in 1656, to prevent a union with St. Nicholas, the parishioners secured a stipend for one. The stipend had lapsed by 1659 when the minister's income was augmented out of the revenues of the impropriate rectory. In 1656 Tuffley, a detached part of St. Mary's parish, was joined to Whaddon.[43]

The ancient parochial framework was re-established at the Restoration. The change was, however, more apparent than real, for no places of worship were provided for five parishes which had lost their churches and another (Holy Trinity) was demolished in 1699. A church was built for St. Aldate's parish in the mid 18th century and for St. Catherine's in the mid 19th. The benefices, most of which depended in the early 18th century on the voluntary contributions of parishioners and payments from prayer or sermon charities, all received augmentations from Queen Anne's Bounty but most remained poor in the early 19th century. From the early 1840s the ancient parish boundaries were affected by the creation of districts for new churches built in the growing suburbs and in Twigworth, and in 1883 Tuffley was transferred to Whaddon.[44] A commission appointed by the bishop in 1906 to look into the spiritual needs of the city recommended that St. Catharine (earlier St. Catherine) be replaced by a new church at Wotton, where the growth of population had been considerable. The commission's other proposals included changes to the boundaries of most parishes in and adjoining the city.[45]

It was acknowledged that the city centre had too many churches in 1927 when a plan was adopted by Order in Council for the closure of St. Aldate and St. Michael and the creation of a united benefice called St. Mary de Crypt with St. John the Baptist.[46] As an interim measure the united benefice of St. Michael with St. John the Baptist was formed in 1931.[47] That of St. Mary de Crypt with St. John the Baptist came into being in 1952.[48] The benefices of St. Mary de Lode and St. Nicholas had been united in 1951. In the 1970s St. John's church, which was shared with Methodists, was renamed St. John Northgate and the benefice of St. Mary de Crypt with St. John the Baptist was reorganized. Of the ancient churches only St. John, St. Mary de Crypt, and St. Mary de Lode were used for services in 1980, although St. Nicholas and the tower of St. Michael also remained standing.

The burial grounds of several ancient parishes, including additional grounds acquired in the 1830s for St. John and St. Michael,[49] had disappeared by 1980, but the churchyard of St. Mary de Crypt survived and those of St. Catherine, St. John, St. Mary de Lode, and St. Nicholas remained with most of the monuments removed. Burials in most city churchyards were discontinued in 1857 when the municipal cemetery was opened.[50] Two 19th-century churchyards remained open, one (St. Luke) being closed in 1873[51] and the other (St. James) used in the 1890s.[52]

ALL SAINTS. No documentary evidence of the church, at the Cross on the south side of Westgate Street,[53] has been found until the mid 12th century, when it was a chapel to St. Mary de Crypt.[54] It was a separate benefice in the gift of Llanthony Priory by the late 12th century, when it had a parson and a vicar; the latter received the profits and 13s. for victuals and paid the vicar of St. Mary's church 2s.[55] All Saints was described as a minster (monasterium) in the early 13th century[56] and the living was a rectory in 1282.[57] In 1648 All Saints was included in the parish served from St. Mary de Crypt[58] and the church was converted as part of the Tolsey.[59] After the Restoration the inhabitants of All Saints' parish continued to attend St. Mary's church and in 1664 the two parishes were united.[60]

Llanthony Priory held the advowson of All Saints' rectory until the Dissolution[61] and the Crown retained it in 1603.[62] The priory had a portion of 2s. in the church in 1291[63] and was later paid that amount as a pension. The rectory was

[39] Hockaday Abs. xlix, state of clergy 1584, f. 4.
[40] Eccl. Misc. 68–9.
[41] Ordinance for uniting certain churches in Glouc. 1648, pp. 3–17: Glos. Colln. 5934 (4).
[42] Hist. MSS. Com. 27, 12th Rep. IX, Glouc. Corp. p. 507.
[43] Hockaday Abs. ccxviii, cccxc.
[44] Lond. Gaz. 7 July 1876, pp. 3884–6; Glos. R.O., P 361/IN 1/6.   [45] Glos. Colln. JF 4.7, p. 14.
[46] Lond. Gaz. 5 July 1927, pp. 4309–11.
[47] Ibid. 9 Oct. 1931, pp. 6456–7.
[48] Citizen, 26 Jan. 1952.
[49] Glos. R.O., P 154/9/IN 3/2; 14/CW 2/4; 14/CH 4/42.
[50] Lond. Gaz. 24 Mar. 1857, p. 1101; above, Public Services.

[51] Lond. Gaz. 11Feb. 1873, pp. 573–4.
[52] Glos. R.O., P 154/8/IN 1/18.
[53] For sites of medieval churches, above, Fig. 4.
[54] Dugdale, Mon. vi (1), 137.
[55] P.R.O., C 115/L 1/6688, f. 54v.
[56] Glouc. Cath. Libr., Reg. Abb. Froucester B, p. 7.
[57] Reg. Giffard, 156.
[58] Ordinance, 1648, pp. 4–5.
[59] Trans. B.G.A.S. xix. 143–9.
[60] G.D.R. vol. 397, f. 44; cf. G.B.R., B 3/3, p. 243.
[61] Cf. Reg. Giffard, 346; Reg. Sede Vacante, 427; Worc. Episc. Reg., Reg. Carpenter, i, f. 226v.
[62] Eccl. Misc. 69.
[63] Tax. Eccl. (Rec. Com.), 224.

worth £6 16s. 6½d. clear in 1535.[64] Later a curate was paid a stipend of £4 6s. 8d. and in 1603 the rectory, valued at £7 0s. 10d., was unfilled.[65] The rectory house, recorded in 1455, stood back from Southgate Street near the church.[66]

A chantry founded in the church by James Ivy and his wife Joan by wills proved 1503 and 1510 respectively was served once a week and its endowments included tenements in Gloucester and a house at Blakeney, in Awre. Known as the feoffees' service, it was dedicated to St. Mary and in 1548 had an income of £4 17s. 4d.[67] Richard Hoare by deed of 1607 gave the parish a rent charge of £2 13s. from several tenements in the city for church repairs, the incumbent, and the poor.[68] After 1648 it was paid to St. Mary de Crypt.[69]

Excavation in 1893 and 1894 revealed that in the later Middle Ages All Saints' church comprised a chancel, a nave on two bays, and a tower and short spire.[70] In 1552 it had three bells and a sanctus.[71] The city corporation, which used the church as a powder store in 1643,[72] incorporated it within the Tolsey at a rebuilding in 1648. The chancel was filled with a staircase leading up to the council chamber.[73] In 1742 the corporation fitted a room next to the council chamber, part of the former church, as a chapel.[74] Timbers from the church were used for the roof when the Tolsey was rebuilt in 1751.[75]

HOLY TRINITY. The church, in the middle of Westgate Street by the entrance to Bull Lane,[76] had been built by 1176[77] and was called a minster (monasterium) in the early 13th century.[78] The rectory was in the gift of the Crown,[79] and Eleanor of Provence presented in 1275 and 1290.[80] In 1291 Holy Trinity and St. Mary de Grace were together worth £5 6s. 8d.[81] In 1391 Richard II granted the advowson to Gloucester Abbey with licence to appropriate the church for the maintenance of lights and ornaments around Edward II's tomb.[82] The abbey had appropriated the church by 1394;[83] at first the cure was served by monks, but in 1403 a vicarage was ordained, with a house and a pension of 12 marks.[84] The abbey,

which paid the bishop a pension of 5s. from the church[85] and remained patron of the vicarage until the Dissolution,[86] granted the vicar a lease of the rectorial tithes and offerings in lieu of his stipend in 1531 but was paying his successor £9 in cash in 1535.[87] The living was valued at £9 in 1603.[88] The vicar instituted in 1618 received personal offerings and tithes of house rents and occasionally of pigs,[89] presumably by the grant of the dean and chapter of Gloucester who had acquired the advowson in 1541.[90]

In 1648 Holy Trinity was included in St. Nicholas's parish,[91] and after the Restoration the inhabitants continued to attend St. Nicholas's church.[92] The vicarage appears to have lapsed, and from 1737 the incumbent of St. Nicholas was licensed to the cure of Holy Trinity, which following endowments from Queen Anne's Bounty was generally described as a perpetual curacy. From 1778 it was held with St. Mary de Lode, with which it was considered united by 1838.[93] An augmentation by lot of £200 in 1743 was laid out on 19 a. in Down Hatherley in 1748, and further augmentations in 1750, 1752, 1787, and 1789 were used to buy 17 a. at Epney, in Moreton Valence, in 1794.[94]

A chantry was founded in the church by John of Sandhurst and its first priest was instituted in 1304. By 1341 the chantry's income from rents had declined so much that it was united with a chantry in St. John's church to support a chaplain serving in each church in alternate years.[95] The chantries had presumably been separated or had lapsed by 1392 when Thomas Pope and six other men were licensed to give the chaplain of a chantry of St. Mary in Holy Trinity 6 messuages, 2 shops, a toft, and a rent of 22s. 8d. in Gloucester and its suburbs for his support.[96] The property held by St. Mary's chantry included tenements in Bull Lane in which the priests serving in the church lived as in a college.[97] The chantry had an income of £8 19s. 8d. in 1548,[98] and its endowments then comprised Trinity College and other property in Gloucester and land in Barton Street.[99]

Thomas Pope by will dated 1400 endowed a

---

[64] Valor Eccl. (Rec. Com.), ii. 498.
[65] Eccl. Misc. 69.   [66] Glouc. Rental, 1455, 5.
[67] Hockaday Abs. ccxiii; Cal. Pat. 1548–9, 266; 1549–51, 200; cf. Glos. R.O., P 154/11/CH 3/1.
[68] G.B.R., J 1/1953A.
[69] Glos. R.O., P 154/11/CW 2/2.
[70] Trans. B.G.A.S. xix. 152–4; Glouc. Rental, 1455, sketch no. 8.
[71] Trans. B.G.A.S. xii. 79.
[72] G.B.R., F 4/5, f. 222.
[73] Trans. B.G.A.S. xix. 143–53; G.B.R., J 1/1977A; above, Public Buildings.
[74] G.B.R., B 3/10, ff. 9v., 18; B 9/3.
[75] Trans. B.G.A.S. xix. 144, 150.
[76] Atkyns, Glos. plate at pp. 82–3; in Speed, Map of Glouc. (1610), the positions of Holy Trinity and St. Mary de Grace have been reversed.
[77] P.R.O., C 115/K 1/6681, f. 82.
[78] Glouc. Cath. Libr., Reg. Abb. Froucester B, p. 464.
[79] Pleas of the Crown for Glos. ed. Maitland, p. 108; Pat. R. 1225–32, 425, 438.
[80] Reg. Giffard, 67, 345.   [81] Tax. Eccl. (Rec. Com.), 224.
[82] Cal. Pat. 1388–92, 406.

[83] Glouc. Cath. Libr., deeds and seals, viii, f. 10.
[84] Cal. Papal Reg. v. 599–600; Worc. Episc. Reg., Reg. Clifford, ff. 72v.–73.
[85] Glouc. Cath. Libr., deeds and seals, ii, f. 21; iii, f. 4; P.R.O., SC 12/38/45.
[86] Worc. Episc. Reg., Reg. Carpenter, i, ff. 167v.–168; Hockaday Abs. ccxiii.
[87] Glouc. Cath. Libr., Reg. Abb. Malvern, ii, ff. 35, 92v.; Valor Eccl. (Rec. Com.), ii. 416, 498.
[88] Eccl. Misc. 68.
[89] Glouc. Cath. Libr. MS. 26; Hockaday Abs. ccxiii; cf. Glos. N. & Q. ii. 248–9.
[90] L. & P. Hen. VIII, xvi, p. 573.
[91] Ordinance, 1648, pp. 6–7.
[92] Atkyns, Glos. 195.
[93] Hockaday Abs. ccxiii, ccxviii.
[94] Hodgson, Queen Anne's Bounty (1845), p. cclxxxvi; G.D.R., V 5/GT 2, 22; Glos. R.O., D 2299/2310.
[95] Reg. Ginsborough, 128; Reg. Bransford, pp. 32–3.
[96] Cal. Pat. 1391–6, 163–4.
[97] Glouc. Rental, 1455, 23.
[98] Hockaday Abs. ccxiii.
[99] Cal. Pat. 1548–9, 264.

guild of St. Thomas of Canterbury with lands and rents to support a chantry priest in the church.[1] The chantry, which was served before the rood and was also known as the Jesus service, in 1548 had an income of £8 10s. from property in Gloucester.[2]

An obit for Walter Froucester, abbot of Gloucester, was supported in the church from the rectory estate until the Dissolution.[3] In the later Middle Ages the churchwardens held property in Gloucester.[4]

The church, which was partly destroyed by fire in 1223,[5] later included chancel, nave with north porch, and west tower with short spire.[6] In 1639 the corporation paid for the upkeep of a new dial on the west face of the tower.[7] Some royalist soldiers taken prisoner at Highnam in 1643 were held in the church;[8] during the Interregnum it was used by the corporation for a school and a store for fire engines, and the bells and some fittings were removed.[9] After the Restoration it was rarely used for services and became dilapidated, and in 1699 it was pulled down.[10] The tower was retained for public use and adapted by the corporation in 1702 as a clock and bell tower.[11] It was demolished in the mid 18th century under the improvement Act of 1750, and the stone was used in rebuilding the church of Upton upon Severn (Worcs.).[12]

The parish registers, which survive from 1557, contain few entries after 1645.[13]

ST. ALDATE. The church, known sometimes as St. Aldhelm,[14] stood on the south side of St. Aldate Street. It may have been built before the Conquest but is not recorded until 1205 when the living was a rectory.[15] In 1387 it was called St. Laurence.[16] In 1648 St. Aldate's parish was included in that served from St. Michael[17] and in the mid 1650s the church was demolished.[18] After the Restoration the inhabitants of St. Aldate's parish continued to attend St. Michael's church and by the 1680s some went to St. John's church.[19] In 1737 the rector of St. John was licensed to the cure of St. Aldate's parish,[20] for which a new church or chapel was opened in 1756.[21] The benefice, which for a time was held in plurality with St. John, was sometimes considered a perpetual curacy from 1768.[22] In 1931 the church was closed and the parish was united with St. John.[23]

The advowson of the rectory belonged to Deerhurst Priory in 1275.[24] During later wars with France it was in the hands of the Crown[25] and by 1481 it had passed to Tewkesbury Abbey.[26] After the Dissolution the patronage was retained by the Crown.[27] In 1768, at the first vacancy in St. John following the building of the new church, the bishop nominated to St. Aldate.[28] The bishop remained patron until 1931.[29]

Deerhurst Priory had a portion of 6s. 8d. in the church in 1291.[30] The rectory was poorly endowed and was valued at £3 17s. 3d. in 1535;[31] in the mid 1540s the rector received £1 13s. 4d. from a chantry in the church to augment his living.[32] By the mid 1560s the churchwardens took those items, including garden tithes and perhaps seat rents, which had made up the rector's income, and paid a priest to officiate in the church. His wages, towards which Luke Garnons gave 8s. a year, were 1s. a week until 1577 when he received 36s. 8d. for the year. In 1594 his annual wage was 34s. 8d.[33] The rectory was vacant in 1603 when the living was said not to exceed £2.[34] In the 1630s the churchwardens paid the minister for three communion services a year.[35]

The benefice, worth £14 in 1750,[36] was augmented by lot from Queen Anne's Bounty in 1746, 1750, and 1756, and was also awarded £200 in 1756 to meet benefactions by Edward Pearson and the trustees of a Dr. Boulter. In 1759 a house and 10½ a. at Wotton were acquired for the living, which was further augmented by lot in 1792.[37] The grants were evidently used to buy more land near Gloucester, for after the inclosure of the fields adjoining the city in 1799 the glebe covered 37 a.[38] It had been reduced to 18 a. by 1910.[39] In the late 18th and early 19th century the rector received quarterly pew rents.[40] The rectory was valued at £154 in 1856.[41]

[1] Rudder, *Glos.* 204; cf. *Glouc. Corp. Rec.* p. 399; *Glouc. Rental, 1455,* 21–3, 37, 53.
[2] Hockaday Abs. ccxiii; *Cal. Pat.* 1548–9, 263–4; cf. *Valor Eccl.* (Rec. Com.), ii. 417.
[3] *Valor Eccl.* (Rec. Com.), ii. 416.
[4] *Glouc. Corp. Rec.* pp. 364, 405.
[5] *Hist. & Cart. Mon. Glouc.* i. 26.
[6] Cf. *Glouc. Rental, 1455,* p. xvi and sketch no. 11; Atkyns, *Glos.* plate at pp. 82–3, detail reproduced above, Fig. 5.
[7] G.B.R., B 3/2, p. 137; F 4/5, f. 128v.
[8] *Bibliotheca Glos.* ii. 373; *V.C.H. Glos.* x. 17.
[9] G.B.R., B 3/2, pp. 453, 677, 801, 852, 859, 864; B3/3, p. 41.
[10] Glos. R.O., P 154/4/IN 1/1; 15/IN 1/1; for the demolition, also ibid. 4/OV 1/9, min. 8 Aug. 1698.
[11] Atkyns, *Glos.* 195; G.B.R., B 3/8, p. 76.
[12] Rudder, *Glos.* 204.
[13] *B. & G. Par. Rec.* 147; Glos. R.O., P 154/4/IN 1/1.
[14] *Glouc. Rental, 1455,* 71–3; *Glouc. Corp. Rec.* p. 442; Glos. R.O., P 154/14/IN 1/2.
[15] *Cal. Papal Reg.* i. 24.
[16] *Reg. Wakefield,* p. 58.
[17] *Ordinance, 1648,* pp. 5–6.
[18] G.B.R., F 4/6, p. 67.
[19] Glos. R.O., P 154/14/IN 1/2–3; 9/IN 1/4–5.

[20] Hockaday Abs. ccxiv.
[21] Rudder, *Glos.* 182; Glos. R.O., P 154/6/IN 1/2.
[22] Hockaday Abs. ccxiv, ccxv.
[23] *Lond. Gaz.* 9 Oct. 1931, p. 6456; Glos. R.O., P 154/6/IN 1/11.   [24] *Reg. Giffard,* 67.
[25] *Reg. Bransford,* p. 418; *Reg. Wakefield,* p. 58.
[26] Worc. Episc. Reg., Reg. Alcock, f. 91; Reg. Ghinucci, f. 69v.
[27] *E.H.R.* xix. 101; Bodl. MS. Rawl. C.790, f. 5v.
[28] Hockaday Abs. ccxiv; cf. ibid. ccxv.
[29] Ibid. ccxiv; *Kelly's Dir. Glos.* (1870 and later edns.).
[30] *Tax. Eccl.* (Rec. Com.), 224.
[31] *Valor Eccl.* (Rec. Com.), ii. 498.
[32] Hockaday Abs. ccxiv, 1546, 1548.
[33] Glos. R.O., P 154/6/CW 1/1–11, 21, 28–33; for Garnons, below, Aldermen of Glouc. 1483–1835.
[34] *Eccl. Misc.* 69.
[35] Glos. R.O., P 154/6/CW 2/7.
[36] G.D.R. vol. 381A, f. 41.
[37] Hodgson, *Queen Anne's Bounty* (1845), pp. cclix, cclxxxiii; Glos. R.O., P 154/6/CW 3/2.
[38] Glos. R.O., Q/RI 70; G.D.R., V 5/GT 4–5.
[39] *Kelly's Dir. Glos.* (1910), 175.
[40] G.D.R., V 5/GT 5.
[41] Ibid. vol. 384, f. 100.

In 1391 the executors of William Heyberare were licensed to grant a messuage to the rector.[42] That may have been the rectory house next to the churchyard[43] which was occupied by several tenants in the later 16th century.[44] The house acquired at Wotton in 1759 was occupied by the rector from 1810[45] and was designated as the glebe house in 1839.[46] It had been sold by the early 1880s.[47]

A chantry of St. Mary had been founded in the church by the mid 13th century when Llanthony Priory undertook to support it with 6d. a year in return for a gift of lands from Richard of Hatherley.[48] The chantry, which was served at its own altar, had in 1548 an income from land of £5 5s. 8d., part of which was used to augment the rectory.[49] In 1455 a guild of St. John, holding eight tenements in the town, supported a chantry in the church.[50]

The anchoress recorded at Gloucester in 1479[51] may have been she who lived in St. Aldate's churchyard in the early 16th century. Her house passed to Sir Thomas Bell who gave it to the parish for church repairs before 1563. From 1594 it was used by the smiths' company for its hall[52] and in the early 18th century vestry meetings were held in it.[53] The parish retained the house in 1823.[54] In the later 16th century another house belonging to the parish provided income for the church.[55]

St. Aldate's church comprised chancel, nave, and tower and short spire in the later Middle Ages.[56] In 1653 the city corporation agreed that the churchwardens of St. Michael's could demolish the church, use the fabric in repairing their church, and inclose the churchyard.[57] The corporation completed the demolition of St. Aldate's church in 1655[58] and the churchwardens were receiving rent for the churchyard in the later 1650s.[59] Of three bells in the church in the late 16th century[60] one was recast at the Purdues' foundry c. 1640.[61] A chalice with cover was sent to St. Michael's church in 1652 and sold the following year.[62]

Elizabeth Aram (d. 1742)[63] left £500 for building a new parish church. Work began in the 1740s and the church, which was on or near the site of the medieval church,[64] was used for services from 1756.[65] It was built of brick and was a single-cell building in a plain gothick style with west bellcot and porch.[66] Some fittings, including a pulpit given by the city corporation and a bell cast at the Rudhall foundry, came from the chapel at the Tolsey, used until 1751.[67] A set of communion plate was given in 1758 by George Cooke.[68] Restoration work was carried out several times, notably in 1876 when the bellcot and porch were rebuilt.[69] A few years later a vestry was added to the north-eastern corner.[70] In the early 1930s the church was converted as a parish hall,[71] and it was demolished in 1963.[72] Some fittings were moved in the early 1930s to the new St. Aldate's church on the outskirts of Gloucester.[73]

The surviving parish registers cover the periods 1572–1646 and 1756–1931.[74]

ST. CATHERINE. The church was part, the north transept and aisle, of the former priory church of St. Oswald.[75] St. Oswald's church, which had been accounted a royal free chapel,[76] had probably provided a place of worship for the people living in its liberty from its beginnings and took the tithes. By the 12th century chapels had been built in those parts of the liberty outside the town and St. Oswald's parish, as defined in the mid 14th century, comprised the northern suburb next to the priory, Brook Street, the house of the Carmelite friars, and Hyde to the east of the town, and parts of Longford and Twigworth to the north;[77] parts of Kingsholm were also in the parish in the mid 16th century.[78] The parish and church were renamed St. Catherine after the Dissolution, although the former name was frequently used.[79] The church was served by a curate in 1536[80] and by a vicar in 1542. The dean and chapter of Bristol cathedral, owners of the impropriate rectory from 1542,[81] appropriated the vicarage and paid curates to serve the living.[82]

In 1648 St. Catherine's parish was included in the parish served from St. John the Baptist.[83] The city corporation pulled down St. Catherine's church in the mid 1650s; parts of the fabric were

---

[42] Cal. Pat. 1388–92, 407.

[43] Glouc. Rental, 1455, 71; Glouc. Cath. Libr., Reg. Abb. Malvern, i, f. 247.

[44] Cf. Glos. R.O., P 154/6/CW 1/1–44.

[45] G.D.R., V 5/GT 5; cf. Hockaday Abs. ccxv, 1811.

[46] Hockaday Abs. ccxiv.

[47] O.S. Map 1/2,500, Glos. XXV. 15 (1886 edn.).

[48] Trans. B.G.A.S. lxiii. 41.   [49] Hockaday Abs. ccxiv.

[50] Glouc. Rental, 1455, 71–5, 81–3.

[51] Worc. Episc. Reg., Reg. Alcock, ff. 58v.–59.

[52] Glos. R.O., P 154/6/CW 1/1–44; CW 2/7; Rudder, Glos. 182.   [53] Glos. R.O., P 154/6/OV 2/3.

[54] Glos. Colln. 18747.

[55] Glos. R.O., P 154/6/CW 3/1; CW 1/3, 5, 28.

[56] Glouc. Rental, 1455, sketch no. 16; cf. Glos. R.O., P 154/6/CW 1/7–11; CW 2/1.

[57] G.B.R., B 3/2, p. 711; cf. Glos. R.O., P 154/14/CW 2/2.

[58] G.B.R., F 4/6, p. 67.

[59] Glos. R.O., P 154/14/CW 2/2.

[60] Cf. ibid. 6/CW 1/32.   [61] Ibid. CW 2/7.

[62] Ibid. 14/CW 2/2.

[63] Fosbrooke, Glouc. 139.

[64] Rudder, Glos. 182; Glos. R.O., P 154/6/OV 2/3.

[65] Glos. R.O., P 154/6/IN 1/2.

[66] Bd. of Health Map (1852); J. Voyce, Glouc. in Old Photogs. (1985), 59.

[67] G.B.R., B 3/10, f. 164; F 4/10, p. 324; Glos. R.O., P 154/6/OV 2/3; Glos. Ch. Bells, 328–9.

[68] Glos. Ch. Plate, 94–5.

[69] Glouc. Jnl. 13 Oct. 1866; 3 June, 28 Oct. 1876.

[70] Ibid. 18 Mar. 1876; O.S. Map 1/2,500, Glos. XXV. 15 (1886 edn.).

[71] Lond. Gaz. 16 Dec. 1932, pp. 8022–3; Glouc. Jnl. 20 Jan. 1934.

[72] Citizen, 22 July 1963.

[73] Lond. Gaz. 9 Oct. 1931, p. 6457.

[74] B. & G. Par. Rec. 148; Glos. R.O., P 154/6/IN 1/1–16.

[75] Antiq. Jnl. lx (2), 216.

[76] V.C.H. Glos. ii. 84.

[77] Trans. B.G.A.S. xliii. 95, 104, 132; in the early 13th cent. St. Oswald's par. was called Hare Lane: ibid. 106 n.

[78] G.D.R. vol. 89, depositions 8 Apr. 1603.

[79] Hockaday Abs. xxviii, 1540 stipendiaries, f. 8; ccxiv.

[80] P.R.O., SC 6/Hen. VIII/1212, rot. 6.

[81] L. & P. Hen. VIII, xvii, pp. 638–9.

[82] E.H.R. xix. 102; Bodl. MS. Rawl. C. 790, f. 6; Eccl. Misc. 68.

[83] Ordinance, 1648, p. 7.

used in building a market house and in repairing the walls of the churchyard, which had been secured by the parishioners of St. John.[84] From 1674 St. Catherine's parish again had a curate who performed baptisms and burials. He also celebrated marriages in nearby churches until c. 1737 when the living was held with St. Mary de Lode. The parishioners were attending St. Mary's church by then and continued to do so after 1788 when the benefices were usually held separately.[85] In 1825 the vicar of St. Mary agreed to perform baptisms and burials for St. Catherine's parish and the perpetual curate of St. Catherine's to take the Sunday morning service in St. Mary's church.[86] St. Catherine's benefice, frequently described as a perpetual curacy from 1735,[87] was called a vicarage in the later 19th century.[88] The patronage belonged to the impropriators[89] until 1867 when it was given to the bishop.[90] A new church built for St. Catherine's parish in the late 1860s[91] and later called St. Catharine[92] was replaced in 1915 by a church at Wotton.[93]

The parish church of St. Oswald was worth £4 5s. 8d. clear in 1535.[94] In 1536 the curate was paid the small tithes and offerings for his stipend,[95] and in 1542 the impropriators were charged with paying 6s. 8d. to augment the vicar's salary.[96] The curate's stipend was £6 in the early 17th century[97] and had been raised to £10 by the early 18th.[98] The perpetual curate received Easter dues, and his stipend, paid by John Pitt from 1801 when he purchased the rectory,[99] was £40 in the early 1860s.[1] The benefice was augmented by lot from Queen Anne's Bounty in 1747 and 1780,[2] and by 1807 the sums received had been laid out on 11½ a. in Eckington (Worcs.).[3] In 1866, following plans to build a church, the Gloucester and Bristol Special Churches Fund granted £1,000 to augment the living.[4] Charles James Monk, the principal benefactor of the new church, gave a tithe rent charge of £20 in Hardwicke in 1868, and in 1869 the Ecclesiastical Commissioners endowed the living with £214 a year.[5] The glebe was sold in 1915.[6] The living was valued at £34 in 1856[7] and c.

£420 in 1885.[8] A house at the corner of London and Heathville Roads became the vicarage house c. 1869.[9]

The medieval parish church included a chantry called the charnel service, which had been founded in the chapel of St. Michael by Edward and William Taverner, John Constable, and Simon Baker c. 1392. They gave six messuages and a rent of 3s. from tenements in the suburbs of Gloucester to support the chaplains serving in it. In 1548 the chantry had an income of £3 14s. from messuages and gardens on the north side of Gloucester.[10]

The parish church, which survived until the mid 17th century, is described above.[11] North of the priory ruins a new parish church was begun in 1867 and consecrated in 1868.[12] The cost was met by a benefaction from C. J. Monk, grants from charities and church building funds, and subscriptions.[13] The church, which was built of brick and designed by M. H. Medland, had a chancel with rounded apse, north vestry, and south organ chamber and a nave with north and south transepts, north porch, and west bellcot.[14] Many of the fittings were given by the Monk family.[15] The vestry was enlarged in 1889[16] and the organ chamber in 1898.[17] Removal of the fittings to the new church at Wotton was authorized in 1914,[18] and the parish church was demolished in 1921.[19]

The surviving parish registers record baptisms in the period 1684–1762 and from 1777 with gaps between 1837 and 1867, marriages in the period 1695–1737 and from 1868, and burials from 1695. The earliest register often notes births rather than baptisms, and the infrequent record of baptisms and marriages before the late 1860s is explained by the lack of a church.[20] A St. Mary de Lode register includes baptisms and burials for St. Catherine's parish in the mid 18th century.[21]

ST. JOHN THE BAPTIST (later St. John Northgate). In 1100 the bishop settled a portion of 20s. in the church, in Northgate Street, on Gloucester Abbey.[22] In 1138 the Crown apparently confirmed

---

[84] G.B.R., B 3/2, pp. 815, 862–3; F 4/6, pp. 74, 82, 110, 136.

[85] Hockaday Abs. ccxiv, ccxviii; Glos. R.O., P 154/7/IN 1/1; cf. G.D.R. vol. 397, f. 45; Rudder, *Glos.* 188.

[86] Glos. R.O., P 154/12/IN 1/2.

[87] Hockaday Abs. ccxiv; G.D.R. vol. 383, no. clxxvii; vol. 384, f. 101.

[88] *Kelly's Dir. Glos.* (1870 and later edns.).

[89] Hockaday Abs. ccxiv; in the early 19th cent. the Pitt fam. was said to hold the patronage under the dean and chapter: Rudge, *Glouc.* 321–2.

[90] *Lond. Gaz.* 1 Jan. 1867, pp. 4–5.

[91] Glos. R.O., P 154/7/VE 2/1.

[92] O.S. Map 1/2,500, Glos. XXV.15 (1886 and 1902 edns.).

[93] *Kelly's Dir. Glos.* (1914), 179; *Glouc. Jnl.* 26 June 1915.

[94] *Valor Eccl.* (Rec. Com.), ii. 487.

[95] P.R.O., SC 6/Hen. VIII/1212, rot. 6; cf. Hockaday Abs. xxviii, 1540 stipendiaries, f. 8.

[96] *L. & P. Hen. VIII*, xvii, p. 639.

[97] *Eccl. Misc.* 68.

[98] Atkyns, *Glos.* 187.

[99] G.D.R., V 5/GT 7–8; Glos. R.O., D 2078, Goodrich fam., deed 1 June 1801.

[1] *Glos. N. & Q.* iv. 484.

[2] Hodgson, *Queen Anne's Bounty* (1845), p. cclxxxiii.

[3] G.D.R., V 5/GT 7–8.

[4] *Lond. Gaz.* 1 Jan. 1867, pp. 4–5.

[5] Ibid. 11 Dec. 1868, p. 6600; 13 Aug. 1869, p. 4570; *Glouc. Jnl.* 18 Apr. 1868.

[6] Ibid. V 6/46.

[7] Ibid. vol. 384, f. 101.

[8] G.D.R., V 5/GT 10.

[9] *Lond. Gaz.* 16 Apr. 1869, p. 2307; 1 July 1870, p. 3233; O.S. Map 1/2,500, Glos. XXV. 15 (1886 edn.).

[10] *Cal. Pat.* 1391–6, 173; 1548–9, 262; Hockaday Abs. ccxiv.

[11] Above, Sites of Religious Houses.

[12] *Glouc. Jnl.* 18 Apr. 1868; O.S. Map 1/2,500, Glos. XXV. 15 (1886 edn.).

[13] Glos. R.O., P 154/7/VE 2/1.

[14] *Glouc. Jnl.* 27 Apr. 1867; 18 Apr. 1868; cf. Glos. R.O., GPS 154/178; above, Plate 51.

[15] *Glouc. Jnl.* 18 Apr. 1868; *Glos. Ch. Plate*, 97.

[16] *Kelly's Dir. Glos.* (1889), 781.

[17] Glos. R.O., P 154/7/VE 2/1; cf. Voyce, *Glouc. in Old Photogs.* 60.

[18] Cf. faculty 29 Dec. 1914, in possession of vicar.

[19] Glos. R.O., D 2689/2/7/1.

[20] Ibid. P 154/7/IN 1/1–17.   [21] Ibid. 12/IN 1/1.

[22] *V.C.H. Glos.* ii. 7.

the whole church to the abbey,[23] which assigned it c. 1163 to support a feast of St. Oswald in the abbey church.[24] St. John's church was described as a chapel in the late 12th and early 13th century but by 1205 the living was a rectory.[25] Plans in 1299 to ordain a vicarage came to nothing.[26] St. John was included in 1931 in the new united benefice of St. Michael with St. John the Baptist, and in 1952 in that of St. Mary de Crypt with St. John the Baptist.[27] St. John's church, which was shared with Methodists from 1972 and renamed St. John Northgate,[28] became a chapel of ease in 1975, when its parish was united with that of St. Mary de Crypt church,[29] and was declared redundant and vested in the Gloucester Diocesan Trust in 1978. The Methodists, who then took a long lease of the building, made a new sharing agreement with the Anglicans.[30]

Gloucester Abbey, which presented to the rectory in 1279,[31] held the patronage until the Dissolution; in 1539 a presentation was made by patrons under a grant from the abbey. From 1546 the patronage was exercised by the Crown,[32] although in 1551 it was said to belong to the dean and chapter of Gloucester cathedral.[33] By the early 18th century the Crown usually presented through the Lord Chancellor,[34] who became patron of the united benefice of St. Michael with St. John the Baptist.[35]

In 1291 the rectory was valued at £6 13s. 4d. over and above the abbey's portion,[36] which was granted to the dean and chapter of Gloucester in 1541.[37] In 1535 the living was worth £14 0s. 10½d. clear[38] and in 1603 the profits did not exceed £7.[39] In the early 18th century the rector's income comprised only voluntary contributions and payments from sermon and prayer charities.[40] In 1737 the rector took tithe pigs from two properties but in 1744 he observed that the living had neither tithes nor glebe.[41] In the late 18th century and the early 19th he received quarterly pew rents.[42] Samuel Palling by will dated 1734 settled the reversion of an inn in Gloucester in trust for the rector[43] and by 1743 the trustees were receiving rent from the property,[44] part of which was exchanged in 1867 for 2½ a. in Down Hatherley. In

1929 the charity's endowments were transferred to the Ecclesiastical Commissioners to augment the benefice.[45] Queen Anne's Bounty awarded it sums of £200 in 1745 and 1755 to meet benefactions by the Revd. Thomas Savage and by William Rogers and John Driver respectively.[46] At inclosure of the fields around Gloucester in 1799 the rector was allotted 8½ a., including 2 a. for part of St. Oswald's tithes.[47] In 1807 the glebe included 18½ a. in Harescombe.[48] The benefice was augmented in 1813 from the parliamentary fund by lot with £400.[49] In 1856 it was worth £127.[50] The Ecclesiastical Commissioners endowed it with £40 a year in 1844, with £20 a year to meet a benefaction of £600 in 1869, and with £86 a year in 1870.[51]

In 1407 Thomas Barse was licensed to alienate to the rector ½ a. near the church on which to build a glebe house and make a graveyard.[52] There was no rectory house in the 18th century and the early 19th[53] but a house near the corner of Heathville and London Roads was acquired for the rector in the early 1870s.[54] It had probably been sold by the early 1920s.[55]

The church had a number of chantries and obits. Two chantries were probably established in the mid 13th century. The income from rents of one, apparently founded by William of Sandhurst, declined so much that in 1341 it was united with a chantry in Holy Trinity church to support a chaplain serving in each church in alternate years.[56] The chantries presumably lapsed or were separated and united with others in their respective churches. Luke of Cornwall, presumably the man who was bailiff in the mid 1250s,[57] founded a chantry in St. John's church,[58] which may have been that served at the altar of St. Mary by its own chaplain in 1383. The chantry of St. Mary, which received several benefactions, had an income from lands and tenements of £13 0s. 8d. in 1548.[59] One of its many messuages and gardens in Gloucester was sold that year to Sir Michael Stanhope and John Bellow. Another messuage, in Hare Lane and known as the College, had been occupied by the priests serving in the church.[60] In the late 15th century Walter

[23] Hist. & Cart. Mon. Glouc. i. 224.
[24] Glouc. Cath. Libr., Reg. Abb. Froucester B, p. 500.
[25] Ibid. Reg. Abb. Froucester A, ff. 86v.–87; Cal. Papal Reg. i. 24.
[26] Reg. Giffard, 517; cf. ibid. 526; Reg. Cobham, 206.
[27] Lond. Gaz. 9 Oct. 1931, pp. 6456–7; Citizen, 26 Jan. 1952.
[28] Notice outside ch.; inf. from dioc. sec.
[29] Lond. Gaz. 24 Oct. 1975, p. 13392; inf. from sec., Church Commissioners, 1 Millbank, London.
[30] Lond. Gaz. 21 Nov. 1978, p. 13929; inf. from rector of St. Mary de Crypt, Canon D. M. Paton.
[31] Reg. Giffard, 108.
[32] Reg. Cobham, 249; Hockaday Abs. ccxv.
[33] E.H.R. xix. 101.
[34] Atkyns, Glos. 186; G.D.R. vol. 285B (3), pp. 51–2.
[35] Lond. Gaz. 9 Oct. 1931, p. 6457; 5 July 1927, p. 4311.
[36] Tax. Eccl. (Rec. Com.), 224.
[37] L. & P. Hen. VIII, xvi, p. 573.
[38] Valor Eccl. (Rec. Com.), ii. 498.
[39] Eccl. Misc. 69.
[40] Atkyns, Glos. 186; G.D.R. vol. 397, f. 41.
[41] Glos. R.O., P 154/9/IN 1/5.
[42] G.D.R., V 5/GT 17.

[43] Glos. R.O., P 154/9/CH 3/1.
[44] G.D.R. vol. 397, f. 41.
[45] Glos. R.O., P 154/9/CH 3/3–4; CH 4/6.
[46] Hodgson, Queen Anne's Bounty (1845), pp. cliv, clviii, cclxxxiv; Savage's gift derived from a legacy by a Mr. Hodges: Rudder, Glos. 183.
[47] Glos. R.O., Q/RI 70.
[48] G.D.R., V 5/GT 16.
[49] Hodgson, Queen Anne's Bounty (1845), p. cclxxxiv.
[50] G.D.R. vol. 384, f. 102.
[51] Lond. Gaz. 3 May 1844, pp. 1505–8; 16 Apr. 1869, p. 2304; 18 Feb. 1870, p. 909.
[52] Cal. Pat. 1405–8, 376.
[53] G.D.R., V 5/GT 15; Hockaday Abs. ccxv, 1811.
[54] Lond. Gaz. 18 Feb. 1870, p. 909; G.B.R., planning dept., file 1873/6.
[55] O.S. Map 1/2,500, Glos. XXV. 15 (1902 and 1923 edns.).
[56] Reg. Bransford, pp. 32–3; for Wm. of Sandhurst, Glouc. Corp. Rec. pp. 209, 227, 262.
[57] Below, Bailiffs of Glouc. 1200–1483.
[58] Reg. Orleton, p. 47.
[59] Hockaday Abs. ccxv.
[60] Cal. Pat. 1548–9, 39, 262–3.

Brickhampton left Brickhampton manor in Churchdown to found a chantry in St. John's church. The chantry, known later as the service of the Holy Cross or of the rood, supported an organist in the church. At its dissolution in 1548 it had an income from the manor of £7 4s. 1½d.;[61] the manor was bought by Thomas Wilkes and Thomas Atkyns.[62]

A chantry of St. Clement had been founded in St. John's church by 1473,[63] presumably by the tanners' company, whose members attended an annual mass in the chantry's chapel in 1542.[64] Richard Warminster by will dated 1473 settled property in Gloucester and Tewkesbury on his mother and his wife Agnes, and after their deaths to support two priests serving at the altars of St. Mary and St. Anne in the church. Agnes married John Bridges and in 1548 the chantry of St. Anne, said to have been founded by her, had an income from lands and tenements of £8 14s. 4d.[65] The chantry's endowments included messuages, gardens, stables, and a dovehouse in Gloucester, and after its dissolution small parts of the property were sold to Sir Miles Partridge and his brother Hugh and to Anthony Bourchier.[66] A messuage which in 1548 brought in an income of 8s. for a lamp in the chancel[67] was sold to Thomas Chamberlayne and Richard Pate.[68]

Alderman Thomas Semys by will dated 1603 left a rent of 10s. for an annual sermon in the church.[69] The rector was paid for the sermon in the early 18th century[70] but later the rent was witheld.[71] Richard Keylock (d. 1637) left £50 to pay the rector a stipend for reading morning prayers. Later that year the principal was vested in the city corporation, which settled £3 a year on the rector.[72] The rector was paid for saying prayers once a week in 1683, twice a week in 1807,[73] and only twice a week during Lent in the 1820s.[74] John Wyman by will dated 1556 left the reversion of a tenement and garden in Gloucester for the use of the church.[75] In 1973, at a reorganization of the ecclesiastical charities of the united benefice, Wyman's and Keylock's charities were united, and the income of Wyman's charity was applied to general church expenses and the rector was paid for reading morning prayers on Lenten weekdays.[76] At a further reorganization in the late 1970s all the ecclesiastical charities of the united benefice were united.[77]

The medieval church of St. John the Baptist comprised chancel, nave with north porch and south aisle, and west tower and spire.[78] The aisle was built for an altar c. 1234.[79] The tower dates from the 15th century. In the later Middle Ages the church had many side altars, and among the lights established by 1368 were those of St. Catherine and St. Nicholas.[80] An altar of St. John was mentioned in 1485.[81] The church was surveyed in 1726 and preparations for rebuilding had started by 1730. Work began in 1732 and the new church was completed in 1734. The cost was met by rates and voluntary contributions.[82]

The south-west respond and the tower and spire were kept and the rest of the church was built to a basilican plan with classical east front[83] and Doric columns between the nave and aisles. The design was evidently by the builders, the brothers Edward and Thomas Woodward of Chipping Campden.[84] The surviving contemporary fittings include a carved oak reredos and communion rails, given by Bridget Price, and a panelled dado around the church. A west gallery was erected in 1826.[85] Two east galleries were taken down in 1874 when the church was restored and largely repewed. Further restoration work was carried out in 1880 and in 1882 when the west gallery was removed.[86] In 1735 three pinnacles were taken down from the tower[87] and in 1910 the top of the spire was removed to the churchyard.[88]

Fittings retained from the medieval church include a font which has been recut, a late medieval chest, many floor slabs, and fragments on the north wall of two brasses, apparently the remains of a memorial to John Semys (d. 1540) and his wives Elizabeth and Agnes. Brasses depicting John Bridges (d. 1483) and his wife Agnes have been lost.[89] On the north wall of the chancel is a monument to Alderman Thomas Price (d. 1679), who appears in an upright half-length effigy. Opposite is a memorial with the figures of his daughters Dorothy and Bridget (d. 1693 and 1753).[90] Several monuments were brought from St. Michael's church in 1953.[91] Of the two rests for churchwardens' staffs, one is dated 1711 and 1842 and the other 1826. The east window contains glass designed by the Camm brothers of Smethwick (Staffs.) as a memorial to Robert Raikes and Thomas Stock on the centenary of the Sunday School movement in 1880.[92] In 1635 the four bells were recast as five, of which three were recast in 1639.[93] The peal and a sanctus bell[94] were

[61] Hockaday Abs. ccxv; *Cal. Inq. p.m. Hen. VII*, iii, pp. 597–8.
[62] *Cal. Pat.* 1547–8, 385.
[63] Hockaday Abs. ccxv.
[64] Glos. Colln. 28652, no. 4.
[65] Hockaday Abs. ccxv; Rudder, *Glos.* 184.
[66] *Cal. Pat.* 1548–9, 110, 263; 1547–8, 328.
[67] Hockaday Abs. ccxv.
[68] *Cal. Pat.* 1548–9, 266.
[69] G.B.R., J 1/1932.
[70] G.D.R., V 5/GT 15; vol. 397, f. 41.
[71] Cf. *16th Rep. Com. Char.* 6.
[72] Glos. R.O., P 154/9/CH 3/1; G.B.R., B 3/2, p. 79.
[73] G.D.R., V 5/GT 12, 16.
[74] *16th Rep. Com. Char.* 9.
[75] Glos. R.O., P 154/9/CH 3/1; G.D.R., V 5/GT 12–13.
[76] Glos. R.O., P 154/11/CH 3/16.
[77] Below, St. Mary de Crypt.

[78] Atkyns, *Glos.* 186; Rudder, *Glos.* 183.
[79] *Close R.* 1231–4, 365.
[80] *Glouc. Corp. Rec.* p. 358; cf. Rudder, *Glos.* 183.
[81] Hockaday Abs. ccxv.
[82] Glos. R.O., P 154/9/CW 2/1; Rudder, *Glos.* 183.
[83] Above, Plate 45.
[84] Colvin, *Biog. Dict. Brit. Architects* (1978), 915.
[85] Glos. R.O., P 154/9/CW 2/1.
[86] Ibid. CW 3/11–12; VE 2/2; *Glouc. Jnl.* 11 Nov. 1882.
[87] Glos. R.O., P 154/9/CW 2/1.
[88] Ibid. CW 3/7.
[89] Davis, *Glos. Brasses*, 149–53; Rudder, *Glos.* 184.
[90] Roper, *Glos. Effigies*, 298–302.
[91] Glos. Colln. NQ 5.1.
[92] Verey, *Glos.* ii. 231; inscr. in ch.
[93] Glos. R.O., P 154/9/IN 1/1.
[94] Cf. G.D.R., V 5/GT 11.

recast as a ring of six by Thomas Rudhall in 1775 and 1776.[95] The tenor had cracked by 1860,[96] and by the end of the century the bells were no longer rung. They were removed in 1976 and the tenor was given to the cathedral, the fourth to a short-lived museum in St. Michael's tower, and the others to Winstone church.[97] The communion plate, given by Thomas Rich in 1660, comprises two chalices and paten covers, two flagons, a credence paten, and an almsdish.[98] The registers survive from 1558.[99]

ST. MARY DE CRYPT. The church, in Southgate Street, was recorded from the early 1140s.[1] It was usually known as St. Mary in the south until the mid 16th century when a crypt served to distinguish it by name.[2] Between the 15th and 17th centuries it was also called Christ Church.[3] In the late 12th century the church had a parson and a vicar; the latter, who paid the parson 2s., received the profits of the living and 2s. from the vicar of All Saints,[4] once a dependent chapelry. The living, which was a rectory in 1274,[5] was united with All Saints in 1664[6] and by the early 18th century St. Owen was considered annexed to it.[7] In 1952 St. Mary de Crypt with All Saints and St. Owen was included in the new united benefice of St. Mary de Crypt with St. John the Baptist,[8] to which Christ Church at the Spa was added in 1979.[9]

The bishop of Exeter held the church in the mid 12th century when he granted a pension of 20s. from it to Godstow Abbey (Oxon.).[10] Soon after, he granted the church with its chapel of All Saints to Llanthony Priory,[11] and in 1241 he quitclaimed the advowson of the church to the priory,[12] which retained it until the Dissolution.[13] A patron for a turn under a grant from the priory made a presentation in 1543. Thereafter the patronage was exercised by the Crown,[14] which by the early 18th century usually presented through the Lord Chancellor.[15] The latter, who became patron of the united benefice of St. Mary de Crypt with St. John the Baptist,[16] shared the right of presentation with the bishop in 1980.[17]

In 1291 the rectory was valued at £5 over and above portions of £1 and 3s. paid to Godstow and Llanthony respectively;[18] Llanthony had earlier received a pension of 3s. 10d. from the church.[19] In 1535 the rectory was worth £14 6s. 6¼d. clear and in 1603 the profits were put at £9, including a pension of 24s. to the Crown, which had evidently retained the portions paid to Godstow and Llanthony.[20] The rector's income by the late 17th century comprised rents from houses on the site of the rectory house, payments from sermon charities, and voluntary contributions;[21] in 1684 it was said that voluntary contributions could raise the value of the living by over £36.[22] The benefice, which in 1743 was valued at £26 besides voluntary contributions,[23] was augmented by lot from Queen Anne's Bounty in 1762 and 1788 and from the parliamentary fund in 1814.[24] In 1856 it was worth £113.[25] The Ecclesiastical Commissioners endowed it with £52 a year in 1844 and with £23 a year in 1872.[26] About 1805 10 a. in Westbury-on-Severn were bought and in 1914 the glebe had c. 28 a. there, including land bought for St. Owen.[27]

Part of the rectory house south of the church was occupied by a tenant in 1455,[28] and by the early 18th century the house had been remodelled as three houses which were let.[29] Another rectory house was used as an inn c. 1775.[30] A house in Brunswick Square was the rectory from the 1870s[31] until the 1950s when the united benefice took over the former rectory house of St. Michael's parish.[32] That house was largely rebuilt in 1985 following its sale.

Several chantries and obits were supported in St. Mary de Crypt church. William of Cheltenham (d. by 1274) left the reversion of some houses in Gloucester to Winchcombe Abbey to support a secular priest celebrating in the church for his soul and that of his wife Alditha.[33] By 1302 the abbey had appropriated the rent from the houses and the chantry was served in the abbey church.[34] A chantry of St. Mary, presumably founded in St. Mary's church long before it was recorded in 1445, was endowed by Richard Manchester by will proved 1454 with two tenements in

---

[95] Glos. R.O., P 154/9/CW 2/1; *Glos. Ch. Bells*, 334–5.
[96] Glos. R.O., P 154/9/VE 2/2.
[97] *Glos. Ch. Bells*, 331, 335; inf. from Miss M. Bliss, of Beech Pike, Winstone.
[98] *Glos. Ch. Plate*, 98–9.
[99] *B. & G. Par. Rec.* 149.
[1] P.R.O., C 115/K 1/6681, f. 76v.
[2] *Tax. Eccl.* (Rec. Com.), 224; *Reg. Wakefeld*, p. 126; *Valor Eccl.* (Rec. Com.), ii. 417, 455; Hockaday Abs. ccxvi; *E.H.R.* xix. 101; G.D.R. vol. 40, f. 2.
[3] Hockaday Abs. ccxix, 1401; *Glouc. Corp. Rec.* pp. 395, 450; *Valor Eccl.* (Rec. Com.), ii. 195, 498; Glos. R.O., P 154/11/CW 2/1; G.B.R., F 4/5, ff. 189v., 250.
[4] P.R.O., C 115/L 1/6688, f. 54v.
[5] *Reg. Giffard*, 65.
[6] G.D.R. vol. 397, f. 44; cf. G.B.R., B 3/3, p. 243.
[7] Atkyns, *Glos.* 188.
[8] Cf. *Lond. Gaz.* 5 July 1927, pp. 4309–10; *Citizen*, 26 Jan. 1952.
[9] Inf. from rector.
[10] *Godstow Reg.* (E.E.T.S. orig. ser. 142), i, p. 138.
[11] Dugdale, *Mon.* vi (1), 137.
[12] P.R.O., CP 25(1)/73/14, no. 269.
[13] *Reg. Giffard*, 248; *Reg. Wakefeld*, p. 126; Worc. Episc. Reg., Reg. Carpenter, i, f. 227v.

[14] Hockaday Abs. ccxvi.
[15] Atkyns, *Glos.* 188; G.D.R. vol. 285B (3), pp. 51–2.
[16] Cf. *Lond. Gaz.* 5 July 1927, p. 4311; 9 Oct. 1931, p. 6457.
[17] *Glouc. Dioc. Year Bk.* (1980), 16–17.
[18] *Tax. Eccl.* (Rec. Com.), 224.
[19] P.R.O., C 115/L 1/6688, f. 76.
[20] *Valor Eccl.* (Rec. Com.), ii. 498; *Eccl. Misc.* 68.
[21] Atkyns, *Glos.* 188–9.
[22] Glos. Colln. NF 5.1.
[23] G.D.R. vol. 397, f. 44.
[24] Hodgson, *Queen Anne's Bounty* (1845), p. cclxxxv.
[25] G.D.R. vol. 384, f. 104.
[26] *Lond. Gaz.* 3 May 1844, pp. 1505–9; 13 Aug. 1872, p. 3655.
[27] G.D.R., V 5/GT 19–20; Glos. R.O., P 154/11/CW 3/6.
[28] *Glouc. Rental, 1455*, 11–13.
[29] Atkyns, *Glos.* 188; G.D.R. vol. 397, f. 44.
[30] Rudder, *Glos.* 191.
[31] Glos. R.O., D 1381/74; *Lond. Gaz.* 13 Aug. 1872, p. 3655; O.S. Map 1/2,500, Glos. XXXIII. 3 (1886 edn.).
[32] Cf. *Lond. Gaz.* 5 July 1927, pp. 4310–11.
[33] *Reg. Mon. Winch.* i. 116–20.
[34] Dugdale, *Mon.* ii. 305; Glouc. Cath. Libr., Reg. Abb. Froucester B, p. 442.

Gloucester.[35] It had an income of £9 3s. 6d. in 1548.[36] Of the endowments, including messuages, gardens, stables, and rents in Gloucester and land in Elmore, Sir Michael Stanhope and John Bellow bought a messuage in 1548.[37]

Garet van Eck by will proved 1506 left 100 marks, a house, vestments, and plate for a chantry at the altar of St. Catherine. The chantry had an income of £7 6s. 4d. in 1548, when its endowments, comprising a stable and garden in Gloucester and property in Lydney and Ripple (Worcs.), were sold to Sir Thomas Bell and Richard Duke.[38] The position of Bell's tomb suggests that the chantry was served in the south chapel. Richard Manchester by will proved 1454 directed his executors to support a chantry at the altar of St. John by selling part of his silver.[39] John Cooke intended the master of the grammar school founded under his will, proved 1528, to celebrate at the same altar, which was on the south side of the church, possibly in the transept.[40] A guild of St. Thomas supported a lamp in the church in 1455.[41] An obit for Richard Manchester was supported by a tenement bringing in an income of 22s. in 1548 when it was sold to Bell and Duke.[42]

Charities founded by Sarah Wright and Daniel Lysons in the late 17th century each provided for payments to the rector for two annual sermons,[43] and those founded by Robert Payne and Thomas Gosling in the early 18th for prayers at Candlemas and an annual sermon respectively.[44] The payments totalled £4 0s. 8d. but in the 19th century the amount received and the number of sermons preached varied.[45] The rent charge of £2 13s. given by Richard Hoare to All Saints' parish was paid to St. Mary's parish after 1648 and used for general church expenses.[46] The payment, which by 1706 was charged on the Tolsey and by 1815 had been reduced to £2 10s., was used for church repairs[47] before 1923 when it was assigned to the united eleemosynary charities.[48] A charity founded for the poor by Walter and Thomas Pury was appropriated for church repairs. Payments to the poor resumed in 1825[49] but in 1910 the income of £1 8s. was used for church repairs, along with an income of £2 1s. 8d. from a gift evidently made for church purposes before 1841.[50] A bequest for church maintenance from William Phelps by will proved 1914[51] produced an income of £11 16s. 4d. in 1923. In that year the charities mentioned above, save that of Richard Hoare, were

reorganized as the United Ecclesiastical Charities, which reserved the payments to the rector and included 18s. for church repairs from the Pury charity. The ecclesiastical charities were further reorganized in 1973 to include those formerly established for St. Michael's church, and the income from the sermon and prayer charities was reserved to the rector on condition that he preached at least ten times a year in St. Mary's church.[52] In the late 1970s the charities were united with those for St. John and in 1980 they had an income of c. £130, of which £18 was paid to the rector and the remainder used for other church expenses.[53]

The church of St. Mary de Crypt comprises chancel with north and south chapels, central tower, transepts, and aisled nave with a south porch with an upper room. The only fragment of the 12th-century church to survive is the hood-mould of the west doorway. By the end of the 13th century the chancel had at least a south chapel, there was presumably a central tower with transepts, and the nave was aisled. During the earlier 14th century new windows were put into the aisles and the east wall of the chapel. Extensive reconstruction took place in the late 14th century when the nave and chancel arcades, the tower, and the east end of the chancel were rebuilt (the north chapel being a possible enlargement of that time), new windows were put into the transepts and west front, and the south porch was added. In 1401 the church was described as new.[54] By the early 16th century the church included several side altars, including one of St. George recorded in 1544.[55] In the 16th century the chancel walls were raised to form a clerestory, probably in the 1520s or 1530s when the walls were painted,[56] and the roof was rebuilt to a higher pitch. In 1642 the city corporation fitted part of the church as a magazine[57] and the building was not considered safe for services.[58] In the early 18th century many seats were made in the aisles and in 1735 a west gallery was built.[59] Side galleries were erected in the aisles in 1820 by subscription, 28 seats being provided for the subscribers and the remaining parts being used by the poor.[60]

The crypt from which the church took its name was either the vaults under the chancel and south chapel, not recorded after c. 1775, or, more probably, the larger space below the west end of the church.[61] That space housed a tavern by 1576

[35] Glouc. Corp. Rec. pp. 135, 395, 401.
[36] Hockaday Abs. ccxvi; Rudder, Glos. 192, suggests the chantry was in the S. chap.
[37] Cal. Pat. 1548–9, 39, 265.
[38] Ibid. 40; Hockaday Abs. ccxvi.
[39] Glouc. Corp. Rec. p. 400.
[40] Hockaday Abs. ccxvi; the transept includes a piscina.
[41] Glouc. Rental, 1455, 23–5.
[42] Hockaday Abs. ccxvi; Cal. Pat. 1548–9, 40; cf. Glouc. Corp. Rec. p. 402.
[43] G.D.R., V 5/GT 18.
[44] Glos. R.O., Q/RNc 4/17; 16th Rep. Com. Char. 14; a sermon founded, according to Rudder, Glos. 193, by Anne Pitt has not been traced.
[45] 16th Rep. Com. Char. 10–14; Glos. R.O., P 154/11/CH 2/1.
[46] G.D.R., V 5/GT 18; Glos. R.O., P 154/11/CW 2/2; 16th Rep. Com. Char. 9–10.

[47] Glos. R.O., P 154/11/CW 2/3–6; CW 3/6.
[48] Ibid. CH 3/14.
[49] 16th Rep. Com. Char. 10; Glos. R.O., P 154/11/CW 2/5.
[50] Glos. R.O., P 154/11/CW 3/6; CH 2/2; CH 3/8.
[51] Ibid. CH 2/8.
[52] Ibid. CH 3/14, 16.
[53] Inf. from rector.
[54] Hockaday Abs. ccxix; cf. Verey, Glos. ii. 233.
[55] Hockaday Abs. ccxvi.
[56] Inf. from Madeleine Katkov, of Newport Pagnell (Bucks.), who restored a painting on the N. wall in 1982.
[57] G.B.R., F 4/5, f. 189v.
[58] Glos. R.O., P 154/11/CW 2/1.
[59] Ibid. 3–4.
[60] Ibid. 5; Hockaday Abs. ccxvi.
[61] Rudder, Glos. 191.

and a timber store during the 1643 siege. It had ceased to be a tavern by the mid 1670s and was let to tenants until the 1840s.[62]

In the early 1840s S. W. Daukes and J. R. Hamilton undertook an extensive restoration of the church, during which the south porch was reopened. The chancel was cleared of monuments and the features revealed, including the east window which had been partly walled up, were restored, and an ancient altar stone was reinstated. The restoration was completed in 1845 when the crypt was arched over, the side galleries, including one in the north transept, were removed, the west gallery was enlarged, and the church repewed. The work, except for that in the crypt, was paid for by the rector and by voluntary contributions, including a gift from the executors of James Wood.[63] Further restoration work was carried out in 1866,[64] in 1876 when the west gallery was taken down, in 1905, and in 1908 when the tower battlements and pinnacles were removed.[65] A carved stone and mosaic reredos was installed in 1889.[66] About 1920 stone screens were built at the west ends of the chapels, one as a parish memorial to the war dead. The south chapel was fitted in the 1930s and dedicated in 1945 as a memorial to Robert Raikes, the promoter of Sunday schools.[67]

The wooden pulpit, which dates from the early or mid 16th century, is carved with Renaissance ornament. From it George Whitefield preached his first sermon and later it was for a time in a Congregationalist chapel at Edge in Painswick.[68] The church has a 17th-century communion table in the south transept and an early 18th-century font. There are several notable monuments. The south chapel contains a tomb recess and the tombchest of Sir Thomas Bell and his wife Joan (d. 1566 and 1567). Two kneeling figures from the Bells' tomb were among monuments placed in the crypt in the early 1840s. Of those moved from the chancel at that time that to Daniel Lysons (d. 1681), which includes a kneeling figure, is in the north chapel.[69] In the north transept are the remains of brasses to Alderman John Cooke and his wife Joan (d. 1528 and c. 1545).[70] Brasses to William Henshaw's wives Alice (d. 1520) and

Agnes, once part of a monument in St. Michael's church, were placed in the north aisle in 1959.[71]

Richard Manchester by will proved 1454 gave his largest brass pot towards the purchase of five bells.[72] In the late 1640s one was replaced by a bell from St. Owen's church and sold to Badgeworth parish, and a clock was erected in the tower. In 1678 William Covey and Richard Purdue of Bristol recast the tenor and a sanctus bell for an enlarged peal. It was recast by Abraham Rudhall in 1686, when the clock was replaced, and again in 1710. Two bells from the Rudhall foundry were added in 1749.[73] The church plate includes a chalice and paten cover given c. 1679 by the rector Abraham Gregory, a salver of 1684, a flagon purchased in 1699, and pieces given anonymously in 1718.[74] The registers survive from 1653 and contain entries for Littleworth.[75]

ST. MARY DE GRACE. The church or chapel, in the middle of Westgate Street near the Cross,[76] had been built by 1176. It was then known as St. Mary in the market[77] but by 1201 it was usually distinguished by its position by the entrance to Grace (later St. John's) Lane;[78] in 1498 it was also called the church or chapel of Graceland.[79] In the early 13th century the church was a separate benefice with parochial rights and in the gift of the Crown.[80] By 1287 it was held with Holy Trinity, presumably because of its poverty,[81] and later it came to be regarded as a chapel to Holy Trinity, with which it was appropriated to Gloucester Abbey in the 1390s.[82] In 1541 St. Mary de Grace was granted to the dean and chapter of Gloucester cathedral.[83]

In 1403 Gloucester Abbey undertook to appoint and support a secular chaplain to serve St. Mary de Grace,[84] and in the early 16th century the chaplain or curate took the profits of the church and paid the abbey a pension of 10s.[85] In 1535 the profits were valued at £5 16s. 1d. from personal tithes and offerings.[86] In 1540 the curate was paid by Alderman Henry Marmion,[87] a leading parishioner,[88] and in 1603 he had a stipend of £6.[89]

In 1648 St. Mary's parish was included in that served from St. Michael[90] and in the mid 1650s

[62] Glos. R.O., P 154/11/CW 2/1–5; G.B.R., F 4/5, f. 250.

[63] Glos. R.O., P 154/11/CW 2/5; CW 3/15; G.D.R., F 1/4; Clarke, *Archit. Hist. of Glouc.* 67, 69 n.; *Gent. Mag.* N.S. xxiii. 198.

[64] *Glos. Ch. Notes*, 2.

[65] Glos. R.O., P 154/11/CW 2/6; *Glouc. Jnl.* 8 July 1876.

[66] *Kelly's Dir. Glos.* (1889), 781.

[67] Glos. Colln. N 5.53 (1); *Kelly's Dir. Glos.* (1939), 181.

[68] *V.C.H. Glos.* xi. 84.

[69] Roper, *Glos. Effigies*, 302–6.

[70] Austin, *Crypt Sch.* 15, 27, 36–7; Hockaday Abs. ccxvi; cf. Davis, *Glos. Brasses*, 154–8.

[71] Verey, *Glos.* ii. 234; Davis, *Glos. Brasses*, 119–22.

[72] *Glouc. Corp. Rec.* p. 400.

[73] Glos. R.O., P 154/11/CW 2/1–4; *Glos. Ch. Bells*, 337–41.

[74] *Glos. Ch. Plate*, 101–2; Glos. R.O., P 154121/CW 2/3–4.

[75] *B. & G. Par. Rec.*, 151; cf. Glos. R.O., P 154/11/IN 1/1.

[76] Glouc. Cath. Libr., Reg. Abb. Malvern, i, f. 198v., where the positions of the ch. and the Cross have been reversed; in Speed, *Map of Glouc.* (1610), the positions of St.

Mary de Grace and Holy Trinity have been reversed.

[77] P.R.O., C 115/K 1/6681, f. 82; cf. *Tax. Eccl.* (Rec. Com.), 224.

[78] *Rot. Chart.* (Rec. Com.), 89; *Cal. Pat.* 1364–7, 91; *Glouc. Rental, 1455*, 31.

[79] Hockaday Abs. xxii, 1498 visit. f. 7; cf. *Valor Eccl.* (Rec. Com.), ii. 416.

[80] *Rot. Chart.* (Rec. Com.), 89; *Pat. R.* 1216–25, 323; cf. P.R.O., C 115/K 1/6681, f. 82v.

[81] P.R.O., JUST 1/278, rot. 66; cf. *Reg. Giffard*, 345; *Tax. Eccl.* (Rec. Com.), 224.

[82] *Cal. Pat.* 1388–92, 406; *Cal. Papal Reg.* v. 599–600.

[83] *L. & P. Hen. VIII*, xvi, p. 572.

[84] Worc. Episc. Reg., Reg. Clifford, ff. 72v.–73.

[85] Glouc. Cath. Libr., Reg. Abb. Braunche, p. 184; Reg. Abb. Newton, ff. 58v.–59; Reg. Abb. Malvern, ii ff. 26v.–27.

[86] *Valor Eccl.* (Rec. Com.), ii. 416.

[87] Hockaday Abs. xxviii, 1540 stipendiaries, f. 3.

[88] *Trans. B.G.A.S.* lxvii. 44–6.

[89] *Eccl. Misc.* 69.

[90] *Ordinance, 1648*, pp. 5–6.

the church was demolished.[91] After the Restoration most inhabitants of St. Mary's parish continued to attend St. Michael's church[92] and made voluntary contributions to the rector of St. Michael.[93] The rector was licensed to the cure of the parish from 1737[94] and the benefice of St. Mary, described as a rectory, was augmented by lot from Queen Anne's Bounty in 1745 and 1750[95] and was considered annexed to St. Michael by 1789.[96]

A chantry of St. Mary had been founded in St. Mary's church by 1328,[97] and in 1365 the rector of Holy Trinity and John Monmouth were licensed to alienate a rent of 33s. 4d. in Gloucester to the chaplain serving it.[98] The chantry had an income from lands and tenements of £8 5s. in 1548 when its endowments included a house called Gracelane College, in Grace Lane, which had been the home of priests.[99] The house was sold in 1548 to Sir Miles and Hugh Partridge. The remaining endowments comprised five messuages and rents totalling 36s. 8d. in Gloucester.[1]

The church of St. Mary de Grace, which was damaged by fire in 1223,[2] later comprised chancel, nave, and west tower and spire.[3] The building, which was in disrepair by the time of the siege of 1643,[4] was used by the city corporation as a magazine until 1651. The corporation, which in 1653 gave the churchwardens of St. Michael's leave to take material from St. Mary's church for repairing their parish church,[5] completed the demolition in 1654 and 1655 and used some stone for a market house.[6] Three bells and a chalice with cover from St. Mary's church, given to St. Michael's church in 1652, were sold and a monument was moved to St. Michael's church c. 1654.[7]

ST. MARY DE LODE. The church, standing just to the west of Gloucester Abbey's precinct, in the later St. Mary's Square, was pre-Conquest in origin. When first recorded, in the mid 12th century, it was subject to the abbey,[8] and it was presumably founded to serve the abbey's extensive estates in and around Gloucester. Its parish later included Tuffley, much of Barton Street and

Wotton, and parts of Kingsholm, Longford, and Twigworth,[9] and the churches of Barnwood, Maisemore, and Upton St. Leonards were originally dependent on it.[10] The present name of the church, recorded from 1523,[11] was taken from a passage of the nearby Old Severn, a channel of the Severn; in the Middle Ages it was usually called St. Mary before the abbey gate[12] and in the 16th century it was also known as St. Mary Broadgate.[13] From 1778 Holy Trinity was held with St. Mary de Lode and by 1838 the benefices were considered united.[14] In 1951 St. Nicholas was united with St. Mary.[15]

In the early 13th century the incumbent of St. Mary's church was called a rector[16] but he received only a portion of the profits of the church.[17] A dispute over the status of the living between the incumbent, who claimed it was a rectory, and the abbey was settled in 1302 when the archbishop's court declared it to be a vicarage.[18] In 1388 the abbey was licensed to appropriate the vicarage and serve the cure by monks.[19] The appropriation had been carried out by 1391 but in 1403 a new vicarage was ordained.[20] The abbey, which by 1394 paid the bishop a pension of 6s. 8d. for the church,[21] retained the advowson of the vicarage until the Dissolution,[22] and in 1541 advowson and impropriate rectory passed to the dean and chapter of Gloucester cathedral.[23] The Crown presented in 1580 and 1697 by reason of lapse.[24] In 1980 the dean and chapter shared the patronage of the united benefice with the bishop.[25]

In 1291 the incumbent's share of the profits of the church was valued at £15 6s. 8d. He also had a portion of 5s. in Matson church. The remaining profits of St. Mary's church were divided between Llanthony Priory, which took £1 6s. 8d. in tithes, and Gloucester Abbey, which received a portion of £3 6s. 8d.;[26] that portion had been confirmed to the abbey between 1164 and 1179.[27] The vicar, who paid the abbey's portion of the profits, was in dispute with the abbey over certain tithes and mortuary payments in 1304. It was then agreed that the vicar would have some tithes of sheep and would continue to receive a corrody in the abbey,

[91] G.B.R., F 4/6, pp. 60–2.
[92] Glos. R.O., P 154/14/IN 1/2–3.
[93] Bodl. MS. Top. Glouc. c. 3, f. 55v.
[94] Hockaday Abs. ccxvii; G.D.R. vol. 381A, f. 41.
[95] Hodgson, *Queen Anne's Bounty* (1845), p. cclxxxv.
[96] G.D.R. vol. 382, f. 22.
[97] *Reg. Orleton*, pp. 4–5.   [98] *Cal. Pat.* 1364–7, 91.
[99] Hockaday Abs. ccxvii.
[1] *Cal. Pat.* 1548–9, 110, 265–6.
[2] *Hist. & Cart. Mon. Glouc.* i. 26.
[3] Cf. *Glouc. Rental, 1455*, sketch no. 10; Speed, *Map of Glouc.* (1610).
[4] *Bibliotheca Glos.* ii. 373.
[5] G.B.R., B 3/2, pp. 628, 700; cf. Glos. R.O., P 154/14/ CW 2/2.
[6] G.B.R., F 4/6, pp. 60–2; cf. ibid. B 3/2, p. 775.
[7] Ibid. B 3/2, p. 677; Glos. R.O., P 154/14/CW 2/2.
[8] Glouc. Cath. Libr., Reg. Abb. Froucester B, p. 56. The abbey claimed liberties in the ch.: Worc. Episc. Reg., Reg. Alcock, f. 63.
[9] Glos. R.O., Q/RI 70 (maps A–H, K–R); G.D.R., T 1/86; cf. Rudder, *Glos.* 196.
[10] Glouc. Cath. Libr., Reg. Abb. Froucester B, p. 56.
[11] Ibid. Reg. Abb. Malvern, i, f. 211.

[12] Ibid. Reg. Abb. Froucester B, p. 56; *Glouc. Corp. Rec.* pp. 104, 157, 299; *Reg. Bransford*, p. 32; Worc. Episc. Reg., Reg. Alcock, f. 151.
[13] Hockaday Abs. ccxviii.
[14] Ibid. ccxiii, ccxviii.
[15] *Glouc. Dioc. Year Bk.* (1951–2), 26–7; (1952–3), 24–5.
[16] Glouc. Cath. Libr., Reg. Abb. Froucester B, p. 346.
[17] Ibid. Reg. Abb. Froucester A, ff. 82v.–83; *Reg. Giffard*, 267.
[18] Glouc. Cath. Libr., Reg. Abb. Froucester A, ff. 83v.–84.
[19] *Cal. Pat.* 1385–9, 458.
[20] *Cal. Papal Reg.* v. 598–600; Worc. Episc. Reg., Reg. Clifford, ff. 71v.–72v.
[21] Cf. Glouc. Cath. Libr., deeds and seals, i, f. 5; ii, ff. 14, 21; iii, f. 4; P.R.O., SC 12/38/45.
[22] Glouc. Cath. Libr., Reg. Abb. Braunche, pp. 32, 148, 159–60; Hockaday Abs. ccxviii.
[23] *L. & P. Hen. VIII*, xvi, p. 572; cf. Bodl. MS. Rawl. C. 790, f. 6.
[24] Hockaday Abs. ccxviii.
[25] *Glouc. Dioc. Year Bk.* (1980), 16–17.
[26] *Tax. Eccl.* (Rec. Com.), 224; cf. Glouc. Cath. Libr., Reg. Abb. Froucester A, f. 82v.
[27] *Hist. & Cart. Mon. Glouc.* i. 327.

where he would also have hospitality for himself, a chaplain, a deacon, and two clerks on feast days and fodder for his horse.[28] The vicarage, which was valued at 10 marks in 1313,[29] was said in 1388 to be endowed with lands.[30] In 1403 the abbey assigned the vicar a pension of £10 and the vicarage house, and undertook to support any other chaplains needed to serve the church and its chapels.[31] The vicar's pension took the form in 1523 of a lease of tithes of calves and dairy produce, personal tithes, and offerings,[32] and in 1535 of a payment of £10 13s. 4d.[33]

The dean and chapter, who continued the same pension, gave the vicar an additional sum of £43 from 1690. In 1697 the increment was reduced to £8 10s., representing small tithes, offerings, and fees with which the living was endowed in 1704. From that time the vicar had a stipend of £21 6s. 8d.,[34] which was paid by the Ecclesiastical Commissioners in the late 19th century.[35] In 1664 and 1670 the impropriators also granted the vicar leases of some corn and hay tithes for terms of 21 years.[36] The vicar's tithes were commuted at inclosure of the fields around Gloucester in 1799 for 41 a. and a corn rent charge of £8 0s. 0½d.[37] The benefice was augmented by lot from Queen Anne's Bounty in 1794[38] and 6 a. at Epney, in Moreton Valence, were bought in 1795.[39] The glebe, which in 1894 covered 89 a.,[40] was sold off piecemeal in the 20th century.[41] The living was valued at £286 in 1856.[42]

The vicarage house was being let at farm in 1535[43] and in 1743 there was no glebe house.[44] By the early 1880s a house in College Green had become the vicarage house.[45] It was replaced, possibly in the late 1930s, by a house in Miller's Green, and in the late 1960s a new vicarage house was built in St. Mary's Square.[46]

There were two chantries in the church. That of St. Mary had been founded by 1331,[47] and in 1392 Richard Barbour was licensed to alienate four messuages and a shop in Gloucester and Leonard Stanley to support the chaplain serving it.[48] In 1548 the chantry had an income from lands and tenements of £4 3s. 4d. The endowments included two burgages sold to Sir Thomas Bell and Richard Duke in 1548, and land in Gloucester, Tredworth, and elsewhere, and a rent of 12d. in Pedmarsh field.[49] The other chantry was supported by the guild of the Holy Trinity,

founded by 1420.[50] Richard Manchester by will proved 1454 left two shops to support its chaplain.[51] The chantry had an income of £3 0s. 1½d. in 1546, and its endowments comprised six messuages in Gloucester, a messuage and land in Minsterworth, and a rent of 12d. in Cheltenham.[52]

An obit for Walter Froucester, abbot of Gloucester, supported from the rectory estate, was celebrated in the church by three priests until the Dissolution.[53]

A charity founded by Edward Nourse in the late 17th century provided for the payment of 10s. a year to the vicar for an annual sermon.[54] In 1971, at a reorganization of charities, including those founded for St. Nicholas's parish, the payment was reserved to the vicar with small sums for five other sermons, and Thomas Withenbury's charity was divided, one part forming a separate charity for general church expenses.[55]

The church of St. Mary de Lode comprises chancel, central tower, and aisled nave with south-east vestry and north and south porches. The chancel and tower survive from the medieval church and the body of the church from a rebuilding of 1825. During the laying of the foundations of the new nave the church was found to be on the site of a Roman building[56] and excavations in the nave in the years 1978–9[57] revealed that there may have been a timber church or oratory on the site as early as the 6th century and that a nave was built there, largely of timber, in the 9th or early 10th century. For a time that nave may have had a west gallery or screen but by the mid 11th century a stone addition had been made to the west end, perhaps to support a gallery. A font stood in the centre of the nave. In the late 11th or early 12th century the church was rebuilt with chancel, central tower, and nave. In the mid 12th century aisles of three bays were added to the nave, which had a west doorway. Later the tower, which probably fell during a fire in 1190,[58] and chancel were rebuilt. In the 13th century the chancel was extended eastwards by a bay and the aisles westwards along the length of the nave.

The chancel was said to have fallen down by 1576 when the church needed repairs.[59] In 1643 the church was used as a prison for royalist soldiers taken at Highnam and, although it fell into disrepair,[60] royalists captured near Stow-on-the-Wold early in 1646 were held in it.[61] By the

[28] Ibid. iii. 228–9.
[29] Glouc. Cath. Libr., Reg. Abb. Froucester B, p. 488.
[30] Cal. Pat. 1385–9, 458.
[31] Worc. Episc. Reg., Reg. Clifford, ff. 71v.–72v.
[32] Glouc. Cath. Libr., Reg. Abb. Malvern, i, f. 211.
[33] Valor Eccl. (Rec. Com.), ii. 416; cf. ibid. 498
[34] Eccl. Misc. 68; Glos. R.O., D 936/A 1/1–8, passim; Glouc. Cath. Libr., Chapter Act bk. ii, f. 44 and v.
[35] Glos. R.O., P 154/12/CW 3/7.
[36] Ibid. D 936/Y 5, Y 8–9.
[37] Ibid. Q/RI 70.
[38] Hodgson, Queen Anne's Bounty (1845), p. cclxxxv.
[39] G.D.R., V 5/GT 22; Glos. R.O., D 2299/2310.
[40] Kelly's Dir. Glos. (1894), 166.
[41] Glos. R.O., P 154/12/IN 3/7; D 2299/2310.
[42] G.D.R. vol. 384, f. 104.
[43] Valor Eccl. (Rec. Com.), ii. 498.
[44] G.D.R. vol. 397, f. 45.
[45] O.S. Map 1/2,500, Glos. XXV. 15 (1886 edn.).
[46] Inf. from vicar, the Revd. S. J. Riggs.
[47] Reg. Orleton, pp. 33, 39.
[48] Cal. Pat. 1391–6, 151.
[49] Hockaday Abs. ccxviii; Cal. Pat. 1548–9, 41, 262.
[50] Hockaday Abs. ccxviii.
[51] Glouc. Corp. Rec. p. 402.
[52] Hockaday Abs. ccxviii; Cal. Pat. 1548–9, 264.
[53] Valor Eccl. (Rec. Com.), ii. 416.
[54] 14th Rep. Com. Char. 46.
[55] Glos. R.O., D 3469/5/67.
[56] Glouc. Jnl. 22 Aug. 1825; for descriptions of ch. before rebuilding, Gent. Mag. xcvi (2), 505–6; Glos. Colln. NQ 5.3.
[57] R. Bryant, 'Excavations at St. Mary de Lode, Glouc., 1978–9' (TS. in possession of ed., V.C.H. Glos.).
[58] Hist. & Cart. Mon. Glouc. i. 22.
[59] G.D.R. vol. 40, f. 6v.
[60] Hist. MSS. Com. 27, 12th Rep. IX, Glouc. Corp. p. 507; cf. V.C.H. Glos. x. 17.
[61] G.B.R., F 4/5, f. 319v.; V.C.H. Glos. vi. 151.

early 18th century a spire which the tower carried had been blown down by a violent storm, perhaps that of 1703,[62] there was a transeptal bay in each aisle, and the vestry had been added.[63] A gallery erected by the early 19th century was paid for with charity money, the seat rents being distributed with another charity.[64]

In the years 1825–6 the nave and vestry were rebuilt and the porches added, all in a stuccoed early Gothic style designed by James Cooke, a local mason. The gallery was moved to the west end.[65] The cost of rebuilding was met partly by loans. In 1845 circular windows were inserted in the nave over the north and south porches, and the tower was restored.[66] The chancel had been restored and the east window replaced by 1850.[67] Further restoration work was carried out in 1865 when the church was repewed, in 1869 when the chancel fabric was partly renewed,[68] c. 1885 when part of the gallery was removed and the vestry enlarged,[69] in 1896 when choir stalls and a low stone screen were placed at the east end of the nave,[70] and c. 1912.[71] The gallery was removed in 1980 when a church hall was built in the west part of the nave.[72]

The most notable monument in the church is an effigy of a priest, which has been reset in a defaced early 14th-century tomb recess on the north wall of the chancel.[73] The carved wooden pulpit dates from the 15th century. The organ, an 18th-century instrument, was brought from St. Nicholas's church in 1972.[74] There are six old bells: (i–iii) 1705 by Abraham Rudhall; (iv–v) 1636 by Roger Purdue; (vi) 1710 by Abraham Rudhall.[75] The church plate includes a paten given in 1724 by Margaret Cartwright, a chalice and paten given in 1736 by Anne Walter, and a chalice of 1756.[76] There is a register for the period 1656–61, and the parish registers, which survive from 1695, contain transcripts of entries for the period 1675–93.[77]

ST. MICHAEL. The church, at the Cross on the south side of Eastgate Street,[78] had been built by the mid 12th century[79] and anciently served a parish which included part of Barton Street.[80] The

living was a rectory in 1263.[81] By 1789 St. Mary de Grace was considered annexed to it[82] and in 1931 the benefice was included in the new united benefice of St. Michael with St. John the Baptist.[83] The church was closed in 1940 as a result of the outbreak of the Second World War,[84] and its parish was united with that of St. Mary de Crypt in 1952.[85]

In the mid 13th century the advowson of St. Michael's church and its dependent chapel of St. Martin belonged to the bishop of Exeter. Gloucester Abbey, which in the 1270s was in dispute with the rector over tithes and claimed the patronage,[86] purchased the advowson from the bishop in 1285. After the Dissolution it was retained by the Crown,[87] which in 1625, following a long vacancy, ordered an inquiry into the patronage.[88] By the mid 18th century the Crown usually presented through the Lord Chancellor,[89] who was patron of the united benefice created in 1931.[90]

The rector took tithes from land east of Gloucester. In the early 1270s Gloucester Abbey claimed that he had deprived it of tithes there, and in 1280 the rector relinquished corn tithes from two strips of land to the abbey.[91] The rector received no mortuary payments before the mid 14th century when land south of the church was dedicated as a graveyard. Before then parishioners had been buried in the abbey churchyard and in 1366 the abbey gave up its right to burials in return for 20s. a year. In 1368 the diocesan bishop lifted an interdict on the new graveyard, which had been dedicated without his authority.[92]

In 1291 the church and its chapel were worth £6.[93] The living was valued at £21 5s. 9½d. clear in 1535[94] but it was said to be worth barely £13 6s. 8d. in 1603[95] and £8 16s. 4d. in 1625. At the last date, when the rectory was vacant, the income comprised tithes, voluntary contributions, and Easter payments.[96] Thomas Woodruffe, who became rector later that year,[97] recovered some tithes and cancelled a modus of 13s. 4d. from 11 a. in Upton St. Leonards,[98] but in 1704 tithes were withheld from c. 30 a.[99] The living's value was £12 excluding voluntary contributions c.

[62] Bodl. MS. Top. Glouc. c. 3, f. 50v. In 1717 it was said that the spire may have been destroyed during the siege of 1643: *Bibliotheca Glos.* ii. 373.

[63] Atkyns, *Glos.* 190 and plate at pp. 82–3; cf. Rudder, *Glos.* 195; R. Dalton and S. H. Hamer, *Provincial Token-Coinage of the 18th Cent.* ii (1911), 35.

[64] *16th Rep. Com. Char.* 17, which suggests incorrectly that the gallery was in St. Mary de Grace ch.

[65] Glos. R.O., D 3117/20–1; *Glouc. Jnl.* 4 Nov. 1826.

[66] Glos. R.O., P 154/12/CW 2/1.

[67] Clarke, *Archit. Hist. of Glouc.* 45 n.

[68] *Glouc. Jnl.* 14 Oct. 1865; 2 Jan. 1869; *Glos. Chron.* 9 Jan. 1869.

[69] Glos. R.O., P 154/12/CW 3/6.

[70] *Glos. N. & Q.* vi. 134, 181; vii. 87–8.

[71] Verey, *Glos.* ii. 235.

[72] Inf. from vicar.

[73] Roper, *Glos. Effigies*, 309–10; cf. Counsel, *Glouc.* 151–2.

[74] Plaque on organ.

[75] *Glos. Ch. Bells*, 341–3.

[76] *Glos. Ch. Plate*, 103–4.

[77] *B. & G. Par. Rec.* 152 and n.; cf. *Rec. of Glouc. Cath.* ed. W. Bazeley, iii (1885–97), 35–57.

[78] *Glouc. Rental, 1455,* 3, 101–3.

[79] *Camd. Misc.* xxii, p. 29.

[80] Atkyns, *Glos.* 191.

[81] *Glouc. Corp. Rec.* p. 239.

[82] G.D.R. vol. 382, f. 22.

[83] *Lond. Gaz.* 9 Oct. 1931, p. 6456.

[84] *Glouc. Jnl.* 2 Mar. 1940.

[85] Cf. *Lond. Gaz.* 5 July 1927, p. 4310; *Citizen*, 26 Jan. 1952.

[86] Glouc. Cath. Libr., Reg. Abb. Froucester A, ff. 89v.–91v.

[87] Ibid. ff. 87–9; *Hist. & Cart. Mon. Glouc.* i. 84; cf. *Reg. Wakefeld*, p. 77; Hockaday Abs. ccxix.

[88] P.R.O., E 337/17, no. 130.

[89] G.D.R. vol. 285B (3), pp. 51–2; Rudder, *Glos.* 197.

[90] *Lond. Gaz.* 5 July 1927, p. 4311; 9 Oct. 1931, p. 6457.

[91] Glouc. Cath. Libr., Reg. Abb. Froucester A, f. 91 and v.

[92] Glos. R.O., P 154/14/CH 3/1–2.

[93] *Tax. Eccl.* (Rec. Com.), 224.

[94] *Valor Eccl.* (Rec. Com.), ii. 498.

[95] *Eccl. Misc.* 68.

[96] P.R.O., E 337/17, no. 130; Rudge, *Glouc.* 332.

[97] Hockaday Abs. ccxix.

[98] Glos. R.O., P 154/14/IN 1/1.

[99] G.D.R., V 5/GT 27.

1708,[1] £50 including £15 from small tithes in 1743,[2] and £235 in 1856.[3] The rector's tithes outside Gloucester were commuted at the inclosure of 1799 for 15 a. and a corn rent charge of £7 2s. 2½d.,[4] and those within the city in 1850 for a corn rent charge of £2 5s.[5] The benefice, which in the early 18th century included voluntary contributions from the inhabitants of St. Mary de Grace parish,[6] was augmented by lot from Queen Anne's Bounty in 1759, 1766, and 1791.[7] The sums received were used to buy 4 a. in the city[8] and in 1795 11 a. at Epney.[9] In 1869 the Ecclesiastical Commissioners endowed the living with £78 a year.[10] The glebe was sold piecemeal in the late 19th century and the early 20th.[11]

In the 18th century and the early 19th the rector received a rent charge of 40s. from an estate in Down Hatherley and Twigworth;[12] it derived from a bequest to the corporation by William Drinkwater to support a public lecturer in the city[13] and had been applied to a weekly lectureship in St. Michael's church.[14]

The chapel of St. Martin, at the Cross on the north side of Eastgate Street,[15] was recorded in the mid 12th century[16] and was a chapel to St. Michael in the mid 13th.[17] The Crown presented a priest to it in 1334.[18] The chapel was closed between 1364 and 1368 by the diocesan bishop, who gave the site to the rector for a dwelling house,[19] and it had been pulled down by 1371.[20] That year the Crown granted the site, called St. Martin's Place, to the burgesses for a clock tower, but in 1372 restored it to the rector.[21] The rectory house built there was apparently in use in 1523[22] but in 1551 the Crown exemplified the grant to the burgesses.[23] Architectural features from the 14th century were discovered at the site in 1894.[24]

Richard Elly by will dated 1754 left a house in Maverdine Lane for the rector. In 1801 it was exchanged for a new house which William Bishop had built on the glebe in the later Brunswick Road.[25] That house passed to the united benefice of St. Mary de Crypt with St. John the Baptist.[26]

Several masses and obits were celebrated in St. Michael's church. A service of the Blessed Virgin Mary was supported by rents in the early 13th century,[27] and in 1321 Andrew of Pendock was licensed to alienate to the rector a messuage adjoining the church for rebuilding as a chapel of St. Mary and a rent of 5s. in Gloucester for supporting a chaplain serving in it daily.[28] The chantry, which may have been endowed with property and rent in the town and Barton Street by William Heyberare and two others in 1364,[29] had an income from lands and tenements of £11 17s. 7d. in 1548.[30] The endowments were sold in 1549, a small part being acquired by Anthony Bourchier.[31] The chantry's goods presumably included the small bell called Pendock in 1611 and sold by the churchwardens in the mid 17th century.[32]

A guild of St. John the Baptist, founded in the church by 1449,[33] supported a chantry which was served in its own chapel and had an income of £9 1s. 6d. in 1548.[34] Its endowments, including St. John's or Brethren Hall in Eastgate Street, messuages, cottages, gardens, stables, and land in Gloucester and Barton Street, and land at Sneedham's Green in Upton St. Leonards, were sold in 1549, a small part being bought by Bourchier.[35]

John Trye and his wife Catherine gave land in Sandhurst for a chantry in the chapel of St. Anne in St. Michael's church,[36] and John by will proved 1485 left the reversion of his estate in Nailsworth to feoffees, including the master and wardens of the weavers' company in Gloucester, to provide a chaplain serving it daily. The chantry may have been refounded in the early 16th century by Margaret van Eck, who gave land to help poor weavers, and the master and wardens acted as proctors of the chantry. Of its income of £9 1s. 4d. in 1548, 8s. was distributed among the poor.[37] The endowments comprised the weavers' hall, a few messuages and gardens, and 1½ a. in and near the city, and property in Sandhurst, King's Stanley, and Nailsworth. They were sold in 1549 and Bourchier bought part including the hall.[38]

In 1499 the abbot of Gloucester at the request of John Hartland gave the church some ornaments and vestments on condition that, among other things, an obit was held on the morrow of St. Kenelm (18 July).[39] A tenement, which in 1548 brought in an income of 10s. to support an

[1] Bodl. MS. Top. Glouc. c. 3, f. 55v.
[2] G.D.R. vol. 397, f. 41. [3] Ibid. vol. 384, f. 105.
[4] Glos. R.O., Q/RI 70.
[5] G.D.R., T 1/87.
[6] Bodl. MS. Top. Glouc. c. 3, f. 55v.
[7] Hodgson, *Queen Anne's Bounty* (1845), p. cclxxxv.
[8] *14th Rep. Com. Char.* 48.
[9] G.D.R., V 5/GT 28; Glos. R.O., D 2299/2310.
[10] *Lond. Gaz.* 18 June 1869, p. 3475.
[11] Glos. R.O., P 154/14/IN 3/4.
[12] *14th Rep. Com. Char.* 33, 51; G.D.R., V 5/GT 28–9.
[13] G.B.R., J 1/1282.
[14] Ibid. B 3/2, p. 504.
[15] *Glouc. Rental, 1455,* 87.
[16] *Camd. Misc.* xxii, p. 29.
[17] Glouc. Cath. Libr., Reg. Abb. Froucester A, ff. 89v.–91; *Hist. & Cart. Mon. Glouc.* i. 84.
[18] *Cal. Pat. 1330–4,* 565.
[19] *Cal. Close, 1369–74,* 391–2.
[20] *Cal. Inq. Misc.* iii, p. 298.
[21] *Cal. Pat. 1370–4,* 178; *Cal. Close, 1369–74,* 391–2.
[22] *Glouc. Rental, 1455,* 87; Glouc. Cath. Libr., Reg. Abb.

Malvern, i, f. 233v.
[23] *Glouc. Corp. Rec.* pp. 29–30.
[24] Glos. Colln. prints GL 15.77; Rob. of Goldhill by will dated 1334 left 40s. towards the repair and decoration of St. Martin: *Glouc. Corp. Rec.* p. 326.
[25] *14th Rep. Com. Char.* 26, 48; Glos. R.O., P 154/14/CH 5; G.D.R., V 5/GT 28–9.
[26] *Lond. Gaz.* 5 July 1927, pp. 4310–11.
[27] Glouc. Cath. Libr., Reg. Abb. Froucester B, p. 349.
[28] *Cal. Pat. 1321–4,* 21.
[29] Ibid. *1361–4,* 459.
[30] Hockaday Abs. ccxix.
[31] *Cal. Pat. 1547–8,* 329; *1548–9,* 260–1.
[32] Glos. R.O., P 154/14/CW 2/1–2.
[33] Ibid. CH 1/5.
[34] Hockaday Abs. ccxix, 1485, 1548.
[35] *Cal. Pat. 1547–8,* 329; *1548–9,* 261; cf. *Glouc. Rental, 1455,* 93.
[36] *Cal. Inq. p.m. Hen. VII,* iii, pp. 597–8.
[37] Hockaday Abs. ccxix.
[38] *Cal. Pat. 1548–9,* 261–2; *1547–8,* 329.
[39] Glos. R.O., P 154/14/CH 3/5.

obit, possibly founded in the late 15th century by Thomas Whitfield,[40] was sold to Thomas Chamberlayne and Richard Pate in 1549.[41]

For several years from 1639 the city corporation paid the rector or a curate £1 for preaching two sermons under the will of Henry Redvern, and from the early 1650s the incumbent had 10s. for one sermon under the same gift.[42] The charity founded by Edward Nourse in the late 17th century provided for a sermon by the rector.[43] From 1733 the corporation also paid the rector for reading prayers twice a day under a bequest from the Revd. Charles Trippet of East Knoyle (Wilts.), and that stipend was increased in 1734 under a bequest by Francis Yate.[44] In the later 18th century and early 19th bequests by Richard Elly and Richard Seyer and an anonymous gift provided for payments to the rector for Sunday services, sermons, and prayers.[45] In 1973 the sermon and prayer charities mentioned above for St. Michael's parish were included with a charity of Jane Punter, who in 1755 gave a house for the parish clerk,[46] in a reorganization which is treated under St. Mary de Crypt.

Bequests by John Browne, Sarah and Giles Marden, and John Blanch of Barton Street in or before the 18th century provided for annual sermons in St. Michael, and the rector held the principals and preached the sermons until at least 1824.[47] The charity founded by Margaret Cartwright before 1704 provided a bible for a poor parishioner each year.[48]

St. Michael's parish was receiving rent in the town by 1364.[49] Feoffees, apparently appointed from 1475, granted leases of tenements belonging to the parish and in 1568 applied the income from three messuages in Eastgate Street to repairing its church, highways, and bridges and to helping its poor.[50] Two houses providing an annual income of £4 for church repairs in 1825[51] were let for £80 from the 1840s and for £92 from 1864.[52]

The medieval church of St. Michael comprised chancel with south chapel, nave with south aisle, and west tower and porch;[53] the porch had an upper room.[54] Architectural evidence suggests that the church was rebuilt in the early 14th century,[55] and the chapel was added in the 1320s to house the chantry of St. Mary.[56] The chancel was reconstructed in 1392.[57] In 1401 a bequest

was made to the fabric of a new belfry,[58] and the west bell tower was built between 1455 and 1472.[59] The church included several side altars in the later Middle Ages when among the lights and images recorded were those of St. Catherine, St. James,[60] and the Holy Rood. There may have been an altar of All Souls.[61]

The chancel was repaired c. 1561.[62] The church underwent a major reconstruction in 1653 and 1654 when the south arcade of four bays was rebuilt. Fabric from the churches of St. Aldate and St. Mary de Grace was used in the rebuilding, some glass from the latter being incorporated in the windows. The cost, almost £200, was met by the sale of materials and fittings from those churches, a rate, and a gift from the corporation.[63] In 1622 the corporation appointed a committee to allot seats in the church to its members,[64] and the mayor and aldermen had seats at the east end in 1704.[65] Repairs to the church were made in 1669, when the parishioners removed the chancel roof without the rector's consent, in 1670, when the church was ceiled, and in 1680, when the aisle was repaired. The chancel and chapel, called the parish chancel in 1704, had ceased to be separate features by then and were described as the pine end, probably from the wainscotting and other fittings, in 1736,[66] when the south-eastern corner was rebuilt and the church refurbished.[67] There was more rebuilding in the late 1770s and extensive repairs were carried out c. 1795 and c. 1802.[68] A gallery had been built by 1648, and in 1678 the seats in the south aisle were set facing the pulpit, in the fashion of a gallery.[69] A gallery in the base of the tower was apparently erected in the early 19th century.[70]

As a result of the many alterations the plan of the church ceased to be rectangular and by 1846 it had been decided to rebuild it except for the tower.[71] Work began in 1849 and the new church, to a design of Thomas Fulljames and F. S. Waller, was consecrated in 1851. It was larger than the old and on a different alignment which permitted a widening of the street. The cost was met by a grant from the Incorporated Church Building Society and subscriptions. The west porch was probably removed at the rebuilding, when the base of the tower was cleared.[72] The

---

[40] Hockaday Abs. ccxix; Fosbrooke, *Glouc.* 176 n.

[41] *Cal. Pat.* 1548–9, 266.

[42] G.B.R., B 3/2, p. 110; F 4/5, ff. 98v., 128v., 152v., 174v., 207v., 240, 453v., 477; *14th Rep. Com. Char.* 39, 44.

[43] *14th Rep. Com. Char.* 46.

[44] G.B.R., B 3/9, f. 335v.; Hockaday Abs. ccxix; Atkyns, *Glos.* 191.

[45] *14th Rep. Com. Char.* 48, 53; G.D.R., V 5/GT 28–9.

[46] *14th Rep. Com. Char.* 48.

[47] G.D.R., V 5/GT 27A, 29; *14th Rep. Com. Char.* 47, 49–50.   [48] G.D.R., V 5/GT 27A; *14th Rep. Com. Char.* 44.

[49] Glos. R.O., P 154/14/CH 2/16.

[50] Ibid. CH 2/1, 9, 11; CH 4/6.

[51] *14th Rep. Com. Char.* 53–4.

[52] Glos. R.O., P 154/14/CW 2/4; VE 2/3.

[53] Plan of ch. 1847, in C. H. Dancey, 'Hist. of St. Michael's Ch.' (MS. in Glos. Colln. 14259).

[54] Glos. R.O., P 154/14/CW 2/2, acct. 1661–2.

[55] Fosbrooke, *Glouc.* plates facing p. 176, one reproduced above, Plate 44; Glos. Colln. prints GL 15.39.

[56] *Cal. Pat.* 1321–4, 21.

[57] *Reg. Wakefeld*, p. 119; cf. Glouc. Cath. Libr., deeds and seals, i, f. 9.

[58] Hockaday Abs. ccxix.

[59] Cf. *Glouc. Rental, 1455*, 3, 101–3; Glos. R.O., P 154/14/CH 4/1.

[60] Glos. R.O., P 154/14/CH 3/3; *Glouc. Corp. Rec.* p. 345.

[61] Hockaday Abs. ccxix, 1485, 1529.

[62] Glos. R.O., P 154/14/CW 1/13.

[63] Ibid. CW 2/2; G.B.R., B 3/2, pp. 700, 711, 753.

[64] G.B.R., B 3/1, f. 484.

[65] Glos. R.O., P 154/14/CW 2/3.

[66] Ibid. 2–3.

[67] Ibid. IN 1/3; Rudder, *Glos.* 198.

[68] Glos. R.O., P 154/14/CW 2/4; VE 2/1.

[69] Ibid. CW 2/2.

[70] Glos. Colln. NR 5.15 (2).

[71] Plan of ch. 1847; Glos. Colln. NR 5.15 (2–3).

[72] *Glouc. Jnl.* 8 Sept. 1849; 3 May 1851; Glos. R.O., P 154/14/VE 2/3; *Church Builder*, v. 158–9.

south chapel housed a vestry and organ loft until 1875 when a south vestry room was added and the organ rebuilt.[73] During a restoration in 1893 the chancel was partly refitted, a carved stone reredos and a stone screen with sedilia being erected.[74] In 1894 an oak screen was placed in the tower arch.[75] After the Second World War the church, which occupied a commercially valuable site projecting into the street, was not reopened and in the years 1955–6 it was demolished except for the tower.[76]

Of the fittings some glass was taken for a church in Bath and the reredos for Saul church.[77] The remains of one memorial were placed in St. Mary de Crypt church and several monuments were moved to St. John's church.[78] The church plate, which included pieces acquired in 1691 with a bequest of Nicholas Webb (d. 1691) and pieces given by his son Alderman Nicholas Webb in 1710, by Elizabeth Austin in 1731, and by Nathaniel Lye in 1749,[79] passed to St. John's and St. Mary's churches.[80]

The 'common' or 'curfew bell' was tolled at St. Michael's church at the borough's expense in 1393,[81] and in 1550 the corporation paid for a bell to be rung at 4 a.m. and 8 p.m.[82] A clock and chimes had been installed in the church by 1546,[83] and in 1612 the common council made a grant towards a dial being erected on the tower by the parish for the public benefit.[84] The corporation contributed to works on the bells and clock.[85] The dial was removed in 1770 because of its disrepair.[86] The 'curfew bell' at 8 o'clock was rung until the Second World War, save in the period 1854–72 when the peal was silent.[87] Between 1752 and 1849 the market (later the fire) bell hung in the tower.[88] In 1611 St. Michael's church had a ring of six bells, which was recast in 1667 by Richard Keene of Woodstock (Oxon.).[89] Two bells were added in 1887,[90] and the corporation gave the fire bell and the mayor, Albert Estcourt, a new bell in 1898 for an enlarged peal.[91] The bells were taken down in 1956, and the treble and second were given to the cathedral and the others sold.[92]

The registers of St. Michael's parish survive from 1553.[93]

ST. NICHOLAS. The church, in lower Westgate Street, had parochial rights by the end of the 12th century[94] and was described as a minster (*monasterium*) in the early 13th.[95] In 1203 the church, which was in the gift of the Crown, was called St. Nicholas of the bridge of Gloucester,[96] and in 1221, when the burgesses claimed it,[97] it was said to have custody of the later Westgate bridge.[98] In 1229 Henry III gave the church to St. Bartholomew's Hospital to support the poor there.[99] The hospital, which was later included in St. Nicholas's parish,[1] appropriated the rectory[2] and served the church through chaplains or stipendiary curates.[3] The right of nomination passed with the governorship of the hospital under a royal grant of 1564 to the city corporation.[4]

The corporation granted leases of the rectory[5] and the curate was the farmer in 1576 and in 1603 when he had a stipend of £10.[6] From c. 1610 the rectory was held by the parishioners who supported a preacher out of the profits.[7] The parishioners claimed a similar arrangement at a vacancy in 1686,[8] but the corporation nominated to the curacy from the next vacancy in 1708.[9] In the early 18th century the curate's income came from voluntary contributions, valued at £60 a year in the 1730s,[10] and sermon charities.[11] Between 1738 and 1742 the corporation, then attending the church during a dispute over its cathedral seats, employed the curate as its chaplain.[12] It also usually paid him, perhaps from 1656, a salary of £6 for services in St. Bartholomew's Hospital.[13] The church was sometimes described in the 18th and 19th centuries as a free chapel annexed to the hospital. By 1735 there was thought to be a perpetual curacy,[14] a status acquired or confirmed through endowments from Queen Anne's Bounty in 1747, 1749, 1781, and 1789 and from the parliamentary fund in 1810 and 1813.[15] Those were laid out on land in Haresfield and Sud Meadow. The glebe, including land in Norton

[73] Glos. R.O., P 154/14/VE 2/3; CH 4/45.
[74] Ibid. CW 3/7; *Glouc. Jnl.* 18 Aug. 1883.
[75] *Kelly's Dir. Glos.* (1894), 166.
[76] *Citizen*, 6 Oct., 17 Nov. 1955; 24 Apr. 1956.
[77] Ibid. 28 Jan., 20 Nov. 1955.
[78] Verey, *Glos.* ii. 234; Glos. Colln. NQ 5.1.
[79] *Glos. Ch. Plate*, 105–6; Glos. R.O., P 154/14/CW 2/3.
[80] Verey, *Glos.* ii. 232.
[81] G.B.R., F 3/2; F 4/2, m. 3.
[82] Ibid. F 4/3, f. 21v.; cf. ibid. B 3/9, f. 238v.
[83] Glos. R.O., P 154/14/CW 1/1.
[84] G.B.R., B 3/1, f. 244.
[85] Ibid. f. 492; 2, pp. 32, 195; 3, pp. 104, 133, 321; 8, p. 355.
[86] Glos. R.O., P 154/14/VE 2/1, p. 62.
[87] *Glos. Chron.* 2 July 1887; *Glouc. Jnl.* 21 Dec. 1872; 16 June 1956.
[88] Glos. R.O., P 154/14/VE 2/1, p. 9; *Glouc. Jnl.* 24 Mar. 1849.
[89] Glos. R.O., P 154/14/CW 2/1–2; *Glos. Ch. Bells*, 40–1.
[90] *Glos. Chron.* 2 July 1887.
[91] Glos. R.O., P 154/14/VE 2/4; *Glos. Ch. Bells*, 320, 331–2.
[92] *Glouc. Jnl.* 16 June 1956; Glos. Colln. N 5.76.
[93] *B. & G. Par. Rec.* 153.
[94] *Glouc. Corp. Rec.* pp. 70, 72.
[95] Glouc. Cath. Libr., Reg. Abb. Froucester B, p. 464.
[96] *Rot. Litt. Pat.* (Rec. Com.), 31, 34.
[97] *Pleas of the Crown for Glos.* ed. Maitland, p. 108.
[98] *Hist. & Cart. Mon. Glouc.* i. 322.
[99] *Cal. Chart. R.* 1226–57, 98.
[1] Cf. *Hist. & Cart. Mon. Glouc.* i. 245; *Valor Eccl.* (Rec. Com.), ii. 488.
[2] *Cal. Pat.* 1401–5, 329; *Valor Eccl.* (Rec. Com.), ii. 490.
[3] Hockaday Abs. ccxx, 1335, 1415; xxv, 1532 subsidy, f. 28; xxviii, 1540 visit. f. 12; 1540 stipendiaries, f. 3; xxx, 1544 stipendiaries, f. 1.
[4] Ibid. ccxxiii.
[5] G.B.R., B 3/1, ff. 126v.–127.
[6] Hockaday Abs. xlvii, 1576 visit. f. 4; *Eccl. Misc.* 68.
[7] Cf. G.B.R., J 3/16, ff. 75v.–77v., 207v.–209.
[8] Ibid. B 3/3, p. 909; cf. Glos. R.O., D 3269, hospitals' lease bk. 1630–1703 (2), ff. 265–266v.
[9] G.B.R., B 3/8, p. 276; 9, f. 365; Glos. R.O., P 154/15/IN 1/1–2; Hockaday Abs. ccxx.
[10] Atkyns, *Glos.* 191; G.D.R. vol. 285B (3), pp. 51–2.
[11] G.D.R., V 5/GT 31.
[12] G.B.R., B 3/9, ff. 412–13, 417 and v., 427v., 437v.; 10, f. 6v.; F 4/9, pp. 192, 224, 259, 298, 389.
[13] G.D.R. vol. 381A, f. 42; cf. G.B.R., B 3/2, p. 887; Glos. R.O., D 3269, St. Barth. Hosp., acct. bk. 1780–9, *passim*; 1797–1817, ff. 1, 5, 10, 15.
[14] Hockaday Abs. ccxx.
[15] Hodgson, *Queen Anne's Bounty* (1845), p. cclxxxv.

given for a weekly lecture, comprised 40 a. in 1828[16] and was sold piecemeal in the 20th century.[17]

Vacancies in the church in 1843 and 1852 were filled by the municipal charity trustees with the concurrence of the city corporation.[18] In 1870 the trustees sold their rights in the living, then called a vicarage, to the incumbent, William Balfour.[19] He transferred them to the bishop in 1871[20] when the benefice, which had been worth £118 in 1856, was endowed with £156 a year by the Ecclesiastical Commissioners.[21] In the mid 19th century the incumbent paid the dean and chapter of Gloucester a pension of 13s. 4d., charged on the impropriate rectory in 1541 and granted to the vicar in 1886.[22] The benefice was united with St. Mary de Lode in 1951[23] and the church, which was closed in 1967,[24] was declared redundant in 1971 when the parish was merged with St. Mary's.[25]

In 1415 the chaplain lived in the church.[26] In 1607 the curate had lodgings in St. Bartholomew's Hospital[27] and after its rebuilding in 1790 he was paid £3 for the loss of his rooms.[28] In 1879 a house in London Road was purchased for a vicarage house.[29] It was replaced in 1924 by a semidetached house in Park Road.[30]

Several chantries and obits were supported in the church. William of Sandford c. 1240 gave his lands and rents to St. Bartholomew's Hospital to provide payments for inmates and to support a secular chaplain celebrating daily in the church, who was to have 20s. a year and accommodation in the hospital. The hospital, which until 1278 appointed one of its own chaplains to serve the chantry, used land in Gloucester, given for a chantry in 1338 by the executors of Owen of Windsor,[31] to augment the chantry priest's stipend. In 1535 he received 100s. and served daily at the altar of St. Thomas of Canterbury.[32]

A chantry of St. Mary was possibly founded by John of Elmore and John Teek who were licensed in 1366 to alienate 2 messuages, ⅓ a., and 12s. rent in Gloucester and its suburbs to a chaplain to serve daily at an altar of St. Mary, presumably in the south aisle.[33] John Cooke by will proved 1528 directed his executors to pay a priest a stipend of £5 to serve the chantry for two years so that the chantry's proctors could augment the endow-

ments to make better provision for services.[34] In 1548 the chantry had an income of £6 9s. 8d.,[35] and its endowments, in the city and including two vacant plots, were sold in 1549, part to Anthony Bourchier.[36]

William Crook by will dated 1401 left the reversion of tenements and rents in Gloucester to support a chaplain celebrating before the Holy Cross in an upper chamber in the church.[37] In 1548 the chantry, called the rood service, had an income of £6 12s. Bourchier bought part of its endowments when they were sold in 1549.[38] Thomas Gloucester by will proved 1447 left land in and around London and in Gloucestershire to found two chantries, one in a London church and the other in St. Nicholas. The priest of the Gloucester chantry was to have a salary of 20 marks and a house and was also to teach grammar for no payment.[39]

An obit for Alderman William Francombe (d. 1488) and his wife Agnes was founded in 1491[40] and one for Walter Beech was mentioned in 1548. A rent of 10s. supported a lamp in the church before 1548,[41] and in the early 18th century the income from three tenements, said to have been given in the mid 15th century to maintain lights at the high altar, was used for church expenses.[42]

Charities founded by John Thorne, Thomas Singleton, William Windowe, Thomas Withenbury, and Sarah Clutterbuck in the 17th and 18th centuries provided for payments for annual sermons, and in the early 1820s the perpetual curate received a total of £3 17s. 8d. for preaching them.[43] The reorganization of those charities in 1971 is treated under St. Mary de Lode. Anthony Ellis gave c. 16 a. in Norton in 1809 to pay the perpetual curate or his nominee for a lecture on Sunday mornings.[44]

The church of St. Nicholas, which is built of oolitic limestone, comprises a chancel with north chapel, a nave with north aisle, south aisle with porch, and south porch with upper room, and a west tower and spire.[45] Two bays of the north arcade and a carved tympanum in the south wall of the nave survive from the 12th-century church, which was rebuilt and enlarged in the 13th century. The 13th-century south aisle was a chapel of St. Mary in 1347. In that year, when a west bell tower was recorded, the south porch was

[16] G.D.R., V 5/GT 32–3.

[17] Ibid. F 4/6/14; Glos. R.O., P 154/15/IN 3/14.

[18] Glos. R.O., D 3269, char. trustees' min. bk. 1836–44, pp. 313, 317–18; 1844–56, f. 292; G.B.R., B 3/16, pp. 313–14; 17, min. 22 Apr. 1852.

[19] Glos. R.O., D 3269, char. trustees' min. bk. 1867–74, pp. 304, 315–16, 335–6, 364; Kelly's Dir. Glos. (1870), 551.

[20] Lond. Gaz. 16 May 1871, pp. 2339–40.

[21] Ibid. 16 June 1871, p. 2805; G.D.R. vol. 384, f. 105.

[22] Glos. R.O., P 154/15/IN 3/12; L. & P. Hen. VIII, xvi, p. 573.

[23] Glouc. Dioc. Year Bk. (1951–2), 26–7; (1952–3), 24–5.

[24] Citizen, 29 Feb. 1968.

[25] Glouc. Dioc. Year Bk. (1980), 16–17; inf. from vicar of St. Mary de Lode.

[26] Hockaday Abs. ccxx.

[27] G.B.R., J 3/16, f. 75v.

[28] Glos. R.O., D 3269, St. Barth. Hosp., ct. bk. 1781–1812, ct. 29 Sept. 1790; acct. bk. 1797–1817, ff. 1, 5, 10, 15.

[29] J. J. Luce, Old Ch. of St. Nicholas (1914), 5: Glos. Colln.

N 5.36; O.S. Map 1/2,500, Glos. XXV. 15. (1886 edn.).

[30] G.D.R., F 4/6/14; Glos. R.O., P 154/15/IN 3/15.

[31] Glouc. Corp. Rec. pp. 164, 263–4, 330–1.

[32] Valor Eccl. (Rec. Com.), ii. 490; G.B.R., K 1/7, m. 2.

[33] Cal. Pat. 1364–7, 228; cf. Glouc. Corp. Rec. pp. 343–4.

[34] Hockaday Abs. ccxvi.

[35] Ibid. ccxx.

[36] Cal. Pat. 1547–8, 329; 1548–9, 264–5.

[37] P.R.O., C 115/K 2/6682, ff. 143v.–144.

[38] Hockaday Abs. ccxx; Cal. Pat. 1547–8, 329; 1548–9, 265; the property acquired by Bourchier was said to have belonged to a chantry in St. Michael's ch.

[39] Glouc. Corp. Rec. p. 398.

[40] Glos. N. & Q. iii. 638–41; cf. Hockaday Abs. ccxx, 1487, 1490; below, Aldermen of Glouc. 1483–1835.

[41] Hockaday Abs. ccxx.

[42] G.D.R., V 5/GT 31.

[43] 16th Rep. Com. Char. 17–22; 14th Rep. Com. Char. 36.

[44] Glos. R.O., P 154/15/IN 3/9.

[45] Illustrated description in Trans. B.G.A.S. xxiii. 109–28.

added to the nave and the ground to the west was built on by the parishioners to provide revenue for church repairs. In 1440 St. Bartholomew's Hospital, which had contested the parishioners' title to the room above the porch and the building to the west, granted those parts on lease for 40 years.[46] In the early 15th century, presumably after the parishioners' acquisition in 1403 of land next to the church for a graveyard,[47] the north aisle was reconstructed and continued alongside the tower (where there may have been a transept), the tower was rebuilt with a spire, incorporating a coronet and surmounted by a ball and cross,[48] and the south windows of the south aisle were replaced. There were many side altars and lights in the church in the later Middle Ages, including those of St. Catherine, St. John the Baptist, Holy Trinity, and the morning mass.[49]

In the 16th century squints were inserted in the north and south walls of the chancel and a small porch and doorway were made on the south side of the south aisle. The north chapel was rebuilt in the 16th or 17th century, apparently as a vestry. A west gallery was erected c. 1621, and in 1622 the city corporation appointed a committee to allot seats in the church to its members.[50] The top of the spire, damaged during the 1643 siege,[51] was in disrepair in 1776, and in 1783 John Bryan removed the part above the coronet, on which he erected pinnacles, battlements, and copper ball finial with weathercock. By then the tower and spire were leaning and poor drainage was causing subsidence. In 1786, when the church was deemed in danger of collapse, services were discontinued and the fittings removed. Repairs were done after a plan to rebuild was dropped.[52] In 1865 at a restoration, apparently by John Jacques & Son,[53] the main south porch was rebuilt, a new window put in the nave wall, and two windows in the south aisle were remodelled. The church was repewed, the gallery was removed and part of it fitted in the tower arch, and the floor was raised.[54] Following a fire in 1901 the church was repaired.[55] The chancel was restored in the early 1920s[56] and the tower strengthened in the mid 1920s. Between 1935 and 1938 the church was reroofed, the north aisle restored, and the south wall strengthened.[57] In the early 20th century a doorway was made at the east end of the north aisle and a vestry room added.[58] The room was demolished in the later 1970s when the redundant church was restored.[59] In 1980 it was used for concerts and exhibitions.[60]

Before 1980 some fittings were removed from the church, including a closing ring on the main south door which incorporated 14th-century bronze work. The front of the gallery, which had been removed from the tower arch in 1924, stood at the east end of the south aisle in 1980.[61] The most notable of many monuments, that to Alderman John Walton and his wife Alice (d. 1626 and 1620), has two full-size recumbent effigies on the tombchest in the south aisle;[62] it was restored in 1980. The chancel has a monument to the Revd. Richard Green (d. 1711) with an upright half-length effigy.[63] A clock had been fixed to the tower by 1716. In 1785 or 1786 the chimes were repaired to play the tune 'Britons Strike Home'[64] but they no longer worked by the 1970s. The church has six bells: (i) 1608 probably by John Baker; (ii-iii) 1636 by Roger Purdue; (iv) 15th century by Robert Hendley; (v) 15th century from a Bristol foundry; (vi) 1725 by Abraham Rudhall the younger, being received from him in exchange for the old tenor in 1726. An early 16th-century sanctus bell was given to the cathedral c. 1973.[65] The church plate included a paten cover dated 1573, which may have belonged to a chalice given away in 1716 in an exchange.[66] Gifts by Alderman Christopher Capel and Ann Robins in 1626 and Alderman Richard Massinger in 1668 were used to buy plate, and other pieces were given by Ann Clayfield in 1716 and Charles Hyett in 1731. By 1970 one flagon had been sold to the city museum.[67]

The parish registers, which contain entries for the castle, survive from 1558.[68]

ST. OWEN. The church, outside the south gate, was probably founded in the late 11th century by Roger of Gloucester who appointed two chaplains to serve it. His son Walter greatly increased the endowments, including St. Kyneburgh's chapel and several chapels outside Gloucester, and the church was dedicated at his request. Its parish on both sides of the town wall may have included one served earlier from St. Kyneburgh. The church, its graveyard, and dependent chapels, including Elmore, Hempsted, and Quedgeley, were part of the endowment of Llanthony Priory made by Walter's son Miles of Gloucester in 1137.[69] A few years later the priory assigned a portion of £1 in St. Owen's rectory to Lire Abbey (Eure) for tithes and land, and at the dispossession of the alien houses in 1414 it passed to Sheen Priory (Surr.).[70] In the late 12th century St. Owen's church had a parson who received the living's revenues and

---

[46] *Glouc. Corp. Rec.* pp. 343-4, 393.

[47] *Cal. Pat. 1401-5*, 329.

[48] *Glouc. Rental, 1455*, sketch no. 11.

[49] *Glouc. Corp. Rec.* p. 361; Hockaday Abs. ccxx, 1485, 1487, 1490.

[50] G.B.R., B 3/1, ff. 482v., 484.

[51] *Bibliotheca Glos.* ii. 373.

[52] Glos. R.O., P 154/15/CW 2/3; *C.J.* xli. 636, 666; G.B.R., B 3/12, ff. 39v.-41v.

[53] Glos. R.O., P 154/15/CW 3/10.

[54] *Trans. B.G.A.S.* xxiii. 117, 126, plan at pp. 120-1; *Glouc. Jnl.* 12 Aug. 1865; 14 Apr. 1866.

[55] *Glos. N. & Q.* ix. 117.

[56] Glos. Colln. NR 5.11 (1, 3).

[57] *Kelly's Dir. Glos.* (1931), 179; (1939), 182; inscrs. in ch.

[58] Cf. *Trans. B.G.A.S.* xxiii, plan at pp. 120-1; plan in ch.

[59] Plan in ch.; 'St. Nicholas Ch.' (Glouc. Folk Mus. inf. sheet).

[60] Inf. from vicar of St. Mary de Lode.

[61] 'St. Nicholas Ch.'

[62] Roper, *Glos Effigies*, 312-14; above, Plate 10.

[63] Roper, *Glos. Effigies*, 314-16.

[64] Glos. R.O., P 154/15/CW 2/1, 3.

[65] *Glos. Ch. Bells*, 343-4, 326; Glos. R.O., P 154/15/CW 2/1.

[66] *Glos. Ch. Plate*, 107; Glos. R.O., P 154/15/CW 2/1.

[67] *Glos. Ch. Plate*, 107-8; Verey, *Glos.* ii. 236 and n.

[68] B. & G. Par. Rec. 155 and n.

[69] *Trans. B.G.A.S.* lxiii. 4-6; *Camd. Misc.* xxii, pp. 17-18, 37 and n., 38, cf. above, A.-S. Glouc..

[70] P.R.O., C 115/K 2/6683, f. 26 and v.; cf. *Tax. Eccl.* (Rec. Com.), 224; *V.C.H. Surr.* ii. 89.

paid Llanthony 2 marks.[71] By the mid 13th century the living was a vicarage in the gift of the priory,[72] which continued to present vicars, notwithstanding a licence in 1395 to appropriate the living and nominate one of its canons to serve the cure.[73] The advowson belonged to the Crown in the early 17th century.[74]

St. Owen's church was pulled down just before the siege in 1643 when the area outside the south gate was fired, and in 1648 its parish was included in that served from St. Mary de Crypt church.[75] After the Restoration the inhabitants of St. Owen's parish continued to attend St. Mary's church[76] and from 1737 the rector of St. Mary was licensed to the cure of St. Owen.[77] The two benefices were later considered united.[78]

In the mid 13th century Llanthony Priory assigned the vicarage a portion comprising the small tithes and offerings of the church, a house once occupied by a chaplain serving the church, and tithes and other property in Elmore, Hempsted, Quedgeley, and Woolstrop. The first vicar to receive that portion claimed that it was insufficient and that the priory was bound by an earlier charter to build a vicarage house, but following arbitration in 1256 he surrendered that charter in return for 6 marks, of which 3½ marks were for providing a house in Hempsted.[79] Elmore, Hempsted, and Quedgeley later won full parochial status and in 1535 St. Owen's vicarage was worth £4 19s. 5½d. clear.[80] Its profits did not exceed £4 10s. in 1603[81] and a payment of £1 from the site of the church was the sole income of the living in the early 18th century.[82] In 1737 the benefice was augmented by lot from Queen Anne's Bounty with £200 which was laid out on 19 a. in Westbury-on-Severn.[83]

A chantry of St. Mary, founded in the church by 1356,[84] had an income of £8 9s. in 1548, when the chantry priest assisted the vicar. Of its endowments, all in Gloucester, part was sold to Sir Thomas Bell and Richard Duke in 1548.[85]

In the early 16th century the church had several side altars and lights, including those of the rood, All Souls, and St. Catherine.[86] The chancel roof was in decay in 1547, and by 1552 the church had been repaired and provided with new seats. A bell was sold in 1551, leaving three bells and a sanctus bell in the church tower.[87] The demolition in 1643 was carried out by the city corporation, which used part of the fabric and fittings for repairs at the Crypt school.[88] Following the corporation's decision in 1648 to develop the waste ground

outside the south gate for public walks and the drying of cloth, the site of the church was cleared, some rubble being used for works at the city quay,[89] but the parishioners of St. Mary de Crypt secured the site in 1650 and let it for £1.[90] Part of the site was taken for an extension of the docks in 1847[91] and St. Owen's parish sold a long lease of another part in 1851 to the Independent chapel, then being enlarged.[92]

MODERN PARISH CHURCHES. The growth of Gloucester in the 19th and 20th centuries was followed by the provision of churches for the new suburbs. The first, Christ Church, opened in 1823 at the Spa, was a proprietary church, unlike those erected later for the working-class suburbs. Those were financed mainly by grants and voluntary contributions and some were left incomplete for lack of funds. The Gloucester and Bristol Diocesan Church Building Association, established in 1836 to further church building in areas inhabited by the poor, helped to complete St. James and planned St. Luke, both consecrated in 1841, and was concerned with St. Matthew at Twigworth (1842) and St. Mark (1847).[93] For the increasing population of the later 19th century the churches of All Saints (1875) and St. Paul (1883) were consecrated, and St. James, St. Luke, and Barnwood church opened missions, those of St. Luke and Barnwood being superseded respectively by St. Luke the Less (1900), later St. Stephen, and Holy Trinity (1934).

The Gloucester Church Extension Society, formed to implement the recommendations of the commission appointed by the bishop in 1906,[94] provided St. Catharine (1915) and the mission church (1907) later replaced by St. Barnabas (1940). Commercial development south of the city centre led in 1934 to the closure of St. Luke and the union of the benefice with Christ Church, which was in turn united in 1979 with St. Mary de Crypt with St. John the Baptist. Suburban development east and south of the city was followed by the consecration of St. Oswald (1939), St. George (1956), and St. Aldate (1964). As in the late 19th century and early 20th those churches superseded mission churches. Other missions were organized by Holy Trinity, St. Barnabas, and Matson church. Both the Holy Trinity and Matson missions were short lived, the latter being provided in 1956 with a hall, dedicated to St. Hilda, in Red Well Road.[95]

[71] P.R.O., C 115/L 1/6688, f. 54v.

[72] Ibid. C 115/K 2/6683, ff. 34v.–35, 43–44v.; *Reg. Giffard*, 175, presumably confused the ch. with that of St. Aldate in the gift of Deerhurst Priory.

[73] *Cal. Papal Reg.* iv. 520; *Cal. Pat.* 1396–9, 342; cf. Worc. Episc. Reg., Reg. Clifford, f. 22; Reg. Polton, ff. 48v., 148v.

[74] *Eccl. Misc.* 68.

[75] *Ordinance, 1648*, pp. 4–5; cf. *Bibliotheca Glos.* i, pp. liv–lv.   [76] Glos. R.O., P 154/11/IN 1/1–2.

[77] Hockaday Abs. ccxi, ccxvi.

[78] Cf. G.D.R. vol. 384, f. 104.

[79] P.R.O., C 115/K 2/6683, ff. 34v.–35, 43–44v.; cf. *Trans. B.G.A.S.* lxiii. 44–6.

[80] *Valor Eccl.* (Rec. Com.), ii. 498.

[81] *Eccl. Misc.* 68.

[82] G.D.R. vol. 285B (2), f. 1v.

[83] Hodgson, *Queen Anne's Bounty* (1845), p. cclxxv; G.D.R., V 5/GT 19–20.

[84] P.R.O., C 115/K 2/6684, f. 174v.

[85] Hockaday Abs. ccxxi; *Cal. Pat.* 1548–9, 40, 266.

[86] G.B.R., B 2/1, f. 237v.

[87] Hockaday Abs. ccxxi; *Trans. B.G.A.S.* xii. 80–1.

[88] G.B.R., B 3/2, pp. 293–4, 314.

[89] Ibid. p. 461; F 4/5, ff. 395–6.

[90] Glos. R.O., P 154/11/CW 2/2.

[91] *Glouc. Jnl.* 10 June 1847; cf. ibid. 7 Oct. 1854.

[92] Glos. R.O., G/GL 8A/6, ff. 57, 67, 126v., 130; *Glouc. Jnl.* 19 Apr. 1851.

[93] G.D.R., F 3/1–2.

[94] For papers of the soc., including *8th Rep. Glouc. Ch. Extension Soc.*, Glos. Colln. NV 5.23.

[95] *Citizen*, 17 Sept. 1956.

ALL SAINTS, lower Barton Street. Begun in 1874 and consecrated in 1875, it was built for the west part of St. James's parish. The cost was met by subscriptions and a benefaction from the family of Thomas Hedley, first perpetual curate of St. James.[96] In 1876 the church was assigned a district chapelry and the living, which was endowed with land in lower Barton Street,[97] became a vicarage (later sometimes called a perpetual curacy) in the gift of the bishop.[98] A vicarage house built on the glebe c. 1877[99] was replaced in the late 1950s by a new house in Derby Road.[1] The church, built of ashlar and designed by Sir George Gilbert Scott in a 14th-century style, comprised a chancel with north vestry rooms and south aisle (later a chapel) and an aisled and clerestoried nave with south porch.[2] In 1887 the north side of the chancel and the vestry rooms were altered to take the organ and a parish room or vestry was built to the north.[3]

All Saints took over from St. James the mission room in Millbrook Street, at the corner of the later Derby Road. The room was rebuilt on a larger scale with two storeys as the Alington Victoria Hall in 1904[4] and was leased to the city corporation for educational use in the 1960s.[5] It was demolished in the 1970s. In 1892 a mission church dedicated to the Good Shepherd was built nearby in Derby Road; the cost was borne by subscriptions and the site was given by Maria Evans. The church, a brick and timber building designed by Waller & Son, was sold in 1974 to a community of Ukrainian Catholics.[6]

CHRIST CHURCH, Brunswick Square. Begun in 1822 and consecrated in 1823,[7] it was built by the residents of the Spa. They subscribed £3,900, of which £3,200 was raised by issuing shares, to meet the cost of construction. The living, in the gift of five trustees appointed by the shareholders or proprietors, was endowed with the dividend from £300 stock and part of the pew rents.[8] It was called a perpetual curacy (later a vicarage)[9] and was worth £135 in 1856.[10] The church, which served an extraparochial area in South Hamlet and Littleworth,[11] was assigned a consolidated

chapelry in 1877, and in 1878 the Ecclesiastical Commissioners endowed it with £200 a year;[12] the patronage passed to the bishop.[13] The benefice was united with St. Luke in 1934[14] and with St. Mary de Crypt with St. John the Baptist in 1979.[15] There was no vicarage house for Christ Church in 1876[16] and the vicar's residence in the 1920s and until 1979 was a semidetached house in Montpellier.[17] The church, built of stuccoed brick and designed in a plain neo-classical style by Thomas Rickman and Henry Hutchinson,[18] comprised small chancel, nave, and west bell turret.[19] In 1865 the chancel was enlarged and a north vestry added. At a restoration in 1883 the division between chancel and nave was moved westwards and a low stone screen erected, and the west gallery was repositioned. In 1899 and 1900 the west end was remodelled, a new front in roughcast and vermilion terracotta being added, the ceiling was given a central barrel vault, and the chancel apse was enlarged.[20] In the apse three windows were fitted with memorial glass in 1908 and the walls and ceiling were decorated in 1911.[21] Elizabeth Waring by will proved 1918 left £400 for the church fabric.[22]

HOLY TRINITY, Longlevens. The church was begun in 1933 and consecrated in 1934.[23] Its origins were in a mission of Barnwood church which opened in Longlevens in 1873. The mission was supported by James Witcombe of Wellsprings, who in 1898 built and later endowed a corrugated iron church of Holy Trinity, south of Church Road.[24] In 1899 a conventional district was attached to that church, which was served by a curate of Barnwood.[25] In 1980 the building was used as a church hall. Plans for a permanent church had been adopted by 1932 when a district called Wotton St. Mary Without and centred on Longlevens was created,[26] and the living was made a perpetual curacy or vicarage in the gift of the bishop.[27] In 1939 a house in Cheltenham Road was the vicarage house[28] but later a house was built in Church Road. The church, designed by Harold Stratton-Davis in a 15th-century style, is built of brick with stone dressings and comprises a

[96] All Saints' Par. Memories (1925), 5–6, 20: Glos Colln. N 5.10; Glouc. Jnl. 6 Nov. 1875.
[97] Lond. Gaz. 26 May 1876, pp. 3166–7; 30 June 1876, p. 3734; 8 Dec. 1876, p. 6833.
[98] Kelly's Dir. Glos. (1879 and later edns.).
[99] All Saints' Memories, 7; Glos. R.O., P 154/1/IN 3/1; cf. O.S. Map 6", Glos. XXXIII. NE. (1891 edn.).
[1] Cf. O.S. Map 1/2,500, SO 8417 (1956 edn.).
[2] Glos. R.O., P 154/1/CW 3/1–2; Glouc. Jnl. 6 Nov. 1875.
[3] Glos. R.O., P 154/1/VE 3/8.
[4] Glouc. Jnl. 29 Oct. 1904; 15 July 1905.
[5] Glos. R.O., P 154/1/CW 3/6.
[6] Kelly's Dir. Glos. (1894), 166; Glouc. Jnl. 17 Dec. 1892; Glos. R.O., P 154/1/CW 3/3.
[7] Glos. R.O., P 154/3/IN 3/1.
[8] Ibid. SP 1/1, 3; G.D.R., V 5/GT 1.
[9] Hockaday Abs. ccxiii; Kelly's Dir. Glos. (1870), 551.
[10] G.D.R. vol. 384, f. 101.
[11] P.R.O., HO 129/336/4/5/5.
[12] Lond. Gaz. 30 Nov. 1877, pp. 6890–2; 10 May 1878, p. 2993.
[13] Cf. Kelly's Dir. Glos. (1870), 551; (1879), 653.
[14] Lond. Gaz. 27 Feb. 1934, pp. 1328–31; Glos. R.O., P

154/3/IN 1/4.
[15] Inf. from rector of St. Mary de Crypt.
[16] Glos. R.O., P 154/3/IN 3/1.
[17] Kelly's Dir. Glos. (1923), 180; inf. from rector.
[18] Glos. R.O., P 154/3/SP 1/2; Colvin, Biog. Dict. Brit. Architects, 690.
[19] Kelly's Dir. Glos. (1870), 551; for a photog. of W. end before 1899, Glos. Colln. 13220, f. 138.
[20] Glouc. Jnl. 14 Oct. 1865; 17 Nov. 1883; 31 Mar. 1900; photog. in vestry shows interior of E. end before 1899.
[21] Glos. R.O., P 154/3/VE 3/1.
[22] Ibid. CW 3/2.
[23] Kelly's Dir. Glos. (1935), 376.
[24] Glos. Colln. R 35.15; O.S. Map 6", Glos. XXV. SE. (1887 and 1902 edns.).
[25] Glos. Colln. JF 4.6, pp. 38–40; Kelly's Dir. Glos. (1919–31 edns.), s.v. Barnwood.
[26] Lond. Gaz. 12 Apr. 1932, pp. 2390–2; Glos. R.O., P 35/IN 3/7; from 1940 the par. included the north end of Churchdown, which later became a separate par.: Glos. R.O., P 84/IN 3/4; H. Oram, Churchdown 1904–54, 52.
[27] Kelly's Dir. Glos. (1935), 376–7.
[28] Ibid. (1939), 384.

chancel with north chapel and south vestry rooms and organ chamber and an aisled nave with east flèche.[29] The main west window and the north windows of the chapel incorporate fragments of ancient stained glass from St. Luke's church which had been collected by Samuel Lysons.[30]

From 1956 a mission to the Innsworth housing estate centred on a new temporary hall, dedicated to St. Francis, in Rookery Road.[31] The mission was later served from the church of St. John the Evangelist, Churchdown, and was ended in 1970.[32] The hall was demolished.

ST. ALDATE, Finlay Road. Begun in 1962 and consecrated in 1964,[33] it replaced a temporary mission church to the south, which was the church hall in 1980. The temporary church, which has timber walls, was dedicated in 1929 and was paid for from an anonymous donation. It was intended as a replacement for the 18th-century parish church of St. Aldate, the rector of which was licensed as curate-in-charge.[34] A parsonage house was built in Finlay Road in 1929.[35] In 1930 the church was given a district, formed out of the parishes of St. James, St. Paul, St. Mary de Lode, Barnwood, Hempsted, and Matson. The living, which was in the gift of the bishop,[36] was made a vicarage.[37] The permanent church, designed by Robert Potter, is built of concrete, faced externally with brick, and is trapezoidal in plan with a parabolic copper roof. It has a west porch surmounted by a skeletal spire.[38]

In 1937 a hall was built in Parry Road for a mission to a council housing estate. The hall, a brick building provided by A. J. Palmer of Fairford, was not used for services for long and in the 1960s was taken over by the city corporation.[39]

ST. BARNABAS, Tuffley. Begun in 1938 and consecrated in 1940,[40] it replaced a temporary church. A school-chapel built at Tuffley in 1874 was used for services by a mission from St. Mary de Lode church.[41] The mission, which from 1882 used the new Tuffley board school,[42] was conducted from 1883 by Whaddon church and from 1885 by St. Paul's church.[43] In 1907 the Gloucester Church Extension Society converted the former board school, west of the Stroud road, as a temporary mission church for a new conventional district.[44] In 1922 the society erected a temporary,

aisled timber and asbestos church of St. Barnabas to the west. A parsonage house was built in Reservoir Road in 1924.[45] The church was assigned a district in 1930[46] and the living became a perpetual curacy (later a vicarage) in the gift of the bishop.[47] In 1980 both temporary churches were used as church halls. The permanent church, on the other side of the road at the corner of Finlay Road, was designed by N. F. Cachemaille-Day,[48] and is built of reinforced concrete, faced externally with brick, and comprises east vestry rooms, chancel with north chapel and south aisle and tower, nave, and west porch. The short tower incorporates an organ loft and carries a crucifix.

In 1941 St. Barnabas's church began a mission to Lower Tuffley; it is treated under the church of St. George. In 1955 a temporary mission hall, dedicated to St. Michael, was built in Lower Tuffley at the corner of Seventh Avenue and Kemble Road. The hall, a Reema system building[49] of pebble-dashed brick, includes vestries and porches.

ST. CATHARINE, Wotton. Begun in 1912 and consecrated in 1915,[50] it was built in London Road by the Gloucester Church Extension Society to serve the reconstructed parish of St. Catharine in place of the church in Priory Road;[51] the cost was met by grants and voluntary contributions.[52] The vicarage house of the original parish was replaced in 1961 by a house at the corner of Denmark and Heathville Roads.[53] The church, built of ashlar and designed by Walter B. Wood in a 14th-century style, has a sanctuary, a chancel with flèche, north vestry rooms and organ chamber, and south chapel, an aisled nave with north and south transeptal bays, and a west porch.[54] By 1980 many fittings brought from the Priory Road church had been replaced but the font and some glass in the chapel and south aisle remained.[55]

ST. GEORGE, Lower Tuffley. The church was built and consecrated in 1956. It had its origins in a mission from St. Barnabas's church begun in 1941. In 1942 Whaddon church hall, a wooden building given to the mission by Mrs. A. M. Jeune of Whaddon, was moved to Grange Road and dedicated to St. George. A temporary church was erected there in 1947 and a conventional district was attached to it in 1948.[56] The per-

[29] *Glouc. Jnl.* 18 Mar. 1933; Verey, *Glos.* ii. 37, 291.
[30] *Glouc. Jnl.* 10 Mar., 7 Apr. 1934; cf. *Trans. B.G.A.S.* xlvii. 321–2.
[31] *Citizen*, 23 Feb. 1956; *Glos. Echo*, 23 Feb. 1956.
[32] Glos. R.O., P 84/2/IN 1/13; cf. *Glouc. Dioc. Year Bk.* (1960–1 and later edns.).
[33] Glos. Colln. N 5.57; NQ 5.8.
[34] *Glouc. Jnl.* 19 Jan. 1929; *Kelly's Dir. Glos.* (1931), 178.
[35] Inf. from vicar.
[36] *Lond. Gaz.* 30 Dec. 1930, pp. 8361–2.
[37] *Kelly's Dir. Glos.* (1939), 181; *Glouc. Dioc. Year Bk.* (1980), 16–17.
[38] Glos. Colln. N 5.57; NQ 5.8.
[39] *Glouc. Jnl.* 16 Oct. 1937; inf. from vicar.
[40] *Glouc. Jnl.* 29 Oct. 1938; 5 Oct. 1940.
[41] Ibid. 26 Dec. 1874; *Kelly's Dir. Glos.* (1879), 772.
[42] *Kelly's Dir. Glos.* (1889), 927.
[43] *Lond. Gaz.* 7 July 1876, pp. 3884–6; 28 Aug. 1885, pp.

4059–61; Glos. R.O., P 361/IN 1/6; Glos. Colln. JF 4.6, p. 17.
[44] Glos. R.O., P 154/19/VE 3/1; Glos. Colln. NV 5.23; O.S. Map 6″, Glos. XXXIII. NE. (1891 edn.).
[45] Glos. R.O., P 154/19/VE 3/2–3; G.D.R., V 6/97.
[46] *Lond. Gaz.* 20 May 1930, pp. 3147–9.
[47] *Kelly's Dir. Glos.* (1931), 180; *Glouc. Dioc. Year Bk.* (1980), 16–17.
[48] Verey, *Glos.* ii. 230.   [49] Inf. from vicar.
[50] *8th Rep. Glouc. Ch. Ext. Soc.*
[51] Kelly's Dir. Glos. (1919), 168; Glos. Colln. JF 4.7, p. 14.   [52] Glos. R.O., GEC 15.
[53] O.S. Map 1/2,500, SO 8318 (1955 edn.); inf. from Mr. F.G. Norman, of Elmbridge Road, a churchwarden.
[54] *Glouc. Jnl.* 26 June 1915: the plans included a SW. tower and spire.
[55] Cf. faculty 29 Dec. 1914, in possession of vicar.
[56] Glos. R.O., P 154/19/VE 3/9–10; Glos. Colln. NQ 9.23.

manent church was assigned a parish in 1967[57] and the living became a vicarage in the gift of the bishop.[58] The vicarage house in Grange Road had been built in 1954. The church, which is built of brick, was designed as a church hall. It was altered in 1970 and 1971 when several rooms, including a hall, were added to the north-east to create a centre for groups involved in church life. The church was enlarged and reoriented in 1981. In the late 1970s two houses were built to the west for clergy.[59]

ST. JAMES, Upton Street. The church, which was begun in 1837 and consecrated in 1841,[60] originated in a plan of 1835 for a chapel of ease to St. Michael's church in the working-class suburb growing up at Barton End but was built by subscription for the whole lower Barton Street area. The funds raised, including a grant from the Incorporated Church Building Society, were insufficient and so the Diocesan Church Building Association paid for the completion of the building.[61] The Revd. S. W. Warneford was a benefactor to the new church.[62] In 1842 the church was given an extensive district south-east of the city.[63] The living, a perpetual curacy (later a vicarage) in the gift of the bishop,[64] was awarded £200 by Queen Anne's Bounty in 1855 to meet benefactions worth £1,300,[65] and the augmentation raised the value of the living to £150.[66] Moses Binning, the principal benefactor of the church, provided a house[67] and in 1856 £2,000 in stock for the incumbent.[68] The house, built in Upton Street in 1854,[69] was demolished in the early 1980s when a new vicarage and other houses were built on the site. The church, built of ashlar and designed by Sampson Kempthorne, son of the rector of St. Michael, in a late 13th-century style, was a single-cell building with north gallery, porch, and bell-cot.[70] A chancel with east vestry and an east aisle with a wooden arcade of four bays were added in 1879.[71] In 1979 the gallery was enlarged and rooms created underneath.

In 1850 John Emeris, perpetual curate of St. James, built a chapel for a mission to Tredworth. The chapel was not open for long, and from 1867 the mission occupied a former Wesleyan chapel in High Street.[72] Anglicans held services there until the mid 20th century.[73] In 1869 a room was built for a school and a mission to the Millbrook Street area. The room, named after Emeris's curate John Alington, was enlarged in 1875 and was in that part of the parish transferred to All Saints' church.[74]

ST. LUKE, High Orchard. The church, which was on the north side of St. Luke's Street,[75] was begun in 1838 and consecrated in 1841. The plan for a church for the area adjoining the docks originated with the Diocesan Church Building Association, which in 1837 handed the project over to Samuel Lysons of Hempsted Court. Lysons, who built and endowed the church at his own expense,[76] became the first minister or perpetual curate.[77] He transferred the patronage to the bishop in 1866.[78] Because of the claims of Christ Church, St. Luke's church, which was in the extraparochial area of South Hamlet,[79] was not assigned a consolidated chapelry until 1868, when one including parts of St. Mary de Lode, St. Michael, Hempsted, and Upton St. Leonards was formed. The living was endowed by the Ecclesiastical Commissioners with £216 a year[80] and became a vicarage worth £250 in 1870.[81] Under a Scheme of 1879 it also received £150 from Silvanus Lysons's charity for the rector of Hempsted.[82] A house in Spa Road was the vicarage house from 1871 to 1898[83] when it was replaced by a new house at the corner of Seymour and Frampton Roads. That house was assigned to the parish of St. Luke the Less in 1909.[84] The church, which was hemmed in by engineering works in the early 20th century,[85] was closed in 1934 and the benefice united with Christ Church.[86] The church, which was built of brick with stone dressings, was designed by Thomas Fulljames in a 13th-century style with sanctuary and nave with south porch and west gallery, vestry, and bellcot.[87] Alterations in the 1870s included a new vestry added to the south-eastern corner in 1874.[88] The church was demolished soon after closure.[89]

In 1884 a corrugated iron room was built for a mission from St. Luke's church to Bristol Road.[90] In 1895 a committee was formed to build a church in the south part of the parish and a site was

[57] *Lond. Gaz.* 3 Aug. 1967, p. 8537.
[58] *Glouc. Dioc. Year Bk.* (1980), 16–17.
[59] Inf. from vicar and Mr. B. C. Frith, of Tuffley.
[60] *Glouc. Jnl.* 6 May 1837; 24 Apr. 1841.
[61] Glos. R.O., P 154/8/SP 1; D 936/A 36.
[62] *Glouc. Jnl.* 24 Apr. 1841.
[63] Glos. R.O., P 154/8/IN 3/1.
[64] Hockaday Abs. ccxv.
[65] Hodgson, *Queen Anne's Bounty* (suppl. 1864), pp. xxxii, lxv.
[66] G.D.R. vol. 384, f. 102.   [67] *Glouc. Jnl.* 13 Oct. 1866.
[68] Hodgson, *Queen Anne's Bounty* (suppl. 1864), p. lxxxv; Glos. R.O., P 154/8/IN 3/4.
[69] Glos. R.O., P 154/8/IN 3/3; O.S. Map 1/2,500, Glos. XXXIII. 3 (1902 edn.).
[70] Glos. R.O., P 154/8/SP 1–2; *Glouc. Jnl.* 24 Apr. 1841.
[71] Glos. R.O., P 154/8/VE 2/1; *Glouc. Jnl.* 10 Apr. 1880.
[72] *Glouc. Jnl.* 13 Oct. 1866; 19 Jan. 1867; Glos. R.O., P 154/8/CW 3/6.
[73] Glos. R.O., P 154/8/VE 3/7.
[74] *Glouc. Jnl.* 29 Oct. 1904; *All Saints' Memories*, 11, 18.

[75] O.S. Map 1/2,500, Glos. XXXIII. 2 (1886 edn.).
[76] G.D.R., F 3/1; *Glouc. Jnl.* 24 Apr. 1841.
[77] Hockaday Abs. ccxv.
[78] *Glos. N. & Q.* ii. 515.
[79] Glos. R.O., P 154/3/SP 3/7, 9; P.R.O., HO 129/336/4/5/6.
[80] *Lond. Gaz.* 10 July 1868, pp. 3867–9; 30 Mar. 1869, p. 2012.
[81] *Kelly's Dir. Glos.* (1870), 551.
[82] Glos. R.O., P 173/CH 4/1.
[83] G.D.R., F 4/6/13.
[84] *Hist. of St. Stephen's Ch.* (1930), 26: Glos. Colln. N 5.48; cf. Glos. Colln. JF 4.7, p. 12.
[85] Cf. O.S. Map 1/2,500, Glos. XXXIII. 2 (1902 and 1923 edns.).
[86] *Lond. Gaz.* 27 Feb. 1934, pp. 1328–31.
[87] Glos. R.O., P 154/22/IN 3/1; photog. of ch. 1899, in Glos. Colln. NQ 5.5.
[88] Glos. R.O., P 154/22/VE 2/1; O.S. Map 1/2,500, Glos. XXXIII. 2 (1886 edn.).
[89] *Glouc. Jnl.* 10 Mar. 1934.
[90] Ibid. 6 Dec. 1884.

acquired in Bristol Road. In 1896 a saw mill in Linden Road, next to the site of the proposed church, was converted as a mission hall, and the mission room was sold. The hall was used for services until 1900 when the new church of St. Luke the Less was consecrated.[91] The church is treated below as St. Stephen, its later dedication.

ST. MARK, Kingsholm. The church, begun in 1846 and consecrated in 1847, was built by the Diocesan Church Building Association; the cost was borne by grants from church building funds and voluntary contributions, including a gift from the Revd. S. W. Warneford.[92] The church served a district created out of the parishes of St. Catherine, St. John the Baptist, and St. Mary de Lode in 1846. The benefice, a perpetual curacy (later a vicarage) to which the bishop nominated,[93] was awarded £200 by Queen Anne's Bounty in 1852 to meet benefactions worth £500 from the bishop and Warneford's trustees.[94] It was valued at £150 in 1856 and had a glebe house by then.[95] A villa in London Road was the vicarage from the early 1880s[96] and until 1932. In 1952 a semidetached house in Tewkesbury Road became the vicarage house.[97] The church is built of coursed ashlar and was designed by Francis Niblett in a 13th-century style with chancel with north vestry and south chapel, aisled and clerestoried nave, and south-west tower and spire.[98] The vestry was enlarged and a room added to the east in 1888, when the body of the church was restored, and the chancel was enlarged and heightened in 1890.[99] The church plate includes a chalice and paten cover of c. 1575.[1]

ST. MATTHEW, Twigworth. Begun in 1841 and consecrated in 1842, it was built for Longford and Twigworth by the Diocesan Church Building Association; the site was given by Brasenose College, Oxford, and the principal lessee of the college's estate there, Walter Hayward de Winton, and the building costs were borne by grants and voluntary contributions, including a gift from the Revd. S. W. Warneford.[2] In 1842 the bishop nominated a perpetual curate,[3] but the church was not assigned a district until 1844,[4] when one was formed from parts of the parishes of St. Catherine

and St. Mary de Lode, and was not licensed for marriages until 1846.[5] The living, later a vicarage, remained in the gift of the bishop[6] and was united with Down Hatherley in 1941 under an Order in Council of 1922.[7] In 1980 the patronage of the united benefice, a rectory, belonged to the Lord Chancellor.[8] The living of Twigworth was worth £70 in 1856.[9] A house, built south of the church in 1858,[10] was replaced as the vicarage c. 1970 by a new bungalow to the east. The church, which is built of lias and in a 13th-century style, originally comprised chancel with north vestry and nave[11] and was designed by Thomas Fulljames.[12] A west tower and spire were added in 1844 at the cost of Benjamin Saunders Claxson, the incumbent,[13] and a north aisle in 1860.[14] In 1890, when the church was restored by Waller & Son, the chancel, vestry, and east walls of nave and aisle were taken down, the chancel was rebuilt on a larger scale, the aisle was extended eastwards to house an organ chamber and vestry, and a north porch was added.[15]

ST. OSWALD, Coney Hill. Begun in 1938 and consecrated in 1939,[16] it replaced a wooden mission church served from Barnwood church. The mission church of St. Oswald, which was opened in 1932, had a conventional district[17] and was assigned a parish in 1935.[18] The patronage of the living, a vicarage, was exercised by the Crown and the bishop alternately[19] but in 1980 belonged solely to the Crown.[20] A vicarage house was built in Coney Hill Road in the mid 1930s.[21] The permanent church, designed by W. E. Ellery Anderson, is built of brick and has a chancel with north chapel and south vestry rooms and an aisled and clerestoried nave with south tower with porch.[22]

ST. PAUL, Stroud Road. The church, begun in 1882 and consecrated in 1883, was built to relieve pressure on the churches of St. James and St. Luke and as a memorial to Robert Raikes on the centenary in 1880 of the Sunday School movement.[23] The cost of building was borne by a grant from the Incorporated Church Building Society and subscriptions, including a large gift from D. H. D. Burr.[24] In 1884 the church was assigned

[91] Hist. of St. Stephen's Ch. 24–7; Glos. Colln. NQ 5.5; (H) E 3.43, 53.
[92] Hist. of St. Mark's Ch. (1947), 7–13: Glos. Colln. NQ 5.6; G.D.R., F 3/1–2; Glos. Colln. NR 5.1.
[93] Lond. Gaz. 10 Feb. 1846, pp. 487–90; Hockaday Abs. ccxv; Kelly's Dir. Glos. (1870), 551.
[94] Hodgson, Queen Anne's Bounty (suppl. 1864), pp. xxvii, lxv.   [95] G.D.R. vol. 384, f. 103.
[96] Glos. R.O., D 2593, private, no. 2 Newland Villas, Glouc.
[97] Inf. from vicar.
[98] Builder, v. 457; Kelly's Dir. Glos. (1879), 653; above, Plate 53.
[99] Glouc. Jnl. 29 Sept. 1888; 24 Jan. 1891.
[1] Glos. Ch. Plate, 100.
[2] G.D.R., F 3/1; Glouc. Jnl. 8 Oct. 1842.
[3] Hockaday Abs. ccclxxxi.
[4] Census, 1871; in 1843 the ch. was described as a district ch. without ch. rates: churchwardens' acct. bk. 1843–1900, in possession of rector.
[5] Glos. R.O., P 342/IN 2/1.
[6] Kelly's Dir. Glos. (1856 and later edns.).
[7] Glos. R.O., P 342/MI 3; Lond. Gaz. 20 June 1922, pp. 4625–6.
[8] Glouc. Dioc. Year Bk. (1980), 20–1.
[9] G.D.R. vol. 384, f. 204.
[10] O.S. Map 6", Glos. XXV. NE. (1883 edn.); date on ho.
[11] Glouc. Jnl. 31 Jan. 1891; cf. Glos. R.O., P 342/CW 3/2–3.
[12] G.D.R., F 3/1.
[13] Inscr. on tower; Kelly's Dir. Glos. (1885), 608.
[14] Glouc. Jnl. 27 Oct. 1860.
[15] Glos. R.O., P 342/CW 3/3; Glouc. Jnl. 31 Jan. 1891.
[16] Glouc. Jnl. 16 July 1938; 22 July 1939.
[17] Ibid. 24 Dec. 1932; Glos. R.O., P 154/20/SP 1.
[18] Lond. Gaz. 31 Dec. 1935, pp. 8377–9.
[19] Kelly's Dir. Glos. (1939), 183.
[20] Glouc. Dioc. Year Bk. (1980), 16–17.
[21] Glos. R.O., P 154/20/SP 1; VE 2/1.
[22] Glouc. Jnl. 22 July 1939.
[23] Ibid. 15 Apr. 1882; 6 Oct. 1883.
[24] Glos. Colln. NV 5.1; inscr. in ch.

a consolidated chapelry which was enlarged by the addition of the north part of Tuffley in 1885.[25] The living was a vicarage (sometimes called a perpetual curacy) in the gift of the bishop. A house, which had been built in Stroud Road opposite the church by 1894,[26] was replaced as the vicarage before 1955 by one in King Edward's Avenue.[27] The church, which is built of lime-stone, was designed by Capel N. Tripp in an Early English style but was unfinished at its consecration. It had sanctuary with north vestry, undivided aisled and clerestoried chancel and nave with east bellcot, the first stage of a south tower, short transeptal outer aisles, and temporary west front.[28] A second north vestry was built in 1931. In 1939 the west end of the church was completed and the east end restored to designs of W. E. Ellery Anderson; the cost was largely met by a bequest of Sarah Critchley. The nave and aisles were extended westwards by a bay, a west porch was added, and a west gallery of stone built in the nave.[29] In the churchyard a stone pulpit with crucifix was erected as a memorial for the First World War.[30]

ST. STEPHEN (formerly St. Luke the Less), Bristol Road. Begun in 1898 and consecrated in 1900, it was built for the south end of St. Luke's parish;[31] the cost was met by subscriptions.[32] It was assigned a consolidated chapelry in 1909,[33] and the living was a vicarage (sometimes called a perpetual curacy) in the gift of the bishop.[34] The vicarage house of St. Luke's parish was assigned to the new parish.[35] The church, which is built of brick with stone dressings, was designed by Walter Planck in late Gothic style but remained incomplete for some time. It originally had a chancel with north vestry rooms and organ chamber and south chapel and an aisled and clerestoried nave[36] with temporary west front. The church was finished between 1928 and 1930 to a modified plan by H. A. Dancey; the cost was borne by subscription and a grant from the Revd. S. W. Warneford's charity. The nave and aisles were extended westwards by two bays, and a bellcot and west front incorporating two porches and polygonal baptistery were added. The church was then dedicated to St. Stephen but the name of the parish remained St. Luke the Less.[37]

NON-PAROCHIAL CHAPELS. Gloucester castle and the hospitals of St. Bartholomew, St. Margaret, and St. Mary Magdalen contained chapels which are treated elsewhere. St. Margaret's and St. Mary's chapels, which were also attended by residents near the respective hospitals, were sometimes described as parish churches.[38] The chapel of St. Bridget, mentioned c. 1220, was within Gloucester Abbey's precinct.[39] The chapel of St. Martin was dependent on St. Michael's church, with which it is treated above.

The chapel of St. Kyneburgh, inside the town wall at the south gate,[40] commemorated a local saint said to have been drowned in a well.[41] It possibly had a parish on both sides of the wall until Walter of Gloucester gave it to St. Owen's church in the late 11th century or early 12th. The chapel later became part of the endowment of Llanthony Priory[42] and was dedicated in 1147 following a rebuilding. In the early 13th century Maud de Bohun confirmed to the priory a rent of 12d. from a fulling mill in Wheatenhurst to maintain a light in the chapel. The rent was remitted in 1272 to Humphrey de Bohun, earl of Hereford and Essex.[43] In 1389 an anchorite was enclosed in a house next to the chapel. St. Kyneburgh's relics, which were moved to the priory church later that year, were replaced in the chapel in 1390.[44] The priory retained the chapel until the Dissolution.[45] Part of it had been demolished by 1543 when the Crown sold the site and an adjoining cottage to Thomas Bell.[46] He built an almshouse on the eastern end of the site next to the cottage, presumably the anchorite's dwelling, which housed a sixth almsman. The body of the chapel, used by the almsmen for prayers, was acquired in 1671 by the cordwainers' company for its hall. The chapel's bell chamber, called the steeple, was a dovecot in 1559.[47] The surviving parts of the former chapel were removed c. 1816 to make room for an extension of the city gaol,[48] which was demolished with the almshouse in the early 1860s.[49]

The chapel of St. Thomas, outside the outer north gate on the north side of the road, was mentioned in the late 12th or early 13th century[50] and was rebuilt in 1454 by Philip Monger and his wife Joan.[51] It was a chantry chapel, possibly that in which in 1324 the rector of St. John agreed to celebrate three days a week for Gloucester

[25] Lond. Gaz. 18 Apr. 1884, pp. 1760–2; 28 Aug. 1885, pp. 4059–61.
[26] Kelly's Dir. Glos. (1885 and later edns.); O.S. Map 1/2,500, Glos. XXXIII. 3 (1902 edn.).
[27] O.S. Map 1/2,500, SO 8317 (1970 edn.).
[28] Glouc. Jnl. 6 Oct. 1883.
[29] Ibid. 25 Feb. 1939; Verey, Glos. ii. 237.
[30] Glos. Colln. N 5.46.
[31] Glouc. Jnl. 20 Oct. 1900; Kelly's Dir. Glos. (1902), 171.   [32] Glos. Colln. (H) E 3.53.
[33] Lond. Gaz. 22 Oct. 1909, pp. 7755–6.
[34] Kelly's Dir. Glos. (1914 and later edns.).
[35] Glos. Colln. JF 4.7, p. 12.
[36] Glouc. Jnl. 20 Oct. 1900; Glos. Colln. (H) E 3.53.
[37] Glos. Colln. NR 5.13, 17; Glouc. Jnl. 19, 26 Apr. 1930.
[38] Above, Glouc. Castle; below, Char. for Poor.
[39] Hist. & Cart. Mon. Glouc. i. 25, 83; cf. Glouc. Cath. Libr., Reg. Abb. Froucester B, p. 463.
[40] Glouc. Rental, 1455, 19.
[41] Hist. & Cart. Mon. Glouc. i, pp. lxvi–lxviii.
[42] Camd. Misc. xxii, pp. 17, 37 and n., 38; cf. above, A.-S. Glouc.
[43] Trans. B.G.A.S. lxiii. 14, 53–4; P.R.O., C 115/K 2/6683, ff. 31v.–32; cf. V.C.H. Glos. x. 295.
[44] P.R.O., C 115/K 2/6684, ff. 132–5; Cal. Pat. 1388–92, 285.
[45] Valor Eccl. (Rec. Com.), ii. 430.
[46] L. & P. Hen. VIII, xviii (2), p. 107.
[47] G.D.R. wills 1566/150; Rudder, Glos. 203–4; cf. Atkyns, Glos. plate at pp. 82–3, detail reproduced above, Fig. 5; below, Char. for Poor.
[48] G.B.R., B 3/13, f. 177v.; F 4/15, pp. 351, 539; G 3/AG 1; cf. Cole, Map of Glouc. (1805).
[49] G.B.R., B 4/1/8, p. 21.
[50] Glouc. Cath. Libr., Reg. Abb. Froucester B, p. 256.
[51] Glouc. Rental, 1455, 99.

Abbey,[52] and in 1576 the Crown granted the building to John and William Marsh.[53]

A church of St. Thomas the Apostle was recorded before 1179.[54] The chapel of St. Thomas the Martyr, which figured in a dispute between Gloucester Abbey and St. Oswald's Priory settled in 1222,[55] was beyond the blind gate, by the road to Kingsholm. It was held by John Tuck under lease from the priory at the Dissolution.[56] The chapel was later used as a house and in 1603 John Wight granted a long lease of it to John Baugh, who converted it as four dwellings and by will proved 1621 left it for an almshouse.[57] The building, which stood on the south side of the Twyver and was known later as Chapel House, was demolished before 1692, probably at the siege of 1643.[58] A new house was built on the site in the early 18th century.[59]

There was a chapel at Kingsholm by 1216 and the Crown had granted St. Oswald's Priory 48 a. at Innsworth to support a chantry priest in it.[60] The chapel, which was at the king's hall, was dedicated to St. Nicholas and was held by the priory in 1221 of the gift of the Crown.[61] In 1228 an anchoress was enclosed there.[62] Later the hall became the Kingsholm manor house and the chapel fell into ruins. The priory, which in 1336 sought to rebuild it on a smaller scale, withdrew the chantry and in 1366 a licence for rebuilding was granted.[63] Nevertheless the chapel was in ruins in 1394 when the priory was given leave to move the chantry to an altar in the priory church.[64]

A chaplain held land in Twigworth before 1216[65] and a chapel was recorded there in 1289. The chapel, which was probably dependent on St. Oswald's church,[66] was apparently in use in the mid 16th century.[67]

A chapel of St. Mary had presumably been built at Saintbridge by 1506 when Garet van Eck left 10s. to the hermit living there.[68] The chapel or hermitage stood a little way north of the Sud brook in St. Mary de Lode parish[69] and at least one of its hermits was buried in the parish church.[70] In 1531 Gloucester Abbey granted a lease of the chapel to the vicar of St. Mary de Lode[71] and in 1546 the Crown sold it to Robert Thornhill and Leonard Warcop.[72] It was later a house and was demolished in the 1920s.[73]

The mariners' chapel, in Gloucester docks, was begun in 1848 and opened in 1849.[74] The cost of building was met by subscriptions and private benefactions[75] and of maintenance by voluntary contributions.[76] The chaplaincy was in the gift of the committee managing the chapel's funds until 1858 when trustees were appointed. The Church Pastoral Aid Society granted £75 a year towards the chaplain's stipend on condition that the same amount was raised locally, but in 1909 the society's grant was only £60 a year.[77] The chapel, built of stone and designed by John Jacques in a 13th-century style,[78] is a single-cell building with east bellcot. When opened it was in the extra-parochial area of South Hamlet and was attended also by people living near the docks for Sunday services[79] and for baptisms.[80] In 1980 services were conducted on Sunday evenings and the first Sunday morning of each month.[81]

ROMAN CATHOLICISM

IN[82] 1577 William Meredith, who lived in the cathedral precincts, was suspected of supporting and visiting Roman Catholics abroad. Of the handful of other Gloucester people described as recusant in 1577[83] Thomas Alfield, the most notable, had visited the English seminary at Douai in 1576[84] and Lewis Vaughan, the wealthiest, was removed in 1581 from the post of physician to St. Bartholomew's Hospital for being a Roman Catholic.[85] Alfield, son of a former master of the

---

[52] Glouc. Cath. Libr., Reg. Abb. Froucester A, f. 86 and v.

[53] P.R.O., C 66/1138, m. 17.

[54] Glouc. Cath. Libr., deeds and seals, iv, ff. 7, 9: both charters are endorsed 'Kingsholm'.

[55] Hist. & Cart. Mon. Glouc. i. 83.

[56] Glouc. Rental, 1455, p. xvi; P.R.O., SC 6/Hen. VIII/1212, rot. 5.

[57] G.B.R., J 1/1952B; G.D.R. wills 1621/53; below, Char. for Poor.

[58] G.B.R., J 3/6, f. 152v. Rudder, Glos. 205, following Furney (Glos. R.O., D 327, p. 147) confuses it with St. Thomas's chapel outside the outer north gate.

[59] G.B.R., J 4/1 (no.1); cf. ibid. J 3/8, ff. 82–83v.

[60] Cal. Pat. 1258–66, 622.   [61] Bk. of Fees, i. 377; ii. 1339.

[62] Close R. 1227–31, 31.

[63] Cal. Pat. 1334–8, 286; 1364–7, 285, 305.

[64] Ibid. 1391–6, 505.

[65] Rot. Litt. Claus. (Rec. Com.), i. 282.

[66] Trans. B.G.A.S. xliii. 110.

[67] G.D.R. vol. 89, deposition of John Parsons 8 Apr. 1603.

[68] Hockaday Abs. ccxvi.

[69] Cf. Glos. Colln. prints GL 65.27; Glos. R.O., Q/RI 70 (map P, no. 136).

[70] Fosbrooke, Glouc. 172; Gent. Mag. xcvi (2), 505.

[71] Glouc. Cath. Libr., Reg. Abb. Malvern, ii, f. 42v.; Hockaday Abs. xxv, 1532 subsidy, f. 28.

[72] L. & P. Hen. VIII, xxi (1), pp. 578–9.

[73] Glos. R.O., GMS 127.

[74] W.H. Whalley, Mariners' Chap. (1909), 18–19.

[75] P.R.O., HO 129/336/4/5/7.

[76] Kelly's Dir. Glos. (1870), 551.

[77] Whalley, Mariners' Chap. 16–19, 26–7.

[78] Glos. Chron. 17 Feb. 1849; Verey, Glos. ii. 230.

[79] P.R.O., HO 129/336/4/5/7.

[80] Glos. R.O., P 154/23/IN 1/1–2.

[81] Inf. from chaplain.

[82] This article was written in 1981.

[83] Trans. B.G.A.S. v. 233–4, 236.

[84] Ibid. lxxxviii. 15–16.

[85] G.B.R., B 3/1, f. 73.

College school, returned in 1580 to the seminary, by then at Rheims, with his relative Thomas Evans. Alfield, whose brother Robert was servant to the Jesuit Robert Parsons, became a priest in 1581 and joined the mission to England. In the latter part of 1583 he was sheltered at Hasfield Court by John Pauncefoot, and he also visited the Gloucester area in 1584. In 1585 he was convicted of importing and distributing seditious books and was hanged at Tyburn. His accomplice Thomas Webley of London came from a Gloucester family.[86] In the mid 1580s two Roman Catholic priests arrested in Gloucestershire were hanged, drawn, and quartered in Gloucester. William Lampley, a Gloucester glover, apparently met a similar end in 1588 for proselytizing some relatives.[87]

In the late 16th and early 17th century Catholic recusancy in Gloucester almost, if not completely, disappeared[88] and in 1676 there was said to be one papist in the city.[89] James II sent a priest to the city[90] but the mission gained few converts. One was Alderman John Hill, who became mayor in 1686. He opened a chapel in the Tolsey,[91] which James attended on his visit to Gloucester in 1687.[92] Other adherents were Anselm Fowler, who succeeded Hill as mayor in 1688, and John Wagstaffe, a former mayor, to whom James entrusted the protection of the priest and his chapel later that year.[93] In the turmoil in the city following William of Orange's invasion the chapel was ransacked, the priest was imprisoned for a time, and Catholic houses, including that of Sir William Compton at nearby Hartpury, were attacked.[94] The mission was ended by those events in 1688, and in 1735 only two papists were recorded at Gloucester.[95]

Mary Webb (d. 1787), daughter of Sir John Webb of Hatherop, left 1,000 guineas to found a mission to the city, and a priest arrived there in late 1788 or early 1789.[96] Tradition states that in the early 1790s mass was said in a house in Berkeley Street used for a Catholic school. From 1790 the mission was undertaken by John Greenway (d. 1800), who bought a house in the later London Road and built a small brick chapel behind it. The chapel was registered in 1792 and had a congregation of 40 in 1813.[97] The mission had close links with a convent established at Hartpury in the mid 1790s, and Robert Canning, who became lord of the manor of Hartpury in the

early 19th century, was the mission's principal benefactor.[98] In 1851 the chapel, which was dedicated to St. Peter ad Vincula, had morning and evening congregations of 110 and 130 respectively.[99] In 1857 Frances Canning gave £1,000 for building a larger church and in 1859 the chapel was demolished and the new church, which was not oriented, was erected in an early 14th-century style to a design by Gilbert Blount. It was not completed until after 1867 when the presbytery was pulled down and the aisled and clerestoried nave was extended southwards by two bays to the street and a south-west tower and spire were built. A new presbytery was built in 1880.[1] On a Sunday in 1881 St. Peter's church had morning and evening congregations of 192 and 248 respectively.[2] From the late 1920s the number of Roman Catholics in the Gloucester area increased, and in the mid 20th century mass centres were established in Brockworth, Churchdown, Matson, and Tuffley.[3] St. Peter's church continued as the parish church for much of the city and the area to the south and west in 1981 when Sunday masses were attended by as many as 1750 people.[4]

In 1862 the Institute of the Blessed Virgin Mary opened a convent school in London Road.[5] It was at Greyfriars in 1870[6] and has not been traced after 1871.[7] In 1940 the Poor Servants of the Mother of God opened a convent in Barnwood Road. They moved it in 1946 or 1947 to a house in Denmark Road. The convent, dedicated to St. Michael, performed educational work in 1981.[8]

At Tuffley mass was said regularly from 1943, at first in a public house and then in an hotel in Southfield Road. In 1946 a hut was purchased and erected elsewhere in Southfield Road for use as a chapel. The chapel, dedicated to the English Martyrs, opened in 1947[9] and was replaced by another building opened there in 1966. In 1968 a mass centre was established at Lower Tuffley,[10] which became the focus for Catholic worship in the south part of the parish. In 1980, when mass was said in the Anglican church of St. George, a chapel was built in Tuffley Lane.[11] The Southfield Road chapel, which it replaced, was sold and demolished. The Tuffley Lane chapel, designed as a hall, was served by a priest from St. Peter's church and had a congregation of 200 in 1981.[12]

Mass was celebrated regularly from 1952 in a temporary building on a new housing estate at

[86] *Trans. B.G.A.S.* lxxxviii. 15–17; *Downside Rev.* xxviii. 19–40.
[87] *Trans. B.G.A.S.* lxxxviii. 21–2; *Eng. Martyrs 1584–1603* (Cath. Rec. Soc. v), 140–2.   [88] Cf. *Eccl. Misc.* 68–9.
[89] *Compton Census*, ed. Whiteman, 533–4.
[90] *Eng. Dominican Rec.* (Cath. Rec. Soc. xxv), 129 and n., 174.
[91] Ripley, 'Glouc. 1660–1740', 150, 187; Bodl. MS. Top. Glouc. c. 3, f. 40.
[92] G.B.R., B 3/6, f. 159v.; F 4/7, pp. 426–7; a room in the Tolsey was known later as the masshouse: ibid. B 3/8, p. 362.
[93] Ripley, 'Glouc. 1660–1740', 188–90, 325; *Cal. S.P. Dom.* 1687–9, p. 342.
[94] *Glouc. Jnl.* 3 Sept. 1881; above, Glouc. 1660–1720, city govt. and politics; for Sir Wm. Compton, Burke, *Ext. & Dorm. Baronetcies* (1838), 124.
[95] G.D.R. vol. 285B (1), f. 25.
[96] Glos. R.O., D 5143/1; for the Webbs, *V.C.H. Glos.* vii. 89, 95.

[97] J. N. Langston, 'Cath. Mission in Glouc.' (1955–7, 4 vols. in Glos. Colln. 31841); G.B.R., G 3/SR, Trin 1792.
[98] Glos. R.O., D 5143/1; PA 165/2; Langston, 'Cath. Mission in Glouc.'
[99] P.R.O., HO 129/336/3/4/9.
[1] Langston, 'Cath. Mission in Glouc.'
[2] *Glouc. Jnl.* 19 Nov. 1881.
[3] Langston, 'Cath. Mission in Glouc.'
[4] Inf. from par. priest.
[5] Langston, 'Cath. Mission in Glouc.'
[6] *Kelly's Dir. Glos.* (1870), 564.
[7] *Census*, 1871.
[8] Langston, 'Cath. Mission in Glouc.'; cf. G.R.O. (General Register Office), Worship Reg. no. 65362.
[9] Langston, 'Cath. Mission in Glouc.'
[10] *Centenary Souvenir Handbook of St. Peter's Ch. Glouc.* (1968), 33: Glos. Colln. NQ 5.16.
[11] Inf. from Mr. B. C. Frith, of Tuffley, Glouc.
[12] Inf. from par. priest; *Citizen*, 5 Jan. 1980.

Matson. Later a community centre was used for worship[13] and then a public house.[14] In 1961 work began on a church in Matson Lane. The church, dedicated to St. Augustine, opened in 1962 and was given a parish.[15] In 1981 the average congregation was 250.[16]

From 1953 St. Peter's church also held mass according to the Eastern Rite for Ukrainian Catholics in Gloucester.[17] In 1974 they bought the church of the Good Shepherd, in Derby Road, from the Church of England[18] and after some alterations opened it for their own use in 1977.[19] In 1981, when a patriarchal dispute divided Ukrainian Catholics in Great Britain, a priest from London said mass twice a month before an average congregation of 80.[20]

An Old Roman Catholic church described as Pro-Uniate worshipped in a room in Brunswick Square for several years. The meeting place, dedicated to St. Clement, was closed in 1941. The spiritual leader of the church, Bernard Mary Williams, lived in Upton St. Leonards.[21]

PROTESTANT NONCONFORMITY

RELIGIOUS nonconformity[22] in Gloucester was insignificant before the early 1640s when it was encouraged by preachers from elsewhere.[23] Baptist and Quaker meetings had been established by the later 1650s when Independents formed a church under James Forbes.[24] Nonconformist groups met with opposition but a report in 1659 of a plan to massacre Independents, Baptists, and other sectaries was denounced by the mayor as a calumny.[25] After the Restoration the tradition of nonconformity was maintained principally by James Forbes and his Independent church, but smaller and less influential groups of Baptists and Quakers continued to hold services. The nonconformist conventicles were persecuted and in 1671 Walter Clements was imprisoned at Gloucester for giving legal advice and encouragement to Baptists and Quakers in the shire and adjoining districts.[26] The Independents registered several meeting places in Gloucester and Longford in 1672 and 1673, but the Baptist church was apparently dissolved soon after 1674. In 1676, when it was reported that conventicles in Gloucester had greatly increased,[27] 110 protestant nonconformists were recorded there.[28] They presumably included Thomas Merrett, a former curate of Churchdown who leaned towards anti-Trinitarianism.[29] The Quakers had opened a new meeting house by 1682 and the Independents built a chapel in 1699. The chapel had become Presbyterian by 1716 and Unitarian by the later 18th century. Although prominent families continued to attend it, it declined in importance. In 1735 membership of the Independent, Presbyterian, and Quaker meetings in Gloucester totalled 220.[30]

In 1708 Samuel Jones came to Gloucester and opened a nonconformist academy.[31] It had attained considerable repute by 1710 when Thomas Secker, later archbishop of Canterbury, entered it, and in 1711 it had 16 students. The following year Jones came under pressure from the ecclesiastical authorities, which accused him of undermining Church and State, and he moved the academy to Tewkesbury.[32] John Alexander, who took over the training of ministers in Gloucester, left the city in 1716.[33] Methodism was introduced to Gloucester by George Whitefield in 1735 when the Independent meeting was already a centre for evangelical revival. Whitefield retained close links with the city, his birthplace, and preached to large crowds there in the late 1730s and early 1740s. In 1739 he was excluded from St. Michael's church on weekdays by opposition to his use of its pulpit during working hours and he preached publicly in the Boothall and in a field belonging to his brother.[34] In 1741 he preached one Sunday in St. John's church, the rector, his opponent, having died recently. By then Whitefield and other revivalist preachers were holding meetings in a barn, which had been enlarged by 1743.[35] In the late 1740s and early 1750s there were several meetings in Gloucester of Calvinistic Methodist preachers[36] but the

[13] Langston, 'Cath. Mission in Glouc.'

[14] *Citizen*, 2 Jan. 1959.

[15] *Centenary Souvenir Handbook of St. Peter's Ch.* 32; *Citizen*, 6 Dec. 1962.

[16] Inf. from par. priest of Glouc.

[17] *Centenary Souvenir Handbook of St. Peter's Ch.* 31.

[18] *Glouc. Jnl.* 19 Oct. 1974.

[19] *Citizen*, 19 Dec. 1977.

[20] Inf. from priest-in-charge; *Cath. Dir.* (1981), 446.

[21] Inf. from Mr. Frith; G.R.O. Worship Reg. no. 59698.

[22] This article was written in 1981 and revised in 1986.

[23] Above, Glouc. 1547–1640, religious and cultural life; Glouc. 1640–60, religious and cultural life.

[24] *Pastoral Instruction: being some remains of the Revd. Jas. Forbes* (Lond. 1713), 8–9.

[25] Glos. Colln. R 33557.

[26] Glos. R.O., D 2052, co. and dioc.

[27] *Cal. S.P. Dom.* 1676–7, 23.

[28] *Compton Census*, ed. Whiteman, 533–4.

[29] *Calamy Revised*, ed. A. G. Matthews, 349.

[30] G.D.R. vol. 285B (1), f. 25.

[31] *Jnl. Eccl. Hist.* xxvii. 374.

[32] *D.N.B.*, s.v. Jones, Sam.; G.D.R., B 4/1/1056; cf. *V.C.H. Glos.* viii. 165–6.

[33] *Jnl. Eccl. Hist.* xxvii. 375.

[34] *G. Whitefield's Jnls.* (1960), 59–61, 80–1, 248–51, 294–8, 304.

[35] *Works of G. Whitefield* (1771), i. 346–7, 361–9; ii. 10–12; *Selected Trevecka Letters 1742–7*, ed. G. M. Roberts (Caernarvon, 1956), 136.

[36] *Works of G. Whitefield*, ii. 224, 438; *Selected Trevecka Letters 1747–94*, ed. G. M. Roberts (Caernarvon, 1962), 3, 9.

Whitefieldian society there has not been traced after 1747, when it was under the stewardship of Gabriel Harris, an alderman.[37] Some members may have drifted towards the Independent chapel. The Wesleyan Methodists, who did not attract much support until the last quarter of the century, opened a chapel in 1787 or 1788. At the same time the countess of Huntingdon provided a meeting place for those who had favoured Whitefield's brand of revivalism. At the end of the century Gloucester had five protestant non-conformist meeting places, each belonging to a different denomination.[38]

In the 19th century Gloucester nonconformity expanded and diversified with the extension of the main denominations into the burgeoning suburbs, the opening of evangelistic missions, and the arrival of many new groups. Between 1811 and 1851 nonconformist groups registered 46 places of worship in Gloucester, Barton Street, Kingsholm, Longford, and Twigworth. Many were small and short lived and the doctrines and even the location of some have not been identified.[39] In 1851 congregations totalling c. 2,802 were claimed for 12 dissenting meetings in the city.[40] At a religious census of the city conducted by the *Gloucester Journal* on 13 November 1881 about half of the worshippers were at nonconformist meeting places, which comprised 16 churches or chapels, belonging to 11 denominations, and 11 mission rooms. In the evening 6,610 people attended nonconformist meetings as opposed to 4,203 at Anglican and 248 at Roman Catholic services.[41]

The main denominations, the Wesleyan Methodists and the Independents or Congregationalists, gained in strength and wealth in the 19th century, and the Baptists, who formed a church in 1813, became an important group. The Countess of Huntingdon's chapel closed in 1869. New churches were formed following schisms in the Baptist and Independent meetings, and there was a division within the Wesleyan Methodist Church in the late 1840s. In the later 19th and early 20th century Wesleyan Methodism, which prospered in the new suburbs, retained the largest nonconformist following in Gloucester. The smaller Methodist denominations made comparatively little impact, although Primitive Methodists built several chapels in the suburbs.

Nonconformists took the lead in opening the Sunday schools and missions which characterized religious work in the slums and working-class suburbs in the 19th century. Most missions evinced a concern for the social and moral welfare of the poor and many, particularly those in which Quakers were involved, were run on non-sectarian lines. Several were directed at particular groups of workers connected with Gloucester's commercial growth. In the later 19th century the Congregationalists and the Wesleyan and Primitive Meth-

odists consolidated the work of missions to the Barton Street, Tredworth, and Bristol Road areas by building chapels,[42] and the Countess of Huntingdon's chapel was reopened for a mission to the St. Mary's Square area. The main chapels were also centres from which outlying villages were evangelized, the Independents having resumed village preaching by the later 1790s and the Wesleyan and Primitive Methodists and the Baptists taking up similar work. New Connexion Methodists and Presbyterians began the evangelizing of areas of growing population outside Gloucester at Longlevens and Coney Hill.

From the early 20th century the older churches declined and new groups started, including fundamentalist and pentecostal sects. The fortunes of the older denominations were in part determined by the movement of people to new residential suburbs east and south of the city and by the growth from the 1950s of a non-Christian population in the Barton Street area. The Baptists opened four churches on new estates between the late 1920s and the 1950s. The Methodist Church, which took over nine chapels in Gloucester, Wotton, and Hucclecote on the union of the Wesleyan, Primitive, and United Methodists in 1932, opened one in 1934. There were then seven Methodist chapels in the south part of the city and five of them, including the new church, were closed between the late 1940s and the mid 1960s. The two Congregational chapels in Gloucester, both of which joined the United Reformed Church, were closed in the mid 1970s. By 1981 all the principal chapels in the central area, save for the former Presbyterian church which belonged to the United Reformed Church, had been demolished, but the Methodists, who took over an Anglican church in 1972, the Baptists, who opened a new church in 1974, and the Quakers continued to meet there. From the late 1950s the new sects, some of which moved from older parts of the city, built meeting places in the expanding residential suburbs to the east and south, and in some older suburbs people of West Indian origin formed pentecostal churches, which in three cases used former Methodist chapels.

BAPTISTS. By 1642 two preachers from London, invited by a nonconformist group under the curate of Whaddon, presumably the Independent John Wells, had gained converts in Gloucester. The converts, who were baptized, many in the river Severn, were later described as Baptists or Anabaptists and their meeting flourished in the mid 1640s.[43] The Gloucester Baptists were evidently drawn from the poorer trades, and their church was without means and on the brink of collapse in 1674 when they made several appeals to the Broadmead church in Bristol to help them carry on meetings in Framilode and

[37] Glos. R.O., D 4248/13/1, vol. of notes on Howell Harris MSS. ff. 32–5; J. Stratford, *Good and Great Men of Glos.* (Ciren. 1867), 260.

[38] For late 18th-cent. meeting places, above, Fig. 8.

[39] Hockaday Abs. ccvi, ccxiii–ccxxi, ccclxxxi; Glos. R.O., Q/RZ 1.

[40] P.R.O., HO 129/336/1/13/11; HO 129/336/2/1/2; 2/3/4;

2/6/6; HO 129/336/3/3/3–4; 3/4/8, 10; 3/5/7; 3/6/12; HO 129/336/4/1/2; 4/2/3.

[41] *Glouc. Jnl.* 19 Nov. 1881.

[42] For chapels in Barton Street and Tredworth areas, above, Fig. 15.

[43] *Trans. Bapt. Hist. Soc.* iv. 207; Glos. Colln. R 33557.

Whitminster. The Gloucester church was apparently dissolved soon afterwards,[44] and in 1735 Baptists were attending the Independent chapel in Gloucester.[45]

In 1813 seven Baptists who had recently settled in Gloucester formed a church worshipping in a room in New Inn Lane. They included George Box Drayton, a surgeon, from whom the room was hired. The church, which opened a Sunday school c. 1815, evangelized outlying villages and hamlets, including Birdwood in Churcham and Hucclecote. Thomas Flint, the minister, discouraged by the smallness of congregations, resigned in 1817. During the next three years there was no minister and the church experienced many difficulties, including disagreements with Drayton over the conduct of its affairs and method of worship. In 1819 there was a reconciliation with Drayton and a management committee was formed.[46] In 1820 Drayton became minister and a chapel was built at his expense in Parker's Row (later Brunswick Road). The chapel, which opened in 1821, included two schoolrooms. Under Drayton the church began a mission to the Barton End suburb and increased its support among the working classes, and by 1824, when he resigned, the congregation at the chapel had risen to over 200. The church also evangelized outlying villages[47] and established a chapel in Little London in Longhope.[48] The continuation of a settled pastorate in the late 1820s was jeopardized by lack of funds and the debt on the Parker's Row chapel, which was mortgaged in 1827 to pay Drayton's building costs.[49] In the early 1830s there was considerable dissatisfaction with the ministry of Edward Elliott, who resigned in 1835, and in 1836 the church was re-formed with 16 members and an open communion. The admission of Paedobaptists to the new church and communion caused dissension and in 1839 the church was re-formed with an adult membership of 38, some drawn from other churches.[50]

The new church prospered and in 1847 the chapel was rebuilt to provide more accommodation.[51] The new chapel, which opened in 1848 and was designed and built by Joseph Sims, had a pedimented street front with round-headed windows and a schoolroom to the south.[52] In the late 1840s the average congregation was c. 450.[53] The church grew during the ministries of William Collings, 1856–69, and John Bloomfield, 1870–86.[54] In 1864 classrooms were built in the chapel and an organ loft and gallery placed over them. The schoolroom was demolished in 1872 and the chapel was enlarged and reoriented. The new building, which opened in 1873 and incorporated external features of the old, was designed by Searle & Son of London with galleries on three sides.[55] It had morning and evening congregations of 375 and 531 in 1881. In 1884 the Baptists built a schoolroom and hall next to the chapel as a memorial to Robert Raikes.[56] J. E. Barton's ministry from 1888 occasioned dissension at the chapel and in 1893 he withdrew with a large part of the congregation to form a separate church.[57] By the 1960s the membership of the Brunswick Road church had declined considerably, partly as the result of the move of population to new suburbs.[58] In 1972 the chapel was sold and the building of a new church in Southgate Street was begun. Known as Brunswick Baptist church it opened in 1974[59] and had an average congregation of c. 135 in 1981.[60] The Brunswick Road chapel was demolished in 1972[61] and the Raikes Memorial Hall later, the sites of both being used for an extension to a shop.

In 1823 the Baptist minister built a small school-chapel in Back Barton Terrace (later Albany Street) for a mission to Barton End.[62] The building was for sale or lease in 1825[63] but was used by Baptists in 1830[64] and was replaced by a new room in Barton Terrace (later the north part of Tredworth High Street) in 1840. Anglicans then used the older room for services until St. James's church was opened.[65] The newer mission room, which was restored in 1878, had morning and evening congregations of 100 and 30 in 1881.[66] It was closed in 1903, when the Sunday school was moved to the Hatherley Road school, and was demolished in 1906.[67]

In the late 1860s the Parker's Row church sent preachers to Little Witcombe, where a preaching station was established, and Matson. A mission to Suffolk Street in Kingsholm, which Baptists had begun by 1870, was at first hampered by lack of a room.[68] Three houses acquired later that year were converted for the mission, which had morning and evening congregations of 44 and 60 in 1881.[69] The buildings were used by the Salvation Army from 1906 and were sold in 1919.[70]

In 1879 Baptists began an undenominational mission to the south part of the city in South End Hall in Weston Road.[71] In 1881 it had morning and evening congregations of 90 and 177.[72] It had

[44] E.B. Underhill, *Rec. of Ch. of Christ meeting in Broadmead, Bristol, 1640–87* (1847), 206–9.

[45] G.D.R. vol. 285B (1), f. 25.

[46] Glos. R.O., D 4373/2/1; for Birdwood and Hucclecote, Hockaday Abs. clii, ccxlviii.

[47] Glos. R.O., D 4373/2/1; 7/3.

[48] Hockaday Abs. cclxiii, 1823–4.

[49] Glos. R.O., D 4373/3/1; 7/1–2.

[50] Ibid. 2/2; 7/3–4.

[51] Ibid. 2/2.

[52] *Glouc. Jnl.* 22 Apr. 1848; Glos. Colln. prints GL 10.2.

[53] P.R.O., HO 129/336/3/3/3.

[54] Glos. R.O., D 4373/2/2–3.

[55] *Brunswick Road Bapt. Ch. Mag.* (July, 1894); *Glouc. Jnl.* 28 June 1873.

[56] *Glouc. Jnl.* 19 Nov. 1881; 22 Nov. 1884; cf. J. Voyce, *Glouc. in Old Photogs.* (1985), 56.

[57] Glos. R.O., D 4373/2/3; *Glouc. Jnl.* 14, 21, 28 Jan. 1893.

[58] Inf. from minister, the Revd. J. Stephens (1981).

[59] *Citizen*, 19 Mar. 1973; 4 Feb. 1974.

[60] Inf. from minister.   [61] *Citizen*, 27 Nov. 1972.

[62] Glos. R.O., D 3117/983, 1101–2; D 4373/8/1/1.

[63] *Glouc. Jnl.* 12 Dec. 1825.

[64] Glos. R.O., D 4373/7/3.

[65] *Glouc. Jnl.* 24 Oct. 1840; cf. Glos. R.O., D 4373/3/4; 8/1/3.

[66] *Glouc. Jnl.* 2 Feb. 1878; 19 Nov. 1881.

[67] Glos. R.O., D 4373/2/4.

[68] Ibid. 2/2–3.

[69] Ibid. 3/3; *Glouc. Jnl.* 3 June 1876; 19 Nov. 1881.

[70] Glos. R.O., D 4373/2/4–5.

[71] *Brunswick Road Bapt. Ch. Mag.* (Dec. 1895); *Kelly's Dir. Glos.* (1879), 674.

[72] *Glouc. Jnl.* 19 Nov. 1881.

closed by 1913,[73] and in 1981 the hall, which had a timber front, was used for commercial purposes.

By 1843 a group of Particular or Calvinistic Baptists had withdrawn from the Parker's Row church and had built a chapel in Worcester Street. The chapel, which had a gallery, was acquired in 1846 by Anglicans and they altered it for use as a school. The Particular Baptists may have moved to a meeting place in Russell Street where Richard Cordwell, who is said to have built a little chapel there called Zoar,[74] registered a room in Russell Terrace in 1847.[75] The Particular Baptists, who had a chapel in Bell Lane by 1894 and had moved to Berkeley Street by 1906, have not been traced after 1923.[76]

Gloucester Baptist Free church, formed in 1893 following the schism at the Brunswick Road church, met at the corn exchange in Southgate Street. It had its own minister and thrived as an open evangelical fellowship.[77] By 1901 it had opened a mission room in Eastgate Street,[78] which was replaced in 1911 by two dwellings, converted as an institute, in Priory Place, Greyfriars.[79] All services were held in the institute from 1938, and in 1940 the congregation moved to a new church, built with the help of the Forward Movement of the Baptist Union, in Kendal Road in Long-levens.[80]

Trinity Baptist church in Finlay Road was formed by the Brunswick Road church in 1929 to serve a new housing estate in Tuffley. A timber Sunday school built near the corner of Selwyn Road that year was used for services and in 1930 a timber hall was erected next to it.[81] A permanent church had been built by 1957.[82] In 1981 it was independent and evangelical.[83]

From 1942 Baptists led by the pastor of Trinity church held services on an estate being built in Lower Tuffley. In 1947 they erected an army hut in Grange Road for worship, and in 1955 they built a permanent church there.[84] It was remodelled in the early 1980s. In the early 1950s the pastor of Trinity Baptist church formed a congregation on an estate being built at Matson, where in 1956 a church was erected in Matson Avenue.[85]

BRETHREN. In 1848 a congregation of Brethren worshipped in the former Quaker meeting house in Park Street[86] and in 1851 it numbered c. 45.[87] The congregation moved to a meeting place in St. John's Lane, where premises were registered in 1854.[88] That place, known as the Ebenezer preaching room in the late 1850s,[89] had morning and evening congregations of 45 and 56 in 1881[90] and ceased to be used by Brethren in the late 1880s.[91] An unidentified group which in 1862 registered a room over a warehouse in Russell Street[92] was presumably the Brethren congregation with a meeting house near the corner with Clarence Street.[93] That meeting house, which had morning and evening attendances of 65 and 57 in 1881,[94] closed in the early 20th century.[95] In the late 1860s there was a Brethren meeting in Whitfield Street[96] and in 1872 a group of Christian Brethren built the Ebenezer Gospel Hall in King Street.[97] The hall, which had morning and evening congregations of 78 and 203 in 1881,[98] was demolished during redevelopment of the area c. 1970 and replaced by a new hall at the corner of Russell and Whitfield Streets registered in 1971.[99]

A group of Brethren met in a room behind a house in Cromwell Street by 1894[1] and until the mid 1960s. From then the room was used by other groups.[2] W. R. Hadwen, a doctor who came to Gloucester in 1896 to champion the anti-vaccination cause, was an active member of the Brethren. He opened a mission in the Glevum Hall in lower Southgate Street and by 1906 he had built Albion Hall, a brick building behind cottages further south, to accommodate the congregation. The new hall, to which two classrooms were added, was later known as Southgate Evangelical church and was in use in 1981. In 1896 Hadwen also organized a mission to Tredworth where he renovated a hall in Nelson Street.[3] That hall, which apparently had been built in 1882,[4] was registered in 1953[5] and called the Nelson Street assembly in 1981. By the early 1940s there was a Brethren meeting place in Bloomfield Road.[6] Christian Brethren registered a meeting room in Brunswick Square in 1956 but had ceased holding services there by 1959.[7]

[73] Brunswick Road Bapt. Ch. Mag. (Sept. 1913).

[74] Ibid. (Sept. 1894); Causton, Map of Glouc. (1843); Nat. Soc. files, Glouc., St. John.

[75] Hockaday Abs. ccxix; cf. Bd. of Health Map (1852). [76] Kelly's Dir. Glos. (1894–1927 edns.).

[77] C. G. Smith, First Glouc. Bapt. Free Ch. (1980), 5–7.

[78] Anct. Order of Foresters' Guide to Glouc. (1901), 97. [79] Glouc. Jnl. 11 Feb. 1911.

[80] Smith, First Glouc. Bapt. Free Ch. 10–15.

[81] Glos. R.O., D 4373/2/5; 3/11; 9/36; Glouc. Jnl. 18 May 1929.

[82] G.R.O. (General Register Office), Worship Reg. no. 66117. [83] Notice outside ch.

[84] Citizen, 17 Oct. 1955; 4 Mar. 1982; cf. G.R.O. Worship Reg. nos. 62211, 62628, 65240.

[85] Citizen, 21 Feb. 1956; 4 Mar. 1982; Glouc. Jnl. 14 July 1956.

[86] F. Bond, Hist. of Glouc. (1848), 104.

[87] P.R.O., HO 129/336/2/6/6.

[88] G.R.O. Worship Reg. no. 5998.

[89] Slater's Dir. Glos. (1858–9), 199.

[90] Glouc. Jnl. 19 Nov. 1881.

[91] Smart's Dir. Glouc. (1886), 86; (1889), 182.

[92] G.R.O. Worship Reg. no. 14762.

[93] Cf. Bretherton's Dir. Glouc. (1879), 55; Smart's Dir. Glouc. (1883), 119. [94] Glouc. Jnl. 19 Nov. 1881.

[95] Cf. Smart's Dir. Glouc. (1910–11), 421.

[96] Bretherton's Dir. Glouc. (1867 and later edns.).

[97] G.B.R., B 4/5/3, min. 16 Feb. 1872; Trans. B.G.A.S. lxxvii. 6 n.; G.R.O. Worship Reg. no. 21975.

[98] Glouc. Jnl. 19 Nov. 1881.

[99] G.R.O. Worship Reg. no. 72433.

[1] Kelly's Dir. Glos. (1894), 175.

[2] G.R.O. Worship Reg. nos. 40063, 69891, 71460.

[3] B. E. Kidd and M. E. Richards, Hadwen of Glouc. (1933), 118, 217–18; Glouc. Jnl. 14 Nov. 1896; 31 Dec. 1932; G.R.O. Worship Reg. no. 45804.

[4] G.B.R., B 4/6/2, improvement cttee. 24 Feb. 1882; cf. O.S. Map 1/2,500, Glos. XXXIII. 3 (1886 edn.).

[5] G.R.O. Worship Reg. no. 64120.

[6] Kelly's Dir. Glouc. (1941–2), A 27.

[7] G.R.O. Worship Reg. no. 65750.

In Hucclecote a group of Christian Brethren, which originated in a Sunday school begun in 1949, held services from 1957 in Colwell Avenue in a former R.A.F. hut, known as Hillview Gospel Hall by 1964. In 1969 the meeting, called Hillview Evangelical church, built a permanent church to replace the hut.[8] In 1954 a group of Exclusive Brethren registered a meeting place in Church Road in Longlevens,[9] and in the 1970s a similar group built a meeting place in Old Painswick Road in Saintbridge.[10]

CONGREGATIONALISTS AND INDEPENDENTS. The Independent or Congregational church, which was the most important dissenting meeting in Gloucester in the later 17th century, was led by James Forbes. Forbes came to Gloucester in 1654 on his appointment by the Council of State as lecturer and minister at the cathedral. He received the stipend which had been paid to augment the living of the minister of St. Mary de Crypt.[11] Forbes's followers formed a nonconformist church, which worshipped in the great hall of Edward Fletcher's house near the little cloister in the college precincts; by will dated 1660 Fletcher, minister of Bagendon, left the reversion of the house in trust to Forbes and five members of the congregation, including inhabitants of Barnwood and Saintbridge. The church, which may have been formed by 1658 when Forbes attended the Savoy Conference, evangelized the countryside[12] and urged Increase Mather to come to Gloucester.[13] Mather, who arrived late in 1659 and became minister of St. Mary de Lode, left early in 1660 and was later prominent in the affairs of the colony of Massachusetts.[14] After the Restoration Forbes was deprived of his lectureship and was twice imprisoned, the second time for a year. By 1664 he had moved to London.[15]

In 1672 Forbes returned to Gloucester[16] and held services in Sampson Bacon's house behind Blackfriars or Greyfriars.[17] At the same time one of his followers, John Badger, was licensed to hold services in a house in Longford; another, Thomas Cole, was also named in the request for

the licence.[18] For a time Congregationalism or Independency enjoyed some security and by February 1673 three more houses in the city, one belonging to John Wall, the ejected minister of Broadwas (Worcs.), had been licensed.[19] Forbes's congregation, which included several prominent citizens,[20] continued to worship in Bacon's house after the renewal of official persecution,[21] and according to one estimate in 1677 numbered over 100.[22] Services were sometimes followed by meetings in Richard Till's house.[23] In late 1680 or early 1681 the mayor imprisoned Forbes under the Five Mile Act and the meeting place was ransacked. On his release Forbes held services outside the city at Elmbridge Court until the owner William Craven, earl of Craven, intervened in 1682 to stop them.[24]

During the reign of James II the meeting's fortunes improved. Forbes, who had left the area, came back to Gloucester in 1687[25] and resumed his work, including visits to outlying villages.[26] In the early 1690s, when he was training students for the ministry, he actively supported the Happy Union of Independents and Presbyterians and was moderator of an association of ministers in Gloucestershire, Somerset, and Wiltshire.[27] In 1692 Forbes and Jonathan Greene, a member of his congregation, entered into a theological debate with the Gloucester Quakers, which was marked by the publication of pamphlets.[28] In 1699 the Independents built a small brick meeting house in Barton Street near the east gate.[29] Forbes, who had an assistant from 1706, remained the minister until his death in 1712 but during his last years factions emerged in the church. Under his successor, Joseph Denham, some members, presumably objecting to changes in church government, withdrew to form a separate church under John Alexander.[30] They took the library and four tankards of 1702 which Forbes had settled on the chapel.[31] The larger part of the congregation remained at the chapel, which was described as Presbyterian by 1716 and later became Unitarian.[32]

In 1716 the secessionists' church, described as Independent, had a congregation of 250 and in 1718 Thomas Cole, a descendant of the Thomas

[8] *Citizen*, 28 Nov. 1969; G.R.O. Worship Reg. no. 69425.

[9] G.R.O. Worship Reg. no. 69784; cf. *Kelly's Dir. Glouc.* (1968), A 8.

[10] Inf. from Mr. G. Whitehead, former minister of Tyndale Cong. ch.

[11] P.R.O., SP 25/75, pp. 483, 512–13, 550; Hockaday Abs. ccx, ccxvi.

[12] *Pastoral Instruction*, 8–11; *Calamy Revised*, ed. A.G. Matthews, 204, 202; for Fletcher's will, Glos. Colln. R 33557.

[13] W. Lloyd, *Hist. of Barton Street Meeting Ho.* (priv. print. 1899), 12.

[14] Hockaday Abs. ccxviii; *Calamy Revised*, ed. A. G. Matthews, 343.

[15] *Pastoral Instruction*, 11; *Calamy Revised*, ed. A. G. Matthews, 204.

[16] *Pastoral Instruction*, 12.

[17] *Cal. S.P. Dom.* 1672, 41; G.D.R. vol. 221, depositions against Jas. Forbes, 13–14 Dec. 1677.

[18] *Cal. S.P. Dom.* 1672, 41, 44; for Badger and Cole, Edw. Fletcher's will, in Glos. Colln. R 33557.

[19] *Cal. S.P. Dom.* 1672, 199; 1672–3, 259, 514; *Calamy Revised*, ed. A. G. Matthews, 507.

[20] Ripley, 'Glouc. 1660–1740', 150–1.

[21] *Pastoral Instruction*, 12; *Calamy Revised*, ed. A. G. Matthews, 205.

[22] G.D.R. vol. 221, deposition of Walter Allard against Jas. Forbes.

[23] Ibid. vol. 232, deposition of Edm. Sturmy against Ric. Till, 6 July 1680.

[24] *Calamy Revised*, ed. A. G. Matthews, 205; for Elmbridge Ct., below, Hucclecote, man.

[25] Lloyd, *Barton Street Meeting Ho.* 13; *Pastoral Instruction*, 12.

[26] T. J. Lander, *Hist. of Southgate Cong. Ch. 1660–1972* (1976), 4.

[27] *Calamy Revised*, ed. A. G. Matthews, 205; A. Gordon, *Freedom after Ejection* (1917), 47.

[28] Ripley, 'Glouc. 1660–1740', 156–7.

[29] Glos. R.O., D 4270/4/1/2–3; G.B.R., G 3/SR, Mich. 1699.

[30] *Jnl. Eccl. Hist.* xxvii. 373–5; Lloyd, *Barton Street Meeting Ho.* 16–17.

[31] Glos. R.O., D 4270/4/1/5; cf. Lander, *Southgate Cong. Ch.* 32, 42; Glos. Colln. N 6.18.   [32] Below, Unitarians.

Cole mentioned above, became its minister.[33] In 1720 the Independents took a lease of a great hall in Blackfriars for services.[34] In 1725, 1728, and 1730 they registered houses in Southgate Street, the last being Cole's house outside the south gate,[35] where later in 1730 they built a meeting house. The site, in front of that of St. Owen's church, was near land which had been used by dissenters as a cemetery.[36] Under Cole the Southgate meeting was an important centre for evangelical revival. From the later 1720s its members registered many houses in outlying towns and villages, especially in the Stroud area, for worship,[37] and in 1735 the chapel, which had a membership of 100, was attended by Baptists.[38] In the late 1730s Cole, whose followers registered four houses in Gloucester between 1736 and 1742,[39] became an important ally of the Methodist movement.[40] He worked in close harmony with George Whitefield and followed his example by attending private religious meetings, holding fortnightly lectures in remote country places, and conducting weekday preaching tours; sometimes he preached in the open air, as at Quarhouse in Stroud. He died in 1742,[41] and in 1768 a testimonial, which Whitefield signed, was published as a model for gospel ministers.[42] The Southgate chapel remained sympathetic to the evangelical revival after Cole's death, and in the later 1740s Howell Harris, a leading Calvinistic Methodist and associate of Whitefield, preached in it several times.[43] In the mid 1730s a vestry was added to the chapel to hold Forbes's library and in the late 1750s a house for the minister was built.[44] In 1744 a house in Barton Street was registered for another group of Independents.[45]

The Southgate meeting declined in the late 18th century but flourished again during the ministry of William Bishop, 1794–1832, who promoted philanthropic ventures in the city and county.[46] The side galleries of the chapel were enlarged in 1803[47] and two schoolrooms were added in 1820; a Sunday school had been held from 1812. The chapel and schoolrooms were enlarged in 1830.[48] Under Bishop the meeting supported missions to outlying villages, where some churches were formed,[49] and its influence reached Newnham and Lydney. Bishop was also active in the Forest of Dean.[50] In 1831 and 1832 Job Bown, a village preacher of the Southgate church, registered several houses in and around the city,[51] and by 1833 the Independents had opened a school in the west part of the city, presumably in the Island where they ran a mission.[52] The growth of the meeting and its involvement in missions continued under Joseph Hyatt, minister 1833–57, and the chapel gave financial help to many smaller churches in the county.[53] In the late 1830s and in the 1840s the average congregation at the chapel was 550.[54] In 1850 the minister's house was demolished and the chapel rebuilt on a larger scale and reoriented. The new chapel, which opened in 1851, was faced with stone and designed by James Medland in a 14th-century style with north and south galleries, vestries, and a schoolroom.[55] The street front was richly decorated.[56] In the late 18th and the early 19th century the meeting received a few gifts to maintain the minister, including in 1770 land at Wotton from John Beale and by 1838 £300 under the will of John Garn (d. 1835). From 1848 the meeting used part of the land as a cemetery.[57]

In 1862 a schism occurred within the Southgate church, and the minister James Kernahan, who wanted a more open communion, and some members resigned.[58] They formed a free church, which leaned towards first Anglicanism and then Presbyterianism.[59] In the 1870s the Southgate Congregational church became involved in evangelizing new working-class areas of the city and the St. Mary's Square area.[60] In 1881 the chapel had morning and evening congregations of 337 and 264. The schoolroom was replaced in 1889 by a larger hall with classrooms on two floors.[61] The church, which had financial problems from the early 20th century, sold James Forbes's tankards in 1923 and his library to Toronto University in 1966. In 1973 it united with the Presbyterian church in Park Road to form the James Forbes United Reformed church, and in 1974 regular services at the Southgate chapel ceased.[62] The chapel was demolished in 1981.

[33] Dr. Williams's Libr., Evans MS. p. 42; cf. Lander, Southgate Cong. Ch. 9.

[34] Ch. min. bk. 1716–1832; lease 25 Mar. 1720. The ch. rec. were in 1981 among W. Midland provincial archives of United Reformed Ch., Leamington Spa.

[35] Hockaday Abs. ccvi; G.B.R., G 3/SR, Epiph. 1729.

[36] Mem. 10 Mar. 1730; draft deed 1730; G.B.R., G 3/SR, Trin. 1730; cf. Bibliotheca Glos. ii. 373.

[37] Hockaday Abs. cviii, cxlviii, ccxlvi, cclxxx, cclxxxiv, cccix, ccclix; for names of members, ch. min. bk. 1716–1832.

[38] G.D.R. vol. 285B (1), f. 25.

[39] Hockaday Abs. ccvi, ccxvi, ccxiii.

[40] Jnl. Eccl. Hist. xxvii. 375–8.

[41] Thos. Hall, Sermon on death of the Revd. Thos. Cole (Lond. 1742), 42–4; Works of G. Whitefield, i. 48, 53–4; ii. 11, 27–8; Glouc. Jnl. 10 Aug. 1742.

[42] Jnl. Eccl. Hist. xxvii. 382–5; for the inscr. on Cole's tomb, Stratford, Good and Great Men of Glos. 253.

[43] Jnl. Eccl. Hist. xxvii. 381–2; for Harris, D.N.B.

[44] Bills and receipts 1733–5, 1758–60; mem. 3 June 1731.

[45] Hockaday Abs. ccxviii.

[46] Evangelical Mag. xi. 45–9.

[47] Ch. min. bk. 1716–1832.

[48] Lander, Southgate Cong. Ch. 18; Glouc. Jnl. 1 Jan. 1821.

[49] Lander, Southgate Cong. Ch. 18–22; cf. P. E. Deggan, Southgate Sun. Sch. Centenary (1913), 6–9.

[50] T. Bright, Rise of Nonconf. in Forest of Dean (Coleford, 1953), 5–6, 16–18; Hockaday Abs. cclxix.

[51] Hockaday Abs. ccvi, ccxiv–v, ccxviii, ccxlviii; cf. ch. min. bk. 1716–1832.

[52] Educ. Enq. Abstract, 316; Causton, Map of Glouc. (1843).

[53] Lander, Southgate Cong. Ch. 21–4.

[54] P.R.O., HO 129/336/3/6/12.

[55] Plan of chap. before Apr. 1850; Glouc. Jnl. 19 Apr. 1851.

[56] Glos. Colln. prints GL 10.10, reproduced above, Plate 52.

[57] Hen. Butler's receipts 1782–3; letter to Char. Com. 11 Apr. 1893; notes on Southgate ch. reg., compiled by the Revd. C. Surman, of Myton Road, Leamington Spa; Char. Com. file 249996.

[58] Deacons' min. bk. 1853–79; Lander, Southgate Cong. Ch. 24–6.

[59] Below, Presbyterians.

[60] Lander, Southgate Cong. Ch. 27–9.

[61] Glouc. Jnl. 19 Nov. 1881; 3 May 1890.

[62] Lander, Southgate Cong. Ch. 40–54; Glos. Colln. N 6.18.

The Independents' mission to the Island, which occupied a schoolroom in Levy's Yard rebuilt c. 1844, had an average congregation of 30 at evening services in 1851.[63] The room, which was reopened for Sunday evening services in 1898,[64] was sold in 1941.[65]

In 1877 Independents converted the St. Mary's Square chapel, which had belonged to the Countess of Huntingdon's Connexion, as a mission hall known as St. Mary's Hall.[66] The mission, which was run by a committee including members of the Southgate Congregational church,[67] had morning and evening attendances of 84 and 220 on the day of the religious census in 1881.[68] In the early 1890s it was led by D.S. Hollies, a Congregationalist minister,[69] and in 1905 it was taken over by the Southgate church, which paid for alterations to the hall;[70] a gallery was replaced by a floor with five classrooms on it.[71] Services were held there until 1958 when the congregation moved to a new building in St. Mary's Street. The old hall was demolished as part of a slum clearance programme.[72] St. Mary's Hall, which became a separate Congregational church in 1974, had an adult membership of 47 in 1981.[73]

Tyndale Congregational chapel originated in 1871 when the Southgate church opened a mission to lower Barton Street and acquired land at the corner of Stratton Road for a chapel. The mission, which William Hurd ran from a room opposite Blenheim Road until 1873, was revived in 1874 under John Bennetts. He held services in a room above the co-operative society's stores in Stratton Road. Tyndale chapel, begun later the year and opened in 1875, was built of brick faced with stone and was designed by James Tait of Leicester in an early 14th-century style. The principal benefactor was William Somerville of Bitton. A Congregational church, which was formed with 37 members in 1876, was reorganized after Bennetts resigned in 1877 and for a time attendance declined.[74] By the day of the religious census in 1881 the morning congregation had risen to 345.[75] At first the chapel, which had a north gallery, was divided by a temporary wall, the south end, including the transepts, being used as a Sunday schoolroom.[76] The partition had been

removed by 1883 to accommodate the congregation,[77] and in 1884 new schoolrooms were opened on the south side of the chapel.[78] In the late 19th century the Tyndale church began missions to Tredworth and Saintbridge and, outside Gloucester, to Bulley[79] and to Cooper's Hill in Brockworth.[80] Congregations at the chapel declined in the mid 20th century and by 1966 winter services were held in a schoolroom. The room, which was refitted as the chapel in 1970, closed in 1975 and the congregation joined the James Forbes United Reformed church.[81] The former Tyndale chapel and schoolrooms were demolished in 1979.

By 1883 the Tyndale church had built a mission room in Wellesley Street in Tredworth. The mission, which from 1887 was run on undenominational lines, had closed by 1964.[82] The building was derelict in 1981. In 1887, following the severing of the connexion with the Wellesley Street mission, the Tyndale church built a mission hall in Saintbridge at the corner of Painswick and Cemetery Roads.[83] Services were held there until 1973,[84] and in 1980 the African Methodist Episcopal Church reopened the hall for services.[85] It was not in use in 1981.

COUNTESS OF HUNTINGDON'S CONNEXION.

Selina Hastings, countess of Huntingdon, acquired a large building on the south side of St. Mary's Square, which was fitted and registered in 1788 as a chapel for followers of George Whitefield.[86] It was of brick and had been erected a few years earlier as a theatre.[87] The chapel was run by local trustees[88] and was supplied by ministers of the Countess of Huntingdon's Connexion, for whom a house was provided at the back.[89] Robert McAll, one of the chapel's earliest ministers, enjoyed a settled pastorate in the later 1790s[90] when he was also working with Independents in the Forest of Dean.[91] The St. Mary's Square chapel, which between 1799 and 1821 was usually served by visiting preachers,[92] was said to be frequented by a large and respectable society in the late 1820s.[93] In 1830, after some internal divisions and at the

[63] Causton, *Map of Glouc.* (1843); P.R.O., HO 129/336/2/1/2.

[64] Glos. Colln. N 6.14.

[65] Lander, *Southgate Cong. Ch.* 49.

[66] *Glos. Chron.* 10 Nov. 1877; *Glouc. Jnl.* 17 Nov. 1877; 2 Feb., 2 Mar. 1878.

[67] Lander, *Southgate Cong. Ch.* 29.

[68] *Glouc. Jnl.* 19 Nov. 1881.

[69] *Kelly's Dir. Glos.* (1894), 175.

[70] Lander, *Southgate Cong. Ch.* 38; Southgate ch. rec., deacons' min. bk. 1881-1914, pp. 343-56.

[71] W. E. James, *Sun. Sch. Movement* (1910), 38; for views of interior c. 1950, photogs. in 1981 in possession of chapel sec.

[72] *Citizen*, 30 July 1958; Lander, *Southgate Cong. Ch.* 49.

[73] Inf. from chapel sec.

[74] *Glouc. Jnl.* 11 Sept. 1875; newspaper cuttings in Tyndale Cong. ch. min. bk. 1898-1913. The ch. rec. were in 1981 among Glos. Colln.

[75] *Glouc. Jnl.* 19 Nov. 1881: the evening service attended by 987 was a funeral.

[76] Ibid. 31 Oct. 1874; 11 Sept. 1875.

[77] Glos. Colln. NV 5.22 (1). For photogs. of chap., *Tyn-*

dale Cong. Ch. Jubilee Souvenir 1875-1925: Glos. Colln. N 6.7.

[78] *Glouc. Jnl.* 5 Apr. 1884; personal observation.

[79] Ch. cttee. min. bk. 1882-8, min. 5 Oct. 1887.

[80] *Tyndale Cong. Ch. Jubilee Souvenir*, 27.

[81] Inf. from Mr. Whitehead.

[82] Glos. Colln. NV 5.22 (1); ch. cttee. min. bk. 1882-8; G.R.O. Worship Reg. no. 30280.

[83] Ch. cttee. min. bk. 1882-8.

[84] Inf. from Mr. Whitehead.   [85] *Citizen*, 21 Apr. 1980.

[86] Hockaday Abs. ccxviii; *Glouc. Guide* (1792), 89.

[87] Rudge, *Glouc.* 336; Voyce, *Glouc. in Old Photogs.* 61; cf. *Glouc. Jnl.* 29 Nov. 1784.

[88] E. Dolby Shelton, 'Notes on Countess of Huntingdon's Connexion Ch. at Glouc.' (TS. in Glos. Colln. NR 6.3).

[89] *Glouc. Jnl.* 21 Apr. 1832; for the ho., *Glos. Chron.* 16 Dec. 1899.

[90] Copy of baptism reg. July 1837. The early ch. rec. were in 1981 among W. Midland provincial archives of United Reformed Ch., Leamington Spa.

[91] Bright, *Nonconf. in Forest of Dean*, 6, 38, 42; Hockaday Abs. cclx, Littledean, 1797.

[92] Copy of baptism reg. July 1837.   [93] Counsel, *Glouc.* 166.

beginning of F. G. White's ministry, the church was re-formed with 30 members.[94] White, who stopped using Anglican liturgy and promoted political and social causes, was minister until his death in 1849.[95] In the late 1830s the chapel supported Sunday schools in Sweetbriar Street and Longford;[96] a Sunday school had been held at the chapel from soon after its inception in 1810.[97] In 1832 the chapel was repaired extensively and the ensuing debt had not been cleared by 1841 when the schoolroom remained dilapidated.[98] Further alterations were made in the mid or late 1840s.[99] In 1851 morning and evening congregations of 200 and 400 were claimed for the chapel,[1] which was refitted in 1863 when more seating for the poor was provided. The growth of slums in the neighbourhood and competition from more imposing chapels contributed to a marked fall in attendance in the late 1860s and the trustees decided to build a memorial church to George Whitefield in Park Road. It had not been started by 1869 when the St. Mary's Square chapel was closed[2] and the congregation united with the Presbyterians.[3]

Later in 1869 the chapel was renovated with the help of the Independents as an interdenominational mission station and an evangelist was appointed. The venture failed but in 1870 the chapel was reopened by J. F. T. Hallowes, a Congregationalist minister who built up a large congregation. Attempts to continue the mission after he left in 1876 were unsuccessful and in 1877 the Countess of Huntingdon's Connexion ended its involvement in the chapel's affairs.[4]

LATTER DAY SAINTS. Mormon missionaries entered Gloucestershire in 1840 and gained converts in villages near Gloucester. Some of them emigrated by way of the city to America in 1841. The same year a Chartist, the first Mormon missionary to Gloucester, preached in a room in Worcester Street and took part in a public debate.[5] The Latter Day Saints, who from 1851 worshipped in a room in a passage off Westgate Street formerly occupied by the mechanics' institution,[6] encountered hostility in Gloucester. In 1855 a lecture on polygamy was broken up and the magistrates dismissed the case against the culprits on the ground that the assembly had not been a religious service.[7] In 1856 the Latter Day Saints registered a building in Worcester Street and although services had ceased there by 1866[8] local people attended a small Mormon conference in the city in 1876.[9] In 1912 a group of Latter Day Saints (Reorganized) registered a mission hall in Stroud Road. In 1942 the same group registered a hall behind Wellington Street and by 1965 it had built a church in Newton Avenue at Coney Hill.[10] In 1963 Mormons registered a house on the main road in Barnwood. In 1970 they moved to a new church next to the house,[11] which they demolished for a car park.

WESLEYAN METHODISTS. John Wesley came to Gloucester with George Whitefield in July 1739 and preached to large crowds.[12] In August Charles Wesley addressed a society, which included three clergymen, and preached to large crowds in a field belonging to Whitefield's brother, but when he returned in 1740 he found his reception lukewarm.[13] Wesleyan Methodism took a long time to become established in the city and John Wesley, who addressed a gathering when he passed through Gloucester in 1744, did not preach there again until 1766.[14] His followers, who were few and poor, were without a permanent meeting place until they took over the cordwainers' hall, in the former St. Kyneburgh's chapel,[15] which John Brown, a local preacher, and others registered in 1767.[16] There was local opposition to the Methodists at that time. In 1768 Wesley was confronted by a hostile mob[17] and in 1769 a preacher was flogged through the streets for disturbing the peace of the city with his rant.[18] From 1777 support for Methodism grew and Wesley preached there regularly. In 1785 his large audience in a public building included many people 'of the better sort'. In 1786 he preached in the chapel of St. Bartholomew's Hospital. The Methodists had opened a subscription for building a chapel by 1787[19] when George Conibere provided a site for it behind cottages in lower Northgate Street.[20] The chapel, which had a gallery, was open by 1788 and Wesley preached in it several times.[21] The chapel became the head of a circuit which covered the north part of Gloucestershire,[22] and in 1795 a house was built alongside it for the use of preachers.[23] The circuit,

[94] Vol. of ch. members, mem.
[95] *Glouc. Jnl.* 24 Feb. 1849; 14 Aug. 1869.
[96] Glos. Colln. NV 5.21 (7–8).
[97] James, *Sun. Sch. Movement*, 35–6.
[98] *Glouc. Jnl.* 21 Apr. 1832; 4 Dec. 1841.
[99] Vol. of ch. members, mem. in burials 1843.
[1] P.R.O., HO 129/336/2/3/4.
[2] Dolby Shelton, 'Notes'; *Glouc. Jnl.* 11 Apr. 1863; 14 Aug. 1869; *Glos. Chron.* 9 Mar. 1867.
[3] F. C. Glover, *Hist. of Presbyterians in Glouc. 1640–1972* (priv. print. 1972), 7–8.
[4] *Glouc. Jnl.* 14 Aug. 1869; 10 Dec. 1870; 15 Jan. 1876; Dolby Shelton, 'Notes'; cf. Southgate ch. rec., deacons' min. bk. 1853–79.
[5] *Glouc. Jnl.* 7 Nov. 1840; 7 Aug., 6 Nov. 1841; Hockaday Abs. ccxv.
[6] Glos. R.O., Q/RZ 1; cf. Causton, *Map of Glouc.* (1843).
[7] *Glouc. Jnl.* 3, 10 Nov. 1855.
[8] G.R.O. Worship Reg. no. 7537.

[9] *Glouc. Jnl.* 19 Aug. 1876.
[10] G.R.O. Worship Reg. nos. 45335, 60132, 70416; *Kelly's Dir. Glouc.* (1965), A 8.
[11] G.R.O. Worship Reg. nos. 69023, 72098; *Glouc. Jnl.* 16 Aug. 1969.
[12] *Works of J. Wesley* (1872), i. 211.
[13] *Jnl. of Chas. Wesley* (1849), i. 163–4, 195.
[14] *Works of J. Wesley*, i. 464; iii. 267, 296.
[15] Rudge, *Glouc.* 140–1; Counsel, *Glouc.* 165.
[16] Hockaday Abs. ccxxi; for Brown, *Glouc. Jnl.* 20 Nov. 1809. [17] *Works of J. Wesley*, iii. 313.
[18] *Glouc. Jnl.* 5 June 1769.
[19] *Works of J. Wesley*, iv. 104, 116, 163, 197, 222, 267, 298, 327, 363.
[20] Glos. R.O., D 2833; Counsel, *Glouc.* 165.
[21] *Glouc. Jnl.* 17 Mar. 1788; *Works of J. Wesley*, iv. 409, 433–4, 447, 481–2.
[22] Glos. R.O., D 2689/1/6/4; D 3187/1/3/6.
[23] Ibid. D 3987/1, pp. 26, 30.

which had two, occasionally three, ministers,[24] was reduced by the creation in the late 18th century and the early 19th of the Stroud, Winchcombe (later Cheltenham), and Tewkesbury circuits.[25] Chapels and meeting places opened in Gloucester's suburbs in the 19th century were attached to the Gloucester circuit, which was re-formed in 1933 to include Primitive and United Methodist chapels.[26]

The Wesleyans began a Sunday school in the Northgate chapel in 1814,[27] and in 1835 they improved the seating and built a schoolroom at the back. In 1840 the chapel was enlarged and more accommodation provided for the poor.[28] At that time local Methodist leaders opposed the involvement of evangelicals, led by William Higgs, in an interdenominational society for young men and in the mechanics' institution, and the replacement of Higgs as a local preacher apparently occasioned a sharp drop in Wesleyan membership.[29] The Wesleyan society divided again during the reform controversy within the Wesleyan Methodist Church in the late 1840s, and the reformers left the chapel in 1850.[30] In 1851 morning and evening congregations of 450 and 650 were claimed for the chapel[31] and the schism proved only a temporary setback. In 1877 the chapel and the buildings in front were pulled down and a new chapel and schoolroom were built. The new chapel, designed in a baroque style, with eclectic detail, by Charles Bell, had twin north spires flanking a semicircular portico, above which was a rose window crowned by an open pediment. It was completed in 1878[32] and the congregation numbered over 400 in 1881.[33] Slum clearance before the Second World War reduced congregations.[34] In 1972 the chapel was closed and the congregation moved to the church of St. John the Baptist, which under a sharing agreement with Anglicans was renamed St. John Northgate.[35] The Northgate Methodist church had a membership of 162 in 1980 and the church had Sunday morning and evening congregations of 111 and 73 respectively.[36] Following its closure the Northgate chapel was demolished[37] and a supermarket built on the site.

In 1816 a Wesleyan minister registered two houses in Gloucester,[38] and perhaps five or those registered in 1821 and 1822 were for Wesleyans.

Two, including one on the quay, were in St. Nicholas's parish[39] where there was a Wesleyan meeting in 1825.[40]

The Wesleyans were particularly active in the Barton Street and Tredworth areas. At Barton End they had opened a Sunday school by 1827. It had closed by 1829 and they began another there in 1834;[41] a minister registered a house in Barton Terrace (later the north part of Tredworth High Street) in 1837.[42] In 1847 the Wesleyans built a schoolroom in Victoria Street to serve an increasingly populous area nearer the city and to relieve pressure on the Sunday school at the Northgate chapel.[43] They used it for services,[44] and in 1851, after part of the congregation had presumably moved to the Wesleyan Reformers' chapel at Ryecroft,[45] it had morning and evening attendances of 50 and 100.[46] By 1851 the Wesleyan Methodists were also holding services in nearby Newtown,[47] and by 1858 they had built a chapel in Tredworth High Street.[48] In 1863 they purchased the Ryecroft chapel and closed those in Victoria and High Streets. The Victoria Street chapel, sold in 1864, was converted as two dwellings,[49] and the High Street chapel was acquired by Anglicans in 1866[50] and used by nonconformist groups from the mid 20th century.

The Wesleyans made the Ryecroft chapel the centre of their work in Barton Street and Tredworth. It was soon too small for the congregation and in 1870 a large brick chapel was built next to it at the corner of Falkner Street. The new chapel, designed by A. W. Maberly with twin towers above the entrance and a gallery on three sides, opened in 1871.[51] In 1876 a house in Falkner Street was bought for its minister.[52] In 1881 the chapel had morning and evening congregations of 356 and 312.[53] The older building, which the Wesleyans turned into a school, was enlarged in 1898.[54] In 1955 the Ryecroft chapel was closed and its members transferred to the former United Methodist church in Stroud Road, which was renamed St. Luke's Methodist church.[55] The Ryecroft school building was sold and the front part demolished in 1957. The chapel, which had been leased to the city education committee for use by the technical college,[56] was used by the Gloucestershire College of Arts and Technology in 1981.

[24] G. R. Hine, *Meth. Ch. Glouc. Circuit Rec.* (1971), 5–8.
[25] Glos. R.O., D 3187/1/3/6; D 2689/1/6/4; G. H. Bancroft Judge, *Origins and Progress of Wesleyan Methodism in Chelt. and District* (Chelt. 1912), 15; *V.C.H. Glos.* viii. 164.
[26] Glos. R.O., D 2689/1/7/1–2.
[27] G. E. Lewis, *Northgate Sun. Sch. Centenary Souvenir* (1914), 18.
[28] *Glouc. Jnl.* 19 Sept. 1835; 4, 25 Apr. 1840.
[29] Glos. Colln. NF 20.1 (3).
[30] Below, United Methodists and their predecessors.
[31] P.R.O., HO 129/336/3/4/8.
[32] Glos. R.O., D 2833; *Glouc. Jnl.* 2 June 1877; 15 July 1878; for photogs. of the street front in 1972, *Glouc., a Pictorial Rec.* (John Jennings Ltd., n.d.), 1, 31.
[33] *Glouc. Jnl.* 19 Nov. 1881.
[34] Glos. R.O., D 2689/2/6/19.
[35] Ibid. D 3987/8; inf. from dioc. sec.
[36] Inf. from superintendent of Glouc. circuit.
[37] *Citizen*, 31 Jan. 1973.
[38] Hockaday Abs. ccxiv, St. Aldate; ccxvi.

[39] Ibid. ccxiv, St. Catherine; ccxviii, ccxx.
[40] G.D.R. vol. 383, no. clxxv.
[41] Glos. Colln. NV 5.20 (3–6, 27).
[42] Hockaday Abs. ccvi.
[43] *Glouc. Jnl.* 28 Aug. 1847.
[44] Glos. R.O., D 2689/1/7/1.
[45] *Glouc. Jnl.* 1 Mar. 1851.
[46] P.R.O., HO 129/336/4/1/2.
[47] Glos. R.O., D 2689/1/7/1.
[48] *Slater's Dir. Glos.* (1858–9), 199.
[49] Glos. R.O., D 2689/2/7/5; *Glouc. Jnl.* 23 Apr. 1864; 16 May 1931.
[50] Glos. R.O., P 154/8/CW 3/6; *Glouc. Jnl.* 19 Jan. 1867.
[51] *Glouc. Jnl.* 13 May 1871; Hine, *Meth. Ch. Glouc. Circuit Rec.* 37, 40.
[52] Glos. R.O., D 2689/2/7/5; cf. ibid. 1.
[53] *Glouc. Jnl.* 19 Nov. 1881.
[54] Glos. R.O., D 2689/2/7/5.
[55] *Citizen*, 10, 30 June 1955.
[56] Glos. R.O., D 2689/2/7/3.

By 1875 the Wesleyan Methodists had moved back into Newtown[57] where they opened a mission room in Tredworth Road.[58] The room, which was attended by 50 people in 1881,[59] went off the circuit plan in 1883.[60]

A Wesleyan meeting place in Westgate Street was recorded in 1875,[61] and a mission room in or near Alvin Street was registered by a minister in 1887 and had closed by 1896.[62] In the 1890s the Wesleyans ran a mission in Goddard's assembly rooms in lower Northgate Street.[63]

The Wesleyans commenced open-air services in Bristol Road in 1891,[64] and later that year they built a temporary wooden mission room at the corner of Clegram Street. In 1892 it was replaced by a brick school-chapel, next to which an iron church was erected in 1897;[65] the iron building had housed an Anglican mission elsewhere in Bristol Road.[66] In 1909 the Wesleyan mission to the Bristol Road area, which had outgrown its accommodation, moved to new buildings, a large brick hall and Sunday school designed by J. Fletcher Trew, at the corner of Seymour and Frampton Roads. The Seymour Road front of the hall was flanked by octagonal towers, that on the south side being carried up to a turret, and had a large semicircular window above the entrance.[67] The hall, known later as Wesley Hall, had 67 members in 1965[68] when it was closed and they were transferred to St. Luke's Methodist church. The school was sold in 1965 and the hall to the city education committee for a youth centre in 1966.[69]

The Methodist church in Lonsdale Road had its origins in a free church which opened in the expanding Wotton suburb in 1909. Its principal benefactor was J. R. Pope, a Wesleyan, and he acquired for it the Bristol Road mission's iron building, which was re-erected in Lonsdale Road as a chapel.[70] The chapel was on the Gloucester Wesleyan Methodist circuit plan from 1913[71] and joined the Wesleyan Methodist Church in 1925.[72] In 1928 a Sunday school, erected at Pope's expense as a memorial to his wife and designed by H. A. Dancey, opened elsewhere in Lonsdale Road.[73] The school, built of brick with stone dressings, was also used for services and the iron chapel was sold to the Rechabites in 1930 and moved to Cromwell Street.[74] With the growth of the Lonsdale Road church in the mid 1950s a manse and a hall were built next to the Sunday

school, which was modified to look more like a church.[75] Membership of the church fell in the later 1970s and was 132 in 1980 when the Sunday morning and evening congregations were 90 and 30 respectively.[76]

In 1934 the Methodists built a small church in Coney Hill, where Primitive Methodists had been holding services in a hall in Newton Avenue. The new church, in Coney Hill Road, was erected at the expense of Elizabeth and Violet Wheeler as a memorial to Daniel Sterry, and in 1939 a schoolroom was added. The hall was sold in 1953 and demolished. The church closed in 1955 and was then used by the Salvation Army, which bought it in 1961.[77]

Wesleyan Methodism was established in the villages and hamlets around Gloucester in the early 19th century.[78] Longford, where William Barber, a Wesleyan minister, ran an academy until 1822,[79] had a Wesleyan Sunday school in 1823.[80] In 1827 a minister registered a house in Twigworth,[81] where cottage services ceased some years later because of opposition from landowners.[82] The meeting at 'Cheltenham Gate' ascribed to the Wesleyan Methodists in the late 1860s[83] was presumably that at Longlevens of New Connexion Methodists and from 1868 of Primitive Methodists.[84]

PRIMITIVE METHODISTS. In 1824 Primitive Methodists, described as Revivalists, held a camp meeting in a field at Longford to pay for the fittings in their chapel in the Dockham area. The chapel, which occupied part of a warehouse in Archdeacon Lane,[85] had closed by 1825. Another short-lived chapel was opened in Clare Street in 1837 when many Primitive Methodists from the Forest of Dean attended a gathering on Town Ham.[86] The meeting in Park Street described in the early 1850s as Primitive Methodist[87] was presumably the nonsectarian group which had morning and evening congregations of 55 and 140 in 1851.[88]

In 1855 a Primitive Methodist mission to Gloucester was established with the help of preachers from Stroud. It covered a large area, including until 1874 Cheltenham, and from 1875 looked after chapels at Broom's Green in Dymock and at Lowbands in Redmarley D'Abitot

[57] Ibid. 1/7/1.

[58] O.S. Map 1/2,500, Glos. XXXIII. 3 (1886 edn.).

[59] *Glouc. Jnl.* 19 Nov. 1881.

[60] Glos. R.O., D 2689/1/7/1.

[61] *Bretherton's Dir. Glouc.* (1875), 58.

[62] G.R.O. Worship Reg. no. 30069; *Smart's Dir. Glouc.* (1889), 181.

[63] *Smart's Dir. Glouc.* (1891), 232; (1897), 123.

[64] Glos. R.O., D 2689/1/7/1.

[65] Ibid. 2/9/1; *Glouc. Jnl.* 29 Oct. 1892.

[66] Glos. R.O., D 2689/2/9/14; cf. *Hist. of St. Stephen's Ch.* (1930), 24: Glos. Colln. N 5.48.

[67] *Glouc. Jnl.* 18 Sept. 1909.

[68] Glos. R.O., D 2689/1/7/2.

[69] Hine, *Meth. Ch. Glouc. Circuit Rec.* 17, 47.

[70] *Glouc. Jnl.* 28 Aug. 1909.

[71] Glos. R.O., D 2689/1/7/1.

[72] Ibid. 2/4/1.

[73] *Glouc. Jnl.* 17 Mar. 1928.

[74] Glos. R.O., D 2689/2/4/1; Hine, *Meth. Ch. Glouc. Circuit Rec.* 21.

[75] *Citizen*, 10 June 1955; Glos. Colln. N 6.24.

[76] Glos. R.O., D 2689/1/7/2; inf. from superintendent of Glouc. circuit.

[77] *Glouc. Jnl.* 6 Oct. 1934; 22 July 1939; Hine, *Meth. Ch. Glouc. Circuit Rec.* 41.

[78] Cf. Hockaday Abs. ccvi, 1814–19.

[79] *Manual of Glos. Lit.* i. 21.

[80] Glos. Colln. NV 5.20 (2).   [81] Hockaday Abs. ccclxxxi.

[82] Glos. R.O., D 2689/1/4/3, enclosed vol. of notes, recollections of Mr. Cullis 18 Sept. 1907.

[83] *Bretherton's Dir. Glouc.* (1867), 48; (1869), 38.

[84] Below, Primitive Methodists.

[85] *Glouc. Jnl.* 15 Dec. 1823; 31 May 1824; Hockaday Abs. ccvi.

[86] *Glouc. Jnl.* 11 Apr. 1825; 10 June 1837.

[87] *Slater's Dir. Glos.* (1852–3), 137.

[88] P.R.O., HO 129/336/1/13/11.

(Worcs., later Glos.). The mission, which held open-air and cottage services in many parts of the city and its suburbs, including Barton Street, Kingsholm, and Bristol Road, was based on two rooms in Ryecroft Street registered in 1856.[89] The proximity of Wesleyan and New Connexion Methodist chapels limited the mission's scope and so in 1858 the Primitives built a chapel in lower Barton Street.[90] Maintenance of the chapel laid a heavy financial burden on the small societies around Gloucester and in the 1860s the mission ceased much of its work. An attempt to hold regular services in Longford in 1862 came to nothing. Bristol Road and Tredworth were dropped from the mission's plan in 1864 and 1865 respectively, both apparently because of a failure to obtain rooms for services, and Union Street in Kingsholm, where the work had been neglected, in 1868. Cheltenham Road also went off the plan in 1868 but later that year the mission took over a chapel at Longlevens formerly used by New Connexion Methodists. It was abandoned for lack of success in 1873.[91]

In 1869 seating in the Barton Street chapel, which had a gallery, was increased. The average attendance at the principal services was 130. From 1875 the chapel, to which a schoolroom had been added, faced competition from an Anglican church and a Congregational chapel[92] and in 1881 it had morning and evening congregations of only 26 and 70.[93] In 1882 the Primitives sold it and moved to a new and much larger chapel on the other side of the road.[94] The new chapel, erected as a memorial to Robert Raikes in brick to a design by Kerridge & Sons of Wisbech (Cambs.), had a street front with tall, recessed round-headed windows and galleries on three sides. The building also contained a schoolroom and several classrooms.[95] In 1883 Gloucester was made a circuit with one, later two, ministers.[96] It included the chapels at Broom's Green and Lowbands and one in Churchdown, and in 1915 the Cheltenham mission was amalgamated with it.[97] After the formation of the Methodist Church the Primitives' chapels in the city were included in the new Gloucester circuit. From the 1960s membership of the Barton Street Methodist church, never large, declined and was 44 in 1980 when the chapel had Sunday morning and evening congregations of 20 and 26 respectively.[98]

The Primitive Methodist mission resumed

evangelical work to the south-east part of the city in the mid 1870s. Cottage services were held in Painswick Road from 1874 but a mission house there went off the plan in 1886 following the opening of a mission by New Connexion Methodists.[99] The Primitives began regular services in Tredworth in 1875 and built a temporary chapel there in 1876. It was in Melbourne Street, where a permanent chapel was built in 1879. The chapel presumably served Barton End, where the Primitives had discontinued Sunday services in 1877,[1] and it had morning and evening congregations of 92 and 88 in 1881.[2] In 1895 an iron schoolroom behind the chapel was replaced by a brick building.[3] The Melbourne Street church had 20 members in 1955 and the chapel was used for Methodist services until 1962.[4] It had been sold to the Church of God of Prophecy by 1966.[5] The Tredworth Gospel Hall, which in 1881 had morning and evening congregations of 58 and 95,[6] was possibly the mission room at Barton End ascribed to the Primitives in 1885 and recorded until 1919.[7]

The Primitives started regular services in the Bristol Road area in 1880. Meetings were held in the open air or in hired rooms,[8] and in 1881 the attendance at an evening service in a room in Philip Street was 37.[9] In 1886 a school-chapel, Gothic in style, was built in Bristol Road, but the Primitives attracted little support there.[10] The growth of the wagon works made the meeting place undesirable and in 1901 it was replaced by a brick and stucco chapel in Stroud Road.[11] The new chapel, designed by H. A. Dancey with a gallery,[12] stood opposite the junction with Seymour Road, in which the Primitives had held services in a reading room of the co-operative society in the mid 1890s.[13] The Stroud Road chapel was sold in 1947,[14] and in 1981 the New Testament Church of God occupied it.

By 1903 Primitive Methodists were holding services in a mission hall in Coney Hill[15] and in the mid 1930s the Methodists built a church there.[16]

UNITED METHODISTS AND THEIR PREDECESSORS. The expulsion of three reforming ministers from the Wesleyan Methodist Conference in 1849 excited feelings in Gloucester where many members of the Wesleyan society favoured changes in Methodist organization. They held meetings in support of reform and in

[89] Glos. R.O., D 2689/1/9/1–2; G.R.O. Worship Reg. no. 7489.

[90] Glos. R.O., D 2689/1/9/1; Glouc. Jnl. 18 Sept. 1858; the chap. was at the corner of Sinope Street: Hine, Meth. Ch. Glouc. Circuit Rec. 19.

[91] Glos. R.O., D 2689/1/9/2, 12; cf. G.R.O. Worship Reg. no. 6497.

[92] Glos. R.O., D 2689/1/9/2.

[93] Glouc. Jnl. 19 Nov. 1881.

[94] Glos. R.O., D 2689/2/20/1.

[95] Glouc. Jnl. 15 Apr. 1882; Hine, Meth. Ch. Glouc. Circuit Rec. 20.   [96] Glos. R.O., D 2689/1/9/9

[97] Ibid. 3, 5.

[98] Cf. ibid. 1/7/1–2; inf. from superintendent of Glouc. circuit.

[99] Glos. R.O., D 2689/1/9/2–3.

[1] Ibid. 2, 8; cf. G.R.O. Worship Reg. no. 24050; Glouc. Jnl. 22 Nov. 1879.

[2] Glouc. Jnl. 19 Nov. 1881.

[3] Ibid. 6 July 1895; Glos. R.O., D 2689/2/5/1.

[4] Glos. R.O., D 2689/1/7/2; Hine, Meth. Ch. Glouc. Circuit Rec. 50.

[5] Glos. R.O., D 2689/2/5/2.

[6] Glouc. Jnl. 19 Nov. 1881.

[7] Kelly's Dir. Glos. (1885–1923 edns.).

[8] Glos. R.O., D 2689/1/9/8–9.

[9] Glouc. Jnl. 19 Nov. 1881.

[10] Glos. R.O., D 2689/1/9/3; Smart's Dir. Glouc. (1891), 232.

[11] Glouc. Jnl. 1 June, 23 Nov. 1901.

[12] Glos. R.O., D 2689/2/8/1A.

[13] Ibid. 1/9/3.

[14] Hine, Meth. Ch. Glouc. Circuit Rec. 49.

[15] Glos. R.O., D 2689/1/9/4.

[16] Hine, Meth. Ch. Glouc. Circuit Rec. 41; above, Wesleyan Methodists.

November two of the expelled ministers addressed a large public gathering in the Baptist chapel in Parker's Row. The reformers were opposed by John Smedley, the superintendent minister, and during 1850 the division within the society widened. Several local preachers were suspended or expelled and at the end of the year 80 Wesleyan Reformers founded a society, which held services in the circular room in Worcester Street and appointed seven local preachers as ministers. In 1851 the society built Ebenezer, a school-chapel at Ryecroft in the later Conduit Street.[17] Later that year, when the society was described as Christian Brethren, morning and evening congregations of 250 and 450 were claimed for the circular room, and Ebenezer had afternoon and evening congregations of 33 and 50.[18] The Ryecroft chapel was replaced by a larger building in 1852.[19] The society, which also had members in Churchdown, Hucclecote, Hartpury, and Minsterworth, did not sustain impetus and members joined the New Connexion Methodists, who registered a meeting place in the city in 1856. Services at the circular room ceased in 1857.[20]

The New Connexion Methodists held services in an inn in Hare Lane[21] until they had built a chapel to the east in Worcester Street.[22] The chapel, which was of brick with stone dressings and was designed by Jones & Son, opened in 1857.[23] In 1859 the schoolroom at the back was enlarged and in the early 1860s the chapel was made the head of a circuit which included Dursley and Saul and had two preachers. Despite initial success the New Connexion was never strong in Gloucestershire and in 1868, when the circuit only had chapels in Worcester Street and Churchdown, Gloucester was made a mission station.[24] The New Connexion had sold the Ryecroft chapel, which it had taken over,[25] to the Wesleyans in 1863,[26] and a small chapel at Longlevens, which it had registered in 1855,[27] was used by the Primitives from 1868. A mission room in Painswick Road, opened by the New Connexion by 1886,[28] was evidently superseded by the mission hall built in Saintbridge by the Tyndale Congregational church in 1887.[29] The Worcester Street chapel, which in 1881 had morning and evening congregations of 65 and 85,[30] closed in the mid 1890s.[31] In 1930 the building was used as a

theatre studio[32] and a few years later the street front was rebuilt. In 1981 it housed a tyre depot.

A group of Bible Christian Methodists, apparently formed in 1901, held services in the Wellington Hall in Longsmith Street until it had built a brick chapel in Stroud Road. The chapel with gallery and schoolroom opened in 1904 and was designed in a 14th-century style by the Revd. V. H. Culliford, a Bible Christian minister.[33] At first it was called Tuffley Bible Christian chapel but after the Bible Christians joined with other groups to form the United Methodist Church in 1907 it was renamed Stroud Road United Methodist church.[34] After the formation of the Methodist Church it was included in the Gloucester circuit.[35] In 1955 the members of the Ryecroft society were transferred to the church, which was dedicated to St. Luke.[36] With the addition of the members of the Wesley Hall society in 1965 St. Luke's church became the centre of Methodism in the south part of the city and in 1967 a new wing of ancillary buildings was opened.[37] Membership of St. Luke's Methodist church was 144 in 1980 when the chapel had Sunday morning and evening congregations of 94 and 41 respectively.[38]

PRESBYTERIANS. The Barton Street chapel, which was described as Presbyterian in 1716, later became Unitarian.[39] The re-establishment of a Presbyterian church in Gloucester was aided by the secession from the Southgate Independent chapel in 1862.[40] The minister James Kernahan and his followers formed a free church which met at the Theatre Royal until 1863 and then at the corn exchange.[41] It leaned first towards Anglicanism[42] but by 1865 Kernahan, who wished to find a home for his congregation, was encouraging the Presbyterian Church in England to open a church in the city.[43]

The Presbyterians set up a preaching station in 1865. Services were held in hired rooms but the congregation dwindled. The cause was revived in 1868 by P. R. Crole,[44] who conducted services in a hall in the co-operative society's Brunswick Road stores,[45] and was further strengthened in 1869 when the congregation of the Countess of Huntingdon's chapel joined the Presbyterians. The latter took over the plan to build a memorial church to George Whitefield in Park Road, and in

[17] Glos. Colln. NQ 6.3–4; cf. *Glouc. Jnl.* 17 Nov. 1849; 1 Mar. 1851.

[18] P.R.O., HO 129/336/3/4/10; HO 129/336/4/2/3.

[19] *Glouc. Jnl.* 16 Oct. 1852; 24 Sept. 1853.

[20] Glos. Colln. NQ 6.4.

[21] Cf. G.R.O. Worship Reg. no. 7396; Bd. of Health Map (1852).

[22] O.S. Map 1/2,500, Glos. XXV. 15 (1886 edn.).

[23] G.B.R., N 2/1/2, min. 27 June 1856; *Glouc. Jnl.* 9, 16 May 1857.

[24] *Glouc. Jnl.* 30 Apr. 1859; *Glos. Chron.* 27 June 1868.

[25] Cf. Glos. Colln. N 6.6 (2).

[26] Glos. R.O., D 2689/2/7/5.

[27] G.R.O. Worship Reg. no. 6497.

[28] Glos. R.O., D 2689/1/9/2–3.

[29] Tyndale Cong. ch. min. bk. 1882–98, min. 18 May 1887.

[30] *Glouc. Jnl.* 19 Nov. 1881.

[31] Cf. *Kelly's Dir. Glos.* (1894), 175; *Glouc. Jnl.* 18 Jan. 1896.   [32] *Smart's Dir. Glouc.* (1930), 411.

[33] Hine, *Meth. Ch. Glouc. Circuit Rec.* 15; *Glouc. Jnl.* 12 Dec. 1903; 28 May, 29 Oct. 1904.

[34] G.R.O. Worship Reg. no. 41338; *Kelly's Dir. Glos.* (1910–31 edns.).

[35] Glos. R.O., D 2689/1/7/1.

[36] *Citizen*, 10, 30 June 1955.

[37] Hine, *Meth. Ch. Glouc. Circuit Rec.* 17; *Citizen*, 4 Sept. 1967.

[38] Inf. from superintendent of Glouc. circuit.

[39] Below.

[40] Cf. Lander, *Southgate Cong. Ch.* 26.

[41] G.R.O. Worship Reg. no. 15304; *Glouc. Jnl.* 11 Apr. 1863.

[42] Glos. Colln., J. J. Powell's newspaper cuttings 1863–6, 205.

[43] *Glouc. Jnl.* 4 Mar. 1865; Glos. Colln. N 6.2.

[44] Glover, *Presbyterians in Glouc.* 5–7; *Glouc. Jnl.* 6 Feb. 1869.

[45] G.R.O. Worship Reg. no. 19229.

1870 the preaching station was raised in status to a fully sanctioned charge.[46] The Whitefield Memorial church, begun in 1870 and opened in 1872, was built of yellow and red brick and was designed in a 14th-century style by Medland and Son on two storeys with vestries, classrooms, and caretaker's accommodation in the lower, and with a tower with ashlar spire.[47] In 1881 it had morning and evening congregations of 253 and 229.[48] An organ loft was added to the church in the late 1880s[49] and the spire was removed in the later 1970s.[50] In 1973 the Presbyterians united with the Congregationalists of the Southgate church to form the James Forbes United Reformed church and from 1974 worship centred on the Park Road church,[51] to which the members of the Tyndale Congregational church were transferred in 1975.[52] There had been a union with the congregation of the Churches of Christ, in Derby Road, by 1981 when the combined membership was 180.[53]

In 1884 the Presbyterians erected a wooden hall at the corner of Newton and Arreton Avenues in Coney Hill[54] and registered it as an undenominational mission.[55] The hall was used by several groups, including Primitive Methodists, and in the mid 20th century the site was confirmed to the Methodists.[56]

SALVATION ARMY. The Salvation Army 'opened fire' in Gloucester in 1879 under the leadership of Pamela Shepherd who held meetings in the Wellington Hall. Some of its early open-air meetings and marches were disrupted,[57] but on the day of the 1881 census of places of worship 246 and 1,200 people attended special morning and evening services in the skating rink at the former Boothall.[58] In 1888 the army built a barracks or citadel in King's Barton Street and in 1890 it registered another in lower Westgate Street, which became the headquarters of a second corps. It moved from the latter in 1914 to the mission room in Suffolk Street in Kingsholm which it occupied until 1919;[59] the army had used that room in 1906 and 1907.[60] The army evangelized outlying areas, including Longford where a company was established in the 1930s,[61] and in 1955 it took over the Methodist church in Coney Hill.[62] The citadel in King's Barton Street was replaced in 1960 by a new building at the corner of Barton Street and Park Road;[63] the old building became a theatre in 1963.[64]

SOCIETY OF FRIENDS. From the mid 1650s Quakers held meetings in Henry Riddall's house in Gloucester where they were occasionally mocked and assaulted.[65] A meeting attended by George Fox in March 1660 was peaceable,[66] but in the early 1660s several meetings in private houses, including one in Maisemore, were broken up and men imprisoned for unlawful assembly and refusal to take the oath of allegiance.[67] A Quaker preacher was fined in 1668. In 1670 the authorities, having failed despite the use of force to stop Quakers from meeting at Henry Engley's house, locked it, imprisoned a few members, and confiscated personal property.[68] Two cottages in Back Hare Lane (later Park Street), said to have been acquired in 1678, had been converted as a meeting house[69] by 1682 when during renewed harassment it was ransacked, the fittings were burned in the adjoining burial ground, and 25 members were imprisoned.[70] The Quakers, who were drawn from the poorer trades, remained a small and uninfluential group.[71] In 1735 only 20 were enumerated in Gloucester.[72]

From 1670 Gloucester was the place of the monthly meeting for the surrounding area, including Churchdown, Taynton, and Westbury-on-Severn, and for Alvington and Aylburton. In 1755 the Gloucester and Stoke Orchard monthly meetings were united because of their smallness.[73] The circular yearly meeting was held in the Boothall in 1739, 1773, 1779, and 1786.[74] By the end of the century the number of Quakers in Gloucester had dwindled and the meeting house, which was repaired in 1800, was seldom used. A regular preparative meeting was resumed in 1812,[75] and in 1834 the Quakers moved to a new meeting house in Greyfriars and sold the Park Street meeting house, which was of one storey with dormer windows above a plain brick front.[76] It was later used for meetings and for worship by other groups,[77] and became a mission room.[78] The Gloucester Quakers, though few in number,

[46] Glover, *Presbyterians in Glouc.* 7–9.
[47] *Glouc. Jnl.* 10 June 1871; 4 May 1872.
[48] Ibid. 19 Nov. 1881.
[49] Glover, *Presbyterians in Glouc.* 17.
[50] Cf. *Citizen*, 7 Aug. 1976.
[51] Lander, *Southgate Cong. Ch.* 54.
[52] Inf. from Mr. Whitehead.
[53] Inf. from minister of James Forbes United Reformed ch.
[54] Glos. R.O., D 4115/13; *Kelly's Dir. Glos.* (1889), 667.
[55] G.R.O. Worship Reg. no. 28036.
[56] Hine, *Meth. Ch. Glouc. Circuit Rec.* 41.
[57] *Glouc. Corps. 90th Anniversary* (1969): Glos. Colln. NR 6.6.
[58] *Glouc. Jnl.* 19 Nov. 1881.
[59] G.B.R., B 4/5/7, p. 216; G.R.O. Worship Reg. nos. 31330, 33271, 46379; *Smart's Dir. Glouc.* (1910–11), 418.
[60] Glos. R.O., D 4373/3/3.
[61] *Glouc. Corps. 90th Anniversary*.
[62] Hine, *Meth. Ch. Glouc. Circuit Rec.* 41.
[63] *Glouc. Corps. 90th Anniversary*; G.R.O. Worship Reg. nos. 31330, 67644.
[64] *Glos. Life*, Oct. 1969, 31.

[65] N. Penney, *First Publishers of Truth* (1907), 109–11.
[66] *Jnl. of Geo. Fox*, ed. J. L. Nickalls (Camb. 1952), 369.
[67] J. Besse, *Abstract of Sufferings of Quakers*, i (1733), 101; ii (1738), 171–4.
[68] G.B.R., G 3/SO 7, ff. 64v., 95v.; *Short Relation of Sufferings of Quakers* (1670), 8–9.
[69] E. Sessions, *Bit of Old Glouc. Made New* (York, 1933), 3.
[70] *Account of Late Hardships Inflicted upon Quakers in City and Co. of Glocester* (Lond. 1682), 1–3.
[71] Ripley, 'Glouc. 1660–1740', 160–1.
[72] G.D.R. vol. 285B (1), f. 25.
[73] Glos. R.O., D 1340/A 1/M 1, M 10.
[74] Ibid. M 10, M 2–3; *Glouc. Jnl.* 4 Sept. 1739; 27 Sept. 1773; 20 Sept. 1779; 11 Sept. 1786.
[75] Glos. Colln. R 35087; *Glouc. New Guide* (1802), 79.
[76] Glos. R.O., D 1340/A 1/M 4; for appearance of Park Street meeting ho. before 1903, photogs. in Sessions, *Bit of Old Glouc. Made New*; Glos. Colln. 13219, f. 16v.
[77] *Glouc. Jnl.* 20 Aug. 1842; Sessions, *Bit of Old Glouc. Made New*, 4; Bond, *Hist of Glouc.* 104; G.R.O. Worship Reg. no. 8741.
[78] Below, undenominational missions.

included several prominent businessmen. One was Samuel Bowly (d. 1884), a supporter of causes such as negro emancipation, temperance, and universal peace, who attended the meeting from 1829.[79] Another was Jesse Sessions (d. 1894), whose family was involved in many philanthropic ventures.[80] The Greyfriars meeting house, which was used for meetings to promote benevolent causes, had a congregation of 36 in 1851[81] and morning and evening attendances of 87 and 79 respectively in 1881.[82] In 1879 a lobby, with a schoolroom over, was added to the front of the meeting house,[83] which with its lodge remained in use in 1981.

UNITARIANS. In 1716 the Barton Street chapel, formerly Independent, from which some members had withdrawn,[84] had a congregation of 400 and was described as Presbyterian. Joseph Denham, minister until 1722,[85] acquired the house next to the chapel in 1715 and conveyed it to Thomas Browne, the leading member of the meeting and a former alderman, in 1721; it later became the manse.[86] The chapel, which in 1735 had a membership of 100,[87] became Unitarian under Joshua Dickinson, minister from 1751.[88] Dickinson, who in 1772 sought to be released from the legal obligation to subscribe to the Thirty Nine Articles,[89] had become infirm by 1784, when an assistant was appointed, but remained minister until his death in 1796. The meeting continued to be supported by prominent city families,[90] and in the late 18th century and the early 19th it received a few legacies to maintain the minister.[91] In 1819 the minister claimed that the Sunday school at the chapel had been started in the 1780s and had been supported by Robert Raikes.[92] For two years in the mid 1820s there was no minister and the chapel was closed for extensive repairs.[93] The street front, of ashlar and with a pediment, probably dated from the 18th century but its windows were altered in 1844 when the chapel, which had a gallery on three sides, was extensively restored; the wall in front was taken down and the vestry, which projected south of the line of the front, was replaced by rooms on two floors for the school and library.[94] At a restoration in 1867 the chapel was repewed.[95]

In 1851 morning and evening congregations of 60 and 80 were claimed for the chapel.[96] In the later 19th century, despite a reorganization of the meeting on free church principles in 1876, the membership dwindled and most ministers stayed only a few years.[97] The morning and evening congregations in 1881 were 63 and 115 respectively.[98] The manse, which had been occupied by tenants from 1875, was pulled down in 1893 and two shops were built in its place to provide more income.[99] Later that year the interior of the chapel was altered to make it more attractive for worship; the gallery was removed from two sides, an extension made on the north side to take the organ and choir, and new fittings and decorations were provided.[1] In the early 20th century the chapel depended on the support of the Price family of Tibberton Court and in 1905 Margaret Price gave it £1,000. The chapel, which from 1956 shared a minister with the Cheltenham Unitarian church,[2] had fallen into serious disrepair and commercial development of the site had been approved by 1963.[3] The remains of James Forbes were removed to the cathedral cloisters in 1966,[4] and the chapel was closed in 1968 and demolished. In 1981 a small meeting, part of the Cotswold group of Unitarian churches, was held twice a month in the Friends' meeting house.[5] The site of the Barton Street chapel was occupied by the offices of a building society.

UNDENOMINATIONAL MISSIONS. Colin Campbell, who in 1831 registered a room in an office at the canal basin for worship, proposed building a chapel for seamen and boatmen frequenting Gloucester's docks and quay. His scheme failed for lack of funds, but a similar idea promoted in 1846 by men connected with the port was supported by the established church and led to the opening of a chapel in the docks in 1849.[6] The chapel is dealt with above.[7] The mission, which occasionally included services in foreign languages, had been extended to Sharpness docks by 1876. The chaplain opened a coffee house and reading room in Gloucester docks in 1877, and from 1885 until c. 1970 the mission used a hall at the corner of lower Southgate Street and Llanthony Road.[8]

[79] D.N.B.; Glouc. Jnl. 4 Jan. 1868; 29 Mar. 1884.
[80] Glouc. Jnl. 21 Apr. 1894; cf. ibid. 23 Aug. 1873; 26 Oct. 1901.　　　[81] P.R.O., HO 129/336/3/5/7.
[82] Glouc. Jnl. 19 Nov. 1881.
[83] Citizen, 24 Aug. 1971; Glos. R.O., D 4335/67.
[84] Above, Congregationalists and Independents.
[85] Dr. Williams's Libr., Evans MS. p. 42.
[86] Glos. R.O., D 4270/4/1/6, 10, 16; for Browne, Ripley, 'Glouc. 1660–1740', 150–1, 314.
[87] G.D.R. vol. 285B (1), f. 25.
[88] J. Murch, Hist. of Presbyt. and General Bapt. Churches in W. of Eng. (1835), 10.
[89] Trans. Cong. Hist. Soc. v. 205–18.
[90] Murch, Presbyt. and Bapt. Churches, 10, 13.
[91] Glos. R.O., D 4270/4/1/14, 16; 2/1/1, pp. 88–96.
[92] Theophilus Browne, Religious Liberty and Rights of Conscience (1819), p. ii.
[93] Murch, Presbyt. and Bapt. Churches, 10.
[94] Ibid. 12–13; Glouc. Jnl. 1 Feb. 1845; Glos. R.O., D 4270/2/1/1, pp. 1–3; for photog. of street front in 1960, Glouc.,

a Pictorial Rec. 2.
[95] Glos. R.O., D 4270/2/1/1, pp. 101–12; Glos. Chron. 20 July 1867.　　　[96] P.R.O., HO 129/336/3/3/4.
[97] Glos. R.O., D 4270/2/1/1–2; 2/2/1.
[98] Glouc. Jnl. 19 Nov. 1881.
[99] Glos. R.O., D 4270/2/1/2–3.
[1] Ibid. 3; 2/2/2; Glouc. Jnl. 20 Jan. 1894; for view of interior before 1893 alterations, Glos. Colln. 10600 (6), reproduced above, Plate 50; for photogs. of interior in 1963, Glos. Colln. prints GL 10.11 (3–4).
[2] Glos. R.O., D 4270/2/2/2–4.
[3] Citizen, 21 Oct. 1968.
[4] Lander, Southgate Cong. Ch. 7.
[5] Inf. from meeting sec.; cf. Citizen, 15 May 1969.
[6] W. H. Whalley, Mariners' Chap. (1909), 6–21; Hockaday Abs. ccvi, 1831.
[7] Above, Churches and Chapels, non-par. chap.
[8] Whalley, Mariners' Chap. 23–45; 28th Rep. Mariners' Chap. Cttee.: copy in Glos. Colln. N 5.7; for work of first chaplain, J. Hollins, Pastoral Recollections (1857).

In 1866 a mission organized in connexion with a sailors' home in Ladybellegate Street was opened at the city quay in an upper room registered by Bible Christians and known as the Gospel Hall.[9] In 1874 the Southgate church withdrew its support from the mission to concentrate its missionary work in the Island,[10] and the room, which may have been that used by the Anglican mariners' chaplain for a mission to boatmen in 1876 and 1877,[11] was disused in 1895.[12]

The Norwegian Seamen's Missionary Society established in 1865 planned occasional services in Gloucester and from the late 1860s they were conducted by a preacher from Bristol whenever there were enough Norwegian seamen in port. With the increase in trade with Norway in the mid 1870s services were held every other Sunday, and in 1878 a small wooden church was built by subscription next to the canal at the wagon works.[13] It apparently closed in the late 1880s.[14]

In 1839 David Nasmith[15] founded the Gloucester City Mission to evangelize the large number of poor which did not attend religious services. It was supported by the main dissenting churches and some members of the established church and was financed by donations. It employed a missionary in the slums in the north and west parts of the city to hold meetings, circulate religious tracts, and visit dwellings. A female missionary had been appointed by 1842. Although its secretary Isaac Cooke registered a house in Longford in 1840, the mission did not have a fixed centre. It also lacked funds and has not been traced after 1842.[16]

Part of its work was continued by the Gloucester Female Mission, which from 1842 held a weekly meeting in the Quakers' former meeting house in Park Street. The work of the mission was expanded to include Sunday services at the Park Street room,[17] which was registered in 1867[18] and had morning and evening attendances of 55 and 83 in 1881.[19] In 1890 Edith Sessions bought the room to ensure that the work of the Park Street mission continued. The room, which was strengthened in 1894, was replaced by a larger brick building in 1903. Two classrooms and a caretaker's cottage were added in 1911.[20] The mission was open in 1981.

In 1840 Charles Jones, a member of a temperance society, registered a room in Bull Lane

for worship.[21] The room was probably in the building used by the mechanics' institution, which was then being revived under evangelical leadership.[22] Other buildings used for missionary work included a working men's hall in Parliament Street, registered between 1865 and 1876 for use by Bible Christians, and the working men's institute in lower Southgate Street, registered in 1881 and with morning and evening attendances of 106 and 570 later that year. The last-mentioned mission ceased some time before 1925.[23]

There was a short-lived interdenominational mission to the Dockham area where a Sunday school was opened in 1846. It received much support from Quakers, and the schoolroom was also used in winter for an evening school supervised by the master of the British school, but it has not been traced after 1847.[24]

St. Aldate's Hall in St. Aldate Square, used by the Gloucester Sunday School Mission from 1879 or 1880, had morning and evening congregations of 60 and 350 in 1881.[25] The hall had been registered for the Gloucester Bible Christians earlier that year and services had ceased there by 1896.[26]

In 1880 Quakers opened a mission in a hall in Sherborne Street in Kingsholm[27] and in 1881 the morning and evening congregations were 60 and 150. The mission prospered and in 1901 the building was enlarged for the third time.[28] The hall was sold to Christadelphians in 1959.[29]

A railway mission was established in Gloucester in 1884. Meetings were held in the co-operative society's hall and later in the British school, and in 1887 a hall was built in Millbrook Street near the railway. A classroom was added in 1888. In 1891, following a dispute over the use of the building,[30] E. H. Spring, the superintendent, and his supporters withdrew to join a congregation of the Churches of Christ and the hall was closed.[31] It was reopened after a while and in the early 1930s was taken over by a pentecostal church.[32]

At Tuffley Alfred Brown, a Quaker, erected an iron building next to a house on the Stroud road in 1896 for a mission to employees of the Robins Wood Hill brickworks. The mission, which provided a coffee house and reading room, had closed by 1921. The building, which was put to other uses, was pulled down in 1980.[33] In the early 20th century there was also a mission room further south on the Stroud road, just within the

[9] G.R.O. Worship Reg. no. 17540; *Glouc. Jnl.* 30 Mar. 1895. [10] Deggan, *Southgate Sun. Sch.* 10–11.
[11] Whalley, *Mariners' Chap.* 42.
[12] *Glouc. Jnl.* 30 Mar. 1895.
[13] *Glos. Chron.* 24 Aug. 1878; O.S. Map 1/2,500, Glos. XXXIII. 2 (1886 edn.).
[14] Cf. *Smart's Dir. Glouc.* (1886 and 1889 edns.).
[15] Cf. *D.N.B.*
[16] *Glouc. Jnl.* 18, 25 Apr. 1840; 30 Oct. 1841; 10 Sept. 1842; Hockaday Abs. ccxiv.
[17] Sessions, *Bit of Old Glouc. Made New*, 4; cf. *Glos. Chron.* 24 May 1873. [18] G.R.O. Worship Reg. no. 17896.
[19] *Glouc. Jnl.* 19 Nov. 1881.
[20] Sessions, *Bit of Old Glouc. Made New*, 4–7; *Glouc. Jnl.* 31 Oct. 1903; 14 Oct. 1911.
[21] Hockaday Abs. ccxvii; Glos. Colln. NQ 20.3.
[22] *Glouc. Jnl.* 23 Oct. 1841; Glos. Colln. NF 20.1 (1, 3).
[23] G.R.O. Worship Reg. nos. 16734, 25625; *Glouc. Jnl.* 19

Nov. 1881; for the institute, above, Glouc. 1835–1985, social and cultural life. [24] *Glouc. Jnl.* 23 Oct. 1847.
[25] Ibid. 25 Dec. 1880; 19 Nov. 1881.
[26] G.R.O. Worship Reg. no. 25803.
[27] Ibid. no. 25197; the hall, which retains a date stone of 1880, may have been that used earlier by the Foresters: *Glouc. Jnl.* 19 Aug. 1876.
[28] *Glouc. Jnl.* 19 Nov. 1881; 26 Oct. 1901.
[29] Inf. from Mr. P. Rowntree, of Stroud Road; G.R.O. Worship Reg. no. 67166.
[30] E.H. Spring, *Hist. of Glouc. Branch of Railway Mission* (1891), 1–20.
[31] *Glouc. Jnl.* 2 Jan. 1892; G. E. Barr, *Edwin Hen. Spring* (1935), 23–6.
[32] *Jennings's Glouc. Guide* (1895), 81; *Glouc. Jnl.* 30 Jan. 1909; below.
[33] Glos. R.O., D 3117/2103; *Citizen*, 3 Dec. 1980; inf. from Mr. Rowntree.

former boundary of Tuffley,[34] and in 1906 Quakers held meetings in the Tuffley school.[35]

OTHER CHURCHES. In 1839 the schoolroom of James Ricketts in Oxford Street was registered for public worship.[36] Ricketts had moved his school by 1853 to Greyfriars, where it was called Abbot's Hall and was similarly registered until 1876.[37]

Christadelphians were holding services in Goddard's assembly rooms in 1881 when the congregation numbered 80.[38] By 1885 they were meeting in a hall in St. Aldate Square and by 1889 in a hall in King Street.[39] In the early 1940s they worshipped in a room in Northgate Mansions, in lower Northgate Street,[40] and from 1959 they used the Sherborne Street mission hall.[41]

In 1890 an evangelist of the Disciples or Churches of Christ began preaching in Goddard's assembly rooms. In 1891 the congregation was joined by E.H. Spring and his followers from the railway mission and Spring became its pastor. At the end of the year the Churches of Christ built a chapel, the East End tabernacle, in Derby Road and in 1896 added a schoolroom to it.[42] In 1981 the congregation held joint services with the James Forbes United Reformed church.[43]

The Labour Church, which held a meeting in a hall in Barton Street in 1904, failed to establish itself in Gloucester.[44]

By 1920 a group belonging to the Pentecostal Churches, later known as the Assemblies of God, was meeting at a house in Blenheim Road. The congregation moved several times: to a house in lower Barton Street, registered for a full gospel mission in 1925; to a room in India Road, registered in 1936; to the chapel in Tredworth High Street, registered in 1957 and formerly used by Anglicans; and in 1978 to the gymnasium of the former army barracks on Robins Wood Hill.[45]

A gospel mission recorded in Commercial Road in 1931[46] may have been the pentecostal church which in 1933 registered Victory Hall, the former railway mission hall, in Millbrook Street. The church joined the Elim Four Square Gospel Alliance in 1934 and the hall, which was destroyed by a bomb in 1941, was replaced by a larger temporary building in 1950. In 1957 the Elim Pentecostal church took over a cinema in Parkend Road to accommodate larger congregations.[47]

Spiritualists in Gloucester were reported in 1876 to be about to form an association[48] but no record of any place of worship has been found before 1939 when the Gloucester Spiritualist church met in Russell Street.[49] By 1959 it had moved to a small meeting place in Montpellier[50] and in 1981 was known as the Gloucester First Spiritualist church. In 1962 another group, the Gloucester National Spiritualist church, registered the room in Brunswick Square formerly used by Christian Brethren.[51]

Zion Hall of the Jehovah's Witnesses recorded in London Road in 1939 was presumably Kingdom Hall,[52] which had closed there by 1952. In 1955 the Jehovah's Witnesses registered Kingdom Hall in Seymour Road.[53]

Christian Science services were held in the early 1940s in Cromwell Street in the iron chapel, moved from Wotton where Wesleyan Methodists had once used it.[54] In 1960 the congregation moved to the new First Church of Christ Scientist, Gloucester, in Cheltenham Road at Longlevens.[55]

A branch of the Seventh Day Adventist Church was using a room in the Good Templars' hall in Park Road by 1959.[56] By 1962 it had taken over the iron chapel in Cromwell Street vacated by the Christian Scientists.[57] The chapel was later replaced by a brick church.[58] In 1980 another group of Seventh Day Adventists opened a new church in Tredworth at the corner of Hatherley and Tarrington Roads.[59]

The Apostolic Church registered two rooms in Stroud Road in 1960. In 1968 the congregation moved to the room behind Cromwell Street, which had earlier been used by Brethren. The New Testament Church of God, which had registered that room in 1965, moved in 1967 to a hall, originally a Primitive Methodist chapel, in Stroud Road.[60] In Tredworth the Church of God of Prophecy purchased the Methodist chapel in Melbourne Street in 1965 or 1966,[61] and in 1981 the Bethel United Church of Jesus Christ (Apostolic) occupied the chapel in High Street, formerly used by the Assemblies of God and built by Wesleyan Methodists.

Two rooms of a Christian youth centre in Denmark Road were registered in 1948. Services had been discontinued by 1964. An unspecified Christian group, which registered a room at Spa Villas, Montpellier, in 1963, had disbanded by 1967.[62]

[34] O.S. Map 1/2,500, Glos. XXXIII. 11 (1903 and 1923 edns.). [35] Glos. Colln. JF 4.6, p. 17.

[36] Hockaday Abs. ccxv.

[37] G.R.O. Worship Reg. no. 1073; Bd. of Health Map (1852); Glouc. Jnl. 6 Jan. 1855.

[38] Glouc. Jnl. 19 Nov. 1881.

[39] Cf. Kelly's Dir. Glos. (1885–1927 edns.).

[40] Kelly's Dir. Glouc. (1941–2), A 27; (1945–6), A 29.

[41] G.R.O. Worship Reg. no. 67166; inf. from Mr. Rowntree.

[42] Barr, E. H. Spring, 24–6, 47; Glouc. Jnl. 2 Jan. 1892.

[43] Inf. from minister of James Forbes United Reformed ch.

[44] Glouc. Jnl. 2 Apr. 1904.

[45] Citizen, 16 Oct. 1978; G.R.O. Worship Reg. nos. 49855, 56479, 65927, 75087.

[46] Kelly's Dir. Glos. (1931), 188.

[47] G.R.O. Worship Reg. no. 54635; Citizen, 21 Oct. 1955; 18 June 1957; 27 Mar. 1974; cf. Citizen, 6 Jan. 1955.

[48] Glouc. Jnl. 23 Sept. 1876.

[49] Kelly's Dir. Glos. (1939), 191; Kelly's Dir. Glouc. (1941–2), A 27.

[50] Kelly's Dir. Glouc. (1959 and later edns.).

[51] G.R.O. Worship Reg. no. 68543.

[52] Kelly's Dir. Glos. (1939), 191; Kelly's Dir. Glouc. (1941–2), A 27.

[53] G.R.O. Worship Reg. nos. 62120, 64914.

[54] Kelly's Dir. Glouc. (1941–2), A 27; (1952), A 16.

[55] G.R.O. Worship Reg. nos. 67220, 67991.

[56] Kelly's Dir. Glouc. (1958), A 8.

[57] G.R.O. Worship Reg. no. 68490.

[58] Cf. Hine, Meth. Ch. Glouc. Circuit Rec. 21.

[59] Inf. from minister (1981).

[60] G.R.O. Worship Reg. nos. 67733, 71460, 69891, 71149; Citizen, 30 Oct. 1967.

[61] Glos. R.O., D 2689/2/5/2.

[62] G.R.O. Worship Reg. nos. 62103, 68968.

OTHER RELIGIOUS BODIES

JUDAISM.[63] An account of the medieval Jewry is given above.[64] Jews reappeared in Gloucester shortly before 1764.[65] They traded as jewellers and silversmiths, some throughout the county and beyond, and as shopkeepers, and in the early 19th century dominated pawnbroking in the city.[66] By 1792 the Jewish community had a synagogue in Barton Street nearly opposite the Unitarian chapel[67] and by 1802 had moved it[68] to a room in Mercy Place, opposite the infirmary in lower Southgate Street.[69] From the mid 19th century the community declined, a fact ascribed to an influx of Quakers with superior business ability.[70] The synagogue may have remained open until the early 1850s[71], but by the mid 1850s Gloucester Jews attended the Cheltenham synagogue.[72] Amelia Abrahams, the last member of the community, died in 1886,[73] and the pawnbroker Samuel Goldberg traded in the city until the end of the century.[74]

By 1785 the Jews had a cemetery to the north of Barton Street, which also served Jewry in Stroud and Ross-on-Wye (Herefs.) and was apparently not used after 1887. In 1938 it was laid out as a playground for St. Michael's school in Russell Street and the remains and monuments were removed to the new municipal cemetery at Coney Hill.[75]

ISLAM. The Muslim community in Gloucester dates from the late 1950s and the Gloucester Muslim Welfare Association, which had been formed by 1965, converted two houses in Ryecroft Street as a prayer hall or mosque,[76] registered for worship in 1968.[77] The Muslim community in the Barton Street area grew during the following years and in 1981 the association demolished the two houses and began a larger mosque on the site. The new mosque, designed by Brian Tait, a local architect,[78] had a dome and minaret and opened in 1983.

From the later 1970s the Gloucestershire Islamic Trust, formed to serve the needs of a separate group of Muslims, held services in a warehouse in All Saints Road.[79] In 1985 the building was demolished and replaced by a mosque.

EDUCATION

THE HISTORY of the Gloucester grammar schools before 1882, including the school run by Llanthony Priory in the Middle Ages, the Crypt school founded by Joan Cooke and entrusted to the city corporation in 1540, and the College school run by the dean and chapter of Gloucester from the 1540s, will be found in another volume.[80] The brief account of Sir Thomas Rich's school included there is amplified here, and details are given of the history of the Crypt school buildings.

The original schoolhouse of the Crypt school, built in 1539,[81] stands in Southgate Street adjoining St. Mary de Crypt church on the south and incorporating a gateway over the entrance to St. Mary's Lane on the north. Above the schoolroom with its two tiers of windows were cocklofts, used as accommodation for the schoolmaster.[82] In the late 18th century or the early 19th the upper row of windows on the street front was replaced by sash windows,[83] but later, possibly at a restoration of the building in 1880,[84] Tudor-style windows, to match the originals, replaced the sashes. A site for a new school, on the south side of inner Barton Street, was acquired by the municipal charity trustees in 1858 but building was delayed because parishioners of St. Mary de Crypt opposed the removal of the school from their parish. The new school, a brick building designed by Medland and Maberly,[85] was opened in 1862. The old school, sold the same year, became the Sunday schoolroom for St. Mary de Crypt parish.[86]

SIR THOMAS RICH'S SCHOOL (OR THE BLUECOAT HOSPITAL) TO 1882. The school was founded by Sir Thomas Rich, Bt., of Sonning (Berks.), a native of Gloucester who

[63] This article on Judaism and Islam was written in 1982 and revised in 1986.

[64] Medieval Glouc., Glouc. 1066–1327.

[65] Glouc. Jnl. 26 Mar. 1764.

[66] G.D.R., B 4/1/1147; Glouc. New Guide (1802), 145, 156–7; Gell and Bradshaw, Glos. Dir. (1820), 61, 78, 81; Glos. N. & Q. iv. 163–4; Jewish Monthly, ii. 473.

[67] Glouc. Guide (1792), 77.

[68] Glouc. New Guide (1802), 79.

[69] Glouc. Jnl. 3 Mar. 1823; Glos. N. & Q. iv. 163.

[70] Jewish Monthly, ii. 474; Glos. N. & Q. iv. 164.

[71] Cf. Slater's Dir. Glos. (1852–3), 127.

[72] Glos. R.O., D 3883/1/7; 2/2.

[73] Glos. N. & Q. iv. 163.

[74] Kelly's Dir. Glos. (1885–1902 edns.).

[75] Glos. N. & Q. iv. 385–7; Glos. R.O., NC 66.

[76] Citizen, 29 June 1965.

[77] G.R.O. (General Register Office), Worship Reg. no. 71508.

[78] Citizen, 23 Sept., 8 Dec. 1981.

[79] Ibid. 19 Sept. 1981.

[80] V.C.H. Glos. ii. 314–37, 342–52. This article was written in 1984–5.

[81] Austin, Crypt Sch. 30.

[82] Ibid. 32, 53–4, 64.

[83] Glos. R.O., A 154/44; Fosbrooke, Glouc. 151.

[84] Plaque on bldg.

[85] Glos. R.O., D 3270/19678, pp. 434, 482; 19679, pp. 3, 57.

[86] Glouc. Jnl. 28 June, 5 July 1862.

became a wealthy London merchant engaged in trade with Turkey.[87] By his will dated 1666 he gave the city corporation a house on the north side of Eastgate Street for the use of the school and £6,000 to be laid out on land. As well as supporting other charities, the endowment was to provide annual payments of £160 for lodging and maintaining 20 poor boys, £20 for the salary of a schoolmaster to teach the boys reading and writing, and £60 for apprenticing and clothing six of the boys each year. The boys, who were to be dressed in the blue uniform of Christ's Hospital, London, were to stay in the school between the ages of 10 and 16; the corporation decided to admit only sons of freemen. The endowment was received in 1668 and laid out on several farms in Awre and Lydney, and the school was started the same year.[88] Until 1804, when a separate management committee of council members was appointed,[89] the school was under the management of the full common council, which appointed the master and the 'motherwoman', or matron, who received the maintenance allowance, and admitted, and occasionally expelled, boys. A rent gatherer, who from 1738 was the city treasurer, submitted annual accounts.[90]

Until the mid 18th century the estates, which extended to 626 a. in 1731,[91] were on long leases and brought in a rental of c. £320. That sum was barely sufficient to meet the expenses of the charity,[92] and the school was aided on several occasions from the corporation's own funds or by interest-free loans from well-wishers.[93] There were some additional endowments. Amity Clutterbuck by will dated 1721 gave £1,000 in stock, received in 1729, and Thomas Browne, a former alderman, gave £400, which was received and invested in stock in 1731. In 1749 £1,000 of the stock was sold[94] and the proceeds used to buy another farm in Awre.[95] Richard Elly by will dated 1754 gave £500 to be applied according to the wishes of the schoolmaster Luke Hook; Hook decided that the interest on £170 should be used each year to buy shoes and stockings for the boys and the interest on the remainder used to repair the school building.[96] In 1766 another farm was added to the endowment,[97] £2,000 of the purchase price being raised by loans from two aldermen and the remaining £700 by the sale of stock.[98]

The new purchases raised the total rental of the school's lands to £452. Tenures were later changed to rack rent, and the rental increased to £975 by 1800 and £1,560 by 1815.[99] In spite of cost of living increases in the matron's allowance,[1] the school enjoyed a considerable surplus of funds during that period. The school was rebuilt between 1806 and 1808 at a cost of £4,000, the sum including the principal of the Elly bequest. The new building, designed by John Wheeler,[2] had an ashlar front with a rusticated ground floor and an upper floor with Ionic pilasters and balustraded parapet.[3] In 1815 part of a substantial balance in funds was used to pay £2,380, for principal and interest, to the city treasury, under the mistaken impression that the £700 used in the 1766 purchase had come from the corporation's own funds.[4] Later a falling rental, which stood at £1,072 in 1825,[5] and expenditure on the farm buildings produced an annual deficit of c. £300. Economies introduced in 1831 included reducing the cost of an annual dinner for the corporation and the recipients of the charity; Sir Thomas Rich had assigned £6 13s. 4d. for that purpose but c. £40 was usually spent.[6]

In the early 19th century the boys were kept in the school for three years and taught reading, writing, arithmetic, grammar, and the elements of religion.[7] There were frequent disciplinary problems: boys often went absent without leave, and in 1827 an inquiry revealed that older boys had been forcing younger ones to steal for them. Feuding between the master and the matron, which was disrupting the running of the school in 1818,[8] led to the appointment of a married couple in 1820.[9]

In 1836 Sir Thomas Rich's school was transferred from the corporation to the new municipal charity trustees. The two bodies later went to law over the mistaken repayment made in 1815, and in 1847 the corporation was directed to pay the trustees £4,778 in respect of it.[10] In 1851 the school was regulated by a Scheme under which 30 boys, sons of city residents, were to be taught and subsequently apprenticed; the annual rental of the estates was then £1,217.[11] The curriculum remained an elementary one in the mid 19th century, though some new subjects were introduced and from c. 1849 examinations by outside examiners were held.[12]

[87] Burke, *Ext. & Dorm. Baronetcies* (1838), 440; D. J. Watkins, 'Hist. of Sir. Thos. Rich's Sch.' (1966, TS. in Glos. R.O. Libr.), 1–2.
[88] *14th Rep. Com. Char.* 21–5; G.B.R., B 3/3, pp. 357, 361, 367.
[89] G.B.R., B 3/13, f. 7v.; Glos. R.O., D 3270/19659.
[90] G.B.R., B 3/6–12, *passim*.
[91] *14th Rep. Com. Char.* 26.
[92] Glos. R.O., D 3270/19672.
[93] G.B.R., B 3/7, ff. 230, 232; B 4/1/2, f. 153.
[94] Ibid. B 3/9, ff. 221v., 268, 309–10; Glos. R.O., D 3270/19662.
[95] *14th Rep. Com. Char.* 26.
[96] G.B.R., B 3/11, ff. 201v.–202.
[97] *14th Rep. Com. Char.* 27.
[98] The stock sold comprised £250-worth, acquired by the corp. under a bequest for another charitable purpose by Thos. Gunter, and other stock vested in the sch., perhaps including

the residue of the Clutterbuck and Browne bequests: Glos. R.O., D 3270/19672, acct. 1766–7; G.B.R., B 3/11, ff. 276v.–277v.; cf. G.B.R., B 3/15, min. 17 Jan. 1837.
[99] Glos. R.O., D 3270/19672.
[1] G.B.R., B 3/12, ff. 42, 223v.; 13, f. 116.
[2] Glos. R.O., D 3270/19659; *14th Rep. Com. Char.* 27–9.
[3] Above, Plate 47; *Glouc. As It Was* (Nelson, 1973), 9. [4] G.B.R., B 4/1/2, ff. 153–4v.; B 3/13, f. 164.
[5] Glos. R.O., D 3270/19672.
[6] G.B.R., B 3/14, ff. 177v.–182.
[7] *14th Rep. Com. Char.* 29. [8] Glos. R.O., D 3270/19659.
[9] *14th Rep. Com. Char.* 28; G.B.R., B 3/13, ff. 288v., 319v.
[10] Glos. R.O., D 3270/19677, pp. 190, 193–4.
[11] Glos. Colln. N 17.82.
[12] Glos. R.O., D 3270/19677, pp. 420, 429–30; 19678, pp. 24, 191.

SECONDARY EDUCATION 1882–1984. Under a Scheme of 1882 the Crypt school and Sir Thomas Rich's school with their ancient endowments were made part of one foundation, the Gloucester United Endowed Schools. The governing body, comprising an equal representation of city councillors, municipal charity trustees, and co-opted members, was empowered to build two new girls' high schools and provide scholarships and exhibitions. Several city charities administered by the charity trustees were annexed to the foundation, together with a charity of William Bond,[13] who by will dated 1823 had given £40 a year to be divided among four Bluecoat boys on completion of their apprenticeships.[14] The Girls' Lower school was opened in 1883 and the two boys' schools were provided with new accommodation in 1889, but the fall in rents caused by the agricultural depression led to the postponement of the building of the fourth school and to a reduction in the scholarships provided under the Scheme of 1882.[15] The King's school (formerly the College school) remained entirely independent of that and all later plans for secondary education in the city. The factors that had thwarted a connexion with the other schools in the early 1870s, opposition by the dean and chapter to any dilution of their control and their determination to preserve it principally as a choir school, continued to limit opportunities for the school's expansion for many years.[16]

In 1906 a Scheme amalgamated the United Schools governors with the governors of the Gloucester municipal schools, who ran the Schools of Science and Art under the city education committee. The new body, comprising 18 city councillors, 3 county councillors, and 6 co-opted members, carried on the Crypt, Sir Thomas Rich's, and the girls' school (renamed the Girls' High) as public secondary schools for 8 to 18 year olds,[17] with an income drawn from the old endowments, local education authority and Board of Education grants, and tuition fees. In 1907 some land was sold to pay for a new building for the Girls' High school, opened in 1909, and further sales were made in 1921 to finance the establishment of a second high school, Ribston Hall. Ribston Hall, though managed by the United Schools governors, was later maintained entirely by the city education committee.[18]

The movement to provide schooling of a more vocational nature led the United Schools governors in 1919 to open a Junior Technical school, in which boys aged from 13 to 15 were taught by the staff of the Technical College. In 1920 the city education committee opened a Girls' Junior Technical school in Brunswick Square, and in 1925 it opened Central schools in Derby Road, providing education with a commercial and industrial bias for children selected from the elementary schools at the age of 11. The Girls' Central school absorbed the Girls' Junior Technical school in 1928.[19]

By the early 1930s the education provided by the Crypt school and Sir Thomas Rich's school, which had adopted a curriculum on the grammar school model, was thought by many to be inappropriate to the needs of their pupils, many of whom joined local engineering firms when they left. Plans for reorganizing secondary education, involving the transformation of Sir Thomas Rich's into a school with a technical and commercial bias, met strong opposition and were abandoned in 1933. The plans had also included measures to bring the United schools under more direct control by the city, which was by then supplying a fairly large share of their costs;[20] in the year 1932–3 government grants provided £11,449, city rates £7,785, and county rates (paid in respect of the considerable number of children from outside the city who attended the schools) £3,664, while tuition fees provided £8,710 and the ancient endowments £3,014.[21] In 1937 the endowments of the United schools were transferred to the direct control of the education committee and the governors were reconstituted as 21 appointees of the city council (including 15 councillors) and 7 appointees of the county.[22] The governors managed the schools until 1945 when a new governing body for all the city's secondary schools was appointed.[23]

At a reorganization under the 1944 Education Act, not completed until 1949, the four United schools lost their preparatory departments and their intake of children from outside the city and became secondary grammar schools; five senior departments of city elementary schools became secondary modern schools; and the two Central schools became secondary technical schools.[24] Between 1957 and 1967 five of the schools and the aided Roman Catholic secondary school were rehoused in new buildings in the outer parts of the city. Under the boundary extension of 1967 two county secondary schools, at Longlevens and Hucclecote, came under the city authority. From 1965 various schemes for a comprehensive system for the city's secondary schools were discussed,[25] and that system was introduced on a limited scale in the early 1970s when a new comprehensive school was built and two other schools were reorganized on comprehensive lines. The county council, which became responsible for education in the city in 1974, decided in 1984 on a comprehensive scheme involving all the schools; it was to take effect in 1987.[26]

The King's school in the late 19th century and the early 20th remained a small, academically

[13] Glos. Colln. NF 17.18.   [14] *14th Rep. Com. Char.* 40–1.
[15] Glos. Colln. NF 17.11; 17.24 (1).
[16] D. Robertson, *King's Sch., Glouc.* (1974), 152–63.
[17] Glos. Colln. NF 17.12.
[18] M. Burden, *My Brook became a River* (Glouc. 1980), 36, 60.
[19] P. G. Rossington, 'Hist. of Glouc. Technical Coll.' (c. 1962, TS. in Glos. Colln. NF 17.461), 77–8, 100–2; G.B.R., B 4/25/70, pp. 55–6, 220–1, 227.
[20] Glos. Colln. NF 17.15 (1–2); Watkins, 'Sir Thos. Rich's

Sch.', 98, 106–11.   [21] Burden, *My Brook became a River*, 83.
[22] G.B.R., B 4/25/15, pp. 21–2; 16, pp. 155–6.
[23] Ibid. 20, p. 62.
[24] Ibid. 25/58; W. C. Charter, 'The Secondary Modern Sch. in Glouc. 1944–64' (Bristol Univ. B. Ed. thesis, 1981), 11–19.
[25] e.g. G.B.R., B 4/25/54, finance and general purposes cttee. 20 July 1965; governors of Glouc. secondary schs. 5 Jan. 1966; 56, sub-cttee. on reorganization of sec. educ. 17 Sept. 1969.   [26] Notices issued by educ. cttee. 30 Nov. 1984.

undistinguished school of 50–60 boys, run by the dean and chapter principally as a choir school. It was housed mainly in the schoolroom built on the north side of the cathedral in 1849 and, from 1891, in Paddock House, in Pitt Street, which was acquired as a headmaster's and boarding house. Frequent applications for aid from the Ecclesiastical Commissioners, under the terms of the Endowed Schools Act of 1869, were unsuccessful; after the 1902 Education Act such aid was likely to involve the inclusion of city councillors on the governing body, an innovation strongly opposed by the dean and chapter. In 1928 a grant was acquired, leading to some expansion and an improvement in standards. New buildings in Pitt Street were opened in 1929, and in the following year there were 150 boys in the school. In 1950 the Ministry of Education's refusal to grant the school official recognition led, following a public appeal, to a major expansion and reorganization. Laymen joined the dean and chapter as governors, and additional accommodation, notably the former bishop's palace acquired in 1954, was found in and around the cathedral close.[27] Several new buildings were added to those on the Pitt Street site in the early 1980s. In 1984 the King's school was classed as an independent cathedral school and was supported almost entirely by fees. There were then c. 500 children on the roll, including boys of preparatory and secondary age and some girls of secondary age.[28]

The Crypt school became one of the United schools in 1882, the governors being required to maintain it as a boys' grammar school for 120 day and 40 boarding pupils aged from 8 to 17.[29] In 1889 it moved from Barton Street to Friars Orchard, where it was housed in a new building, designed by Medland and Son, and in the former Bowling Green House which became the headmaster's residence and boarding house.[30] The falling attendance evident before 1882 continued for some years, but in the early 20th century the school expanded[31] and had 401 on its roll in 1932.[32] It moved to new premises on part of the Podsmead estate in 1943, though the buildings there were not completed until several years later.[33] Reorganized as a secondary grammar school under the 1944 Act, it had 508 boys on the roll in 1984.[34]

Sir Thomas Rich's school became one of the United schools in 1882 for 200 boys aged from 8 to 15.[35] In 1889 it moved from the old Bluecoat Hospital building in Eastgate Street to the former Crypt school in Barton Street, where new classrooms were added; the old building was sold

to the city council and replaced by the Guildhall.[36] The school expanded in the early 20th century, taking many boys from outside the city; the buildings were enlarged in 1911–12 and the former British school nearby was taken over in 1932.[37] There were 340 boys on the roll in 1932.[38] It became a secondary grammar school under the 1944 Act, and moved to new buildings at Elmbridge in 1964.[39] There were 562 boys on the roll in 1984. Parts of the old buildings in Barton Street were then in use as a youth centre and for adult education purposes.

Denmark Road High school originated as the *Girls' Lower* school, opened by the United Schools governors in 1883 for girls aged from 8 to 16. Drawing pupils from a wide area of the county, it had 220 by 1894. It was renamed the *Girls' High* school in 1906. Housed at first in Mynd House, Barton Street, it moved in 1904 to Bearland House and in 1909 to a new building in Denmark Road, designed in Queen Anne style by Walter B. Wood. Numbers rose to 488 by 1919, but were reduced after Ribston Hall opened[40] and there were 449 on the roll in 1932.[41] The school became a secondary grammar school under the 1944 Act. The buildings were enlarged in the late 1950s,[42] and there were 533 girls on the roll in 1984.

Ribston Hall High school was opened by the United Schools governors in 1921 as a second girls' high school. It was housed in Ribston Hall, Spa Road, and later expanded into other houses in the area.[43] There were 259 on the roll in 1932.[44] It became a secondary grammar school under the 1944 Act, and moved to new buildings in Stroud Road in 1961.[45] There were 534 girls on the roll in 1984.

Derby Road Central schools were opened by the city education authority in 1925 in former council elementary school buildings. Separate boys' and girls' schools provided education with a commercial bias for children of 11 and over.[46] In 1932 there were 267 boys and 276 girls on the rolls.[47] The schools became secondary technical schools under the 1944 Act. The Boys' Central school moved to new buildings at Saintbridge in 1957 and was renamed *Saintbridge* school in 1969. It was reorganized as a comprehensive school in 1972[48] and had 987 boys on the roll in 1984. The Girls' Central school remained at Derby Road, where the buildings were extended and modernized c. 1970.[49] In 1974 it was reorganized as a grammar school and renamed *Colwell School for Girls*;[50] there were 492 on the roll in 1984.

Linden Road schools. The former senior boys'

[27] Robertson, *King's Sch.* 152 sqq.
[28] Inf. from headmaster's sec.
[29] Glos. Colln. NF 17.18.
[30] Glos. R.O., D 3270/19655, pp. 434, 484, 487, 533–4; cf. Glos. Colln. N 17.185.
[31] Austin, *Crypt Sch.* 75–7; Glos. R.O., D 3270/19655.
[32] Glos. Colln. NF 17.15 (1).
[33] *Glouc. Jnl.* 18 Sept. 1943; *Glos. Countryside*, Jan.–Mar. 1951, 376–8.
[34] Numbers for 1984 given in this section are for Jan. of that year, taken from list of schs. 1984: co. educ. cttee.
[35] Glos. Colln. NF 17.18.
[36] Glos. R.O., D 3270/19655, pp. 416, 470, 480; *Glouc. Jnl.* 21 Sept. 1889; 16 July 1892.

[37] Watkins, 'Sir Thos. Rich's Sch.', 99, 104–5, 116.
[38] Glos. Colln. NF 17.15 (1).
[39] Ibid. NF 17.64.
[40] Burden, *My Brook became a River*, 7–60.
[41] Glos. Colln. NF 17.15 (1).
[42] Burden, *My Brook became a River*, 112–13.
[43] Glos. Colln. N 17.146.
[44] Ibid. NF 17.15 (1).
[45] Ibid. N 17.204.
[46] Above.
[47] Glos. Colln. NF 17.15 (1).
[48] Ibid. NF 17.204, 383.
[49] *Glouc. Official Guide* (1972), 43.
[50] Glos. Colln. 40972.

and girls' departments at the council elementary school became separate secondary modern schools under the 1944 Act. They were united as a single mixed school in 1973,[51] and had 556 on the roll in 1984.

Hatherley Road schools. The former senior boys' and girls' departments at the council elementary school became separate secondary modern schools under the 1944 Act. The boys' school moved to new buildings at Estcourt Close in 1967 and was later renamed *Oxstalls Boys' Secondary* school;[52] there were 408 on the roll there in 1984. The girls' school remained at Hatherley Road and was closed in 1981.[53] In 1984 the buildings were being converted as a day centre for physically handicapped people.

Kingsholm school, a former council senior elementary school in Worcester Street, became a mixed secondary modern school under the 1944 Act. In 1957 the girls were moved to new buildings at Barnwood as the *Winifred Cullis* school. In January 1984 it had 460 girls on its roll. Kingsholm remained as a boys' school until it was closed in 1973.[54] The building became the county record office in 1979.

Longlevens school, a former county council senior elementary school in Church Road, Longlevens, became a mixed secondary modern school in 1945 under the 1944 Act.[55] It moved to new buildings in Paygrove Lane in 1963,[56] and in 1967 was transferred to the city education authority.[57] In 1984 there were 520 on the roll.

St. Peter's Roman Catholic school. In 1957 the buildings of the former Roman Catholic all-age school in London Road became a mixed aided secondary modern school. The school moved to new buildings at Tuffley in 1964 and its catchment area was widened to include Stroud, Woodchester, and Nympsfield.[58] In 1973 the comprehensive system was introduced and the school was renamed *St. Peter's R.C. High* school.[59] In 1984 there were 1,013 on the roll.

Hucclecote school, a new county council mixed secondary modern school, was opened in 1960.[60] It was transferred to the city education authority in 1967.[61] In 1984 there were 559 on the roll.

Beaufort school, a new mixed comprehensive school at Tuffley, was opened by the city education authority in 1971.[62] In 1984 there were 1,008 on the roll.

ELEMENTARY EDUCATION. Apart from the 20 boarding places at Sir Thomas Rich's school, the earliest provision of free elementary education was in the Poor's school founded in 1700 and later carried on by the governors and guardians of the poor. More significant were the Sunday schools started in 1780 by Robert Raikes and the Revd. Thomas Stock, curate of St. John's parish. Through the publicity that Raikes gave to the venture, mainly through his newspaper, the *Gloucester Journal*, those Schools provided the impetus for the national Sunday School movement, but they were not, as was sometimes claimed, the first such schools in the country; in Gloucester itself one was recorded in 1777. Raikes and Stock employed women to teach four small schools in poor areas of the city, including the northern suburb in St. Catherine's parish, where the poverty of many families had first prompted the idea. Children aged between 5 and 14 were admitted, attending both in the morning and in the afternoon, when they were taken to church. The schools taught reading and spelling as well as giving religious instruction.[63] Most of the city parishes ran their own Sunday schools from the early 19th century. Three parishes had them by 1818[64] and five by 1833.[65] Among the nonconformists the earliest Sunday schools were those run by the Countess of Hungtindon's chapel in St. Mary's Square from 1810 and by the Wesleyans of Northgate Street from 1814. Sunday schools in outlying areas included those run by the Wesleyans at Longford, Twigworth, and Barton End from the 1820s.[66]

The provision of weekday education for the poor was much increased by the reorganization of the Poor's school in 1813 and the opening of a National school for the city in 1817. Otherwise the demand was met in the early 19th century by small dame schools, of which there were 14 in the city and the hamlets in 1818.[67] From the 1830s parish National schools were established. Between 1833 and 1848 in at least seven parishes, including the newly populated outer areas of St. Mark's, St. Luke's, and St. James's, school buildings were provided, usually with the help of government and National Society grants.[68] The most ambitious project, which the bishop of Gloucester at the opening in 1844 is said to have described as too elaborate and costly for its surroundings,[69] was the St. James's school; it cost £2,345, of which the government provided £565 and the National Society £400, while the remainder was raised locally. That school had separate departments for boys, girls, and infants;[70] most of the other parish schools built at the period took only infants or girls and infants, the boys attending the city National school in London Road. British, Wesleyan, and Roman Catholic schools were opened at the same period, and, among the outlying villages Hempsted, Twigworth, and Hucclecote built new National schools

[51] Ibid. NF 17.204.
[52] Ibid.; *Glouc. Official Guide* (1972), 171; (1976), 49.
[53] Glos. R.O., S 154/2/1/3.
[54] Glos. Colln. NF 17.204; NR 17.115.
[55] G.B.R., B 4/25/58, min. 19 Mar. 1945.
[56] Glos. Colln. NQ 17.45.
[57] G.B.R., B 4/25/54, governors of Glouc. secondary schs. 15 Mar. 1967.
[58] *St. Peter's Sch., Glouc., 1864–1964*, 22–3: copy in Glos. Colln. N 17.151.
[59] Glos. Colln. NV 17.7; ibid. 40972.
[60] Ibid.
[61] G.B.R., B 4/25/54, governors of Glouc. secondary schs. 15 Mar. 1967.
[62] *Glouc. Official Guide* (1972), 45.
[63] F. Booth, *Rob. Raikes of Glouc.* (1980).
[64] *Educ. of Poor Digest*, 308–9.
[65] *Educ. Enq. Abstract*, 315–16.
[66] Above, Prot. Nonconf.
[67] *Educ. of Poor Digest*, 301, 308–9.
[68] *Rep. of Educ. Cttee. of Council, 1862–3* [3171], pp. 405–6, H.C. (1863), xlvii.
[69] Glos. R.O., P 154/8/SC 17.
[70] Nat. Soc. files, Glouc., St. James.

in the early 1850s. A more unusual venture was the Ragged school begun in 1852 to provide free education for children in one of the poorest areas of the city.

The parish schools, drawing their income from annual subscriptions and other contributions, from school pence, and, after the 1850s, in most cases from capitation grants, were chronically short of funds. They were usually dependent on the energy and fund-raising abilities of the local incumbents, who in most cases supplied a deficiency in funds from their own resources.[71] Between 1868 and 1876, however, six city parishes were able to raise the funds to build larger school premises. The total cost of the six schools was £8,824, of which £5,868 was raised locally, while £1,616 was supplied by government grants, £730 by diocesan grants, £590 by National Society grants, and £20 by the S.P.C.K.[72] The increased accommodation provided in the city still fell far short of what was required under the 1870 Education Act. Following the Act the city council proposed the formation of a school board, possibly to cover areas outside the city boundary, but the scheme was postponed after causing much controversy.[73] By October 1875 the shortage of school places had become critical: some schools had been forced to close departments because of lack of funds and the accommodation at others was no longer recognized by the Education Department, while the city by then included the populous lower Barton Street area. The Department's final notice, giving the six-month time limit for making good the deficiency before a board was formed, recognized that places existed in the city for 3,780 children with another 1,715 being needed.[74] A total of 19 voluntary schools then served the city: they were 12 National schools, 2 Wesleyan, a British, a Baptist, a Roman Catholic, and, soon to be merged, the Endowed Free and Ragged schools. The two largest schools were then those serving the outer areas of St. Luke's and St. James's; some of the parish schools in the inner city were very small.[75]

The school board, formed in 1876,[76] began to supply some of the shortage of school places in the lower Barton Streeet area by opening a temporary school in a former church school at Tredworth in 1877, and in 1878 it opened its first new school building in Widden Street. The board and the Education Department later disagreed strongly about the needs of the eastern part of the city and also debated over which of the city's private schools could be counted in the total accommodation figures. After several years of pressure by the Department, the board agreed to provide a new school at Tredworth,[77] opened in 1887. Later

the growth of the Bristol Road area and the raising of the school-leaving age in 1891, was met by a new school at Linden Road, opened in 1895. Irregular attendance was a major preoccupation of the board in its early years.[78] Its original attendance officer was joined by a second in 1878 and a third in 1883, from which time the city was divided into three districts each supervised by a separate attendance committee of the board.[79] In 1891 the board, in association with the voluntary schools, opened classes for training pupil teachers.[80]

In the years after the board was formed a few of the smaller voluntary schools closed, and some of the others only narrowly survived financial crises.[81] The voluntary schools continued, however, to provide the bulk of the school places in the city until the beginning of the 20th century. In 1891 the total average attendance at the voluntary schools was 3,953 and at the board schools 1,201.[82] By 1900 average attendance at the 13 voluntary schools was 4,130 and at the 5 board schools 2,582; the recognized accommodation at the former was then 5,191 and at the latter 2,784.[83] A joint association of the managers of the voluntary schools met from c. 1891.[84]

At the boundary extension of 1900 the city school board assumed responsibility for an area on the south that since 1876 had been the responsibility of the Barton St. Mary United District school board, which had maintained a school at Tuffley.[85] Two city schools, the Endowed Free in 1899 and the British in 1900, were also taken over by the city board, and in 1901, when the Widden Street and Tredworth schools were much overcrowded, it opened another school for the Tredworth area, at Hatherley Road.

In 1903, under the 1902 Act, responsibility for elementary education in the city passed to the city council[86] and in the outlying areas, of which Hucclecote had had a board from 1880,[87] to the county council. The city education committee took over the two former Wesleyan schools in 1904 and in the next few years it completed two building projects that had been started by the board. In 1907 the Board of Education placed a time limit on its recognition of three old inner city schools, leading to the opening of some new temporary and permanent buildings in the following years.[88] In 1931, in accordance with the recommendations of the Hadow Committee of 1926,[89] the city's schools were reorganized to provide separate senior departments for children over 11 at four of the schools. All the non-provided schools except the Roman Catholic were included in the scheme, under which c. 2,000

[71] P.R.O., ED 7/35/335; ED 7/36/3, 10–14; *Rep. of Educ. Cttee. of Council, 1862–3*, pp. 405–6.

[72] Nat. Soc. files, Glouc., St. Mary de Lode; St. Aldate; St. Luke; St. Nic.; St. Mark; St. Cath.

[73] *Glouc. Jnl.* 28 Jan., 11 Mar., 8 Apr. 1871.

[74] Ibid. 17, 24 July, 30 Oct. 1875.

[75] Ibid. 14 Oct. 1876; Glos. R.O., SB 20/1/1, pp. 72–3.

[76] Glos. R.O., SB 20/1/1, p. 2.

[77] Ibid. 2, pp. 58, 115–16, 122, 128, 235; 3, pp. 11–12.

[78] Ibid. 1–2, *passim*.

[79] Ibid. 1, p. 317; 2, p. 124; 5, pp. 13–14.

[80] Ibid. 4, pp. 263–4, 275–7, 383.

[81] *Glouc. Jnl.* 12 Feb.; 23 Apr., 28 May, 12 Nov. 1881; Glos. Colln. (H) E 3.4; Nat. Soc. files, Glouc., St. Mark.

[82] *Glouc. Sch. Bd. Rep.* (1891), 4–5: copy in Glos. R.O., SB 20/1/4.

[83] Ibid. (1900), 20: copy in Glos. R.O., SB 20/1/7.

[84] Glos. Colln. NQ 17.4.

[85] Glos. R.O., SB 20/1/8, pp. 231, 237, 269–70; *Glouc. Jnl.* 29 Apr., 13 May 1876.

[86] G.B.R., B 4/25/1, pp. 1–2.

[87] *Kelly's Dir. Glos.* (1885), 507.

[88] G.B.R., B 4/25/65, pp. 144–5, 155, 162, 224–5; below.

[89] Cf. Glos. Colln. NF 17.204.

children changed their schools.[90] At the same period schools were built for the new estates in the Finlay Road and Coney Hill areas, and under the 1935 boundary extension schools at Matson and Tuffley came under the city education authority. In 1938 within the city there were 12 council elementary schools and 9 non-provided schools; the schools had a total average attendance of 6,510.[91] In the outlying areas county council schools at Longlevens (which some city children attended) and Hucclecote and church schools at Twigworth, Barnwood, and Hempsted had a total average attendance of 784.[92]

Between the late 1950s and early 1970s the city and county authorities provided new schools, sometimes separate infant and junior schools on adjoining sites, for the new estates at Tuffley, Matson, Hucclecote, and Innsworth. Under the boundary extension of 1967 schools at Longlevens and Hucclecote passed from county to city, and in 1974 the county council assumed responsibility for all primary education in the area. In the inner city area the main development was the closure of the remaining church schools to be replaced by a new C. of E. school at Kingsholm. In January 1984 the primary schools in the city with Twigworth and Innsworth were 32 county council schools, 6 aided or controlled C. of E. schools, and 2 aided Roman Catholic schools; the total number of children on the rolls was then 8,100.[93]

Note. For sites of defunct schools in the following accounts, see Causton, *Map of Glouc.* (1843); Bd. of Health Map (1852); O.S. Maps 1/2,500, Glos. XXV. 14–15; XXXIII. 3, 7 (1886 edn.). For the reorganization of city schools in 1931, see *Glouc. Educ. Week Handbk.* (1933), 23–5: copy in Glos. Colln. N 17.4.
Sources for the attendance figures are as follows:
1847   Nat. Soc. *Inquiry, 1846–7,* Glos. 10–11, 18–19 (average attendance).
1877   Glos. R.O., SB 20/1/1, pp. 72–3 (attendance May 1877).
1904   *Public Elem. Schs. 1906,* 190, 199 (average attendance 1903–4).
1938   *Bd. of Educ., List 21, 1938* (H.M.S.O.), 128, 134 (average attendance 1937–8).
1984   List of schs. 1984: co. educ. cttee. (number on roll Jan. 1984).

The Poor's, later the *Endowed Free* school. In 1700 a group of subscribers opened a charity school, known as the Poor's school, in the city bridewell at the east gate.[94] Considerable numbers of children were being taught in 1703 when the school was placed under the newly constituted

governor and guardians of the poor. It continued after the failure of the first workhouse scheme and in 1711 85 children were being taught and given clothes at Christmas.[95] Alderman John Hyett (d. 1711) left legacies totalling £1,500 to support the school and build a new schoolroom; most of the sum was contingent on the death before 21 of his son Joseph,[96] but Joseph, who died in 1714 having reached that age, redirected the full sum for the school.[97] The guardians received £1,004 for the legacies in 1733[98] and used part to buy an estate at Miserden.[99] Dorothy Cocks by will dated 1711 left land at Taynton to support poor children at the school and at a school in Dumbleton.[1] Under the new workhouse Act of 1727 it was assumed that the Hyett and Cocks endowments were to support the general functions of the guardians,[2] who later applied the proceeds indiscriminately. In 1727 the school was transferred to the new workhouse. In 1737 the guardians were employing a schoolmaster and schoolmistress,[3] and the school seems to have had a continuous existence. At the beginning of the 19th century it was teaching only 20 children[4] and it was later said to have been only the shadow of a school, taught by an illiterate pauper.[5]

In 1810 the misdirection of the Hyett and Cocks legacies became evident and it was decided to apply the rents of the Miserden and Taynton estates to support an enlarged Poor's school on the British system. It was opened in 1813 with accommodation for 200 boys in a building in lower Northgate Street, built by the Revd. Richard Raikes and leased by him to the guardians. The master was paid an annual salary of £63,[6] a sum thought substantial enough to make it unnecessary for him to take private pupils;[7] the first master, Thomas Holmes, remained in the post for 57 years.[8] The pupils, aged between 6 and 15, benefited from a clothing scheme, under which the guardians matched parents' contributions.[9] Later usually known as the Free school, the school had an average attendance of 115 in 1843[10] and c. 140 in 1877.[11] In 1874 the inadequacy of the building prompted plans for a new one, and in 1877 the Education Department refused to recognize the school. In the latter year, however, the guardians were offered the Ragged school building in Archdeacon Street.[12]

The school reopened at Archdeacon Street in 1878, as the Endowed Free school, with c. 100 boys, the numbers rising to c. 140 by 1881. Most of the pupils came from the old Free school, but some who were not from the poorest class were debarred under the terms of the Ragged school trust deed. In 1891 an 'industrial training school'

[90] *Glouc. Educ. Week Handbk.* (1933), 23–5: copy in Glos. Colln. N 17.4.
[91] *Bd. of Educ., List 21, 1938* (H.M.S.O.), 134.
[92] Ibid. 125, 127–8.
[93] List of schs. 1984: co. educ. cttee.
[94] G.B.R., B 3/7, f. 237v.; 8, p. 100.
[95] Ibid. B 6/5; Rudder, *Glos.* 129.
[96] G.D.R. wills 1711/212.
[97] Ibid. 1713/42; Fosbrooke, *Glouc.* 177.
[98] Glos. R.O., D 214/T 20; D 3270/19712, pp. 192–4, 203.
[99] Ibid. D 3270/19712, p. 204; *16th Rep. Com. Char.* 27, where the date 1717, given for the purchase of the est., is a mistake or misprint.

[1] *16th Rep. Com. Char.* 26.
[2] Glouc. Poor-Relief Act, 13 Geo. I, c. 19.
[3] Above, Glouc. 1720–1835, city govt.; Glos. R.O., D 3270/19712, pp. 17, 272.
[4] *Poor Law Abstract, 1804,* 186–7; *Evangelical Mag.* xi. 48.   [5] *Evangelical Mag.* xi. 48.
[6] Ibid.; *Glouc. New Guide* (c. 1817), 87.
[7] Counsel, *Glouc.* 179.
[8] Glos. R.O., D 3270/19713, min. 17 Feb. 1871.
[9] *16th Rep. Com. Char.* 28.
[10] *Glouc. Jnl.* 17 June 1843.
[11] Glos. R.O., SB 20/1/1, pp. 72–3.
[12] Ibid. D 3270/19713.

was opened in a new building adjoining the schoolroom, where boys were employed in chopping and tying bundles of wood. A government grant was received from 1879,[13] but the school was in financial difficulties in 1891 through the fall in the rents of the guardians' estates, and the introduction of fees was planned.[14] The institution of fee-grants in 1891, under the Act abolishing fees, enabled the school to recover and a new infants' classroom was added.[15] In 1899 further difficulties led the guardians to transfer the school to the Gloucester school board[16] and the building later housed a board school. The corporation of the governor and guardians of the poor was dissolved in 1907 and the income from the Miserden and Taynton estates applied to exhibitions at the United schools.[17]

The Industrial Ragged school. In 1851 subscriptions were raised to provide free education for the children of the poorest part of the city, the streets around St. Mary's Square and the Island. The school, known as the Industrial Ragged school, was begun in 1852 in a granary at the quay,[18] moving the next year to a building in Archdeacon Street by the entrance to Clare Street. The site was given by the dean and chapter and vested in the city corporation as trustees, and building was aided by a government grant.[19] The trust deed specified that the school should teach reading, writing, arithmetic, geography, and undenominational bible study, to the most destitute class of children.[20] A field in Stroud Road, given by the corporation, was used for vegetable gardening, and a house for the schoolmaster was built on part of it.[21]

The Ragged school had an average attendance of 85 boys in 1853; a plan to take girls also was never realized.[22] The master Edward Perry, who gained a high reputation for his work at the school,[23] described his first pupils as 'perfect strangers to discipline, and. . .determined to dispute all authority'.[24] In 1857 he reported that he gave some boys three meals a day simply to keep them at school; otherwise they would have to resort to begging or stealing.[25] Annual subscriptions were at first supplemented by a government grant, which was reduced gradually and in 1862, when the Revised Code made grants dependent on examinations, ended altogether;[26] additional subscriptions were then found. The school had an average attendance of 200 in 1866.[27] A scheme to

charge fees to those children who could afford them was unsuccessful in 1872,[28] and in 1876 the school's financial position led to a move to close it and transfer the building to the new school board. The board was, however, unwilling to be bound by the terms of the trust deed,[29] and in 1877 the school was accepted instead by the governor and guardians of the poor,[30] who carried it on as the Endowed Free school.

VOLUNTARY SCHOOLS. *Alington* school, an additional school for St. James's parish, named after the curate J. W. Alington, opened in 1869 in a new building in Millbrook Street. The building, also used for general parish purposes, had accommodation for *c*. 130 children,[31] and in 1877 there was a mixed attendance of 120. The school closed *c*. 1878.[32]

Baptist. By 1868 the Baptists of the Brunswick Road church held a day school in a mission room in Barton Terrace (later part of Tredworth High Street).[33] The accommodation was not recognized by the Education Department in 1875.[34] In 1877 there was a mixed attendance of 70. The school closed at the end of that year.[35]

Barnwood National, see below, Barnwood, educ.

British. A British school with boys' and girls' departments opened in 1841 in a new building in Wellington Street (then Hampden Place).[36] In 1843 it had an average attendance of 320,[37] and in 1877 the attendance was 380. The building was enlarged in 1883.[38] In 1900 the managers, unable to finance additional accommodation required by the Education Department, handed it over to the school board.[39] In 1904 attendance was 342. The school was renamed *Wellington Street Council* school in 1905.[40] After the accommodation had been condemned, it was reorganized as a mixed school in 1908, and it became a boys' school in 1915.[41] It closed at the reorganization of schools in 1931.[42]

Christ Church National school was opened as a girls' school before 1842 in a new building at the corner of Park Road and Brunswick Road. It was then managed by the perpetual curate Robert Holmes, whose wife is said to have supported it as a private charity and clothed the girls in uniform.[43] In 1847, when there was an attendance of 60 girls, Holmes transferred the site to the parish.[44] In 1877, when there was probably also an

[13] Ibid.   [14] Ibid. 19714.
[15] Ibid. 19715.
[16] Ibid.; cf. ibid. S 154/14/2, p. 305.
[17] Glos. Colln. NF 17.13.
[18] *Glouc. Jnl.* 2 Aug. 1851; 4 Sept. 1852.
[19] *Glouc. Ragged Sch. Rep.* (1852; 1853): copies of the reps. for 1852–66 are in Glos. Colln. 24099.
[20] Glos. R.O., D 3270/19713, mins. 27 July 1877, 28 Feb. 1878.
[21] *Glouc. Ragged Sch. Rep.* (1852; 1854).
[22] Ibid. (1852; 1853).
[23] Ibid. (1854); *Glouc. Jnl.* 12 Feb. 1853.
[24] *Glouc. Ragged Sch. Rep.* (1852).
[25] Ibid. (1857).
[26] Ibid. (1860; 1863).
[27] Ibid. (1866).
[28] *Glouc. Jnl.* 18 May 1872.

[29] Ibid. 7 Oct. 1876; 24 Feb., 31 Mar., 12 May 1877.
[30] Glos. R.O., D 3270/19713, min. 27 July 1877.
[31] *Glouc. Jnl.* 20 Nov. 1869.
[32] Glos. R.O., SB 20/1/7, p. 34.
[33] *Slater's Dir. Glos.* (1868), 204; cf. above, Prot. Nonconf., Baptists.
[34] *Glouc. Jnl.* 14 Oct. 1876.
[35] Glos. R.O., D 4373/2/3, mins. 5 Sept., 7 Nov. 1877.
[36] *Glouc. Jnl.* 17, 24 Apr. 1841.
[37] Ibid. 17 June 1843.
[38] Ibid. 4 Aug. 1883; Glos. R.O., SB 20/1/2, p. 123.
[39] Glos. R.O., SB 20/1/8, pp. 125–6, 239.
[40] G.B.R., B 4/25/65, pp. 11, 13.
[41] Ibid. pp. 155, 225, 231; *Kelly's Dir. Glos.* (1927), 197.
[42] G.B.R., B 4/25/12, p. 77.
[43] Nat. Soc. files, Glouc., Christ Church.
[44] G.B.R., L 7, Christ Church sch. trust deed.

infants' department, the attendance was 162. A new infants' room was added in 1893–4.[45] Attendance was 112 girls and infants in 1904. In 1931 it became an infants' school only, and in 1938, as *Christ Church C.E.* school, had an attendance of 86. It closed in 1958.[46]

Hempsted National, see below, Hempsted, educ.

Hucclecote National (later *Hucclecote Council*, later *Larkhay*), see below, Hucclecote, educ.

Independent. In 1833 Independents ran a day and boarding school for boys in the west part of the city.[47] It was perhaps continued as the infants' day school run by that sect in a room built *c*. 1844 at Levy's Yard in the Island. In 1871 it had an attendance of 94.[48] It closed soon afterwards, probably before 1877.[49]

Kingsholm C.E. school, a controlled junior school, was opened in new buildings in Guinea Street in 1962, taking the junior children from four old church schools.[50] In 1973 it was enlarged to take infants also, with a total accommodation of *c*. 600.[51] In 1984 it had 335 children on the roll.

Matson National, see below, Matson, educ.

National (London Road). A National school, situated in St. Catherine's parish but intended to serve the whole city, was opened in 1817, with *c*. 300 boys and girls on the roll, in a new building in London Road.[52] It was promoted and managed by a diocesan society for church education, led by the bishop, Henry Ryder,[53] who, with the National Society, the city corporation, the Revd. Richard Raikes, and Mary Pitt, was a chief subscriber to the building fund.[54] The school later took boys only, probably from *c*. 1835,[55] and in 1847 had an attendance of 173. As other National schools opened in the city numbers fell, reaching 40 in 1872,[56] but there was a revival to 184 by 1877. Enlarged in 1879 and 1895,[57] the school had an attendance of 289 in 1904. After 1931 it took only junior boys and in 1938, as *London Road C.E.* school, had an attendance of 221. It became a controlled school in 1956 and closed in 1962, when the children were transferred to the new Kingsholm C.E. school.[58]

Northgate Street Wesleyan. In 1863 the Wesleyans of Northgate Street opened a school in a new building on the site of the 'round house' in Worcester Street.[59] It had a mixed attendance of 392 in 1877. In 1878 it moved to a building adjoining the new Northgate Street chapel.[60] In 1904, when the attendance was 366 in mixed and infants' departments, the school was handed over to the city education authority and became *Northgate Council* school.[61] The building was judged to be below standard by the Board of Education in 1907,[62] but the school remained open until 1926, when 216 children were transferred to the new Kingsholm council school.[63]

Quaker. A 'ragged' Sunday school opened by Quakers in White Swan (or Dockham) Lane *c*. 1846 also gave secular teaching. A weekday evening school was started in conjunction with it in 1847.[64] The school probably closed *c*. 1852 when the Industrial Ragged school opened.[65]

Ryecroft Wesleyan. In 1847 the Wesleyans opened an infants' day school in a new building in Victoria Street.[66] In 1871 a new school was opened in the former Wesleyan chapel in Ryecroft Street,[67] where there was a mixed attendance of 295 in 1877. In 1904, when it had an attendance of 410 in mixed and infants' departments, the school was handed over to the city education authority and became *Ryecroft Council* school.[68] It was closed in 1908 after the accommodation was condemned by the Board of Education.[69]

St. Aldate's National. St. John's National school, established in 1847, also served St. Aldate's parish,[70] but by 1868 an infants' school for St. Aldate's was being held in a cottage in St. Aldate Square.[71] A National school, established through the efforts of the rector H. M. Bowles, opened in 1869 in a new building on the west side of the square; it had accommodation for *c*. 120 girls and infants.[72] Attendance was 97 in 1877. The school closed between 1885 and 1888.[73]

St. Catherine's National school opened in 1835 or 1836 in a new building in Water Street (later part of Priory Road), north of the remains of St. Catherine's church. It seems originally to have been run as the girls' department of the London Road school and to have been under the same management, but later it served only St. Catherine's and, until 1868, St. Mary de Lode parishes. In 1847 130 girls attended.[74] In 1876 a new parish National school, designed by Medland and Son, opened on a site west of the new St. Catherine's church given by Charles Walker, of Hillfield House; it had accommodation for 195 girls and infants,[75] and in 1877 the attendance was 145. A new infants' room was added in 1887, and the school was again enlarged in 1901 when it

[45] Nat. Soc. files, Glouc., Christ Church.
[46] Glos. R.O., S 154/11/3, p. 75.
[47] *Educ. Enq. Abstract*, 316.
[48] P.R.O., HO 129/336/2/1/2; Causton, *Map of Glouc.* (1843); *Glouc. Jnl.* 7 Jan. 1871.
[49] Cf. Glos. R.O., SB 20/1/1, pp. 72–3.
[50] G.B.R., B 4/25/30, pp. 168, 224; 31, pp. 7, 93; Glos. Colln. NQ 17.44.   [51] Glos. Colln. NF 17.204, 242.
[52] *Glouc. New Guide* (*c*. 1817), 86.
[53] *Trans. B.G.A.S* lxxxix. 140; cf. P.R.O., ED 7/36/6A.
[54] *Glouc. Jnl.* 17 June 1816.   [55] Below, St. Cath. National.
[56] *National Sch., Glouc.* (1936), 10: copy in Glos. Colln. N 17.25.
[57] Ibid. 13; *Kelly's Dir. Glos.* (1906), 182.
[58] Glos. Colln. NQ 17.44.
[59] *Glouc. Jnl.* 28 Sept. 1861; Glos. R.O., S 154/17/1, p. 1.
[60] G. E. Lewis, *Northgate Sun. Sch. Centenary Souvenir* (1914) 45.

[61] G.B.R., B 4/25/64, p. 199.
[62] Ibid. 65, pp. 155, 225.
[63] Ibid. 71, p. 214; Glos. Colln. NR 17.115.
[64] *Glouc. Jnl.* 23 Oct. 1847.
[65] Cf. ibid. 2 Aug. 1851; *Slater's Dir. Glos.* (1852–3), 129.
[66] *Glouc. Jnl.* 28 Aug. 1847.
[67] Ibid. 19 Mar. 1870; 18 Nov. 1871.
[68] G.B.R., B 4/25/64, pp. 74, 247.
[69] Ibid. 65, pp. 155, 224; 66, p. 31.
[70] Nat. Soc. files, Glouc., St. John.
[71] Ibid. St. Aldate; *Slater's Dir. Glos.* (1868), 204.
[72] *Glouc. Jnl.* 7 Aug. 1869; 1 Jan. 1870.
[73] *Kelly's Dir. Glos.* (1885), 477; Glos. R.O., SB 20/1/3, p. 341.
[74] Hockaday Abs. ccxiv, 1835; Nat. Soc. Inquiry, *1846–7*, Glos. 10–11; P.R.O., ED 7/37, Glouc. Girls' National Sch.
[75] *Glouc. Jnl.* 2 Oct. 1875; 10 June 1876; Nat. Soc. files, Glouc., St. Cath.

Fig. 23. St. Luke's National school, as built in 1870

amalgamated with St. Mary de Lode school, from which the older girls were transferred.[76] In 1904 the enlarged school had an attendance of 347 girls and infants. It ceased to take infants in 1910 when Mount Street Temporary school opened,[77] and in 1931 it became a junior girls' school. In 1938, as *St. Catherine's C.E.* school, it had an attendance of 207. From 1921 it was managed by St. Mary de Lode parish alone, ecclesiastical boundary changes of 1916 having placed the building in that parish.[78] The school took infants again from 1955 when Mount Street school closed.[79] The junior girls left for the new Kingsholm C.E. school in 1962[80] and the infants followed in 1973 when the St. Catherine's school closed.[81]

St. James's National school opened in 1844 in a new building in the later St. James's Street at Barton End with accommodation for 486 children in boys', girls', and infants' departments. It was built through the efforts of the perpetual curate Thomas Hedley, who took responsibility for a considerable deficit in the finance.[82] In 1852 he gave two houses as an endowment.[83] Attendance was 244 in 1847, 493 in 1877, and 469 in 1904. The building was enlarged in 1894,[84] and again in 1909.[85] From 1931 the school had junior mixed and infants' departments, and from 1935 junior mixed alone.[86] In 1938, as *St. James's C.E.* school, it had an attendance of 324. It became a controlled school in 1949,[87] and in 1984 had 103 children on the roll.

St. John's National school was opened in 1847 by the rector F.T. Bayley in a converted non-conformist chapel on the west side of Worcester Street;[88] it began with an attendance of 120 girls and infants. In 1877 the attendance was 63. By 1870 the parish also ran a National boys' school in Black Dog yard;[89] that was presumably the building at the Worcester Street end of the yard that was marked as a school for boys and girls in 1883, when the original school may have closed.[90] There was apparently no school for St. John's parish in existence by 1885.[91]

St. Luke's National school was opened by the perpetual curate Samuel Lysons in 1843 in a new building in Bristol Road by the Sud brook.[92] In 1847 it was attended by 93 boys and girls. In 1870 it was replaced by a new school in New Street, designed by A. W. Maberly, with accommodation for 580 in boys', girls', and infants' departments; Daniel Higford Burr, owner of the Llanthony manor estate, was a chief subscriber to the building fund.[93] The attendance in 1877 was 662 and in 1904, after the addition of a new classroom in 1888,[94] 746. In 1931 the school was reorganized with junior mixed and infants' departments. In 1934, when St. Luke's church closed, the management was transferred to St. Paul's parish,[95] and in 1938, as *St. Paul's C.E.* school, it had an attendance of 318. In 1984, as a controlled primary school, it had 205 children on the roll.

St. Mark's National. An infants' school opened in Columbia Street *c.* 1841 was by 1853 being run as a parish school.[96] Later it also took older girls. It was replaced in 1873 by a new school in Sweetbriar Street, designed by Medland and Son, with accommodation for 500 in boys', girls', and infants' departments.[97] The boys' and girls'

[76] Nat. Soc. files, Glouc., St. Cath.; Glos. R.O., S 154/21/1, pp. 426–8.

[77] G.B.R., B 4/25/66, pp. 53, 121.

[78] Nat. Soc. files, Glouc., St. Cath.

[79] Glos. R.O., S 154/8/3, pp. 39–40.

[80] G.B.R., B 4/25/30, p. 168; 31, p. 93.

[81] Glos. Colln. NF 17.204, 242.

[82] Nat. Soc. files, Glouc., St. James; *Glouc. Jnl.* 27 July 1844. Part of the deficit was met by the sale of medals and lithographs of the new sch.: cf. Glos. R.O., A 154/45, reproduced above, Plate 49.

[83] Glos. R.O., P 154/8/CH 1.

[84] Nat. Soc. files, Glouc., St. James.

[85] *Kelly's Dir. Glos.* (1927), 198.

[86] G.B.R., B 4/25/14, pp. 134, 177.

[87] Glos. R.O., P 154/8/SC 17.

[88] Nat. Soc. files, Glouc., St. John.

[89] *Kelly's Dir. Glos.* (1870), 557.

[90] O.S. Map 1/2,500, Glos. XXV. 15 (1886 edn.).

[91] *Kelly's Dir. Glos.* (1885), 198.

[92] Nat. soc. files, Glouc., St. Paul; *Glouc. Jnl.* 11 June 1870.

[93] *Glouc. Jnl.* 11 June 1870.   [94] Ibid. 7 July 1888.

[95] G.B.R., B 4/25/13, p. 133.

[96] P.R.O., ED 7/36/12; *Pigot's Dir. Glos.* (1842), 109; *Slater's Dir. Glos.* (1852–3), 129.

[97] Nat. Soc. files, Glouc., St. Mark; *Glouc. Jnl.* 14 June 1873.

departments had closed through lack of funds by 1875 but reopened in 1877.[98] The attendance in 1904 was 519, and in 1938, after being reorganized in 1931 as junior mixed and infants' departments, *St. Mark's C.E.* school had an attendance of 327. By 1952 it was organized as separate junior and infants' schools.[99] The juniors were transferred to the new Kingsholm C.E. school in 1962[1] and the infants followed in 1973 when the St. Mark's school closed.[2]

St. Mary de Lode National. Children of the parish attended the National schools in London Road and St. Catherine's churchyard[3] before 1868 when a new school for 120 girls and infants opened at the corner of Mount Street and Priory Road (later part of St. Oswald's Road). Originally called the *Sydney Reynolds Memorial* school, it was built largely at the cost of Joseph Reynolds in memory of his son.[4] Attendance in 1877 was 74. After amalgamation with St. Catherine's school in 1901 it housed only infants.[5] After being condemned by the Board of Education the building was leased to the city education authority and used from 1910 by Mount Street Temporary school.[6]

St. Michael's National school was opened in 1848 in a new building in Russell Street, designed by S. W. Daukes. It had girls' and infants' departments,[7] attended by 144 children in 1877 and by 159 in 1904. From 1931 it took junior girls and infants and in 1938, as *St. Michael's C.E.* school, had an attendance of 86. The school closed in 1962 when the older children were transferred to the new Kingsholm C.E. school.[8]

St. Nicholas's National. In 1830 the vicar John Davies started an infants' school and in 1833 a new National schoolroom was built for it on the corner of Castle Lane and Bearland;[9] 80 children attended in 1847. In 1872 it was replaced by a new school on the corner of Quay Street and Upper Quay Lane. It had accommodation for 380 in boys', girls', and infants' departments,[10] but lack of funds had forced the boys' department to close by 1875. It was reopened in 1877,[11] when the school had an attendance of 322. The boys' department closed through lack of funds in 1898, the boys transferring to Archdeacon Street board school the following year,[12] and 247 girls and infants attended in 1904. The school took only infants from 1931 and closed in 1933.[13]

St. Paul's C.E., see above, St. Luke's National.

St. Peter's Roman Catholic. In 1835 the parish priest Abbé Josse opened a school in a loft over the sacristy of the Catholic church in London Road. Later the school occupied other premises near the church and in 1864 it moved to a new building by the north end of the church, built through the efforts of the priest Leonard Calderbank. The school, which for a few years in the mid 1860s, was taught by the nuns of the London Road convent,[14] had a mixed attendance of 95 in 1877. In 1893 it was enlarged and reorganized as mixed and infants' departments.[15] Attendance was 144 in 1904 and 143 in 1938. Various adjoining properties were acquired in the mid 1930s and four new classrooms were opened in 1939. St. Peter's remained an all-age school until the early 1950s when it was attended by over 400 children. In 1953 the infants moved to a new school in Horton Road and in 1957 the juniors moved to a new school on an adjoining site, the London Road building becoming a secondary school. St. Peter's R.C. junior and infants' schools, which served Gloucester, Churchdown, Brockworth, and Innsworth,[16] had respectively 294 and 204 children on the rolls in 1984.

Sydney Reynolds Memorial school, see above, St. Mary de Lode National.

Tredworth. A former Wesleyan chapel in Tredworth High Street was acquired by St. James's parish in 1866 as an additional day school and for other parish purposes.[17] The school closed through lack of funds in 1875[18] and the building was later used by the school board and the city education authority.

Twigworth National. A church school was held at Twigworth from soon after the opening of the new church in 1842,[19] and in 1847 had an attendance of 56 boys and girls. In 1854 a new National school was built on the main road between Twigworth and Longford, which it also served. The chief promoters, the perpetual curate Benjamin Claxson and Mrs. Clarence Saunders, gave a small endowment. The school had an average attendance of 60 in 1885,[20] and in 1904, after the completion of a new infants' classroom the previous year,[21] 103 children attended in mixed and infants' departments. In 1938, as *Twigworth C.E.* school, it had an attendance of 74, and in 1984, when it was a controlled primary school, it had 72 children on the roll.

BOARD AND COUNCIL SCHOOLS. *Archdeacon (Deacon) Street.* The former Endowed Free school was taken over by the school board in 1899 and enlarged to accommodate a board school for boys.[22] In 1904 it had an attendance of 209. After

[98] *Glouc. Jnl.* 30 Oct. 1875; 28 Oct. 1876; 21 July 1877.

[99] *Glouc. Official Guide* (1952), 191.

[1] G.B.R., B 4/25/30, p. 168; 31, p. 93.

[2] Glos. Colln. NF 17.204, 242.

[3] Nat. Soc. *Inquiry, 1846–7,* Glos. 10–11; *Kelly's Dir. Glos.* (1856), 305; *Glouc. Jnl.* 24 Oct. 1868.

[4] *Glouc. Jnl.* 24 Oct. 1868.

[5] Nat. Soc. files, Glouc., St. Cath.; Glos. R.O., S 154/21/1, p. 426; G.B.R., B 4/25/65, p. 155.

[6] Nat. Soc. files, Glouc., St. Mary de Lode; G.B.R., B 4/25/66, pp. 53, 121; below.

[7] *Glouc. Jnl.* 27 May 1848; Nat. Soc. files, Glouc., St. Mic.

[8] G.B.R., B 4/25/31, pp. 6, 114.

[9] Nat. Soc. files, Glouc., St. Nich.; Glos. Colln. 13219, f. 56; *Glouc. Jnl.* 18 Dec. 1830.

[10] *Glouc. Jnl.* 1, 8 June 1872.

[11] Ibid. 30 Oct. 1875; 28 Oct. 1876.

[12] Glos. R.O., SB 20/1/7, pp. 283, 318; *Glouc. Sch. Bd. Rep.* (1900), 6.

[13] G.B.R., B 4/25/13, pp. 17, 54.

[14] *St. Peter's Sch., Glouc., 1864–1964,* 4, 8–10.

[15] J. N. Langston, 'Cath. Mission in Glouc.' i: Glos. Colln. 31841.   [16] *St. Peter's Sch.* 16–19, 22, 46.

[17] Glos. R.O., P 154/8/CW 3/6; *Glouc. Jnl.* 19 Jan. 1867; 17 Apr. 1869.

[18] Ibid. 30 Oct. 1875; 14 Oct. 1876.

[19] P.R.O., ED 7/35/335.

[20] *Kelly's Dir. Glos.* (1885), 608.

[21] Nat. Soc. files, Twigworth.

[22] Glos. R.O., SB 20/1/7, p. 438; *Glouc. Sch. Bd. Rep.* (1900), 6.

the old building had been condemned by the Board of Education, a new building, designed by Fletcher Trew, was opened in 1911.[23] From 1931 it took only senior boys and in 1938 had an attendance of 171. The school closed in 1939 when the boys were transferred to Kingsholm school.[24]

Calton Road school was planned by the board in 1903[25] and opened by the city education authority in 1906; designed by Walter B. Wood, the building had accommodation for 810 children in mixed and infants' departments.[26] From 1931 it had junior mixed and infants' departments. Attendance in 1938 was 226. By 1952 the two departments had become separate schools,[27] and in 1984 the junior school had 366 children on the roll and the infants' school 184.

Coney Hill. In 1933 the city education authority planned to re-erect a temporary school building from Finlay Road on the new housing estate at Coney Hill.[28] It opened an infants' school in a new building at Coney Hill in 1935;[29] it had an attendance of 156 in 1938. In 1952 a junior school was opened on an adjoining site with 291 children on the roll.[30] In 1984 the junior school had 270 children on the roll and the infants' school 197.

Derby Road school was planned by the board in 1903[31] and opened by the city education authority in 1907; designed by Fletcher Trew, the building had accommodation for 1,100 children in boys', girls', and infants' departments.[32] In 1925 the boys' and girls' departments were replaced in the building by the Central schools and the infants' department continued as a separate school,[33] having an attendance of 121 in 1938. It closed in 1957.[34]

Dinglewell school at Hucclecote was opened as a primary school by the county education authority in 1966, passing to the city in 1967. In 1970, after the addition of new buildings, it was reorganized as separate junior and infants' schools.[35] In 1984 the junior school had 242 children on the roll and the infants' school 163.

Elmbridge school, in Elmbridge Road, originated in 1947 with the children of pre-secondary age removed from Denmark Road High school. The school, which had 200 children in 1948, was at first housed in temporary buildings.[36] With the provision of more permanent buildings in 1952 separate junior and infants' schools were created.[37] In 1984 the junior school had 300 children on the roll and the infants' school 196.

Finlay Road school was opened with junior mixed and infants' departments in temporary timber buildings at the reorganization of city schools in 1931. It was transferred to new buildings in 1933.[38] There was an attendance of 656 in 1938. By 1952 the school was organized as separate junior and infants' schools.[39] In 1984 the junior school had 257 children on the roll and the infants' school 184.

Grange schools, see below, Lower Tuffley.

Harewood infants' school, at Lower Tuffley, was opened by the city education authority in 1966, and Harewood junior school was opened on an adjoining site the following year.[40] In 1984 the junior school had 296 children on the roll and the infants' school 176.

Hatherley Road school was opened by the board in 1901; the building designed by Alfred Dunn, had accommodation for 890 in mixed and infants' departments.[41] The attendance in 1904 was 803. In 1905 the school was reorganized as senior mixed, junior mixed, and infants' departments and the accommodation increased to 1,028;[42] in 1915 it was reorganized as boys', girls', and infants' departments;[43] and in 1931 it was enlarged and reorganized as senior boys', senior girls', and infants' departments. The attendance in 1938 was 724. After the senior departments became secondary schools under the 1944 Act the infants' department continued as a separate school. In 1984 it had 92 children on the roll.

Heron school, a primary school on the Heron Park estate at Saintbridge, was opened by the education authority in 1977.[44] In 1984 it had 234 children on the roll.

Hillview school, at Hucclecote, was opened by the county education authority in 1957,[45] taking the junior children from the old Hucclecote (later Larkhay) school. It passed to the city in 1967, and in 1982 became a primary school, taking the infants from Larkhay school.[46] In 1984 it had 253 children on the roll.

Innsworth primary school, in Rookery Road, was opened by the county education authority in 1958.[47] In 1984, when it took only juniors, it had 139 children on the roll. Innsworth infants' school, in Mottershead Drive, was opened in 1974,[48] and in 1984, recently renamed *Larkfield* school, had 97 children on the roll.

Kingsholm school was planned by the city education authority from *c.* 1908 as a replacement for Northgate Council school,[49] and the site, east of Worcester Street, was bought in 1914,[50] but the school was not completed and opened until 1926. Designed by Walter B. Wood,[51] the school had

[23] G.B.R., B 4/25/65, pp. 155, 224; 66, p. 6; 67, pp. 14, 23.
[24] Glos. R.O., S 154/14/4, pp. 103, 250.
[25] Ibid. SB 20/1/9, pp. 142, 190, 206.
[26] *Glouc. Jnl.* 3 Mar. 1906.
[27] *Glouc. Official Guide* (1952), 191.
[28] *Glouc. Educ. Week Handbk.* (1933), 24.
[29] G.B.R., B 4/25/14, pp. 131, 198.
[30] Ibid. 25, p. 246.
[31] Glos. R.O., SB 20/1/9, p. 244.
[32] Glos. Colln. N 17.23.
[33] *Kelly's Dir. Glos.* (1927), 197.
[34] G.B.R., B 4/25/29, p. 13; Glos. Colln. NF 17.204.
[35] G.B.R., B 4/25/54, primary sch. sub-cttee. 14 Mar. 1967; 56, primary sch. sub-cttee. 7 Oct. 1969.
[36] Glos. Colln. N 17.341.
[37] G.B.R., B 4/25/24, p. 66; 25, pp. 55, 246.
[38] *Glouc. Educ. Week Handbk.* (1933), 24.
[39] *Glouc. Official Guide* (1952), 191.
[40] Glos. Colln. 40972.
[41] Glos. R.O., SB 20/1/8, pp. 362–3.
[42] *Public Elem. Schs. 1906*, 199.
[43] *Kelly's Dir. Glos.* (1927), 197.
[44] Inf. from head teacher.
[45] Glos. Colln. NF 17.204.
[46] Inf. from head teacher; G.B.R., B 4/25/54, primary sch. sub-cttee. 14 Mar. 1967.
[47] Inf. from head teacher.   [48] Inf. from head teacher.
[49] G.B.R., B 4/25/65, p. 225; 66, p. 216.
[50] Ibid. 68, p. 33.
[51] Ibid. 71, pp. 130, 200, 214.

accommodation for 564. Originally a mixed and infants' school,[52] it became a senior girls' and infants' school in 1931, and in 1938 it had an attendance of 335. In 1939, when the boys from Archdeacon Street school were transferred there, it became a senior mixed and infants' school.[53] After the senior department became a secondary school under the 1944 Act the infants' department continued as a separate school, closing in 1962.[54]

Larkfield school, see above, Innsworth.

Linden Road school was opened by the board in 1895 in buildings, designed by Medland and Son, with accommodation for 813 in mixed and infants' departments.[55] From 1901 until 1906, when the opening of Calton Road school eased the over-crowding, some pupils were housed in the nearby St. Luke's mission hall.[56] In 1903 the school was reorganized as senior mixed, junior mixed, and infants' departments and a new building for the infants was opened.[57] The attendance in 1904 was 937 and the recognized accommodation 1,210. In 1931, when the building was enlarged, the school was reorganized as senior boys', senior girls', and infants' departments. The attendance in 1938 was 760. After the two senior departments became secondary schools under the 1944 Act the infants' department continued as a separate school. It had 109 children on the roll in 1984.

Longlevens. In 1930 the county education authority opened an all-age elementary school under the official title of *Wotton St. Mary (Without) Council* school; sited in Church Road (then Longlevens Lane), the building had accommodation for 312.[58] After the boundary extension of 1935 the school took considerable numbers of city children and there was later much discussion between the two authorities on the provision of an additional school for the area.[59] Longlevens school had an attendance of 389 in mixed and infants' departments in 1938. Later that year it became a senior school when the county opened a new school for juniors and infants in Paygrove Lane; the city authority was represented on the managing bodies of the two schools.[60] In 1945 the senior school became a secondary modern school. The primary school, transferred to the city authority in 1967,[61] was reorganized in 1969 as separate junior and infants' schools,[62] the former in the Church Road building (vacated by the secondary school) and the latter in the Paygrove Lane building. In 1984 Longlevens junior school had 388 children on the roll and Longlevens infants' school had 248.

Lower Tuffley infants' school, in Grange Road,

was opened by the city education authority in 1951,[63] and Lower Tuffley junior school was opened nearby, in Holmleigh Road, in 1953.[64] The names of the schools were changed before 1972 to *Grange* junior and infants.[65] In 1984 the junior school had 285 children on the roll and the infants' school 171.

Moat junior school, in Juniper Avenue, Matson, was opened by the city education authority in 1959, and Moat infants' school was opened on an adjoining site in 1960, replacing the old Matson C.E. school.[66] In 1984 the junior school had 317 children on the roll and the infants' school 207.

Mount Street Temporary school was opened by the city education authority in 1910 in the former St. Mary de Lode school; it took 108 infants from St. Catherine's school.[67] In spite of the intended temporary nature and the limited recognition given to the building by the Board of Education,[68] the school survived for many years. It had an attendance of 83 in 1938. In 1948, still an infants' school, it moved to part of the Archdeacon Street school buildings.[69] It closed in 1955 when the children were transferred to St. Catherine's school.[70]

Northgate Council, see above, voluntary sch., Northgate Street Wesleyan.

Robinswood junior and infants' schools, on adjoining sites in Matson Avenue, Matson, were opened by the city education authority in 1955.[71] In 1984 the junior school had 224 children on the roll and the infants' school 168.

Ryecroft Council, see above, voluntary sch., Ryecroft Wesleyan.

Tredworth (High Street). The mission hall and former church school in Tredworth High Street was reopened as a board school in 1877,[72] when it had an attendance of 120. After the opening of Widden Street school in 1878 it took only infants[73] and it closed c. 1887.[74] It was again used by the board for a few years after 1898 to ease overcrowding at Widden Street and Tredworth schools,[75] and the city education authority used it for a few years after 1904 as an overflow school for Hatherley Road.[76]

Tredworth school, at the corner of Tredworth Road and Tredworth High Street, was opened by the board in 1887; the building, designed by Medland and Son, had accommodation for 684 in boys', girls', and infants' departments.[77] By 1891 attendance in two departments was in excess of the recognized accommodation and the school was still severely overcrowded in 1896.[78] Attendance

[52] Glos. Colln. N 17.24.
[53] Glos. R.O., S 154/14/4, pp. 103, 250.
[54] Glos. Colln. NR 17.115.
[55] Glos. R.O., SB 20/1/6, p. 376.
[56] Ibid. 8, pp. 281–2, 338; G.B.R., B 4/25/65, p. 32.
[57] Glos. R.O., SB 20/1/9, p. 50; *Kelly's Dir. Glos.* (1927), 197.
[58] *Glouc. Jnl.* 18 Jan. 1930.
[59] G.B.R., B 4/25/14, pp. 64–5, 146–7, 169, 192, 194, 221.
[60] Ibid. 16, p. 25; 17, p. 18.
[61] G.B.R., B 4/25/54, primary sch. sub-cttee. 14 Mar. 1967.
[62] Glos. Colln. NF 17.204.
[63] G.B.R., B 4/25/25, pp. 43, 105.
[64] Ibid. 26, pp. 24, 98.
[65] *Glouc. Official Guide* (1972), 171.
[66] G.B.R., B 4/25/30, pp. 27, 40, 60–1.
[67] Ibid. 66, pp. 53, 121.
[68] Ibid. 68, p. 28.
[69] Glos. R.O., S 154/8/2, pp. 279–80.
[70] Ibid. 3, pp. 39–40.
[71] G.B.R., B 4/25/27, p. 234.
[72] Glos. R.O., SB 20/1/1, pp. 30–2, 61, 65, 119.
[73] Ibid. pp. 191–2.
[74] *Kelly's Dir. Glos.* (1885), 477; Glos. R.O., P 154/8/SC 5.
[75] Glos. R.O., SB 20/1/7, p. 328; *Glouc. Sch. Bd. Rep.* (1900), 5.
[76] G.B.R., B 4/25/64, pp. 45, 61; *Kelly's Dir. Glos.* (1906), 182.
[77] Glos. R.O., SB 20/1/3, pp. 11–12, 155–6.
[78] Ibid. 4, p. 290; 7, pp. 25–6, 186.

in 1904 was 770. The buildings were enlarged in 1911.[79] After 1931 the school took junior boys, junior girls, and infants, and in 1938 attendance was 621. In 1952 it was reorganized as separate junior and infants' schools[80] and in 1970 the infants' school moved to a new building in Victory Road.[81] In 1984 the junior school had 184 children on the roll and the infants' school 201.

Tuffley. The Barton St. Mary United District school board formed in 1876[82] opened a school that year in the mission chapel at Tuffley.[83] The building was unsafe by 1881 and the school moved out to temporary accommodation.[84] In 1882 the board opened a new school, also used as a mission chapel, on the Stroud road south of the railway; it had accommodation for 90.[85] The school passed to the city board in 1900,[86] and in 1904 had an attendance of 109 in mixed and infants' departments. It closed in 1906.[87]

Wellington Street Council, see above, voluntary sch., British.

Whaddon school was opened by the county education authority in temporary premises in 1905 and moved into a new building in 1908. Sited by the Stroud road just within the former boundary of Tuffley, the school was apparently intended to serve Whaddon village and the part of Tuffley transferred to Whaddon parish in 1900.[88] It passed to the city authority in 1935 and had an attendance of 79 in junior mixed and infants' departments in 1938. A separate infants' school, to serve Lower Tuffley east of the railway line, was opened on an adjoining site in 1958.[89] In 1984 Whaddon junior school had 156 children on the roll and Whaddon infants' school 87.

Widden Street school was opened by the board in 1878 in a new building, designed by Medland and Son, with accommodation for 660. In June 1879 it was attended by 466 children in boys', girls', and infants' departments.[90] The school was enlarged in 1892[91] but it was overcrowded in the late 1890s with the attendance more than the recognized accommodation.[92] In 1904 778 children attended. From 1931 it was organized as junior mixed and infants' departments, and attendance in 1938 was 392. The school was reorganized as separate junior and infants' schools before 1952.[93] In 1984 the junior school had 120 children on the roll and the infants' school 106.[94]

Wotton St. Mary (Without) Council, see above, Longlevens.

SPECIAL SCHOOLS. *The Open Air* school, at Oak Bank house in Tuffley, was opened by the city education authority in 1936, having been planned in 1930. Originally for delicate children, needing fresh air,[95] it later took physically handicapped children. It was renamed *Oak Bank* school in 1957,[96] and in 1976 it moved to a new building in Longford Lane and was renamed *Chamwell* school.[97] In 1984 it had 72 children, aged from 2 to 16, on the roll.

Archdeacon junior school for educationally subnormal children was opened by the city authority in the Archdeacon Street buildings in 1949.[98] It closed in 1963 when the children were transferred to Longford school.[99]

Longford school, for educationally subnormal children of secondary age, was opened by the city authority in Longford Lane in 1957.[1] It also took children of junior age from 1963. In 1984 there were 122 children, aged from 7 to 16, on the roll. A department of the school moved in 1983 to an adjoining site as a separate school called *The Hawthorns*;[2] in 1984 it had 63 children, aged from 2 to 16, on the roll.

HIGHER EDUCATION. In 1859 a committee of subscribers opened a School of Art at Bearland House; its leading promoter was Thomas Gambier Parry, of Highnam Court,[3] who remained its chairman until his death in 1888.[4] Evening classes in science were begun in the city in 1867 and later moved[5] with the art classes to the new Schools of Science and Art opened in Brunswick Road in 1872.[6] In 1881 262 students were attending the Schools. Later there was a fall in numbers as evening classes in science and art were started at some of the city elementary schools,[7] notably at the National school, in London Road, in 1884.[8] Following the Technical Instruction Act of 1889 and the grant of surplus excise duties, known as the 'whisky money', to local authorities in aid of technical education, the city council made grants in support of the Schools and the London Road classes in 1892, and in 1896 it took over the management of both ventures.[9] In 1906 the Schools became the responsibility of the reconstituted United Schools governors,[10] under whom they remained until 1933 when the education committee assumed direct control.[11]

The curriculum at the Science School included

[79] G.B.R., B 4/25/66, p. 215.
[80] Glos. Colln. N 17.347; *Glouc. Official Guide* (1952), 191.
[81] Glos. Colln. NF 17.204.
[82] *Glouc. Jnl.* 29 Apr., 13 May 1876.
[83] *Kelly's Dir. Glos.* (1879), 772; P.R.O., ED 7/37, Tuffley Board sch.
[84] *Glouc. Jnl.* 5 Feb. 1881.
[85] Glos. R.O., D 4335/108; *Kelly's Dir. Glos* (1885), 607.
[86] Glos. R.O., SB 20/1/8, pp. 237, 269–70.
[87] G.B.R., B 4/25/65, pp. 82–3.
[88] P.R.O., ED 7/35/360; cf. *Kelly's Dir. Glos.* (1910), 359.
[89] G.B.R., B 4/25/29, p. 110; cf. Glos. Colln. NF 17.7.
[90] Glos. R.O., SB 20/1/1, pp. 81–2, 181, 250–1, 317.
[91] *Kelly's Dir. Glos.* (1906), 182.
[92] Glos. R.O., SB 20/1/7, pp. 186, 427.
[93] *Glouc. Official Guide* (1952), 191.
[94] In 1985 new sch. bldgs. were under construction nearby, at the end of Sinope St.

[95] *Glouc. Jnl.* 6 Feb. 1937.
[96] G.B.R., B 4/25/29, p. 62.
[97] Inf. from head teacher.
[98] G.B.R., B 4/25/22, p. 196; 23, p. 109.
[99] Inf. from head teacher, the Hawthorns.
[1] G.B.R., B 4/25/28, pp. 178, 238.
[2] Inf. from head teacher, the Hawthorns.
[3] *Glouc. Coll. of Art, 1858–1958* (Glouc. 1958), 10–13: copy in Glos. Colln. N 17.134.
[4] Ibid. 15–18, 20, 23.
[5] Rossington, 'Glouc. Technical Coll.' 18, 31.
[6] *Glouc. Jnl.* 13 July, 14 Sept. 1872; 19 Apr. 1873; cf. above, Plate 48.
[7] *Glouc. Coll. of Art,* 16–19.
[8] Rossington, 'Glouc. Technical Coll.' 33, 37.
[9] Ibid. 26–7, 40–3.
[10] Glos. Colln. NF 17.12.
[11] *Glouc. Coll. of Art,* 25.

from the 1870s building, machine construction, and agricultural science, and *c.* 1900 new courses, including telegraphy and plumbing, were introduced, to be followed in the next few years by an expansion of commercial and clerical training. The School, known successively as the Technical School and Technical College, co-operated with local firms, some of which gave day release to their apprentices from 1920. Aeronautical engineering and industrial drawing were among new courses introduced in the 1930s.[12] At the Art School courses in industrial design were developed in the 1920s and 1930s, and following the 1944 Education Act its activities took on a strong industrial bias.[13]

In 1941 the Technical College moved to a new building on the part of the Friars Orchard site that fronted Brunswick Road. Extensions to the building were opened in 1967 and 1974, temporary accommodation having been used meanwhile.[14] The Art School, carried on in the original building and other temporary accommodation, was renamed the College of Art in 1952.[15] In 1968 it moved into new buildings on the east side of Brunswick Road,[16] and in the same year it was amalgamated with the art college at Cheltenham to form the Gloucestershire College of Art and Design.[17] In 1981 the Art and Technical Colleges were amalgamated with the North Gloucestershire College of Technology at Cheltenham to form the Gloucestershire College of Arts and Technology, housed in the Brunswick Road buildings, the former College of Education buildings in Oxstalls Lane, and buildings at the Park and Pittville in Cheltenham.[18]

A college for training teachers of domestic science, the Gloucestershire School of Cookery and Domestic Economy (renamed in 1900 the Gloucestershire School of Domestic Science),[19] was opened at Gloucester in 1891, largely through the efforts of Mary Playne of Longfords, Minchinhampton, a daughter of Richard Potter and sister of Beatrice Webb. It was opened with the aid of a grant from the 'whisky money', and Gloucestershire county council agreed to pay the salary of its organizing secretary, who was also to have general responsibility for domestic science teaching in the county. From 1903 it was run by a domestic economy sub-committee of the county education committee, which had a majority of co-opted members and Mrs. Playne as its first chairman; in 1920 the education committee took more direct control. The school was at first housed in part of the old gas company offices in Quay Street, moving in 1894 to the nearby bar-

racks, to which additional buildings were added in the early 20th century. Under its first organizing secretary, Florence Baddeley (d. 1923), the school grew to become one of the largest domestic science schools in the provinces. The students were housed in a number of hostels in the city. Wotton House was bought for that purpose in 1925 and a large new building was completed there in 1931.[20]

The school was renamed the Gloucestershire Training College of Domestic Science in 1925. Degree courses were introduced in association with Bristol University in 1926, and from 1947 the college was affiliated to the university's Institute of Education. A new curriculum, including general subjects as well as domestic science, was introduced in 1950. Plans for new premises were discussed from the late 1930s,[21] but were not realized until 1958 when the college moved to extensive new buildings at the junction of Cheltenham Road and Oxstalls Lane.[22] From 1962 the college provided general teacher training and it was renamed the Gloucestershire College of Education in 1967. It was closed in 1980.[23]

A school of dairying was established at Gloucester in 1889 by Dr. F. T. Bond in association with the Bath and West of England Society. Held at first in a building in Station Road,[24] it moved by 1899 to the barracks.[25] The county council, which aided the school from 1891,[26] took it over before 1906 and ran it, as the Gloucestershire County Council Diary School, until the late 1920s.[27]

From the mid 1850s or earlier some of the city's elementary schools, including St. Luke's and St. Mark's, ran evening classes.[28] The chaplain of the mariners' chapel was organizing classes for dock workers in the late 1860s.[29] An evening school for boys of over school age, started by the headmaster of Widden Street board school in 1879,[30] was apparently short lived. In the 1890s, however, evening classes were started at all the city's board schools; the board provided the rooms, fuel, and grant aid, leaving the teachers to organize the classes and take the fees (and the government grants for students aged under 21).[31] Evening classes at the council schools were continued by the city education committee after 1903.[32] After the Second World War they were organized as the Gloucester Evening Institute, which held classes at the secondary schools and prepared students for specific examinations, and the Gloucester Adult Institute, which was open to people of all ages and where the work was not directed to any particular qualifications. From the late 1960s the

[12] Rossington, 'Glouc. Technical Coll.' 29, 49, 53, 104, 122.

[13] *Glouc. Coll. of Art*, 26, 31.

[14] Rossington, 'Glouc. Technical Coll.' 131–2, 169; *Glouc. Official Guide* (1972), 47; (1976), 53.

[15] *Glouc. Coll. of Art*, 31.

[16] G.B.R., B 4/25/55, governors of Glouc. Technical Coll. and Coll. of Art, 12, 14 Mar. 1968.

[17] Ibid. 28 May 1968.

[18] Inf. from admin. dept., Glos. Coll. of Arts and Technology.   [19] Glos. Colln. JX 15.1.

[20] M. B. T[aylor], *Glos. Training Coll. of Dom. Science* (4th edn., *c.* 1956), 1–17.

[21] Ibid. 13, 23–4, 35–6.   [22] *Citizen*, 28 May 1959.

[23] Inf. from Mrs. E. A. Christmas, a former member of staff.

[24] Glos. Colln. (H) C 30.61; J 10.74.

[25] Glos. R.O., CE/M 8/1, p. 8.   [26] Ibid. M 7B/1, p. 3.

[27] *Kelly's Dir. Glos.* (1906 and later edns.).

[28] P.R.O., ED 7/36/11–12; *Glouc. Jnl.* 1 Oct. 1853; 23 Jan. 1869; 19 Mar. 1870.

[29] *Glouc. Jnl.* 11 May 1867; 19 Feb. 1870.

[30] Glos. R.O., SB 20/1/1, pp. 222–3, 317.

[31] Ibid. 5, pp. 29–30, 37–9; *Glouc. Sch. Bd. Rep.* (1900), 11–12, 26.

[32] G.B.R., B 4/25/64, p. 194; 65, p. 31; *Glouc. Educ. Week Handbk.* (1933), 21.

Evening Institute (renamed the Adult College in 1968) also held classes in outlying areas, such as Hucclecote and Longlevens. Other bodies organizing courses in adult education in the mid 20th century were the Gloucester branch of the W.E.A., which received grant aid from the education committee, and Bristol University's extramural department.[33] The education committee opened a language centre for immigrants in 1970.[34]

More short-lived establishments recorded in the city included a Domestic Training Institution opened in 1868, which trained girls from the poorer classes in domestic science,[35] and a Gloucester Commercial College founded at the custom house c. 1930 to provide training for careers in business and the civil service.[36]

PRIVATE SCHOOLS. From the earlier 18th century Gloucester had a number of private schools, most of them boarding academies for young ladies.[37] Typical was one kept at a house in College Green from 1743 by Ann Counsel; the girls were taught needlework, music, and dancing and a writing master attended.[38] There were four such establishments in the city in 1791.[39] Private schools for boys included a nonconformist academy of considerable reputation held in the city by Samuel Jones between 1708 and 1712.[40] Another boys' school was kept from 1748 by Thomas Rudge, writing master and accountant, in a house in St. Mary's Square, the curriculum including book keeping and accounting.[41] The Revd. Thomas Rudge, who was later master of the Crypt school,[42] was offering private tutition for up to six boys at his house in Kingsholm in 1778.[43]

During the 19th century private schools proliferated in the city. There were at least 11 in 1823[44] and at least 26 in 1842;[45] In 1881 there were 44, teaching a total of 994 pupils.[46] Schools providing education of a sectarian nature included an academy at Longford run by William Barber, a Wesleyan, in 1822[47] and a Roman Catholic convent school for girls opened in London Road in 1862.[48] Many of the large houses in the city were used for private schools at some time, those at former monastic sites being found particularly suitable for the purpose. Priory House at St. Oswald's[49] and part of Blackfriars[50] housed schools in the late 18th and early 19th centuries. Suffolk House at Greyfriars housed a succession of schools for some 65 years from c. 1825,[51] and in the mid 19th century a girls' school, called Abbot's Hall, was held in one of the houses in the ruins of the priory church[52] and another in Bowling Green House, briefly renamed Brunswick House.[53] Also used for many years by girls' schools was the former Spa hotel in Spa Road, which was renamed Ribston Hall when a school moved there from Suffolk House in 1867.[54]

The most ambitious venture in private education was begun in 1886, prompted by the depressed state of the King's school and the feeling that the city should have a first-class independent school, such as existed in Cheltenham and Malvern. The chief promoter was the Revd. Joseph Brereton who had been involved in setting up 'county schools' in Norfolk and Devon.[55] An association of subscribers opened three schools in 1887, a boys' school under Brereton's headmastership at Hempsted Court and girls' schools at Suffolk House and Ribston Hall.[56] A company to carry on the schools was floated in 1888 as the Gloucestershire County Schools Association,[57] but the enterprise was unsuccessful and was wound up in 1891.[58]

In the 20th century, with the development of the grammar and high schools run by the United Schools governors, private education played a dwindling role. There were c. 8 private schools in the city and suburbs in 1931[59] and c. 5 in 1966.[60] There were usually two or three private preparatory schools; the proximity of Cheltenham, supporting a large number of such establishments, probably helped to restrict their number. A convent school was opened in Denmark Road in 1951,[61] and in 1958 Selwyn school, an Anglican foundation, opened at Matson House. The latter, which for some purposes was regarded as a 'sister school' of the King's school but was under quite separate management, took boarders from 1962, and in 1984 had c. 280 girls of primary and secondary age on the roll.[62]

[33] Glos. Colln. N 17.7; G.B.R., B 4/25/55, further educ. sub-cttee. 2 Feb., 15 Mar., 25 Oct. 1968.
[34] Glos. Colln. NF 17.204.
[35] Kelly's Dir. Glos. (1870), 553; Glouc. Jnl. 14 Dec. 1867.
[36] Glos. Colln. N 17.116.
[37] e.g. Glouc. Jnl. 12 Mar. 1728; 23 Dec. 1740.
[38] Ibid. 1 Mar. 1743; 9 Apr. 1751; 31 Aug. 1756.
[39] Univ. Brit. Dir. iii (1794), 192–4.
[40] Above, Prot. Nonconf., intro.
[41] Glouc. Jnl. 8 Mar. 1748; 6 Jan. 1756.
[42] I. Gray, Antiquaries of Glos. and Bristol (B.G.A.S. 1981), 72; Austin, Crypt Sch. 116.
[43] Glouc. Jnl. 6 July 1778.   [44] Pigot's Dir. (1822–3), 56.
[45] Pigot's Dir. Glos. (1842), 109.
[46] Glos. R.O., SB 20/1/1, p. 344.
[47] Glouc. Jnl. 21 Jan. 1822; 29 Nov. 1828.
[48] Langston, 'Cath. Mission in Glouc.' i.

[49] Glouc. Jnl. 19 Sept. 1796; G. A. Howitt, Gloucester's Ancient Walls and Gate Houses (1890), 24.
[50] Glouc. Jnl. 23 Mar. 1795; 25 Dec. 1815; 15 July 1848.
[51] Ibid. 23 Mar. 1844; 21 Dec. 1867; 4 Jan. 1873; Kelly's Dir. Glos. (1885), 754; (1889), 1074.
[52] Glouc. Jnl. 5 July 1862; cf. Bd. of Health Map (1852).
[53] Glos. Colln. N 17.140.
[54] Glouc. Jnl. 29 Dec. 1866; Kelly's Dir. Glos. (1885), 754.
[55] Glouc. Jnl. 30 Oct., 11 Dec. 1886.
[56] Ibid. 27 Nov., 4 Dec. 1886; 22 Jan. 1887.
[57] Glos. Colln. NF 17.91 (1–3).
[58] Glouc. Jnl. 12 Sept. 1891.
[59] Kelly's Dir. Glos. (1931), 547.
[60] Glouc. Official Guide (1966), 191.
[61] Langston, 'Cath. Mission in Glouc.', i.
[62] A. Jennings, Hist. of Matson House (1983), 25–6: copy in Glos. Colln. R 201.5; inf. from sch. sec.

CHARITIES FOR THE POOR

ALMSHOUSES AND ALMSHOUSE CHARITIES

THREE ancient hospitals, St. Bartholomew, St. Margaret, and St. Mary Magdalen,[63] whose medieval history is given in another volume,[64] had all passed into the control of the corporation by the end of the 16th century, and were placed under a joint system of administration in 1636. A fourth hospital, St. Kyneburgh, founded in the 1560s, also passed to the corporation.

In 1636 statutes for the government of the three ancient hospitals were promulgated by the common council.[65] A board of governors, comprising a president, a treasurer, two surveyors, two almoners, and two scrutineers, was to be elected annually and was to hold monthly meetings at St. Bartholomew, the chief hospital; the board was to include the mayor, two aldermen, and other corporation members. Salaried officers — a minister, physician, surgeon, rent gatherer, and 'overseer of the manners of the poor' — were to be appointed and given residence at St. Bartholomew, while separate ministers and readers were to be appointed for the two smaller hospitals and paid at the same rate as the almspeople there. The three hospitals were to maintain a total of 77 almspeople aged at least 52 years, precedence being given to burgesses and their wives. Detailed regulations covering behaviour and religious observance were to be enforced.[66] By the early 18th century a single reader was usually appointed for all three hospitals[67] and the office of minister was by then usually held by the incumbent of St. Nicholas's church.[68] In 1779 an attempt to tighten up the administration was made by the common council, which ordered the statutes to be printed and the rules of behaviour to be posted up in the almspeople's rooms.[69] New statutes, differing little from those of 1636, were enacted by the council in 1830.[70] The hospitals continued to be financed for the most part by their medieval endowments, which were administered and leased under the same policy as the corporation property. Occasionally, however, the revenues were found insufficient: in 1641 because of debts it was decided that each new board of governors should collectively supply each year a loan of £40 to supplement the hospitals' finances,[71] and in 1719, when large sums had been borrowed at interest, the corporation decided to apply some of its own income to the hospitals.[72]

In 1836, under the provisions of the Municipal Corporations Act, the three ancient hospitals and St. Kyneburgh were placed under the management of the Gloucester municipal charity trustees.[73] In 1861 St. Margaret and St. Mary Magdalen were amalgamated as the United Hospitals and the following year moved to a new building at the St. Margaret's site on London Road. The Gothic-style brick building, designed by Fulljames and Waller, comprised two quadrangles, one occupied by the United Hospitals and the other by St. Kyneburgh's Hospital.[74] The United Hospitals were regulated by a Scheme of 1875, under which they were to house 21 almspeople aged at least 60,[75] and in 1882 they were amalgamated with St. Kyneburgh to form a single institution, supporting 31 almspeople.[76] In 1890 St. Bartholomew was also united with it, though the old St. Bartholomew's building in the Island remained in use. The united hospital was to have a total of 71 inmates, paid weekly stipends of 8–12s., and any surplus of income was to be paid to out-pensioners. Its revenues were still drawn largely from land, comprising house property in the city and farmland in various parishes in the county.[77] Much land, including most of the city property, was sold between 1917 and 1927.[78] A Scheme of 1934 fixed the number of inmates at 61, and in 1959 31 people were housed at each of the two sites and there were 81 out-pensioners. The annual income in 1959 comprised £3,508 drawn from stocks and shares and £1,867 rental of farmland.[79] Alice Poulton by will proved 1954 gave the residue of her personal estate, amounting to c. £5,000 in stock and bonds, to provide coal, clothing, and provisions for the almspeople, and a Scheme of 1971 applied that charity and three others administered by the municipal charity trustees to the general support of the almshouses.[80] In the mid 20th century the almspeople also received aid from parish charities of St. Nicholas and St. Catharine.[81] The St. Bartholomew's building was given up in 1971 and the hospital concentrated on the London Road site, where a new block of flats, behind the 19th-century almshouses, was opened in 1978. In 1982

[63] This article was written in 1985.

[64] *V.C.H. Glos.* ii. 118–22; cf. above, Medieval Glouc., Glouc. 1066–1327; town and religious communities.

[65] G.B.R., B 3/2, pp. 51–3, records that they were drawn up by a cttee. appointed by the council, but they were later attributed to Abp. Laud: *14th Rep. Com. Char.* 7.

[66] Glos. Colln. NQ 12.1.

[67] G.B.R., B 3/9, ff. 159, 380v.; 10, ff. 157v., 164v., 175.   [68] G.D.R. vol. 381A, f. 42.

[69] G.B.R., B 3/11, f. 259.

[70] Ibid. 14, ff. 41, 130; Glos. Colln. NQ 12.2.

[71] G.B.R., B 3/2, p. 203.

[72] Ibid. 9, ff. 65v.–66, 71v.

[73] Glos. R.O., D 3270/19677, pp. 1, 373.

[74] Ibid. 19679, pp. 121–2, 129, 150, 172, 208, 235, 262; *Glouc. Jnl.* 8 Sept. 1860.

[75] Glos. Colln. N 12.39 (4).   [76] Ibid. N 12.35 (1).

[77] Ibid. N 12.257.

[78] Glos. R.O., D 3269, Schemes and orders 1865–1934.

[79] T. Hannam-Clark, *Glouc. Municipal Char. Handbk.* (1959), 12–13, 24, 35–6.

[80] Glos. R.O., D 3469/5/67, file marked 'almshouses and general'.

[81] Ibid. file marked 'Edw. Nourse and others'; CH 21, Glouc. co. boro. pp. 19, 30.

the charity opened another new block of flats, in Philip Street in the upper Bristol Road area, and a third new block, in Sherborne Street west of London Road, was opened in 1984. In 1985 a total of 84 flats for old people was maintained at the three sites.[82]

ST. BARTHOLOMEW'S HOSPITAL, the largest and wealthiest of the three ancient hospitals, stood in the Island between Westgate bridge and the Foreign bridge. In 1535 it supported a master, 5 priests, and 32 almspeople out of its extensive property in Gloucester and outlying parishes, which brought in an annual income of £95 7s. 1d.[83] The Crown appointed governors for the hospital in 1547 and 1549,[84] and in 1564 Queen Elizabeth granted the patronage and the reversion of the hospital at the death of the incumbent governor, John Mann, to the corporation; it was to maintain a priest, physician, surgeon, and 40 almspeople and was to be styled the Hospital of St. Bartholomew 'of the foundation of Queen Elizabeth'.[85] An Act of Parliament confirming the grant in 1566 made the bishop of Gloucester visitor to the hospital, and successive bishops exercised that right, notably Martin Benson who made some new regulations in 1745.[86] The corporation took possession of the hospital on the resignation of Mann[87] and in the years 1569–70 rebuilt 19 of the 40 almspeople's rooms and made considerable improvements to other parts of the building.[88]

Under the statutes of 1636 St. Bartholomew was to maintain 50 almspeople (20 men and 30 women) at the weekly pay of 2s. 6d.[89] William Capel then undertook to build six additional rooms for men, and the full complement was apparently made up in 1648 when the common council decided to place another four women in the hospital. The council planned to build four new rooms in 1655,[90] and at the start of the 18th century, the hospital housed 24 men and 30 women.[91] In 1767 Jane Punter gave £500 stock to endow rooms for six additional women, to be paid 1s. a week. In 1781 £500 came to the hospital under the will of Thomas Ratcliffe dated 1761 and it was decided to use it to add 6d. a week to the pay of Jane Punter's women and add two men.[92] In 1825, however, there were 23 men and the 36 women in the hospital.[93] The pay of the almspeople was increased by 1s. in 1805, that of the Punter women being apparently equalized with

that of the others.[94] By 1830 the weekly pay had been increased to 5s. 6d.[95]

Apart from those of Punter and Ratcliffe, other grants supplemented the hospital's medieval endowments. A rent charge of 3s. 4d. a week was distributed to the almspeople under the Crypt school charity established by Joan Cooke in 1540,[96] and in 1859 £78 a year was assigned from that foundation.[97] A payment of 5s. a year was received under the charity established by Sir Thomas Bell in 1562,[98] and Henry Cugley by will dated 1594 gave £10 a year to buy provisions. William Goldstone by will dated 1569 gave the hospital houses and lands in St. Catherine's parish, Richard Pate in 1576 gave houses in St. Mary de Lode parish, and Henry Brown by will dated 1659 gave 8 a. in Walham.[99] The ancient endowments of the hospital included small farms in Uley, Brimpsfield, Coaley, Hardwicke, Longdon (Worcs.), Castle Moreton (Worcs.), and Minety (Glos., later Wilts.) with a total area of 431 a. in 1731, together with parcels of land in several other parishes and extensive property in the city; c. 62 houses belonged to the hospital in 1781 but the number was reduced to 48 by the 1820s as the result of sales for land-tax redemption and demolitions under city improvement Acts. The total rental of the hospital's lands was £504 in 1781, rising to £889 by 1822 when fines, timber sales, and a small income from stock brought its annual income up to c. £1,070.[1] Additional land, mainly in Awre, was bought for the hospital in the late 1870s and early 1880s.[2]

The hospital was regulated by a Scheme of 1872 under which the number of almspeople was to be allowed to fall to 40 people, aged at least 60, and any surplus income used to support non-resident pensioners.[3] In 1890 St. Bartholomew was amalgamated with the United Hospitals.[4]

The first buildings at the site of St. Bartholomew's Hospital apparently dated from Henry II's reign.[5] A chantry chapel was added c. 1230,[6] and in 1265 the Crown gave land for enlarging the chancel.[7] A 'great house' of the poor on the west part of the site was mentioned in 1380.[8] Andrew Whitmay, prior of the hospital from 1510 and suffragan bishop of Worcester diocese,[9] rebuilt the hospital on higher foundations to raise it above flood level, adding also a 'fair lodging' for his own use.[10] Presumably that work was carried out after 1528 when John Cooke bequeathed £9 to secure the hospital against

---

[82] Inf. from Mr. A. G. Keddie, clerk to the trustees of Glouc. municipal char.

[83] *Valor Eccl.* (Rec. Com.), ii. 488–9.

[84] *Cal. Pat.* 1547–8, 193; 1548–9, 244.

[85] Ibid. 1563–6, pp. 71–2; the full title does not seem to have been used later.

[86] Hockaday Abs. ccxxiii, 1669; *14th Rep. Com. Char.* 6–7. The new statutes made for the three hospitals in 1830 were submitted to the bp. for his approval, presumably in acknowledgement of that right: G.B.R., B 3/14, f. 130.

[87] Rudder, *Glos.* 161, 202.

[88] G.B.R., K 1/14; cf. ibid. J 3/16, f. 61v.

[89] Glos. Colln. NQ 12.1.

[90] G.B.R., B 3/2, pp. 53, 479, 853.

[91] Atkyns, *Glos.* 192.

[92] G.B.R., B 3/11, ff. 81v.–82, 291v., 296.

[93] *14th Rep. Com. Char.* 12; the commissioners were at

Glouc. in Mar. 1825: G.B.R., B 3/14, ff. 24–25.

[94] *14th Rep. Com. Char.* 11; G.B.R., B 3/13, f. 8v.

[95] Glos. Colln. NQ 12.2.

[96] Austin, *Crypt Sch.* 153–4.

[97] Glos. Colln. NQ 17.2.

[98] Hockaday Abs. ccxxiii.

[99] *14th Rep. Com. Char.* 9–10; G.B.R., J 3/16, f. 36 and v.

[1] *14th Rep. Com. Char.* 7–9.

[2] Glos. R.O., D 3269, Schemes and orders 1865–1934.

[3] Glos. Colln. N 12.35 (2).

[4] Above.

[5] *Cal. Inq. Misc.* iii, p. 80.

[6] *Hist. & Cart. Mon. Glouc.* (Rolls. Ser.), i. 245.

[7] *Cal. Pat.* 1258–66, 450.

[8] Ibid. 1377–81, 578.

[9] *V.C.H. Glos.* ii. 121.

[10] Leland, *Itin.* ed. Toulmin Smith, ii. 59.

winter floods.[11] The buildings were said to be ruinous at the time of the grant of 1564,[12] following which considerable work on them was undertaken by the corporation.[13] In the 18th century the chapel, evidently not included in Whitmay's rebuilding, remained a substantial building, mainly of the late 13th century or early 14th.[14] Between 1787 and 1790 the hospital was completely rebuilt by the corporation. The new building, designed in gothick style by William Price, had a road front with blind arcading, the central bays projecting,[15] and a semicircular bay at the rear which housed the chapel.[16] Following its sale by the municipal charity trustees, it was restored in the early 1980s as a shopping and craft centre.

ST. MARGARET'S HOSPITAL, which stood outside the city boundary on the south-east side of the London road, had passed into the control of the burgess community by the late Middle Ages and leading burgesses were appointed to the post of master.[17] In 1546 the hospital had an annual income of £8 12s.,[18] and in 1563 the inmates were a reader and 10 poor men.[19] Under the statutes of 1636 it was to support a reader and 8 men at the weekly pay of 2s. a week each[20] and its complement of almspeople remained unchanged. In 1805 their pay was increased by 1s. a week,[21] and they were receiving 4s. a week in 1825. Those almsmen who were married at the time of their election were allowed to bring their wives into the hospital.[22]

The hospital's ancient endowments included houses in the city and parcels of land in the outlying hamlets and other parts of the county. The total rental was £58 in 1781 and £137 in 1822, when the number of houses owned, recently increased by new building, was 22.[23] Under the will of Thomas Horton, dated 1735 but not confirmed until 1763, St. Margaret's and St. Mary Magdalen's hospitals shared in a rent charge of £10, given for provisions and for a sermon and prayers, and in the proceeds of £100.[24] Alderman John Hayward (d. 1758) gave a rent charge of 40s. to be distributed among the almsmen of St. Margaret at Christmas, and they also received any residue of £15 which was to be paid every five years for repairing Hayward's tomb and part of the pavement in the hospital chapel.[25] In 1822 the total annual income of the hospital was £170.[26] St. Margaret's Hospital was united with St. Mary Magdalen in 1861.[27]

The hospital was founded before the mid 12th century[28] and the surviving two-celled chapel incorporates 12th-century masonry in its west wall. The chapel appears, however, to have been rebuilt in the early 14th century, and new windows were put into the nave in the 15th. The chapel was restored in 1846 and again in 1875;[29] a south vestry was added, the roof was renewed, and the interior was refitted. As well as serving the inmates of the hospital the chapel was used over the centuries by inhabitants of the neighbouring suburbs. That was possibly the reason why in the late Middle Ages the chantry priest maintained by Gloucester Abbey in the chapel was sometimes styled rector[30] and why in the mid 16th century the chapel was said to be parochial.[31] The registers, which survive from the 1790s, include baptisms and burials of residents of the neighbouring London road area.[32] Use of the chapel by outsiders was probably encouraged by the fact that parts of the area belonged to the extraparochial North and South Hamlets and other parts to St. Catherine's parish,[33] which had no church after 1655. The chapel remained in use by the almspeople in 1985.

In 1560 the domestic buildings included the former prior's lodging, then leased, and the almsmen's lodgings.[34] An old hall is said to have been converted to a barn c. 1589.[35] In the early 19th century the buildings comprised a single tall range, partly timber-framed and partly stone-built, fronting the main road east of the chapel.[36] It was demolished in 1862 when the new United Hospitals were opened on an adjoining site.[37]

ST. MARY MAGDALEN'S HOSPITAL, known alternatively from 1617 as King James's Hospital, stood on the south side of the London road, further out than St. Margaret, near Wotton Pitch. In 1546 it had annual revenues of £3 6s. 8d.[38] and in 1563 maintained a reader and six poor men and women.[39] The Crown, which had assumed rights as patron exercised before the Dissolution by Llanthony Priory,[40] appointed governors of the hospital in the later 16th century. In 1573, when John Fenner (or Spring) was appointed,[41] the

[11] Austin, *Crypt Sch.* 138.
[12] *Cal. Pat.* 1563–6, p. 72.
[13] Above.
[14] Glos. Colln. prints GL 45.8.
[15] G.B.R., B 3/12, ff. 78v., 84v.–85, 119, 133v.; above, Plate 57.
[16] Cf. Glos. R.O., D 3269, bk. of plans of hosp. property 1826, no. 14.
[17] Above, Medieval Glouc., town and religious communities.
[18] Hockaday Abs. ccxxiii.
[19] Ibid. xlii, 1563 dioc. surv., f. 15.
[20] Glos. Colln. NQ 12.1.   [21] G.B.R., B 3/13, f. 8v.
[22] *14th Rep. Com. Char.* 15.   [23] Ibid. 12–13.
[24] Ibid. 13–14; cf. below, Outlying Hamlets, man.
[25] *14th Rep. Com. Char.* 14. Hayward's tomb was removed from the chap. in 1846, and in 1857 the municipal char. trustees bought the est. on which the payments were charged: Glos. R.O., D 3270/19678, pp. 430, 471, 475–6.
[26] *14th Rep. Com. Char.* 13.

[27] Above.
[28] *V.C.H. Glos.* ii. 121.
[29] *Glouc. Jnl.* 15 Aug. 1846; Verey, *Glos.* ii. 232.
[30] Worc. Episc. Reg., Reg. Lynn, f. 5v.; Reg. Alcock, ff. 119v., 143v.
[31] Hockaday Abs. ccxxiii, 1546, 1558.
[32] Glos. R.O., D 3269.
[33] Cf. Causton, *Map of Glouc.* (1843).
[34] G.B.R., B 2/2, ff. 118v.–119v.
[35] Rudder, *Glos.* 186.
[36] Clarke, *Archit. Hist. of Glouc.* plate facing p. 55; Glos. Colln. prints GL 15.5, reproduced above, Plate 55; cf. G.B.R., J 4/1, no. 20, which shows other bldgs. E. of that range in 1731.
[37] *Glouc. Jnl.* 21 June 1862; above.
[38] Hockaday Abs. ccxxiii.
[39] Ibid. xlii, 1563 dioc. surv., f. 15.
[40] *Glouc. Corp. Rec.* p. 119; P.R.O., C 115/K 2/6684, f. 90v.
[41] *Cal. Pat.* 1553–4, 406; 1572–5, p. 162.

hospital and all its revenues were held by John Norris under a lease from an earlier governor and the almspeople were left unsupported. After an inquiry Norris was ordered to give up the hospital in 1576.[42] In 1598 the hospital was said to be in ruins and Elizabeth I granted the patronage to the corporation so that they could carry out repairs.[43] By 1614 an additional 13 almspeople were being maintained at St. Mary Magdalen by its governor, Alderman Thomas Machen, and at his death that year he left £100 to the corporation to support a payment of 6d. a quarter to each of them.[44] In 1617 James I granted the governorship of the hospital and its lands and revenues, including a pension of £13 from the Crown, to the corporation; the hospital was to continue to maintain 19 almspeople and was to be renamed the Hospital of King James (though the old name also remained in use).[45]

The statutes of 1636 provided for 10 men and 9 women to be maintained at the weekly pay of 1s. 6d.,[46] and the number of almspeople remained unchanged. The weekly pay was increased by 6d. in 1805,[47] but in 1824, as an economy measure, the pay of newly elected inmates was set at 1s. 6d.[48] In 1827 the sum of £4 a year, an ancient bequest to the city poor by Leonard Tarne, was added to the weekly pay,[49] and from 1838 the almspeople at St. Mary Magdalen and St. Kyneburgh had an additional 6d. a week, the proceeds of £1,500 received under the will of John Garn (d. 1835).[50]

The ancient endowments comprised a farm at Hayden, in Cheltenham parish, which covered 58 a. in 1731, some parcels of land in the outlying hamlets of Gloucester, and a few houses in the city. In 1822 the total rental was £155 and the total annual income of the hospital c. £170. The hospital was by then in an impoverished state, a debt of £522 having accumulated. It was hoped that building then in progress on some of the hospital's land in the London road would eventually improve the finances, but it was still in debt and its buildings ruinous in 1833.[51] St. Mary Magdalen was united with St. Margaret's Hospital in 1861.[52]

St. Mary Magdalen's Hospital was probably founded in the early 12th century[53] and its small two-celled chapel dating from that period survived relatively unaltered until the mid 19th century. A lancet window was put into the north wall of the chancel in the 13th century, the east window was enlarged in the 15th, and the chancel roof was renewed and a new window put in the south side in the 16th. A west porch of brick was added in the late 18th century or the early 19th, and a small west bellcot contained a bell cast by John Rudhall in 1793.[54] By the 1840s the inmates of the hospital attended St. Margaret's chapel and St. Mary Magdalen's chapel became dilapidated.[55] In 1861 the nave was demolished but the richly ornamented south doorway was reset, facing east, in the chancel arch, and the north doorway was set in the south wall of chancel.[56] The east window was probably restored at that time. The chapel contains the recumbent effigy of a lady, said to have been brought from St. Kyneburgh's chapel.[57] The chapel was no longer used in 1985.

St. Mary Magdalen's chapel, like St. Margaret's, was said to serve a separate parish in the mid 16th century.[58] From at least the early 18th century inhabitants of Wotton, including members of the Blanch family, were buried in the chapel and its burial ground[59] and burials and baptisms of people from various neighbouring areas were being registered there in the 1790s.[60] John Blanch (d. 1756) of Barton Street devised £300 in reversion to maintain a minister to read service and preach in the chapel on Sundays; the gift was conditional on the inhabitants of Wotton raising another £100[61] and was apparently never implemented.

The main London road formerly ran close to the north side of the chapel[62] but in 1821 it was diverted to the south side,[63] dividing the chapel from the domestic buildings of the hospital which formed a quadrangle some way to the south.[64] The buildings, which were wholly or partly timber-framed,[65] were refronted following the road diversion,[66] and were demolished in or soon after 1862.[67]

ST. KYNEBURGH'S HOSPITAL, commonly called the Kimbrose, was founded by Sir Thomas Bell, the wealthy Gloucester capper, on the site of St. Kyneburgh's chapel at the south gate. Bell had built an almshouse there by 1559 when he drew up his will leaving it, with endowments, to the city corporation.[68] In 1562, however, he settled it

[42] Acts of P.C. 1571–5, 391, 399; 1575–7, 126–7.
[43] Hockaday Abs. ccxxiii.
[44] G.B.R., G 12/1, f. 275 and v.; cf. ibid. B 3/1, f. 198 and v.
[45] 14th Rep. Com. Char. 15–16. The new name was sometimes given incorrectly as St. James's Hosp.: Atkyns, Glos. 186; G.D.R. vol. 381A, f. 43.
[46] Glos. Colln. NQ 12.1.
[47] G.B.R., B 3/13, f. 8v.
[48] Ibid. 14, f. 213.
[49] Ibid. B 4/1/4, f. 14 and v.
[50] He left £2,000 but only £1,500 was received: Glouc. Jnl. 12 Dec. 1835; G.B.R., B 3/15, mins. 10 Apr., 10 July 1837, 26, 30 Apr., 5 Dec. 1838; Char. Com. file 249996. The char. was transferred from the corp. to the char. trustees in 1878 and merged in the general funds of the United Hospitals in 1882: Glos. R.O., D 3269, Schemes and orders 1865–1934.
[51] 14th Rep. Com. Char. 16–17; G.B.R., B 3/14, ff. 25v., 212v.–213.
[52] Above.
[53] E. J. Kealey, Medieval Medicus (1981), 112.
[54] Glos. Colln. prints GL 15.25–7, 37, one reproduced

above, Plate 56; H. T. Ellacombe, Ch. Bells of Glos. (Exeter, 1881), 48.
[55] Glouc. Jnl. 15 Aug. 1846; 6 July 1850; Glos. R.O., D 3270/19678, p. 359.
[56] Glos. Colln. prints GL 15.21; cf. ibid. GL 15.25, 37.
[57] Roper, Glos. Effigies, 316–17.
[58] Hockaday Abs. ccxxiii, 1546, 1565; cf. P.R.O., E 134/6 & 7 Geo. I Trin./1, referring to a deed of 1623 mentioning St. Mary Magdalen's par.
[59] Fosbrooke, Glouc. 154–5.
[60] Glos. R.O., D 3269.
[61] P.R.O., PROB 11/830 (P.C.C. 182 Herring), f. 327v.; Glouc. Jnl. 21 Dec. 1756.
[62] G.B.R., J 4/1, no. 14.
[63] Glos. R.O., D 204/3/3.
[64] Ibid. D 3269, bk. of plans of hosp. property 1824, no. 33.
[65] Glos. Colln. prints GL 45.10A–B.
[66] G.B.R., F 4/15, p. 579.
[67] Glos. R.O., D 3270/19679, p. 262.
[68] G.D.R. wills 1566/150.

on a body of trustees, who took possession after the deaths of Bell and his wife Joan[69] in 1566 and 1567 respectively.[70] Under the terms of the trust deed the hospital was to maintain six poor people, one of them to be if possible a burgess. It gave the site of Whitefriars, Morin's Mill in Brook Street, six houses, and the rent of another house, having a total annual value of £16 0s. 4d., to support a quarterly payment of 13s. 4d. to each of the almspeople, and gave substantial endowments for other charitable purposes and to provide for property repairs. The trustees did not, as was intended, fill vacancies in their own number and only two remained in 1598 when they acquired licence to transfer the hospital and its endowments to the corporation. The transfer, which was prompted by the corporation's energetic management of St. Bartholomew's Hospital after 1564, was completed in 1603[71] and the corporation retained St. Kyneburgh under its direct management until 1836.

The original endowment was supplemented by the gift of a house from Thomas Hobbs in 1608,[72] and Margaret Norton by will dated 1689 gave the interest on £30,[73] for which £1 a year was received in the 1820s. In 1763 Susanna Cooke gave £40 for provisions on St. Thomas's day, and £2 in cash was distributed for that gift in the 1820s.[74] In 1833 the annual income of the hospital was £42. The inmates, whose number remained at six, were then receiving 1s. 6d. a week each and an annual sum of £10 7s. divided amongst them.[75] A plan in 1835 to use surplus funds to buy stock and raise the weekly pay by 6d. a week[76] may not have been implemented but an increase at that rate was made in 1838 under John Garn's bequest.[77]

In the mid 19th century the almshouse remained as built by Bell, comprising a low range of building with five doorways to the almsrooms.[78] An older building, which survived adjoining the west end, housed the sixth almsman.[79] The almshouse was demolished after 1862 when the inmates were rehoused in the new building on London Road.[80] A Scheme of 1861 increased the number of almspeople to 10, who were to be aged at least 60 and receive between 7s. 6d. and 10s. a week.[81] St. Kyneburgh was amalgamated with the United Hospitals in 1882.[82]

OTHER ALMSHOUSES. A number of other almshouses were established in Gloucester in the late 16th century and the 17th but some were short lived, probably as a result of lack of endowment.

Alderman *William Hill* (d. 1636) left £80 to build a house outside the south gate in which six poor people of the south ward were to be placed by the corporation.[83] The house was built and almspeople were regularly maintained there by the corporation,[84] though there was apparently no endowment for repairs or weekly pay. Sarah Wright by will dated 1667 gave 6s. a year to buy coal for the almspeople.[85] The house was demolished at the same time as the south gate in 1781 and the existing almspeople were found other lodgings. They were not, however, replaced when they died and only two remained c. 1811.[86]

Alderman *John Baugh* (d. 1621) devised the remainder of his 300-year lease of the former St. Thomas's chapel, by the river Twyver in the later Dean's Walk, for an almshouse and devised an adjoining orchard to provide for maintenance of the building, which was divided into four tenements; the master and four almsmen of St. Bartholomew's Hospital were to settle poor burgesses there. In 1631, however, the administrator of Baugh's will assigned the lease to a Gloucester mercer,[87] and following a Chancery suit brought by the corporation it was conveyed in 1633 to a group of common councillors who were to implement the will.[88] It is not known whether almsmen were ever settled in the building, which was demolished before 1692, probably at the siege of 1643.[89]

Alderman *John Hayward* (d. 1640) built two almshouses near St. John's church and left other property to St. John's parish as an endowment.[90] Two widows were housed there in 1738 when Alderman Samuel Browne left a rent charge of 10s. to help support them.[91] The houses were pulled down in 1804 and the widows were moved to two new houses built on parish property adjoining lower Northgate Street. The widows each received an annual pension of 50s. in the early 19th century[92] and £16 in the 1890s.[93] The houses were apparently sold c. 1934, and by the early 1960s the proceeds of the endowment were being applied for general charitable purposes in the parish.[94]

Almshouses founded by *Mr. Pate*, presumably Richard Pate (d. 1588), and by Alderman *Thomas Semys* (d. 1603) were said to have existed in 1643, and *Richard Keylock*, presumably the man who served as sheriff in 1627, was said to have provided houses for two men in St. John's parish. Nothing was known of those three foundations in the mid 18th century.[95] Almshouses recorded in Holy Trinity parish between 1614 and 1645[96] were

[69] Hockaday Abs. ccxxiii. [70] Fosbrooke, *Glouc.* 165–6.
[71] Hockaday Abs. ccxxiii, which gives full transcripts of the trust deeds.
[72] Ibid.
[73] P.R.O., PROB 11/397 (P.C.C. 180 Ent), f. 330 and v.
[74] *14th Rep. Com. Char.* 21; G.B.R., B 3/11, f. 34.
[75] G.B.R., B 3/14, f. 213.
[76] Ibid. f. 258v.
[77] Above, St. Mary Magdalen's Hosp.
[78] Drawing (reproduced above, Plate 54) in copy of Fosbrooke, *Glouc.*, in Glos. Colln. 10675.
[79] G.D.R. wills 1566/150; cf. Rudder, *Glos.* 204.
[80] Glos. R.O., D 3270/19679, pp. 249, 262.
[81] Glos. Colln. N 12.37.   [82] Above.
[83] G.D.R. wills 1636/120.

[84] G.B.R., G 12/1, f. 200; Rudder, *Glos.* 204.
[85] *16th Rep. Com. Char.* 11–12.
[86] Rudge, *Glouc.* 141.
[87] G.D.R. wills 1621/53; G.B.R., J 1/1958B.
[88] G.B.R., J 1/1959.
[89] Below, Churches and Chapels, non-par. chap.
[90] G.D.R. wills 1640/113.
[91] Ibid. 1738/159.
[92] *16th Rep. Com. Char.* 7.
[93] Glos. R.O., P 154/9/CH 1/1.
[94] Ibid. 2; cf. ibid. CH 10/1, Scheme 1972.
[95] Glos. R.O., D 327, p. 374; and for those three men, Fosbrooke, *Glouc.* 136, 209, 211; below, Aldermen of Glouc. 1483–1835.
[96] G.D.R. wills 1614/21; Glouc. Cath. Libr. MS. 26.

apparently four houses in Bull Lane given by a *Mr. Peach*,[97] and *John Cromwell* by will dated 1679 left two houses in Hare Lane to be used, after the deaths of the tenants, to house poor people of St. John's parish;[98] no later record has been found of those almshouses in use. *John Harvey Ollney* (d. 1836) left £8,000 to the city

corporation to found an almshouse for 18 poor people and provide them with a weekly allowance.[99] The corporation obtained a site for the house, apparently as a gift, in 1846[1] but Chancery proceedings begun in 1848 to secure the legacy and similar gifts to Tewkesbury, Cheltenham, and Winchcombe were unsuccessful.[2]

OTHER CHARITIES

CITY CHARITIES MANAGED BY THE OLD CORPORATION.[3] The minor charities controlled by the city corporation before 1835 were mainly tradesmen's loan charities and apprenticeship charities, most of them given in the later 16th century or the earlier 17th. The funds given for tradesmen, which were lent, usually free of interest, on bond and surety for periods of a few years, were much underused *c.* 1695 when only £302 of a total of £1,095 were out. Later most of the loan funds were lost, either not recovered from borrowers or absorbed into the general corporation funds; by 1825 only the charity of Sir Thomas White, which was periodically augmented, survived. It, Sir Thomas Rich's, and three apprenticeship charities, were transferred to the municipal charity trustees in 1836 and applied to educational purposes in 1882.

Hugh Atwell, rector of St. Tew (Cornw.), *c.* 1601 gave £3 11*s.* 7*d.* a year to keep the poor at work. About 1695, when the proceeds were said to be £3 6*s.* 8*d.*, it was regarded as a loan charity. It had been lost by 1825.

Sir Thomas Bell, alderman, by his trust deed of 1562, endowing St. Kyneburgh's Hospital, gave annual rent charges totalling £6 10*s.* for the poor of the four wards of the city and the prisoners in the county and city gaols. The charity became the corporation's responsibility in 1603.[4] The sums were distributed regularly up to 1825 but have not been found recorded later.

Abraham Blackleech (d. 1639)[5] gave £50 for apprenticeships. The capital was probably distributed as a principal sum.[6]

Sarah Browne, widow of Alderman John Browne,[7] by will dated 1643 gave her lease of property held under the corporation, part of the Bell charity estate; the profits were to be used for paying the chief rent, renewing the lease, and apprenticing three boys each year. The property was producing a rent of £25 in 1825. From 1836 the charity was administered by the municipal

charity trustees.[8] It was apparently discontinued *c.* 1851 in the course of a Chancery suit over the arrangements for leasing the Bell charity property.[9]

Jasper Clutterbuck, alderman, by will dated 1658 gave leasehold land, £10 of the profits to be used for apprenticing two boys each year. The charity, if ever applied,[10] presumably lapsed on expiry of the lease.

Giles Cox, of Abloads Court, Sandhurst, by will dated 1620 gave £100 for loans to five impoverished clothiers.[11] The charity was in operation *c.* 1695 but had been lost by 1825.

Henry Ellis by will dated 1647 gave £500 from his share of the cargo of a ship, if it returned safely from its voyage, to provide loans to citizens involved in overseas trade. About 1695 £50 in the chamberlain's hands was said to represent the charity but no record has been found of it in operation.

Dame Eleanor Fettiplace in 1625 gave £40 to set the poor to work.[12] It was used for loans to tradesmen[13] until *c.* 1695 or later and had been lost by 1825.

Helpe Foxe, incumbent of St. Nicholas,[14] in 1669 offered £100 for apprenticeships. Attempts to acquire the sum were made in 1678, after Foxe's death,[15] but no record has been found of the charity in operation.

Thomas Gloucester of London, presumably a native of Gloucester, by codicil to his will proved 1447 gave 500 marks for loans to young tradesmen of the town or the county.[16] By 1503 keepers of the fund were being appointed annually and had £108 3*s.* 4*d.* in their hands; £80 was lent in 1529 for rebuilding the Boothall, to be repaid out of the profits of the weighing beams kept there. No record of the fund has been found after 1539, when £95 6*s.* 4*d.* was in hand.[17]

Joan Goldstone by will dated 1578 gave £20 to provide wood and coal for the poor. In 1612 the corporation assigned the principal sum together with a lease of its storehouse near the Foreign

[97] Bodl. MS. Top. Glouc. c. 3, f. 50.
[98] G.D.R. wills 1680/75.
[99] *Glos. Chron.* 30 Jan. 1836; 24 Nov. 1838.
[1] *Glouc. Jnl.* 17 Jan. 1846; G.B.R., B 4/1/6, p. 231.
[2] G.B.R., B 4/1/6, pp. 343, 359, 389; B 3/17, f. 378.
[3] This section is based on *14th Rep. Com. Char.* 21–2, 30–41 (compiled in 1825); G.B.R., G 12/1 (a reg. of early gifts and bequests to the corp.); and ibid. B 3/7, ff. 254–5 (a rep. on the loan charities, *c.* 1695).
[4] Cf. above, almshouses.   [5] Fosbrooke, *Glouc.* 138.
[6] As were probably small sums given for the poor of the city parishes by Blackleech: P.R.O., PROB 11/181 (P.C.C.

194 Harvey), ff. 451v.–452.
[7] Cf. *V.C.H. Glos.* x. 17.
[8] Glos. R.O., D 3270/19677, pp. 76, 127.
[9] Ibid. D 3269, legal papers 1853–6.
[10] G.B.R., B 3/3, p. 162; P.R.O., PROB 11/300 (P.C.C. 180 Nabbs), f. 160 and v.
[11] G.D.R. wills 1621/23.
[12] G.B.R., B 3/1, ff. 509v.–510.   [13] Cf. ibid. 3, p. 146.
[14] Fosbrooke, *Glouc.* 182.
[15] G.B.R., B 3/3, pp. 405, 717.
[16] Ibid. J 1/1134.
[17] Ibid. B 2/1, ff. 14, 208v.–224.

bridge, the lessee being required to sell fuel to the poor at fixed prices,[18] and in 1825 the charity was considered to be met in the subsidized coal supply.[19]

Thomas Gunter of Massachusetts, a native of Gloucester, by will dated 1760 gave £1,000 for loans to tradesmen. Only £333 was received, all but £83 of which was used in 1766 to buy additional land for the Bluecoat school endowment. In 1780 the corporation agreed to pay interest on the £333 to Gunter's poverty-stricken residuary legatees during their lives.[20] The eventual use of the residue of the principal received has not been discovered.

William Halliday, alderman of London, by will dated 1623 and modified by his later spoken wishes,[21] gave £500 for apprenticeships; it was to be laid out on land so as to produce a rent of £30, and the corporation later decided that six boys should benefit each year. The principal was not laid out but kept in hand by the corporation until 1835 when part of its property was charged with a payment of £30 for it.[22] From 1792 the charity was applied with Sarah Browne's, providing a total premium of £9 for each boy.[23] From 1836 the charity was administered by the municipal charity trustees,[24] and in 1882 it was annexed to the United Schools foundation to provide scholarships at Sir Thomas Rich's school.[25]

John Heydon, a London mercer, by will dated 1580 gave £100 for loans to young Gloucester merchants trading overseas; interest was to be charged at £3 6s. 8d. a year and distributed among the prisoners in the city gaol.[26] Loans were made at least once, in 1585, but c. 1695 the principal, though still accounted for, was not in use. The loan charity had lapsed altogether by 1825 but a payment was still made to the prisoners in respect of it.

William Huntley gave £10 for loans to set poor men to work. The sum was received by the corporation in 1632[27] but had apparently been lost by c. 1695.

John Langley by will proved c. 1657 gave £20 for loans to young tradesmen. The charity was in operation in 1673 but has not been found recorded later.

Thomas Machen, alderman,, by will dated 1614 gave £100 for loans at interest to mercers. The charity was in operation c. 1695 but had been lost by 1825.

John Morris by will dated 1626 gave £10 for loans to poor burgesses; interest at 13s. 4d. a year was to be charged and given to the poor at Christmas.[28] The principal was accounted for but not in use c. 1695. It had been lost by 1825 but

12s. was paid to the poor each year in respect of the interest.

Richard Pate, recorder of the city, by will dated 1588 gave a rent charge of £1 to the poor for a term of 20 years after his death.

Robert Pettifer by will dated 1612 gave the herbage of a piece of land for the use of the poor during the remainder of his lease.

Thomas Poulton of Tewkesbury by will dated 1607[29] gave £60 for loans to young tradesmen. The charity was in operation at least until 1787[30] but had been lost by 1825.

John Powell (d. 1666),[31] alderman, gave £100, the proceeds to be used to apprentice two or more boys each year. The charity was in operation in 1682[32] but has not been found recorded later.

Jane Punter by will dated 1767 gave the residue of her personal estate to apprentice as many boys at £10 each as the interest on the sum would allow; £2,523 was received and invested in stock. Later the stock was sold and the principal merged in the general funds of the corporation, which made itself liable to interest of £79 a year. By 1825 there was an accumulation of £715, few apprenticeships having been made since 1805, and it was planned to use the fund in conjunction with other apprenticing charities. From 1836 the charity was administered by the municipal charity trustees,[33] and in 1882 it was annexed to the United Schools foundation to provide scholarships at Sir Thomas Rich's school.[34]

Sir Thomas Rich by will dated 1666 charged his Bluecoat school endowment[35] with £30 a year to provide clothes for 10 poor men and 10 poor women; he also gave the residual income of the endowment for distribution to young tradesmen and to poor maidservants when they married or, failing suitable recipients, to poor and sick householders. The clothing charity was distributed in blue gowns, the recipients being required to attend the mayor to church on Sundays and festivals.[36] The other charities were being distributed irregularly in the early 19th century, whenever there was a surplus of funds.[37] As part of the school foundation, the charities were administered from 1836 by the municipal charity trustees.[38] Under a Scheme of 1851 the payments to tradesmen, maidservants, and householders were placed on a regular basis, at a fixed rate every five years, while the clothing charity was to continue annually, the recipients to be known as Blue Gowns.[39] The Scheme for the United Schools in 1882 provided only for the continuance of the clothing charity, at £40 a year,[40] and it was made a separate foundation in 1906.[41] The charity operated until 1971 when the

[18] Ibid. B 3/1, f. 240v.
[19] Cf. above, Glouc. 1720–1835, city govt.
[20] G.B.R., B 3/11, ff. 276v.–277Av., 301–2.
[21] Cf. ibid. J 1/1701A–B.
[22] Ibid. B 3/14, f. 260v.
[23] Ibid. 12, ff. 168v., 331v.
[24] Glos. R.O., D 3270/19677, p. 76; 19679, p. 36.
[25] Glos. Colln. NF 17.18.
[26] G.B.R., J 1/1931.
[27] Ibid. B 3/1, f. 559.
[28] G.D.R. wills 1626/111.
[29] Cf. *21st Rep. Com. Char.* H.C. 349, p. 196 (1829), vii (1).

[30] G.B.R., B 3/3, p. 265; F 4/13, p. 329.
[31] Below, Aldermen of Glouc. 1483–1835.
[32] G.B.R., B 3/3, p. 819.
[33] Glos. R.O., D 3270/19677, pp. 76, 127.
[34] Glos. Colln. NF 17.18.
[35] Cf. above, Educ., Sir Thos. Rich's sch.
[36] G.B.R., B 3/3, pp. 378, 464.
[37] Glos. R.O., D 3270/19659, mins. 22 Feb. 1805, 4 Aug. 1806, 18 Dec. 1809, 14 Dec. 1820.
[38] Ibid. 19677, pp. 212, 405.
[39] Glos. Colln. N 17.82.
[40] Ibid. NF 17.18.
[41] Glos. R.O., D 3269, Schemes and orders 1875–1927.

proceeds were assigned to the general fund of the United Hospitals.[42]

Miles Smith (d. 1624), bishop of Gloucester, gave £20 for setting the poor to work. It was on loan to a tradesman in 1629,[43] but has not been found recorded later.

Leonard Tarne, alderman, by will dated 1641 gave a rent charge of £4 a year to be distributed among 40 poor people.[44] In 1827 it was assigned to the inmates of St. Mary Magdalen's Hospital[45] and later remained part of the endowments of the almshouses.[46]

Sir Thomas White, a London clothier, by will dated 1566[47] included Gloucester among the 23 towns which (with the London merchant tailors' company) were in turn to receive from Bristol corporation an annual payment of £104; after the deduction of £4 for management expenses, the sum was to be used for loans to young tradesmen, with preference to clothiers. Gloucester took its first turn in 1581. About 1695, when it had received the charity five times, £62 of the fund had been lost, and in 1825 only £400 remained of the £1,100 received. Part of the fund was used on litigation between 1816 and 1818 when Gloucester joined other towns in an unsuccessful attempt to get Bristol corporation to share out a large surplus of rents from the endowment; the city declined to join another attempt in 1831.[48] From 1836 the charity was administered by the municipal charity trustees,[49] and in 1882 it was annexed to the United Schools foundation.[50]

Gregory Wilshire by will dated 1585 gave £100 for loans to clothiers. At least £20 remained and was out on loan in 1746 but the whole sum had been lost by 1825.

Sarah Wright by will dated 1669 and codicil dated 1670 gave £10 for loans to young tradesmen, with preference to saddlers. The charity was still in operation in 1765; no later record could be found in 1825 but the corporation admitted liability for the charity. The same donor, by an earlier will dated 1667 and ratified by that of 1669, charged two houses with 3s. a year for the sick or poor of the city, with doles in bread for the prisoners in the city and county gaols, and with various parish charities. The corporation were named as trustees[51] but in 1674, finding that the property would not support the full value of the bequests, it transferred the trust to St. Mary de Crypt parish.[52] In 1825 the bread was being distributed but not the 3s., which it was planned to restore.[53]

Isabel Wytherston gave £20 to support a distribution of 40s. among 40 poor people. The corporation was trying to secure payment of the interest in 1676,[54] but the charity has not been found recorded later.

OTHER CITY CHARITIES. *A. E. Allen* (d. 1946) gave £1,000 to be invested and the proceeds used to provide pensions or grants for poor freemen of the city or their relatives; an additional £214 was also received by lapse of other legacies under his will. The charity was placed under the management of the freemen's committee,[55] and in 1971 had an annual income of £100.[56]

F. H. Collins by declaration of trust of 1926 gave £1,000 stock to the city corporation, the proceeds to be distributed to the blind or aged poor in December in food, clothing, fuel, or other necessaries. In 1972 the charity became part of the Charity of John Ward and Others.[57]

William Johnston-Vaughan by will proved 1928 gave the residue of his personal estate, after the death of his wife, to the municipal charity trustees to support annual payments of £1 each to poor people of the city aged over 60. In 1962 the charity had an endowment of £18,815 in stock and bonds, producing an annual income of £588. In 1971 it was applied to the support of the United Hospitals.[58]

Ann Lysons of Hempsted[59] by will dated 1705 gave £120 to produce £6 a year for clothing six poor widows; the sum was charged on land in 1707. The charity was managed by private trustees[60] until 1890 when it was transferred to the municipal charity trustees,[61] and in 1971 it was applied to the support of the United Hospitals.[62]

John Ward, who died in 1895 while mayor of the city, left £6,000 to the city corporation to support annual payments, totalling £170, for dinners for the poor, a tea for schoolchildren, and an outing for the paupers of Gloucester union; the residual income was to be distributed to the poor at Christmas in the form of clothing vouchers. In 1972 the charity became part of the Charity of John Ward and Others.[63]

The Freemen's Compensation Fund. By a trust deed of 1903 £7,095, awarded in compensation for the extinction of common rights of the freemen in the city's meadows, was invested for the benefit of poor, aged, or sick freemen.[64] A Scheme of 1906, placed the fund under the management of a body formed of appointees of the freemen's committee, the municipal charity

[42] Ibid. D 3469/5/67, file marked 'almshouses and general'.
[43] G.B.R., B 3/1, f. 531v.
[44] G.D.R. wills 1642/67.
[45] G.B.R., B 4/1/4, f. 14 and v.
[46] Glos. R.O., D 3269, Schemes and orders 1865–1934.
[47] D.N.B.
[48] G.B.R., B 3/13, ff. 97v.–98v., 186, 197v.–238; 14, f. 183v.; *Glouc. Jnl.* 16 Nov. 1818.
[49] Glos. R.O., D 3270/19677, pp. 76, 370–1.
[50] Glos. Colln. NF 17.18.
[51] Glos. R.O., P 154/11/CH 3/3; cf. G.D.R. wills 1673/137.
[52] G.B.R., B 3/3, p. 600.
[53] *16th Rep. Com. Char.* 11–12.
[54] G.B.R., B 3/3, p. 646.

[55] *Freemen of Glouc.* (1950), 14: copy in Glos. R.O., GMS 110.
[56] Glos. R.O., CH 21, Glouc. co. boro. p. 9.
[57] Ibid. D 3469/5/67, file marked 'city general'; below, par. char., Holy Trinity.
[58] Glos. R.O., D 3469/5/67, file marked 'almshouses and general'; P 154/8/CH 1.
[59] She was the widow of Dan. (d. 1681), donor of the bread char.: *Trans. B.G.A.S.* vi. 323; Glos. R.O., D 750.
[60] *20th Rep. Com. Char.* H.C. 19, pp. 7–8 (1829), viii (1).
[61] Glos. R.O., D 3269, Schemes and orders 1875–1927.
[62] Ibid. D 3469/5/67, file marked 'almshouses and general'.
[63] Ibid. files marked 'city general', 'almshouses and general'; below, par. char., Holy Trinity.
[64] Glos. R.O., D 4430/12/11.

trustees, and the city corporation, and applied it to provide pensions for freemen and their widows.[65] Additional endowments were received in 1930, 1940, and 1942 in compensation for the remaining common rights.[66] In 1971 the fund had an annual income of £394.[67]

PAROCHIAL CHARITIES.[68] ALL SAINTS.

Richard Hoare by deed of 1607 gave a rent charge of 53s. for the poor, church repairs, and the incumbent. After 1648 it was used for general church repairs and other expenses by St. Mary de Crypt, into which All Saints was absorbed. Reduced to 50s. by 1815, it was included as one of the United Charities for the Poor in 1923.[69]

ALL SAINTS (the new parish created in 1876). *W. R. Voller* in 1935 gave a bequest for the poor,[70] which in 1971 had an income of £5 a year, derived from stock.[71]

HOLY TRINITY. *Mary Broad* by will dated 1682 gave from her personal estate a sum sufficient to buy land to produce 40s. a year for the poor. In 1825 it was distributed with other parish charities in cash and bread.

Elizabeth Gregory by will dated 1742 gave £10 to provide 10s. a year for the poor. In 1746 her executor *George Worrall* added another £5 and invested the whole £15 with the city corporation. In 1825 the 12s. interest paid by the corporation was distributed with other parish charities in cash and bread. The charity has not been found recorded later.

Daniel Lysons by will dated 1678 and codicil dated 1681 charged lands with sums, totalling £16, to provide bread for the poor of nine city parishes, for the poor of Barton Street, and for the prisoners in the city gaol.[72] The charity was regulated by a Scheme of 1894, which appointed the town clerk and chamberlain of the city as trustees.[73] Holy Trinity received 20s. from the charity, which was apparently later included in the sum of £4 10s. received by St. Mary de Crypt parish as part of its United Charities for the Poor of 1923.

A *Mrs. Norton*[74] gave a bequest for the poor, in respect of which the corporation was paying the parish 18s. a year in 1825. It has not been found recorded later.

Alice Whitfield by will dated 1693 gave a rent charge of 20s. a year for the poor.[75]

Samuel Willetts (d. c. 1673) left £10 to the corporation in trust for the poor of the parish.[76] In 1825 the corporation paid 8s. for that charity,

which was distributed in cash and bread. The charity has not been found recorded later.

In 1957 the Broad and Whitfield charities were formed into the *Holy Trinity Poor Charities* and applied to the general benefit of the city poor, with preference to those living within the area of the ancient parish of Holy Trinity. In 1972 the charity was amalgamated with the city charities of F. H. Collins and John Ward to form the *Charity of John Ward and Others*, applied to the general relief in need of residents of the city.

ST. ALDATE. *George Cooke*, before 1825, gave a house, the rent to be distributed in bread to the poor.[77]

Daniel Lysons, see above, Holy Trinity. The parish received 30s. for bread.

William Miles by will proved 1842 gave £110, the proceeds to be distributed among six poor men aged over 70.[78]

St. Aldate's ecclesiastical parish having ceased to exist in 1931, the Cooke and Miles charities were transferred in 1955 to the municipal charity trustees and applied to the general benefit of the city poor.[79] The Lysons charity was administered by St. John's parish after 1931 and included in 1972 in the United Charity of Palling, Burgess, and Others.

ST. CATHERINE. *Daniel Lysons*, see above, Holy Trinity. The parish received 40s. for bread.

Thomas Machen by will dated 1614 gave part of the interest on his city loan charity to provide 12 poor people of the parish with 6d. a quarter each. The corporation continued the payment to the parish after the principal was lost.[80]

Timothy Nourse by will dated 1698 gave a rent charge of £12 10s. to St. Catherine and St. Mary de Lode parishes: £10 was to be used to place five apprentices and £2 10s. to provide gowns for three poor people.[81] The charity came into operation c. 1732,[82] and in 1825 the parishes were taking equal shares and using the whole to provide clothing.

The three charities were amalgamated in 1969 as the *Charities of Thomas Machen and Others* and applied to the relief of residents of the ecclesiastical parish in cash or kind. In 1971 part of the income was being distributed to the inmates of the United Hospitals.[83]

ST JAMES. *Mary Comley* by will proved 1883 gave £200, the proceeds to be distributed to the poor on Christmas Eve.

Thomas Hart by will dated 1963 gave £70, the proceeds to be distributed among the aged and poor.[84]

[65] Ibid. D 3269, Schemes and orders 1875–1927.
[66] *Freemen of Glouc.* 13.
[67] Glos. R.O., CH 21, Glouc. co. boro. p. 10.
[68] This section is based on *14th Rep. Com. Char.* 41–54; *16th Rep. Com. Char.* 5–26; and Glos. R.O., D 3469/5/67 (files of char. review organizer for Glos.).
[69] Above, Churches and Chapels, ancient par. ch., St. Mary de Crypt.
[70] No governing instrument exists: Char. Com. file 231102.
[71] Glos. R.O., CH 21, Glouc. co. boro. p. 14.
[72] P.R.O., PROB 11/372 (P.C.C. 22 Drax), ff. 169–72.
[73] Glos. R.O., P 154/15/CH 11.

[74] Possibly the donor to St. Mary de Crypt, but her will makes no mention of the char. for Holy Trinity.
[75] G.D.R. wills 1695/75.
[76] G.B.R., B 3/3, p. 561.
[77] Cf. Hannam-Clark, *Char. Handbk.* 14; Glos. R.O., P 154/6/CW 2/8.
[78] Hannam-Clark, *Char. Handbk.* 14.
[79] Ibid.
[80] *14th Rep. Com. Char.* 32–3.
[81] G.D.R. wills 1700/57.
[82] Fosbrooke, *Glouc.* 138.
[83] Glos. R.O., CH 21, Glouc. co. boro. p. 19.
[84] Ibid. P 154/8/CH 1.

James King by will proved 1855 gave the residue of his real and personal estate to be invested in stock and the proceeds distributed among 30 poor people; £208 was received under the bequest. By 1971 the proceeds of the Comley and King charities, *c.* £15 a year, were jointly distributed in particular cases of need.[85]

ST. JOHN THE BAPTIST. *Samuel Browne*, alderman, by will dated 1738 gave a rent charge of 10*s.* for bread. The charity had been lost by 1825 and may never have operated.

John Burgess by will proved 1882 gave £1,000 to be invested in stock and the proceeds distributed to the poor in bread and coal.[86]

Elizabeth Clarke by will dated 1752 gave £80, the proceeds to be distributed among poor householders. The principal was a debt owed by the parish to her brother *Thomas Webley* (d. 1751),[87] to whom the bequest was later attributed.[88]

John Cromwell by will dated 1679 gave land, the rent to be distributed in coal to six poor people in the winter months.[89] In 1825 the rent was 5 guineas.

Samuel Flower by will dated 1777 gave £20, the proceeds to be distributed in bread to poor people attending church at Christmas. The charity lapsed *c.* 1815 when the principal was lost.

A charity for almshouses given by *John Hayward* was applied as an eleemosynary charity from the mid 20th century.[90]

Daniel Lysons, see above, Holy Trinity. The parish received 30*s.* for bread.

Samuel Palling by will dated 1734 gave a house, the rent to provide cloth gowns for the poor.

Thomas Semys, alderman, by will dated 1602 gave the rent of a stable and garden, to be distributed, after payment of a sermon charity, to the poor.[91] The charity had been lost by 1825.

Sarah Wright, see above, city charities. By her will of 1667 she gave a rent charge of 16*s.* for clothing widows and orphans in St. John's and St. Mary de Crypt parishes, another of 10*s.* for bread for the poor of St. John, and another of 10*s.* for bread for the poor of St. Mary de Crypt. In 1714, when each parish took the 16*s.* in alternate years, it was being used in St. John for bread.[92] In 1825 it had not been paid for many years and was to be restored, but it has not been found recorded later. The rent charges for bread in the two parishes were redeemed and replaced by stock in 1892.[93]

Francis Yate by will dated 1733 gave £20, the proceeds to be distributed in bread for the poor;[94] the charity was later met by a rent charge of £1.

In 1972 the eight charities still active were amalgamated, together with the charities of St. Mary de Crypt and St. Michael, to form the *United Charity of Palling, Burgess, and Others*.

The income was to be applied in cases of need in cash, goods, or services to residents of the city, with preference to inhabitants of the three ancient parishes.

ST. LUKE. By a Scheme of 1889 part of the annual income of a charity of *Mary Harris* for Hempsted was applied to St. Luke's parish, £6 for apprenticing and educational purposes and £4 for clothing elderly men. A Scheme of 1972 assigned part of the endowment of the Harris charity to Christ Church parish, which had absorbed St. Luke: £114 stock was to support a charity for the poor and £171 stock a charity for educational purposes.[95]

ST. MARK. *Hartley K. Butt* by will proved 1933 gave £2,000, from after his wife's death, to be invested and the proceeds used to provide food, fuel, and clothing for the poor. In 1971 the charity had an annual income of £60.[96]

ST. MARY DE CRYPT. *Sir Thomas Bell* (d. 1566) gave £10 for the poor. The principal was invested with the corporation, and in 1825 the interest was distributed by the parish in bread.

Samuel Burroughs, the elder, gave £40, the interest to be distributed among eight poor householders. The principal was invested in stock in 1808.

Samuel Burroughs, the younger, by will dated 1753 gave £60 for the same purpose.[97] It was apparently never received.

Charles Glanville gave £50, the interest to be distributed to the poor in bread. The principal was invested with the corporation.

Thomas Gosling by will dated 1721, as interpreted by a trust deed of 1752, gave land, the annual rent, after payment of £1 for a sermon charity, to be given to poor householders attending church to hear the sermon.[98] In 1825, when the rent was £8, the rector was taking £3 for the sermon.

Sarah Harris by will dated 1811 gave £10, the interest to be distributed to the poor in bread. In 1825 the charity was not in operation through a misunderstanding, and, though intended to be restored, it has not been found recorded later.

John Hill before 1683[99] gave £10 for the poor. The principal was invested with the corporation, and in 1825 the parish was distributing the interest in bread.

Phyllis Lewis before 1683[1] gave £40, the interest to be distributed to the poor of St. Mary de Crypt and St. Owen's parishes, and £10, the interest to be distributed among four poor householders of St. Mary de Crypt. Both principal sums were invested with the corporation, and in 1825 part of the interest was being used to buy coal for the almspeople of St. Kyneburgh's Hospital and the

85 Ibid. CH 21, Glouc. co. boro. p. 20.
86 Ibid. P 154/9/CH 2/1.
87 G.D.R. wills 1753/79; cf. ibid. 1751/29.
88 Cf. Glos. R.O., P 154/9/CH 4/1.
89 G.D.R. wills 1680/75.
90 Above, almshouses, other almshouses.
91 G.B.R., G 12/1, f. 82v.
92 Bodl. MS. Top. Glouc. c. 3, f. 53v.

93 Glos. R.O., P 154/11/CH 3/14.
94 G.D.R. wills 1734/259.
95 Glos. R.O., D 3469/5/76.
96 Ibid. CH 21, Glouc. co. boro. p. 28.
97 P.R.O., PROB 11/893 (P.C.C.497 Caesar), f.66.
98 Glos. R.O., Q/RNc 4/17.
99 Ibid. P 154/11/CH 3/4.
1 Ibid.

remainder distributed by the rector of St. Mary de Crypt to the poor of the two parishes.

Daniel Lysons, see above, Holy Trinity. The parish received 40s. in bread.

Margaret Norton by will dated 1689 gave £80, the interest to be distributed among poor householders.[2] The principal was invested with the corporation.[3]

Robert Payne (d.1713), alderman, gave 23s. 4d. a year, apparently in the form of a rent charge, to be distributed in bread to the poor of St. Mary de Crypt and St. Owen's parishes. In 1825 the churchwardens of St. Mary de Crypt distributed it in the two parishes.

William Henry Phelps by will proved 1914 gave £150, the interest to be distributed to the poor at Easter in bread and other necessaries.[4]

Thomas Pury, alderman, by deed of 1647 gave £8 a year to be distributed in bread to the poor of St. Mary de Crypt and St. Owen's parishes and the prisoners in the city gaol. It was charged on Vineyard hill at Over, a forfeited estate of the bishop of Gloucester. It and another charge on the estate, made by Pury in 1650 for bread for prisoners in the county gaol,[5] presumably lapsed at the Restoration.

Walter Pury by his will gave a house to support a distribution of 10s. a year among 10 aged poor people; his son *Thomas Pury*, the alderman, settled the property for that use by a trust deed of 1629 and was later credited as founder of the charity. The payment ceased in 1763 and all the profits of the house applied to church repairs. Payment of the 10s. to the poor was restored in 1825,[6] but by 1910 and until 1923 it was again misappropriated to church repairs.[7]

Josias Randall by will dated 1708[8] gave £50 for loans to five tradesmen and also gave houses, after the deaths of his wife and nephew, to be sold and the proceeds invested for the benefit of the poor. Only the loan charity apparently ever operated. Loans ceased c. 1878 when £30 had been lost; the remaining £20 was invested and from 1907, when the sum had accumulated to £54, the interest was distributed to the poor.[9]

Mary Shaile by will dated 1734 gave £50 each to St. Mary de Crypt, St. Michael's, and St. Nicholas's parishes, the proceeds to be distributed in each among 10 or 12 poor householders.[10] The St. Mary's principal was invested in stock in 1808.

John Tunks before 1683[11] gave £10 for the poor. The principal was invested with the corporation, and in 1825 the parish was distributing the interest in bread.

Eleanor (or ? *Anne*) *Weaver* before 1705 gave £100, the interest to be distributed among five poor women at Christmas.[12] The principal was invested with the corporation.

Alice Whitfield by will dated 1693 gave a rent charge of £3 to be distributed to the poor during the remainder of a lease.[13]

Sarah Wright, see above, St. John the Baptist.

The Revd. Matthew Yate by will dated 1713 gave £100, the interest to be distributed among five poor householders.[14] The principal was invested with the corporation.

In 1923 the 17 charities still active (including those parts originally assigned for St. Owen's parish) and the Richard Hoare charity for All Saints were amalgamated as the *United Charities for the Poor*, with an annual income of £62, to be used for the general benefit of the poor of St. Mary's parish in subscriptions to hospitals or provident clubs, grants for medical aid, or goods. In 1972 the United Charities became part of the United Charity of Palling, Burgess, and Others (see above, St. John the Baptist). The same year the city corporation redeemed the annual payments with which it was charged in respect of interest for various parish charities, including eight of St. Mary de Crypt.

ST. MARY DE GRACE. *Daniel Lysons*, see above, Holy Trinity. The parish was assigned 20s. in bread, which, failing suitable recipients, was to be given to the poor of Littleworth hamlet. It was included in 1972 in the endowments of the United Charity of Palling, Burgess, and Others, having earlier been distributed with the sum for St. John's parish.[15]

ST. MARY DE LODE.[16] *George Coulstance* by will dated 1626 gave a rent charge of 20s. for the poor.

John Dupree by will dated 1744 gave £30, the interest to be distributed to the poor at Christmas.[17] The principal was later used to build a gallery in the church and the rent of the sittings, c. 2 guineas a year in 1825, was distributed. The charity lapsed later, presumably when pew rents were ended.

Mary Jones by will proved 1871 gave £100 to be invested and the proceeds used to provide blankets for the poor.

Daniel Lysons, see above, Holy Trinity. The parish received 40s. in bread.

Edward Nourse by will dated 1674 gave £100 to be laid out on land, the rent, after payments for sermons, to be distributed among the poor of St. Mary de Lode and St. Michael's parishes. Land was bought in 1678, and in 1823, when St. Michael was taking the bulk of the rent, it was agreed to divide it equally between the two parishes.

Timothy Nourse, see above, St. Catherine.

James Sayer by will dated 1713 gave a rent charge of 40s. to be distributed among 40 poor

[2] P.R.O., PROB 11/397 (P.C.C. 180 Ent), f. 330 and v.
[3] G.B.R., B 3/6, f. 269v.
[4] Glos. R.O., P 154/11/CH 2/8.
[5] *Glouc. Corp. Rec.* pp. 453–4.
[6] Cf. Glos. R.O., P 154/11/CW 2/5.
[7] Above, Churches and Chapels.
[8] Cf. G.D.R. wills 1709/36.
[9] Glos. R.O., P 154/11/CH 2/1.
[10] G.D.R. wills 1735/94.

[11] Glos. R.O., P 154/11/CH 3/4.
[12] Bodl. MS. Top. Glouc. c. 3, ff. 51v., 60; cf. G.D.R., V 5/GT 31.
[13] G.D.R. wills 1695/75.
[14] Ibid. 1717/166.
[15] Glos. R.O., CH 21, Glouc. co. boro. p. 20.
[16] *16th Rep. Com. Char.* lists the charities for St. Mary de Lode under St. Mary de Grace.
[17] G.D.R. wills 1747/199.

widows.[18] No record has been found of the charity in operation.

Thomas Singleton of London, a native of Gloucester,[19] by will dated 1656 gave £150 to support payments of £3 each for the poor of St. Mary de Lode and St. Nicholas's parishes. The principal was invested with the corporation.

Alice Whitfield by will dated 1693 gave a rent charge of 20s. to be distributed to the poor during the remainder of a lease.[20]

By 1971 the six charities still active were being jointly administered. In that year they were amalgamated with the charities of St. Nicholas's parish to form the *St. Mary de Lode and St. Nicholas Relief in Need Charity* and applied to the general relief of inhabitants of the area of the two ancient parishes.

ST. MICHAEL. *Elizabeth Austin c.* 1731 gave £5 for the poor; in 1820 it could not be traced and was thought to have been disposed of as principal.[21]

Thomas Barnes of London, a native of Gloucester,[22] by will dated 1700 gave £100 to support payments of 20s. a year each to four poor people. In 1706 the charity was charged on land, bought with the principal and £30 principal of the charities of Phyllis Lewis and Margaret Cartwright. In 1858 an annual surplus of rent from the land, remaining after the three charities had been met, was applied in aid of the parish's National school.[23]

John Blanch by will dated 1756 gave £50, the interest to be distributed among 10 poor householders.[24] Part of the principal was lost through the insolvency of a tradesman to whom it was lent; the remainder was later used with other parish money to buy stock, and 50s. of the annual dividends was applied to the charity.

Margaret Cartwright gave £10, the interest, after providing a bible for a poor person, to be distributed at 12d. each among six poor people. The charity was charged on land in 1706 (see above, Thos. Barnes).

George Coulstance by will dated 1626 gave a rent charge of 20s. for the poor.

John Falconer, alderman, by will dated 1545 gave £40 to the weavers' company to be used for loans to poor tradesmen and others of the parish. It was being used for loans in the early 18th century, when it was administered by trustees for the parish,[25] but later, that form of application being thought too risky, the principal was invested in stock and the proceeds distributed to the poor.

Samuel Flower by will dated 1777 gave £20, the interest to be distributed in bread to poor people attending church at Christmas; the principal was invested in stock in 1797. Later regarded as an

ecclesiastical charity,[26] it was included in 1973 in a Scheme for the ecclesiastical charities of the old city parishes.[27]

Joseph Horner by will dated 1683 gave a rent charge of £4 to be distributed among eight poor householders.[28]

Job Jefferies by will dated 1824 gave £300 stock, the proceeds to be distributed in coal among 30 poor householders.

Phyllis Lewis before 1683[29] gave £20, the interest to be distributed to the poor. It was lent out until 1706 when it was charged on land at 20s. a year[30] (see above, Thos. Barnes).

Daniel Lysons, see above, Holy Trinity. The parish received 40s. a year in bread.

Frances Mann by will dated 1769 gave £20, the interest to be distributed to the poor in bread.

Edward Nourse, see above, St. Mary de Lode.

Richard Seyer by will dated 1815 gave the interest on £500 for three poor men and two poor women.[31] His estate proved inadequate to support his legacies, and, following a Chancery suit, the parish received only £23 12s. 10d. for the charity; it was invested in stock in 1830.[32]

Mary Shaile, see above, St. Mary de Crypt. In 1825 the principal was held by the rector who distributed interest for it.

John Spillman by will dated 1809 gave £100 stock, the proceeds to be distributed among 12 poor people.

John Webb, alderman, by will dated 1686 gave a rent charge of 20s. to be distributed among 10 poor men and 10 poor women.[33]

Nicholas Webb by will dated 1691 gave a rent charge of 30s. for the poor.[34] The house on which it was charged was demolished in the late 18th century and the payment charged on stock, bought with the compensation and other charity money. In 1825 half the sum was distributed in bread.

Nicholas Webb by will dated 1769 gave £50 stock, the proceeds to be distributed among six poor householders.

Thomas Webb, alderman, by will dated 1734 gave £20, the interest to be distributed among four poor householders. The corporation, the intended trustees, declined to accept it, and his son, the last-mentioned *Nicholas Webb*, gave by his will £25 stock to the parish in its place.

Thomas Webb by will dated 1751 gave £20, the interest to be distributed among the poor.[35]

John Wintle by will proved 1847 gave £300 stock, the proceeds to be given to two blind men and two blind women; failing suitable recipients in the parish they were to be found in the city as a whole or in the county.[36]

In 1915 the 20 charities still active were amalgamated under the title of the *Consolidated Charities*; of the total annual income of £55, £34 was assigned in fixed payments for specific chari-

18 Ibid. 1713/24.
19 Ibid. V 5/GT 21.
20 Ibid. wills 1695/75.
21 Glos. R.O., P 154/14/CH 9.
22 Ibid.
23 Ibid. CH 10.
24 P.R.O., PROB 11/830 (P.C.C. 182 Herring), ff. 327–9.
25 Cf. G.D.R., V 5/GT 27A.
26 Glos. R.O., P 154/14/CH 11/3.
27 Ibid. 11/CH 3/16.
28 G.D.R. wills 1684/178.
29 Glos. R.O., P 154/11/CH 3/4.
30 Cf. ibid. 14/CH 10.
31 G.D.R. wills, 31 Jan. 1817.
32 Glos. R.O., P 154/14/CH 10.
33 G.D.R. wills 1686/361.
34 Ibid. 1691/160.
35 Ibid. 1751/29.
36 P.R.O., PROB 11/2049 (P.C.C. 84), ff. 263v.–266v.

table purposes, £16 5s. in weekly allowances to 10 poor people during the first 13 weeks of the year, and the residue to be distributed in goods or, in bad weather, in coal. In 1972 the Consolidated Charities became part of the United Charity of Palling, Burgess, and Others (see above, St. John the Baptist).

ST. NICHOLAS. *Jasper Clutterbuck*, alderman, by will dated 1658 gave the poor a portion of the rent[37] from leasehold land. The charity, if ever applied, probably lapsed on expiry of the lease.[38]

Sarah Clutterbuck by will dated 1748 gave £50, the interest, after payments for a sermon and to the parish clerk, to be distributed to the poor in bread.[39] The principal was invested in stock.

The Revd. Richard Green (d. 1711)[40] gave £50 to support a payment of 12d. a week to the poor. The charity was at first distributed in bread by the donor's father, Alderman Richard Green;[41] after the alderman's death it was distributed by the parish, which put the principal out on mortgage and later invested it in stock.

William Lisle of Longford by will dated 1723 gave a portion of the rent of land to provide bread for the poor.[42] A trust deed of 1726, following a Chancery suit, set the uses as providing clothes and fuel, but in 1825 the £38 a year received was being used with other charity money on bread, beef, and coal.

Daniel Lysons, see above, Holy Trinity. The parish received 40s. in bread.

Samuel Mee by will dated 1744 gave a rent charge of £4 to be distributed among 10 poor people. The payment, charged on leasehold property, was discontinued c. 1820.

Thomas Mee in 1722[43] gave £50, the interest to be distributed among 10 poor householders. The parish abandoned a suit for obtaining the principal c. 1785 and the charity apparently never operated.

Elizabeth Morris by will dated 1679 gave £50, the proceeds to be distributed among 20 poor householders. Of that sum £40 was used in 1701 to renew a lease of property held by the parish; in 1808 the lease was sold and the profits invested in stock. The remaining £10 was out at interest in 1705.[44] In 1825 the parish was distributing £2 10s. a year in respect of the charity.

Joseph Reeve by will dated 1716 gave £85, the interest to be distributed in bread, beef, and coal to 20 poor householders. The principal was invested with the governor and guardians of the poor until 1787 when it was placed in stock.

Mary Shaile, see above, St. Mary de Crypt. The principal was invested in stock in 1813.

Thomas Singleton, see above, St. Mary de Lode.

Mary Smith by trust deed of 1805 gave £333

stock to support a distribution of £10 in coal among 40 poor people.

John Thorne, alderman, by will dated 1618 gave a rent charge of 6s. 8d. to be distributed among 20 poor people.[45]

Thomas Wadley by will dated 1770 gave a rent charge of 20s. to be distributed to the poor in bread. The charity was discontinued in 1797.

Eleanor (or ? *Anne*) *Weaver* gave £100, the interest to be distributed among five poor women at Christmas. In 1705 the principal was invested with the corporation.[46]

Henry (or ? *John*) *Windowe* before 1705 gave a rent charge of 50s. to be distributed in coal[47] among 12 poor people who attended church. In 1825 it was being used with other charity money on bread, beef, and coal.

William Windowe before 1705[48] gave a rent charge of £5 4s. to be distributed in bread among 12 poor people who attended church.

Thomas Withenbury by will dated 1720 gave a rent charge of 40s. to be distributed to the poor in bread.

For some years before 1971 the charities of Sarah Clutterbuck, Green, Morris, and Reeve were jointly administered and much of the income distributed among the inmates of St. Bartholomew's Hospital who by then formed a large proportion of the parish's population. In 1971 all 14 charities still active were included in the St. Mary de Lode and St. Nicholas Relief in Need Charity (see above, St. Mary de Lode).

ST. OWEN. See above, St. Mary de Crypt: Phyllis Lewis, Rob. Payne, Thos. Pury.

OUTLYING HAMLETS. A trust deed of 1633, settling lands purchased under the will of *Giles Cox*, of Abloads Court, Sandhurst, to support annual rent charges for the various parishes of Dudstone and King's Barton hundred, assigned any surplus of rents to be distributed from time to time to the poor of the hamlets of Kingsholm, Longford, Twigworth, Wotton, and Tuffley (and Woolstrop in Quedgeley). From 1821 the hamlets each received a regular annual sum from the charity, initially £2 10s. for Longford, £2 for Wotton, and £1 10s. each for Kingsholm, Twigworth, and Tuffley.[49] A Scheme of 1892 applied the income of the charity at the trustees' discretion to a wide range of charitable purposes in the 29 places benefiting, and in 1957 the foundation was divided to form separate charities for each place, each being given an endowment of £256 stock and a small sum in cash.[50]

J. T. Dorrington by will proved 1921 gave £1,000, from after his wife's death, to be invested and the proceeds used to buy goods for poor inhabitants of Twigworth and Longford.[51] In 1971 the charity had an annual income of £34.

[37] Ibid. PROB 11/300 (P.C.C. 180 Nabbs), f. 160 and v.
[38] Cf. G.B.R., B 3/3, p. 162.
[39] G.D.R. wills 1750/54.
[40] Fosbrooke, *Glouc.* 182.   [41] Cf. G.B.R., B 3/8, p. 564.
[42] G.D.R. wills 1724/84.
[43] Glos. R.O., D 327, p. 440.
[44] G.D.R., V 5/GT 31.
[45] Glos. R.O., P 154/15/CH 15; cf. P.R.O., C 142/377, no. 96.
[46] G.D.R., V 5/GT 31.
[47] Ibid.   [48] Ibid.
[49] *16th Rep. Com. Char.* 38–41.
[50] Glos. R.O., D 2695/3–4; in 1957 Wotton was omitted.
[51] Ibid. D 3469/5/160; his bequest of another £1,000 to assist women in childbirth in the two hamlets was revoked by his wife.

NONCONFORMIST CHARITIES. *William Bird* (d. 1871) left £50 for poor members of the Southgate Independent church; £45 of it was put out on mortgage and the proceeds used with John Garn's charity.[52]

John Garn by will proved 1836 gave £500 to be invested in stock and the proceeds distributed among poor members of the same church. Only £375 was received for the charity.[53] In 1971 the charity had an annual income of £16.[54]

Edwin Harris by will proved 1882 gave £100 to be invested in stock and the proceeds distributed among aged members of the Baptist church in Gloucester.[55] In 1971 the charity had an annual income of £2.[56]

For charities for the prisoners in the city and county gaols, see above, city charities: Sir Thos. Bell, John Heydon, and Sarah Wright; parochial charities, Holy Trinity: Dan. Lysons; St. Mary de Crypt: Thos. Pury. Sermon charities are included above, in the account of churches and chapels.

STREET NAMES

THE following list[57] is of streets which existed before 1800 within the old city boundary. The modern name of each street, and the first date at which that name has been found, is followed by earlier variations, with dates to indicate when they were in use. As will be seen, some streets had two or more names at the same time. Posts displaying the street names, set up in 1671 'for preserving of the ancient names',[58] seem to have done little to standardize the usage. For the location of the streets, see Figs. 4, 8, 16.

Principal sources used are as follows; other sources are given in footnotes.

1455	*Glouc. Rental, 1455*
1535	Llanthony rental (*Glouc. Rental, 1455*, pp. xv–xxi)
1649	Dean and chapter survey (Glos. R.O., D 936/E 1)
1714	Wantner's MS. (Bodl. MS. Top. Glouc. c. 3, ff. 44–5)
1743	Furney's MS. (Glos. R.O., D 327, pp. 9–11)
1780	Hall and Pinnell, *Map of Glouc.*
1826	Plans of city and hospital property (G.B.R., J 4/12; Glos. R.O., D 3269)
1843	Causton, *Map of Glouc.*
1852	Bd. of Health Map

Abbey Lane, see College Street; St. Mary's Street.

Alvin Street, 1831:[59] *Fete*, or *Vete*, *Lane*, c. 1220, 1799;[60] *Alngate*, or *Onnyat*, *Lane*, 1810, 1825.[61]

Ailesgate Street, see Eastgate Street.

Anchor Alley, see Turnstile Alley.

Archdeacon (or *Deacon*) *Street*, c. 1230,[62] from house of archdeacon of Glouc.: *Leather Bottle Lane*, 1767, 1852,[63] from inn.

Barbican Road (or *Alley*), 1843,[64] from Barbican hill, site of the first castle. Mentioned 1694 as a way leading from the city towards Hempsted.[65]

Barton Street, c. 1260,[66] from the bartons of the king's and Glouc. Abbey's manors.

Bearland (formerly *The Bareland*), 1301:[67] *New Street*, 1714, having been newly built up in the mid 17th cent.

Bell Walk, 1960s, when made into a covered shopping street: *Travel Lane*, c. 1160,[68] 1826; *Bellman's Lane*, 1680,[69] 1743; *Bell Lane*, 1826, 1960s.

[52] Southgate ch. rec. (in possession of United Reformed Ch. provincial archives, Leamington Spa), letter to Char. Com. 11 Apr. 1893.

[53] Char. Com. file 249996.

[54] Glos. R.O., CH 21, Glouc. co. boro. p. 8.

[55] Char. Com. file 241831.

[56] Glos. R.O., CH 21, Glouc. co. boro. p. 9.

[57] The list was compiled in 1984.

[58] G.B.R., B 3/3, p. 479.

[59] Glos. R.O., D 3117/1690.

[60] *Ciren. Cart.* ii. p. 388; Glouc. Cath. Libr., Reg. Abb.

Froucester B, p. 177; Glos. R.O., D 3117/992; G.B.R., J 6/3, f. 44.

[61] Glos. R.O., D 3117/996, 1688.

[62] Glouc. Cath. Libr., Reg. Abb. Froucester B, p. 13.

[63] Glos. R.O., D 3117/1891; *Glouc. Jnl.* 4 Dec. 1852.

[64] Cf. Glos. R.O., DC/F 7, deeds 1851, 1906.

[65] Ibid. D 326/X 3; cf. ibid. Q/CL 1/6.

[66] *Glouc. Corp. Rec.* p. 223.

[67] Ibid. p. 295.

[68] P.R.O., C 115/K 1/6681, f. 79.

[69] Glos. R.O., D 3117/503.

Berkeley Street, 1780: *Broadsmith Street*, 1301, 1805;[70] *Little Smith Street*, 1726;[71] *Catherine Wheel Lane*, 1694, 1795,[72] from inn.

Blackfriars, 1843, from former Dominican friary. Apparently built 1246.[73]

Bolt Lane, see Longsmith Street.

Bride Lane, 1312,[74] 1535. Ran parallel to, and *c.* 70 yd. west, of Park Street. Closed by 1598, but still visible in 1743.[75]

Broadsmith Street, see Berkeley Street.

Brook Street, see Station Road.

Brunswick Road, 1864:[76] *Parker's Row*, 1814, 1862.[77] Mentioned 1455 as site of tenements by Goose ditch.

Bulgeres Lane, *c.* 1285.[78] Unidentified.

Bull Lane, 1708,[79] from inn: *Gore Lane*, *c.* 1260, 1830.[80]

Butchers' Row, see Westgate Street.

Castle Lane, early 13th cent.[81] The continuation of Upper Quay Street through to the castle. Destroyed for new Shire Hall complex 1960s.

Catherine Wheel Lane, see Berkeley Street.

Clare Street, 1834:[82] *Dockham Lane*, 1722, 1834.[83]

College Court, given that name 1778:[84] *Craft's Lane*, 1333,[85] 1535; *Ironmongers' Row*, 1455, 1523;[86] *Turries Lane*, 1455, 1544;[87] *St. Peter's Lane*, 1509,[88] 1743; *Upper College Lane*, 1714, 1778.[89]

College Street (formerly *Lane*), 1780: *Lich Lane*, 1276, 1509,[90] because it gave access to the abbey burial ground; *Abbey Lane*, 1455, 1649; *St. Edward's Lane*, 1509, 1544,[91] perhaps from an unofficial canonization accorded to Edward II after his burial in the abbey; *King Edward's Lane*, 1551, 1784,[92] from the abbey gate, said to have been built by Edward I; *Lower College Lane*, 1714, 1795.[93] The name King Edward's Lane was used later (1826) for an alley, also called Upper George Passage, on the east side of College Street.

Constitution Walk, 1779.[94]

Cordwainers' Row, see Northgate Street.

Craft's Lane, see College Court.

Cross Keys Lane, 1780, from inn: *Scrudde Lane*, 1312,[95] 1535; *Crud Lane*, 1649, 1789.[96]

Crypt Alley, see St. Mary's Lane.

Crypt Lane, see Greyfriars.

Dean's Walk, 1803:[97] *Chapel House Walk*, 1843. Existed from medieval times as part of a way from the blind gate to St. Thomas's chapel and Kingsholm palace (e.g. 1535).

Dockham Lane, used for various streets which led to Dockham ditch (formerly the Old Severn), see Clare Street; Mount Street; White Swan Lane.

Dog Lane, 1780: *Brook Lane*, 1832.[98] Mentioned 1455 as the way leading from outside the east gate to Brook Street. Destroyed 1970s for new shopping precinct.

Dolphin Lane, 1843, from inn. Led off Northgate Street, north of the Oxbode. Closed during redevelopment of the area 1926.

Eastgate Street, 1473:[99] *Jews'*, or *Jewry*, *Street*, 1310;[1] *Ailesgate Street*, 1330, 1709.[2]

Ebridge Street, see Westgate Street.

Fete Lane, see Alvin Street.

Fish Street, 1395.[3] Unidentified.

Fox Entry, see Mercers' Entry.

Gore Lane, see Bull Lane.

Goseyrote Lane, 1277.[4] Unidentified.

[70] *Glouc. Corp. Rec.* p. 295; Glos. R.O., D 3117/415.
[71] Glos. R.O., D 3117/408.
[72] Ibid. 407; *Glouc. Jnl.* 26 Oct. 1795.
[73] *Cal. Lib.* 1245–51, 65.
[74] Glouc. Cath. Libr., Reg. Abb. Froucester B, p. 442.
[75] G.B.R., J 3/1, f. 17; J 4/1, at end.
[76] *Glouc. Jnl.* 23 July 1864.
[77] Ibid. 28 Nov. 1814; 5 Apr. 1862.
[78] *Glouc. Corp. Rec.* p. 278.
[79] Glos. R.O., D 3117/3861.
[80] P.R.O., C 115/K 1/6681, f. 84; G.B.R., B 3/14, f. 141.
[81] Glouc. Cath. Libr., Reg. Abb. Froucester B, p. 180.
[82] Glos. R.O., P 154/12/VE 2/1.
[83] Ibid.; ibid. D 936/E 12/9, f. 15.
[84] *Glouc. Jnl.* 7 Sept. 1778.
[85] P.R.O., C 115/K 1/6681, f. 133v.
[86] Glouc. Cath. Libr., Reg. Abb. Malvern i, f. 213v.
[87] G.B.R., J 5/1.

[88] Ibid. 3.
[89] *Glouc. Jnl.* 7 Sept. 1778.
[90] *Glouc. Corp. Rec.* p. 263; G.B.R., J 5/3.
[91] G.B.R., J 5/3, 5.
[92] Ibid. F 4/3, f. 29v.; Glos. R.O., D 936/E 12/15, f. 20v.
[93] G.B.R., B 3/12, f. 223v.
[94] Ibid. 11, f. 263.
[95] P.R.O., C 115/K 1/6681, f. 163v.
[96] Glos. R.O., D 936/E 12/15, f. 214v.
[97] Ibid. E 114.
[98] Ibid. D 4453, deeds 1758–1886.
[99] *Rot. Parl.* vi. 49.
[1] *Glouc. Corp. Rec.* pp. 303, 338.
[2] P.R.O., C 115/K 1/6681, f. 107; Glos. R.O., D 3117/512.
[3] Glos. R.O., P 154/14/CH 2/20.
[4] Glouc. Cath. Libr., Reg. Abb. Froucester B, p. 206.

Grace Lane, see St. John's Lane.

Grant Lane, see New Inn Lane.

Great Western Road, given that name 1889.[5] The northern part was *Hyde Lane*, 1589,[6] 1826; it was lengthened 1830s to give access to union workhouse and called *Union Lane*.[7] A street further east later took the name Hyde Lane.

Green Dragon Lane, see Parliament Street.

Greyfriars, 1843, from Franciscan friary: *Friars Street*, or *Lane*, before 1714, 1743; *Crypt Lane*, 1714, from church of St. Mary de Crypt.

Half Street, see St. Mary's Street.

Hare Lane, 1301:[8] 'the tanners' street', *c.* 1235.[9] The southern part, between Pitt Street and Northgate Street, was called *Tewkesbury Street*, 1843.

Hare Lane, Back or *Little*, see Park Street.

Hyde Lane, see Great Western Road.

Ironmongers' Row, see College Court.

Island, The, see Westgate Street.

Jewry or *Jews' Street*, see Eastgate Street.

Kimbrose (formerly *St. Kyneburgh's*) *Lane*, 1743, from almshouse, formerly chapel.

King's Walk, 1970s, when the surviving part of the old street was redeveloped as a covered shopping area: *King Street*, 1780, 1970s. The north part was removed in the late 1920s when King's Square was laid out.

Ladybellegate Street, 1843, from a gate to Blackfriars at its northern end, which was called after Joan (d. 1567), wife of Sir Thomas Bell.

Leather Bottle Lane, see Archdeacon Street.

Lich Lane, see College Street.

Longsmith Street, 1549:[10] 'the smiths' street', 1215;[11] *Old Smiths' Street*, 1390,[12] 1535; *Schoolhouse Lane*, 1535, from school kept there by Llanthony Priory; *Bolt Lane*, 1714, 1843, from inn.

Love Alley, see Mercers' Entry.

Maverdine Lane, 1455, 1799[13] (name no longer in use). The alley running along the east side of no. 26 Westgate Street.[14]

Mercers' Entry (or *Alley*), *c.* 1770, 1875[15] (name no longer in use): *Love Alley*, before 1714; *Fox Entry*, 1855.[16] Runs between upper Westgate Street and Cross Keys Lane.

Mercers' Row, see Westgate Street.

Milk Street, 1620, 1732.[17] Unidentified, in St. Mary de Crypt parish.

Mill Lane, see Station Road.

Mitre Street, see the Oxbode.

Mount Street, 1883:[18] *Dockham*, 1843, 1852.

Myende Lane, *c.* 1270.[19] Unidentified, in lower Westgate Street area.

New Inn Lane, 1549:[20] *Grant Lane*, *c.* 1190,[21] 1649; *Rosse Lane*, 1342,[22] 1455. Also said to have been called *Pilgrims' Lane*, before 1714.

New Street, see Bearland; Queen Street.

Northgate Street, 1455. The part between the north gate and outer north gate was usually distinguished as *lower Northgate Street*, e.g. 1649, 1780. The west side of the upper part of the street was called *Cordwainers' Row*, 1392, *c.* 1740.[23]

Onnyat Lane, see Alvin Street.

Oxbode, The (or *Oxbode*, or *Oxbody, Lane*), 1263:[24] *Mitre Street*, 1836, 1896,[25] from inn. The street was widened and truncated in the late 1920s.

Park Street, 1843: 'the middle lane' called *Hare Lane*, 1535; *Little Hare Lane*, 1598;[26] *Back Hare Lane*, 1743, 1805.[27]

Parker's Row, see Brunswick Road.

Parliament Street, 1860:[28] *Green Dragon*, or *Dragon Lane*, 1756, 1860,[29] from inn.

Pilgrims' Lane, see New Inn Lane.

[5] *Glos. Chron.* 9 Nov. 1889.
[6] P.R.O., E 134/31 Eliz. East./15.
[7] O.S. Map. 1/2,500, Glos. XXV. 15 (1886 edn.).
[8] Glouc. Cath. Libr., Reg. Abb. Froucester B, p. 191.
[9] *Ciren. Cart.* ii, p. 391.
[10] *Cal. Pat.* 1548–9, 263.
[11] Glouc. Cath. Libr., Reg. Abb. Froucester B, p. 1.
[12] P.R.O., C 115/K 2/6684, f. 138.
[13] G.B.R., J 6/3, f. 22.
[14] Cf. P.R.O., C 115/K 1/6678, f. 57v.
[15] Rudder, *Glos.* 85; Glos. R.O., D 3117/2344.
[16] G.B.R., B 3/18, p. 24.

[17] Ibid. J 3/1, f. 139; 9, f. 1v.
[18] O.S. Map 1/2,500, Glos. XXV. 15 (1886 edn.).
[19] *Glouc. Corp. Rec.* pp. 251, 262.
[20] *Cal. Pat.* 1548–9, 261.
[21] P.R.O., C 115/K 1/6681, f. 118.
[22] Ibid. f. 145.
[23] *Glouc. Corp. Rec.* p. 369; G.B.R., J 5/2.
[24] *Hist. & Cart. Mon. Glouc.* (Rolls Ser.), ii. 198.
[25] Glos. R.O., D 3117/2597, 2620.
[26] G.B.R., J 3/1, f. 17.
[27] Cole, *Map of Glouc.* (1805).
[28] *Glouc. Jnl.* 13 Oct. 1860.
[29] Ibid.; Glos. R.O., HO 19/11/9.

Pitt Street, 1843, from the Pitt family, which had a house there: *Behind the Walls*, 1536, 1766;[30] the west part was called *College Wall* and the east part *Beast Market*, 1780, 1805.[31]

Portcullis Lane, see St. Mary's Street.

Powke (or *Puke*) *Lane*, early 13th cent.,[32] 1455. On the north side of lower Westgate Street. Closed by 1544.[33]

Quay Court or *Little Quay Lane*, see Turnstile Alley.

Quay Street (or *Lane*), 1714. Apparently unnamed 1633 when mentioned as the 'street leading by the Marybone Park rails'.[34]

Quay Street, Lower (formerly *Lane*), 1733;[35] 'the fullers' street', early 13th cent.;[36] *Walkers' Lane*, early 13th cent.,[37] 1535; *Quay Lane*, 1535, 1714.

Quay Street, Upper (formerly *Lane*), 1630.[38] Sometimes regarded as part of *Castle Lane*, e.g. *c.* 1770, 1829.[39]

Queen's Walk, 1970s, when redeveloped as a covered way: possibly *New Street*, near the east gate, 1746;[40] named as part of *Travel Lane* in 1780; *Queen Street*, 1817,[41] 1970s.

Rosse Lane, see New Inn Lane.

St. Aldate Street (formerly *Lane*), 1544,[42] from church: *St. Aldhelm's Lane*, 1455, when that was an alternative dedication of the church.

St. Catherine Street, 1714, from church. *Wateringstead*, or *Watering*, *Street*, 1350, 1728, from a watering place on the Old Severn, was used for the whole street from the blind gate to Alvin gate;[43] later, 1780, 1843, the southern part near St. Oswald's was called *Water Street* and the rest St. Catherine Street.

St. Edward's (or *King Edward's*) *Lane*, see College Street.

St. John's Lane, 1714, from church: *Grace Lane*, late 13th cent., 1814,[44] from church of St. Mary de Grace.

St. Mary's Lane (*Marylone*), 1316,[45] from church of St. Mary de Crypt: *Crypt*, or *St. Mary de Crypt*, *Alley*, 1714, 1826.

St. Mary's Street, 1883,[46] from church of St. Mary de Lode. The southern part was called *Abbey Lane*, 1316,[47] 1649, *Portcullis Lane*, 1649, 1721,[48] from inn, and *Three Cocks Lane*, 1743, 1867,[49] from inn. The northern part was called *Half Street*, 1589,[50] 1852.

St. Peter's Lane, see College Court.

Saters Lane, 1455. Ran from Longsmith Street to Blackfriars, east of Ladybellegate Street. Closed by 1535.

Schoolhouse Lane, see Longsmith Street.

Scrudde Lane, see Cross Keys Lane.

Severn Street, 1295, 1643.[51] Ran from the Bristol road to the Severn at the south boundary of the city. The houses there were destroyed at the siege of 1643, but it survived until the building of the canal basin in the 1790s.

Sheep Lane, mid 13th cent.,[52] 1535. Ran from Greyfriars to the south wall of the city, parallel to Southgate Street. It was partly built on, and probably closed, by 1641, and part was used as a garden in 1760.[53]

Shipsters Lane. Ran along the south wall of the city, west of the south gate. Mostly destroyed by the enlargement of the ditch 1260s.[54]

Small Lane, 1354,[55] 1535. Ran from St. Owen's church to Severn Street, parallel to lower Southgate Street. Probably destroyed 1643.

Smith Street, Little, see Berkeley Street.

Southgate Street, c. 1141.[56] The part outside the south gate, as far as Severn Street, was sometimes distinguished as *lower Southgate Street*, e.g. 1535, 1780.

Station Road, 1883;[57] *Brook Street*, early 13th cent.,[58] 1649; *Mill Lane*, 1843, 1852. In 1883 only the west part was called Station Road and the east part was called *Market Street*; the

[30] P.R.O., SC 6/Hen. VIII/1212, rot. 4d.; Glos. R.O., D 936/L 6.   [31] Cole, *Map of Glouc.* (1805).
[32] *Hist. & Cart. Mon. Glouc.* i. 186.
[33] G.B.R., J 5/5.
[34] Ibid. J 3/3, f. 83.
[35] *Glouc. Jnl.* 28 Aug. 1733.
[36] *Glouc. Corp. Rec.* p. 131.
[37] Ibid.
[38] G.B.R., J 5/6.
[39] Rudder, *Glos.* 85; G.B.R., B 3/14, f. 115v.
[40] *Glouc. Jnl.* 4 Nov. 1746.
[41] Glos. R.O., P 154/14/VE 2/2.
[42] G.B.R., J 5/5.
[43] Glouc. Cath. Libr., deeds and seals, viii, f. 17; G.B.R., J 3/8, f. 230v.; P.R.O., SC 6/Hen. VIII/1212, rot. 4; *Glouc. Rental, 1455*, p. xvi.

[44] *Hist. & Cart. Mon. Glouc.* i. 194; Glos. R.O., D 3117/1644.
[45] P.R.O., C 115/K 2/6682, f. 98v.
[46] O.S. Map. 1/2,500, Glos. XXV. 15 (1886 edn.).
[47] P.R.O., C 115/K 1/6681, f. 135v.
[48] G.B.R., J 3/8, f. 147.
[49] Ibid. B 4/5/2.
[50] P.R.O., E 134/31 Eliz. East./15.
[51] Ibid. C 115/K 1/6681, f. 41v.; *Bibliotheca Glos.* ii. 219.
[52] P.R.O., C 115/K 1/6681, f. 74v.
[53] G.B.R., J 3/3, ff. 163–4; 10, f. 49.
[54] P.R.O., C 115/K 2/6685, ff. 9, 10v.
[55] Ibid. C 115/K 1/6681, f. 155.
[56] Ibid. f. 76v.
[57] O.S. Map 1/2,500, Glos. XXV. 15 (1886 edn.).
[58] *Glouc. Corp. Rec.* p. 170.

whole became Station Road after the building of Eastgate station in 1896.[59] The houses in Brook Street were destroyed at the siege of 1643.

Tewkesbury Street, see Hare Lane.

Three Cocks Lane, see St. Mary's Street.

Travel Lane, see Bell Lane.

Turnstile Alley, 1795, 1862:[60] *Anchor Alley*, 1714; *Little Quay Lane*, 1780, 1826; *Quay Court*, 1843. Ran from lower Westgate Street to the north end of the quay. Destroyed early 20th cent.

Turries Lane, see College Court.

Vete Lane, see Alvin Street.

Walkers' Lane, see Lower Quay Street.

Water, Watering, Wateringstead Street, see St. Catherine Street.

Westgate Street, 1312:[61] *Ebridge Street*, early 13th cent., 1595.[62] The western end, beyond the Old Severn, once described as 'between the bridges', early 13th cent.,[63] 1743, became known as *The Island*, 1728,[64] 1843. The eastern end was once divided by a central line of buildings into two lanes, that on the south side called *Butchers' Row*, 1522, 1836, and that on the north side called *Mercers' Row*, 1522, 1843.[65]

White Swan (or *Swan*) *Lane*, 1843, from inn: *Dockham Lane*, 1455, 1826; *Dock Lane*, 1455, 1714. Ran from lower Westgate Street to the Old Severn. Destroyed for redevelopment 1970s.

ARMS, SEALS, INSIGNIA, AND PLATE

ARMS.[66] Several different coats of arms used by Gloucester after its charter of 1483 depicted a sword between horseshoes and nails, a reference to the town's principal trade. One such coat was displayed on a mayoral seal used in 1492[67] and another on the Crypt school building of 1539.[68] The charges on the latter, a sword with a cap of maintenance on the point, between two horseshoes and six nails, were incorporated in arms granted to the town in 1538. Those arms, obtained through the efforts principally of Alderman Thomas Bell, also referred to Richard III and his violent death and to the Lancastrian and Yorkist houses.[69]

Another coat of arms, believed to have been borne by Gloucester before 1538, was made up of charges from the blazons of the de Clares, earls of Gloucester, and of Worcester diocese.[70] It appeared on the monument in Gloucester cathedral to John Jones (d. 1630), a former mayor,[71] and was adopted by the corporation in place of the Tudor arms in 1647.[72] In 1652 the city acquired a grant of the new blazon, which had as supporters lions rampant and guardant holding broadswords and on the crest a third lion holding a sword and a trowel, probably to recall Gloucester's part in the Civil War. The motto *fides invicta triumphat* was adopted at the same time. After the Restora-

Fig. 24. TOWN OF GLOUCESTER. *Vert, on a pale or a sword azure, bezanted, the hilt and pommel gules, upon the point a cap of maintenance purpure lined ermine, all between two horseshoes argent pierced sable, each between three nails in triangle argent; on a chief per pale or and purpure a boar's head couped argent, in his mouth a queen apple gules, between two demi-roses, the dexter gules, the sinister argent, both rayed or.* [Granted 1538; surrendered 1647]
CITY OF GLOUCESTER. *Or, three chevrons between ten torteaux, 3, 3, 3, 1, all gules.* [Granted 1652, 1945, and 1974]

tion Gloucester continued to use those arms[73] but, in the absence of any new grant, its right to crest and supporters was challenged.[74] The full armorial achievement was conferred on the city in 1945 and was confirmed at local government reorganization in 1974 when Gloucester was accorded honorary borough status.[75]

[59] O.S. Map 1/2,500, Glos. XXV. 15 (1902 edn.).
[60] Glos. R.O., D 3117/535, 362.
[61] Glouc. Cath. Libr., Reg. Abb. Froucester B, p. 1.
[62] *Glouc. Corp. Rec.* p. 83; Glos. R.O., D 936/E 12/1, f. 121.   [63] *Glouc. Corp. Rec.* p. 92.
[64] Glos. R.O., D 936/E 12/9, f. 129v.
[65] Glouc. Cath. Libr., Reg. Abb. Malvern, i, f. 198v.; Glos. R.O., D 936/E 12/19, ff. 99, 158.
[66] This article was written in 1986.
[67] B.M. *Cat. of Seals*, ii. p. 81.
[68] Cf. above, Educ.
[69] G.B.R., B 3/50, pp. 209–10 (a transcript of original grant in Bodl. MS. Chart. Glos. 13); the apple has sometimes been described erroneously as a quince: Rudder, *Glos.* 124; *Glouc.*

Official Guide (1980), 128.
[70] G.B.R., B 3/2, p. 625; Rudder, *Glos.* 125.
[71] Roper, *Glos. Effigies*, plate facing p. 275; the arms granted in 1538 were used on mons. of c. 1614 and c. 1626: ibid. 266, 313; Fosbrooke, *Glouc.* plate facing p. 138.
[72] G.B.R., B 3/2, pp. 413, 625.
[73] Ibid. F 4/5, f. 456; Rudder, *Glos.* 125; C. W. Scott-Giles, *Civic Heraldry in Eng. and Wales* (1953), 149; the crest and supporters in J. Dorney, *Certain Speeches* (Lond. 1653), *frontispiece*, differ from those displayed later.
[74] *Trans. B.G.A.S.* xxx. 111.
[75] *Glouc. Official Guide* (1980), 45, 128–9; Local Govt. Act, 1972, c. 70, ss. 245–7; inf. from chief executive, Glouc. city council.

SEALS.[76] The town's common seal in use by 1245[77] was round, $2\frac{3}{8}$ in. in diameter, with the device of a triangular citadel by a river and the legend, in lombardic lettering, SIGILL*VM* B[*VR*]GE*N*SIV*M* D[E GILD*A* MERC]ATO-[*RVM* GLOVCE]STRIE. The seal remained in use in 1364[78] but had been replaced by 1398 by a circular seal,[79] $2\frac{1}{4}$ in., bearing a similar device with a castellated gateway and the same legend in black letter. The latter seal was in use in 1550.[80] In 1564 the matrix was struck in silver for a new common seal.[81] That seal, $2\frac{5}{8}$ in. in diameter, showed the arms of the city on a shield between two pairs of maces in saltire and bore the legend, in renaissance lettering, SIGILLVM MAIORIS ET BVRGENSIVM DE GILDA MERCATORVM CIVITATIS GLOVCESTRIÆ.[82] In 1654 the corporation broke and sold the matrix[83] and adopted a new seal depicting the arms granted in 1652 and bearing a different legend.[84] Its matrix was in turn sold in 1661 when the corporation made a large oval seal,[85] $3\frac{1}{4}$ in. × $2\frac{1}{4}$ in., displaying the arms on a shield with elaborate scroll work and the legend, in renaissance lettering, SIGILL*VM* MAIORIS ET BVRGENSIVM CIVIT*ATIS* GLOVCESTRIÆ IN COMIT*ATV* CIVIT-*ATIS* GLOV*C*ESTRIÆ. From 1800 or 1801[86] the corporation used a smaller circular seal, $2\frac{1}{8}$ in., with the same legend and an unadorned blazon, and at local government reorganization in 1974 the city council acquired a new seal showing the arms on a shield and the legend THE COMMON SEAL OF THE COUNCIL OF THE CITY OF GLOUCESTER.[87] In 1986 the city museum kept the silver matrices struck in 1661 and 1800.

From 1565 the corporation used a new seal for St. Bartholomew's Hospital,[88] which had come under its control the previous year and remained so until 1836.[89] The matrix, which was in the city museum in 1986, was made of silver from a cup given to the corporation by Sir Thomas Bell.[90] The seal, $2\frac{1}{2}$ in. in diameter, bore the legend, in renaissance lettering, SIGIL*LVM* HOS-*PITALIS* S*ANCTI* BARTHO*LOMEI* GLO-VC*ESTRIÆ* EX S*ECVNDA* FVNDAC*IONE* ELISABETH*Æ* REGINE and depicted St. Bartholomew holding a large knife and a whip, symbols of his martyrdom.[91] It was also used for the hospitals of St. Margaret and St. Mary Mag-

dalen[92] and was replaced in 1800 or 1801[93] by a smaller seal, 2 in. in diameter, bearing the same device and legend. That seal was in use in 1818 but the corporation had adopted the city's common seal for the hospitals by 1820.[94]

In 1302 the town's bailiffs used a circular seal,[95] $1\frac{3}{8}$ in., with the device of a castellated gateway by a river and the legend, in lombardic lettering, SIGILL*VM* PREPOSITOR*VM* GLOVCES-TRIE. By 1334 they had adopted an almost identical seal[96] with the legend SIGILL*VM* BALLIVOR*VM* GLOVCESTRIE; its silver matrix was preserved in the city museum in 1986. A fragmentary impression of the mayor's seal, presumably made when the office was created in 1483, is attached to a deed of 1492. The seal, also employed in 1582 and 1609,[97] was round, $1\frac{5}{8}$ in., depicting a shield, charged with a sword in bend between six horseshoes and ten nails, and a lion couchant guardant and bearing the legend, in black letter, S*IGILLUM* OFFICII MAIOR-ALITATIS VILLE GLOUCESTRIE. The matrix may have been replaced in the early 17th century, for an old mayoral seal was for sale in 1642 to help pay for the city's fortifications,[98] and one matrix was broken and sold in 1654.[99] In the late 19th century the mayoral seal was a circular one, $1\frac{3}{16}$ in., bearing as a device the city arms on a shield and the legend, in roman lettering, SIGILL*VM* MAIORAT*VS* CIVITATIS GLO-VCESTRIÆ. The matrix was in the mayor's office in 1986.[1]

Gloucester was granted a statute merchant seal in 1348.[2] Of the seal's two pieces that known as the king's seal was round, $2\frac{1}{2}$ in., and showed a half-length figure of the monarch, full-faced and crowned, with a border of annulets on the neck and the lion of England couchant guardant on the breast, and, in an allusion to Gloucester's trade, two horseshoes and thirteen nails in the field. The legend, in lombardic lettering, was S*IGILLVM* EDWARDI REG*IS* ANGL*IE* AD RECOG-N*ICIONEM* DEBITOR*VM* APVD GLO-VCESTRI*AM*. The bronze or latten matrix was in the city museum in 1986. Clerks were appointed regularly to keep the smaller counter-seal[3] and that used in 1590 was $\frac{7}{8}$ in. in diameter and bore a shield of the city arms granted in 1538.[4]

[76] Unless otherwise stated the accounts of seals, insignia, and plate are based on Ll. F. W. Jewitt and W. H. St. John Hope, *Corp. Plate and Insignia* (1895), i. 221–34; C. H. Dancey, 'Silver Plate and Insignia of City of Glouc.' *Trans. B.G.A.S.* xxx. 91–122.

[77] G.B.R., J 1/351.

[78] Ibid. 981.

[79] Ibid. 1038.

[80] Ibid. 1245.

[81] Ibid. F 4/3, f. 107; date on seal.

[82] e.g. G.B.R., J 1/1265, 1277, 1282.

[83] Ibid. F 4/6, p. 4.

[84] Ibid. B 3/2, pp. 625, 771.

[85] Ibid. F 4/6, pp. 390, 408; B 3/3, p. 206.

[86] Ibid. B 3/12, f. 325; F 4/14, p. 305.

[87] Inf. from chief executive, Glouc. city council.

[88] Date on seal; cf. G.B.R., J 1/1269–70, 2080B.

[89] Above, Char. for Poor, almshouses.

[90] G.B.R., F 4/3, ff. 97, 100 and v., 113.

[91] The device copied that on the former seal of the hosp.:

ibid. J 1/1209; cf. *V.C.H. Glos.* ii. 121 and plate opposite p. 98.

[92] Cf. Glos. R.O., D 3269, St. Marg. Hosp., leases 1757–1815; the medieval seal of St. Marg. Hosp. was in use in 1559: G.B.R., J 1/1256.

[93] G.B.R., B 3/12, f. 325; Glos. R.O., D 3269, St. Barth. Hosp., acct. bk. 1797–1817, f. 18.

[94] Glos. R.O., D 3269, St. Mary Magd. Hosp., leases 1762–1878; St. Barth. Hosp., Hare Lane leases 1812–56.

[95] G.B.R., J 1/762.

[96] Ibid. 873; B.M. *Cat. of Seals*, ii, p. 81; the seal was probably used by the sheriffs after the charter of 1483: *Glouc. Corp. Rec.* p. 18.

[97] B.M. *Cat. of Seals*, ii, p. 81; G.B.R., J 1/1269, 1277.

[98] G.B.R., B 3/2, p. 230.   [99] Ibid. F 4/6, p. 4.

[1] Inf. from chief executive, Glouc. city council.

[2] *Cal. Pat.* 1348–50, 14.

[3] Cf. ibid. 48; 1364–7, 211; 1367–70, 206; 1446–52, 3.

[4] B.M. *Cat. of Seals*, i, p. 144; the clerk's seal had changed by 1640: Glos. R.O., D 4431, bond 27 Jan. 1640.

INSIGNIA.[5] The insignia include two swords, a cap of maintenance, four serjeants' maces, chains and badges for the mayor and sheriff, and an oar for the water bailiff. The charter of 1483 provided for a sword to be carried before the mayor in the same manner as in other boroughs and cities.[6] A sword had presumably been acquired by 1486, when the office of sword bearer was mentioned,[7] and the city had two swords by 1560. The principal sword, which was redecorated to mark the visit of Elizabeth I in 1574,[8] was lost in the 19th century.[9] The other sword, perhaps the first acquired, was known as the mourning sword in 1584.[10] It is 3 ft. 11½ in. long and has been painted black, retaining the original blade and hilt with curved quillons. A third sword, made for the corporation in 1567 and given a red scabbard,[11] had become the principal sword by the mid 17th century and was depicted on the monument to John Jones (d. 1630).[12] It is 4 ft. 3½ in long and retains its original blade and hilt. With the scabbard it was altered in London in 1652 to carry the Commonwealth arms. In 1660 those were replaced by Charles II's arms and the scabbard was partly redecorated, some royal badges being reinstated soon afterwards.[13] A cap of maintenance, recorded on the arms granted to the borough in 1538,[14] was replaced several times.[15] It was identified, questionably, as the sword bearer's hat by the mid 19th century and until 1933 when W. L. Edwards, the mayor, gave the city a new cap of maintenance.[16]

The town's two serjeants carried maces by 1392[17] and their right to bear them before the bailiffs within the precinct of Gloucester Abbey was confirmed in 1429.[18] Under the charter of 1483 four serjeants-at-mace were appointed, two to serve the mayor and two the two sheriffs.[19] A mace was purchased for one of the serjeants in 1494[20] and repairs to the maces were a frequent item of expenditure for the corporation.[21] The four maces depicted on the common seal used from 1564 had conical heads and shafts with central knobs.[22] By the 1620s another four silver maces, having crested heads and long shafts with central encircling bands, had been acquired,[23] and the older set was sold in 1642 to raise funds for fortifying the city.[24] The new maces were refashioned in 1652 as Commonwealth maces, apparently by Thomas Maundy of London whose mark appears on two of them.[25] Four little pocket maces purchased for the serjeants later that year[26] were sold in 1660 to help pay for the conversion in London of the principal maces back to royal maces by remaking the heads as open crowns surmounted by orbs and crosses and decorated with royal badges.[27] The maces, which are 2 ft. 5 in. long, were represented in a carving of the city arms and insignia on the new Tolsey in 1751.[28] All four maces remained in use after the reform of the corporation in 1835 when the number of sheriffs was reduced to one.[29]

The mayor's gold chain and badge were bought by subscription in 1870. The chain, formed of two rows of links with a horseshoe motif, displays the cap of maintenance on the ornament connecting it to the enamelled badge, which bears the city arms with supporters.[30] The sheriff's chain and badge, also of gold, were purchased by local freemasons in 1883 for Henry Jeffs, who gave it to the corporation at the expiry of his term of office. Enamelled shields incorporated in the chain include references to a bailiffs' seal and the arms of Gloucester diocese and the enamelled badge shows the city arms with crest and supporters. Freemasons presented badges for the mayoress and sheriff's lady in 1932, and in 1937 a badge was provided for the deputy mayor.[31] The water bailiff's oar is 4½ in. long and of silver. It was made in 1807 or 1808 for William Brown[32] and was carried by his successors in that office.[33] It belonged to Caroline Brain in 1852 when the corporation hired it, probably for the presentation of an address to Queen Victoria, then passing through Gloucester.[34] Gloucester retained its mayor and sheriff and the use of its civic insignia following the local government reorganization of 1974.[35]

PLATE.[36] The corporation built up a collection of plate mostly from gifts, the earliest known being a cup from Sir Thomas Bell in 1563.[37] Pieces were given by William Guise of Elmore in 1615, by

[5] Above, n. 76.   [6] *Glouc. Corp. Rec.* p. 17.
[7] G.B.R., B 2/1, f. 1; cf. ibid. f. 2; F 4/2.
[8] Ibid. F 4/3, ff. 78v., 107v., 159; Rudder, *Glos.* 113.
[9] Cf. Fosbrooke, *Glouc.* 203; *Kelly's Dir. Glos.* (1889), 783.
[10] G.B.R., F 4/3, f. 232v.
[11] Ibid. ff. 118, 314v.
[12] Roper, *Glos. Effigies*, plate facing p. 275; ibid. 276, mistakes the sword for that lost in the 19th cent.
[13] G.B.R., F 4/5, f. 456; 6, pp. 370, 443; B 3/3, p. 136.
[14] Above.
[15] G.B.R., F 4/3, f. 113; 5, ff. 138v., 489; 6, p. 367; 8, p. 41; 11, p. 341.
[16] *Glouc. Jnl.* 4 Sept. 1852; 30 Sept. 1933.
[17] P.R.O., C 115/K 2/6684, f. 159.
[18] G.B.R., B 2/1, ff. 195v., 197.
[19] *Glouc. Corp. Rec.* p. 18.
[20] G.B.R., F 4/2.
[21] Ibid. 3–16, *passim.*
[22] Cf. ibid. J 1/1265.
[23] Ibid. F 4/5, f. 34; description from maces shown on mon. to John Jones (d. 1630): Roper, *Glos. Effigies*, plate facing p. 275.
[24] G.B.R., F 4/5, ff. 168, 202; B 3/2, p. 230.

[25] Cf. ibid. B 3/2, p. 685; F 4/5, ff. 456, 471v.; W. J. Cripps, *Old Eng. Plate* (1967), 408–9.
[26] G.B.R., B 3/2, p. 689; F 4/5, ff. 486v., 496v.
[27] Cf. ibid. B 3/3, p. 136; F 4/6, pp. 339, 370; the mayoral and shrieval maces were apparently altered separately, a fact which may explain why two maces are dated 1652 and two 1660.
[28] Ibid. B 3/10, f. 148; *Trans. B.G.A.S.* xix, plate facing p. 144.
[29] Municipal Corporations Act, 5 & 6 Wm. IV, c. 76, s. 61.
[30] Above, Plate 23.
[31] *Glouc. Municipal Year Bk.* (1964–5), 94.
[32] Cf. G.B.R., F 4/15, p. 2.
[33] The oar is engraved with inits. W.B. and S.C., the latter presumably for Stephen Creed, water bailiff in 1836 and 1852: G.B.R., treasurer's acct. bk. 1836–8, f. 27; 1851–5, f. 75.
[34] Ibid. B 4/1/7, f. 39; *Glouc. Jnl.* 4 Sept. 1852.
[35] *Glouc. Official Guide* (1980), 45, 129; Local Govt. Act, 1972, c. 70, ss. 245–7; cf. *Citizen*, 18 Aug. 1986.
[36] Above, n. 76.
[37] G.B.R., F 4/3, f. 100 and v.; Bell had redeemed plate pawned by the Dominican friars of Glouc.: *Trans. B.G.A.S.* liv. 171 n.

Thomas Varnam on his appointment in 1617 as surveyor of the city's works, and by Walter Huntley in 1625.[38] Alderman John Baugh (d. 1621) left a set of apostle spoons[39] and Richard Keylock (d. 1637) £20 to buy plate for the mayor.[40] Other donors at that time were Alderman John Thorne (d. 1618), Gervase Smith (d. 1626), Lady (Anne) Porter, James Clent, and John Hanbury, M.P. for the city 1628–9.[41] In 1642 and 1643 the corporation sold several pieces to help pay for the city's fortifications.[42] In 1648, when it exchanged the two flagons remaining from Keylock's bequest for smaller vessels,[43] Captain John Evans gave a bowl and Thomas Barrett, a local cutler, a set of apostle knives.[44] The knives had been lost by 1675.[45]

In 1700 the corporation bought a large salver using the recorder's salary repaid by John Somers, Lord Somers, for that purpose.[46] Between 1742 and 1751 part of the plate, including two salvers of 1743 obtained in exchange for two bowls, was used for holy communion in the corporation's Tolsey chapel.[47] In 1767 Charles Barrow, M.P. for the city, gave a loving-cup and the following year George Selwyn,

his fellow member,[48] presented a punch bowl, for which a ladle was bought in 1790. The flagons derived from Keylock's gift were replaced in 1713,[49] the apostle spoons were remade between 1729 and 1732, and the remaining pieces of plate acquired before 1700 were sold or were exchanged for sets of forks and spoons in 1818.[50] Among plate acquired later by the corporation are pieces originally presented to the prominent London politician Sir Matthew Wood, Bt. (d. 1843), who acquired an estate at Down Hatherley;[51] to Robert Bransby Cooper, M.P. for Gloucester 1818–30;[52] to David Mowbray Walker, a local newspaper owner and civic leader, in 1857;[53] to James Bruton, the mayor, in 1909; and to George Sheffield Blakeway, the town clerk, in 1919. Three silver-gilt roundels given to the corporation in 1906 had evidently once adorned part of the civic insignia or plate. Two display Gloucester's Tudor arms, on one impaling an unidentified blazon. The third roundel, bearing the arms of Sir Thomas Bell and the date 1563, has an inscription evidently marking his gift to the city of a cup. The plate and insignia were displayed at the Guildhall until 1986.

BAILIFFS OF GLOUCESTER 1200–1483

GLOUCESTER had two bailiffs under its charter of 1200; they were evidently elected each year from that time, taking office within a few days of Michaelmas.

A list of bailiffs, which can be amplified and corrected from original sources, was compiled by Furney (Glos. R.O., D 327, pp. 12–19) and was used by Rudder (*Glos.* 113–15) and Fosbrooke (*Glouc.* 206–8). Entries from Furney's list for which no supporting evidence has been found but which there is no obvious reason to doubt are enclosed in brackets in the following list.

Recurrent sources are abbreviated as follows:

A (with page number)
D (with volume and folio number)
G (with page number)
L (with folio number)

Glouc. Cath. Libr., Reg. Abb. Froucester B
Glouc. Cath. Libr., deeds and seals
Glouc. Corp. Rec.
P.R.O., C 115/K 1/6681

Undated, 1200 × c. 1228
Wal. Cadivor; Rob. Calvus (G 81)
Arnold; Rob. Calvus (G 82)
Wm. de Fovis; John the younger (A 298)
Ellis Goodman; Wm. the burgess (G 83)
Ellis the palmer; Ralph of Tidenham (G 84)
John Rufus; Adam the Welshman (A 178)
Ric. son of William; Maur. Palmer (G 83)
Hen. the burgess; John of Goose ditch (G 116)
John of Goose ditch; Ric. son of Walter (G 141)
Thos. Oye; Adam son of Roger (L 106)
John the draper; Thos. Oye (G 156)
Ric. the burgess; Thos. Oye (L 126v.)

Ric. the burgess; Maur. son of Durand (G 132)
John the draper; Maur. son of Durand (L 80v.)
David Dunning; Wal. Hoth (A 9)
John the draper; David Dunning (G 99)
Maur. son of Durand; John the weaver (A 264)
Maur. son of Durand; John the dyer (L 81)
Maur. son of Durand; Gilb. the tailor (G 133)
Wal. Hoth; Wal. Payn (G 159)

Undated, c. 1228 × c. 1240 (while Ric. the burgess was mayor)
John the draper; Wm. of Sandford (D vi. 9)
David Dunning; Wal. Payn (G 143)

---

[38] G.B.R., B 3/1, ff. 270v., 444v.–445, 506.
[39] G.D.R. wills 1621/53. The spoons, said in Baugh's will to be a dozen, numbered thirteen: G.B.R., F 4/5, f. 119v.
[40] Glos. R.O., P 154/9/CH 3/1; G.B.R., B 3/2, p. 79.
[41] G.B.R., F 4/5, f. 119v.; for Thorne, P.R.O., C 142/377, no. 96; for Smith, son of Miles Smith, bp. of Glouc., Fosbrooke, *Glouc.* 135; for Lady Porter and Clent, below, Outlying Hamlets, man.; for Hanbury, Williams, *Parl. Hist. of Glos.* 193.
[42] G.B.R., B 3/2, pp. 230, 240, 253, 257–8, 270–1.
[43] Ibid. p. 476; F 4/5, f. 391Av.

[44] Ibid. F 4/5, ff. 365, 384v.; a bowl lost by the mayor in 1648 had been replaced by 1650: ibid. 384v., 422v.
[45] Cf. ibid. F 4/7, p. 83.
[46] Ibid. B 3/7, f. 232; F 4/7, pp. 723, 731.
[47] Ibid. F 4/10, p. 43; above, Glouc. 1720–1835, city govt.; Churches and Chapels, ancient par. ch., All Saints.
[48] Williams, *Parl. Hist. of Glos.* 210–11.
[49] Cf. G.B.R., B 3/8, p. 526. [50] Cf. ibid. 13, f. 231v.
[51] D.N.B. [52] Williams, *Parl. Hist. of Glos.* 213.
[53] *Glouc. Jnl.* 15 July 1871.

David Dunning; Thos. Oye (G 144)
Wal. Payn; Hugh of king's hall (G 135)
Wal. Payn; Ric. of the cellar (G 160)
Hugh the tailor; Wal. Kentwine (G 133)
Wal. Hoth; Geof. Cuttestich (P.R.O., C 115/L 1/6687, f. 108)
Adam Crook; ———— (L 80)

Undated, c. 1240 × c. 1265
Hugh the girdler; Alex. of the brook (G 184)
Ric. of the cellar; Egeas the fisher (G 190)
Wm. de Sumery; Egeas the fisher (G 199)
Wm. de Sumery; Steph. of Cornwall (A 459)
Wm. de Sumery; John son of Roger Simon (A 9)
John son of Simon; Rog. le Wyse (G 207)
Ric. le Blunt; Rob. of Putley[54] (G 234)
Wm. of Cheltenham; Herbert the mercer (A 436)

Undated, c. 1265 × c. 1285
Wm. of Cheltenham; John Payn (G 232)
Phil. the spicer;[55] John Payn (A 194)
John Payn; Rob. of Cheltenham (G 244)
John Payn; John the draper[56] (G 264)
John Payn; Alex. of Bicknor[57] (G 267)
Alex. of Bicknor; Wal. Sevare (G 278)
Alex. of Bicknor; Ralph of Putley (G 272)
John the draper; Wm. Chose (D i.29)
John the draper; Alex. of Bicknor (G 251)
John the draper; Ralph of Andover (G 243)
John of Worcester;[58] Rob. of Sandhurst (G 248)
John Payn; Wal. Sevare (L 137v.)
Wal. Sevare; John Sage (G 271)
Wal. of Sandon; Wm. Chose (G 265)
Ralph of Andover; Peter Flori (G 251)
John Payn; Rob. de Honsum[59] (A 193)
Wal. Sevare; Wal. of Bicknor (G 277)

Dated (years beginning at Michaelmas)
1244 Wm. de Sumery; Rog. le Wyse (A 9)
1245 Wm. de Sumery; ———— (L 113v.)

1247 Wm. de Sumery; Thos. of Evesham (*Hist. & Cart. Mon. Glouc.* iii, p. xxiii)
1248 or 1249 Wm. de Sumery; Ric. Francis[60] (A 443)

1253 or 1254 Egeas the fisher; Luke of Cornwall (P.R.O., C 115/K 2/6682, f. 105)

1255 John son of Simon; Wm. of Cheltenham (G 213)

1258 Wm. of Cheltenham; Rog. le Wyse (*Cal. Lib.* 1251–60, 468)

1260 Wm. of Cheltenham; John son of Simon (*Cal. Lib.* 1260–7, 44)

1262 Rob. of Putley; Rob. Sely (G 238)

1263 or 1264 Wm. of Cheltenham; Phil. the spicer (A 3)

1268 John Payn; Rob. le Wyse (L 162v.)
1269 Wm. of Cheltenham; John of Cornwall (A 238)

1273 Rob. the clerk; Alex. of Bicknor (A 295)
1274 Rob. the clerk; Wm. Chose (L 94v.)

1276 John the draper; Wal. Sevare (A 259)

1282 Phil. the spicer; John the draper (L 48)
1283 John of Worcester; Ralph of Putley (G 275)

1286 Alex. of Bicknor; Germain of Tunbridge (P.R.O., JUST 1/278, rot. 65)
1287 Wal. Sevare; Wm. Staward (G 280)
1288 Wal. Sevare; Jas. of Longney (G 282)
1289 Hugh the clerk; Hen. the draper (L 41)
1290 John of the garden; Rob. of Standish (L 41)
1291 Alex. of Bicknor; Hugh the clerk (A 288)
1292 John the draper; Wal. Sevare (G 286)
1293 Hugh the clerk; Rob. of Standish (G 287)
1294 Hen. del Oke; Steph. Brown (A 234)
1295 John Lucas;[61] Wm. Crook (G 289)
1296 Hugh the clerk; Hen. the draper (A 284)
1297 (Wal. Sevare; Wm. of Wightfield)

1299 Wal. of Bicknor; Rog. le Heyberare (A 490)
1300 Rog. le Heyberare; Rob. the spicer[62] (G 295)

1302 Rob. of Standish; Rob. the spicer (G 297)
1303 Alex. of Bicknor; Wm. de Riouns[63] (L 127)
1304 (Wm. of Wightfield; Wm. of Hertford)
1305 John le Bole;[64] Wm. of Hertford (L 163v.)
1306 John of Combe; John of Northwich (A 291)
1307 Rob. Pope;[65] Rob. of Goldhill (L 163)
1308 Wal. the spicer; Thos. of Barnwood (G 302)
1309 Wal. the spicer; Peter of the hill (G 303)
1310 Wal. the spicer; Peter of the hill (G 305)
1311 Wal. the spicer; Nic. Honsum (L 66)
1312 Wm. of Aston; Edm. of Baverton (L 165)
1313 Wm. of Marcle; Wm. of Aston (G 306)
1314 Rob. of Goldhill; John of Northwich (G 308)
1315 And. of Pendock; Owen of Windsor[66] (G 308)
1316 And. of Pendock; Ric. of Aston (G 310)
1317 Steph. Brown;[67] John the tanner (G 313)
1318 And. of Pendock; John the tanner (G 315)

1320 John the tanner; Ranulph the wheeler (G 316)
1321 Adam of Hill; Wal. the spicer (A 378)
1322 And. of Pendock; Wal. le Southern (L 140v.)
1323 John of Boyfield;[68] Rog. Head (G 318)

---

[54] A mercer: A 9.
[55] Also called Phil. the apothecary: A 6; L 48, 161v. He also traded as a merchant: P.R.O., JUST 1/278, rot. 66; Glos. R.O., D 4431 (no. 24006).
[56] Probably the same man as John of Worcester: below, and cf. G 251, 268, 272.
[57] A merchant: *Cal. Pat.* 1292–1301, 300.
[58] See n. 56.
[59] A merchant: *Cal. Pat.* 1281–92, 201.
[60] A mercer or merchant: L 84, 98v.

[61] Probably the same man as John le Bole: L 163; below.
[62] Also called Rob. the apothecary: A 193–4.
[63] A merchant: L 41v.
[64] See n. 61. Replaced by July 1306 by Rob. of Goldhill: A 292.
[65] Perhaps a draper: *Reg. Mon. Winch.* i. 262–3.
[66] A merchant: L 165, 167. Also called Owen of the Boothall: A 467.
[67] A merchant: *Cal. Pat.* 1330–4, 514.
[68] A tanner: L 155.

1324 John of Chedworth; Thos. of Foxcote (G 319)
1325 John of Chedworth; Wm. the spicer (G 320)
1326 And. of Pendock; John of Marcle[69] (*Cal. Mem. R.* 1326–7, pp. 3, 360)
1327 John King; Wm. of Lindsey (L 166)
1328 Edw. the taverner;[70] Ric. le Recevour[71] (L 39v.)
1329 Laur. of Severn; Wm. Crisp[72] (G 323)
1330 And. of Pendock; Ranulph the wheeler (G 324)
1331 Ric. le Recevour; John of Boyfield (A 437)
1332 Steph. Brown; Rog. Head (A 263)
1333 Ric. le Recevour; Edw. the taverner (G 326)
1334 Ric. le Recevour; John the dyer (A 369)
1335 Ric. Shot; Wm. Brown (G 327)
1336 And. of Pendock; Ric. of Aston (G 328)
1337 Rog. of King's Lane; John Cluet (G 330)
1338 Wm. Crisp; Rob. Hendy (G 332)
1339 Wm. Ragoun; Hen. the draper (G 333)
1340 John Cheverel; Rob. le Walour (D iii.2)
1341 Hen. the draper; Hugh of Chew (G 335)
1342 Adam of Hope; Nic. atte Boure (G 336)
1343 Hen. the draper; Hugh of Chew (G 337)
1344 Rog. of King's Lane; Wm. of 'Kingeshagh' (G 339)

1346 Wm. of 'Kingeshagh'; Rob. le Walour (L 167v.)

1348 Ric. Shot;[73] Hen. the draper (G 344)
1349 Wm. of Leadon; Thos. of Monnington (D iv.5)

1352 Wm. of Leadon; Edm. of Chedworth (G 349)
1353 Wm. of Leadon; Thos. of Monnington (G 350)

1355 Edm. of Chedworth; Rob. of Aston (G 351)
1356 Thos. of Monnington; John of Hazleton (G 352)
1357 Rob. le Walour; Hugh the parker (G 353)
1358 Wm. of 'Kingeshagh'; Hugh the parker (G 354)
1359 Thos. of Ledbury; Thos. of Stoke (G 354)
1360 Hugh the parker; Wm. of Trewsbury (G 355)
1361 Wm. Crook; Wm. Heyberare (G 356)
1362 Wm. Crook; Wm. Heyberare (G 356)

1367 Thos. of Bisley; John of Anlep (G.B.R., J 1/1934E)

1369 Thos. Styward; John of Elmore (G 359)
1370 Wm. Heyberare; Thos. of Bisley (D iii.7)
1371 Thos. Styward; John Monmouth (G 360)
1372 Wm. Heyberare; John Pope (G 360)

1374 Thos. of Bisley; Wm. Foliot (A 215)

1375 Edw. the taverner; Nic. Birdlip (G.B.R., J 1/998)
1376 Wm. Heyberare; Thos. of Bisley (G 362)
1377 John Compton; Rob. Pope (G 363)
1378 John Ruseby; Wm. Crook (P.R.O., C 115/K 2/6685, f. 13)
1379 John Pope; Wm. Crook (G 363)
1380 Rog. Recevour; Ric. Ashwell (G 364)
1381 Ric. Barret;[74] Ric. Ashwell (G 364)
1382 (Ric. Barret; Wm. Wightfield)
1383 John Ruseby; Rob. Pope (G 365)
1384 Wm. Heyberare; Wm. Crook (G 365)
1385 Wm. Crook; Rog. Recevour (G 366)
1387 John Head;[75] Rog. Recevour (G 366)
1388 John Head; ——— (G 368)
1389 John Banbury;[76] Rob. Pope (P.R.O., C 115/K 2/6684, f. 139)
1390 Ric. Ashwell; Wm. Crook (P.R.O., C 115/K 2/6684, f. 145)
1391 Rob. Pope; John Pope (G 368)
1392 John Ruseby; Thos. Pope[77] (G 369)
1393 John Bisley; Thos. Pope (G 371)
1394 John Pope; Rog. Ball (*Cal. Inq. Misc.* vi, p. 39)
1395 (Ric. Ashwell; Wm. Crook)
1396 Thos. Pope; Rog. Ball (G.B.R., C 9/2)
1397 Rog. Ball; Rob. Swansea[78] (G 371)
1398 Wm. Crook; Rog. Ball (G.B.R., C 9/3)
1399 Rob. But; Simon Brook (G 373)
1400 Ric. Barret; Rog. Ball (G 374)
1401 John Bisley; Rog. Ball (G 375)
1402 Rob. But; Thos. Compton (*Cal. Close*, 1402–5, 117)
1403 Rob. But; Wm. Birdlip (G 376)
1404 Rog. Ball; Simon Brook (G 376)
1405 Simon Brook; Thos. Compton (A 341)
1406 Rog. Ball; Thos. Compton (G 378)
1407 John Pope; Simon Brook (P.R.O., C 115/L 1/6687, f. 24v.)
1408 Thos. Compton; Thos. Salisbury (G 379)
1409 Rob. But; Wm. Birdlip (G 379)
1410 (Rog. Ball; Ric. Chamberlain)

1412 Rog. Ball; Wm. Birdlip (G 380)
1413 Rob. But; Thos. Moore[79] (G 381)
1414 Rog. Ball; Thos. Moore (G 382)

1417 John Bisley the elder; Rog. Ball (G 382)
1418 John Strensham; Mic. Salisbury (G 384)
1419 (Ric. Chamberlain; Thos. Hughes)

1421 Rog. Ball; John Hamlyn (P.R.O., C 115/K 2/6682, f. 148v.)
1422 (Rog. Ball; Thos. Compton)
1423 John Bisley the elder; Ric. Dalby (G 384–5)
1424 (Rob. Gilbert;[80] John Hamlyn)
1425 (John Bisley the elder; Ric. Dalby)
1426 (Thos. Guildford; Hen. Salisbury)
1427 Wm. Butler; Thos. Hughes (G.B.R., B 2/1, f. 139)[81]

[69] A merchant: *Cal. Pat.* 1330–4, 232.
[70] Also called Edw. of Ley: G 322.
[71] Also called Ric. of Bramshall: G 322, 327.
[72] A merchant: P.R.O., C 115/L 1/6687, f. 74v.
[73] Replaced early in 1349 by Wal. of Elmore: A 379; G 347.
[74] A draper: G.B.R., C 9/1; Hockaday Abs. ccxix, 1401.
[75] A draper, and probably merchant: A 481; Hockaday Abs. ccxiii, 1390; *Cal. Close*, 1389–92, 483.

[76] A merchant: *Cal. Pat.* 1385–9, 128; 1401–5, 148.
[77] A merchant: *Cal. Close*, 1389–92, 482–3.
[78] A mercer: P.R.O., C 115/K 1/6678, f. 60.
[79] A mercer: D v.18.
[80] A lawyer: *Trans. B.G.A.S.* lxxiv. 87–9; *Glouc. Rental, 1455*, 93.
[81] Given as bailiffs in Mar. 1428 (cf. also P.R.O., C 115/K 2/6685, f. 60), but G.B.R., J 1/1091 has John Bisley and Rog. Ball in June.

1428 John Strensham; Ric. Dalby (G 387)
1429 Rob. Gilbert; Thurstan Power[82] (P.R.O., C 115/L 1/6687, f. 82)

1431 John Reed; Wm. Oliver[83] (G 388)
1432 Rob. Gilbert; John Strensham (G 389)
1433 John Hamlyn; John Luke[84] (G 57)
1434 (John Strensham; Thos. Hughes)

1436 Wm. Oliver; Phil. Monger[85] (G 391)
1437 John Strensham; Ric. Dalby (G 391)

1439 John Reed; Wm. Oliver (Cal. Pat. 1441–6, 134)
1440 Thurstan Power; Wal. Banknot[86] (G 393)
1441 (Wm. Eldersfield;[87] Wal. Chantrel[88])
1442 Wm. Oliver; Wal. Banknot (G 395)

1444 John Luke; John Heydon (G 395)
1445 Wal. Chantrel; Wm. Saunders[89] (G 395)
1446 Wm. Oliver; Hen. Dood[90] (Cal. Pat. 1446–52, 126)
1447 John Heydon; Wm. Boneson (ibid.)
1448 (Thos. Hilley; Wm. Newman[91])
1449 (Wm. Nottingham;[92] Hen. Dood)
1450 John Andrew;[93] Thos. Bridge (G 397)

1452 Wm. Eldersfield; Thos. Bye (G 398)

1455 Wm. Eldersfield; Ric. Skidmore (P.R.O., C 115/K 2/6685, f. 17)
1456 Maur. Andrew; John Kilroy[94] (G 403)
1457 Thos. Buckland;[95] John Hilley (G 60)
1458 Maur. Andrew; John Joliffe (G 404)

1460 Ric. Russell; Nic. Hill (Glos. Colln. 28652, no. 1)
1461 John Grove;[96] Wm. Francombe (D x.15)

1463 Wm. Brookwood; Wm. Gram. . . (G.B.R., J 1/1149)
1464 John Chantrel; John Poole (G 405)

1466 Nic. Hill; Wm. Perkins (G 408)

1474 John Farley;[97] John Hartland the elder[98] (Glos. R.O., P 154/14/CH 2/1)
1475 (John Barton; John Capel)
1476 (John Farley; Wm. Poole)

1478 John Farley; Wm. Cole (G 412)

1481 Wm. Francombe; Hen. Richards[99] (G.B.R., C 9/5)
1482 Alex. Sely; Thos. Fairford (ibid. B 1/1)

ALDERMEN OF GLOUCESTER 1483–1835

UNDER its charter of 1483 Gloucester had 12 aldermen, who were to hold office for life and one of whom was to serve each year as mayor. Under the Municipal Corporations Act the existing bench of aldermen retired from office at the end of 1835.

The list is based on G.B.R., B 2/1, ff. 26v.–31, 36–39v., 60–63v.; on the records of elections and the lists of the common council in ibid. B 3/1–14; and on Ripley, 'Glouc. 1660–1740', App. XXV. Other sources are given in the footnotes. There are probably some names missing in the period 1483–1503. An asterisk indicates where the appointment or removal of an alderman was the result of government intervention.

Most of the aldermen served two terms as sheriff before their appointment and one or two terms as mayor after it. For a list of mayors and sheriffs during the period, see Fosbrooke, Glouc. 208–11 (which can be completed up to 1835 from G.B.R., B 3/13–14).

---

[82] Also called Thurstan Southern; he was probably a mercer like his son John, to whom he gave shops in the mercery: P.R.O., C 115/K 1/6678, f. 57.
[83] A chaloner: Cal. Pat, 1446–52, 126.
[84] A brazier: ibid. 1441–6, 8.
[85] A merchant: Brokage Bk. of Southampton, 1439–40 (Southampton Rec. Soc. xl), 77, 113, 136, 143, 148, 155–6.
[86] A mercer: Glouc. Rental, 1455, 29.
[87] A mercer: ibid. 31.
[88] A brewer: ibid.
[89] A brewer: ibid. 17.

[90] A merchant: Cal. Pat. 1446–52, 126.
[91] A dyer: G 396.
[92] A lawyer: Glouc. Rental, 1455, 77.
[93] A lawyer: ibid. 93.
[94] A fishmonger: P.R.O., C 115/K 2/6685, f. 17.
[95] A lawyer: Glouc. Rental, 1455, 75.
[96] A draper and hosier: ibid. 73.
[97] A mercer, Cal. Close, 1476–85, p. 160.
[98] A mercer, also called John Porter: P.R.O., C 115/K 2/6685, f. 56v.; cf. Hockaday Abs. ccxv, 1474.
[99] A brewer: Cal. Close, 1476–85, p. 21.

Election (or, in brackets, first occurrence)		Occupation (where known)	Death, Resignation, or Removal
1483[1]	John Trye		d. 1485[2]
(1484)	John Capel[3]		d. 1505
(1485)	Wm. Francombe		d. 1488[4]
(1486)[5]	John Hilley	wiredrawer	d. 1494[6]
(1486)	John Poole		(by 1503)
(1486)	Ric. Russell		(by 1503)
(1486)	And. Bye		(by 1503)
(1486)	Thos. Long		(by 1503)
(1486)	Thos. Bower		(by 1503)
(1486)	Wm. Cole	mercer[7]	d. 1517
(1486)	Thos. Fairford		d. 1487[8]
(1486)	Rob. Cuff	draper	d. 1496[9]
(1486)	Thos. Hart	mercer[10]	(by 1503)
(1489)[11]	Rob. Poole		(by 1503)
(1491)[12]	Wal. Rowden	lawyer[13]	d. 1513
(1492)	Wm. Cooke		d. 1494[14]
(1492)	Phil Pridith		(by 1503)
(1492)	John Elliott	tanner	(d. 1497)[15]
(1495)[16]	Rob. Rawlings	draper	d. 1497[17]
(1499)	Garet van Eck	merchant[18]	d. 1506
(1501)	John Cooke	mercer	d. 1528[19]
(1503)	Wm. Henshaw	bellfounder[20]	d. 1522
(1503)	Wm. Marmion		res 1530
(1503)	Thos. Asplyn		res. 1510/11
(1503)	Thos. Tayloe	clothier[21]	d. 1531
(1503)	Thos. Lane		d. 1504
(1503)	John Natton	mercer[22]	d. 1519
(1503)	David Vaughan	merchant[23]	d. 1504
1504	Wm. Goldsmith (or Smith)	goldsmith[24]	d. 1517
1504	Thos. Studley		d. 1511/12[25]
1505	Nic. Elliott		d. 1517
1506	Ric. Rowden	mercer[26]	d. 1517
1510/11	Ralph Sankey	capper[27]	d. 1524
1511/12	Rob. Plavis		d. 1519
1513	John Hawkins	brewer[28]	d. 1523
1517	Thos. Porter (or Hartland)[29]	draper[30]	d. 1522
1517	Wm. Jordan	cutler[31]	d. 1545
1517	Ralph Halsey		d. 1519
1517	John Allen	tanner[32]	d. 1524
1519	John Falconer	capper[33]	d. 1545
1519	John Rawlings	draper[34]	d. 1532
1519	Wm. Hazard	dyer[35]	d. 1543
1522	Thos. Osborne	mercer[36]	d. 1541

[1] For date of occurrence of first three, Fosbrooke, *Glouc.* 208.

[2] Hockaday Abs. ccxix.

[3] Possibly a lawyer, for he was retained 'at counsel' by the corporation in 1493: G.B.R., F 4/2.

[4] Hockaday Abs. ccxx.

[5] For date of occurrence of him and next nine, G.B.R., B 2/1, f. 1.   [6] Hockaday Abs. ccxxi.

[7] Ibid. ccxv, 1518.

[8] Ibid. ccxvi.

[9] Ibid. ccxiii.

[10] G.B.R., G 10/1, p. 175.

[11] Fosbrooke, *Glouc.* 208.

[12] For date of occurrence of him and next three, B.L. Add. Ch. 23845.

[13] Glouc. Cath. Libr., Reg. Abb. Newton, ff. 48–9.

[14] Hockaday Abs. ccxix.

[15] Ibid. ccxx.

[16] For date of occurrence of him and next two, Fosbrooke, *Glouc.* 208.

[17] Hockaday Abs. ccxiii.

[18] *L. & P. Hen. VIII,* i (1), p. 239.

[19] Austin, *Crypt Sch.* 15.

[20] *L. & P. Hen. VIII,* i (1), p. 346.

[21] Ibid. p. 265.

[22] Ibid. p. 257.

[23] *Cal. Pat.* 1494–1509, 270.

[24] *L. & P. Hen. VIII,* i (1), p. 247; G.B.R., F 4/2.

[25] Worcs. R.O., Worc. dioc. wills, vol. ii, f. 39v.

[26] *L. & P. Hen. VIII,* i (1), p. 252.

[27] Ibid. p. 229.

[28] G.B.R., G 10/1, p. 93.

[29] Cf. Glouc. Cath. Libr., Reg. Abb. Malvern, i, f. 41; G.B.R., B 2/1, f. 211v.

[30] Draper and hosier: G.B.R., B 2/1, f. 194v.

[31] Hockaday Abs. ccxiii, 1547.

[32] No conclusive evidence, but he devised a lease of the tanners' company hall to his son Edm., a tanner, and was buried in the company's chap. of St. Clement: Hockaday Abs. ccxv, 1524, 1547.

[33] G.B.R., C 9/6, freemen's admissions 1535–6, 1537–8.

[34] Ibid. G 10/1, f. 288.

[35] Hockaday Abs. ccxx, 1543.

[36] G.B.R., B 2/1, f. 221v.

Election (or, in brackets, first occurrence)		*Occupation* (where known)	*Death, Resignation, or Removal*
1522	John Chapman		res. 1527/8
1523	John Semys		d. 1540
1524	John Rastell		d. 1533
1524	Thos. Massinger		d. 1534
1527/8	Wm. Matthews	tanner[37]	d. 1539
1528	Adam ap Howel		d. 1546
1530	Hen. Marmion		d. 1542
1531	Thos. Bell (later Kt.)	capper[38]	d. 1566
1532	Lewis ap Rice		d. 1533
1533	Thos. Payne	draper[39]	d. 1560
1533	Rob. Poole	merchant[40]	d. 1545
1534	Thos. a Morgan		d. 1534
1534	Phil. Redvern	mercer[41]	d. 1549
1539	Thos. Loveday		d. 1558
1540	Thos. Bell		d. 1560/1[42]
1541	Maur. Vaughan	mercer[43]	d. 1542
1542	John Huggins	capper[44]	d. 1544
1542	Ralph Rawlings		d. 1548
1543	David Lewis	draper[45]	d. 1545
1544	Thos. Clutterbuck	merchant[46]	res. 1557
1545	John Rastell	draper[47]	d. 1558
1545	John Sandford	clothier[48]	res. 1554
1545	Wm. Traherne		d. 1549
1545	Wm. Mitchell	draper[49]	d. 1555
1546	Thos. Pury	mercer	d. 1579
1548	Wm. Hazard	draper[50]	res. 1555
1549	Rob. Moreton	vintner[51]	d. 1571
1549	Wm. Jenkins		d. 1566/7
1554	John ap Richard		d. 1558
1555	Wm. Bond	goldsmith[52]	d. 1565
1555	Hen. Machen		d. 1567
1557	Thos. Massinger		d. 1565
1558	Thos. Hyde	tanner	d. 1574
1558	Lawr. Singleton	draper	res. 1593
1558	John Woodward	mercer	d. 1575
1560/1[53]	Hen. King	mercer	d. 1571
1560	Thos. Semys	clothier	d. 1603
1565	Wm. Massinger		d. 1594
1565	John Kirby	clothier	d. 1578
1566/7	Hen. ap Rice	vintner	d. 1569
1566	Luke Garnons	draper	d. 1615
1567	Thos. Wicks		d. 1572
1569	Wm. Sandford	clothier	d. 1570
1570	Peter Romney	clothier	d. 1577
1571	Ric. Cugley	baker	d. 1586
1571	Thos. Francombe	merchant	d. 1579
1572	Jas. Morse	tanner	d. 1578
1574	Thos. Machen	mercer	d. 1614
1575	Thos. Lane	maltster	d. 1584
1577	John Smith	brewer	d. 1586
1578	Lawr. Holliday	mercer	d. 1587
1578	John Webley	dyer	d. 1588
1579	Thos. Best		d. 1587
1579	John Cowdale	tanner, later maltster	d. 1607

[37] Ibid. C 9/6, freemen's admissions 1537–8; Hockaday Abs. ccxx, 1540.
[38] Glouc. Cath. Libr., Reg. Abb. Malvern, ii, f. 111v.; P.R.O., E 134/25 Eliz. Hil./3. In 1539 he was described as a clothmaker: *L. & P. Hen. VIII*, xiv (1), p. 590.
[39] G.B.R., C 9/6, freemen's admissions 1543–4.
[40] P.R.O., C 142/74, no. 77 (2).
[41] Glos. R.O., D 2957/201.16, 19.
[42] G.D.R. wills 1561/120.
[43] Hockaday Abs. ccxiii, 1543.

[44] Ibid. 1544.
[45] G.B.R., C 9/6, recognition of debt 1545.
[46] Ibid. B 2/1, f. 153v.
[47] Ibid. 2, ff. 30v.–31.
[48] Ibid. f. 34 and v.
[49] Ibid. C 9/6, recognition of debt 1546.
[50] *Cal. Pat.* 1548–9, 141.
[51] Ibid. 1555–7, 232.
[52] Ibid. 1547–8, 329.
[53] G.B.R., B 2/1, f. 29v.; cf. G.D.R. wills 1561/120.

Election (or, in brackets, first occurrence)		Occupation (where known)	Death, Resignation, or Removal
1584	John Browne	mercer	d. 1593
1586	Ric. Coxe	maltster	d. 1605
1586	Rob. Walkeley	mercer, later brewer	rem. 1604
1587	Ric. Webb	baker, later brewer	d. 1598
1587	John Rastell		d. 1587
1587	Ric. Ward	upholsterer	d. 1593
1588	John Taylor	maltster	rem. 1615
1593	Hen. Hazard	maltster	res. 1616
1593	Ric. Hands	diocesan registrar	d. 1593
1593	Grimbald Hutchins	draper	rem. 1602
1593	Wal. Nourse	mercer	rem. c. 1606
1594	John Jones	diocesan registrar	d. 1630
1598	Chris. Capel	mercer	d. 1626[54]
1602	Thos. Rich	mercer	d. 1607
1603	John Payne	innkeeper	d. 1605
1604	Hen. Darby	baker	d. 1614
1605	Lawr. Wilshire	clothier[55]	d. 1612
1605	John Baugh	mercer	d. 1621
c. 1606	John Brewster	furrier	d. 1610
1607	John Thorne	brewer	d. 1618[56]
1607	John Browne	brewer	d. 1638
1610	Wm. Hill	mercer	d. 1636
1612	Thos. Adams	clothier	d. 1621
1614	Edm. Clements	mercer	d. 1633[57]
1614	Ric. Smith	tanner	d. 1637
1615	Mat. Price	tanner	d. 1635
1615	Geof. Beale	mercer	res. 1635
1616 (2nd term)	John Taylor	maltster	d. 1626
1618[58] (2nd term)	Hen. Hazard	maltster	d. 1625[59]
1621	Ric. Beard	mercer	d. 1638
1621	John Walton	goldsmith	d. 1626
1625	Wm. Price	mercer[60]	d. 1640
1625	Hen. Browne		d. 1637
1626	Ant. Robinson		d. 1641
1626	Toby Bullock		d. 1641
1630	John Brewster	maltster[61]	d. 1649
1633	John Webb		d. 1643
1635	Wm. Lugg	tanner[62]	d. 1646
1635	Wm. Singleton	draper[63]	rem. 1662*
1636	Wm. Capel		rem. 1662*
1637	Jas. Powell		d. 1646
1637	John Hayward		d. 1640
1638	Thos. Hill		d. 1652
1638	Thos. Pury	attorney[64]	res. 1662
1640	John Scriven	ironmonger[65]	d. 1645
1640	Dennis Wise	mercer[66]	rem. 1662*
1641	Nic. Webb		d. 1647
1641	Leon. Tarne	vintner[67]	d. 1642
1642	Luke Nourse		rem. 1662*
1643	Lawr. Singleton	draper[68]	rem. 1662*
1645	Jasper Clutterbuck		d. 1659[69]
1646	Jas. Wood		d. 1646
1646	John Madock		d. 1657/8
1646	Hen. Cugley		d. 1669
1647	Jas. Stephens	tanner, later maltster[70]	rem. 1672*

[54] For correction of the date given in G.B.R., B 2/1, f. 60v., cf. ibid. B 3/1, ff. 509, 510v., 514v.
[55] Rudder, *Glos.* 176.   [56] P.R.O., C 142/377, no. 96.
[57] G.B.R., B 2/1, f. 60; cf. Glos. R.O., P 154/14/IN 1/1, burials 1632–3.
[58] G.B.R., B 2/1, f. 60; cf. P.R.O., C 142/377, no. 96.
[59] G.B.R., B 2/1, ff. 38v., 60; cf. G.D.R., wills 1625/53.
[60] G.B.R., C 10/1, p. 342.
[61] Ibid. p. 481.

[62] Ibid. p. 476.
[63] Ibid. 2, p. 16.
[64] *Cal. S.P. Dom.* 1639–40, 582.
[65] G.B.R., C 10/1, p. 397.
[66] Ibid. p. 548.
[67] Glos. R.O., D 326/T 15.
[68] G.B.R., C 10/2, p. 3.
[69] Fosbrooke, *Glouc.* 183–4.
[70] G.B.R., C 10/2, pp. 56, 172, 323.

Election (or, in brackets, first occurrence)		Occupation (where known)	Death, Resignation, or Removal
1649	Ant. Edwards		d. 1660
1652	Edm. Collett	tanner[71]	res. 1658
1657/8	Rob. Tyther	tanner[72]	d. 1660[73]
1658	Toby Jordan	bookseller	rem. 1663*
1659	Rob. Payne		rem. 1662*
1660	Thos. Pierce		rem. 1663*
1660	Thos. Lugg	mercer	rem. 1662*
1661/2	Wm. Clarke		rem. 1662*
1662*	Wm. Russell	furrier	d. 1682
1662*	John Powell		d. 1666
1662*	Thos. Yate	apothecary	d. 1668
1662*	Thos. Price		d. 1679
1662*	John Woodward		d. 1667
1662*	Ant. Arnold	attorney[74]	rem. 1672
1662	Rob. Fielding	physician	rem. 1671
1662	Nic. Webb		rem. 1663*
1663*	Hen. Ockhold		d. 1669
1663*	John Wagstaffe		res. 1689
1663*	Hen. Fowler	physician	d. 1685
1666/7	Wm. Bubb		rem. 1672*
1666/7	Ric. Massinger	brewer[75]	d. 1668
1668	Wm. Scudamore		rem. 1672*
1668	Toby Langford	bookseller	rem. 1672*
1669	Wm. Hodges		rem. 1672*
1669	Rob. Longden		rem. 1672*
1672*	Hen. Norwood	landowner[76]	d. 1689
1672*	Wm. Cooke	landowner[77]	d. 1703
1672*	Duncombe Colchester (later Kt.)	landowner[78]	d. 1694
1672*	Hen. Brett	landowner[79]	d. 1674
1672*	Wm. Selwyn	landowner[80]	d. 1679
1672*	John Gythins	draper	d. 1690
1672*	Thos. Aram	mercer	d. 1679
1672*	John Rogers	baker	d. 1694
1674	John Webb	mercer[81]	d. 1686
1679	Rob. Halford		d. 1683
1679	Francis Singleton	ironmonger[82]	d. 1682
1679	John Price		d. 1687
1682	Wm. Lambe	chapter registrar	res. 1691
1682	Wm. Jordan	apothecary	rem. 1687*
1683	John Hill		res. 1689
1685	Benj. Hyett	attorney[83]	rem. 1687*
1686	John Smallwood		rem. 1687*
1687*	Anselm Fowler	landowner[84]	res. 1688
1687*	John Essington	landowner[85]	rem. 1689
1687*	Thos. Browne		res. 1712
1687*	Thos. Snell		rem. 1690
1689	Wm. Hodges		d. 1703
1689	Rob. Payne	mercer	d. 1713
1689	John Ewens	draper	d. 1696
1689	Wm. Nicholls	tanner	d. 1693
1690	Sir John Guise, Bt.	landowner[86]	d. 1695
1690	Wm. Corsley	goldsmith	d. 1691
1690	Wm. Taylor	ironmonger	d. 1706
1691	John Hyett	mercer	d. 1711

[71] Ibid. p. 204.
[72] Ibid. p. 251.
[73] Fosbrooke, *Glouc.* 184.
[74] *Cal. S.P. Dom.* 1671–2, 24.
[75] 'Freemen of Glouc. 1653–1838', ed. P. Ripley (1984, TS. in Glos. R.O. Libr.), 6.
[76] Rudder, *Glos.* 521.
[77] *V.C.H. Glos* x. 19.
[78] Ibid. 87.
[79] P.R.O., PROB 11/345 (P.C.C. 69 Bunce), ff. 123–4; cf. *V.C.H. Glos.* vii. 194; *Visit. Glos. 1682–3*, 25.
[80] Rudder, *Glos.* 542.
[81] 'Freemen of Glouc.', 18; cf. G.D.R. wills 1686/361.
[82] G.B.R., C 10/3, p. 137; cf. P.R.O., PROB 11/372 (P.C.C. 27 Drax), f. 136v.
[83] F. A. Hyett, 'Hyetts of Painswick' (1907, TS. in Glos. R.O., Libr.), 26.
[84] *V.C.H. Glos.* x. 275; G.D.R. wills 1701/48.
[85] *Visit. Glos. 1682–3*, 61.
[86] Rudder, *Glos.* 313, 440, 622.

Election (or, in brackets, first occurrence)		Occupation (where known)	Death, Resignation, or Removal
1691	Thos. Longden	ironmonger	d. 1702
1693	Wm. Scudamore	draper[87]	d. 1695
1694	Giles Rodway	mercer	d. 1729
1694	Thos. Willcocks		d. 1699
1695 (2nd term)	Thos. Snell		d. 1706
1695	Thos. Webb	mercer	d. 1734
1696	Nic. Webb		d. 1712
1699	Sam. Eckley (later Kt.)	landowner[88]	rem. 1705
1702	Nic. Lane	apothecary	d. 1718
1703	Sam. Palmer		rem. 1707
1703	Sam. Lye	grocer	d. 1712
1705	John Bell	mercer	d. 1719
1706	Capel Payne	mercer	d. 1743
1706	Wm. Nicholls		d. 1721
1707	Edm. Gregory	furrier	d. 1720
1711	Sam. Hayward	grocer	d. 1715
1712	Jas. Furney	ironmonger	d. 1737
1712	Ric. Green	maltster	d. 1729
1712	Sam. Browne	maltster	d. 1738
1713	Thos. Ludlow	draper	d. 1734
1715	Thos. Nicholls	plumber	d. 1719
1719	Ric. Corsley	goldsmith	d. 1742
1719	John King	dyer	d. 1730
1719	Gabriel Harris	bookseller	d. 1744
1720	Dan. Washbourne	maltster	res. 1727
1721	John Rodway	mercer	d. 1736
1727	John Selwyn	landowner[89]	d. 1751
1729	Thos. Carill	hosier	d. 1736
1729	John Small	landowner[90]	d. 1739
1730	Wm. Bell	landowner, tax collector[91]	d. 1768
1734	John Hayward	mercer	d. 1758
1734	Ric. Lewis	goldsmith	d. 1745
1736	Thos. Hill	apothecary	d. 1760
1736	Chas. Selwyn	landowner[92]	res. 1740
1737	Wm. Nicholls	postmaster[93]	d. 1769
1738	Edw. Machen		d. 1740
1739	Sam. Worrall	proctor[94]	d. 1745
1740	Ric. Finch		res. 1749
1740	Thos. Hayward		d. 1781
1742	Lawr. Crump	upholder[95]	d. 1776
1744	John Blackwell		d. 1760
1745	Benj. Saunders	wine merchant, former innkeeper[96]	d. 1763
1745	Gabriel Harris	bookseller[97]	d. 1786
1747	Mic. Bailey		d. 1749
1749	Sam. Farmer	apothecary[98]	d. 1778
1749	Ric. Roberts		d. 1757
1751	Jas. Herbert		d. 1758
1757	Geo. Augustus Selwyn	landowner[99]	d. 1791
1758	Jos. Cheston	apothecary[1]	d. 1779
1758	Ric. Webb	grocer[2]	d. 1772
1760	John Baylis	woolstapler[3]	d. 1772
1760	Edw. Baylis	woolstapler[4]	d. 1775
1764	Thos. Branch		d. 1784

[87] *Visit. Glos 1682-3*, 159.   [88] *V.C.H. Glos.* x. 292.

[89] Williams, *Parl. Hist. of Glos.* 209-10.

[90] G.B.R., B 3/9, f. 217; cf. *V.C.H. Glos.* xi. 297.

[91] P.R.O., PROB 11/936 (P.C.C. 49 Secker), ff. 42v.-46v.; Rudder, *Glos.* 640.

[92] Williams, *Parl. Hist. of Glos.* 209.

[93] *Glouc. Jnl.* 20 Feb. 1769.

[94] He also held various posts in Chancery, King's Bench, and Exchequer: *Glouc. Jnl.* 4 Jan. 1737.

[95] G.D.R. wills 1776/196.

[96] *Glouc. Jnl.* 3 Sept. 1722; 25 May 1731; 5 Mar. 1764.

[97] Ibid. 24 Apr. 1744.

[98] Ibid. 9 Sept. 1760.

[99] Williams, *Parl. Hist. of Glos.* 211.

[1] Glos. R.O., D 936/E 12/11, f. 17v.

[2] Ibid. 12, f. 21.

[3] Ibid. D 1886, Packer fam. deeds.

[4] Ibid. D 936/E 12/11, f. 242.

379

Election (or, in brackets, first occurrence)		Occupation (where known)	Death, Resignation, or Removal
1768	John Jefferies	pinmaker[5]	d. 1778
1769	John Webb	grocer[6]	d. 1785
1772	Benj. Baylis	woolstapler[7]	d. 1777
1772	Abraham Saunders	wine merchant[8]	d. 1793
1775	Wm. Crump	surgeon[9]	d. 1784
1776	John Box	pinmaker[10]	res. 1783
1777	Jas. Sadler	woolstapler[11]	d. 1779
1778	Wm. Lane	attorney[12]	d. 1789
1778	John Bush	woolstaper[13]	d. 1781
1779	Thos. Weaver	pinmaker[14]	d. 1805
1779	Wm. Cowcher	pinmaker[15]	d. 1785
1781	Ric. Webb		d. 1787
1781	Chas. Howard, earl of Surrey (later duke of Norfolk)	landowner[16]	d. 1815
1783	Sam. Colborne	apothecary[17]	d. 1813
1784	Edwin Jeynes (later Kt.)	mercer, later banker[18]	d. 1810
1784	Sir John Guise, Bt.	landowner[19]	d. 1794
1785	John Webb	landowner[20]	d. 1795
1785	John Jefferies	pinmaker[21]	d. 1818
1786	Sam. Woodcock	Post Office surveyor[22]	d. 1829
1787	Jas. Sadler	mercer[23]	d. 1810
1789	Giles Greenaway	landowner, former innkeeper[24]	d. 1815
1791	Wm. Middleton		d. 1793
1793	Thos. Mee	landowner[25]	d. 1812
1793	John Turner	banker[26]	res. 1812
1794	John Ready		res. 1806
1795	John Cooke	wine merchant[27]	res. 1808
1805	Ric. Nayler	surgeon[28]	d. 1816
1806	Dan. Willey	landowner[29]	d. 1817
1808	David Arthur Saunders	wine merchant	d. 1828
1810	Sir Berkeley Wm. Guise, Bt.	landowner[30]	d. 1834
1810	Thos. Commeline	former attorney[31]	d. 1830
1812	John Pleydell Wilton	surgeon	(1835)
1812	Edw. Weaver	pinmaker	res. 1819
1813	Jas. Jelf (later Kt.)	banker	res. 1815
1815	Sam. Ricketts	attorney	d. 1820
1815	Thos. Washbourne	druggist, later banker[32]	d. 1824
1815	David Walker	printer	res. 1829
1816	Chas. Weaver	pinmaker	res. 1818
1817	Ralph Fletcher	surgeon	(1835)
1818	John Phillpotts	barrister	res. 1823
1818	John Baron	physician	res. 1821
1819	Sam. Jones	brushmaker	(1835)
1820	Jas. Wood	banker, mercer	(1835)
1821	Hen. Wilton	attorney	d. 1822
1822	Wm. Price	timber merchant	(1835)
1823	Thos. Smith	attorney	res. 1825

[5] Ibid. D 3117/3953, 3955.
[6] Ibid. D 936/E 12/13, f. 124v.
[7] P.R.O., PROB 11/1033 (P.C.C. 301 Collier), ff. 46–49v.
[8] G.B.R., B 3/10, f. 248v.; P.R.O., 11/1239 (P.C.C. 570 Dodwell), ff. 72v.–73v.
[9] G.D.R. wills 1786/119.   [10] G.B.R., B 3/10, f. 223.
[11] G.D.R. wills 1779/181.
[12] Glouc. Jnl. 21 Dec. 1789.
[13] G.B.R., B 3/11, f. 71.
[14] Glos. R.O., D 3117/3957.
[15] Ibid. D 936/E 12/12, f. 197v.
[16] Cf. below, Outlying Hamlets, man.
[17] G.B.R., B 3/11, f. 161v.
[18] Ibid.; Glos. Colln., Hannam-Clark papers, TS. notes on Glouc. bankers: 'Turner and Morris'.
[19] V.C.H. Glos. x. 19.
[20] Williams, Parl. Hist. of Glos. 211.

[21] Glos. R.O., D 3117/3957.
[22] G.B.R., B 3/14, f. 215.
[23] Ibid. 11, f. 187v.
[24] P.R.O., PROB 11/1565 (P.C.C. 80 Pakenham), ff. 169–72; V.C.H. Glos. vi. 20; G.B.R., G 3/AV 4.
[25] Below, Outlying Hamlets, man.
[26] G.B.R., B 3/12, f. 11.
[27] Ibid.
[28] Unless another reference is given, occupations of aldermen appointed from 1805 are from G.B.R., B 3/14, f. 215.
[29] Glos. Colln. 13221, f. 80v.; V.C.H. Glos. x. 210.
[30] V.C.H. Glos. x. 19.
[31] Glouc. Jnl. 27 July 1789; cf. ibid. 14 July 1888, rep. of presentation to T. Commeline.
[32] Glos. Colln., Hannam-Clark papers, TS. notes on Glouc. bankers: 'Wilton & Co.'.

ALDERMEN OF GLOUCESTER 1483–1835

Election (or, in brackets, first occurrence)		Occupation (where known)	Death, Resignation, or Removal
1824	John Cooke	attorney	res. 1829
1825	Shadrach Charleton	grocer[33]	res. 1831
1828	David Mowbray Walker	printer	(1835)
1829	Alex. Walker	printer	(1835)
1829	Wm. Hen. Hyett	landowner[34]	res. 1834
1829	Edw. Bower	currier	(1835)
1830	John Wm. Wilton	surgeon	(1835)
1831	Wm. Morgan Meyler	surgeon	(1835)
1834	Thos. Russell	banker[35]	(1835)
1834	Elisha Farmer Sadler	land surveyor[36]	(1835)

[33] 'Freemen of Glouc.', 174, 236. On his resignation he became master of the Bluecoat sch.

[34] V.C.H. Glos. xi. 68.

[35] Glos. Colln., Hannam-Clark papers, TS. notes on Glouc. bankers: 'Wilton & Co.'.

[36] Pigot's Dir. (1830), 375.

OUTLYING HAMLETS

OUTSIDE Gloucester but included in the parishes of some of its churches lay the hamlets of Barton Street, Kingsholm, Longford, Tuffley, Twigworth, and Wotton.[1] With the extraparochial places of Littleworth, North Hamlet, South Hamlet, and the vill of Wotton, which intermixed with them, they comprised an area of over 5,000 a. (2,023 ha.) in the early 19th century. It was irregular in shape and had many detached pieces, the complex boundary arising from the sharing of common fields and meadows with neighbouring parishes, particularly Barnwood and Upton St. Leonards. The main part, within which were many detached pieces of neighbouring parishes, lay east of the river Severn's eastern channel and in the south took in the west side of Robins Wood Hill. In places it was bounded by watercourses, including the Hatherley or Broadboard brook on parts of the north, the Sud brook on the south-east at Saintbridge, and Daniel's brook on part of the south-west.[2]

The origins of the hamlets are obscure. The complex boundaries between them suggest an early division of land between the six principal settlements in the area. Except in the case of Tuffley they correlated little with the parochial and manorial boundaries, which evidently derived from ancient divisions of land between the Crown, Gloucester Abbey, and St. Oswald's church. Much, though not all, of the extraparochial land belonged at one time to Llanthony Priory. The account printed here covers the hamlets, the extraparochial places, and Saintbridge, which was anciently part of Upton St. Leonards but was later absorbed by the city. Some pieces of South Hamlet islanded within or closely interconnected with Hempsted are treated with that parish below. This account describes the history of manors, agriculture, mills, and early local government. It also deals with early settlement in the area, apart from the suburbs of Gloucester in inner Barton Street and Littleworth, which are treated above. Suburban growth of Gloucester into the hamlets after c. 1800 and related aspects of their history, including churches, schools, and public services, are also treated above.

The boundaries of the hamlets were defined at inclosure in 1799 and later. The parochial division within them was complex: Tuffley, most of Barton Street and Wotton, and parts of Kingsholm, Longford, and Twigworth were in St. Mary de Lode parish; most of Kingsholm and Twigworth and parts of Longford and Wotton were in St. Catherine's (earlier St. Oswald's) parish; and parts of Barton Street were in St. Michael's parish.[3] St. Mary de Lode parish originally represented the lands of Gloucester Abbey[4] but the intricate boundary in Kingsholm, Longford, and Twigworth between it and St. Catherine's, confirmed in a mid 16th-century perambulation, was achieved by a division between the land belonging to houses respectively east and west of the main road leading northwards from Gloucester.[5]

In Barton Street the boundary between St. Mary de Lode and St. Michael's parishes, said in the early 18th century to follow the main road leading south-eastwards from the city,[6] was also irregular[7] and was used to divide Barton Street for civil purposes by the late 17th.[8] Barton St. Mary, the part of Barton Street in St. Mary's parish, contained c. 700 a. (c. 283 ha.) and took in much of the land on both sides of the road in an area extending from Gloucester to the Sud brook. It also had detached pieces at Saintbridge and elsewhere around the city, including some within Churchdown to the north-east, and part of Oxlease on Alney Island, west of Gloucester, belonged to it.[9] Barton St. Michael, the part of Barton Street in St. Michael's parish, comprised c. 500 a. (c. 202 ha.). It intermingled with Barton St. Mary and had detached pieces within Upton St. Leonards to the south-east.[10]

Kingsholm included c. 160 a. (c. 65 ha.) north of Gloucester and in detached pieces to the north and north-east, to the south-east at Wotton, and within Upton.[11] Longford comprised 897 a. (363 ha.); most of it lay north of Kingsholm in an area including several pieces of Sandhurst and extending eastwards to Innsworth and Longlevens, and there were detached pieces to the north, to the south and south-east of Gloucester, and within Upton.[12] Twigworth covered 426 a. (172.5 ha.) in a compact area north of Longford and in detached pieces to the south near Kingsholm, to the north between Norton and Sandhurst, and to the east within Down Hatherley.[13]

Wotton took in much land north-east of Gloucester in an area extending to Longlevens and Innsworth and had detached pieces around the city, within Barnwood to the south-east, and within Upton, Churchdown, and Sandhurst. Wotton St. Mary, the part of the hamlet in St. Mary de Lode parish, covered 826 a. (334.5 ha.), while Wotton St. Catherine, the part in St.

---

[1] This account, written in 1983 and revised in 1986, does not include the Vineyard and Woolstrop, which were sometimes accounted among the hamlets: Atkyns, *Glos.* 584, 677; Rudder, *Glos.* 577, 680; the Vineyard, which was in St. Mary de Lode parish, has been treated under Churcham, and Woolstrop under Quedgeley, to which it belonged: *V.C.H. Glos.* x. 15, 216.

[2] Glos. R.O., Q/RI 70 (maps); 79; G.D.R., T 1/86; Causton, *Map of Glouc.* (1843).

[3] Glos. R.O., Q/RI 70 (maps); G.D.R., T 1/86.

[4] Above, Churches and Chapels.

[5] G.D.R. vol. 89, depositions 8 Apr. 1603; vol. 205, depositions 30 June – 1 July 1641.

[6] Atkyns, *Glos.* 254.   [7] Causton, *Map of Glouc.* (1843).

[8] Cf. Glos. R.O., P 154/14/CW 2/2–3.

[9] Ibid. Q/RI 70 (maps B–D, F–G, L–N, P–R); Causton, *Map of Glouc.* (1843).

[10] Glos. R.O., Q/RI 70 (maps C, K–N, P–R); *Kelly's Dir. Glos.* (1870), 471.

[11] Glos. R.O., Q/RI 70 (maps B–G, K).

[12] Ibid. (maps A–H, K–L, Q–R); *Kelly's Dir. Glos.* (1870), 591–2.

[13] Glos. R.O., Q/RI 70 (maps A, C–G); *Kelly's Dir. Glos.* (1870), 663.

Catherine's parish, had only a few houses at Wotton.[14] Under the Extraparochial Places Act of 1857 some extraparochial houses and land at Wotton were annexed to Wotton St. Mary,[15] which at an inclosure in 1867 was allotted new pieces of land within Sandhurst.[16]

Tuffley lay 3 km. south of Gloucester, apart from the other hamlets, and shared open fields with neighbouring parishes. In the early 19th century it covered c. 770 a. (c. 312 ha.), the main part running up the west side of Robins Wood Hill to just below the summit. There were detached pieces on the east side of the hill, to the north and north-west, and within Quedgeley to the south and south-west.[17] The southern boundary was regularized at inclosure in 1866 to leave Tuffley with 765 a. (309.5 ha.).[18]

The extraparochial places of Littleworth, North Hamlet, South Hamlet, and the vill of Wotton became parishes under the Extraparochial Places Act of 1857.[17] Littleworth, recorded from 1665,[20] covered 12½ a. (4.25 ha.) south of Gloucester in and east of the Bristol road;[21] described sometimes as a hamlet, it was also known as Lower Southgate Street in the later 17th century and in the 18th.[22] The vill of Southgate Street mentioned c. 1500[23] was probably the area called Southgate which by 1558 formed a separate tithing with Woolstrop, a hamlet of Quedgeley.[24] Both Littleworth and Southgate may once have belonged to St. Owen's parish.[25]

North Hamlet, recorded from the early 18th century,[26] comprised miscellaneous parts, namely Gloucester castle (later the county prison) on the south-west side of Gloucester, a small island called the Naight in the Severn's eastern channel just below the castle, part of Pool Meadow on Alney Island, pieces at Wotton including the hospitals of St. Margaret and St. Mary Magdalen,[27] and a piece near Over Mill.[28] The area in 1870 was 26 a. (10.25 ha.).[29] In the early 19th century part of Castle Meads on Alney Island and the tithes of Meanham north of Gloucester paid land tax as parts of North Hamlet, but Castle Meads belonged to St. Nicholas's parish and Meanham to St. Catherine's.[30]

South Hamlet, recorded from 1755,[31] had an area of 634 a. (260 ha.).[32] It was formed principally by land of the Llanthony and Sheephouse estates, which had once belonged to Llanthony Priory and presumably to the parish of St. Owen.[33] The main part, irregular in shape, lay south of Gloucester and Littleworth and centred on the site of the priory. To the west a large portion extended to the river Severn north and west of Hempsted village and to the south-east a detached portion extended beyond the Gloucester–Bristol road towards Tuffley. The many detached pieces also included parts of Sud Meadow, south-west of Gloucester, and land south-west of Hempsted village and near Wotton.[34] The Llanthony estate, which in the 18th century was sometimes treated on its own for civil purposes,[35] paid tithes to Hempsted from 1662, and in the early 19th century South Hamlet was occasionally described as a hamlet of that parish.[36]

The vill of Wotton, which may once have been part of Wotton hamlet,[37] had been formed by 1776 from small fragments of land belonging to St. Bartholomew's Hospital; most were at Wotton and some within Barnwood and Sandhurst.[38] At inclosure in 1799 small pieces, mostly allotted for tithes belonging to St. Mary Magdalen's Hospital, were assigned to the vill,[39] which in the early 19th century had 59 a. (24 ha.).[40]

Much of the land in the hamlets and extraparochial places was added to Gloucester in the 19th and 20th centuries. Littleworth and parts of Barton St. Mary, Barton St. Michael, Wotton St. Mary, and South Hamlet came within the city in 1835 when its boundary was extended on the south and south-east.[41] All the hamlets except Twigworth and all the former extraparochial places lost parts to the city in 1874, when the county asylum and prison remained in Gloucestershire, forming within the city islands of 42 a. and 4 a. respectively.[42] The boundaries of the hamlets and former extraparochial places and those of adjoining parishes were rationalized in 1882 and 1885. At the latter date Barton St. Michael, North Hamlet, and the vill of Wotton were dismembered and Kingsholm St. Mary, which had anciently been attached to St. Mary de Lode, and Longford St. Catherine and Longford St. Mary, into which Longford had been divided for civil purposes, also disappeared; Barton St. Mary, St. Catherine with Kingsholm St. Catherine, South Hamlet, and Wotton St. Mary were re-formed as civil parishes within the municipal boundary, with Wotton St. Mary being

[14] Glos. R.O., Q/RI 70 (maps B–H, L–R); G.B.R., L 22/1/121, pp. 1–74, 97–112.

[15] Glos. R.O., P 154/12/VE 2/3; Census, 1861.

[16] Glos. R.O., Q/RI 122.   [17] G.D.R., T 1/86.

[18] Glos. R.O., Q/RI 32; Kelly's Dir. Glos. (1870), 662.

[19] Census, 1851–61.   [20] Glos. R.O., P 154/11/IN 1/1.

[21] Causton, Map of Glouc. (1843); O.S. Area Bk. Glouc. (1886).

[22] Glos. R.O., Q/SO 1, ff. 210v., 224v.; Glouc. Poor-Relief and Lighting Act, 4 Geo. III, c. 60.

[23] G.B.R., B 2/1, f. 230v.

[24] Ibid. f. 77v.; Glos. R.O., Q/SO 1, f. 101v.; V.C.H. Glos. x. 216.

[25] Cf. Glos. R.O., Q/SO 1, ff. 101v., 105v.; 2, f. 220v.

[26] Bodl. MS. Top. Glouc. c. 3, f. 197v.

[27] Glos. R.O., Q/RI 70 (maps D, N); Causton, Map of Glouc. (1843); Hall and Pinnell, Map of Glouc. (1780).

[28] Census, 1891.

[29] Kelly's Dir. Glos. (1870), 575.

[30] Glos. R.O., Q/REl 1A, Dudstone & King's Barton 1821; Causton, Map of Glouc. (1843); cf. Rudder, Glos. 577; Rudge, Hist. of Glos. ii. 150.   [31] Glos. R.O., Q/AV 2, rot. 8.

[32] Kelly's Dir. Glos. (1870), 575.

[33] Cf. P.R.O., C 115/K 2/6682, f. 107v.

[34] Glos. R.O., Q/RI 70 (maps D, P–R); 79; G.D.R., T 1/99; Causton, Map of Glouc. (1843).

[35] Glos. R.O., Q/SR 1773 D; Atkyns, Glos. 676.

[36] Scudamore Churches Endowment Act, 13 & 14 Chas. II, c. 11 (Priv. Act); Census, 1801; cf. G.D.R., T 1/99.

[37] Cf. G.D.R. vol. 397, f. 34.

[38] Glos. R.O., D 936/E 147; Poor Law Abstract, 1804, 176–7.

[39] Glos. R.O., Q/RI 70 (maps C–H, L–N, P, R).

[40] G.B.R., L 22/1/121, pp. 77–94, 115–20.

[41] Glos. Colln. NF 12.59; cf. Causton, Map of Glouc. (1843).

[42] Glouc. Extension and Improvement Act, 1874, 37 & 38 Vic. c. 111 (Local); O.S. Area Bk. Glouc. (1886).

designated Wotton St. Mary (Within); the areas north and north-east of the city were included in the new civil parishes of Longford and Wotton St. Mary (Without); and Tuffley and Twigworth formed civil parishes. Walham and Sud Meadow, the principal meadows in which several hamlets had shared, were included in Longford and Hempsted respectively, and that part of Oxlease outside the city in Maisemore.[43] In 1896 Gloucester's civil parishes and St. Nicholas Without, a parish created from the prison in 1894, were merged in a single parish. The asylum had been detached from Wotton St. Mary (Within) in 1894 to form the civil parish of Wotton Vill; a small part was added to Gloucester in 1910 and the rest in 1951.[44]

Tuffley parish was dismembered in 1900 when the northern part was absorbed by Gloucester. The rest, transferred to Quedgeley and Whaddon,[45] was added to Gloucester in 1935 along with parts of Longford, Maisemore, and Wotton St. Mary (Without). The remainder of Wotton St. Mary (Without), save for a few acres given to Barnwood and Churchdown, was included with parts of Barnwood, Churchdown, and Hucclecote in the new civil parish of Longlevens, north-east of Gloucester. Parts of Longlevens were added to Gloucester in 1951 and in 1967 when the remainder was re-formed as Innsworth civil parish. In 1967 part of Longford was also transferred to Gloucester and a minor boundary adjustment made to the remainder.[46] In 1983 most of the land of the former hamlets and extraparochial places not absorbed by Gloucester was in Innsworth, Longford, and Twigworth civil parishes.

Upton St. Leonards, which lies south-east of Gloucester, anciently extended north-westwards to the Sud brook at Saintbridge and had many detached pieces around Gloucester, including several in Barton Street and Sud Meadow.[47] The irregularities in its boundaries were removed in 1882 and 1885; at the latter date the pieces within the city boundary from 1874 were transferred to Barton St. Mary. Land at Saintbridge was added to Gloucester in 1900 and 1935.[48]

The area is flat and lies at under 30 m., except in the south-east where it included part of a low rise at Coney Hill and in the south where it runs up almost to the summit at 198 m. of Robins Wood Hill, an outlier of the Cotswolds. The land lies mostly on the Lower Lias, on which are large deposits of gravel, but bordering the Severn, which is liable to flood, it is formed by alluvium. Robins Wood Hill is formed by strata of Marlstone, the Upper Lias, sand, and the Inferior Oolite. At Saintbridge (formerly Sandbridge) is a small area of alluvium.[49] The gravel at Kingsholm was worked for many years before 1819.[50]

The names of Tuffley and Wotton indicate that parts of the area were once thickly wooded.[51] Sutgrove or Sudgrove, recorded in the mid 12th century, was a wood south of Gloucester towards Tuffley. It had disappeared by 1593.[52] In 1086 Gloucester Abbey had a wood measuring 5 furlongs by 3 furlongs near Gloucester.[53] It probably represented woodland in Tuffley in which the abbot claimed free warren in 1287.[54] In the later 17th century Tuffley manor had a park on the south-west side of Robins Wood Hill.[55] In the early 18th century Tuffley remained heavily wooded and there were many woods and groves north-east of Gloucester,[56] where a small wood was recorded at Paygrove in the early 12th century.[57] At Twigworth a park mentioned in 1437 belonged to Kingsholm manor.[58] Much of the land of the hamlets was in open fields and common riverine meadows, principally Walham and Sud Meadow to the north and south-west of Gloucester respectively. Inclosure was a gradual process, which culminated in 1799 in parliamentary inclosure of a large area north and east of Gloucester. It was completed south and southwest of the city in 1815 and in Tuffley in 1866.[59] In 1983 the land in agricultural use was mainly pasture.

Above Gloucester the easternmost of the Severn's three channels, flowing near Kingsholm, was allowed to silt up at an early date and in 1799 was represented east of Walham by a strip of land called Tween Dyke and west of Kingsholm by a brook called the Old Severn;[60] Tween Dyke was in 1607 described as a highway but later was a common meadow, sometimes called Queen Dyke.[61] Just below Gloucester the Naight ceased to be an island during the building of a canal basin in the late 18th century.[62] The hamlets were drained by streams and ditches falling into the Severn. The river Twyver, the principal stream, divided into two channels east of Gloucester, one emerging from the town near Alvin gate before joining the Old Severn near Kingsholm.[63] The Sud brook, which ran south of Gloucester, was called Mare brook at Saintbridge in 1290.[64] The

[43] Census, 1891; Local Government Board's Confirmation Act, 47 & 48 Vic. c. 82 (Local); O.S. Area Bk. Glouc. (1886); Hempsted (1886); Longford (1886); Maisemore (1886); Tuffley (1886); Twigworth (1885); Wotton St. Mary (Without) (1885).
[44] Census, 1901–11; 1951.
[45] Ibid. 1901; O.S. Map 6″, Glos. XXXIII. NE. (1891 and 1903 edns.); NW. (1888 and 1903 edns.).
[46] Census, 1931 (pt. ii); 1951; 1971.
[47] G.D.R., T 1/189.
[48] Census, 1871–1931; O.S. Map 6″, Glos. XXXIII. NE. (1903 edn.).
[49] Geol. Surv. Map 1″, solid, sheet 43 SE. (1855 edn.); sheet 44 (1856 edn.); ibid. 1/50,000, solid and drift, sheet 234 (1972 edn.); P.N. Glos. (E.P.N.S.), ii. 141.
[50] Fosbrooke, Glouc. 11.
[51] P.N. Glos. (E.P.N.S.), ii. 142, 158.
[52] Ibid. 140–1; P.R.O., E 134/35 Eliz. I East./23.
[53] Dom. Bk. (Rec. Com.), i. 165v.
[54] Plac. de Quo Warr. (Rec. Com.), 247.
[55] Glos. R.O., D 3117/11; Atkyns, Glos. 677; cf. G.D.R., T 1/86.
[56] Bodl. MS. Top. Glouc. c. 2, f. 125 and v.
[57] Hist. & Cart. Mon. Glouc. (Rolls Ser.), i. 59.
[58] P.R.O., C 139/79, no. 14; Glos. R.O., D 326/E 1, f. 55.
[59] Glos. R.O., Q/RI 70, 79, 32.
[60] Ibid. 70 (maps B, no. 43; C, nos. 33–5, 90–2, 99–100, 126; D, nos. 75–8).
[61] Ibid. D 326/E 1, f. 59v.; M 24; G.B.R., J 4/2.
[62] Hall and Pinnell, Map of Glouc. (1780); Cole, Map of Glouc. (1805).
[63] Hall and Pinnell, Map of Glouc. (1780); cf. Trans. B.G.A.S. lxxxiii. 80.
[64] Glouc. Corp. Rec. p. 283.

course of the Wotton brook north-east of Gloucester was known as the Winter ditch in the early 14th century.[65]

Main roads radiating from Gloucester ran through the hamlets. The Roman Ermin Street to Cirencester ran eastwards from the outer north gate to Wotton Pitch where it joined the route from Kingsholm;[66] the latter was known in 1799 as Gallows Road or Lane[67] and later as Denmark Road. Ermin Street has remained an important thoroughfare, linking Gloucester with London and Oxford,[68] and in the mid 13th century Wotton and Barnwood were responsible for, and travellers contributed to, the repair of a bridge over the Wotton brook.[69] Under an Act of 1698 the section between Gloucester and Birdlip together with the Oxford road climbing Crickley Hill in Badgeworth was a turnpike for 20 years, tolls being collected by the county justices to supplement parish highway rates. Those roads were turnpiked again between 1723, when trustees were appointed to administer them,[70] and 1871.[71] Gloucester corporation was responsible for maintaining the section between the city boundary and Wotton Pitch by 1651[72] and until 1848.[73]

Gloucester was linked with Cheltenham and Winchcombe by a road leading north-eastwards from Ermin Street at Wotton Pitch.[74] In the mid 13th century Gloucester Abbey and the archbishop of York had responsibility for maintaining Cole bridge, which carried the road over the Wotton brook.[75] The road, which in the mid 16th century provided an alternative route to Tewkesbury,[76] was called Gallows Lane in the late 17th century,[77] a gallows standing near Cole bridge.[78] The Cheltenham road was turnpiked between 1756 and 1871.[79] The Innsworth road, which branched from it near Cole bridge, was known in its south part as Winterditch Road in 1799[80] and as Oxstalls Lane later.

The Tewkesbury road ran northwards from Alvin gate through the settlements of Kingsholm, Longford, and Twigworth.[81] In Kingsholm it was joined by a road from the blind gate,[82] which in its south part was known in 1803 as Dean's Walk and

in its north part in 1722 as Snake Lane (later Edwy Parade).[83] Bridges and a causeway carried the Tewkesbury road over water courses and low-lying meadows in Longford, which took its name from the crossing.[84] There was possibly a medieval chapel at the south end of the crossing, where a close east of the road was called Chapel Hay.[85] Offerings at a wayside cross, recorded nearby from 1501,[86] belonged to St. Mary de Lode rectory.[87] In the mid 13th century Longford was responsible for repairing a bridge and the lord of Kingsholm manor one near Twigworth.[88] The causeway was maintained in 1541 by two men, to whom Robert Gibbs left the reversion of a house.[89] The Twigworth bridge, for the repair of which Henry III, after crossing it, authorized the levying of tolls in 1251,[90] presumably spanned the Hatherley brook at the site of Broadboard bridge, recorded in 1824.[91] The Tewkesbury road was turnpiked between Gloucester and Norton Mill in 1756 under the same Act as the Cheltenham road and ceased to be a turnpike in 1871.[92] A road which leaves it at Twigworth was part of a lower road to Tewkesbury through Bishop's Norton until the 19th century.[93]

The Bristol road ran south-westwards from the south gate of Gloucester and in the mid 13th century Llanthony Priory was responsible for repairing the bridge which carried it across the Sud brook.[94] The road was a turnpike from 1726, when it also linked Gloucester with Bath,[95] until 1877.[96] South of the Sud brook a road called Sandy Lane in 1777 branched eastwards to join an old route from Barton Street.[97] That route, known in its north part as Barton Lane (later Park Road and Parkend Road),[98] ran south-westwards to Tuffley, where it crossed the lower slopes of Robins Wood Hill, and on to Edge in Painswick and Paganhill in Stroud.[99] Millbrook Street, which runs northwards from Barton Street, follows the line of Goosewhite Lane, recorded in the early 13th century and known later as Goose Lane.[1]

The road running south-eastwards from Gloucester's east gate along Barton Street once forked just north of the Sud brook at Saintbridge

[65] Glouc. Cath. Libr., deeds and seals, ii, f. 20; cf. Glos. R.O., Q/RI 70 (map E, nos. 144–5).

[66] Margary, *Rom. Roads*, i. 123.

[67] Glos. R.O., Q/RI 70; Causton, *Map of Glouc.* (1843).

[68] e.g. *Cal. Papal Reg.* v. 390; Glos. Colln. prints GL 65.27.

[69] P.R.O., C 115/K 2/6684, f. 127v.

[70] Glouc. Roads Act, 9 & 10 Wm. III, c. 18; 9 Geo. I, c. 32.

[71] Annual Turnpike Acts Continuance Act, 34 & 35 Vic. c. 115.

[72] Above, Public Services, paving, cleaning, and lighting.

[73] G.B.R., B 3/17, pp. 285–6.

[74] Glos. Colln. prints GL 65.27; Glos. R.O., D 184/M 2, ct. 11 Sept. 1480.

[75] P.R.O., C 115/K 2/6684, f. 127v.

[76] *Trans. B.G.A.S.* lxvii. 276–8.

[77] Glos. R.O., Q/SIb 1, ff. 40v., 92v.; G.B.R., B 3/3, pp. 505–6.

[78] Glos. R.O., D 3117/128; D 2957/192.72.

[79] Glouc. Roads Act, 29 Geo. II, c. 58; Annual Turnpike Acts Continuance Act, 34 & 35 Vic. c. 115.

[80] Glos. R.O., Q/RI 70.

[81] Cf. Hockaday Abs. ccxvi, 1546, will of Joan Cooke.

[82] *Glouc. Rental, 1455*, p. xvi.

[83] Glos. R.O., D 936/E 114; E 12/9, f.8v.; Causton, *Map of Glouc.* (1843).

[84] *P.N. Glos.* (E.P.N.S.), ii. 149.

[85] Glos. R.O., Q/RI 70 (map B, nos. 92–3).

[86] Ibid. P 329/MI 1, rot. 44; Glouc. Cath. Libr., Reg. Abb. Braunche, p. 8.

[87] *Valor Eccl.* (Rec. Com.), ii. 416.

[88] P.R.O., C 115/K 2/6684, f. 127v.

[89] Hockaday Abs. ccxiv.

[90] *Close R.* 1251–3, 9.

[91] Greenwood, *Map of Glos.* (1824).

[92] Glouc. Roads Act, 29 Geo. II, c. 58; Annual Turnpike Acts Continuance Act, 34 & 35 Vic. c. 115.

[93] Glos. R.O., Q/RI 70; O.S. Map 6", Glos. XXV. NE. (1883 edn.).

[94] P.R.O., C 115/K 2/6684, f. 127v.

[95] Glos. Roads Act, 12 Geo. I, c. 24; *V.C.H. Glos.* x. 170.

[96] Annual Turnpike Acts Continuance Act, 39 & 40 Vic. c. 39.

[97] Taylor, *Map of Glos.* (1777).

[98] Bd. of Health Map (1852).

[99] Glos. Colln. prints GL 65.27; Taylor, *Map of Glos.* (17777).

[1] Glouc. Cath. Libr., deeds and seals, v, f. 17; Causton, *Map of Glouc.* (1843).

with one road, perhaps that known as Dancers Lane in the late 13th century,[2] apparently running south-eastwards over the Wheatridge towards Upton St. Leonards. The other, more important, road ran southwards to cross the brook, some way beyond which it forked in Upton for Cranham and Painswick.[3] In the mid 13th century Upton, Saintbridge, Matson, Sneedham, and Cranham were responsible for, and travellers contributed to, the repair of the bridge at Saintbridge.[4] Nearby, at a fork just north of the brook, the road passed a chapel or hermitage,[5] the lessee of which under a grant of 1531 was to spend 26s. 8d. a year on repairs to the highway between the town gate and Upton church.[6] The bridge presumably took the name of Mary bridge, recorded in 1589,[7] from the chapel. From c. 1672 the rent of a house left by John Wyman was used for the repair of the road between the bridge and the site of Abbot's Barton manor nearer the city[8] and in 1860 the county justices ordered repairs to be made to the bridge.[9] The Painswick road, which also linked Gloucester with Stroud, was administered as a turnpike by the trustees of the 1726 Act but their powers were disputed. An Act of 1746 confirmed the turnpiking of the section between the east gate and the top of Painswick Hill,[10] and in 1778 the road was placed under a separate trust.[11] The road was a turnpike until 1876,[12] but because of its steepness carriage traffic between Gloucester and Stroud at the beginning of the 19th century preferred the longer route by way of the Bristol road and Stonehouse.[13] A new Stroud road through Pitchcombe was built under an Act of 1818.[14] It left the Bristol road at the Sud brook, Sandy Lane being closed in 1822, and followed the Tuffley road for part of its course.[15] It remained a turnpike until 1875.[16]

The low-lying land outside Gloucester was not suitable for early settlement, which until the early 19th century remained small and mostly restricted to the main roads.[17] KINGSHOLM, which had been the site of a Roman military base at a passage of the Severn before the foundation of Gloucester,[18] lies 1 km. NNE. of the Cross. It was also the site of an Anglo-Saxon royal palace, which stood between the Old Severn and the Sandhurst road. The palace later became a manor house and was demolished before 1591.[19] In 1327 three men were assessed for the subsidy in Kingsholm,[20] which in the later 13th century included several houses scattered along the Tewkesbury road, then known as Kingsholm Street.[21] That occupied by a man surnamed 'atte vineyard' in 1304 presumably stood north of the river Twyver, where a vineyard was later recorded.[22] Most building took place around the junction of the Tewkesbury road with the Sandhurst and Wotton roads where settlement remained predominantly rural in the early 17th century. It included the medieval White Barn north of the Wotton road[23] (later Gallows Lane), at the entrance to which had once been a green,[24] perhaps that belonging to the lord of Kingsholm manor in 1304.[25] To the south-west, by the road to the blind gate, was Tulwell, the site of a manor[26] described in the mid 14th century as a hamlet of St. Oswald's parish.[27] At the beginning of the siege of 1643 eleven houses and a barn at Kingsholm were fired or pulled down along with houses nearer the city,[28] and in 1672 only eight houses, one of them new, were assessed for hearth tax in Kingsholm.[29] In 1801 Kingsholm had a population of 139 in 30 houses,[30] most of which were replaced or demolished when the area was absorbed by Gloucester. The oldest surviving buildings are an 18th-century cottage on the Sandhurst road and a house, which dates from the 18th century, north of Kingsholm Square. A pound in the angle of the Tewkesbury and Sandhurst roads, recorded from 1607,[31] was maintained by the lord of King's Barton manor.[32] Following the erection of a tollhouse on that corner in 1822 the pound was moved to Gallows Lane.[33] In 1755 Kingsholm had two victuallers;[34] one kept the White Hart in 1778[35] and the other presumably the Red Lion, recorded from the early 18th century.[36]

On the Sandhurst road outside Kingsholm a cottage was remodelled in the 1830s.[37] Further

[2] Glouc. Cath. Libr., Reg. Abb. Froucester B, p. 275; cf. Glos. R.O., Q/RI 70 (map L, nos. 97–9, 123).

[3] Glos. Colln. prints GL 65.27; G.D.R., T 1/189.

[4] P.R.O., C 115/K 2/6684, f. 127v.

[5] Glos. R.O., Q/RI 70 (map P, no. 136); above, Churches and Chapels, non-par. chap.

[6] Glouc. Cath. Libr., Reg. Abb. Malvern, ii, f. 41v.

[7] Glos. R.O., P 347/MI 1.

[8] G.D.R. wills 1640/84; G.B.R., B 3/3, pp. 548, 562; 14th Rep. Com. Char. 38; cf. Glos. R.O., D 3270/19679, pp. 18, 131, 489; Abs. of City Treasurer's Acct. 1879–80: copy in G.B.R.

[9] Glos. R.O., Q/CI 2, p. 18.

[10] Glos. Roads Act, 12 Geo. I, c. 24; 19 Geo. II, c. 18.

[11] Glouc. and Stroud Road Act, 18 Geo. III, c. 98.

[12] Annual Turnpike Acts Continuance Act, 39 & 40 Vic. c. 39.

[13] V.C.H. Glos. xi. 101.

[14] Glouc. and Stroud Road Act, 58 Geo. III, c. 1 (Local and Personal).

[15] Bryant, Map of Glos. (1824); Glos. R.O., Q/SRh 1822 D/5.

[16] Annual Turnpike Acts Continuance Act, 36 & 37 Vic. c. 90.

[17] Below, Figs. 25–6.

[18] Antiq. Jnl. lv (2), 267–8.

[19] Below, man.; Glos. R.O., D 326/E 1, ff. 53v., 58v.; Q/RI 70 (map C, no. 122).

[20] Glos. Subsidy Roll, 1327, 6.

[21] Glouc. Cath. Libr., Reg. Abb. Froucester B, pp. 208–26.

[22] P.R.O., C 133/113, no. 5; Glos. R.O., D 936/E 118/43.

[23] Glos. R.O., D 326/E 1, ff. 53v.–56v., 58v.–59v.; G.B.R., J 4/1, no. 18.

[24] Cf. Glos. R.O., Q/RI 70 (map D, no. 70); Causton, Map of Glouc. (1843).

[25] P.R.O., C 133/113, no. 5.

[26] Below, man.; Glouc. Rental, 1455, p. xvi; Glos. R.O., D 936/E 114; Q/RI 70 (map D, no. 87).

[27] Inq. Non. (Rec. Com.), 415.

[28] G.B.R., H 2/3, pp. 211, 214.

[29] P.R.O., E 179/247/14, rot. 31d.

[30] Census, 1801.

[31] Glos. R.O., D 326/E 1, f. 54; Q/RI 70 (map C, no. 140).

[32] Ibid. D 45/M 3; E 6; D 326/M 1, ct. 21 Oct. 1790.

[33] Ibid. D 204/1/2; Causton, Map of Glouc. (1843).

[34] Glos. R.O., Q/AV 2, rot. 8.

[35] Ibid. D 326/E 4, ff. 38–9; Q/RI 70 (map C, no. 148).

[36] Bodl. MS. Top. Glouc. c. 3, f. 41v.; G.B.R., King's Barton ct. bk. 1769–1810.

[37] Cf. Glos. R.O., Q/RI 70 (map B, no. 137).

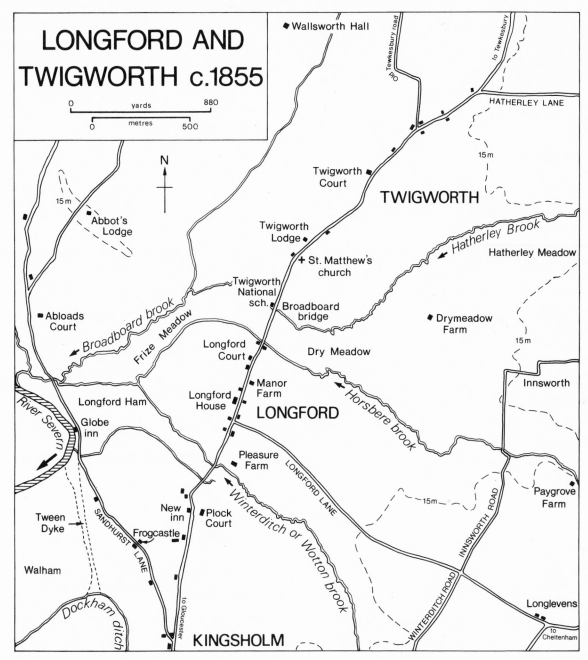

Fig. 25

north two houses called Frogcastle in 1745[38] formed a single dwelling by the end of the century.[39] It was destroyed by fire in 1983. A farmstead opposite dates from the 19th century. To the west in Walham in the early 19th century a farmstead was built where the Twyver joined the Severn,[40] and in the late 1830s there was a riverside inn higher up called the Jolly Waterman[41] and probably another, later called the Globe, at a public wharf alongside the Sandhurst road.[42] The latter inn closed in the 1970s.[43]

On the Tewkesbury road north of Kingsholm a house was converted into three cottages in the early 19th century.[44] Further north in LONGFORD there was a small early settlement at the south end of the causeway, where a medieval cross and possibly a chapel stood. There was evidently a house there by the early 13th century, when a man surnamed of the plock was recorded,[45] and Plock Court, east of the road, occupied the site of a medieval manor house.[46] In the later 18th century the buildings opposite included a farm-

[38] Glouc. Jnl. 5 Nov. 1745.
[39] Glos. R.O., Q/RI 70 (map B, no. 114).
[40] Ibid. (map C, no. 80); G.D.R., T 1/16.
[41] G.B.R., L 22/1/121, pp. 3–4.
[42] G.D.R., T 1/156; G.B.R., L 6/4/9; Glos. R.O., Q/RI 70.

[43] Cf. O.S. Map 1/2,500, SO 8220 (1970 edn.).
[44] Glos. R.O., Q/RI 70 (map B, no. 112); G.D.R., T 1/156.
[45] Glouc. Corp. Rec. pp. 122, 179.
[46] Below, man.

house belonging to the Gloucester poor-relief corporation and an inn recorded in 1799.[47]

The main part of Longford village lies 2 km. NNE. of Gloucester Cross along the causeway carrying the road between the Wotton and Horsbere brooks. It presumably included most of the 18 people assessed for the subsidy in Longford in 1327[48] and most of the 26 houses assessed for hearth tax there in 1672.[49] The village had several farmhouses and other substantial residences in the late 18th century,[50] when R. B. Cheston, a Gloucester surgeon and aspiring landowner, built his seat there and the road and the village's appearance were improved.[51] In the north Manor Farm includes a timber-framed farmhouse with an early 18th-century brick wing. Longford Court dates from a late 18th-century rebuilding of the Olive family's farmhouse, which had been an inn.[52] Longford Lodge also dates from the 18th century when it was the centre of an estate which the Hyett family had inherited from the Webbs.[53] In the south Pleasure Farm, an early 18th-century brick farmhouse which in 1799 belonged to Anthony Ellis,[54] was used as a lorry depot for several years before 1983 when it was demolished to make room for a housing estate. In 1801 Longford St. Catherine and Longford St. Mary together had 36 houses with a population of 166.[55] Many buildings in Longford village date from the 19th century, including the Queen's Head inn, which had opened by 1851,[56] and in the 20th century the village's appearance was much altered by the building of houses for people working in Gloucester.

TWIGWORTH village, which is scattered along the Tewkesbury road 4 km. NNE. of the Cross, had been founded by the early 13th century[57] and had a medieval chapel.[58] In 1327 only four people were assessed for the subsidy in Twigworth,[59] and the village remained small. In 1672 there were 13 houses assessed for hearth tax[60] and in 1801 there were 13 houses with a population of 59.[61] The main concentration of buildings, at the fork of the former lower road to Tewkesbury, includes a thatched timber-framed farmhouse of the early 17th century called the Manor House,[62] and a brick farmhouse of the 18th century. Opposite is a 17th-century timber-framed cottage. Some way north-east of the main group Court Farm comprises a timber-framed farmhouse and barn of the 17th century. Twigworth Court, the largest

house, stands south-west of the main group and dates from a rebuilding of a farmhouse; it has large ranges of farm buildings.[63] The Dayhouse, a farmhouse recorded from 1607, was 1 km. to the south-west on the site of Twigworth Lodge,[64] which dates from a 19th-century rebuilding and was a hotel by the late 1970s. A number of houses were added to Twigworth in the 19th century, and a church was built on the main road towards Longford in 1842 and a vicarage house and school were built nearby in the 1850s. In the early 1980s, though there was a large caravan park in the village, Twigworth remained rural in character.

WOTTON was an early settlement on Ermin Street 1.5 km. ENE. of the Cross. In 1327 fourteen people were assessed for the subsidy in Wotton.[65] Wotton Pitch, where Ermin Street is joined by the Kingsholm and Cheltenham roads, was originally called Dudstone and was evidently the ancient meeting place of that hundred.[66] The hospital of St. Mary Magdalen stood to the south and that of St. Margaret lower down towards Gloucester.[67] By the early 18th century two mansions had been built near Wotton Pitch, Wotton Court to the east and Wotton House to the south-east. John Blanch, a clothier who bought the Wotton Court estate in 1683,[68] had by 1723 advanced a scheme to make Wotton a centre for the cloth and stocking trade and built at Wotton Pitch five houses and, for use as an exchange, a large inn. The inn, on the corner of the Cheltenham road and known in 1726 as the Golden Fleece[69] (later the Fleece), was of three storeys. The houses formed a brick terrace north of the Cirencester road;[70] later in the century the east part was replaced by a grander house and the west part was used as a tollhouse until 1792.[71] A house built south of Wotton Court in the 18th century was enlarged to the south in the 19th.[72]

Wotton, which in the mid 16th century included a great messuage called Seger's Lane or Place,[73] expanded eastwards along Ermin Street towards Barnwood at an early date. The Old Rectory, in the east end of Wotton, occupies the site of a farmhouse called Colliers, which belonged in the early 17th century to the Capel family[74] and was acquired for St. Aldate's rectory in 1759.[75] It was rebuilt in the mid 19th century, and some fittings were brought from the Tolsey in the early 1890s.[76] Further east the Old House incorporates a 17th-century timber-framed farmhouse,

[47] Glos. R.O., Q/RI 70 (map C, nos. 17–23).
[48] *Glos. Subsidy Roll, 1327*, 7, 32.
[49] P.R.O., E 179/247/14, rot. 31d.
[50] Glos. R.O., D 6/E 4, no. 16; Q/RI 70 (maps B and E).
[51] *Glouc. New Guide* (1802), 111–12; below, man.
[52] Glos. R.O., Q/REl 1A, Dudstone & King's Barton 1779 and 1790, Longford; Q/RI 70 (map B, no. 21).
[53] Ibid. D 6/E 4, no. 16; G.D.R. wills 1715/85.
[54] Glos. R.O., Q/RI 70 (map B, no. 72).
[55] *Census*, 1801.
[56] P.R.O., HO 107/1961.
[57] *Glouc. Corp. Rec.* pp. 128, 156.
[58] *Trans. B.G.A.S.* xliii. 110.
[59] *Glos. Subsidy Roll, 1327*, 6.
[60] P.R.O., E 179/247/14, rot. 31d.
[61] *Census*, 1801.
[62] Cf. Glos. R.O., D 1297, Twigworth, Herbert fam., deeds 1729–1929; Q/RI 70 (map A, no. 22).

[63] Below, man.
[64] Glos. R.O., D 326/E 1, f. 52v.; Bryant, *Map of Glos.* (1824).
[65] *Glos. Subsidy Roll, 1327*, 6, 33.
[66] *Glouc. Corp. Rec.* p. 119; *Public Works in Med. Law*, i (Selden Soc. xxxii), p. 104; *P.N. Glos.* (E.P.N.S.), ii. 137.
[67] Glos. R.O., Q/RI 70 (map D, nos. 119–29).
[68] Below, man.
[69] *Glouc. Jnl.* 9 Sept. 1723; 28 Dec. 1725; G.B.R., J 3/8, ff. 211v.–216. [70] G.B.R., J 4/1, no. 15.
[71] Glos. R.O., Q/RI 70 (map G, nos. 90–1); D 204/3/2.
[72] Ibid. Q/RI 70 (map G, nos. 92–3).
[73] P.R.O., SC 6/Hen. VIII/1212, rot. 6; *L. & P. Hen. VIII*, xvii, p. 638; Glos. R.O., D 936/L 11, abs. of deeds 11 July 1774.
[74] Glos. Colln. prints GL 65.27; Glos. R.O., D 3117/1207.
[75] Glos. R.O., P 154/6/CW 3/2; Q/RI 70 (map M, no. 5).
[76] Ibid. D 2299/3893; Verey, *Glos.* ii. 254.

once probably L-shaped in plan, and 18th-century brick additions to the front and back. In 1755 Wotton had five victuallers.[77] The Plough alehouse recorded in 1750 was probably in Wotton.[78] The Swan at Wotton, which by 1750 occupied a building west of Colliers belonging to Barnwood,[79] closed in the late 1780s.[80] It had been the home of Mary Cole, who married Frederick Augustus Berkeley, earl of Berkeley, in 1796, an alleged earlier marriage resulting in the Berkeley peerage case of 1810.[81] Wotton, which had 28 houses with a population of 156 in 1801,[82] was thereafter subject to suburban development and most earlier buildings disappeared. The Fleece was demolished in 1964.[83]

On the Cheltenham road north-east of Wotton there was a farmhouse at Wellsprings in 1722.[84] The place was known as Puckstool in the mid 1780s when the farmhouse, which had been rebuilt, was an inn.[85] Early settlement at Innsworth north-east of Gloucester may have included the Norman's house recorded in 1126;[86] it presumably stood near the Horsbere brook, which was called Norman's brook in the early 16th century.[87] There were two early farmsteads at Innsworth. Drymeadow Farm was called Wicks Hay in 1640 when it belonged to Edward Capel, a Bristol merchant.[88] It was later rebuilt in brick and in 1983 the buildings were mainly derelict. Paygrove or Plackets Farm, by the Horsbere brook,[89] may have belonged to James Elly, an attorney, in 1724.[90] In 1779 its owner was Luke Hook,[91] master of Sir Thomas Rich's school, Gloucester.[92] In the 19th century several farmhouses and cottages were built at Innsworth, including Innsworth Farm,[93] demolished in the mid 20th century to make room for a housing estate, and Innsworth House Farm, which was new in 1870.[94] Field Farm, east of Longford, had been built by the early 1880s.[95]

BARTON STREET grew up outside Gloucester's east gate along the road on which were the bartons of manors of the Crown and Gloucester Abbey.[96] The inner part west of the Tuffley road formed an early suburb of Gloucester with which it is treated

above. Settlement further out on Barton Street had apparently started by the 13th century when the Fokett family owned land there.[97] In the 1590s it extended beyond a bend in the road at the junction of a lane (later India Road), where several dwellings belonged to Upton St. Leonards.[98] One called the World's End in 1658 was later divided into three dwellings, which included the Red Lion inn in 1780;[99] by that time the World's End was used as the name of the area.[1] The India House, recorded there in 1780, was later an inn.[2] A house in which Alderman Lawrence Wilshire (d. 1612) lived[3] was probably that east of Goose Lane (later Millbrook Street) which Robert Halford had acquired by 1653.[4] Known later as Lower Barton House, it was demolished in the mid 1880s.[5] In the mid 18th century two farmhouses were built in outer Barton Street,[6] where in the 1770s houses were strung out along the road to the World's End. Further out was a dwelling called the Rudge House in 1789 and cottages extended along the south-west side of the road as far as one which in 1799 was the Chequers inn. There were also a few cottages in nearby Mop Lane (later Upton Street).[7] The pound in Barton Street in 1637[8] may have been that for Dudstone hundred moved to waste ground opposite the Tuffley road in 1778.[9] On the Tuffley road there was an outlying homestead south of the Sud brook in 1731.[10] In 1801 Barton St. Mary and Barton St. Michael together had 136 houses with a population of 697,[11] most of it presumably in the city's older suburbs. In outer Barton Street, where there was considerable suburban development from the mid 19th century, the only early dwelling to survive in 1983 was an 18th-century brick building.

Further along the road at Saintbridge there was a small settlement south of the Sud brook in Upton parish in the late 12th century.[12] In 1327 ten people were assessed for the subsidy at Saintbridge,[13] which was described as a vill c. 1500[14] and was joined temporarily to Matson parish between 1656 and 1660.[15] At the junction of a road known in 1290 as Bull Lane (later Cottes-

[77] Glos. R.O., Q/AV 2, rot. 8.
[78] Ibid. D 1740/E 3, list of copyholds.
[79] Ibid. ff. 14, 25; Q/RI 70 (map M, no. 4).
[80] Ibid. D 936/M 1/2; D 326/M 24.
[81] Ibid. Q/REl 1A, Dudstone & King's Barton 1780, Barnwood; Complete Peerage, ii. 142–3.
[82] Census, 1801.
[83] Citizen, 29 July 1964.
[84] Fosbrooke, Glouc. 154.
[85] Glos. R.O., D 2957/192.79, 84; Q/RI 70 (map G, no. 60).
[86] Hist. & Cart. Mon. Glouc. ii. 89; cf. Earldom of Glouc Charters, ed. Patterson, pp. 85–6.
[87] Glouc. Cath. Libr., Reg. Abb. Malvern, ii, ff, 5v.–6.
[88] Glos. R.O., D 3117/1207; D 1406, Wood fam., misc. est. papers 1799–1830, agreement 1799.
[89] O.S. Map 1″, sheet 44 (1828 edn.).
[90] G.D.R. wills 1728/296.
[91] Glos. R.O., Q/REl 1A, Dudstone & King's Barton 1779, Wotton.
[92] G.B.R., B 3/10, ff. 5v., 70; 11, f. 262.
[93] Below, man.
[94] O.S. Map 1″, sheet 44 (1828 edn.); Glos. R.O., D 2299/367.
[95] O.S. Map 6″, Glos. XXV. SE. (1887 edn.).

[96] Below, man.
[97] Glos. R.O., D 3117/257–61; Glouc. Cath. Libr., Reg. Abb. Froucester B, pp. 271–8.
[98] Glos. R.O., P 347A/FM 1; cf. ibid. Q/RI 70 (map M).
[99] Ibid. D 3117/272, 283; G.B.R., King's Barton ct. bk. 1769–1810, ct. 23 Oct. 1780.
[1] Rudder, Glos. 206.
[2] Glos. R.O., D 6/E 4, no. 13.
[3] Glos. Colln. prints GL 65.27; above, Aldermen of Glouc. 1483–1835.
[4] Glos. R.O., D 6/T 1; P.R.O., C 78/1104, no. 2.
[5] All Saints' Par. Memories (1925), 11: Glos. Colln. N 5.10.
[6] Glouc. Jnl. 26 Jan. 1742.
[7] Rudder, Glos. 206; Glos. R.O., Q/RI 70 (map M–N, P, and R); D 3117/563; D 6/E 4, no. 13.
[8] Glos. R.O., D 45/M 1.
[9] Ibid. D 326/M 22.
[10] G.B.R., J 4/1, no. 31(2).
[11] Census, 1801.
[12] Glouc. Corp. Rec. pp. 73–4.
[13] Glos. Subsidy Roll, 1327, 31; cf. G.D.R., T 1/189.
[14] G.B.R., B 2/1, f. 230v.
[15] Cal. S.P. Dom. 1655–6, 336.

wold Road)[16] stands a large house, partly timber-framed and partly brick and probably 17th century in origin. East of the main road Saintbridge House dates from an early 19th-century rebuilding.[17] Several buildings, including a farmhouse north of Saintbridge House, were demolished in the mid 20th century to make way for housing estates.[18] West of Saintbridge there was evidently a dwelling below Robins Wood Hill in 1531 on the site of the farmhouse called Boddenhams[19] in 1619, when John Robins bought it from the owners of Upton St. Leonards manor.[20] It later belonged to the Hyett family and was known as Starveall or Tredworth Farm in 1780.[21] It was demolished in the mid 20th century to make way for housing.[22] In the north-east corner of Upton towards Hucclecote a farmstead called the New House in 1799[23] was presumably on the site of a tenement of the same name, which belonged to St. Oswald's Priory in 1498[24] and was described as in Hucclecote when the Crown alienated it in 1575.[25] In the 19th century it was known as Botton Farm[26] and in the early 20th included a brick farmhouse.[27]

There was little early settlement in the area included in South Hamlet, which in 1801 had 8 houses and a population of 60.[28] The principal buildings were those at the site of Llanthony Priory, west of the Bristol road,[29] and, some way east of the road, the priory's sheephouse which later became the centre of an estate.[30] Of the farmhouses of that estate[31] one near the Tuffley road, described in 1632 as new and known later as the Upper Sheephouse, was cased in brick *c.* 1800 when the west end was extended or rebuilt[32] and later became a private residence. Another to the north on the Tuffley road at Sutgrove, where there had been an habitation in the early 13th century,[33] was built in the 18th century. It was demolished in 1984 following a fire. Opposite a farmstead belonging to Tuffley manor[34] included a 19th-century farmhouse, which survives as a private residence. Further south a small farmhouse built for the rector of Matson's glebe estate in the early 19th century[35] was demolished in the 20th.

Early settlement in TUFFLEY, which lies 3.5 km. south of Gloucester Cross, was scattered. In 1672 it included 17 houses assessed for hearth tax[36] and *c.* 1710 it comprised 26 houses with an estimated population of 110.[37] In 1801 Tuffley had 18 houses with a population of 112.[38] Most of the dwellings were strung out along the road crossing the west side of Robins Wood Hill,[39] where a 17th-century farmhouse, which became a lodge to a late 19th-century house,[40] comprises a long timber-framed range with a south cross wing. The focal point was at the junction with Tuffley Lane, from which a green extended southwards along the main road until inclosure in 1866.[41] Near the junction was Tuffley Court, a farmhouse which replaced an ancient manor house higher up the hill.[42] An inn recorded from 1779 opposite Tuffley Lane[43] was presumably kept by the victualler licensed in Tuffley in 1755.[44] There were some cottages at the south end of the green by 1824.[45] In the west at Lower Tuffley there were several farmhouses and cottages by the mid 17th century.[46] Most of the early houses in Tuffley were replaced or rebuilt following the break-up of the Tuffley Court estate in 1867.[47] In the 20th century Tuffley was subject to considerable suburban development, and in 1983 only one farmhouse, a 19th-century building south-east of Lower Tuffley, remained in use.

MANORS AND OTHER ESTATES. A statement that Offa, king of the Mercians, gave 10 hides at Innsworth to Glastonbury Abbey (Som.) in 794 is uncorroborated.[48]

The royal manor of BARTON comprised 9 hides without its members in 1066 and included ½ hide in Droitwich (Worcs.), said in 1086 to belong to the hall of Gloucester.[49] By 1244 the manor was held at farm by Gloucester Abbey[50] and was called KING'S BARTON to distinguish it from the Barton estate held by the abbey in its own right. It included property in many of the hamlets and parishes outside Gloucester.[51] In 1265, the abbey having failed to pay the farm because of the civil wars, the Crown granted King's Barton at farm to Roger de Clifford.[52] The abbey became the farmer again in 1267 but in 1273 the estate was assigned with the town and castle in dower to Henry III's widow, Eleanor of Provence,[53] under whom it was known as Queen's Barton.[54] In 1299 it was included in the dower of Queen Margaret. Edward II made a grant of the

[16] *Glouc. Corp. Rec.* p. 283.
[17] Below, man.
[18] Cf. O.S. Map 6″, Glos. XXXIII. NE. (1903 edn.).
[19] Glouc. Cath. Libr., Reg. Abb. Malvern, ii, ff. 43v.–44; cf. Glos. R.O., P 347A/FM 1, rott. 1d., 4.
[20] Glos. R.O., D 6/T 16.   [21] Ibid. E 4, no. 13.
[22] Cf. O.S. Map 6″, Glos. XXXIII. NE. (1903 edn.).
[23] Glos. R.O., Q/RI 70 (map I, no. 134).
[24] P.R.O., SC 6/Hen. VIII/1212, rot. 7.
[25] Ibid. C 66/1135, m. 25.
[26] Bryant, *Map of Glos.* (1824).
[27] Glos. R.O., D 2299/1753, 6517.
[28] *Census,* 1801.
[29] Above, Sites of Religious Houses.
[30] Below, man.; Glos. R.O., Q/RI 70 (map Q, no. 26).
[31] Cf. Glos. R.O., Q/RI 70 (map Q, nos. 7, 34).
[32] Ibid. D 3117/3; D 936/E 149; *Glevensis,* xiii. 12.
[33] *Glouc. Corp. Rec.* p. 117.
[34] Glos. R.O., D 936/E 5, p. 26; E 110.
[35] Ibid. Q/RI 70 (map Q, nos. 1–6); P 215/IN 3/4, 9.

[36] P.R.O., E 179/247/14, rot. 34.
[37] Atkyns, *Glos.* 677.
[38] *Census,* 1801.
[39] G.D.R., T 1/86.
[40] Glos. R.O., D 2299/3433.
[41] Ibid. Q/RI 32.
[42] Below, man.; Glos. Colln. prints GL 65.27.
[43] Glos. R.O., Q/REl 1A, Dudstone & King's Barton 1779; D 936/E 3/1, p. 181.
[44] Ibid. Q/AV 2, rot. 8.
[45] Bryant, *Map of Glos.* (1824).
[46] Glos. R.O., D 936/M 27/1–2; G.D.R., T 1/86.
[47] Below, man.
[48] Finberg, *Early Charters of W. Midlands,* p. 42.
[49] *Dom. Bk.* (Rec. Com.), i. 162v., 172v.
[50] *Cal. Lib.* 1240–5, 280.
[51] *Hist. & Cart. Mon. Glouc.* iii. 67–76, 149.
[52] *Cal. Pat.* 1258–66, 520–1; *Close R.* 1264–8, 200–1.
[53] *Cal. Pat.* 1266–72, 117; 1272–81, 27.
[54] P.R.O., JUST 1/278, rot. 62d.

estate in 1318 to his brother Edmund of Woodstock,[55] and in 1322 committed it during pleasure to Gilbert Talbot and appointed Hugh le Despenser the younger to a superior custody.[56] King's Barton was granted for life to Queen Isabella in 1327 and the reversion for life to Thomas de Bradeston in 1330. He held it in 1331[57] and until 1345 when Edward III granted the manor to Gloucester Abbey at fee farm.[58] The abbey, which from 1316 also held Dudstone hundred at fee farm,[59] was granted free warren on the demesne in 1354[60] and retained the estate until the Dissolution.[61]

The Crown, which sold part of the estate to Robert Milner in the later 16th century, granted the manor and the hundred or hundreds of King's Barton and Dudstone in March and August 1611 respectively to the brothers George and Thomas Whitmore of London.[62] Later that year George apparently released his interest to Thomas (d. c. 1612), who was succeeded by their brother Sir William Whitmore.[63] Because of his royalist sympathies Sir William's estates were sequestered in 1645. He recovered them and at his death in 1648 King's Barton passed to his second son Richard, who was discharged from the sequestration in 1653.[64] From Richard (d. 1667) the manor passed to his daughter Catherine. In 1694 she and her husband George Walcot, a London merchant, sold it to her cousin Sir William Whitmore and her nephew William Whitmore of Lower Slaughter, to whom Sir William released his interest in 1695. After William Whitmore's death in 1725 the manor passed first to his widow Elizabeth (d. 1735) and then to his second son William,[65] who sold it in 1754 or 1755 to Samuel Blackwell of Northaw (Herts.).[66] By 1769 King's Barton had been acquired by William Singleton (d. 1777), who left it to his widow Anne. In 1780 John Price and Thomas Mitchell held the manor as assignees of Messrs. Walker and Singleton, bankrupts, and by 1784 Edmund Probyn, a mortgagee, was in possession.[67] The manor, which comprised mainly rents from freehold and copyhold estates and fishing rights in the river Leadon, was sold under a Chancery decree in 1786.[68] The purchaser was Sir John Guise, Bt., with whose nearby Highnam

estate it descended to Sir John Wright Guise.[69] After his death in 1865 King's Barton passed in the direct line to Sir William Vernon Guise (d. 1887), Sir William Francis George Guise (d. 1920), and Sir Anselm William Edward Guise, who relinquished the remaining manorial rights in 1946.[70]

The site of King's Barton manor, recorded in Barton Street in the early 13th century,[71] was let at farm at the Dissolution when it comprised a court house.[72] It has not been identified.

In the mid 13th century the king's hall at Kingsholm was the centre of an estate held under King's Barton manor by the serjeanty of keeping the door of the king's pantry.[73] The estate, which was known as the manor of *KINGSHOLM* by 1287,[74] included land in Kingsholm, Longford, and Twigworth.[75] Wybert of the king's hall may have held it in the early 12th century[76] and Peter of Kingsholm, who was also surnamed of the king's hall, gave it to his son William of Kingsholm in or before 1239.[77] From William, who was also called William Daubeney, the estate, extended at 2 ploughlands, passed to his son John Daubeney,[78] who performed the serjeanty at Edward I's coronation.[79] John Daubeney (d. c. 1304) was succeeded by his son John, a minor.[80] He settled the manor in 1333 on his marriage,[81] and his wife Cecily survived him and died in 1345. She was succeeded by John's son Ellis Daubeney,[82] but William Marsh, whom she had married by 1337, retained a moiety of the manor for life. In 1359 Ellis was licensed to grant his moiety to his son and daughter-in-law, Richard and Joan Daubeney.[83] They both died in 1361 and were succeeded by Richard's sister Elizabeth, a minor,[84] to whom William Marsh's moiety had reverted by 1364.[85] Elizabeth, who married Gilbert Giffard (d. 1373)[86] and Andrew Walton, had forfeited the manor and been executed by 1388 on conviction for Walton's murder.[87] Her son and heir John Giffard died a minor in 1392[88] and the Crown, which granted Kingsholm manor in 1394 to John Luffwyk and William Gold,[89] divided it in 1395 between Elizabeth's surviving heirs, Cecily Sage, Nicholas Matson Droys, John Swonhongre, and Eve wife of Simon Cadle.[90]

[55] *Cal. Pat.* 1292–1301, 452; 1317–21, 105.

[56] Ibid. 1321–4, 214; *Cal. Fine R.* 1319–27, 182.

[57] *Cal. Pat.* 1327–30, 69; 1330–4, 6, 43.

[58] Ibid. 1343–5, 551; *Cal. Chart. R.* 1341–1417, 40.

[59] *Cal. Fine R.* 1307–19, 304.

[60] *Cal. Chart. R.* 1341–1417, 142.

[61] *Valor Eccl.* (Rec. Com.), ii. 416.

[62] Glos. R.O., D 317; G.B.R., J 1/1954.

[63] Cf. *Reg. Mon. Winch.* i, p. lxx.

[64] Glos. R.O., D 45/E 1; for the Whitmores, Burke, *Land. Gent.* (1937), 2424–5.

[65] Glos. R.O., D 45/T 1/6–12; cf. *V.C.H. Glos.* vi. 130.

[66] Glos. R.O., D 45/M 3.

[67] Ibid. D 326/M 21; *Glouc. Jnl.* 5 Jan. 1778.

[68] Glos. R.O., SL 196.

[69] Ibid. D 326/M 21; T 13; *V.C.H. Glos.* x. 19.

[70] Glos. R.O., D 2078, Guise fam., King's Barton ct. bk. 1854–1946; Burke, *Peerage* (1963), 1087–8.

[71] Glouc. Cath. Libr., Reg. Abb. Froucester B, pp. 264, 269.

[72] Ibid. Reg. Abb. Malvern, ii, ff. 173v.–174; P.R.O., SC 6/Hen. VIII/1248, rot. 5d.

[73] *Hist. & Cart. Mon. Glouc.* iii. 69; *Cal. Pat.* 1364–7, 285, 305.

[74] P.R.O., JUST 1/278, rot. 64.

[75] Glos. R.O., D 326/E 1, ff. 50–62.

[76] *Hist. & Cart. Mon. Glouc.* i. 106.

[77] *Ex. e Rot. Fin.* (Rec. Com.), i. 322; *Glouc. Corp. Rec.* pp. 101, 116, 128.

[78] *Bk. of Fees*, ii. 1407; *Cal. Inq. p.m.* i, p. 311.

[79] P.R.O., JUST 1/278, rot. 64.

[80] *Cal. Inq. p.m.* iv, p. 146.

[81] P.R.O., CP 25(1)/77/60, no. 112.

[82] *Cal. Inq. p.m.* viii, p. 412; Ellis held land in Twigworth, Down Hatherley, and Sandhurst in 1343: B.L. Add. Ch. 6028.

[83] *Cal. Pat.* 1334–8, 395; 1358–61, 318.

[84] *Cal. Inq. p.m.* xi, p. 445.

[85] *Cal. Fine R.* 1356–68, 285.

[86] *Cal. Inq. p.m.* xiv, p. 28.

[87] *Cal. Fine R.* 1383–91, 206; 1391–9, 169.

[88] P.R.O., C 136/75, no. 13.

[89] *Cal. Pat.* 1391–6, 470.

[90] *Cal. Fine R.* 1391–9, 169–70.

Kingsholm manor was fragmented further by divisions among coheirs, the parts being held from the Crown for fractions of knights' fees. Eve Cadle's quarter was divided after her death in 1413 between her five surviving daughters, including Alice wife of John Adams and Emme wife of John Hyett, and the son, a minor who died soon afterwards, of a sixth.[91] The share of Nicholas Matson Droys, later called Nicholas Matson, passed at his death in 1435 to his son Robert Matson.[92] Robert died in 1459 leaving a third of the manor to five coheirs, including Isabel wife of Walter Brickhampton.[93] Isabel, who in 1460 inherited the quarter of the manor once held by her grandmother Cecily Sage, was succeeded at her death in 1488 by William Hartland.[94]

John Swonhongre's share of the manor was divided in 1398 between his sisters Elizabeth, wife of James Gayner (d. 1434), and Isabel, later wife of John Thorpe (d. 1440). Both parts passed to Isabel's son John Thorpe,[95] who inherited another part from Robert Matson.[96] John died in 1469 seised of a third of the manor which passed to his son Richard.[97] Richard (d. 1514) was succeeded by his son Thomas but his wife Margery (d. 1517) retained a third of the estate in freebench.[98] From Thomas (d. 1525) the estate evidently passed in the direct line to Thomas (d. 1543), Nicholas (d. 1600), and George. George sold it in 1606 or 1607 to Sir William Cooke, who held another third of the manor in the right of his wife Joyce.[99]

Joyce's interest derived from a grant of the reversion of a moiety of a third of the manor by Hugh Griffith to John Arnold in 1529.[1] John, who acquired Highnam manor, died in 1545 and his son Nicholas, who was knighted before 1552, settled part of Kingsholm manor in 1557 on his son Rowland. Rowland (d. 1559) was survived by his wife Margaret and infant daughter Dorothy (d. 1580), and Dorothy's husband Thomas Lucy, who was knighted in 1593, retained a third of Kingsholm with the Highnam estate until his death in 1605 when it passed to his daughter Lady (Joyce) Cooke (d. 1613). After Sir William Cooke's death in 1619[2] his Kingsholm estate, later described as a manor, descended with Highnam. Parts were sold in the 1760s and early 1770s.[3] In 1782 John Guise exchanged part with John Pitt,[4] to whom he sold the manor in 1783.[5] Pitt (d. 1805)[6] left it to his daughter Mary and her husband, the Revd. James Pitt (d. 1806), and Mary (d. 1836) to William Goodrich.[7] William (d. 1845) left his estates in trust for his son James, after whose death in 1890 the site of the ancient Kingsholm manor was offered for sale.[8] No later record of the manor has been found.

Fractions of the ancient manor of Kingsholm descended to Thomas Adams and Arthur Porter,[9] who sold them to Brasenose College, Oxford, in 1527 and 1533 respectively.[10] The college, which thereby acquired land in Kingsholm, Longford, and Twigworth[11] and in 1607 held a third of the manor,[12] retained land north of Gloucester until c. 1920.[13]

The royal palace at Kingsholm was recorded from 1051 and described as the king's hall and chamber in 1086. Excavations at the site have revealed timber buildings dating from before the Conquest. By the reign of Henry III the king had ceased to stay at the hall,[14] which by the late 13th century had become the Kingsholm manor house.[15] It had been demolished by 1591.[16] The chapel at the hall is treated above.[17]

By 1221 Maud had inherited a yardland in Twigworth, held from the Crown by the service of 5s., from her father Thomas of Twigworth.[18] She married Robert Marsh, apparently also called Robert Savage, whose service for the land included carrying royal writs in the county to the sheriff.[19] The writ-carrying service was remitted in 1251.[20] Henry Lovel, the king's cook, held the land in 1260,[21] and Robert Savage's son Robert had granted it by 1287 to John Daubeney,[22] after which it presumably merged with Kingsholm manor.

Eldred, under-king of the Hwicce, granted Gloucester Abbey 120 or 100 hides outside Gloucester in or before 767.[23] The abbey's estate, extended with its members at 22 hides less a yardland in 1086, was known as the manor of *BARTON*[24] and later as *ABBOT'S BARTON*. It included land in Barton Street, Longford, and Wotton, and in parishes outside Gloucester.[25] Among lands added to the estate were 6 a. in Longford granted in the late 12th or early 13th century by Wymark, widow of John Frenchevaler, for mending the ironwork of horses of monks visiting the hospice; a similar grant of that land was made by Ralph of Willington, who married Wymark's granddaughter Olympia and to

[91] Ibid. 1413–22, 21, 67–8; cf. ibid. 1430–7, 47, 320–1.
[92] P.R.O., C 139/74, no. 25.
[93] *Cal. Fine R.* 1452–61, 224–5.
[94] P.R.O., C 139/181, no. 67; cf. *Cal. Pat.* 1485–94, 115.
[95] *Cal. Fine R.* 1391–9, 288; P.R.O., C 139/68, no. 9; C 139/102, no. 4.
[96] *Cal. Fine R.* 1452–61, 224–5.
[97] P.R.O., C 140/31, no. 13.
[98] Ibid. C 142/29, no. 116; C 142/33, no. 66.
[99] Ibid. C 142/44, no. 163; C 142/69, no. 74; C 142/262, no. 121; Glos. R.O., D 326/E 1, ff. 50–59v.
[1] *L. & P. Hen. VIII*, iv (3), p. 2376.
[2] *V.C.H. Glos.* x. 18; P.R.O., C 142/126, no. 78; C 142/378, no. 146; Glos. R.O., D 326/E 1, ff. 50–5.
[3] *V.C.H. Glos.* x. 19; Glos. R.O., D 626, Twigworth deeds 1736–65; Longford deeds 1754–72; D 2957/192.28.
[4] Glos. R.O., D 326/E 4, f. 82.   [5] Ibid. D 936/M 11.
[6] *Glouc. Jnl.* 15 July 1805.
[7] Glos. R.O., D 3269, St. Marg. Hosp, Longford deeds 1846–76, abs. title 1846.
[8] Ibid. D 3117/3662, 3666; D 326/E 1, f. 53v.
[9] P.R.O., C 140/49, no. 31; C 142/44, no. 164.
[10] Glos. R.O., EL 134, pp. 30–2, 34.
[11] *Valor Eccl.* (Rec. Com.), ii. 272.
[12] Glos. R.O., D 326/E 1, f. 50.
[13] Cf. *Kelly's Dir. Glos.* (1919), 334; (1923), 350.
[14] *Antiq. Jnl.* lv (2), 267–94; *Dom. Bk.* (Rec. Com.), i. f. 162.
[15] P.R.O., C 133/113, no. 5; *Cal. Pat.* 1364–7, 285, 305.
[16] Glos. R.O., D 326/E 1, ff. 53v., 58v.
[17] Above, Churches and Chapels, non-par. chap.
[18] P.R.O., E 372/65, rot. 16.
[19] *Bk. of Fees*, i. 377; ii. 1407.
[20] *Cal. Chart. R.* 1226–57, 357. [21] *Cal. Pat.* 1258–66, 131.
[22] *Plac. de Quo Warr.* (Rec. Com.), 258.
[23] Finberg, *Early Charters of W. Midlands*, p. 41; *Hist. & Cart. Mon. Glouc.* i. 4, 64.
[24] *Dom. Bk.* (Rec. Com.), i. 165v.
[25] *Hist. & Cart. Mon. Glouc.* iii. 67, 149–64.

whose Sandhurst fee it belonged.[26] The abbey, which was granted free warren on the demesne in 1354,[27] retained Abbot's Barton until the Dissolution together with the manors of Longford and Wotton created out of it.[28] Other property in Longford and Twigworth was administered with the abbey's Sandhurst estate.[29]

In 1540 the Crown granted a lease of the site of Abbot's Barton manor and over 300 a. to John ap Rice, who retained his interest after that estate was granted to Gloucester corporation in 1542.[30] From 1560 John Kirby held a lease of the estate,[31] which became known as Barton farm. Kirby's mortgagee Peter Romney acquired an absolute title to the leasehold but in 1578 Romney's widow Elizabeth assigned the estate in trust for Kirby's widow Bridget (d. 1579) with remainder to her son Thomas Kirby, who took the profits from c. 1585.[32] In 1604 the corporation granted Thomas a lease for 41 years,[33] but from 1621, when it bought out his widow Margaret who was also the widow of Roger Batherne, the farm was divided between leaseholders immediately under the corporation.[34] In 1731 the farm comprised c. 400 a. of the c. 505 a. belonging to the corporation in the hamlets.[35] The corporation, which sold some land c. 1800 to redeem land tax,[36] sold more in the mid 1850s to pay a debt to the municipal charity trustees and for public works.[37] The site of the manor in Barton Street, where buildings were destroyed at the beginning of the siege of 1643,[38] comprised in 1731 a house connected to a range of farm buildings on the east by a gateway to the Tuffley road (Barton Lane). South of the range were a barn and a bowling green.[39] The house, which was called the Court House or Barton House in 1773 when the Dudstone hundred court met there,[40] was demolished in the early 19th century, after the Gloucester–Cheltenham tramway and Tuffley road had encroached on the bowling green.[41] Most of the farm buildings had been pulled down by the early 1820s when the land fronting Barton Street east of the tramway was divided into building lots.[42]

The Crown broke up the rest of the Abbot's Barton estate in the mid 16th century[43] and

granted the manor in 1557 to Dame Anne Fortescue, wife of Thomas Parry, with remainder to John Fortescue.[44] John, later Sir John (d. 1607), was succeeded by his son Sir Francis Fortescue[45] and both father and son claimed property in Longford, Wotton, Barnwood, and Upton St. Leonards for the manor.[46] Sir Francis (d. 1624) was succeeded by his son John,[47] who in 1632 was party to a grant of the manor for 70 years to Robert Halford, a London fishmonger (fl. 1651). Halford's estate passed to his nephew Robert Halford (d. 1683) of Barton Street, who was succeeded by his son William. Trustees under William's will dated 1695 sold land north of the city in 1700.[48] The manor has not been traced later.

Gloucester Abbey's manor of LONGFORD, recorded from 1520,[49] formed part of the endowment of the new bishopric of Gloucester in 1541.[50] The manor, which in the mid 17th century comprised leasehold and copyhold estates,[51] was transferred to the Ecclesiastical Commissioners in 1856.[52] In 1858 it covered 162 a., mostly leasehold belonging to the Longford House estate.[53] In 1904 the commissioners in an exchange with the trustees of that estate acquired 132 a. at Longford, including Manor Farm.[54] The commissioners, who bought the adjoining Drymeadow farm (66 a.) in 1940, retained their Longford estate until 1963 when they sold 235 a. to the tenants, J. W. and G. W. Sivell.[55]

The abbey's manor of WOTTON, recorded from 1519,[56] passed to the dean and chapter of Gloucester in 1541[57] and was held on lease from them with Barnwood and Cranham manors,[58] save in 1638 when a lease of Wotton was granted to Edward Stephens's cousin Nathaniel Stephens (d. 1660) of Eastington.[59] From the late 18th century land in Wotton was held by lease or copy directly from the dean and chapter, who took the manorial rights in hand in 1783.[60] In 1855 the dean and chapter's reversionary interest in leasehold and copyhold estates covering c. 406 a. in and near Gloucester was transferred to the Ecclesiastical Commissioners, who had enfranchised that land by the late 1880s;[61] part had belonged to the dean

[26] Ibid. i. 353–4.   [27] Cal. Chart. R. 1341–1417, 142.
[28] Valor Eccl. (Rec. Com.), ii. 415–16; cf. Glouc. Cath. Libr., Reg. Abb. Malvern, i, ff. 126 and v., 157, 167 and v.; ii, ff. 24 and v., 121 and v.
[29] Hist. & Cart. Mon. Glouc. iii. 165, 169; Glouc. Cath. Libr., Reg. Abb. Froucester B, pp. 331–2, 335–6.
[30] L. & P. Hen. VIII, xv, p. 566; xvii, p. 488.
[31] G.B.R., B 2/2, ff. 107v.–110.
[32] P.R.O., REQ 2/54/77; REQ 2/132/15; G.D.R. wills 1579/14.
[33] G.B.R., J 1/1953.
[34] Ibid. 1956; B 3/1, ff. 480–1.
[35] Ibid. J 4/1, nos. 15, 17–18, 21, 30, 31(2), 35.
[36] Ibid. J 4/8; J 6/1.
[37] Glos. R.O., D 3117/761–3; Glouc. Jnl. 28 Apr., 5 May 1855.   [38] G.B.R., H 2/3, p. 213.
[39] Ibid. J 4/1, no. 31(2); Glos. R.O., Q/RI 70 (map R, nos. 21–3).
[40] G.B.R., Dudstone ct. bk. 1769–1810; F 4/12, p. 188.
[41] Cf. Glos. R.O., Q/RUm 26; Causton, Map of Glouc. (1843).
[42] G.B.R., J 3/13, pp. 327–35; F 4/15, pp. 509, 650.
[43] L. & P. Hen. VIII, xviii (1), p. 536; (2), p. 53; xxi (1), pp. 578–9; cf. P.R.O., C 142/122, no. 63.

[44] Cal. Pat. 1557–8, 197.
[45] P.R.O., C 142/305, no. 132.
[46] Ibid. E 123/38, ff. 27–8; E 134/40 Eliz. Hil./3; E 134/14 Jas. I East./4; REQ 2/415/25.
[47] Ibid. C 142/407, no. 105.
[48] Glos. R.O., D 2957/192.101, 103–4; deeds in possession of Mrs. G. Sykes, of Westfield Terrace, Glouc.; for Rob. (d. 1683), above, Aldermen of Glouc. 1483–1835.
[49] Glouc. Cath. Libr., Reg. Abb. Malvern, i, f. 167 and v.
[50] L. & P. Hen. VIII, xvi, p. 572.
[51] G.D.R., G 3/19.
[52] Glos. R.O., D 2957/192.279–80.
[53] Church Com. MSS., Glouc. and Bristol bishopric est. surv. M 1, pp. 540–1.
[54] G.D.R., G 2/3/304716.
[55] Church Com. MSS., file 66698; Glouc. and Bristol bishopric est. surv. M 1, p. 565.
[56] Glouc. Cath. Libr., Reg. Abb. Malvern, i, f. 126.
[57] L. & P. Hen. VIII, xvi, p. 572.
[58] Below, Barnwood, man.
[59] Glos. R.O., D 936/E 12/2, ff. 361–4; Visit Glos. 1682–3, 174–6.   [60] Glos. R.O., D 936/E 38; M 1/1–2.
[61] Kirby, Cat. of Glouc. Dioc. Rec. ii, p. xiii; Church Com. MSS., Glouc. chapter est. surv. M 4, pp. 357–436, 461–87.

and chapter's Sandhurst estate[62] and part represented tithes commuted in 1799.[63]

An estate at Tuffley, said to have been given to Gloucester Abbey by Osbern, bishop of Exeter from 1072,[64] was a member of the abbey's Barton manor in 1066[65] and was known as *TUFFLEY* manor by the early 13th century.[66] The abbey, which was granted free warren on the demesne in 1354,[67] retained the manor until the Dissolution.[68] In 1541 it passed to the dean and chapter of Gloucester,[69] from whom it was farmed in 1552 by Thomas Winston. Winston was followed as farmer in 1560 or 1561 by Edward and Richard Stephens.[70] By 1583 the farmer was Richard Atkyns of North Ockendon (Essex), whose father Thomas (d. 1552) had been granted a lease of the manor, presumably in reversion, by the dean and chapter. Richard, who sought to recover the demesne held by Thomas Hale under a lease of 1536,[71] was a justice in Welsh courts and lord of Hempsted manor.[72] He died at Tuffley in 1610 and his interest in Tuffley manor passed to his son Richard.[73] In 1636 the latter died and the dean and chapter granted his son and heir Richard a lease of the manor for 21 years.[74] Thereafter the estate was held under leases renewed every few years.[75] Richard Atkyns, who fell heavily into debt, raised a troop for the royalist cause in the early 1640s and his estates were sequestered.[76] He recovered Tuffley after being pardoned in 1646[77] and sold it in 1670 to Henry Norwood,[78] who became M.P. for Gloucester in 1675 and a landowner in Leckhampton.[79] Norwood was followed as lord farmer of Tuffley manor in 1676 by Sir Paul Whichcot of Hendon (Mdx.), who inherited a baronetcy the next year, and in 1683 by Sir Thomas Hanbury of Little Marcle (Herefs.).[80] Sir Thomas (d. 1708) left the estate to his second son Thomas.[81] Samuel Mee, the lord farmer in 1717, left it at his death in 1749 to his son Thomas. From Thomas (d. 1757) it passed in turn to his widow Barbara (d. 1788) and son Thomas.[82] In 1792 the dean and chapter took the manorial rights in hand and thereafter land in Tuffley was

held under them by lease or copy;[83] they enfranchised some in 1799 and 1800 to redeem land tax.[84] The manorial rights passed in 1855 to the Ecclesiastical Commissioners,[85] who enfranchised much of the land.[86] In 1868 the commissioners sold the manorial rights to Henry Cecil Raikes and he to Richard William Attwood, owner of the Tuffley Court estate.[87]

From 1792 Thomas Mee held a lease of Tuffley Court and the manorial demesne.[88] He enlarged the estate, which at his death in 1812 passed to his brother-in-law, the Revd. Richard Raikes.[89] Richard (d. 1823)[90] was succeeded by his nephew, the Revd. Henry Raikes[91] (d. 1854). Tuffley Court passed to Henry's son Henry (d. 1863), who was succeeded by his son H. C. Raikes. H. C. Raikes sold the estate of 480 a. to Joseph Lovegrove in 1867.[92] Lovegrove broke up the estate, selling most of it that year when R. W. Attwood bought the house and 270 a.;[93] Attwood offered his estate for sale in lots in 1872[94] and sold the house and 109 a. to E. T. Bullock in 1873. Bullock sold that estate to the guardians of the Gloucester poor-law union in 1896,[95] and in 1930 it passed to Gloucester corporation,[96] which used it for housing after the Second World War.[97]

By the early 13th century Gloucester Abbey had built an oratory at the site of Tuffley manor.[98] In the early 17th century the manor house, Tuffley Court, was a substantial residence sometimes occupied by tenants under the Atkyns family. It was damaged by fire c. 1640 and had been repaired by Richard Atkyns for his residence by 1650[99] when it comprised six bays and two storeys and the outbuildings included a barn of nine bays.[1] In 1672 Henry Norwood was assessed on 13 hearths for it.[2] The house, which probably stood in the park on Robins Wood Hill,[3] was uninhabited in 1764 and was demolished by the dean and chapter before 1785. It was replaced by a farmhouse below the hill in Tuffley Lane.[4] That house, which became a boys' home in the late 1890s,[5] was demolished in the mid 20th century.

Copyhold land in Tuffley, which John Morris

[62] Cf. Glos. R.O., D 936/E 3/2, ff. 5–6; E 80–1.
[63] Below. [64] *Hist. & Cart. Mon. Glouc.* i. 116.
[65] *Dom. Bk.* (Rec. Com.), i. 165v.
[66] Glouc. Cath. Libr., Reg. Abb. Froucester B, p. 346.
[67] *Cal. Chart. R.* 1341–1417, 142.
[68] *Valor Eccl.* (Rec. Com.), ii. 414.
[69] *L. & P. Hen. VIII*, xvi, p. 572.
[70] Glos. R.O., D 1815, Barnwood, Wotton, Cranham, and Tuffley ct. rolls 1558–71.
[71] P.R.O., C 2/Eliz. I/A 6/21; C 142/95, no. 86; Glouc. Cath. Libr., Reg. Abb. Malvern, ii, ff. 119v.–120.
[72] *Trans. B.G.A.S.* l. 238.
[73] P.R.O., C 142/318, no. 148; Glos. R.O., D 936/A 1/1, pp. 5, 27.
[74] *Inq. p.m. Glos.* 1625–42, ii. 24–6; Glos. R.O., D 936/E 12/2, ff. 342–3. [75] Glos. R.O., D 936/E 110.
[76] *Vindication of Ric. Atkyns* (1669): Glos. Colln. 8975.
[77] *D.N.B.*; cf. *Cal. Cttee. for Compounding*, i. 86; ii. 1086; Glos. R.O., D 936/M 27/1.
[78] Glos. R.O., D 3117/145.
[79] *Trans. B.G.A.S.* xlvii. 120; Rudder, *Glos.* 521.
[80] Glos. R.O., D 936/A 1/3, pp. 308, 330, 462, 486; D 3117/152–4; Burke, *Peerage* (1889), 1456–7.
[81] Glos. R.O., D 3117/155–7; Bigland, *Glos.* iii, no. 205.
[82] Glos. R.O., D 936/A 1/5, p. 287; D 3117/1943–6; P 154/15/IN 1/2; 12/IN 1/1, 31.

[83] Ibid. D 936/Y 21; E 111; M 27/1–2.
[84] Ibid. D 123, Tuffley deeds 1807–52; D 177, Lysons fam., Hempsted and Tuffley deeds 1751–1809.
[85] Kirby, *Cat. of Glouc. Dioc. Rec.* ii, p. xiii.
[86] Church Com. MSS., Glouc. chapter est. surv. M 5.
[87] Glos. R.O., D 1388, Attwood fam., Tuffley deeds 1859–72.
[88] Ibid. D 936/E 111.
[89] Ibid. D 3117/142, 168–9, 171–3; G.B.R., B 3/13, f. 111v.
[90] Mon. in Glouc. cath.
[91] Glos. R.O., D 4115/9, abs. title 1866.
[92] Ibid. D 3117/1761, 1766–7, 2098, 2100.
[93] Ibid. 1166, 1768, 2100; D 4115/9; SL 538.
[94] Ibid. D 1388/SL 5/62.
[95] Ibid. G/GL 8A/23, pp. 105–7, 167.
[96] G.B.R., B 3/64, p. 307.
[97] *Glouc. Municipal Year Bk.* (1964–5), 89–91.
[98] Glouc. Cath. Libr., Reg. Abb. Froucester B, p. 346.
[99] *Vindication of Ric. Atkyns*; cf. Glos. Colln. prints GL 65.27. [1] Glos. R.O., D 1740/E 1, f. 90.
[2] P.R.O., E 179/247/14, rot. 34.
[3] Atkyns, *Glos.* 677; G.D.R., T 1/86.
[4] Glos. R.O., D 936/E 110; Y 21; Taylor, *Map of Glos.* (1777); cf. S. Eward, *No Fine but a Glass of Wine* (1985), 301–2.
[5] Cf. Glos. R.O., G/GL 8A/25, p. 166.

held from 1768, passed to his son Robert. He enlarged the estate and in 1792 conveyed it to his brother William, later of Sevenhampton. William (d. 1834) was succeeded by his son Walter Lawrence, who had changed his surname to Lawrence and who owned c. 150 a. in the hamlet in 1840. In 1844 W. L. Lawrence sold his Tuffley estate, which included a reversionary right to other copyhold land, to John Curtis-Hayward.[6] John inherited an estate in Quedgeley with which the Tuffley land passed. His son John Frederick Curtis-Hayward[7] sold a farm with 56 a. at Tuffley in 1922.[8]

An estate of 2 hides at Wotton was held by Godric in 1066 and by William Froisselew in 1086.[9] It may have passed to Richard son of Niel, who in 1126 gave land, a mill, and tithes in Wotton to Gloucester Abbey;[10] that grant was confirmed by Robert, earl of Gloucester, and by Walter of Holcombe.[11]

A hide at Utone or Wotton, held by Pain in 1066 and by Hunfrid de Medehal in 1086,[12] possibly gave the name *HYDE* to the area between Wotton and Gloucester. In the early 13th century several tenants held land in Hyde under Walter of Hyde,[13] but the later descent of that lordship is unknown.

Land in Hyde held c. 1270 by Peter son of Herbert from Churchdown barony as ⅕ knight's fee[14] was presumably among the lands of St. Oswald's church which had passed to the archbishop of York.[15] St. Oswald's Priory, which was given 48 a. at Innsworth by the Crown before 1216, acquired other land near Gloucester[16] and was one of the lords of Wotton in 1316.[17] Most of the priory's land was included in *TULWELL* manor, which at the Dissolution was held under lease by John a' Deane and his wife Anne. In 1546 the Crown granted the manor to the dean and chapter of Gloucester.[18] They granted leases in reversion to Thomas Davis, who may have married Anne a'Deane, in 1547 and to George Hatton in 1558. Eleanor Wannerton held the estate in 1650 when it was extended at 86 a.[19] In 1662 Robert Halford of Barton Street and Alderman Henry Cugley of Longford took leases for 21 years of 70 a. and 16 a. respectively; thereafter both parts were held under leases renewed every few years. From 1781 the land was in three tenan-

cies.[20] Presumably the land was in that which the Ecclesiastical Commissioners had enfranchised by the late 1880s.[21] St. Oswald's Priory had built an oratory at the site of the manor by 1309.[22] The buildings, some of which were in ruins before being replaced in 1615,[23] were burnt at the beginning of the siege of 1643 when they comprised a house called Tulwell or Tully Court and a large barn.[24] The house was replaced by one, which in 1799 was held under lease by the dean Josiah Tucker[25] and later was known as Castle Grim.[26] It was demolished after the site was bought for Gloucester Football Club in 1891.[27]

St. Oswald's Priory had property also in Longford and Wotton, which was sold off by the Crown in the later 16th century.[28] By 1446 the priory paid Godstow Abbey (Oxon.) 10s. rent for land in Longford.[29]

In the late 11th century Walter of Gloucester held land outside the town, presumably held before him by his two predecessors as hereditary sheriffs and castellans of Gloucester. Walter's son Miles included part in his endowment of Llanthony Priory in 1137, and Miles's daughter Margaret de Bohun[30] had overlordship of land in Longford and Sud Meadow in the later 12th century.[31] Miles of Gloucester's endowment of Llanthony Priory included Castle Meads and a hide of land south of Gloucester.[32] The priory, which acquired more land,[33] retained *LLANTHONY* manor until the Dissolution when it covered over 390 a.[34] In 1540 the Crown granted the priory and its land near Gloucester to Arthur Porter.[35] After his death in 1558 or 1559 the estate, including Newark House and land in Hempsted, passed in the direct line to Sir Thomas Porter (d. 1597) and to Arthur Porter, who had married Anne, daughter of Sir John Danvers.[36] In 1609 Arthur, who was also knighted, conveyed the estate for the payment of his debts and a settlement on his wife and daughter Elizabeth to Henry Danvers, Lord Danvers. Danvers sold part to Leonard Bennett of Ebley in 1611 and settled the remainder, including the priory, on Anne Porter in 1615. From Anne (fl. 1630) it had passed to Elizabeth and her husband John Scudamore, Viscount Scudamore,[37] by the mid 1640s when he was in prison for his support of the royalist cause.

[6]. Ibid. D 936/M 27/1–2; G.D.R., V 1/Sevenhampton 1834; T 1/86.

[7] V.C.H. Glos x. 218–19; Kelly's Dir. Glos. (1885), 607.

[8] Glos. R.O., D 2299/6406.

[9] Dom. Bk. (Rec. Com.), i. 167v.

[10] Hist. & Cart. Mon. Glouc. i. 107, 118, 319; ii. 89.

[11] Earldom of Glouc. Charters, ed. Patterson, pp. 85–6; Glouc. Cath. Libr., deeds and seals, iii, f. 13.

[12] Dom. Bk. (Rec. Com.), i. 170.

[13] Glouc. Corp. Rec. pp. 80, 91, 110–12, 152–7; J. S. Moore in Dom. Bk. Glos. (Chich. 1982) suggests that Utone was in Upton St. Leonards. [14] Reg. Giffard (Surtees Soc. cix), 19.

[15] Cf. Taylor, Dom. Glos. 14.

[16] Cal. Pat. 1258–66, 622; 1281–92, 471; 1301–7, 396; 1340–3, 409. [17] Feud. Aids, ii. 265.

[18] P.R.O., SC 6/Hen. VIII/1212, rot. 10; L. & P. Hen. VIII, xxi (1), p. 486.

[19] Glos. R.O., D 1740/E 1, ff. 124–125v.

[20] Ibid. D 936/E 114–15; E 3/2, ff. 1–3.

[21] Cf. Church Com. MSS., Glouc. chapter est. surv. M 4,

pp. 357–436, 461–87.

[22] Trans. B.G.A.S. xliii. 113.

[23] Glos. R.O., D 936/E 12/1, f. 320v.

[24] Ibid. D 1740/E 1, f. 124; G.B.R., H 2/3, p. 214.

[25] Glos. R.O., Q/RI 70 (map D, no. 87).

[26] Ibid. D 936/E 3/1, pp. 85–6.

[27] Glos. Colln. 10691.

[28] Glos. R.O., D 2957/192.37; Cal. Pat. 1557–8, 135; 1572–5, pp. 547–8; cf. Valor Eccl. (Rec. Com.), ii. 487; B.L. Add. Ch. 66800.

[29] P.R.O., SC 6/1108/3, m. 2; Valor Eccl. (Rec. Com.), ii. 195. [30] Camd. Misc. xxii, pp. 1, 4–5, 9, 16–17, 37–8.

[31] Cur. Reg. R. Ric. I (Pipe R. Soc. N.S. xxxi), 105; Hist. & Cart. Mon. Glouc. ii. 180–1. [32] Camd. Misc. xxii, p. 17.

[33] Trans. B.G.A.S. lxiii. 24, 40, 51.

[34] Valor Eccl. (Rec. Com.), ii. 430.

[35] L. & P. Hen. VIII, xvi, pp. 383–4.

[36] P.R.O., C 142/118, no. 56; C 142/253, no. 97; cf. G.D.R., T 1/99.

[37] Inq. p.m. Glos. 1625–42, i. 128–9; Glos. R.O., D 3117/1.

Elizabeth died in 1651 and John, who under a private Act of 1662 endowed Hempsted church with tithes from the estate, in 1671.[38] The estate evidently passed with the viscounty in turn to his grandson John Scudamore (d. 1697) and to the latter's son James (d. 1716). James's daughter Frances, heir to his lands, married first Henry Somerset, duke of Beaufort, who divorced her, and second Charles Fitzroy, who took the name Scudamore. She died in 1750 when Llanthony became the inheritance of Frances, child of her second marriage.[39] In 1771 Frances married Charles Howard, who inherited the dukedom of Norfolk in 1786.[40] The duke, who in 1802 bought part of Sud Meadow from Giles Greenaway,[41] died without issue in 1815 and Frances, a lunatic, in 1820.[42] At the partition of her lands in 1829 the Newark and Llanthony estate went to John Higford (formerly Parsons) (d. 1852), who left it to Daniel Higford Davall Burr (d. 1885) of Aldermaston (Berks.). He was succeeded by his son, who was called Higford Higford[43] and who sold the site of Llanthony Priory in 1898 to the chemicals company of J. M. Collett.[44] After Higford's death in 1906 the estate passed to his wife Julia, and in 1919, when it comprised 428 a., mostly riverine meadow land with Newark House, it was put up for sale.[45] The site of the priory, which was acquired in 1908 by the G.W.R. and in 1974 by Gloucester city council,[46] is treated above.[47]

The estate bought by Leonard Bennett in 1611 comprised over 200 a. centred on the *SHEEP-HOUSE*.[48] At his death in 1621 it passed to his daughter Edith (d. 1632), wife of William Selwyn.[49] In 1635 William (d. 1643) inherited an estate in Matson,[50] with which the Sheephouse descended.[51] In 1799 Thomas Townshend, Viscount Sydney, exchanged the freehold of most of the Sheephouse estate for that of the part of his Matson estate belonging to Upton St. Leonards parish. The freehold land he retained at Sutgrove[52] was sold in 1912 at the final break-up of the Matson estate and 18 a. were bought in 1922 by Gloucester corporation.[53] The Sheephouse estate which the dean and chapter of Gloucester acquired at the exchange in 1799[54] was held under lease by the owners of the Matson estate until

1861 when the lease was assigned to E. S. J. Griffiths. He surrendered it in 1869 to the Ecclesiastical Commissioners who sold off the land between 1874 and 1876.[55] The Sheephouse incorporated a long range of one storey with an open roof in which lofts were created for hay storage, possibly by Llanthony Priory before 1507 when it was also called Shepherds Elms. In the early 17th century a small house adjoining a room at the east end of the range was used as a farmhouse.[56] The building, which by 1683 was known as the Lower Sheephouse,[57] was occupied as cottages in 1851.[58] In 1876 the Ecclesiastical Commissioners sold it with 34 a. to William Hemmings[59] and c. 1919 Gloucester corporation bought the site for housing.[60]

In the late 12th century Roger son of Nicholas held 2 ploughlands in Longford under Margaret de Bohun.[61] The estate, to which Bertram Mare had a claim, was assessed at $\frac{1}{2}$ fee[62] and in 1214, when Roger sought a grant of it at farm from the Crown, was called *LONGFORD* manor;[63] later it was known as *PLOCK COURT*. In 1198 the overlordship belonged to Margaret's grandson Henry de Bohun, who was created earl of Hereford in 1200.[64] The overlordship passed with the earldom and in 1384 was assigned to Humphrey de Bohun's daughter Mary and her husband Henry of Lancaster, later Henry IV.[65] A mesne lordship was exercised by Henry son of Nicholas in 1236,[66] by the heirs of John de Burgh c. 1275, by Nicholas son of Ralph in 1301, and by John son of Nicholas in 1351.[67] In the early 16th century the manor was said to be held under Gloucester Abbey.[68]

In the early 13th century Ralph Avenel (d. by 1223) and his wife Margaret (d. by 1236) held the manor in demesne. In 1236 it formed part of the inheritance of Douce, the infant daughter of Ralph's son William Avenel. Later that year Roger of Lockington claimed land in Longford in marriage by the grant of Margaret Avenel, his mother-in-law.[69] The manor, which John de Mucegros held at his death c. 1275,[70] was the inheritance of his wife Cecily (d. c. 1301), who was succeeded by her granddaughter Hawise de Mucegros.[71] Hawise's second husband, John de Ferrers, was assessed at $\frac{1}{3}$ fee in Longford in 1303,

[38] *D.N.B.*; Scudamore Churches Endowment Act, 13 & 14 Chas. II, c. 11 (Priv. Act).
[39] *D.N.B.* s.v. Scudamore, John; cf. Atkyns, *Glos.* 501; Rudder, *Glos.* 515.   [40] Burke, *Peerage* (1963), 1808.
[41] Glos. Colln. NQ 28.51; cf. Glos. R.O., Q/RI 70 (map R).
[42] Burke, *Peerage* (1963), 1808; *D.N.B.* s.v. Scudamore, John.
[43] Glos. R.O., EL 201, p. 133; D 4791, Glouc. Railway Carriage & Wagon Co., deeds 1886–1919; Burke, *Land. Gent.* (1898), i. 726–7.
[44] *Ind. Glos. 1904*, 58: copy in Glos. Colln. JV 13.1.
[45] Glos. R.O., D 2299/1685; P 173/MI 3/3; *Kelly's Dir. Glos.* (1910), 218; Burke, *Land. Gent.* (1898), i. 726.
[46] Inf. from Mr. J. F. Rhodes, curator of Glouc. Mus.
[47] Above, Sites of Religious Houses.
[48] Glos. R.O., D 3117/1.
[49] P.R.O., C 142/391, no. 49; *Trans. B.G.A.S.* xlvi. 346.
[50] Below, Matson, man.
[51] Glos. R.O., D 3117/5–6; cf. Rudge, *Hist. of Glos.* ii. 172–3.
[52] Glos. R.O., Q/RI 70.

[53] Ibid. GMS 128; *Glouc. Jnl.* 6 June 1912.
[54] Glos. R.O., Q/RI 70.
[55] Ibid. D 936/E 118/166; D 1740/E 50; T 48–9.
[56] P.R.O., C 115/L 2/6691, f. 61 and v.; Glos. R.O., D 3117/4.
[57] *Glos. N. & Q.* iv. 377.
[58] P.R.O., HO 107/1962.
[59] Glos. R.O., D 1740/T 49.
[60] Ibid. GMS 24; G.B.R., B 3/53, pp. 44, 207.
[61] *Cur. Reg. R. Ric. I* (Pipe R. Soc. N.S. xxxi), 105.
[62] *Abbrev. Plac.* (Rec. Com.), 99.
[63] *Pipe R. 1214* (P.R.S. N.S. xxxv), 58.
[64] *Cur. Reg. R. Ric. I* (Pipe R. Soc. N.S. xxxi), 105; *Camd. Misc.* xxii, pp. 4, 10 n.; *Complete Peerage*, vi. 457–9.
[65] P.R.O., CP 25(1)/73/7, no. 91; *Cal. Close, 1381–5*, 513.
[66] *Close R. 1234–7*, 297.
[67] *Cal. Inq. p.m.* ii, pp. 80–1; iv, p. 8; ix, p. 402.
[68] P.R.O., C 142/27, no. 47.
[69] *Glouc. Corp. Rec.* pp. 92–3; *Ex. e Rot. Fin.* (Rec. Com.), i. 109; *Close R. 1234–7*, 297, 303–4.
[70] *Cal. Inq. p.m.* ii, pp. 80–1.
[71] Ibid. iv, p. 8; *Cal. Close, 1272–9*, 172.

and her third husband, John de Bures, was described as lord of Longford in 1316.[72] The manor descended with Hawise's estate in Boddington to Richard Beauchamp, Lord Beauchamp of Powicke (d. 1503), who also held an estate called Twigworth manor. His lands passed to his daughter Anne, wife of Richard Lygon (d. 1512), and his grandsons Richard Read and Edward Willoughby.[73]

Although Anne's grandson William Lygon quitclaimed an interest in the estate in 1560,[74] Longford manor passed to Richard Read's son William, who was described in 1558 as one of the lords of Longford, Twigworth, and Kingsholm.[75] William and his brother and heir John both died in 1570, John having settled Longford on his wife Margaret and daughter Dorothy.[76] In 1588 the manor was held by Dorothy and her husband Oliver St. John,[77] who became Lord St. John of Bletsoe in 1596. Dorothy died in 1605, and by 1612 Plock Court manor had passed to her second son, Sir Anthony St. John, and his wife, Catherine.[78] They sold part to John Showle in 1614,[79] and another part, including the manor house, to Robert Dobbs (fl. 1656), a local landowner. Dobbs's estate passed to his son Thomas, who was dead by 1676 when it was settled on the marriage of his daughter Anne and William Jones of Usk (Mon.). In 1699 Anne, a widow, released the estate to her eldest son Thomas,[80] but in 1709 she and her son William sold it to Miles Beale of Newent (d. 1713), who was succeeded by his son Miles (d. 1748).[81] The estate presumably passed in turn to the latter Miles's son John (d. 1775), to John's uncle Thomas Beale (d. 1784), and to Thomas's son the Revd. Thomas Beale, who enlarged it and died in 1805.[82] He left Plock Court to his nephew Thomas Beale Cooper, who in 1852 sold the estate of 112 a. to the Revd. Thomas Sherwood (d. 1871). In 1890 Sherwood's daughter Anna, widow of the Revd. William Hedley (d. 1884), sold her interest in the estate to her brother Thomas.[83] From Thomas (d. 1891) the estate passed to his wife Anne, who died in 1912 soon after taking the additional surname Hale. In 1920 the estate was sold to Ernest Cloke, who broke it up by sales.[84] In 1936 Gloucester corporation bought the manor house and 57 a., part of which it used for playing fields.[85] The manor house, called Plock Court in 1540,[86] was occupied as a farmhouse by 1607.[87] It was rebuilt in the 17th century and cased in brick in the 19th. It housed two dwellings in 1852[88] and had been uninhabited for several years when, following damage by fire, it was demolished in 1986. Its grounds, which the corporation had used as a nursery garden, were covered by houses in the mid 1980s.

Tewkesbury Abbey acquired a small estate in Longford, including a yardland confirmed to it by Henry I in 1106[89] and a messuage and 7 a. quitclaimed to it by Cecily, countess of Hereford, in 1201.[90] At the Dissolution the abbey's land was called the Plocks.[91] Deerhurst Priory may have had land in Longford and Twigworth.[92] The Carmelite friars of Gloucester acquired land in Twigworth and, by the grant of Llanthony Priory, in Barton Street.[93] The Knights Hospitallers apparently had land in Twigworth, Down Hatherley, and Sandhurst attached to their preceptory at Quenington.[94]

St. Bartholomew's Hospital, Gloucester, acquired lands and rents outside the town, mostly to the north and east.[95] In 1311 it was said to have a manor at Kingsholm,[96] the site of which was presumably the White Barn from which over 35 a. were farmed in 1505.[97] The hospital acquired 4 a. at Saintbridge by exchange in the mid 13th century,[98] and in 1731 Gloucester corporation as the hospital's trustee held 52 a. in the hamlets and Saintbridge.[99] The White Barn appears to have survived the firing of Kingsholm in 1643,[1] and in 1731 there were two houses and outbuildings on the site.[2]

St. Margaret's Hospital at Wotton acquired land north and east of the town, including in Longford and Twigworth.[3] St. Mary Magdalen's Hospital at Wotton was granted a yardland there by Henry III.[4] In 1731 Gloucester corporation as the hospitals' trustee held 31 a. and 27 a. respectively in the hamlets.[5] Under the Municipal Corporations Act of 1835 control of the endowments of the three hospitals passed to a new body, the municipal charity trustees.[6]

[72] *Feud. Aids*, ii. 253, 265.

[73] *V.C.H. Glos.* viii. 190; *Cal. Inq. p.m.* ix, p. 402; B.L. Add. Ch. 72646; P.R.O., C 142/27, nos. 47, 125.

[74] P.R.O., CP 25(2)/141/1774, no. 2; for the Lygons, below, Matson, man.

[75] *V.C.H. Glos.* viii. 190–1; G.B.R., B2/1, f.77v.

[76] P.R.O., C 142/153, no. 59; C 142/157, no. 75.

[77] Ibid. SC 2/175/16.

[78] Burke, *Peerage* (1963), 2144; Glos. R.O., D 6/T 18; D 928, Longford deeds 1607–99.

[79] Glos. R.O., D 2957/192.2.

[80] Ibid. D 928, Longford deeds 1607–99.

[81] Ibid. Longford deeds 1718–1850, deed 1718; Bigland, *Glos.* ii. 241.

[82] Cf. *V.C.H. Glos.* x. 40; Glos. R.O., D 928, abs. of Revd. T. Beale's title.

[83] Glos. R.O., D 2078, Hale (Sherwood) fam., Plock Ct. papers 1859–93.

[84] Ibid. D 2299/2286; D 3117/2888, 2890.

[85] G.B.R., B 3/70(2), pp. 1227–8, 1353; 71(1), pp. 284, 990.

[86] Glos. R.O., P 329/MI 1, rot. 44.

[87] Ibid. D 928, Longford deeds 1607–99.

[88] Ibid. D 2078, Hale (Sherwood) fam., Plock Ct. papers.

[89] *Cal. Pat.* 1494–1509, 104.

[90] *Rot. Cur. Reg.* (Rec. Com.), 82, 279; *Camd. Misc.* xxii, p. 41.

[91] Glos. R.O., P 329/MI 1, rot. 44.

[92] *Cal. Pat.* 1569–72, p. 342.

[93] P.R.O., SC 6/Hen. VIII/7407, rot. 4.

[94] *Cal. Pat.* 1557–8, 317.

[95] Cf. *Glouc. Corp. Rec.* pp. 92–3, 182–3, 218–19, 223–5, 283, 307.

[96] Glouc. Cath. Libr., deeds and seals, ix, f. 2.

[97] G.B.R., B 2/1, ff. 237v.–239.

[98] *Glouc. Corp. Rec.* p. 186.

[99] G.B.R., J 4/1, nos. 17–18, 34, 36.

[1] Cf. Glos. R.O., D 326/E 78; D 936/E 118/52.

[2] G.B.R., J 4/1, f. 18.

[3] Cf. *Glouc. Corp. Rec.* pp. 94, 107, 151, 155–6, 323, 381–2, 399, 415; *Cal. Fine R.* 1485–1509, p. 193.

[4] *Cal. Pat.* 1317–21, 576.

[5] G.B.R., J 4/1, nos. 14, 20, 23.

[6] Above, Char. for Poor; cf. Glos. R.O., D 3269, vol. of plans 1848.

The estates of Sir William Nottingham (d. 1483) included land in Twigworth, called Twigworth manor in 1480, and Wotton. Richard Poole, who married Sir William's widow Elizabeth and bought the estates from trustees in 1487, was later said to hold an estate called Wotton manor.[7] The descent of an estate known sometimes as Down Hatherley and Twigworth manor[8] is reserved for a later volume.

Many estates were built up in the hamlets, comprising land held under a variety of tenures from the ancient manors. The *WOTTON COURT* estate had its origins in a small estate which had been divided by the early 16th century. A moiety belonged to George Twissell (d. 1534) of King's Stanley, whose son Edward sold it in 1542 to John Falconer.[9] Falconer left his property to Gloucester corporation, to which his widow Margaret released her life interest in 1546.[10] In 1608 Grey Brydges, Lord Chandos, and others sold the other moiety including a house at Wotton called Spencers to Lewis Roberts.[11] Lewis (d. 1629) was succeeded by his son Lewis[12] (d. 1679), whose daughters, Elizabeth Atkyns, Mary, and Hester, sold the property in 1683 to John Blanch of Eastington, a clothier.[13] Blanch, M.P. for Gloucester 1710–13,[14] bought 36 a. near Wotton for his daughter Mary Horton in 1715.[15] He died in 1725[16] and his estate passed to his nephew William Blanch. William, who held part of the house with 57 a. by lease under the corporation, enlarged the estate, Mary Horton's land being settled in 1728 on his marriage. He died in 1758 and his son and heir William (d. 1766) left his estates for life to his widow Anne with reversion to James Rogers.[17] Anne married Samuel Walbank and in 1776 they and Rogers's heirs conveyed the estate of over 200 a. to trustees for sale.[18] Walbank purchased the house and much of the land in 1777 and sold them to Thomas Cother in 1779.[19] Cother, who had bought much land in the hamlets, particularly at Longford and Wotton in the 1770s, died in 1781 leaving the house for life to his widow Sarah (d. 1786) and the estate in trust for his sons William, Thomas, and Charles.[20] In 1790 George Caesar Hopkinson, an army officer, bought the house, known later as Wotton Court, and some land.[21] Hopkinson, who by 1812 had bought c. 95 a. in the adjoining part of

Barnwood from Robert Morris,[22] died in 1825 and the estate passed in the direct line to Charles (d. 1830) and Charles (d. 1882).[23] Parts of the estate adjoining the Barnwood road were sold off at the end of the century leaving 208 a., which Ralph Fream bought in 1899.[24] In the early 20th century the land, title of which was vested in 1905 in a limited company, was used for residential development.[25] In the early 18th century Wotton Court, which incorporated the house called Spencers, was of two storeys with attics and tall cross wings at each end of the main south front. There were formal gardens to the north and south and a short avenue led westwards to Wotton Pitch.[26] In 1799 the landscaped grounds, in which another house had been built, included a short canal.[27] In the 19th century the front of the centre range of Wotton Court was cased in brick and heightened to three storeys. The house was demolished c. 1900[28] and part of the fabric may have been used in a new building nearby. A lodge on the Cheltenham road at Cole bridge was standing in 1925.[29]

In 1791 the remaining part of Thomas Cother's estate was divided between his sons. Most of the Wotton land was assigned to William, the eldest, most of the Longford land to Thomas, and a few acres at Wotton to Charles, the youngest. William, who in 1795 bought much of Thomas's land and sold it to the Revd. Thomas Beale,[30] enlarged his own estate[31] and at his death in 1838[32] left it, including a farm at Puckstool, to Charles.[33] Charles died in 1855[34] and under his will the Puckstool or Wellsprings land passed in 1873 to Thomas Commeline, who sold it that year to James Witcombe[35] (d. 1899).[36] In 1913 Thomas Witcombe's Wellsprings estate covered 54 a. It was sold in 1916[37] and was later broken up.

A small estate was attached to *WOTTON HOUSE*, which in the early 18th century was the seat of Thomas Horton, John Blanch's son-in-law and owner of the Combend estate in Elkstone.[38] Thomas (d. 1727), a lunatic, was succeeded by his son Thomas, who was declared a lunatic in 1746. His estates, which were placed in the custody of his brothers-in-law, were disputed after his death in 1755, for, although by will dated 1735 he had devised them to members of the Brereton family, in 1739 he had settled them on his two sisters. Agreement for a threefold parti-

[7] *Trans. B.G.A.S.* l. 193–201; P.R.O., REQ 2/6/228.
[8] P.R.O., C 142/91, no. 113; cf. Glos. R.O., D 160/T 1; *Inq. p.m. Glos.* 1625–42, iii. 17–18.
[9] P.R.O., C 2/Eliz. I/T 5/9; G.B.R., J 1/1940/1–2; *V.C.H. Glos.* x. 247.
[10] *Glouc. Corp. Rec.* pp. 435–7.
[11] Glos. R.O., D 547A/T 15.
[12] *Inq. p.m. Glos.* 1625–42, ii. 181–2.
[13] Glos. R.O., D 547A/T 15; *V.C.H. Glos.* x. 191.
[14] Williams, *Parl. Hist. of Glos.* 207.
[15] Glos. R.O., D 2957/192.88.
[16] Bigland, *Glos.* ii. 154.
[17] Glos. R.O., D 2957/192.69–70, 72, 76; G.B.R., J 4/1, no. 15; J 3/8, ff. 211v.–216.
[18] Glos. R.O., D 134/T 57; D 936/E 147.
[19] Ibid. D 2957/192.77–8.
[20] Ibid. D 928, abs. of Revd. T. Beale's title; G.D.R. wills 1781/121.
[21] Burke, *Land. Gent.* (1937), 1152; cf. Glos. R.O., Q/RI 70 (map G).
[22] Glos. R.O., D 936/E 3/2; E 119/10.

[23] Burke, *Land. Gent.* (1937), 1152; cf. Glos. R.O., D 936/E 119/24, 31.
[24] Glos. Colln. (H) G 4.16; *Glouc. Jnl.* 20 May 1899.
[25] Glos. R.O., D 2299/5726.
[26] Atkyns, *Glos.* plate at pp. 428–9.
[27] Glos. R.O., Q/RI 70 (map G, nos. 92–3).
[28] Glos. Colln. (H) G 4.16; O.S. Map 1/2,500, Glos. XXV. 15 (1902 edn.).
[29] Glos. R.O., D 2299/5726.
[30] Ibid. D 928, abs. of Revd. T. Beale's title; Q/RI 70.
[31] Cf. ibid. D 2957/192.84; Q/RI 70.
[32] *Glouc. Jnl.* 2 June 1838.
[33] G.D.R. wills, 4 July 1838; G.B.R., L 22/1/121, pp. 35–6.
[34] *Glouc. Jnl.* 27 Jan. 1855.
[35] Glos. R.O., D 3117/1159–60.
[36] *Glouc. Jnl.* 11 Nov. 1899.
[37] Glos. R.O., D 2299/1298.
[38] Bodl. MS. Top. Glouc. c. 3, f. 199v., where Thomas is mistakenly called John.

tion was reached in 1758, and in 1763 Wotton House was confirmed as part of the share of the Revd. Richard Brereton,[39] who enlarged the estate[40] and died in 1801. The estate passed to his son Thomas, who had changed his name to Westfaling, and with the latter's Edgeworth estate to the Revd. Edward Colston Greville (d. 1830), who left it to be sold for the benefit of his seven children.[41] In 1838 Kitty Niblett owned the Wotton House estate[42] and it passed to her son D. J. Niblett (d. 1862).[43] Trustees under his will sold the house in 1873 to C. B. Walker.[44] Wotton House, which is dated 1707,[45] was built for Thomas Horton. It is of two storeys with attics and originally had outbuildings flanking a small forecourt on the east and a large walled garden on the west.[46] Many original fittings, including two staircases with twisted balusters, remain. The house was extended and some rooms were redecorated in the early 19th century by which time the formal garden had been destroyed, although part of the outer walls remains.[47] In 1925 it was acquired by Gloucestershire county council and converted as a hostel for its school of domestic science;[42] a large extension was made on the north in 1931.[49] Gloucestershire area health authority bought the house in the late 1970s.

In the mid 18th century Joseph Cheston, a Gloucester apothecary, acquired land north-east of the city[50] and after his death in 1779[51] it passed to his son Richard Browne Cheston, a surgeon. R. B. Cheston acquired piecemeal an estate of over 300 a.[52] centred on *LONGFORD HOUSE*, which he built for his residence.[53] He left the estate at his death in 1815 to his son, the Revd. Joseph Bonnor Cheston (d. 1829), from whom it passed first to his wife Rebecca (d. 1838) and then to his daughters Mary and Maria, wife of Robert Canning (d. 1843) of Hartpury.[54] Mary's undivided moiety passed at her death in 1844 to Maria, who later married Alexander Wright Daniel. Daniel retained that interest at her death in 1868 when the other moiety passed to her daughters by her first marriage, Maria, whose husband Patrick Gordon had taken the additional surname of Canning, and Frances, who later married Edmund Herbert. Daniel (d. 1882) left his interest to Frances and to trustees for Maria (d. 1887)

and some of her children including Robert (d. 1900) and William. Patrick Gordon-Canning died in 1893.[55] The estate was broken up by sales in the early 20th century.[56] Longford House was built in brick west of the Tewkesbury road before 1799.[57] In 1811 R. B. Cheston granted a lease of the house for five years.[58] It was demolished c. 1916.[59] Part of the stabling remained in 1983.

A small freehold estate based on the *MAYHOUSE* in Twigworth was settled in 1631 on Robert Herbert and in 1639 the reversion was bought by James Clent. In 1723 Samuel Mee bought the estate and in 1726 he settled it with other lands on the marriage of his son Thomas.[60] Thomas sold it in 1750 to Samuel Hayward, formerly a London linen draper, who under his marriage settlement was enlarging an estate centred on Sandhurst.[61] He purchased other land at Twigworth and Longford[62] and after his death in 1790 his land there descended with Wallsworth Hall in Sandhurst to Thomas de Winton (d. 1901).[63] J. T. Dorrington bought some Twigworth land with Wallsworth Hall in 1904, but most passed to de Winton's son Henry and was acquired c. 1920 by Frank Vines and in the later 1930s by Walter Cooke.[64] In 1945, following Cooke's death, 236 a. were sold with Twigworth Court to Percy House, whose son Frederick was the owner in 1983.[65] The Mayhouse evidently occupied the site of the farmhouse, which was rebuilt c. 1840 and renamed Twigworth Court.[66]

Land at Saintbridge belonged to the manor of Upton which Robert son of Henry inherited and in 1239 granted to his younger brother William.[67] The descent of the estate has not been traced, but it may have been included in Abbot's Barton and in the manor of Upton St. Leonards or Barton Upton, which had been formed from Abbot's Barton by 1536 and had land at Saintbridge.[68] The descent of Upton St. Leonards manor is reserved for a later volume. The Saintbridge tithing of Upton was described as a manor in 1541.[69]

A copyhold estate held by Margery Webley from Upton St. Leonards manor in 1589[70] formed the basis of the estate later attached to *SAINTBRIDGE HOUSE*. Margery's son John Webley[71] sold the freehold to John Badger in 1620, and Joseph Phelps, who acquired land at

[39] *Wilts. Arch. Mag.* v. 325–7; xli. 262; *V.C.H. Glos.* vii. 213.   [40] Glos. R.O., D 936/E 32.

[41] Ibid. D 1801/13–14; *V.C.H. Glos.* xi. 43.

[42] G.B.R., L 22/1/121, pp. 61–2.

[43] *V.C.H. Glos.* x. 191–2; Glos. R.O., D 936/E 119/35, 42.

[44] Deed in 1981 in possession of Glos. area health authority, Burlington Ho., Chelt.

[45] Rainwater head on N. end.

[46] Atkyns, *Glos.* 586 and plate at pp. 428–9.

[47] Cf. Causton, *Map of Glouc.* (1843).

[48] Land certificate 1979, in possession of Glos. area health authority; *Kelly's Dir. Glos.* (1927), 212.

[49] Date on rainwater heads; cf. *Glouc. Jnl.* 11 June 1932.

[50] Glos. R.O., D 2957/192.28, 74, 111.

[51] Ibid. P 154/9/IN 1/5.

[52] Ibid. D 3101/1; cf. ibid. D 2957/192.29, 34–55, 86, 89, 96–9, 172, 273; G.D.R., G 2/3/15669–70.

[53] *Glouc. New Guide* (1802), 111–12.

[54] G.D.R., G 2/3/304722; Glos. R.O., P 154/9/IN 1/21; D 2557/T 3.

[55] G.D.R., G 2/3/304722, 304719.

[56] Ibid. 304716; Glos. R.O., D 2299/6865.

[57] Glos. R.O., Q/RI 70 (map E, no. 113); D 2299/3621.

[58] Ibid. D 2957/192.57.

[59] Ibid. D 2299/3621; cf. *Kelly's Dir. Glos.* (1914), 245; (1919), 230.   [60] Glos. R.O., D 3117/238–40; cf. ibid. 135.

[61] Ibid. D 1326/T 41A.

[62] Ibid. D 626, Twigworth deeds 1736–65; Longford deeds 1754–72.

[63] Ibid. D 1297, Roberts fam., abs. of title 1857; Burke, *Land. Gent.* (1937), 611; mon. to Sam. and Cath. Hayward in Glouc. cath.; cf. Glos. R.O., Q/RI 70; *Kelly's Dir. Glos.* (1870–97 edns.), s.vv. Twigworth and Sandhurst.

[64] *Glouc. Jnl.* 31 Dec. 1904; *Kelly's Dir. Glos.* (1906 and later edns.).

[65] Glos. R.O., D 2299/7692; inf. from Mr. F.A. House, of Twigworth Ct.

[66] Cf. Glos. R.O., D 3117/240; Q/RI 70 (map A, no. 73).

[67] *Ciren. Cart.* ii, pp. 363–4.

[68] *Hist. & Cart. Mon. Glouc.* iii. 149–51; *Valor Eccl.* (Rec. Com.), ii. 416; Glos. R.O., P 347/MI 1; P 347A/FM 1–2.

[69] *L. & P. Hen. VIII*, xvi, p. 573; cf. G.D.R., T 1/189.

[70] Glos. R.O., P 347/MI 1.

[71] P.R.O., E 134/4 Jas. I Mich./18.

Saintbridge in 1704, bought the Badger family's land in 1706. In 1735 Phelps sold the estate to the printer Robert Raikes[72] (d. 1757), from whom it passed in turn to his wife Mary and his son Robert. In 1809 the estate was broken up by sale, the largest part being bought by James Wintle.[73] Wintle's purchase included Saintbridge House, which he had rebuilt by 1835.[74] In the late 1860s the house and 110 a. were owned together with a mill in Barnwood by Arthur Stewart (d. 1879).[75] Saintbridge House and its land, which Charles Brown bought in 1887, later belonged to J. D. Birchall of Bowden Hall in Upton St. Leonards. He sold most of the land in 1908, when Gloucestershire county council bought 76 a. for its asylum in Barnwood, and in 1912 he sold the house to his brother E. V. D. Birchall. After the latter's death in 1916 the house passed to his sisters Violet and Linda, wife of the Revd. C. H. Verey.[76] Gloucester corporation made it into a home for the elderly in 1954. A new wing was opened in 1962.[77]

Gloucester Abbey, which appropriated St. Mary de Lode rectory,[78] took the tithes of Abbot's Barton by the later 12th century.[79] In the early 16th century it granted leases of tithes for years or lives.[80] The abbey's possessions granted to the dean and chapter of Gloucester in 1541 included the impropriate rectory and tithes from Abbot's Barton, Wotton, and land called king's furlong which belonged to the King's Barton demesne.[81] The dean and chapter also acquired corn and hay tithes in the hamlets and Sandhurst known as the Kingsholm tithing, which had belonged to the abbey,[82] and they granted leases of corn and hay tithes for 21 years renewed every few years. James Elly (d. 1728), an attorney who acquired several leases, became the principal tithe holder.[83] The dean and chapter's tithes in the hamlets except Tuffley were commuted at inclosure in 1799 for land and corn rent charges. Of the lessees John Pitt received 14 a. and rent charges for that part of the Kingsholm tithing commuted. John Whithorne, the principal lessee, received 116 a. at Innsworth and rent charges.[84] That land, on which Innsworth Farm was built, passed in 1808 to William Ireland Newman and in 1816 to Samuel Lovesy. Lovesy's mortgagee, Esther Har-

tlebury, sold it to John Aubrey Whitcombe, a solicitor, in 1830. Whitcombe enlarged the estate in 1854,[85] and in 1863 it was broken up by sale.[86]

The tithes of Tuffley manor belonged to Gloucester Abbey, which in 1536 granted a lease of them to Thomas Hale.[87] They passed with St. Mary de Lode rectory to the dean and chapter of Gloucester under whom Richard Arden and John Morse claimed to hold them in the mid 1590s.[88] Later the tithes were held under leases for 21 years renewed every few years. By 1706 the lord farmer of the manor was lessee and from 1792 the tithes were held with the Tuffley Court estate.[89] In 1840 the tithes from c. 636 a. were commuted for a corn rent charge of £141 to the Revd. Henry Raikes as lessee, and those from another 70 a. at Tuffley, said to be tithable to Whaddon, were commuted for a corn rent charge of £13 13s. to Thomas Lediard.[90]

Gloucester Abbey also took the Upton tithes,[91] and in 1541 those of the Saintbridge tithing scattered throughout that parish were granted to the dean and chapter of Gloucester.[92] By the mid 17th century the Saintbridge corn and hay tithes were held under leases for 21 years renewed every few years.[93] In 1842, when they were leased to the landowners, they were commuted for a corn rent charge of £46 3s. 6d.[94]

Llanthony Priory acquired corn and hay tithes in Longford valued as a portion of St. Mary de Lode church at £1 6s. 8d. in 1291.[95] By the Dissolution, when those tithes were held with Hempsted rectory, the priory paid part to the inmates of St. Mary Magdalen's Hospital.[96] In 1609 the Crown granted the priory's Longford and Wotton tithes to Francis Morris and Francis Phillips.[97] They were later bought by Henry Cugley,[98] whose descendant John Twyning sold them in 1729. They were sold three more times before 1774[99] when Thomas Cother bought them. At the division of his estate they were assigned to his son Thomas but in 1795 Thomas's brother William acquired them[1] and sold parts to two other landowners, the Revd. Thomas Beale and Anthony Ellis. The tithes were commuted at inclosure in 1799 for land and corn rent charges.[2]

The bishop of Gloucester acquired corn and

[72] Glos. R.O., D 2957/321.110; D 134/T 17.
[73] Ibid. D 309/T 5; D 936/E 119/6; F. Booth, *Robert Raikes of Glouc.* (1980), 30–9.
[74] Glos. R.O., Q/RI 70 (map L, no. 112); G.D.R., T 1/189; view of the ho. dated 1835, in *Diary of a Cotswold Parson*, 96.
[75] Glos. R.O., D 1746/E 2; DC/F 3/3.
[76] Ibid. D 2299/338, 10844; ibid. HO 23/11/1; *Diary of a Victorian Squire*, ed. D. Verey (1983), pp. xii–xiii.
[77] *Glouc. Municipal Year Bk.* (1964–5), 96.
[78] Above, Churches and Chapels.
[79] *Hist. & Cart. Mon. Glouc.* i. 327.
[80] Cf. Glouc. Cath. Libr., Reg. Abb. Braunche, pp. 128–9; Reg. Abb. Malvern, i, ff. 151v.–153.
[81] *L. & P. Hen. VIII*, xvi, pp. 572–3; cf. Glouc. Cath. Libr., Reg. Abb. Malvern, i, f. 152.
[82] Glos. R.O., D 936/Y 19; Q/RI 70; cf. P.R.O., C 66/1193, m. 6, where the Crown in 1579 granted the Kingsholm tithing and the Abbot's Barton demesne tithes to John Farnham.
[83] Glos. R.O., D 936/E 12/1, ff. 45, 219 and v.; Y 3–9, Y 15–17, Y 19; P 154/14/IN 1/3; G.D.R. wills 1728/296.
[84] Glos. R.O., Q/RI 70.

[85] Ibid. D 2079/III/23–4; for Whitcombe, *Glouc. Jnl.* 21 Dec. 1872.
[86] Glos. R.O., D 1388/SL 4/85; *Glouc. Jnl.* 1 Aug. 1863.
[87] Glouc. Cath. Libr., Reg. Abb. Malvern, ii, ff. 119v.–120.
[88] P.R.O., E 134/35 & 36 Eliz. I Mich./33; E 123/22, f. 178v.; E 123/23, f. 255v.
[89] Glos. R.O., D 936/Y 21; E 12/2, ff. 68 and v., 313; E 110–11; E 119/24.
[90] G.D.R., T 1/86; G.B.R., L 22/1/111.
[91] *Hist. & Cart. Mon. Glouc.* i. 327.
[92] *L. & P. Hen. VIII*, xvi, p. 573; G.D.R., T 1/189.
[93] Glos. R.O., D 936/E 12/2, ff. 160v.–161, 195, 375 and v.; Y 18. [94] G.D.R., T 1/189.
[95] *Tax. Eccl.* (Rec. Com.), 224.
[96] *Valor Eccl.* (Rec. Com.), ii. 424; cf. *Trans. B.G.A.S.* lxiii. 41. [97] P.R.O., C 66/1798, mm. 1–28.
[98] Ibid. E 126/17, ff. 105v.–106.
[99] Glos. R.O., D 928, Longford deeds 1724–50, 1718–1850.
[1] Ibid. abs. of Revd. T. Beale's title.
[2] Ibid. Q/RI 70.

hay tithes from 51 a. near Longford.[3] In 1720 they were held under lease by Charles Hyett[4] and at inclosure were commuted for 9 a.[5]

St. Oswald's Priory took the tithes of St. Oswald's (later St. Catherine's) parish.[6] In 1542 the impropriate rectory and tithes in Longford, Twigworth, and Wotton were granted to the dean and chapter of Bristol cathedral.[7] The rectory and corn and hay tithes were held under lease from the dean and chapter, the leasehold passing in the early 18th century to James Elly.[8] In the late 18th century the dean and chapter and John Pitt, the lessee in 1771, claimed for the rectory the Tulwell tithes which had been included in leases of that estate from the mid 16th century.[9] The dean and chapter's tithes in the hamlets were commuted at inclosure in 1799 when Pitt received 45 a. and corn rent charges and William Jackson, lessee of tithes in Twigworth, 24 a.[10] Pitt bought the rectory except for its tithes in Sandhurst from the dean and chapter in 1801.[11]

In the later 16th century the Crown sold tithes in Wotton which had belonged to St. Oswald's Priory.[12] Those bought in 1577 by Peter Grey and his son Edmund passed to Benjamin Burroughs, who owned tithes from 120 a. in the mid 1780s.[13] James Laurence, William Cother, Robert Hopton, and the rector of St. John the Baptist owned St. Oswald's tithes at inclosure in 1799 when those tithes were commuted for 13 a. in Barton St. Mary and Wotton and for corn rent charges, one of which was claimed by a lessee of the bishop of Bristol.[14] Outside the hamlets St. Oswald's Priory's tithes in Meanham were granted in 1540 to John Jennings[15] and were commuted in 1850 for a corn rent charge of £12 to the Revd. John Fendall Newton.[16]

Tithes in Longford, apparently acquired by St. Augustine's Abbey, Bristol, were granted to the bishop of Bristol in 1542.[17] They were held under lease with Sandhurst rectory and were commuted in 1799 for 8 a. and a corn rent charge. That land passed to the Ecclesiastical Commissioners in 1856.[18]

St. Mary Magdalen's Hospital acquired tithes, including by 1265 hay tithes from Sud Meadow.[19] At inclosure in 1799 the tithes, which were held under Gloucester corporation as the hospital's trustee, were commuted for small plots of land and corn rent charges.[20]

AGRICULTURE. There was extensive arable farming outside Gloucester in the early Middle Ages. In 1066 there were 12 ploughteams on King's Barton manor, of which 3 belonged with 7 *servi* to the demesne. The manor rendered £9 5s. and 3,000 loaves for the king's hunting dogs. The king's reeve had added a team and more tenants and mills by 1086 when the manor, which apparently had 22 teams, rendered £20, 20 cows, 20 pigs, and 16s. for bread. In 1086 the number of teams on Abbot's Barton manor was 54, of which 9 were in demesne with 12 *servi*. The manor's value had trebled from £8 in 1066. Of the two estates in Wotton surveyed in 1086 that of William Froisselew, which had doubled in value since 1066, had 4 teams in demesne with 4 *servi*, and that of Hunfrid de Medehal, which had fallen in value by a third, 1 team in demesne with 3 *servi*.[21] In 1220 there were 17 teams in King's Barton, 3 in Twigworth, 2 in Longford, and 1½ in Wotton.[22]

In the 1260s the King's Barton demesne comprised 275 a. of arable, 58 a. of meadow, and 4½ a. of pasture in a moor. The king also took the profits of a beech wood, which contained c. 30 a. and was subject to common pasture rights; it was evidently on the Cotswold escarpment near Pincott in Upton St. Leonards. The king had 15 oxen, 1 cow, and 1 heifer on the manor and Gloucester Abbey was required to supplement the small amount of demesne pasture, which could support only 12 oxen for a month, by finding pasturage for 18 oxen, 2 cows, and 2 horses before haymaking. The manor could keep 200 wethers and 24 pigs between Easter and Martinmas.[23] The demesne of Kingsholm manor in 1304 included 155 a. of arable, 28 a. of meadow, 11 a. of pasture, and pastures called the Stath and Kingsholm green.[24] In 1607 the demesne on Sir William Cooke's two parts of the manor was extended at 224 a., of which only 18 a. were in hand and the rest was held as 14 tenements ranging from 1 a. to 40 a.[25]

In 1291 there were 6 and 2 ploughlands in Abbot's Barton and Tuffley respectively. Tulwell manor included 1½ ploughland.[26] In 1535, following the creation of manors at Longford and Wotton, the demesne of Abbot's Barton, part of which lay outside the hamlets, included 266 a. of arable, 117 a. of meadow, and 42 a. of pasture. The Tuffley demesne comprised 125 a. of arable, 53 a. of pasture, and 33 a. of meadow excluding Monk Meadow which had been let at farm.[27] In 1536 the demesne remaining in hand was let at farm with pasture rights and 10 loads of firewood a year from Standish wood.[28] Arable husbandry was relatively less important on the demesne of Llanthony Priory's estate which in 1535 included 102 a. of arable, 160 a. of meadow, and 130 a. of

[3] Ibid. D 6/E 4; T 5.
[4] P.R.O., E 134/6 & 7 Geo. I Trin./1.
[5] Glos. R.O., Q/RI 70.
[6] Above, Churches and Chapels.
[7] L. & P. Hen. VIII, xvii, pp. 638–9.
[8] Glos. R.O., D 936/L 11; cf. P.R.O., REQ 2/100/24; REQ 2/80/1; REQ 2/117/11.
[9] Glos. R.O., D 936/L 11–12.
[10] Ibid. Q/RI 70.
[11] Ibid. D 2078, Goodrich fam., deed 1 June 1801.
[12] Rudder, Glos. 578.
[13] Glos. R.O., D 2957/192.37, 41–2, 84.
[14] Ibid. Q/RI 70.
[15] L. & P. Hen. VIII, xv, p. 592.

[16] G.D.R., T 1/85.
[17] L. & P. Hen. VIII, xvii, p. 257.
[18] Glos. R.O., Q/RI 70; D 936/Y 35, Y 38.
[19] Trans. B.G.A.S. lxiii. 51.
[20] Glos. R.O., Q/RI 70.
[21] Dom. Bk. (Rec. Com.), i. 162v., 165v., 167v., 170.
[22] Bk. of Fees, i. 307.
[23] Hist. & Cart. Mon. Glouc. iii. 67, 71, 73.
[24] P.R.O., C 133/113, no. 5.
[25] Glos. R.O., D 326/E 1, ff. 50–61v.
[26] Tax. Eccl. (Rec. Com.), 231, 233.
[27] Valor Eccl. (Rec. Com.), ii. 414–16.
[28] Glouc. Cath. Libr., Reg. Abb. Malvern, ii, ff. 119v.–120.

pasture.[29] The priory had a sheephouse at Shepherds Elms[30] and the meadows around Llanthony were used for dairy farming and cheese making.[31]

After its inclusion in the Barnwood estate the demesne of Wotton manor was not distinguished in estate surveys from that of Barnwood.[32] In 1650 the demesne of Tuffley manor, represented by 236 a. extended with Tuffley Court and comprising more pasture than arable, was evidently grouped as holdings of 190 a., 27 a., 13 a., and 6 a. The largest was farmed with Tuffley Court which had a large buttery. The Tulwell estate remained mainly arable.[33]

The tenants on King's Barton manor in 1066 were 14 *villani* and 10 bordars with 9 ploughs. Eight bordars had been added by 1086 when 2 freemen held 2 hides with 9 ploughs.[34] In the 1260s there were 38 free tenements of varying sizes on the manor, excluding those in Gloucester's suburbs, and most were ancient tenures. Many represented estates in parishes outside the hamlets and there was also a salt pan at Droitwich for which Gloucester Abbey rendered a fixed quota of salt. Save for the Kingsholm estate, which was a serjeanty, the tenements were of three yardlands or less. Most owed cash rents and several also customary payments or else some specific service; six were held by the service of carrying writs through the county. One tenant had to supply an archer in war, a smith owed 200 arrows, and one tenant surnamed of Pincott kept the king's wood. The customary payments included *wiveneweddinge* on the eve of the feast of St. John the Baptist and a hen at Christmas. One tenant owed bedrips.[35] The customary tenants on the manor were 6 holding ½ yardlands, 4 pairs holding ½ yardlands jointly, 3 holding ¼ yardlands, and 1 holding 9 a. Most half-yardlanders paid cash rents and were required to work four days and plough ½ a. every other week. They also owed ploughing boonwork and bedrips, performed a custom called *benherthe* by which they cultivated ½ a. and received a sheaf, and paid the customary payments mentioned above; for the Christmas hen they received a load of wood. The tenant of 9 a. worked four days a week from July to September and two days a week for the rest of the year.[36] The rents of assize said to belong to King's Barton manor in 1535 may have included payments from tenants of Abbot's Barton manor.[37] Copyhold tenure had been introduced in King's Barton manor by the mid 16th century.[38] In 1637, when some copyholders claimed never to have received copies, some tenants at rack rent in Barton Street were granted leases for 21 years.[39] In the later 18th century the manor comprised freehold and copyhold estates, cottages on waste ground in many parishes and hamlets near Gloucester, and fishing rights in a stretch of the river Leadon.[40]

In 1304 Kingsholm manor had 26 free tenants, most paying cash rents. One held a ploughland and one a yardland, but most, including a smith, a few acres or a cottage. There were also 6 villeins, who held 12 a. or 8 a. and paid cash rents. They each spent 1½ day in digging and treating loam, mowed for 10 days, and provided a man to reap and work during the autumn for 32 days.[41] In 1607 Sir William Cooke's Kingsholm estate had free tenements of 52 a. and 17 a. on one part and copyholds of 11½ a. and 1½ a. on the other.[42] Copyhold tenure in Kingsholm had been extinguished by the end of the 18th century.[43]

The tenants on Abbot's Barton manor and its members in 1086 were 42 *villani* and 21 bordars with 45 ploughs.[44] In the 1260s Abbot's Barton included 51 holdings of varying sizes, some being estates in parishes outside the Gloucester hamlets. The two largest were each a ploughland, held by the serjeanty of providing a squire equipped with a horse and harness and owing heriots and reliefs. Two of a yardland, one of which was held by two tenants, owed the same service for half a year, and another tenant provided a squire for two holdings of ½ yardland. Cash rents owed by four holdings of ½ yardland and two of ¼ yardland possibly represented that service commuted. Three holdings, ¾, ½, and ¼ yardland, owed cash rents and customary payments, and tenants of several mills owed heriots. The other holdings, which owed cash rents and aid, included five ½ yardlands, of which one was held with two mondaylands, and nine ¼ yardlands, of which three were held with a mondayland.[45] A ½ yardland was apparently also included among the customary tenements. Those included thirty of ½ yardland (a ½ yardland being 32 a.), fifteen of ¼ yardland, and thirty-two mondaylands, each of 4 a. There were also 6 cottars. Most half-yardlanders were apparently required to work three days a week from October to July and five days every other week in August and September. The one day owed by the mondaymen was increased (except in the case of one tenant) to two in the harvest months. Other customs included two heriots to Gloucester Abbey, one as lord and the other as rector of St. Mary de Lode, and pannage.[46]

In the early 16th century the abbey granted leases of demesne and other land held under the manors of Abbot's Barton, Longford, Wotton, and Tuffley for terms of years or lives with heriots payable. Some Abbot's Barton and Wotton tenants were required to carry several loads of firewood a year to the abbey from Buckholt wood, which centred on Cranham, and a Longford tenant to collect timber in the abbey's wood at

---

[29] *Valor Eccl.* (Rec. Com.), ii. 430.
[30] P.R.O., C 115/L 2/6691, f. 61 and v.
[31] *L. & P. Hen. VIII*, v, pp. 750, 758; Leland, *Itin.* ed. Toulmin Smith, ii. 63.
[32] Below, Barnwood, econ. hist.
[33] Glos. R.O., D 1740/E 1, ff. 90–1, 124 and v.
[34] *Dom. Bk.* (Rec. Com.), i. 162v.
[35] *Hist. & Cart. Mon. Glouc.* iii. 67–71; for the salt pan, ibid. ii. 143; *Ex. e Rot. Fin.* (Rec. Com.), i. 110.
[36] *Hist. & Cart. Mon. Glouc.* iii. 71–2.

[37] *Valor Eccl.* (Rec. Com.), ii. 415–16.
[38] P.R.O., C 3/14/99.
[39] Glos. R.O., D 45/M 1.
[40] Ibid. M 3; D 326/M 24; T 13; SL 196.
[41] P.R.O., C 133/113, no. 5.
[42] Glos. R.O., D 326/E 1, ff. 54 and v., 60–1.
[43] Ibid. Q/RI 70; Rudge, *Hist. of Glos.* ii. 144.
[44] *Dom. Bk.* (Rec. Com.), i. 165v.
[45] *Hist. & Cart. Mon. Glouc.* iii. 149–54.
[46] Ibid. 158–64.

Woolridge between Maisemore and Hartpury for repairs.[47] In 1535 Longford, Wotton, and Tuffley manors had customary tenants owing rents of assize.[48] Barton farm, the Abbot's Barton land which passed to Gloucester corporation, was held by leaseholders under the corporation's lessee and from 1621 under the corporation itself.[49] In 1650 the Barnwood estate included nine copyholds in Wotton, of which two had been divided. They ranged from 4 a. to 41½ a. The surviving customs included pannage in Buckholt wood.[50] In later surveys the Barnwood and Wotton copyholders were not usually distinguished[51] and at inclosure in 1799 most were said to be in Barnwood.[52] Only 28 a. in Wotton remained copyhold in 1856.[53] On Tuffley manor there were 6 freeholders and 15 copyholders in 1650. Of the copyholders five had c. 25 a. (described as ½ yardland), two c. 20 a., and eight 10–17 a. The surviving customs included swine tack or pannage, and every tenant owning a cart had to fetch wood once a year from Buckholt for the dean and chapter.[54] Three were 10 copyholders on the manor in 1760. Several extensive copyhold estates were built up in the 18th century and a large part of Tuffley continued to be copyhold until the mid 19th.[55] The bishop's Longford manor in 1647 comprised nine tenements held by lease for terms of years or lives and six held by copy. Of the leaseholds one had 28 a., four 10–20 a., and four less than 10 a., and of the copyhold two had 18 a. and the others less than 9 a.[56] In 1858 the manor comprised 127 a. held under leases for lives, 16 a. under leases for 21 years, and only 19 a. under copy.[57] Much land in Longford continued to be held under leases for lives until 1904.[58]

The tenants on the two Wotton estates in 1086 were 4 bordars on that of William Froisselew and 4 bordars with 2 ploughteams on that of Hunfrid de Medehal.[59]

Open-field land outside Gloucester is recorded from the 13th century.[60] There had been major changes in the fields by the 16th century, including the absorption of a field at Paygrove by another and the division of a north field at Wotton.[61] There had also been piecemeal inclosure, some of which accompanied consolidation of the demesne of Abbot's Barton, and much land near Gloucester was in several meadows or pasture.[62] In the 16th century areas of open-field

land remained near Gloucester's suburbs, including one at Ryecroft near Barton Street, but the main fields lay further away.[63] There is no evidence that the fields, apart from those at Tuffley, formed groups. Orders regulating the use of fields near Longford and Wotton were made in Plock Court and Barnwood manor courts,[64] but the land of the hamlets and manors mingled in the fields, in which neighbouring parishes shared.[65] There were at least 12 fields to the north and north-east of Gloucester, namely West and Pedmarsh fields north and east of Kingsholm respectively; Apperley and Longford fields at Longford; Twigworth or Brook, Burcott, and White Cross fields at Twigworth; Chamwell, Wyatts, and Innsworth fields east of Longford; and Colebridge and Elbridge fields north of Wotton. East of Gloucester was Windmill field, which covered a large area extending south-eastwards from Wotton to the Twyver at Coney Hill. There were several small fields by the Painswick road north-west of Saintbridge, including Sand field and Tween Brooks. South of Gloucester there was open-field land at Drakes Croft south of the Sud brook, and further out Tredworth field included a large area stretching to the lower slopes of Robins Wood Hill; the areas east and west of the Tuffley road were known by 1699 as Upper and Lower Tredworth fields respectively.[66] There was open-field land to the west at Madleaze and to the south at Shepherds Elms in the early 16th century.[67]

Tuffley had at least eight open fields which were shared not with other hamlets but with neighbouring parishes, for example West field with Quedgeley and Hempsted and Whaddon's Hill with Quedgeley and Whaddon. Markham field, which was on the south side of Robins Wood Hill and was recorded from the mid 13th century,[68] was shared with Matson, Upton St. Leonards, and Whaddon. Tuffley also had fragments in Tredworth field and in two fields within Quedgeley to the south-east.[69]

Most of the 120 a. of meadow recorded in 1086 in Abbot's Barton and its members[70] presumably comprised Oxlease and other meadows north-west of Gloucester in which the burgesses shared commoning rights with the abbey and its Maisemore tenants.[71] Oxlease, which passed with the site of the manor, covered 39 a. on Alney

[47] Glouc. Cath. Libr., Reg. Abb. Braunche, pp. 8, 19, 55, 164–5; Reg. Abb. Malvern, i, ff. 36v.–277; ii, ff. 3–143v.

[48] Valor Eccl. (Rec. Com.), ii. 414–16.

[49] G.B.R., J 1/1956; B 3/1, ff. 480v.–1; J 4/1, nos. 18, 31 (2).

[50] Glos. R.O., D 1740/E 1, ff. 15–17v., 20.

[51] Cf. ibid. E 3, ff. 27–92.

[52] Ibid. Q/RI 70.

[53] Church Com. MSS., Glouc. chapter est. surv. M 4, p. 358.

[54] Glos. R.O., D 1740/E 1, ff. 91v.–96.

[55] Ibid. D 936/M 27/1–2; E 3/2, ff. 52–3; Rudge, Hist. of Glos. ii. 178.

[56] G.D.R., G 3/19, pp. 38–54.

[57] Church Com. MSS., Glouc. and Bristol bishopric est. surv. M 1, p. 540.

[58] G.D.R., G 2/3/304716.

[59] Dom. Bk. (Rec. Com.), i. 167v., 170.

[60] Glouc. Corp. Rec. pp. 117, 151, 203, 219, 263; Glouc.

Cath. Libr., deeds and seals, ii, f. 3.

[61] Glouc. Corp. Rec. pp. 223–4, 292–3; P.R.O., SC 6/Hen. VIII/1248, rott. 3d.–4.

[62] Glouc. Cath. Libr., Reg. Abb. Malvern, i. ff. 36v.–37, 121, 270v.–271; ii, ff. 129v.–130.

[63] Ibid. i, ff. 36v.–277; ii, f. 31 and v.; Glos. R.O., P 347/MI 1; G.B.R., B 2/1, f. 238v.

[64] P.R.O., SC 2/175/16; Glos. R.O., D 1815, Barnwood, Wotton, Cranham, and Tuffley ct. rolls 1558–71.

[65] Glos. R.O., D 326/E 1, ff. 50–61; D 1740/E 1, ff. 12–17v., 90–94v., 124–5; G.D.R., G 3/19, pp. 38–45.

[66] Cf. Glos. R.O., Q/RI 70 (maps); Q/RI 79; D 1809/T 1.

[67] Valor Eccl. (Rec. Com.), ii. 430.

[68] P.R.O., C 115/K 1/6681, f. 187v.

[69] Glos. R.O., Q/RI 32; G.D.R., T 1/86, 195.

[70] Dom. Bk. (Rec. Com.), i. 165v.

[71] Glouc. Corp. Rec. pp. 421–6; above, Medieval Glouc., town and religious communities.

Island.[72] Two large common meadows, Walham with *c.* 100 a. and Sud Meadow with *c.* 180 a., bordered the Severn north and south-west of Gloucester respectively.[73] That part of Walham known as Coberley's dole in the early 16th century had presumably been attached to Gloucester Abbey's manor in Coberley parish.[74] A dole stone recorded in 1607 marked the boundary of eight holdings in the meadow.[75] In the late 18th century pasture rights in Walham after haymaking were enjoyed without stint by landholders in the neighbouring hamlets.[76] In 1304 the lord of Kingsholm manor had the right to pasture a foal in Walham[77] and in 1607 Sir William Cooke by ancient right ran two horses in the same from the feast of St. George (23 April) until it had been mown.[78] That right, which adversely affected the hay crop, was commuted at inclosure in 1799.[79] Much of Sud Meadow belonged to Llanthony Priory after an exchange with the Crown in 1265,[80] and in 1416 the priory claimed that Gloucester Abbey's tenants had overburdened the meadow.[81] The meadow included parts which were lot meadow.[82] By the mid 17th century the lord of Llanthony had exclusive pasture rights over Sud Meadow between the feasts of All Saints and St. George,[83] a custom which inhibited the growth of grass. After the hay harvest in the late 18th century landholders in the meadow observed a stint of 2 cows to the acre and the duke of Norfolk, owner of the Llanthony estate, also had unstinted pasture rights for horses and sheep.[84]

There were small common meadows at Longford and Twigworth, including Hatherley Meadow, Dry Meadow, and Frize Meadow between the Horsbere and Hatherley brooks.[85] In the early 16th century a flock of ewes from Gloucester Abbey's estate at Sandhurst had winter pasture in Walham and Frize Meadow.[86] Monk Meadow with *c.* 18 a. between Gloucester and Hempsted belonged to the Tuffley demesne[87] and in 1535 was in the hands of a tenant or tenants.[88] Under an agreement of 1287 Llanthony Priory enjoyed common of pasture and a right of way in the meadow after haymaking,[89] but in the early 15th century it was again in dispute with Gloucester Abbey over the meadow, parts of

which had been brought under the plough.[90] In the mid 17th century the lessee of Tuffley manor shared the aftermath with the lord of Llanthony. As well as in Sud Meadow, Tuffley manor had pieces in Coberley Meadow and Long Meadow, two small common meadows south-west of Gloucester.[91]

The times at which the common meadows were opened and closed to livestock varied.[92] In the early 16th century Frize Meadow was opened at Michaelmas.[93] In the mid 17th century the Wotton leaseholders and copyholders had common of pasture in the open fields, Walham, and Dry Meadow at the rate of 80 sheep and 16 cows or horses for the yardland; some copyholders had additional rights for cattle in Walham or Sud Meadow from haymaking to the feast of All Saints. The lessee of the Tulwell estate had common of pasture in Walham for 16 cattle.[94] Some Longford landholders had common of pasture for cattle in Longford Ham, bordering the Severn west of Longford.[95] Sheep farming was carried on near Gloucester in the Middle Ages and a sheep pen was recorded in Wotton in 1330.[96]

In 1547 the demense of Abbot's Barton included four areas of open-field land, at Ryecroft and elsewhere, which were cropped each year and were described as every year's land.[97] The practice of annual cropping, also followed in Longford field in 1534,[98] resulted from the high rent of land near Gloucester and was observed in most if not all the open fields outside the city in the late 18th century, when corn and pulses were grown alternately.[99] The area under arable declined from the 16th century and the estates, particularly in Tuffley, included a large proportion of permanent pasture in closes in the early 17th century.[1] The Sheephouse estate south of Gloucester was formed in 1611 mostly from meadow and pasture closes.[2] The piecemeal inclosure of the open fields continued in the 17th and 18th centuries.[3] By 1762 meadow and pasture closes covering 48 a. had been created in the open fields at Innsworth.[4] By 1799 some smaller open fields had disappeared and part of West field adjoining Walham had been laid down as grassland, known as Green West field.[5] In the late 18th century much of the

[72] Glos. R.O., D 326/T 144; G.B.R., J 4/1, no. 31(2); Causton, *Map of Glouc.* (1843).

[73] Glos. R.O., AP 85; ibid. Q/RI 70 (maps C–D, R); Q/RI 79.

[74] Glouc. Cath. Libr., Reg. Abb. Malvern, i, f. 121.

[75] Glos. R.O., D 326/E 1, f. 52.

[76] *Trans. B.G.A.S.* lxiv. 32. [77] P.R.O., C 133/113, no. 5.

[78] Glos. R.O., D 326/E 1, f. 62.

[79] Ibid. Q/RI 70; W. Marshall, *Rural Econ. of Glos.* (1789), i. 198; cf. *V.C.H. Glos.* x. 22, where the right is said mistakenly to belong to Highnam manor.

[80] *Trans. B.G.A.S.* lxiii. 50–1.

[81] P.R.O., C 115/K 2/6682, ff. 107–8.

[82] Glos. R.O., D 326/E 35; D 1740/E 3, f. 66.

[83] Scudamore Churches Endowment Act, 13 & 14 Chas. II, c. 11 (Priv. Act).

[84] Marshall, *Rural Econ. of Glos.* i. 198; *Trans. B.G.A.S.* lxiv. 32.

[85] Glos. R.O., D 326/E 1, ff. 51–60v.; D 1740/E 1, ff. 12–17v., 124; G.D.R., G 3/19, pp. 41–4; G.B.R., J 4/1, no. 31(2).

[86] Glouc. Cath. Libr., Reg. Abb. Braunche, p. 109; *Hist. & Cart. Mon. Glouc.* iii. 291–2.

[87] Glos. R.O., D 1740/E 1, f. 90; D 936/E 110–11; Q/RI 79.

[88] *Valor Eccl.* (Rec. Com.), ii. 414; cf. Glouc. Cath. Libr., Reg. Abb. Malvern, ii, f. 119v.

[89] *Hist. & Cart. Mon. Glouc.* iii. 244–5.

[90] P.R.O., C 115/K 2/6682, ff. 107, 181.

[91] Glos. R.O., D 1740/E 1, ff. 90–94v.; G.D.R., T 1/86.

[92] Marshall, *Rural Econ. of Glos.* i. 198.

[93] Glos. R.O., D 326/T 144.

[94] Ibid. D 1740/E 1, ff. 15–17v., 20, 124v.

[95] Ibid. D 326/E 1, ff. 51–2; G.D.R., G 2/3/15667, 16046; cf. Glos. R.O., Q/RI 70 (maps B–C).

[96] *Glouc. Corp. Rec.* p. 323.

[97] G.B.R., B 2/1, f. 31v.

[98] Glouc. Cath. Libr., Reg. Abb. Malvern, ii, ff. 86v.–87.

[99] Marshall, *Rural Econ. of Glos.* i. 65–6; Rudge, *Agric. of Glos.* 150.

[1] Glos. R.O., D 326/E 1, ff. 50–61; D 1740/E 1, ff. 12–17v., 90–94v., 120, 124–5; G.D.R., G 3/19, pp. 38–44.

[2] Glos. R.O., D 3117/1.

[3] Cf. ibid. D 6/T 17; D 936/E 115; E 118/161; E 171, terrier of Edw. Driver's land 1772.

[4] Ibid. D 936/E 38.

[5] Ibid. Q/RI 70 (award and map B, nos. 123–4).

countryside around Gloucester was devoted to dairy farming and some large farms were made up entirely of grassland.[6] Some closes were leased by city butchers and innkeepers.[7]

An orchard was recorded at Wotton in 1429.[8] In the 17th and 18th centuries there were numerous orchards around Gloucester, where several varieties of apple and pear were raised.[9] In the hamlets the number of market and nursery gardens supplying the needs of the city increased. In 1653 a nursery of fruit trees was recorded in outer Barton Street,[10] and in the 1790s James Wheeler, a leading Gloucester nurseryman, had several nurseries in Kingsholm.[11]

The inclosure of the open fields and common meadows in the hamlets, excluding most of Tuffley and meadows in which the Gloucester burgesses had common rights, was largely completed in 1799 under an Act of 1796 which also covered the vill of Wotton, Barnwood, and Matson. The award re-allotted many existing inclosures. In the hamlets allotments were made, some for tithes, to 108 proprietors holding under a variety of tenures. Nearly a quarter of them each received less than 2 a. Each landholder's share of the inclosure cost was met by the sale of a small part of his or her allotted land. Property exchanges under the award included land in South Hamlet and Upton St. Leonards and led to the acquisition of 53 a. in South Hamlet by the rector of Matson.[12]

Sud Meadow was inclosed in 1815 under an Act of 1814. The award, which also dealt with Coberley Meadow and open-field land in Lower Tredworth field, re-allotted a few existing inclosures and gave Monk Meadow, an adjoining meadow called Little Coberley Meadow, and part of Coberley Meadow to the duke of Norfolk. He was also awarded a group of former common meadows lying west of Hempsted in which the rights had been shared between his Llanthony estate and estates in Hempsted.[13] Of Sud Meadow 140 a. were allotted to the duke and the rest was divided between seven other landholders. Seven people received land in Lower Tredworth ranging from ¼ a. to 18½ a. Exchanges of land under the award made for the consolidation of a few holdings in Tuffley.[14] Inclosure in Tuffley was piecemeal and by 1802 had reduced Markham field to two separate areas.[15] Parts of the park had been inclosed by 1684.[16] Tuffley's inclosure was completed with that of adjoining parishes in 1866. The award, which re-allotted many existing closes, dealt with a green, five or six areas of open-field land in the south and west of Tuffley,

Long Meadow, and an adjoining meadow. Of the eight people receiving allotments in Tuffley, J. Curtis-Hayward had 50 a., H. C. Raikes 23½ a., and the others less than 10 a. each.[17]

In the early 19th century most agricultural land near Gloucester was under grass and supported cattle, some of which were fattened for London's Smithfield market, and flocks of Ryeland sheep.[18] In 1801 the parishes of St. Mary de Lode and St. Michael had 821 a. under crops, mainly wheat, barley, and beans, with some peas, vetches, and potatoes.[19] Tuffley in 1840 had 600 a. of meadow and pasture compared with 120 a. of arable.[20] In 1866 most agricultural land in the hamlets was devoted to permanent grassland and only southeast of Gloucester in Barton St. Mary was as much land under arable crops as under grass. The hamlets returned 562 cattle, including 190 milk cows, 685 sheep, of which Longford accounted for 415, and 672 pigs, most of them in Barton St. Mary, Longford, and Wotton. The principal arable crops were wheat and potatoes, and significant acreages in Longford were also used for other roots and in Tuffley for beans.[21] The land remained principally meadow and pasture and the parishes of Gloucester, Longford, Twigworth, and Wotton St. Mary (Without), which in 1905 included 2,372½ a. of permanent grass compared with 575 a. of arable,[22] returned 734 cattle, including 283 milk cows, 538 sheep, and 800 pigs in 1926, as well as large numbers of poultry.[23] Orcharding, which was increased at Innsworth in the mid 19th century,[24] remained an important feature and in 1896 covered at least 172 a. in the parishes of Gloucester, Longford, Tuffley, Twigworth, and Wotton St. Mary (Without).[25] The demands of Gloucester's growing population in the 19th century increased market gardening in the hamlets and by 1843 J. C. Wheeler's nurseries included a large area between Kingsholm and Wotton.[26] In 1851 market gardeners were fairly numerous in Longford and Twigworth,[27] and later there were several market gardens and nurseries at Longlevens (called Springfield) and Innsworth.[28] In 1896 at least 84 a., most of them in Longford parish, were devoted to such use.[29]

In the 19th century there were many small farms in the hamlets where few had over 150 a.[30] In 1896 a total of 112 agricultural occupiers was returned for Gloucester, Longford, Tuffley, Twigworth, and Wotton St. Mary (Without),[31] and of a total of 81, not including Tuffley, returned in 1926 67 had less than 50 a. and only 1 in Longford, 1 in Twigworth, and 3 in Wotton more than 150 a.[32] Several farms, including

[6] Marshall, *Rural Econ. of Glos.* i. 48.

[7] G.B.R., B 3/9, ff. 136v., 162v., 315, 431v.; 10, f. 270.

[8] Glos. R.O., D 326/T 142.

[9] Ibid. E 1, ff. 50–59v.; D 134/T 17; cf. Rudge, *Agric. of Glos.* 209–32.

[10] Glos. R.O., D 6/T 1; above, Glouc. 1660–1720, econ. development.

[11] Glos. R.O., D 936/M 11.

[12] Ibid. Q/RI 70.

[13] Below, Hempsted, econ. hist.

[14] Glos. R.O., Q/RI 79. [15] G.B.R., L 6/27/18.

[16] Glos. R.O., D 936/M 27/1.

[17] Ibid. Q/RI 32.

[18] Rudge, *Agric. of Glos.* 190–1, 195.

[19] *List & Index Soc.* clxxxix, p. 172. [20] G.D.R., T 1/86.

[21] P.R.O., MAF 68/25/13; MAF 68/26/4–5, 19–21.

[22] Acreage Returns, 1905.

[23] P.R.O., MAF 68/3295/9–10.

[24] Glos. R.O., D 2299/367, 1567.

[25] P.R.O., MAF 68/1609/12–13.

[26] Causton, *Map of Glouc.* (1843).

[27] P.R.O., HO 107/1961–2.

[28] *Kelly's Dir. Glos.* (1863–1939 edns.), s.vv. Barnwood, Longford, and Wotton St. Mary (Without).

[29] P.R.O., MAF 68/1609/12–13.

[30] Cf. Glos. R.O., D 936/E 3/1; P.R.O., HO 107/1961–2.

[31] P.R.O., MAF 68/1609/12–13.

[32] Ibid. MAF 68/3295/9–10.

Manor farm at Longford with *c.* 200 a., supplied milk for sale in the city.[33] In the late 1930s inhabitants included a dairyman in Longford and a poultry farmer and 4 dairymen in the former Wotton St. Mary (Without).[34] There were several farms in Tuffley, of which one belonged to a Gloucester butcher.[35] In the mid 20th century the appropriation of land for housing steadily reduced the number and size of farms.

TRADES AND FISHERIES. The few trades recorded in the hamlets before they were affected by the growth and commercial development of Gloucester from the early 19th century were those usual for small agricultural settlements. Longford had a carpenter, a smith, and a tailor in 1608[36] and two smithies were worked there in the 1750s.[37] Twigworth had a carpenter in 1729.[38] In 1327 a wheelwright was apparently assessed for tax in Wotton,[39] which with Barnwood included several tradesmen in 1608.[40] Most of the tradesmen listed in Barton Street in 1608 presumably lived in the inner suburban part.[41] In the outer part there was at least one smith's shop in the mid 18th century[42] and a glue yard nearby in 1750.[43] A fisherman lived at Saintbridge in 1327[44] and another at Longford in 1720.[45]

The principal source of fish was the Severn. Gloucester Abbey claimed fishing rights in stretches of the river touching its lands under a grant of William I, and in the later 13th century the lord of Kingsholm manor enjoyed the right to fish in the river with appropriate nets and two small boats, though not near the abbey's two fishing weirs above Westgate bridge. The higher weir, known as Each weir[46] and held under lease from the dean and chapter of Gloucester in the early 17th century,[47] was at or near Walham,[48] where a weir house was apparently standing in 1610.[49] Fishing rights in the stretch of the Severn below Gloucester castle belonged to the lord of Llanthony in the late 16th century.[50] They extended for 3½ miles (5.6 km.) and their own-

ership passed with Newark House until *c.* 1914.[51]

MILLS. In 1086 King's Barton manor included three mills, of which two had been built since 1066, and Abbot's Barton manor one.[52] In the 1260s King's Barton had two mills, of which one was apparently in Upton St. Leonards, and Abbot's Barton had six.[53] In 1291 five were recorded on Abbot's Barton manor and one at Tuffley,[54] where a millward was assessed for the subsidy in 1327.[55] There was a mill in Walham in the later 13th century[56] but many of the mills mentioned were on the river Twyver above Gloucester. Five mill sites have been identified on the river between Saintbridge and Barton Street.

North of Saintbridge were two corn mills, presumably among those held from Abbot's Barton in the 1260s. The higher mill, standing at the east end of the lane later called Highfield Road,[57] was possibly Budel's Mill, which the abbey granted for life in the mid 1260s to Agnes the beadle and in 1277 to Walter Sevare, its agent for buying fish,[58] and of which William Jenkins acquired a lease in reversion in 1537.[59] In 1589 the mill belonged to a small copyhold estate held from Upton St. Leonards manor by William Barnes.[60] It had been enfranchised by 1618,[61] and later may have been acquired by Henry Nourse, after whose death it was sold in 1706 to John Garnons.[62] John Fisher bought it in 1805[63] and it remained in use in the early 20th century.[64] The buildings had been removed by the late 1970s.

The lower mill, standing south of the road later called Coney Hill Road,[65] may have been that called Savage's Mill in the early 13th century[66] and Stone Mill in the mid 14th.[67] In the early 16th century it was called White's Mill[68] and in 1589 John White held it from Upton manor.[69] In 1592 the copyhold was granted to Humphrey Haynes[70] who had sold the mill to Richard Wood by 1632.[71] In 1838 it was a farmhouse held under John Higford,[72] and in 1864 it was owned by Thomas Higford Burr. Known as Wood's Mill,[73] it was

[33] Church Com. MSS., file 66698.
[34] *Kelly's Dir. Glos.* (1939), 251, 362, 385.
[35] Ibid. 203, 371.
[36] Smith, *Men and Armour*, 18.
[37] Glos. R.O., D 2957/192.25; G.D.R., G 2/3/15667.
[38] Glos. R.O., D 45/M 3.
[39] *Glos. Subsidy Roll, 1327*, 6.
[40] Below, Barnwood, econ. hist.
[41] Smith, *Men and Armour*, 27–8; cf. ibid. 18.
[42] G.B.R., J 1/2065.
[43] Glos. R.O., D 1740/E 3, list of leases and f. 20.
[44] *Glos. Subsidy Roll, 1327*, 31.
[45] P.R.O., E 134/6 & 7 Geo. I Trin./1.
[46] *Hist. & Cart. Mon. Glouc.* ii. 79–80, 186.
[47] Glos. R.O., D 936/E 12/1, ff. 187–8.
[48] *Glouc. Corp. Rec.* p. 250.
[49] Speed, *Map of Glouc.* (1610); the ho. may have been that recorded in 1573 downstream in Archdeacon Meadow: Glos. R.O., D 936/E 12/1, f. 26.
[50] P.R.O., C 142/253, no. 97.
[51] Glos. R.O., D 2299/1685.
[52] *Dom. Bk.* (Rec. Com.), i. 162v., 165v.
[53] *Hist. & Cart. Mon. Glouc.* iii. 67–9, 151; cf. P.R.O., C 139/16, no. 8.
[54] *Tax. Eccl.* (Rec. Com.), 231.

[55] *Glos. Subsidy Roll, 1327*, 31.
[56] *Glouc. Corp. Rec.* p. 250.
[57] Glos. R.O., Q/RI 70 (map L, no. 56).
[58] *Hist. & Cart. Mon. Glouc.* i. 219; ii. 204, 239–41; iii. 151; cf. *Glos. Subsidy Roll, 1327*, 31.
[59] Glouc. Cath. Libr., Reg. Abb. Malvern, ii, f. 130 and v.; Jenkin's Mill, acquired by Jas. Commeline in 1653, was probably upstream at Bondend in Upton St. Leonards: *Glouc. Jnl.* 19 Nov. 1831; 10 May 1834; Glos. R.O., D 127/933; *Trans. B.G.A.S.* lxxxiii. 79–81.
[60] Glos. R.O., P 347/MI 1.
[61] P.R.O., C 142/377, no. 103.
[62] Glos. R.O., D 177, Wilton fam., mill deeds 1711–1827.
[63] Ibid. D 3117/4069.
[64] O.S. Map 6", Glos. XXXIII. NE. (1903 edn.).
[65] Glos. R.O., Q/RI 70 (map L, no. 53).
[66] *Glouc. Corp. Rec.* p. 117; cf. *Hist. & Cart. Mon. Glouc.* iii. 151.
[67] *Glouc. Corp. Rec.* p. 346.
[68] G.B.R., B 2/1, f. 230v.
[69] Glos. R.O., P 347/MI 1.
[70] Ibid. P 347A/FM 1, rot. 3d.
[71] Ibid. D 3117/3867.
[72] G.B.R., L 22/1/121, pp. 63–4.
[73] Glos. R.O., Q/SRh 1864 C/2.

licensed in 1874 for the manufacture of gun-cotton,[74] but later in the century it became a private residence.[75] It was demolished apparently during the construction of a road bypassing Gloucester in the 1930s.

There were three mills north of Barton Street. In descending order they were sometimes called Third, Second, and First Mill in the 18th and 19th centuries. The highest, at the east end of the lane later called India Road,[76] was held from Upton manor by John Windowe in 1540[77] and by John Thorne in 1589.[78] In 1591 the copyhold was granted to William Frankis but in 1593 it was granted again to Thorne,[79] before whose death in 1618 the mill was enfranchised.[80] About 1741 the mill was probably rebuilt as a cloth mill by the clothier Benjamin Gegg, who had moved to Barton Street from Woodchester.[81] In the 1820s and 1830s it was used as a grinding house by the Gloucester firm of Cox & Buchanan, edgetool makers.[82] In the late 19th century, when it was a corn mill known as Brown's Mill, it incorporated a timber-framed house of the late 16th century.[83] The mill ceased operating c. 1910.[84]

Goosewhite or Whitegoose Mill, the next below, stood a little way east of Goose Lane (later Millbrook Street).[85] It was first recorded in 1219 when William of Gloucester held it for life from King's Barton manor.[86] In the 1260s the mill was said to have once belonged to a writ-carrying serjeanty of the manor.[87] In the early 1220s it was held by Alfred of the barton, who granted it to Reynold le Deveneis. Alfred's interest descended to his granddaughter Denise, a minor, and by 1239 William son of Henry, to whom Henry III had granted Denise's marriage, had ejected Reynold le Deveneis from the mill.[88] Denise married Henry of Lasborough[89] but the mill was considered as an escheat in 1251 when it was granted for life to William Daubeney.[90] Edward I granted the mill and land in dower to his queen, Margaret, who in 1313 was ordered to release them to Robert Mayel and his wife Cecily, daughter and heir of Denise.[91] By the early 16th century ownership of the mill was divided with that of the small estate of which George Twissell had a moiety,[92] and in the mid 17th the grist mill was part of the estate of Lewis Roberts, who held one moiety under Gloucester corporation.[93] It had been converted into a snuff mill by 1790 when the owner was Powell Chandler, a Gloucester tobacconist.[94] It was for sale in 1805.[95] The Gloucester pinmaking firm of Hall and Lander, founded in 1813, evidently worked it as a wire mill[96] and it continued as a wire mill in 1838 when it belonged to Maria Martin.[97] Richard Cherrington and Emanuel Wilesmith, who bought the mill in 1862, had sold the site by 1865 when the development of the area for housing had begun.[98] The mill was evidently demolished at that time.[99]

Morin's Mill, downstream at the east end of Brook Street (later Station Road),[1] was named after the family which held it in the early 13th century. Roger Morin held it under the lordship of Hyde[2] and Geoffrey Morin from William of the park, who in 1220 granted 6s. rent from the mill to Gloucester Abbey.[3] Later John son of Roger son of Simon held it under Nicholas Morin.[4] In 1289 Thomas of Cossington and his wife Emme quitclaimed the mill to Richard Gabriel and his wife Joan.[5] Richard granted it to Robert de Honsum and he sold it in 1315 to John of Frocester and his wife Joan. They sold it in 1316 to John Tormarton, who granted it to Gloucester Abbey in 1318.[6] At the Dissolution Thomas Pincott held a lease of the mill[7] and Thomas Bell a lease in reversion.[8] In 1544 the Crown granted the mill to Richard Andrews and George Lisle,[9] but Bell owned it in 1559 and after his widow Joan's death in 1567 it passed to trustees for maintaining his St. Kyneburgh's almshouse. Gloucester corporation held the mill for that use from 1603 until 1836 when it passed to the municipal charity trustees.[10] The mill, the leasehold of which was acquired by the Tarne family before 1641, was known also as Pincott's Mill.[11] It was evidently destroyed at the beginning of the siege of 1643[12] but had been rebuilt by 1649 when it was a grist

[74] *Glouc. Jnl.* 14 Mar. 1874.

[75] Cf. O.S. Map 6″, Glos. XXXIII. NE. (1891 and 1903 edns.).

[76] *Glouc. Jnl.* 13 Jan. 1783; Causton, *Map of Glouc.* (1843).

[77] P.R.O., SC 6/Hen. VIII/1248, rot. 4d.

[78] Glos. R.O., P 347/MI 1.

[79] Ibid. P 347A/FM 1, rott. 2, 5.

[80] P.R.O., C 142/377, no. 96.

[81] *Glouc. Jnl.* 20 Jan. 1741; 9 Mar. 1742.

[82] Glos. R.O., D 3117/988; *Glos. Chron.* 14 Feb. 1885; *Suppl. to 56th Rep. Glouc. Chamber of Commerce* (1897), 29: Glos. Colln. N 15.6.

[83] O.S. Map 6″, Glos. XXXIII. NE. (1891 edn.); Glos. Colln. 36297 (37).

[84] O.S. Map 6″, Glos. XXXIII. NE. (1903 and 1924 edns.).

[85] Causton, *Map of Glouc.* (1843).

[86] *Pipe R. 1219* (P.R.S. N.S. xlii), 12.

[87] *Hist. & Cart. Mon. Glouc.* iii. 69.

[88] *Cal. Inq. Misc.* i, p. 3; *Close R. 1242–7*, 32–3, 85.

[89] *Hist. & Cart. Mon. Glouc.* iii. 69.

[90] *Cal. Inq. Misc.* i, p. 33; *Cal. Pat. 1247–58*, 107.

[91] *Cal. Close, 1307–13*, 503.

[92] P.R.O., C 2/Eliz. I/T 5/9.

[93] Cf. *Inq. p.m. Glos. 1625–42*, ii. 181–2; G.B.R., B 3/2, p.

672; Glos. R.O., D 547A/T 15.

[94] G.B.R., B 3/12, f. 132; Glos. R.O., Q/RI 70 (map M, no. 64).

[95] *Glouc. Jnl.* 14 Oct. 1805.

[96] *Business Hist.* xviii. 37–9.

[97] G.B.R., L 22/1/121, pp. 89–90.

[98] Glos. R.O., DC 2/30.

[99] Cf. Causton, *Map of Glouc.* (1843); O.S. Map 6″, Glos. XXXIII. NE. (1891 edn.).

[1] Glos. R.O., D 3117/930; Causton, *Map of Glouc.* (1843).

[2] *Glouc. Cath. Libr., Reg. Abb. Froucester B*, p. 300.

[3] *Hist. & Cart. Mon. Glouc.* ii. 30; cf. ibid. iii. 151.

[4] *Glouc. Cath. Libr., Reg. Abb. Froucester B*, pp. 299–300.

[5] P.R.O., CP 25(1)/75/35, no. 141.

[6] *Glouc. Cath. Libr., Reg. Abb. Froucester B*, pp. 320, 333–4, 337.

[7] P.R.O., SC 6/Hen. VIII/1248, rot. 4.

[8] *Glouc. Cath. Libr., Reg. Abb. Malvern*, ii, f. 132.

[9] *L. & P. Hen. VIII*, xix (2), p. 76.

[10] G.D.R. wills 1566/150; Hockaday Abs. ccxxiii; Fosbrooke, *Glouc.* 165–6.

[11] Glos. R.O., D 326/T 15.

[12] G.B.R., H 2/3, p. 213.

mill.[13] William Binning and John Whitehead, Gloucester dyers who bought the leasehold in 1782, converted part of the mill as a dyeworks and in 1785 sold it to John Harvey Ollney, a Gloucester woolstapler.[14] Later the property, said to contain a grist mill and a dyehouse, changed hands several times, the Gloucester pinmakers Richard Goodwin and William Marsh acquiring the leasehold in 1811 and James Hall in 1834,[15] and by 1831 Edwin Jones worked it as a flock mill. A steam engine had been installed and part converted into three cottages by the early 1850s, when it also included a saw mill. In 1856 the charity trustees sold the mill, sometimes called the Puff Mill, to the Midland Railway.[16] In 1859 it was occupied by Benjamin Wheeler, a woolstapler,[17] but later the site was taken for railway development.[18]

The mill of Wotton, or of the ford, which Richard son of Niel granted to Gloucester Abbey in 1126,[19] was presumably on the Wotton or Horsbere brook north-east of Gloucester. Its site has not been identified.

By 1615 there was a corn mill on the Sud brook at Elming Row, west of the Bristol road. It adjoined the site of Llanthony Priory[20] and had been demolished by the mid 18th century.[21]

In 1885 Henry Smith owned and worked a corn mill, on a stream in Lower Tuffley, powered by steam and water. It was unused in 1896[22] when the poor-law guardians adapted the mill house as a children's home during the smallpox epidemic in Gloucester.[23] The mill site has not been identified.

Several windmills were built near Gloucester. That recorded in 1310 presumably gave its name to the large open field east of the town[24] and occupied the site of the mill by the road from Wotton to Barton Street in 1686.[25] By 1750 that windmill had been replaced by another on a nearby site,[26] which may have been the large brick mill built by John Blanch and described in 1725 as new.[27] It had been removed by 1799.[28] A windmill in Pedmarsh field in 1604[29] was presumably one of two on Barton farm in 1621.[30] In 1734 there was a windmill near the outer north gate of the city.[31] A windmill east of the Bristol road in 1624[32] was presumably that in Tredworth belonging to the Llanthony estate in 1648.[33]

LOCAL GOVERNMENT. King's Barton manor or liberty, which was part of Dudstone hundred in the 13th century,[34] had frankpledge jurisdiction over the estates held from it.[35] The liberty, which was regarded as a separate hundred in 1316[36] but was held with Dudstone hundred from 1345,[37] included, in the hamlets, Barton Street, Kingsholm, Twigworth, and parts of Longford and Wotton.[38] Kingsholm and Twigworth formed a single tithing in the early 17th century.[39] Court books survive for King's Barton court leet for the period 1769–1841 and for 1851. It was held in October[40] with the manor court at inns in Barton Street, except in the mid 1770s when it met at the Red Lion in Kingsholm.[41] It had jurisdiction over Barton St. Michael, Kingsholm, Southgate and Woolstrop, and Twigworth, while the Dudstone court had jurisdiction over Barton St. Mary, Longford, Tuffley, Wotton, Littleworth, North Hamlet, South Hamlet, and the vill of Wotton. Each hamlet was policed by a constable and most had a tithingman and a hayward; Walham was looked after by its own or the Kingsholm hayward, and Wotton sometimes shared a hayward with Barnwood.[42] Surviving court books of King's Barton court baron cover the period 1769–1946 during which it dealt mainly with copyhold matters in Upton St. Leonards.[43]

The lord of Kingsholm manor exercised frankpledge jurisdiction by the later 18th century; a court book for the period 1783–1835 records the maintenance of paths, bridges, watercourses, and drains and the regulation of common rights in Walham. The court appointed the constable, tithingman, and hayward for Kingsholm hamlet, the hayward for Walham, and sometimes haywards for open fields and other common meadows.[44] In 1607 Sir William Cooke's bailiff had looked after Walham.[45] Presentments to a session of Brasenose College's court for Kingsholm in 1789 survive.[46]

For Abbot's Barton manor court rolls, dealing with estate matters, survive for 1291–2 and for 1351 when presentments for Longford and Wotton were recorded separately.[47] The court, which was held in a barn at the manor site, was attended by the tenants of the abbey's Longford

[13] Ibid. B 3/2, pp. 512, 519.
[14] Glos. R.O., D 3117/930.
[15] Ibid. Q/RI 70 (map N, no. 21); G.B.R., B 3/13, f. 110 and v.; 14, ff. 159v., 219, 246.
[16] Glouc. Jnl. 19 Nov. 1831; 10 May 1834; Glos. R.O., D 3269, Kimbrose Hosp., mill sale papers 1853–7; leases 1816–55.
[17] Slater's Dir. Glos. (1858–9), 199.
[18] O.S. Map 1/2,500, Glos. XXV. 15 (1886 edn.).
[19] Hist. & Cart. Mon. Glouc. i. 107, 118.
[20] Inq. p.m. Glos. 1625–42, i. 128–9; Scudamore Churches Endowment Act, 13 & 14 Chas. II, c. 11 (Priv. Act); cf. Glos. R.O., Q/RI 79.
[21] Glos. R.O., D 327, p. 339.
[22] G.B.R., L 22/1/112–19; Kelly's Dir. Glos. (1885), 607.
[23] Glos. R.O., G/GL 8A/22, pp. 448, 463.
[24] Glouc. Cath. Libr., deeds and seals, ii, f. 20; Glouc. Corp. Rec. p. 351.   [25] Glos. R.O., D 3117/947.
[26] Ibid. D 1740/E 3, f. 15.
[27] Glouc. Jnl. 28 Dec. 1725.
[28] Glos. R.O., Q/RI 70.
[29] G.B.R., J 1/1953.   [30] Ibid. B 3/1, f. 481v.

[31] Glos. R.O., A 154/83.
[32] Glos. Colln. prints GL 65.27.
[33] Scudamore Churches Endowment Act, 13 & 14 Chas. II, c. 11 (Priv. Act).
[34] Bk. of Fees, i. 307; P.R.O., JUST 1/278, rott. 62d.–63d.
[35] Rot. Hund. (Rec. Com.), i. 180–1; Cal. Inq. p.m. ii, p. 80; iv, p. 146.
[36] Feud. Aids, ii. 264, 274.
[37] Cal. Chart. R. 1341–1417, 40; Cal. Fine R. 1307–19, 304.
[38] Glos. Subsidy Roll, 1327, 6–7; cf. G.B.R., B 2/1, f. 230v.
[39] G.D.R. vol. 89, deposition of John Parsons 8 Apr. 1603.
[40] Glos. R.O., D 326/M 21.
[41] Ibid. M 25, M 27; G.B.R., King's Barton ct. bk. 1769–1810.
[42] Glos. R.O., D 326/M 21–2; G.B.R., Dudstone ct.bk. 1769–1810; King's Barton ct.bk. 1769–1810.
[43] G.B.R., King's Barton ct. bk. 1769–1855; Glos. R.O., D 326/M 25; D 2078, Guise fam., King's Barton ct. bk. 1854–1946.   [44] Glos. R.O., D 936/M 11.
[45] Ibid. D 326/E 1, f. 62.
[46] Ibid. EL 134, p. 103.
[47] Ibid. D 936A/M 1, rott. 1, 6; M 2, rot. 16.

and Wotton manors in the early 16th century. After the Dissolution the fragmentation of Abbot's Barton manor caused the demise of its court; Longford manor had its own court and the Wotton tenants attended the Barnwood court.[48] Sessions of the Longford court are recorded in court books of the bishop's Maisemore manor for the period 1753–1867.[49] For Tuffley manor court, held by the farmer of the manor in 1552 and until 1792, there are court rolls for 1558–68 when it usually met once a year to deal with estate matters, including the collection of pannage. There are also court books for 1647–1860 when its business was mostly tenurial.[50] Court rolls for Plock Court manor survive for 1588–92, 1595, and 1598.[51]

The hamlets, which were in the county of the city from 1483 until 1662,[52] were units for poor-law and other civil purposes.[53] For poor relief Kingsholm, rated with the inhamlets, or city parts, of St. Catherine and St. Mary de Lode by the late 17th century, was treated as part of Gloucester.[54] The other hamlets, which evidently each had an overseer of the poor and levied their own rates, resisted attempts to make them support the city poor, but in 1705, when a poor rate was made for the whole of St. Catherine's parish, the overseers of Longford and Twigworth were ordered to make payments to the inhamlet's overseers.[56] In Barton Street, where in 1676 the poor were too numerous for the inhabitants to maintain,[57] Barton St. Michael had its own overseer by the 1680s. It also had a wayman or surveyor of the highways, who by 1690 received a rent charge of £1 left by George Coulstance for repairing the main road.[58]

From 1727 the hamlets sent their poor to the Gloucester workhouse[59] and collected rates for the city poor-relief corporation. Parochial divisions were used for rating purposes, Wotton St. Catherine being assessed with Longford St. Catherine and Twigworth St. Mary with Longford St. Mary.[60] The hamlets, except for Kingsholm, maintained their poor from the closure of the workhouse in 1757 and were excluded from the scheme which revived the workhouse in 1764.[61] Barton St. Michael, which had resumed responsibility for maintaining its poor by 1755,

employed a salaried assistant overseer by 1818 and retained the services of a doctor from 1827.[62] Barton St. Mary had opened a workhouse in Barton Street by 1786.[63] In Tuffley in the period 1789–1835 relief took the usual forms and the number of people of weekly pay rose from 2 in 1798 to 7 in 1816. The hamlet had a poorhouse in the early 1830s.[64] Wotton St. Mary, Longford St. Catherine, and Longford St. Mary were separate poor-law units in the later 18th century.[65] Kingsholm continued to be treated as part of the city for poor relief and with North Hamlet[66] presumably comprised that part of the county which an Act of 1781 brought under the jurisdiction of the city magistrates and guardians for poor-law purposes.[67]

In the extraparochial places provisions for poor relief varied. North Hamlet was evidently rated with the inhamlet of St. Catherine by the early 18th century.[68] Littleworth was unable to support its poor in the later 1670s when the hundred of Dudstone and King's Barton was charged with part of the cost.[69] From 1727 Littleworth sent its poor to the Gloucester workhouse but the city's poor-relief corporation returned them several times because of the non-payment of Littleworth's rates.[70] From 1757 Littleworth maintained its poor.[71] In the period 1793–1834 relief took the usual forms and in the mid 1790s, when 2 or 3 families received regular help, the annual cost rose from under £10 to over £20.[72] In South Hamlet, where only one person received permanent help in 1803, the principal landholder, presumably the owner of the Llanthony estate, supported the poor before 1813, when five people were on permanent and nine on occasional relief.[73] In 1773 Giles Greenaway, tenant of the estate, had paid for road repairs at Llanthony.[74] The vill of Wotton, which in 1777 was said to repair parts of the turnpike roads leading from Wotton Pitch towards Cirencester and Cheltenham, maintained its poor;[75] only one person was given regular and one occasional assistance in 1803 and no help was provided in the years 1813–15.[76]

The cost of poor relief in the hamlets and extraparochial places rose in the later 18th and early 19th century and, excluding Kingsholm and North Hamlet, was £699 in 1803. There were few

[48] P.R.O., E 134/40 Eliz. I Hil./3; 14 Jas. I East./4; below, Barnwood, local govt.

[49] G.D.R., G 3/7, 9–11.

[50] Glos. R.O., D 1815, Barnwood, Wotton, Cranham, and Tuffley ct. rolls. 1558–71; D 936/M 27/1–2.

[51] P.R.O., SC 2/175/16.

[52] Dudstone and King's Barton Act, 13 & 14 Chas. II, c. 12 (Priv. Act).

[53] Cf. Glos. R.O., Q/SO 1, ff. 16, 31v., 61v., 106, 108, 142v., 162, 224, 230, 233v.; 2, ff. 179v., 188; 3, pp. 40, 456.

[54] Cf. ibid. 3, pp. 150–1, 161; G.B.R., G 3/SO 8, 13 Jan. 1766.

[55] G.B.R., B 3/3, p. 292.

[56] Glos. R.O., Q/SO 3, pp. 150–1, 161.

[57] Ibid. 1, f. 106.

[58] Ibid. P 154/14/CW 2/2–3; OV 2/2; 14th Rep. Com. Char. 44: for a period from 1719 the rent charge was used for highway repairs by the city part of St. Michael's par.

[59] Glouc. Poor-Relief Act, 13 Geo. I, c. 19; above, Glouc. 1720–1835, city. govt.

[60] Glos. R.O., D 3270/19712, pp. 9, 46, 65–6, 77, 186–7.

[61] Glouc. Poor-Relief and Lighting Act, 4 Geo. III, c. 60.

[62] Glos. R.O., P 154/14/OV 2/2; OV 1/10: which together comprise overseers' accounts for Barton St. Michael for the periods 1716–17, 1723–43, 1755–9, and 1818–38.

[63] Glouc. Jnl. 19 June 1786.

[64] Glos. R.O., P 154/12/OV 2/3.

[65] Poor Law Abstract, 1804, 176–7; cf. Poor Law Com. 1st Rep. p. 251.

[66] G.B.R., G 3/SO 8, 13 Jan. 1766; Glos. Colln. NQ 12.60.

[67] Glouc. Gaol and Improvement Act, 21 Geo. III, c. 74.

[68] Bodl. MS. Top. Glouc. c. 3, f. 197v.; cf. Glos. Colln. NQ 12.60.

[69] Glos. R.O., Q/SO 1, f. 158v.; 2, ff. 3, 10.

[70] Glouc. Poor-Relief Act, 13 Geo. I, c. 19; Glos. R.O., D 3270/19712, pp. 205, 220, 305, 319.

[71] Glouc. Poor-Relief and Lighting Act, 4 Geo. III, c. 60.

[72] Glos. R.O., P 154/5/OV 1/1–2.

[73] Poor Law Abstract, 1804, 176–7; 1818, 148–9.

[74] Glos. R.O., Q/SR 1773 D.

[75] Ibid. D 936/E 147.

[76] Poor Law Abstract, 1804, 176–7; 1818, 150–1.

poor save in the Barton hamlets which accounted for 31 of the 68 paupers on regular aid in 1803. Apart from Littleworth and Longford the numbers on both permanent and occasional relief had risen by 1813.[77] Annual expediture on relief in the area in the later 1820s averaged £1,039, nearly half of which was incurred by the Barton hamlets. In the early 1830s it averaged £1,209 with the greatest increases sustained by Littleworth and South Hamlet,[78] both areas affected by the development of Gloucester's docks.[79] From 1835 the hamlets and extraparochial places were in the Gloucester poor-law union.[80]

In the 19th century the need for public services in the area of the hamlets was usually met by bodies acting for the city and its suburbs.[81] Local boards of health were established for the county parts of Barton St. Mary and Barton St. Michael in 1863 and for Kingsholm St. Catherine in 1865.

Mainly because of boundary complexities they were ineffective, even though the Barton boards acted together.[82] Powers under an Act of 1871 to replace the Kingsholm St. Catherine board by one for a district north-east of the city were not used.[83] The three boards were dissolved when the Gloucester city boundary was extended in 1874 and those parts of their districts not in the enlarged city were transferred to the rural sanitary authority.[84] Also dissolved in 1874 was a sanitary committee for South Hamlet formed in 1873 to deal principally with the polluted Still ditch.[85] After 1885 there were several reorganizations of the civil parishes covering the area of the former hamlets and extraparochial places. Those remaining outside the city were included in Gloucester rural district until 1974[86] when Innsworth, Longford, and Twigworth parishes became part of Tewkesbury district.

BARNWOOD

THE ancient parish of Barnwood lay ESE. of Gloucester and its church stands 2.75 km. from the city's central crossroads.[87] The proximity of the city and the course of the Roman Ermin Street, the road from Gloucester to Cirencester, through the middle of the parish influenced Barnwood's early development. In the later 19th century two mental hospitals opened there. Barnwood remained predominantly rural in character until the 20th century when it was absorbed by Gloucester.

The ancient parish, which was not clearly defined until parliamentary inclosure in 1799, contained 1,439 a. and was irregularly shaped.[88] It had many detached parts, most resulting from holdings in open fields and common meadows shared with other parishes, hamlets, and extraparochial places outside Gloucester. The complexity was increased by the existence within the main part of Barnwood of a few detached pieces belonging to the hamlet and vill of Wotton. The boundary of the main part of Barnwood was marked by the Horsbere brook in the north-east, the river Twyver in the south-east, and, for a short distance, the Sud brook in the south-west beyond Coney Hill towards Saintbridge. The northern boundary followed parts of the Gloucester–Cheltenham road and the later Elmbridge Road. The detached parts included several pieces within Wotton to the west, one west of Saintbridge, and one at Longlevens to the north.

In the south-east small pieces of Barnwood lying intermingled with Upton St. Leonards and detached parts of neighbouring hamlets represented old closes and holdings in shared open fields that were inclosed in 1897.[89] Barnwood also had pieces in meadows bordering the Severn north and south-west of Gloucester, including Maisemore Meadow, on Alney Island, which had been inclosed in 1794.[90]

Parts of Barnwood were taken into Gloucester in 1874 when the city's eastern boundary was extended to the Wotton brook and a railway line (then disused) bypassing Gloucester.[91] The irregularities in the parish boundary were adjusted in 1882 and 1885 when the detached parts were transferred to other parishes, the northern boundary was made to follow the Gloucester–Cheltenham road, and an extension of the parish south-westwards brought Coney Hill completely within Barnwood, giving it an area of 1,411 a. east of Gloucester.[92] In 1900 70 a. at Coney Hill were added to Gloucester, and in 1935 Barnwood lost 419 a. to the city and 92 a. in the north to the new civil parish of Longlevens and gained 2 a. from Wotton St. Mary (Without). In 1951 a further 52 a. were transferred to Gloucester, which in 1967 absorbed the remaining 780 a. (315.6 ha.) save for small areas in the east and south-east added to Hucclecote and Upton St. Leonards.[93] The following account of Barnwood, which relates to the ancient parish

[77] Ibid. *1804*, 176–7; *1818*, 148–51.
[78] *Poor Law Returns* (1830–1), 68; (1835), 66–7.
[79] Above, Glouc. 1720–1835, topog.
[80] *Poor Law Com. 1st Rep.* p. 251.
[81] Above, Public Services.
[82] Above, Glouc. 1835–1985, city govt.
[83] Kingsholm District Act, 34 & 35 Vic. c. 54.
[84] Glouc. Extension and Improvement Act, 1874, 37 & 38 Vic. c. 111 (Local).
[85] Glos. R.O., P 154/25/VE 2/1.

[86] *Census*, 1891–1971.
[87] This account was written in 1979 and revised in 1986.
[88] G.D.R., T 1/16; Glos. R.O., Q/RI 70 (maps C–D, G–I, K–N, P, R).
[89] Glos. R.O., Q/RI 149.
[90] Ibid. 94; cf. ibid. 70 (map C, nos. 1–5).
[91] Glos. Colln. NF 12.7; cf. O.S. Map 6″, Glos. XXV.SE. (1887 edn.); XXXIII. NE. (1891 edn.).
[92] *Census*, 1891; *O.S. Area Bk.* (1885).
[93] *Census*, 1891–1971; *Kelly's Dir. Glos.* (1902), 31.

except for those detached parts on Alney Island and to the south-east transferred to Maisemore and Upton respectively in 1882, does not cover those aspects of its history from the mid 19th century connected with its transformation to a suburb of Gloucester.

The land of Barnwood is generally flat, rising at its highest only to 54 m. in the south-east and including, in the south-west, part of a low rise at Coney Hill, formerly known as Blake Hill.[94] Barnwood is on the Lower Lias, on which are large sand and gravel patches.[95] The parish name indicates that it was once thickly wooded[96] but by the mid 17th century the soil was cultivated as open-field land or grassland. Inclosure of most of the common land was completed in 1799. Market gardening became important in the 19th century. The land is drained by small streams, including the river Twyver in the south and the Wotton brook, which crosses the middle of the parish.

Ermin Street has remained an important thoroughfare and by the mid 13th century Barnwood shared responsibility for maintaining a bridge carrying the road over the brook at Wotton.[97] The road, which linked Gloucester with London and Oxford,[98] was a turnpike through the parish between 1698 and 1718 and between 1723 and 1871[99]. Upton Lane running south from it near the eastern side of the parish is presumably an ancient route. Church Road further west was a track leading to open fields before 1799[1] when it was confirmed as part of a road to Matson, turning westwards at Coney Hill.[2] The Gloucester–Cheltenham road was a turnpike from 1756 until 1871.[3]

Barnwood church, which had been built by the 12th century, and the site of Barnwood manor are close together 300 m. south of Ermin Street. In the later 16th century there was a church house north of the churchyard.[4] Barnwood village developed as a roadside settlement, which with Wotton was strung out along Ermin Street by the early 17th century.[5] In the late 18th century the main part of Barnwood had c. 35 houses on the road, many set in small orchards and several with farm buildings.[6] Most of those houses were replaced in

the later development of the village, which from 1860 was dominated by a private mental hospital.[7] New buildings in brick included many villas, a vicarage house and school of the mid 1870,[8] and a parish room opened in 1898 in memory of G. F. Riddiford, a former resident who had been active in county government.[9] The older surviving buildings include the 18th-century brick Manor House, which once belonged to the Bubb family's estate.[10]

Apart from mills on the Twyver there was no ancient outlying settlement in Barnwood. In the north two post-inclosure farmsteads, on Elm-bridge Road and by the Horsbere brook respectively,[11] were removed to make way for housing in the 20th century and Hillview Farm, a cottage built by 1901,[12] was demolished in 1964.[13] Lobley's Farm in the south-east is a brick building recorded from 1841.[14] In the early 1880s the county built an asylum in the south of Barnwood near Coney Hill.[15]

Nine people in Barnwood were assessed for the subsidy in 1327.[16] There were c. 117 communicants in the parish in 1551[17] and 133 in 1603;[18] 25 householders were recorded in 1563.[19] The estimated population c. 1710 was 180[20] and by 1801 it had risen to 309. Between 1811 and 1831 the population rose from 306 to 419. By 1851 it had fallen to 358 but by 1861, following residential development and the opening of the private mental hospital, it had risen to 507.[21]

Barnwood had at least one alehouse in the mid 1660s.[22] The Salutation, which was assessed on 11 hearths in 1672,[23] stood north of Ermin Street by a footpath to Churchdown.[24] It closed after 1817.[25] Another alehouse, formerly the glebe house, had closed by 1807.[26] The village blacksmith ran a beer shop in the 1850s.[27]

Barnwood was the birthplace of the judge Sir Edmund Saunders (d. 1683)[28] and of the physicist Sir Charles Wheatstone (1802–75).[29]

MANOR AND OTHER ESTATES. *BARN-WOOD*, which in 1066 was a member of Gloucester Abbey's Barton manor,[30] became a

[94] G.D.R., T 1/16; Glos. R.O., D 1740/E 1, f. 1v.; cf. Glos. R.O., D 1815, Barnwood, Wotton, Cranham, and Tuffley ct. rolls 1558–71, rot. 19, for the name Coney Hill in 1565.

[95] Geol. Surv. Map 1", solid, sheet 44 (1856 edn.); Richardson, *Wells and Springs of Glos.* 54.

[96] *P.N. Glos.* (E.P.N.S.), ii. 117.

[97] P.R.O., C 115/K 2/6684, f. 127v.

[98] Glos. Colln. prints GL 65.27.

[99] Glouc. Roads Act, 9 & 10 Wm. III, c. 18; 9 Geo. I, c. 31; Annual Turnpike Acts Continuance Act, 34 & 35 Vic. c. 115.

[1] Cf. Glos. R.O., D 6/E 4, no. 15.

[2] Ibid. Q/RI 70.

[3] Glouc. Roads Act, 29 Geo. II, c. 58; Annual Turnpike Acts Continuance Act, 34 & 35 Vic. c. 115.

[4] P.R.O., E 134/40 Eliz. I Hil./3; Glos. R.O., Q/RI 70 (map L, no. 35).

[5] Glos. Colln. prints GL 65.27.

[6] Glos. R.O., D 6/E 4 , no. 15; Q/RI 70 (maps H–I, L).

[7] Above, Hosp.

[8] *Glos. Chron.* 11 Aug. 1877.

[9] *Glouc. Jnl.* 29 Jan. 1898; *Kelly's Dir. Glos.* (1889), 646, 667.

[10] Taylor, *Map of Glos.* (1777).

[11] Cf. Glos. R.O., Q/RI 70 (map H, nos. 9, 15–16); O.S. Map 1", sheet 44 (1828 edn.).

[12] O.S. Map 6", Glos. XXV. SE. (1903 edn.).

[13] Glos. R.O., D 3725, Barnwood Ho. Trust, rep. 1964.

[14] G.D.R., T 1/16.

[15] Above, Hosp.

[16] *Glos. Subsidy Roll, 1327*, 33.

[17] *E.H.R.* xix. 103.

[18] *Eccl. Misc.* 70.

[19] Bodl. MS. Rawl. C. 790, f. 6v.

[20] Atkyns, *Glos.* 251.

[21] *Census*, 1801–61.

[22] Glos. R.O., Q/SIb 1, ff. 36, 84; cf. *Trans. B.G.A.S.* c. 212.

[23] P.R.O., E 179/247/14, rot. 34d.

[24] Glos. R.O., Q/RI 70.

[25] Ibid. D 936/M 1/2.

[26] G.D.R., V 5/35T 4.

[27] Glos. R.O., D 1388/SL 4/24; *Kelly's Dir. Glos.* (1856), 225.

[28] *D.N.B.*

[29] J. Stratford, *Glos. Biog. Notes* (1887), 188–200.

[30] *Dom. Bk.* (Rec. Com.), i. 165v.

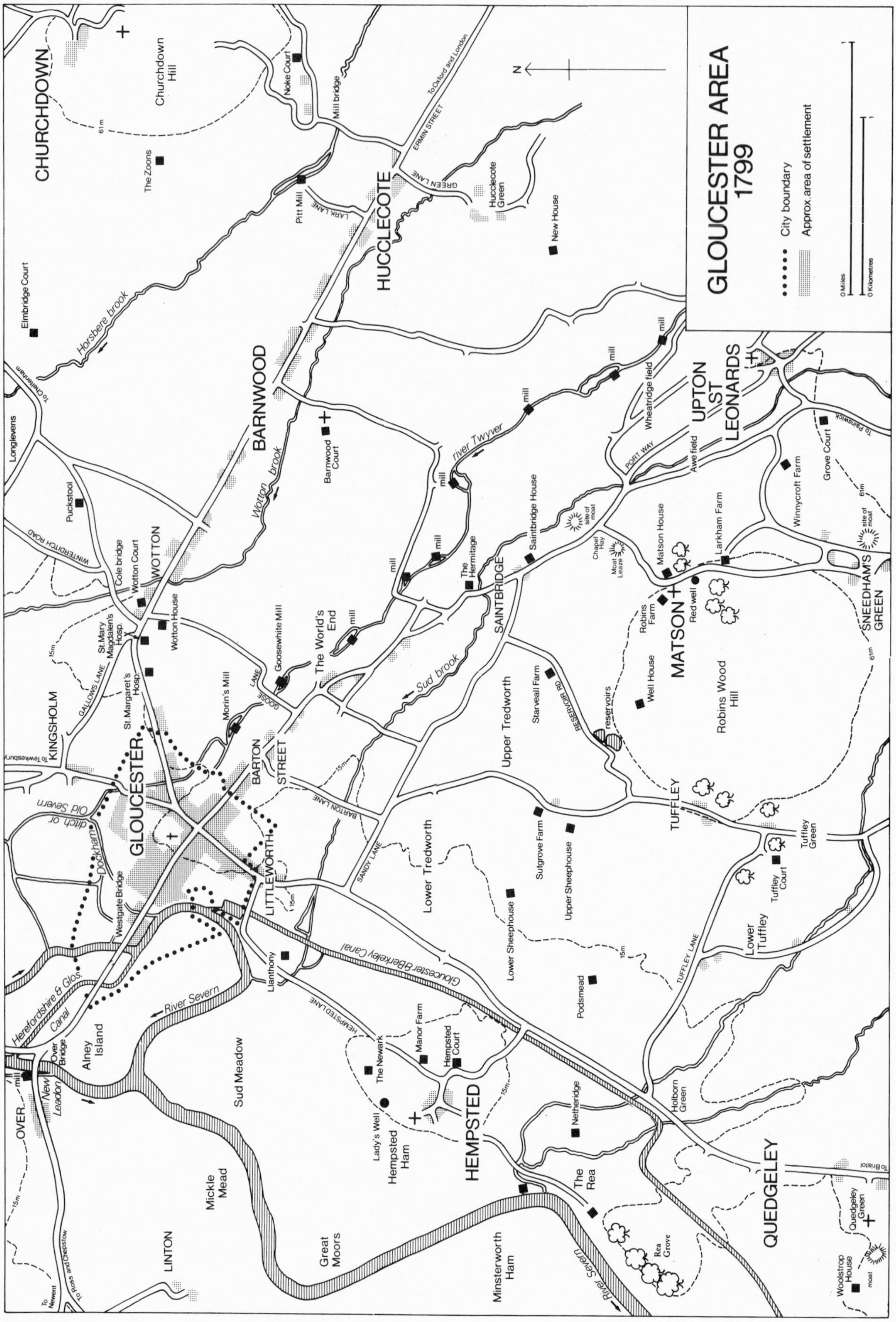
GLOUCESTER AREA
1799
City boundary
Approx. area of settlement
0 Miles
0 Kilometres
N
CHURCHDOWN
Churchdown Hill
The Zoons
Noke Court
Mill bridge
To Oxford and London
ERMIN STREET
Pitt Mill
LARK LANE
GREEN LANE
HUCCLECOTE
Hucclecote Green
New House
Elmbridge Court
Horsbere brook
To Cheltenham
Longlevens
BARNWOOD
Barnwood Court
Wotton brook
river Twyver
mill
Wheatridge field
PORT WAY
Awe field
UPTON ST LEONARDS
To Painswick
Grove Court
Winnycroft Farm
site of moat
Larkham Farm
SNEEDHAM'S GREEN
Puckstool
WINTERDITCH ROAD
Cole bridge
Wotton Court
WOTTON
Wotton House
St. Mary Magdalen's Hosp.
St. Margaret's Hosp.
GALLOWS LANE
KINGSHOLM
To Tewkesbury
Goosewhite Mill
GOOSE LANE
The World's End
Morin's Mill
The Hermitage
SAINTBRIDGE
Saintbridge House
Chapel Hay
Moat Leaze
Matson House
Robins Farm
MATSON
Red well
Robins Wood Hill
Well House
Starveall Farm
RESERVOIR RD
reservoirs
Upper Tredworth
Sud brook
GLOUCESTER
Old Severn
ditch or
Dockham
BARTON STREET
BARTON LANE
LITTLEWORTH
Westgate Bridge
SANDY LANE
Lower Tredworth
Sutgrove Farm
Upper Sheephouse
TUFFLEY
Tuffley Green
Tuffley Court
Lower Tuffley
TUFFLEY LANE
Lower Sheephouse
Podsmead
Gloucester & Berkeley Canal
Llanthony
HEMPSTED LANE
Herefordshire & Glos. Canal
River Severn
Over Bridge
Alney Island
OVER
New Leadon
Sud Meadow
The Newark
Manor Farm
Hempsted Court
Lady's Well
Hempsted Ham
HEMPSTED
Netheridge
Holborn Green
QUEDGELEY
To Bristol
The Rea
Rea Grove
Mickle Mead
LINTON
Great Moors
Minsterworth Ham
River Severn
To Newent
To Ross and Chepstow
Woolstrop House
moat
Quedgeley Green
15m
61m

Fig. 26

separate manor.[31] The abbey, which was granted free warren on the demesne in 1354[32] and administered its Cranham land with Barnwood, retained the manor until the Dissolution.[33] In 1541 it was given to the dean and chapter of Gloucester cathedral[34] and by c. 1547, when a lease was granted to Sir Thomas Seymour, was held with Cranham and Wotton manors. The lease passed before 1550 to Thomas Winston, who was followed as lessee in 1560 or 1561 by Edward and Richard Stephens. Edward (d. 1587) devised his lease to his son Thomas,[35] later of Over Lypiatt in Stroud, who was succeeded, presumably at his death in 1613, by his son Edward Stephens of Little Sodbury. The estate, later farmed from the dean and chapter on leases for 21 years renewed every few years,[36] belonged in 1661 to Edward's son, Sir Thomas Stephens, and in 1674 to George Johnson of Bowden Park near Chippenham (Wilts.). Under George's will dated 1680 it passed in turn to his wife Mary and his second son William on reaching the age of 24. Mary, William, and Mary Wright, whom William made his trustee in 1707, later defended a Chancery action concerning legacies left by George to other sons, and in 1714 William conveyed the estate to his son William.[37] The younger William, who became a Bristol merchant, died in 1750 and the estate passed to his wife Elizabeth. Her father Anthony Edwards of Little Shurdington was the leaseholder until his death in 1760. Elizabeth (d. 1773)[38] was succeeded by her daughters Elizabeth, wife of John Jones, Hester, wife of the Revd. William Walbank, and Sarah, widow of Henry Wyatt[39] and from 1782 wife of Thomas Wathen.[40] The dean and chapter, who curtailed the lords farmers' rights over the demesne in the mid 1770s,[41] took the manorial rights in hand in 1783.[42] In 1855 the manor passed to the Ecclesiastical Commissioners,[43] and in 1857 it covered 506 a. in Barnwood, mostly belonging to leaseholders. The commissioners, who in 1867 endowed the bishopric of Gloucester and Bristol with 276 a. in Barnwood, sold off parts of the estate, mostly to the leaseholders.[44] In 1932 the remaining 303 a. were bought by Gloucester corporation for housing and a cemetery.[45]

In 1501 Gloucester Abbey granted a lease of the manorial demesne, including the site of the manor west of the church, known later as Barnwood Court, to Lady (Margaret) Bridges; the rent included 40 measures of wheat a year to the warden of Buckholt wood, centred on Cranham.[46] Humphrey Parker, lessee from 1517, and his sons William and John became wardens in 1519. John was granted a lease of the demesne in 1538,[47] and in 1543 the dean and chapter granted him and his wife Isabel one for 90 years. At Isabel's death in 1559 or 1560 Barnwood Court passed to her son John Parker, whose wife Margery had a lease in reversion from her brother Thomas Stephens, the lord farmer, in 1587. John by will dated 1602 devised his estate to his son Richard and a life interest in a moiety to Margery.[48] Richard's widow Mary married George Worrall,[49] who c. 1631 sold Barnwood Court and the lease in reversion to William Capel.[50] In 1659 Capel settled the estate on the marriage of his son William.[51] From 1778 the lords farmer of the manor held a lease of Barnwood Court and part of the demesne. The lessee from 1784 was John Morris[52] (d. 1788),[53] who was succeeded by his son Robert. The latter, who conveyed c. 64 a. in Wotton to his brother William, enlarged the estate considerably and in 1799 it covered over 720 a. in Barnwood.[54] Robert, M.P. for Gloucester, died in 1816 leaving the estate to his son Robert and a life interest in the house to his widow Mary[55] (d. 1828).[56] The son, like the father, was a partner in a Gloucester bank, which failed in 1825.[57] He was declared bankrupt and in 1829 Barnwood Court and 200 a. were bought by Samuel Charles Turner (d. 1833). In 1838 Turner's widow Susannah sold most of the estate, but not the house, to Robert Witcomb,[58] who owned 192 a. in 1841.[59] Witcomb died in 1846, and in 1867 his son Robert surrendered the estate to the Ecclesiastical Commissioners.[60]

Barnwood Court, which contained eight bays in 1650,[61] dates from the 17th century and probably had an L-shaped plan. It was the residence of the Johnson family from the late 17th century[62] and of Thomas Cother in the 1770s.[63] The house, from which a straight avenue led to Ermin Street,[64] was

---

[31] Glouc. Cath. Libr., Reg. Abb. Froucester A, f. 26 and v.; *Hist. & Cart. Mon. Glouc.* (Rolls Ser.), ii. 41.

[32] *Cal. Chart. R. 1341–1417*, 142.

[33] *Valor Eccl.* (Rec. Com.), ii. 415, 418.

[34] *L. & P. Hen. VIII*, xvi, p. 572.

[35] P.R.O., REQ 2/162/119; Glos. R.O., D 1815, Barnwood, Wotton, Cranham, and Tuffley ct. rolls 1558–71; for the Stephenses, *Visit. Glos. 1682–3*, 174–7.

[36] Glos. R.O., D 936/E 12/2, ff. 361–4.

[37] Ibid. E 17; D 1815, Barnwood, Wotton, and Cranham deeds 1723–6, deed 21 Sept. 1726.

[38] Glos. R.O., D 936/E 17; D 1740/E 3, ff. 1–5; Bigland, *Glos.* i. 118, 131.   [39] Glos. R.O., D 936/E 18, E 38.

[40] Ibid. P 35/IN 1/1.

[41] Glouc. Cath. Libr., Chapter Act bk. iv, pp. 1–2, 18–22, 38–9; below, econ. hist.

[42] Glos. R.O., D 936/M 1/1–2.

[43] Kirby, *Cat. of Glouc. Dioc. Rec.* ii, p. xiii.

[44] Church Com. MSS., Glouc. chapter est. surv. M 3, pp. 9–107; *Lond. Gaz.* 23 Aug. 1867, pp. 4680–2; Glos. R.O., D 2957/35.2.

[45] Church Com. MSS., deeds 379935–6.

[46] Glouc. Cath. Libr., Reg. Abb. Braunche, p. 20.

[47] Ibid. Reg. Abb. Malvern, i, ff. 93–4, 153v.–156v.; ii, ff. 178–9.

[48] Glos. R.O., D 340A/T 1; G.D.R. wills 1559/92; 1602/42.

[49] *Visit. Glos. 1623*, 189.

[50] Glos. R.O., D 936/E 148.

[51] Ibid. D 2440, Capel fam. deeds 1659–1873.

[52] Ibid. D 936/E 18.

[53] *Glouc. Jnl.* 9 June 1788.

[54] Glos. R.O., D 936/E 18, E 35; M 1/2; Q/RI 70.

[55] Ibid. D 1740/T 20; *Glouc. Jnl.* 9 Sept. 1816.

[56] Glos. R.O., P 35/IN 1/5.

[57] Cf. *Glouc. Jnl.* 10 Sept. 1859.

[58] Ibid. 18 Apr. 1829; Glos. R.O., D 1740/T 21.

[59] G.D.R., T 1/16.

[60] Glos. R.O., D 1740/T 21.

[61] Ibid. E 1, f. 1v.

[62] Ibid. D 870/T 1; Atkyns, *Glos.* 251.

[63] Glos. R.O., D 936/E 18, E 171.

[64] Ibid. D 6/E 4, no. 15.

greatly improved c. 1800 by Robert Morris,[65] who squared off the plan and added a south front of five bays. In 1841 the house and a few acres belonged to the Revd. William Spencer Phillips[66] and thereafter had a succession of owners, including James Henry Dowling who bought the freehold in 1871.[67] In 1937 the house was bought for the vicarage,[68] which it remained until the mid 1970s. It had been sold by the early 1980s when it was converted as flats.

In 1692 a small estate, held under William Johnson and centred on a farmhouse at the west end of Barnwood village, was bought from Giles Roberts, a clothier, by Nicholas Webb.[69] Nicholas (d. 1712) was succeeded by his son Nicholas (d. 1714 or 1715), who left the estate in turn to his wife Joyce and his nephew Nicholas Hyett.[70] Hyett (d. 1777) was succeeded by his son Benjamin,[71] who sold the estate to Robert Morris c. 1797.[72] In 1799, after inclosure, Morris sold the estate of c. 70 a. to Thomas Herbert (d. 1810), whose son Edward sold it in 1821 to Jane Trimnell (d. 1856). In 1858 her administrators surrendered the estate to the Ecclesiastical Commissioners[73] and in 1932 the land was part of that bought by the corporation.[74] The farmstead was burnt down in 1855[75] and the house replaced in 1861 by a pair of cottages later called Bridge Farm.[76] It was demolished in the 1950s.[77]

In the early 19th century the Walters family built up a large estate centred on *BARNWOOD HOUSE*. David Walters bought the house and 32 a., formerly copyhold land owned by Sir Charles Hotham, Bt. (d. 1811), in 1813.[78] He added to the estate,[79] which passed at his death in 1833 to his son James Woodbridge Walters.[80] James owned 719 a. in Barnwood,[87] was high sheriff of Gloucestershire in 1841,[82] and died in 1852 heavily in debt to the County of Gloucester Bank, which took over the estate the following year and sold off the land in the late 1850s and 1860s. Large parts were acquired by Arthur Stewart and J. H. Dowling.[83] The subscribers to the Gloucester asylum bought the house, landscaped gardens, and 48 a. in 1858 and converted the house as a private asylum, later known as Barnwood House Hospital. The hospital's trustees, who in the mid 1870s bought 166 a. in Barnwood,[84] had by 1935 acquired over 300 a. there. From 1967 land was sold for development[85] and in 1982 the trustees retained c. 80 ha. (c. 200 a.), some of it let for commercial purposes.[86] Barnwood House dated from the early 19th century.[87]

The County of Gloucester Bank sold Barnwood Mill and 119 a. in 1866 to the trustees of the marriage settlement of Walter and Mary Wilkins. In 1878 the county magistrates bought that land for the site of a new county asylum.[88] The estate was enlarged and from 1908 covered over 310 a. in Barnwood and adjoining parishes.[89] Much of the land was sold after the early 1960s for housing.[90] The asylum, known as Coney Hill Hospital, remained in use in 1986.

Gloucester Abbey was taking the Barnwood tithes before c. 1171 when they were confirmed to it.[91] In 1517 the tithes were leased with the manorial demesne but by 1519 the abbey had reserved the small tithes, evidently all tithes other than those of corn and hay. Of the corn and hay tithes of Barnwood and Wotton manors those of the demesne were known by 1527 as the little tithing and the rest as the great tithing. The abbey had reserved part of the corn and hay tithes by 1538.[92] The tithes and possibly some land[93] were granted with the manor in 1541 to the dean and chapter of Gloucester[94] and the corn and hay tithes were leased with the demesne in 1543.[95] In the early 1630s the leasehold of those tithes was separated from that of the demesne, and James Mitchell[96] by will dated 1698 left it to three grandchildren.[97] The following year the dean and chapter leased part of the corn and hay tithes to James's son-in-law James Small and part to Christopher Capel.[98] Another part was leased to James Elly (fl. 1721). From 1721 Capel's tithe portion was leased with the small tithes to the curate[99] and in 1767 the living was endowed with both.[1] The remaining corn and hay tithes were held under leases renewed every few years and Robert Morris, who acquired a lease in 1797,[2]

---

[65] Rudge, *Hist. of Glos.* ii. 133.
[66] G.D.R., T 1/16; Glos. R.O., D 1740/E 13.
[67] Glos. R.O., D 1388/SL 6/104; *Kelly's Dir. Glos.* (1885), 359.
[68] Glos. R.O., P 35/IN 3/10; *Glouc. Jnl.* 24 July 1937.
[69] Glos. R.O., D 2957/35.23; cf. ibid. Q/RI 70 (map L, no. 5).
[70] G.D.R. wills 1713/211; 1715/85; Fosbrooke, *Glouc.* 179.
[71] F. A. Hyett, 'Hyetts of Painswick' (1907, TS. in Glos. R.O.), 39–42; Glos. R.O., D 6/E 4, nos. 14–15.
[72] Glos. R.O., D 936/E 31.
[73] Ibid. D 1740/T 20.
[74] Above.
[75] Church Com. MSS., Glouc. chapter est. surv. M 3, p. 124.
[76] G.B.R., B 6/33/1, pp. 247–8; cf. *Kelly's Dir. Glos.* (1889), 667.
[77] Local inf.
[78] Glos. R.O., D 936/M 1/2; *Glouc. Jnl.* 15 June 1812; Burke, *Peerage* (1963), 1259.
[79] Glos. R.O., D 936/M 1/2; D 1297, Barnwood, Churchdown, and Upton deeds 1823–5.
[80] Ibid. DC/F 3/2.
[81] G.D.R., T 1/16.

[82] *Glos. N. & Q.* iii. 416.
[83] Glos. R.O., DC/F 3/1–3; Glos. Colln. JR 13.7 (6); *Glouc. Jnl.* 1 Aug. 1863.
[84] Glos. R.O., D 3725, Barnwood Ho. Trust, min. bks. 1856–77.
[85] Ibid. rep. 1879, 1890, 1893, 1928, 1935, 1967–73.
[86] Inf. from sec., Barnwood Ho. Trust.
[87] Above, Hosp.
[88] Glos. R.O., DC/F 3/1; HO 23/1/1, pp. 2–6.
[89] Ibid. HO 22/25/1.
[90] Ibid. 8/19.
[91] *Hist. & Cart. Mon. Glouc.* i. 327–8.
[92] Glouc. Cath. Libr., Reg. Abb. Malvern, i, ff. 93–4, 153v.–156, 267v.–268v.; ii, ff. 178–9.
[93] Cf. *Valor Eccl.* (Rec. Com.), ii. 415.
[94] *L. & P. Hen. VIII*, xvi, p. 572.
[95] Glos. R.O., D 340A/T 1.
[96] Cf. ibid. D 936/A 1/1, pp. 218, 240, 262; 2, pp. 2, 138, 170, 200, 324.
[97] Hockaday Abs. ccxxxii.
[98] Glos. R.O., D 936/E 20.
[99] Ibid. Y 2; G.D.R., V 5/35T 5.
[1] Glos. R.O., D 936/Y 64; Glouc. Cath. Libr., Chapter Act bk. iii, p. 167.
[2] Glos. R.O., D 936/E 20.

414

took them from 968 a. in 1801.[3] In 1841 the tithes held under the dean and chapter mainly by the landowners were commuted for a corn rent charge of £350.[4]

ECONOMIC HISTORY. The manorial demesne at Barnwood was worked by four ploughteams in 1291.[5] In the early 16th century much of it was farmed with the site of the manor[6] and the remainder by tenants on leases for lives or years.[7] In 1650 the demesne of the Barnwood estate in Barnwood and Wotton comprised 731 a. in common fields and meadows and pasture closes. It was evidently grouped as farms of 200 a. held with Barnwood Court, 152 a., 119 a., 104 a., 81 a., 58 a., and 18 a.,[8] probably held by tenants on leases or at will. By the late 17th century the lords farmer of Barnwood and Wotton manors granted leases of demesne land for terms of 20 years and 11 months,[9] and in 1750, when Elizabeth Johnson had 431 a., mostly meadow and pasture, in hand, 22 tenants on leases held 410 a., predominantly arable. Of their holdings the largest was 80 a. and half were less than 8 a. each.[10] In the years 1776–8 the leaseholders surrendered their leases and with the agreement of the lords farmer became tenants of the dean and chapter on leases for terms of 21 years renewed every few years.[11]

The tenants and services recorded on the Barnwood estate in the 1260s are mentioned under Cranham, where the estate included heavily wooded land;[12] the customary tenements and those of the mondaymen were evidently in Barnwood as were eight of the holdings owing cash rents and bedrips, including a ½ yardland, 2 mills, and a smithy.[13] In 1650 the tenants on the Barnwood part of the estate included 4 freeholders and 18 copyholders. The latter held 20 tenements, ranging from 2¼ a. to 57½ a. and made up mainly of open-field land with small pasture closes and common meadow land. The copyholders also had common pasture rights and the surviving customs included pannage in Buckholt wood in Cranham.[14] In 1750 there were 39 copyhold tenements, ranging from less than ¼ a. to 105 a., on the estate in Barnwood and Wotton. They covered 938 a., of which Elizabeth Johnson had 422 a., representing 10 tenements, in hand.[15] By 1799 Robert Morris, owner of the Barnwood Court and another leasehold estate, had acquired 16 copyhold estates.[16]

Of the copyhold land some was enfranchised c. 1800[17] and only 27 a. remained unenfranchised in Barnwood in 1857.[18]

Barnwood's open fields were small and in the late 18th century included in the north Badnum field, Sand field in which Wotton hamlet had a small share, and Wellfurlong, and in the south Ash field, Church field, and Redding field. Lilly field, east of Upton Lane, probably originated as part of a field in which neighbouring Hucclecote had shared. Barnwood also shared larger fields with neighbouring hamlets and Upton St. Leonards, including Colebridge field, Elbridge field, and Chamwell field to the north-west, Windmill field and Upper Tredworth field to the west, and Bottom field and Nuthill field to the south-east.[19] There had been some consolidation of the Barnwood demesne in the shared fields by the early 16th century[20] but much of the land lay in small pieces in 1650 when a three-course rotation was apparently followed on the Barnwood estate.[21]

The main common meadows in which Barnwood shared were Walham and Sud Meadow, beside the Severn north and south-west of Gloucester respectively.[22] In 1650 the Barnwood estate also had small pieces at Wickham in Maisemore Meadow on Alney Island, in Dry Meadow and Frize Meadow between Longford and Twigworth, and in a common meadow in Upton bottom south-east of Barnwood. Three tenants took hay from ½ a. in Wickham every other year and another from ½ a. in Walham and Dry Meadow every alternate two years.[23] In 1780 a piece in Walham was said to be changeable every other year for ½ a. in Dry Meadow.[24] Stints of 3 horses and 48 sheep to the yardland in 1559 and 1571 respectively apparently applied to common in the open fields. In 1571 two men were appointed to ensure that pigs, which also fed in the fields, were ringed.[25] In 1650 the tenants' common rights in the open fields were stinted at 80 sheep and 16 cattle for every yardland held. After the hay harvest they also had common rights in Walham and Dry Meadow, and three tenants could graze cattle in Sud Meadow until All Saints.[26] Barnwood had a small common at Wotton containing less than ¼ a. It lay east of the brook and had been taken into an adjoining pasture close by 1750.[27]

In the mid 17th century many of the houses in Barnwood had orchards, and cider was

[3] Ibid. E 5, pp. 32–4.
[4] G.D.R., T 1/16.
[5] *Tax. Eccl.* (Rec. Com.), 231.
[6] Above, man.
[7] Glouc. Cath. Libr., Reg. Abb. Malvern, i, ff. 36v.–37, 85v.–86, 157 and v., 259v.–260; ii, ff. 22 and v., 63 and v., 166; cf. *Valor Eccl.* (Rec. Com.), ii. 415.
[8] Glos. R.O., D 1740/E 1, ff. 1–5, 12–15.
[9] Ibid. D 2957/35.23–5.
[10] Ibid. D 1740/E 3, ff. 1–26.
[11] Ibid. D 936/E 38; cf. ibid. E 21–37; Glouc. Cath. Libr., Chapter Act bk. iv, pp. 1–3, 18–22.
[12] Cf. Glos. R.O., D 936A/M 1, rot. 3d.
[13] *V.C.H. Glos.* vii. 205; *Hist. & Cart. Mon. Glouc.* iii. 120–6.
[14] Glos. R.O., D 1740/E 1, ff. 1, 6–12, 19–20.
[15] Ibid. E 3, list of copyholds and ff. 27–92.

[16] Ibid. Q/RI 70.
[17] Rudge, *Hist. of Glos.* ii. 133.
[18] Church Com. MSS., Glouc. chapter est. surv. M 3, p. 9.
[19] Glos. R.O., D 6/E 4, nos. 14–15; Q/RI 70 (maps D, G–I, K–L, P).
[20] Glouc. Cath. Libr., Reg. Abb. Malvern, i, ff. 36v., 121v., 157.
[21] Glos. R.O., D 1740/E 1, ff. iv.–12.
[22] Ibid.; cf. ibid. Q/RI 70 (maps C–D, R); 79; above, Outlying Hamlets, agric.
[23] Glos. R.O., D 1740/E 1, ff. iv.–12; cf. ibid. Q/RI 94.
[24] Ibid. D 6/E 5.
[25] Ibid. D 1815, Barnwood, Wotton, Cranham, and Tuffley ct. rolls. 1558–71.
[26] Ibid. D 1740/E 1, ff. iv.–12, 20.
[27] Ibid. E 3, f. 74; Q/RI 70 (map M, nos. 11–12).

produced.[28] In the early 18th century the parish was said to be rich in arable and pasture.[29] Market gardens had probably been established there by 1769, when two small nurseries were recorded on the manorial demesne.[30] Open-field land probably decreased in the 18th century, at the end of which Barnwood had more pasture than arable.[31]

The inclosure of the Barnwood fields was completed, with that of most fields and meadows which the parish shared with Wotton and other hamlets, in 1799 under an Act of 1796. The award allotted commonable land and old inclosures in Barnwood to 21 landholders, who with one exception were tenants of the dean and chapter and met their share of the inclosure cost by the sale of part of the land allotted them. Robert Morris, the principal beneficiary received 761 a. and John Jordan 134 a. Three others received between 11 a. and 43 a., nine between 1 a. and 10 a., and seven fractions of 1 a.[32] The award dealt with pieces of Barnwood in Sud Meadow, which was inclosed in 1815.[33]

In the early 19th century c. 96 a. of arable in the north were laid down as pasture[34] and in 1838 Barnwood had 989 a. permanently under grass and 450 a. under crops.[35] Dairying was carried on,[36] and in 1866 the parish returned 144 cattle, both beef and dairy, 307 sheep, and 108 pigs. Leys of clover and lucerne were part of the crop rotation which included wheat, barley, beans, potatoes, and other roots.[37] Market and nursery gardens in the parish, including Longlevens (called Springfield),[38] catered for Gloucester's growing population, and by 1863 one farm's 86 a. of arable had been adapted for market gardening and its 34 a. of grassland partly planted with fruit trees.[39] Orchards covered at least 44 a. of the parish in 1896.[40] Before 1901 the Gloucester firm of J. C. Wheeler and Son laid out extensive nurseries north of Barnwood[41] and from the late 1920s a firm of rose growers was recorded.[42] Dairying remained important, and Barnwood, which in 1905 had 765 a. of permanent grassland and 240 a. of arable land,[43] returned 320 cattle, including 137 milk cows, 167 sheep, and 300 pigs in 1926, as well as a large number of poultry.[44]

In 1856 five farmers were listed in the parish

and in 1863 six.[45] The number of farms, including smallholdings, was evidently higher, for in 1896 a total of 24 agricultural occupiers was returned.[46] The number returned in 1926 was 13, of whom 8 had less than 50 a., two more than 150 a., and another more than 300 a.[47] In 1881 the farmland of Barnwood House Hospital was taken in hand and placed under the management of a bailiff.[48] The county asylum's estate was also farmed directly in the early 20th century, and in 1932 a dairy herd was established. The farm supplied both county mental hospitals and after the introduction of the National Health Service produce was also sold to other hospitals. In the late 1950s and early 1960s direct management was gradually abandoned and the land granted to tenants, including the county council which took c. 60 a. in the south-east for smallholdings.[49] Barnwood House Hospital, which began releasing land for building in 1967, ended direct farming in 1971 and sold grazing rights over agricultural land.[50] From the late 1960s much land in Barnwood was taken for houses and factories and most of that remaining in agricultural use in the early 1980s provided grazing.

Three corn mills were recorded in Barnwood on the river Twyver. The highest, in the south-east corner,[51] was probably that held by Robert the sheriff in 1221[52] and called Sheriff's Mill in the 1260s.[53] It was later held by copy[54] and in 1775 was granted to James Wintle, a Gloucester pinmaker, who sold it to William Green in 1793.[55] The mill was later part of J. W. Walters's estate[56] and was sold with some land in 1862 to Arthur Stewart (d. 1879), who also acquired the nearby Saintbridge House estate. In 1887 the county magistrates bought the mill and 85 a. for their asylum estate.[57] The mill had ceased working by 1921[58] and the building, incorporating an 18th-century house and a 19th-century brick mill, was used as a farmhouse in 1983.

Barnwood Mill, downstream,[59] was that held in the 1260s by Joan of Clayford.[60] It was later held by copy[61] and was bought in 1783 by John Morris.[62] It later belonged to J. W. Walters.[63] The county magistrates, who acquired the mill with an estate for their new asylum in 1878,[64] converted

[28] Ibid. D 1740/E 1, ff. iv.–12; cf. Hist. MSS. Com. 29, 13th Rep. II, Portland, ii, p. 295.

[29] Atkyns, Glos. 251.

[30] Glos. R.O., D 936/E 143.

[31] Bigland, Glos. i. 130.

[32] Glos. R.O., Q/RI 70.

[33] Ibid. 79.

[34] Ibid. D 1740/E 13, deed 24 Nov. 1841.

[35] G.D.R., T 1/16.

[36] Glos. R.O., D 2080/383.

[37] P.R.O., MAF 68/25/13; MAF 68/26/4, 19.

[38] Kelly's Dir. Glos. (1863 and later edns.).

[39] Glos. R.O., D 2299/303.

[40] P.R.O., MAF 68/1609/12.

[41] O.S. Map 6″, Glos. XXV. SE. (1903 edn.); Kelly's Dir. Glos. (1906), 31.

[42] Kelly's Dir. Glos. (1927), 38; (1931), 36.

[43] Acreage Returns, 1905; cf. P.R.O., MAF 68/1609/12.

[44] P.R.O., MAF 68/3295/9.

[45] Kelly's Dir. Glos. (1856), 225; (1863), 202.

[46] P.R.O., MAF 68/1609/12.

[47] Ibid. MAF 68/3295/9.

[48] Glos. R.O., D 3725, Barnwood Ho. Trust, rep.

1881.

[49] Ibid. HO 22/8/19; 26/13.

[50] Ibid. D 3725, Barnwood Ho. Trust, rep. 1967–73; PA 35/3, p. 30.

[51] Ibid. Q/RI 70 (map I, no. 117).

[52] P.R.O., CP 25(1)/73/4, no. 12.

[53] Hist. & Cart. Mon. Glouc. iii. 120; cf. Glouc. Cath. Libr., deeds and seals, x, ff. 23–4.

[54] Glos. R.O., D 1815, Barnwood, Wotton, Cranham, and Tuffley ct. rolls 1558–71, rot. 36; D 1740/E 1, f. 10v.

[55] Ibid. D 936/M 1/1–2.

[56] G.D.R., T 1/16.

[57] Glos. R.O., DC/F 3/3; HO 22/8/6; D 1746/E 2; above, Outlying Hamlets, man.

[58] O.S. Map 6″, Glos. XXXIII. NE. (1924 edn.).

[59] Glos. R.O., Q/RI 70 (map I, no. 81).

[60] Hist. & Cart. Mon. Glouc. iii. 120; cf. Glouc. Cath. Libr., deeds and seals, x, f. 25.

[61] Glos. R.O., D 1815, Barnwood, Wotton, Cranham, and Tuffley ct. rolls 1558–71, rot. 26d.; D 1740/E 1, f. 8v.

[62] Ibid. D 936/M 1/1.

[63] G.D.R., T 1/16.

[64] Above, man.

the buildings, including a farmhouse, as patients' cottages[65] and the mill ceased working.[66] The buildings were demolished after 1950.

The lowest mill of the three, standing southeast of Coney Hill,[67] was leased with the demesne from 1501 when it was a customary messuage called Holder's Mill.[68] In 1750 it was held under lease with 26 a. by Thomas Blizard.[69] From 1838 the mill was in Robert Witcomb's estate[70] and by 1851 its house was a farmhouse.[71] It was known as Court Farm in 1882 when the mill was no longer working,[72] and was demolished after 1937.[73]

The great majority of people listed in Barnwood and Wotton in 1608 were engaged in agriculture, including 35 husbandmen or husbandmen servants, and trades were represented by 4 millers, 2 tailors, a wheeler, and a carpenter.[74] Barnwood had a cordwainer in 1669[75] and the usual village trades were recorded there in the 18th century.[76] In 1811 agriculture provided a livelihood for 51 families out of 73 and in 1831 for 41 families out of 83, the change reflecting the gradual transformation of Barnwood from a village to a suburb of Gloucester.[77]

LOCAL GOVERNMENT. A court roll of Barnwood manor survives for 1292, when the court was attended by the abbey's Cranham tenants and dealt with estate matters, including the care of woodland.[78] By 1558 the court was held, sometimes in the church house,[79] by the lord farmer and was attended by the Wotton and Cranham tenants, who made their presentments separately. In the period 1558–71 the court usually met twice a year and was concerned with tenures, the collection of pig tack or pannage, the maintenance of ditches, driftways, and footbridges, and infringement of common pasture rights.[80] In the years 1726–47 and 1774–1867, for which there are court books and a record of a 1796 court of survey, the court's business was almost exclusively tenurial. The court met frequently at the Salutation inn and from 1783 was held by the dean and chapter.[81] In 1821 Dudstone hundred court ordered the dean and chapter to provide stocks and a pound at Barnwood.[82]

The parish had two churchwardens in 1543[83] and two surveyors of the highways in 1665.[84] The churchwardens received the rent from Barnwood common in the mid 18th century.[85] The accounts of the two overseers of the poor for the years 1705 and 1709–11 survive.[86] Annual expenditure on poor relief rose from £110 in 1776 to £292 in 1803. In the early 19th century the number of persons receiving regular help, 30 in 1803, fell and the cost of relief was kept down despite a considerable increase in the number receiving aid occasionally, 16 in 1803 and 105 in 1815.[87] In the early 1830s the annual cost averaged £139.[88] The parish, which until 1799 had used the church house as a poorhouse,[89] built ten small poorhouses with gardens at the east end of the village in the early 19th century. Those houses were sold to J. W. Walters[90] after the parish joined the Gloucester poor-law union in 1835.[91] Barnwood was later part of Gloucester rural district until absorbed by the city in 1967.[92]

CHURCH. In the mid 12th century Barnwood church was dependent on St. Mary de Lode church, Gloucester, which had been appropriated by Gloucester Abbey.[93] Barnwood church was described as a chapel in 1315[94] and 1498. At the latter date it had a chaplain and a stipendiary priest.[95] In the early 16th century it was served by curates appointed for life.[96] Later the dean and chapter of Gloucester, owners of the tithes, appointed curates[97] and by 1735 the living was called a perpetual curacy.[98] Following a fuller endowment in the later 18th century[99] it became known as a vicarage and was first recorded as such in 1799.[1] It has remained in the gift of the dean and chapter.[2]

In the early 16th century the curate received offerings and all tithes save those of corn and hay for his salary, which was valued at £5 8s. in 1535, and he paid Gloucester Abbey a pension of 6s. 8d.[3] From 1538 he received 20s. a year for his tithes from the demesne[4] and in 1603 his tithes were worth £8.[5] Payment of tithes in kind had ceased by 1704 when the curate apparently received £10 a year in composition from the

[65] Glos. R.O., HO 22/8/6.
[66] O.S. Map 1/2,500, Glos. XXXIII. 8 (1885 edn.).
[67] Glos. R.O., Q/RI 70 (map L, no. 72).
[68] Glouc. Cath. Libr., Reg. Abb. Braunche, p. 20; Glos. R.O., D 340A/T 1.
[69] Glos. R.O., D 1740/E 3, f. 21.
[70] Ibid. T 21.
[71] P.R.O., HO 107/1961.
[72] O.S. Map 6″, Glos. XXXIII. NE. (1891 edn.).
[73] Glos. R.O., D 2299/6520.
[74] Smith, *Men and Armour*, 19–20.
[75] Glos. R.O., D 177/III/13.
[76] Ibid. D 936/M 1/1, cts. 23 Apr., 1 Nov. 1734, 31 Mar. 1736, 13 Jan. 1775.
[77] *Census*, 1811, 1831.
[78] Glos. R.O., D 936A/M 1, rot. 3d.
[79] P.R.O., E 134/40 Eliz. I Hil./3.
[80] Glos. R.O., D 1815, Barnwood, Wotton, Cranham, and Tuffley ct. rolls 1558–71.
[81] Ibid. D 936/M 1/1–3; M 5.
[82] Ibid. D 326/M 22.
[83] Hockaday Abs. xxix, 1543 subsidy, f. 5; xliv, 1572 visit. f. 14.

[84] Glos. R.O., Q/SIb 1, f. 69.
[85] Ibid. D 1740/E 3, f. 74.
[86] Ibid. P 35/IN 1/1.
[87] *Poor Law Abstract, 1804*, 176–7; *1818*, 150–1.
[88] *Poor Law Returns* (1835), 67.
[89] Glos. R.O., Q/RI 70; cf. ibid. (map L, no. 35); P 35/IN 1/1, bapt. 22 Mar. 1785.
[90] Ibid. Q/RI 70 (map I, no. 21); G/GL 8A/3, p. 81.
[91] *Poor Law Com. 1st Rep.* p. 251.
[92] *Census*, 1961–71.
[93] Glouc. Cath. Libr., Reg. Abb. Froucester B, p. 56.
[94] Worc. Episc. Reg., Reg. Maidstone, f. 25.
[95] Hockaday Abs. xxii, 1498 visit. f. 10.
[96] *Valor Eccl.* (Rec. Com.), ii. 415.
[97] Glos. R.O., D 936/E 20; Y 2.
[98] Hockaday Abs. cxii.
[99] Glos. R.O., D 936/Y 64.
[1] Ibid. Q/RI 70.
[2] *Glouc. Dioc. Year. Bk.* (1979), 16–17.
[3] *Valor Eccl.* (Rec. Com.), ii. 415.
[4] Glouc. Cath. Libr., Reg. Abb. Malvern, ii, ff. 178–9; cf. Glos. R.O., D 936/E 20, deed 2 Dec. 1664.
[5] *Eccl. Misc.* 70.

impropriators.[6] From 1721 the curate had a lease of the small tithes and Capel's tithe portion, the corn and hay tithes from 166 a.,[7] and in 1750 the living was worth £35.[8] Its value increased following an allotment in 1765 of £200 from Queen Anne's Bounty, and in 1767 the impropriators endowed the living with the small tithes and Capel's tithe portion to obtain a further award of £200 in 1769.[9] The grants were used to buy 17 a. in Minchinhampton.[10] The vicar's tithes were commuted for a rent charge of £176 in 1841,[11] and in 1856 the vicarage was worth £195.[12]

A small glebe house recorded in 1704 stood north of Ermin Street. It was later used as an alehouse and by 1799 had been converted as four tenements, which were demolished c. 1810.[13] In 1872 an area of 5½ a. south of Ermin Street was acquired for the glebe,[14] and in 1873 a vicarage house to designs of F. S. Waller & Son was built on it some way from the road.[15] That house was standing in the mid 1980s. Barnwood Court, next to the church, was the vicarage from 1937 to the mid 1970s, when a bungalow was built in its grounds for the vicar.[16]

In 1548 Thomas Baskerville, a former monk of Gloucester Abbey, was curate. George Cooper, a former Franciscan and curate of Cowley, was curate the following year[17] and in 1551 was found unable to repeat the Ten Commandments.[18] In 1563 the curate, Lewis Evans, who also held the livings of Churchdown and Upton St. Leonards, was unable to serve Barnwood and Upton at appropriate times.[19] William Perkins, curate by 1572,[20] was not preaching quarterly sermons in 1576[21] and was described as a sufficient scholar but no preacher in 1593.[22] He retained the living until 1634 or 1635.[23] There is evidence of puritan feeling in the parish in the later 1630s when the churchwardens were dilatory in moving the altar to the east end of the chancel and one parishioner went to sermons in Gloucester in preference to attending the parish church.[24] In 1648 the minister of Barnwood, William Edwards, was a signatory of the *Gloucestershire Ministers' Testimony*.[25]

Curates in the later 17th century often held livings nearby[26] and Thomas Merrett, curate by 1690,[27] was usher of the Crypt grammar school, Gloucester.[28] In 1705 the parishioners raised a subscription to pay his successor Richard Eaton for a weekly sermon and provide an annuity of £5 for Merrett.[29] For much of the 18th and 19th centuries the living was served by non-resident incumbents or stipendiary curates, most of whom lived in Gloucester. John Longdon, who became perpetual curate in 1741,[30] moved to Winstone when he became rector there in 1742. For a time he served Barnwood in person[31] but from 1787 he employed stipendiary curates, including from 1790 Arthur Benoni Evans,[32] headmaster of the College school, Gloucester. Evans, who succeeded Longdon as vicar in 1809 and was also rector of Coln Rogers in 1814, employed curates at Barnwood from 1822. The latter included his nephew Thomas Evans, who became his assistant at the school in 1826. A. B. Evans retained the living until his death in 1841.[33] A later headmaster, Hugh Fowler, became vicar of Barnwood upon his retirement in 1872 and in a few years built a vicarage house, restored the church, and promoted the building of a National school.[34] The opening of missions in those parts of the parish affected by the suburban growth of Gloucester from the later 19th century is discussed above.[35]

A small piece of land which had supported an anniversary in the parish was sold in 1553.[36]

The parish church had been dedicated to *ST. LAWRENCE* by the mid 12th century,[37] although a dedication to St. Margaret was recorded in 1287[38] and one to St. Michael and All Saints in the early 18th century.[39] It comprises chancel with north chapel, nave with east bellcot and north aisle and porch, and west tower. Parts of the nave and the chancel arch are of the later 12th century. The north arcade and aisle were added in the early 13th century and some decorative painting of that date survives on the arcade. The bellcot was placed over the chancel arch in the 14th century. In the early 16th century the chapel and tower were built and the nave was reroofed.[40] The chancel was said to be in decay in 1548 and also in

---

[6] G.D.R., V 5/35T 3; a payment of £12 from the impropriation is mentioned in Atkyns, *Glos.* 251; Rudder, *Glos.* 261.

[7] Glos. R.O., D 936/Y 2; cf. G.D.R., V 5/35T 5.

[8] G.D.R. vol. 381A, f. 34.

[9] Hodgson, *Queen Anne's Bounty* (1845), pp. clxviii, cclxxxiii; Glos. R.O., D 936/Y 64; Glouc. Cath. Libr., Chapter Act bk. iii, p. 167.

[10] G.D.R., V 5/35T 4.

[11] Ibid. T 1/16.

[12] Ibid. vol. 384, f. 14.

[13] Ibid. V 5/35T 3–5; F 1/4; Glos. R.O., Q/RI 70 (map H, no. 86).

[14] Glos. R.O., P 35A/PC 3/5.

[15] G.D.R., F 4/1; cf. *Glos. Chron.* 11 Aug. 1877.

[16] *Glouc. Jnl.* 24 July 1937; *Citizen*, 21 Jan. 1977.

[17] Hockaday Abs. xxxi, 1548 visit. f. 9; cxii; *Trans. B.G.A.S.* xlix. 82, 96.

[18] *E.H.R.* xix. 103.

[19] Bodl. MS. Rawl. C. 790, f. 6v.; Hockaday Abs. cxii.

[20] Hockaday Abs. xliv, 1572 visit. f. 14.

[21] G.D.R. vol. 40, f. 13v.

[22] Hockaday Abs. lii, state of clergy 1593, f. 12.

[23] Glos. R.O., D 936/A 1/1, p. 265; 2, pp. 5, 29.

[24] Ibid. D 2052.

[25] *Calamy Revised*, ed. A.G. Matthews, 555.

[26] Glos. R.O., D 936/A 1/3, pp. 5, 47, 111, 442, 466; 4, pp. 5, 30; Hockaday Abs. clxxiii.

[27] G.D.R., V 1/25.

[28] Rudder, *Glos.* 129.

[29] Glos. R.O., P 35/IN 1/1.

[30] Ibid. D 936/Y 2; Hockaday Abs. cxii.

[31] *V.C.H. Glos.* xi. 150; G.D.R. vol. 319; vol. 320; vol. 381A, f. 34.

[32] Glos. R.O., P 35/IN 1/1.

[33] Hockaday Abs. cxii; *V.C.H. Glos.* ii. 333; D. Robertson, *King's Sch., Glouc.* (1974), 101.

[34] Robertson, *King's Sch.* 111–13; *Glos. Chron.* 11 Aug. 1877.

[35] Churches and Chapels, mod. par. ch., Holy Trinity; St. Oswald.

[36] *Cal. Pat.* 1553, 154.

[37] Glouc. Cath. Libr., Reg. Abb. Froucester B, p. 56.

[38] P.R.O., JUST 1/278, rot. 62d.

[39] Atkyns, *Glos.* 251.

[40] The additions were probably made for William Malvern or Parker, abbot of Glouc., whose arms appear on the tower above the west doorway: Verey, *Glos.* ii. 96; *V.C.H. Glos.* ii. 61.

1563 when the windows were out of repair.[41] The nave roof was ceiled in 1730, and pews and a communion table, the object of a bequest by Elizabeth Whitehead (née Johnson), were provided in 1756.[42] By the mid 19th century the ceiling had been removed, a west gallery erected, and the south doorway blocked. The chancel, which probably dated from the 13th century, was heavily restored in the 1850s or early 1860s. The lancet east window was replaced by a three-light window, and a piscina, sedilia, and a credence were renewed. A nave window was altered then. The church was restored in 1873 and 1874 to the designs of F. S. Waller and, in the chancel, Ewan Christian. The south wall of the nave was rebuilt and the doorway opened up, and the north wall of the aisle was partly rebuilt. The north porch was presumably rebuilt at the same time. Several windows were replaced and the aisle was reroofed. The gallery was removed, the church repewed, and other new fittings included a stone pulpit.[43] A screen was installed in the tower arch after 1914.[44]

The appearance of the interior of the church was much altered during the incumbency of M. O. Seacome, vicar 1958–84.[45] Most of the 19th-century innovations were removed and the chancel cleared of monuments. The organ and choir stalls were moved to the nave where new furnishings were introduced, including late 18th-century pews, formerly in St. Mary's church, Woolwich (Kent), and a pulpit of similar date which was restored and painted. The floors of the chancel and chapel were paved with stone and that of the nave retiled. In 1966 a fibre-glass sculpture of Christ in Majesty, by Darsie Rawlins, was placed over the chancel arch.[46]

The octagonal font is richly carved and is contemporary with the early 16th-century additions to the church.[47] The north chapel contains monuments to members of the Parker and Johnson families and other memorials are in the base of the tower, which was used as a vestry in 1983. The chancel, nave, and aisle contain stained-glass memorial windows of the 19th and 20th centuries. The tower's four bells were recast by Abraham Rudhall in 1698 or 1699 as a peal of six,[48] of which one was removed shortly afterwards.[49] In 1873 a treble was given as a memorial to Mary Dowling,[50] and in 1913 two more were added.[51] The plate includes a chalice and paten of

1761 and a chalice of 1863.[52] The registers survive from 1651 and contain entries for Wotton.[53]

The churchyard has the base of an ancient cross, which in 1911 was in the garden of Barnwood Court,[54] and two carved tombchests of the 18th century. A lich gate erected south-east of the church in 1921 as a memorial to the dead of the First World War[55] had been taken down by 1979.

NONCONFORMITY. In 1676 eight protestant nonconformists were recorded at Barnwood.[56] Thomas Shipton, one of several people presented between 1679 and 1685 for not attending the parish church,[51] belonged by 1660 to the Independent church in Gloucester led by James Forbes.[58] The two Presbyterians recorded at Barnwood in 1735 were presumably members of the Barton Street chapel in Gloucester.[59] There is no evidence of any nonconformist meeting in Barnwood before the mid 19th century.

EDUCATION. A charity school for Barnwood and Wotton had been founded in Barnwood, apparently with a gift of £100 from Mary Wright, by 1716 when the dean and chapter, in whom the gift was vested, decided to pay £3 a year to it.[60] From 1754 the lord farmer paid the dean and chapter £5 a year for the school's support.[61] The Barnwood school teaching 35 children in 1818 presumably derived from the charity school, though subscriptions were the only source of income mentioned.[62] In 1833 it was supported entirely by D. or J. W. Walters, apart from the dean and chapter's £5 a year,[63] payment of which was charged on the Barnwood Court estate in 1821 and on Robert Witcomb's estate in 1843.[64] The school, which was held in a cottage north of Ermin Street,[65] was also supported by subscriptions and other payments in 1847 when, with one teacher and 50 children, mostly girls, it was insufficient for the population.[66]

It was replaced by a National school opened in 1874 in a new building, incorporating a schoolhouse, south of Ermin Street on land given by the vicar. The National school had mixed and infants' departments[67] with an average attendance in 1885 of 76, including children from Wotton.[68] Beginning in 1893 it was enlarged several times[69] and in 1904 it had an average attendance of 169.[70] Attendance had declined to 143 by 1938.[71] As

[41] Hockaday Abs. cxii.

[42] Bigland, *Glos.* i. 130; mon. in ch.

[43] R. & J. A. Brandon, *Par. Churches* (1848), views of ch. at pp. 70–1; F. G. Baylis, *Ancient Churches of Glos.* (1865), i. 4–6; *Glos. Chron.* 24 Jan. 1874.

[44] Cf. Glos. Colln. R 35.15.

[45] *Crockford* (1985–6), 433.

[46] Inf. from the Revd. M. O. Seacome; *Cotswold Life*, May 1975, 31; the pulpit was bought in Camberwell (Lond., formerly Surr.) and is said to have come from Lambeth Palace chapel (Lond., formerly Surr.).

[47] *Trans. B.G.A.S.* xlvi, plates II–III at pp. 140–1.

[48] *Glos. Ch. Bells*, 135–6; G.D.R., C 6/1.

[49] Cf. Bodl. MS. Rawl. B. 323, f. 133; Bigland, *Glos.* i. 130.

[50] *Glos. Ch. Bells*, 135.

[51] Glos. Colln. R 35.15.

[52] *Glos. Ch. Plate*, 15.

[53] B. & G. Par. Rec. 59; Glos. R.O., P 35/IN 1/1–5.

[54] Glos. Colln. R 35.15.

[55] *Glouc. Jnl.* 29 Oct., 5 Nov. 1921.

[56] *Compton Census*, ed. Whiteman, 534.

[57] Glos. R.O., D 2052.

[58] Glos. Colln. R 33557.

[59] G.D.R., vol. 285B (1), f. 24.

[60] *16th Rep. Com. Char.* 43; ct. Glos. R.O., D 936/A 1/5,

[61] Glos. R.O., D 936/E 17.

[62] *Educ. of Poor Digest*, 291.

[63] *Educ. Enq. Abstract*, 302.

[64] Glos. R.O., D 936/E 119/18; D 1740/E 13.

[65] Ibid. D 1388/SL 4/24; cf. G.D.R., T 1/16.

[66] Nat. Soc. *Inquiry, 1846–7*, Glos. 2–3.

[67] P.R.O., ED 7/34/29; Glos. R.O., P 35A/PC 3/4.

[68] *Kelly's Dir. Glos.* (1885), 359, 628.

[69] Ibid. (1906), 31.

[70] *Public Elem. Schs. 1906*, 181.

[71] *Bd. of Educ., List 21, 1938* (H.M.S.O.), 125.

Barnwood C. of E. Primary school it had 148 pupils in 1984.[72]

CHARITIES FOR THE POOR. Barnwood benefited from the charity established under the will of Giles Cox of Abload's Court, Sandhurst, dated 1620. The trust deed of 1633 assigned 40s. a year of the profits of the charity estate to help householders not receiving poor relief,[73] but the parish apparently received £1 10s. a year in the late 18th century[74] and persons on poor relief received doles before 1826 when the original

amount was being distributed every few years.[75] The charity, which was regulated by a Scheme of 1892, allotted Barnwood £9 16s. in its distribution for 1897.[76] The separate Barnwood charity established in 1957 on the division of the Cox charity[77] had an income in 1971 of £7, which was distributed among the poor whenever necessary.[78]

Jasper Clutterbuck, a Gloucester alderman, by will dated 1658 gave the poor of Barnwood a portion of the rent from land in the parish which he left to the city corporation.[79] The charity, if ever applied, probably lapsed on expiry of the lease by which he had held that land.[80]

HEMPSTED

THE parish of Hempsted[81] lay by the river Severn south-west of Gloucester city, its parish church 2.3 km. from Gloucester Cross. The boundaries of the ancient parish were very irregular. On the north side Hempsted was intertwined with the extraparochial South Hamlet and on the south side with Quedgeley; in the Middle Ages all three places were estates of Llanthony Priory, and Hempsted and Quedgeley were chapelries to its church of St. Owen, Gloucester. The main body of Hempsted parish, including the village and, east of the Gloucester–Bristol road, Podsmead farm, extended from the Severn on the north-west to the boundaries of Tuffley hamlet, near the course of the Bristol railway line, on the south-east. A southern peninsula of the parish extended between the river and the Netheridge estate in Quedgeley to include the area known as Lower Rea. The largest detached part of Hempsted lay in a bend of the river west of the village, divided from the main body by a spur of South Hamlet. Smaller detached parts, representing land in shared common meadows and open fields, lay to the north in Sud Meadow, to the north-east in the Bristol road and Tredworth areas, to the east on the slopes of Robins Wood Hill, and to the south-east in the Lower Tuffley area.[82] In 1879 the parish was estimated to contain 904 a.[83]

In 1882 Hempsted absorbed two detached parts of South Hamlet and lost a detached part to Tuffley. In 1885 there was a major rationalization of its boundaries. The north boundary was fixed on the Gloucester city boundary: detached parts in the upper Bristol Road and Tredworth areas, which had been taken into the city in 1874 and had a population of 344, were transferred to South Hamlet, while a large part of South Hamlet in the Sud Meadow area, with a population of 33,

was transferred to Hempsted, giving it all the land lying within the broad loop of the Severn south-west of the city. In the south the parish boundary was fixed on the Gloucester and Berkeley canal and Tuffley Lane: the Netheridge area of Quedgeley north-west of the canal was transferred to Hempsted, while Quedgeley took land lying south-east of the canal near Sims bridge and Tuffley took land in the Lower Tuffley area. The alterations left Hempsted with an area of 1,495 a.[84] Gloucester city absorbed land adjoining Bristol Road and the canal in 1900, the Podsmead area in 1935, and Netheridge and Middle and Upper Rea in 1951; by the last extension Lower Rea was left as a detached part of Hempsted[85] until it was transferred to Quedgeley in 1954. The remainder of Hempsted, including the village, was absorbed by the city in 1967.[86] The account given here covers the parish as it was before the late 19th-century boundary changes, together with some parts of South Hamlet which were islanded within or closely interconnected with the parish. Aspects of Hempsted's history which relate to Gloucester's industrial and suburban development, affecting mainly the area adjoining the canal and Bristol Road, are treated above with the city.

The west part of the parish comprises a tract of meadow land lying at below 15 m., defended from the river by a continuous earthen bank; in the mid 1980s the level of parts of the area was being raised by tipping refuse. The village sits on a low but pronounced hill in the centre of the parish, rising to c. 27 m. above the meadows, and a low ridge runs alongside the river in the Rea area in the south part of the parish. The low-lying land is formed by alluvial soils and the higher ground by the Lower Lias clay, which is capped by gravel at the village site.[87] At Lower Rea the clay was fairly

---

[72] List of schs. 1984: co. educ. cttee.
[73] 16th Rep. Com. Char. 38–9.
[74] Bigland, Glos. i. 130.
[75] 16th Rep. Com. Char. 43, which suggests that Barnwood's share of the char., unlike those of other pars., had not been doubled in 1822: cf. ibid. 41.
[76] Glos. R.O., D 2695/1–2.   [77] Ibid. 4.
[78] Ibid. CH 21, Glouc. co. boro., p. 15.
[79] P.R.O., PROB 11/300 (P.C.C. 180 Nabbs), f. 160 and v.
[80] Cf. G.B.R., B 3/3, p. 162.
[81] This account was written in 1986.

[82] G.D.R., T 1/99.
[83] Kelly's Dir. Glos. (1879), 683.
[84] Census, 1891; O.S. Area Bk. (1886). The land at Netheridge given to Hempsted also included a small detached part of Harescombe: cf. Glos. R.O., D 177, Hempsted leases 1850–92, lease 1880.
[85] Census, 1901, 1931 (pt. ii), 1951; O.S. Map. 1/25,000, SO 81 (1952 edn.).
[86] Census, 1961–71.
[87] Geol. Surv. Map 1/50,000, solid and drift, sheet 234 (1972 edn.).

extensively worked for brickmaking in the late 19th century.[88] The parish was predominantly grassland; some small open fields in the east and central parts were inclosed during the 17th and 18th centuries.[89] The only known woodland, recorded from 1615, was Rea Grove (a detached part of South Hamlet), which crowned the ridge above the Severn between Middle and Lower Rea. It covered 7 a. in 1839,[90] and was felled before 1883.[91]

The north end of the hill at the centre of the parish is partly occupied by the earthworks of a Roman military camp, evidently built to command the approach to Gloucester from the south.[92] Its site (in South Hamlet) was later known as the Coneygar,[93] having been preserved by Llanthony Priory as a rabbit warren in the Middle Ages.[94] A spring rising on the west side of the camp is enclosed by a small ashlar-built wellhouse of the 14th century.[95] There is a figure, now defaced, carved in the east gable, and the name Lady's well, recorded from the late 18th century,[96] presumably recalls an ancient invocation to the Virgin Mary.

The main Gloucester–Bristol road, running north-south through the parish, was a turnpike from 1726 until 1877.[97] From Hempsted village two lanes ran down the hill to meet the main road,[98] and the village was also connected to Gloucester by Hempsted Lane, running north-wards past the site of Llanthony Priory and sometimes known in the 19th century as Llanthony Road.[99] Rea Lane, running south from the village to the houses at Upper and Middle Rea, was formerly known as Horsepool Street (or Lane).[1] The Gloucester and Berkeley canal, running alongside and west of the Gloucester–Bristol road, was built in the 1790s but not fully opened until 1827.[2] Hempsted bridge, a wooden swing bridge, was built to carry the southern of the two lanes leading from the village to the Bristol road, and the northern lane was closed. Two other swing bridges, Sims bridge and Rea bridge (within the ancient parish of Quedgeley), were built where minor lanes linked the south part of the parish to the Bristol road.[3]

The village, whose name means the 'high homestead',[4] occupies the south end of the hill at the centre of the parish. Most of the houses were built along a single street crossing the top of the hill.[5] The parish church at the west end was founded in early Norman times. In 1671 a substantial rectory house (in 1986 a private house called Hempsted House) was built adjoining the churchyard,[6] and a village school was added nearby in 1851.[7] Further east at the junction with Rea Lane is a late-medieval village cross, presumably that which originally standing in the churchyard for which William Franklin left money in 1417 before setting out on pilgrimage to Compostella.[8] In the early 19th century only the steps survived. The shaft, found buried in the churchyard, was restored to its place in 1839 by the lord of the manor, the Revd. Samuel Lysons, who provided a new top stage in 1850.[9]

Some small 17th-century farmhouses survive in the village, including Church Farm near the west end and Home Farm near the east, which both have later brick casings. There are also a few cottages of the late 18th century or the early 19th, mainly in the north-west part of the village. In the late 17th century a large new house, Hempsted Court, was built for the Lysons family on the east side of the village overlooking the Bristol road.[10] In the early 19th century, before 1835, two villas with large gardens, Elm Lodge and Willow Lodge, were built on the south side of the village street, east of its junction with Rea Lane.[11] Several other substantial private residences were added in the later 19th century and the early 20th, including Milocroft, at the junction with Hempsted Lane, built for a Gloucester solicitor c. 1890, and Dudstone (later Fairmead House) built further east before 1901.[12] In spite of the proximity of the growing city, Hempsted village retained its rural character in the late 19th century, when it was a favourite destination of Gloucester people out for a Sunday walk.[13] Its character was transformed in the 1960s when Hempsted Court, Elm Lodge, and Willow Lodge were demolished and their grounds developed for housing.[14]

Some way north of the village by Hempsted Lane the large house called the Newark was established as a residence for the priors of Llanthony in the late Middle Ages.[15] Newark Farm nearer the village was built (in part of South Hamlet) by the owners of the Newark and Llanthony estate in the earlier 19th century, probably soon after 1815 when the estate was reorganized at an inclosure.[16] Podsmead, a grange of Llanthony and the ancient site of Hempsted

[88] O.S. Map 1/2,500, Glos. XXXIII. 5 (1885 edn.).
[89] Below, econ. hist.
[90] *Inq. p.m. Glos.* 1625–42, i. 129; G.D.R., T 1/99.
[91] O.S. Map 1/2,500, Glos. XXXIII. 5 (1885 edn.).
[92] S. Lysons, *Romans in Glos.* (1860), 47–50; *Trans. B.G.A.S.* xcv. 35.
[93] G.D.R., T 1/99.   [94] *Trans. B.G.A.S.* lxiii. 119.
[95] R. C. Walters, *Ancient Wells of Glos.* (Bristol, 1928), 63–5.
[96] Bigland, *Glos.* ii, plate facing p. 65; G.D.R., T 1/99.
[97] Glos. Roads Act, 12 Geo. I, c. 24; Annual Turnpike Acts Continuance Act, 39 & 40 Vic. c. 39.
[98] Glos. R.O., D 134/Z 10.
[99] Ibid. P 173/VE 2/1, min. 26 Mar. 1857; MI 3/1–2.
[1] Ibid. D 177, Hempsted fishery deeds, deed 1683; P 173/VE 2/1, min. 23 Mar. 1849.
[2] C. Hadfield, *Canals of S. and SE. Eng.* (1969), 343–4, 347.

[3] G.D.R., T 1/99.
[4] *P.N. Glos.* (E.P.N.S.), ii. 166.
[5] Cf. Glos. R.O., D 134/Z 10; above, Fig. 26.
[6] Below, ch.
[7] Below, educ.
[8] Hockaday Abs. ccxl, 1420.
[9] C. Pooley, *Old Crosses of Glos.* (1868), 15–16.
[10] Below, man.
[11] Glos. R.O., D 177, Hempsted man. deeds 1668–1835; G.D.R., T 1/99; O.S. Map 1/2,500, Glos. XXXIII. 2 (1886 edn.).
[12] R. P. Smith, *Hempsted: the Village and Church* (Chelt. 1983), 17; *Kelly's Dir. Glos.* (1889 and later edns.); O.S. Map 1/2,500, Glos. XXXIII. 2 (1902, 1923 edns.).
[13] Glos. Colln. RX 159.2.
[14] Smith, *Hempsted*, 19.
[15] Below, man.
[16] Glos. R.O., Q/RI 79; G.D.R., T 1/99.

manor, occupied a moated site in an isolated position beyond the Bristol road in the south-east part of the parish.[17]

A scattered group of small farms stood in the part of the parish known as the Rea, where there were some dwellings by the mid 15th century[18] and five houses *c.* 1710.[19] A small farm at Middle Rea was alienated from Hempsted manor in 1683, and in the 18th century was owned by the Payne family;[20] the brick house is apparently a rebuilding of the late 18th century but has a 17th-century plan. Sims Farm, which stood on the lane east of Sims bridge until replaced by new housing in the 20th century, was presumably the house sold by the lord of the manor to Joanna and Hannah Sims in 1700.[21] Both farms were once more part of the manor by 1839.[22] At Lower Rea on the south boundary of the ancient parish stands a small timber-framed house of the late 17th century or the early 18th. A short row of brick cottages was built beside it in the mid 19th century, and other new dwellings added in the south part of the parish at that period included the Bungalow, between Middle and Lower Rea,[23] which was replaced by a modern house in the mid 20th century.

Twenty-five inhabitants of Hempsted were assessed for the subsidy of 1327.[24] About 100 communicants were enumerated in 1551[25] and 31 households in 1563.[26] About 1710 there were said to be *c.* 140 inhabitants in 30 houses,[27] and about 1775 *c.* 129 inhabitants.[28] In 1801 there were 159 inhabitants and 22 houses in the parish. By 1811 the population had fallen to 128, but it had risen again to 251 in 51 houses by 1851. There was then a rapid rise to 424 in 88 houses by 1861 as parts of the parish near the canal and Bristol Road began to be affected by the growth of Gloucester.[29]

There was an alehouse in Hempsted in 1667.[30] There is no later record of a public house in the village,[31] and in 1883 when the Lysons family put their estate, including the bulk of the village, up for sale potential purchasers were required to convenant not to open one.[32] Waterworks, which pumped supplies from a spring in Rea Lane up to a reservoir in the village,[33] were constructed by the Revd. Samuel Lysons in 1871 to serve the village and a suburban area of Gloucester on Bristol Road.[34] A parish room was put up in the school

playground in 1902[35] and replaced by a village hall adjoining the churchyard in 1929.[36]

John of Hempsted (d. 1240), prior of Llanthony, was presumably a native of the parish.[37] From the late 17th century to the late 19th Hempsted was the home of the Lysons family, leading Gloucestershire landowners, whose members also followed antiquarian pursuits and professions in the church, medicine, and the law.[38]

MANOR AND OTHER ESTATES. In Edward the Confessor's reign the manor of *HEMPSTED* was held by Edric Lang, a thegn of Earl Harold. After the Conquest it was acquired by William FitzOsbern (d. 1071), earl of Hereford, who held it in demesne. On his son Roger's rebellion in 1075 it was taken by the Crown.[39] The manor was apparently granted after 1086 to Henry de Beaumont, earl of Warwick, whose heirs had rights as overlords.[40] It was later held in demesne by Walter of Gloucester who gave the chapel and tithes there to St. Owen's church, Gloucester.[41] Walter's son Miles, earl of Hereford, gave the manor in 1141 to his foundation, Llanthony Priory.[42] William (d. 1184), earl of Warwick, later confirmed that grant and released the heirs of Miles from relief and other services; the prior of Llanthony was to continue to provide a service of hospitality for the earl and his retinue twice a year. The service of hospitality had lapsed by 1236 when the prior acknowledged the obligation to Thomas, earl of Warwick, and the following year the earl quitclaimed the service.[43]

Llanthony Priory held the manor until the Dissolution. In 1545 the Crown sold it to Thomas Atkyns (d. 1552) of London and his wife Margaret, who survived him. It passed in direct male line of descent to Richard Atkyns[44] (d. 1610) of Tuffley, a justice of sessions in North Wales, Richard[45] (d. 1636), and Richard.[46] The last Richard sold it, apparently in 1653,[47] to his cousin Robert, later Sir Robert Atkyns of Sapperton. Sir Robert gave it to his son Sir Robert, the historian of Gloucestershire, on the latter's marriage in 1669.[48] In 1699 the younger Sir Robert sold part of the estate to Daniel Lysons and another part to Thomas Lysons,[49] whose family had held leas-

---

[17] Below, man.
[18] P.R.O., C 115/K 2/6685, f. 11.
[19] Atkyns, *Glos.* 473.
[20] Glos. R.O., D 177, Hempsted fishery deeds; D 2525, Ciren., Hempsted, and Daglingworth deed 1716; Bigland, *Glos.* ii. 66.
[21] Glos. R.O., D 1809/T 1, deed 1710.
[22] G.D.R., T 1/99.
[23] O.S. Map 1/2,500, Glos. XXXIII. 5–6 (1885–6 edn.).
[24] *Glos. Subsidy Roll, 1327,* 32.
[25] *E.H.R.* xix. 102.
[26] Bodl. MS. Rawl. C. 790, f. 7.
[27] Atkyns, *Glos.* 473.
[28] Rudder, *Glos.* 491.
[29] *Census,* 1801–61.
[30] Glos. R.O., Q/SIb 1, f. 113.
[31] Cf. Glos. Colln. RX 159.2; *Kelly's Dir. Glos.* (1863), 293.
[32] Glos. R.O., D 2299/1583.
[33] O.S. Map 1/2,500, Glos. XXXIII. 2 (1886 edn.).
[34] G.B.R., B 4/5/3, min. 2 Mar. 1871.
[35] Glos. R.O., P 173/CW 3/15; cf. O.S. Map. 1/2,500,

Glos. XXXIII. 2 (1923 edn.).
[36] Glos. R.O., P 173/MI 14.
[37] *V.C.H. Glos.* ii. 91.
[38] Below, man.; *D.N.B.* s.v. Lysons.
[39] *Dom. Bk.* (Rec. Com.), i. 164; *Complete Peerage,* vi. 447–9.   [40] Below.
[41] *Camd. Misc.* xxii, pp. 37–8.
[42] Ibid. pp. 13–14.
[43] D. Walker, 'Hospitium: a Feudal Service of Hospitality', *Trans. B.G.A.S.* lxxvi. 48–61.
[44] *L. & P. Hen. VIII,* xx (2), pp. 446–7; P.R.O., C 142/95, no. 86. For the Atkyns fam., J. D. Thorp, 'Hist. of Man. of Coates', *Trans. B.G.A.S..* l. 236–46, where, however, some details of the Hempsted descent are incorrect.
[45] P.R.O., C 142/318, no. 148.
[46] *Inq. p.m. Glos.* 1625–42, ii. 24–6.
[47] Glos. R.O., D 1809/T 1. Reynold Graham of London, described as lord of the man. in 1649, was apparently a trustee for Ric. Atkyns: ibid. D 177, Hempsted fishery deeds.
[48] Ibid. D 444/T 70.
[49] Ibid. D 1809/T 1.

ehold estates from the manor since the 1630s or earlier.[50] On Sir Robert's death in 1711 the manor passed to his wife Louise for life, and in 1716 she and Sir Robert's trustees sold it to Allen Bathurst, Lord Bathurst.[51] In 1721 Lord Bathurst sold it to Daniel Lysons, the owner of part of the estate since 1699.[52]

From Daniel Lysons (d. 1736)[53] the manor passed to his son Daniel (d. 1773) and to that Daniel's son Daniel (d. 1800), a physician.[54] The last Daniel was succeeded by his brother the Revd. Samuel[55] (d. 1804). The manor then passed in direct male line of descent to the Revd. Daniel (d. 1834), the antiquary and joint author with his brother Samuel of *Magna Britannia*, to the Revd. Samuel (d. 1877), who like his father and grandfather was rector of Rodmarton, and to Lorenzo George Lysons, later Col. Lysons.[56] In 1883 the estate, comprising c. 580 a. with Hempsted Court, most of the village, and five farms, was offered for sale.[57] Part was sold then or soon afterwards but the bulk of the estate remained in possession of the trustees for sale and was again offered for sale in 1918. By 1923 the farmers were the chief landowners in the parish.[58]

Under Llanthony Priory the manor was administered from Podsmead, which passed into separate ownership at the Dissolution.[59] No later lords of Hempsted resided on the manor until Daniel Lysons became owner in 1721. Hempsted Court, which then became the manor house, was apparently begun by his father Daniel Lysons, a Gloucester draper, who bought leasehold lands in the parish a few years before his death in 1681. The house is said to have been completed during the younger Daniel's minority.[60] It was of two storeys and attics, having a main, east, front of seven bays and a low service wing on the south-west. It stood within a walled enclosure surrounding formal gardens, and adjoining on the north-west was a large walled kitchen garden.[61] At the beginning of the 19th century the house was refronted and the attics brought into the elevation,[62] apparently to the designs of Robert Smirke.[63] The house and grounds, and apparently also the manorial rights,[64] were bought from the Lysons trustees c. 1887 by the Revd. Joseph

Brereton, who opened a boys' school, later transferred to the Gloucestershire County Schools Association. The school closed in 1891[65] and some additions made to the house for it were pulled down soon afterwards.[66] Later owners of Hempsted Court included from c. 1914 Arnold Hurry (d. 1927), who was regarded as squire of the village,[67] and from 1928 C. B. Trye (d. c. 1961).[68] The house was demolished in 1962[69] and the site used for a housing estate. When the house was built in the late 17th century a small park was laid out east of it with a broad double avenue of elms and a series of ornamental gates, leading down to the Bristol road.[70] The eastern end of the avenue was destroyed when the canal was built in the 1790s but the remainder of it survived in 1839, by which time a drive had been constructed branching from it to a lodge on the lane west of Hempsted bridge.[71] Parts of the avenue had been felled by the early 1880s and a more irregular pattern of planting adopted in the park,[72] but some trees survived until the outbreak of Dutch elm disease in the early 1970s.[73]

The lands bought from the manor by Thomas Lysons in 1699 apparently comprised *MANOR FARM*, based on a house in Hempsted Lane on the north side of the village. Thomas (d. 1714) left his Hempsted lands to his wife Mary[74] who was succeeded before 1716 by his son Silvanus.[75] Silvanus Lysons (d. 1731) left Manor farm to his wife Mary and after her death, which occurred in 1750, for charitable purposes.[76] The farm comprised 64 a. following inclosure in 1815.[77] Some land was sold in 1979, and in 1986 the charity trustees retained the farmhouse, which had been rebuilt in the early 20th century, a cottage, and 29 a.[78]

By 1291 and until the Dissolution Hempsted manor was administered from Llanthony Priory's grange of *PODSMEAD*, lying east of the Bristol road, and Podsmead was sometimes used as an alternative name for the manor. The priory granted a 60-year lease of Podsmead to Richard Partridge and his family in 1507.[79] The freehold was bought from the Crown in 1539 by Joan Cooke, who that year granted a new lease for 99 years to John Partridge, son of Richard, and his

[50] Ibid. P 173/IN 1/1; D 892/T 37.

[51] Ibid. D 2525, Ciren., Hempsted, and Daglingworth deed 1716.

[52] Ibid. D 177, Hempsted man. deeds 1668–1835.

[53] For the Lysons fam., *Trans. B.G.A.S.* vi. 323.

[54] Rudder, *Glos.* 489–90.

[55] Rudge, *Hist. of Glos.* ii. 169.

[56] Glos. R.O., P 173/CH 5/1; *Glos. N. & Q.* ii. 514–16.

[57] Glos. R.O., D 1809/E 1.

[58] *Kelly's Dir. Glos.* (1885 and later edns.); Glos. R.O., D 2299/1583.

[59] Below.

[60] P.R.O., PROB 11/372 (P.C.C. 22 Drax), ff. 169–72; Bigland, *Glos.* ii. 66.

[61] Painting c. 1700, at Glos. R.O., detail reproduced above, Plate 58.

[62] *Delineations of Glos.* 154 and plate facing; Glos. R.O., D 1809/Z 2.

[63] Glos. R.O., D 1809/E 1, where the date 1802 given for the work is too early; c. 1810 or later is more likely: cf. *Delineations of Glos.* 154; Colvin, *Biog. Dict. of Brit. Architects* (1978), 740–3.

[64] *Kelly's Dir. Glos.* (1889), 816.

[65] *Glouc. Jnl.* 12 Sept. 1891; above, Educ., private schs.; cf. Glos. R.O., D 177, Hempsted leases 1850–92, lease 1886.

[66] Glos. Colln. (H) G 4.9; *Glos. Countryside*, Oct. 1936, 176.

[67] *Kelly's Dir. Glos.* (1914), 224; Smith, *Hempsted*, 19.

[68] *Glos. Countryside*, Oct. 1936, 176; Glos. Colln. RR 159.4.

[69] Smith, *Hempsted*, 19.

[70] Painting c. 1700; Glos. R.O., D 134/Z 10.

[71] G.D.R., T 1/99.

[72] O.S. Map 1/2,500, Glos. XXXIII. 2 (1886 edn.).

[73] Smith, *Hempsted*, 17.

[74] G.D.R. wills 1713/58; Bigland, *Glos.* ii. 67.

[75] Glos. R.O., D 2525, Ciren., Hempsted, and Daglingworth deed 1716.

[76] *16th Rep. Com. Char.* 54–5; Bigland, *Glos.* ii. 67; below, char.

[77] Glos. R.O., D 134/P 7; cf. ibid. Q/RI 79.

[78] Inf. from Mr. G. M. T. Fowler, clerk to the Lysons char. trustees.

[79] *Tax. Eccl.* (Rec. Com.), 232; *Valor Eccl.* (Rec. Com.), ii. 423; *Cal. Pat. 1350–4*, 456; P.R.O., C 115/L 2/6691, f. 61 and v.

family. In 1540 Joan Cooke settled the estate on Gloucester corporation as part of the endowment of the Crypt school; her trust deed directed that after the expiry of the existing lease the corporation was to grant 31-year leases at fixed rents and fines, giving preference to the heirs of her relation Margaret Woodward, a stepdaughter of John Partridge.[80] In 1633 the lessee of Podsmead was Henry Holman, a grandson of Margaret, and his son Richard held it in 1652.[81] In 1690 a lease was granted to Richard's daughters Elizabeth Hoskins and Sarah Evans. Elizabeth's son Holman Hoskins later acquired, reputedly by dubious means, the interest of Sarah's son George Evans of Tewkesbury, and in 1715 surrendered the lease in return for a new one naming him as sole lessee. Holman, who lived at Podsmead, died in 1717. Chancery suits later were brought involving Ann Russell, who had succeeded to Holman's interest, Elizabeth Hope, another heir of Elizabeth Hoskins, and George Evans; the suits were finally resolved in 1732 when the corporation was directed to grant a new joint lease to Ann Russell and George Evans.[82] Between the mid 18th century and the early 19th members of the Phelps family, heirs of George Evans, and the Hope family were joint lessees of the Podsmead estate,[83] which covered c. 220 a.[84] The interest of both lessees was bought c. 1815 by Samuel Jones,[85] later an alderman of Gloucester, who farmed Podsmead and was succeeded there at his death in 1844 by his son Samuel.[86]

From 1844 Gloucester corporation's right to the freehold of Podsmead and the other Crypt school endowments was challenged in Chancery by the municipal charity trustees for the city who established their right in 1851,[87] though a further suit brought by the Hope family delayed the transfer of the estate until 1857.[88] Subsequently the estate was leased to farmers for short terms, the restrictive provisions of the trust having been set aside.[89] It passed with the other Crypt endowments to the governors of the United Schools in 1882 and back to the city corporation in 1937. Part of the estate became the site of the new Crypt school in 1939[90] and most of the remainder was used for council housing in the 1940s and 1950s.[91]

The house at Podsmead was built on a moated site. Work on a servants' hall and barn there was carried out in the time of William of Cherington, prior of Llanthony 1377–1401.[92] The lease of 1507

reserved to the prior, when he wished to lodge there, chambers, study, chapel, underparlour, hall, kitchen, pantry, and buttery, and lodgings for his servants.[93] In 1731 the house, standing within its square moat, was a gabled building, apparently with a detached gatehouse.[94] It was rebuilt as a small brick farmhouse c. 1867.[95] It was demolished in 1985 and the site, where part of the moat had still survived,[96] was used for new houses.

The house called *THE NEWARK*, later Newark House, north of Hempsted village, was recorded on Llanthony Priory's estates in 1507,[97] and, according to tradition, was built by a 14th-century prior to rival the Vineyard, the abbot of Gloucester's house on a similar site at Over west of the Severn.[98] After the Dissolution the house with some lands in the parish descended with the Llanthony manor estate in the Porter, Scudamore, and Higford families.[99] The bulk of that estate lay in South Hamlet, though John Scudamore, Viscount Scudamore, made the whole of his land tithable to Hempsted church in 1662,[1] and a reorganization of the estate at inclosure in 1815 increased its holding of land in Hempsted parish.[2] The Newark was described c. 1540 as a pretty stone house.[3] It was rebuilt by Viscount Scudamore in the mid 17th century[4] and was described c. 1710 as a handsome, beautiful house.[5] It is said, however, to have remained unfinished until c. 1830 when John Higford rebuilt it[6] as a plain ashlar-faced mansion, incorporating part of the old foundations. In the early 1860s it was occupied by a private school.[7] From 1883 until c. 1910 it housed a branch of St. Lucy's Home, Gloucester, training girls for domestic service.[8] In 1986 it was occupied as flats.

The rectory of Hempsted was held by Llanthony Priory before the Dissolution, and in the late 16th century the great and small tithes from the relatively small area of the parish that remained tithable were leased from the Crown.[9] In 1603 the rectory was valued at £30.[10] By 1628, comprising the tithes, two houses, and a small parcel of land, it was owned by Richard Powle who on his death that year was succeeded by a kinsman Henry Powle.[11] Henry's younger son, Henry Powle of Williamstrip, Coln St. Aldwyns,[12] sold the rectory in 1662 to Viscount Scudamore, who gave it as part of his endowment of the living of Hempsted.[13]

[80] Austin, *Crypt Sch.* 144–58; Glos. R.O., D 3270/C 18.

[81] Glos. R.O., D 3270/C 19; P.R.O., C 3/447/144; cf. Glos. R.O., D 3270/C 20.

[82] Glos. R.O., D 3270/C 21; G.D.R. wills 1717/286.

[83] Glos. R.O., D 3270/C 23–4; C 25/1.

[84] |Ibid. D 3270/19678, p. 315; G.B.R., J 4/1 (no. 32A).

[85] Glos. R.O., D 3270/C 25/2, 9–10, 19.

[86] Ibid. C 25/14; D 3117/3469.

[87] Ibid. D 3270/19677, pp. 190–1, 373–6, 521–2.

[88] *V.C.H. Glos.* ii. 350; G.B.R., L 6/11/11.

[89] Glos. R.O., D 3270/C 90; 19678, p. 315.

[90] Above, Educ., secondary educ. 1882–1984; Austin, *Crypt Sch.* 134.

[91] *Glouc. Municipal Year Bk.* (1964–5), 89–91.

[92] P.R.O., C 115/K 2/6684, f. 8.

[93] Ibid. C 115/L 2/6691, f. 61 and v.

[94] G.B.R., J 4/1 (no. 32A). [95] Glos. R.O., D 3270/C 26/1.

[96] Cf. Glos. Colln., G. M. Davies papers, notes on moats.

[97] P.R.O., C 115/L 2/6691, f. 61 and v.

[98] Atkyns, *Glos.* 584; Glos. R.O., D 327, p. 173; cf. *Hist. & Cart. Mon. Glouc.* (Rolls Ser.), i. 48.

[99] Above, Outlying Hamlets, man.

[1] M. Gibson, *View of the Ancient and Present State of the Churches of Door, Home-Lacy, and Hempsted* (1727), 206–16; cf. G.D.R., T 1/99. [2] Glos. R.O., Q/RI 79.

[3] Leland, *Itin.* ed. Toulmin Smith, ii. 63.

[4] Glos. R.O., D 327, p. 173. [5] Atkyns, *Glos.* 501.

[6] Glos. Colln. RX 159.2.

[7] *Glouc. Jnl.* 19 Jan. 1861; *Kelly's Dir. Glos.* (1863), 293.

[8] Glos. Colln. R 159.6; *Kelly's Dir. Glos.* (1885 and later edns.); cf. above, Hosp., children's hosp.

[9] *Cal. Pat.* 1560–3, 68–9; 1572–5, p. 328.

[10] *Eccl. Misc.* 71.

[11] P.R.O., C 142/718, no. 149.

[12] Cf. *V.C.H. Berks.* iii. 164; *V.C.H. Glos.* vii. 48.

[13] Gibson, *Ch. of Door*, 169–71.

ECONOMIC HISTORY. In 1086 the demesne of Hempsted manor was worked by 3 plough-teams and employed 6 *servi*. The tenants of the manor were 6 *villani* and 8 bordars, having 6 ploughteams between them.[14] In 1291 the manor had 4 ploughlands in demesne.[15] The demesne farm of Podsmead was leased from Llanthony Priory before 1507 for a rent in produce, and in 1535 there were also pieces of demesne land leased at cash rents.[16] Bondmen of the manor were given manumission by the priory in 1503 and 1506.[17] In 1535 there were free tenants owing rents of 13s. and customary tenants owing rents of £27 0s. 9¾d.[18]

After the Dissolution, when the Podsmead estate passed into separate ownership, Hempsted manor apparently had no demesne farm until the mid 18th century when the Lysonses kept some land in hand.[19] In 1699 the manor estate comprised c. 26 small holdings, some held by copy but most of them leased for 60 years or lives.[20]

In the late 17th century the parish contained a number of small open fields. A field called Streetley lay north-east of the village and one called Hill field was probably represented later by the close called Hill Ground lying to the south-east; Oakley and Whitcroft adjoined the east side of the Bristol road at its junction with Tuffley Lane; and South field lay near Lower Rea at the south end of the parish. Hempsted tenants also had land in Upper and Lower Tredworth fields south of Gloucester,[21] and in West field near Quedgeley.[22] Exchanges and inclosures were carried out in Oakley and Hill field before 1686[23] and all the fields were inclosed by such private agreement before the early 19th century, some of the land being turned to pasture and orchard.[24]

West of Hempsted village, bounded by a bend of the river Severn, was a large tract of common meadow land. After the Dissolution much of it, comprising Oxlease and Cowlease (both in South Hamlet), Great Moors, and some smaller parcels, was subject to a division of rights between the various estates which derived from Llanthony's demesnes south of Gloucester. Oxlease and Cowlease were said to belong to Llanthony manor in 1662, but Hempsted manor was entitled to the latter math of Oxlease. In 1759 Great Moors, covering 59 a., lay in 31 parcels for the purposes of the first mowing, the bulk of them belonging to Hempsted manor, Podsmead farm, and the Silvanus Lysons charity estate (an offshoot of Hempsted manor); two of the parcels changed ownership each year. The whole of the latter math

of Great Moors was taken by Llanthony manor. The winter pasture of the three large meadows belonged to Hempsted manor, but Llanthony manor and Podsmead each had the right to pasture 21 beasts in Great Moors and Oxlease during part of the summer and autumn, rights which the owner of Hempsted, Daniel Lysons, rented from them each year in the 1750s.[25] The meadows were inclosed in 1815 by Act of Parliament. Most of the land, including the three large meadows, was awarded to the owner of Llanthony manor, the duke of Norfolk, who gave up some of his old inclosures to Hempsted manor, Podsmead, and the Lysons charity estate in return for the extinction of their rights. The Act also inclosed Sud Meadow, lying further north, where a few parcels belonged to Hempsted parish.[26] Another large common meadow called Hempsted Ham lay between the village and Oxlease and Cowlease. Apart from Podsmead's right to one horse pasture, extinguished in 1815,[27] it belonged wholly to Hempsted manor after the Dissolution. Some of the tenants had rights of common there, mainly for sheep, in the late 17th century,[28] but the Lysons family inclosed the meadow before 1796, taking 68 a. while the Lysons charity estate took 6 a.[29]

The bias towards pasture farming in Hempsted was already evident by 1553 when 65 a. of Podsmead farm had been recently converted from arable.[30] In 1731 only 28 a. of the 213-a. farm were arable.[31] About 1775 the parish was said to comprise rich pasture and orchard, producing excellent cheese and cider.[32] In 1839 the parish together with the tithable parts of South Hamlet adjoining it contained 188 a. of arable compared with 1,106 a. of pasture and meadow.[33] In 1866 94 a. in Hempsted parish were returned as under crops and 669 a. as permanent grassland;[34] 130 dairy cows, 253 other cattle, 259 sheep, and 45 pigs were then kept in the parish.[35] By 1926 the arable had shrunk to a few acres and the farms of the enlarged parish (including former parts of South Hamlet and Quedgeley) were given over to dairying, raising cattle and sheep, and keeping poultry.[36]

In the 19th century and the earlier 20th the land was divided among six or seven farms, of which only Podsmead, which remained a compact farm of c. 220 a.,[37] was large. The land of the Llanthony manor estate in Hempsted, with some land in South Hamlet, was farmed from Newark Farm, built north of the village in the early 19th century, and Manor farm, belonging to the Lysons charity, was a small farm of c. 30 a.[38] On

---

[14] *Dom. Bk.* (Rec. Com.), i. 164.
[15] *Tax. Eccl.* (Rec. Com.), 232.
[16] P.R.O., C 115/L 2/6691, f. 61 and v.; *Valor Eccl.* (Rec. Com.), ii. 423.
[17] P.R.O., C 115/L 2/6691, ff. 18 and v., 38v.
[18] *Valor Eccl.* (Rec. Com.), ii. 423.
[19] Glos. R.O., D 750.
[20] Ibid. D 1809/T 1, deed 1699.
[21] Ibid.; cf. ibid. D 134/Z 10; G.D.R., T 1/99.
[22] Glos. R.O., D 123/T 12; D 750, est. ptic. 1769.
[23] Ibid. D 892/T 37.
[24] Ibid. D 750, est. ptic.; G.D.R., T 1/99.
[25] Gibson, *Ch. of Door*, 208–9; Glos. R.O., D 750; D 1233/10; D 177, deeds of Hempsted and Haresfield 1698–

[26] Glos. R.O., Q/RI 79.
[27] Ibid.; G.B.R., B 2/1, f. 35.
[28] Glos. R.O., D 891/T 37.
[29] Ibid. D 1233/10; D 177, deeds of Hempsted and Haresfield 1698–1808, mortg. 1808; cf. G.D.R., T 1/99.
[30] G.B.R., B 2/1, f. 34v.
[31] Ibid. J 4/1 (no. 32A).
[32] Rudder, *Glos.* 489.
[33] G.D.R., T 1/99.
[34] P.R.O., MAF 68/26/20.
[35] Ibid. MAF 68/25/13.
[36] Ibid. MAF 68/3295/9.
[37] Glos. R.O., D 3270/C 90.
[38] G.D.R., T 1/99; Glos. Colln. RX 159.1; Glos. R.O., D 134/Z 10.

1808, mortg. 1808; G.B.R., B 2/1, f. 35v.

the Hempsted manor estate in 1839 the farms were Church farm with 99 a., Hill farm with 96 a., and 116 a. in the south part of the parish held with the houses and buildings at Sims Bridge Farm and Middle Rea.[39] In the 1850s and 1860s the Revd. Samuel Lysons carried out drainage and other improvements on the farms, using loans from the Land Improvement Co.[40] In 1882 the main farms on the estate were Church farm (82 a.) and Middle Rea farm (102 a.). Sims Bridge farm (25 a.) was held with Netheridge farm in Quedgeley, which had been added to the estate, and there were various smallholdings, including Upper Rea farm (19 a.).[41] In 1926 in the enlarged parish there were 12 agricultural holdings, of which two were over 150 a. and four were 100–150 a.[42] The farms still working then included Podsmead, Newark, Manor, Hill, Church, and Middle Rea, and other land was farmed from the Bungalow at the Rea.[43] By 1986 the Bungalow was the only working farm based in the ancient parish. The land in the south part was then mainly under crops, while the meadows of the north part were used by small-holders for grazing sheep.

Llanthony Priory apparently held a market and fairs on the manor in the late Middle Ages. They were included as an item in the bailiff's account at the dissolution of the priory in 1539 but no profits were received that year.[44]

In 1608 the inhabitants of Hempsted included a weaver, a cordwainer, and a sailor.[45] Among the very few parishioners later recorded as following a trade were fishermen, a smith in 1669,[46] and the tenant of a coalyard recorded in 1750 and 1808, apparently at Lower Rea[47] where there was later a wharf on the river.[48] In 1831 only two families of the parish were supported by trade compared with 26 supported by agriculture.[49]

Half of a fishery called Horsepool weir, situated at the bend in the river at Upper Rea,[50] was given to Llanthony Priory with the manor in 1141.[51] The priory apparently acquired the other half by grant from Henry II c. 1173.[52] It was among weirs in the Severn below Gloucester whose owners were indicted in the 1390s for taking fish of too small a size,[53] and in 1502, when the priory granted it on lease together with the lops of riverside willows for its repair, possibility of its destruction by royal officials was mentioned.[54] After the Dissolution the fishing rights in the river

above the site of Horsepool weir descended with Llanthony manor,[55] while Hempsted manor had the rights in the stretch adjoining the south part of the parish.[56] The latter were held with the small farm at Middle Rea until that was sold by the manor in 1683, and were later granted on short leases. In 1731, when it was worked with a boat and nets, the fishery was leased together with another owned by the Lysons family in Minster-worth at an annual rent of £40 and 30 lb. of salmon.[57] In the late 19th century it was known as Foxhole salmon fishery.[58]

LOCAL GOVERNMENT. In 1287 the prior of Llanthony claimed view of frankpledge, waif, and gallows on his manor of Hempsted; the Hempsted view was also attended by his tenants from Qued-geley and Elmore.[59] In 1456 or 1457 the priory claimed assize of bread and of ale in addition to the other liberties.[60] The lords of the manor continued to exercise leet jurisdiction after the Dissolution, but the courts leet and baron were not recorded after the early 18th century.[61] No court rolls are known to survive.

No parish government records survive before the mid 19th century. Two churchwardens were recorded from 1498.[62] Women held the office fairly regularly in the late 16th century and the early 17th. It was served in rotation by houses, as were the offices of overseers and highway surveyors which were recorded from the mid 17th century. In 1663 and 1673, and possibly on a regular basis, the parish constable was appointed by the county magistrates.[63] Poor relief was prob-ably never a severe burden in Hempsted, with usually no more than 10 people on permanent relief during the early 19th century,[64] and the rise in expenditure only a gradual one until the last years of the old poor law.[65] In the depressed years of the mid 1780s Daniel Lysons excused his tenants a large part of their rents and he and another resident, Charles Tyrell Morgan, provided aid for the poor.[66] In the 19th century the Hempsted poor continued to enjoy the ben-evolent attention of local landowners, as well as benefiting from the substantial parish charities.[67] Hempsted became part of the Gloucester poor-law union in 1835[68] and remained in the Gloucester rural district[69] until the residue of the parish was absorbed by the city in 1967.

[39] G.D.R., T 1/99.
[40] Glos. R.O., D 177, Hempsted papers 1837–77.
[41] Ibid. trust deed of Hempsted man. 1882; V.C.H. Glos. x. 219.
[42] P.R.O., MAF 68/3295/9.
[43] Kelly's Dir. Glos. (1927), 234.
[44] P.R.O., SC 6/Hen. VIII/1224, rot. 19.
[45] Smith, Men and Armour, 25.
[46] Glos. R.O., D 892/T 37.
[47] Ibid. D 750, rental 1750–1; D 177, deeds of Hempsted and Haresfield 1698–1808.
[48] G.D.R., T 1/99.   [49] Census, 1831.
[50] Inq. p.m. Glos. 1625–42, i. 128; Glos. Colln. RX 159.1; cf. also a mention of Clipsmead (G.D.R., T 1/99, no. 292) as lying between the village and Horsepool, in P.R.O., C 115/K 2/6683, f. 29v.
[51] Dugdale, Mon. vi. 137.
[52] Pipe R. 1173 (P.R.S. xix), 151; cf. Rot. Chart. (Rec. Com.), 7.

[53] Trans. B.G.A.S. lxii. 142–51.
[54] P.R.O., C 115/L 2/6691, ff. 51v.–52.
[55] Inq. p.m. Glos. 1625–42, i. 128; Glos. Colln. RX 159.1.
[56] P.R.O., C 142/95, no. 86.
[57] Glos. R.O., D 177, Hempsted fishery deeds; Hempsted man. deeds 1668–1835.
[58] Ibid. D 1809/E 1.
[59] Plac. de Quo Warr. (Rec. Com.), 244.
[60] P.R.O., C 115/K 2/6685, f. 11.
[61] Ibid. E 134/5 Jas. I Mich./24; Glos. R.O., D 892/T 37; Atkyns, Glos. 472.
[62] Hockaday Abs. xxii, 1498 visit. f. 10.
[63] Glos. R.O., P 173/IN 1/1; Q/SO 1, f. 29v.
[64] Poor Law Abstract, 1804, 176–7; 1818, 148–9.
[65] Ibid.; Poor Law Returns (1830–1), 68; (1835), 66.
[66] Glouc. Jnl. 16 Feb. 1784.
[67] Glos. N. & Q. iii. 84; Kelly's Dir. Glos. (1870), 579.
[68] Poor Law Com. 1st Rep. p. 251.
[69] Census, 1911.

CHURCH. A church was built at Hempsted soon after the Norman Conquest, and Walter of Gloucester granted it with the tithes of the *villani* there to St. Owen's church, Gloucester.[70] In 1137 it passed with St. Owen's church to Llanthony Priory,[71] which soon afterwards, in return for an annual payment of 16s., had a grant of tithes and a small piece of land in Hempsted held by Lire Abbey (Eure).[72] Some of the profits of the chapelry were assigned as part of the portion of the vicar of St. Owen in the mid 13th century, by which time the chapel had acquired burial rights.[73] By 1428 a separate vicarage of Hempsted had been ordained and Llanthony presented a priest to it.[74] In 1513, however, the living had only the status of a chaplaincy, though endowed with certain tithes and offerings,[75] and from the mid 16th century it was called a curacy.[76] In 1662 it was newly endowed with tithes by John Scudamore, Viscount Scudamore, and became a rectory.[77] In 1984 the living was placed in the care of a priest-in-charge while plans for its future were considered.[78]

After the Dissolution the curates were appointed, and presumably paid, by the owners or lessees of the rectory estate. At the endowment of the living in 1662 the advowson was assigned to Viscount Scudamore[79] and it descended with Llanthony manor.[80] In 1920 trustees for the Higford family transferred it to the bishop of Gloucester.[81]

In 1540 the curate was said to receive a tenth of the profits of the church,[82] and in 1603 his stipend was £9 10s.[83] In 1653 he was receiving £12, to which the trustees for the maintenance of ministers added £20; a further £5 was added in 1657.[84] The living owed its endowment to Viscount Scudamore's unease over lay ownership of tithes, which also led him to endow several livings in Herefordshire. His Llanthony manor estate had been tithe free since the Dissolution but he charged himself with arrears of tithes from the time he took possession of it, using them during the Interregnum in aid of a fund for dispossessed clergy. In 1662 he gave all the tithes from Llanthony manor together with the Hempsted rectory estate, which he bought from the lay owner for £376, to the living of Hempsted.[85]

The new rectory thus became possessed of the tithes of a large part of South Hamlet and

Hempsted, but 316 a. of Hempsted, comprising Podsmead, Great Moors, and Hempsted Ham, as former Llanthony demesne, remained tithe free and another considerable area of the parish was free of great tithes by ancient custom. In 1796 the rector leased the tithes owed from the Hempsted manor estate to the owner Daniel Lysons for £52 10s. a year. The rector's tithes from Hempsted and South Hamlet were commuted for a corn rent charge of £286 in 1839.[86] A small parcel of glebe land, a house called the vicarage house, apparently that built beside the churchyard for the vicar of St. Owen in the mid 13th century, a church house, and a barn passed to the living among the assets of the lay rectory in 1662.[87] The glebe was sold in 1899.[88]

About 1710 the rectory was worth £80 a year.[89] From 1750 it was much augmented from the charity founded by Silvanus Lysons, who by will dated 1731 left the rector the surplus rent of lands in Hempsted and elsewhere after the provision of £180 a year in pensions to clergy widows of the diocese. In 1825 the rectory was worth c. £400 a year, drawn about equally from the Lysons charity and from the other endowments,[90] and in 1856 it was worth £449.[91] A Scheme of 1879 gave the rector a fixed annual sum of £860 from the charity[92] and in 1885 the rectory was worth £1,000 a year.[93] The Lysons charity, which retained its land, became very wealthy in the mid 20th century. A Scheme of 1962 assigned to the rector half of the large annual surplus left after payment of the pensions,[94] and one of 1980 awarded him £6,000 a year or a sum exceeding by at least 25 per cent the minimum clerical stipend for the diocese.[95]

Under the Lysons charity the rector received 21s. for a sermon and prayers on Ascension day; the payment was increased to £5 in 1980.[96] Under a charity of Mary Harris established in 1721 he received 20s. for preaching a sermon and administering communion on the anniversary of the founder's death.[97]

The curates of Hempsted before 1662 were possibly allowed to use the house called the vicarage house belonging to the lay rectory.[98] Viscount Scudamore began building a large new rectory house on the south side of the churchyard and it was completed by his trustees in 1671 after his death.[99] It is of brick with stone-framed win-

[70] *Camd. Misc.* xxii. pp. 37–8.
[71] Dugdale, *Mon.* vi. 136.
[72] P.R.O., C 115/K 2/6683, f. 26 and v.
[73] Gibson, *Ch. of Door*, 231–4; P.R.O., C 115/K 2/6683, ff. 34v.–35, 46v.
[74] Worc. Episc. Reg., Reg. Polton, f. 48v.
[75] P.R.O., C 115/L 2/6691, f. 57.
[76] e.g. Hockaday Abs. xxv, 1532 subsidy, f. 29; xlix, state of clergy 1584, f. 4; *Eccl. Misc.* 71. [77] Below.
[78] Inf. from the Revd. J. E. Newell, of Hempsted House.
[79] Gibson, *Ch. of Door*, 170, 212, 215.
[80] Hockaday Abs. cclx; *Kelly's Dir. Glos.* (1870 and later edns.); cf. above, Outlying Hamlets, man.
[81] *Lond. Gaz.* 24 Dec. 1920, p. 12588.
[82] Hockaday Abs. xxviii, 1540 stipendiaries, f. 5.
[83] *Eccl. Misc.* 71.
[84] Hockaday Abs. ccxl.
[85] Gibson, *Ch. of Door*, provides a full account of Vct. Scudamore and his endowment of Hempsted.

[86] G.D.R., T 1/99; Glos. R.O., D 1233/10.
[87] Gibson, *Ch. of Door*, 170, 233–4; P.R.O., C 115/K 2/6683, f. 46v.
[88] Glos. R.O., P 173/IN 3/11.
[89] Atkyns, *Glos.* 472
[90] *16th Rep. Com. Char.* 54–5; Hockaday Abs. ccxl, 1825.
[91] G.D.R. vol. 384, f. 115.
[92] Glos. R.O., P 173/CH 4/1.
[93] *Kelly's Dir. Glos.* (1885), 502.
[94] Glos. R.O., D 3469/5/76; CH 21, Glouc. rural district, p. 23.
[95] Char. Com. Scheme 3 Mar. 1980. In 1986 the priest-in-charge received the minimum stipend from the char., the additional 25 per cent going to a diocesan training fund for ordinands: inf. from Mr. Fowler.
[96] *16th Rep. Com. Char.* 54; Char. Com. Scheme 3 Mar. 1980.
[97] *16th Rep. Com. Char.* 51.
[98] Above. [99] *Trans. B.G.A.S.* xiii. 151–2.

dows and has two storeys and attics. The symmetrical design has an east front of five bays and a long rear wing. The doorcase, though renewed in gothick style in the mid 18th century, repeats the date 1671 and a couplet that was inscribed on the original doorway:[1]

'Who 'ere doth dwell within this door,
thank God for Viscount Scudamore'

Most of the interior fittings of the house were renewed in the early 19th century, and later in the century bays were added to the south side. The rectory was sold in 1954 and became a private house called Hempsted House; a new rectory was built on part of its garden.[2]

Among 16th-century curates of Hempsted were Robert Nash, who in 1551 could repeat the Articles and Lord's Prayer but not the Commandments,[3] and John Gravestock, described in 1593 as a poor old man, unlearned but honest in life.[4] Curates during the Interregnum included William Warren in 1653 and Jonathan Smith, who was appointed in 1658[5] and ejected in 1660. Smith later led Congregationalist groups at Tetbury and at Ross-on-Wye (Herefs.), where his father had been rector before the Restoration.[6] The first rector of Hempsted after the re-endowment of the living was George Wall. He was succeeded in 1669[7] by John Gregory (d. 1678), archdeacon of Gloucester,[8] whose son John succeeded him in 1679 and died in 1708. John Webb, rector 1737–53,[9] was also rector of Great Rissington and employed a curate at Hempsted.[10] John Taylor, rector 1753–92,[11] was living at Clifton in 1784 when Thomas Stock, master of the College school, Gloucester, served as curate.[12] Thomas Jones, instituted as rector in 1826, was presented by his father Samuel Jones, alderman of Gloucester, who had bought the patronage for one turn.[13] Jones, who died in 1867, was absent because of ill-health during much of his incumbency.[14]

The church of ST. SWITHUN, so called by 1417,[15] is built of ashlar, and comprises a chancel, central tower, and nave with north vestry and south porch. The oldest parts of the building, including the south doorway, the porch, and the lowest stage of the tower are of the 14th century, as were the chancel windows before restoration in the 19th century.[16] The upper stages of the tower and the windows and roof of the nave appear to have been rebuilt in the 15th century. Between 1837 and 1839, to the designs of G. V. Maddox, a vestry room was added on the north side of the

nave, a west gallery with an external entrance was inserted, the church was repewed, and the nave was reroofed. The cost was met from subscriptions, principally £200 given by the patron John Higford, and church rates.[17] In 1885 during a restoration carried out under F. S. Waller the vestry was replaced by a new one, connected to the east end of the nave by a cloister, the gallery was removed, the nave was extended westwards and its roof altered, a new east window was inserted, and the interior was refitted. The cost was met by subscriptions, the patron Daniel Higford Burr giving £500.[18]

The font is of Transitional date, having a cylindrical bowl on a pedestal with clustered shafts.[19] The tomb of Richard Atkyns (d. 1610) bears his effigy in his judge's robes.[20] There are wall monuments to members of the Lysons family, including the antiquary Samuel Lysons (d. 1819). A bishop's head in a north aisle window is the only fragment surviving of the more substantial remains of medieval glass recorded in the late 18th century.[21] A peal of five bells was cast by Abraham Rudhall in 1694; one was recast by Thomas Rudhall in 1764 and two by John Rudhall, at the cost of Samuel Lysons, in 1817.[22] In 1885 the peal was restored and a treble, given by the rector Benjamin Dawson, was added by the Whitechapel foundry.[23] The peal was rehung in 1979.[24] The plate includes a salver of 1697, and a chalice, paten, and flagon of 1721 acquired with a gift from Mary Harris.[25] The parish registers survive from 1558.[26]

NONCONFORMITY. None known.

EDUCATION. The curate Thomas Stock, the joint founder of the Gloucester Sunday schools, had started a Sunday school at Hempsted by 1784,[27] and it continued to be held in 1818.[28] By 1833 there was also a small dame school teaching nine children.[29]

A parish school was held in a cottage before 1851 when a new church school was built east of the churchyard; the site was given by the Revd. Samuel Lysons and the cost met by subscriptions raised by the rector Thomas Jones. In 1877, when the average attendance was 42, voluntary contributions provided the bulk of the income and pence were also charged.[30] A new classroom was added

[1] Gibson, *Ch. of Door*, 173–4.
[2] Inf. from the Revd. Newell.
[3] *E.H.R.* xix. 102.
[4] Hockaday Abs. lii, state of clergy 1593, f. 12.
[5] Ibid. ccxl.
[6] *Calamy Revised*, ed. A. G. Matthews, 447; cf. Rudder, *Glos.* 696–7.
[7] Hockaday Abs. ccxl.   [8] Bigland, *Glos.* ii. 67.
[9] Hockaday Abs. ccxl.
[10] G.D.R. vol. 397, f. 36; 381A, f. 36; cf. Hockaday Abs. cccxxiii.   [11] Hockaday Abs. ccxl.
[12] G.D.R. vol. 319; *V.C.H. Glos.* ii. 332–3.
[13] Hockaday Abs. ccxl; *Diary of a Cotswold Parson*, 58–9.
[14] Hockaday Abs. ccxl; mon. in ch.
[15] Hockaday Abs. ccxl; cf. Worc. Episc. Reg., Reg. Polton, f. 48v.
[16] Bigland, *Glos.* ii, plate facing p. 65.

[17] Glos. R.O., P 173/CW 3/1; cf. *Glos. N. & Q.* iii. 605.
[18] *Glos. N. & Q.* iii. 606–8; Glos. R.O., P 173/CW 3/2.
[19] *Trans. B.G.A.S.* xxxvii. 109.
[20] Roper, *Glos. Effigies*, 331–3.
[21] Bigland, *Glos.* ii. 65.
[22] *Glos. Ch. Bells*, 375–6; cf. Bodl. MS. Rawl. B. 323, f. 151.
[23] Glos. R.O., P 173/CW 3/3.   [24] *Glos. Ch. Bells*, 376.
[25] *Glos. Ch. Plate*, 118; cf. Glos. R.O., P 173/CH 2/1; *16th Rep. Com. Char.* 51.
[26] *B. & G. Par. Rec.* 167; the first volume ends in 1701 not 1661 as listed: Glos. R.O., P 173/IN 1/1.
[27] *Glouc. Jnl.* 16 Feb. 1784.
[28] *Educ. of Poor Digest*, 301.
[29] *Educ. Enq. Abstract*, 317.
[30] Glos. R.O., D 177, Hempsted papers 1837–77; P.R.O., ED 7/34/164.

in 1880, the cost being met partly by grants from the trustees of the Mary Harris and Parish Allotment charities.[31] The school, which was united with the National Society before 1889,[32] had an average attendance of 51 in a single mixed department in 1904.[33] In 1938, as the Hempsted C.E. school, it had an average attendance of 70 in mixed and infants' departments.[34] In 1949 a large bill for repairs forced the managers to accept controlled status for the school. It passed from the county to the city education authority in 1967.[35] The school was rebuilt on a site further north in 1976.[36] In 1984 it was a primary school with 122 children on the roll.[37]

CHARITIES FOR THE POOR. Hempsted was one of the parishes benefiting under the charity of Giles Cox, established by will dated 1620 and trust deed dated 1633; its poor received £1 a year, which was increased to £2 for several years in the 1820s.[38] A Scheme of 1892 applied the charity to a wide range of purposes throughout the benefiting parishes generally, and another of 1957 created separate charities for each parish, each with an endowment of £256 stock and a small sum in cash.[39]

Mary Harris, sister of Silvanus Lysons, by will dated 1721 gave £1,000 to buy land to support charities in Hempsted and Whaddon. In Hempsted four poor widows were to be clothed each year at a cost of 25s. each and part of the residual income was to be used to apprentice boys of the parish or, failing suitable candidates, to provide gowns for old men. The £900 received under the will was used in 1728 to buy a small farm in Upton St. Leonards. In the mid 1820s, when the rent was £60, Hempsted's share was used generally for clothing and apprenticing within the parish.[40] By a Scheme of 1889 the surplus income after the fixed payments under the will was assigned to Hempsted and Whaddon at the rate of two thirds and a third respectively and Hempsted was required to make payments from its share to St. Luke's ecclesiastical parish, Gloucester, which included former parts of Hempsted in the Bristol Road area. Part of the surplus income was to be used for apprenticing or educational purposes and part for clothing old men.[41] In 1918 the farm was sold for £1,800, which was invested in stock.[42] In 1970 Hempsted received c. £22 a year from the charity.[43]

John Higford by will and codicil proved 1852 gave £600 to be invested in stock and the proceeds distributed in blankets and coal for the poor.[44] In 1970 the income was £15 a year.[45]

In 1972 a Scheme amalgamated the endowments of the Cox, Harris, and Higford charities to create three new charities for the parish. A relief in need charity, endowed with £446 stock, was to help the poor with cash, goods, and services; an educational foundation, endowed with £455 stock, was to help young people entering higher education or starting work; and an ecclesiastical charity, endowed with £39 stock, was to make a payment for a sermon under Mary Harris's will and help the work of the ecclesiastical parish.[46]

Richard Atkyns (d. 1636), lord of the manor, left £5 for the poor; it was placed as parish stock in the hands of the churchwardens who were to distribute 8s. a year for it,[47] but it has not been found recorded later.

At the inclosure of the common meadows in 1815 1 a. of land was awarded to the parish officers for the benefit of the poor.[48] The income was used in aid of the poor rates before 1867, when it was applied instead to the parish school.[49] In 1878 the land was sold for £1,250, which was invested in stock and administered by trustees as the Parish Allotment charity.[50] In the late 19th century and the 20th the annual income, £32 in 1970,[51] was applied to various parish purposes, including a clothing club, the village school, and church repairs.[52]

In 1962 part of a large annual residue of funds from the wealthy charity of Silvanus Lysons was applied to religious and charitable purposes within the ecclesiastical parish.[53] From 1980 the trustees were empowered to use the surplus funds within the diocese generally, giving preference to the needs of Hempsted;[54] the church fabric, the repair of the village hall, and help in providing scholarships for Hempsted boys at the King's school, Gloucester, were among objects of the charity at the period.[55]

[31] Glos. R.O., P 173/SC 3; CH 2/1; CH 6/1.
[32] *Kelly's Dir. Glos.* (1889), 816; cf. Nat. Soc. files, Hempsted.
[33] *Public Elem. Schs.* 1906, 185.
[34] *Bd. of Educ., List 21, 1938* (H.M.S.O.), 127.
[35] Glos. R.O., P 173/SC 7.
[36] Glos. Colln. N 17.346.
[37] List of schs. 1984: co. educ. cttee.
[38] *16th Rep. Com. Char.* 38–42, 54.
[39] Glos. R.O., D 2695/3–4.
[40] *16th Rep. Com. Char.* 51–4.
[41] Glos. R.O., D 3469/5/76.
[42] Ibid. P 173/CH 2/1, 3.

[43] Ibid. CH 21, Glouc. rural district, pp. 21–2.
[44] Ibid. P 173/CH 3/1.
[45] Ibid. CH 21, Glouc. rural district, p. 22.
[46] Ibid. D 3469/5/76.
[47] Ibid. P 173/IN 1/1, mem. at end.
[48] Ibid. Q/RI 79.
[49] Ibid. P 173/CW 3/2.
[50] Ibid. CH 5/1; D 3469/5/76.
[51] Ibid. CH 21, Glouc. rural district, p. 22.
[52] Ibid. P 173/CH 6/1.
[53] Above, ch.; Glos. R.O., D 3469/5/76.
[54] Char. Com. Scheme 3 Mar. 1980.
[55] Inf. from Mr. Fowler.

HUCCLECOTE

HUCCLECOTE, which was formerly a hamlet in the ancient parish of Churchdown, lies ESE. of Gloucester.[56] Its main settlement grew up 4.25 km. from the city's central crossroads on Ermin Street, the Roman road between Gloucester and Cirencester. Hucclecote maintained its own poor by the later 17th century and was regarded as a separate civil parish by the mid 19th.[57] Its development has been greatly influenced by the course of Ermin Street through its middle and by the proximity of Gloucester. From the late 1890s many houses were built for people working in the city[58] but parts of Hucclecote still retained a predominantly rural character in the 1980s.

Hucclecote formed the south part of Churchdown parish and was an irregularly shaped area defined in 1807 by hedges and watercourses. In the north the hamlet took in the summit of Churchdown or Chosen Hill and on the north-west it included a peninsula containing Elmbridge and bounded on the south-west by the Horsbere brook.[59] In 1066 Hucclecote and Churchdown were distinct manors belonging to St. Oswald's church, Gloucester, and later they were part of the archbishop of York's barony of Churchdown.[60] The existence of separate rectory estates for Hucclecote and Churchdown[61] suggests that the churches or chapels in both places were once equal in status. Churchdown church, which was in Hucclecote on the top of Churchdown Hill,[62] became the parish church and Hucclecote chapel was abandoned after 1289.[63] Elmbridge, which was another manor of the Churchdown barony,[64] evidently paid its tithes to the Churchdown rectory estate.[65]

After 1844 some minor alterations in the boundary between Hucclecote and Churchdown were made, the most substantial being east of Churchdown Hill, and in the early 1880s Hucclecote contained 1,437 a.[66] In 1935 Hucclecote lost 42 a. on the top of Churchdown Hill to Churchdown and 199 a. at Elmbridge to the new civil parish of Longlevens. In 1967 Gloucester took from Hucclecote 419 a. in the south-west, including the old village and most of the built-up area, and the parish was left with 853 a. (345 ha.), including a small area in the north-west taken from Barnwood.[67] The following account deals with Hucclecote as constituted in the early 19th century, save for that part transfer-

red to Churchdown in 1935. Those aspects of its history from the late 1890s connected with Gloucester's suburban growth are discussed above with the general history of the city.

Most of Hucclecote lies at over 30 m. on the Lower Lias clay, on which there are patches of gravel or sand; in the north-west at Elmbridge the land falls to 15 m. The land is generally flat, save in the north where the slopes of Churchdown Hill, an outlier of the Cotswolds rising to 154 m., are formed by successive strata of Marlstone and the Upper Lias.[68] Quarrying on the hill had started by 1453.[69] Drainage was principally by two streams flowing north-westwards across the hamlet, in the centre the Horsbere brook, presumably that called Huccle brook in 1486,[70] and in the south the Wotton brook. Woodland, once a dominant feature, measured a league by ½ league in 1086.[71] Cowsley wood, recorded in 1399, was in the south-east between Ermin Street and the Wotton brook[72] and was the principal wooded area in the mid 15th century when it was managed for the archbishop of York with other woods belonging to Churchdown barony. The archbishop may then have had a warren on the upper slopes of Churchdown Hill,[73] where a warren for coneys and a lodge were recorded in 1622.[74] The land of the hamlet was suited to pasture and the inclosure of its open fields was completed by 1727.[75]

Hucclecote village, the principal settlement in the hamlet, grew up on Ermin Street. The road, which linked Gloucester with Oxford and London,[76] was a turnpike through Hucclecote between 1698 and 1718 and between 1723 and 1871.[77] Two lanes ran northwards from it.[78] In the east Churchdown Lane, possibly that called Court Lane in 1451 and Green Street in 1598, ran east of Churchdown Hill, having crossed the Horsbere brook by a wooden bridge called Mill bridge in 1451.[79] North of the crossing the course of the lane was moved eastwards during the construction in the mid 1960s of a bypass road for Hucclecote. Further west Larkhay Road, called Lark Lane in 1591,[80] was presumably once part of a common way between the village and the hilltop church, crossing the brook at Pitt Mill, apparently by a bridge in 1486.[81] A ford below Pitt Mill was replaced in 1886 by a bridge provided largely at the expense of the owner of Zoons Court, a nearby farmstead.[82] Green Lane, which ran

[56] This account was written in 1985; the hist. of Churchdown is reserved for a later vol.

[57] Below; *Kelly's Dir. Glos.* (1856), 313.

[58] Cf. G.B.R., B 6/33/1, pp. 65, 143.

[59] Bristol R.O., DC/E/17/4.

[60] *Dom. Bk.* (Rec. Com.), i. 164v.; Taylor, *Dom. Glos.* 14; *L. & P. Hen. VIII*, xx (1), p. 214.

[61] *L. & P. Hen. VIII*, xvii, p. 638.

[62] Bristol R.O., DC/E/17/4.

[63] Below, ch.

[64] Glos. R.O., D 621/M 1, rot. 9; M 4, rot. 5.

[65] Cf. P.R.O., SC 6/Hen. VIII/1212, rot. 7.

[66] Cf. Bristol R.O., DC/E/17/4; Glos. R.O., Q/RI 44; *O.S. Area Bk.* (1885).

[67] *Census*, 1931 (pt. ii); 1971; cf. Glos. R.O., PA 183/1, map 4.

[68] Geol. Surv. Map 1″, solid, sheet 44 (1856 edn.); for sand, *Glouc. Corp. Rec.* pp. 123, 228.

[69] Glos. R.O., D 621/M 1, rot. 6.

[70] Ibid. M 2, rot. 1d.   [71] *Dom. Bk.* (Rec. Com.), i. 164v.

[72] Glos. R.O., D 621/M 7; cf. Bristol R.O., DC/E/17/4.

[73] Glos. R.O., D 621/M 1, rot. 4; M 10.

[74] P.R.O., E 134/20 Jas. I Mich./17.

[75] Glos. R.O., Q/RI 82.

[76] Cf. Glos. Colln. prints GL 65.27.

[77] Glouc. Roads Act, 9 & 10 Wm. III, c. 18; 9 Geo. I, c. 31; Annual Turnpike Acts Continuance Act, 34 & 35 Vic. c. 115.

[78] Bristol R.O., DC/E/17/4.

[79] Glos. R.O., D 621/M 1, rot. 3; M 6, rot. 13.

[80] Ibid. M 6, rot. 4; cf. Bristol R.O., DC/E/17/4.

[81] Glos. R.O., D 621/M 2, rot. 1d.

[82] Ibid. HB 8/M 1/4, pp. 120–72.

southwards from Ermin Street to a settlement called Wood Hucclecote, crossed the Wotton brook by a wooden bridge known as Pill bridge in 1424.[83] The main road from Gloucester to Cheltenham, which ran across the distant north-western peninsula of Elmbridge[84] and in 1480 linked Gloucester with Winchcombe,[85] was a turnpike between 1756 and 1871.[86] A tramway ran beside the road between 1811 and 1861,[87] and to the south-east a railway was opened in 1840 as part of a line between Gloucester and Birmingham.[88]

Settlement in the hamlet was scattered and the names Noke and Wood Hucclecote given to two clusters of houses indicate the once wooded nature of the landscape.[89] Hucclecote village grew along Ermin Street west of Churchdown Lane[90] and had a chapel at least until 1289.[91] Eight people at Hucclecote were assessed for the subsidy in 1327.[92] The village later included several farmhouses, one of which was called Garbage (later Gartage) Hall in 1824.[93] The village pound recorded from 1597 was to the south in Green Lane;[94] after it fell into ruin the site was taken into private ownership c. 1903.[95] In the later 18th century two substantial houses were built on the south side of Ermin Street for Gloucester men, Chosen House in the 1760s for the attorney James Elly[96] and Hucclecote Court further west in the early 1770s for Sir William Strachan, Bt. Part of the cost of the latter was paid by Samuel Hayward, the landowner.[97] Many cottages and villas were added to the village in the early 19th century. Several, including Chosen or Coles Villa, west of Chosen House, and Larkhay Villa (later the Cedars), north of Ermin Street, were built by John Major, a landowner, in the mid 1820s.[98] By 1807 building had begun west of the village towards Barnwood with a group of cottages, possibly an early encroachment, on the north side of the highway and a dwelling south of the Wotton brook at Dinglewell.[99] The village was given a new focus in the early 1850s by the building of a church and school in Larkhay Road.[1] From the late 1890s the size and character of the village was substantially transformed by Gloucester's suburban development,[2] and many

older buildings were replaced in the 1950s and later.[3] The few 17th- and 18th-century houses remaining in 1985 included two timber-framed cottages north of Ermin Street. Another, west of Green Lane, which belonged to the rectory estate in 1598,[4] has framing that was altered at an early date. East of the village a house had been built on Ermin Street at Fair Mile, on the boundary of Hucclecote with Brockworth, by 1807.[5] In the mid 19th century one or two cottages were built next to the house,[6] which was later replaced by terraced dwellings. A farmhouse was built between the village and Fair Mile c. 1860.[7]

In the south-east the settlement of Wood Hucclecote, where four people were assessed for the subsidy in 1327,[8] was perhaps that called Little Hucclecote in 1243.[9] It grew up south of the Wotton brook around a green,[10] recorded in 1597,[11] and in 1807 contained seven houses, including several farmhouses.[12] Some were later replaced and in 1985 the green, known as Hucclecote Green, remained largely undeveloped.

Noke, where four people were assessed for the subsidy in 1327,[13] was a loose collection of farmsteads and cottages at the foot of Churchdown Hill on lanes leading from the village to Churchdown and the hilltop church.[14] One house, presumably that occupied before 1318 by Richard of the hall,[15] was called Hall Place in 1453.[16] Noke Court, a farmstead on the Churchdown road, was part of an estate acquired by Samuel Hayward under his marriage settlement in 1751[17] and it was included in his Wallsworth Hall estate until at least the mid 1850s.[18] The house, which was rebuilt in the 19th century, and the farm buildings were derelict in 1985. The farmhouse at Noke Farm, to the west, dates from the late 18th century and was probably that called Noke Place in 1870.[19] A house north-east of Mill bridge incorporates a timber-framed building of the 17th or 18th century and was occupied as several cottages in the mid 19th. South-west of the bridge a timber-framed house was rebuilt in brick and was converted as three cottages by 1848.[20] West of Churchdown Hill a farmstead had been built at Zoons Court by 1689.[21] Known also as the Zoons, it was part of a

[83] Ibid. D 621/M 1, rot. 13; cf. Bristol R.O., DC/E/17/4.
[84] Glos. Colln. prints GL 65.27.
[85] Glos. R.O., D 184/M 2.
[86] Glouc. Roads Act, 29 Geo. II, c. 58; Annual Turnpike Acts Continuance Act, 34 & 35 Vic. c. 115.
[87] D. E. Bick, *Glouc. and Chelt. Railway* (1968, Locomotion Papers, no. 43), 4, 10, 28–9. [88] *Glouc. Jnl.* 7 Nov. 1840.
[89] *P.N. Glos.* (E.P.N.S.), ii. 147–8.
[90] Cf. Glos. Colln. prints GL 65.27; above, Fig. 26.
[91] *Trans. B.G.A.S.* xliii. 110.
[92] *Glos. Subsidy Roll, 1327,* 34.
[93] Bryant, *Map of Glos.* (1824); Glos. R.O., PA 183/1, pp. 100–42.
[94] Glos. R.O., D 621/M 6, rot. 12; Bristol R.O., DC/E/17/4.
[95] Glos. R.O., HB 8/M 1/5, pp. 81–2, 98; P 183A/PC 1/1, p. 137.
[96] Ibid. D 2714, Churchdown deeds 1756–1895; for photogs. of ho., demolished in 1968, Glos. Colln. prints 156.5.
[97] Glos. R.O., D 626, Churchdown deeds 1754–1806; Bigland, *Glos.* i. 332; cf. Taylor, *Map of Glos.* (1777).
[98] Glos. R.O., D 2714, Churchdown deeds 1756–1895; cf.

ibid. PA 183/1, p. 116; G.D.R., T 1/54.
[99] Bristol R.O., DC/E/17/4.
[1] *Glouc. Jnl.* 3 May 1851; Glos. R.O., D 531.
[2] Above, Glouc. 1835–1985, topog.
[3] Glos. R.O., PA 183/1, pp. 100–42.
[4] Ibid. D 2957/201.51; cf. Bristol R.O., DC/E/3/1, f. 12.
[5] Bristol R.O., DC/E/17/4; Bryant, *Map of Glos.* (1824).
[6] *Glouc. Jnl.* 13 Oct. 1838.
[7] Glos. R.O., PA 183/1, pp. 120–1.
[8] *Glos. Subsidy Roll, 1327,* 34.
[9] *Glouc. Corp. Rec.* p. 183.
[10] Cf. Glos. R.O., D 2714, Churchdown deeds 1756–1895, deed 22 Aug. 1761.   [11] Ibid. D 621/M 6, rot. 12.
[12] Bristol R.O., DC/E/17/4.
[13] *Glos. Subsidy Roll, 1327,* 34.
[14] Cf. Bristol R.O., DC/E/17/4.
[15] *Glouc. Corp. Rec.* p. 314.
[16] Glos. R.O., D 621/M 1, rot. 6.
[17] Ibid. D 1326/T 41A; cf. ibid. photocopy 342.
[18] Ibid. D 2299/7824; Burke, *Land Gent.* (1937), 611–12.
[19] *Kelly's Dir. Glos.* (1870), 583.
[20] Glos. R.O., PA 183/1, pp. 142–4; D 3106/4.
[21] W. T. Swift, *Hist. of Churchdown* (1905), 47.

large estate belonging to Mary Holcomb in the late 18th century.[22] The farmhouse, which has a 17th-century south front, was remodelled in the later 19th century when a rear wing was removed.[23] It had been derelict for several years by 1985 when the farmstead included a bungalow.[24] In the early 19th century a small group of cottages was established above Zoons Court on the side of the hill,[25] where there was scattered building above Noke in the later 19th century and the early 20th.[26]

A small settlement had grown up at Elmbridge (formerly Telbridge or Elbridge),[27] east of the Horsbere brook on the Gloucester–Cheltenham road, by the mid 12th century when it included a chapel.[28] A bridgewright living there in the early 13th century[29] was evidently responsible for maintaining bridges there by virtue of the land he held.[30] In 1327 only three people at Elmbridge were assessed for the subsidy,[31] and by the later 18th century the settlement comprised only the ancient manor house of Elmbridge Court, southeast of the road.[32] A cottage north of the road was the only other dwelling at Elmbridge in the mid 19th century.[33]

In 1801 Hucclecote's population was 234. By 1831, following the building of many new houses, it had risen to 465, but in the mid 19th century it fell a little and in 1871 was 429. In 1891, when the village was becoming primarily a dormitory of Gloucester, 459 people lived in Hucclecote.[34]

As a village with much passing road traffic Hucclecote had several inns. A man was brewing and selling ale there in 1451,[35] and inns were recorded from 1598[36] with names that included the Fiery Beacon in 1638[37] and the General Wood in 1726.[38] The latter may have had an outdoor bowling alley[39] and was possibly the inn called the Royal Oak in 1841.[40] Further east the Wagon and Horses, recorded in 1767,[41] was evidently kept by one of three victuallers licensed in the hamlet in 1755.[42] At Fair Mile the Victoria inn had opened by 1846[43] and at Elmbridge there was a beer retailer in 1863.[44] The Royal Oak, which in 1957 changed premises, and the Wagon and Horses and Victoria, both rebuilt c. 1900,[45] survived in 1985.

The antiquary Richard Furney (1694–1753),

archdeacon of Surrey and a native of Gloucester, became a landowner in Hucclecote where he died.[46] The poet Sydney Dobell (1824–74) lived for a time at Noke Place.[47]

MANORS AND OTHER ESTATES. An estate of 4 hides in Hucclecote was among the lands of the minster of St. Oswald, Gloucester, that were held in 1066 by Stigand, archbishop of Canterbury, and in 1086 by the archbishop of York.[48] Known as *HUCCLECOTE* manor, the estate was retained by the archbishop of York as a member of the barony of Churchdown until 1545 when the manors of the barony were exchanged with the Crown.[49] In 1552 the barony was granted to Sir Thomas Chamberlayne[50] (d. 1580), whose eldest son John succeeded to the manors of Churchdown and Hucclecote. John had been knighted by 1607 and had died without issue[51] by 1622 leaving both manors encumbered with debts,[52] for which his brother Edmund Chamberlayne was imprisoned in the Fleet.[53] After Edmund's death in 1634 both manors descended, evidently with Maugersbury manor in Stow-on-the-Wold, in the Chamberlayne family.[54] In 1875 Henry Ingles Chamberlayne sold his lands in Churchdown and Hucclecote to Joseph Lovegrove, a Gloucester solicitor.[55] On Lovegrove's death in 1883 the manorial rights passed to trustees, including his brother-in-law Frederick Smithe, vicar of Churchdown, after whose death in 1900 they were sold to John Handcock Selwyn-Payne of Badgeworth Court.[56] A later owner John Jones apparently relinquished the remaining manorial rights in 1935.[57]

In 1327 John Browning held 2 ploughlands and 20 a. of meadow at Noke from the archbishop of York by knight service.[58] The estate was probably that called *NOKE* manor, part of which was held by Thomas Kemyll (fl. 1434) and by Thomas Feld (d. c. 1511). The latter's son and heir Giles was a minor and the estate has not been traced after 1515.[59]

St. Margaret's Hospital at Wotton acquired land in Hucclecote and Elmbridge in the 13th

[22] Glos. R.O., Q/REl 1A, Dudstone & King's Barton 1780; Rudge, *Hist. of Glos.* ii. 139.

[23] Cf. Glos. R.O., D 1388/SL 4/18.

[24] Cf. ibid. D 2299/1791.

[25] Cf. Bristol R.O., DC/E/17/4; G.D.R., T 1/54.

[26] Cf. G.D.R., T 1/54; O.S. Map 6″, Glos. XXVI. SW. (1885 and later edns.).

[27] *P.N. Glos.* (E.P.N.S.), ii. 147.

[28] *Trans. B.G.A.S.* xliii. 112.

[29] *Glouc. Corp. Rec.* pp. 126–7, 152.

[30] P.R.O., C 115/K 2/6684, f. 127v.

[31] *Glos. Subsidy Roll, 1327*, 34.

[32] Glos. R.O., D 184/P 1, f. 109.

[33] Cf. Bristol R.O., DC/E/17/4; G.D.R., T 1/54.

[34] *Census*, 1801–91.

[35] Glos. R.O., D 621/M 1, rot. 3.

[36] Ibid. M 6, rot. 13.

[37] Ibid. M 18; cf. G.D.R. wills 1636/52.

[38] Glos. Colln. RF 77.4.

[39] G.B.R., J 4/1, no. 16.

[40] Glos. R.O., PA 183/1, p. 46; D 2079/III/166.

[41] Ibid. D 626, Churchdown deeds 1754–1806.

[42] Ibid. Q/AV 2, rot. 8.

[43] Ibid. PA 183/1, suppl. f. 21.

[44] *Kelly's Dir. Glos.* (1863), 297.

[45] Glos. R.O., PA 183/1, pp. 114, 116, 122.

[46] Ibid. D 626, Churchdown deeds 1754–1806; I. Gray, *Antiquaries of Glos. and Bristol* (B.G.A.S. 1981), 59–61.

[47] *D.N.B.*

[48] *Dom. Bk.* (Rec. Com.), i. 164v.; Taylor, *Dom. Glos.* 14.

[49] *L. & P. Hen. VIII*, xx (1), p. 214.

[50] *Cal. Pat.* 1550–3, 357.

[51] *Visit. Glos. 1682–3*, 37; Hockaday Abs. cccxv, 1580; Smith, *Men and Armour*, 13–14.

[52] P.R.O., E 134/20 Jas. I Mich./17; E 159/461, Recorda 20 Jas. I East. rot. 84. [53] *Cal. S.P. Dom.* 1627–8, 496.

[54] *V.C.H. Glos.* vi. 152; cf. *Cal. Cttee. for Compounding*, iii, p. 1981; Rudder, *Glos.* 339–40; Glos. R.O., D 626, Churchdown deeds 1754–1806; G.D.R., T 1/54.

[55] Glos. R.O., D 1410, Hucclecote deeds 1805–89; *Kelly's Dir. Glos.* (1870), 583; (1879), 687.

[56] Glos. R.O., D 3117/839; Swift, *Churchdown*, 13, 33; *Kelly's Dir. Glos.* (1885–1902 edns.).

[57] Glos. R.O., D 2299/5559.

[58] *Trans. B.G.A.S.* x. 181.

[59] Glos. R.O., D 621/M 3, rot. 3; M 8, rot. 4.

century and the early 14th.[60] In the mid 17th century the hospital's possessions included c. 3 a. in Hucclecote,[61] which were exchanged under an inclosure Act of 1726 for a close of 3 a.[62] The close was retained by the Gloucester municipal charity trustees in 1848.[63]

There were several estates at Elmbridge in the 13th century, including one belonging in the 1230s to John of Elmbridge, described as lord of Elmbridge, and his wife Alice.[64] Land at Elmbridge and Brickhampton in Churchdown, held c. 1270 by Geoffrey de Longchamp from Churchdown barony as ⅛ knight's fee,[65] formed the estate later known as the manor of ELBRIDGE or ELMBRIDGE, which also included land in Down Hatherley and Innsworth.[66] That estate probably passed to William de Gardinis (fl. 1299), a landowner at Matson, from whom land at Elmbridge was held by St. Bartholomew's Hospital, Gloucester,[67] and by Walter of Gloucester (d. c. 1311). Walter's estate, comprising a capital messuage and 35 a., was held by the yearly service of ½ mark and passed to his son Walter, a minor.[68] The hospital acquired land there piecemeal in the 13th century and the early 14th and exchanged some of it with Thomas de la Mare in 1347.[69]

Elmbridge manor passed to the de la Mare family and was held jointly by Robert de la Mare (d. 1382) and his wife Maud who survived him.[70] In 1394 Maud's daughter William de la Mare and son-in-law John Roach quitclaimed their rights in the estate to Roger Pirton.[71] He or another Roger Pirton did homage for the manor in 1426 and died in 1453, having granted it to feoffees. His widow Elizabeth married John Bradston[72] and in 1455 they granted the manor for the term of her life to William Nottingham,[73] to whom Walter Grey and his wife Margaret quitclaimed rights in it in 1467.[74] Nottingham held the manor with other feoffees, including John Dodyng to whom Thomas Aleyn and his wife quitclaimed an interest in it in 1457.[75] Nottingham, a lawyer and a former M.P. for Gloucester and for the county, was knighted and appointed Chief Baron of the Exchequer. He died in 1483 having granted Elmbridge manor and other estates to trustees, from

whom they were bought in 1487 by Richard Poole, husband of his widow Elizabeth.[76] After Poole's death in 1517 Elmbridge manor descended with Sapperton, from the mid 16th century together with Pirton manor in Churchdown,[77] and in 1622 Henry Poole sold Elmbridge and Pirton to Elizabeth Craven, widow of Sir William Craven.[78] Both manors passed to her son William, who was created Lord Craven in 1627 and earl of Craven in 1665. After his death in 1697 over 200 a. descended with Elmbridge Court and the Craven barony to William Craven (d. 1791).[79] Elmbridge Court passed to his second son Henry Augustus Berkeley Craven[80] (d. 1836), who was succeeded by a younger brother Richard Keppel Craven. After Richard's death in 1851[81] the Elmbridge Court estate, which including Pirton manor comprised 759 a., reverted to the representative of the main line, William Craven, earl of Craven.[82] In 1853 he sold the estate,[83] and Francis Leyborne-Popham, of Littlecote in Ramsbury (Wilts.), the owner in 1870, was succeeded at his death in 1880 by his son Francis William Leyborne-Popham.[84] Elmbridge Court and 240 a. were bought, probably in 1890, by Frederick Harvey (d. 1908), a cattle breeder and horse dealer.[85] By 1937 Elmbridge Court had been purchased by Colborne Estates Ltd. and new houses had been built on part of its land.[86] Government offices were also built there in the mid 20th century.[87]

Elmbridge Court, which was on an ancient moated site,[88] was occupied as a farmhouse by 1478.[89] The house was possibly partly rebuilt in the 16th century or the early 17th, and in 1652 had several outbuildings, all within the moat and including two milkhouses above which were six lodging rooms and three corn lofts.[90] By 1769 outbuildings had been erected beyond the moat.[91] Following additions and remodelling by Frederick Harvey in 1896,[92] the house was mainly of brick and retained a central range with two cross wings.[93] It was demolished with the farm buildings c. 1960 when the site was included in a new housing estate.[94]

[60] Glouc. Corp. Rec. pp. 75–6, 101, 159, 168, 190, 228–30, 259, 311.   [61] Hockaday Abs. ccxxiii.

[62] G.B.R., J 4/1, no. 16.

[63] Glos. R.O., D 3269, bk. of plans of hosp. property 1848, f. 28.

[64] P.R.O., CP 25(1)/73/10, no. 164; Glouc. Corp. Rec. p. 121.

[65] Reg. Giffard (Surtees Soc. cix), 19.

[66] Glos. R.O., D 621/M 1, rot. 9; M 4, rot. 5; D 184/M 2.

[67] Glouc. Corp. Rec. p. 291; below, Matson, man.

[68] Cal. Inq. p.m. v, p. 199.

[69] Glouc. Corp. Rec. pp. 50, 109, 123–4, 127, 153, 182–3, 243, 266, 342.

[70] Cal. Inq. p.m. xv, pp. 215–16; Cal. Close, 1381–5, 148.

[71] P.R.O., CP 25(1)/78/82, no. 122; V.C.H. Glos. xi. 168.

[72] Glos. R.O., D 621/M 1, rott. 6, 9, 20.

[73] Ibid. D 281.

[74] P.R.O., CP 25(1)/79/93, no. 13.

[75] Glos. R.O., D 184/M 2; P.R.O., CP 25(1)/79/92, no. 142.

[76] Trans. B.G.A.S. l. 185–6, 193–4, 201; P.R.O., C 1/57, no. 239.

[77] V.C.H. Glos. xi. 91; P.R.O., C 142/79, no. 294; C 142/222, no. 45; C 142/365, no. 153.

[78] Glos. R.O., D 184/T 16.

[79] Ibid. T 18, T 100; for the Craven fam., Burke, Peerage (1963), 614.

[80] Rudge, Hist. of Glos. ii. 138.

[81] G.D.R., T 1/54; Burke, Peerage (1889), 349.

[82] Glos. R.O., D 4769.

[83] Ibid. D 1388/SL 7/31.

[84] Kelly's Dir. Glos. (1870), 516, 583; (1885), 419, 507; V.C.H. Wilts. xii. 29; Burke, Land. Gent. (1937), 1831.

[85] Kelly's Dir. Glos. (1894), 213; Glouc. Jnl. 25 Feb. 1899; 25 Jan. 1908; Glos. R.O., D 2299/443.

[86] G.B.R., B 3/72 (1), pp. 130–1, 661–2.

[87] Cf. Glouc. Jnl. 26 Aug. 1961.

[88] Trans. B.G.A.S. xxi. 60; cf. Glos. R.O., D 184/P 1, f. 109.

[89] Glos. R.O., D 184/M 2; cf. ibid. T 16, T 18–19; M 24, p. 199.

[90] Ibid. M 4, rot. 2; cf. Kelly's Dir. Glos. (1885), 507.

[91] Glos. R.O., D 184/P 1, f. 109.

[92] Ibid. D 2299/443; Glos. Colln., G. M. Davies papers, notes on moats.

[93] Swift, Churchdown, 24–5.

[94] Glos. Colln., G. M. Davies papers, notes on moats; Glouc. Jnl. 26 Aug. 1961.

The rectory of Hucclecote, which included the tithes of Hucclecote, Wood Hucclecote, and Noke, belonged to St. Oswald's Priory, Gloucester, and under a lease of 1498 was farmed by John Lewis.[95] In 1542 it was settled with the priory's other rectories on the dean and chapter of Bristol cathedral,[96] who treated it as part of the rectory of Churchdown.[97] The farmer of Churchdown rectory granted a lease of a house in Hucclecote and of the Hucclecote, Wood Hucclecote, and Noke tithes in 1598 to Richard Bishop[98] and a lease of the Elmbridge tithes in 1768 to John Allen, whose right to take milk tithes was confirmed in 1773.[99] The dean and chapter of Bristol retained the freehold of the Hucclecote house in 1858.[1] The tithes from the Hucclecote land inclosed under the Act of 1726 were commuted for a rent charge of 2s. 6d. an acre. The hamlet's other tithes were commuted with those of Churchdown in 1840 when Edmund Hopkinson of Edgeworth, Thomas Dancey, and Joanna Matthews held them under the dean and chapter.[2] Land near Wood Hucclecote owned by St. Oswald's Priory in 1316[3] was presumably held with a tenement called the New House in 1498.[4] Although said to be in Hucclecote,[5] the house stood in Upton St. Leonards to the south.[6]

ECONOMIC HISTORY. In 1086 there were 2 ploughteams on the demesne of the archbishop of York's Hucclecote estate.[7] That estate was later administered with the archbishop's lands in Churchdown and by 1399 the demesne had been leased, with customary tenants, including several in Hucclecote, holding small shares known as pennyland.[8] The vineyard belonging to the archbishop in the later 12th century[9] was at Noke and by 1506 had become a pasture.[10] In 1538 the Churchdown estate was leased for 21 years to six husbandmen, including three Hucclecote men,[11] and in the mid 17th century the Hucclecote demesne was held by a tenant for £10 a year.[12] Elmbridge comprised 2 ploughlands in 1220.[13] The demesne of Elmbridge manor was leased with Elmbridge Court as one farm by 1478,[14] and in 1630 was extended at 218 a.[15]

In 1086 there were 11 villani and 5 bordars working 11 teams on the archbishop's Hucclecote estate.[16] By 1399 the archbishop had commuted the labour services of the customary tenants holding yardlands, half-yardlands, and fardels on his Churchdown estate but he could still require them to perform bedrips and make hay in Meanham, his meadow by the Severn on the north side of Gloucester.[17] The customary tenants, several of whom held mondaylands in Hucclecote, also owed pannage and heriots and until the mid 16th century needed the lord's licence to live elsewhere.[18] In the later Middle Ages the archbishop's Churchdown estate also included a few free tenants in Hucclecote,[19] who c. 1552 owed 24s. 9d. in assized rents while the customary tenants there owed £17 17s. 4d.[20] In the late 16th century the lord of the manor denied the claim of tenants to inherit copyholds,[21] and in 1637 most tenancies in Hucclecote and Noke were leaseholds, of which 11, including the demesne, were on fixed rents and another 16 were described in 1644 as fee farms.[22] Both fee-farm and copyhold tenure persisted in Hucclecote until after the First World War.[23] The tenants on Elmbridge manor in 1630 comprised one leaseholder for lives with 10¾ a., one tenant at will with 6 a., and four copyholders with 38 a. including a former mondayland, 19¾ a., 14 a., and 6 a. respectively.[24]

In the 13th century the settlements of Hucclecote, Wood Hucclecote, and Noke shared open fields,[25] and in 1340 a third of the arable on the archbishop's estate was left fallow each year.[26] In 1442 part of a field on Churchdown Hill called the Breach[27] may have been taken into cultivation recently. In the early 18th century eight areas of open field remained in the main part of Hucclecote.[28] One, Outhill, was on Churchdown Hill and another, Pittmill field, lay north of the Horsbere brook. There were five fields beside Ermin Street. To the north Brook and Windmill fields, respectively east and west of the village, extended to the Horsbere brook. To the south Cowsley and Huckley fields, respectively east and west of Green Lane, reached to the Wotton brook, and Foxall covered a small area between Ermin Street and the stream on the west side of the hamlet. South of the Wotton brook Lillys field, recorded from 1432,[29] may have once included Goose Acre, a small area of land to the east,[30] and probably originated as a fragment of a field shared

[95] P.R.O., SC 6/Hen. VIII/1212, rot. 7.
[96] L. & P. Hen. VIII, xvii, p. 638.
[97] Glos. R.O., D 936/Y 27–31; Bristol R.O., DC/E/3/1, f. 12; DC/E/17/1.
[98] Glos. R.O., D 2957/201.51; cf. ibid. D 184/T 17.
[99] P.R.O., E 126/30, 1772 Mich. no. 7, 1773 East. no. 6.
[1] Glos. R.O., D 936/Y 31.
[2] Glos. Colln. RF 77.4; G.D.R., T 1/54.
[3] Glouc. Corp. Rec. p. 309.
[4] P.R.O., SC 6/Hen. VIII/1212, rot. 7.
[5] Ibid. C 66/1135, m. 25.
[6] Glos. R.O., Q/RI 70 (map I, no. 134); above, Outlying Hamlets, intro.
[7] Dom. Bk. (Rec. Com.), i. 164v.
[8] Glos. R.O., D 621/M 7–8, M 13.
[9] Trans. B.G.A.S. lvii. 74.
[10] Glos. R.O., D 621/M 2, rot. 13; cf. Bristol R.O., DC/E/17/4.
[11] Glos. R.O., D 621/M 15.
[12] Ibid. M 16, M 18.

[13] Bk. of Fees, i. 307.
[14] Glos. R.O., D 184/M 2.
[15] Ibid. M 24, p. 199.
[16] Dom. Bk. (Rec. Com.), i. 164v.
[17] Glos. R.O., D 621/M 7.
[18] Ibid. M 1–4.
[19] Ibid. M 7.
[20] Ibid. M 15.
[21] P.R.O., C 2/Eliz. I/D 6/46; C 2/Eliz. I/T 3/47; cf. Willcox, Glos. 1590–1640, 278 n.
[22] Glos. R.O., D 621/M 18.
[23] Ibid. D 2299/1172, 5559.
[24] Ibid. D 184/M 24, pp. 200–5.
[25] Cf. Glouc. Corp. Rec. pp. 101, 183, 210, 213, 229–30, 309.
[26] P.R.O., C 145/140, no. 7.
[27] Glos. R.O., D 184/M 2; cf. ibid. M 24, p. 200.
[28] Ibid. Q/RI 82; PA 183/1, map 9 (1).
[29] Ibid. D 621/M 1, rot. 25d.
[30] Ibid. Q/RI 82.

with neighbouring Barnwood.[31] The low-lying land in Hucclecote was unsuited to arable farming and in 1442 part of Cowsley field was called watery land. There were then many small closes of pasture and meadow.[32] With the exception of Hucclecote Green no permanent common pastures have been identified in the main part of the hamlet.[33] After the harvest the open fields were grazed by the tenants' cattle and pigs and in 1451 two haywards were appointed to deal with offenders pasturing sheep in the stubble. The commoning of sheep was stinted at 40 to the yardland in 1486. In 1516 pulses were growing in one field.[34] At Elmbridge, where open-field land was recorded from the 13th century,[35] the manorial demesne was evidently inclosed shortly before 1489 when the commoners pulled down several hedges and pastured sheep and oxen among crops growing on it.[36] In 1630 Elmbridge manor included part of Gunsmoor, a meadow north-east of the Horsbere brook at Innsworth, in which some of Gloucester's hamlets also shared. Elmbridge Court farm comprised 218 a. mostly in large meadows and pasture closes[37] and was given over mainly to dairying.[38] In 1699 it was leased to a grazier.[39] An unusual feature of local husbandry was the vineyard owned by Nathaniel Matthews near the Zoons in 1733.[40]

Hucclecote was inclosed under an Act of 1726 by agreement between the 29 landholders, not all of them freeholders, sharing in the 436 a. of remaining open-field land. Their allotments were described in a deed of 1727 and ten comprised 5 a. or less and another thirteen 20 a. or less. The principal beneficiary, with 93 a., was Nathaniel Matthews.[41] In 1831 there were in the hamlet 12 farmers employing a total of 63 labourers and 5 employing none.[42] The largest farms were Elmbridge Court and Zoons Court, with 230 a. and 216 a. respectively in 1861.[43] Smallholdings remained a significant feature in Hucclecote in the late 19th century and the early 20th: in 1896 a total of 33 agricultural occupiers was returned and in 1926 a total of 29, of whom 24 had less than 50 a. and 9 less than 5 a.[44] The largest farms in the 1930s still centred on Elmbridge Court and Zoons Court.[45]

Hucclecote had a large area of arable land in 1840,[46] but permanent grassland, which covered at least 571 a. in 1866, was predominant and became even more significant in the late 19th century as cereal and other arable cultivation declined.[47] In 1905 the amounts of permanent grass and arable were 1,175 a. and 175 a. respectively.[48] More cattle, sheep, and pigs were raised and dairying assumed greater significance in local farming; the number of milk cows returned was 44 in 1866 and 118 in 1896.[49] In the early 20th century arable farming continued to decline and the number of pigs reared fell, but more sheep and poultry were introduced and were returned at 586 and 3,265 respectively in 1926.[50] Hucclecote's inhabitants included in 1863 a farmer who was also a butcher, in 1889 dealers in cattle and pigs and a dairyman, and in 1906 a poultry farmer.[51] The area of orchards, which in 1840 covered 70 a. mostly around the village and green, had increased to at least 95 a. by 1896 and to 135 a. by 1933.[52] The needs of Gloucester encouraged market gardening, and in Hucclecote five market gardens were recorded in 1885[53] and at least 11 a. were so used in 1896.[54] A nursery including greenhouses was laid out on 16 a. north of Ermin Street in or before 1858.[55] The area of farmland declined in the 20th century as land was taken for building and in the 1960s and early 1970s for main roads. The area of orchards was more than halved between 1956 and 1970 and the nursery closed c. 1964.[56] Three or four outlying farms remained in 1985 when farming was mixed.

There were several mills on the Horsbere brook. That from which Mill bridge, on the road between Hucclecote and Churchdown, was named apparently belonged in 1320 to St. Margaret's Hospital at Wotton. It probably stood downstream from the bridge[57] but no other mention of it has been found. The millward living at Noke in 1327[58] may have worked it or Pitt Mill, recorded from 1399 on a site downstream and north of the village.[59] Pitt Mill, called Horsemans Mill in 1840[60] and presumably the mill belonging to the archbishop of York in 1086 and 1340,[61] was always a corn mill. It may have been burnt in 1634, allegedly in divine punishment on the miller for sabbath breaking.[62] With a windmill built nearby before 1610,[63] it was bought in 1675 by Nicholas Lane, a Gloucester apothecary, and in 1713 by Richard Harding, a Tetbury mercer.[64]

[31] Above, Barnwood, econ. hist.
[32] Glos. R.O., D 184/M 2.
[33] Cf. G.D.R., T 1/54.
[34] Glos. R.O., D 621/M 1, rott. 2, 31d.; M 2, rot. 1d.; M 3, rot. 4.
[35] Glouc. Corp. Rec. pp. 90–1, 96–7, 123–5, 342.
[36] Glos. R.O., D 184/M 2.
[37] Ibid. M 24, p. 199; P 1, f. 109; for Gunsmoor, cf. ibid. D 1740/P 2; Q/RI 70 (map F, nos. 50–64).
[38] Cf. ibid. D 184/M 4, rot. 2.
[39] Ibid. T 18.
[40] Glouc. Jnl. 18 Sept. 1733.
[41] Glos. R.O., Q/RI 82; Trans. B.G.A.S. lxiv. 46, 65; cf. G.B.R., J 4/1, no. 16.
[42] Census, 1831.
[43] Glos. R.O., PA 183/1, pp. 62–70.
[44] P.R.O., MAF 68/1609/13; MAF 68/3295/9.
[45] Kelly's Dir. Glos. (1931), 230; (1939), 236.
[46] G.D.R., T 1/54; Glos. R.O., PA 183/1, p. 10, map 6(2).
[47] P.R.O., MAF 68/26/4, 20; MAF 68/1609/13.

[48] Acreage Returns, 1905.
[49] P.R.O., MAF 28/25/13; MAF 68/1609/13.
[50] Ibid. MAF 68/3295/9.
[51] Kelly's Dir. Glos. (1863), 297; (1889), 822; (1906), 221.
[52] Glos. R.O., PA 183/1, p. 10, maps 6 (2–3); P.R.O., MAF 68/1609/13.
[53] Kelly's Dir. Glos. (1885), 508.
[54] P.R.O., MAF 68/1609/13.
[55] Glos. R.O., PA 183/1, pp. 26–7, 113; Glouc. Jnl. 21 Apr. 1877.
[56] Glos. R.O., PA 183/1, pp. 10, 113.
[57] Glouc. Corp. Rec. p. 316; cf. Bristol R.O., DC/E/17/4.
[58] Glos. Subsidy Roll, 1327, 34.
[59] Glos. R.O., D 621/M 7.
[60] G.D.R., T 1/54.
[61] Dom. Bk. (Rec. Com.), i. 164v.; P.R.O., C 145/140, no.7.
[62] Glos. N. & Q. ii. 222.
[63] Cf. P.R.O., CP 43/111, rot. 182d.; Glos. R.O., D 184/M 24, p. 202.
[64] Glos. R.O., D 531.

The water mill, which in 1840 belonged to John Matthews,[65] was acquired by Gloucester corporation in 1856 during the construction of waterworks at the brook's source.[66] The corporation sold the mill in 1861 to Joshua Dowdeswell[67] of Noke Court farm, but the reduction in the stream's flow sometimes made milling impossible. The mill, which was unoccupied in 1881, was not worked after the early 1920s. The leat was filled in c. 1958 and the buildings, comprising a brick mill and a mill house with some timber framing, fell into ruins and were demolished after 1971.[68]

A mill had been built at Elmbridge by the early 13th century.[69] In 1236 John of Elmbridge and his wife Alice granted it to Walter, son of Walter of Banbury.[70] The mill, which has not been found recorded after 1347,[71] evidently stood upstream from the Cheltenham road.[72] Withygun Mill, mentioned in 1320 and 1480,[73] was apparently some way below the road where a meadow of the same name, once part of Down Hatherley manor, was included in the Elmbridge estate in 1574.[74]

The inhabitants of Hucclecote included a smith in 1545,[75] and a smith, a tailor, a cordwainer, and a weaver in 1608.[76] Gravel working had started by 1819[77] and important brick and tile works had been established at Fair Mile by 1856.[78] In 1831 trade supported 13 families compared with 77 supported by agriculture.[79] The village had a blacksmith's shop in 1840,[80] and in 1856 the basic village trades of carpenter, cooper, shoemaker, and tailor were also represented. Those of blacksmith and bootmaker continued until after the First World War. Two shops were open in 1870.[81]

LOCAL GOVERNMENT. Frankpledge jurisdiction over Hucclecote and Elmbridge was exercised by the court held at Churchdown by the lords of the barony of Churchdown. That court, in which the Hucclecote and Churchdown homages made their presentments separately, also acted as the court baron for Hucclecote manor, and court rolls, including one for a court of survey in 1426, survive for many years in the periods 1423–57, 1486–7, 1497–1549, and 1590–1600. The maintenance of watercourses, roads and lanes, and bridges was an important part of its business. The Hucclecote homage in 1516 elected a constable.[82] In the 18th century and the early 19th the court sometimes met in one of

Hucclecote's inns.[83] Court rolls for Elmbridge manor, which had its own court, survive for 1442, when the rental was renewed, and for several years in the period 1457–89 when its work included the maintenance of watercourses and rights of way. In 1489 it dealt with the destruction of hedges and forcible pasturing of sheep and oxen among crops growing on the demesne.[84] There are also court rolls for 1664–1702 and estreat rolls for 1664 and 1684–5.[85] The tenants of the Hucclecote rectory estate in the early 16th century owed suit to Parton manor court in Churchdown.[86]

Hucclecote hamlet had its own churchwarden, one of two for Churchdown parish,[87] and his account for 1684 has survived.[88] The hamlet maintained its own poor and highways by the 1670s, and in 1675 was involved in a settlement dispute with Churchdown.[89] Expenditure on poor relief rose from £52 in 1783 to £110 in 1803 and £398 in 1813. The number of persons receiving regular help was 9 in 1803 and 34 in 1813.[90] Annual expenditure fell after 1813 and averaged £204 in the late 1820s and early 1830s.[91] Hucclecote joined the new Gloucester poor-law union in 1835.[92] Later it was in Gloucester rural district, and that part not absorbed by Gloucester city in 1967[93] was included in Tewkesbury district in 1974.

CHURCH. There was a chapel at Hucclecote in 1289. It was under the jurisdiction of the archbishop of York and evidently originated as a chapel of the minster (later priory) of St. Oswald, Gloucester.[94] It presumably served the settlements at Hucclecote, Wood Hucclecote, and Noke, the tithes of which belonged to the priory's Hucclecote rectory estate[95] granted in 1542 to the dean and chapter of Bristol cathedral.[96] No record of the chapel has been found after 1289 and Hucclecote probably became part of Churchdown parish soon afterwards.[97] A chapel at Elmbridge, one of several built in the priory's liberty in the mid 12th century, has not been traced.[98] Later Elmbridge evidently paid its tithes to the rectory of Churchdown.[99]

A church was built at Hucclecote in 1850. The cost was borne by voluntary contributions and by grants from, among others, the Gloucester and Bristol Diocesan Church Building Association, the Revd. S. W. Warneford, and the dean and

[65] G.D.R., T 1/54.
[66] G.B.R., N 2/1/2, mins. 18 Sept.–18 Dec. 1856.
[67] Ibid. N 2/1/3, min. 25 June 1861.
[68] Glos. R.O., PA 183/1, pp. 3, 62, 140; suppl. ff. 12, 23v.; Glos. Colln., G. M. Davies papers, photogs. of mills.
[69] Cf. *Glouc. Corp. Rec.* pp. 124–5.
[70] P.R.O., CP 25(1)/73/10, no. 164.
[71] *Glouc. Corp. Rec.* p. 342.
[72] Cf. Glos. R.O., D 184/M 24, p. 199; P 1, f. 109.
[73] *Glouc. Corp. Rec.* p. 316; Glos. R.O., D 184/M 2.
[74] Glos. R.O., D 184/T 22; cf. ibid. M 24, p. 199.
[75] Hockaday Abs. cliii. [76] Smith, *Men and Armour*, 14–15.
[77] *Glouc. Jnl.* 22 Mar. 1819.
[78] *Kelly's Dir. Glos.* (1856), 313; Glos. R.O., PA 183/1, pp. 47, 65.
[79] *Census*, 1831. [80] G.D.R., T 1/54.
[81] *Kelly's Dir. Glos.* (1856 and later edns.).
[82] Glos. R.O., D 621/M 1–6.
[83] Ibid. D 626, Churchdown deeds 1754–1806; D 177/VII/

8; cf. ibid. D 2079/III/166.
[84] Ibid. D 184/M 2.
[85] Ibid. M 3, M 23.
[86] P.R.O., SC 6/Hen. VIII/1212, rot. 7.
[87] Cf. Hockaday Abs. xxix, 1543 subsidy, f. 6; lxviii, 1661 visit. f. 42. [88] G.D.R., C 6/3.
[89] Glos. R.O., Q/SO 1, ff. 24, 32, 63v., 79, 164, 183v.
[90] *Poor Law Abstract, 1804*, 176–7; *1818*, 150–1.
[91] *Poor Law Returns* (1830–1), 68; (1835), 67.
[92] *Poor Law Com. 1st Rep.* p. 251.
[93] *Census*, 1961–71.
[94] *Trans. B.G.A.S.* xliii, 95, 98, 110.
[95] P.R.O., SC 6/Hen. VIII/1212, rot. 7.
[96] *L. & P. Hen. VIII*, xvii, p. 638.
[97] *Trans. B.G.A.S.* xliii, 110; cf. *Tax. Eccl.* (Rec. Com.), 224; Glos. R.O., D 621/M 2, rot. 1d.
[98] *Trans. B.G.A.S.* xliii. 112.
[99] Cf. P.R.O., SC 6/Hen. VIII/1212, rot. 7; E 126/30, 1772 Mich. no. 7.

chapter of Bristol, and the site was given by Edmund Hopkinson.[1] In 1851 the church was assigned those parts of Hucclecote south of the Horsbere brook and at Noke as a district chapelry.[2] A house was acquired for the living, which was otherwise poorly endowed and in 1856 was worth £32. The living was called a perpetual curacy[3] (later a vicarage) and has remained in the gift of the bishop.[4] In 1862 Chosen Villa was purchased for the vicar's residence, and another house bought for the same purpose in 1952 was similarly replaced after 1968.[5]

The church, which was dedicated in 1851 to *ST. PHILIP AND ST. JAMES*,[6] was built of stone in a 13th-century style to a design by John Jacques & Son of Gloucester. It comprised chancel with north vestry and nave with south porch and west bellcot.[7] In 1886 the easternmost bay of the nave was adapted to accommodate the choir, the floor being raised and a low stone screen built to divide it from the rest of the nave. A north aisle with an arcade of five bays was added to the nave in 1911[8] and the vestry was enlarged in 1927.[9] A set of plate made in 1849 by John Keith was acquired for the church.[10]

NONCONFORMITY. In 1790 a house in Hucclecote was registered for nonconformist worship and in 1817 the ministers of the Baptist and Independent churches in Gloucester each registered a building in the village. Other houses there were registered in 1820 and 1831, the latter by a preacher from the Gloucester Independent church.[11]

Wesleyan Methodists in Hucclecote used buildings registered in 1834 and 1842, the latter being the house of Richard Colwell, a local preacher.[12] In 1848 the Wesleyans built a chapel to a plain classical design of John Jacques.[13] Paid for largely by William Wingate, the builder,[14] it was on the south side of Ermin Street[15] and for a few years was the only permanent place of worship in the village. In 1851, after several Wesleyan Reformers had recently left the meeting,[16] it had Sunday afternoon and evening congregations of 40 or more.[17] With the growth of the village the meeting flourished and in 1915 a resident minister was

appointed.[18] The chapel, which had become unsafe as well as too small, was replaced in 1929 by a new church, built further east, in the later Carisbrooke Road, to a design of William Leah. The older chapel was demolished, and the site, including a cemetery, was retained.[19] By 1981 membership of the Hucclecote Methodist church had risen to 220 and the congregation had outgrown the accommodation.[20]

EDUCATION. Hucclecote had at least two schools in 1819. One, begun that year, was a day and boarding school teaching 19 children in 1833 and remained open until 1841 or later. In 1833 there were two other day schools in Hucclecote where children were educated at the parents' expense; one begun in 1832 taught 10 girls and the other 5 children.[21]

In 1852 a small National school was built north of the churchyard on land given by Edmund Hopkinson.[22] Its income from voluntary sources[23] became insufficient and in 1880 a school board was compulsorily formed to run it. The board had five members representing Anglicans and Wesleyan Methodists.[24] The building continued to be used for an Anglican Sunday school[25] and in 1888 the Wesleyans erected their own Sunday school south of Ermin Street.[26] The board school, which in 1885 had an average attendance of 55,[27] later held some classes in the Wesleyans' building and was moved in 1900 to a new building north of the former National school.[28] In 1904, under the county council, it had an average attendance of 98.[29] Later the Anglican and Wesleyan Sunday schools were sometimes used for classes[30] and in 1938 the day school's average attendance was 108.[31] It became an infants' school on the opening in 1957 of a school in Hillview Road[32] and was renamed Larkhay infants' school in 1966.[33] Between 1967 and 1974 it was run by the city education authority.[34] In 1982 it was closed, the children were transferred to Hillview school, and the building was used by the county council for an information technology centre.[35]

CHARITIES FOR THE POOR. Hucclecote

[1] G.D.R., F 3/1–2; *Glouc. Jnl.* 3 May 1851.
[2] *Lond. Gaz.* 27 June 1851, p. 1668; Glos. R.O., P. 183/IN 3/3.
[3] *Glouc. Jnl.* 3 May 1851; G.D.R. vol. 384, f. 121.
[4] Hockaday Abs. ccxlviii; *Glouc. Dioc. Year Bk.* (1985), 18–19.
[5] Glos. R.O., P 183/IN 3/1–2, 8.
[6] Glos. Colln. R 169.1.
[7] *Glouc. Jnl.* 3 May 1851; Glos. R.O., P 183/CW 3/5; *Slater's Dir. Glos.* (1852–3), 129.
[8] Glos. R.O., P 183/CW 3/1, 3, 5; *Glouc. Jnl.* 23 Dec. 1911.
[9] Glos. R.O., PA 183/1, p. 181.
[10] *Glos. Ch. Plate*, 124.
[11] Hockaday Abs. cliii, ccxlviii; above, Prot. Nonconf.
[12] Hockaday Abs. ccxlviii; cf. *Glouc. Jnl.* 11 Apr. 1914.
[13] *Glouc. Jnl.* 30 Oct. 1847; 7 Oct. 1848; *Pigot's Dir. Glos.* (1842), 109; for a photog. of exterior, G. R. Hine, *Meth. Ch. Glouc. Circuit Rec.* (1971), 23.
[14] *Glos. Chron.* 20 July 1867.
[15] O.S. Map 6″, Glos. XXXIII. NE. (1891 edn.).
[16] Glos. Colln. NQ 6.4.
[17] P.R.O., HO 129/336/1/15/15.
[18] Glos. R.O., PA 183/1, p. 184.
[19] *Glouc. Jnl.* 25 May, 16 Nov. 1929; Glos. R.O., D 2689/2/11/3.
[20] Inf. from minister.
[21] Glos. R.O., PA 183/1, p. 186; *Educ. Enq. Abstract*, 311.
[22] Glos. R.O., D 531; Nat. Soc. files, Hucclecote.
[23] *Kelly's Dir. Glos.* (1856), 313; (1879), 687.
[24] *Lond. Gaz.* 20 Apr. 1880, p. 2601; Glos. R.O., PA 183/1, pp. 186, 205.
[25] Glos. R.O., D 531.
[26] *Glouc. Jnl.* 8 Sept. 1888; inscr. on bldg.
[27] *Kelly's Dir. Glos.* (1885), 507.
[28] Glos. R.O., PA 183/1, p. 186; SB 25/1, pp. 82, 91–104, 125–6.
[29] *Public Elem. Schs. 1906*, 185.
[30] Glos. R.O., PA 183/1, pp. 187–8.
[31] *Bd. of Educ., List 21, 1938* (H.M.S.O.), 127.
[32] Inf. from head teacher, Hillview Co. Primary sch.; above, Educ., elem. educ.
[33] G.B.R., B 4/25/54, primary schs. sub-cttee. 20 Sept. 1966.
[34] Local inf.
[35] Inf. from head teacher, Hillview Co. Primary sch.

benefited from the eleemosynary charities established for Churchdown ancient parish[36] and some time before 1905 was assigned by Churchdown two fifths of the income from those of Giles Cox and William Stansby.[37] Hucclecote's share of the Cox charity, valued at £3–4 in 1885,[38] was distributed under a Scheme of 1892 by a coal, drapery, and boot club[31] and was received directly from the charity's trustees from 1915, when it was £6 5s.[40] On the division of the

charity in 1957 a separate Hucclecote charity was formed. In 1971 its income of £6 was paid to needy students and apprentices.[41] Until 1936 Hucclecote regularly received £1 4s. from the Stansby apprenticing charity.[42] In 1971 Hucclecote continued to benefit from Richard Holford's Churchdown charity.[43]

A charitable trust established for Hucclecote in 1944 as a memorial to George Kingscote (d. 1942) provided £14 for the poor at Christmas.[44]

MATSON

THE small ancient parish of Matson lay SSE. of Gloucester, its church 3.5 km. from the city's central crossroads.[45] The parish boundaries as defined at a parliamentary inclosure in 1799 were extremely complex. They included much of the land on the east side of Robins Wood Hill, which Matson shared with Upton St. Leonards and, to a much lesser extent, with Tuffley and Whaddon, and touched the Gloucester–Painswick road to the east at three points. Matson also had land on the north-west and south-west sides of the hill and several detached pieces to the east and south within the main part of Upton parish. Most of the detached pieces represented holdings in open fields which Upton shared with neighbouring parishes and hamlets. To the south-east, on the Cotswold escarpment above Prinknash, Pope's wood belonged to Matson.[46] Following a minor adjustment of its boundary at another parliamentary inclosure in 1866[47] Matson covered 466 a.[48] The compactness of the combined area of Matson and Upton St. Leonards on Robins Wood Hill and the irregularity of their shared boundaries suggest that they may originally have been a single parish and that the parochial division followed the establishment of a church on an estate at Matson. The tenurial pattern at Matson in the Middle Ages was very fragmentary and much of Upton's land there belonged to an estate acquired by Gloucester Abbey in 1470.[49] Upton's boundaries, which were described in a manorial survey of 1589,[50] also took in Saintbridge on the Painswick road north-east of Robins Wood Hill,[51] and in 1608 Upton, Matson, and Saintbridge were described as a single tithing.[52] Upton's land at Matson and Saintbridge was united with Matson parish between 1656 and 1660.[53]

The irregularities in the boundaries of Matson, Upton St. Leonards, and neighbouring parishes were removed in 1882 and 1885. Matson, which lost Pope's wood and many other pieces to Upton,[54] was given a compact area of 655 a. comprising the east side of Robins Wood Hill and land to the north, including Starveall Farm and bounded by the G.W.R. line from Swindon (Wilts.) to Gloucester and by the later Cotteswold Road.[55] The Painswick road was included in a north-western peninsula of Upton parish, extending beyond Saintbridge to the same railway line and bounded on the east mostly by the river Twyver and at Saintbridge by the Sud brook.[56] In 1900 Gloucester took 154 a. at Starveall from Matson and part of Saintbridge from Upton. In 1935 the city absorbed the rest of Matson, save for 15 a. in the south added to Brookthorpe and Upton, and also the rest of Saintbridge and much of the Painswick road east of Matson. Upton also lost to Gloucester 22 a. between Matson and Sneedham's Green to the south in 1957 and a large area at the Wheatridge east of the Painswick road in 1967.[57] The following history of Matson relates to those parts both of the ancient parish and of Upton St. Leonards, on Robins Wood Hill and by the Painswick road, which were absorbed by Gloucester, apart from Saintbridge which is dealt with above.[58] The other parts of Matson are reserved for treatment in a later volume. The following account does not deal with suburban development of the city from the late 19th century, particularly the growth from the 1950s of large housing estates which destroyed the predominantly rural character of the Matson area.[59]

Matson lies on ground rising steeply to the

---

[36] Cf. *16th Rep. Com. Char.* 44–6.

[37] Swift, *Churchdown*, 73–4.

[38] *Kelly's Dir. Glos.* (1885), 507.

[39] Glos. R.O., P 183A/CH 1/1.

[40] Ibid. D 2695/1–2.

[41] Ibid. 4; CH 21, Glouc. rural district, p. 25.

[42] Ibid. P 183/CH 1–2.

[43] Ibid. CH 21, Glouc. rural district, p. 13.

[44] Ibid. D 3469/5/80; CH 21, Glouc. rural district, p. 25.

[45] This account was written in 1986.

[46] Glos. R.O., Q/RI 70 (maps K–L, O–P); cf. G.D.R., T 1/86, 189, 195.

[47] Glos. R.O., Q/RI 32.

[48] *Kelly's Dir. Glos.* (1870), 597. Sometimes the area was given as 463 a.: ibid. (1879), 702; cf. Glos. R.O., P 215/VE 2/1, p. 12. A figure of 323 a. in Rudge, *Hist. of Glos.* ii. 171,

apparently derived from the areas of pasture and arable given in Bigland, *Glos.* ii. 200.

[49] Below, man.

[50] Glos. R.O., P 347/MI 1.

[51] G.D.R., T 1/189.

[52] Smith, *Men and Armour*, 29–30.

[53] *Cal. S.P. Dom.* 1655–6, 336.

[54] O.S. Map 6", Glos. XXXIII. SE. (1884 edn.); NE. (1891 edn.); *Census*, 1891, which does not mention parts of Matson and Upton transferred to Whaddon: cf. G.D.R., T 1/195.

[55] *O.S. Area Bk.* Matson (1886).

[56] Ibid. Upton St. Leonards (1885).

[57] *Census*, 1901–71.

[58] Outlying Hamlets.

[59] Cf. above, Glouc. 1835–1985, topog.

summit of Robins Wood Hill at 198 m. By 1553 the summit was the site of a beacon[60] and in 1588 a small house was built nearby for watchmen waiting to signal the approach of the Spanish Armada.[61] The hill, formerly called Matson Hill or Knoll, presumably took the name of the Robins family, which held land there from the early 16th century,[62] though the form Robin Hood's Hill was recorded from 1542.[63] East of the hill the land rises from 30 m. at Saintbridge to over 46 m. at the Wheatridge in the south and lies on the Lower Lias clay, on which there are sand and gravel patches. The hill, an outlier of the Cotswolds, is formed by successive strata of Marlstone, the Upper Lias, sand, and the Inferior Oolite.[64] The Red quarry, of which Gloucester Abbey granted a lease to St. Bartholomew's Hospital in 1522, was possibly on the hill.[65] The hill included open fields, parts of which survived until 1866. In 1753 Horace Walpole described it as 'a mountain of turf to the very top' with 'wood scattered all over it',[66] and in the later 18th century George Selwyn, the owner of much of it, improved the plantations.[67] The lower land to the east, which was drained by the Sud brook, was mostly open arable land until inclosure in 1897.

The complex pattern of landholding on Robins Wood Hill was presumably connected with an early division of ownership of the many copious springs there. Waterworks serving Gloucester Abbey were constructed in the early 13th century and may have been visited in the mid 14th by the prince of Wales, whose intervention led the abbey and the Franciscan friars of Gloucester to settle a dispute over a spring in 1357.[68] The principal works, on the north side of the hill, included two small medieval wellhouses;[69] that called the Well House in 1589[70] remained in place in 1986. Two open reservoirs built there in the mid 18th century were used until 1946, though the springs ceased to feed Gloucester's water supply in 1924.[71] On the east side of the hill the Red well, fed by a chalybeate spring south of Matson village,[72] was much frequented by Gloucester citizens for medicinal purposes in the early 18th century.[73] Gloucester people made use of the hill for their recreation,[74] and an inn was opened at the reser-

voirs before 1820,[75] and perhaps by 1755 when a victualler was licensed in Matson parish.[76] The inn, where a bowling green was apparently laid in 1859,[77] was closed by the magistrates in 1876[78] and became a private residence.[79] It was later demolished and the emptied reservoirs, one of which was filled in, became part of a country park opened on the hill in 1975.[80]

South of Saintbridge the Painswick road for a distance follows the course of an ancient route between Gloucester and Cranham[81] known as the Port way.[82] In the mid 13th century Upton, Saintbridge, Matson, Sneedham, and Cranham were responsible for, and travellers contributed to, the repair of a bridge which carried that route over the Sud brook in Awe field.[83] East of the crossing the Port way ran along a straight causeway below the Wheatridge towards Upton village.[84] That section had ceased to be of major importance by the later 18th century[85] and part was a footpath in 1840.[86] The Painswick road, which left the Port way on Awefield Pitch just west of the Sud brook crossing,[87] also linked Gloucester with Stroud and was administered as a turnpike from 1726 until 1876.[88] In 1854 the tollgate was moved from the city boundary to north of the junction of the lane to Matson (later Matson Lane).[89] The route of Reservoir Road running along the north side of Robins Wood Hill was specified at the inclosure of 1799.[90]

Two moated sites have been identified by the Painswick road north-east of Robins Wood Hill, one on the east side. The other, on the west side and to the north of Matson Lane,[91] included a medieval building, perhaps a manor house,[92] and gave the name Moat Leaze to the field in which it lay. Between it and the main road a small close called Chapel Hay presumably marked the site of a chapel on the Port way.[93]

There was little early building in the area and Matson parish had only 9 houses c. 1710 and 8 in 1801.[94] The diminutive village stood on the side of Robins Wood Hill where Matson Lane turned southwards towards Sneedham's Green.[95] In the 17th century it probably comprised the church, a rectory house, two manor houses, and several farmsteads.[96] In 1556 there had been a church

[60] G.B.R., F 4/3, f. 44.
[61] Ibid. H 2/1, ff. 13v.–14.
[62] P.N. Glos. (E.P.N.S.), ii. 168.
[63] Glos. N. & Q. iv. 45.
[64] Geol. Surv. Map 1", solid, sheet 43 SE. (1855 edn.); sheet 44 (1856 edn.); Trans. B.G.A.S. cii. 26–7.
[65] Glouc. Cath. Libr., Reg. Abb. Malvern, i, ff. 189v.–190.
[66] Horace Walpole's Correspondence, ed. W. S. Lewis, xxxv. 152.
[67] Glouc. Jnl. 4 Aug. 1788; Selwyn proposed moving Llanthony Priory's gatehouse to the summit: H. Walpole's Correspondence, xxxv. 154–5.
[68] Above, Public Services.
[69] Trans. B.G.A.S. lxxxvii. 116 and plates VII–VIII.
[70] Glos. R.O., P 347/MI 1.
[71] Above, Public Services; cf. Taylor, Map of Glos. (1777).
[72] Glos. R.O., Q/RI 70 (map O, nos. 57–8); Richardson, Wells and Springs of Glos. 116, 265.
[73] Bodl. MS. Top. Glouc. c. 3, f. 198v.
[74] Fosbrooke, Glos. i. 274–5.
[75] Gell and Bradshaw, Glos. Dir. (1820), 107; Glos. R.O., D 3117/677–9; the inn occupied the ho. at the reservoirs in 1780: Glos. R.O., D 6/E 4, no. 13.
[76] Glos. R.O., Q/AV 2, rot. 8.

[77] G.B.R., N 2/6/1.
[78] Diary of a Victorian Squire, ed. D. Verey (1983), 84.
[79] Glos. Colln. R 201.2; G.B.R., N 2/4/5.
[80] Glos. Colln. N 3.61, p. 20.
[81] Ibid. prints GL 65.27.
[82] Glos. R.O., P 347A/FM 3, ct. roll 24 Oct. 1765.
[83] P.R.O., C 115/K 2/6684, f. 127v.
[84] O.S. Map 6", Glos. XXXIII. NE. (1891 edn.); Trans. B.G.A.S. cii. 23–72; the crossing may have been that called Wickham bridge in 1552: Glos. R.O., D 2957/201.22.
[85] Taylor, Map of Glos. (1777).
[86] G.D.R., T 1/189.
[87] Glos. Colln. prints GL 65.27; for Awefield Pitch in 1800, Glos. R.O., P 347A/FT 2.
[88] Above, Outlying Hamlets, intro.
[89] Glouc. Jnl. 16 Dec. 1854.
[90] Glos. R.O., Q/RI 70.
[91] O.S. Map 6", Glos. XXXIII. NE. (1891 edn.).
[92] Citizen, 4 May 1953; below, man.
[93] Glos. R.O., Q/RI 70 (map P, nos. 30–1).
[94] Atkyns, Glos. 552; Census, 1801.
[95] Above, Fig. 26.
[96] One farmhouse had probably once been a manor ho.: below, man.

house.[97] One manor house, Matson House, is a substantial building dating from the late 16th century. In the later 18th century its grounds took in the site of the other manor house to the north-east; the latter had possibly replaced the building in Moat Leaze on the opposite side of Matson Lane.[98] Apart from Matson House the only house surviving near the church in 1799 belonged to the farmstead a short distance to the north-west, called in 1788 Robin Hood's Farm and later Robins Farm.[99] Scattered building elsewhere on the east side of the hill included a row of timber-framed cottages called Hammershall north-west of the village.[1] There was a dwelling on the site of Larkham Farm, at a fork in the road to Sneedham's Green, by the mid 13th century and it was part of a small estate purchased in 1525 by Philip Redvern, a Gloucester mercer, and in 1552 by John Robins.[2] Larkham Farm probably dates from the 17th century and has a timber-framed range of two storeys with a short rear wing and, in the angle, a brick addition dated 1866. In the 1970s the farmstead was converted as a country club for which there was much new building to the north-east.[3] Further south on the road a pair of farm cottages was built in the early 1890s.[4] Winnycroft Farm south-east of the hill had apparently been established by 1681 for a holding with six closes called the Vine crofts.[5] The farmhouse was later rebuilt in brick. On the north side of the hill two houses were built in Reservoir Road east of the reservoirs in the early 19th century.[6]

In the 19th century most building in the Matson area took place on the west side of the Painswick road north-east of Robins Wood Hill. Among cottages built there in the early 19th century was a row, south of the junction of Matson Lane, called Trafalgar Place.[7] By the later 19th century the settlement had become the most populous in the district and in 1892 it was transferred with Saintbridge for ecclesiastical purposes from Upton St. Leonards to Matson.[8] In the late 1870s a rectory house was built on Matson Lane midway between Matson church and the main road, where new buildings included a school in 1881 and a church room or hall in 1905.[9] Further south building was barred by the open field called Awe field, through which the main road ran, but by 1840 encroachments on the field had resulted

in two small groups of cottages east of the road. A cottage on the Wheatridge in 1773 had been removed.[10] Some scattered building had taken place on the main road by 1897 when the inclosure of Upton's open fields released land there and on the Wheatridge for house building.[11]

Three people in Matson were assessed for the subsidy in 1327.[12] There were said to be c. 28 communicants in the parish in 1551,[13] 7 households in 1563,[14] and 37 communicants in 1603.[15] Later estimates of the population included 50 c. 1710 and 45 c. 1775.[16] In 1801 the population of Matson parish was 51 and in the following eighty years the lowest number recorded was 32 in 1861 and the highest 73 in 1881.[17]

For several centuries Matson had imported resident landholders in the Robins family, established there in the early 16th century, and the Selwyn family, owners of Matson House from 1600. The last Selwyn, sole landholder from 1766, died in 1791[18] and for over a century no lord of the manor lived at Matson House,[19] but the Misses Rice, who occupied it in the later 19th century, were a dominant influence on Matson's life.[20]

MANORS AND OTHER ESTATES. None of the three manors of Matson has been found recorded before the 14th century, and the earlier descent of estates at Matson is obscured by a complex pattern of landholding. In the mid 13th century much land was held under either King's Barton or Abbot's Barton manor.[21] King's Barton, which included all of Matson parish,[22] had overlordship of the Matson manor acquired by the Lygon family[23] and in the mid 1630s of the Selwyn family's estate.[24] Some land in Matson was held in 1239 from Herbert FitzPeter and later from Reynold FitzPeter.[25] The manor of Upton St. Leonards or Barton Upton, which had been formed from Abbot's Barton by 1536, included land at Matson.[26] Its descent is reserved for a later volume.

Among the principal landholders at Matson in the early 12th century were presumably Ralph and his son Ernulf, who granted the church or chapel there to Gloucester Abbey.[27] Ernulf, whose estate included land on the Cotswold escarpment, was described both as of Matson and Prinknash. The estate evidently passed to Philip of Matson

[97] Glos. R.O., D 2957/201.37.
[98] Below, man.
[99] Glos. R.O., D 2957/321.106; Q/RI 70 (map P, no. 19).
[1] Ibid. Q/RI 70 (map P, no. 25); Glos. Colln. N 3.61, p. 27.
[2] Glos. R.O., D 2957/201.2–7, 11–16, 19–20, 22; Q/RI 70 (map O, no. 28).
[3] Glos. and Avon Life, Jan. 1984, 36–7.
[4] Glos. R.O., D 2299/116.
[5] Glos. Colln. RF 201.3 (3); cf. Glos. R.O., D 2957/321.105.
[6] Glos. R.O., D 3117/677–8.
[7] Cf. ibid. Q/RI 70 (maps O–P); G.D.R., T 1/189; the date on Trafalgar Place is probably 1805.
[8] Lond. Gaz. 12 July 1892, pp. 4000–5.
[9] Glouc. Jnl. 19 Dec. 1908; Glos. R.O., P 215/CW 3/7; VE 2/6.
[10] G.D.R., T 1/189; Glos. R.O., D 127/893.
[11] Glos. Colln. RF 321.3, p. 17; Glos. R.O., Q/RI 149.
[12] Glos. Subsidy Roll, 1327, 6.
[13] E.H.R. xix. 103.
[14] Bodl. MS. Rawl. C. 790, f. 8.
[15] Eccl. Misc. 71.
[16] Atkyns, Glos. 552; Rudder, Glos. 542.
[17] Census, 1801–81.
[18] Below, man.
[19] A. Jennings, Hist. of Matson Ho. (1983), 12–13: Glos. Colln. R 201.5.
[20] Glouc. Jnl. 4 Mar. 1905.
[21] Cf. Hist. & Cart. Mon. Glouc. (Rolls Ser.), iii. 67–71, 149–51.
[22] Glos. R.O., D 326/M 24.
[23] Cal. Inq. p.m. xiv, p. 28; Cal. Inq. p.m. Hen. VII, iii, p. 184.
[24] Inq. p.m. Glos. 1625–42, i. 229–30; iii. 142.
[25] P.R.O., C 115/K 1/6681, ff. 187v.–188v.
[26] Valor Eccl. (Rec. Com.), ii. 416; Glos. R.O., P 347/MI 1; P 347A/FM 1–2.
[27] Hist. & Cart. Mon. Glouc. i. 100; ii. 259.

(fl. 1159), the son of either Ralph or Ernulf,[28] and possibly to Simon of Matson, whose son and heir John of Matson in 1239 sold half of it, with land for building a barn or oxhouse, to Llanthony Priory. John, whose mother held some land in dower,[29] had fallen into debt. He paid his relief to the Crown in 1242, and by 1246 he had given the rest of his estate to his son Philip of Matson.[30] Philip, who granted Llanthony Priory 15½ a.[31] and held a yardland under King's Barton by the servide of 5s.,[32] was evidently the father of Philip of Matson,[33] who in the 1260s, when a minor, held a ploughland, in which his mother had dower, under Abbot's Barton by the service of a squire equipped with a horse and harness and of a heriot and relief.[34] The younger Philip was probably the knight (fl. 1284),[35] who later enlarged his estate in Matson and Upton St. Leonards.[36]

In 1329 Philip's son William of Matson[37] and others granted the manor of MATSON to Ellis Daubeney and his wife Agnes.[38] Gilbert Giffard (d. 1373) later held the manor, comprising a messuage and a ploughland, by knight service in right of his wife Elizabeth,[39] daughter of Ellis Daubeney.[40] In 1415 John Giffard of Leckhampton granted a lease of the manor to Roger Ball, a Gloucester burgess,[41] and in 1460 Nicholas Giffard and his wife Margery settled it for life on Margaret, wife of Richard Cheke.[42] By the marriage of Nicholas's daughter Anne the manor passed to the Lygons of Madresfield (Worcs.). Anne's husband Thomas Lygon (d. 1507) was succeeded by his son Richard[43] (d. 1512). Richard's son and heir, also Richard, who was knighted in 1533, died seised of the manor in 1557, but in 1552 his son and heir William,[44] then described as of Arle, had granted a lease of part, including the site of the manor, for 50 years to John Robins;[45] John's father Thomas (d. 1550) had held land under Sir Richard Lygon.[46] William Lygon (d. 1567) was succeeded by his son Richard (d. 1584), who left the manor for life to his second son Henry[47] (fl. 1609). In 1597 Henry's older brother William sold his reversionary right to Jasper Selwyn, a lawyer[48] who built up a large estate in Matson and Upton,[49] as mentioned

below. The house, which Philip of Matson had next to Matson church in the mid 12th century[50] and John of Matson retained in 1239,[51] was presumably occupied by tenants in the later Middle Ages.[52] It evidently stood north or west of the church, where a farmhouse on the Selwyn family's estate in 1671 was demolished before 1799.[53]

Llanthony Priory, which in the mid 1260s held a yardland under King's Barton,[54] had a plough-land at Matson in 1291.[55] That land, called the manor of MATSON by 1378,[56] was administered with the priory's Hempsted estate at the Dissolution.[57] In 1542 the Crown granted the site of the manor, including a house, to the mayor and burgesses of Gloucester, who granted it in 1543 to Thomas Lane,[58] the city's recorder. Lane (d. 1544) left the house to his wife Maud for life with reversion to his son Thomas.[59] By 1547 Maud had married Richard Pate, a lawyer who became recorder of and M.P. for Gloucester.[60] Pate, who in 1561 acquired a 200-year lease of the reversion,[61] built Matson House and died in 1588. Later, at Maud's death, the house and grounds passed to their granddaughter Susan Brook. Susan married Ambrose Willoughby, who fell into debt and from whom she was legally separated in 1598.[62] They sold the house in 1600 to Jasper Selwyn.[63]

Selwyn also acquired land in Matson by his marriage in 1591 or 1592 to Margaret Robins;[64] land bought in 1552 by her grandfather John Robins (d. 1563)[65] was left to her by her father Thomas (d. 1577) subject to the life interest of his widow Joan (d. 1605), who married John Walkley.[66] At Jasper Selwyn's death in 1635 his Matson estate passed to his son William, who inherited his mother's land in 1636.[67] William, who by marriage had acquired the nearby Sheephouse estate,[68] died in 1643 and was succeeded by his son William (d. 1679). That William's son and heir William became a major-general and in 1701 was appointed governor of Jamaica, where he died in 1702, leaving part of the Matson estate in jointure to his wife Albinia (d. 1737).[69] His son and heir John became a

[28] Ibid. i. 63, 180; ii. 259.
[29] P.R.O., C 115/K 1/6681, ff. 187–188v.
[30] Ex. e Rot. Fin. (Rec. Com.), i. 457; Pipe R. 1242 (ed. H. L. Cannon), 253.
[31] P.R.O., C 115/K 1/6681, f. 187v.
[32] Hist. & Cart. Mon. Glouc. iii. 68; cf. Close R. 1253–4, 121.
[33] Glouc. Cath. Libr., deeds and seals, iii, f. 8.
[34] Hist. & Cart. Mon. Glouc. iii. 150.
[35] Cal. Close, 1279–88, 300.
[36] Glouc. Cath. Libr., deeds and seals, vi, f. 5; Glos. R.O., D 3117/312.   [37] Cal. Close, 1327–30, 568.
[38] Glouc. Cath. Libr., deeds and seals, iii, f. 13.
[39] Cal. Inq. p.m. xiv, p. 28; P.R.O., CP 25(1)/78/76, no. 519.
[40] Above, Outlying Hamlets, man.
[41] Glos. R.O., D 2957/201.9.
[42] P.R.O., CP 25(1)/79/92, no. 148.
[43] Trans. B.G.A.S. xlvi. 332; Cal. Inq. p.m. Hen. VII, iii, p. 184.
[44] P.R.O., C 142/27, no. 125; C 142/148, no. 1; V.C.H. Worcs. iv. 120–1.
[45] Glos. R.O., D 2957/201.23.
[46] Ibid. P 347/IN 1/1; G.D.R. wills 1550/82.
[47] P.R.O., C 142/148, no. 1; C 142/206, no. 8.

[48] Glos. R.O., D 2957/201.37, 54.
[49] Cf. Glos. Colln. RF 321.11.
[50] Hist. & Cart. Mon. Glouc. ii. 259.
[51] P.R.O., C 115/K 1/6681, f. 187.
[52] Cf. Glos. R.O., D 2957/201.23.
[53] Ibid. 67; Q/RI 70 (map P, no. 17).
[54] Hist. & Cart. Mon. Glouc. iii. 68.
[55] Tax. Eccl. (Rec. Com.), 232.
[56] P.R.O., C 115/K 2/6684, f. 30v.; cf. Glos. Colln. 27077 (2), p. 134.   [57] P.R.O., SC 6/Hen. VIII/1224, rot. 18d.
[58] G.B.R., B 2/2, ff. 31v.–33v.
[59] Trans. B.G.A.S. xlvi. 328–9; V.C.H. Glos. x. 276.
[60] Cal. Pat. 1547–8, 11; Trans. B.G.A.S. lvi. 201–21.
[61] Glos. R.O., D 2957/201.26; cf. Cal. Pat. 1558–60, 6.
[62] Trans. B.G.A.S. xlvi. 333–8; lvi. 219–25
[63] Glos. R.O., D 2957/201.44–50.
[64] Ibid. 35; V.C.H. Glos. x. 276.
[65] Glos. R.O., D 2957/201.20; P.R.O., E 150/383, m. 2; according to Glos. R.O., P 215/IN 1/1, John died in 1564.
[66] P.R.O., C 142/181, no. 108; Trans. B.G.A.S. xlvi. 331–2.
[67] Inq. p.m. Glos. 1625–42, i. 229–30; iii. 142.
[68] Above, Outlying Hamlets, man.
[69] Trans. B.G.A.S. ii. 259–64; Williams, Parl. Hist. of Glos. 204; Glos. Colln. RF 201.3 (3).

colonel in the army and later a royal courtier. The estate passed at his death in 1751 to his son George Augustus Selwyn,[70] a bachelor and a noted wit in London society.[71] George, who like his father and paternal grandfather represented Gloucester in parliament,[72] acquired the only other sizeable estate at Matson, the Robins family's manor held under the dean and chapter of Gloucester cathedral, in 1766.[73] At his death in 1791 his enlarged estate passed to his nephew Thomas Townshend,[74] Viscount Sydney, who upon an exchange in 1799 acquired the dean and chapter's freehold interest over part.[75] After his death in 1800 the estate passed with the viscounty in the direct line to John Thomas Townshend (d. 1831) and John Robert Townshend, who was created Earl Sydney in 1874. On the latter's death in 1890 the peerage became extinct and the estate passed in turn to his widow Emily (d. 1893)[76] and nephew Robert Marsham, afterwards Marsham-Townshend.[77] In 1912 Robert broke up the estate[78] and sold Matson House to the occupant, George Dunstan Timmis, with much of the surrounding land.[79] Timmis died in 1954 leaving his estate in trust for his wife Sybil (d. 1961) and daughters.[80] From 1950 Gloucester corporation bought a large part of the former Matson estate piecemeal for housing and a country park[81] and in the mid 1970s Larkham farm was used for a country club and sporting activities.[82]

Richard Pate's house, east of the church, is of stone and has a U-shaped plan open to the south-west. Much 16th- and early 17th-century panelling survives, although some of it has been reset. There was a newel stair adjacent to the north corner of the central hall and a gallery in the attic. Charles I lodged in the house while his troops laid siege to Gloucester in 1643,[83] and in 1672 William Selwyn's eldest surviving son Edward was assessed on 13 hearths for it.[84] A succession of alterations in the early and mid 18th century included the arcading of the south-west and north-east sides of the hall, the relocation of several internal doorways, some new panelling, and the fitting of a staircase in the east corner of the hall. By the mid 18th century all but a few windows had been sashed and later in the century the frames were remade with gothick glazing bars, an embellishment probably influenced by the work at Strawberry Hill in Twickenham (Surr.) of Horace Walpole, who visited George Selwyn at Matson several times.[85] Selwyn, who apparently adapted one room as a Roman Catholic oratory for his adopted daughter Maria Fagnani,[86] illustrated the house's history, particularly its role during the siege of Gloucester, with works of art, including a bust of Charles I by Louis Roubiliac.[87] He entertained George III and Queen Charlotte at Matson during their visit to Cheltenham in 1788.[88] For over a century after Selwyn's death in 1791 tenants lived in the house,[89] and in the early 19th century the two drawing rooms on the south-east side were refitted,[90] being connected through wide doors, and the gallery was divided into three rooms. A short 18th-century brick service wing on the north-west side[91] was rebuilt to a greater length in the earlier 19th century.[92] In 1869 Viscount Sydney's six cousins, the Misses Rice, took up residence in the house; Maria, the youngest sister, survived until 1905.[93] From 1958 Matson House was occupied by Selwyn school, an independent girls' school, the trustees of which bought the house in 1972.[94]

In 1651, in an exchange of land, William Selwyn gave part of the garden, including a pond, to John Robins, whose manor house stood north-east of Matson House.[95] The garden of Matson House retains walls, terraces, and a canal of the earlier 18th century.[96] A bowling green laid out at the same period was apparently incorporated before 1799 in a shrubbery with a serpentine walk,[97] but was restored to its former use before 1825.[98] George Selwyn, who acquired the Robins family's house in 1766, demolished it and in its grounds, which also included a canal, planted a grove with an avenue leading from Matson House to Matson Lane.[99] The demolished house provided stone for Tudor-style stables and servants' cottages in the courtyard north of Matson House.[1] Older outbuildings, perhaps including

[70] Trans. B.G.A.S. ii. 264; Williams, Parl. Hist. of Glos. 209–10.
[71] D.N.B.; Geo. Selwyn: Letters and Life, ed. E. S. Roscoe and H. Clergue (1899), 6.
[72] Williams, Parl. Hist. of Glos. 204, 209–11.
[73] Glos. R.O., D 936/E 73.
[74] Trans. B.G.A.S. ii. 268, 271.
[75] Glos. R.O., Q/RI 70.
[76] Complete Peerage, xii(1), 590–3; Fosbrooke, Glos. i. 273; Kelly's Dir. Glos. (1856), 326; (1885), 524; Glos. R.O., D 2299/116.
[77] Burke, Peerage (1900), 1286–7; Glos. R.O., D 2299/116.
[78] Cf. Glos. R.O., D 2299/950.
[79] Jennings, Matson Ho. 13; G.B.R., L 6/27/8; cf. Glos. R.O., P 215/VE 2/1, p. 51.
[80] Citizen, 12 Jan., 1 May 1954; inscr. in Matson churchyard.
[81] Country Life, 8 Dec. 1950, pp. 1990; Glos. Colln. N 3.61, p. 8; above, Glouc. 1835–1985, topog.
[82] Citizen, 17 July 1967; Glos. and Avon Life, Jan. 1984, 36–7.
[83] Bibliotheca Glos. ii, p. lx.
[84] P.R.O., E 179/247/14, rot. 33d.; Trans. B.G.A.S. ii. 260.
[85] Hist. MSS. Com. 42, 15th Rep. VI, Carlisle, pp. 277–8; H. Walpole's Correspondence, i. 341; xxx. 275; xxxv. 152; for Walpole, D.N.B.
[86] Jennings, Matson Ho. 11–12; cf. Verey, Glos. ii. 298.
[87] Bigland, Glos. ii. 201; H. Walpole's Correspondence, i. 341; xxxiv. 16 and n.; Verey, Glos. ii. 298.
[88] Glouc. Jnl. 4 Aug. 1788.
[89] Glos. Colln. RF 201.1; Delineations of Glos. 94–6; Jennings, Matson Ho. 12.
[90] Cf. Diary of a Cotswold Parson, 132.
[91] Cf. views of ho. in S. P. Kerr, Geo. Selwyn and the Wits (1909), plate facing p. 20; Country Life, 8 Dec. 1950, p. 1993.
[92] Cf. above, Plate 59.
[93] Burke, Peerage (1889), 472, 1338–9; Glouc. Jnl. 4, 11 Mar. 1905: the other sisters were Frances (d. 1884), Cecil (d. 1882), Harriet (d. 1879), Caroline (d. 1878), and Katharine (d. 1887).
[94] Jennings, Matson Ho. 13, 25.
[95] Glos. R.O., D 2957/201.64–5; 321.59.
[96] One wall is dated 1755.
[97] Cf. Glos. R.O., Q/RI 70 (map O, no. 50).
[98] Delineations of Glos. plate facing p. 94.
[99] Jennings, Matson Ho. 29; Glos. R.O., Q/RI 70 (map O, no. 54).
[1] The stables were apparently built in 1780: Kerr, Geo. Selwyn and the Wits, 307–8.

Llanthony Priory's house, were demolished in the late 18th century.[2] In the 1970s and early 1980s Selwyn school put up many new buildings in the grounds north-east of the house.[3] An early 19th-century entrance lodge in Matson Lane[4] was rebuilt in the late 19th century or the early 20th.

The Robinses' manor of *MATSON* lay in Upton St. Leonards.[5] It possibly originated in the estate of William Geraud of Matson (fl. 1238 and 1266),[6] who held ½ virgate from Abbot's Barton by the service of 12*d.* and a heriot and relief.[7] William de Gardinis, who in 1299 was described as lord of Matson,[8] held ¼ knight's fee there in 1303.[9] William Geraud, who is said to have settled Matson manor on his marriage in 1314 or 1315,[10] may have been the same man as the William de Gardinis to whom the ¼ knight's fee had passed by 1346. In 1402 Thomas Bridges held it.[11] By 1399 John of Matson, a London dyer, had conveyed land in Matson claimed by his creditor Edmund Francis, a London grocer, to Hugh of Bisley.[12] In 1414 Hugh gave land at Matson and Saintbridge to John Geraud.[13] John may have been the same man as John Crofton, who in 1458 quitclaimed the manors of Matson and Sneedham to William Nottingham and others.[14] In 1470 William gave both manors to Gloucester Abbey in return for the establishment of a chantry in the abbey church.[15] The abbey retained Matson manor until the Dissolution,[16] and it passed to the dean and chapter of Gloucester cathedral in 1541.[17] From 1526 Thomas Robins held a lease of the demesne for 70 years.[18] Thomas, whose family also used the surname of Butcher in the mid 16th century,[19] died in 1550 and the lease passed in turn to his son Richard (d. 1586)[20] and to Richard's son John. The dean and chapter later granted leases of the whole manor to John (d. 1646) and from 1626 to his son Henry. The leases, for terms of 21 years, were renewed every few years. Henry was succeeded at his death in 1646 by his son John[21] and the manor comprised 180 a. in 1649.[22] John (d. 1691) was succeeded by his daughter Mary (d. 1735), wife of Gilbert Ironside (d. 1701), bishop of Hereford. Mary's nephew William Robins, who was the lessee in 1725,[23] became high sheriff of

Gloucestershire in 1737 and a landowner in Cromhall.[24] In 1760, after his death, Jane Clarke of Walford (Herefs.) was granted a lease, and from 1766 the manor formed part of George Selwyn's estate.[25] The dean and chapter relinquished their interest upon an exchange in 1799.[26]

William Geraud's house in the mid 13th century[27] may have been on the moated site in Moat Leaze[28] or on the site of the Robinses' manor house to the south-west.[29] The Robinses' house, including a hall and parlour, comprised five bays in 1649[30] and was occupied by tenants in the 1670s.[31] George Selwyn pulled it down before 1777.[32]

The rectory of Matson may have been appropriated by Gloucester Abbey, to which the church had been granted by the earlier 12th century. In later periods, however, the tithes and a rectory house with 3 a. were usually, if not always, occupied by the parish priest, who was normally styled rector and by the 18th century was regarded as having the freehold of the tithes and 3 a.[33] If the glebe had earlier been larger, the balance may have been added to the abbey's manor of Matson.

ECONOMIC HISTORY. Llanthony Priory granted its Matson manor with 2 a. of meadow land in Hempsted at farm in 1378 for 48 years or lives and in 1517 for 60 years or lives.[34] On Gloucester Abbey's manor, the demesne of which was farmed by 1526, the rents of the free and customary tenants were valued in 1535 at £4 19*s.* 7½*d.* One tenant, who also held part of the Barnwood demesne, had to supply the abbot's house at Prinknash with firewood from nearby Buckholt wood.[35]

Other evidence for tenant holdings at Matson is almost entirely lacking until the later 18th century, by which time most of the land belonged to a single estate. Land ownership had been very fragmented until the 16th century when the Robins and Selwyn families began consolidating estates.[36] In the late 17th century and the early 18th there were at least seven small tenant farms on the Selwyns' estate, on which some land was

[2] Cf. Jennings, *Matson Ho.* 29; Glos. R.O., Q/RI 70 (map O, no. 50).

[3] Jennings, *Matson Ho.* 25–6; Glos. Colln. RR 201.3, pp. 41–2.

[4] Cf. Glos. R.O., Q/RI 70 (map O, no. 54); G.D.R., T 1/189.

[5] Cf. *Cal. S.P. Dom.* 1655–6, 336.

[6] *Close R.* 1237–42, 69; *Cal. Pat.* 1258–66, 648.

[7] *Hist. & Cart. Mon. Glouc.* iii. 150.

[8] *Glouc. Corp. Rec.* p. 291; cf. P.R.O., C 115/K 2/6683, f. 36.

[9] *Feud. Aids*, ii. 253.

[10] Atkyns, *Glos.* 552.

[11] *Feud. Aids*, ii. 290, 296.

[12] *Cal. Close,* 1399–1402, 186–7; P.R.O., C 1/3, no. 68.

[13] Glouc. Cath. Libr., deeds and seals, vii, f. 10.

[14] Ibid. ix, f. 16; cf. Glos. R.O., D 2957/321.36.

[15] Glouc. Cath. Libr., deeds and seals, vii, f. 14.

[16] *Valor Eccl.* (Rec. Com.), ii. 415.

[17] *L. & P. Hen. VIII*, xvi, p. 572.

[18] Glouc. Cath. Libr., Reg. Abb. Malvern, i, ff. 248–9.

[19] *Valor Eccl.* (Rec. Com.), ii. 415; P.R.O., E 150/383, m. 2.

[20] G.D.R. wills 1550/82; Glos. R.O., P 347/IN 1/1

[21] *Trans. B.G.A.S.* xlvi. 349–50; Glos R.O., p 347/IN 1/1–2; D 936/E 12/2, ff. 121v.–122v., 308 and v.

[22] Glos. R.O., D 1740/E 1, ff. 120–121v.

[23] Ibid. D 936/E 73; *Trans. B.G.A.S.* xlvi. 350–1; for Ironside, *D.N.B.*

[24] Rudder, *Glos.* 54; Glos. R.O., D 654/IV/67.

[25] Glos. R.O., D 936/E 73; D 2957/201.71–3.

[26] Ibid. Q/RI 70.

[27] P.R.O., C 115/K 1/6681, f. 187v.

[28] Glos. R.O., Q/RI 70 (map P, no. 30); *Citizen*, 4 May 1953.

[29] Cf. Jennings, *Matson Ho.* 29; Glos. R.O., Q/RI 70 (map O, no. 54).

[30] Glos. R.O., D 1740/E 1, f. 120.

[31] Ibid. Q/SO 1, ff. 106, 138v.

[32] Cf. Taylor, *Map of Glos.* (1777); above.

[33] Below, ch.

[34] P.R.O., C 115/K 2/6684, f. 30v.; SC 6/Hen. VIII/1224, rot. 18d.

[35] *Valor Eccl.* (Rec. Com.), ii. 415; Glouc. Cath. Libr., Reg. Abb. Malvern, i, ff. 248–60.

[36] Above, man.

held for terms of one or two lives;[37] copyhold tenure in Matson was mentioned in 1552.[38] In the later 18th century there were 11 or 12 tenants on the leasehold part of George Selwyn's estate,[39] and in the 1790s the same part included 47 a. of plantations and arable in hand, tenant holdings of 102 a., 34 a., and 18 a., and another five holdings of 6 a. or less.[40] Some of those holdings were possibly part of four farms which in the early 1770s had between 173 a. and 75 a. each in Matson parish.[41] In 1788 Robins and Winnycroft farms comprised 253 a. and 133 a. respectively.[42]

The slopes of Robins Wood Hill once included several open fields which Matson and Upton shared with neighbouring parishes and hamlets. Inclosure of those fields and the creation of pasture closes evidently began before 1589, when one close on the hill was called Deep Furrows.[43] The upper slopes possibly retained open-field land in 1651 when strips in Hill field were included in an exchange of land between John Robins and William Selwyn.[44] The laying down as pasture of arable on the hill continued in the later 17th century,[45] and by the 18th century open-field land was confined to the lowest slopes, in Tredworth and Markham fields on the north and south sides respectively. Matson and Upton shared Markham field with Tuffley and Whaddon and shared Tredworth field, which also took in much land between the hill and Gloucester, with many parishes and hamlets; that part covering the foot of the hill became known as Upper Tredworth field.[46] Below the hill to the east two large open fields belonging principally to Upton, but shared by Matson and other parishes and hamlets, were recorded from 1221.[47] Awe field lay on either side of the Sud brook and Wheatridge field to the east had the river Twyver for its eastern boundary. To the south within Upton parish Matson also had a share in Brimps field.[48]

Sheep were kept on Robins Wood Hill in the mid 16th century[49] and in the mid 17th when dairy farming was important there.[50] In 1681 a farmhouse was called the Dayhouse.[51] By the mid 18th century the hill was predominantly grassland,[52] and in 1788 Robins farm had 220 a. of pasture and meadow and 33 a. of arable, and Winnycroft farm had respectively 111 a. and 22 a.[53] All the farms depended on dairying and they kept some beef cattle, a few sheep, and poultry.[54] In 1830 their chief produce was cheese, butter, meat, and wool.[55]

Though it included little open-field land by 1796 Matson parish was covered by the Act under which large tracts of land near Gloucester were finally inclosed in 1799. The award, which re-allotted several existing inclosures, dealt with Upper Tredworth field, and benefited Viscount Sydney, the principal landholder, and the rector of Matson, who received land for his Matson glebe and tithes. Eight other landowners also received allotments in Upper Tredworth for land belonging to Upton, including the owners of Tuffley Court, Saintbridge House, Starveall Farm, and Grove Court. Under the Act Viscount Sydney consolidated his Matson estate by exchanges of land, in which the dean and chapter of Gloucester relinquished their freehold interest in part of it and the rector acquired 53 a. in South Hamlet.[56] The inclosure of Markham field was completed in 1866.[57] Despite encroachments, the fields east of the hill were largely untouched and were cultivated in strips and used for common pasture after the harvest until their inclosure under the award for Upton in 1897.[58] Following that the Matson estate was further consolidated by exchanges with the Grove Court estate.[59]

In the later 19th century and the early 20th the Matson estate included in Matson three large farms, Larkham, Robins, and Winnycroft,[60] and in 1896 five agricultural occupiers were returned for Matson parish.[61] The three principal farms each had over 150 a. in the 1930s.[62] Matson remained predominantly grassland and in 1866 the parish returned 124 cattle, both dairy and beef, and 135 sheep.[63] A dairyman, principally a milk seller, lived at the reservoirs in the late 19th century.[64] The area of permanent pasture apparently increased in the later 19th century, and in 1905 Matson parish had 492 a. of permanent grass to 57 a. of arable. In the later 19th century leys of clover and grass were part of the crop rotation which included wheat, barley, beans, peas, and turnips,[65] arable farming being more important in the Painswick road area with its open fields than on Robins Wood Hill.[66] In 1896 orchards covered at least 32 a. of Matson parish.[67] From the 1950s much farmland, including the lowest slopes of the hill, disappeared under housing estates.[68] The higher land was taken for recreational use in the 1970s[69] but grazing continued over part in the mid 1980s

[37] Glos. Colln. RF 201.3 (2–3).
[38] Glos. R.O., D 2957/201.22.
[39] Ibid. D 936/E 180.
[40] Glos. Colln. RX 201.1.
[41] P.R.O., E 126/30, 1772 Hil. no. 8.
[42] Glos. R.O., D 2957/321.105–6.
[43] Ibid. P 347/MI 1, pp. 82–8, 108.
[44] Ibid. D 2957/321.59; cf. ibid. D 1740/E 1, f. 121.   [45] Ibid. D 2957/201.67.
[46] Ibid. Q/RI 70 (maps P–Q); cf. ibid. Q/RI 32; G.D.R., T 1/86, 195.
[47] P.R.O., CP 25(1)/73/4, no. 12.
[48] G.D.R., T 1/189; cf. Glos. R.O., P 347/MI 1.
[49] Glos. R.O., D 2957/201.22.
[50] Ibid. D 1740/E 1, f. 120.
[51] Glos. Colln. RF 201.3 (3).
[52] Above, intro.
[53] Glos. R.O., D 2957/321.105–6.

[54] P.R.O., E 126/30, 1772 Hil. no. 8.
[55] Glos. Colln. RF 201.2 (6).
[56] Glos. R.O., Q/RI 70.
[57] Ibid. 32; above, Outlying Hamlets, agric.
[58] Glos. Colln. RF 321.1; Glos. R.O., Q/RI 149.
[59] Glos. R.O., D 140/Z 6; P 347B/PC 41/2.
[60] Ibid. D 2299/116; G.B.R., L 6/27/8.
[61] P.R.O., MAF 68/1609/13.
[62] Kelly's Dir. Glos. (1935), 255, 357.
[63] P.R.O., MAF 68/25/13; MAF 68/26/20.
[64] Kelly's Dir. Glos. (1889), 840; (1894), 233; Glos. Colln. R 201.2.
[65] P.R.O., MAF 68/26/20; MAF 68/1609/13; Acreage Returns, 1905.
[66] Cf. Glos. Colln. RF 321.1.
[67] P.R.O., MAF 68/1609/13.
[68] Above, Glouc. 1835–1985, topog.
[69] Ibid. social and cultural life.

when Robins Farm remained the centre of a working farm.

A corn mill on the river Twyver at Elm Court, east of the Wheatridge in Upton St. Leonards,[70] may have been on the site of that held in 1221 by Reynold Leviet[71] and in the 1260s under Abbot's Barton manor by William Leviet.[72] In the 1820s it was called Lodge Mill[73] and belonged to a small farm held under John Owen (d. by 1825) and acquired by Ralph Fletcher. The mill apparently ceased working in the 1840s. The former mill house has a brick south front and stable block dating from *c.* 1820.[74]

Early references to tradesmen in the Matson area are lacking, and in 1831 only one family in Matson parish was supported by trade and five by agriculture.[75]

LOCAL GOVERNMENT. The farmer of Llanthony Priory's Matson manor in 1378 owed suit to the court of King's Barton manor,[76] which exercised view of frankpledge over Matson parish.[77] No records of manorial government are known to survive for the parish. King's Barton and Upton St. Leonards manors each had leet jurisdiction in the parts of Matson belonging to Upton parish,[78] and the former also dealt with tenurial matters there.[79] The Upton manor court regulated the use of open-field and waste land by the Painswick road until the inclosure of 1897. Inhabitants of Matson contributed towards the expenses of the Upton pound in the mid 19th century.[80]

Matson parish had two churchwardens in the 16th century[81] but later there was sometimes only one.[82] The parish had a constable in 1715.[83] The annual cost of poor relief in the late 18th century and the early 19th rarely rose above £43, there being usually only two or three people on permanent relief.[84] The parish was included with Upton St. Leonards in the Gloucester poor-law union in 1835.[85] Later the Matson area was in Gloucester rural district until Gloucester city absorbed Matson and the Painswick road area in 1935 and the Wheatridge in 1967.[86]

CHURCH. There was a church or chapel at Matson by 1100 when the bishop granted Gloucester Abbey a pension of 10s. from it.[87] In the second quarter of the 12th century Ernulf, apparently in confirming a grant by his father Ralph, gave the church with its tithes and graveyard to the abbey, and Philip of Matson (fl. 1159) later confirmed the grant.[88] Priests appointed by the abbey to serve the church or chapel paid the pension[89] and also a portion of 5s. settled by 1291 on the rector of St. Mary de Lode, Gloucester.[90] The living, although occasionally described as a vicarage,[91] was by 1349 more usually called a rectory,[92] presumably because the priest took the profits of the church. Uncertainty over the living's status continued, but by the 18th century it was generally regarded as a rectory.[93]

The advowson of the church or rectory passed together with the 10s. pension as former possessions of the abbey to the dean and chapter of Gloucester cathedral in 1541.[94] In 1556 Thomas Hale was patron for one turn under a grant from the abbey,[95] and at consecutive vacancies in 1571 and 1626 the patronage was exercised respectively by Richard Robins and his son John as lessees of the dean and chapter.[96] The dean and chapter made later presentations, though the bishop collated through lapse in 1695 and the Crown acting through the Lord Chancellor was patron for a turn in 1747.[97] In 1986 the patronage remained with the dean and chapter.[98]

In 1291 the living's annual income was too small to be assessed for tax;[99] the ninth of grain, wool, and lambs in 1340 was valued at 16s.[1] The priest, who presumably received the tithes and other profits,[2] occupied a house and 3 a. by the late 16th century.[3] His living, including tithes, was worth £3 16s. 5½d. clear in 1535[4] and £3 6s. 1½d. in 1603.[2] In 1651 the trustees for the maintenance of ministers assigned the Matson priest the rent of £26 paid by the lessee of the tithes and glebe, which had come to them as former possessions of the dean and chapter.[6] Later the incumbent was regarded as having the freehold of the tithes and 3 a., which by 1718 and until 1745 he let at farm for £19 a year.[7] The complex parish boundary made

[70] Glos. R.O., D 6/4, no. 14; Q/RI 70 (map K).
[71] P.R.O., CP 25(1)/73/4, no. 12.
[72] *Hist. & Cart. Mon. Glouc.* iii. 151.
[73] Bryant, *Map of Glos.* (1824); *Glouc. Jnl.* 1 Aug. 1829.
[74] Glos. R.O., D 127/897-9; D 1388/SL 6/67; G.D.R., T 1/189.
[75] *Census*, 1831.   [76] P.R.O., C 115/K 2/6684, f. 30v.
[77] Glos. R.O., D 326/M 24; for rec. of King's Barton ct., above, Outlying Hamlets, local govt.
[78] Glos. R.O., D 326/M 21, M 24; P 347A/FM 2-3.
[79] Ibid. D 2078, Guise fam., King's Barton ct. bk. 1854-1946.   [80] Ibid. P 347A/FM 2-7; FT 2.
[81] Hockaday Abs. xxxi, 1548 visit. f. 9; xlvii, 1576 visit. f.12.
[82] Ibid. lxviii, 1661 visit. f. 41; G.D.R., C 4/1.
[83] Glos. R.O., Q/SO 4.
[84] *Poor Law Abstract, 1804,* 176-7; *1818,* 148-9; *Poor Law Returns* (1830-1), 68; (1835), 66.
[85] *Poor Law Com. 1st Rep.* p. 251.
[86] *Census*, 1931 (pt. ii); 1961-71.
[87] *Hist. & Cart. Mon. Glouc.* ii. 41.
[88] Ibid. i. 100, 180; ii. 258-9.
[89] Ibid. i. 327-8; Glouc. Cath. Libr., Reg. Abb. Froucester B, p. 501; cf. Glos. R.O., D 936/A 1/1, p. 8.

[90] *Tax. Eccl.* (Rec. Com.), 224; *Valor Eccl.* (Rec. Com.), ii. 499: the abbey received the 5s. portion following its appropriation of St. Mary's rectory.
[91] *Hist. & Cart. Mon. Glouc.* i. 327-8; *Reg. Giffard,* 346; *Valor Eccl.* (Rec. Com.), ii. 499.
[92] *Reg. Bransford,* pp. 402, 414; *Reg. Wakefeld,* p. 34; Worc. Episc. Reg., Reg. Bourchier, ff. 68, 90.
[93] Hockaday Abs. cclxxviii; G.D.R., V 5/201T 3.
[94] *L. & P. Hen. VIII,* xvi, p. 573.
[95] Hockaday Abs. cclxxviii; Glouc. Cath. Libr., Reg. Abb. Malvern, ii, f. 111.
[96] Hockaday Abs. cclxxviii; P.R.O., IND 17004, p. 54; above, man.
[97] Hockaday Abs. cclxxviii; P.R.O., IND 17014, p. 219.
[98] *Glouc. Dioc. Year Bk.* (1986), 18-19.
[99] *Tax. Eccl.* (Rec. Com.), 224.
[1] *Inq. Non.* (Rec. Com.), 417.
[2] Cf. *Reg. Bransford,* p. 402; Worc. Episc. Reg., Reg. Winchcombe, f. 3.
[3] G.D.R., V 5/201T 1.
[4] *Valor Eccl.* (Rec. Com.), ii. 499.   [5] *Eccl. Misc.* 71.
[6] Hockaday Abs. cclxxviii; Glos. R.O., D 1740/E 1, f. 122; cf. Glos. R.O., P 215/IN 3/1.
[7] Glos. Colln. RF 201.5; cf. Atkyns, *Glos.* 552.

tithe collection difficult and in the early 1770s landholders claimed that for many years they had paid a modus of £20.[8] The rectory house, which stood south or east of the churchyard, comprised three bays and was in serious disrepair in 1649. After a rebuilding in the early 1650s it was of three storeys with a thatched roof.[9] It was later abandoned and demolished, apparently in the early 18th century.[10] To meet a benefaction from the Revd. Thomas Savage, Queen Anne's Bounty in 1745 awarded the living £200[11] which was used to buy 30 a. in Westbury-on-Severn for the incumbent's glebe.[12] At the inclosure of 1799 the rector acquired 53 a. in South Hamlet in composition for his Matson glebe and tithes, save those of Pope's wood for which he was assigned a corn rent charge of 18s.[13] The living remained poor and was worth £185 in 1856.[14] The glebe, to which 11 a. at Sneedham's Green were added in 1889, was sold between 1918 and 1921.[15] In 1878 and 1879 a rectory house was built on Matson Lane northeast of the church to a design of F. S. Waller & Son largely at the expense of the Misses Rice.[16] Selwyn school bought the house in 1962 and a new house was built for the rector in the grounds; the older rectory was converted, and in the early 1980s enlarged, as a boarding house for the school.[17]

The living was filled in 1325 and 1382 on exchanges of benefices,[18] and in 1395 the rector had leave to absent himself for a year and to let the church at farm.[19] A Dominican friar became rector in 1443.[20] Richard Brook, rector by 1532, was decrepit in 1551.[21] Lewis Evans, whose incumbency lasted from 1571 to his death in 1626,[22] was neither a graduate nor a preacher but was deemed a sufficient scholar in 1593.[23] In 1648 the church was served by Thomas Jennings, a signatory of the *Gloucestershire Ministers' Testimony*.[24] In 1649 and in 1661 there was no incumbent.[25] In the later 17th century several rectors also held the living of Barnwood,[26] and in the early 18th, when the rector was non-resident, Albinia Selwyn employed Samson Harris, a friend of George Whitefield and vicar of Stonehouse from 1727, as her private chaplain at Matson.[27] Edward Nicholls, rector of St. Mary de

Crypt, Gloucester, was licensed to the curacy of Matson in 1735 and was rector from 1747 to his death in 1763.[28] He held services every Sunday morning except the last in the month.[29] The poverty of the living and the lack of accommodation made Matson an unattractive benefice and between 1763 and 1788 eight men were instituted as rector; five of them resigned to become vicar of St. Mary de Lode, Gloucester.[30] In the later 18th century and the early 19th the rector usually lived in or near Gloucester, where a house in Wellington Parade was designated the glebe house in 1839. Under Robert Clifton, rector 1817–31, who was dispensed in 1819 to hold a living in Worcester, a curate conducted a Sunday service and four communion services a year. Matson was also served occasionally by stipendiary curates in the mid 19th century.[31] William Bazeley, rector 1875–1924, took up residence in the parish and assisted the Misses Rice in improvements to the church and school; his antiquarian interests resulted in several publications.[32] A mission church on the Matson housing estate from the mid 1950s is mentioned above.[33]

In 1427 Philip of Matson gave 3 a. for the repair of Matson church.[34] The land formed the endowment of the Matson visitation lands charity, the trustees of which were allotted land at the Wheatridge at the inclosure of 1799.[35] A small piece of land which had supported a lamp in the church was sold in 1549.[36]

Matson church was largely rebuilt in 1739 and again in 1893. When completed in 1894 it was dedicated to *ST. KATHARINE*[37] and comprised a chancel with north vestry and former south organ chamber and a nave with north porch, south organ chamber, and east bellcot.[38]

Barely any architectural evidence survives of the small medieval church. Fabric dating from the 13th and 15th centuries was discovered during the rebuilding of 1893,[39] and some fragments were incorporated in the porch.[40] Royalists used the church as a magazine during the siege of Gloucester in 1643,[41] and the chancel was in serious disrepair in 1649[42] and in 1661 when the dean and chapter of Gloucester ordered repairs to be made.[43] In 1739 the church, which was in

[8] P.R.O., E 126/30, 1772 Hil. no. 8.
[9] Glos. R.O., D 1740/E 1, f. 122; P 215/IN 3/1.
[10] *Trans. B.G.A.S.* ii. 263; G.D.R. vol. 397, f. 37.
[11] Hodgson, *Queen Anne's Bounty* (1845), pp. cliv, cclxxxv; Savage's benefaction derived from a legacy by a Mr. Hodges: Rudder, *Glos.* 542.
[12] Glos. R.O., P 215/IN 3/2.
[13] Ibid. Q/RI 70 (award and map Q, nos. 1–6); G.D.R., V 5/201T 4.
[14] G.D.R. vol. 384, f. 142.
[15] Glos. R.O., P 215/IN 3/10; VE 2/1, mem. at end.
[16] Ibid. D 1381; *Glouc. Jnl.* 4 Mar. 1905; 19 Dec. 1908.
[17] Jennings, *Matson Ho.* 25–6; Glos. Colln. RR 201.3, p. 49; inf. from rector.
[18] *Reg. Cobham*, 244; *Reg. Wakefield*, p. 34.
[19] Worc. Episc. Reg., Reg. Winchcombe, f. 3.
[20] Ibid. Reg. Bourchier, f. 90.
[21] Hockaday Abs. xxv, 1532 subsidy, f. 29; *E.H.R.* xix. 103.
[22] Hockaday Abs. cclxxviii; Glos. R.O., P 215/IN 1/1.
[23] Hockaday Abs. xlix, state of clergy 1584, f. 5; lii, state of clergy 1593, f. 12.
[24] *Calamy Revised*, ed. A. G. Matthews, 297.
[25] Glos. R.O., D 1740/E 1, f. 122; Hockaday Abs. lxviii, 1661 visit. f. 41.
[26] Glos. R.O., D 936/A 1/3, pp. 5, 111, 442, 466; 4, pp. 5, 30.
[27] *Trans. B.G.A.S.* ii. 263; *V.C.H. Glos.* x. 286.
[28] Hockaday Abs. cclxxviii, ccxvi.
[29] G.D.R. vol. 397, f. 37.
[30] Hockaday Abs. cclxxviii, ccxviii.
[31] G.D.R. vol. 319; vol. 382, f. 25; vol. 383, no. clviii; Hockaday Abs. cclxxviii.
[32] *Glouc. Jnl.* 19 Dec. 1908; 18 July 1925.
[33] Churches and Chapels, mod. par. ch., intro.
[34] Glos. R.O., D 2957/201.10.
[35] Ibid. Q/RI 70.
[36] *Cal. Pat.* 1549–51, 100; P.R.O., E 301/23, rot. 11d.
[37] *Glos. Chron.* 26 May 1894; no earlier dedication has been recorded.
[38] The alignment of ch. is SE.–NW.
[39] *Glouc. Jnl.* 12 Dec. 1908.
[40] Glos. Colln. RR 201.2.
[41] *Bibliotheca Glos.* ii, p. lx.
[42] Glos. R.O., D 1740/E 1, f. 122.
[43] Glouc. Cath. Libr., Chapter Act bk. i, f. 104.

Fig. 27. Matson church: the north side before the rebuilding of the nave and tower in 1893

danger of collapse, was rebuilt except for the small chancel with money left by Albinia Selwyn.[44] The new parts, in brick, comprised a square nave with large round-headed windows and north doorway and a small west tower. They contrasted with the chancel,[45] which the rector Robert Anwyl Pritchard rebuilt in the early 1850s on a larger scale with a vestry and to a design in a 13th-century style by F. S. Waller.[46] The arrival of the Misses Rice at Matson House was followed by extensive improvements in the church; many fittings were replaced in 1872, a small organ chamber was added to the chancel, the chancel arch was widened in a 13th-century style in 1877, and the vestry was enlarged in 1888.[47] With the enlargement of its parish in 1892[48] the church became too small, and in 1893 the nave and tower were pulled down to be replaced by a larger stone nave with porch, organ chamber, and bellcot designed by F. S. Waller & Son to match the chancel. The rebuilding was financed principally by Maria Rice in memory of her sister Katharine, whose name suggested the choice of dedication.[49]

The church retains some fittings from the earlier buildings, notably several monuments to members of the Selwyn family.[50] The bellcot houses a bell of the 15th century or early 16th, probably from the Bristol foundry, and the church also has a bell cast by Abel Rudhall in 1739.[51] The plate includes a paten of 1699 and a chalice of 1717 given by Albinia Selwyn in 1717, and a chalice and paten from a church in Havana, Cuba, given by George Selwyn (d. 1791).[52] The parish registers, which survive from 1553, contain few entries in the periods 1648–71 and 1687–1721.[53] The churchyard, which was enlarged in 1788 and 1894,[54] has a war memorial built in 1920.[55]

NONCONFORMITY. In 1676 one Matson parishioner was said to be a nonconformist.[56] In 1853 a house in Trafalgar Place on the Painswick road was registered for use by Wesleyan Methodists. That meeting lapsed before 1876.[57] In the late 1860s Baptist preachers from Gloucester visited Matson but no other evidence of nonconformist meetings there before the 1950s has been found.[58]

[44] *Trans. B.G.A.S.* ii. 263–4; Bigland, *Glos.* ii. 200.

[45] Elevation in Glos. R.O., P 215/CW 3/3, reproduced above, Fig. 27.

[46] Glos. Colln. RF 201.6; *Kelly's Dir. Glos.* (1856), 325; *Glouc. Jnl.* 12 Dec. 1908.

[47] Glos. R.O., P 215/CW 3/1–3; IN 4/4, f. 96; *Glouc. Jnl.* 19 Dec. 1908.

[48] *Lond. Gaz.* 12 July 1892, pp. 4000–5.

[49] Glos. R.O., P 215/CW 3/2–3; *Glos. Chron.* 26 May 1894; cf. *Glouc. Jnl.* 19, 26 Dec. 1908.

[50] Cf. Bigland, *Glos.* ii. 202–3; Roper, *Glos. Effigies*, 335–8

[51] *Glos. Ch. Bells*, 426–7.

[52] *Glos. Ch. Plate*, 144–6.

[53] *B. & G. Par. Rec.* 190; Glos. R.O., P 215/IN 1/1.

[54] Hockaday Abs. cclxxviii; *Glouc. Jnl.* 19 Dec. 1908.

[55] Glos. R.O., P 215/IN 4/6.

[56] *Compton Census*, ed. Whiteman, 545.

[57] G.R.O. (General Register Office), Worship Reg. no 669.

[58] Above, Prot. Nonconf., Baptists.

EDUCATION. There was no school in Matson parish in 1818 when the only three children receiving education did so at the expense of a parishioner, possibly the curate's sister,[59] and in the mid 19th century children went to school in Upton St. Leonards.[60] A Sunday school in Matson teaching 10 children in 1825[61] had lapsed by 1833 when another was started.[62]

An infants' school opened at Matson before 1875 was supported by pence, subscriptions, and payments from Matson church funds.[63] It was held in a cottage on the Painswick road until 1881 when it moved with 20 children to a new building provided on an adjacent site by the Misses Rice in memory of their sisters Harriet and Caroline. The Misses Rice built a schoolhouse to the north in 1884,[64] and in 1885 they endowed the school with £25 a year in stock.[65] In 1886 the school was reorganized as a National school and the older children of the area ceased to attend Upton National school.[66] Matson school, which was enlarged in 1897, had an average attendance of 50 in 1889[67] and 86 in 1904,[68] and as Matson C. of E. school taught 39 children in 1938.[69] With the growth of the Matson housing estate in the 1950s the number of children on the roll increased rapidly and from 1952 the juniors went to a school in Finlay Road. The Matson school, where the number of children fell from 206 to 140 on the opening in 1955 of Robinswood infants' school in Matson Avenue, was replaced in 1960 by Moat infants' school in Juniper Avenue. Of the buildings, which included huts added in 1953 and the adjacent Matson church hall,[70] only the former schoolhouse was standing in 1986.

CHARITY FOR THE POOR. The trust deed of 1633 for the charity founded by Giles Cox of Abload's Court, Sandhurst, by will dated 1620, assigned Matson parish 15s. a year to help householders not receiving poor relief.[71] Payment had apparently lapsed by 1683[72] but resumed before 1822 when the amounts received by Matson and other parishes, including Upton St. Leonards, were doubled for several years. In Matson the charity was generally shared among four or five householders.[73] By 1896 Matson's share of the charity had risen to £3 16s., which under a Scheme of 1892 was distributed by a clothing club, but from 1903 it was 10s.[74] Residents of those parts of the Matson area (including Saintbridge) belonging to Upton received no payments from Upton's share of the charity for many years before 1890 when £1 13s. 4d. was given to Matson parish for their benefit. That and later payments were distributed by a coal club[75] and from 1914 Matson received £3 of the Upton share directly from the charity's trustees.[76] On the division of the charity in 1957 a separate charity was established for Matson.[77] In the early 1970s it distributed its income of £4 occasionally.[78]

[59] *Educ. of Poor Digest*, 303; Hockaday Abs. cclxxviii.
[60] Nat. Soc. *Inquiry, 1846–7*, Glos. 12–13.
[61] G.D.R. vol. 383, no. clviii.
[62] *Educ. Enq. Abstract*, 320.
[63] Glos. R.O., P 215/IN 4/4, ff. 58–67.
[64] Nat. Soc. files, Matson; *Glouc. Jnl.* 17 Dec. 1881; 19 Dec. 1908; E. S. Bazeley, *Recollections of a Forester* (1970), 26.
[65] Glos. R.O., D 3469/5/67; P 215/IN 4/4, f. 60.
[66] Ibid. S 215/1; P.R.O., ED 7/35/214.
[67] *Kelly's Dir. Glos.* (1889), 840; (1906), 243.
[68] *Public Elem. Schs.* 1906, 187.

[69] *Bd. of Educ., List 21, 1938* (H.M.S.O.), 134.
[70] Glos. R.O., S 215/4; above, Educ., elem. educ.
[71] *16th Rep. Com. Char.* 38–9.
[72] G.D.R., V 5/201T 3.
[73] *16th Rep. Com Char.* 39, 41–2, 57–8.
[74] Glos. R.O., P 215/IN 4/4, ff. 91–3, 98–100, 102–3; D 2695/1–2.
[75] Ibid. P 215/VE 2/1, mins. 9 Apr. 1885, May 1894; IN 4/4, ff. 33, 88–93.
[76] Ibid. D 2695/1–2; P 215/CW 2/1.
[77] Ibid. D 2695/4.
[78] Ibid. CH 21, Glouc. co. boro., p. 19.

INDEX

INDEX